may be kept

W9-CLZ-905

A History of
Medieval Civilization

JOSEPH H. DAHMUS
The Pennsylvania State University

The Odyssey Press • New York

TO MY PATIENT WIFE AND FAMILY

Photo on title page of Ekkehart and Uta by permission
of Bildarchiv Foto Marburg

Library of Congress Catalog Card Number: 64 – 15005

Foreword

Two features in particular justify the appearance of this textbook. There are, first, the READINGS from contemporary sources which accompany each of the fifteen chapters. These READINGS serve to supplement the textual material, to elucidate, illustrate, and to enrich it. The instructor who teaches with the aid of documents and the instructor who employs a "problems approach" will especially appreciate this feature. And because students will find the READINGS generally interesting and frequently provocative, a greater measure of class participation can be expected. While the documents are self-explanatory, constant reference is made to them in the text in order to enhance their value.

A second feature which justifies the text is its untraditionally heavy emphasis upon the literature, thought, and art of the Middle Ages. The farther a period recedes into the past, the greater the demand that the history of that period tell the whole story, and this is becoming increasingly true of the Middle Ages. Why should the student not be told as much about scholasticism as about feudalism, as much about medieval literature and Romanesque architecture as about medieval agriculture and the "just price"? Nevertheless, the text's treatment of such topics as feudalism and manorialism remains as extensive as that provided by conventional textbooks. By eliminating dates and details which contribute nothing to the history of medieval ideas and institutions, it has been possible to give considerably more space to the cultural facets of the Middle Ages without neglecting the political, economic, and social.

Another feature which may appeal to the instructor, surely to the student, is the bold type in which the phrases introducing each succeeding paragraph are printed. Modern textbooks often sacrifice such study-aids to economy, but it is an economy the average student can ill afford. Since history consists of men as much as movements, important figures like Justinian, Charlemagne, Henry II, and St. Louis receive proportionately greater attention than they could expect in a five-volume study of the Middle Ages. Only by bringing men of this stature out from the shadow cast by their lesser contemporaries can the instructor be reasonably confident that two years after taking a course in medieval history, the student will be retaining more vital memories of that period than banalities and the long bow.

Even a Solomon with Aristotle at his elbow could not organize the matter of the Middle Ages to suit the preferences of every instructor. The number of chapters has been kept down to fifteen, partly because most semesters run fifteen weeks, partly because the fewer the chapters (within limits), the greater the odds that at the end of the term the student will still be able to see the woods despite the trees. The material presented in these chapters follows both a chronological and topical pattern. Because France, England, and Germany were the principal countries of medieval Europe, they carry the story; and rather than devote a paragraph to Poland in chapter four, another paragraph in chapter eight and so on, countries of lesser importance in the Middle Ages receive brief but unified coverage in chapter fifteen, the concluding chapter. The bibliography, in giving priority to paperbacks, accepts the fact that only the superior student will consult a bibliography unless it lists books which are both readable and available.

Several good friends and scholars have come to my aid in those areas where my deficiencies are most marked. I should like to acknowledge the assistance of Professor Robert Kaske in matters concerned with literature; the counsel of Professors Finch and John Mourant in science and philosophy; the advice of Professor Paul Norton in my discussion of medieval art; and the immense good will of Professor William Furlong for his painstaking reading of the manuscript.

Contents

Readings

1. THE ROMAN WORLD AND ITS DECLINE

2. THE RISE AND EARLY DEVELOPMENT OF CHRISTIANITY

3. THE BARBARIZATION OF THE WEST

4. THE BYZANTINE WORLD

5. ISLAM

6. THE FRANKISH KINGDOMS

7. FEUDALISM

8. THE MEDIEVAL MANOR

9. THE REVIVAL OF TRADE;
THE RISE OF TOWNS; THE CRUSADES

10. THE RISE OF FEUDAL MONARCHIES

11. THE CHURCH OF THE HIGH MIDDLE AGES

12. MEDIEVAL THOUGHT AND LEARNING

13. THE LITERATURE AND ARTS
OF THE HIGH MIDDLE AGES

14. RELIGIOUS AND CULTURAL DEVELOPMENTS OF THE LATE MIDDLE AGES

15. POLITICAL DEVELOPMENTS OF THE LATE MIDDLE AGES

Illustrations

Maps

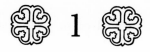

1

THE ROMAN WORLD AND ITS DECLINE

Introduction

No True Breaks in History. For some three hundred years historians have been labeling the thousand or more years which elapsed between Ancient and Modern History as the period of the Middle Ages. How much justification can be offered for thus marking off these particular centuries as a formal division of history? No more than can be suggested for establishing Early Modern Europe or the History of the United States since the Civil War as distinct periods of history. The people who lived in the transitional decades between one period and another had little reason to believe that future historians would designate those decades as transitional. For the vast majority of Europeans who lived in 1500, conditions did not change so perceptibly between the years 1495 and 1505 as to justify later historians in singling out the year 1500 as marking the end of one era and the beginning of another. Yet these same historians will be the first to admit that when they periodize history, they are violating one of the axioms of history. This is the law that says history moves smoothly, that it flows like a river, without sudden stops, reversals, or forward lunges. Nevertheless, while mores and institutions are today what they were yesterday and what they will be tomorrow, few people will deny that the passage of twenty-five years will alter them. It would be remarkable, indeed, if the course of a generation did not witness measurable modification in the way people think, in the way they live, in short, in their civilization. It is to take note of such

1

changes, and also to make history more digestible, that historians chop it up into eras and periods.

Events and Developments Setting Off the Middle Ages.   Granted the need for reducing the immense sweep of history into smaller periods, what events or developments present themselves to justify setting off the particular centuries of the Middle Ages as distinct from the centuries immediately preceding and from those that followed? One might note first the decline and disintegration (in the west) of the Roman Empire which had dominated the Mediterranean world for five hundred years. Next there was the Christianization of this empire, a religious development which gradually transformed its thoroughly pagan civilization. Convincing symptoms of profound change in the course of history, too, are suggested by the transferal of the capital of the Roman Empire from Rome on the Tiber to Constantinople on the Bosporus. Helping to set off the Middle Ages from modern times which traditionally began in 1500 were the discoveries of America and the all-water route to India, the fall of Constantinople to the Ottoman Turks, the passing of maritime supremacy from Italian waters to the Atlantic, and the disruption of the universal Catholic Christian church.

When Did the Middle Ages Begin?   While little argument rises over designating 1500 A.D. as the logical terminus of the Middle Ages, no equally round and convenient date offers itself to introduce the period. Shall we take the accession of the Emperor Diocletian in 285 A.D., since the empire which he re-established after fifty years of relative anarchy was no longer the classical world of Augustus and Trajan? Or shall we prefer as a point of departure the extension of toleration to the Christians early in the fourth century which prepared the ground for the Christian Middle Ages? Some scholars suggest the death of Theodosius the Great in 395 A.D. as a good dividing year since Theodosius was the last Roman emperor to exercise control over both western and eastern parts of the empire. Even a date as late as Charlemagne's coronation in 800 A.D. appeals to certain scholars as marking the true break between the world of antiquity and the Middle Ages.

The Year 400 A.D. as the Beginning of the Middle Ages.   Although historians will probably never agree on any date to usher in the Middle Ages, there is much to recommend the year 400 A.D., particularly if one is seeking as round a date as the 1500 A.D. with which the medieval period ends. By 400 A.D., the Christian and barbarian (principally Germanic) ingredients which eventually fused with the classical element to produce the civilization of the Middle Ages, had clearly asserted themselves. By 400 A.D., the classical, pagan culture of the Roman Empire had been largely replaced by a culturally decadent, predominantly Christian civilization. By 400 A.D., too, the political character of the Roman Empire had been radically altered. Until the turn of the fourth century, Roman rule had remained a fact in the west; shortly after the death of Theodosius in 395 A.D., however, it became a myth. True, these three ingredients, the classical, Christian, and barbarian, had been present before 400 A.D. But until 400 A.D. the Roman element had been generally in command and had ordinarily determined the rate of fusion with the other two ingredients. After 400 A.D. the initiative in the fusing process passed to the Germans, and, for better or for worse, western Europe of the Middle Ages was a Germanic world.

Classical Element. Now to take a closer look at the three ingredients of medieval civilization, let us consider first the classical tradition. By this is understood the ideas, institutions, and techniques which the medieval west inherited from the dying Roman Empire. Part of this tradition was Rome's own, but most of it the Romans had inherited from the Greeks, and how much of theirs the Greeks in turn owed to the more ancient peoples of Egypt, Syria, and Mesopotamia is difficult to say. It must have been considerable. Yet few will quarrel with Professor Toynbee's statement that Hellenic civilization was "perhaps the finest flower of the species that has ever come into existence up to the present." And so it is to the Greeks that we credit our criteria of what is best in literature and what is beautiful in art; our conception of law; much of our political thought; our introduction to science; and above all, the bases of our philosophy. The Romans themselves we credit first with having preserved the civilization of the Greeks and the ancient Near East. The Romans superimposed upon this civilization the idea of universality, the principle that many if not all peoples might live under the same law, accept the same religion, respect the same government. The Romans revealed peculiar talents as builders and an equally unique skill in the development of law and in the application of legal principles. Rome's achievement in establishing the conception of the rule of law "is indeed rightly claimed as the outstanding contribution of Rome to the development of civilization."*

Christian Element. A second ingredient in the medieval civilization which emerged in western Europe during the thousand years following the passing of the Roman Empire was that provided by the Christian or Catholic Church. This Christian ingredient was, in fact, the most distinctive element in medieval civilization and, at the same time, the most persuasive. In the words of Professor Lea: "The history of mankind may be vainly searched for another institution such as that of the Latin Church, which has exercised so vast an influence on human destinies." Apart from the role of churchmen in salvaging a considerable portion of classical thought and tradition, it was primarily in the realm of ideas that the Christian Church left its mark. It preached a moral code based upon the Ten Commandments and the Sermon on the Mount (Reading 10), and a way of life which gradually transformed the barbarous German into a reasonably civilized individual. It insisted upon the recognition of an authority above that of the state to which all men, all institutions, all other authorities must give precedence. The principle of natural rights, of the essential equality of all

* Percy Neville Ure, *Justinian and His Age* (Penguin Books, 1951), p. 139.

men, even of men and women (Reading 136), the dignity and spiritual value of labor—these and other ethical ideas have come down to us through the medium of the medieval church. Without the contribution of the Christian Church, the Declaration of Independence might not have opened with these ringing claims: "We hold these truths to be self-evident, that all men are created equal, that they are endowed by their Creator with certain unalienable rights . . . that to secure these rights governments are instituted among men."

German Element. The semicivilized Germans provided a third element. The German invader was the raw material, as it were, who was to be civilized through the agency of classical and Christian ideas. All the countries of modern Europe saw their rise in the Middle Ages, and a large portion of the earth's peoples have since been Europeanized by the descendants of these medieval folk. If there is any cogency in the claim of certain ethnologists that peoples, just as persons, decline and die, then we would have to admit the possibility that classical civilization might have disappeared with the Romans had it not been for the appearance of these rough peoples north of the Roman frontier who accepted it before it had passed away. For as we shall find, Rome was far advanced in her decline before the Germans possessed themselves of her empire. Yet the Germans, and the Celts and Slavs to a lesser degree, can claim contributions all their own. Whether it was accident or the achievement of their peculiar genius, it is generally agreed that we must credit them and the Middle Ages with the rise of towns, of the bourgeoisie, of capitalism with all its manifold derivatives, of parliamentary government, of the modern jury, and of as enterprising and energetic a collection of nations as history has ever encountered.

Fusing Process Long and Difficult. These three ingredients were a long time in producing medieval civilization. Any civilization alters its mold grudgingly. Civilization's most abiding characteristic, in fact, is its reluctance to change. It may be likened to a tremendous mass moving at a glacial pace. Medieval society was especially sluggish in adopting the higher forms of classical and Christian civilization. There was, first, the great gap which yawned between the pagan barbarous German on the one hand and the sophisticated Christian Roman on the other. Then, for the greater part of the Middle Ages travel was difficult and dangerous. Neither goods, persons, nor ideas circulated freely. Furthermore, several of man's strongest loyalties, those to religion and tribe, had frequently to be extinguished before the peoples who moved into the Roman Empire and into western Europe became receptive to different ideas and ways. Then there appeared periodic invasions of uncivilized peoples from Asia and northern Europe which partly unmade the slow, painful progress of preceding generations. So it was a long time before classical and Christian agencies succeeded in making over the rude German into a civilized person and a Christian. The record of that struggle is the story of medieval history.

Why Medieval History?   The story of this fusing is not only intriguing; it is important. For a study of medieval history will reveal the wellsprings from which so many principles and practices of our present civilization have originated. Surely it is principally what happened in the Middle Ages which makes our civilization so different from that of the Orient. The Athenian was perhaps the world's greatest individualist and the sober Roman of the early Republic was not greatly different from ourselves. But most of that individualism disappeared during the last centuries of the Empire. Had it not been for the Christian insistence upon natural rights and upon the sanctity of the individual, we might today attach as little value to human life as do many Orientals. The medieval period was an institutional epoch when the modern state took form, when Christian society arose, when family life as we know it took root, when the university was born, when town life and modern representative government originated, when our present art forms were molded, when trade and agriculture and industry as we know them came into existence. The Middle Ages established the criteria of a Christian civilization which ours is, they brought forth the capitalistic system, they ushered on to the stage of history all the modern nations of the most important continent on the face of the earth. If history is important, then no part of it is more worthy of our consideration than the medieval period.

Geography of Medieval Europe.   Because geography exercises a varying, though frequently significant, influence upon history, it is well to take a look at the physical world of the Middle Ages. The area with which we shall concern ourselves is not exclusively that of Europe and, in some cases, parts of Europe will not even receive primary emphasis. Eastern Europe, that is, Russia and its eastern neighbors, will come in for but little attention. That huge area enjoyed but few ties with the west during the Middle Ages. It developed a distinctly inferior and essentially nonwestern culture. And as it happened, geography was largely responsible for this condition. For through the wide gap between the Ural Mountains and the Caspian Sea to the south, successive waves of Asiatic conquerors swept into Russia and isolated that country from the west for long periods of time. Furthermore, Russia was closer geographically, therefore culturally, to Constantinople than to Rome. The consequence was the "backwardness" of Russia about which we still read today. Yet though we shall give little attention to eastern Europe, we must familiarize ourselves with the lands bordering the Mediterranean to the east (Asia Minor and Syria) and to the south (north Africa). Here flourished Byzantine and Islamic cultures, both of which heavily influenced the culture of the west, and here the most dramatic spectacles of the Middle Ages, the Crusades, were staged.

Western and Southern Europe.   The most vital portions of Europe under consideration during the medieval period are those of the west. These are divided by a line of mountains running roughly from the Atlantic to the

PHYSICAL MAP OF EUROPE,
MEDITERRANEAN WORLD,
AND NEAR EAST

ARCTIC OCEAN

ATLANTIC OCEAN

Tundras

Steppes

Urals

Altai Mts.

Ural R.

Volga R.

Don R.

ARAL SEA

CASPIAN SEA

Caucasus

Euphrates R.

Tigris R.

Syrian Desert

Arabian Tableland

PERSIAN GULF

ARABIAN SEA

G. OF ADEN

RED SEA

Nile R.

Indus R.

BLACK SEA

Dnieper R.

Dniester R.

Pripet Marshes

Vistula R.

Oder R.

Elbe R.

Carpathian Mts.

Danube R.

BALTIC SEA

NORTH SEA

Rhine R.

Seine R.

Loire R.

Alps

Po R.

Pyrenees

Tagus R.

Atlas Mts.

MEDITERRANEAN SEA

Sahara Desert

Niger R.

Black Sea, starting with the Pyrenees of Spain and terminating with the Carpathian chain in Hungary. The highest and most formidable barrier, the Alps, lies in the middle of this line. The lands to the south of this line are mountainous and peninsular, all jutting out into the Mediterranean. These are Spain, Italy, and the Balkans. To the north of the line lie France, Germany, Poland, and the Baltic areas. Topographically these are largely plains and, because of their heavy rainfall, densely forested. The chief physical facts of this extensive region are not mountains but rivers: the Loire, Seine, Rhine, Elbe, Oder, and Vistula, all running more or less in a northwesterly direction. The forest which blanketed the area militated against the evolution of a uniform culture, as did also the marshes of Germany and Poland and the smaller mountain clusters scattered about southern France and Germany. The insular positions of Ireland and England proved of great significance in the medieval period, as did also the maritime areas of Scandinavia. Of primary importance in the movements of peoples and of trade, and the location of cities, were medieval rivers. They were the principal and frequently the only avenues men could use in moving goods from place to place. A large proportion of medieval history took place along the Loire, the Rhone, the Po, the Rhine, and the Danube.

The Peoples of Europe. Geography continues to affect the course of European history. Certainly much less influential is the racial distribution of Europe's peoples. Yet mention must be made of these, if for no other reason than the fact that foolish claims have occasionally been advanced for the alleged superiority of this or that group. Anthropologists classify the peoples of Europe into three groups: the Nordic, the Alpine, and the Mediterranean. All three groups belong to the white race. In arriving at this differentiation, anthropologists employ as criteria such physical characteristics as the shape of the skull, stature, and pigmentation, characteristics which they claim were the result of environmental differences of thousands of years duration. One division of these peoples is tall, muscular, large-boned, fair, with either gray or blue eyes, and has skulls which are long and massive. This group is called the Nordic. It can be recognized most easily in Scandinavia and along the shores bordering the North Sea. A second group or type is the Alpine, which is found in the highlands of central Europe. These people have short, broad heads, set upon bodies of medium stature. Their eyes are brown and their hair dark. In this category belong both Celts and Slavs, the most populous of the peoples of Europe. To the south, from Spain to Syria along the shores of the Mediterranean, the third group made its home. Their bodies are short and slender, their eyes and hair black, and their color swarthy, while their skulls are long and narrow. These three races probably constituted fairly distinct groups some thousands of years ago, but so great has been the mingling and scattering of peoples during subsequent millennia, that no pure specimens exist today. A German may be a Nordic, so might a Russian, or a Frenchman, or an Italian.

Indo-Europeans. Somewhat less susceptible to misuse than such terms as Nordic and Alpine, is the word Indo-European. This is a linguistic classification which philologists give to the family of languages spoken by most of the peoples of Europe. Actually only four minor languages fall without this classification: the Basque, Finnish, Turkish, and Magyar. The first two languages, the Basque and Finnish, are spoken by peoples who entered Europe at a very early age and who managed somehow to retain their own idiomatic speech. The Turks and Magyars crossed over into Europe from Asia in medieval times. Although the differences among many of the languages of Europe may appear stupendous, at least to the student who is introduced to them for the first time, the fact is that for certain common words such as father, mother, sister, and brother, all the languages employ phonologically related sounds: e.g. Greek *pater*, Latin *pater*, Italian and Spanish *padre*, French *père*, German *Vater*, English *father*. Yet here again one must remember that the Indo-European label connotes no intellectual eminence. The term is of some value to philologists. To historians it provides additional material to confute the vagaries of racial purists who like to think of their peoples as still enjoying in unadulterated vigor the unusual talents they had from the gods.

Roman Civilization

Medieval History Begins with Rome. A history of the Middle Ages begins necessarily with the decline of the Roman Empire and the passing of classical civilization. As mentioned above, the practice of periodizing history is more convenient than it is logical, since the culture of one period melts unobtrusively into that of another. This is particularly true of medieval history since medieval Europe inherited two of the three basic ingredients of its civilization from antiquity, namely, the classical and the Christian elements. It was actually a long time before the Middle Ages recognized the fact that so radically had conditions changed since Cicero's day that theirs was no longer a Roman world. We shall see that, as late as the year 800 A.D., the people of Rome hailed Charlemagne, the Frankish king, as "emperor of the Romans." (See page 244.)

Universality of Roman Civilization. The Roman Empire was unique in history. Neither before nor since has there existed so extensive a state to which so many different peoples paid voluntary homage for so long a period of time; nor a state which purveyed so high a civilization to so many. The Romans, like the Normans whom we shall meet in the Middle Ages, permitted no foolish national pride to blind them to the ways of other peoples which were superior. The Romans adopted what they could use, whether it was the weapons of the Italic Samnites or the culture of the Greeks. To these alien borrowings they added the products of their own sober, industrious, somewhat unimaginative natures, as well as the knowledge gained from ruling so many peoples for so many years. They did not force their language, laws, or religion upon the conquered. History has seldom realized so tolerant a mistress. Yet in the course of centuries, a civilization grew up in the lands bordering the Mediterranean and along the Rhine and in Britain, which, though sufficiently diversified to reflect local cultures, bore nevertheless the unmistakable stamp of Rome.

Pax Romana.   It is traditional to single out the age of Augustus (31 B.C. to 14 A.D.) as reflecting the Roman Empire at its best. The interminable wars of expansion were past and the internal strife bred by the ambitions of Pompey and Caesar, Octavian and Antony, had come to an end. With the defeat of Antony and Cleopatra at Actium in 31 B.C., there broke upon the Mediterranean world the dawn of a peace which was to endure for two hundred years. Two centuries without a major conflict—the famous *Pax Romana!* Even when this halcyon period was already on the wane, Tertullian could write (*ca.* 200 A.D.):

Surely a glance at the world shows that it is daily being more cultivated and better peopled than before. All places are now accessible, well known, open to commerce. Delightful farms have now blotted out every trace of the dreadful wastes; cultivated fields have supplanted woods; flocks and herds have driven out wild beasts; sandy spots are sown; rocks and stones have been cleared away; bogs have been drained. Large towns now occupy land hardly tenanted before by cottages. Islands are no longer dreaded as abodes of pirates; houses, people, civil rule, civilization are everywhere.

This was the world which Augustus ushered in and which the *Pax Romana* that he also initiated helped so powerfully to Romanize.

Extent of Roman Empire.   How large a world did Augustus rule? He ruled almost the whole of the civilized world known to the people of the Mediterranean. His empire stretched from the Euphrates to the Atlantic and from the sands of the Sahara to the Rhine. It comprised some three and one-half million square miles and boasted a population of fifty millions. With the exception of Mesopotamia and Persia, all the civilizations of the ancient "Western" world were there gathered up: Egypt, Palestine, Syria, Asia Minor, Greece, and Carthage. Britain would be added by Claudius in 45 A.D. and what passes roughly for Roumania today by Trajan in 117 A.D. Mesopotamia alone of the civilized areas of antiquity eluded Roman control. Though the Roman soldier proved himself indomitable whether fighting the civilized Macedonian or the more backward German, he found himself seriously handicapped against the armed horsemen out of Persia who ranged so swiftly over the semi-arid reaches of Mesopotamia. Yet

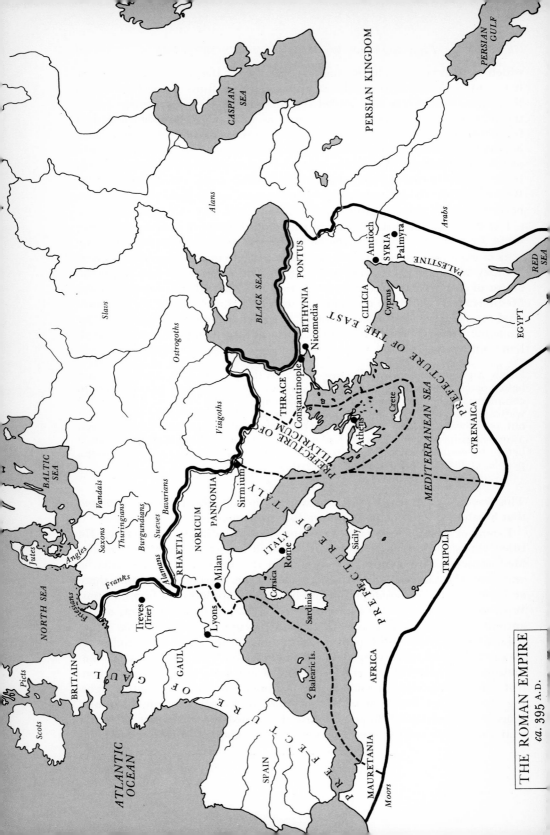

THE ROMAN EMPIRE
ca. 395 A.D.

PERSIAN GULF

PERSIAN KINGDOM

CASPIAN SEA

Alans

RED SEA

Arabs

Antioch
SYRIA
Palmyra

PALESTINE

PONTUS
BITHYNIA

Nicomedia

CILICIA

Cyprus

EGYPT

BLACK SEA

PREFECTURE OF THE EAST

Slavs

Ostrogoths

THRACE

Constantinople

Crete

Visigoths

PREFECTURE OF ILLYRICUM

Athens

MEDITERRANEAN SEA

PREFECTURE

CYRENAICA

BALTIC SEA

Vandals

Saxons
Thuringians
Burgundians
Sueves
Bavarians

Sirmium

PANNONIA

NORICUM

RHAETIA

Alamans

Franks

Milan

ITALY

Rome

Sicily

PREFECTURE OF ITALY

TRIPOLI

Angles
Jutes

NORTH SEA

Frisians

Treves
(Trier)

GAUL

Lyons

Corsica

Sardinia

Balearic Is.

AFRICA

Picts

BRITAIN

Scots

ATLANTIC OCEAN

PREFECTURE OF GAUL

SPAIN

MAURETANIA

Moors

Mesopotamia was at best an uninviting corner of the world to the Roman, who found richer and more cultured lands within his immediate orbit.

Position of the Emperor. Augustus' government was almost as simple as one-man rule generally was in antiquity. Officially the Republic continued to function through the medium of the august senate and the assemblies. The power of the latter, however, was entirely nominal and soon disappeared completely. The senate, on the other hand, continued to enjoy real governing authority in the city of Rome, in Italy, and in those provinces of the empire which did not require the presence of legions. But any independence the senate might have attempted to exercise during the closing decades of the Republic died with that Republic at Actium. Augustus thought it prudent to share the administration of the empire with the senate, but how much responsibility and authority the senate would enjoy, even in the so-called senatorial provinces, was his to decide. Because he was anxious to preserve as much of the atmosphere of a republic as was feasible, he referred to himself as the *princeps,* that is, the first citizen. This was no mere lip service, and historians customarily designate his regime as the Principate, rather than Empire. His successors, who were less concerned about disguising their autocracy under republican forms, are known simply as emperors. As time went on the absolute power of the emperor grew progressively more evident, and reached its official culmination in the Oriental despotism of Diocletian (285-305 A.D.). (See page 25.)

The Roman Municipality. A bulwark of the empire was the municipality or *civitas* through which the imperial administrative system functioned. The original plan of the *civitas* may have been Julius Caesar's, but it remained for Augustus and his successors to bring it to fruition. In the municipality lay much of the strength of the Empire and the popularity of imperial rule. The *civitas* was essentially a city or urban community which enjoyed autonomy in matters of local government, and which administered not only its own affairs but those of the surrounding countryside as well. Two major advantages commended the system: first, it left undisturbed for the most part local traditions and practices, despite acceptance of Roman rule; second, it relieved the imperial government of the necessity of providing for local administration in an age when the science of government was still not sufficiently advanced to have made this successful on so large a scale. No other system would have worked, but this worked admirably. The municipal system drew its vitality from the wealthier and more prominent citizens in the community. Those freemen who met certain property qualifications were listed officially as curials because of their membership in or eligibility to serve as members of the *curia* (council). The *esprit de corps* of this group was excellent during the first century of the Empire. Though the offices which the curials vied for were nonsalaried—in fact, the successful candidate was expected to make a generous contribution to the community upon his election—the municipal system did provide the means for satisfying the aspirations of the politically ambitious, even to the extent of winning them possible imperial notice and promotion.

Imperial Succession.   The eminent success of the municipal system, however, was not shared by the system of imperial succession, if something so irregular may be called a system. Augustus established the principle of dynastic succession, but the failure of most emperors to leave a son damned the system from the beginning. The tragic consequence was that the praetorian guard and then the provincial armies began to take a hand in the question of succession. Vespasian, the commander of the Syrian legions, took over in 69 A.D., and although he left two sons, neither of these had an heir. In 96 A.D. Nerva adopted a mature man, Trajan, to succeed him, because he lacked a son of his own. Trajan did the same for the same reason, so also Hadrian and Antoninus Pius. As misfortune would have it, the man whom Antoninus Pius adopted, the famous Marcus Aurelius, had a son, the infamous Commodus, or else the system of adoption might have continued on its unique and highly successful course.

Imperial Finance.   The financial problem of the Empire proved almost as vexing and insoluble as that of imperial succession. Gladstone's statement that "Athens perished because of its poor public finance" might have applied with equal force to Rome. The existence of several treasuries under Augustus, such as the military and senatorial treasuries, was not especially serious, since the emperor controlled them all in the last analysis. In fact, the emperors were usually obliged to supplement public revenues from their own purses, and all treasuries had been absorbed into his own by the close of the third century. Roman public finance suffered the same serious weaknesses common to all ancient fiscal systems. It lacked the bases which could be tapped to produce sufficient revenue; it depended principally upon land assessments when agriculture was generally noncapitalistic; it could not fall back upon credit to meet extraordinary demands since credit was relatively unknown; and it was without the administrative machinery requisite to collecting efficiently the revenues owing to it. Under the circumstances few emperors could withstand the temptation to debase the coinage, while a number such as Nero, Domitian, and Commodus, even stooped to confiscating property under guise of punishing real or alleged crimes. Port duties, income from state properties (e.g. mines), an inheritance tax from citizens, and a tax on manumissions completed the list of imperial revenues. The provincials paid property, poll, and personal taxes. Under the early emperors these taxes were not excessive, but they mounted steadily with the cost of government, until by the close of the second century they were draining the economic lifeblood of the Empire. The most onerous tax suffered by the provincials involved the right of the army to commandeer food and services for its use.

Roman Army.   The army played a much more influential role in the Roman Empire than it commonly does in the modern state. The Roman army policed a long and dangerous frontier; it might decide who would succeed upon the death of an emperor; and it proved the most effective Romanizing agency in the provinces. Throughout the period of the Empire the army represented the real source of power. As long as the emperor controlled it, it proved the mainstay of the Empire; when it in turn became master of the emperor, the army became a Frankenstein and threatened the very existence of the state. However, Augustus' settlement worked out satisfactorily for two hundred years. He set up two categories of troops, one the legionaries who were citizens, the other the auxiliaries who were recruited from provincials and noncitizens. Each numbered some 125,000 men. Both were ordinarily deployed along the extensive frontiers of the empire. A third category, the praetorian guard of 9,000 troops, was quartered in the vicinity of Rome to serve as the imperial bodyguard. Conditions in the service were generally hard, which made it imperative that discipline be kept at a high level or the army would get out of hand.

Agriculture. The economic backbone of the Roman Empire was agriculture. That fact—and the same holds true of all ancient states—is apt to escape the student since the textbook he reads normally devotes as much attention to Roman industry, trade, and finance, as to agriculture. The great majority of Roman citizens and noncitizens lived in rural areas and drew their sustenance either directly or indirectly from the soil. By ancient standards, agriculture of the first two hundred years of the Empire was reasonably satisfactory. Though modern farmers would not stomach the Roman farmer's hard life of heavy toil, excessive taxes or rents, and the profound cultural backwardness which marked the life of the rustic, the ancient husbandman knew nothing better. Much of the same contrast between the small and large farmer existed in ancient Rome as does today. Then too as now, extensive tracts were held by absentee landlords whose only physical contact with their acres was the sumptuous country home or villa which they visited on occasion. The small farmer, where he could still be found, farmed as his forefathers had done hundreds of years before. Still it is evident from the writings of Columella and Vergil (*Georgics*) that the "modern" farmer in Roman times had a fair knowledge of fertilization, rotation of crops, and stock breeding.

Latifundia: The Landed Estates. The tendency toward larger and fewer farms which appears to be endemic in human history plagued agriculture under the emperors, who did not even make the attempt to halt the trend as had the Republic, albeit ineffectually. Only in Spain, northern Italy, and Gaul did the small farm exist in any numbers. The large estate (*latifundia*, Latin, pl.) might be operated by a resident owner, but more probably was not. The owner normally made his home in Rome, where the emperor, the largest single landowner of the Empire, was also located. The imperial estates, and those of other absentee owners, were handled by agents, who in turn let them out to free tenants (*coloni*) at a rental amounting to one half the crop. Many slaves continued to be employed on the land, although their number fell off gradually with the end of warfare, the principal source of their supply. By the close of the first century it had become more profitable to lease to *coloni* than to keep slaves. Landholding was as much the mark of the gentleman in ancient Rome as it was in the Middle Ages, but in neither age did this distinction extend to those who actually worked the soil.

Industry and Commerce. To say that industry and trade grew under the Empire may be misleading, since they never bulked as large as we would deem essential to the economic well-being of so large an empire. But they did tend to increase, due partly to the growth of the empire itself, partly to the blessings of peace, partly to the success of the emperors in curbing extortion in the provinces on the part of imperial officials. We read of commercial contacts with central Russia, with China and India, and even with Malaya. Emperors such as Claudius (d. 57 A.D.) undertook extensive road-building programs which should have proved a much greater boon to commerce than they did. Actually only purveyors of commodities of small volume and high value made any use of these roads, for which a special license had to be procured. Most goods moved by ship, but the ships were small and slow and sailed only during the summer months. Typical of Roman industrial organization was the small shop, of which an abundance existed in Italy and Gaul in the first century of the Empire. Larger establishments might be found engaged in the production of bronze and metal ware, of pottery, bricks, and textiles. Yet for all its relative activity during the first century, industry never established itself as a major occupation. The majority of both industrial workers and traders remained Syrians and Greeks, even in Italy and Gaul. More serious deterrents to the expansion of industry and commerce were the relative isolation of the rural population, the tendency of great households to become self-sufficient, the low purchasing power of the masses, the absence of patent laws, the illegality of corporations, and the adverse balance of trade suffered by the west, which purchased more from the east than the east wanted in return. Roman industry lacked the incentive to improve its processes or its efficiency, and it never sloughed off its social stigma.

Social Classes. It is usual to distinguish three social classes under the Empire: the senatorial order, the equestrian, and the *populares* or common people. These three represented inheritances from the Republic, and as such, only the first had changed appreciably. The senatorial aristocracy no longer enjoyed the political ascendancy it had exploited under the Republic. It continued, nevertheless, to hold the most important posts in the government, to invest heavily in land, and to engage in financial operations not too conspicuously demeaning. Between its wealth which some senators delighted to display, and its servility to the emperor, the senatorial aristocracy was not a constructive force in Roman society. Neither was the

equestrian class. This class was composed of businessmen, financiers, indus-
trialists, in general of men with wealth but without the sobering traditions
of the senatorial aristocracy to temper its rapaciousness in the search for
greater wealth. Equestrians shared the higher imperial offices with the
senators, the emperor frequently preferring them since they lacked any
tradition of political importance. The *populares* were limited to the city of
Rome. They comprised an assortment of groups: a large number of slaves
whose influence was as hostile to industrial development as it was degrading
to moral life; an increasing number of freedmen or ex-slaves; and freemen.
Many freedmen and freemen had gainful employment of one kind or
another in the city, but an unfortunately large number were forced to take
up the demoralizing life of a client. As such they attached themselves to
some wealthy Roman aristocrat, accompanied him wherever he went, performed odd tasks for him, and eked out an existence from the casual
employment they might find and the pittances their patron might give
them. The emperors kept their potential turbulency in hand by means of
the traditional "bread and circuses." To this melancholy view of the moral
side of Roman society under the Empire, many contemporaries have left
eloquent testimony.

Roman Religion. The people of the early Empire professed the same
confusing variety of religious beliefs as under the late Republic. Most
people dismissed as myths the ancient stories about Jupiter, Mars, and the
other gods in the Roman pantheon, although emperors might still erect
huge edifices in their honor. Even the worship of such peculiarly Roman
divinities as the *lares* and *penates* was generally limited to the rural districts.
The masses preferred to become initiated into one or another of the mystery
cults from the eastern Mediterranean, whose elaborate liturgies, doctrines
of moral regeneration, and promise of a happy hereafter they found more
appealing. These cults had been introduced in the west as early as the third
century B.C. Their great popularity, however, came only with the Empire,
when men and their ideas could circulate more freely about the Roman
world. A new cult, Mithraism, was imported into the west in the first century A.D. and proved a powerful rival to such older mystery religions as
those of Cybele and Isis. Mithraism became Christianity's principal rival in
the third century. Those Romans who were skeptical of all supernatural
existence found a measure of satisfaction in the naturalistic ethics which
Stoicism and Epicureanism preached. A somewhat larger number took refuge
in the escapist idealism of Neoplatonism and Neopythagoreanism. Superstition was rampant during the period of the Empire, and persons of all
classes, from the emperor Marcus Aurelius down to the dullest peasant,
permitted themselves to be duped by the wild claims of astrologers. The
next chapter will consider the most significant development in the realm
of religion during the period of the Empire, that is, the rise of Christianity.

Roman Jurisprudence. To the modern reader Roman law and juris-

prudence present an infinitely more rewarding study than Roman religion.
Here the Roman proved himself capable of making an original contribution to western civilization, as significant in its way as the Greek achievement in the field of philosophy. It is true that Roman law was less a conscious product than a legal accretion due to circumstance, to time, to some
ethical ideas, and to experience. But in Rome's development of a legal
system to whose principles many peoples of the modern world still subscribe, a great deal must be credited to the practical mind of the Roman
and to his pragmatic approach to problems. If something worked and was
reasonable, it was right. With the varied sources of Roman law which
produced an enormous volume of legal literature over the centuries, we
need not presently concern ourselves. (See page 147.) Still we can wonder what gave Roman law its flexibility, its vitality, its reasonableness,
together with those other qualities which led so many different peoples to
accept it. We can, in short, ask why Roman law became so universal. To
two factors in particular may this quality of universality in Roman law be
traced. One was the writings of eminent jurists such as Sulpicius Rufus
and Scaevola of the Republic, of Julian and Papinian of the Empire, whose
opinions were accorded the highest respect in the courts. These jurists
based their interpretation and application of law upon reason, upon equity,
and, to a degree, upon the ethical doctrines of Stoic philosophers. The
Stoics made something of a god out of reason. They argued that the law of
the universe was reason, that all men must live by reason, and that the
same justice must be meted out to all alike since all men are brothers.

The other factor which contributed to the universality of Roman law
was the practice of laying down rules of law which could be applied in
disputes between Romans and non-Romans or between aliens of different
nationality who brought their suits to Roman courts. It was inevitable that
this kind of law, the *ius gentium* or Law of Nations as the Romans called
it, should be based upon reason, more specifically upon a rational compromise between the legal principles and usages of the Romans and those of
non-Romans, notably those of the Greeks. It was similarly inevitable that
the very reasonableness and fairness of this law should force its gradual
assimilation into the body of Roman civil law, especially as citizenship
came to be extended to more and more provincials. Because of this continuing process of adapting foreign legal principles to their own, the
Romans found themselves able to bequeath to posterity a law which was
so universally acceptable only because it had already proved itself universal
in Roman times. (Reading 3)

Roman Literature.   In literature the achievement of the Roman Empire
was second in antiquity only to that of the Greeks. Their inferiority to the
Greeks the Romans themselves were ready to admit. Indeed, it is entirely
possible that the high esteem in which they held Greek literary norms may
have hampered the fuller development of their own potentialities. Though

the greatest master of Latin prose, Cicero, died before Augustus assumed control, distinguished prose writers were not wanting during the first two centuries of the Empire. Livy, the national historian of the Republic, might incur some criticism for his fondness for the state, but none certainly for the literary excellence of the style in which he expressed this. Of an entirely different mold was the historian Tacitus, whose impassioned indictment of the crimes and tyranny of the emperors Tiberius, Nero, and Domitian, retains something of its pungency even in translation. Posterity is also grateful for the unpretentious *Letters* of Pliny the Younger, for he helps reassure us that there were people living in the early second century A.D. who were not greatly different from ourselves. Seneca composed moral essays which are still read and tragedies which are not. The poetry of the early Empire was the best that Rome produced. The greatest single poem was the *Æneid*, Vergil's long epic, descriptive of the legendary founding of Rome. Vergil retained his fame as Rome's leading poet down through the Middle Ages. He was also considered the highest authority in questions of grammar, and his popularity can be used as a criterion of the popularity of classical studies in the Middle Ages. Dante paid him the highest honor in his power when he selected him to be his guide through the *Inferno*. (See page 691.) Horace's odes and particularly his satires continue to attract many modern readers. Ovid's extraordinarily beautiful verses about love and about mythology assured him a popularity which carried through the Middle Ages. Two lesser poets, Martial and Juvenal, set the norms for two literary types, Martial for the epigram, Juvenal for the satire. Several Greek writers enjoyed wide popularity in the west. Chief among these was the prose satirist Lucian and the biographer Plutarch. Probably no writer from antiquity continues to reach more modern readers than the latter through his moral essays and his *Parallel Lives*.

Learning.   While one may compare Latin literature with the best offerings of the Greeks, in the field of pure learning no comparison is possible. The Romans produced no philosopher, no scientist, no mathematician. And Cicero, at least in the field of mathematics, was not at all apologetic over this deficiency, for he commends his fellow Romans that they, unlike the Greeks, limited their study of that science to its strictly practical applications. The best the Romans could do in the field of philosophy was to ponder over what the Greeks had written and to select what they could put to everyday use. Like Cicero, Seneca (d. 65 A.D.) was primarily a moralist. Epicureanism degenerated during the second and third centuries of the Empire into sheer hedonism, although that other philosophy of life which the Romans inherited from the Greeks, Stoicism, attained a level of humanitarianism in the *Meditations* of Marcus Aurelius (Reading 2) far above that preached by its original founder.

The most distinguished names in the field of scholarship during the period of the Empire were those of Greeks. There was Ptolemy, a learned mathematician in his own right, who gathered together the knowledge of the ancient world in the fields of geography and astronomy. Had Ptolemy given his blessing to the heliocentric theory of Aristarchus rather than to the geocentric views of Hipparchus, the world might never have heard of Copernicus and Galileo. Ptolemy's contemporary Galen, another Greek, prepared an encyclopedia of medicine in which he recorded alongside the work of Hippocrates and later Hellenistic physicians a great deal that he himself had learned as a perceptive physician and surgeon. In Pliny the Elder the Romans found their own encyclopedist of scientific information. His *Natural History* embraces an enormous store of information on an astounding variety of subjects. Unfortunately, Pliny was neither critical in his collection of this information nor systematic in its organization. The bulk of the pseudo-science of the Middle Ages can be traced back to his *Natural History*. (Reading 1)

Roman Art. The Romans proved themselves the greatest builders of antiquity. With the Greek sense of what was beautiful, they combined their own genius for what was practical. To erect the enormous structures with which they graced Rome and most of the cities of the empire, they had a huge supply of cheap labor at hand and an inexhaustible quantity of building materials. The Romans were the first to use concrete and also the first to exploit to their fullest extent the engineering possibilities of the arch and vault. They covered the empire with a network of excellent roads; they built aqueducts, sewers, and bridges, some of which continue in use to this day; they erected temples, baths, civic buildings, amphitheatres, and circuses in all the principal cities. The traveler may admire their classical columns almost everywhere in the Mediterranean world, in the excavated city of Palmyra on the edge of the Arabian desert, in North Africa, in Spain, and in France. We shall consider later the influence of the Romans upon early Christian architecture. (See page 619.) In sculpture the Romans did not venture far beyond the Greeks. Most of their work was actually done by Greek artists. But Roman sculpture did achieve real excellence in the fields of portraiture and in historical relief. Finally, there have probably never been homes in the western world more luxurious in their proportions and appointments than those which wealthy Romans erected and which they adorned with sculptures, mosaics, and frescoes.

The Decline of the Roman Empire

The Problem. Such in brief was Roman civilization during approximately the first two centuries of imperial rule, that is, from the reign of

Augustus down to the death of Marcus Aurelius (d. 180 A.D.). Unfortunately, this sketchy survey is apt to be misleading. It suffers the weakness of all summaries which would present in a few paragraphs the civilization of so long a period. Institutions and mores do not remain static for long, and a mere mention of them does not constitute an appreciation. Yet granting the validity of such criticism, the survey will have revealed one striking truth, which is, that Rome was not entirely healthy long before the traditional decline of the third century. This suggests one of the circumstances which renders so complex the problem of Rome's decline. Not all phases of Roman civilization declined at the same time nor at the same rate. Some students maintain, for instance, that southern Italy has never recovered from the ravaging effects of Hannibal's devastation suffered back in the third century B.C. And again, every student of political science must admit that no Roman government ever functioned so effectively and so democratically as did the Roman Republic during that same third century.

Significant Decline before Third Century A.D.   Then there is the moral issue which insists on intruding itself when one speaks of decline. For when we speak of decline, we unconsciously set up criteria of values. Yet are these criteria absolute and do all men accept them? Take Edward Gibbon for example, whose famous *Decline and Fall of the Roman Empire* remains the most widely read history of Rome. Gibbon was an agnostic and probably wrote as one. In any event, he maintained that Christianity was chiefly responsible for the decline and eventual collapse of the Roman Empire, and he, accordingly, mourned its appearance as an unqualified tragedy. Most scholars would hold Gibbon wrong on at least two counts: first, the rise of Christianity had little to do with the collapse of Rome's political power as such; second, Gibbon either conveniently overlooked serious weaknesses which were already sapping the strength of the empire of the second century or he was unaware of them. Roman industry and commerce never developed sufficiently to provide the west with the degree of economic stability enjoyed by the east,—a stability which enabled the east to outlive the west for so many centuries. Nor could agriculture of the first centuries of the Empire be considered a healthy institution, when the most common unit was the large estate farmed by slaves or sharecroppers. Neither could the "bread and circuses" which the emperors were obliged to dispense on a progressively larger scale to keep the huge population of marginally employed Romans quiet, be classified as anything but an unwholesome situation. As a matter of fact, the so-called Good Emperors of the second century, whose epoch Gibbon proclaimed the most glorious in the history of mankind,* earned that title partly because of the extensive relief they

---

* Few scholars today would endorse Gibbon's famous boast: "If a man were called to fix the period in the history of the world during which the condition of the human race was most happy and prosperous, he would without hesitation name that which elapsed from the death of Domitian to the accession of Commodus." (96 A.D. to 180 A.D.)

felt impelled to dole out to homeless children, poverty-stricken farmers, and bankrupt municipalities. By no stretch of the imagination could Roman paganism of the first two centuries of the Empire be judged superior to the continued growth of Christianity in the third and fourth centuries, even though these were centuries of decline in other respects.

Decline in the Arts. Even in the arts the picture of Rome's decline is confused. The literature and secular learning (as opposed to theological) of the third and fourth centuries were distinctly inferior to those of the first and second. Claudian, a Greek, composed unusually beautiful Latin verse, but he could not rise above the emptiness of his theme: the eternity and grandeur of Rome—which were no more or were fast departing. Ausonius is equally uninspiring, except for such rare occasions as when he describes the river and scenery of the Moselle. The poetry of the Christian Prudentius, on the other hand, while not artistically superior to that of Ausonius, reflects the vigor and enthusiasm born of the hope of a new world, not the despair of one that was waning. The one noteworthy prose writer (secular) was the historian Ammianus Marcellinus (Reading 23) who sought unsuccessfully to match the matchless prose of Tacitus (Reading 20), although he did reasonably well in presenting an honest record of the events of the third quarter of the fourth century. In jurisprudence, the writings of eminent jurists such as Papinian and Ulpian forbid the designation of the early third century as one of decline. In architecture, the baths of Caracalla and the basilica of Maxentius demonstrate the continued ability of the Roman engineer to erect impressive structures, even to incorporate in them principles new to the Romans, such as groined vaults and clerestory windows. (See page 620.) Yet a closer look at these structures would reveal the use of less finely hewn stone, of a correspondingly greater amount of mortar, and a lack of finished detail. This last suggests that convincing evidence of decline would be visible in the finer arts of sculpture and painting, and such is the case. The arch of triumph which Constantine erected provides a striking illustration of this decline. In order to embellish his arch of triumph with beautiful sculptures, Constantine's architects found it necessary to remove pieces from earlier buildings.

No System of Succession. Many questions still badger the student who investigates the problem of Rome's decline. As to the immediate, possibly even major, factor which aggravated this decline and brought Rome to the brink of complete collapse, there is little disagreement. That was the failure of the Roman Empire to establish a workable system of imperial succession. As noted above, imperial succession had always been something of a makeshift and one which, accordingly, might at any moment invite the intrusion of the praetorian guard or the army. Where luck had been with Rome during the first and second centuries, except for the year's interlude between the death of Nero and the accession of Vespasian when three short-lived emperors rose and fell, in the third century that luck ran out. Commodus, the degenerate son of Marcus Aurelius, was strangled in 193 A.D., an event which normally could be accounted a capital bit of fortune, except that it reminded the praetorian guard and the provincial armies of their opportunities. In this instance, the praetorian guard was closest at hand and managed to step into the breach first. It set up as the imperial successor an elderly senator named Pertinax, but cut him down again in less than three months when he attempted to introduce economies and discipline into the service. Then it auctioned off the imperial office, but the unfortunate senator who made the highest bid had but three months to enjoy it before he too was murdered. (Reading 5) What precipitated his death was the revolt of several of the provincial armies, which now moved in to determine the matter of succession. The nominee of the troops along the Danube, Septimius Severus (193 A.D. to 211), eventually won out. From now on for almost a hundred years, it was the army which generally controlled the succession.

Greed of the Armies. Army rule would not necessarily have proved disastrous for the state had there been but one Roman army, centrally controlled and administered, to make the decision as to who would succeed. Unfortunately this was not the case. Instead there existed a number of great army corps, quite independent of one another, stationed in different parts of the Empire, as in Syria, along the Danube, the Rhine, and in Britain. Each of these had to be convinced that the new emperor would look with favor upon its particular demands for more pay and less discipline, or it would seek to replace him. This was an assignment few emperors were capable of handling. Economic conditions, as we shall presently see, were most unfavorable, and taxes were already at a confiscatory level. If this emperor proved able to meet the demands of the particular army corps responsible for his accession, almost certainly there would be another army which felt it could do better with its own appointee on the throne. The result would be assassination and civil war. Then when a new emperor would finally emerge from the chaos and destruction, he would find that while the rapaciousness of armies had not slackened, there was now even less revenue available with which to satisfy it. The inevitable would be more civil war. Such was generally the order of political events for much of the third century. From 192 A.D. until 284, thirty-three emperors ascended the throne. Of the eighteen who preceded Diocletian (285 A.D. to 305), seventeen were murdered or executed. Is there any need to look further for the major immediate cause of Rome's decline?

Less Discipline in the Army. The student may ask, if the problem of succession had always been present to vex the Empire, how is it that it was not until the third century that it almost brought about the destruction of the Roman state. The answer to that question lies in the altered character of the Roman army. As a matter of fact, had the army of the third century been the army of the first, the tragic period of the "barrack emperors" from

235 A.D. to 285 would never have happened. Had a well-disciplined army, loyal to the state, replaced a vicious ruler like Caracalla (d. 217) with its own capable general, Rome would have been the gainer. That is how Vespasian (69 A.D. to 79) rose to the emperorship. Yet so thorough and solid were the measures of reform Vespasian introduced and carried through, that he has been called the second founder of the Empire. But this army of the third century was a far cry from Vespasian's legions of the first. Gone was the renowned discipline of the Roman army of the Republic which had fought Hannibal so valiantly. To gain the support of the soldiers, successive emperors had relaxed rules and granted privileges not conducive to high morale. The laborious job of setting up a semi-permanent camp each afternoon, for example, in order to reduce the danger from night attacks, had long since been abandoned, together with the heavy defensive armor and pack which the soldier had carried.

The Army Less Roman. This relaxation of discipline was a reflection of a more ominous change which had come over the Roman army. To put it bluntly, the army was a Roman army only in a narrow sense. Since the time of Augustus, its personnel had been completely transformed. Even Augustus had failed to replace the three legions ambushed by the Germans in the Teutoberg woods in 9 A.D. because of his inability to recruit citizens willing to serve. This difficulty in recruiting had increased with time. The consequence was greater reliance upon noncitizens, first upon noncitizens who had been within the Empire for generations, then upon noncitizens who had but recently crossed the frontier. By the third century the Roman armies were largely Germanic. Even the word *barbarus*, which originally meant barbarian, took on the connotation of soldier. These soldiers had little love for Roman traditions and institutions, and they acknowledged no responsibility for preserving the state. Discovering that they could make and unmake emperors, coddled by emperors like Septimius Severus who admonished his son on his deathbed, "Take care of the army," (Reading 5) they quite naturally concluded that the state was their servant, not the reverse. Such soldiers became a law to themselves. This, then, was the kind of Roman army which felt no compunction at exploiting its power during the third century, even though in so doing it might threaten the very foundations of the state.

Economic Decline. The economic havoc which followed in the wake of the wars of the third century was profound. The movement of goods, already difficult and inconsiderable, almost halted. Wide stretches of the empire lay ravaged and desolate, numerous cities including Lyons, the largest city of Gaul, and Antioch, the largest city of Syria, were in ruins. With no demand for its products, industry withered to where it became provincialized and served only the needs of the immediate area. The absence of competition which accompanied the loss of markets led inevitably to the loss of technical skills and the production of inferior goods.

Agriculture shared in the general collapse of economic life. Caught between the harsh demands of the tax collector on the one hand, the cruelties of war on the other, the farmer found life intolerable. To gain a measure of security, he surrendered his economic freedom and joined the ranks of the sharecroppers on the estates of influential landowners, who could better contend with the tax collector and with the soldiery. Agriculture lost what commercial character it still retained and became a way of life. Large areas, once cultivated by farmers or grazed by their stock, were left depopulated by the war, and either reverted to thicket or were handed over to semi-civilized immigrant Germans.

Debasement and Inflation. Contributing measurably to the economic distress of the third century were rampant inflation and confiscatory taxation. The raising of sufficient revenue to meet the normal needs of government, as we have seen, had always been a formidable task. The frequent and extended wars of the third century made that task now impossible. Yet over and above the larger expenditures these wars entailed, many emperors were pledged to reward their troops with handsome bonuses, while others appreciated the necessity of doing so in order to prevent revolution. Methods, therefore, which had heretofore been employed only on occasion by desperate or unscrupulous emperors, now became common. Debasement of the coinage, for instance, was carried to such lengths that by the middle of the third century ninety-eight percent of the imperial currency had become alloy. Debasement fed the forces of inflation, which in turn completed the ruin of many people already brought to impoverishment by the exorbitant rate of taxation. Taxes, indeed, rose so high as to ruin those classes which could not hide their wealth. This included the small free farmer whose plight we have already noted, and the curial as well. Once the responsibility of the curial to gather the taxes which the municipality had been assessed had been one of simple administrative routine. In the third century it proved his destruction, since deficiencies owing to the government had to be covered by himself.

Demoralization. Morale was low and still falling. The backbone of provincial administration, that is, the municipality, which had nourished civic responsibility and love of Rome, weakened during the second century under stress of bankruptcy and collapsed during the civil wars of the third. An especially ominous sign of the deterioration of morale was provided by the indifference which greeted Caracalla's decree of 212 A.D. extending Roman citizenship to all freemen, the same citizenship which once had drawn the Apostle Paul's boast and which the auxiliaries in Augustus' army had looked forward to as the principal boon of their twenty-five years of long service. Even nature appeared to conspire against mankind. Terrible plagues ravaged the empire in the second and third centuries, with the same horrifying ease and devastating consequences as the more famous Black Death of 1348. (See page 741.) Two scourges in particular might be singled out, the smallpox epidemic of 166 A.D. which the army of Marcus Aurelius brought back with it from the east, and a similar plague which endured for fifteen years around the middle of the third century. Throughout much of the second and third centuries the danger of semicivilized Germans sweeping away life and property was not limited to the frontier areas. Aurelian (270 A.D. to 275) gave orders to fortify Rome since the army could no longer guarantee to hold the Germans beyond the confines of the empire. Occasional famines brought misery and starvation to scattered provinces. A falling birth rate which can be traced back as far as the Good Emperors contributed, with the wars, to a general decline in population and to actual depopulation in certain areas. On many grave markers of the early third century the passer-by might read the disquieting inscription: "This man was the last of his house." All these evils, together with those noted above, exerted a grievously depressing influence upon morale during the late second and third centuries. (Reading 9)

The Empire Rights Itself

Darkness before the Dawn.   These factors and others conspired to bring Rome to her knees in the third century. The century actually opened with some hope of a return to normalcy after the violent deaths of Commodus, Pertinax, and his successor. For the next emperor, Septimius Severus, eliminated the last of his rivals in 197 A.D. and established a powerful, albeit brutal, regime which endured for fourteen years, and a dynasty which lasted another twenty-four. Yet with the assassination of the last of the Severi in 235 A.D., military anarchy ensued and for fifty years spread desolation over the empire. This period, which extended from 235 A.D. to 285, has been called the era of the "barrack emperors." (Reading 6) During these fifty years the army or armies put up their generals as emperors, only to pull them down almost immediately again when they proved too conscious of their imperial responsibilities. That was the fate of all but two emperors, whose deaths from other sources serve to dramatize the foreign peril which menaced the state from without as seriously during these years as did civil war threaten its existence from within. The Goths slew Decius in 251 A.D. in Thrace and annihilated his army; his successor, Valerian, died a prisoner of the Sassanid Persians. Worse was yet to come. A few years later an independent Gallic state arose in the west, while in the east, at Palmyra, the beautiful widow Zenobia set up a short-lived state which included Syria, Asia Minor, and Egypt. Aurelian, the general hailed as emperor by the army in 270, proved himself equal to the crisis. He destroyed the Gallic state and Zenobia's as well, thereby earning for himself the title "Restorer of the World." Yet no sooner had he accomplished this, than he too fell victim to a military conspiracy. Fortunately for Rome, Diocletian shortly after in 285 made himself master of the empire, and with him dawned a new era for Rome.

Diocletian's Military Measures. Diocletian was a rough Dalmatian soldier of humble birth, energetic and resolute, with the foresight to share the administration of the weakening empire with others and the strength of character to command their loyalty. In medieval times his name was execrated for ordering a particularly harsh persecution of the Christians; but students of history are more concerned with the measures he took to rehabilitate the empire. Few of these were actually new with him. The elaborate ceremonials of eastern potentates, which he introduced to lend an awesome atmosphere to his court and enhance his own exalted position, had been employed by several of his immediate predecessors. His most pressing problem was a military one: to bolster the sagging frontier and to re-establish law and order within the empire. To aid him in this work he made a number of wise appointments. He first chose a junior Augustus, Maximian, to direct the pacification of the west. Next he selected two generals, to whom he gave the title Caesar, the one, Galerius, to assist him in the east, the other, Constantius, to support Maximian in the west. Diocletian's most revolutionary step was to move his capital to Nicomedia, to point up the vital importance to the Empire of the east and the greater vulnerability of its frontiers. In fact, it was the peril along the frontier which guided the assistants of Diocletian in their choice of capitals. The western Augustus established headquarters at Milan, the western Caesar at Treves (Trier), in order to better guard the Alpine passes and Rhine respectively. The Caesar in the east established his base at Sirmium near the Danubian frontier. To bolster the northern defenses, Diocletian expanded the army to 450,000 men. To cope with the Persians he developed a powerful cavalry force, and he organized mobile units to handle those German groups which might succeed in breaking through the frontier.

Edict of Prices and Reorganization of Empire. Among Diocletian's reform measures was his famous Edict of Prices (301 A.D.), with which he hoped to halt inflation and stabilize the economy of the empire. The edict attempted to place ceilings on wages, services, and prices. Though it carried the sanction of capital punishment, it was so poorly executed and so inefficiently administered that it proved a complete failure. More successful was Diocletian's reorganization of the empire. In the interest of administrative efficiency, he divided the empire into approximately one hundred provinces, grouped these into thirteen districts called dioceses, and these in turn into four praefectures. The administrative head of each of these districts was the highest civil official in that area, although none of them exercised military authority. Implicit in Diocletian's selection of two Caesars as subordinates to himself and his co-Augustus was the expectation that they would succeed him, which they did. Diocletian retired to his vegetable garden in 305 A.D. and forced Maximian to abdicate with him. Unfortunately, his plan of succession proved as much a failure as his Edict of Prices, although it would have been difficult to devise any better scheme with greater promise under the circumstances.

Caste System. The most oppressive of Diocletian's reform measures were those aimed at raising revenues and procuring the services which the government and army required. How distasteful these proved to the people on the one hand, and how critically essential Diocletian and his successors considered them to the well-being of the state on the other, is attested to by the frequency with which the measures were re-enacted. For the bulk of its revenues the government had traditionally depended upon the land tax. But hard times and high taxes were causing many tenant farmers to throw up their leases and abandon the land, making it impossible for the government to collect the tax assessed against the estates of the large landowners. So in order to assure the latter full production and the treasury its taxes, the government decreed that the tenant farmer and sharecropper must remain on the land. The farmer, in effect, ceased being a free agent. That so revolutionary a measure proved effective is demonstrated by the new meaning the term *colonus* acquired. Originally it meant simply farmer. From the third century, it denoted a farmer who was bound to the soil, one who had lost his ability to bargain and to move.

A similar fate awaited the tradesman and artisan. Such services as transportation or the manufacture of military equipment were as essential to the state as the land tax. They were also just as likely to fall short of requirements because of the same troublesome times. Rather than deal with individual merchants or artisans, which would have been impractical, the government ordered all men who were engaged in certain occupations to become permanent members (*corporati* or *collegiati*) of industrial corporations or colleges. With these corporations the government could more conveniently do business. A third group, the curials, suffered a similar fate. The government had desperate need of the taxes assessed against their municipalities. To prevent them from evading their responsibility to deliver over this tax to the imperial treasury by surrendering their positions, the government froze them in their profession. Thus the larger portion of the empire's population found themselves permanently restricted, and their children after them, to their respective occupations and professions. (Reading 4)

Constantine. Diocletian's successors pursued in general the course he had laid down. His plan of succession worked only once, the first time. Five years after his abdication, there were five rulers, all Augusti. Fortunately imperial rivalry which threatened to reproduce the situation of the third century happily terminated in 324 A.D. when Constantine emerged as sole ruler. After Constantine succession usually went to the son if the family was sufficiently powerful; if not, the army decided who should succeed. Constantine (d. 337) meantime proved the ablest of Diocletian's successors. He was a man of tireless energy and vaulting ambition and he directed the administration of the empire with a vigor which at times bordered on ruthlessness. Constantine gave the empire a sound currency, a gold coin stamped with his own seal. Christian apologists conferred on him the title "Great" because of his legalization of Christianity. Though he has long since lost this title, no single act by any emperor, before or after Constantine, proved so epochal in its consequences as that granting the Christians toleration. (See page 55.) Constantine revealed his statesmanship in his selection of the old Greek city of Byzantium as the site of his new capital. The location was not only a healthful one, but it enjoyed greater advantages with respect to trade and military strength than any other city of the ancient Mediterranean. Constantine strove earnestly to make his capital the "New Rome." He gave it a senate, created festivals similar to those observed in Rome on the Tiber, distributed free grain, erected comparable buildings and amusement centers, and even introduced horse races and their colors from Rome. (Reading 8) Posterity remembers him, however, for beginning a new era, not for extending an old.

Empire Restored But Not in Good Health. While the site of Constantinople proved of the utmost importance in the life of the empire in the east (see page 139), the imperial policy of the emperors of the fourth century contributed significantly to the early death of that empire in the west. For this they cannot be held overly culpable. It is an easy matter to indict as unwise, acts whose lack of wisdom is only revealed by time. To recognize the imprudence of such acts before their evil consequences make it manifest, calls for the highest statesmanship, and these emperors of the fourth century were not geniuses. As noted above, they continued Diocletian's policies for the most part, largely for want of anything better. Of these, Diocletian's military reforms proved least questionable, although the policy of placing increasing reliance upon Germans invited trouble. More insidious in its ultimate consequences was the policy of freezing farmers, artisans, and curials in their jobs. Though some economic stability was surely achieved thereby, it came at the cost of what love and loyalty these elements of the population might have had for the state. As has been stated with considerable cogency, Rome fell to the numerically and culturally inferior Germans because the Roman citizenry did not feel their empire was worth fighting to preserve. What added to their indifference was the growth of a huge, often irresponsible bureaucracy, whose foundations were laid in Diocletian's reform measures. Only one group in the empire, the smallest, was content. This was the class of landed magnates, the powerful landlords who were sufficiently strong to bargain with or to defy the government officials. This group was not strong enough to save the empire.

 READINGS

No. 1. Pliny's *Natural History*

(*The Natural History of Pliny*, tr. Bostock & Riley. London, 1855.)

Bk. II. Ch. 39. It is obvious that there are causes of the seasons and of other things which have been stated, while there are some things which are casual, or of which the reason has not yet been discovered. For who can doubt that summer and winter, and the annual revolution of the seasons are caused by the motion of the stars. As therefore the nature of the sun is understood to influence the temperature of the year, so each of the other stars has its specific power, which produces its appropriate effects. Some abound in a fluid retaining its liquid state, others, in the same fluid concreted into hoar frost, compressed into snow, or frozen into hail; some are prolific in winds, some in heat, some in vapours, some in dew, some in cold. . . .

Ch. 40. Who is there that does not know that the vapour of the sun is kindled by the rising of the Dog-star? The most powerful effects are felt on the earth from this star. When it rises, the seas are troubled, the wines in our cellars ferment, and stagnant waters are set in motion. There is a wild beast, named by the Egyptians Oryx, which, when the star rises, is said to stand opposite to it, to look steadfastly at it, and then to sneeze, as if it were worshiping it. There is no doubt that dogs, during the whole of this period, are peculiarly disposed to become rabid.

Ch. 41. There is moreover a peculiar influence in the different degrees of certain signs, as in the autumnal equinox, and also in the winter solstice, when we find that a particular star is connected with the state of the weather. It is not so much the recurrence of showers and storms, as of various circumstances, which act both upon animals and vegetables. Some are planet-struck, and others, at stated times, are affected in the bowels, the sinews, the head, or the intellect. The olive, the white poplar, and the willow turn their leaves round at the summer solstice. The herb pulegium [fleabane], when dried and hanging up in a house, blossoms on the very day of the winter solstice, and bladders burst in consequence of their being distended with air. One might wonder at this, did we not observe every day, that the plant named heliotrope always looks towards the setting sun, and is, at all hours, turned towards him, even when he is obscured by clouds. It is certain that the bodies of oysters and of whelks [cockles], and of shell-fish generally, are increased in size and and again diminished by the influence of the moon. Certain accurate observers have found out, that the entrails of the field-mouse correspond in number to the moon's age, and that the very small animal, the ant, feels the power of this luminary, always resting from her labours at the change of the moon. . . .

Ch. 43. It cannot therefore be denied, that fire proceeding from the stars which are above the clouds, may fall on them, as we frequently observe on serene evenings, and that the air is agitated by the impulse, as darts when they are hurled whiz through the air. And when it arrives at the cloud, a discordant kind of vapour is produced, as when hot iron is plunged into water, and a wreath of smoke is evolved. Hence arise squalls. And if wind or vapour be struggling in the cloud, thunder is discharged; if it bursts out with a flame, there is a thunderbolt; if it be long in forcing out its way, it is simply a flash of lightning. By the latter the cloud is simply rent, by the former it is shattered. Thunder is produced by the stroke given to the condensed air, and hence it is that the fire darts from the chinks of the clouds. It is possible also that the vapour, which has risen from the earth, being repelled by the stars, may produce thunder, when it is pent up in a cloud; nature restraining the sound whilst the vapour is struggling to escape, but when it does escape, the sound bursting forth, as is the case with bladders that are distended with air. . . .

Ch. 45. But there is a great difference between a gale and a wind. The former are uniform and appear to rush forth; they are felt, not in certain spots only, but over whole countries, not forming breezes or squalls, but violent storms. Whether they be produced by the constant revolution of the world and the opposite motion of the stars, or whether they both of them depend on the generative spirit of the nature of things, wandering, as it were, up and down in her womb, or whether the air be scourged by the irregular strokes of the wandering stars, or the various projections of their rays, or whether they, each of them, proceed from their own stars, among which are those that are nearest to us, or whether they descend from those that are fixed in the heavens, it is manifest that they are all governed by a law of nature, which is not altogether unknown, although it be not completely ascertained.

Ch. 46. More than twenty old Greek writers have published their observations upon this subject. And this is the more remarkable, seeing that there is so much discord in the world, and that it is divided into different kingdoms, that is into separate members, that there should have been so many who have paid attention to these subjects, which are so difficult to investigate. Especially when we consider the wars and the treachery which everywhere prevail; while pirates, the enemies of the human race, have possession of all the modes of communication, so that, at this time, a person may acquire more correct information about a country from the writings of those who have never been there, than from the inhabitants themselves. Whereas, at this day, in the blessed peace which we enjoy, under a prince who so greatly encourages the advancement of the arts, no new inquiries are set on foot, nor do we even make ourselves thoroughly master of the discoveries of the ancients. Not that there were greater rewards held out, from the advantages being distributed to a greater number of persons, but that there were more individuals who diligently scrutinized these matters, with no other prospect but that of benefiting posterity. It is that the manners of men are degenerated, not that the advantages are diminished. All the seas, as many as there are, being laid open, and a hospitable reception being given us at every shore, an immense number of people undertake voyages; but it is for the sake of gain, not of science. Nor does this understanding, which is blinded and bent only on avarice, perceive that this very thing might be more safely done by means of science. Seeing, therefore, that there are so many thousands of persons on the seas, I will treat of the winds with more minuteness than perhaps might otherwise appear suitable to my undertaking.

No. 2. The *Meditations* of Marcus Aurelius

(*The Thoughts of Marcus Aurelius*, tr. George Long. London, 1903.)

Sect. 1. From my grandfather Verus [I learned] good morals and the government of my temper. From the reputation and remembrance of my father, modesty and a manly character. From my mother, piety and beneficence, and abstinence, not only from evil deeds, but even from evil thoughts; and further, simplicity in my way of living, far removed from the habits of the rich. From my great-grandfather, not to have frequented public schools, and to have had good teachers at home, and to know that on such things a man should spend liberally. From my governor, to be neither of the green nor of the blue party at the games in the Circus, nor a partizan either of the Parmularius or the Scutarius at the gladiators' fights; from him too I learned endurance of labour, and to want little, and to work with my own hands, and not to meddle with other people's affairs, and not to be ready to listen to slander.

From Diognetus, not to busy myself about trifling things, and not to give credit to what was said by miracle-workers and jugglers about incantations and the driving away of daemons and such things; and not to breed quails [for fighting], nor to give myself up passionately to such things; and to endure freedom of speech; and to have become intimate with philosophy; and to have been a hearer, first of Bacchius, then of Tandasis and Marcianus; and to have written dialogues in my youth; and to have desired a plank bed and skin, and whatever else of the kind belongs to the Grecian discipline. . . .

From Apollonius I learned freedom of will and undeviating steadiness of purpose; and to look to nothing else, not even for a moment, except to reason; and to be always the same, in sharp pains, on the occasion of the loss of a child, and in long illness; and to see clearly in a living example that the same man can be both most resolute and yielding, and not peevish in giving his instruction; and to have had before my eyes a man who clearly considered his experience and his skill in expounding philosophical principles as the smallest of his merits; and from him I learned how to receive from friends what are esteemed favours, without being either humbled by them or letting them pass unnoticed.

Sect. II. Begin the morning by saying to thyself, I shall meet with the busybody, the ungrateful, arrogant, deceitful, envious, unsocial. All these things happen to them by reason of their ignorance of what is good and evil. But I who have seen the nature of the good and it is beautiful, and of the bad that it is ugly, and the nature of him who does wrong, that it is akin to me, not [only] of the same blood or seed, but that it participates in [the same] intelligence and [the same] portion of the divinity, I can neither be injured by any of them, for no one can fix on me what is ugly, nor can I be angry with my kinsman, nor hate him. For we are made for co-operation, like feet, like hands, like eyelids, like the rows of the upper and lower teeth. To act against one another then is contrary to nature; and it is acting against one another to be vexed and to turn away. . . .

Since it is possible that thou mayest depart from life this very moment, regulate every act and thought accordingly. But to go away from among men, if there are gods, is not a thing to be afraid of, for the gods will not involve thee in evil; but if indeed they do not exist, or if they have no concern about human affairs, what is it to me to live in a universe devoid of gods or devoid of providence? But in truth they do exist, and they do care for human things, and they have put all the means in man's power to enable him not to fall into real evils. And as to the rest, if there was anything evil, they would have provided for this also, that it should be altogether in a man's power not to fall into it. Now that which does not make a man worse, how can it make a man's life worse? But neither through ignorance, nor having the knowledge, but not the power to guard against or correct these things, is it possible that the nature of the universe has overlooked them; now is it possible that it has made so great a mistake, either through want of power or want of skill, that good and evil should happen indiscriminately to the good and the bad. But death certainly, and life, honour and dishonour, pain and pleasure, all these things equally happen to good men and bad, being things which make us neither better nor worse. Therefore they are neither good nor evil.

Sect. III. We ought to consider not only that our life is daily wasting away and a smaller part of it is left, but another thing also must be taken into the account, that if a man should live longer, it is quite uncertain whether the understanding will still continue sufficient for the comprehension of things, and retain the power of contemplation which strives to acquire the knowledge of the divine and the human. For if he shall begin to fall into dotage, perspiration and nutrition and imagination and appetite, and whatever else there is of the kind, will not fail; but the power of making use of ourselves, and filling up the measure of our duty, and clearly separating all appearances, and considering whether a man should now depart from life, and whatever else of the kind absolutely requires a disciplined reason, all this is already extinguished. We must make haste then, not only because we are daily nearer to death, but also because the conception of things and the understanding of them cease first.

Sect. V. In the morning when thou risest unwillingly, let this thought be present—I am rising to the work of a human being. Why then am I dissatisfied if I am going to do the things for which I exist and for which I was brought into the world? Or have I been made for this, to lie in the bed-clothes and keep myself warm?—But this is more pleasant—Dost thou exist then to take thy pleasure, and not all for action or exertion? Dost thou not see the little plants, the little birds, the ants, the spiders, the bees working together to put in order their several parts of the universe? And art thou unwilling to do the work of a human being, and dost thou not make haste to do that which is according to thy nature?—But it is necessary to take rest also—It is necessary: however nature has fixed bounds to this too: she has fixed bounds both to eating and drinking, and yet thou stoppest short of what thou canst do. So thou lovest not thyself, for if thou didst, thou wouldst love thy nature and her will. . . .

No. 3. Roman jurisprudence

(*The Institutes of Gaius*, tr. James Muirhead. Edinburgh, 1880.)

1. All peoples that are under the government of laws and customs use in part their own law, in part what is common to mankind; for what each people has established on its own account is peculiar to itself, and is called its civil law, in the sense of being the proper law of the particular state or *civitas;* whereas what its natural reasonableness has caused to be received by mankind generally is observed by all peoples alike, and is called the law of nations,—that, as it were, which all nations make use of. The Roman people, therefore, employs a body of law which is partly its own, partly common to all men. What each branch includes will be explained in due course.

2. The laws of the Roman people are the product of *leges* [i.e. comitial enactments], plebiscits, senatusconsults, imperial constitutions, edicts of those enjoying the *ius edicendi*, and responses of the jurisprudents. 3. A *lex* is a law enacted and established by the whole body of the people; a plebiscit, one enacted and established by its plebeian members. The difference between *plebs* and *populus* is this,—that the latter denotes the whole mass of the citizens, patricians included, whereas the former denotes only the citizens who are not patricians. It was because of this distinction that of old the patricians maintained that plebiscits were not binding upon them, because enacted without their authorisation. But in the course of time the Hortensian law was passed, declaring that plebiscits should be of force universally; and thus they were put on a par with *leges.* 4. A senatusconsult is a law enacted and established by the senate, and, although at one time doubted, has all the force of statute. 5. An imperial constitution is what the emperor has established by decree, edict, or letter. It has never been disputed that such a constitution has the full force of a *lex;* for it is by a *lex* that the emperor is invested with the *imperium.* 6. The *ius edicendi* [or right to publish edicts] is an attribute of the magistrates of the Roman people. Nowhere has it a more ample exponent than in the edicts of the two praetors, the urban and the peregrin, whose jurisdiction is exercised in the provinces by the provincial governors; as also in that of the curule aediles, whose jurisdiction is exercised in the popular provinces by the quaestor: (there are no quaestors sent to the imperial provinces, where, consequently, the aeditilian edict is not propounded. 7. The responses of the jurisconsults are the decisions and opinions of individuals licensed to

lay down the law. If those consulted be unanimous, their decision or opinion has the force of statute; but if they differ, the judge may adopt any of their opinions he pleases; so it is declared in a rescript of our late emperor Hadrian's.

8. The whole body of law in use amongst us relates either to persons, things or actions. Let us first turn our attention to persons.

9. The primary division of the law of persons is this,—that all men are either free or slave. 10. Next, free men are either *ingenui* (freeborn) or *libertini* (freedmen). 11. *Ingenui* are those born free, *libertini* those manumitted from lawful slavery. 12. Again, of *libertini* or freedmen there are three classes; for they may be either Roman citizens, or latins, or classed with the dediticians. Let us deal with these separately, beginning with the last. 13. By the Aelia-Sentian law it is provided in regard to slaves who have been put in chains or branded by their masters by way of punishment, or who have been put to the torture on account of some offence of which they have been eventually convicted, or who have been given up to fight in the arena either with men or beasts, or who have been committed either to a gladiatorial training school or to prison, that if afterwards they be manumitted either by the owner who has dealt with them or by a later one, they shall as freemen be of the same condition as the *peregrini dediticii*. 14. Those are called *peregrini dediticii* who, having taken up arms and made war against the Roman people and been vanquished, have afterwards unconditionally surrendered. 15. Slaves disgraced in any of the ways described, no matter how or at what age they may have been manumitted, and even though their manumitter may have held them in full ownership [i.e. both bonitarian and quiritarian], can never become either Roman citizens or latins, but must ever be classed as dediticians. 16. If, however, no such disgrace attach to a slave, he becomes on manumission sometimes a Roman citizen, sometimes a latin. 17. He becomes a Roman citizen in whose person these three requisites concur,—that he is above thirty years old, that he is held by his owner on quiritarian title, and that he is freed by a legally recognized mode of manumission, i.e. by *vindicta*, census, or testament; if any of these requisites fail he will be a latin.

No. 4. The principle of hereditary compulsory service

(*Codex Theodosianus*, ed. Gustavus Haenel. Bonn, 1842. Translation.)

Emperors Arcadius and Honorius to Eutychianus, Praetorian Prefect:
    . . . we command that curials be warned under threat of punishment not to flee or desert their municipalities (*civitates*) in order to live in the

country. Any farm which they may prefer to the city they should know will be confiscated to the fisc, and they will be deprived of that law to whose cause they showed themselves impious by fleeing their homes. 396 A.D. (p. 1307)

Emperor Constantine to the Provincials:
   Coloni who meditate flight shall be reduced to slavery and be bound by chains, so that the duties which are suited to freemen they will be compelled to perform as a punishment of their servile condemnation. 332 A.D. (p. 471)

Emperors Honorius and Theodosius to Palmatus, Prefect of the City:
   It is the responsibility of the governors of the provinces that members of the gilds of the city of Rome who have crossed over into foreign parts be forced to return, and that they perform those services which ancient custom has ordained. 412 A.D. (p. 1375)

No. 5. Degradation of the imperial office

(*Dio's Roman History*, IX, tr. Earnest Cary. Reprinted by permission of the publishers from the Loeb Classical Library. Cambridge, Mass.: Harvard University Press, 1926.)

(Pp. 141-143) The soldiers on seeing him (Pertinax) were at first abashed, all save one, and kept their eyes on the ground, and they thrust their swords back into their scabbards; but that one man leaped forward, exclaiming, "The soldiers have sent you this sword," and forthwith fell upon him and wounded him. Then his comrades no longer held back, but struck down their emperor together with Eclectus. The latter alone had not deserted him, but defended him as best he could even wounding several of his assailants; hence I, who felt that even before that he had shown himself an excellent man, now thoroughly admired him. The soldiers cut off the head of Pertinax and fastened it on a spear, glorying in the deed. Thus did Pertinax, who undertook to restore everything in a moment, come to his end. He failed to comprehend, though a man of wide practical experience, that one cannot with safety reform everything at once, and that the restoration of a state, in particular, requires both time and wisdom. He had lived sixty-seven years, lacking four months and three days, and had reigned eighty-seven days.
   When the fate of Pertinax was noised about, some ran to their homes and others to those of the soldiers, all taking thought for their own safety.

But Sulpicianus, who had been sent by Pertinax to the camp to set matters in order there, remained on the spot, and intrigued to get himself appointed emperor. Meanwhile Didius Julianus, at once an insatiate money-getter and a wanton spendthrift, who was always eager for revolution and hence had been exiled by Commodus to his native city of Mediolanum (Milan), now, when he heard of the death of Pertinax, hastily made his way to the camp, and, standing at the gates of the enclosure, made bids to the soldiers for the rule over the Romans. Then ensued a most disgraceful business and one unworthy of Rome. For, just as if it had been in some market or auction-room, both the City and its entire empire were auctioned off. The sellers were the ones who had slain their emperor, and the would-be buyers were Sulpicianus and Julianus, who vied to outbid each other, one from the inside, the other from the outside. They gradually raised their bids up to twenty thousand sesterces per soldier. Some of the soldiers would carry word to Julianus, "Sulpicianus offers so much; how much more do you make it?" And to Sulpicianus in turn, "Julianus promises so much; how much do you raise him?" Sulpicianus would have won the day, being inside and being prefect of the city and also the first to name the figure twenty thousand, had not Julianus raised his bid no longer by a small amount but by five thousand at one time, both shouting it in a loud voice and also indicating the amount with his fingers. So the soldiers, captivated by this excessive bid and at the same time fearing that Sulpicianus might avenge Pertinax (an idea that Julianus put into their heads), received Julianus inside and declared him emperor.

(Pp. 269-273) On another occasion, when both were riding forward to meet the Caledonians, in order to receive their arms and discuss the details of the truce, Antoninus [Caracalla] attempted to kill his father outright with his own hand. They were proceeding on horseback, Severus also being mounted, in spite of the fact that he had somewhat strained his feet as the result of an infirmity, and the rest of the army was following; the enemy's force were likewise spectators. At this juncture, while all were proceeding in silence and in order, Antoninus reined in his horse and drew his sword, as if he were going to strike his father in the back. But the others who were riding with them, upon seeing this, cried out, and so Severus turned at their shout and saw the sword, yet he did not utter a word, but ascended the tribunal, finished what he had to do, and returned to headquarters. Then he summoned his son, together with Papinian and Castor, ordered a sword to be placed within easy reach, and upbraided the youth for having dared to do such a thing at all and especially for having been on the point of committing so monstrous a crime in the sight of all, both the allies and the enemy. And finally he said: "Now if you really want to slay me, put me out of the way here; for you are strong, while I am an old man and prostrate. For, if you do not shrink from the deed, but hesitate to murder me with your own hands, there is Papinian, the prefect, standing beside you, whom you can order to slay me; for surely he will do anything that you command, since you are virtually emperor." Though he spoke in this fashion, he nevertheless did Antoninus no harm, and that in spite of the fact that he had often blamed Marcus for not putting Commodus quietly out of the way and that he had himself often threatened to act thus toward his son. Such threats, however, were always uttered under the influence of anger, whereas on the present occasion he allowed his love for his offspring to outweigh his love for his country; and yet in doing so he betrayed his other son, for he well knew what would happen.

When the inhabitants of the island again revolted, he summoned the soldiers and ordered them to invade the rebels' country, killing everybody they met; and he quoted these words:

> Let no one escape sheer destruction,
> No one our hands, not even the babe in the womb of the mother,
> If it be male, let it nevertheless not escape sheer destruction

When this had been done, and the Caledonians had joined the revolt of the Maeatae, he began preparing to make war upon them in person. While he was thus engaged, his sickness carried him off on the fourth of February, not without some help, they say, from Antoninus. At all events, before Severus died, he is reported to have spoken thus to his sons (I give his exact words without embellishment): "Be harmonious, enrich the soldiers, and scorn all other men." After this his body, arrayed in military garb, was placed upon a pyre, and as a mark of honour the soldiers and his sons ran about it; and as for the soldiers' gifts, those who had things at hand to offer as gifts threw them upon it, and his sons applied the fire. Afterwards his bones were put in an urn of purple stone, carried to Rome, and deposited in the tomb of the Antonines. It is said that Severus sent for the urn shortly before his death, and after feeling of it, remarked: "Thou shalt hold a man that the world could not hold."

No. 6. The "barrack emperors"

(*Scriptores Historiae Augustae*, III, tr. David Magie. Reprinted by permission of the publishers from the Loeb Classical Library. Cambridge, Mass.: Harvard University Press, 1932.)

The Thirty Pretenders by Trebellius Pollio (pp. 65-66)

After having written many books in the style of neither an historian nor a scholar but only a layman, we have now reached the series of years in which the thirty pretenders (*ca.* A.D. 258-261) arose—the years when the Empire was ruled by Gallienus and Valerian (A.D. 253-268), when Valerian was busied with the great demands of the Persian War and Gallienus, as will be shown in the proper place, was held in contempt not only by men but by women as well. But since so obscure were these men, who flocked in from divers parts of the world to seize the imperial power, that not much concerning them can be either related by scholars or demanded of them, and since all those historians who have written in Greek or in Latin have passed over some of them without dwelling even on their names, and, finally, since certain details related about them by many have varied so widely, I have therefore gathered them all into a single book, and that a short one, especially as it is evident that much concerning them has already been told in the Lives of Valerian and Gallienus and need not be repeated here.

Regalianus (pp. 85-91)

It was the public destiny that in the time of Gallienus whosoever could, sprang up to seize the imperial power. And so Regalianus, who held the command in Illyricum, was declared emperor, the prime movers being the Moesians, who had previously been defeated with Ingenuus and on whose kinsmen Gallienus had vented his anger severely. He, indeed, performed many brave deeds against the Sarmatians, but nevertheless, at the instigation of the Roxolani and with the consent of the soldiers and the provincials, who feared that Gallienus might, on a second occasion, act even more cruelly, he was put to death.

It may perhaps seem a matter for wonder if I relate the origin of his rule, for it was all because of a notable jest that he gained the royal power. For when some soldiers were dining with him and a certain acting-tribune arose and said, "Whence shall we suppose that Regalianus gets his name?" another replied at once, "I suppose from his regal power." Then a schoolmaster who was present among them began, as it seemed, to decline grammatically, saying "Rex, regis, regi, Regalianus," whereupon among the soldiers—a class of men who are quick to express what they have in mind—one cried out, "So, then, can he be regal?" another, "So, then, can he hold regal sway over us?" and again another, "God has given you a regent's name." Why should I then say more? The next day after these words were spoken, on going forth in the morning he was greeted as emperor by the front-line troops. Thus what was offered to others through daring or reasoned choice was offered to him through a clever jest.

It cannot, indeed, be denied that he had always won approbation in warfare and had long been suspected by Gallienus because he seemed worthy to rule; he was, moreover, a Dacian by birth and a kinsman, so it was said, of Decebalus himself. . . .

It was not, indeed, from Gallienus that Regalianus received his promotion, but from his father, Valerian, as did also Claudius, Macrianus, Ingenuus, Postumus, and Aureolus, who all were slain while they held the imperial power, although they deserved to hold it. It was, moreover, a matter for marvel in Valerian as emperor, that all who were appointed commanders by him, afterwards, by the voice of the soldiers, obtained the imperial rule, so that it is clear that the aged emperor, in choosing the generals of the commonwealth, was, in fact, such an one as the felicity of Rome—could it only have been permitted by fate to continue under a worthy prince—ever required. Oh that it might have been possible either for those who seized the imperial power to rule for a longer time, or for this man's son to rule less long, that somehow our commonwealth might have kept itself in its proper position! But Fortune claimed for herself too much indulgence, when with Valerian she took away our righteous princes, and preserved Gallienus for the commonwealth longer than was meet.

The Deified Aurelian by Flavius Vopiscus of Syracuse
(pp. 233-237, 257-263)

Aurelian, however, since he wished, by massing his forces together, to meet all the enemy at once, suffered such a defeat near Placentia that the empire of Rome was almost destroyed. This peril, in fact, was caused by the cunning and perfidy of the barbarians' mode of attack. For, being unable to meet him in open battle, they fell back into the thickest forests, and thus as evening came on they routed our forces. And, indeed, if the power of the gods, after the Sibylline Books had been consulted and the sacrifices performed, had not confounded the barbarians by means of certain prodigies and heaven-sent visions, there would have been no victory for Rome.

When the war with the Marcomanni was ended, Aurelian, over-violent by nature, and now filled with rage, advanced to Rome eager for the revenge which the bitterness of the revolts had prompted. Though at other times a most excellent man, he did, in fact, employ his power too much like a tyrant, for in slaying the leaders of the revolts he used too bloody a method of checking what would have been cured by milder means. For he even killed some senators of noble birth, though the charges against them were trivial and could have been held in disdain by a more lenient prince, and they were attested either by a single witness or by one who was himself trivial or held in but light esteem. Why say more? By the blow of a graver ill-repute he then marred that rule which had previously been great and of which high hopes were cherished, and not without reason. Then men ceased to love and began to fear an excellent prince, some asserting that such an emperor should be hated and not desired, others that he was a good physician indeed, but the methods he used for healing were bad.

Then, since all that happened made it seem possible that some such thing might occur again, as had happened under Gallienus, after asking advice from the senate, he extended the walls of the city of Rome. . . .

And so Aurelian, now ruler over the entire world, having subdued both the East and the Gauls, and victor in all lands, turned his march toward Rome, that he might present to the gaze of the Romans a triumph over both Zenobia and Tetricus, that is, over both the East and the West.

It is not without advantage to know what manner of triumph Aurelian had, for it was a most brilliant spectacle. There were three royal chariots, of which the first, carefully wrought and adorned with silver and gold and jewels, had belonged to Odaenathus, the second, also wrought with similar care, had been given to Aurelian by the king of the Persians, and the third Zenobia had made for herself, hoping in it to visit the city of Rome. And this hope was not unfulfilled; for she did, indeed, enter the city in it, but vanquished and led in triumph. There was also another chariot, drawn by four stags and said to have once belonged to the king of the Goths. In this —so many have handed down to memory—Aurelian rode up to the Capitol, purposing there to slay the stags, which he had captured along with this chariot and then vowed, it was said, to Jupiter Best and Greatest. There advanced, moreover, twenty elephants, and two hundred tamed beasts of divers kinds from Libya and Palestine, which Aurelian at once presented to private citizens, that the privy-purse might not be burdened with the cost of their food; furthermore, there were led along in order four tigers and also giraffes and elks and other such animals, also eight hundred pairs of gladiators besides the captives from the barbarian tribes. There were Indians, Bactrians, Hiberians, Saracens, and Persians, all bearing their gifts; there were Goths, Alans, Roxolani, Sarmatians, Franks, Suebians, Vandals and Germans—all captive, with their hands bound fast. There also advanced among them certain men of Palmyra, who had survived its fall, the foremost of the State, and Egyptians, too, because of their rebellion. There were led along also ten women, who, fighting in male attire, had been captured among the Goths after many others had fallen; these a placard declared to be of the race of the Amazons—for placards were borne before all, displaying the names of their nations. In the procession was Tetricus also, arrayed in scarlet cloak, a yellow tunic, and Gallic trousers, and with him his son, whom he had proclaimed in Gaul as emperor. And there came Zenobia, too, decked with jewels and in golden chains, the weight of which was borne by others. There were carried aloft golden crowns presented by all the cities, made known by placards carried aloft. Then came the Roman people itself, the flags of the guilds and the camps, the mailed cuirassiers, the wealth of the kings, the entire army, and, lastly, the senate (albeit somewhat sadly, since they saw senators, too, being led in triumph)—all adding much to the splendor of the procession. Scarce did they reach the

Capitol by the ninth hour of the day, and when they arrived at the Palace it was late indeed. On the following days amusements were given to the populace, plays in the theatres, races in the Circus, wild-beast hunts, gladiatorial fights and also a naval battle.

No. 7. A Christian view of Diocletian and Constantine

(Lactantius' *On the Manner in Which the Persecutors Died. The Ante-Nicene Fathers*, VII. New York, 1926, pp. 303-304, 318.)

While Diocletian, that author of ill, and deviser of misery, was ruining all things, he could not withhold his insults, not even against God. This man, by avarice partly, and partly by timid counsels, overturned the Roman empire. For he made choice of three persons to share the government with him; and thus, the empire having been quartered, armies were multiplied, and each of the four princes strove to maintain a much more considerable military force than any sole emperor had done in times past. There began to be fewer men who paid taxes than there were who received wages; so that the means of the husbandmen being exhausted by enormous impositions, the farms were abandoned, cultivated grounds became woodland, and universal dismay prevailed. Besides, the provinces were divided into minute portions, and many presidents and multitude of inferior officers lay heavy on each territory, and almost on each city. There were also many stewards of different degrees, and deputies of presidents. Very few civil causes came before them: but there were condemnations daily, and forfeitures frequently inflicted; taxes on numberless commodities, and those not only often repeated, but perpetual, and, in exacting them, intolerable wrongs.

Whatever was laid on for the maintenance of the soldiery might have been endured; but Diocletian, through his insatiable avarice, would never allow the sums of money in his treasury to be diminished: he was constantly heaping together extraordinary aids and free gifts, that his original hoards might remain untouched and inviolable. He also, when by various extortions he had made all things exceedingly dear, attempted by an ordinance to limit their prices. Then much blood was shed for the veriest trifles; men were afraid to expose aught to sale, and the scarcity became more excessive and grievous than ever, until, in the end, the ordinance, after having proved destructive to multitudes, was from mere necessity abrogated. To this there were added a certain endless passion for building, and on that account, endless exactions from the provinces for furnishing wages to labourers and artificers, and supplying carriages and whatever else was requisite to the works which he projected. Here public halls, there a circus, here a mint, and there a workhouse for making implements of war; in one place a habitation for his empress, and in another for his daughter. Presently a great part of the city was quitted, and all men removed with their wives and children, as from a town taken by enemies; and when those buildings were completed, to the destruction of whole provinces, he said, "They are not right, let them be done on another plan." Then they were to be pulled down, or altered, to undergo perhaps a future demolition. By such folly was he continually endeavouring to equal Nicomedia with the city Rome in magnificence. . . .

But the other Maximian [Galerius], chosen by Diocletian for his son-in-law, was worse, not only than those two princes whom our own times have experienced, but worse than all the bad princes of former days. In this wild beast there dwelt a native barbarity and a savageness foreign to Roman blood; and no wonder, for his mother was born beyond the Danube, and it was an inroad of the Carpi that obliged her to cross over and take refuge in New Dacia. The form of Galerius corresponded with his manners. Of stature tall, full of flesh, and swollen to a horrible bulk of corpulency; by his speech, gestures, and looks, he made himself a terror to all that came near him. His father-in-law, too, dreaded him excessively. The cause was this. Narseus, king of the Persians, emulating the example set him by his grandfather Sapores, assembled a great army, and aimed at becoming master of the eastern provinces of the Roman empire. Diocletian, apt to be low-spirited and timorous in every commotion, and fearing a fate like that of Valerian, would not in person encounter Narseus, but he sent Galerius by the way of Armenia, while he himself halted in the eastern provinces, and anxiously waited the event. It is the custom amongst the barbarians to take everything that belongs to them into the field. Galerius laid an ambush for them, and easily overthrew men embarrassed with the multitude of their followers and with their baggage. Having put Narseus to flight, and returned with much spoil, his own pride and Diocletian's fears were greatly increased. For after this victory he rose to such a pitch of haughtiness as to reject the appellation of Caesar; and when he heard that appellation in letters addressed to him, he cried out, with a stern look and terrible voice, "How long am I to be Caesar?" Then he began to act extravagantly, insomuch that as if he had been a second Romulus, he wished to pass for and to be called the offspring of Mars; and that he might appear the issue of a divinity, he was willing that his mother Romula should be dishonoured with the name of adulteress. But, not to confound that chronological order of events, I delay the recital of his actions; for indeed afterwards, when Galerius got the title of emperor, his father-in-law having been divested of the imperial purple, he became altogether outrageous, and of unbounded arrogance.

While by such a conduct, and with such associates, Diocles—for that was the name of Diocletian before he attained sovereignty—occupied himself in subverting the commonweal, there was no evil which his crimes did not deserve: nevertheless he reigned most prosperously, as long as he forbore to defile his hands with the blood of the just; and what cause he had for persecuting them, I come now to explain. . . .

And now a civil war broke out between Constantine and Maxentius. Although Maxentius kept himself within Rome, because the soothsayers had foretold that if he went out of it he should perish, yet he conducted the military operations by able generals. In forces he exceeded his adversary; for he had not only his father's army, which deserted from Severus, but also his own, which he had lately drawn together out of Mauritania and Italy. They fought, and the troops of Maxentius prevailed. At length Constantine, with steady courage and a mind prepared for every event, led his whole forces to the neighborhood of Rome, and encamped them opposite to the Milvian bridge. The anniversary of the reign of Maxentius approached, that is, the sixth of the kalends of November, and the fifth year of his reign was drawing to an end.

Constantine was directed in a dream to cause the heavenly sign to be delineated on the shields of his soldiers, and so to proceed to battle. He did as he had been commanded, and he marked on their shields the letter X, with a perpendicular line drawn through it and turned round thus at the top ☧, being the cipher of CHRIST. Having this sign, his troops stood to arms. The enemies advanced, but without their emperor, and they crossed the bridge. The armies met, and fought with the utmost exertions of valour, and firmly maintained their ground. In the meantime a sedition arose at Rome, and Maxentius was reviled as one who had abandoned all concern for the safety of the commonweal; and suddenly, while he exhibited the Circensian games on the anniversary of his reign, the people cried with one voice, "Constantine cannot be overcome!" Dismayed at this, Maxentius burst from the assembly, and having called some senators together, ordered the Sibylline books to be searched. In them it was found that:—"On the same day the enemy of the Romans should perish." Led by this response to the hopes of victory, he went to the field. The bridge in his rear was broken down. At the sight of that the battle drew hotter. The hand of the Lord prevailed, and the forces of Maxentius were routed. He fled towards the broken bridge; but the multitude pressing on him, he was driven headlong into the Tiber.

No. 8. Constantinople, the "New Rome"

(Sozomen's *Ecclesiastical History. A Select Library of Nicene and Post-Nicene Fathers*, II. New York, 1890.)

Bk. II. Ch. III. The emperor [Constantine], always intent on the advancement of religion, erected the most beautiful temples to God in every place, particularly in metropolises, such as Nicomedia in Bithynia, Antioch on the river Orontes, and Byzantium. He greatly improved this latter city, and constituted it the equal of Rome in power, and participation in the government; for, when he had settled the affairs of the empire according to his own mind, and had rectified foreign affairs by wars and treaties, he resolved upon founding a city which should be called by his own name, and should be equal in celebrity to Rome. With this intention, he repaired to a plain at the foot of Troy, near the Hellespont, above the tomb of Ajax, where, it is said, the Achaians had their naval stations and tents while besieging Troy; and here he laid the plan of a large and beautiful city, and built the gates on an elevated spot of ground, whence they are still visible from the sea to those sailing by. But when he had advanced thus far, God appeared to him by night, and commanded him to seek another spot. Led by the hand of God, he arrived at Byzantium in Thrace, beyond Chalcedon in Bithynia, and here he was desired to build his city and to render it worthy of the name of Constantine. In obedience to the words of God, he therefore enlarged the city formerly called Byzantium, and surrounded it with high walls. He also erected magnificent dwelling houses southward through the regions. Since he was aware that the former population was insufficient for so great a city, he peopled it with men of rank and their households, whom he summoned hither from the elder Rome and from other countries. He imposed taxes to cover the expenses of building and adorning the city, and of supplying its inhabitants with food, and providing the city with all the other requisites. He adorned it sumptuously with a hippodrome, fountains, porticos, and other structures. He named it New Rome and Constantinople, and constituted it the imperial capital for all the inhabitants of the North, the South, the East, and the shores of the Mediterranean, from the cities on the Ister and from Epidamnus and the Ionian gulf, to Cyrene and that part of Libya called Borium.

He constructed another council house which they call senate; he ordered the same honors and festal days as those customary to the other Romans, and he did not fail studiously to make the city which bore his name equal in every respect to that of Rome in Italy; nor were his wishes thwarted;

for by the assistance of God, it had to be confessed as great in population and wealth. I know of no cause to account for this extraordinary aggrandizement, unless it be the piety of the builder and of the inhabitants, and their compassion and liberality towards the poor.

No. 9. A Christian accounts for the "fall" of Rome

(Salvian's *On the Government of God.* Migne, *Patrologia Latina,* LIII, 1847. Translation.)

Bk. V. 8. Just as the poor are the first to be oppressed, so are they the last to receive relief. For when, as happened recently, the government decided to reduce somewhat the tax burden of bankrupt cities, the relief which was intended for all was divided by the wealthy among themselves. Who then remembers the poor? Who summon the humble and needy to share in the common benefits? Who permits him who is always first to want to be last in securing relief? And what more? The poor are never considered taxpayers except when the burden of taxation is being laid upon them, never among the company of taxpayers are they counted when relief is being distributed.

Can we consider ourselves undeserving of the punishment of the divine vengeance when we thus ever mistreat the poor? Or do we believe that God will not visit his justice upon us since we are constantly unjust? For where or in whom are these evils to be found except among the Romans? Whose injustice is so enormous as ours? For the Franks do not know this vice; the Huns are immune to these crimes. None of these exist among the Vandals, neither among the Goths. So far indeed are the Goths from tolerating such crimes that even the Romans who live among them do not accept them. Wherefore, universal is the hope of those Romans that they may never have to pass under the jurisdiction of the Romans. One and universal is the prayer of the Roman people living there that it be permitted them to live their lives among the barbarians.

Yet we wonder why the Goths are not overcome by our peoples, when Romans prefer to live with them rather than with us? Therefore, not only do our brothers not choose to flee from them to us, but they rather leave us to take refuge with them. And indeed I would wonder why not all the poor and needy taxpayers do not do the same were it not for the fact that they cannot take with them their few possessions, homes, and families. For since very many abandon their tiny fields and shops in order to escape the enforced payment of tax, why would they not wish to take with them, if this were possible, that which they are obliged to leave behind? Therefore, because they perhaps are not able to do that which they prefer, they do the one thing they can. They surrender themselves into the care and protection of the powerful, they make themselves captives of the rich, and pass as it were under their jurisdiction. Yet I should not consider this serious nor intolerable, in fact, would even commend the generosity of the powerful to whom the poor had entrusted themselves if they did not sell that patronage, if the defense they give the poor were sprung from charity rather than from greed. It is a grave and grievous thing, that by this law the poor appear to be protected that they may be exploited; that by means of this law they defend the miserable so that by defending them they can make them yet more miserable.

Bk. VII. 23. . . . And how can there be any hope, I ask, for the Roman state, when the barbarians are more chaste and pure than the Romans? There is little we can say. What hope of life or of pardon is there for us, I ask, in the sight of God, when we see chastity among the barbarians and are not willing to be chaste ourselves? Should we not blush, I ask, and be ashamed? Already among the Goths none are immodest except Romans, none among the Vandals other than Romans. So much has the zeal for chastity accomplished among them, so much the austerity of their morals, that not only are they themselves chaste, but to say a new thing, something incredible, something almost unimaginable, they have even made the Romans chaste! If human weakness would permit, I should like to shout beyond my powers so that my voice would re-echo throughout the world: Be ashamed of yourselves, Roman people wherever you are; be ashamed of the lives you lead! Almost no cities are free of debauchery, none whatever of immorality, excepting only those in which barbarians have begun to live. And do we still wonder then why we are miserable who are so impure; wonder why we are overcome by the enemy who surpasses us in uprightness; wonder why they have taken over our possessions who execrate our wickedness? It is not the native strength of their bodies which enables them to conquer, nor the infirmity of our nature that we are overcome: it is only our vices that have conquered us.

2

THE RISE AND EARLY DEVELOPMENT OF CHRISTIANITY

The Birth of Christianity

Of the three medieval ingredients of western civilization, the classical, Germanic, and Christian, the most pervasive and enduring in its influence was Christianity. Religious beliefs have usually left a deeper mark upon the lives of people and upon their civilization than have material and cultural circumstances. A striking illustration of this fact is revealed in the history of the lands of the eastern Mediterranean. Though the entire littoral from the Bosporus to the Nile was at one time more or less Hellenized, the mores and institutions of those peoples which adopted and retained Christianity are fundamentally different from those which are Mohammedan, for reasons beyond the peculiarities of the particular nationality involved. Because historic Christianity has generally required greater conformity from its membership in matters of faith and morals than have other religions, its influence has been correspondingly more extensive. For this reason no factor in the history of the western world has exercised greater influence upon its course and the development of ideas and institutions than has the doctrine of Jesus of Nazareth.

Sources. With the exception of a few isolated though significant references in such pagan writings as those of Tacitus and Pliny the Younger, almost all that is known about Christ and the rise of the Christian church

47

is based upon the New Testament and the writings of the church fathers.*
Because the New Testament represented to the early Christians the fulfillment of the promise of the Old Testament as interpreted by the prophets,
it was designated at least from the fourth century on as the second part of
the Bible. It consists of the four gospels of the evangelists, Matthew, Mark,
Luke, and John; the epistles or letters of a number of the apostles; the Acts
of the Apostles; and the Apocalypse or Revelation of John. (Reading 10)
The gospels, which were written during the latter half of the first century,
describe events in the life of Christ, particularly his years of preaching and
his death. Though reflecting differences in style and emphasis, the four
accounts largely parallel and supplement one another. Somewhat apart is
the gospel of John. Its opening words: "In the beginning was the Word
and the Word was with God and the Word was God," are suggestive of
John's interest in the spiritual and mystical character of Christ's mission.
He was also more concerned than the other evangelists in affirming the
divinity of Christ. The epistles consist of letters which several of the
apostles, notably St. Paul, sent to different churches and Christian leaders
of the Mediterranean world for the purpose of instructing them in the
proper interpretation and application of Christ's teachings. The Acts of the
Apostles records the events which followed immediately upon the death of
Christ, such as the descent of the Holy Spirit upon the apostles, the first
proselytizing activities of the disciples, and the conversion of Paul. The
Book of Revelation is the only prophetic book of the New Testament. It
was written to encourage those Christians suffering persecution with a
reminder of the glorious hereafter which awaited the sanctified in heaven.
Because of its abstruse and prophetical language, it remains the most controversial of the books of the Bible, and pious people and scholars still
wrangle over the meaning of its mysterious language.

Christ's Life. It would be inaccurate to say that the gospels furnish the
reader a history of the life of Christ. They provide almost nothing concerning his early life beyond the story of his birth in a stable near Bethlehem, his flight into Egypt with his parents to escape the anger of King
Herod, and his visit to Jerusalem at the age of twelve when he was lost to
his parents for three days. The evangelists are principally concerned with
Christ's public life of preaching which began for him at about the age of
thirty, and with the circumstances which attended his crucifixion. Though
Christ's early years were apparently spent in the quiet obscurity of a carpenter's shop, once he left his home at Nazareth, he seems never once to
have ceased from preaching, from working miracles, or from denouncing
the Pharisees, until death cut short his career at approximately the age of

* An intriguing new source pertinent to the origins of Christianity came to light with
the discovery in 1947 of the first of the Dead Sea Scrolls. It is still too early to speak
definitively of their importance, although it is agreed that it will be significant since some
of the manuscripts recovered date from the second century B.C.

thirty-three. Christ's zeal took him back and forth across Palestine, and he preached as he went, now in the temple, now on the highway or, because of the pressure of the crowd, from a boat off the shore of the Sea of Galilee. His words stirred many people, particularly the poor, and his fame as healer and prophet drew considerable numbers to accept his doctrines. Other listeners, however, were offended by his words, influential people like the chief priests and the Pharisees whom he accused of self-righteousness and of perverting the prophecies and traditions of the Old Law. These groups prevailed upon Pontius Pilate, the Roman procurator of Judea, to have Christ executed as a threat to the peace of that province, and he was crucified as a common criminal between two thieves. The final act of Christ's career, according to the evangelists, was his resurrection from the grave. For those who believed in him, this miracle was the most crucial of all, since it placed the stamp of divinity upon his claims and upon his promises.

Christ's Doctrines. Since Christ was raised an orthodox Hebrew, his teachings rested quite understandably upon the basic monotheistic precept of the Mosaic law: "I am the Lord Thy God." Christ assured his listeners that he had come, not to destroy, but rather to fulfill the law. But in contrast to the law of Moses which was expressed in the negative: "Thou shalt not," Christ's first law was a positive injunction: "Thou shalt love the Lord thy God with thy whole heart, and with thy whole soul, and with thy whole mind." His second law represented a fundamental departure from the Old Law. To supersede the Mosaic law of revenge—"an eye for an eye and a tooth for a tooth"—and the prohibition against associating with the Gentile, Christ issued an uncompromising command to love everyone: "Thou shalt love thy neighbor as thyself." For all men are children of God, whether they be Jew or Gentile, rich or poor, white or black, and to all is given the same opportunity of saving their souls. In place of the God of the Hebrews whose sternness appeared somewhat to hide his love, Christ introduced the merciful God of the New Law, who would deal patiently with sinful man so long as man acknowledged his own inadequacy and forgave those who offended him. Since all men are sinners, so Christ insisted, the most detestable of sins was pride, while the antithesis of pride, that is, humility, was the virtue most essential to spiritual progress. Yet God's justice demanded that erring man show in his behavior his desire to please his maker. "By their fruits you shall know them."

St. Paul. Of the scores of great thinkers who have interpreted and given application to the principles which Christ enunciated, none has left a deeper mark upon Christianity than St. Paul. Saul, as Paul was known before his miraculous conversion, was a well-educated, Hellenized Jew of Tarsus, who carried over into Christianity all the fiery zeal which had motivated him as an orthodox Hebrew. Above any of the other apostles, he was most anxious to cut Christianity free of its Jewish moorings and to set it upon its own independent course. This he accomplished in his own lifetime; in fact, when the Roman state finally came to recognize these Christians as a distinctly non-Judaic sect, Paul was among the first group of martyrs it executed. Paul proved himself an indefatigable missionary. He visited most of the Christian centers as they sprang up in the Roman Empire; some biblical scholars believe his fervor carried him as far west as Spain. As vital to the unity of the early church as his extensive travels was his famous correspondence, which was most persuasive in molding Christian thought and practice during these formative years. While he insisted that the faithful exemplify in their everyday lives the virtues which Christ had instructed them to practice, Paul appeared most convinced of the fundamental importance of charity. As he wrote to the Corinthians: "and now there remain faith, hope, charity, these three: but the greatest of these is charity." Paul stands apart from the other apostles because of his superior education and his knowledge of Greek philosophy. He was thus able to attract the attention of the intellectually sophisticated who might otherwise have remained indifferent to Christianity as a creed of the lower classes.

Spread and Persecution of Christianity

Why Christianity Spread. The zeal which men like Paul displayed in disseminating the teachings of Jesus contributed powerfully to the rapid spread of Christianity. Never in the two thousand years since these early days of the apostles has there been so enthusiastic a response to the obligation with which Christ charged his disciples, to "go and teach all nations, baptizing them in the name of the Father, and of the Son, and of the Holy Spirit." When such enthusiasm was coupled with a heroic disregard for the tortures and death with which hostile authorities sought to suppress these ideas, the pagan world could not help but take notice. The Roman state discovered to its chagrin much truth in the defiant boast of Tertullian, that "the blood of martyrs is the seed of the church." The Christian promise of immortality and of a happy hereafter proved all the more persuasive as stories of miracles performed by its leaders appeared to corroborate the divine claims of its founder. To a society morally weary, to men searching aimlessly for a more satisfactory answer to the problems of existence, the high ethical appeal of Christianity provided a powerful attraction. The presence of Hebrews in most of the cities of the empire (the *Diaspora* or Dispersion) provided Christian ideas a favorable climate in which to take root, particularly in the beginning before differences between Judaism and

Christianity had become clearly defined and irreconcilable. Finally, the superior organization of the Christian church served to channel the industry of individual leaders and to harmonize their ideas, while it prevented their energies from being dissipated into the formation of isolated sects. Early Christianity possessed, in short, an admirable combination of enthusiasm, idealism, and organization, qualities which any voluntary association must possess if it is to succeed.

Christianity vs. Eastern Mystery Cults. It would be a mistake to omit mention of such secondary factors in the spread of Christianity as the existing opportunity for peaceful travel throughout the length and breadth of the Mediterranean world, and the facility almost everywhere of making oneself understood in either Latin or Greek. Yet these circumstances were surely as favorable to the dissemination of the tenets of competing religions, such as the Oriental mystery cults. These cults, those of Cybele, Isis, Serapis, and Mithra, for example, offered certain of the same inducements that attracted men to Christianity, that is the promise of immortality, regeneration often by means of a divine intermediary, and a rich ritual. The cults lacked, however, significant advantages which Christianity enjoyed. Christianity was able to point to a founder who had actully lived, not just a character drawn from mythology or a spirit such as Mithra who was born of a mother-rock and a river. As opposed to the fantastic exploits of such legendary founders, the Christians had the appealing story of the barefooted Galilean to offer. Where the mystery cults emphasized the cleaning efficacy of their ritual largely independent of any interior compunction, the Christian insisted that a spiritual regeneration must accompany the rite in order to make it efficacious. The exclusive claims which Christianity made upon the spiritual loyalties of its members inspired greater admiration than the easy, tolerant attitude of the cults, which permitted their initiates to belong to other sects as well, even to worship the entire Roman pantheon if they so chose. As might be suspected, no martyrologies memorialize the passing of these cults. They disappeared or were suppressed without great effort.

Extent of Spread. For these reasons Christianity spread rapidly despite its hunted existence and the efforts of the state to suppress it. Pliny the Younger, a governor of the province of Bithynia in Asia Minor, wrote to the Emperor Trajan early in the second century that "the contagious superstition is not limited to cities, but has spread through the villages and countryside." Toward the close of the same century, Tertullian announced that all the world, excepting only the pagan temples themselves, was fast becoming Christian. Even these temples would have very soon been deserted, such was the warning of the augur to Emperor Alexander Severus (d. 235), were he to persist in his plan of erecting a shrine to Christ and placing his image in the Roman pantheon. By the end of the third century Christian churches could be found in all the principal communities of the

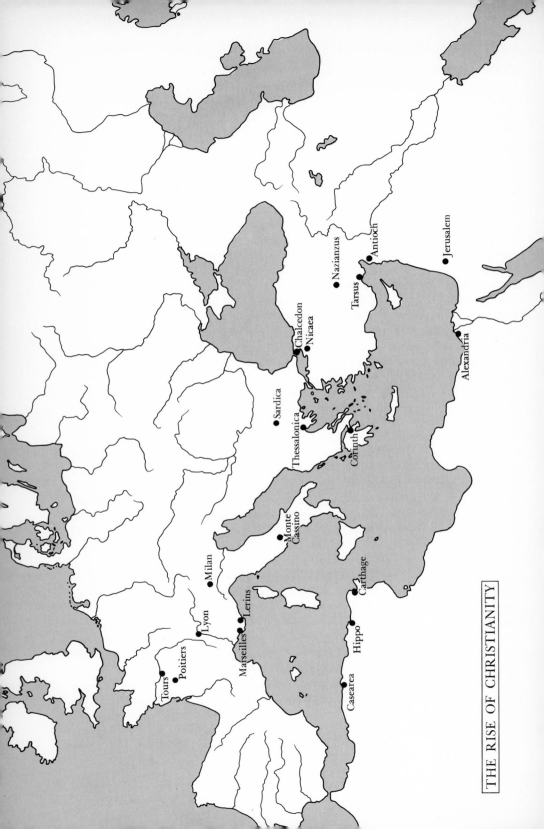

THE RISE OF CHRISTIANITY

empire, with more than forty in Rome alone. It was only in the outlying areas where a stolid peasantry clung to its ancient superstitions, that the spread of Christianity made little headway. The Latin word *paganus* furnishes philological corroboration of this fact. In the first century of the Christian era *paganus* simply meant a rustic. By the close of the fourth century, it had taken on the connotation it has today.

Persecution.   While Christianity spread rapidly, its eventual triumph came only after a long history of persecution. The first persecutors to oppress the Christian community were the Hebrews, the first martyr, Stephen, who was slain by them at Jerusalem. The hostility of the Hebrews actually proved something of a blessing, since for a generation it led the Roman government to dismiss the Christians as nothing more than a Jewish sect. The first persecution of Christians undertaken by the Roman state came in the year 64 A.D. during the reign of Nero. According to the pagan historian Tacitus, Nero used the Christians on this occasion as scapegoats in order to free himself from the charge of having fired a large part of Rome in order to make room for a new palace. Tradition has it that the two apostles Peter and Paul lost their lives during this persecution. From the reign of Domitian (81 A.D. to 96), some form of persecution was the order of the day, even under the Good Emperors. Polycarp, for example, was beheaded during the reign of Antoninus Pius, Justin Martyr under Marcus Aurelius. The persecution of the Emperor Decius in 249 A.D. was the first to be carried out on an empire-wide scale. Until then the prosecution of Christians as traitors of the state had been generally left to the discretion of local law-enforcement agencies. Under pressure of his son-in-law Galerius, the Emperor Diocletian decreed the last general and, as it proved, the most severe of all the persecutions.

Severity of Persecutions.   The severity of the persecutions varied from emperor to emperor and from province to province. Thus Constantius ignored Diocletian's edict in the provinces of Gaul and Britain which were under his control. The Emperor Philip (244 A.D. to 249) was even believed by some to be a Christian. Though the machinery of law enforcement in antiquity was grossly inefficient by modern standards, it could prove reasonably effective especially when abetted by a hostile public opinion. The usual punishment suffered by the Christian amounted to loss of the privileges of citizenship and the imposition of civil disabilities. It was difficult, if not impossible, for Christians to use the law courts for redress of grievances, while Diocletian's decree had the effect of formally outlawing them. Yet under normal circumstances, it was only the Christian leader who stood in any great danger, for the procedure laid down by the Emperor Trajan was that ordinarily observed. As Trajan explained in a famous letter to Pliny the Younger, the state would prosecute those accused of being Christians and demand their execution, but it would not ferret them out. (Reading 12) Still, Christians everywhere and at all times were in danger of the same sort of mob violence which has been the lot of the Hebrew throughout much of his history. As Tertullian wrote: "If the Tiber overflows, if the Nile does not overflow, if there is a drought, an earthquake, a scarcity, a pestilence, straightway the people cry: 'The Christians to the lions'."

Why Rome Persecuted Christians. That Rome undertook to suppress Christianity by force requires some explanation, since few states have shown themselves more tolerant toward alien creeds and institutions. In fact, apart from a few cults which practiced grossly immoral rites, it was only Judaism and Christianity which ever suffered persecution during Rome's long history. It is one of the ironies of history that these same early Christians who today receive universal commendation for their virtues, were held in the lowest repute by many of their contemporaries and classified as a horribly debased sect, guilty of cannibalism and other vicious practices. Suetonius described the religion as a "depraved superstition," and Tacitus classified the Christian community as the deserved target of general abomination. The origin of these charges can doubtless be traced to the clandestine character of the meetings of the Christians and to their "love feast" (communion), which provided rich store for hostile tongues. How much credence the government gave them is questionable, although the unpopularity of the Christians would have reassured the authorities that a policy of repression had popular support. For their part, the Christians contributed to their unpopularity by failing to participate in many civic festivals because of their semireligious or immoral character, by refusing to hold office since religious duties were often entailed, and, in general, by keeping themselves aloof from their pagan neighbors. Many Christians considered it criminal to serve in the army and consequently incurred the odium usually attaching to conscientious objectors.

The Cult of Augustus. While the state must have been concerned about these evidences of Christian non-conformity, it was principally exercised over the refusal of Christians to pay homage to the cult of Augustus. This cult, though nondogmatic and nonmoral, had become identified in the course of time with the Roman state, and the act of homage, which consisted of dropping a bit of incense into an urn placed before the emperor's image, might be required of the subject as proof of his allegiance. So simple, indeed, were the external manifestations of the act, that the Roman government could not understand why Christians refused to perform it. Yet though the state attached such high political significance to the act, the Christians could see only its religious implications. One has difficulty explaining the failure of the government to accept the insistence of the Christian apologists that refusal to perform the rite in no way reflected upon the Christian's civic loyalty. So ancient and time-honored was the association of the ancient state with pagan worship, however, that the emperors could not conceive of the continued existence of the one without the other. The only group which the state relieved of the obligation of paying homage to the cult of Augustus were the Hebrews, and this concession had been wrung from an unsympathetic government only after harsh measures had failed to force them into line. What inclined the authorities to waive the obligation of homage in the case of the Jews was their limited numbers; they would never constitute a menace to the state. The number of Christians, on the other hand, was constantly swelling, and it was the fear that they would in time develop into a real threat to the existence of the state that led to the cruel persecutions of the third century.

Toleration.   In the end it was the state that capitulated. In 311 A.D. the Emperor Galerius formally decreed the end of persecution. He admitted his failure "to bring all things into conformity with the ancient laws," and, accepting the futility of employing force any longer against the foolish and arrogant Christians, he was willing "that the Christians might again exist and might have their meetings." In their appreciation of this indulgence, he instructed them "to pray to their God for our welfare, for that of the commonwealth, and for their own." Since Galerius' order which he issued on his deathbed was generally ignored throughout the empire, credit for finally terminating the hostile policy of the Roman state toward Christianity is traditionally given the co-emperors Constantine and Licinius. The decree which they issued to that effect in 313 A.D. is called, somewhat inaccurately, the Edict of Milan. Constantine is considered the moving force behind the decree, if for no other reason than that Licinius later reintroduced persecution in his part of the empire. Once the latter had been defeated and eliminated in 323, persecution ceased completely and permanently, with the exception of the repressive measures taken against Christianity by Julian (361-363).

Constantine's Position.   The motives which inspired Constantine to end the persecution of Christianity have received conflicting interpretations. That he considered such action politically wise can hardly be denied, since it was what Galerius and Licinius had likewise deemed advisable. Personal conviction, on the other hand, was just as surely present in his decision. His mother, Helena, for whom he had the deepest affection, was a devout Christian. His father, Constantius, had refused to honor Diocletian's decree of persecution in his prefecture. According to a story preserved by Lactantius, Constantine may have accepted the god of the Christians as early as 312. Lactantius states that just before the crucial battle of Milvian Bridge with Maxentius, Constantine, in obedience to a vision, ordered his soldiers to place "the heavenly sign" of the Christians, presumably the Chi Rho monogram, on their shields. There is an even more dramatic story told by Eusebius, of how immediately before the battle Constantine and his army beheld the sign of the cross in the sky with the inscription, "Conquer by this" (*Hoc vince*). That Constantine retained the title of Pontifex Maximus, that he even presided on occasion in the role of pagan high priest, might be attributed either to his fear of alienating his numerous pagan subjects or to his rationalization that such ritual was solely political in character and entirely bereft of its earlier religious implications. Constantine did eschew any claim to divinity; he prohibited the worship of his image, and he was baptized on his deathbed. No special significance need be attached to his tardy baptism, incidentally, since at this time many convinced Christians delayed baptism until late in life. Finally, in calling the bishops to Nicaea in order to resolve the controversy over Arianism (see page 69), Constantine appears to have assumed a position of leadership in the Christian church analogous to that earlier held by his predecessors in pagan Rome. Whatever may have been the motive behind Constantine's conversion, that act remains "the most important fact in the history of the Mediterranean world beween the establishment of the hegemony of Rome and the setting up of Islam."*

Julian. Christianity suffered a last persecution during the brief reign of Julian (361-363). Julian's hatred of Christianity might have sprung from the ill treatment he suffered at the hands of Constantine's sons (Julian's cousins). Whatever its origin, he announced upon his accession that he had always been a pagan at heart, in fact, an initiate in the cult of Mithra. Not only did he repudiate Christianity, but he sought to introduce a kind of paganism which he hoped would wean people away from Christianity. What he proposed was a curious amalgam of Stoic philosophy and Neoplatonism, to which he added something of the Christian hierarchic system, together with the Christian interest in charity and asceticism, on the theory that it was these latter features which afforded Christianity its vigor. He also withdrew the privileges his predecessors had bestowed upon the Christian church and its officials, and decreed such discriminatory measures as the exclusion of Christians from schools. Julian's efforts to reintroduce paganism scarcely had time to bear fruit before a Persian arrow cut short his career during a campaign against the Sassanids in Mesopotamia. Julian's successors restored Christianity to its privileged position and saddled pagan worship with increasing restrictions until it was officially proscribed in a series of decrees issued in 391-392 by the Emperor Theodosius. Already in 380, this same Theodosius had proclaimed Christianity the official religion of the empire.

Organization of Early Christianity

Leadership of the Apostles. One of the major factors in the growth of Christianity, as we have seen, was its efficient organization. According to

* Ferdinand Lot, *The End of the Ancient World* (New York, 1931), p. 39.

the accounts of the evangelists, the basis of this organization had already been prepared by Christ when he conferred the highest spiritual authority in the church he was founding upon Peter and the apostles. That was the construction, in any event, which these apostles placed upon Christ's words: "Whatsoever you shall bind upon earth, shall be bound also in heaven: and whatsoever you shall loose upon earth, shall be loosed also in heaven." Thus Christ's commission, as interpreted and applied by the apostles, assured a reasonably compact, integrated organization, with the apostles retaining control over the administration of the early Christian communities, the selection of assistants, their ordination by means of the imposition of hands, and, finally, over the interpretation of doctrine. Because of the high esteem in which the apostles were held by the early Christian community, they encountered no difficulty in prevailing upon their followers to accept this interpretation and to respect their authority and leadership. As time went on and as the number of Christians and Christian communities grew larger, such factors as the force of tradition and the constant threat of persecution tended to increase the cohesiveness of the organization and to counteract tendencies toward decentralization. A unique and particularly important feature which played a significant part in giving coherence and stability to the early Christian organization was the rite involving the imposition of hands. For whatever the means by which the priest (*presbyter* or elder) or bishop (*episcopus*) had been selected, whether by the members of the local community, by his superiors, or by a political official, it was universally agreed that the candidate did not acquire the proper faculties to carry out the duties of his office until he had been ordained. His authority, it was believed, came from God rather than from men, and the imposition of hands symbolized the transfer of this authority from above. So when the need arose for assistants to the apostles to help in the distribution of food, the apostles instructed their disciples to select seven men qualified to do this work. "And they chose Stephen" and six others. "These they set before the apostles; and they praying, imposed hands upon them."

The Hierarchy. From the very beginning of its history, therefore, the Christian church was blessed with an astonishingly efficient system of control and administration. Though at first there was little to distinguish the priest from the bishop, by the close of the first century the latter had come to be considered superior to, and as having authority over, the priest. Similarly by the end of the first century, the priest and bishop, who earlier had been largely itinerant, had become localized, the priest in his parish, the bishop in his see or diocese. The diocese was usually coterminous with the *civitas* or city-state which had long constituted the backbone of the Roman imperial administrative structure. The bishops who resided in the larger cities gradually acquired jurisdiction over bishops in smaller communities and were called metropolitans as a consequence, later archbishops. The incumbents of such old and honored sees as Jerusalem, Antioch, Alexandria, and Rome, came to be classified as patriarchs, to which select group Constantinople was later added because of the political eminence enjoyed by that city. This arrangement of metropolitan, bishop, and priest (the deacon entrusted with responsibilities such as the distribution of alms, was an important though minor official in the early church organization) is known as the hierarchy, that is, a body of ecclesiastical administrators ranked according to authority.

Primacy of Bishop of Rome. The final step yet remaining to be taken in the development of a completely centralized hierarchy came with the emergency of the bishop of Rome or pope to leadership in the church. The term pope is derived from the Latin word for father. As a title it was applied to priests and bishops somewhat indiscriminately in the early centuries. Only after the sixth century did it come to be restricted to the bishop of Rome. Though the primacy of the bishop of Rome hardly became an accomplished fact prior to the forceful and brilliant pontificate of Leo (I) the Great (440-461), it was persistently urged, and in progressively greater measure realized, by Leo's predecessors from the first century onward. Clement, for example, addressed a strong letter to the Christians of Corinth in 95 A.D., in which he reminded them that they were to respect his admonitions since these were divinely inspired. A century later Victor excommunicated the bishops of Asia Minor for refusing to accept the date of Easter which he had approved. The Council of Sardica (343) formally accorded the bishop of Rome certain appellate powers, and in 385 Pope Siricius issued the first decretal or papal directive addressed to the whole of Christendom. Probably the clearest and sharpest affirmation of the claim of the bishop of Rome to primacy was made by Leo in 451, when he denounced the Council of Chalcedon for daring to rank the church of Constantinople as the equal of Rome. He announced: "The assenting votes of the bishops . . . we render void, and by the authority of the blessed Apostle Peter we do nullify in absolutely unqualified terms." Yet the success of the bishop of Rome came only after a protracted and acrimonious struggle with the patriarchs of the east who contested his claims. Historically the most vocal of the opponents to the primacy of the bishop of Rome was the patriarch of Constantinople, whose claims to equality were strongly endorsed for political reasons by the emperor. (See page 160.)

How Pope Justified Claim. The bishop of Rome based his claim to primacy upon the so-called Petrine doctrine. According to this theory, Christ designated Peter as the head of his church when he said to him: "Thou art Peter, and upon this rock I will build my church." Since according to accepted tradition, Peter had established his see at Rome and was there martyred, the champions of Roman primacy argued that Peter's successor in that city, that is, the bishop of Rome, had fallen heir to the authority Peter had exercised over the entire church. This doctrine carried considerable weight, particularly in the west. Thus Irenaeus, the bishop of Lyons, writing toward the close of the second century, insisted that because of this principle of apostolic succession, "every church should agree with this church (Roman), on account of its preeminent authority." Apart from this Petrine theory, there existed several circumstances which contributed to the emergence of the bishop of Rome. One was the unquestioned eminence enjoyed by the city of Rome in the west and its long tradition as the capital of the empire. That the emperor no longer resided there served to enhance the position and fame of its bishop who was now second to none in prestige. Furthermore, since the bishop of Rome was so much more influential than the other bishops of the west who recognized him as their superior, he was on occasion appealed to as arbiter by the patriarchs of the east when they found themselves embroiled in bitter theological controversy. In any event, the primacy of the bishop of Rome had become an established fact by the end of the sixth century and never was to be seriously disputed again in the west prior to the sixteenth century. Few developments during the medieval period have held more far-reaching consequences for the course of western European history during the Middle Ages.

The Pope's Civil Authority. During the period in which the bishop of Rome was advancing his claims to primacy in the ecclesiastical order, he discovered that his powers and responsibilities in the temporal sphere were also mounting. To understand how this latter came to pass, it is necessary, first of all, to appreciate the fact that neither the ancient nor the medieval world possessed our sensitiveness on the question of separation of church and state. These worlds were convinced rather that the union or close cooperation of the two institutions was an entirely normal, if not necessary, arrangement. It was considered in no way unusual for Constantine to assign an increasing variety of civil duties to Christian bishops, especially since they were held in so high repute by their communities. He not only entrusted them with the distribution of charity and the care of widows and orphans, but even permitted them to serve in the capacity of appellate judges in purely civil disputes. Constantine's practice was followed and expanded by his successors, partly because of their inability to find competent officials of their own to handle all phases of imperial administration, partly in order to relieve the hard-pressed treasury of the expense of financing such activities.

Temporal Sovereignty. In time the bishop of Rome acquired powers in the temporal sphere which went far beyond those enjoyed by other bishops. From the close of the sixth century, he began to exercise temporal sovereignty, that is, the power to direct subjects in strictly civil matters and to deal with foreign states as though he were a king. Two factors in the main accounted for this development. The first was the pope's position as landlord of extensive estates in Italy and Sicily, the so-called patrimony of St.

Peter. These estates had been accumulating over a period of centuries principally in the form of gifts and bequests from pious Christians. The not inconsiderable income which the pope realized from these lands enabled him to wield powerful influence in political circles. Futhermore, because of the perennial absence of adequate imperial bureaucracy, the ownership of extensive land holdings usually entailed wide jurisdictional rights of a civil nature over the people living on these lands. The second factor which helped establish papal temporal sovereignty was the more compelling. This was the inability of the emperor at Constantinople or his representative at Ravenna to exercise any real authority in Italy from within a few years of the death of Justinian in 565. Because of imperial impotence, the onus of providing effective government for the city of Rome and of maintaining the city's defenses against the Lombards devolved by default upon the pope. And since the weakness of the eastern emperor increased with the passage of time, the bishop of Rome found himself to all intents and purposes *de facto* ruler of Rome and its environs long before 756 when he was officially recognized as such by the Franks. (See page 240.)

Doctrine and the Church Fathers

Doctrinal Uniformity. According to the belief of Christians, Christ left with the apostles the original deposit of faith which has never required any addition in fundamental matters. Yet the deposit of faith was one thing, the interpretation and application of what must be believed and practiced by the faithful Christian was quite another. Such theological problems as fundamental as the mystery of the Trinity and the nature of Christ remained to perplex the hierarchy and church. Until these and other profoundly important doctrinal questions had been satisfactorily clarified and generally accepted, they posed a very real threat to the unity of the church. Fortunately for the stability and continued growth of the institution, there existed from the beginning of the church a number of centripetal forces, as it were, which served to prevent dissension over doctrinal differences from leading to that ecclesiastical fragmentation which has characterized Christianity since the sixteenth century. Prior to the period of toleration which came early in the fourth century, persecution at the hands of the Hebrews and the Roman government tended to encourage cooperation among the several groups and to reduce disagreements. From the time of Constantine, the emperor usually took a hand, for better or worse, in the interest of doctrinal unity and conformity. The use of the same sacraments (for the sacraments, see page 505), together with the practice of requiring converts to Christianity to accept a succinct formula or creed before baptism, also helped to standardize doctrine. Traditionally the oldest of these creeds was the Apostles' Creed. The most famous historically is the Nicene (Constantinopolitan) Creed which embodied the formula adopted by the First Ecumenical (general) Council at Nicaea in 325 A.D. Meetings such as this one at Nicaea which were often attended by hundreds of bishops and theologians from widely separated areas, proved most effective in resolving doctrinal controversies and preventing schism. But the most successful instrument in checking the development of doctrinal divergencies, especially in the west, was, once it came to be accepted, the primacy of the bishop of Rome.

The Church Fathers. The most constructive force which promoted both the unity of the church during the first five or six centuries of its existence and the evolution of a logical and well-integrated system of theology as well, was the work of the church fathers. These men were eminent theologians who earned the title "father" because of their conspicuous contribution to the clarification, defense, and development of Christian doctrine. The earliest of the fathers of the patristic age are called apostolic because they lived so close to the apostles. Their writings frequently throw important light on questions of doctrine and practice in the first hundred years or so of the history of the church. The apologists wrote principally during the second half of the second century, their objective being to convince the pagans that the state had no cause to persecute Christians. Typical of such writing was the *Apology* of Justin Martyr (d. 165) which he addressed to Marcus Aurelius in the hope of persuading the emperor that Christians were an asset, not a source of weakness, to the empire.

Unlike Justin's conciliatory *Apology,* that of Tertullian (d. 222) fairly bristles with denunciation of the Roman state while boasting of the infinite superiority of Christianity and its inevitable victory. Tertullian, who was the first product of the Christian center at Carthage in North Africa, permitted his puritanism to take him first to the heretical Montanists whose extreme rigorism attracted him, then to establishing his own sect when the Montanists proved too moderate. Although Tertullian was condemned as a heretic, he provided Latin Christianity its theological terminology and its first important influence. Tertullian's later writings classify him with the controversialists, the term which is applied in a general way to the fathers of the third century because of their major concern with differences among Christians themselves. The most noted of these fathers was Origen (d. 254) who was also the greatest scholar early Christianity produced and its most prolific writer as well. Of Origen's industry Jerome is said to have remarked: "Who of us can read all he has written?" Only a handful remain of the 6,000 works attributed to him. Origen was a profound thinker and thoroughly instructed in Greek philosophy. His theological treatises reflect strong Neoplatonist influences, and these, together with his own many errors and those of his scribes, evoked ecclesiastical condemnation of several of his works. Origen himself was never condemned. Origen produced the first critical and systematic study of the Bible, while his voluminous commentaries on the Scriptures constituted his most popular works. His search for higher meanings to supplement the literal sense of the biblical text helped establish such investigations as a favorite exercise for medieval theologians. (Reading 136)

Eastern Fathers of the "Golden Age." The "golden age" of patristic writing covered the fourth and first half of the fifth century. Listed among the most distinguished fathers of eastern Christendom during this period were St. Athanasius (d. 373), St. Basil (d. 379), St. Gregory Nazianzen (d. 390), and St. John Chrysostom (d. 407). Athanasius was born and reared in Alexandria when that city ranked as the intellectual center of the world in both secular and religious learning. As a youth Athanasius became devoted to the divinity of Christ and before he was ordained priest composed two erudite treatises on the mystery of the incarnation. He accompanied Bishop Alexander to Nicaea, where his convictions and learning qualified him as the principal champion of "orthodoxy" to lead the dispute against the views of Arius. (For Arianism, see page 69.) Upon Alexander's death, Athanasius succeeded him as bishop of Alexandria. His forty-five year episcopacy proved a most hectic one, for on five different occasions he was forced into exile by emperors sympathetic to Arianism. Athanasius' most influential writings were his *Discourses Against the Arians* and his *Life of St. Anthony*, the latter work gaining wide popularity and contributing to the acceptance of monasticism in the west.

The most important of the eastern fathers in point of influence was Basil. Not only did he prove a fearless opponent of Arianism when it was dangerous to oppose a doctrine supported by the emperor, but his writings on the subject of monasticism found such acceptance that eastern monasticism remains Basilian to this day. (For his contribution to monasticism, see page 73.) The martyrdom suffered by his parents helped mold the seriousness of his character and led him to dedicate his life to prayer and the practice of asceticism. One of the earliest eleemosynary establishments was the one he erected near his bishop's residence in Caesarea which administered to the friendless, sick, and poor, and provided industrial training for the unemployed. Included in Basil's extant writings are numerous commentaries on the Scripture, homilies, and letters. (Reading 16)

Gregory of Nazianzen was a close friend of Basil, and although the course of their friendship proved stormy, among Gregory's most beautiful poems are epitaphs he composed on the occasion of Basil's death. Like Basil, Gregory was versed in Greek philosophy and literature. His writings possessed a literary polish which recommended them to the attention of cultured circles. His religious poetry, too, was the best to appear in the patristic age. Basil was responsible for forcing Gregory to accept short public careers as bishop of Constantinople, then of Nazianzen, posts for which Gregory was hardly suited by temperament. Gregory proved himself most successful in preaching and writing. His sermon on the priesthood left a deep impression on Gregory the Great (see page 67), and it has been said of his writings that they "summed up and closed the controversy of a whole century."

John, surnamed Chrysostom, the "golden mouthed," for his extraordinary eloquence, acquired his deep knowledge of Greek philosophy and culture at Antioch. The influence of Antioch's theological schools is also reflected in his exegetical writing, for he is inclined to limit his interpretation of biblical passages to their historical or literal sense. As bishop of Constantinople, John Chrysostom revealed himself so outspoken a critic of extravagance and loose morals, that powerful opponents, including the empress, had him exiled to the wild Caucasus. The hardships of the journey killed him. Next to Origen, John Chrysostom was the most prolific of the eastern fathers. Among his extant writings are 240 letters, 100 sermons, and 700 homilies. In his writings and sermons, he showed himself most concerned with Christian morality and practice, rather than in speculative theology. Eastern Christianity has always revered him as the most authoritative of the fathers. In the later iconoclastic controversy (see page 161), when a statement by John Chrysostom was read at the Seventh Ecumenical Council (787 at Constantinople and Nicaea) which expressed his acceptance of the veneration of images, the bishop of Nicomedia exclaimed: "If John Chrysostom speaks in that way of images, who would dare to speak against them?"

Western Fathers of the "Golden Age": Ambrose.   The four great church fathers of the Latin west were St. Ambrose (d. 397), St. Jerome (d. 420), St. Augustine (d. 430), and St. Gregory the Great (d. 604). It would be difficult to overestimate the mark they left upon Christianity. Though their writings, particularly those of Augustine, are not without philosophical depth, the western fathers in general were less concerned with the interpretation and elaboration of doctrine (Augustine excepted) than they were with the practical application of Christian principles. This was especially true of Ambrose. Ambrose was a member of one of Italy's most respected families, his father was the pretorian prefect of Gaul. He received an excellent education and entered the imperial service, where he rose quickly, as much by reason of his native talents and his high sense of justice as by his family's prestige. As governor of two north Italian provinces, he was at Milan seeking to maintain order between Arian and Catholic factions over the selection of a new bishop, when the people prevailed upon him to accept the post. Though only a catechumen, that is, preparing himself for baptism, he was moved in rapid sequence through orders to the rank of bishop within a few days. His deficiencies in sacred learning he more than corrected through a lifelong study of the Bible and the writings of the fathers, particularly the eastern fathers. Ambrose was, incidentally, one of the last western scholars who had a command of both Latin and Greek. For twenty years he served the faithful of Milan, not with aloofness from his episcopal palace, but with the door of his study always open so that people might approach him at any time. Augustine speaks of the "multitudes of busy people whose weaknesses he served." On Sundays immense crowds filled the great cathedral to hear him preach. Among his favorite themes was virginity, and so eloquently did he extol this virtue that mothers hesitated to permit their daughters to hear him for fear they would remain unwed.

Ambrose proved himself an admirable administrator and a statesman. Three emperors sought his advice which he gave frankly and, on occasion, without being asked. His most famous controversy with an emperor came when he refused to read mass in the cathedral upon the arrival of the emperor Theodosius, until the latter had publicly confessed and lamented his part in the slaughter of several thousand Thessalonians. Ambrose's writings, which include letters, dogmatic works, and homilies, reveal a deeply sincere yet practical Christianity, little concerned with speculative theology but expressing thoughts which humble minds could appreciate. Surely his most popular compositions were his hymns, several of which continue to provide various Christian denominations appealing reminders of the vigor and beauty of this early age. Augustine confesses how he was moved when "those voices flowed into his ears and the truth permeated his heart." Ambrose has, indeed, been called the "father of Latin hymnody." In his most influential work, *On the Duties of the Clergy*, he presented a program of Christian morality which both priests and laity could embrace, while pointing up the superiority of Christian ethics to those of the pagan Stoics.

St. Jerome. Jerome was the greatest scholar among the western fathers. His teachers included the famous grammarian Donatus and the learned Gregory of Nazianzen. Jerome was thoroughly versed in Greek and Latin scholarship and literature, and his writings abound with classical allusions. This deep interest in classical learning we have on his own admission. In a somewhat jocular mood he tells of a vision he experienced, of how he found himself hailed before the judgment seat of God where he was asked what he was. When he replied that he was a Christian, he received the stern rebuke: "Thou liest. Thou art a Ciceronian, not a Christian; for where thy treasure is, there shall thy heart be also." Jerome was a man of extraordinary vitality and he appears never to have permitted himself a moment's relaxation. His voluminous writings include letters, treatises on a wide variety of religious subjects, and biographies of early churchmen. His great fame derives principally from the monumental character of his biblical work. Because of the existence of serious discrepancies among the different versions of the Bible in use at that time, Pope Damasus commissioned Jerome, who was his secretary, to prepare a new Latin translation. To this prodigious task Jerome devoted twenty of the most active years of his life, working from the oldest Greek, Hebrew, and Chaldaic manuscripts he could locate. So thorough a job did he do and so clear and straightforward was the style he employed, that his version, commonly called the Vulgate, gradually forced other Latin translations of the Bible out of use (hence the term Vulgate from vulgar, meaning common). In addition to facilitating later exegetical study of the Bible, Jerome's Vulgate proved a powerful agency in establishing the foundations of medieval Latin. (See page 598.)

Two qualities stand out in Jerome's stern character: his love of asceticism and the sharpness of his tongue. He has been aptly called the "irascible hermit." Though personally humble and most charitable toward the poor, he was quick with his denunciations of clerical laxity and pretense and was often capable of criticizing with a venom that could hardly be characterized as Christian. Of those, for example, who were wont to let their whiskers grow as a mark of sanctity, he observed: "If there is any holiness in a beard, nobody is more holy than a goat." So vitriolic and general were his attacks on the deficiencies of ecclesiastics, that he was practically forced to flee Rome after the death of his protector Pope Damasus. He eventually made his home in Bethlehem, where he devoted the last thirty-five years of his life to study and to the practice of asceticism. Jerome was among the first to acquaint the west with the monastic life and to recommend among the occupations of monks the copying of manuscripts. (Reading 17)

St. Augustine.   The greatest of all the church fathers was St. Augustine. No one after the first century exerted anything approaching his influence upon the development of Christianity in the west. Perhaps the observation of Frank J. Sheed is no overstatement, that "Every man living in the Western world would be a different man if Augustine had not been, or had been different." In his *Confessions*, surely the most famous and popular autobiography ever written, Augustine sketches the wonderfully moving story of his life. Born near Hippo in North Africa to a pagan father and a devout Christian mother, he received a classical education, and excelled in the study of grammar and rhetoric. To the anguish of his pious mother Monica, he gradually lost all interest in Christianity and drifted into the ways of a libertine. A chance reading of Cicero's *Hortensius* (now lost) led him to the study of philosophy, and he became first a free-thinker, then an admirer of the pagan Greek philosophers, and for a time even a champion of Manichaeism. (For Manichaeism, see page 70.) In the end he found all this to be nothing more than empty learning or deluding error, and his questions about himself and the world as unanswered as before. The best he could say of Faustus, the Manichaean authority, for example, was that "he was not altogether ignorant of his own ignorance." To ease his mental and spiritual turmoil, Augustine decided to turn to teaching and opened a school of rhetoric, first at Rome, later at Milan. In the latter city he learned of Ambrose's fame and he writes how he dropped in to hear him preach in order to discover "whether his eloquence measured up to his fame." He found Ambrose fully deserving of his reputation and it was Ambrose's insistence that divine truth could often be found in the spirit rather than in the letter of biblical passages, that prompted him to return to the study of the Bible. Shortly thereafter, he was converted in most dramatic fashion (Reading 13), was ordained priest, and eventually became bishop of Hippo. He turned his episcopal residence into a monastery, and for the remaining thirty-four years of his life, he and his priests lived together as a monastic community. His rule, known as the Rule of St. Augustine, provided his clergy a practical compromise between the contemplative and the pastoral life.

Augustine's Theology. Augustine's principal achievement in the realm of theology consisted of clarifying the essential role of the church in the salvation of souls. Though he left untouched scarcely any major philosophical or theological question, he wrote most definitely about the church. He described its authority, its inherent marks (one, holy, catholic, and apostolic), and its mission in the distribution of grace through the intermediary of the mass and the sacraments. Reflected throughout Augustine's writings is the deep feeling of his naturally emotional nature. Actually it was the intense conviction with which he wrote, as much as the logic of his thought, that caused his writings to inscribe themselves so indelibly upon the western mind. Because he found himself unable to accept Christianity even after long search and study had convinced him of the reasonableness of its doctrines, he is inclined to stress the compelling importance of God's grace in the salvation of the soul. As he writes in his *Confessions*, only after he had acknowledged his complete unworthiness and helplessness—"How long, O Lord, how long?"—did faith finally come to him. Augustine's insistence upon the indispensable nature of God's grace has led some theologians to ascribe to him a belief in predestination, an interpretation with which other scholars have taken issue. This and other controversies concerning Augustine's position on theological issues arise in part from the nature of his writing. Augustine is seldom the cold theorist; rather he writes more frequently as a rhetorician or polemicist, as one rising to a challenge. In his eagerness to convince, his language assumes an extravagance on occasion which invites varying interpretations, particularly when studied out of context.

The City of God. Almost as well known as Augustine's *Confessions* is his *City of God.* Of the two books, the *City of God* was the more popular in the Middle Ages and exerted the greater influence for its theme held a special fascination for the medieval mind. Augustine explains how he came to write the book: "Rome had been overthrown by a raid of Goths, led by King Alaric, a most destructive invasion. The polytheistic worshippers of false gods, whom we commonly call 'pagans,' endeavoured to bring this overthrow home to the Christian religion, and began to blaspheme the true

God with unusual sharpness and bitterness." To acquit Christianity of this charge, he devoted the leisure hours of fifteen years to the composition of perhaps literature's longest apologia, undoubtedly its most famous. Augustine ridicules the idea that the craven, degenerate lot of Roman gods, assuming for the sake of argument that they had any existence, could have afforded Rome any protection. The city fell because of its vices. Yet he reminds his readers that they must not permit this catastrophe to obscure their sense of values. Rome was, after all, but a material city. As such it enjoyed no privileged place in the divine plan of the universe. The only city of any moment was the City of God. God intended the world only as a place where men should have the opportunity of proving their fitness to become permanent residents of this eternal city. All change, whether individual or affecting many, will be made to serve this higher end. While "God maketh the sun to rise upon the good and the bad" alike, what fortune befalls the wicked will do them no good in the end, though the misfortunes which are the lot of the virtuous will ultimately be revealed as blessings.

Augustine's argument is substantially that announced in the gospels, namely, that all material values are fleeting and that God rules the world. Because Augustine fits the historical fall of Rome into that context, he has been credited with proposing the first Christian philosophy of history. While Augustine may not deserve this distinction, his *City of God* surely did inspire most later medieval writers to assume a teleological approach in their analysis of history. Even kings like Charlemagne were deeply impressed with its argument. (Reading 14)

St. Gregory the Great.   The last of the church fathers of the west was St. Gregory the Great. It is proof of the enormous measure of the influence which he exerted upon Christianity, that he is listed with the greatest of the church fathers even though he lived a century and a half after Augustine. For were it not for the supreme importance of Gregory's contribution, Augustine would ordinarily be credited with having closed the patristic age and the formative period of the church. Gregory was born of a wealthy, distinguished family in Rome, entered the imperial service, and became prefect of the city at the age of thirty. He held this, the highest civil office in the city, hardly more than a year, for when his father died, he turned his back on political life to devote himself wholly to God. He used his patrimony to found six monasteries in Sicily, while he remained a monk in his residence in Rome, a residence he turned into a monastery. Gregory of Tours expresses the wonder of Gregory's contemporaries at the abruptness and magnitude of the step: "He who had before gone about the city clad in the trabea and in silk and jewels, now clothed in a humble garment consecrated himself to the service of God." The austere life of a contemplative is what Gregory would have preferred, and he reminisces in his later troubled years on how happy he was during those short months when he could give undisturbed worship to God. Twice he was persuaded by the pope to leave his monastic retreat, on one occasion to go to Constantinople as papal ambassador where he acquired a knowledge of Byzantine affairs which proved of vital importance to his subsequent career. In 590 Gregory accepted with reluctance his election as pope, and for the fourteen years of his pontificate devoted himself to the cares of office with an energy which belied his poor health. (He had injured his health by the rigors of his austerities.) These cares he made heavier by assuming responsibility for tasks and services other popes would have considered outside their province or have delegated to subordinates. For example he kept a personal watch on the administration of the extensive estates of the church, directed the distribution of alms, organized the defenses of the city against the Lombards, and handled negotiations with the enemy.

So comprehensive was Gregory's influence upon the medieval church that it is not easy to single out the areas where he left the deepest marks. Partly because of his own firmness, partly because Byzantine power had waned perceptibly since the time of Justinian, Gregory succeeded in almost completely eliminating imperial interference in papal and ecclesiastical affairs in the west. At the same time he made significant progress in strengthening his own papal authority in the west through an extensive correspondence with the bishops of the area and by means of appeals to their kings. Though the times were critical, he did not neglect the spread of Christianity, but sent out missionaries, notably to England, while nearer home he directed the extinction of the last islands of heresy in Spain (Arianism) and in Africa (Donatism). The pretensions of the patriarch of Constantinople he rejected outright. To Benedictine monasticism he extended his positive endorsement and thus assured the papacy a powerful ally in the west. In the interest of uniformity, he regularized liturgical practices, and while his part in the reform of church music is not entirely clear, Gregorian chant continues to bear his name.

Gregory's Writings.   Despite Gregory's constant harassment by a never ending series of vexing problems, he found time for the composition of several of the most influential books of the Middle Ages. Foremost among these was his *Pastoral Rule* (Reading 19), a handbook of instructions for bishops and priests, outlining their responsibilities and directing them on how they might best discharge them. Another book, the *Moralia,* is a commentary on the Book of Job in its application to Christian ethics. Gregory's *Dialogues* consists of a collection of edifying stories about saintly men and women. If the stories leave something to be desired in point of historical accuracy, it should be remembered that to Gregory it was principally the moral that mattered. Gregory was the first pope to use the traditional papal title, "the servant of the servants of the Lord." In view of his deep faith and utter dedication to the salvation of men, no one can deny the complete appropriateness of the title. Most expressive of Gregory's practical sense on the one hand and, on the other, his acute perception of true Christianity, were his instructions to Augustine and his band of monks as they were about to leave Rome to labor among the pagan Angles and Saxons: "Remember that you are not to interfere with any traditional belief or religious observance that can be harmonized with Christianity." Few administrators have maintained so admirable a balance between religious idealism and hard common sense.

Heresies

Rise of Heresies.   Probably the bulk of patristic literature grew out of efforts to clarify or defend doctrines which had been brought into dispute. Since the fathers ordinarily expressed the accepted or official opinion of the church in such doctrinal controversy, those Christians who proposed interpretations deemed inconsistent with that position were called heretics and their view heresies. A Christian heresy may be therefore defined as a belief which is at variance with recognized doctrines of Christianity. Nothing disturbed the tranquillity of the early church nor impeded its progress more seriously than the rise of heresies. One of them, Arianism, grew so powerful that it even threatened to subvert the institution. Among the various factors which contributed to the rise of heresy were the absence of an accepted theological terminology, the lack of definitive pronouncements on certain fundamental doctrines, laxity and indifference on the part of both clergy and laity, and even the individual preferences of the emperor.

Arianism.   Most of the heresies which beset the unity of the early church had their origin in the east where Christianity was more highly developed and where the Greek mind was more given to theological speculation. One of the earliest heresies to appear there and, as it proved, the most dangerous, was Arianism. This heresy had its inception in the query posed by Arius, a priest of Alexandria, as to whether the Father had not existed before the Son as a strictly human understanding of the two terms, father and son, would seem to imply. Faced with an episcopal order to curb his discussions, Arius boldly announced his conviction that Christ, though now God, had not always been God, and that, consequently, he was not equal to the Father but simply his creature. What future turn Christianity would have taken had Arius' position prevailed, remains a matter of conjecture. It is doubtful, however, whether Christ, the Redeemer, would have remained the motivating soul of the institution. The council of Nicaea declared Arius' views heretical and confirmed instead the opposing position defended by Athanasius, namely, that the Son is equal to and consubstantial with the Father. (Reading 11) Despite this condemnation, Arianism did not disappear, partly because to many church-men Arius' views appeared reasonably acceptable in an area where precise theological terms were lacking. The heresy waxed strong and arrogant under the tutelage of Constantine's son, Constantius II, and several of his successors, and not only continued to plague the eastern church for almost a century, but left to the west a heritage of heretical Germanic tribes to convert. As we shall see, most of the Germans owed their conversion from paganism to the Arian missionary Ulfilas.

Nestorianism and Monophysitism.   Two other heresies developed over the thorny problem of Christ's nature, one almost the reverse of the other. Nestorianism, deriving its name from Nestorius, bishop of Constantinople, proposed two completely distinct persons in Christ which were united in little more than a moral union. Nestorius preached that God did not die and that Mary was only the mother of the human person, for had she been the mother of God, one would have to call her a goddess. The Monophy-sites, on the other hand, sought to solve the problem of Christ's dual na-ture by admitting the existence of only one, the divine. The Monophysites found themselves becoming wedded to this view as their anxiety to com-bat Nestorianism led them to contemplate too exclusively the divine na-ture of God. The Nestorians would have robbed the redemption of Christ of its efficaciousness in the salvation of souls; the Monophysites in denying the reality of Christ's human nature would have made his death impossible and the example of Christ's human life valueless to men. Both sects re-flected the mind of the Near East in its tendency to view the material world as evil in itself and therefore not worthy of the Godhead. Nestorian-ism lingers on in Iran, while Monophysitism counts large numbers among the Christian elements of Egypt and the Near East.

Other Heresies.   In Donatism we have an example of a sect which found orthodox Christian practice too lenient. The Donatists would have ex-cluded from the church all who had sinned grievously, particularly those who had once apostatized. In pursuing the strict logic of their premises, they also denied the validity of sacraments administered by unworthy priests. Quite different in premises was Pelagianism which had its name from Pelagius, a British monk, who attacked the doctrine of original sin. Pelagius insisted that man was wholly good and that he could save his soul and gain eternal happiness without God's grace. To Augustine fell the task of confuting the views of Pelagius and also those of the Mani-chaeans, a sect to which he had at one time adhered. The Manichaeans be-lieved that there were two forces in the universe, one good and one evil, both equally powerful and eternal, the first spiritual, the second material. The world and all that was in it of a material character were of their very natures evil. Man if he wished to be saved must subordinate, as far as humanly possible, his physical being to the spiritual. This heresy was akin to Gnosticism, which in turn had so many points of similarity with Christianity, that it left large numbers of Christians confused. While the majority of these heresies had disappeared or spent themselves by the close of the fifth century, several left scars, especially between eastern and western Christendom, which were never obliterated. (See page 161.)

Monasticism

If the early church encountered in heresies the most serious threat to its existence, it drew its principal nourishment from monasticism. No other development within the organization of the church proved so effective an instrument in furthering the work of the church, in converting the pagan and inspiring the Christian to a more Christlike practice of his religion, than did the self-sacrificing monk in his threadbare habit. Though in its origins Christian monasticism was not unlike that of similar ascetical movements found in both Judaism* and paganism, as an institution it represents an entirely independent development, and it attained proportions and exerted an influence far beyond the monasticism of any other religious group.

Motives: Closer Union with God.   The words monasticism and monk are derived from the Greek root meaning alone. The first monks were strikingly solitary figures, hermits or anchorites as they are commonly called, who withdrew from society to some desolate spot in order to be alone with their God. And while monasticism early developed a communal organization, the monastic community continued to live as much apart from the bustle and distractions of the world as possible, in order the better to achieve its spiritual ends. For it was this motive above all others, that of attaining a more intimate union with God, which impelled thousands of men and women to take up the monastic life. "If thou wouldst be perfect," Christ told the rich young man, "sell all thou hast and follow me." It is true that the rigor of the austerities practiced by the first hermits tends to obscure in the modern mind their more conventional activities of worship and contemplation. Yet this mortification of the flesh was ordinarily considered simply a means to a higher end, which was to free the soul of the physical demands of the flesh in order to permit it the more readily to commune with God. As the Apostle Paul had written: "The flesh lusteth against the spirit, and the spirit against the flesh: for these are contrary

---

* The Essenes, a Hebrew sect known for the piety and asceticism of its members, maintained the monastery at Qumran where the Dead Sea Scrolls were discovered. The parchments had, indeed, belonged to the monastery.

one to another"; and again, "They who belong to Christ have crucified their flesh with its passions and desires." Once the demands of the flesh had been harnessed, they would no longer hamper the monk in his meditations and prayers.

Other Motives. There were additional factors which led men (and women) to take up the life of a hermit. Before Christianity became a tolerated religion, some men fled to the desert to escape persecution. When persecution ended and Christianity became instead the religion of the emperors, the influx of thousands whose conversion stemmed from self-interest rather than conviction deprived the Christian community of something of its pristine virtue. Now men might flee society to escape, not persecution, but the corrupting influences of everyday life. It was, for example, to escape the contagion of licentious Rome that Benedict withdrew to a cave east of the city. During the first centuries the expectation of the early dissolution of the world prompted some to assume the rigors of eremitical life. Others gave up lives of relative comfort and the society of friends in order to do penance for their sins. Such, we read, was the motive which impelled Mary of Egypt to abandon Alexandria and a life of sin for the desert. As monasticism came to be recognized as a highly meritorious vocation, wealthy men and women lent their encouragement to the movement with gifts of money and estates. Finally, the extreme character of the austerities undertaken by a number of hermits suggests that they hoped by way of such mortifications to emulate the heroic sacrifice of martyrs, now that toleration had closed the door to actual martyrdom.

Pillar Saints. The most unique of this last group were the Pillar Saints of whom Simeon Stylites is the best known. In order to live apart from men, he hunted out a rocky prominence some forty miles east of Antioch and built himself a tower which finally reached an eminence of fifty feet. There upon a narrow platform, too small to permit him to lie down, he lived out the last thirty-six years of his life, worshipping God and preaching to the multitudes who flocked to the desert to hear him. His apologists would justify the appalling nature of his mortifications by his conversion of thousands of wild tribesmen whom more conventional methods would have left untouched.

Founders of Eastern Monasticism. St. Anthony (d. 356), who devoted more than eighty years of his long life to the practice of asceticism may be regarded as the father of monasticism. (Reading 15) This honor is given him because he was the first hermit to assume the spiritual guidance of other anchorites. The fame of his holiness had attracted these to his retreat east of the Nile in such numbers that he felt a measure of supervision was imperative. A further step in the direction in which monasticism eventually developed was taken by Anthony's contemporary, St. Pachomius, also of Egypt, who organized the first actual community of hermits. The hermits could occupy individual huts, but they were obliged to accept the direction of a superior who would lay down a simple routine of worship, private prayer, and physical labor. The greatest name in the history of eastern monasticism is that of the church father St. Basil. Basil recognized the superiority of community or cenobitic monasticism, and centralized far beyond Pachomius the spiritual and material activities of the monastic community. Basil erected the first formal monastery, that is, a common building housing all the members of the community. Because Basil was a most influential bishop and, at the same time, the author of extensive ascetical literature, he left such a mark upon eastern monasticism that it has remained Basilian to this day. It should be noted that a parallel monastic movement took place among women. Both Pachomius and Basil had sisters who organized ascetical orders.

Founders of Western Monasticism. The west learned of monasticism through a visit of Athanasius, so the story goes, and through the popular *Life of St. Anthony* which he composed. Among the important names in the history of early monasticism in the west are those of John Cassian (d. *ca.* 435) who established two houses in Marseilles and left voluminous writings on asceticism; St. Augustine, who required the clergy of his diocese of Hippo to follow a monastic routine; St. Martin (d. *ca.* 397), bishop of Tours, whose monastery near Poitiers was the first actually established in the west; and St. Patrick (d. 461). According to the traditional accounts, Patrick was born in Celtic Britain, where he was captured by Irish raiders who kept him a slave for six years before he managed to make good his escape to France. There he studied at the monastery of Lerins, became monk, priest, and bishop, and then returned to the land of his captivity, which he practically converted by the time of his death. Western monasticism in this early period reflected the austerity of its eastern antecedents, but lacked its vitality. Though many monasteries took root, monasticism in general languished except in Ireland, where an astonishing degree of missionary zeal appears to have preserved its high morale. In any event, the real founder of western monasticism was St. Benedict. What had been a moribund institution blossomed out under his inspiration into the most powerful single monastic movement in the history of asceticism. The "matrix of Western Christendom," so Professor Toynbee calls Benedictine monasticism.

Life of St. Benedict. Benedict (d. 543) was born of a good family at Nursia some seventy miles northeast of Rome about the year 480. His parents sent him to Rome for an education, but the profligate life of the city disgusted him, and he sought out a cave at Subiaco forty miles east of the city. His retreat soon lost its isolation when other ascetically minded men hunted him out, and some who were not so ascetically minded. For when he sought to hold them to a strict regimen of fasting and prayer, some of his monks attempted to poison him. He managed to set up a dozen small monastic centers in the area and then traveled southward to a mountain overlooking the village of Monte Cassino which lay halfway on the road between Rome and Naples. Here he founded the most famous mother-house of all monastic orders (*ca.* 520), and here he composed his *Rule* and lived out the remaining years of his life.

The Rule. As the word suggests, the purpose of Benedict's *Rule* was to prescribe the spiritual and social routine the community of monks was to observe in its practice of monasticism. Though Benedict did not intend that the *Rule* itself should serve as a source of spiritual inspiration, he does single out the virtues which the members of the monastic community should seek to develop and the means they should employ in their quest for Christian perfection. The monks must lead lives of self-denial, they must give up personal possessions, they must be celibate, they must submit themselves to their superiors, they must pray and they must work. Because the life of a monk was hard and, from the world's viewpoint, uninviting and drab, only those who persevered in their original intention after a year of probation (novitiate) were to be accepted as monks. The members of the community were required to respect with unquestioning obedience the absolute authority of their abbot, whom they would elect, but who would guide their destinies as a father, with only their counsel and the fear of God to restrain him. For "let him know that he who undertakes to rule souls must prepare to render an account." (Reading 18)

The Monastic Day. The most important feature of Benedict's *Rule* was the care with which the day's activities were set down. The *Rule* called for about five hours of community worship and prayer, allotted a somewhat shorter period to spiritual reading and meditation, approximately six hours to manual labor, and some eight hours to sleep. The material well-being of the monastery required that the members engage in manual labor, but it is entirely possible that Benedict recognized the value of such work to the physical and mental health of the community. Yet all labor, even of the most menial sort, was to be done for the love of God, and represented, therefore, but another form of prayer. Labor would furthermore, keep the devil on the defensive, for, as Benedict wrote, "Idleness is the enemy of the soul." The *Rule* directed that food be simple though adequate, and that the monks observe silence at all times, except when necessity required them to speak. Finally, the monk was to remain a permanent member of the particular community he joined (the vow of stability). It is in the more careful regulation of the monastic day and the reasonableness and moderation of its requirements, that students are inclined to find the secret of the extraordinary popularity and success of the *Rule* of Benedict. Few documents have had a greater impact upon civilization, few have reflected a deeper understanding of human nature, especially of human nature bent on spiritual advancement.

The Achievement of Monasticism. Modern writers, whatever their religious convictions, have universally acknowledged the great achievement of medieval monasticism. Among its many contributions to society are enumerated the care of the sick and destitute, the distribution of charity, the maintenance of schools, the collection of libraries and the copying of manuscripts, the keeping of records and historical chronicles, the clearing of land and draining of swamps, the stimulation of agriculture and the development of certain industrial arts, and, in general, the conversion and civilizing of the barbarians of western Europe. Yet these accomplishments were for the most part peripheral to the principal objectives of monasticism, which were the community worship of God through the mass and the divine office, and the assistance of the individual monk in his work of personal sanctification. Even the work of civilizing and converting the pagan German, Celt, and Slav, devolved upon the monk principally because of the absence, or the inadequate number, of priests. Monasticism formalized in time the ascetic ideal in terms of the triple vow of chastity, poverty, and obedience, which served to pedestal these rules of self-abnegation as the highest of all Christian virtues. Probably the most significant contribution which monasticism made to medieval Christianity was that of providing the secular clergy, the laity, and non-Christians, an example of what constituted the ideal in Christian living. In doing this monasticism not only served as a stimulant to the moral conscience of Christendom, but it tended also to absorb within itself waves of protest and reform which periodically swept western Europe and which otherwise might have swung outside the Christian community as heretical movements. Monasticism in its origins was a reform movement, and so it remained. (For later developments in monasticism, see page 496.)

 READINGS

No. 10. The New Testament

(The New Testament of Our Lord and Savior Jesus Christ, tr. **F. A.** Spencer. New York, 1951. Reprinted by permission of The Macmillan Co.)

The Sermon on the Mount (Matthew, 5:1-12)

Now, seeing the crowds He ascended the mountain; and when He had seated Himself, His disciples came to Him. Then, opening His mouth, He taught them, saying:

"Blessed are the poor in spirit; for theirs is the kingdom of Heaven.

"Blessed are the meek; for they shall inherit the earth.

"Blessed are the mourners; for they shall be comforted.

"Blessed are they who hunger and thirst after righteousness; for they shall be filled.

"Blessed are the merciful; for they shall obtain mercy.

"Blessed are the pure in heart; for they shall see God.

"Blessed are the peacemakers; for they shall be called children of God.

"Blessed are they who suffer persecution for the sake of righteousness; for theirs is the kingdom of Heaven.

"Blessed are you when men revile you and persecute you, and say everything evil against you falsely, for My sake. Be glad and rejoice, because your reward will be abundant in heaven; for so they persecuted the prophets who were before you."

Manner of Almsgiving (Matthew, 6:1-4)

"Take care not to perform your religious duties before men in order to be observed by them; for if you do, you will have no reward with your Father who is in heaven. When, therefore, thou givest alms, do not have a trumpet blown before thee, as the hypocrites do in the synagogues and in the streets, that they may be honored by men. Indeed, I tell you, they have received their reward! But when thou givest alms, do not let thy left hand know what thy right hand is doing, so that thine almsgiving may be in secret; and thy Father, who sees in secret, will reward thee."

True Riches to be Stored in Heaven (Matthew, 6:19-21)

"Do not lay up for yourselves treasures upon the earth, where moth and rust consume, and where thieves break through and steal; but lay up for yourselves treasures in heaven, where neither moth nor rust consumes, and where thieves do not break through nor steal. For where thy treasure is, there will thy heart be also."

Trust in Divine Providence (Matthew, 6:25-34)

"I say to you, therefore, do not be anxious about your life, what you shall eat or what you shall drink; nor about your body, what you shall wear. Is not the life of more consequence than the food, and the body than the clothing? Look at the birds of the sky, how they neither sow nor reap nor gather into barns; yet your heavenly Father feeds them! Are you not of much more value than they? Yet who among you, by anxious thought, is able to add a single span to his life? And why should you worry about clothing? Observe the field-lilies, how they grow; they neither toil nor spin; yet I tell you that even Solomon in all his magnificence was not arrayed like one of them. But if God so clothes the grass of the field, which exists today and is thrown into the oven tomorrow, will He not much rather clothe you, O you of little faith? Do not therefore worry, saying, 'What shall we eat?' or, 'What shall we drink?' or, 'What shall we wear?' for the heathen seek after all these things; and your heavenly Father knows that you need them all. But seek first the kingdom of God and His holiness, and all these things shall be given you besides. Do not then be anxious about tomorrow, for tomorrow will take care of itself. Quite enough for the day is its own trouble."

Parable of the Sower and the Seed (Luke, 8:4-15)

Now when a great crowd was gathering, and people from every town were resorting to Him, He addressed them in a parable: "The sower went out to sow his seed; and as he sowed, some seed fell along the roadside, where it was trodden upon, and the birds of the air devoured it. And some fell upon the rock; but on sprouting it withered for lack of moisture. And some fell amid the briers, and the briers grew up with it and choked it. And some fell upon good soil; and springing up it yielded a hundred-fold crop." As He said this He cried out, "He that has ears to hear, let him hear!"

His disciples then asked Him what this parable meant. "It is granted to you," He replied, "to know the mysteries of the kingdom of God; but to the rest in parables, so that seeing they may not see, and hearing may not understand. Now the parable means this: the seed is THE WORD OF GOD. And those along the roadside are they that have heard; then comes the devil, and takes away THE WORD from their heart, that they may not believe and be saved. And those upon the rock are they who, when they hear, receive THE WORD with delight; yet these have no root: they believe for a while, and in the hour of trial fall away. And that falling among the briers are they that have heard; yet, as they go on their way, are choked by the anxieties and riches and pleasures of life, and bring no fruit to maturity. But that upon the good soil are they who, with a noble and generous heart, having heard THE WORD, hold it fast, and yield fruit with endurance."

First Epistle of St. Paul to the Corinthians (13:1-13)

If I spoke the languages of men and of angels, but had not love, I should sound as a blaring trumpet, or a clashing cymbal. And if I possessed prophetic powers, and knew all mysteries and all science, and if I possessed entire faith, so as to remove mountains, but had not love I should be nothing. And if I gave bit by bit all my possessions to feed the poor, and if I delivered up my body to be burned, but had not love, it would avail me nothing.

Love is long-suffering, is kind; love envies not, boasts not of itself, is not arrogant, is not rude, is not self-seeking, is not provoked to anger, takes no account of evil treatment, rejoices not over wickedness, but rejoices with the truth. Love bears everything, believes everything, hopes everything, endures everything.

Love never fails; but whether there be prophetic powers, they shall come to an end; or languages, they shall cease; or knowledge, it shall be rendered useless. For we know but partially, and we prophesy but partially; but when the perfect arrives, then the partial shall come to an end. When I was a child I spoke as a child, I felt as a child, I thought as a child; now that I have become a man I have discarded childish ways. For now I know partially; but then I shall know completely, even as I am completely known. And now there remain faith, hope, love—these three; but the greatest of these is love.

No. 11. The Nicene Creed

(Translations and Reprints from the Original Sources of European History, University of Pennsylvania, Philadelphia, 1898, IV, No. 2, pp. 3, 11.)

We believe in one God, the FATHER Almighty, Maker of all things visible and invisible. And in one Lord, JESUS CHRIST, the Son of God, begotten of the Father, the only-begotten; that is, of the essence of the Father, God of God, Light of Light, very God of very God, begotten, not made, being of one substance with the Father; by whom all things were made, both in heaven and on earth; who for us men, and for our salvation, came down and was incarnate and was made man; he suffered, and the third day he rose again, ascended into heaven; from thence he shall come to judge the quick and the dead. And in the HOLY GHOST. But those who say: 'There was a time when he was not;' and 'He was not before he was made;' and 'He was made out of nothing,' or 'He is of another substance' or 'essence,' or 'The Son of God is created,' or 'changeable,' or 'alterable' —they are condemned by the holy catholic and apostolic church.

The Creed as Revised by the Council of Constantinople (381 A.D.)
(Translations and Reprints, IV, No. 2, p. 11)

We believe in one God, the FATHER Almighty, Maker of heaven and earth and of all things visible and invisible. And in one Lord JESUS CHRIST, the only-begotten Son of God, begotten of the Father before all worlds, Light of Light, very God of very God, begotten, not made, being of one substance with the Father; by whom all things were made; who for us men, and for our salvation, came down from heaven, and was incarnate by the Holy Ghost of the Virgin Mary, and was made man; he was crucified for us under Pontius Pilate, and suffered, and was buried, and the third day he rose again, according to the Scriptures, and ascended into heaven, and sitteth on the right hand of the Father; from thence he shall come again, with glory, to judge the quick and the dead; whose kingdom shall have no end. And in the HOLY GHOST, the Lord and Giver of life, who proceedeth from the Father, who with the Father and the Son together is worshipped and glorified, who speak by the prophets. In one holy catholic and apostolic church; we acknowledge one baptism for the remission of sins; we look for the resurrection of the dead, and the life of the world to come. Amen.

No. 12. The persecution of Christians

(The *Letters* of Pliny the Younger, Nos. 96, 97.)

Letter No. 96, to Emperor Trajan

It is my invariable rule, sir, to refer to you in all matters where I feel doubtful; for who is more capable of removing my scruples, or informing my ignorance? Having never been present at any trials concerning those who profess Christianity, I am unacquainted not only with the nature of their crimes, or the measure of their punishment, nor how far it is proper to enter into an examination concerning them. Whether, therefore, any difference is usually made with respect to ages, or no distinction is to be observed between the young and the adult; whether repentance entitles them to a pardon, or if a man has been once a Christian it avails nothing to desist from his error; whether the very profession of Christianity, unattended with any criminal act, or only the crimes themselves inherent in the profession, are punishable,—on all these points I am in great doubt.

In the meanwhile, the method I have observed towards those who have been brought before me as Christians is this: I asked them whether they were Christians: if they admitted it, I repeated the question twice and threatened them with punishment; if they persisted, I ordered them to be at once punished,—for I was persuaded, whatever the nature of their opinions might be, a contumacious and inflexible obstinacy certainly deserved correction. There were others also brought before me possessed with the same infatuation; but being Roman citizens, I directed them to be sent to Rome.

But this crime spreading (as is usually the case), while it was actually under prosecution several instances of the same nature occurred. An anonymous information was laid before me, containing a charge against several persons, who upon examination denied they were Christians, or had ever been so. They repeated after me an invocation to the gods, and offered religious rites with wine and incense before your statue (which for that purpose I had ordered to be brought, together with those of the gods), and even reviled the name of Christ; whereas there is no forcing, it is said, those who are really Christians into any of these compliances: I thought it proper, therefore, to discharge them. Some among those who were accused by a witness in person at first confessed themselves Christians, but immediately after denied it; the rest owned indeed that they had been of that number formerly, but had now (some above three, others more, and a few above twenty years ago) renounced that error. They all worshiped your statue and the images of the gods, uttering imprecations at the same time against the name of Christ.

They affirmed that the whole of their guilt, or their error, was, that they met on a stated day before it was light, and addressed a form of prayer to Christ as to a divinity, binding themselves by a solemn oath, not for the purpose of any wicked design, but rather never to commit any fraud, theft, or adultery, never to falsify their word, nor deny a trust when they should be called on to deliver it up; after which it was their custom to separate, and then re-assemble, to eat in common a harmless meal. From this custom, however, they desisted after the publication of my edict, by which, according to your commands, I forbade the meeting of any assemblies. After receiving this account I judged it so much the more necessary to endeavor to extort the real truth, by putting two female slaves to the torture, who were said to officiate in their religious rites; but all I could discover was evidence of an absurd and extravagant superstition. I deemed it expedient therefore to adjourn all further proceedings, in order to consult you. For it appears to be a matter highly deserving your consideration, more especially as great numbers must be involved in the danger of these prosecutions, which have already extended, and are still likely to extend, to persons of all ranks and ages, and even of both sexes. In fact, this contagious superstition is not confined to the cities only, but has spread its infection among the neighboring villages and country. . . .

Letter No. 97, Trajan to Pliny

You have adopted the right course, my dear Pliny, in investigating the charges against the Christians who were brought before you. It is not possible to lay down any general rule for all such cases. Do not go out of your way to look for them. If indeed they should be brought before you, and the crime is proved, they must be punished; with the restriction, however, that where the party denies he is a Christian, and shall make it evident that he is not, by invoking our gods, let him (notwithstanding any former suspicion) be pardoned upon his repentance. Anonymous informations ought not to be received in any sort of prosecution. It is introducing a very dangerous precedent, and is quite foreign to the spirit of our age.

No. 13. St. Augustine's *Confessions*

(The Confessions of St. Augustine, tr. Marcus Dods. Edinburgh, 1896.)

Ch. VIII. 19. In the midst, then, of this great strife of my inner dwelling, which I had strongly raised up against my soul in the chamber of my heart, troubled both in mind and countenance, I seized upon Alypius, and exclaimed: "What is wrong with us? What is this? What heardest thou? The unlearned start up and 'take' heaven, and we, with our learning, but wanting heart, see where we wallow in flesh and blood! Because others have preceded us, are we ashamed to follow, and not rather ashamed at not following?" Some such words I gave utterance to, and in my excitement flung myself from him, while he gazed upon me in silent astonishment. For I spoke not in my wonted tone, and my brow, cheeks, eyes, colour, tone of voice, all expressed my emotion more than the words. There was a little garden belonging to our lodging, of which we had the use, as of the whole house; for the master, our landlord, did not live there. Thither had the tempest within my breast hurried me, where no one might impede the fiery struggle in which I was engaged with myself, until it came to the issue that Thou knewest, though I did not. But I was made that I might be whole, and dying that I might have life, knowing what evil thing I was, but not knowing what good thing I was shortly to become. Into the garden, then, I retired, Alypius following my steps. . . .

Ch. XII. 28. But when a profound reflection had, from the secret depths of my soul, drawn together and heaped up all my misery before the sight of my heart, there arose a mighty storm, accompanied by as mighty a shower of tears. Which, that I might pour forth fully, with its natural expressions, I stole away from Alypius; for it suggested itself to me that solitude was fitter for the business of weeping. So I retired to such a distance that even his presence could not be oppressive to me. Thus was it with me at that time, and he perceived it; for something, I believe, I had spoken, wherein the sound of my voice appeared choked with weeping, and in that state had I risen up. He then remained where we had been sitting, most completely astonished. I flung myself down, how, I know not, under a certain fig-tree, giving free course to my tears, and the streams of mine eyes gushed out, an acceptable sacrifice unto Thee. And, not indeed in these words, yet to this effect, spake I much unto Thee,—"But Thou, O Lord, how long?" "How long, Lord? Wilt Thou be angry for ever? Oh, remember not against us former iniquities;" for I felt that I was enthralled by them. I sent up these sorrowful cries,—"How long, how long? Tomorrow, and tomorrow? Why not now? Why is there not this hour an end to my uncleanness?"

29. I was saying these things and weeping in the most bitter contrition of my heart, when, lo, I heard the voice as of a boy or girl, I know not which, coming from a neighbouring house, chanting, and oft repeating, "Take up and read; take up and read." Immediately my countenance was changed, and I began most earnestly to consider whether it was usual for children in any kind of game to sing such words; nor could I remember ever to have heard the like. So, restraining the torrent of my tears, I rose up, interpreting it no other way than as a command to me from Heaven to open

the book, and to read the first chapter I should light upon. For I had heard of Antony, that, accidentally coming in whilst the gospel was being read, he received the admonition as if what was read were addressed to him, "Go and sell what thou hast, and give it to the poor, and thou shalt have treasure in heaven; and come and follow me." And by such oracle was he forthwith converted unto Thee. So quickly I returned to the place where Alypius was sitting; for there had I put down the volume of the apostles, when I rose thence. I grasped, opened, and in silence read that paragraph on which my eyes first fell,—"Not in rioting and drunkenness, not in chambering and wantonness, not in strife and envying; but put ye on the Lord Jesus Christ, and make not provision for the flesh, to fulfill the lusts thereof." No further would I read, nor did I need; for instantly, as the sentence ended,—by a light, as it were, of security infused into my heart,—all the gloom of doubt vanished away.

No. 14. St. Augustine's *The City of God*

(*The City of God of St. Augustine*, tr. Marcus Dods. Edinburgh, 1888.)

Bk. 1. Of the advantages and disadvantages which often indiscriminately accrue to good and wicked men.

There is, too, a very great difference in the purpose served both by those events which we call adverse and those called prosperous. For the good man is neither uplifted with the good things of time, nor broken by its ills; but the wicked man, because he is corrupted by this world's happiness, feels himself punished by its unhappiness. Yet often, even in the present distribution of temporal things, does God plainly evince His own interference. For if every sin were now visited with manifest punishment, nothing would seem to be reserved for the final judgement; on the other hand, if no sin received now a plainly divine punishment, it would be concluded that there is no divine providence at all. And so of the good things of this life: if God did not by a very visible liberality confer these on some of those persons who ask for them, we should say that these good things were not at His disposal; and if He gave them to all who sought them, we should suppose that such were the only rewards of His service; and such a service would make us not godly, but greedy rather, and covetous. Wherefore, though good and bad men suffer alike, we must not suppose that there is no difference between the men themselves, because there is no difference in what they both suffer. For even in the likeness of the sufferings, there remains an unlikeness in the sufferers; and though exposed to the same anguish, virtue and vice are not the same thing. For as the same fire causes gold to glow brightly, and chaff to smoke; and under the same flail the straw is beaten small, while the grain is cleansed; and as the lees are not mixed with the oil, though squeezed out of the vat by the same pressure, so the same violence of affliction proves, purges, clarifies the good, but damns, ruins, exterminates the wicked. And thus it is that in the same affliction the wicked detest God and blaspheme, while the good pray and praise. So material a difference does it make, not what ills are suffered, but what kind of man suffers them. For, stirred up with the same movement, mud exhales a horrible stench, and ointment emits a fragrant odour.

Bk. 11. Of this part of the work, wherein we begin to explain the origin and end of the two cities.

The city of God we speak of is the same to which testimony is borne by that Scripture, which excels all the writings of all nations by its divine authority, and has brought under its influence all kinds of minds, and this not by a casual intellectual movement, but obviously by an express providential arrangement. For there it is written, "Glorious things are spoken of thee, O city of God." And in another psalm we read, "Great is the Lord, and greatly to be praised in the city of our God, in the mountain of His holiness, increasing the joy of the whole earth." And, a little after, in the same psalm, "As we have heard, so have we seen in the city of the Lord of hosts, in the city of our God. God has established it for ever." And in another, "There is a river the streams whereof shall make glad the city of our God, the holy place of the tabernacles of the Most High. God is in the midst of her, she shall not be moved." From these and similar testimonies, all of which it were tedious to cite, we have learned that there is a city of God, and its Founder has inspired us with a love which makes us covet its citizenship. To this Founder of the holy city the citizens of the earthly city prefer their own gods, not knowing that He is the God of gods, not of false, i.e. of impious and proud gods, who, being deprived of His unchangeable and freely communicated light, and so reduced to a kind of poverty-stricken power, eagerly grasp at their own private privileges, and seek divine honours from their deluded subjects, but of the pious and holy gods, who are better pleased to submit themselves to one, than to subject many to themselves, and who would rather worship God than be worshipped as God. But to the enemies of this city we have replied in the ten preceding books, according to our ability and the help afforded by our Lord and King. Now, recognizing what is expected of me, and not unmindful of my promise, and relying, too, on the same succour, I will endeavour to treat of the origin, and progress, and deserved destinies of the two cities (the earthly and the heavenly, to wit), which, as we said, are in this present world commingled, and as it were entangled together. And, first, I will explain how the foundations of these two cities were orginally laid, in the difference that arose among the angels.

No. 15. The first Christian hermits

(*The Life of Paulus the First Hermit* by St. Jerome. *A Select Library of Nicene and Post-Nicene Fathers*, VI. New York, 1912.)

It has been a subject of wide-spread and frequent discussion what monk was the first to give a signal example of the hermit life. For some going back too far have found a beginning in those holy men Elias and John [Baptist], of whom the former seems to have been more than a monk and the latter to have begun to prophesy before his birth. Others, and their opinion is that commonly received, maintain that Antony was the origina-tor of this mode of life, which view is partly true. Partly I say, for the fact is not so much that he preceded the rest as that they all derived from him the necessary stimulus. But it is asserted even at the present day by Amathas and Macarius, two of Antony's disciples, the former of whom laid his mas-ter in the grave, that a certain Paul of Thebes was the leader in the move-ment, though not the first to bear the name. . . . So then inasmuch as both Greek and Roman writers have handed down careful accounts of Antony, I have determined to write a short history of Paul's early and latter days, more because the thing has been passed over than from confidence in my own ability. What his middle life was like, and what snares of Satan he experienced, no man, it is thought, has yet discovered.

During the persecutions of Decius and Valerian [249-251, 253-258], when Cornelius at Rome and Cyprian at Carthage shed their blood in blessed martyrdom, many churches in Egypt and the Thebaid were laid waste by the fury of the storm. . . . While such enormities were being perpetrated in the lower part of Thebaid, Paul and his newly married sister were bereaved of both their parents, he being about sixteen years of age. He was heir to a rich inheritance, highly skilled in both Greek and Egyptian learn-ing, gifted with a gentle disposition and a deep love for God. Amid the thunders of persecution he retired to a house at a considerable distance and in a more secluded spot. But to what crimes does not the "accursed thirst for gold" impel the human heart? His brother-in-law conceived the thought of betraying the youth whom he was bound to conceal. The young man had the tact to understand this, and, conforming his will to the necessity, fled to the mountain wilds to wait for the end of the persecution. . . . At length he found a rocky mountain, at the foot of which, closed by a stone, was a cave of no great size. He removed the stone (so eager are men to learn what is hidden), made eager search, and saw within a large hall, open to the sky, but shaded by the wide-spread branches of an ancient palm. The tree, however, did not conceal a fountain of transparent clearness. . . .

Accordingly, regarding his abode as a gift from God, he fell in love with it, and there in prayer and solitude spent all the rest of his life. The palm afforded him food and clothing. And, that no one may deem this impossible, I call to witness Jesus and His holy angels that I have seen and still see in that part of the desert which lies between Syria and the Saracens' country, monks of whom one was shut up for thirty years and lived on barley bread and muddy water, while another in an old cistern kept himself alive on five dried figs a day. What I relate then is so strange that it will appear incredible to those who do not believe the words that "all things are possible to him that believeth."

But to return to the point at which I digressed. The blessed Paul had already lived on earth the life of heaven for a hundred and thirteen years, and Antony at the age of ninety was dwelling in another place of solitude (as he himself was wont to declare), when the thought occurred to the latter, that no monk more perfect than himself had settled in the desert. However, in the stillness of the night it was revealed to him that there was farther in the desert a much better man than he, and that he ought to go and visit him. So then at break of day the venerable old man, supporting and guiding his weak limbs with a staff, started to go: but what direction to choose he knew not. . . . Antony traversed the region on which he had entered, seeing only the traces of wild beasts, and the wide waste of the desert. What to do, whither to wend his way, he knew not. Another day had now passed. One thing alone was left him, his confident belief that he could not be forsaken by Christ. The darkness of the second night he wore away in prayer. . . . At length through the fearful midnight darkness a light appeared in the distance. In his eager haste he struck his foot against a stone and roused the echoes; whereupon the blessed Paul closed the open door and made it fast with a bar. Then Antony sank to the ground at the entrance and . . . craved admission. . . . Paul gave him access, and, the door being opened, they threw themselves into each other's arms, greeted one another by name, and joined in thanksgiving to God. After the sacred kiss Paul sat down and thus began to address Antony. "Behold the man whom you have sought with so much toil, his limbs decayed with age, his gray hairs unkempt. You see before you a man who ere long will be dust. But love endures all things. Tell me therefore, I pray you, how fares the human race? Are new homes springing up in the ancient cities? What government directs the world? Are there still some remaining for the demons to carry away by their delusions?"

No. 16. St. Basil on the monastic life

(*The Letters of St. Basil. A Select Library of Nicene and Post-Nicene Fathers*, VIII. New York, 1895.)

No. XXII. On the Perfection of the Life of Solitaries

Many things are set forth by inspired Scripture as binding upon all who are anxious to please God. But, for the present, I have only deemed it necessary to speak by way of brief reminder concerning the questions which have recently been stirred among you, so far as I have learnt from the study of inspired Scripture itself. I shall thus leave behind me detailed evidence, easy of apprehension, for the information of industrious students, who in their turn will be able to inform others.

The Christian ought to be so minded as becomes his heavenly calling, and his life and conversation ought to be worthy of the Gospel of Christ. The Christian ought not to be of doubtful mind, nor by anything drawn away from the recollection of God and of His purposes and judgements. The Christian ought in all things to become superior to the righteousness existing under the law, and neither swear nor lie. He ought not to speak evil; to do violence; to fight; to avenge himself; to return evil for evil; to be angry. The Christian ought to be patient, whatever he have to suffer, and to convict the wrong-doer in season, not with the desire of his own vindication, but of his brother's reformation, according to the commandment of the Lord. The Christian ought not to say anything behind his brother's back with the object of calumniating him, for this is slander, even if what is said is true. He ought to turn away from the brother who speaks evil against him; he ought not to indulge in jesting; he ought not to laugh nor even to suffer laugh makers.

He must not talk idly, saying things which are of no service to the hearers nor to such usage as is necessary and permitted us by God; so that workers may do their best as far as possible to work in silence; and that good words be suggested to them by those who are intrusted with the duty of carefully dispensing the word to the building up of the faith, lest God's Holy Spirit be grieved. . . .

The Christian ought not to be enslaved by wine; nor to be eager for flesh meat, and as a general rule ought not to be a lover of pleasure in eating or drinking, "for every man that striveth for the mastery is temperate in all things." The Christian ought to regard all the things that are given him for his use, not as his to hold as his own or to lay up. . . . No

Christian ought to think of himself as his own master, but each should rather so think and act as though given by God to be slave to his like minded brethren. . . .

The Christian ought never to murmur either in scarcity of necessities, or in toil or labour, for the responsibility in these matters lies with such as have authority in them. There never ought to be any clamour, or any behaviour or agitation by which anger is expressed, or diversion of mind from the full assurance of the presence of God.

The voice should be modulated; no one ought to answer another, or do anything, roughly or contemptuously, but in all things moderation and respect should be shewn to every one. No wily glances of the eye are to be allowed, nor any behaviour or gestures which grieve a brother and shew contempt. Any display in cloak or shoes is to be avoided; it is idle ostentation. Cheap things ought to be used for bodily necessity; and nothing ought to be spent beyond that is necessary, or for mere extravagance; this is a misuse of our property. The Christian ought not to seek for honour, or claim precedence. Every one ought to put all others before himself. . . .

The Christian ought not to grudge another's reputation, nor rejoice over any man's faults; he ought in Christ's love to grieve and be afflicted at his brother's faults, and rejoice over his brother's good deeds. He ought not to be indifferent or silent before sinners. He who is proved wrong or rebuked ought to take it willingly, recognizing his own gain in being set right.

No. 17. St. Jerome on the monastic life

(*The Letters of St. Jerome. A Select Library of Nicene and Post-Nicene Fathers*, VI. New York, 1893.)

No. XXII. To Eustochium (excerpts)

I would have you draw from your monastic vow not pride but fear. You walk laden with gold; you must keep out of the robber's way. To us men this life is a race-course: we contend here, we are crowned elsewhere. No man can lay aside fear while serpents and scorpions beset his path. The Lord says: "My sword hath drunk its fill in heaven," and do you expect to find peace on the earth? No, the earth yields only thorns and thistles, and its dust is food for the serpent. "For our wrestling is not against flesh and blood, but against the principalities, against the powers, against the world-rulers of this darkness, against the spiritual hosts of wickedness in the heavenly places." We are hemmed in by hosts of foes, our enemies are upon every side. The weak flesh will soon be ashes: one against many, it fights against tremendous odds. . . . So long as we are held down by this frail body, so long as we have our treasure in earthen vessels; so long as the flesh lusteth against the spirit and the spirit against the flesh, there can be no sure victory. "Our adversary the devil goeth about as a roaring lion seeking whom he may devour."

I would begin by urging you and warning you as Christ's spouse to avoid wine as you would avoid poison. For wine is the first weapon used by demons against the young. Greed does not shake, nor pride puff up, nor ambition infatuate so much as this. Other vices we easily escape, but this enemy is shut up within us, and wherever we go we carry him with us. Wine and youth between them kindle the fire of sensual pleasure. There are, in the Scriptures, countless divine answers condemning gluttony and approving simple food. But as fasting is not my present theme and an adequate discussion of it would require a treatise to itself, these few observations must suffice of the many which the subject suggests. By them you will understand why the first man, obeying his belly and not God, was cast down from paradise into this vale of tears; and why Satan used hunger to tempt the Lord Himself in the wilderness; and why the apostle cries: "Meats for the belly and the belly for meats, but God shall destroy both it and them;" and why he speaks of the self-indulgent as men "whose God is their belly." For men invariably worship what they like best. Care must be taken, therefore, that abstinence may bring back to Paradise those whom satiety once drove out.

Do not court the company of married ladies or visit the houses of the high-born. Do not look too often on the life which you despised to become a virgin. Women of the world, you know, plume themselves because their husbands are on the bench or in other high positions. Let your companions be women pale and thin with fasting, and approved by their years and conduct. Be subject to your parents, imitating the example of your spouse. Take food in moderation, and never overload your stomach. When you rise at night to pray, let your breath be that of an empty and not that of an overfull stomach. Read often, learn all that you can. Let sleep overcome you, the roll still in your hands; when your head falls, let it be on the sacred page. Let your fasts be of daily occurrence and your refreshment such as avoids satiety. It is idle to carry an empty stomach if, in two or three days' time, the fast is to be made up for by repletion. When cloyed the mind immediately grows sluggish, and when the ground is watered it puts forth the thorns of lust.

It is hard for the human soul to avoid loving something, and our mind must of necessity give way to affection of one kind or another. The love of the flesh is overcome by the love of the spirit. Desire is quenched by desire. What is taken from the one increases the other. Therefore, as you lie on your couch, say again and again: "By night have I sought Him whom my soul loveth."

Some one may say, "So you dare detract from wedlock, which is a state blessed by God?" I do not detract from wedlock when I set virginity before it. No one compares a bad thing with a good. Wedded women may congratulate themselves that they come next to virgins. I praise wedlock, I praise marriage, but it is because they give me virgins. I gather the rose from the thorns, the gold from the earth, the pearl from the shell. Why, mother, do you grudge your daughter her virginity? Your watchful affection has kept her a virgin. Are you angry with her because she chooses to be a king's wife and not a soldier's? She has conferred on you a high privilege; you are now the mother-in-law of God.

Emerge, I pray you, for a while from your prison-house, and paint before your eyes the reward of your present toil, a reward which "eye hath not seen, nor ear heard, neither hath it entered into the heart of man." What will be the glory of that day when Mary, the mother of the Lord, shall come to meet you, accompanied by her virgin choirs! As often as this life's idle show tries to charm you; as often as you see in the world some vain pomp, transport yourself in mind to Paradise, essay to be now what you will be hereafter. . . .

No. 18. The Rule of St. Benedict

(*Select Historical Documents of the Middle Ages,* tr. Ernest F. Henderson. London, 1896, pp. 274-314 *passim.*)

Prologue. . . . we are about to found, therefore, a school for the Lord's service; in the organization of which we trust that we shall ordain nothing severe and nothing burdensome. But even if, the demands of justice dictating it, something a little irksome shall be the result, for the purpose of amending vices or preserving charity;—thou shalt not therefore, struck by fear, flee the way of salvation, which can not be entered upon except through a narrow entrance. But as one's way of life and one's faith progresses, the heart becomes broadened, and, with the unutterable sweetness of love, the way of the mandates of the Lord is traversed. Thus, never departing from His guidance, continuing in the monastery in His teaching until death, through patience we are made partakers in Christ's passion, in order that we may merit to be companions in His kingdom.

An abbot who is worthy to preside over a monastery ought always to remember what he is called, and carry out with his deeds the name of a Superior. For he is believed to be Christ's representative, since he is called by His name, the apostle saying: "Ye have received the spirit of adoption of sons, whereby we call Abba, Father." Therefore, when any one receives the name of abbot, he ought to rule over his disciples with a double teaching; that is, let him show forth all good and holy things by deeds more than by words. So that to ready disciples he may propound the mandates of

God in words; but, to the hard-hearted and the more simple-minded, he may show forth the divine precepts by his deeds. He shall make no distinction of persons in the monastery. One shall not be more cherished than another, unless it be the one whom he finds excelling in good works or in obedience. A freeborn man shall not be preferred to one coming from servitude, unless there be some other reasonable cause. As often as anything especial is to be done in the monastery, the abbot shall call together the whole congregation, and shall himself explain the question at issue. And, having heard the advice of the brethren, he shall think it over by himself, and shall do what he considers most advantageous. And for this reason, moreover, we have said that all ought to be called to take counsel: because often it is to a younger person that God reveals what is best.

The first grade of humility is obedience without delay. This becomes those who, on account of the holy service which they have professed, or on account of the fear of hell or the glory of eternal life consider nothing dearer to them than Christ. Let us do as the prophet says: "I said, I will take heed to my ways that I sin not with my tongue, I have kept my mouth with a bridle: I was dumb with silence, I held my peace even from good; and my sorrow was stirred." And everywhere, sitting or walking or standing, let him always be with head inclined, his looks fixed upon the ground; remembering every hour that he is guilty of his sins.

If when to powerful men we wish to suggest anything, we do not presume to do it unless with reverence and humility: how much more should we supplicate with all humility, and devotion of purity, God who is the Lord of all.

They [the monks] shall sleep separately in separate beds. They shall receive positions for their beds, after the manner of their characters, according to the dispensation of their abbot. They shall sleep clothed, and girt with belts or with ropes; and they shall not have their knives at their sides while they sleep, lest perchance in a dream they should wound the sleepers. And let the monks be always on the alert; and, when the signal is given, rising without delay, let them hasten to mutually prepare themselves for the service of God. . . . And when they rise for the service of God, they shall exhort each other mutually with moderation, on account of the excuses that those who are sleepy are inclined to make.

As cellarer of the monastery there shall be elected from the congregation one who is wise, mature in character, sober, not given to much eating. . . . All the utensils of the monastery, and all its substance, he shall look upon as though they were the sacred vessels of the altar. The brothers shall so serve each other in turn that no one shall be excused from the duty of cooking, unless either through sickness, or because he is occupied in some important work of utility.

We believe, moreover, that, for the daily refection of the sixth as well as of the ninth hour, two cooked dishes, on account of the infirmities of the different ones, are enough for all tables: so that whoever, perchance, can not eat of one may partake of the other. Therefore let two cooked dishes suffice for all the brothers: and, if it is possible to obtain apples or growing vegetables, a third may be added. But the eating of the flesh of quadrupeds shall be abstained from altogether by every one, excepting alone the weak and the sick. Each one has his own gift from God, the one in this way, the other in that. Therefore it is with some hesitation that the amount of daily sustenance for others is fixed by us. Nevertheless, in view of the weakness of the infirm we believe that a pint of wine a day is enough for each one.

Idleness is the enemy of the soul. And therefore, at fixed times, the brothers ought to be occupied in manual labour; and again, at fixed times, in sacred reading.

All guests who come shall be received as though they were Christ: for He Himself said: "I was a stranger and ye took me in." And to all, fitting honour shall be shown; but, most of all, to servants of the faith and to pilgrims. Chiefly in the reception of the poor and of pilgrims shall care be most anxiously exhibited: for in them Christ is received the more. For the very fear of the rich exacts honour for them.

A monastery, moreover, if it can be done, ought so to be arranged that everything necessary,—that is, water, a mill, a garden, a bakery,—may be made use of, and different arts be carried on, within the monastery; so that there shall be no need for the monks to wander about outside. For this is not at all good for their souls. We wish, moreover, that this Rule be read very often in the congregation; lest any of the brothers excuse himself on account of ignorance.

No. 19. The *Pastoral Rule* of St. Gregory the Great

(The Book of Pastoral Rule. A Select Library of Nicene and Post-Nicene Fathers, XII. New York, 1895.)

Pt. I. Ch. X. What manner of man ought to come to rule

That man, therefore, ought by all means to be drawn with cords to be an example of good living who already lives spiritually, dying to all passions of the flesh; who disregards worldy prosperity; who is afraid of no adversity; who desires only inward wealth; whose intention the body, in good accord with it, thwarts not at all by its frailness, nor the spirit greatly by its disdain: one who is not led to covet the things of others, but gives freely of his own; who through the bowels of compassion is quickly moved to pardon, yet is never bent down from the fortress of rectitude by pardoning more than is meet; who perpetrates no unlawful deeds, yet deplores those perpetrated by others as though they were his own; who out of affection of heart sympathizes with another's infirmity, and so rejoices in the good of his neighbour as though it were his own advantage; who so insinuates himself as an example to others in all he does that among them he has nothing, at any rate of his own past deeds, to blush for; who studies so to live that he may be able to water even dry hearts with the streams of doctrine; who has already learnt by the use and trial of prayer that he can obtain what he has requested from the Lord, having had already said to him, as it were, through the voice of experience, *While thou art yet speaking, I will say, Here am I* (Isai. LVIII. 9). For if perchance any one should come to us asking us to intercede for him with some great man, who was incensed against him, but to us unknown, we should at once reply, We cannot go to intercede for you, since we have no familiar acquaintance with that man. If, then, a man blushes to become an intercessor with another man on whom he has no claim, with what idea can any one grasp the post of intercession with God for the people, who does not know himself to be in favour with Him through the merit of his own life? And how can he ask of Him pardon for others while ignorant whether towards himself He is appeased? And in this matter there is yet another thing to be more anxiously feared; namely, lest one who is supposed to be competent to appease wrath should himself provoke it on account of guilt of his own. For we all know well that, when one who is in disfavour is sent to intercede with an incensed person, the mind of the latter is provoked to greater severity. Wherefore let one who is still tied and bound with earthly desires beware lest by more grievously incensing the strict judge, while he delights himself in his place of honour, he become the cause of ruin to his subordinates.

Pt. II. Ch. 1. How one who has in due order arrived at a place of rule ought to demean himself in it.

The conduct of a prelate ought so far to transcend the conduct of the people as the life of a shepherd is wont to exalt him above the flock. For one whose estimation is such that the people are called his flock is bound anxiously to consider what great necessity is laid upon him to maintain rectitude. It is necessary, then, that in thought he should be pure, in action chief; discreet in keeping silence, profitable in speech; a near neighbour to every one in sympathy, exalted above all in contemplation; a familiar friend of good livers through humility, unbending against the vices of evildoers through zeal for righteousness; not relaxing in his care for what is inward from being occupied in outward things, nor neglecting to provide for outward things in his solicitude for what is inward. But the things which we have thus briefly touched on let us now unfold and discuss more at length.

3

THE BARBARIZATION
OF THE WEST

Celts, Slavs, Huns

No Racially Pure Nations. We must now introduce the different peoples who forced their way into the Roman empire between the fourth and sixth centuries and merged with its subjects to produce the varied cultures of modern Europe. We can enumerate the names of these peoples—Celts, Germans, Slavs, and Asiatic nomads—more readily than we can describe their respective mores, and this for two reasons. In the first place, many scholars hesitate to associate a particular set of qualities or institutions with any of these different peoples, on the theory that even as early as the fourth century A.D. none of them was sufficiently pure and isolated to justify such differentiation. Historians point to the Romans, for example, who were a hopelessly composite people as early as 509 B.C. when they ousted the Etruscans and established the Roman Republic. Even the most savage of conquerors whose barbarities history has exposed usually spared the lives of the women and children of the conquered. Thus long before the names of individual racial strains had grown sufficiently distinct for historians to make them out, a ceaseless sharing of physical and cultural traits between conqueror and conquered had been in progress.

Inadequacy of Sources. Scholars speak with considerable caution about the characteristics of these different peoples, the Celts, Germans, Slavs, and Asiatic nomads, for yet another reason. Even accepting the possibility that the mores of this or that group had remained free of "contamination" from foreign influences and could present the world a pure civilization, the scholar in attempting a study of this civilization would find but meager and often uncritical evidence upon which to base his investigations. The most informative source about any of the peoples noted above is a brief treatise by Tacitus concerning the Germans, but to say this is the best is not to say that it is dependable. Though a serious historian, Tacitus never saw the Germans whom he described, and those he described lived fully two hundred and fifty years before the Germans who penetrated the empire in the late fourth century. How applicable to ourselves, for instance, would a characterization be which a foreign writer who had never visited our shores drew up about Americans in 1700? Furthermore, there is good reason to suspect Tacitus of magnifying the virtues of the Germans in order to arouse the Romans to the threat of the warlike peoples north of the Rhine and Danube. However, lean the historian must upon Tacitus, for all else that is available is Caesar who lived considerably farther from the scene than did Tacitus; Jordanes whose *History of the Goths* is note-worthy chiefly for its unreliability; and scattered but occasionally revealing references in Orosius, Procopius, and Ammianus Marcellinus.

Celts. The Celts figured least prominently in the invasions of the fourth to the sixth centuries which transformed or overwhelmed Roman civilization. Most of them had already been living either with or near the Romans for so many centuries that they had assimilated a great deal of Roman culture. The Celts whom Caesar fought in France could scarcely be distinguished four hundred years later from the descendants of his own veterans who had settled there. These Celts of France, together with those who occupied Spain and Britain, were among the invaded rather than invaders. The Celts of western England, Wales, Scotland, and Ireland retained their pristine Celtic ways in large measure, but except for pirate raids from Ireland, only the Picts and Scots in their highland fastnesses in Scotland posed any kind of a threat to the Roman empire in that part of the world. These Celts have been called fierce, restless, and imaginative, but if they were tall and fair as early writers attest, it was only those of the outlying areas who retained into medieval times those qualities in any purity. The humbler native stock of shorter and darker men whom the Celts found in western Europe, altered substantially, if it did not engulf, the proud physical characteristics of its conqueror.

Slavs. Of the early Slavs even less is known than of the Celts and Germans, despite their overwhelming numbers today. They were blocked from immediate contact with the Romans who might otherwise have noticed them, by Germanic and Asiatic tribes who were no more literate than they were. So it is not until the sixth century when we learn some-thing about them from the pen of Byzantine historian Procopius. He pictures them as a peace-loving people and as perennially abused and enslaved by their more warlike neighbors. It may be significant that early

Slavic reveals no word for weapons. Some philologists say it was the ease with which they permitted themselves to be enslaved that gave the Slavs their name. What we know of their social and political organization and of their material advancement suggests a civilization distinctly inferior to that of their Germanic neighbors. It is said that the Slavs had no choice but to be vegetarians since the tribes around them kept them robbed of their cattle. Still if the vegetarianism of the Slavs was a dietary trait, it might as readily be laid to their teeming numbers. Surely it was their high birth rate which saved them from extinction, and which enabled them in time to absorb almost without trace their less prolific conquerors. From their original home among the woodland marshes of the Pripet River (or the Vistula River) where nature afforded a measure of protection denied them by temperament, they spread out quietly in all directions, into open country and into areas vacated by their enemies. Today they cover two thirds of Europe.

The Huns. The most fearsome of the different peoples who contributed to the destruction of the Roman empire and civilization were the Huns. So at least is the impression one gains from the few western writers who mention them. For was it not the terror of these Huns which drove the powerful Visigothic nation in panic across the wide Danube to seek the protection of Rome? Seventy-five years later, it was the approach of these same Huns westward which impelled Celt, German, and Roman to forget mutual animosities for the moment in 451 A.D. and join hands against this terrible menace. (See page 110.) And if some doubt lingers regarding the savagery of these people, one need but consult Jordanes who considered them so brutish and subhuman as to have been sired by the devil himself. They were small, foul, and skinny, low-browed, high-cheeked, and scar-faced. "They made their foes flee in horror because their swarthy aspect was fearful, and they had, if I may call it so, a sort of shapeless lump, not a head, with pin-holes rather than eyes." But such a view, the traditional one, is undoubtedly overdrawn. It rests solely on the Latin sources which of all are the least reliable. The Romans knew the Huns only by hearsay, and from those who had fled their approach in fear of their lives. Even we, to our subsequent confusion, are inclined to paint our war-time enemies as something less than human. Recent scholars as they dig deeper into Byzantine, Hungarian, and Armenian sources find the Huns a less frightening people than did their contemporaries. One may wonder how so mild a picture of Attila and his Huns could have found its way into the *Nibelungenlied* (see page 606), had they been as ferocious as the historical sources declare. (Reading 23)

Their Habitat. The homeland of these yellow-faced nomads is the least controversial question concerning them. It is believed that they lived originally in the vast reaches which lay between the Ural Mountains on the west, the Altai Mountains to the east, and the Caspian Sea to the south.

Here nature reveals herself in one of her fiercest moods. Man must contend with the greatest extremes of heat and cold, with bitter winds that freeze him to the marrow in winter, and with hot scorching heat waves that sear his flesh in the summer. Underfoot stretches in all directions a limitless expanse of unproductive sand and gravel. Life is always harsh, for it means following the weather northward in the spring with the deer to the grasslands on the edge of Siberia, to return again with them in the fall to the southern steppes of Turkestan. The livelihood of these nomads was linked to that of their flocks of sheep. Their fare, except for a little millet which can mature in a short growing season, consisted primarily of fermented milk and cheese and whatever game they might stumble upon. Always on the move as their flocks ate up the pasturage, they almost lived out their lives on the backs of their wiry steeds, both man and beast the products of the unfriendly elements. For sheer toughness, endurance, and mobility, there never was so indomitable a pair as the Mongol astride his horse—as so many peoples discovered to their woe.

Hunnish Expansion.   From this inhospitable habitat in west-central Asia these nomads needed little encouragement to impel them to seek better homes elsewhere. Already as early as the third century B.C., the Chinese emperor in desperation threw up that tremendous chain of fortifications known as the Great Wall to keep them out of his country. These nomads spilled southward into Afghanistan and Persia, into northern Mesopotamia, Syria, and Asia Minor, and through the gap between the Ural Mountains and the Caspian Sea into the steppes of southern Russia. Where they found more sedentary life possible, they ceased being nomads and erected villages. In time these herdsmen came to possess social institutions, a well-developed political organization, and a formidable military machine. Of the efficiency of the latter, the pages of medieval history provide constant evidence, as Hun, Bulgar, Avar, Mongol, Tartar, Turk, and others poured out from this same general habitat to carry rapine and desolation westward. Much of the military prowess of these nomads can be laid to their speed—they seldom gave their enemies time to concentrate. So inured was the nomad to the normal demands of human nature, that he could outlast his stronger opponent as inexorably as his horse could wear down the heavier charger his enemy rode. His strategy was to avoid frontal attacks where his small horse, his bow, arrows, and spears were no match for the heavier armor and weapons of the foe. The Huns preferred by means of fierce raids or feints of retreat, to lead the enemy to break formation so that they could then pick off and destroy the smaller, disorganized and demoralized units with relative ease. Fearsome, indeed, were the Asiatic invaders, but the fact that Bulgar, Magyar, and Turk have left their blood and names to Europe suggests that they came less in the guise of marauding nomads than as migrants on the lookout for a home. In this respect they would have differed little from the Germans who fled in terror before them.

The Germans

Social Traits. The most numerous and most important of all the invaders to cross the frontiers of the Roman empire were the Germans. The Germans may have been the original inhabitants of Scandinavia. In any event, as early as the sixth century B.C., they began to find the bleak shores of the North Sea and Baltic too confining for their increasing numbers, and we see them moving southward and westward in the wake of the migrating Celts. By 200 B.C. they had extended their power as far west as the Rhine. Though Tacitus was able to identify more than fifty Germanic tribes, he considered them all equally "pure and untainted by intermarriage with other peoples," for "who would leave Asia, Africa, or Italy in order to visit Germany, with its unlovely scenery, its bitter climate, its general dreariness to sense and eye?" What most impressed the dark-eyed and moderate-statured Roman about these Germans were their tall, muscular frames, their blue eyes and blonde or red hair. Tacitus draws, probably overdraws, a vivid picture of a virile, gifted folk with many of the virtues and vices of primitive civilizations. The men were fierce and quarrelsome. When not away on a campaign or hunting, they trifled away their time in sloth, gambling, and drunkenness. "They are so strangely inconsistent," wrote Tacitus. "They love indolence, but they hate peace." Martial virtues of courage and loyalty they held in the highest honor, and they buried the infamy of the coward in the mire of a swamp. Though hostile to others, toward visitors and guests they were most hospitable. Monogamy was the rule except with chieftains. Tacitus has special commendation for the German wife and mother, prolific and hardworking, and devoted equally to children as to the husband whom she might accompany into battle. (Reading 20)

Their Homes and Fare. Owing partly to their semi-migratory character, partly to the indolence of the men, the homes of the early Germans proved no more comfortable than the climate. Until they were influenced by contact with a higher civilization, interwoven branches plastered with mud sufficed for the sides of their huts, with a roof of thatched straw and a floor of ground. A particularly severe winter might drive them into caves or burrows. They lived in villages where each hut stood somewhat apart from its neighbors. The German woman had learned to weave wool and linen long before encountering the Roman, although furs remained a common clothing material because of the harsh climate. German women also knew how to make soap, and to fashion vessels of earthenware in which to store food. Strikingly beautiful ornaments and utensils of gold and silver attest to the aesthetic instincts of the race. The fare of the German was simple, although it actually included more meat than that contained in the average Roman diet. The German villager ate pork, horsemeat, products of the hunt, cheese, and cakes of grain meal, and fish whenever available. His food he washed down with a fermentation of wheat and barley which has ever since remained the most popular beverage of the land east of the Rhine. Only a small measure of agriculture did the all-embracing forest permit, and the wealth of the individual was counted not in grain but in cattle, sheep, and horses. Cattle actually served as a kind of currency. Despite the primitiveness of German civilization, social stratification was already visible in Tacitus' day. There were a few noble families, a small number of slaves and of freedmen. Most of the villagers were freemen. The distinction between slave and freedman was more apparent than real. The freedman did not bear arms which was the mark of the true German, while the slave normally had a plot of land to work from which he paid his owner a portion of the grain produced.

Political Institutions.   The political institutions of these early Germans resembled those of similarly primitive peoples. A number of families formed a clan and several of these would constitute a tribe, which in time of war might find it necessary to ally itself with other tribes. Chieftains or kings enjoyed positions of leadership in the tribe, not of control. The chieftain or king was always elected, although his family might claim almost hereditary possession of the office. Yet it was the chief's or king's ability as a warrior that commanded the respect of the tribesmen, not any authority which more advanced civilizations might consider implicit in that office. These Germans lacked any conception of the state or of any impersonal authority for that matter, a trait some scholars believe was conducive several centuries later to the rise of feudalism. (See page 285.) Final authority in the German tribe was vested in the assembly of freemen, whose ability to bear arms, no less than their freedom, qualified them for membership. This assembly met at full or new moon to consider proposals presented by the chief or king. If the members approved such proposals they would clash their weapons, otherwise they would shout them down. Disputes might be settled before this group, and it was also customary for the young freeman entering manhood to be formally invested with his weapons before this assembly. The young warrior might immediately attach himself to some band (*comitatus*) and take service with a chieftain whom he admired. "To defend and protect him, to put down one's own acts of heroism to his credit—that is what they really mean by 'allegiance.' "

Judicial Institutions.   The judicial practices of these Germans deserve special attention for they proved more enduring than most of their other institutions. As with other early peoples, the Germans originally recognized the primitive law of personal revenge. But already by Tacitus' day this had been replaced with a system of justice administered through the popular court (usually the hundred court which ordinarily served a number of villages). "Even homicide can be atoned for by a fixed number of cattle or sheep, and the satisfaction is received by the whole family." Custom determined the size of the fines, which would vary with the rank of the parties to the dispute, particularly that of the defendant. By the fifth century A.D., Germanic custom had evolved an elaborate schedule of fines which appears to have covered every conceivable kind of crime for so simple a society, from calling a man a fox to stealing a hive of bees. The sum required to be given to the relatives of a man to satisfy for his murder was called a wergeld (literally "man money"). This would vary with the man's social rank. In Anglo-Saxon England we read of botless crimes, that is, crimes for which no bot (wergeld) short of execution could be accepted (e.g. the murder of a king). For the great majority of offenses, however trifling the injury to person, animal, or property, a fine was specified and normally accepted. A further development of this system of fines saw the payment of an additional fee to the king, in recognition of his role as protector of the peace which the offender had disturbed. This was as far as the early German, who was apt to view all relationships and obligations in personal terms, could be expected to go. (Reading 26)

Compurgation. Equally peculiar to the German were his methods of establishing the innocence or guilt of the defendant in any judicial dispute. He was not interested in the evidence as we understand it. He based judgment rather upon the sworn testimony of the parties involved in the dispute or upon that of their "oath-helpers." Neither did these oath-helpers or compurgators concern themselves directly with the evidence. They simply swore that in their judgment the oath of their client was a true one. It followed necessarily that the number of compurgators needed to establish a man's innocence would be determined by their prestige and rank and by those of the defendant. The oath of a nobleman might of itself suffice to clear himself of a charge, while his oath in support of the validity of someone else's oath might be decisive.

The Ordeal. In the event of more serious crimes or where a decision could not be reached by compurgation, appeal was made to the procedure known as the ordeal. This involved one of a variety of tests. The defendant might be required to carry a hot iron for a few paces or plunge his hand into boiling water. Should the wound be healing properly when it was examined after an interval of a few days, the defendant was declared to have proved his innocence. If the wound were infected, the judgment would be "Guilty." The ordeal of cold water involved tying the defendant's hands and feet and casting him into a lake. If he sank, he was considered innocent, inasmuch as water being pure would not accept anything defiled. It must be assumed that the defendant was removed from the water before he drowned! In fact, we must also assume that those in charge of conducting the ordeal of hot iron or water would have pretty well decided beforehand whether the defendant was innocent or guilty, and judge accordingly. Trial by combat was a form of ordeal, and we even hear of armed contests between men and women, with the man given the handicap of fighting from the bottom of a three-foot hole. However administered, the ordeal always constituted an appeal to the supernatural to intervene and vindicate the righteousness of the cause of the innocent party. (Reading 27)

German Religion. The Germans accepted the existence of many gods, both good and evil, all able and willing to do man injury or bring him blessing. To some of these gods they had given names, while many more continued to roam the forests and fens as unidentified spirits of nature. It is probable that some of these spirits were believed to be the departed souls of their ancestors. No organized religion existed so far as can be determined, and the German was under no compulsion to accept any particular creed. Priests enjoyed a privileged status, although nothing comparable to that of the Druids among the Celts. Old women had the reputation of possessing prophetic powers. Human sacrifice was not unknown, although the common holocaust was the horse. The bulk of the carcass would be consumed by the faithful after some token offering had been made to the gods. Because of the universality of this practice among the pagan Germans, Christian Europe long identified the eating of horsemeat as an infallible sign of paganism. Several individual gods were accorded special recognition. Among these were Wotan (Odin or Woden), the sky god and god of war; Thor, the god of thunder; Frigg, the wife of Wotan; and Tiw, a war god. These four deities give their names to our Wednesday, Thursday, Friday, and Tuesday respectively. The Germans practiced the universal pagan custom of divination and based their forecasts customarily on the flight of birds or the neighing of the sacred white horses. Views concerning the afterlife were vague and not reassuring, and the purpose of religion was principally that of averting harm which neglected gods might otherwise cause to befall man. No moralizing influence can be credited to German paganism.

Early Contacts Between Germans and Romans

A glance at the history of Roman-German relations prior to the final collapse of the northern frontier before waves of these Germans in the early fifth century, will place these invasions in their proper perspective. In order to describe these folk movements, which they actually were, ethnographers traditionally prefer the term migration to invasion, since the movement of Germans into the empire was not that of alien conquerors riding roughshod across largely unknown frontiers. It resembled rather a human river which had been flowing slowly over this particular barrier long before the dam had finally given way. For several centuries before the Germans had broken down the northern frontiers to roam at will within what were once the sacred reaches of the Roman empire, a constant and extensive kind of peaceful infiltration had been in progress. This is, of course, what one would expect in view of the fifteen-hundred-mile frontier which extended from the mouth of the Rhine to the Black Sea, along which Roman and German had rubbed shoulders for almost five hundred years. This frontier had never been so sealed as those we hear of in these days of modern efficiency. Furthermore, since this was also the day before "fifth columns," the Romans had never interfered when individual Germans and entire families had drifted over, bent only on peaceful occupation of the lands to the south.

Roman Camps. The central nucleus from which radiated both Roman and German influences, and where the greatest amount of mutual assimilation between Roman and barbarian customs took place during Roman times, was the Roman frontier camp. A veritable chain of these army camps had gradually sprung up all along the frontier. Between these camps and along the military roads leading directly to the frontier, there had passed continuously for several centuries a motley assortment of humanity: soldiers, peddlers, immigrants, hangers-on of every sort, at first fairly distinct by nationality and custom, but gradually merging into a reasonably homogeneous type, the semi-Romanized German. Many of these army camps developed into actual cities, populated by Romans and Germans, who had been attracted there by the protection the camps afforded and by their trade advantages. Such modern cities as Strasbourg, Cologne, Coblenz, Utrecht, Trier, Mainz, Vienna, and Budapest, were once Roman army camps which had grown into sizeable communities already by the fourth century, fed by the constant recruitment of soldiers and by a similarly constant influx of nonmilitary elements. Here the German peddled his precious amber, his furs, goose feathers, beets, soap, cattle, and slaves, and took back with him to dispose of among his less sophisticated tribesmen a store of Roman products more fascinating than they were useful.

Germans as Soldiers and Farmers. While the Roman state offered no objection to the movement of such German vagrants, it actually welcomed Germans who were willing to take service as either soldiers or farmers. We read in Caesar's *Commentaries on the Gallic Wars* how at that early date Caesar had been obliged to recruit German horsemen to assist his legions against the rebellious Celts. From the time of Caesar, the demand for non-Roman recruits mounted steadily as the frontier grew more sensitive and as the problem of filling military needs with Roman citizenry proved ever more difficult. Military service began to assume a distinctly professional character as early as 100 B.C., and its increasingly low-cast character repelled the war-weary Roman already suspicious of the motivation behind the interminable warfare in Spain, Africa, Greece, and the Near East. From the time of Augustus, half of the army, that is, the auxiliaries, had been recruited from provincials who were noncitizens. This non-Roman element swelled ever larger, until by the fourth century the army was predominantly German. The very word "barbarian" had taken on the meaning of soldier. From the time of Jovian in the middle fourth century, the Roman soldiers would hail their new emperor by raising him aloft on their shields, a peculiarly Germanic practice. With Marcus Aurelius began the practice of settling thousands of Germans within the empire, on lands unused or depopulated, with the dual responsibility of tilling the soil and of helping protect the frontier. In the third and fourth centuries increasingly large areas of land belonging to the state or falling by default under government control, were turned over to Germans on these terms. Enormous numbers of Germans and Sarmatians were settled in the Balkans and northern Gaul. Finally, the Roman government might permit entire tribes to come across the frontier where they enjoyed the status of *foederati* (allies) and served as buffers against more dangerous Germans beyond. This was done, for example, by the emperor Julian in 358 A.D. when he defeated the Salian Franks and gave them lands just inside the frontier on the south bank of the lower Rhine.

Germans as Officers. It was inevitable that if lowly peasants such as Aurelian and Diocletian could rise to positions of prominence in the army, so would also in time the more aggressive and talented of these German warriors. Their striking physique and the ease with which their loyalty could be purchased won them an early welcome into the imperial guard. They gradually made their way into the higher eschelons of the army, until by the close of the fourth century the leading generals were frequently barbarians. Arbogast, a Frank, was *magister militum* (commander-in-chief) under Valentinian I; Stilicho, a Vandal, under Honorius; Richimer, a Frank, under Valens. Intermarriage with influential Romans followed in time. Valentinian married the daughter of his German chieftain Bauto, while Honorius wed the daughter of his general Stilicho. Particularly common was intermarriage between the lower class Romans and Germans. By 350 A.D. it would have been difficult except for the "purists" to distinguish in the frontier provinces between Roman, Celt, and German.

Appearance of the Huns. This largely peaceful infiltration of the Germans into the Roman Empire had been proceeding at an ever accelerating pace for several hundreds of years before the frontier actually collapsed. It is easy to see, therefore, that these "Roman" soldiers who were sent northward to shore up the sagging frontier in the late fourth and early fifth centuries were only to a degree less German than those Germans to the north who sought to breach it. It is also evident that this infiltration had been accepted by the Romans, for the most part as a matter of indifference, if they did not view it as beneficial to the empire. Given no untoward event which would alter radically the rate with which these Germans were crossing the frontier, their gradual assimilation into the empire might be reasonably expected to follow in the course of time. One might even venture the thought that had this movement been held to a slow infiltration, the substance of Roman culture would not have been fatally diluted. But the onrushing Huns introduced an entirely new and explosive element into the picture. Their onslaught changed infiltration to invasion. Not only could the Romans no longer determine the rate of movement into the empire, but their initiative in European affairs passed irrevocably into the hands of the invaders.

Larger Reason for Migrations. Before passing on to actual invasions themselves, it might be well to consider more specifically the motivation which impelled these Germanic tribes to seek entry into the empire. To the ethnographer who sees nothing smaller than races, nor anything shorter than centuries, such considerations as the respective military prowess of the peoples involved or their cultural level are largely of passing importance. He only knows that, on the basis of meager but fairly conclusive evidence, there has been from very early times a generally westward movement of people from Asia into southern Europe, and another southward from out of the northern areas of Europe. The twin movements tend to merge somewhere in east-central Europe, and to carry from there in a generally southwestwardly direction toward the Atlantic. Since such movements are tremendous in their scope and involve thousands of square miles of moving folk, the ethnographer considers questions of politics and of individual leaders as largely idle. To him the movement of the Germans southward was as inexorable as it was inevitable.

Motive of the Germans. While respecting the interpretation of the ethnographer, the historian finds his analysis too broad in terms of time and too cosmic in terms of peoples to explain more time-limited developments. So he suggests more immediate factors in the movement of the Germans southward and westward. The most pressing of these was land hunger. It is true that some of the areas which the Germans vacated, such as the south Baltic shoreland, are today among the world's heaviest producers of food. But until the tenth and eleventh centuries these areas were still blanketed with forests and the terrain left doubly unattractive to settlement because of extensive marshlands and bitter winters. Paul the Deacon tells how the Lombards, while still in Scandinavia, divided their nation into three parts and took lots to determine which third would emigrate, so precarious had the food supply grown because of their increasing numbers. Yet the fact remains that once the movement of German tribes had gathered momentum, it carried them almost clear of the land east of the Elbe, farther than they had any immediate need to go. Thus we must suggest, in addition to land hunger as impelling the German to move southward, such added incentives as the promise of a higher civilization to the south, together with its broader acres, warmer climate, and sunnier skies. There were, of course, Germans who crossed into the empire to plunder. The final and immediate factor, however, which activated a general movement southward that surged across the Roman frontier was the appearance of the terrible Hun.

The Rise of Germanic Kingdoms

Location of German Tribes. Of the large number of Germanic tribes that Tacitus catalogs in his *Germania*, only a few can be identified among those who took part in the invasions of the fourth and fifth centuries. The greater number had probably been subjugated by and assimilated into one or the other of the large groups of later German tribes which we find pressed against the northern frontier in 375 A.D. Scattered along the banks of the lower Rhine and the south shore of the North Sea lay the Salian branch of the powerful Frankish confederation. Moving up the river we find the Ripuarian Franks roughly opposite to Cologne, and the Burgundians near the confluence of the Main and the Rhine. Farther up the river, in the triangle between the Rhine and the Danube, the formidable Alamans made their home, while behind them ranged from the North Sea southward the Saxons, the Thuringians, Vandals, and Lombards. Along the great length of the turgid Danube lay the most powerful and populous of all Germanic groups, the Gothic tribes. Many of these were descendants of those Goths who had surged momentarily across the Roman frontier into Greece and Macedonia in the third century. (See page 24.) From the Danube the Goths had spread in the only direction permitted them, that is toward the east, where they found and overwhelmed the unmilitaristic Slavs. The west Goths or Visigoths occupied the lands roughly up to the Dniester, the east Goths or Ostrogoths those beyond. Still farther east were the Sarmatian Alans and the approaching Mongol Huns.

Visigoths Cross the Danube. The impulse which precipitated the Germanic invasions started with the Huns. About the year 375, they fell upon the Ostrogoths after having subjugated the Alans and incorporated these into their army. Most of the Ostrogoths appear to have accepted Hunnish domination, but a number of them, together with some Sarmatians, joined the Visigoths in their flight westward to the Danube. There they sought asylum within the empire. Emperor Valens hesitated, but finally granted them permission to cross the river. A negative reply might have precipitated a battle with them, while he could use their help against the approaching Huns. Yet he was troubled at the thought of so large a barbaric element within the empire, so he required them to lay down their arms. It appears that the Roman officials entrusted with the resettlement of the Visigoths failed to disarm them. Instead they subjected them to various kinds of abuse, even that of enslaving their children. So at least did the Visigoths charge in justifying their decision to plunder the countryside. Emperor Valens undertook to chastise them, but he fatally underestimated their power. Refusing to await the arrival of his nephew and co-emperor Gratian from the west, he attacked them in August, 378 near Adrianople, and he and all his generals were slain and his army annihilated.

Significance of Adrianople. This catastrophe at Adrianople was long classified as one of the truly decisive battles of history, since it presumably sounded the death rattle of the Roman Empire. Though modern scholars assess it as somewhat less, the destruction of a Roman army at the hands of German invaders does mark a point of departure in Roman history. It is true that more than a hundred years earlier (251 A.D.), the Roman army had suffered a similar disaster when the emperor Decius was killed by these same Goths and his army destroyed. The empire at that time, however, had demonstrated that it still possessed the vitality to recover, and a generation later it had righted itself. After the battle of Adrianople, on the other hand, it soon became painfully clear that the empire had lost its powers of recuperation. The soldiers recruited to replace those lost at Adrianople were more Germanic and less loyal than those killed, and the narrow line which divided invader and invaded came just so much closer to disappearing. From now on the German invader usually had the upper hand. The powerful Visigothic nation was within the empire to stay, and other Germans were soon to follow. The battle of Adrianople also holds some significance in the history of the art of war. Because of the decisive role played by the Ostrogothic and Sarmatian cavalry in the victory, horsemen dominate the battle field for the next thousand years.

Theodosius Quiets Goths. Epochal as their victory at Adrianople may have been, the Visigoths were not aware they were making history, and after several years spent in plundering Macedonia and Thessaly, they accepted the terms offered them by Emperor Theodosius. They were to make their home in the unoccupied areas lying between the lower Danube and the Balkans, and to retain their own laws and ruler, and, in return for an annual subsidy of food, to assist in bolstering the frontier. This was the best arrangement Theodosius could make under the circumstances. But it required his constant vigilance to keep the Visigoths reasonably quiet. If Theodosius was the last Roman emperor to rule both east and west, he was able to accomplish this only because he commanded the respect of several powerful Germanic chieftains. This respect his incompetent sons, Arcadius and Honorius, were unable to earn, and upon the death of Theodosius in 395, imperial power passed into the hands of the German generals who commanded the Roman armies.

Stilicho. Honorius inherited Theodosius' position in the western half of the empire, although the power behind the throne was Stilicho, a Vandal, who had proved his worth under Theodosius. Upon the death of Theodosius he had assumed the direction of military affairs, as much for Honorius' deficiencies as for his own aggressiveness. Since he was a German and a barbarian, he did not covet the imperial title for himself, although he married two daughters in succession to Honorius. He aspired rather to exercise the real power in the state, not only over the west but over the east as well. The principal obstacle to his ambition was not the eastern emperor Arcadius, but the Visigothic chieftain and king, Alaric. Alaric was busy despoiling Greek cities and countryside since being denied a position in the east similar to that held by Stilicho in the west. When Arcadius found himself unable to halt this plundering directly, he commissioned Alaric to take over the province of Illyricum on the Adriatic which Stilicho considered within his orbit. There followed several confusing years of warfare and intrigue between the two German leaders. Stilicho managed to maintain the upper hand at both games, but at the price of fatally depleting the defenses along the frontiers in Britain and the Rhine. In what looked like an abandonment of the west in order to advance his ambitions in the east, Stilicho overreached himself. Upon the insistence of a number of western soldiers, Honorius had him executed for treason (408 A.D.).

The "Sack of Rome." Stilicho had been little more than a scheming adventurer, but he had kept Alaric out of Italy. With Stilicho now out of the way, the Visigothic chieftain found nothing to prevent his leading his people across the Alps and southward against Rome. The city might have been able to offer strong resistance had it not failed to lay in a store of food. Alaric simply cut off the grain supply and starved the city into paying a huge ransom which included three thousand pounds of pepper! But this proved just a respite. With the promise of eastern troops making Honorius still more uncompromising from behind the lagoons of Ravenna where he had taken refuge, Alaric marched back against Rome a second time and after a three-day siege forced it to open its gates. This calamity, which came on August 24, 410 A.D., is known traditionally as the "Sack of Rome." The phrase reflects, however, more the horrified manner in which the entire Roman world recoiled at the thought that the Eternal City had fallen to barbarians, than the actual savagery of the Gothic occupation. St. Augustine in his *City of God* (see page 66), speaks of the orderly manner in which the Goths looted the city, how they even advised the populace to betake themselves to churches where they would not be molested. Subsequent history has proved that the "Sack of Rome" was not the earth-shaking catastrophe that its contemporaries believed. It did, however, signal in most dramatic fashion the passing of the western empire. (Reading 24)

The Visigothic Kingdom. In view of the fact that within a short time Germanic kingdoms would have taken over most of the Roman west, one may wonder why Alaric did not seize the opportunity and establish himself as ruler of 'he city of Rome and of Italy. What deterred the Germanic invader was the awe in which he stood of the Roman state. It would be two generations yet before any German would dare take that step. Furthermore, populous Rome with its urban civilization did not appeal to the semi-nomadic Visigothic nation which was still looking for the homeland Honorius had foolishly refused it. So after collecting all they wanted or could conveniently remove from the city, the Visigoths moved southward with the hope of crossing over the Mediterranean to the fertile and less populated lands beckoning in north Africa. But a storm destroyed the fleet which they started to assemble and a fever carried off Alaric. His devoted followers buried their great chieftain where they thought his body would be safe, beneath the waters of the Busento River. Then under the leadership of Alaric's brother-in-law Athaulf, they retraced their steps to north Italy and from there moved westward into southern Gaul. After further vicissitudes which found them now fighting Honorius, now fighting other Germans such as his *foederati,* they eventually carved out a kingdom which included southern France and most of Spain. (Reading 21)

The Vandals. On the last day of 406 A.D., the Vandals, Sueves, and Alans crossed the Rhine frontier which had been stripped of troops to meet the Visigothic peril in Italy. They plundered and looted almost at will in Gaul and then climbed the Pyrenees into Spain. The Roman emperor put on the only face possible under the circumstances and accepted them as *foederati.* When the Visigoths in turn began elbowing out a home for themselves in Gaul, he commissioned them to destroy the Spanish intruders. This the Visigoths were well on the way to accomplishing, when they were recalled to Gaul. The Suevi managed to maintain themselves in the mountains of Galicia. What was left of the Vandal nation crossed over into Africa under Gaiseric as allies of the rebellious military governor of Africa. Finding the land rich and the step from allies to conquerors an easy one, they soon made themselves masters of the country. Even more astonishing was the powerful naval force which this semi-nomadic German tribe quickly created, with which they ravaged both eastern and western Mediterranean, conquered the Balearic Islands, Sardinia, and Corsica, established a foothold in Sicily, and carried out a famous raid on the city of Rome (455 A.D.). Though they looted and plundered for two solid weeks, modern historians regret as an injustice to them the act of the eighteenth-century scholar in making their name the synonym for wanton destruction.

The Burgundians. Another Germanic group which was able to carve out a state for themselves within the confines of the empire were the Burgundians. They crossed the Rhine in 413 A.D. and occupied the area of

Upper Germany about Strasbourg and Worms. Honorius was forced to recognize them as *foederati*. In 436 A.D. a Hunnish army in the pay of Rome overthrew this first Burgundian kingdom. A distorted echo of this event found immortal literary fame in the *Nibelungenlied*. (See page 606.) In 443 the scattered Burgundians were permitted to settle as *foederati* in Savoy, whence they extended their control over the greater length of the Rhone river valley.

The Franks. More powerful than the Burgundians and destined to have a much greater future were the Salian Franks. They crossed the lower Rhine before the middle of the fourth century into the territory between the Scheldt and Meuse. There the emperor Julian was able to halt their farther progress, although he permitted them to remain in the area as his *foederati*. During the troublous times of the fifth century, they threw off Roman control and extended their power first to the Somme, then under their greatest king Clovis, to the Loire. The Ripuarian Franks pushed westward from Cologne and captured Treves (Trier), the largest city of the Rhineland area. Farther up the river, the Alamans crossed over to occupy Strasbourg and Switzerland.

The Angles and Saxons. Britain meantime had been left to its own resources which were pitifully inadequate. The last Roman legion left the island in 406 A.D., never to return. For many decades before 406, Roman garrisons had been hard pressed to keep the Picts and Scots north of Hadrian's wall, and to drive off Saxon raiders from Germany and Irish pirates from the west. (Patrick was captured in one of their raids. See page 73.) According to tradition, the Britons, realizing their helplessness, invited the Germans in to aid them against the Picts and Scots who were pressing southward from Scotland. But if the German Saxons, Angles, and Jutes were invited in, they soon forgot they were guests, and history has drawn a merciful curtain over their destructive progress across the island. Only in the highland fastnesses of Wales and Cornwall and across the sea in Brittany where they left their name, did the native Britons find refuge.

The Huns. It now becomes necessary to consider the movements of the Huns, the nation which was responsible, directly or indirectly, for causing these other peoples to move at this time. When we last saw the Huns, they were moving westward from the Crimea, after overwhelming the Ostrogothic nation. For all the terror they were supposed to have aroused on their progress westward, they appear to have proceeded at a rather modest pace. Seventy-five years after they first attacked the Ostrogoths, they had extended their control over the regions of Hungary, Rumania, and the Ukraine. No physical remains help the archaeologists locate their nondescript capital of tents and wooden buildings on the Theiss River. Their army included thousands of Germans: Gepids, Ostrogoths, Sueves, Thuringians, and others, while thousands of their own people fought as mercenaries in the service of Rome. Actually it was largely through the aid of Hunnish soldiers that Aetius, called somewhat generously the "last of the Romans," had been able to preserve a semblance of Roman rule in central and southeastern Gaul during the third and fourth decades of the early fifth century. And it was largely the annual tribute of seven hundred pounds or more of gold, which the eastern emperors paid to the Huns, that helped them preserve their own eastern territories from molestation.

Attila and the Battle of Châlons. About 450 A.D. the eastern emperor cut off this tribute, whereupon the Huns started westward seeking plunder under the command of their king Attila. Attila was one of those organizing geniuses which the Mongol nation produced on rare occasion, who was able to win and hold in his iron hand the unstable loyalties of his rough tribesmen. Contemporaries called him the "Scourge of God," and from their accounts he and his army appear to have richly deserved the title. According to a contemporary story, Attila took his army of Huns and Germans westward in order to force Valentinian III (the successor of Honorius) to give him the hand of his willing sister Honoria, with half of the western empire as her dowry. Actually the impregnable walls of Constantinople provide a more convincing, if less romantic, explanation for Attila's decision to go west, together with the promise of richer and easier loot in that direction.

Attila crossed the Rhine into Gaul and ravaged Trier, Metz, Reims, but found the defenses of Orleans too stout. Upon the approach of Aetius with a large "Roman" army and with supporting contingents led by the kings of the Franks, Visigoths, and Burgundians, Attila fell back toward Troyes in Champagne. Here at Mauriacus in 451 A.D. was fought what has since been known as the "Battle of Châlons," another of history's traditionally "decisive" battles. Modern historians are apt to question the crucial character of the battle. The fact that Roman and German could forget their own quarrels for the moment in order to draw together against what they considered a common threat to them all, however, emphasizes how grave they must have considered the emergency. Attila sustained no staggering defeat at Châlons, but the setback was sufficient to lead him to retrace his steps to Hungary. The following year he invaded northern Italy. Of the thousands of refugees who fled his approach, some made their way into the swamplands of the northern Adriatic, where, according to tradition, they laid the foundations of Venice. Tradition also has it that Attila abandoned his projected march southward against Rome upon the personal appeal of Pope Leo I. Whether it was the force of the pope's appeal, or the threat of plague and famine, or disaffection among his German mercenaries, all we know for certain is that Attila returned to his Hungarian headquarters where he died the following year. Shortly after, these mercenaries revolted, crushed the Huns at Nedad in 454 A.D., and brought the short though terrifying episode of these Asiatic nomads to an abrupt end. As a nation, nothing more was heard of the Huns.

Odoacer. Though the Hunnish peril ceased of a sudden, the power of the Roman emperor continued as shadowy as before. True, Valentinian stabbed Aetius (454 A.D.) because he mistrusted his powerful savior—he "used his left hand to cut off his right" as a contemporary described his act—but his own death followed a few months later at the hands of Aetius' avenging officers. Germanic control moved perceptibly closer, and the successors of Valentinian were even more the creatures of their German generals. A Sueve, Ricimer by name, made emperors from 456 A.D. until his death in 472, and unmade them when he felt they were presuming too much on their titles. Orestes, an erstwhile officer in Attila's army, ruled through his son Romulus Augustulus until 476 A.D., when he was killed and his son deposed by the German mercenary leader Odoacer. Because Odoacer dispensed with the formality of ruling through a Roman puppet, writers in bygone centuries have accorded his assumption of power a significance it did not deserve. They declared that his deposition of Romulus in 476 A.D. marked the end of the Roman Empire in the west. Actually the last Romulus' power had been no less mythical than that of his legendary namesake and predecessor, the first Romulus.

Theodoric the Ostrogoth. There is this minor significance which attaches to the rise of Odoacer to power: he sent the imperial insignia to Constantinople whence they never returned. Zeno, the emperor in the east, was content for the moment to recognize Odoacer as patrician, and to view Italy as just another administrative unit of his domain. Of course, in assuming that he exercised any real imperial control in Italy, Zeno was deluding few, surely not Odoacer. This rough chieftain maintained a vigorous rule over Italy for a dozen years, after which he was murdered (493) and replaced by another German chief, Theodoric, king of the Ostrogoths. This Theodoric was undoubtedly the most civilized and administratively astute of these early Germanic conquerors. Ten years as a hostage in Constantinople had given him a high regard for Roman culture, but neither this nor the high honors pressed upon him by the emperor had dulled his love for his people. Although his Ostrogoths found themselves free with the collapse of Hunnish power and had settled as *foederati* south of the Danube, they were disgruntled and rebellious. Because of what they considered intolerable conditions, they had followed Theodoric on a pillaging campaign through the eastern provinces and had even marched against Constantinople. Here Theodoric soon learned how difficult it would be to take the city, so he readily accepted a commission from Zeno to go to Italy and drive out Odoacer. This he was able to accomplish with a combination of hard fighting and treachery. After a long siege, he lured Odoacer from his stronghold at Ravenna and invited him to a banquet to cement their co-regency. There he murdered him instead, and struck him so devastating a blow with his sword, that he remarked, "he must have no bones." Odoacer's followers were systematically hunted down and murdered.

The Lombards.   There will be more about Theodoric later. This will suffice for the moment, that he maintained himself in Italy without serious threat for almost thirty-five years until his death in 526 A.D. Theodoric's less capable successors experienced increasing difficulty holding on to their thrones, but it, nevertheless, required almost twenty years of bloody fighting before the armies of Emperor Justinian forced the country back under imperial control. (See page 145.) As we shall see, Justinian's tremendous exertions proved largely wasted in the end, since the imperial rule which he established proved of short duration. In 568, just three years after the death of Justinian, the Lombards, the last of the Germanic invaders, began moving into Italy. Like so many of their Germanic predecessors, they had also served as Roman *foederati*. Unlike these earlier *foederati*, however, they assumed a distinctly hostile attitude toward things Roman. Scholars have traced this unfriendliness to their lack of acquaintance with Roman institutions, to the ferocity of such of their more barbarous allies as the Saxons, and to their inability to conquer the country at one sweep. Whatever may have been the source of their anti-Roman bitterness, they undoubtedly caused greater injury to classical civilization than any of their Germanic predecessors. The Lombards were never able to conquer the entire peninsula. Important enclaves such as Rome, Naples, Venice, and Ravenna, and the heel and toe of the peninsula were able to repel their most persistent efforts. One might note that beginning with the Lombard failure to conquer the peninsula, Italy remained what Metternich called "a geographical expression" until the culmination of Italian unification in 1870.

Impact of German Upon Roman Civilization

Germanic Kingdoms.   In this manner the great part of the Roman west was lost to the German invaders. By the close of the fifth century Visigothic rule extended over southern Gaul and most of Spain. Behind the mountains of northwestern Spain in Galicia, the Sueves had barricaded themselves. The Vandal kingdom stretched along the coast of north Africa and included the island of the western Mediterranean. Though we know little about the situation in England, we do know that now Angle, Saxon, and Jute roamed where for centuries the Roman eagles had marched. The expansive Franks ruled over central and northern Gaul, the Burgundians over the valley of the Rhone in southeastern Gaul. The Alamans occupied roughly the area of Switzerland, while a variety of Germanic peoples shared control of the upper Danube. Italy, Sicily, Provence, and the lands

THE GERMANIC KINGDOMS AND BYZANTIUM *ca.* 486 A.D.

east of the Adriatic to the Danube comprised the Ostrogothic kingdom. By 500 A.D. almost two thirds of the former Roman empire was lost to Constantinople.

How Much Classical Culture Preserved. To what extent did Roman civilization suffer in these territories from the invasions of the Germans? (Reading 22) Did it continue to exist or did it tend to disappear? No simple answer can be given to these questions. We must ask ourselves in the first place, how truly Roman was the culture of Gaul, for instance, when the frontier gave way to the Germans in the early fifth century? If one may call that culture Roman, it was certainly not the classical culture characteristic of the worlds of Cicero and Horace. The anarchy of the third century and the thousands upon thousands of Germans who had preceded Alaric into the empire had seen to that. Then in the second place, we must recall that German invaders were not alike either in their willingness to accept or in their ability to assimilate Roman culture. Some like the Ostrogoths preserved all they could. As Theodoric declared: "Yours the work of peace, ours of war." Other Germans like the Lombards and Vandals cared little for what Roman culture they found and treated the Romans as subject people. Many Germans, like the Arab in Libya today who prefers his ragged tent to the modern structures the Italians left behind, had no taste for a higher culture. In certain areas the German invader left no mark, as in north Africa, while in others, as in Britain, Latin civilization disappeared almost without trace. As a result, the question of how much Roman civilization was salvaged from the period of Germanic migrations cannot be answered by any general statement true of every part of the west.

Numbers Important. Possibly the factor which exerted most influence in determining the extent of de-Romanization consequent upon the movement of Germans into the empire was that of numbers. Where Germans were in a majority, the culture took on a marked Germanic character; where the Romans remained predominant, so also did their mores. Thus the insignificant Germanization consequent upon the Vandal conquest of north Africa can best be explained in terms of the small number Gaiseric led across the straits at Gibraltar. He had with him a people that numbered no more than 80,000, counting women and children. What impression could this small number have made upon a population of cultured Romans which must have numbered more than a million? How many Goths and Lombards and other Germans made permanent homes in Italy cannot be estimated, but it was surely less than one tenth of the six or more millions of Romans already living there. In central and western Spain, on the other hand, the Romans had never established themselves in any number, nor had they plentifully established themselves in northern Gaul, Britain, or in Germany. Here Germans engulfed or exterminated the Romanized element. Little remained likewise of Roman civilization along the upper Danube after that area had suffered successive devastations at the hands of marauding Germans and Huns.

Other Factors. The factor of comparative numbers was not the only one which determined the extent to which Roman civilization suffered consequent upon the Germanic invasions. Under ordinary circumstances, a higher civilization conquers one that is inferior. In its material manifestations, even decadent Roman civilization was markedly superior to the Germanic. This fact the invader was quick to appreciate. With the exceptions noted above, he generally sought to adopt those Roman practices which he admired, since his unsophisticated society still boasted no apostles of national purity. Even when a leader appeared who might have wished to eradicate Roman civilization, he would either find this impossible or not politic. So the hostile Visigothic successor of Alaric was obliged to confess: "Once I sought eagerly to efface the name of Rome and to transform the Roman Empire into a Gothic empire. . . . But a long experience has taught me that the unbridled barbarism of the Goths is not compatible with law. Without law there is no state. I have therefore decided to play the part of restorer of the Roman name in its integrity by Gothic strength. I hope to be known to posterity as the restorer of Rome, since I can not supplant her." So the German home came to resemble the more substantial stone dwelling of the Roman. The German took over the better weapons of the Roman and began to learn his language. Roman superiority he also recognized in the fields of administration and taxation. Such Roman conventions as keeping records and recording laws appealed to him, but lacking a script of his own, he had perforce to use the Latin. Roman scribes did the writing for him. Because of these considerations, Roman civilization continued viable in a large portion of the western empire, in decline to be sure, but far from fatally crippled.

Theodoric and Roman Civilization. Of all the western provinces, Italy suffered the smallest amount of barbarization. This fortunate fact can be attributed above all else to the peninsula's heavy Roman population and to its large and numerous cities. It was also due to the friendly attitude of rulers like Theodoric the Ostrogoth, who made every effort to preserve Roman civilization. Theodoric retained the Roman administrative and fiscal systems almost without change. He was able to do this because he left the civil bureaucracy to the Romans as before, and even forbade Goths from entering the civil service. Only the army did he reserve for his Goths. He even provided the city of Rome its traditional bread and circuses, and he permitted the Roman senate to function with a respect and authority that body had not known since the days of the Good Emperors. He kept the two leading intellectual lights of the west near his own person, Cassiodorus as his secretary, Boethius as his principal adviser. While he established a capital at Ravenna, he claimed to exercise authority only in the name of the emperor at Constantinople. Actually his position was analogous to that of an imperial colleague, and on several occasions the German kings of the west accorded him that recognition. Theodoric assumed responsibility for repairing important buildings which had fallen into a state of disrepair, of erecting new ones, and of maintaining the public schools of rhetoric and grammar. It is possible that this German proved himself more Roman in his anxiety to preserve things Roman than had any ruler of Italy since the time of Marcus Aurelius. (Reading 25)

German Administrative System. Unhappily for medieval culture, no other Germanic chieftain approached Theodoric in his efforts to preserve the Roman way of life. These rulers did content themselves for a time with the title of patrician or master of the troops, probably as much from force of tradition as with the hope of rendering their rule more acceptable to the natives. However, such sham proved no less temporary than the trappings of the imperial palace they adopted for their own, or the high-sounding titles they borrowed from the imperial court for their courtiers. Accustomed to rule by personal direction, the German king learned early that neither he nor his men possessed the ability to operate the relatively complex administrative machinery of the Roman government. So what had begun to bog down already in Roman hands, they let die of its own weight. The German king ruled rather through his counts (from the Latin *comes*, meaning companion) to whom he gave rights of jurisdiction over areas roughly coterminous with the Roman *civitas*. These counts he selected, not for their administrative skill of which they were as innocent as he was, but for their loyalty and military prowess. On his part, he gradually assumed the unlimited powers of a Roman emperor. Where once he was merely a chieftain, he now claimed to exercise legislative and executive powers in his own name. Yet his ambitions did him no good. Because of the turbulency of the times and the progressively worsening communications, government became more and more a local matter under control of practically autonomous counts. The king might have been able to partially neutralize the evil consequences of this provincialism upon his power had he possessed ample revenue. As it was, almost the first branch of the Roman administrative system to go by the board was the land tax which had provided the bulk of the imperial revenues. From the close of the sixth century the German king had perforce to depend principally on his own lands for his resources. Whatever his personal pretensions to power, this fact above all others prevented their fulfillment.

Developments in Realm of Law. In the realm of law, two major obstacles retarded the fusion of Roman and German principles and procedures: first, the generally accepted rule that each nation should enjoy its own peculiar law; second, the fact that Germanic law was based upon custom, Roman upon statute. Yet neither obstacle proved insuperable. The Franks actually permitted intermarriage from the beginning and this opened the door to early fusion in that part of the west between the native and invader. The other German states sought for a time to maintain two completely distinct civilizations with each group having its own laws, but the second generation was already finding such division well-nigh impossible. As the line distinguishing Roman from German grew ever less distinct, it eventually became impossible to apply separate law codes. By the middle seventh century, Romans and Visigoths were using the same law. By the time this happened, the gap separating the two law codes had steadily narrowed, the Roman becoming barbarized, the Germanic reflecting strong Roman influences. The ultimate result of this fusion, however, was a law that was more Germanic than Roman, despite the vast superiority of the latter. The explanation for this strange and unfortunate development is to be found in the progressive deterioration of western European civilization. Under the primitive conditions which existed in western Europe in the sixth, seventh, and eighth centuries, men discovered that the relatively simple Germanic system could be more readily employed than the comparatively complex Roman. Even in Italy the crude Germanic devices of the ordeal and compurgation came to replace enlightened Roman judicial procedure.

Social Fusion. Although the invader made no effort to force the Roman into his own social mold, something approximating that is what transpired. As has been noted, the German restricted to himself the exercise of military and political power. The Roman landed aristocrat, therefore, had no choice, if he wished to retain his own social eminence or to share with his conqueror the prestige that accompanied the latter's political supremacy, but to adopt the ways of the German and to give him his daughter in marriage. Never so chary over differences in rank or excellence as their betters, social levelling came without effort to the lower classes. This was especially true since both found themselves, whether Roman or German, in pretty much the same condition. The Roman was generally a *colonus*, while the German, if free in the fifth century, had since lost his freedom. He was now quite as unfree as his Roman neighbor and subject to the same aristocratic landowner. The result was that Roman and German social conventions and usages fused without great reluctance into a homogeneous cast. Those of the upper classes assumed more the pattern of a German artistocracy, those of the lower classes the indistinctive features of the unfree.

Religion as a Fusing Agent. In the fusion of Roman and German, religion first served as a bar except among the Franks who had been converted directly from paganism to Catholic Christianity. All the other Germanic invaders were Arian Christians. They traced their faith back to the Arian missionary Ulfilas who had worked so successfully among the Goths in the fourth century. Arian Germans and Christian Romans did not fuse easily. The gulf between them in the early sixth century was quite as difficult to bridge as that yawning between Catholic and Protestant in the sixteenth. Once Arianism, however, had lost its favored position at the emperor's court in Constantinople, its demise came quickly. Goths and Burgundians had repudiated it by the close of the sixth century and the Lombards shortly thereafter. Whereupon religious uniformity now became as effective a fusing agent between Roman and non-Roman as religious differences had previously served the reverse.

Economic Change. The advent of the German may have produced its most far-reaching consequences in the economic order. It was not that the German introduced any revolutionarily novel trends; rather that his coming accelerated those already under way. Thus the movement toward a natural and closing economy which can be traced back as far as the end of the second century, received sharp encouragement from the German whose entire civilization had been built around land. The agricultural economy itself was affected very little. The invader demanded from one third to two thirds of the soil, but in many areas expropriation proved unnecessary since sufficient land was lying idle. On the other hand, urban life suffered seriously. The German had no love for cities, and those which had miraculously escaped looting and destruction decayed rapidly for want of peace and trade. The Germans also had little taste for many of the luxury articles which had been moving to the west and had appealed to a higher culture. How drastic was the decline of cities is illustrated by the fate of Arles in France whose entire sixth-century population could have taken refuge within the ruined walls of its amphitheatre. Rome sank from a city of one million to one less than 50,000. With no demand for a city's manufactures beyond its immediate vicinity, with little fluid capital to wet the arteries of trade, with growing instability due to war, industry became localized where it did not completely disappear. Western economy in general took on a more agrarian complexion.

Impact of the German upon Culture.   The arrival of the illiterate German dealt a staggering blow to a Roman culture already far advanced in decline. Only where the Germans did not penetrate, that is, in the eastern half of the empire and in Ireland, did learning and letters continue undisturbed. The lament of Gregory of Tours would apply to most of western Europe: "Woe to us, for the study of letters has disappeared from amongst us." Had it not been for the Christian church, which salvaged the language of the past and some of its learning, we would not speak of the decline of Roman civilization—we would rather announce its disappearance. However, we shall peer at more of this cultural darkness later. For the moment it will be sufficient to note that the coming of the Germans helped precipitate western Europe into the gloom of the Dark Ages which would not begin to lift again before the close of the eighth century. It would take that long before Roman and German, and German and German, could compose their differences and begin to produce a new and vigorous civilization eager to learn again the ways of their more cultured forbears.

READINGS

No. 20. Tacitus' views of the early Germans

(*The Works of Tacitus.* Bohn's Classical Library, II. London, 1872.)

Ch. 4. I concur in opinion with those who deem the Germans never to have intermarried with other nations; but to be a race, pure, unmixed, and stamped with a distinct character. Hence a family likeness pervades the whole, though their numbers are so great: eyes stern and blue; ruddy hair; large bodies, powerful in sudden exertions, but impatient of toil and labour, least of all capable of sustaining thirst and heat. Cold and hunger they are accustomed by their climate and soil to endure. . . .

Ch. 7. In the election of kings they have regard to birth; in that of generals, to valour. Their kings have not an absolute or unlimited power; and their generals command less through the force of authority, than of example. If they are daring, adventurous, and conspicuous in action, they procure obedience from the admiration they inspire. None, however, but the priests are permitted to judge offenders, to inflict bonds or stripes; so that chastisement appears not as an act of military discipline, but as the instigation of the god whom they suppose present with warriors. They also carry with them to battle certain images and standards taken from the sacred groves. It is a principal incentive to their courage, that their squadrons and battalions are not formed by men fortuitously collected, but by the assemblage of families and clans. Their pledges also are near at hand; they have within hearing the yells of their women, and the cries of their children. These, too, are the most revered witnesses of each man's conduct, these his most liberal applauders. To their mothers and their wives they bring their wounds for relief, nor do these dread to count or to search out the gashes. The women also administer food and encouragement to those who are fighting. . . .

Ch. 11. On affairs of smaller moment, the chiefs consult; on those of greater importance, the whole community; yet with this circumstance, that what is referred to the decision of the people, is first maturely discussed by the chiefs. They assemble, unless upon some sudden emergency, on stated days, either at the new or full moon, which they account the most auspicious season for beginning any enterprise. Nor do they, in their computation of time, reckon, like us, by the number of days, but of nights. In this way they arrange their business; in this way they fix their appointments; so that, with them, the night seems to lead the day. An inconvenience produced by their liberty is, that they do not all assemble at a stated time, as if it were in obedience to a command; but two or three days are lost in the delays of convening. When they all think fit, they sit down armed. Silence is proclaimed by the priests, who have on this occasion a coercive power. Then the king, or chief, and such others as are conspicuous for age, birth, military renown, or eloquence, are heard; and gain attention rather from their ability to persuade, than their authority to command. If a proposal displease, the assembly reject it by an inarticulate murmur; if it prove agreeable, they clash their javelins; for the most honourable expression of assent among them is the sound of arms.

Ch. 12. Before this council, it is likewise allowed to exhibit accusations, and to prosecute capital offences. Punishments are varied according to the nature of the crimes. Traitors and deserters are hung upon trees; cowards, dastards, and those guilty of unnatural practices, are suffocated in mud under a hurdle. This difference of punishment has in view the principle, that villainy should be exposed while it is punished, but turpitude concealed. The penalties annexed to slighter offences are also proportioned to the delinquency. The convicts are fined in horses and cattle; part of the mulct goes to the king or state; part to the injured person or his relations. . . .

Ch. 15. During the intervals of war, they pass their time less in hunting than in a sluggish repose, divided between sleep and the table. All the bravest of the warriors, committing the care of the house, the family affairs, and the lands, to the women, old men, and weaker part of the domestics, stupify themselves in inaction; so wonderful is the contrast presented by nature, that the same persons love indolence, and hate tranquillity! . . .

Ch. 18. The matrimonial bond is, nevertheless, strict and severe among them; nor is there anything in their manners more commendable than this. Almost singly among the barbarians, they content themselves with one wife; a very few of them excepted, who, not through incontinence, but because their alliance is solicited on account of their rank, practise polygamy. The wife does not bring a dowry to her husband, but receives one from him. The parents and relations assemble, and pass their approbation on the presents—presents not adapted to please a female taste, or decorate the bride; but oxen, a caparisoned steed, a shield, spear, and sword. By virtue of these, the wife is espoused; and she in her turn makes a present of some arms to her husband. This they consider as the firmest bond of union: these, the sacred mysteries, the conjugal deities. That the woman may not think herself excused from exertions of fortitude, or exempt from the casualties of war, she is admonished by the very ceremonial of her marriage, that she comes to her husband as a partner in toils and dangers; to suffer and to dare equally with him, in peace and in war; this is indicated by the yoked oxen, the harnessed steed, the offered arms. Thus she is to live; thus to die. She receives what she is to return inviolate and honoured to her children; what her daughters-in-law are to receive, and again transmit to their grandchildren.

Ch. 19. They live, therefore, fenced around with chastity; corrupted by no seductive spectacles, no convivial incitements. Men and women are alike unacquainted with clandestine correspondence. Adultery is extremely rare among so numerous a people. Its punishment is instant, and at the pleasure of the husband. He cuts off the hair of the offender, strips her, and in the presence of her relations expels her from his house, and pursues her with stripes through the whole village. Nor is any indulgence shown to a prostitute. Neither beauty, youth, nor riches can procure her a husband; for none there looks on vice with a smile, or calls mutual seduction the way of the world. Still more exemplary is the practice of those states in which none but virgins marry, and the expectations and wishes of a wife are at once brought to a period. Thus, they take one husband as one body and one life; that no thought, no desire, may extend beyond him; and he may be loved not only as their husband, but as their marriage. To limit the increase of children, or to put to death any of the later progeny, is accounted infamous; and good habits have there more influence than good laws elsewhere. . . .

Ch. 21. It is an indispensable duty to adopt the enmities of a father or relation, as well as their friendships; these, however, are not irreconcilable or perpetual. Even homicide is atoned by a certain fine in cattle and sheep; and the whole family accepts the satisfaction, to the advantage of the public weal, since quarrels are most dangerous in a free state. . . .

Ch. 22. As soon as they arise from sleep, which they generally protract till late in the day, they bathe, usually in warm water, as cold weather chiefly prevails there. After bathing they take their meal, each on a distinct seat, and at a separate table. Then they proceed, armed, to business; and not less frequently to convivial parties, in which it is no disgrace to pass days and nights, without intermission, in drinking. The frequent quarrels that arise amongst them, when intoxicated, seldom terminate in abusive language, but more frequently in blood. In their feasts, they generally deliberate on the reconcilement of enemies, on family alliances, on the appointment of chiefs, and finally on peace and war; conceiving that at no time the soul is more opened to sincerity, or warmed to heroism. These people, naturally void of artifice or disguise, disclose the most secret emotions of their hearts in the freedom of festivity. The minds of all being thus displayed, without reserve, the subjects of their deliberation are again canvassed the next day; and each time has its advantages. They consult when unable to dissemble; they determine when not liable to mistake.

Ch. 23. Their drink is a liquor prepared from barley or wheat brought by fermentation to a certain resemblance of wine. Those who border on the Rhine also purchase wine. Their food is simple; wild fruits, fresh venison, or coagulated milk. They satisfy hunger without seeking the elegances and delicacies of the table. Their thirst for liquor is not quenched with equal moderation. If their propensity to drunkenness be gratified to the extent of their wishes, intemperance proves as effectual in subduing them as the force of arms.

Ch. 24. They have only one kind of public spectacle, which is exhibited in every company. Young men, who make it their diversion, dance naked amidst drawn swords and presented spears. Practice has conferred skill at this exercise, and skill has given grace; but they do not exhibit for hire or gain; the only reward of this pastime, though a hazardous one, is the pleasure of the spectators. What is extraordinary, they play a dice, when sober, as a serious business; and that with such a desperate venture of gain or loss, that, when everything else is gone, they set their liberties and persons on the last throw. The loser goes into voluntary servitude; and, though the youngest and strongest, patiently suffers himself to be bound and sold. Such is their obstinacy in a bad practice—they themselves call it honour. The slaves thus acquired are exchanged away in commerce, that the winner may get rid of the scandal of his victory.

No. 21. The Visigoths, Alaric, and the "Sack of Rome"

(From Jordanes' *The Origin and Deeds of the Goths. Readings in European History*, ed. James Harvey Robinson, I. Boston, 1904, pp. 39-44.)

The West Goths [terrified by the victories of the Huns over the East Goths] requested Emperor Valens to grant them a portion of Thrace or Moesia south of the Danube in which to settle. They promised to obey his laws and commands and, in order still further to gain his confidence, they engaged to become Christians if only the emperor would send to them teachers who knew their language. When Valens heard this he readily agreed to a plan which he might himself have proposed. He received the Goths into Moesia and erected them, so to speak, into a sort of rampart to protect his empire against the other tribes.

Now, since Valens was infected with the heresy of the Arians and had closed all the churches which belonged to our party [i.e. the orthodox], he sent the Goths preachers of his own infection. These missionaries poured out for the newcomers, who were inexperienced and ignorant, the poison of their own false faith. So the West Goths were made Arians rather than Christians by Emperor Valens. Moreover, in their enthusiasm they converted their kinsmen, the East Goths and the Gepidae, and taught them to respect this heresy. They invited all nations of their own tongue everywhere to adopt the creed of this sect.

The Battle of Adrianople

When news of this (the revolt of the Visigoths) reached the emperor Valens at Antioch, he hastened with an army into Thrace. Here it came to a miserable battle in which the Goths conquered. The emperor fled to a peasant's hut not far from Adrianople. The Goths, according to the custom of the raging enemy, set fire to the buildings, having no idea that there was an emperor hidden in the little hut, and so he was consumed in his kingly pomp. This was in accordance with God's judgment that he should be burned with fire by them, since when they asked for the true faith he misled them with false teaching and changed for them the fire of love into the fire of hell.

After the great and glorious victory, the West Goths set themselves to cultivate Thrace and the Dacian river valley as if it were their native soil of which they had just gained possession.

Theodosius invites Athanaric, king of the Visigoths, to visit him

When the West Goth [Athanaric] entered the royal city [Constantinople] he was astounded. "Now I see what I have often heard without believing—the glory of this great city." Looking here and there, he admired the site of the city, and the number of ships, and the magnificent walls. He saw people of many nations, like a stream flowing from different sources into one fountain. He marveled at the martial array of the soldiers and exclaimed, "Doubtless the emperor is a god of this earth, and whoever has raised his hand against him is guilty of his own blood."

A few months later, Athanaric, upon whom the emperor heaped his favors, departed from this world, and the emperor, because of his affection for Athanaric, honored him almost more in death than he had done in life, gave him worthy burial, and was himself present beside the bier at the funeral.

After the death of Athanaric, all his army remained in the service of the emperor Theodosius, submitted to the Roman power, and formed, as it were, one body with its soldiers. They resembled the allies whom Constantine had had, who were called *Foederati*.

Alaric and the "Sack" of Rome

After Theodosius, who cherished both peace and the Gothic people, had departed this life, his sons [Honorius and Arcadius], through their lives of indulgence, began to bring ruin down upon their empires and withdrew from their allies, the Goths, the accustomed gifts. The Goths soon grew disgusted with the emperors, and since they were fearful lest their bravery in war should decline by too long a period of peace, they made Alaric their king. . . . So, since the said Alaric was chosen king, he took counsel with his fellows and declared to them that it was preferable to conquer a kingdom through one's own force rather than to live under the yoke of strangers.

He thereupon took his army and advanced, during the consulate of Stilicho and Aurelianus, through Pannonia and Sirmium into Italy. This country was so completely deprived of forces that Alaric approached without opposition to the bridge over the Candiano, three miles from the imperial city of Ravenna. . . .

Finally they entered the city of Rome and sacked it at Alaric's command. They did not, however, set fire to the city, as is the custom of the wild peoples, and would not permit that any of the holy places should be desecrated. They then proceeded into Campania and Lucania, which they likewise plundered, and came then to Britii. . . .

Alaric, the king of the West Goths, also brought hither the treasures of all Italy which he had won by plunder, and determined to cross from here over to Sicily and thence to Africa, which would offer him a final abode. But a number of his ships were swallowed up by that fearful sea, and many were injured; for man is unable to carry out his wishes when they are opposed to God's will.

While Alaric, discouraged by this misfortune, was considering what he should do, he was struck down by an early death and departed this world. His followers mourned the loss of him they had so dearly loved. They diverted the river Busento from its ordinary bed near the town of Consentia— this river, it may be added, brings salubrious water from the foot of the mountains to the town—and had a grave dug by captives in the middle of the channel. Here they buried Alaric, together with many precious objects. Then they permitted the water to return once more to its old bed. Moreover, in order that the place might never be found, they killed all those who had helped dig the grave.

The Goths transferred the rule to Atavulf, a relative of Alaric's, and a man of fine figure and lofty spirit, who, although he was not distinguished for his size, was remarkable for his figure and face. When Atavulf had assumed the rule he turned back again to Rome, and what had been left there from the first sack was now swept clean away, as a field might be devastated by grasshoppers. He robbed not only individuals of their wealth in Italy, but he also took that of the state, and Emperor Honorius was able in no way to restrain him. He even led away prisoner from Rome Placidia, the sister of Honorius, and daughter of Emperor Theodosius by his second wife.

No. 22. The destructiveness of the German invasions

(St. Jerome's lament. Robinson's *Readings*, pp. 44-45.)

Nations innumerable and most savage have invaded all Gaul. The whole region between the Alps and the Pyrenees, the ocean and the Rhine, has been devastated by the Quadi, the Vandals, the Sarmati, the Alani, the Gepidae, the hostile Heruli, the Saxons, the Burgundians, the Alemanni and the Pannonians. O wretched Empire! Mayence (Mainz), formerly so noble a city, has been taken and ruined, and in the church many thousands of men have been massacred. Worms has been destroyed after a long siege. Rheims, that powerful city, Amiens, Arras, Speyer, Strasbourg,—all have seen their citizens led away into Germany. Aquitaine and the provinces of Lyons and Narbonne, all save a few towns, have been depopulated; and these the sword threatens without, while hunger ravages within. I cannot speak without tears of Toulouse, which the merits of the holy Bishop Exuperius have prevailed so far to save from destruction. Spain, even, is in daily terror lest it perish, remembering the invasion of the Cimbri; and whatsoever the other provinces have suffered once, they continue to suffer in their fear.

I will keep silence concerning the rest, lest I seem to despair of the mercy of God. For a long time, from the Black Sea to the Julian Alps, those things which are ours have not been ours; and for thirty years, since the Danube boundary was broken, war has raged in the very midst of the Roman Empire. Our tears are dried by old age. Except a few old men, all were born in captivity and siege, and do not desire the liberty they never knew. Who could believe this? How could the whole tale be worthily told? How Rome has fought within her own bosom not for glory, but for preservation—nay, how she has not even fought, but with gold and all her precious things has ransomed her life. . . .

Who could believe that Rome, built upon the conquest of the whole world, would fall to the ground? that the mother herself would become the tomb of her peoples? that all the regions of the East, of Africa and Egypt, once ruled by the queenly city, would be filled with troops of slaves and handmaidens? that today holy Bethlehem should shelter men and women of noble birth, who once abounded in wealth and are now beggars?

No. 23. The Huns

(The Roman History of Ammianus Marcellinus, tr. C. D. Yonge. London, 1862.)

Bk. XXXI. Ch. 2. The people called Huns, slightly mentioned in the ancient records, live beyond the Sea of Azov, on the border of the Frozen Ocean [Maeotic Sea], and are a race savage beyond all parallel. At the very moment of their birth the cheeks of their infant children are deeply marked by an iron, in order that the usual vigour of their hair, instead of growing at the proper season, may be withered by the wrinkled scars; and accordingly they grow up without beards, and consequently without any beauty, like eunuchs, though they all have closely-knit and strong limbs, and plump necks; they are of great size, and low legged, so that you might fancy them two-legged beasts, or the stout figures which are hewn out in a rude manner with an axe on the posts at the end of bridges.

They are certainly in the shape of men, however uncouth, but are so hardy that they neither require fire nor well-flavoured food, but live on the roots of such herbs as they get in the fields, or on the half-raw flesh of any animal, which they merely warm rapidly by placing it between their own thighs and the backs of their horses.

They never shelter themselves under roofed houses, but avoid them as people ordinarily avoid sepulchres as things not fitted for common use. Nor is there even to be found among them a cabin thatched with reed; but they wander about, roaming over the mountains and the woods, and accustom themselves to bear frost and hunger and thirst from their very cradles. And even when abroad they never enter a house unless under the compulsion of some extreme necessity; nor, indeed, do they think people under roofs as safe as others.

They wear linen clothes, or else garments made of the skins of field-mice: nor do they wear a different dress out of doors from that which they wear at home; but after a tunic is once put round their necks, however it becomes worn, it is never taken off or changed till, from long decay, it becomes actually so ragged as to fall to pieces.

They cover their heads with round caps, and their shaggy legs with the skins of kids; their shoes are not made on any lasts, but are so unshapely as to hinder them from walking with a free gait. And for this reason they are not well suited to infantry battles, but are nearly always on horseback, their horses being ill-shaped, but hardy; and sometimes they even sit upon them like women if they want to do anything more conveniently. There is not a person in the whole nation who cannot remain on his horse day and night. On horseback they buy and sell, they take their meat and drink, and there they recline on the narrow neck of their steed, and yield to sleep so deep as to indulge in every variety of dream.

And when any deliberation is to take place on any weighty matter, they all hold their common council on horseback. They are not under the authority of a king, but are contented with the irregular government of their nobles, and under their lead they force their way through all obstacles.

Sometimes when provoked, they fight; and when they go into battle, they form in a solid body, and utter all kinds of terrific yells. They are very quick in their operations, of exceeding speed, and fond of surprising their enemies. With a view to this, they suddenly disperse, then reunite, and again, after having inflicted vast loss upon the enemy, scatter themselves over the whole plain in irregular formations: always avoiding a fort or an entrenchment.

And in one respect you may pronounce them the most formidable of all warriors, for when at a distance they use missiles of various kinds tipped with sharpened bones instead of the usual points of javelins, and these bones are admirably fastened into the shaft of the javelin or arrow; but when they are at close quarters they fight with the sword, without any regard for their own safety; and often while their antagonists are warding off their blows they entangle them with twisted cords, so that, their hands being fettered, they lose all power of either riding or walking.

None of them plough, or even touch a plough-handle: for they have no settled abode, but are homeless and lawless, perpetually wandering with their waggons, which they make their homes; in fact they seem to be people always in flight. Their wives live in these waggons, and there weave their miserable garments; and here too they sleep with their husbands, and bring up their children till they reach the age of puberty; nor, if asked, can any one of them tell you where he was born, as he was conceived in one place, born in another at a great distance, and brought up in another still more remote.

In truces they are treacherous and inconstant, being liable to change their minds at every breeze of every fresh hope which presents itself, giving themselves up wholly to the impulse and inclination of the moment; and, like brute beasts, they are utterly ignorant of the distinction between right and wrong. They express themselves with great ambiguity and obscurity; have no respect for any religion or superstition whatever; are immoderately covetous of gold; and are so fickle and irascible, that they very often on the same day that they quarrel with their companions without any provocation, again become reconciled to them without any mediator.

No. 24. Orosius on the "Sack of Rome"

(Orosius' *Seven Books Against the Pagans*. Migne, *Patrologia Latina*, XXXI, 1846. Translation.)

Bk. VII. Ch. 38. Meanwhile Count Stilicho who was of the Vandal nation, a race unwarlike, greedy, treacherous, and crafty, not satisfied that he was the power behind the emperor, sought by every possible means to elevate his son, Eucherius, to the throne, who according to common report had planned a persecution of the Christians even when he was yet a boy and a private citizen. For this reason, when Alaric and the whole Gothic nation had asked humbly and simply for a lasting peace and a place to settle, Stilicho favored with a secret alliance, while publicly denying them the opportunity to make either war or peace, in order to reserve them for wearing down and terrorizing the state. Moreover, he aroused other tribes, irresistible in number and resources, who are now pressing upon the frontiers of Gaul and Spain, that is, the Alans, Suevi, Vandals, and also the Burgundians who were driven forward by the same movement, and encouraged them to take up arms once their fear of the name of Rome had been lost. Stilicho meanwhile planned to attack the Rhine frontiers and to strike at the Gallic provinces, hoping, that miserable wretch, under the pressure of this necessity, to be able to wrest the imperial dignity from his son-in-law in favor of his son, and to find it as easy to pacify the barbarous tribes as it had been once to arouse them. Therefore, when the nature of these crimes had been revealed to the Emperor Honorius and the Roman army, the army quite justifiably mutinied and killed Stilicho, who had endangered the blood of the entire human race so that he might invest one boy with the purple. Eucherius was also slain, who, in order to gain the favor of the pagans, had promised to restore the temples upon his accession and destroy the churches. And a few accomplices in these plots were also punished. So with a minimum of trouble and the punishment of a few, the churches of Christ and the pious emperor were freed and avenged. Therefore, after such an increase in blasphemies with no evidence of penitence, that long-delayed punishment finally overwhelmed the city.

Ch. 39. Alaric appeared, laid siege to terrified Rome, threw all into confusion and then broke into the city. Yet he first gave orders that those people who had fled to holy places, specifically to the basilicas of the holy apostles Peter and Paul, were not to be molested but would be safe; furthermore, that while his men might plunder as they wished, they were to refrain from bloodshed. It also happened, in order the better to prove that the storming of the city had been occasioned by the anger of God rather than by the bravery of the enemy, that the holy Innocent, bishop of the church of Rome, like to the just Lot who had withdrawn from Sodom, by the hidden providence of God was then at Ravenna and did not witness the ruin of the sinful populace. . . .

On the third day after the barbarians had broken into the city, they left of their own accord, having fired indeed some buildings, but not so many as had been burned in the fire which an accident had started in the seven hundredth year of Rome's existence. For if I recall the conflagration which took place during the spectacles of Nero, her emperor, there is no doubt that this fire which the anger of the conqueror caused cannot compare with that which the wantonness of the prince had kindled. Neither, indeed, in this connection need I recall the Gauls who after burning and razing the city camped on its burned out ashes for almost an entire year. And lest anyone, perchance, doubt that the enemy was permitted to chastize the proud, lascivious, and blasphemous city, it should be noted that at that very same time the most famous sites in the city which the enemy had not been able to fire were destroyed by lightning.

No. 25. Theodoric and Roman culture

(*The Letters of Cassiodorus*, tr. Thomas Hodgkin. London, 1886. Cassiodorus was Theodoric's secretary.)

Bk. I, 21. King Theodoric to Maximian . . .

If the people of Rome will beautify their City we will help them.

Institute a strict audit (of which no one need be ashamed) of the money given by us to the different workmen for the beautification of the City. See that we are receiving money's worth for the money spent. If there is embezzlement anywhere, cause the funds so embezzled to be disgorged. We expect the Romans to help from their own resources in this patriotic work, and certainly not to intercept our contributions for the purpose.

The wandering birds love their own nests; the beasts haste to their own lodgings in the brake; the voluptuous fish, roaming the fields of the ocean, returns to its own well-known cavern. How much more should Rome be loved by her children!

Bk. I, 31. King Theodoric to the Roman People . . .

The Circus, in which the King spends so much money, is meant to be for public delight, not for stirring up wrath. Instead of uttering howls and insults like other nations [the populace of Byzantium?], whom they have despised for doing so, let them tune their voices, so that their applause shall sound like the notes of some vast organ, and even the brute creation delight to hear it.

Anyone uttering outrageous reproaches against any Senator will be dealt with by the Praefectus Urbis.

Bk. I, 41. King Theodoric to Agapitus . . .

The dignity of the Senate makes it necessary to be unusually careful who is admitted into that body. Let other orders receive middling men: the Senate must receive none but those who are of proved excellence.

Therefore let your Illustrious Magnificence cause those enquiries to be made concerning Faustus, the grown-up son of the Illustrious Faustus, which the Senate hath ordered to be made concerning all persons who are to be enrolled in its council. In thus confirming and ratifying the proceedings of the Senate we are in no degree trenching on the accustomed authority of that sacred order.

Bk. II, 7. King Theodoric to Sura . . .

Let nothing lie useless which may redound to the beauty of the City. Let your Illustrious Magnificence therefore cause the blocks of marble which are everywhere lying about in ruins to be wrought up into the walls by the hands of the workmen whom I send herewith. Only take care to use only those stones which have really fallen from public buildings, as we do not wish to appropriate private property, even for the glorification of the City.

Bk. II, 7. King Theodoric to Agapitus . . .

We have decided to send you on an embassy to the East [Constantinople]. Every embassy requires a prudent man, but here there is need of especial prudence, because you will have to dispute against the most subtle persons—artificers of words, who think they can foresee every possible answer to their arguments. Do your best therefore to justify the opinion which I formed of you before full trial of your powers.

Bk. II, 12. King Theodoric to the Count of the Siliquatarii (Customs Officers) . . .

Italy ought to enjoy her own products, and it is monstrous that anything which she produces should be wanting to her own children.

Therefore let no lard be exported to foreign parts, but let it by God's grace be all kept for consumption at home.

Now take care not to incur the slightest blame in this matter. It is a very serious fault even in trifles to disobey orders. Sin consists in quality, not in quantity; and injustice cannot be measured. A command, if it be despised in one part, is violated in the whole.

Bk. II, 29. King Theodoric to Adila . . .

We wish to protect all our subjects, but especially the Church, because by so doing we earn the favour of heaven. Therefore, in accordance with the petition of the blessed Eustorgius, Bishop of Milan, we desire to accord all necessary protection to the men and farms belonging to the Milanese Church in Sicily: always understanding, however, that they are not to refuse to plead in answer to any public or private suit that may be brought against them. They are to be protected from wrong, but are not themselves to deviate from the path of justice.

Bk. III, 31. King Theodoric to the Senate of the City of Rome . . .

Our care is for the whole Republic, in which, by the favour of God, we are striving to bring back all things to their former state; but especially for the City of Rome. We hear that great depredations are being committed on public property there.

(1) It is said that the water of the aqueducts is being diverted to turn mills and water gardens—a thing which would not be suffered even in the country districts. Even in redressing this wrong we must be observant of law; and therefore if it should be found that those who are doing this can plead thirty years' prescription, they must be bought off, but the misuser must cease. If the diversion is of less ancient date, it must of course be at once stopped without compensation.

(2) Slaves assigned by the forethought of previous rulers to the service of the aqueducts have passed under the sway of private masters.

(3) Great weights of brass and lead (the latter very easy to steal, from its softness) have been stripped off from the public buildings. Now Ionos, King of Thessaly, is said to have first discovered lead, and Midas, King of Phrygia, brass. How grievous that we should be handed down to posterity as neglecting two metals which they were immortalised by discovering!

(4) Temples and other public buildings, which at the request of many we have repaired, are handed over without a thought to spoliation and ruin.

We have appointed the Spectabilis John to enquire into and set straight all these matters. *You* ought to have brought the matter before us yourselves: at least, now, support him with the necessary "solatia."

No. 26. The Salic Law

(Henderson's *Historical Documents*, pp. 176-189 *passim*.)

Title I. Concerning Summonses

If any one be summoned before the "Thing" [the court] by the king's law, and do not come, he shall be sentenced to 600 denars, which make 15 shillings.

But he who summons another, and does not come himself, shall, if a lawful impediment have not delayed him, be sentenced to 15 shillings, to be paid to him whom he summoned.

And he who summons another shall walk with witnesses to the home of that man, and, if he be not at home, shall bid the wife or any one of the family to make known to him that he has been summoned to court.

But if he be occupied in the king's service he can not summon him.

But if he shall be inside the hundred seeing about his own affairs, he can summon him in the manner explained.

Title II. Concerning Thefts of Pigs, etc.

If any one steal a sucking pig, and it be proved against him, he shall be sentenced to 120 denars, which make three shillings.

If any one steal a pig that can live without its mother, and it be proved on him, he shall be sentenced to 40 denars—that is, 1 shilling.

If any one steal 25 sheep where there were no more in that flock, and it be proved on him, he shall be sentenced to 2500 denars—that is, 62 shillings.

Title III. Concerning Thefts of Cattle

If any one steal that bull which rules the herd and never has been yoked, he shall be sentenced to 1800 denars, which make 45 shillings.

But if that bull is used for the cows of three villages in common, he who stole him shall be sentenced to three times 45 shillings.

If any one steal a bull belonging to the king he shall be sentenced to 3600 denars, which make 90 shillings.

Title XI. Concerning Thefts or Housebreakings of Freemen

If any freeman steal, outside of the house, something worth 2 denars, he shall be sentenced to 600 denars, which made 15 shillings.

But if he steal, outside of the house, something worth 40 denars, and it be proved on him, he shall be sentenced, besides the amount and the fines for delay, to 1400 denars, which make 35 shillings.

If a freeman break into a house and steal something worth 2 denars, and it be proved on him, he shall be sentenced to 15 shillings.

But if he shall have stolen something worth more than 5 denars, and it have been proved on him, he shall be sentenced, besides the worth of the object and the fines for delay, to 1400 denars, which make 35 shillings.

Title XIV. Concerning Assault and Robbery

If any one have assaulted and plundered a free man, and it be proved on him, he shall be sentenced to 2500 denars, which make 63 shillings.

If a Roman have plundered a Salian Frank, the above law shall be observed.

But if a Frank have plundered a Roman, he shall be sentenced to 35 shillings.

If any man should wish to migrate, and has permission from the King, and shall have shown this in the public "thing": whoever, contrary to the decree of the king, shall presume to oppose him, shall be sentenced to 8000 denars, which make 200 shillings.

Title XXX. Concerning Insults

If any person shall have called another "fox," he shall be sentenced to 3 shillings.

If any man shall have called another "hare," he shall be sentenced to 3 shillings.

If any man shall have brought it up against another that he have thrown away his shield, and shall not have been able to prove it, he shall be sentenced to 120 denars, which make 3 shillings.

If any man shall have called another "spy" or "perjurer," and shall not have been able to prove it, he shall be sentenced to 600 denars, which make 15 shillings.

Title XLI. Concerning the Murder of Free Men

If any one shall have killed a free Frank, or a barbarian living under the Salic law, and it have been proved on him, he shall be sentenced to 8000 denars.

But if he shall have thrown him into a well or into the water, or shall have covered him with branches or anything else, to conceal him, he shall be sentenced to 24000 denars, which make 600 shillings.

But if any one has slain a man who is in the service of the king, he shall be sentenced to 24000 denars, which make 600 shillings.

But if he have put him in the water or in a well, and covered him with anything to conceal him, he shall be sentenced to 72000 denars, which make 1800 shillings.

If any one have slain a Roman who eats in the king's palace, and it have been proved on him, he shall be sentenced to 12000 denars, which make 300 shillings.

But if the Roman shall not have been a landed proprietor and table companion of the king, he who killed him shall be sentenced to 4000 denars, which make 100 shillings.

But if he shall have killed a Roman who was obliged to pay tribute, he shall be sentenced to 63 shillings.

If any one have thrown a free man into a well, and he have escaped alive, he (the criminal) shall be sentenced to 4000 denars, which make 100 shillings.

Title LIX. Concerning Private Property

If any man die and leave no sons, if the father and mother survive, they shall inherit.

If the father and mother do not survive, and he leave brothers or sisters, they shall inherit.

But if there are none, the sisters of the father shall inherit.

But if there are no sisters of the father, the sisters of the mother shall claim that inheritance.

If there are none of these, the nearest relatives on the father's side shall succeed to that inheritance.

But of Salic land no portion of the inheritance shall come to a woman: but the whole inheritance of the land shall come to the male sex.

Title LXII. Concerning Wergeld

If any one's father have been killed, the sons shall have half the compounding money (wergeld); and the other half the nearest relatives, as well on the mother's as on the father's side, shall divide among themselves.

But if there are no relatives, paternal or maternal, that portion shall go to the fisc.

No. 27. Ordeal of hot water

(Thatcher and McNeal, *A Source Book for Mediaeval History*. New York, 1905, pp. 401-404.)

1. When men are to be tried by the ordeal of hot water, they shall first be made to come to church in all humility, and prostrate themselves, while the priest says these prayers:

First prayer. Aid, O God, those who seek thy mercy, and pardon those who confess their sins. . . .

2. After these prayers, the priest shall rise and say the mass before all the

men who are to be tried, and they shall take part in the mass. But before they take the communion, the priest shall adjure them in these words: I adjure you, by the Father, Son, and Holy Spirit, by your Christianity, by the only begotten Son of God, whom you believe to be the Redeemer of the world, by the holy Trinity, by the holy gospel, and by the relics of the saints which are kept in this church, that you do not come to the holy communion and take of it, if you have done this offence, or consented to it, or if you know who committed it, or anything else about it.

3. If they all keep silence and no one makes any confession, the priest shall go to the altar and take communion, and then give it to the men; but before they take it he shall say: Let this body and blood of our Lord Jesus Christ be today a trial of your guilt or innocence.

4. After the mass the priest shall go to the place where the ordeal is to be held, bearing with him the book of the gospels and a cross, and he shall say a short litany. After the litany he shall exorcise the water before it becomes hot, as follows:

5. I exorcise thee, water, in the name of the omnipotent God, and in the name of Jesus Christ, his Son, our Lord, that you may become exorcised and freed from the power of the enemy and the wiles of the devil; so that, if this man who is about to put his hand in you is innocent of the crime of which he is accused, he may escape all injury through the grace of omnipotent God. If he is guilty either in deed or knowledge of the offence of which he is accused, may the power of omnipotent God prove this upon him, so that all men may fear and tremble at the name of our Lord Jesus Christ, who lives and reigns with God.

6. Prayer. Lord Jesus Christ, who art a just judge, strong and patient, plenteous in mercy, by whom all things are made, God of gods, Lord of lords, who didst come down from the bosom of the Father for us and our salvation, and wast born of the Virgin Mary; who by thy passion on the cross didst redeem the world . . . we beseech thee, O Lord, to send down from heaven thy Holy Spirit upon this water, which is now hot and steaming from the fire, that through it we may have a just judgment upon this man. O Lord, who didst turn the water into wine in Cana of Galilee as a sign of thy power, who didst lead the three children Meshach, Shadrach, and Abednego, through the fiery furnace without harm . . . we, thy suppliants, beseech thee not to have regard for the errors in our prayer, but to make known to us before all men thy true and righteous judgment; so that if this man who is accused of fornication, *or* theft, *or* homicide, *or* adultery, *or* any other crime, and who is about to put his hand into the hot water, is not guilty of that crime, thou wilt so guard him that no harm or injury shall happen to that hand.

7. Omnipotent God, we, thy unworthy and sinful servants, again beseech thee to make manifest to us thy true and righteous judgment, so that this man, who is accused and is about to undergo the ordeal, is guilty of that

crime, by act or consent, because of the instigation of the devil or through his own cupidity or pride, and expects to escape or to circumvent the ordeal by some trick, his guilt may be made known upon him by thy power, and may be shown upon his hand, in order that he himself may be brought to confession and repentance, and that thy holy and righteous judgment may be made manifest to all people.

8. [Another exorcism of the water.]

9. Then the priest takes off the garments of each of the men and clothes them in the clean robes of an exorcist or deacon, makes them each kiss the gospel and cross of Christ, and sprinkles them with holy water. Then he makes them each take a drink of the holy water, saying to each one: I give you this water as a trial of your guilt or innocence. Then the wood is placed under the caldron and lighted, and when the water begins to get hot the priest says these prayers:

10. In the name of the holy Trinity. God the just Judge, etc. [Similar to No. 6.]

11. Let us pray. God, who didst free St. Susanna from the false accusation; God, who didst free St. Daniel from the lions' den, and the three children from the fiery furnace: free now the innocent, and make known the guilty.

12. The man who is to undergo the ordeal shall say the Lord's prayer and make the sign of the cross; then the caldron shall be taken from the fire, and the judge shall suspend a stone in the water at the prescribed depth in the regular manner, and the man shall take the stone out of the water in the name of the Lord. Then his hand shall be immediately bound up and sealed with the seal of the judge, and shall remain wrapped up for three days, when it shall be unbound and examined by suitable persons.

4

THE BYZANTINE WORLD

Continued Existence of Roman Empire in the East

As we have seen, Roman power was hardly more than a memory in the West by 450 A.D. Within a few generations, a number of Germanic kingdoms had established regimes to replace the one Roman Empire: an Ostrogothic in Italy, a Vandal in North Africa, a Visigothic in Spain, Burgundian and Frankish states in Gaul, and a number of Anglo-Saxon kingdoms in Britain, to mention the more important. Yet a glance at the map will reveal the astonishing fact that the eastern half of the empire had meantime remained intact, while a closer look at this state will show that a Roman emperor in Constantinople continued to rule this half with reasonable effectiveness. The western half of the empire gone, the eastern relatively unchanged: how can we account for this phenomenon? Why did not Roman rule crumble in the east simultaneously with its disintegration in the west? Why did fortune vouchsafe almost a thousand years of further existence to the eastern half of the empire after the western half had disappeared?

West Most Seriously Affected. One can suggest a number of reasons to explain the astonishing vitality of the eastern half of the empire. It must be remembered, in the first place, that since the days of Diocletian the empire had usually been administered as two parts. One half might have a history apart from the other, and that is precisely what happened. The west had been left to its own resources, which had proved inadequate for self-preservation; those of the east were more than ample to assure its continued existence. The east had always enjoyed a favorable balance of trade, with the west suffering the evils of an adverse balance. The large landed estate with its depressing effect upon industry and its debilitating influence upon government had become common in the west while it remained relatively unknown in many parts of the east. Several of the major factors in the decline of the empire had affected the western portion far more seriously than they had the eastern. The economic depression of the second and third centuries had proved less severe in the east, and so had also the depopulation which had followed in the wake of plague, famine, warfare, and falling birth rate. Though the Balkans suffered disastrously at the hands of the Visigoths and Ostrogoths, it was the west which bore the brunt of the barbarian invasions. Even had the west been spared these misfortunes, it is doubtful whether, without the assistance of the east, it possessed sufficient wealth and manpower to maintain itself and defend its thousand-mile frontier.

East More Prosperous. The east had always been a different world from the west, even though for centuries it had been ruled from the same Rome on the Tiber. The east already had several millenia of advanced culture behind it when the future mistress of the Mediterranean was still desperately struggling for supremacy among the semicivilized Latin groups of central Italy. The east could claim a half-dozen cities—Constantinople, Antioch, Alexandria, Damascus, Tarsus, Pergamum—none so large as Rome of the first century A.D., but each of them more alive economically. Rome was an economic parasite, eternally harassed with the problem of keeping a large unproductive populace quiet, while the eastern metropolises hummed with the industry and trade of centuries-long standing. Even the decline of the west had not struck a serious blow at the east's economy, since only luxury commodities and these in limited quantity had ever found a market there. Sufficient to the prosperity of the eastern Mediterranean were the large cities scattered the length of its littoral, many of which enjoyed important trade connections with India and the Orient. In contrast to the relative poverty of the west, the wealth of the east was incredible, despite the enormous quantities carried off during the corrupt days of the Roman Republic by Roman governors, officials, tax collectors, and moneylenders. Actually the thought of the vast sums emperors like Justinian and Heraclius must have expended in the defense of the empire almost staggers the imagination.

Strong Government. Considerable credit for the survival of the eastern empire must be given its emperors and generals. While the clash of their ambitions occasionally erupted in violence and civil war, they usually proved themselves capable of throwing back any threat from without the empire's frontiers, while maintaining an efficient administration at home. Particularly successful were they in their dealings with the dangerous barbarians strung along the Danubian frontier. If they could not persuade them as had Zeno to go west and occupy the broad acres of Italy, so much more productive than the semiarid hills of the east, they fell back on their huge store of gold and bought them off. If this failed, they might sow dissension among the ranks of their enemies, for at this game of making friends and corrupting enemies one would have to go to the Orient to find the equal of the Byzantines. To satisfy the enormous demands of the

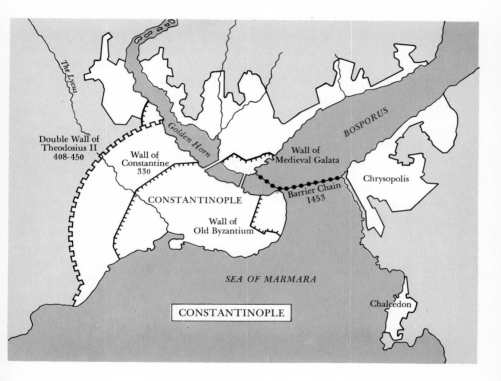

CONSTANTINOPLE

army for recruits, the empire discovered a rich source in the sturdy, loyal peasantry of Anatolia. Furthermore, as we shall see, the eastern empire boasted the services of the most efficient and well-trained bureaucracy in either the ancient or medieval worlds.

Constantinople.   A decisive share in the credit for the survival of the eastern empire must be reserved to its capital city, Constantinople. Its location on the narrow nexus connecting Europe and Asia, at the end of a peninsula jutting out into the Bosporus between the Golden Horn and the Sea of Marmora, assured it unsurpassed commercial and military advantages. A bay seven miles in length provided it a magnificent harbor which for many centuries attracted more ships and cargo than any other city in the world. The strategic superiority of Constantinople's site proved even greater. Until the city rose to block their passage, many peoples had crossed at will between Europe and Asia Minor. But now Constantinople commanded these waters, the most vital crossroads of the Mediterranean world, and it was not until late in the Middle Ages that a hostile force managed to effect a crossing. The city of Constantinople was itself practically impregnable. To the north, east, and south, water and its own fleet provided security against sea attack and against starvation. To the west on the only land approach to the city (about three miles from the eastern tip of the peninsula) Constantine had erected a wall. A mile farther west Theodosius II threw up a double wall in 413, and a third wall running the entire distance from the Sea of Marmora to the Black Sea was constructed by the emperor Anastasius in 500 A.D. Only an enemy capable of mounting a powerful sea and land attack simultaneously could hope to storm the city, as the Turks eventually did in 1453.

The Term "Byzantine Empire." For these reasons, then, the Roman empire survived in the east. Yet the state that lived on for another thousand years is known today as the Byzantine rather than the Eastern Roman Empire. The longer phrase, the Eastern Roman Empire, is linguistically cumbersome and historically misleading. Except in a narrow sense, the civilization which characterized the lands of the eastern Mediterranean was scarcely Roman any longer within a century or two after Constantine's death. True, the official title of the ruler from the ninth century onward was "Emperor of the Romans," and so sensitive were easterners on this score that they incarcerated the envoys of the pope in the tenth century when these dared address Nicephorus II simply as "Emperor of the Greeks." Still no amount of protesting could obscure the fact that within a generation of the death of Justinian, who was the last emperor to speak Latin, the sloughing off of Roman practices and institutions had proceeded apace. Sharply expediting this process were the invasions of the Avars and Slavs who swept away Latin civilization in the Balkan peninsula, thereby erecting a land barrier between the Greek east and the Roman west. A striking illustration of the rapid decline of Roman influences is provided by the *Corpus Juris Civilis*. Whereas the first three and older parts of the *Corpus* are in Latin, the commentaries and the fourth part, which includes the new laws, are in Greek. As Justinian explained: "We did not write this law in the national language [Latin], but in the common language, which is Greek, so that it may be known by all because of the ease with which it will be understood."

Mingling of Cultures. The civilization of the Eastern Roman Empire represents a mingling of eastern cultures, of which the most fundamental was the Hellenistic. Superimposed upon this Greek base were Semitic and Iranian influences, some Slavic and a few Roman. Because of the heterogeneous nature of this culture, its thoroughly Christian character which was wholly incompatible with the classical Rome of the Caesars, and, withal, the modest proportions of the Roman ingredient compared with the Greek, scholars prefer to give this civilization a label other than Roman. Actually this eastern empire produced within a short time a set of wholly non-Roman political institutions, a distinct Christianity, a unique art, and a peculiarly "eastern" literature. In short, it developed its own culture. The label which most modern scholars employ to identify this new civilization is "Byzantine," a word derived from Byzantium, the name of the old Greek city which Constantine selected as the site for his capital.

Justinian

Christopher Dawson has said that the history of the Byzantine Empire "has suffered more from depreciation and neglect than that of any other phase of European culture."* Were it not for the Emperor Justinian who reigned from 527 to 565 A.D., he might have written that this stretch of history had been completely ignored. For Justinian's stature bulks so large, he forces himself and his age upon the historian. While Justinian remains something of a controversial figure because of the dubiousness of much of the limited evidence, he has the distinction of being one of that very small group of men who have given their names to an age. All students of history, whatever their particular prejudices, recognize Justinian as the leading secular figure of the sixth century. And though much of what he accomplished proved impermanent, possibly even unwise, few men have left so enduring and impressive memorials as the *Corpus Juris Civilis* and Hagia Sophia.

Justinian the Man. Justinian was of medium height and average build. Abstemious by nature, he would have passed for an unusually virtuous man even in a less dissolute age. Few kings would have bothered with what he considered indispensable: that the commoner he loved become his wife and empress. Although of an emotional nature, he appears to have borne himself with the dignity befitting the successor of Augustus and Constantine. His vices, if this is not too strong a term to employ, included a measure of irresolution and a willingness to accept flattery and the tales of informers. His critics charged him, also, with devoting too much time to theological problems in face of the overwhelming pressure of administrative and military responsibilities. He was, on the other hand, a most indefatigable worker. "The Emperor never sleeps," so went the word at the court.

Though of Illyrian peasant stock, he received an excellent classical education which helped instil in him a deep sense of Rome's greatness and of

* *The Making of Europe* (New York, 1938), p. 103.

its mission. To restore the empire's frontiers as they had existed under Constantine, and to unite all its subjects in the worship of the one, triune God: these two objectives he made the goals of his driving ambition. In the attainment of his objectives, we see him but infrequently, and then busied with the administrative details many men consider nonessential. But if Justinian rarely carried out any of his projects personally, he possessed a happy faculty for selecting singularly able men to do so. What sustained Justinian throughout his long career of almost fifty years was the burning conviction that God was pleased with his motives and would support him. "Governing under the authority of God our empire, which was delivered to us by His Heavenly Majesty . . . we so lift up our mind in contemplation of the aid of the Omnipotent Deity, that we do not put our trust in our arms nor in our soldiers nor in our own skill, but we rest all our hopes in the providence of the Supreme Trinity alone."*

Theodora. Of the group of extraordinarily capable individuals who helped Justinian place his stamp on this era, none was probably more indispensable, surely none so intriguing, as a woman, the Empress Theodora. Procopius, our chief source, sought to destroy her name, but his malice is so patent scholars discount his testimony. There is little reason to doubt Theodora's low birth, even her dubious reputation as a girl. Procopius credits her with possessing remarkable intelligence, and he compliments her on her unusual beauty "she was fair of face and charming as well, but short and inclined to pallor, not indeed completely without colour but slightly sallow. The expression of her eyes was always grim and tense." Justinian first met her while his uncle Justin occupied the throne. So enamored was he of her, that once his unbending aunt died, he persuaded his sympathetic uncle to have the law changed to enable him to marry one of so low a station. Whatever the nature of her antecedents and her life before her marriage, Theodora proved a most devoted wife. Justinian and Theodora, in fact, present a picture of connubial fidelity and concord scarcely matched in the annals of royalty. Theodora is said to have stated that the emperor never decided anything without consulting her, which was probably true, and fortunate for Justinian. For with her own abundant courage she supplied his want of resolution and decision. On at least one famous occasion her firmness saved him his throne. The violent Nika riots which the rapacious policies of several departments of the government had provoked, had raged out of control and were even threatening the palace. Justinian and his court were for fleeing, but Theodora refused to budge. She reminded them that it was only proper for men who wore the crown not to survive its loss, and that she herself accepted the old proverb which recommended the purple as the most noble winding sheet. Her unyielding stand revived the courage of Justinian and his councilors, and a last desperate attempt to put down the riot succeeded. Theodora's enemies charged

* Quoted in Ure, *op. cit.*, p. 17.

her with having abused her hold upon the emperor to further favorites and destroy those she disliked. If the charge is valid, it is doubtful whether she ever indulged her personal prejudices to the injury of the realm. Because of her lowly origin and her generosity—she founded hospitals, orphanages, even a home for fallen women—Theodora was immensely popular with the people. Whatever the verdict concerning Theodora's place in political history, her position in the history of womankind is assured: no woman has ever risen quite so high socially.

Military History of Reign. Justinian's military activities bulk largest in a remarkably crowded career. We can distinguish three phases of their history, in ascending order of importance: the defensive operations along the lower Danube, those against the Persians in Asia Minor, and, above all, the mighty offensive aimed at recovering the western provinces. Though history questions the wisdom of these western campaigns, it is easy to understand why Justinian did not hesitate to commit so many years and so vast an amount of the empire's resources to achieve this objective. As pointed out above, he conceived it his first duty as Roman emperor to restore the empire and to destroy Arianism in Africa, Spain, and Italy. Furthermore, Justinian no more than his predecessors ever accepted the legal separation of the western provinces. As he affirmed: "God has given us to subdue the Vandals, Alans, and Moors . . . and we have taken hope that the Lord will grant us the rest of the Empire, which the Romans of old extended to the bounds of the two oceans, and which they lost through indolence." If the antithesis of indolence was required to win back the empire, Justinian was the man to undertake the job.

Justinian's Army. Justinian had the best soldiers in the world to carry out his plans and the ablest generals to execute them. The most effective fighter of the era was the *cataphract* (from the Greek verb meaning to clothe with mail). The history of this soldier's evolution went back at least to the Parthians who had destroyed Julius Caesar's colleague, Crassus, in 53 B.C., and defeated Mark Antony some years later. What made the *cataphract* such a formidable warrior were his maneuverability and speed. In the semiarid country of the Near East and North Africa which were ideally suited to a mobile type of warfare, the *cataphract* had proved himself invincible. He wore a close-fitting steel helmet, a shirt of mail, bore a small shield for protection, and carried what amounted to a small arsenal of offensive weapons: lance, broadsword, dagger, bow, and arrows. The powerful charger he rode was said to have been produced on the rolling plains of upper Mesopotamia. Heavy-armed infantry made up the great part of Justinian's armies, but they always played a subordinate role except in sieges. The major weaknesses in Justinian's armies were two: first, there were insufficient troops to wage offensive warfare on a broad western front while attempting at the same time to maintain vulnerable frontiers along the Danube and in the east; second, his armies were Roman only in the technical sense of being in the service of Rome. The majority of his "Roman" soldiers were actually recruited from the fiercer tribes located along the frontier and beyond. These tribesmen took service simply because they liked to fight and to plunder. Only by pressing tribal chieftains with their bands of armed retainers (*bucellarii*) into personal service, could Justinian's generals assure themselves of the loyalty of the rank and file. But Justinian's own distrust of his generals led him in turn to be niggardly in providing them the authority and money they required to be victorious. Nevertheless, in Belisarius and Narses Justinian possessed as superb a pair of generals as any ruler in history.

Danube Frontier. The fighting along the Danube was strictly defensive. Justinian would gladly have accepted that river as his frontier since the constant pressure of German and Hunnic tribes seriously hampered the success of his arms elsewhere. Strung out along the middle Danube were the Germanic Lombards, Heruli, and Gepids, and farther down the river the more dangerous Slavs and such Hunnic tribes as the Bulgars and Avars who carried their plundering raids far down into the Balkans. Belisarius' last assignment as an old man was that of throwing back a Bulgar attack which had carried to the very walls of Constantinople. Justinian used both arms and diplomacy to fight these semicivilized tribes. His agents discovered that the rapaciousness of the tribal leaders and their quarrelsome natures left them especially receptive to imperial offers of gold and honors. Justinian took occasional tribes into his service as *foederati*.

Campaigns Against the Persians. The fighting in Asia Minor and northern Mesopotamia against the Persians presents a confusion of economic, religious, and imperialist considerations. The most crucial area contested between Byzantium and Persia was Lazica, a small Christian state in northern Armenia which bordered on the Black Sea. The Romans were anxious to hold the area in order to develop direct connections eastward with the silk trade of China, and so bypass the Persian monopoly. The Persians for their part would find the occupation of Lazica immensely valuable in prosecuting the war against Byzantium since it fronted on the Black Sea. Friction had likewise developed between Constantinople and Persia over the joint responsibility they had assumed of guarding the Caspian Gates against Hunnic tribes which were a threat to both of them. Religious factors too played a part since Christian proselytizing and penetration eastward had led to retaliatory persecution on the part of the Persians. Regardless of the considerations involved, Justinian always viewed the east as a secondary front, and would willingly have accepted the status quo had the Persian king, Chosroes I, done the same. This Chosroes, the ablest of the Sassanid monarchs, was as treacherous as he was cruel. His armies ravaged Syria, Armenia, and Asia Minor and slaughtered and enslaved on a scale unparalleled since the days of the ancient Assyrians. The largest city of the Near East, Antioch, he left a smouldering ruin, its huge population sold into slavery. Despite Chosroes' ruthless savagery, however, Justinian's armies and his Hunnic and Arab allies, usually had the better of the fighting. Belisarius won his spurs as a young man of twenty-five with a tremendous victory at Daras in 528. But war blazed for another thirty-five years before a relatively permanent peace was concluded, which permitted the Romans to hold Lazica at the price of 30,000 pieces of gold annually. An amount covering the payments for the first seven years, that is to say, 210,000 pieces of gold, was paid on the spot, an eloquent commentary on the wealth of Byzantium.

Conquest of Vandal Kingdom. Justinian wisely opened his campaign to recover the western provinces with an attack on their most vulnerable area, the Vandal kingdom of north Africa. Not only were the Vandals the least numerous of the Germanic invaders, but probably the most unpopular as well. Their harsh rule had earned them the hatred of the Afro-Romans; at the same time they had permitted themselves to become enervated by the wealth and climate of the country. Justinian was presented a convenient pretext for interfering when the Vandal king, Hilderic, who happened to be his friend, appealed to him for aid against a usurper. So unsuspecting was Amalasuntha, the Ostrogothic regent of Italy, of Justinian's ultimate designs on her own country, that she permitted him to use Italy as a base. Justinian's general Belisarius landed his army without opposition and with his six thousand *cataphracts* cut the Vandal armies to pieces in two engagements. Within the brief space of six months the Vandal kingdom was extinguished and with its people disappeared into the pages of history. But the Berbers (Moors) proved as indomitable a foe against Belisarius as they had against earlier invaders. It required fourteen years of fighting before they accepted a measure of submission. Justinian knew better than to attempt the subjugation of Mauretania (Algiers and Morocco).

Conquest of Italy. The major objective in the west was, of course, Italy, and here again Justinian was not wanting a pretext. Amalasuntha, daughter of the great Theodoric and a pro-Roman by sympathy, had sought to shore up her unsteady throne by marrying her cousin, a member of the Gothic faction, only to be strangled for her pains. Ostensibly to avenge her death, Justinian sent one army westward through Dalmatia, another his general Belisarius brought in by way of Sicily. Rome fell with astonishing ease, and within five years the entire peninsula had been pacified, or so at least it appeared. Hardly had Belisarius moved the bulk of his troops eastward to fight the Persians, however, than the Goths rallied under their new chieftain, Totila. This Gothic king is perhaps the most attractive personality we meet with among the early Germanic leaders in the west. Even his enemies respected him for his bravery and his sense of justice. After capturing Rome, he was deterred from razing the city by a letter from Belisarius which asked: "Did Totila wish to go down to pos-

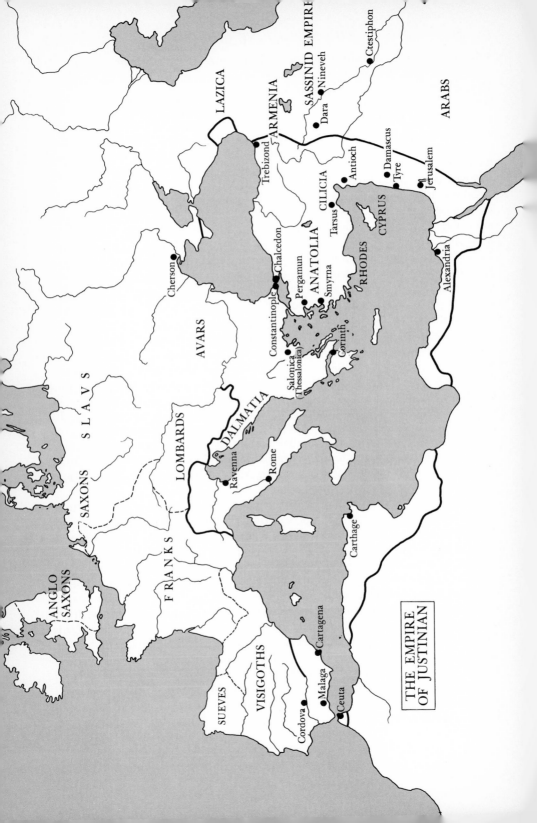

THE EMPIRE
OF JUSTINIAN

ANGLO
SAXONS

SAXONS

SLAVS

FRANKS

AVARS

Cherson

LOMBARDS

DALMATIA

Ravenna
Rome

SUEVES

VISIGOTHS

Cordova
Malaga
Cartagena
Ceuta

Carthage

Salonica
(Thessalonica)

Constantinople
Chalcedon

Pergamun
Smyrna

Corinth

ANATOLIA

RHODES

CYPRUS

CILICIA

Tarsus

Antioch

Damascus
Tyre
Jerusalem

Alexandria

LAZICA

Trebizond

ARMENIA

SASSINID EMPIRE

Nineveh

Dara

Ctesiphon

ARABS

terity as the man who had destroyed the most glorious city in the world?" Belisarius returned to Italy, but he lacked the troops to undo Totila's success. Upon his request, Justinian replaced him with the wily Narses whom he supplied with 35,000 troops, most of them Lombards. Totila fell in battle and within three years Narses had subdued the Goths together with the Franks and Alamans who had crossed the Alps. Justinian's forces moved next against Spain where they exploited the dissension among the Visigothic chieftains to capture such coastal towns as Cordova, Cartagena, and Malaga. (Reading 28)

An Evaluation. How does history assess Justinian's military achievement? Justinian and his contemporaries were most impressed with the territories the imperial armies had recovered: the Roman provinces of Africa, Dalmatia, Italy, southeastern Spain, Ceuta which guarded Gibraltar, and the islands of the western Mediterranean. Though Mauretania, most of Spain, and Gaul remained outside the empire, the Mediterranean was again a Roman lake. Unfortunately it remained a Roman lake very briefly, the student of history protests in announcing his sharply critical evaluation of Justinian's military policies. Within a century all these newly won territories had slipped away save for Sicily and a few points in Italy such as Rome and Ravenna which the Lombards failed to capture. True, these enclaves proved valuable economic and cultural links between Constantinople and Italy for five hundred years to come. Still the price paid for these benefits was high, too high. The tremendous military exertions which Justinian's wars necessitated depleted the economic resources of the Byzantine east and, what was equally as serious, alienated many of his subjects in Syria and Egypt because of the high taxes the wars entailed. The sufferings of Italy during the twenty years of cruel warfare (the entire population of Milan, for example, was massacred by the Goths) reminds one of Tacitus' indictment of ancient Rome's "pacification" of Britain: "They made it a desert and called it peace." That the Goths disappeared so completely as not to leave even a single word in the Italian language can be accounted no great loss; that classical civilizaion which had somehow managed to weather the invasions of Visigoths, Vandals, and Ostrogoths, should have all but perished, must be appraised a calamity. These wars radically altered the cultural, economic, and political character of the peninsula. The city of Rome, subjected to five sieges and captured and recaptured several times, scarcely remained a city, with its population decimated and impoverished. Hopeless confusion and desolation reigned from the Po valley to Sicily while Lombard chieftains quarreled over the remnants of a glorious past.

The Codification of Roman Law: the Great Need. It is the codification of Roman law, not his recovery of important provinces of the western empire, which entitles Justinian to his niche in history. That several of his predecessors, including Julius Caesar, had contemplated carrying out this project, which two, Hadrian and Theodosius II had actually attempted on a limited scale, emphasized the grave urgency for such a codification. For Roman law was gradually passing into disuse because of the confusion which confronted at every turn the judge who would apply it. As a matter of fact, because of the difficulty of using Roman law, it had become common for judges to base their decisions on what they deemed proper and reasonable, rather than upon legal precedent or statute. Since 451 B.C. when the first laws were inscribed on the famous Twelve Tables, legal precedents, opinions, and laws had been accumulating at a steady rate. The Republican assemblies, the senate, praetors, emperors, and jurisconsults, all had contributed to the mounting mass of legal literature. Some of the laws hearkened back to the days of the early Republic when Rome was but a diminutive agrarian state on the Tiber, ruled by custom. Many more dated from the period of Rome's might, when her empire stretched from the Atlantic to Mesopotamia. Most of the laws and legal literature bore the stamp of a pagan civilization, while those since the early fourth century were Christian in tone. Not only had this mass of laws and legal writing reached a tremendous volume over the period of a thousand years, but the degree of duplication, confusion, and inconsistency must have been equally profound.

Work of Codification. Justinian appreciated the enormity of the project and wisely instructed the distinguished jurist Tribonian and his commission of ten, to begin their work with those imperial edicts still considered pertinent and applicable. The group decided to go back as far as Hadrian's reign, and after a year's work (529 A.D.) compiled a volume known officially as the *Codex Constitutionum* or *Book of Constitutions*. This volume included 4652 enactments which are organized into twelve books, after the manner of the original Twelve Tables. Four years later a second compilation appeared called the *Digest* (Greek *Pandects*), which summarized the legal writings of eminent jurists of both republican and imperial Rome, notably those, however, of the second and third centuries A.D. This task of summarizing legal opinion represented the most extensive phase of the entire work of codification. When completed, it constituted a reduction of some three million lines of legal literature to 150,000. The organization of this material follows the same pattern as that of the *Codex*.

The Corpus Juris Civilis. A relatively short work, the *Institutes*, which appeared with the *Digest*, was intended to serve as a manual for the use of law students and civil servants. As Justinian announced in the Preface: "Receive then these laws with your best efforts and with an enthusiasm for study, and show yourselves so learned as to be encouraged to hope that when you have compassed the whole field of law you may have the ability to govern such portions of the state as may be entrusted to you."* Justinian declared these three parts, the *Codex*, *Digest*, and *Institutes*, to be the sole

* Quoted in Ure, *op. cit.*, p. 143.

law of the empire, while designating them at the same time the subject matter to be studied in the imperial law schools. A fourth compilation known as the *Novels* consisted simply of an appendix of 154 ordinances which Justinian had issued after the appearance of the *Codex* in order to supplement or modify its enactments. These four parts make up what is known as the *Corpus Juris Civilis* (Body of Civil Law) or more commonly (though erroneously) Justinian's Code.

Importance of the Corpus. The *Corpus* is a lengthy work which runs some 2,000 closely printed pages in a modern edition. As might be expected of a work of such scope, the value of the four parts varies sharply. The *Novels* are least important since they reflect the legal thought of one reign, even of one man. For "What gives the *Corpus* its unique value is its singular freedom from the delusion that all Roman wisdom was to be found in any one age or period. The result of this enlightened traditionalism is that the *Code* and *Digest* embody the accumulated experience and wisdom of centuries."* This statement applies particularly to the *Digest*, which has been called the most important law book the world has ever seen. For the *Digest* comprises not actual laws which must be constantly adjusted to changing conditions, but legal principles which have met the test of time. The *Institutes* enjoy in more modest fashion some of the timelessness of the *Digest*. Justinian's codification of Roman law preserved for the West Rome's most precious legacy from a glorious past. For his own Byzantine state it proved a powerful agent in establishing the centralized administration which he demanded. (Readings 31, 32)

Justinian and the Church. Justinian's attitude toward the Church is deserving of special attention, both for its own interest as well as for the fact that it set the pattern generally followed by his successors. Three circumstances conditioned Justinian's religious policy. There was first the principle inherited from Constantine and his pagan predecessors that the head of the state was also head of the church. According to this principle, the emperor's power, which was of divine origin, was absolute and unquestioned in all things touching the common welfare of his subjects and of the empire, be these of a secular or religious character. This policy or attitude is commonly called Caesaropapism, that is, it is based on the theory that the head of the state is both Caesar and pope. As Emperor Leo III reminded the pope: "I am emperor and priest whom God has ordered to feed his flock like Peter, prince of the Apostles." A second circumstance affecting Justinian's policy toward the church followed logically from the first. Partly because of the tradition that the emperor was supreme in civil as well as in religious affairs, partly because neither the ancient world nor the medieval subscribed to the principle of separation of church and state, it was common practice for Justinian and his successors to confer wide civil responsibilities upon bishops and other ecclesiastical officials. Bishops

* Ure, *op. cit.*, p. 145.

often acted as heads of municipal government; they served as judges of last appeal; they were given jurisdiction over widows, orphans, and the poor. That Chosroes negotiated with the local bishop over the ransom of the captured city of Sura was not considered exceptional in the sixth century. Even if the bishop's authority did not normally embrace high civil prerogatives, in those troublous times he was frequently the only one willing to assume a position of responsibility when disaster struck or threatened.

Presence of Heretical Groups. A third circumstance which prompted Justinian to assume a leading role in religious affairs was the existence of large heretical groups within the empire. While religious communities with conflicting doctrinal convictions have learned to live next to one another in harmony today, this was not so until recent centuries, surely not in the sixth. To aggravate the danger of strife in Justinian's day was the national character of several of the religious sects within the empire. Thus the Monophysite bishops of Egypt and Syria were the real rulers of those areas. Unless the emperor succeeded in conciliating their religious prejudices, he could not count on their political loyalty. Actually the people of the east showed an even greater interest in affairs of the church and in religious controversy than they did in matters of state. What Gregory of Nyssa said of Constantinople of the fourth century was as readily applicable in the sixth, namely: "This city is full of mechanics and slaves who are all of them profound theologians and preach in the shops and the streets. If you want a man to change a piece of silver, he tells you in what way the Son differs from the Father; if you ask the price of a loaf of bread, you are told by way of reply that the Son is inferior to the Father; and if you inquire whether the bath is ready, the answer is that the Son was made of nothing." Is it any wonder, then, that in a nation of theologians Justinian should have been referred to as a "crowned theologian"?

Religious Uniformity Impossible. Justinian's chief concern in religious matters was that of bringing all minds into conformity, as much to please God as to stabilize his regime. Thus in referring to an edict condemning heretical bishops, he announced: "This we enact on behalf of the peace of our most holy churches, that the whole hieratical order may henceforth abide in peace and quiet. For if it is kept in peace, the state at large will flourish . . . possessed of the peace from on high which our great God and Saviour Jesus Christ bestows on those found worthy to glorify and adore Him in sincerity and truth."* For all of Justinian's conviction and persistence, he found it just as difficult to legislate religious conformity into existence as had his predecessors. Anastasius (d. 518) had been frankly Monophysite in his sympathies, Justin (d. 527), on the other hand, just as vigorously orthodox. Though Justinian's own preference was for ortho-

* Ure, *op. cit.*, pp. 126-127.

thousands of skilled workmen were busily engaged producing some of the world's finest silks and brocades, glass and enamelware, jewelry and ivory carvings. Few cities have rivaled the commercial activity of this bustling entrepôt on the Bosporus, or have offered so great a variety of goods as could be obtained in its vast open-air bazaars. Nor could a more magnificent city be found west of the largely unknown Orient unless it were Islamic Baghdad on the Tigris. What treasure and unrivaled workmanship could accomplish to make their capital the wonder of the world the Byzantine emperors expended without stint. Few of the luxurious commodities gathered up out of the east and south passed through and beyond the Golden Horn. They were kept there in Constantinople to grace the imperial palace or the homes of the aristocracy or the city's many churches and shrines. There has never been a city in Christendom which could approach Constantinople in the richness of its mosaics, its inlaid furniture, tapestries, rugs, silks, in the beauty and wealth of its liturgical and religious articles (vestments, crucifixes, reliquaries) or illuminated manuscripts. In the center of the city and dominating its social and political life were the splendid church of Hagia Sophia, the sumptuous Great Palace, and the stupendous Hippodrome (Circus). To the awestricken European from the west who knew only ruined and decayed communities, Constantinople was truly the fabulous city of the world.

Commerce and Industry. After the fifth century western Europe could boast of not one active industrial center; the Byzantine world could enumerate a series: Constantinople, Alexandria which was second only to the city on the Golden Horn, Thessalonica, Antioch, Tyre, Damascus, Smyrna, Trebizon, and Corinth. Because of the revenues and resources such thriving cities supplied the imperial coffers, anxious emperors gave constant attention to the problem of fostering trade and industry. It was preeminently Byzantine trade, in fact, that enabled the empire to absorb the huge costs of government and war. In their efforts to stimulate industry and commerce, the Byzantine emperors maintained protective tariffs, they opened trade routes to Ethiopia and Russia, they negotiated commercial treaties with anyone who had anything to trade, and they circulated the most widely accepted coin in the medieval world, the bezant (from Byzantine). Though Justinian failed in his efforts to break the Persian monopoly of the silk trade with the east, he did better in the end. In 552 two monks smuggled silk worms out of China in the hollow stems of bamboo rods. Within a few years mulberry groves were covering the hills of Syria, and the Greek peninsula had developed into a major silk-weaving area. Through gilds which the government carefully supervised and controlled, the emperors were usually successful in assuring continuous production to industry and a price system conducive to the general well being. These gilds, like those in the west which we shall consider later, procured their own raw materials, processed and sold the finished products, and regulated wages and hours of labor. In certain industries such as those producing silk and armaments, the state exercised a veritable monopoly. Yet for all the attention paid to industry and trade, agriculture remained the principal means of livelihood for most people of the empire. At a time when the west was slipping ever deeper into a state of agrarian self-sufficiency, Byzantine agriculture was offering for export a diversity of commodities which included sugar cane, cotton, mulberries, dye plants, citrus fruits, flax, and medicinal herbs.

Learning, Literature, and Art

Byzantine learning and literature ranked first in Europe until the thirteenth century when the west assumed the leadership it has never relinquished. This leadership, first of Byzantium, then of the west, rested substantially upon the same base, that is, the classical heritage of Greece and Rome. Byzantium enjoyed an unbroken classical tradition which extended back to the Hellenic world of the sixth century B.C. Thanks to this tradition and to its interest in scholarship, the Byzantine empire boasted a remarkably high ratio of educated people and of scholars. In no medieval city was a good education within easier reach than in Constantinople; no medieval state produced more able scholars and writers. "Byzantium stood for a thousand years as the most important stronghold of culture and learning," declares Professor Ostrogorski. That Byzantine scholarship failed to proceed far beyond the level of classical antiquity may be attributed partly to enemy invasions which constantly threatened the state, partly to its deep veneration for tradition. For Byzantine scholarship seemed content to preserve, not to build upon, its rich heritage. Yet the true eminence of Byzantine culture, even though lacking in originality, has only recently attracted the attention of modern scholarship which so long accepted Edward Gibbon's false indictment of that civilization as "the triumph of barbarism and religion."

Historians.   The Byzantine world produced a vast amount of hagiography, theological learning, and even some classical poetry, but all of this the modern world is apt to find uninviting. More appealing are the pungent writings of Procopius, the historian of Justinian's reign. Procopius' *Wars* describe Justinian's efforts to recover the west while maintaining the Danube and eastern frontier; his *Buildings* describes the extensive work of construction and reconstruction Justinian undertook throughout the empire; his *Secret History* or *Anecdota* relates the chief characters, notably the emperor and Theodora, to the events of that day. Though

Procopius may have captured some of the literary verve of Thucydides whom he admired, he falls woefully short of that historian's extraordinary objectivity. So marked indeed is the contrast between the incomparable Justinian of the *Buildings* and the diabolical Justinian of the *Secret History*, that Procopius' authorship of the latter work has often been disputed. (Readings 28-30) Several minor historians continued Procopius' account of Justinian's reign, the most important of these being the lawyer Agathias.

Apart from the preparation of historical compilations which he encouraged, Constantine VII's own writings constitute our best source of information concerning Byzantine administration and court ceremonials; we also learn much about the peoples who bordered Byzantium in the tenth century. Leo the Deacon has left a reasonably honest, though uninspiring, history of his own times, the third quarter of the tenth century. A highly literary, somewhat colored, account of the subsequent hundred years (997-1077) by an eyewitness comes from the prolific pen of Michael Psellus, statesman, universal scholar, and encyclopedist. (Reading 35) Deserving to be ranked with the best of Byzantine historians is a princess, Anna Comnena, whose epic-like poem, the *Alexiad*, which combines literary talent with historical ability, has as its theme the exploits of her father, Alexius I, and the events of the First Crusade. (See page 405.) Less literary, accurate, and unprejudiced, although frequently supplying valuable information where none other is available, are a number of chronicles, such as that of George the Monk (to 842) and of Theophanes (to 813).

Other Scholars and Literary Figures. Byzantine's foremost theologian (post patristic era) was St. John Damascene (d. 750) whose *Fount of Knowledge* represents the first systematic presentation of Christian theology which attempted to incorporate Aristotelian philosophy. Theologians of the Orthodox churches have always recognized his writings as definitive. This John of Damascus also contributed to Byzantine's imposing treasury of sacred poetry, whose heaviest contributor was Romanus the Melodus (sixth century), said to have composed a thousand hymns. What endeared Romanus' verse to his contemporaries were both the pious sentiments he expressed and his rhythm which was based upon accent rather than upon quantity. (On accentual verse, see page 602.) The leading "Byzantine" novel was the religious romance of Barlaam and Josaphat. This story started out as an Indian tale relating to the life of Buddha, but in its Greek and Western adaptations in the Middle Ages, the hero is converted not to Buddhism but to Christianity and lives his last edifying years as a hermit.

Without question the name of the patriarch Photius (d. 891) stands forth as the most illustrious of all Byzantine scholars. He was called the most learned man since Aristotle, and so he must have appeared to his colleagues and students at the school Caesar Bardas (regent for Michael III) maintained at the palace. Photius' best known work, entitled *Myrio-*

biblon, consists of an abridgement of ancient and later scholarly writings, some of which we know only by means of this compendium. (Reading 33) Two contemporaries of Photius, Leo the Mathematician and John the Grammarian, have left no writings to substantiate their high reputations. We do know that the caliph Al Mamun offered the Byzantine emperor two thousand pounds of gold and perpetual peace if he would induce Leo to make his home in Damascus. The refusal of the Byzantine emperor to accept the offer was not the act of an eccentric. Several Byzantine emperors proved themselves generous patrons of the arts, and the eminence of Byzantine scholarship particularly in the ninth century was due to their encouragement.

Though the record of Byzantine achievement in literature and learning is high, modern critics generally agree that more should have been accomplished given the rich heritage from the past, the patronage of the court, the wealth of the empire, and the high level of scholarship. If the criticism is justified, Byzantine deficiencies might be traced to the strength of the classical tradition and the love of antique culture. For all the glory they brought Byzantium, these proved mixed blessings in the end. They discouraged creative scholarship and literary originality, they hampered progress in philosophy and the sciences, in literature they led poets to express themselves in classical rather than in vernacular Greek, which soon lost them their contact with the people.

Art. The Byzantine Empire developed a distinctive and truly admirable art. Of the major contributing influences which were active in the evolution of that art, the inspiration of the Greek genius was most important. Yet this had to be modified to a considerable degree before Byzantine culture would accept it. The Greek temple, which was essentially the deity's shrine, was quite unsuited to serve as a shelter for a large Christian congregation engaged in rich liturgical service. Equally unsuited was the Greek mind which had gloried in the human and finite and had feared the supernatural and the infinite. The Christian easterner had instead a deep and abiding interest in the mystical and eternal. So the Byzantine architect wanted a lofty and spacious interior and employed the vaulted or domed structure which had proved its suitability to the east in Mesopotamia and to the west in Rome. In place of the Hellenic and pagan tradition of portraying the human form in all its natural beauty, the Byzantine artist chose rather to subordinate his art forms to the service of religion. Yet, though he preferred the Syrian love of symbolism and religious didactic art to Greek naturalism, he did preserve in his carved relief, paintings, and especially in his mosaics, something of the Hellenic representation element. The exterior of the Byzantine church was austere in its simplicity, but the interior, where the faithful assembled for worship, was alive with light and color and glowed with the brilliance of multicolored marbles, paintings, and mosaics.

Byzantine Mosaics. The lavish use of mosaics for interior decoration is as characteristic of Byzantine art as is the dome. This exquisite art form Byzantine workmanship carried to perfection. Infinite patience is required in fitting the tiny bits (tesserae) of glass, marble, porphyry, and other colored stones into which gold or silver leaf has been fused, into their proper place in the soft plaster and at the proper angle so that the reflected light and color of each particle blend into the design. So masterfully did the Byzantine artist accomplish this feat, that the deep, rich, never-fading colors of his mosaics give almost the expressiveness of three dimensions. The vigor and glow of Byzantine mosaics more than compensate for any lack of realism.

Influence of Byzantine Art Forms. Famous churches in other countries of Europe attest to the wide influence of Byzantine art. Among these are structures in Ravenna, San Apollinare in Classe and San Vitale, which date from Justinian's own day. Gracing opposite sides of the choir walls of

Mosaic of Theodora (San Vitale, Ravenna)　　*Italian State Tourist Office*

the latter church are two famous mosaics, the one a magnificent portrait of Justinian attended by his clergy, the other of Theodora with her ladies-in-waiting. The mosaic of the apse narrates the story of Abraham, Sarah, and Isaac. The five domes and elaborate mosaic and metal work of St. Mark's in Venice reflect Byzantine influence of the eleventh century. In far off Moscow the traveler will recognize Byzantine influence in the bulbous domes of St. Basil's, in Sicily he can see it in the splendid interior of Monreale, and in the United States he can find it revealed in the churches which Slavic immigrants erected.

The Byzantine Contribution. Of Byzantium's great and varied contributions to civilization perhaps the most significant was not strictly her own. The work of preparing the monumental *Corpus Juris Civilis* which has proved of inestimable importance to western culture was that of Justinian's

Sarcophagus of Theodorus

Alinari—Art Reference Bureau

lawyers, but the matter codified was principally Roman. We have just noted the pervasiveness of Byzantine art and how its influences are reflected in such widely separated worlds as Venice, Moscow, and Hazleton (Pennsylvania). In the realm of military science the Byzantine *cataphract* expedited the evolution of the feudal knight, while Byzantine knowledge of Near Eastern warfare afforded significant aid to the Crusaders during the period of the Crusades. (See page 401.) That most sensational product of Byzantine chemistry, Greek fire, remained war's most spectacular weapon until gunpowder and artillery superseded it in the fourteenth century. Constantinople continued as chief carrier of the trade of the eastern Mediterranean and Black Sea areas until the twelfth century when its protégé, Venice, replaced it. The medieval west was indebted to Byzantium for the drawloom used in silk weaving and for lateen sails. The west also learned much from Byzantine craftsmen concerning the manufacture of glass and enamelware. Valuable knowledge continued to seep into western Europe until the eleventh century through the windows Constantinople maintained in Italy. Though Byzantium added only in limited measure to the immense store of learning inherited from antiquity, it is to its eternal credit that it preserved this with care and pride and shared it subsequently with the west. As late as the fifteenth century western humanists were drawing upon Constantinople for Greek teachers and Greek manuscripts. The role of Byzantium as a bulwark against the Ottoman Turks will be considered in a later chapter. On this point we might ponder the assertion of a noted Byzantine authority: "it is hardly an exaggeration to say that the civilization of western Europe is a by-product of the Byzantine Empire's will to survive."* History may one day establish that Constantinople's most vital and enduring contribution was that of civilizing and converting the Slavs of the Balkans and Russia. While Rome was placing its stamp upon western Europe, the "New Rome" on the Bosporus was providing eastern Europe its cultural and spiritual inspiration.

* Norman Baynes in *Byzantium*, ed. N. H. Baynes and H. Moss (Oxford 1961, p. xxxi).

San Apollinare in Classe, Ravenna

Anderson—Art Reference Bureau

READINGS

No. 28. The wars of Justinian

(Procopius' *History of the Wars*, III, tr. H. B. Dewing. Reprinted by permission of the publishers from the Loeb Classical Library. Cambridge, Mass.: Harvard University Press, 1919, pp. 171-179.)

On the following day the Goths destroyed the gates of the tower with no trouble and made the crossing, since no one tried to oppose them. But Belisarius, who had not as yet learned what had happened to the garrison, was bringing up a thousand horsemen to the bridge over the river, in order to look over the ground and decide where it would be best for his forces to make camp. But when they had come rather close, they met the enemy already across the river, and not at all willingly they engaged with some of them. And the battle was carried on by horsemen on both sides. Then Belisarius, though he was safe before, would no longer keep the general's post, but began to fight in the front ranks like a soldier; and consequently the cause of the Romans was thrown into great danger, for the whole decision of the war rested with him. But it happened that the horse he was riding at that time was unusually experienced in warfare and knew well how to save his rider; and his whole body was dark grey, except that his face from the top of his head to the nostrils was the purest white. Such a horse the Greeks call "phalius" (white-face) and the barbarians "balan." And it so happened that the mob of the Goths threw their javelins and other missiles at him and at Belisarius for the following reason. Those deserters who on the previous day had come to the Goths, when they saw Belisarius fighting in the front ranks, knowing well that, if he should fall, the cause of the Romans would be ruined instantly, cried aloud urging them to "shoot at the white-faced horse." Consequently this saying was passed around and reached the whole Gothic army, and they did not question it at all, since they were in a great tumult of fighting, nor did they know clearly that it referred to Belisarius. But conjecturing that it was not by mere accident that the saying had gained such currency as to reach all, the most of them, neglecting all others, began to shoot at Belisarius. And every man among them who laid any claim to valour was immediately possessed with a great eagerness to win honour, and getting as close as possible they kept trying to lay hold of him and in a great fury kept striking with their spears and swords. But Belisarius himself, turning from side to side, kept killing as they came those who encountered him, and he also profited very greatly by the loyalty of his own spearmen and guards in this moment of danger. For they all surrounded him and made a display of valour such, I imagine, as has never been shewn by any man in the world to this day; for, holding out their shields in defence of both the general and his horse, they not only received all the missiles, but also forced back and beat off those who from time to time assailed him. And thus the whole engagement was centered about the body of one man. In this struggle there fell among the Goths no fewer than a thousand, and they were men who fought in the front ranks; and of the household of Belisarius many of the noblest were slain, and Maxentius, the spearman, after making a display of great exploits against the enemy. But by some chance Belisarius was neither wounded nor hit by a missile on that day, although the battle was waged around him alone.

Finally by their valour the Romans turned the enemy to flight, and an exceedingly great multitude of barbarians fell, until they reached their main army. For there the Gothic infantry, being entirely fresh, withstood their enemy and forced them back wihout any trouble. And when another body of cavalry in turn reinforced the Goths, the Romans fled at top speed until they reached a certain hill, which they climbed, and there held their position. But the enemy's horsemen were upon them directly, and a second cavalry battle took place. There Valentinus, the groom of Photius, the son of Antonina, made a remarkable exhibition of valour. For by leaping alone into the throng of the enemy he opposed himself to the onrush of the Goths and thus saved his companions. In this way the Romans escaped, and arrived at the fortifications of Rome, and the barbarians in pursuit pressed upon them as far as the wall by the gate which has been named the Salarian Gate. But the people of Rome, fearing lest the enemy should rush in together with fugitives and thus get inside the fortifications, were quite unwilling to open the gates, although Belisarius urged them again and again and called upon them with threats to do so. For, on the one hand, those who peered out of the tower were unable to recognise the man, for his face and his whole head were covered with gore and dust, and at the same time no one was able to see very clearly, either, for it was late in the day, about sunset. Moreover, the Romans had no reason to suppose that the general survived; for those who had come in flight from the rout which had taken place earlier reported that Belisarius had died fighting bravely in the front ranks. So the throng of the enemy, which had rushed up in strength and possessed with great fury, were purposing to cross the moat straightway and attack the fugitives there; and the Romans, finding themselves massed along the wall, after they had come inside the moat, and so close together that they touched one another, were being crowded into a small space. Those inside the fortifications, however, since they were without a general and altogether unprepared, and being in a panic of fear for themselves and for the city, were quite unable to defend their own men, although these were now in so perilous a situation.

Then a daring thought came to Belisarius, which unexpectedly saved the day for the Romans. For urging on his men he suddenly fell upon the enemy. And they, even before this, had been in great disorder because of the darkness and the fact that they were making a pursuit, and now when, much to their surprise, they saw the fugitives attacking them, they supposed that another also had come to their assistance from the city, and so were thrown into a great panic and all fled immediately at top speed. But Belisarius by no means rushed out to pursue them, but returned straightway to the wall. And at this the Romans took courage and received him and all his men into the city.

No. 29. Hagia Sophia

(Procopius' *Buildings*, tr. H. B. Dewing. Reprinted by permission of the publishers from the Loeb Classical Library. Cambridge, Mass.: Harvard University Press, 1940, pp. 25-33.)

The whole ceiling of Hagia Sophia is overlaid with pure gold, which adds glory to the beauty, yet the light reflected from the stones prevails, shining out in rivalry with the gold. And there are two stoa-like colonnades, one on each side, not separated in any way from the structure of the church itself, but actually making the effect of its width greater, and reaching along its whole length, to the very end, while in height are they less than the interior of the building. And they too have vaulted ceilings and decorations of gold. One of these two colonnaded stoas has been assigned to men worshippers, while the other is reserved for women engaged in the same exercise. But they have nothing to distinguish them, nor do they differ from one another in any way, but their very equality serves to beautify the church and their similarity to adorn it. But who could fittingly

describe the galleries of the women's side, or enumerate the many colonnades and the colonnaded aisles by means of which the church is surrounded? Or who could recount the beauty of the columns and the stones
with which the church is adorned? One might imagine that he had come
upon a meadow with its flowers in full bloom. For he would surely marvel
at the purple of some, the green tint of others, and at those on which the
crimson glows and those from which the white flashes, and again at those
which Nature, like some painter, varies with the most contrasting colours.
And whenever anyone enters this church to pray, he understands at once
that it is not by any human power or skill, but by the influence of God,
that this work has been so finely turned. And so his mind is lifted up toward God and exalted, feeling that He cannot be far away, but must
especially love to dwell in this place which He has chosen. And this does
not happen only to one who sees the church for the first time, but the same
experience comes to him on each successive occasion, as though the sight
were new each time. Of this spectacle no one has ever had a surfeit, but
when present in the church men rejoice in what they see, and when they
leave it they take proud delight in conversing about it. Furthermore, con-
concerning the treasures of this church—the vessels of gold and silver and
the works in precious stones, which the Emperor Justinian has dedicated
here—it is impossible to give a precise account of them all. But I shall
allow my readers to form a judgment by a single example. That part of the
shrine which is especially sacred, where only priests may enter, which they
call the Inner Sanctuary is embellished with forty thousand pounds' weight
of silver.

So the church of Constantinople (which men are accustomed to call the
Great Church), speaking concisely and merely running over the details with
the fingertips, as it were, and mentioning with a fleeting word only the
most notable features, was constructed in such a manner by the Emperor
Justinian. But it was not with money alone that the Emperor built it, but
also with the labour of the mind and with the powers of the soul, as I
shall straightway shew. One of the arches which I just now mentioned
(*lori*, the master-builders call them), the one which stands toward the
east, had already been built up from either side, but it had not yet been
wholly completed in the middle, and was still waiting. And the piers, above
which the structure was being built, unable to carry the mass which bore
down upon them, somehow or other suddenly began to crack, and they
seemed on the point of collapsing. So Anthemius and Isidorus, terrified at
what had happened, carried the matter to the Emperor, having come to
have no hope in their technical skill. And straightway the Emperor, impelled by I know not what, but I suppose by God (for he is not himself a
master-builder), commanded them to carry the curve of this arch to its final
completion. "For when it rests upon itself," he said, "it will no longer
need the props beneath it." And if this story were without witness, I am

well aware that it would have seemed a piece of flattery and altogether incredible; but since there are available many witnesses of what then took place, we need not hesitate to proceed to the remainder of the story. So the artisans carried out his instructions, and the whole arch then hung secure, sealing by experiment the truth of his idea. Thus, then, was the arch completed; but in the process of building the other arches, indeed, those namely which are turned toward the south and the north, the following chanced to take place. The so-called *lori* had been raised up, carrying the masonry of the church, but everything underneath was labouring under their load, making the columns which stood there throw off tiny flakes, as if they had been planed. So once more the master-builders were dismayed at what had happened and reported their problem to the Emperor. And again the Emperor met the situation with a remedy, as follows. He ordered them immediately to remove the upper parts of the masonry which were strained, that is, the portions which came into contact with the arches, and to put them back much later, as soon as the dampness of the masonry should abate enough to bear them. These instructions they carried out, and thereafter the structure stood secure. And the Emperor, in this way, enjoys a kind of testimonial from the work.

No. 30. Procopius attacks the character of Justinian

(Procopius' *Anecdota*, tr. H. B. Dewing. Reprinted by permission of the publishers from the Loeb Classical Library. Cambridge, Mass.: Harvard University Press, 1954, pp. 3-7, 91-103.)

All that has befallen the Roman Nation in its wars up to the present day has been narrated by men, as far as it proved possible, on the plan of arranging all the accounts of its activities in accordance with their proper time and place. Henceforth, however, this plan of composition will be followed by me no longer, for here shall be set down everything that came to pass in every part of the Roman Empire. The reason for this is that it was not possible, as long as the actors were still alive, for these things to be recorded in the way they should have been. For neither was it possible to elude the vigilance of multitudes of spies, nor, if detected, to escape a most cruel death. Indeed, I was unable to feel confidence even in the most intimate of my kinsmen. Nay, more, in the case of many of the events described in the previous narrative I was compelled to conceal the causes which led up to them. It will therefore be necessary for me in this book to disclose, not only those things which have hitherto remained undivulged, but also the causes of those occurrences which have already been described.

As I turn, however, to a new endeavour which is fraught with difficulty and is in fact extraordinarily hard to cope with, being concerned, as it is, with the lives lived by Justinian and Theodora, I find myself stammering and shrinking as far from it as possible, as I weigh the chances that such things are now to be written by men as will seem neither credible nor probable to men of a later generation; and especially when the mighty stream of time renders the story somewhat ancient, I fear lest I shall earn the reputation of being even a narrator of myths and shall be ranked among the tragic poets. But I shall not flinch from the immensity of my task, basing my confidence on the fact that my account will not be without the support of witnesses. For the men of the present day, being witnesses possessing full knowledge of the events in question, will be competent guarantors to pass on to future ages their belief in my good faith in dealing with the facts.

And yet there was still another consideration which very often, when I was eager to undertake my narrative, held me back for a very long time. For I conceived the opinion that for men of future generations such a record as this would be inexpedient, since it will be most advantageous that the blackest deeds shall if possible be unknown to later times, rather than that, coming to the ears of sovereigns, they should be imitated by them. For in the case of the majority of men in power their very inexperience always causes the imitation of the base actions of their predecessors to be easy, and they ever turn with greater ease and facility to the faults committed by the rulers of an earlier time. But afterwards I was brought to write my history of these events by the thought that it will assuredly be clear to those who hereafter shall hold sovereign power that, in the first place, punishment will in all probability overtake them likewise for their misdeeds, just as befell these persons; and, in the second place, that their own actions and characters will likewise be on record for all future time, so that consequently they will perhaps be more reluctant to transgress. For what men of later times would have learned of the licentious life of Semiramis or of the madness of Sardanapalus and of Nero, if the records of these things had not been left behind by the writers of their times? And apart from these considerations, in case any should chance to suffer like treatment at the hands of their rulers, this record will not be wholly useless to them. For those who have suffered misfortunes are wont to receive consolation from the thought that not upon themselves alone have cruel disasters fallen. For these reasons, then, I shall proceed to relate, first, all the base deeds committed by Belisarius; and afterwards I shall disclose all the base deeds committed by Justinian and Theodora.

. . . .

These things, then, were being enacted both in Byzantium and in every other city. For the evil, like any other malady, beginning there fell like a scourge upon every part of the Roman Empire. But the Emperor Justinus

[A.D. 518-527] paid not the slightest heed to what was passing, for he, in fact, had no power of perception at all, though he was an eye-witness at all times of what was being done in the hippodromes. For he was extraordinarily simple-minded and exceedingly like a stupid donkey, inclined to follow the man who pulls the rein, his ears waving steadily the while. And Justinian was not only doing the things described but was also throwing everything else into confusion. Indeed, as soon as this man laid hold of the Government of his uncle [Justinus], he straightway was eager to squander the public funds with complete recklessness, seeing he had become master of them. For he kept squandering very great sums for service to the State on those of the Huns who chanced from time to time to meet him; and as a result of this the land of the Romans came to be exposed to frequent inroads. For when once these barbarians had tasted the wealth of the Romans, they could no longer keep away from the road leading to Byzantium. . . .

And I think it not inappropriate to describe the appearance of this man. He was neither tall in stature nor particularly short, but of a medium height, yet not thin but slightly fleshy, and his face was round and not uncomely; for his complexion remained ruddy even after two days of fasting. . . .

Such was Justinian in appearance; but his character I could not accurately describe. For this man was both an evil-doer and easily led into evil, the sort of a person whom they call a mere pervert, never of his own accord speaking the truth to those with whom he conversed, but having a deceitful and crafty intent behind every word and action, and at the same time exposing himself, an easy prey, to those who wished to deceive him. And a certain unusual mixture had developed in him, compounded of both folly and wickedness. And possibly this illustrated a saying uttered by one of the Peripatetic philosophers in earlier times, to the effect that the most opposite elements are found in man's nature, just as in mixed colours. (I am now writing, however, of matters in which I have not been able to attain competency.) But to resume, this Emperor was insincere, crafty, hypocritical, dissembling his anger, double-dealing, clever, a perfect artist in acting out an opinion which he pretended to hold, and even able to produce tears, not from joy or sorrow, but contriving them for the occasion according to the need of the moment, always playing false, yet not carelessly but adding both his signature and the most terrible oaths to bind his agreements, and that too in dealing with his own subjects. But he departed straightway from his agreements and his oaths, just like the vilest slaves, who, through fear of the tortures hanging over them, are induced to make confession of acts which they had denied on oath. He was a fickle friend, a truceless enemy, an ardent devotee of assassination and of robbery, quarrelsome and an inveterate innovator, easily led astray into wrong, but influenced by no counsel to adopt the right, keen to conceive and execute base designs, but looking upon even the hearing about old things as distasteful. How could any man be competent to describe adequately the character of Justinian? These faults and many others still greater he manifestly possessed to a degree not in accord with human nature. On the contrary, Nature seemed to have removed all baseness from the rest of mankind and to have concentrated it in the soul of this man.

No. 31. The *Corpus Juris Civilis:* the Institutes

(*The Four Books of Justinian's Institutions*, tr. George Harris. London, 1761.)

In the name of our Lord Jesus Christ. The Emperor Caesar Flavius Justianus, vanquisher of the Alamani, Goths, Franks, Germans, Angles, Alani, Vandals, Africans, pious, happy, glorious, victor and conqueror, ever august, to the youth desirous of studying the law, greeting.

The imperial majesty should be not only made glorious by arms, but also strengthened by laws, that, alike in time of peace and in time of war, the state may be well governed, and that the emperor may not only be victorious in the field of battle, but also may by every legal means repel the iniquities of men who abuse the laws, and may at once religiously uphold justice and triumph over his conquered enemies.

By our incessant labours and great care, with the blessing of God, we have attained this double end. The barbarian nations reduced under our yoke know our efforts in war; to which also Africa and very many other provinces bear witness, which, after so long an interval, have been restored to the dominion of Rome and our empire, by our victories gained through the favour of heaven. All nations moreover are governed by laws which we have already either promulgated or compiled.

When we had arranged and brought into perfect harmony the hitherto confused mass of imperial constitutions, we then extended our care to the vast volumes of ancient law; and, sailing as it were across the mid-ocean, have now completed, through the favour of heaven, a work that once seemed beyond hope.

When by the blessing of God this task was accomplished, we summoned the most eminent Tribonian, master and ex-quaestor of our palace, together with the illustrious Theophilus and Doretheus, professors of law, all of whom have on many occasions proved to us their ability, legal knowledge, and obedience to our orders; and we have specially charged them to compose, under our authority and advice, Institutes, so that you may no more learn the first elements of law from old and erroneous sources, but apprehend them by the clear light of imperial wisdom; and that your minds and ears may receive nothing that is useless or misplaced, but only what obtains in actual practice. So that, whereas, formerly, the junior students could scarcely, after three years' study, read the imperial constitutions, you may now commence your studies by reading them, you who have been thought worthy of an honour and a happiness so great as that the first and last lessons in the knowledge of the law should issue for you from the mouth of the emperor.

When, therefore, by the assistance of the same eminent person Tribonian and that of other illustrious and learned men, we had compiled the fifty books, called Digests or Pandects, in which is collected the whole ancient law, we directed that these Institutes should be divided into four books, which might serve as the first elements of the whole science of law.

In these books a brief exposition is given of the ancient laws, and of those also which, overshadowed by disuse, have been again brought to light by our imperial authority.

These four books of Institutes thus compiled, from all the Institutes left us by the ancients, and chiefly from the commentaries of our Gaius, both in his Institutes, and in his work on daily affairs, and also from many other commentaries, were presented to us by the three learned men we have above named. We have read and examined them and have accorded to them all the force of our constitutions.

Receive, therefore, with eagerness, and study with cheerful diligence, these our laws, and show yourselves persons of such learning that you may conceive the flattering hope of yourselves being able, when your course of legal study is completed, to govern our empire in the different portions that may be entrusted to your care.

Given at Constantinople on the eleventh day of the kalends of December, in the third consulate of the Emperor Justinian, ever August (533).

Of Justice and Law

Justice is the constant and perpetual wish to render every one his due.
1. Jurisprudence is the knowledge of things divine and human; the science of the just and the unjust. . . . 2. Having explained these general terms, we think we shall commence our exposition of the law of the Roman people most advantageously, if our explanation is at first plain and easy, and is then carried on into details with the utmost care and exactness. For, if at the outset we overload the mind of the student, while yet new to the subject and unable to bear much, with a multitude and variety of topics, one of two things will happen—we shall either cause him wholly to abandon his studies, or, after great toil, and often after great distrust of himself (the most frequent stumbling block in the way of youth), we shall at last conduct him to the point, to which, if he had been led by a

smoother road, he might, without great labour, and without any distrust of his own powers, have been sooner conducted. 3. The maxims of law are these: to live honestly, to hurt no one, to give every one his due. 4. The study of law is divided into two branches: that of public and that of private law. Public law is that which regards the government of the Roman Empire; private law, that which concerns the interests of individuals. We are now to treat of the latter, which is composed of three elements, and consists of precepts belonging to natural law, to the law of nations, and to the civil law.

Of Natural Law, of Nations and Civil Law

The law of nature is that law which nature teaches to all animals. For this law does not belong exclusively to the human race, but belongs to all animals, whether of the air, the earth, or the sea. Hence comes that yoking together of male and female, which we term matrimony; hence the procreation and bringing up of children. We see, indeed, that all the other animals besides man are considered as having knowledge of this law.

1. Civil law is thus distinguished from the law of nations. Every community governed by laws and customs uses partly its own law, partly laws common to all mankind. The law which a people makes for its own government belongs exclusively to that state, and is called the civil law, as being the law of the particular state. But the law which natural reason appoints for all mankind obtains equally among all nations, and is called the law of nations, because all nations make use of it. The people of Rome, then, are governed partly by their own laws, and partly by the laws which are common to all mankind. What is the nature of these two component parts of our law we will set forth in the proper place.

2. Civil law takes its name from the state which it governs, as, for instance, from Athens; for it would be very proper to speak of the laws of Solon or Draco as the civil law of Athens. And thus the law which the Roman people make use of is called the civil law of the Romans, or that of the Quirites, as being used by the Quirites; for the Romans are called Quirites from Quirinus. But whenever we speak of the civil law, without adding of what state we are speaking, we mean our own law: just as when "the poet" is spoken of without any name being expressed, the Greeks mean the great Homer, and we Romans mean Virgil. The law of nations is common to all mankind, for nations have established certain laws, as occasion and the necessities of human life required. Wars arose, and in their train followed captivity and then slavery, which is contrary to the law of nature; for by that law all men are originally born free. Further, from this law of nations almost all contracts were at first introduced, as, for instance, buying and selling, letting and hiring, partnership, deposits, loans returnable in kind, and very many others.

3. Our law is written and unwritten, just as among the Greeks some of their laws were written and others not written. The written part consists of law, *plebiscita, senatus-consulta*, enactments of emperors, edicts of magistrates, and answers of jurisprudents.

4. A law is that which was enacted by the Roman people on its being proposed by a senatorial magistrate, as a consul. A *plebiscitum* is that which was enacted by the plebs on its being proposed by a plebeian magistrate, as a tribune. The *plebs* differs from the people as a species from its genus; for all the citizens, including patricians and senators, are comprehended in the people; but the *plebs* only includes citizens, not being patricians or senators. But *plebiscita*, after the Hortensian law had been passed, began to have the same force as laws.

5. A *senatus-consultum* is that which the senate commands and appoints: for, when the Roman people was so increased that it was difficult to assemble it together to pass laws, it seemed right that the senate should be consulted in the place of the people.

6. That which seems good to the emperor has also the force of law; for the people, by the *lex regia*, which is passed to confer on him his power, make over to him their whole power and authority. Therefore whatever the emperor ordains by rescript, or decides in adjudging a cause, or lays down by edict, is unquestionably law; and it is these enactments of the emperor that are called constitutions. Of these, some are personal, and are not to be drawn into precedent, such not being the intention of the emperor. Supposing the emperor has granted a favour to any man on account of his merits, or inflicted some punishment, or granted some extraordinary relief, the application of these acts does not extend beyond the particular individual. But the other constitutions, being general, are undoubtedly binding on all. . . .

9. The unwritten law is that which usage has established; for ancient customs, being sanctioned by the consent of those who adopt them, are like laws.

10. The civil law is not improperly divided into two kinds, for the division seems to have had its origin in the customs of the two states of Athens and Lacedaemon. For in these states it used to be the case, that the Lacedaemonians rather committed to memory what they were to observe as law, while the Athenians rather kept safely what they had found written in their laws.

11. The laws of nature, which all nations observe alike, being established by a divine providence, remain ever fixed and immutable. But the laws which every state has enacted undergo frequent changes, either by the tacit consent of the people, or by a new law being subsequently passed.

12. All our laws relate either to persons, or to things, or to actions. Let us first speak of persons; as it is of little purpose to know the law, if we do not know the persons for whom the law was made.

No. 32. The *Corpus Juris Civilis:* the Digest

(*The Digest of Justinian,* tr. Charles Henry Monro, I. Cambridge, 1904.)

Fourth Book: I. On Restitutions *in integrum*

1. Ulpianus: The practical character of this title need not be dwelt on, it is plain in itself. Under this title the praetor gives relief on a number of different occasions to persons who have made a mistake or have been circumvented, whether they were put to a disadvantage by intimidation, or craft, or their youth, or their absence.

2. Paulus: —or a change of status, or excusable error.

3. Modestinus: Wherever restitution *in integrum* is promised by the praetor it is always on the cause shown, so that he may examine into the sufficiency of the causes alleged, and see whether the particular case is of a kind in which he gives relief.

4. Callistratus: I know it is the practice of some magistrates not to listen to one who asks for restitution *in integrum* in respect of any very trivial matter or amount, if this would prejudge the case of some matter or amount of more importance. . . . (p. 201)

Fourth Book: IX. Seamen, Innkeepers, Stablekeepers, To Restore What They Receive

1. Ulpianus: The praetor says:—"Where seamen, innkeepers, or stablekeepers have received the property of anyone on the terms of safe custody, then, unless they restore it, I will allow an action against them." 1. This Edict is highly beneficial, as it is very often necessary to rely on the engagements of the persons mentioned and to commit things to their custody. And no one need think that the above Edict bears hardly on them, as it is open to them, if they like, to refuse to receive anyone, and, unless this rule were laid down, they would have it in their power to conspire with thieves against the persons they took in; in fact, even as it is, they are not always innocent of dishonest machinations of this kind. 2. Let us consider first then, first of all, who the persons are that are held liable. The praetor uses the word "seamen" (*nautae*). By seaman we must understand a person who has the management of the ship, though, as a matter of fact, anybody is

called a seaman who is on board the ship to aid in navigation; however, the praetor is only thinking of the *exercitor* (owner or charterer). It is clear, Pomponius says, that the *exercitor* ought not to be bound by the act of some oarsman or man before the mast, but only by his own act or that of the master; though, no doubt, if he himself told anyone to commit something to the care of one of the sailors, he must himself be liable.   3. There are particular officers on board vessels who exercise authority in the ship with a view to the proper custody of goods, such as the *nauphylai* (ship's guard) and the *dioetarius* (steward); so if one of these receives anything, I should say there ought to be an action allowed against the *exercitor*, because a man who gives the above officers the conduct of any such department as described authorizes things being committed to their charge, though it is the owner (*navicularius*) or the master who does what is called the cheirembolon (taking charge). Even if he does not do this, still the owner will be liable for what is received. . . . (pp. 294-295)

No. 33. Photius' *Myriobiblon*

(Ancient India as described by Ktesias the Knidian, being a translation of his *Indika* by Photius, tr. J. W. McCrindle, London, 1882.)

Another work was read—the Indika of Ktesias, contained in a single book wherein the author has made more frequent use of Ionic forms. He reports of the river Indus that, where narrowest, it has a breadth of forty stadia, and where widest of two hundred; and of the Indians themselves that they almost outnumber all other men taken together. He mentions the *skolex,* a kind of worm bred in the river, this being indeed the only living creature which is found in it. He states that there are no men who live beyond the Indians, and that no rain falls in India but that the country is watered by its river. . . . (p. 7)

He notices also the elephants that demolish walls; the kind of small apes that have tails four cubits long; the cocks that are of extraordinary size; the kind of bird called the parrot and which he thus describes: it has a tongue and voice like the human, is of the size of a hawk, has a red bill, is adorned with a beard of black colour, while the neck is red like cinnabar, it talks like a man in Indian, but if taught Greek can talk in Greek also. . . . (p. 8)

He writes that in the middle of India are found swarthy men called Pygmies, who speak the same language as the other Indians. They are very diminutive, the tallest of them being but two cubits in height, while the majority are only one and a half. They let their hair grow very long—down to their knees, and even lower. They have the largest beards anywhere to be seen, and when these have grown sufficiently long and copious, they no longer wear clothing, but, instead, let the hair of the head fall down their backs far below the knee, while in front are their beards trailing down to their very feet. When their hair has thus thickly enveloped their whole body, they bind it round them with a zone, and so make it serve for a garment. . . . (p. 15)

The Indians are not afflicted with headache, or toothache, or ophthalmia, nor have they mouthsores or ulcers in any part of their body. The age to which they live is 120, 130, and 150, though the very old live to 200. . . . (p. 18)

Ktesias thus writing and romancing professes that his narrative is all perfect truth, and, to assure us of this, asseverates that he has recorded nothing but what he either saw with his own eyes, or learned from the testimony of credible eye-witnesses. He adds moreover that he has left unnoticed many things far more marvellous than any he has related, lest any one who had not a previous knowledge of the facts might look upon him as an arrant story-teller. . . . (pp. 33-34)

And Ktesias (if any one consider him a competent authority) asserts that the distance from the one bank of the Indus to the other where the stream is narrowest is 40 stadia. . . . (p. 34).

No. 34. A Western view of Byzantium

(Liutprand's report of his mission to Constantinople. A.D. 968. Henderson's *Historical Documents*, pp. 446-448. Liutprand was a legate from the court of Otto I.)

May nothing keep me from describing this procession, and my masters from hearing about it! A numerous multitude of tradesmen and low-born persons, collected at this festival to receive and to do honour to Nicephorus, occupied both sides of the road from the palace to St. Sophia like walls, being disfigured by quite thin little shields and wretched spears. And it served to increase this disfigurement that the greater part of this same crowd in his (Nicephorus') honour, had marched with bare feet. I believe that they thought in this way better to adorn that holy procession. But also his nobles who passed with him through the plebeian and barefoot multitude were clad in tunics which were too large, and which were torn through too great age. It would have been much more suitable had they marched in their everyday clothes. There was no one whose grandfather had owned one of these garments when it was new. No one there was adorned with gold, no one with gems, save Nicephorus alone, whom the imperial adornments, bought and prepared for the persons of his ancestors, rendered still more disgusting. By thy salvation, which is dearer to me than my own, one precious garment of thy nobles is worth a hundred of these, and more too. I was led to this church procession and was placed on a raised place next to the singers.

And as, like a creeping monster, he proceeded thither, the singers cried out in adulation: "Behold the morning star approaches; Eos rises; he reflects in his glances the rays of the sun—he the pale death of the Saracens, Nicephorus the ruler." And accordingly they sang: "Long life to the ruler Nicephorus! Adore him, ye people, cherish him, bend the neck to him alone!" How much more truly might they have sung: "Come, thou burnt-out coal, thou fool; old woman in thy walk, wood-devil in thy look; thou peasant, thou frequenter of foul places, thou goatfoot, thou horn-head, thou double-limbed one; bristly, unruly, countrified, barbarian, harsh, hairy, a rebel, a Cappadocian!" And so, inflated by those lying fools, he enters St. Sophia, his masters the emperors following him from afar, and, with the kiss of peace, adoring him to the ground. His armour-bearer, with an arrow for a pen, places in the church the era which is in progress from the time when he began to reign, and thus those who did not then exist learn what the era is.

On this same day he ordered me to be his guest. Not thinking me worthy, however, to be placed above any of his nobles, I sat in the fifteenth place from him, and without a tablecloth. Not only did no one of my suite sit at table, but not one of them saw even the house in which I was a guest. During which disgusting and foul meal, which was washed down with oil after the manner of drunkards, and moistened also with a certain other exceedingly bad fish liquor, he asked me many questions concerning your power, many concerning your dominions and your army. And when I had replied to him consequently and truly, "Thou liest," he said, "the soldiers of thy master do not know how to ride, nor do they know how to fight on foot; the size of their shields, the weight of their breast-plates, the length of their swords, and the burden of their helmets permits them to fight in neither one way nor the other." Then he added, smiling: "Their gluttony also impedes them, for their God is their belly, their courage but wind, their bravery drunkenness. Their fasting means dissolution, their sobriety panic. Nor has thy master a number of fleets on the sea. I alone have a force of navigators; I will attack him with my ships, I will overrun his maritime cities with war, and those which are near the rivers I will reduce to ashes. And how, I ask, can he even on land resist me with his scanty forces? His son was there, his wife was there, the Saxons, Swabians, Bavarians, were all with him: and if they did not know enough and were unable to take one little city that resisted them, how will they resist me when I come . . . ?"

When I wished to reply to him and to give forth an answer worthy of his boasting, he did not permit me; but added as if to scoff at me: "You are not Romans but Lombards." When he wished to speak further and was waving his hand to impose silence upon me, I said in anger: "History teaches that the fratricide Romulus, from whom also the Romans are named, was born in adultery; and that he made an asylum for himself in which he received insolvent debtors, fugitive slaves, homicides, and those who were worthy of death for their deeds. And he called to himself a certain number of such and called them Romans. From such nobility those are descended whom you call world-rulers, that is, emperors; whom we, namely the Lombards, Saxons, Franks, Lotharingians, Bavarians, Swabians, Burgundians, so despise, that when angry we can call our enemies nothing more scornful than Roman—comprehending in this one thing, that is in the name of the Romans, whatever there is of contemptibility, of timidity, of avarice, of luxury, of lying: in a word, of viciousness. But because thou dost maintain that we are unwarlike and ignorant of horsemanship, if the sins of the Christians shall merit that thou shalt remain in this hard-heartedness: the next battle will show what you are, and how warlike we."

Nicephorus, exasperated by these words, commanded silence with his hand, and bade that the long narrow table should be taken away, and that I should return to my hated habitation—or, to speak more truly, my prison. . . .

No. 35. From Psellus' history

(*The Chronographia of Michael Psellus*, tr. E. R. Sewter. New Haven, 1953, pp. 11-19. By permission of the Yale University Press.)

The circumstances in which the emperor John Tzimisces met his death have already been described (in the history of Leo Diaconus). Basil and Constantine . . . were now the legitimate heirs to an Empire which through the efforts of their predecessor had won many triumphs and greatly increased its power.

Both princes had seen the last of their boyhood days, but their interests lay far apart, for whereas Basil, the elder of the two, always gave an impression of alertness, intelligence, and thoughtfulness, his brother was to all appearances apathetic, passing a lazy existence, and devoted to a life of luxury. It was natural, therefore, that they should abandon the idea of a diarchy. By mutual consent all real power was vested in Basil, and Constantine was associated with him as emperor in name only. . . .

Once invested with the supreme power over the Romans, Basil was

loath to share his designs with anyone else or to accept advice on the conduct of public affairs. On the other hand, having had no previous experience of military matters or of good civil administration, he discovered that
he was unable to rely on his own judgment alone, and he was therefore
compelled to turn for assistance to the Lord Chamberlain Basil. Now this
man happened to be at that time the most remarkable person in the Roman Empire, both for the depth of his intellect and for his bodily stature
and regal appearance. Although he was born of the same father as the
father of Basil and Constantine, on his mother's side he came of different
stock. In early infancy he had suffered castration—a natural precaution
against a concubine's son, for under those circumstances he could never
hope to usurp the throne from a legitimate heir. Actually he was resigned
to his fate and was genuinely attached to the imperial house—after all, it
was his own family. He was particularly devoted to his nephew Basil, embracing the young man in the most affectionate manner and watching
over his progress like some kindly fosterparent. It is not surprising, then,
that Basil placed on this man's shoulders the burden of Empire. . . .

To most men of our generation who saw the emperor Basil he seemed
austere and abrupt in manner, an irascible man who did not quickly
change his mind, sober in his daily habits and averse to all effeminacy, but
if I am to believe the historians of that period who wrote about him, he
was not at all like that when his reign began. A change took place in his
character after he acceded to the throne, and instead of leading his former
dissolute, voluptuous sort of life, he became a man of great energy. It was
the pressure of events that brought about this complete alteration in the
course of his life. . . . The complete change in his mode of living dates
from the attempted revolution of the notorious Sclerus and of Phocas. . . .

Sclerus' attempted *coup d'etat* found considerable support. It was the
first of these daring efforts to depose Basil, but the pretender was very confident of victory. He marched against the emperor in full force, with cavalry and foot-soldiers, thinking he had but to stretch forth his hand to
seize the Empire. Actually, the heavy-armed infantry had rallied to Sclerus
en bloc and the emperor's advisers, knowing this, at first believed their
cause to be hopeless. On second thoughts, however, they changed their
minds and the whole affair took on a different aspect. Despair gave way
to courage when in a certain Bardas they thought they had discovered a
worthy opponent for the rebel. To them Bardas represented a safe anchor-
age, a shelter from the storm. He was, indeed, a man of noble birth and
great valour, nephew of the emperor Nicephorus. So they entrusted to this
Bardas whatever forces still remained. He was made commander-in-chief
and set forth to do battle with the common enemy.

Their immediate difficulties were thus overcome, but their new general
was no less formidable than Sclerus. He was descended from an emperor.
In all probability he would never be content to occupy a subordinate

position. So they stripped him of his citizen's robes and all insignia of royalty, and forced him to enter the Church. They bound him by the most fearful oaths never to be guilty of treason, never to transgress the promises he had made. Having taken these precautions against any ambitious schemes he might entertain in the future, they sent him out with the whole of the emperor's forces. . . .

Each side was confident in face of its foes, and the two leaders, by common consent, decided to engage in single combat. So, riding out to the space that divided the two lines of battle, they spied one another and without more ado came to close quarters. The rebel Sclerus, unable to curb his natural impetuosity, broke the rules of this kind of fighting, and as he approached Phocas struck him with all his might on the head. The blow gained additional power because it was delivered on the charge. Phocas, dumbfounded at the unexpectedness of this stroke, momentarily lost control of his reins, but collecting his wits again, he returned the blow, on the same part of his adversary's body. The latter thereupon lost interest in the combat and rode away in flight.

Both patriots and rebels were convinced that here was the decisive point in the war. Certainly no event contributed more to the emperor's victory, for Sclerus was completely embarrassed. He could no longer withstand Phocas in battle. He was too ashamed to beg terms from the emperor. In these circumstances he adopted a policy which was neither very wise nor very safe, transferring his whole army from Roman territories to Assyria. There he made himself known to the king Chosroes and roused his suspicions, for Chosroes feared the great numbers of his army, and possibly he was nervous, too, in case the Romans planned some sudden attack on himself. The upshot of the matter was that all Sclerus' men were made prisoners. . . .

Phocas, after receiving high honours when he first returned to Byzantium, later found himself neglected. His ambitions appeared to be once more slipping from his grasp. This kind of treatment, in his opinion, was undeserved. He had not betrayed the trust reposed in him: he had entered into an agreement, on specific terms, and he had faithfully kept it. So, disgruntled, he broke away in revolt . . . with the greater part of the army ranged beside him in opposition to Basil. . . .

The emperor Basil was well aware of the disloyalty among the Romans, but not long before this a picked band of Scythians had come to help him from the Taurus, and a fine body of men they were. He had these men trained in a separate corps, combined with them another mercenary force, divided by companies, and set them out to fight the rebels. . . .

So the two faced one another: on the one side, by the sea, the emperor's forces; on the higher parts, the rebels, with a great space between. When Phocas discovered that Basil and Constantine were in the enemy's rank, he no longer put off the battle. That day, he decided, was to be the turning-point of the war, the day which was to determine the future of the Empire. So he committed his cause to fortune. It was contrary to the advice of the astrologers in his retinue, for they would have dissuaded him from fighting. Their sacrifices clearly showed the folly of it, but he gave rein to his horse and obstinately refused to listen. . . . Gathering speed, he made straight for the emperor with a wild war-cry, his sword uplifted in his right hand, as if he intended to kill the emperor there and then.

While Phocas was so boldly charging towards him, Basil rode out in front of his army too. He took his stand there, sword in hand. In his left hand he clasped the image of the Saviour's Mother, thinking this ikon the surest protection against his opponent's terrific onslaught. Phocas swept on, like a cloud driven on by violent winds, whirling over the plain. Meanwhile those who were stationed on either flanks hurled their javelins at him. Among others, slightly in front of the main army, was the emperor Constantine, brandishing a long spear. After he had galloped forward some distance from his own men, Phocas suddenly slipped from his saddle and was thrown to the ground. At this point the accounts of different authors become contradictory. Some contend that he was hit by the javelin-throwers and fell mortally wounded. Others aver that he was overcome by a sudden faintness, the effect of a stomach disorder, and so fell down from the saddle. What the true explanation may have been, Constantine arrogated to himself the proud distinction of having slain the rebel. The usual story, however, and the one considered to be most probable, is that the whole affair was the result of an intrigue. Poison was mixed, Phocas drank it, and when he moved about, the potion became suddenly effective, deprived him of his powers of reason, and caused the giddiness that led to his downfall. The original idea was Basil's, the ministering hand that of Phocas' cupbearer. For my own part, I prefer to express no opinion on the subject and ascribe all the glory to the Mother of the Word. . . .

The complete change in the emperor's character dates from that time. While he rejoiced at the death of his enemy, he was no less grieved by the sad condition of his own affairs, with the result that he became suspicious of everyone, a haughty and secretive man, ill-tempered, and irate with those who failed to carry out his wishes.

5

ISLAM

As we have seen in the preceding chapter, the life of the Byzantine Empire was constantly threatened by the expansive energies of a great Mohammedan state which gradually engulfed its north African possessions and all but a small portion of Asia Minor to which the successors of Justinian managed to cling. This Mohammedan world, commonly known as Islam, constituted the third part of that huge area once encompassed within the frontiers of the Roman Empire or lying immediately adjacent to them. Like the other two parts, the German west and the Byzantine center, Islam was from its very origins closely identified with a religion from which it drew much of its character and motivation. So militant was this religion and so hostile its relationship with Christianity, that the rise of Islam completely disrupted the century-old unity of the Mediterranean world and severed as the German invaders had never done the religious, economic, and political ties which had bound the area together. It is to the land which cradled mighty Islam, to isolated, forbidding, and mysterious Arabia, that we must now direct our attention.

Arabia before Mohammed

Geography. Arabia is one of the driest and hottest countries in the world. Geographically it consists of a tremendous peninsula, about one third the size of the United States, bounded on the north by the lands of the Fertile Crescent (Palestine, Syria, and Mesopotamia) and on the other sides by the Red Sea, Indian Ocean, and Persian Gulf. Although almost surrounded by water, most of the country remains an uninhabitable and unexplored desert. Only along the slopes of the tableland, which is the principal configuration of the country, is any kind of cultivation possible, except for the occasional oasis which breaks the awful monotony of the trackless expanse. In antiquity, Arabia was known as the land of frankincense, precious stones, and spices. The camel, "the special gift of Allah," was and remains the land's most useful beast. For both man and beast the date serves as staple. "Honor your aunt, the palm which was made of the same clay as Adam," the Prophet is said to have enjoined.

The Arabs. With the exception of a few strangers who had settled along the caravan routes in Hejaz, the inhabitants of Arabia were of Semitic origin and so they remained. For such was the isolation and uninviting character of the country, that Arabia was left largely untouched by ancient civilizations, and even today the Arab provides in physique and language, as well as in psychological traits, the purest example of pristine Semitism. A few loosely organized kingdoms could be found along the western and southern coasts and in the north. But a majority of the peninsula's scattered population preferred to acknowledge the easier restraint of tribal membership. Even this was reasonably effective only in time of war. The natives, never numerous because of the poverty of the country, engaged in several simple pursuits. In Yemen, Nejd, and the northern part of Hejaz, some marginal agriculture was possible. An active merchant class could be found in the larger communities of the west such as Mecca, Medina, and Ta'if. The largest and most typical segment of the population lived in the desert, whence their name Bedouins, or desert-dweller.

The Bedouins. Alone or in the company of a few families, the Bedouin usually spent his life roaming about the desert from oasis to oasis with almost the same restless constancy as the shifting sands themselves, seeking out and fighting over the meager sustenance an unpropitious nature had provided. Unaffected for the most part by alien cultures, the Bedouin grew up a child of his naturally harsh environment. He was lean, tough, and wiry, short of stature, his curly hair matching in color the blackness of his eyes. Fighting and feuding were the necessary heritage of a bountyless land. Although without pity for the stranger whose property he coveted, to the traveler who sought lodging for the night his hospitality knew no bounds. A fierce individualist, this barefoot, often hungry, near-naked desert rat as he must have appeared to others, was as proud of his race and ancestry as any Oriental prince. No other people in history has shown more devotion to the preservation of genealogies. Though able neither to read nor write, the mysteries of the desert and the wonders of the starry heavens made something of a poet of him. He stood bemused with all of primitive man's awe for the natural phenomena he could not explain, and he discovered as a result a multitude of spirits, some good, others wicked, in the stars, rocks, oases, winds, and storms. Yet above an amazing host of supernatural spirits and forces, of nymphs, djinns, gods, and goddesses, many of his fellows recognized the superior majesty and power of Allah.

Mecca. For most Arabs, Mecca was the "holy city." Each spring during the four-month truce period, thousands journeyed there from all corners of the peninsula to worship and pray. Even at other times Mecca was a busy town since through it a considerable amount of trade moved by caravan between the Mediterranean and the Indian Ocean. The principal structure of the city was a temple called the Kaaba (cubical in shape, hence the name) in which were placed physical representations of several hundred native gods including even an image of Christ. Embedded in one of the walls of the Kaaba was a black stone, the most sacred object of all, which was reputed to have come from heaven and to have been revered by Abraham. Its highly polished surface bore eloquent witness to the frequency with which it had been kissed by reverent pilgrims. The possibility of trade had attracted a number of Jews and Christians to Mecca, and their religion in turn had attracted the attention of, and gained acceptance by, many natives. It was this dusty, sprawling, pilgrim center along a cara-

Kaaba
Arab Information Center

van route in far-off Arabia which was destined to revolutionize the course of history for the greater part of the civilized world.

Isolation of Arabia.   The Arabs were a backward and largely unknown people. With the exception of the few tribes which occupied the northern and southwestern fringes of the country, they had lived the millenia prior to the seventh century of the Christian era largely outside the sweep of civilization. And this isolation, strangely enough, had tended to deepen with time. For since the extension of Roman rule to Egypt in the last century before Christ, some of the trade which had earlier moved along the Arabian side of the Red Sea had shifted to the western bank. Prior to 630 A.D., it would have been the height of fancy to suggest that from this despised corner of the world would emerge a power so formidable that it would destroy one empire of the Near East (the Persian), fatally cripple the other (the Byzantine) and which would, within less than a century, engulf more than half of the known world. What made such a miracle possible was the appearance of a religious leader whose dynamic gospel welded together into a tremendous force the dissipated energies of the peninsula and whose name is reverenced yet by some half billion followers. That man was Mohammed.

Mohammed

Mohammed's Early Years.   So humble were Mohammed's origins that the year of his birth can only be guessed. He was born about 570 into a poorer branch of the powerful Kuraish tribe which dominated Mecca. Left an orphan at an early age, he was raised by his grandfather and uncle and as a boy spent many hours watching herds of sheep, goats, and camels. It is improbable that he received any formal education. He did acquire some knowledge of writing and reckoning, and as a young man became the commercial agent of a wealthy widow, Khadijah by name, whose caravans he directed northward out of Mecca. This position proved of great importance in his subsequent career and the associations he made with Hebrews and Christians in the course of his travels left a deep mark upon the impressionable youth. Of possibly even greater importance was the impression Mohammed made upon his employer, for he eventually married her, and in so doing gained the leisure to devote himself to his religious interests.

His Personality.   Mohammed's physical appearance was typical of that of his countrymen. He was of average height, had a large head, flashing black eyes, and dark, long hair and beard. His hands were those of a woman rather than a man, and he had the love of neatness one commonly associates with women. His tastes were simple—he mended his own clothes —and until Khadijah died he was content with one wife. Probably lest he antagonize her whose wealth and influence proved so essential to his mission, he did not practice, until after her death, the polygamy common to Arabia. He accumulated in time nine wives and many concubines. His apologists would insist that most of these wives were either widows of deceased friends who would otherwise have suffered want, or that the marriages were politically inspired. At the age of fifty-three he married his favorite wife, Aishah, the nine-year-old daughter of his friend and successor, Abu Bakr. Of a nervous and retiring nature, Mohammed experienced now periods of depression, now moments of wild hysteria. Though lacking both the physique and temperament of a warrior, he possessed, nevertheless, a great deal of personal courage and determination which showed to good advantage during his early years of preaching in Mecca. Toward his intimates he was kind and affectionate; toward his enemies he could be cruel and vengeful. It was this last trait and his sexual life which distinguished him most sharply from Christ with whose religion his own was soon to collide.

Origin of Mohammed's Ideas. From his boyhood Mohammed was subject to sieges of unconsciousness which continued to afflict him throughout his life. While these lapses from consciousness have been diagnosed variously by scholars as epileptic fits or hallucinations, to the faithful they were nothing less than holy trances or ecstasies which served to provide the media for Mohammed's communications from God through the instrumentality of the Angel Gabriel. For it was God, so Mohammed insisted, who was the ultimate source of his ideas and the instigator of his reforms. Since the society Mohammed planned to establish would be a thoroughgoing theocracy, these divine revelations extended far beyond purely religious matters. Actually on the conviction that all his views, regardless of their nature, derived from the Almighty, Mohammed felt free to pronounce with equal finality upon social, agricultural, medical, military, even astronomical problems. What he had to say on these subjects did not set him markedly above his countrymen. As for the evolution of his religious ideas, Mohammed found at least the proper atmosphere conducive to contemplative thought in the desert to which it was his custom to retire for a month at a time, during his fifteen years of married life with Khadijah. Since Mohammed was neither a scholar nor a trained theologian, his ideas were limited to his experiences with Arabic polytheism and what he had learned of the ideas of Judaism and Christianity in Mecca and on his caravan trips. Mohammed began to preach at the age of forty, and he continued to receive divine communications for the balance of his life. His critics suggest the pragmatic opportuneness of these revelations and even their occasional inconsistency.

Mohammed as Preacher. For Mohammed the path of the religious innovator proved no smoother than other zealots have found it. Four years of effort brought him scarcely forty converts. Among these were his wife, Khadijah, and a wealthy cloth merchant by the name of Abu Bakr. These two, together with his loyal though unbelieving uncle, Abu Talib, proved indispensable to his cause in these early years by furnishing him protection against the hostility of the powerful Kuraish leaders. The latter were at first inclined to dismiss Mohammed as just another religious fanatic. But they grew alarmed as the number of his adherents increased since the Prophet's monotheism appeared to pose a serious threat to Mecca's prosperity and to their own. For once Mecca ceased being the "holy city," it might lose many of its pilgrims upon whose purchases the prosperity of the community depended. That the majority of Mohammed's proselytes were of the lower classes and included many who had joined in the hope of improving their material position, likewise aroused uneasiness. While Mohammed himself was largely secure from molestation, his followers were frequently subjected to harsh treatment, and a group of them fled to Abyssinia to escape persecution. When Khadijah and Abu Talib died, Mohammed's own position grew so perilous that he decided to accept the offer of asylum and leadership which the city of Medina had offered him. Medina was a smaller community that lay two hundred miles north of Mecca, but it enjoyed a more advanced culture because of the large number of Jews and Judaized Arabs who made their home there. Some of these had been attracted to Mohammed's monotheism, while a few even saw in him the promised Messiah. Factional strife had left the city in turmoil, and it was the hope that Mohammed might bring peace to the troubled community that had inspired the invitation.

The Hejira. In September, 622 Mohammed and a few followers fled Mecca and escaped to Medina. This flight or Hejira proved to be such a momentous event in the life of the Prophet and in the history of Islam that it was early accepted as the base year in the Mohammedan calendar. The flight seemed to transform Mohammed almost overnight from a peaceful missionary into a ruthless theocrat. Those Jews who refused to accept his views, he exiled or massacred, and a holy war was declared against Mecca and unfriendly desert tribes in the vicinity. For ten years the Medinites plundered the caravans moving to and from Mecca and skirmished, generally with success on their side, against that city's troops. As losses in lives and business mounted, the Meccans became disheartened. Meantime the number of Mohammed's adherents inside the city continued to grow, while Mohammed's own assurances tended to dissipate the fear that Mecca would cease to be the "holy city" once it accepted his views. Organized resistance finally collapsed and in 630, almost without opposition, the Prophet and his troops rode into the city. His chief enemies he executed, others he permitted to escape. He likewise destroyed the idols in the Kaaba, though not the building itself which he believed had been erected by Abraham. He also retained the famous black stone "whose cult the Prophet felt constrained to adopt into the ritual of Islam where it still lingers as a weird testimonial to Islam's failure to rid itself of the crude associations of its origins."* Success came rapidly after Mecca's capitulation. Within the year Mohammed began to organize raids against the powerful Byzantine Empire which presented the first and principal obstacle in the way of Arabic expansion. When he died in 632 the greater part of Arabia had accepted his doctrines.

The Religion of Islam

The Koran. The substance of Mohammed's teachings is found in the Koran (Arabic for book or reading). This book was compiled a year after the Prophet's death from records kept by his associates, of what he had said. Its contents consist of a variety of elements, from doctrinal discussions and moral injunctions to parables and fables. Compared to the Bible, the Koran is a short book, in volume actually smaller than the New Testament. Even then it abounds in repetitions and includes tales and legends such as that of the Seven Sleepers, along with many observations and regulations, which are quite extraneous to religion. If these were eliminated to leave only the strictly sacred content, the Koran would shrink to no more than a hundred pages. The organization of the Koran is unusual. After a long introductory prayer, the one hundred and fourteen chapters or surahs which comprise the whole follow neither chronologically nor logically, but in order of length with the longest first. Many stories from both the Old and New Testaments, often with curious twists, attest to Mohammed's acquaintance with the Bible. Actually Mohammed held the Bible in the highest esteem. He regarded it as inspired, although falsified, and, therefore, superseded by what he said. The Koran is written in beautiful rhythmic prose, and pious Moslems often commit all or large portions of it to memory. Since Mohammedans must always read the Koran in the Arabic, it has served as a powerful influence in stabilizing the language and in assuring its use throughout the length and breadth of the Moslem world. The Koran has been criticized for its lack of organization, the tedious recurrence of certain themes, and its somewhat wild flavor. One might point out in Mohammed's defense that as a teacher of primitive folk he must have appreciated the necessity of constant repetition; that he was a self-made, not trained, theologian; that he lacked a speculative mind; and

* Gustave E. Von Grunebaum, *Medieval Islam* (Chicago, 1947), p. 68.

that he found difficulty in expressing theological and juristic ideas in Arabic, which possessed no such terminology. And, of course, neither did Mohammed write nor organize the Koran. (Reading 36)

Faith. The religious requirements which Mohammed placed upon his followers are commonly classified under five headings, the so-called "Five Pillars of Islam." Though Mohammedans, like Christians, today divide into differing sects, all hold implicitly to these same five basic tenets which Mohammed laid down. The first and foremost obligation is that of faith, the substance of which is expressed in the formula: "There is no god but Allah, and Mohammed is His Prophet." A good Moslem can accept the patriarchs and prophets of the Old Testament and even Christ, as did Mohammed, but he must of necessity accord Mohammed the rank of final and definitive "Prophet." On the question of Allah, not the slightest compromise is tolerated. Total, unquestioning, and exclusive worship is to be paid to him. Mohammed, in fact, reserved his sharpest blasts for polytheists. "Slay the idolators wherever ye find them," he instructed the faithful. While he declared unrelenting warfare against pagans, to Jews and Christians, that is, to monotheists who revered a "Book," he was ready to offer toleration. Mohammed indeed considered his mission to be principally one of purifying the religion the ancient Hebrews had practiced, but which they had permitted to become corrupted since Abraham's time, chiefly through idolatry. Faith is so important that only Moslems may enter heaven. Those whom Mohammed relegated to hell were assigned to one or the other of its seven tiers largely on the basis of their faith or rather their lack thereof. No idea so dominates and pervades the Koran as that of the omnipotence and omnipresence of Allah. "His is the kingdom of the Heavens and of the Earth; He maketh alive and killeth; and He hath power over all things!"

Prayer. A second obligation which rested upon the Moslem was that of praying five times each day. The faithful were instructed to face Mecca during their prayers and to precede these with a ceremonial act of ablution with water or, if this was not available, with sand. In the larger communities prayers were preferably to be said in common under the direction of a prayer-leader called the imam. In place of the church bells of the west, it was the cry of the muezzin from his lofty minaret which summoned the Moslem faithful to prayer. These five prayers, which were to be distributed over the entire day beginning with sunrise and ending in the evening, consisted in the main of Koranic formulas expressive of worship and subjection to the will of Allah. Accompanying the prayers and forming an essential part of the act of worship were elaborate prostrations which had to be performed in a liturgically correct manner in order to make the prayers themselves efficacious. An interesting by-product of the ritual of ablution was its encouragement to personal cleanliness, while certain salubrious values have been attributed to the ritualistic prostrations. Formal attendance and participation of the faithful in religious services were required only on Friday, which was, however, not respected as a day of rest and prayer.

Other Requirements. The faithful Moslem was further required to abstain, during the holy month of Ramadan, from anything that might please his senses from early morning as soon as "the white thread becometh distinct to you from the black thread" until nightfall. A fourth injunction commanded the faithful to give alms, an injunction second only in the frequency with which Mohammed insisted upon it to the obligation of faith itself. "So give to the kinsman his due, and to the needy, and to the wayfarer. That is best for those who seek Allah's countenance." Since according to Mohammed's theocratic plan there was to be no distinction between church and state, and since an adequate system of taxation could scarcely have functioned in so primitive a society, it was principally through the obligation of giving alms that hospitals, orphanages, and mosques were to be erected and maintained. Finally, if humanly possible, every Moslem was expected to make a pilgrimage to Mecca at least once during his lifetime. Whether the duty of prosecuting a holy war (*jihad*) of subjection or extermination against the unbeliever was incumbent upon the Moslem is not entirely clear from the Koran, although ample justification for such was to be found there for those who wished to do so. "O ye who believe! Fight those of the disbelievers who are near to you, and let them find harshness in you, and know that Allah is with those who keep their duty unto him."

Moral Injunctions. Supplementing these fundamental duties were a variety of moral injunctions, several of them reminiscent of the Mosaic law. Pork, for example, was classified as unclean and declared forbidden. The good Moslem was enjoined to shun gambling and the use of intoxicating beverages. "In both is great sin, and some utility for men; but the sin in them is greater than their usefulness." Condemned likewise were sexual irregularities, murder, the use of faulty weights and measures, perjury, the taking of interest, and infanticide. "Slay not your children because of penury. We provide for you and for them." Children were exhorted to be kind to their parents, husbands to love their wives, and all were admonished to avoid giving offense to or injuring their neighbors. While slavery was condoned and remained an important phase of Islamic civilization, manumission was commended as a meritorious act. Feuding, long the bane of Arabian life, was somewhat restricted by requiring the aggrieved party to accept compensation, although retaliation was not entirely ruled out. "If ye punish, then punish with the like of that wherewith ye were afflicted. But if ye endure patiently, verily it is better for the patient." Elaborate rules governing the inheritance of property tended to improve the position of orphans and women, but left the rights of the latter distinctly inferior to those of men. Mohammed's limitation of four wives to those who could afford them similarly raised the lot of women, but only to a minor degree, since no limit was placed on the number of concubines a man might keep, and since a man could divorce his wife simply by stating publicly, "I divorce you." It is worth noting, furthermore, that what improvement Mohammed may have been able to effect in the status of women was largely undone by the subsequent interpretations of Moslem casuists.

Islam vs. Christianity. A number of interesting parallels on the one hand and contrasts on the other, between Islam and Christianity, offer themselves for consideration. The most fundamental similarity between the two groups lay in their insistence upon monotheism. Because of the prevalence of idolatry in Arabia, the Mohammedan position is fanatically sensitive on this issue. While both Islam and Christianity accepted the existence of one God whom they declared to be omnipotent, omniscient, and omnipresent, the God of Mohammed resembled more the stern Jehovah of the Old Testament rather than the loving, merciful father of the New. Mohammed, it must be emphasized, never claimed to be divine, nor even to be able to work miracles. Both Christ and Mohammed insisted upon man's responsibility to his creator for his actions, and both accepted the doctrine of a final judgment with heaven the reward of the just and hell the punishment of the wicked. Both spoke of angels and evil spirits, the first capable of helping men, the latter of doing him injury. Both recommended the practice of such virtues as patience and charity, although there is nothing in the Koran which approaches the force of Christ's counsel with regard to taking revenge: "If one strike thee on the right cheek, turn to him also the other." Furthermore, where Mohammed encouraged his followers to use the sword in spreading his gospel, Christ ordered his disciples to preach. And again, while both Christ and Mohammed commanded their followers to give alms, Mohammed expected the Moslem to be reasonable in this, while Christ would require absolute poverty of those who sought perfection. On the other hand, while both Moslem and Christian were instructed to accept with resignation the day's trials and misfortunes as the will of God, it was the Mohammedan who provided most evidence in his own life of observing this rule. It is not just an interesting coincidence that the word Islam means submission, while a Moslem is one who submits. One may well wonder whether it is not this blind acceptance of what happens as God's will, against the background of the grinding poverty of the Near East, which explains in large measure the fatalism peculiar to the world of Islam.

Other Contrasts. The Koran provides for no ordained priesthood and, consequently, for no sacramental system. For this reason, the Moslem ritual, in contrast to the Christian, is extremely simple. It consists of readings from the Koran, prayers with prostrations, and observations by the reader in charge. No day is holy to the Mohammedan, although all Moslems are expected to attend the noon-day service on Friday. In sharp contrast to the spiritual heaven where the Christian will experience such joys as only a mystic can appreciate, Mohammed promised his faithful a material paradise with everything their carnal natures might crave, from cool shade and exhilarating beverages to luscious fruits and beautiful maidens. This material conception of the pleasures of the hereafter exercised a depressing effect upon the development of monasticism in Islam. And it is interesting to note that when religious asceticism did finally take root and flower in the twelfth century into what is known as Sufism (from the undyed garments of wool the members wore), although it esteemed the practice of poverty, obedience, and other forms of self-abnegation much like the west, it shunned celibacy as a means of personal sanctification. Mohammed's own example and his clear and frequent strictures on the subject proved too emphatic. As the Prophet directed: "Ye that are unmarried shall marry." The greatest name, incidentally, in the history of Sufism, is that of Al Ghazali (d. 1111), unquestionably Islam's leading mystic and theologian. (Reading 38) It is significant that like monasticism in the west, Sufism became the principal missionary agency in the Mohammedan world.

In the social order the most striking contrast between Islam and Christianity was to be found in the family. For the virile monogamous unit of the Christian west in which the wife and mother enjoyed a position of honor, Islam presented by contrast a polygamous group in which the women and girl children occupied an inferior, if not despised, status. Finally, the stamp of divine authority which Mohammed claimed for his pronouncements, and his insistence that these defined for all time the gamut of man's spiritual and material problems, not only blighted the growth of theological studies, but frequently served to erect a rigid barrier to social and economic progress. Christ's pronouncements, on the other hand, did not extend beyond the realm of faith and morals, and even here frequently invited considerable latitude in interpretation and application.

Expansion of Islam

Early Victories. The occasion of Mohammed's death was seized upon by many tribes to repudiate Islam, and the Prophet's immediate successor, Abu Bakr, was obliged to devote all his efforts to recovering lost ground. Once this had been accomplished and the tribes of Arabia welded for the first time in their history into a unified force, the robust energies of the peninsula spilled outside to engulf within an amazingly short space of time more than one half of the Mediterranean and Near Eastern worlds. It would, in fact, have been impossible to have held these warlike tribes in check for any period of time had they not been able to substitute for their petty raids at home the infinitely more profitable "holy war" against the foreign unbeliever. Damascus, the capital of Syria, fell in 635, and after Khalid's crushing victory over the forces of the Byzantine Empire at Yarmuk the following year, all the populous cities of Syria and Palestine rapidly capitulated. The Persian Empire fared even worse. The Moslem host annihilated the Persian army at Kadesiya (637) and seized the capital, Ctesiphon, whereupon the once-powerful empire of the Sassanids ceased to exist. Within another half-dozen years the frontiers of India and Turkestan had been reached and penetrated.

Westward Expansion. In the other direction, toward the west, the story was not appreciably different. Alexandria fell in 642, whence the Moslem flood rolled westward to engulf Cyrenaica and Tripoli. The great city of Carthage, second only to Rome in the west, was levelled because of its courageous resistance and disappeared for the last time from the face of the earth. Stiffer resistance was encountered from the wild Berbers whose country and customs most resembled those of the Arabs. It required fifty years of fighting and diplomacy, together with the prospect of participating in plundering raids to the west, to induce them to accept Moslem hegemony. In 711 a Moslem chieftain, Tarik by name, led a raiding party composed chiefly of Berbers (Moors as they came to be called) across into Spain and captured the rock which still bears his name (Gibraltar from gib-al-Tarik or Tarik's Hill). What started as a minor raid proved so successful, that Tarik's commanding general, Musa, came over in person to gain for himself the glory of conquering the peninsula. Had Spain been united this would have been impossible. As it was, the natives hated their Visigothic lords and aided the invaders, as did likewise a large number of embittered Hebrews who had suffered persecution at the hands of the Christians. Even with this assistance and the lack of unity among the Visigothic chieftains, the Moslems were nine years at completing the conquest of the peninsula. Only in the extreme northwestern corner, in Galicia, were the Christians able to cling to a foothold. Though Musa reaped the glory he had anticipated, it proved his undoing in the end. After carrying back tremendous loot to Damascus together with hundreds of captive Visigothic princes and thousands of beautiful girls to grace the harems of the east, he found himself broken and degraded by the jealous caliph and ended his days a beggar.

The Moslem drive had meantime carried across the Pyrenees and over much of southwestern France. It suffered its first serious reverse at Toulouse which the Moors failed to capture, and shortly after, somewhere between Tours and Poitiers, in October 732, they were defeated by the Franks

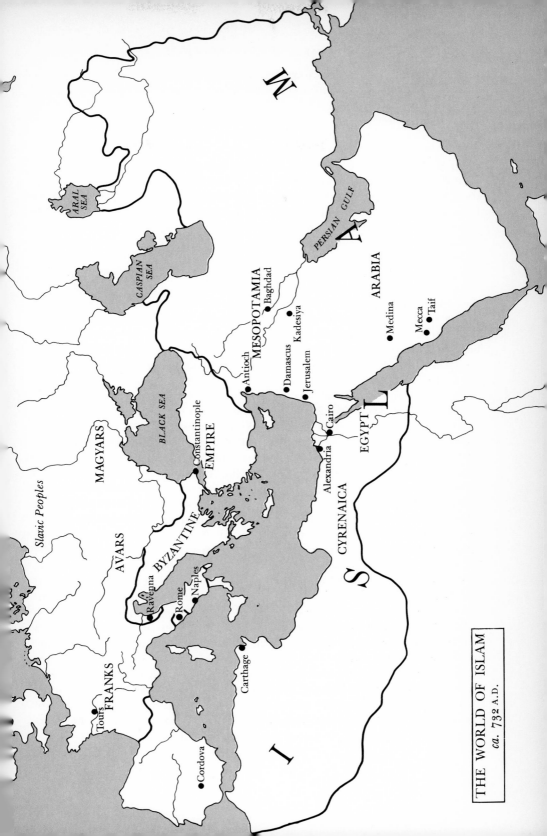

THE WORLD OF ISLAM
ca. 732 A.D.

under Charles Martel and forced to pull back. Modern scholars do not agree with Edward Gibbon and older historians who label Tours one of the truly decisive· battles of history. In their opinion the Moslem push had already pretty well spent itself and, in any event, could not have penetrated much farther because of the revolt of the Berbers in north Africa. By this time the Moslems had constructed fleets, had manned them with Greek and Syrian sailors, and had captured the major islands of the Mediterranean and carried the war directly to the gates of Constantinople. We have already seen how this city just barely managed to beat off these attacks, including a last powerful thrust which came in 717-718. After this final lunge in which Islamic power seems to have attained its peak, it receded and remained relatively dormant for several centuries to come.

Negative Factors in the Expansion of Islam. A variety of factors accounted for the spectacular success of the Moslem armies. First and foremost was the weakness of the once mighty Byzantine and Persian empires whose long, destructive wars against each other had left both exhausted. Had these two states still enjoyed the vitality which was theirs at the beginning of Justinian's reign, the expansion of Islam would have been inconceivable. Further reducing the resistance which these two states could offer the Arabs was the presence in each of large disaffected elements, alienated in the case of Persia by oppressive and incompetent rulers, in the case of the Byzantine Empire by heavy taxation and religious persecution. The majority of Christians in Syria, Palestine, and Egypt, for instance, were Monophysites who considered their Byzantine persecutors nothing more than heretics. We have seen how misgovernment and oppression had similarly smoothed the way for the invader in Spain.

Positive Factors in the Success of Islam. Important positive factors contributed to the success of Moslem arms. Some scholars maintain, for instance, that even without the mighty inspiration of Mohammed, Arabia would have driven beyond its frontiers at this time because a growing population and further desiccation of the land made expansion inevitable. Militarily the Arab horsemen with their speed, enthusiasm, and numbers proved well-nigh irresistible, particularly when led by geniuses like Khalid and Muawiyah. Yet it was their fanatical courage, not their arms or organization, since these were usually inferior, that gave them their victories. What always made the Moslems a dangerous foe, even after this fanaticism had lost its early ardor, was their numbers and the speed with which they maneuvered. Futhermore, the prospect of rich plunder if he lived and instant paradise if he were killed made the Moslem a most formidable enemy. And once the first excesses of victory were past, the Moslem conqueror showed himself a reasonably tolerant lord. He exacted only a moderate tribute from the many peoples he conquered and permitted them the practice of their religion if they were Hebrews or Christians.

Attractiveness of Mohammedanism. Mohammedanism proved an easy religion for nonbelievers to accept. For the Arabs themselves, the doctrines of the Prophet constituted the most advanced system that people had ever known, and one admirably suited to the mores of the nation. The confidence with which Mohammed promised heaven to the faithful proved a powerful magnet to those who had any real fear of hell. By accepting the legitimacy of the Jewish patriarchs and of Christ and claiming only that he was bringing the series of prophets to its logical conclusion, Mohammed facilitated the acceptance of Islam by many Hebrews and Christians. The simplicity of the religion of Islam, the modest liturgical requirements it placed upon the Moslem, the opportunity of practicing polygamy and concubinage with the blessing of the Almighty, these all proved strong inducements to many people, whether Arab or otherwise. Finally, one should not forget that many accepted Mohammedanism in order to escape payment of the tribute and to qualify for a share in the spoils of government and expansion. For these reasons and others, the number of converts to Islam grew rapidly, so rapidly indeed, that the burden of taxation had eventually to be placed upon everyone regardless of his faith.

Consequences of Expansion. Whatever the causes explaining the phenomenal speed with which the followers of Mohammed established the Islamic empire, there is no doubting the far-reaching consequences of that development. In the sphere of religion, for example, it meant the immediate severance and eventual loss to Christianity of the oldest lands of Christendom, lands in which the Christian religion was most deeply entrenched and most highly developed. North Africa, Egypt, and Syria, the latter two countries no less vital to eastern Christianity than Asia Minor, Constantinople, and the Balkans, were irretrievably lost. Surely this crippling loss in the east helped assure the Latin west of leadership in medieval Christendom. Politically, the rise of Islam radically altered the relationship between Byzantium and the west. For better or worse, Byzantine influence steadily declined and shortly vanished. It is entirely possible that the marriage of Rome to the Frankish kingdom which we shall presently discuss would not have taken place had not the rise of Islam so crippled Byzantine power. In the economic order the repercussions of the rise of Islam were far-reaching. During Roman times and until the appearance of the Islamic empire, the Mediterranean had served as the principal economic nexus uniting the lands lying about its shores. Now for the first time since the rise of Augustus who had completed the conquest of the area, that unity had been shattered and would remain so throughout the balance of the medieval period. Industry and trade, already languishing because of the invasions of the Germans, suffered further depression and decline. Cities dwindled in size and number; many ceased to exist; while provincialism and an agrarian economy spread their stupefying influences over western Europe.

Problem of Succession

The Ommiads. Islam meantime had experienced a number of changes in leadership which frequently interrupted the force of its drives. Though Mohammed had legislated on a great many matters, he failed to provide for a successor (caliph), and despite his many wives, he left only a daughter, Fatima. Because Abu Bakr, the father of his favorite wife, Aishah, was one of Mohammed's oldest and most devoted followers and had led in prayer when the Prophet was sick, the choice fell upon him. Abu Bakr proved an excellent selection, as did Omar as well whose rule of ten years (634-644) witnessed the period of greatest expansion. Dissension appeared under Othman (644-656) who was a member of the powerful Ommiad family. Once the Ommiads had been numbered among Mohammed's most implacable foes. Now they appeared well on their way to securing control of all the important offices in Islam. Ali, the Prophet's nephew and son-in-law, led the revolt of the "legitimists" who based their claims to succession on the grounds of blood relationship. Othman was assassinated, but Muawiyah, the head of the Ommiad clan, refused to recognize Ali and civil war ensued. Ali was shortly murdered, whereupon Muawiyah moved the capital from the small provincial community of Medina to Damascus, a huge city lying athwart the caravan route between Mesopotamia and Egypt. For the next ninety years the caliphate remained hereditary in the Ommiad family, whose caliphs introduced a more advanced administrative system patterned after the Byzantine. Though the Arab aristocracy continued to dominate the government, both non-Arabs and non-Moslems came to be used extensively in the army and in the different branches of the bureaucracy. Islam was fast becoming less a theocracy and more an empire.

Rise of the Abbasids. The "legitimists" who insisted that the succession should remain in the family of Mohammed, did not approve of the use of non-Mohammedans in the government. They further maintained that the sayings (*hadith* or *sunna*) traditionally attributed to Mohammed were spurious and that Islam should limit its creed to what was contained in the Koran. Since their views were not shared by the majority of believers, the "legitimists" came to be known as Shiites (*shia* or sect), while the traditionalists, because they accepted the traditions, were called Sunnites. The Shiites repudiated the rule of the Ommiad dynasty and threw their support to the Abbasids, a group which championed the claims of a descendant of Abbas, the uncle of Mohammed. With the assistance of non-Arab Moslems particularly Persians, who resented the domination of Islam by the Arab-Syrian element, they brought about the overthrow of the Ommiad dynasty in 750. Every last member of the family was hunted down and murdered save one. This one was Abd ar Rahman who after five years of incredible adventures, which included fleeing his pursuers by swimming the Euphrates, managed to make his way to Spain where he set up an autonomous state with Cordova as his capital. Once in power, the Abbasids moved the capital from Damascus farther east to the new city of Baghdad on the Tigris, thereby announcing the future cosmopolitan character Islam was soon to assume. Within a few years the former Arab aristocracy and theocracy were completely submerged. The Abbasid caliphate gradually assumed the characteristics of an Oriental despotism and adopted to a considerable extent the old Persian administrative system and court etiquette. While the move ushered in the most brilliant period in the history of Islamic culture, the ties of the empire began to loosen almost immediately as distinctions between Arab and non-Arab, between Moslem and non-Moslem, lost their meaning. By the middle of the ninth century most of the provinces of the empire had become autonomous and the caliph, who had originally wielded autocratic power over matters of church and state, degenerated because of over-luxurious living into nothing better than a puppet subject to the will of more virile viziers and generals.

Harun al Rashid. It would be unfortunate were we to pass by without comment the two caliphs traditionally singled out as the most illustrious during the most brilliant period of the Islamic caliphate. These two were Harun al Rashid (786-809) and his son, Al Mamun (813-833). Harun earned the title "al Rashid," (the Straightforward) from his father in recognition of his prowess against the Byzantine army. As for Harun's military record as caliph, it was good though not remarkable. He was usually victorious against both the Byzantine armies as well as the Hunnic hordes that kept pressing southward out of Armenia. Embassies passed between him and Charlemagne, one of them bringing the wondrous elephant, Abu-Lubabah (father of intelligence) as a gift to the Frankish capital. During most of his reign Harun collected tribute from Constantinople. He was outwardly at least a religious person, being most generous in his distribution of alms, performing one hundred prostrations each day, and making a number of pilgrimages to Mecca. Yet those of the faithful who knew, did not approve of his seven wives (in addition to a well-filled harem), nor his love of wine, nor the images of birds, beasts, and men he kept in his palace. Harun might be counted among the best of the caliphs were it not for the dark spots of treacherous cruelty that stain his whole career. Much of the vast treasure he dispensed he had amassed by oppressive and unscrupulous means. The clue to Harun's immense fame can be traced to the magnificence of Baghdad in his day, to that of his own court in particular, to his princely munificence, and to the host of scholars and writers he patronized.

To one poet who composed a sonnet in his honor he gave a purse of 5000 gold pieces, a robe of honor, ten Greek slave girls, and one of his steeds. Small wonder that the principal glory of Harun's reign was the literary revival it inspired!

Al Mamun. Al Mamun emerged as sole ruler after six years of destructive warfare with an elder brother, which left a large portion of Baghdad in ruins. War, in fact, was the chief concern of his reign, and he was constantly called upon to put down revolts which became increasingly difficult to suppress. Al Mamun's rule was generally just and efficient, although like his father he cannot be entirely acquitted of charges of brutal and capricious cruelty. In religious matters he demanded that his own liberal interpretation of controversial passages in the Koran be accepted. His own fame, again like that of his father, sprang from the display of wealth and luxury which lent his reign its fabulous character, and from the men of science, letters, and philosophy whom he entertained and who eulogized him in return. It is said that on the occasion of his marriage to the daughter of his vizier, a thousand pearls of extraordinary size were showered on the couple from a golden tray as they stood on a golden mat studded with pearls and sapphires. History is more impressed with the observatory Al Mamun constructed for the study of astronomy, and with his House of Wisdom, the first true institution of higher learning in the Islamic world.

Prosperity of Islam

Why Islam Prospered. However checkered the careers and accomplishments of the different caliphs, the economic life of the Moslem empire remained strangely undisturbed by political and dynastic upheavals. It prospered as it had never prospered before, or would ever prosper again. Several factors contributed to Islam's material wealth. Some of its basis may have been prepared by Mohammed who was himself a merchant and who left a number of injunctions in the Koran to protect the mercantile profession. Surely the vastness of the Moslem world, extending as it did from the Atlantic to central India and embracing all the ancient civilizations of the Near East and Egypt would have provided an ideal climate for the development of industry and trade. Within this huge dominion flourished such great cities as Baghdad, Antioch, Damascus, Alexandria, Cairo, and Cordova. Over this vast area ships and caravans carried their varied cargos, hampered by no tolls, boundary restrictions, or language barriers. This last, a common language, represented one of the few contributions the Arabs themselves made to the economic revival of the world of Islam. The other contribution was their religion which together with their Arabic language provided powerful cohesive bonds which served to unify the polyglot peoples enclosed in so far-flung an empire. Finally, the duty of every Moslem, whether in Spain or India, to visit Mecca once in a lifetime, must have done much to reduce political antipathies and to promote social and economic intercourse.

Commercial Wealth of Islam. The spread of Islam tapped the resources of three continents and brought access to the commodities of lands hitherto unknown. The eastern reaches of the empire drew exotic merchandise from China and the Indies; across the Black and Caspian Seas moved the raw products of the Baltic countries and Russia; while through Egypt and beyond the Sahara came strange exports from tropical Africa. The various fruits, vegetables, grains, and mineral wealth of dozens of countries and climes, together with the industrial products of ingenious hands and minds from China to the Pyrenees, were placed before the customer who visited the crowded bazaars of Baghdad and the other large cities of Islam. While the communities of western Europe had to be content generally with what could be produced in their immediate vicinities, a staggering list of goods and commodities were available throughout most of the Moslem world: muslin (Mosul), damask (Damascus), silks, brocades, rugs, and tapestries; metalware, weapons, coats of mail, steel mirrors, and glassware; jewels, rubies, gold, and silver; perfumes, flowers, and spices; melons, oranges, figs, apricots, and peaches; asparagus, spinach, and artichokes; flax, hemp, rice and wheat; furs and leather goods. Never before in the history of luxury did the sophisticated have as much to tickle their palates or adorn their bodies. Yet no description, however extravagant, of the amazing array of marvellous items to be had in the world of Islam, can suppress one hollow note. Though the home of the western king was pitiful by contrast to the sumptuous palace of the caliph in Baghdad, his subjects usually had more to eat than the wretched masses who lived under the crescent.

Flowering of Islamic Culture

Factors in this Flowering. Even more impressive than the material wealth of the Moslem world during the early Abbasid period was its achievement in science and thought. Several of the same factors which shared in effecting Islam's economic prosperity contributed likewise to the flowering of its culture. As the vastness of the empire made possible the exchange of a rich variety of goods, so similarly did it bring together the minds and books of many different peoples and ages. The best that the Persian and Hindu savants had to offer was compared with or added to the work of the ancient Greeks and that of the more recent Hellenized scholars of the eastern Mediterranean. Again, the knowledge of one language expedited the exchange of ideas and their assimilation. Even religion played a significant though negative role. Where the best minds of the west concentrated their efforts on the clarification and rationalization of Christian theology, the relative simplicity of Moslem religion and the difficulty of harmonizing this with philosophy (see below), discouraged scholarly analysis and left many eastern minds free to devote themselves to subjects which modern man considers more practical. Finally, under the first of the Abbasid caliphs, particularly Harun al Rashid and Al Mamun whom we have met, scholars and scholarship from whatever race or creed enjoyed a patronage never again equalled before fifteenth-century Italy.

Moslem Philosophers. Preparing the way for the achievement of Islamic scholars was the work of an active coterie of translators. Though the translation of Greek philosophical and scientific works was far advanced in Mesopotamia and Persia by the time of Mohammed's birth, it was sharply accelerated under the patronage of the early Abbasids. Once these translations had been made available, the work of synthesizing the materials and preparing commentaries commenced. The ancient philosopher most highly regarded by Moslem scholars was Aristotle. Leading an array of eminent Moslem thinkers in analyzing his metaphysical disquisitions was the Spaniard Averroës (d. 1198). Because of the scope and high order of his commentaries, Averroës was held in great esteem in the west and exerted considerable influence upon the development of scholastic philosophy and theology. He more than any one else was responsible for the cult of Aristotle which flourished in the west in the thirteenth century. (See page 558.) Western scholars referred simply to Averroës as "the Commentator," although only a few of them were willing to accept his unqualified endorsement of Aristotle. For it was Averroës' conviction that Aristotle was always right. As he wrote: "Aristotle's doctrine is the sum of truth because his was the summit of all human intelligence." Yet while the west honored Averroës' philosophical writings, Islam burned them and disgraced and banished their author as a heretic. (Reading 40) Al Kindi, Al Farabi, and Avicenna rank next to Averroës among the leading philosophers which Islam produced. All four scholars were concerned with substantially the same problem, that of harmonizing Greek philosophy with the Koran, more specifically with the orthodox view concerning the nature of God, creation, prophecy, and the immortality of the individual soul. Because all four philosophers found this an impossible task, they tended to become rationalists. Since other Islamic philosophers revealed this same tendency, philosophy itself became an object of suspicion to Islamic theologians. Significantly, the Arabic term for philosophers, that is, *falasifa*, carries the connotation of persons who teach heresy.

Islamic Medicine. The same high authority which Aristotle enjoyed among Islamic philosophers was accorded Galen by Islam's physicians. While a religious prohibition against dissection prevented their making any appreciable progress in surgery, they did assemble and reorganize all available medical knowledge and even added a small but significant contribution of their own. Islamic physicians were the best practitioners of the age and the most learned writers. Most voluminous of all writers was Al Razi. Included among his hundred and forty books was the most scientific essay on smallpox to appear before the eighteenth century. (Reading 43) The most eminent of all Islamic physicians was Avicenna, the philosopher, who has been called the greatest clinician of Islam and the Middle Ages. Avicenna's ninety-nine volumes of scholarly writing covered the fields of geography, physics, law, theology, metaphysics, and medicine. His *Canon* constituted the most systematic and complete syllabus of medical knowledge available to the medieval world. (Reading 39) Because of the prevalence of eye disorders in the east, some advance over antiquity was achieved by Islamic medicine in the science of ophthalmology.

Geography and Science. Significant advance was made in the field of descriptive geography with the help of knowledge gained by merchants who now found it safe to make regular trips into lands scarcely heard of before. Among Moslem visitors to these strange countries and peoples were geographers themselves, who used the knowledge they acquired to revise old maps and draw new ones. The best known of Islamic geographers was Idrisi, whose map of the world was rightly judged by his twelfth-century contemporaries to be the most advanced in existence. While most Islamic scholars were also astrologers, this did not prevent them from correcting tables and measurements and improving upon such astronomical instruments as the astrolabe and sextant. Rather characteristic, however, of the essential conservatism of Islamic scholarship and science and of the inability of Islam's scholars to introduce revolutionary departures in any field of knowledge, was their failure to recognize the basic error in the Ptolemaic theory of the universe. Some progress was accomplished in the field of optics and even in chemistry or alchemy as that science was known, despite the scholar's obsession with the hope of discovering an elixir of life or a formula which would enable him to transmute baser metals into gold. The experimentations of the alchemist with metals, acids, and various substances did contribute in the end to a greater knowledge of techniques and of the chemical properties of elements and compounds.

Mathematics. Islamic scholars left their greatest mark in mathematics and related fields. Their accomplishment here can be attributed to two factors in the main: to their ability to supplement the basic work of Euclid and Hipparchus in geometry and trigonometry with the arithmetic and algebra of the Hindus; second, to their own computations which were marvelously facilitated by the introduction of "Arabic" numerals, the cipher, and the decimal from India. Islam's leading mathematician was Al Khwarizmi who was most successful in fusing Hindu and Greek mathematical knowledge. He was the first mathematician to describe the function of the zero for the Near East and to organize that branch of mathematics which we know today as algebra. It was his work and that of other Islamic scholars which was responsible for the classification of the different branches of mathematics as clearly defined and exact sciences.

Literature and History. In literature Islam's achievement was modest. Its best-known contribution to the western world was the *Rubaiyat* of Omar Khayyam (Reading 41) who was not only a mathematician and astronomer of note, but something of a philosopher as well. There can be little question that his principal claim to fame should not be the melancholic wisdom which he expounded in some of literature's most famous quatrains, but rather his reformed calendar of the eleventh century which is considered superior to the Gregorian of the sixteenth, and his geometrical algebra which anticipated that of Descartes by five hundred years. The most popular stories to come out of Islam are found in the fourteenth-century collection known as the *Arabian Nights*. Some of these stories go back as early as the tenth century. While they scarcely provide a true picture of Baghdad in the days of Harun al Rashid as they pretend, they do reflect the Moslem's persuasion of the omnipresence of Allah, his fatalism, and his rather childish fascination with magic, precious stones, savory dishes, and beautiful girls.

Moslem historians usually began their accounts with the Creation since that is where they believed history began and because they were convinced God continued to take an occasional hand in human affairs. To most Islamic historians, therefore, events prior to Mohammed were strictly preliminary. While this religious orientation in their analysis of events would not have divided them from the chroniclers of the west, their record for objectivity and accuracy was generally above that of their Christian contemporaries. Especially noteworthy were the two tenth-century scholars Al Tabari and Al Masudi. Al Tabari produced the first monumental world history with Islam at its center. While Al Tabari's organization, a strictly annalistic one which records events by the year, lacks that interpretative organization the modern reader demands, he did bring to his task a high degree of accuracy and a vast store of information gained through travel, reading, and study. (Reading 42) Al Masudi contributed a massive thirty-volume world history whose volume and rich variety of information explain his reputation as the "Herodotus of the Arabs." Adding to the appeal of his work is his practice of organizing events around kings, dynasties, and peoples, instead of simply listing them as they happened. Islam's foremost historian was Ibn Khaldun (d. 1406), traveler, politician, and scholar. In his discussion of historical developments, Ibn Khaldun not only considered factors such as climate, environment, geography, and mores to which earlier historians had usually given scant attention, but he analyzed these with a perceptiveness which would do credit to a modern sociologist, economist, or historian. "No Arab writer, indeed no European, had ever taken a view of history at once so comprehensive and philosophic. By the consensus of critical opinion, Ibn Khaldun was the greatest historical philosopher Islam produced and one of the greatest of all time."* (Reading 37)

Islamic Architecture. Islam's art reflected the same borrowing from older and higher civilizations which characterized its achievements in other fields. This was particularly evident in the early period when the Moslem conquerors had no choice but to recruit Greek and Syrian architects and technicians to construct their first buildings since they lacked trained men of their own. Because of certain Koranic prescriptions, notably that condemning the representation of human and animal figures as conducive to idolatry, there evolved in time an art peculiar to the Moslem world although heavily influenced by Iranian, Egyptian, Syrian, and, especially, Byzantine forms and inspirations. Perhaps the most peculiarly Islamic architecture is to be found in the mosque, the physical structure the Mohammedans used for worship. Since Moslem liturgy placed few demands upon the artist and architect, and since the climate throughout Islam permitted gatherings under the open sky, the central unit of the mosque was ordinarily the open courtyard. This was surrounded on its four sides by a covered arcade, to which was adjoined a tower or minaret from which the muezzin called the faithful together for services. A fountain placed inside the entrance where the Moslem performed his ritualistic ablution, together with a niche in the wall of the interior court toward Mecca to indicate the direction the faithful were to face during their prayers, completed the essential features of the mosque. From a distance its most impressive elements were the lofty, graceful minaret and the huge bulbous dome with which the most pretentious mosques were covered.

Islamic Art. A number of decorative forms are commonly associated with Islamic art. These include the cupola, alcove, pointed and horseshoe-shaped arches, and cusped window opening and doorway. The cusped window opening is frequently adorned with stone or stucco tracery. The Moslem architect made extensive use of a wide variety of columns, ranging in size from the heavy pier to a cluster of slender supports. These re-

* Philip K. Hitti, *History of the Arabs* (London, Macmillan 1960), p. 568.

Hall of Ambassadors: Granada

flected principally Byzantine and Persian influences in their general outline and elaborateness of detail. The most striking feature of the Moslem
interior was the richness of the wall decoration. This consisted in the main
of an amazing diversity of formalized designs, some linear and geometric,
others of naturalistic and conventionalized representations of flowers, trees,
and shrubs. Even human and animal forms began to creep into such patterns under the Abbasids who showed less concern for the Prophet's prohibitions. So characteristic of Moslem art did such grouping of animal and
plant forms within a myriad of interlacing lines become, that it has been
given the name of Arabesque. Painted wood carvings, mosaics, marble,
stone, and tile of various colors provide a richness to the interior never
equalled in the Christian west. While the Moslem interior resembled the
Byzantine in the lavishness of its color, intricacy of detail, and in its lack
of a third dimension, there remained a striking contrast between the two
with respect to the purpose served by this decoration. With the exception
of an occasional passage from the Koran which might be inscribed on the
wall, Moslem decoration was wholly devoid of religious or symbolic significance. This lack has been traced to the comparatively simple and materialistic appeal of the Mohammedan creed, and, to some degree, to the Koranic
prohibition of images. Mention should be made of the many examples of
exquisite calligraphy found in illuminated copies of the Koran and of the
marvelous designs executed in the pottery, rugs, and embroidery of Islamic
Persia.

Conclusion. It is dangerous to speak with assurance of the nature of the
achievement of Islam in the arts and sciences. There is, first of all, the im-
possibility of comparing cultures in the absence of agreement as to what
constitute objective criteria of excellence. There exists also the language
barrier which has obstructed deeper study of Moslem scholarship and literature, a fact which similarly prevents any definitive evaluation of the Byzantine contribution with which one might then compare that of Islam.
Very real, indeed, and distinctive was the contribution of Islam in the field
of art. Equally impressive are the learned commentaries Islamic savants
prepared on Greek philosophy. The medieval world of the west was also
indebted to Islam for what advances Islamic scholars effected in the fields
of medicine and optics. Undoubtedly the west profited materially from
Islam's superior knowledge in the realm of nautical science and geography.
Islamic mathematicians left a very deep mark in the area of mathematics,
especially in algebra.

And yet, significant though Islamic cultural achievement was, when one
considers the immense store of learning Islamic scholars inherited from
classical antiquity and what they drew from contemporary civilizations in
Egypt, Syria, Persia, and India, one is almost forced to this conclusion:
that Islam's role in the history of culture was less in the nature of an origi-

Court of Lions: Alhambra

nal contribution than one of organizing the knowledge and ideas sprung from these various sources. Impressive as was the work of Islamic scholars and scientists, there is no hiding a very definite lack of imagination and of creative talent. Islamic scholars were best at improving, at clarifying, at preparing commentaries, at synthesizing and reclassifying knowledge, not at introducing new principles or embarking upon uncharted seas. It is significant that within two or three generations of acquiring the learning of the east, the west had equalled and within a short time far outdistanced its erstwhile cultural superior. And the cultural pall which began to settle upon Islam at about the time the medieval west was entering its most brilliant era has never lifted. One last note concerning Islamic culture: with the exception of Al Kindi, the names of the most eminent philosophers, scientists, mathematicians, and literary figures, are those of non-Arabs. Furthermore, just as most of these scholars learned Arabic and assumed Arabic names, so similarly did they conform outwardly to the more formal requirements of the Mohammedan religion. Their Arabic nationality and Mohammedanism were usually no more genuine than Islam's "Arabic" numerals.

⬣ READINGS ⬣

No. 36. The *Koran*

(*The Meaning of the Glorious Koran,* tr. Mohammed Marmaduke Pick-thall. Mentor, 1953. By permission of George Allen & Unwin Ltd., London.)

Surah I

In the name of Allah, the Beneficent, the Merciful.

Praise be to Allah, Lord of the Worlds, the Beneficent, the Merciful. Owner of the Day of Judgment, Thee (alone) we worship, Thee (alone) we ask for help. Show us the straight path, the path of those whom Thou hast favoured; not (the path) of those who earn Thine anger nor of those who go astray.

Surah III

In the name of Allah, the Beneficent, the Merciful.

Allah! There is no God save Him, the Alive, the Eternal. He hath revealed unto thee (Muhammad) the Scripture with truth, confirming that which was (revealed) before it, even as He revealed the Torah and the Gospel aforetime, for a guidance to mankind; and hath revealed the Criterion (of right and wrong). Lo! those who disbelieve the revelations of Allah, theirs will be a heavy doom. Allah is Mighty, Able to requite (the wrong). Lo! nothing in the earth or in the heavens is hidden from Allah. He it is who fashioneth you in the wombs as pleaseth Him. There is no God save Him, the Almighty, the Wise. He it is Who hath revealed unto thee (Muhammad) the Scripture wherein are clear revelations. They are the substance of the Book—and others (which are) allegorical. But those in whose hearts is doubt pursue, forsooth, that which is allegorical seeking (to cause) dissension by seeking to explain it. No one knoweth its explanation save Allah. And those who are of sound instruction say: We believe therein; the whole is from our Lord; but only men of understanding really heed.

Our Lord! Cause not our hearts to stray after Thou hast guided us, and bestow upon us mercy from Thy Presence. Lo! Thou, only Thou art the Bestower. Our Lord! it is Thou Who gatherest mankind together to a Day of which there is no doubt. Lo! Allah faileth not to keep the tryst. (On that day) neither the riches nor the progeny of those who disbelieve will aught avail them with Allah. They will be fuel for fire. . . .

Surah IV

In the name of Allah, the Beneficent, the Merciful.

. . . And Serve Allah, Ascribe no thing as partner unto Him. (Show) kindness unto parents, and unto near kindred, and orphans, and the needy, and unto the neighbour who is of kin (unto you) and the neighbour who is not of kin, and the fellow-traveller and the wayfarer and (the slaves) whom your right hands possess. Lo! Allah loveth not such as are proud and boastful. Who hoard their wealth and enjoin avarice on others, and hide that which Allah hath bestowed upon them of His bounty. For disbelievers We prepare a shameful doom; and (also) those who spend their wealth in order to be seen of men, and believe not in Allah nor the Last Day. Whoso taketh Satan for a comrade, a bad comrade hath he.

What have they (to fear) if they believe in Allah and the Last Day and spend (aright) of that which Allah hath bestowed upon them, when Allah is ever Aware of them (and all they do)? Lo! Allah wrongeth not even of the weight of an ant; and if there is a good deed, He will double it and will give (the doer) from His presence an immense reward. But how (will it be with them) when We bring of every people a witness, and We bring thee (O Muhammad) a witness against these? On that day those who disbelieved and disobeyed the messenger will wish that they were level with the ground, and they can hide no fact from Allah. . . .

Wheresoever ye may be, death will overtake you, even though ye were in lofty towers. Yet if a happy thing befalleth them they say: This is from Allah; and if an evil thing befalleth them they say: This is of thy doing (O Muhammad). Say (unto them): All is from Allah. What is amiss with these people that they come not nigh to understand a happening? Whatever of good befalleth thee (O man) it is from Allah, and whatever of ill befalleth thee it is from thyself. We have sent thee (Muhammad) as a messenger unto mankind and Allah is sufficient as witness. . . .

Surah XLVIII

In the name of Allah, the Beneficent, the Merciful.

There is no blame for the blind, nor is there blame for the lame, nor is there blame for the sick (that they go not forth to war). And whoso obeyeth Allah and His messenger, He will make him enter Gardens underneath which rivers flow; and whoso turneth back, him will He punish with a painful doom. Allah was well pleased with the believers when they swore allegiance unto thee beneath the tree, and He knew what was in their hearts, and He sent down peace of reassurance on them, and hath rewarded them with a near victory; and much booty that they will capture. Allah is ever Mighty, Wise. Allah promiseth you much booty that ye will capture, and hath given you this in advance, and hath withheld men's hands from you, that it may be a token for the believers, and that He may guide you on a right path. And other (gain), which ye have not been able to achieve, Allah will compass it. Allah is able to do all things. . . .

Surah LVI

In the name of Allah, the Beneficent, the Merciful.

When the event befalleth—there is no denying that it will befall—abasing (some), exalting (others); when the earth is shaken with a shock and the hills are ground to powder so that they become a scattered dust, and ye will be three kinds: (first) those on the right hand; what of those on the right hand? And (then) those on the left hand; what of those on the left hand? And the foremost in the race, the foremost in the race: those are they who will be brought nigh in gardens of delight; a multitude of those of old and a few of those of later time, on lined couches, reclining therein face to face. There wait on them immortal youths with bowls and ewers and a cup from a pure spring wherefrom they get no aching of the head nor any madness, and fruit that they prefer and flesh of fowls that they desire. And (there are) fair ones with wide, lovely eyes, like unto hidden pearls, reward for what they used to do. There hear they no vain speaking nor recrimination (naught) but the saying: Peace, (and again) Peace.

And those on the right hand; what of those on the right hand? Among thornless lote-trees and clustered plantains, and spreading shade, and water gushing, and fruit in plenty neither out of reach nor yet forbidden, and raised couches. Lo! We have created them a (new) creation and made them virgins, lovers, friends, for those on the right hand; a multitude of those of old and a multitude of those of later time.

And those on the left hand; what of those on the left hand? In scorching wind and scalding water and shadow of black smoke, neither cool nor refreshing. Lo! heretofore they were effete with luxury and used to persist in the awful sin. And they used to say: When we are dead and have become dust and bones, shall we then, forsooth, be raised again, and also our fore-fathers? Say (unto them, O Muhammad): Lo! those of old and those of later time will all be brought together to the tryst of an appointed day. Then lo! ye, the erring, the deniers, ye verily will eat of a tree called Zaq-qum and will fill your bellies therewith; and thereon ye will drink boiling water, drinking even as the camel drinketh. This will be their welcome on the Day of Judgment. . . .

Surah LVII

In the name of Allah, the Beneficent, the Merciful.

All that is in the heavens and the earth glorifieth Allah; and He is the Mighty, the Wise. His is the sovereignty of the heavens and the earth; he quickeneth and He giveth death; and He is able to do all things. He is the First and the Last, and the Outward and the Inward; and He is Knower of all things. He it is Who created the heavens and the earth in six days; then He mounted the throne. He knoweth all that entereth the earth and all that emergeth therefrom and all that cometh down from the sky and all that ascendeth therein; and He is with you wheresoever ye may be. And Allah is Seer of what ye do. His is the sovereignty of the heavens and the earth, and unto Allah (all) things are brought back. He causeth the night to pass into the day, and He causeth the day to pass into the night, and He is Knower of all that is in the breasts. Believe in Allah and His messenger, and spend of that whereof He hath made you trustees; and such of you as believe and spend (aright), theirs will be a great reward. . . .

No. 37. Ibn Khaldun

(*An Arab Philosophy of History*—Selections from the *Prologomena* of Ibn Khaldun of Tunis, tr. Charles Issawi. London, 1950. "The Wisdom of the East Series." By permission of John Murray, London.)

The Arabs

Arabs are, of all peoples, the least versed in the crafts. The reason for this is that they are deeply rooted in nomadism, far removed from seden-tary society and its accompanying crafts and other activities. Non-Arabs, on the other hand, whether they are the inhabitants of the East or the Chris-tians dwelling north of the Mediterranean, are, of all peoples, best fitted for practicing the crafts, since they have a long tradition of sedentary life and are so far removed from nomadism that the camels which have helped the Arabs to remain in a state of nomadism and savagery and the pastures and sands in which camels thrive, are not to be found among them. This is why the lands of the Arabs, and those conquered by them under Islam, are so deficient in crafts that they, i.e. crafts or their products, are imported from abroad. Notice on the other hand how abundant are the crafts in non-Arab lands such as China, India, the land of the Turks, and the lands of the Christians, which export to other lands.

When the Arabs conquer a country ruin quickly descends upon it. This is because the Arabs are a fierce people, their character having been thus moulded by the rough life they lead, until roughness has become a second nature to them. In fact they positively enjoy a rough life, because it enables them to shake off the yoke of authority and to escape political domination.

Now such a character is opposed and contrary to the spread of civilization. Thus their favourite occupation is trekking and roaming in the desert, and this is opposed to the establishment of a quiet and sedentary life, on which the growth of civilization depends. Thus, for instance, they will meet their need for stones to prop up their cooking vessels by demolishing a building. In the same way they will get their tent poles and pegs from the roof of a house. As a result of their mode of living, their very presence is inimical to the existence of buildings, which are the very foundation of civilization.

Scholars and Politicians

Scholars are of all men those least fitted for politics and its way. The reason for this is that they are accustomed to intellectual speculation, the search for concepts, and their abstraction from sense-data and clarification in the mind. All these operations aim at attaining the universal aspect of things, not those particular to their material content, or to a person, generation, nation, or particular class of men. They then seek to apply these universal concepts to external objects; moreover, they judge things by analogy with similar things, as they are accustomed to do in jurisprudence. Their judgments and views, then, remain purely speculative and do not seek to conform themselves to things until after the thought process is complete.

Now those who engage in politics must pay great attention to what goes on outside and to all circumstances that accompany and succeed an event. For politics are tortuous and may contain elements which prevent the subsumption of a given event under a universal concept or maxim or its comparison with another similar event. In fact, no social phenomenon should be judged by analogy with other phenomena, for if it is similar to them in certain respects it may yet differ from them in many others. Hence men of learning, who are accustomed to generalizations and the extensive use of analogy, tend, when dealing with political affairs, to impose their own framework of concepts and deductions on things, thus falling into error—hence their unreliability.

Public Finance

Now where taxes and imposts are light, private individuals are encouraged to engage actively in business; enterprise develops, because business men feel it worth their while, in view of the small share of their profits which they have to give up in the form of taxation. And as business prospers the number of taxes increases and the total yield of taxation grows. But when taxes rise too high business men are soon discouraged by the comparison of their profits with the burden of their taxes, and between their output and their net profits. Consequently production falls off, and with it the yield of taxation.

God's Existence

All objects in the created world, whether they are things or acts (human or animal) presuppose prior causes which bring them into being. And each of these causes is in its turn an event which presupposes prior causes. Hence the series of causes ascends until it culminates in the Cause of causes, their Maker and Creator—praised be His name, than whom there is no other God.

Limits of Knowledge

Do not trust the claims of thought to be able to comprehend beings and their causes and to follow out the ramifications of existence, this is sheer nonsense.

For every percipient imagines the world to be restricted to his range of perceptions, which is far from being true. Notice the deaf, for whom the world is confined to the four senses and reflection and for whom no sounds exist. In the same way the blind lack knowledge of visible things. It is only the traditions they take over from their parents, teachers, and acquaintances that make them admit the existence of what they do not perceive. In other words their belief is founded on the general opinion around them, not on their instinct or sense perceptions. Similarly animals, if they could answer our questions, would be found to deny the possibility of intellectual, reflective acts of the mind.

This point being established, it is probable that there is a kind of perception superior to our own; for our perceptions are created and cannot comprehend the vast range of beings. God's creation, being vaster than man's, is outside man's range of comprehension; He alone comprehends all. . . .

This does not impugn the validity of the mind or its apprehensions. The mind is an accurate scale, whose recordings are certain and reliable; but to use it to weigh questions relating to the Unity of God, or the after life, or the nature of prophecy or of the divine qualities, or other such subjects falling outside its range, is like trying to use a goldsmith's scale to weigh mountains. This does not mean that the scale is in itself inaccurate.

The truth of the matter is that the mind has limits within which it is rigidly confined; it cannot therefore hope to comprehend God and His qualities, itself being only one of the many atoms created by God.

No. 38. Al Ghazali

(*The Alchemy of Happiness by Mohammed Al-Ghazali*, tr. Henry A. Holmes. Albany, 1873, pp. 13-16.)

Ch. 1. On Knowledge of the Soul, and How Knowledge of the Soul Is the Key to the Knowledge of God.

O seeker after the divine mysteries! know thou that the door to the knowledge of God will be opened to a man first of all, when he knows his own soul, and understands the truth about his own spirit, according as it has been revealed, "he who knows himself knows his Lord also." And God proclaims in his holy book: "We will display our miracles in the different countries of the world, till it shall be demonstrated to them that the Koran is the truth," that is, let us show men in the visible world, and in their own souls, the wonderfulness of our works and the perfection of our power, that they may learn to know that the Lord God is Almighty and true and that everything else is vanity.

O seeker of the mysteries! since there is nothing nearer to thee than thyself, and that still with thy soul alone, thou canst not discriminate anything, and art impotent to find out and know thyself, in what way canst thou become acquainted with anything else, and with that which is even separate from thyself? And how should'st thou be able to comprehend God, who in his nature cannot be comprehended, and of whose absolute essence it is not possible to give thee any explanation. If thou should'st say, "I perfectly know myself," we reply that we have no doubt that what you are acquainted with is your own hand and foot, with your eye and mouth, and animals even have this kind of knowledge. You know also that if you are hungry, your stomach craves food, and that if you are cold, you desire clothing; but other animals also understand these things.

However, that knowledge of the soul which leads to the knowledge of God, is not of this kind. The knowledge which you need to possess is, to know what you are; how you are created; whence you are; for what you are here; whither you are going; in what your happiness consists, and what you must do to secure it; in what your misery consists, and what you must do to avoid it. And further, your internal qualities are distributed into animal, ferocious, demoniacal and angelic qualities. You need to know, therefore, what qualities predominate in your character, and in the predominance of which your true happiness consists. If your qualities are chiefly animal, the essence of which is to eat and drink, you will day and night seek these things. If your qualities are of the ferocious kind, the essence of which is to tear and rend, to injure and destroy, you will act accordingly. If you are endowed chiefly with the qualities of devils, which consist in evil machinations, deceit, and delusion, then you should know and be aware of it, that you may turn towards the path of perfection. And if you possess angelic qualities whose nature it is to worship God in sincerity and continually to await the vision of His beauty, then like them you should unceasingly, resting neither day nor night, be zealous and strive that you may become worthy of the vision of the Lord. For know, O student of the mysteries! that man was created to stand at the door of service in frailty and weakness, and wait for the opening of the door of spiritual union, and for the vision of beauty, as God declares in his holy word: "I have not created the genii and men except that they should worship me."

These qualities, whether animal or ferocious or demoniacal have been bestowed upon men, that by their means the body might be adapted to be a vehicle for the spirit, and that the spirit, by means of the body which is its vehicle, while here in this temporary home of earth, might seek after the knowledge and love of God, as the huntsman would seek to make the phoenix and the griffin his prey. Then, when it leaves this strange land for the region of spiritual friendship, it shall be worthy to partake of the mystery contained in the invitation, "enter in peace, O believers!" and which is in the homage, "Peace is the word they shall hear from the merciful Lord." People in general suppose that this refers to Paradise. Woe to him who has no portion in this knowledge! There is great danger in his path. The way of faith is veiled from his eyes.

If you wish, O seeker of the way! to know your own soul, know that the blessed and glorious God created you of two things: the one is a visible body, and the other is a something internal, that is called spirit and heart, which can only be perceived by the mind. But when we speak of heart, we do not mean the piece of flesh which is in the left side of the breast of a man, for that is found in a dead body and in animals: it may be seen with the eyes, and belongs to the visible world. That heart, which is emphatically called spirit, does not belong to this world, and although it has come to this world, it has only come to leave it. It is the sovereign of the body, which is its vehicle, and all the external and internal organs of the body are its subjects. Its especial attribute is to know God and to enjoy the vision of the beauty of the Lord God. The invitation to salvation is addressed to the spirit. The commandment is also addressed to it, for it is capable of happiness or misery. The knowledge of what it is in reality, is the key to the knowledge of God. Beloved, strive to obtain this knowledge, for there is no more precious jewel. In its origin it comes from God, and again returns to him. It has come hither but for a time for intercourse and action.

Be sure, O seeker after knowledge! that it is impossible to obtain a knowledge of the heart, until you know its essence and its true nature, its faculties, and its relations with its faculties,—nor until you know its attributes, and how through them the knowledge of God is obtained, and what happiness is, and how happiness is to be secured. Know then, that the existence of the spirit is evident and is not involved in doubt. Still, it is not body, which is found in corpses and in animals generally. If a person with his eyes open should look upon the world and upon his own body, and then shut his eyes, everything would be veiled from his view, so that he could not see even his own body. But the existence of his spirit would not be at the same time shut out from his view. Again, at death, the body turns to earth, but the spirit undergoes no corruption. Still it is not permitted to us to know what the spirit is in its real nature and in its essence, as God says in his Holy Word: "They will ask you about the spirit. Answer, the spirit is a creation by decree of the Lord."

No. 39. Avicenna

(*Avicenna on Theology*, tr. Arthur J. Arberry. London, 1951. "The Wisdom of the East Series." By permission of John Murray, London.)

Autobiography of Avicenna (pp. 9-13)

My father was a man of Balkh, and he moved from there to Bukhara . . . where I was put under teachers of the Koran and of letters. By the time I was ten I had mastered the Koran and a great deal of literature, so that I was marvelled at for my aptitude.

Now my father was one of those who had responded to the Egyptian propagandist (who was an Ismaili); he, and my brother too, had listened to what they had to say about the Spirit and the Intellect, after the fashion in which they preach and understand the matter. They would therefore discuss these things together, while I listened and comprehended all that they said; but my spirit would not assent to their argument. Presently they began to invite me to join the movement, rolling on their tongues talk about philosophy, geometry, Indian arithmetic; and my father sent me to a certain vegetable-seller who used the Indian arithmetic, so that I might learn it from him. Then there came to Bukhara a man called Abū 'Abd Allāh al-Nātilī who claimed to be a philosopher; my father invited him to stay in our house, hoping that I would learn from him also. Before his advent I had already occupied myself with Muslim jurisprudence, attending Ismā'īl the Ascetic; so I was an excellent enquirer, having become familiar with the methods of postulation and the techniques of rebuttal according to the usages of the canon lawyers. I now commenced reading the *Isagoge* (of Porphyry) with al-Nātilī: when he mentioned to me the definition of *genus* as a term applied to a number of things of different species in answer to the question "What is it?" I set about verifying this definition in a manner such as he had never heard. He marvelled at me exceedingly, and warned my father that I should not engage in any other occupation but learning; whatever problem he stated to me, I showed a better mental conception of it than he. So I continued until I had read all the straightforward parts of Logic with him; as for the subtler points, he had no acquaintance with them.

From then onward I took to reading texts by myself; I studied the commentaries, until I had completely mastered the science of Logic. Similarly with Euclid I read the first five or six figures with him, and thereafter undertook on my own account to solve the entire remainder of the book. Next I moved on to the *Almagest* (of Ptolemy); when I had finished the prolegomena and reached the geometrical figures al-Nātilī told me to go on reading and to solve the problems by myself; I should merely revise what I read with him, so that he might indicate to me what was right and what was wrong. The truth is that he did not really teach this book; I began to solve the work, and many were the complicated figures of which he had no knowledge until I presented them to him, and made him understand them. Then al-Nātilī took leave of me, setting out for Gurganj.

I now occupied myself with mastering the various texts and commentaries on natural science and metaphysics, until all the gates of knowledge were open to me. Next I desired to study medicine, and proceeded to read all the books that have been written on this subject. Medicine is not a difficult science, and naturally I excelled in it in a very short time, so that qualified physicians began to read medicine with me. I also undertook to treat the sick, and methods of treatment derived from practical experience revealed themselves to me such as baffle description. At the same time I continued between whiles to study and dispute on law, being now sixteen years of age.

The next eighteen months I devoted entirely to reading; I studied Logic once again, and all the parts of philosophy. During all this time I did not sleep one night through, nor devoted my attention to any other matter by day. I prepared a set of files; with each proof I examined, I set down the syllogistic premises and put them in order in the files, then I examined what deductions might be drawn from them. I observed methodically the conditions of the premisses, and proceeded until the truth of each particular problem was confirmed for me. Whenever I found myself perplexed by a problem or could not find the middle term in any syllogism, I would repair to the mosque and pray, adoring the All-Creator, until my puzzle was resolved and my difficulty made easy. At night I would return home, set the lamp before me, and busy myself with reading and writing; whenever sleep overcame me or I was conscious of some weakness, I turned aside to drink a glass of wine until my strength returned to me; then I went back to my reading. If ever the least slumber overtook me, I would dream of the precise problem which I was considering as I fell asleep; in that way many problems revealed themselves to me while sleeping. So I continued until I had made myself master of all the sciences; I now comprehended them to the limits of human possibility. All that I learned during that time is exactly as I know it now; I have added nothing more to my knowledge to this day.

I was now a master of Logic, natural sciences and mathematics. I therefore returned to metaphysics; I read the *Metaphysica* (of Aristotle), but did not understand its contents and was baffled by the author's intention; I read it over forty times, until I had the text by heart. Even then I did not understand it or what the author meant, and I despaired within myself, saying, "This is a book which there is no way of understanding." But one day at noon I chanced to be in the bookseller's quarter, and a broker was there with a volume in his hand which he was calling for sale. He offered it to me, but I returned it to him impatiently, believing that there was no use in this particular science. However he said to me, "Buy this book from me: it is cheap, and I will sell it to you for four dirhams. The owner is in need of the money." So I bought it, and found that it was a book by Abū Nasr al-Fārābī *On the Objects of the Metaphysica*. I returned home and hastened to read it; and at once the objects of that book became clear to me, for I had it all by heart. I rejoiced at this, and upon the next day distributed much in alms to the poor in gratitude to Almighty God.

Now the Sultan of Bukhara at that time was Nūh ibn Mansūr, and it happened that he fell sick of a malady which baffled all the physicians. My name was famous among them because of the breadth of my reading; they therefore mentioned me in his presence, and begged him to summon me. I attended the sick-room, and collaborated with them in treating the royal patient. So I came to be enrolled in his service. One day I asked his leave to enter their library, to examine the contents and read the books on medicine; he granted my request, and I entered a mansion with many chambers, each chamber having chests of books piled one upon another. In one apartment were books on language and poetry, in another law, and so on; each apartment was set aside for books on a single science. I glanced through the catalogue of the works of the ancient Greeks, and asked for those which I required; and I saw books whose very names are as yet unknown to many—works which I had never seen before and have not seen since. I read these books, taking notes of their contents; I came to realize the place each man occupied in his particular science.

So by the time I reached my eighteenth year I had exhausted all these sciences. My memory for learning was at that period of my life better than it is now, but today I am more mature; apart from this my knowledge is exactly the same, nothing further having been added to my store since then.

No. 40. Averroës on Aristotle's preeminence

(Robinson's *Readings*, p. 456.)

Aristotle was the wisest of the Greeks and constituted and completed logic, physics, and metaphysics. I say that he constituted these sciences, because all the works on these subjects previous to him do not deserve to be mentioned and were completely eclipsed by his writings. I say that he put the finishing touches on these sciences, because none of those who have succeeded him up to our time, to wit, during nearly fifteen hundred years, have been able to add anything to his writings or find in them any error of any importance. Now that all this should be found in one man is a strange and miraculous thing, and this privileged being deserves to be called divine rather than human.

No. 41. The *Rubaiyat* of Omar Khayyam (Excerpts)

(Tr. Edward Fitzgerald.)

> Come, fill the Cup, and in the fire of Spring
> Your Winter-garment of Repentance fling:
> The bird of Time has but a little way
> to Flutter—and the Bird is on the Wing.

> Some for the Glories of This World; and some
> Sigh for the Prophet's Paradise to come;
> Ah, take the Cash, and let the Promise go,
> Nor heed the rumble of a distant Drum!

The Worldly Hope men set their Hearts upon
Turns Ashes—or it prospers; and anon,
Like Snow upon the Desert's dusty Face,
Lighting a little hour or two—is gone.

Ah, make the most of what we yet may spend,
Before we too into the Dust descend;
Dust into Dust, and under Dust to lie,
Sans Wine, sans Song, sans Singer, and—sans End!

There was a Door to which I found no Key:
There was the Veil through which I could not see:
Some little talk awhile of Me and Thee
There was—and then no more of Thee and Me.

Oh, threats of Hell and Hopes of Paradise!
One thing at least is certain—*This* life flies:
One thing is certain and the rest is Lies;
The Flower that once is blown forever dies.

Strange, is it not? that of the myriads who
Before us passed the door of Darkness through
Not one returns to tell us of the Road,
Which to discover we must travel too.

We are no other than a moving row
Of Magic Shadow-shapes that come and go
Round with this Sun-illumined Lantern held
In Midnight by the Master of the Show.

Impotent Pieces of the Game He plays
Upon this Chequer-board of Nights and Days;
Hither and thither moves, and checks, and slays;
And one by one back in the Closet lays.

The Ball no Question makes of Ayes and Noes,
But Here or There as strikes the Player goes;
And He that tossed you down into the Field,
He knows about it all—*He* knows—*He* knows!

The moving Finger writes; and having writ,
Moves on: nor all your Piety nor Wit
Shall lure it back to cancel half a Line,
Nor all your Tears wash out a Word of it.

And that inverted Bowl they call the Sky,
Whereunder crawling cooped we live and die,
Lift not your hands to *It* for help—for It
As impotently rolls as you or I.

Yesterday *This* Day's Madness did prepare;
Tomorrow's Silence, Triumph, or Despair:
Drink! for you know not whence you came, nor why:
Drink! for you know not why you go, nor where.

No. 42. *The Chronicle of Al Tabari*

(Translated by E. W. Brooks, *English Historical Review*, XV, pp. 741-746.)

A.H. 182 (A.D. 799) And in it 'Abd Al Rahman the son of 'Ahd Al Malik the son of Salih made the summer-raid and reached Dafasus [Ephesos], the city of the inmates of the cave. [i.e. the Seven Sleepers]

And in it the Romans put out the eyes of their king, Constantine the son of Leo, and they confirmed his mother Rina [Irene] in the kingdom, and she was surnamed Ughutash Augustua. . . .

A.H. 187 (A.D. 803) And in it Al Rashid sent his son Al Kasim on the summer-raid; and he gave him to God and made him an oblation for himself and a propitiation; and he appointed him wali of Al 'Awasim. . . .

And in this year Al Kasim the son of Al Rashid entered the land of the Romans in Sha'ban and besieged Kurra [Koron] and blockaded it; and he sent Al 'Abbas the son of Ga'far the son of Mahomet the son of Al Ash'ath, and he besieged the fort of Sinan until they were sore distressed. And the Romans sent to him offering him 320 Moslem prisoners if he would retire from them. And he accepted their offer and retired from Kurra and the fort of Sinan in peace. And 'Ali the son of 'Isa the son of Moses died on this raid in the land of the Romans, and he was with Al Kasim.

And in this year the ruler of the Romans broke the peace made between his predecessor and the Moslems, and refused what their previous king had undertaken to pay.

And the reason of this was that peace had been made between the Moslems and the ruler of the Romans (and their ruler at that time was Rina, and we have recorded above the reason of the peace made between the Moslems and her): and the Romans turned against Rina and deposed her and made Nikephoros king over them. And the Romans record that this Nikephoros was a descendant of Gafna of Ghassan, and that before his accession he was comptroller of the revenue-accounts. Then Rina died five months after the Romans had deposed her. And it is recorded that, when Nikephoros became king, and the Romans were confirmed in allegiance to him, he wrote to Al Rashid:

The queen (Irene) considered you as a rook, and herself as a pawn.

That pusillanimous female submitted to pay a tribute, the double of which she ought to have exacted from the barbarians. Restore therefore the fruits of your injustice, or abide the determination of the sword.

He says: And, when Al Rashid read the letter, his wrath was roused so much that no one could look at him, much less speak to him; and his household separated, fearing to increase it by any speech or action on their part; and the wazir was in doubt whether to give him advice or to leave him to his own deliberations without him. And he called for an inkpot and wrote on the back of the letter:

In the name of the most merciful God, Harun al Rashid, commander of the faithful, to Nicephorus, the Roman dog. I have read thy letter, O thou son of an unbelieving mother. Thou shalt not hear, thou shalt behold, my reply.

Then he set out the same day and marched until he reached the gate of Herakleia; and he made captures and took spoil and carried off the best of everything and slew and wasted and burnt and extirpated. And Nikephoros asked for a treaty on condition of paying annual tribute, and he accepted his offer. And, when he had returned from his raid and reached Al Rakka [Kallinikos], Nikephoros broke the treaty and violated the compact. And the cold was severe, and Nikephoros made sure that he would not return against him. And the news came that he had gone back from the conditions which he laid upon him, and it was not easy for any one to tell him this through fear of returning at such a season on his account and their own. And an artifice was used with him by means of a poet, a man of Gada called Abu Muhammad 'Abd Allah the son of Joseph (and it is said that he was Al Haggag the son of Joseph), and Taimi; and he said: [here are given three poems.]

And, when he had finished his recital, he said, "The action of Nikephoros has kindled this;" and he knew that the wazirs had used an artifice with him in this matter. And he retraced his steps amidst the greatest hardships and the sorest fatigues, until he encamped in his possessions, and he did not return until he was satisfied and went as far as he wanted. . . .

A.H. 188 (A.D. 804) And among the events of the year was the summer-raid of Abraham the son of Gabriel and his invasion of the land of the Romans by the pass of Al Safsaf.

And Nikephoros came out to meet him, but there was brought to him from behind the news of an event which caused him to turn aside from coming to meet him, and he fell in with a party of Moslems and received three wounds and was routed. And there was slain of the Romans, as is recorded, 40,700 men, and 4,000 beasts of burden were captured.

A.H. 189 (A.D. 805) And in this year was the ransoming between the Moslems and the Romans, and no Moslem remained in the land of the Romans who was not ransomed, as is recorded. And Marwan the son of Abu Hafsa said of this:

And through thee were the captives freed, for whom high prisons were built, wherein was no friend to visit them, for so long as the price of their redemption passed the Moslems' power to pay. And they said, "The prisons of the polytheists [Christians] are their graves."

A.H. 190 (A.D. 806) And this year Al Rashid made the summer-raid. . . . And in it the Romans went out to Anazarbos and Kanisa Al Saudaa and overran the country and took prisoners: the men of Mopsouestia recovered all that were in their hands. And in it Al Rashid took Herakleia and dispersed his troops and his horsemen over the land of the Romans; and he entered it, as is recorded, with 135,000 regularly paid men besides the camp-followers and volunteers and those who were not registered. . . . And Al Rashid's capture of Herakleia was in Shawwal [20 Aug.-17 Sept.]; and he laid it waste and carried its people into captivity after remaining before it thirty days. And he appointed Humaid the son of Ma'yuf wali of the coast of the sea of Al Sham as far as Egypt, and Humaid reached Cyprus and destroyed and burnt and carried 16,000 of its people captive; and he brought them to Al Rafika; and Abu'l Bakhtara the judge was appointed to sell them, and the bishop of Cyprus fetched 2,000 denarii. And Aaron's entry into the land of the Romans was on 20 Ragab [11 June]; and he made a pointed cap on which was written "Raider and pilgrim," and wore it. And Abu'l Mu'ali the Kilabi said:

And who would seek or wish to contend with thee, whether in the holy cities or on the farthest frontier, whether in the enemy's land on a high-bred horse or in the land of ease upon a camel's saddle? And none beside thee subdued the frontiers, of those that were appointed to rule over affairs.

Then Al Rashid went to Tyana and encamped there. Then he removed from it and left 'Ukba the son of Ga'far in command of it and ordered him to build a station there. And Nikephoros sent Al Rashid the contribution and tribute for himself and his successor-designate and his patricians and the other inhabitants of his country, 50,000 denarii, of which 4 denarii were for his own person and 2 denarii for that of his son Stauracius. And Nikephoros wrote a letter and sent it by two of his chief patricians about a female slave among the captives of Herakleia, which I have copied:

To God's slave, Aaron, Commander of the believers, from Nikephoros, king of the Romans. Peace to you. To proceed, O King, I have a request to make of you that will not injure you in your religious or your worldly life, a small and easy matter, that you will give my son a female slave, one of the inhabitants of Herakleia, whom I had sought as a wife for my son; and, if you think good to perform my request, do so. And peace be to you and God's mercy and blessing.

And he also asked him for some perfume and one of his tents. And Al Rashid ordered the slave to be sought, and she was brought and decked out and seated on a throne in his tent in which he was living; and the slave was handed over, and the tent with all the vessels and furniture in it, to the envoy of Nikephoros.

And he sent him the scent which he asked, and he sent him some dates and figs and raisins and treacle. And Al Rashid's envoy handed over all this to him, and Nikephoros gave him a load of Islamic drachmai upon a bay horse, the amount of which was 50,000 drachmai, and 100 silk garments and 200 embroidered garments and 12 falcons and 4 hunting dogs and 3 horses. And Nikephoros had stipulated that he should not lay waste Dhu'l Kila' or Samaluh or the fort of Sinan; and Al Rashid stipulated with him that he should not restore Herakleia, and that Nikephoros should undertake to pay him 300,000 denarii.

No. 43. Al Razi on smallpox

(*A Treatise on the Small-Pox and Measles*, by Abú Becr Mohammed Ibn Zacaríyá Ar-rází, commonly called Rhazes, tr. William A. Greenhill. London, 1848, pp. 23-30.)

Author's Preface

In the name of GOD, the Compassionate, the Merciful.

Abú Becr Mohammed Ibn Zacaríyá says:—It happened on a certain night at a meeting in the house of a nobleman, of great goodness and excellence, and very anxious for the explanation and facilitating of useful sciences for the good of mankind, that, mention having been made of the Small-Pox, I then spoke what came into my mind on that subject. Whereupon our host (may GOD favour men by prolonging the remainder of his life) wished me to compose a suitable, solid, and complete discourse on this disease, because there has not appeared up to this present time either among the ancients or the moderns an accurate and satisfactory account of it. And therefore I composed this discourse, hoping to receive my reward from the Almighty and Glorious GOD, and awaiting His good pleasure.

The plan of my undertaking, and the subject of the chapters is as follows:

Ch. 1. Of the causes of the Small-Pox, and how it comes to pass that hardly any one escapes the disease.   Ch. 2. A specification of those habits of body which are most disposed to the Small-Pox; and also of the seasons in which the disease is most prevalent.   Ch. 3. Of the symptoms which indicate the approaching eruption of the Small-Pox and Measles.   Ch. 4. A specification of the articles of the regimen or treatment of the Small-Pox in general.   Ch. 5. Of the preservation from the Small-Pox before the symptoms of the disease appear, and the way to hinder the multiplying of the pustules after the appearance of the symptoms.   Ch. 6. Of those things which accelerate the pustules of the Small-Pox and their appearance externally, and which assist Nature herein.   Ch. 7. Of the care to be taken of the eyes, throat, joints, ears, and those parts of which it is necessary to take care upon the appearance of the symptoms of the Small-Pox.   Ch. 8. Of those things which hasten the ripening of those pustules which can be ripened.   Ch. 9. Of the drying of those pustules which are ripened.   Ch. 10. Of those things which take away the scabs of the Small-Pox and eschars.

Ch. 11. Of those things which take away the marks of the Small-Pox from the eyes and the rest of the body.   Ch. 12. Of the regulating the patient's food in the Small-Pox.   Ch. 13. Of the regulating the patient's bowels in the Small-Pox.   Ch. 14. Of the mild and the fatal species of Small-Pox.

Ch. 1. Of the causes of the Small-Pox; how it comes to pass that hardly any one escapes the disease; and the sum of what Galen says concerning it.

As to any physician who says that the excellent Galen has made no mention of the Small-Pox, and was entirely ignorant of this disease, surely he must be one of those who have either never read his works at all, or who have passed over them very cursorily. For Galen describes a plaster in the first book of his treatise *Kata Genos,* and says that it is useful against this and that disease, "and also against the Small-Pox." . . .

We will now begin therefore by mentioning the efficient cause of this distemper, and why hardly any one escapes it; and then we will treat of the other things that relate to it, section by section: and we will (with GOD'S assistance) speak on every one of these points with what we consider to be sufficient copiousness.

I say then that every man, from the time of his birth till he arrives at old age, is continually tending to dryness; and for this reason the blood of children and infants is much moister than the blood of young men, and still more so than that of old men. And besides this it is much hotter; as Galen testifies in his Commentary on the "Aphorisms," in which he says that "the heat of children is greater in quantity than the heat of young men, and the heat of young men is more intense in quality." And this also is evident from the force with which the natural processes, such as digestion and growth of body, are carried on in children. For this reason the blood of infants and children may be compared to must, in which the coction leading to perfect ripeness has not yet begun, nor the movement towards fermentation taken place; the blood of young men may be compared to must, which has already fermented and made a hissing noise, and has thrown out abundant vapours and its superfluous parts, like wine which is now still and quiet and arrived at its full strength; and as to the blood of old men, it may be compared to wine which has now lost its strength and is beginning to grow vapid and sour.

Now the Small-Pox arises when the blood putrefies and ferments, so that the superfluous vapours are thrown out of it, and it is changed from the blood of infants, which is like must, into the blood of young men, which is like wine perfectly ripened: and the Small-Pox itself may be compared to the fermentation and the hissing noise which take place in must at that time. And this is the reason why children, especially males, rarely escape being seized with this disease, because it is impossible to prevent the blood's changing from this state into its second state, just as it is impossible to prevent must (whose nature it is to make a hissing noise and to ferment) from changing into the state which happens to it after its making a hissing noise and its fermentation. And the temperament of an infant or child is seldom such that it is possible for its blood to be changed from the first state into the second by little and little, and orderly, and slowly, so that this fermentation and hissing noise should not show itself in the blood: for a temperament, to change thus gradually, should be cold and dry; whereas that of children is just the contrary, as is also their diet, seeing that the food of infants consists of milk; and as for children, although their food does not consist of milk, yet it is nearer to it than is that of other ages; there is also a greater mixture in their food, and more movement after it; for which reason it is seldom that a child escapes this disease. . . .

6

THE FRANKISH KINGDOMS

The Merovingians

The Germanic West *ca.* 500 A.D.   We must now turn our attention back to western Europe, to the Germanic nations which had established themselves there in the fifth and sixth centuries. The principal Germanic states, as we have seen, were the Frankish in north-central Gaul, the Visigothic in southern France and Spain, the Vandal in north Africa, the Anglo-Saxon in England, the Burgundian in the valley of the Rhone, and the Ostrogothic in Italy. The first of these kingdoms to disappear had been that of the Vandals, which Belisarius destroyed in a campaign of a few months duration. Next passed the Ostrogothic kingdom, but only after twenty years of bitter, destructive warfare with Justinian's armies. In both these instances, Byzantine success had proved short-lived. By 700 the Moslems had overrun north Africa, while even earlier the empire had surrendered large portions of Italy to the Lombards. The Visigothic kingdom disappeared into history early in the eighth century, and all of Spain with the exception of Galicia passed under control of the Moslems. It remains for us to consider the fortunes of the Franks, Burgundians, and the Angles and Saxons, those Germans, as it happened, who were destined to leave the most enduring marks upon western Europe.

Clovis: His Character.   The first man we meet is Clovis, the most important of the Germanic chieftains, and one of the true founders of western European history. More French kings have borne his name, spelled Louis in modern times, than any other. Clovis was just one of a number of kinglets among the Salian Franks when in 481 A.D. at the age of fifteen, he assumed control of his group, the Sicambri. By the time he died in 511, he had managed, through cunning and ruthlessness, to extend his authority over two thirds of historical France. The dynasty he founded is called the Merovingian, after its legendary ancestor Meroveg. About the methods Clovis employed to establish his power, however, there was nothing nebulous. Medieval history reveals few statesmen who were more forthright and unscrupulous. So it comes as something of a shock to find the only historian of the time, and a saintly one at that, Gregory, bishop of Tours, bestowing upon Clovis the most generous encomia. Of Clovis he wrote: "The Lord cast his enemies under his power day after day and increased his kingdom, because he walked with a right heart before Him, and did that which was pleasing in His sight." One might posit fear as explaining this astonishing observation had not Clovis been dead when Gregory began to write. It was rather Clovis' acceptance of Christianity and his attacks on pagans and Arians, that won him Gregory's acclaim. These were brutal times, and the good bishop must have argued that God had perforce to rely upon violent men to do his will.

The Conversion of Clovis. Clovis' first major victory after establishing himself as king of the Salians was over Syagrius, whom Gregory called somewhat euphemistically "king of the Romans." Syagrius ruled over the land between the Seine and the Loire. With the annexation of this area, Clovis secured possession of such traditionally French cities as Reims and Paris. The latter city he made his capital. Next he forced the Thuringians across the Rhine, and then the Alamans after a bloody victory near Strasbourg. Gregory says that it was during this battle, when his Franks began to give way and his own pagan deities appeared to have failed him, that Clovis appealed to the God of the Christians for aid. According to Gregory, God hearkened to the prayer of Clovis and gave him the victory, whereupon after the battle the Frankish king and three thousand of his warriors were baptized. Clovis' Christian wife, the Burgundian princess Clotilda, must have enjoyed unusual influence over her rough husband, for he had earlier permitted their children to be baptized. Yet his principal motive in becoming a Christian must have been his realization that such a step would assure him the support of the Catholic hierarchy and Gallo-Roman population against his heathen and Arian neighbors. Whatever the circumstances attending Clovis' conversion, that fact proved most far-reaching in its consequences for medieval France. (Reading 44)

Conquests of Clovis. Clovis next moved against the Burgundians, but here he had to rest content for the moment with an alliance. Then, with his southern frontier protected, he proceeded to dispose finally of the powerful Alamans, which he did with such thoroughness that this proud German nation all but disappeared. In his following campaign he struck at the Visigoths to the south and would have annexed the whole of their

Gallic possessions had it not been for the intervention of Theodoric, the Ostrogothic ruler of Italy. Septimania was saved for the Visigoths for a few more years, while Theodoric himself laid claim to Provence. Clovis also subjugated the Bavarians and Thuringians to his rule, and forced several Saxon tribes to pay tribute. He closed his reign on the same barbarous note with which he had inaugurated it. A series of assassinations eliminated the last of the Salian princes, and he took over the lands of the Ripuarian Franks after executing the son of the Ripuarian king, because he had taken his (Clovis') suggestion and murdered his own father.

The Success of Clovis. The success of Clovis and the Franks in establishing such a large and powerful state must be attributed above all else to the genius and talents of Clovis. Without so forceful a character to assume the leadership, France like Italy might have remained disunited for many centuries to come. Powerfully supplementing Clovis' personal qualities was the overt encouragement, if not direct assistance, of the Catholic hierarchy. The Catholic bishops were inclined to clothe his wars in the garb of crusades, since his enemies were usually pagans or Arians. The success of the Franks must be credited next to the fact that the Franks had not migrated from northwestern Germany—they had simply expanded. In contrast, therefore, to the other Germanic invaders of the Roman Empire, the Frankish nation had never pulled up its roots, and therefore retained a stability seemingly denied its cousins. It was also most fortunate for the Franks that they never once encountered during this early period of expansion, so formidable a foe as Justinian or the Moslems, or that their path was never crossed by such Asiatic invaders as the ferocious Avars and Bulgars.

Division of Frankish Kingdom. The stature of Clovis stands out all the more sharply against the background of the incompetence of his Merovingian successors. None of these approached him in ability, although several surpassed him in savagery. It is true that the sons of Clovis inherited enough of their father's aggressiveness to conquer Burgundy, Provence, and Septimania, and thus carry the frontiers of France to the Rhine, Alps, and Pyrenees. Yet a fatal principle almost doomed their best efforts to failure, while it contributed in the end to the destruction of the dynasty. That was the practice of the Salians of dividing the kingdom as so much property among the surviving sons of the king. The inevitable consequence was that the death of the king signaled the outbreak of civil war, for even if the sons might conceivably have been satisfied with the portions assigned them, their wives were not. Partly as a consequence of these conflicts, France tended to break up into four separate states: Burgundy to the southeast, Aquitaine to the southwest, Austrasia (the eastern part) on both sides of the lower Rhine, and Neustria (the newest part) the western section about Paris. Bavarians, Saxons, and Thuringians exploited the differences among the Frankish kings and recovered their independence. In time racial differences came to sanctify the new frontiers within France. The southern provinces, Burgundy and Aquitaine, remained predominately Celtic-Roman in culture, while the two northern provinces, particularly Austrasia, became largely German. Thus France appeared headed toward permanent partition.

Decline of the Merovingian Dynasty.   There were other factors, in addition to the Salic principle of inheritance, which hastened the decline of Merovingian power. One was the moral and physical weakness of the Merovingian monarchs. Merovingian history reveals in general a sequence of kings guilty of all the moral excesses of semicivilized brutes. Several died in their youth of what has been aptly styled precocious debauchery. Dagobert (d. 639), the last Merovingian to exercise any semblance of power, had three wives at the same time. Not only was the monarchy devoid of honor, it was without funds as well. Industry and trade had fallen to a point where they would have yielded little revenue even had the administrative machinery existed to collect it. A large portion of the income from crown lands in outlying districts had been surrendered to buy the loyalty of the counts and landed aristocracy in those areas. What remained to the king could not readily be translated into fluid capital, to be used when and where circumstances might recommend. Actually if the king wished to enjoy the products of the crown lands still remaining in his possession, he and his court had normally to visit these lands and personally consume the products. The landed aristocracy and higher officialdom had capitalized on the wars among the heirs of the king by selling their services to the highest bidder. The price they asked invariably entailed a reduction of royal power in their provinces. It might mean more crown lands for themselves, it might mean selecting the royal officials from the localities they served, it might mean making those offices hereditary. At every turn the king found himself relinquishing powers to this group, the landed aristocracy, which would eventually encompass his destruction.

Mayor of the Palace.   That the extreme decentralization which we associate with feudalism did not settle upon France one hundred and seventy-five years before it did, was due in large measure to the emergence of one of the royal officials, the mayor of the palace, to a position of such power that he was able to replace the king before all royal power had been dissipated. This official was the most powerful of the royal assistants in late sixth-century France. He was always with the king, he represented him on occasion, he administered the royal estates, and he supervised the other officials of the court. As much because of his own aggressiveness as of the incompetency of the king, the mayor of the palace had become the actual ruler by the close of the seventh century. The monarch had meantime degenerated into a mere puppet, into a "do-nothing king." In the words of the chronicler: "There was nothing left for the King to do but to be content with his name of King, his flowing hair and long beard; to sit on his throne and play the ruler." In 687 A.D., the Austrasian mayor of the palace, Pepin II, defeated the Neustrian mayor of the palace and extended his rule over both countries. His illegitimate son, the famous Charles Martel whom we met earlier, reestablished the France of the earlier Merovingians by forcing Burgundy and Aquitaine to accept his authority. With so much power again concentrated in one hand, it was only natural that Martel's son, Pepin III, should wish to unseat the last Merovingian and reign in his stead. To this step the pope and the great assembly of Frankish nobles gave their ready approval, and in the year 752 St. Boniface, the apostle of the Germans, solemnly anointed Pepin king of the Franks. It was not necessary to execute the last Merovingian—he was so much a puppet. Pepin simply ordered his long hair cut off, a Merovingian mark of power, and stuck him in a monastery. (Reading 47)

The Carolingian Dynasty

Pepin III, King of the Franks. Pepin III (741-768) founded what is known in history as the Carolingian dynasty, the name deriving from its most illustrious member, Pepin's own son Charles (Latin *Carolus*). Pepin continued the work of his father by further extending Frankish dominion. Long years of fighting were required before Aquitaine was entirely pacified and the Moslems driven across the Pyrenees. Pepin also warred to the north and east against the Saxons, Bavarians, and Frisians, and incorporated the lands of the latter people directly into his kingdom. In the area of his greatest success, he kept nothing for himself. This success was against the Lombards in Italy. It so happened that the Lombards had finally succeeded in snuffing out the chief center of Byzantine rule in Italy with the capture of Ravenna in 751. They then marched on Rome and laid siege to the city when the pope refused to surrender. Charles Martel had ignored earlier papal appeals for help against the threatening Lombards, because of his friendly alliance with that people. And it was no easy matter for the pope to gain Pepin's promise of succor, since relations between the Franks and Lombards had continued most amicable. Pepin's two sons, in fact, were wed to daughters of the Lombard monarch. But Pepin's sense of obligation to the church and to the pope proved too strong. The pope, Stephen II, had come across the Alps in person in 754 to Metz to solicit his aid. While there he had improved upon the occasion by solemnly reconsecrating Pepin king of the Franks, adding somewhat gratuitously the imperial dignity of patrician of the Romans. So upon the Lombard king's refusal to lift the siege of Rome, Pepin marched south. He drove the Lombards back after two successful campaigns, and turned over to the pope the lands he had conquered, including the exarchate of Ravenna.

Donations of Pepin and Constantine. This act, known in history as the Donation of Pepin, rightly deserves all the attention paid it. It sealed, first of all, the alliance between the Christian Church in the west and the Franks, which alliance had originated with Clovis. It thereby served to implement in fact what might otherwise have remained only a theory, namely, that the medieval Christian state lay under divine obligation to assist the church. It also established the pope as a formal temporal ruler, a status he held until 1870. Whether Pepin's action in thus transferring the control of Rome to the pope was in any way influenced by the so-called Donation of Constantine is improbable. This last was a document, usually assigned to this very same period, which recorded the presumed transfer of political supremacy in Italy and the west by Constantine to the pope, together with the spiritual dominion over all of Christendom. What had prompted Constantine to make this handsome present to the pope was his gratitude to Pope Sylvester I for having miraculously cleansed him of leprosy. Whose fertile imagination conjured up this fantastic tale is unknown, neither are the motives which might have prompted it. Its authenticity was occasionally questioned in the centuries following, although it was not finally proved a forgery until the fifteenth. The first record of an appeal being made to it on behalf of the papacy came in the eleventh century, when it was used to repulse the pretensions of the patriarch of Constantinople. (Reading 53)

Pepin's Work. Pepin proved himself a thoroughly loyal son of the church. He restored some of the lands his father had seized at its expense and added estates of his own. He actively supported the efforts of St. Boniface and other missionaries in reforming and reorganizing the church in France and in spreading the faith eastward among the pagan Frisians. It was he, as we have seen, who founded the temporal state of the church and then guaranteed its existence by means of an alliance with his own state. Some credit is due Pepin for preparing the ground for the revival of learning which brightened the reign of his famous son Charlemagne. He may also lay claim to some share of Charlemagne's achievement in establishing the Carolingian state, although contemporary writers do not make clear what it was. Pepin is one of those unfortunate kings whose achievement is thrown into shadow by the more spectacular accomplishments of their sons. As if this were not bad enough, he has come down in history with a title which did not fit him, namely Pepin "the Short."

Charlemagne the Man. Pepin was succeeded by two sons, but the Frankish realm escaped the evils of the Salic principle of succession upon the death of the elder. The surviving son, Charles, proved himself the most illustrious monarch of the Middle Ages. His epithet "the Great," has stood the test of time as successfully as that of any other "great" in history, and French and English speaking countries know him as Charlemagne. Though like most of the other "greats" in history he owed his title to his martial exploits, there was much more to his claim to fame than mere military achievement. Before considering the unique accomplishments of this king, let us have a look at his royal person as described by his loyal secretary Einhard.

Charles was large and robust, of commanding stature and excellent proportions, for it appears that he measured in height seven times the length of his own foot. The top of his head was round, his eyes large and animated, his nose somewhat long. He had a fine head of gray hair, and his face was bright and pleasant; so that, whether standing or sitting, he showed great presence and dignity. Although his neck was thick and rather short, and his belly too prominent, still the good proportions of his limbs concealed these defects. His walk was firm, and the whole carriage of his body was manly. His voice was clear, but not so strong as his frame would have led one to expect.

His health was good until the last four years of his life, when he was attacked with frequent fevers, and latterly walked lame on one foot. Even then he relied more on his own judgement than on the advice of physicians, whom he almost hated because they used to recommend him to leave off roasted meats, which he preferred, and to accustom himself to boiled.

He took constant exercise in riding and hunting. . . . He also delighted in the natural warm baths, frequently exercising himself by swimming, in which he was very skillful, no one being able to outstrip him. It was on account of the warm baths at Aix-la-Chapelle that he built his palace there and lived there constantly during the last years of his life and until his death. . . .

In his eating and drinking he was temperate; more particularly so in his drinking, for he had the greatest abhorrence of drunkenness in anybody, but more especially in himself and his companions. . . . While he was dining he listened to music or reading. History and the deeds of men of old were most often read. He derived much pleasure from the works of St. Augustine, especially from his book called *The City of God*.

Motives for his Wars. Charlemagne's contemporaries were most impressed with his victories, and understandably so. Though detailed descriptions of his campaigns are lacking, the very scope of the victories he won over a group of powerful foes establishes him as an outstanding general. Martial tales fill the annals of his reign. Most of his campaigns were across the Frankish frontier against pagan or Moslem foes. This was partly due to circumstances, since few of his neighbors were Christian. Yet the motives which inspired his conquests sprang as frequently from higher considerations as from personal ambition. Thus he attacked the Lombards only after offering their king an indemnity if he would surrender the territories he had taken from the pope (Donation of Pepin). When the Lombard king refused this offer and persisted in his siege of Rome, Charlemagne reluctantly hearkened to the appeal of the pope, destroyed the Lombard army and kingdom and added Lombardy to his realm. His prolonged and bitter campaigns against the Saxons—"no war undertaken by the Franks was so protracted or so fierce, or so full of toil and hardship" —were waged as much to convert them as to subjugate this last most powerful of German tribes that threatened his realm from the northeast. (Reading 48) Charlemagne and his contemporaries were convinced that one could not be accomplished without the other, that is, that a foe was only conquered when he was converted. Coexistence between Christian and non-Christian nations was considered impossible.

Other Campaigns. Charlemagne's campaigns against the Avars effected the destruction of one of the most brutal peoples ever to terrorize eastern Europe. Einhard comments upon the enormity of the plunder which the Avars had accumulated over a period of generations. In their barbarism they could do little with it but keep it in a horde, which fell intact into the hands of the Franks. Charlemagne also fought pagan Slavs along the eastern frontier, and to the north Danes who were just beginning their raids upon western Europe. Had Charlemagne been a boy rather than an old man when he encountered these Vikings, the course of French history might have been altered. The most renowned of his campaigns, and most disastrous, was that which he undertook across the Pyrenees into Spain. Moslem chieftains friendly to the Abbasid caliph ruling in Baghdad had offered him their assistance, if he would come down and attack the sole remaining Ommiad emir at Cordova. Yet when Charlemagne did appear, neither this Moslem aid nor that of Christian elements in Spain material- ized. In fact, Christian Basques fell upon the rear guard and baggage train of his army at Roncesvalles as it was making its way back through the Pyrenees into France, an incident immortalized in the famous *Song of Roland*. (See page 607.) Some years later local chieftains friendly to Charlemagne established a Frankish state under his control which included the city of Barcelona. This was reoccupied by the Saracens, but again reconquered by Charlemagne and gradually expanded.

Military Accomplishments: An Evaluation. Einhard states that Charle- magne almost doubled the extensive kingdom he had inherited from his father Pepin. To the south, just beyond the Pyrenees, lay this last added area, the Spanish march as it was known (from the German *Mark*, mean- ing frontier). To the north he added Saxony, to the southeast in Italy the former lands of the Lombards (he also claimed a protectorate over the papal states), and to the east the entire northern littoral of the Adriatic with the exception of Venice. Along the eastern frontier he established a tier of loosely held marches, running all the way from Denmark on the North Sea to the middle Adriatic in Croatia. Denmark preserves in its name its early historical function as the Danish march. These marches, which were entrusted to loyal vassals called margraves (German *Markgraf*, that is, count of the frontier province), served principally as buffer states against pagan Slavs and Danes. The marches may also be viewed as poten- tial springboards for future German expansion eastward, which here received its first strong impulse from Charlemagne. Thus Charlemagne can count in his military achievement a number of highly significant accomplishments: the final destruction of the Lombards both as a state and as a century-old threat to the papacy; the destruction of German heathen- ism and Saxon independence; the annihilation of the Avar terror state; the initiation of the movement in Spain which would eventually lead to the expulsion of the Moslem; the reversing of a Slavic westward movement by an opposing German *"Drang nach Osten."*

Charlemagne's Coronation as Roman Emperor. Before proceeding to a consideration of other phases of Charlemagne's career, it will be well to discuss first his coronation as Roman emperor. For if this act did not influence his subsequent actions to the extent that the historical impor- tance of the title might suggest, it was hailed by contemporaries at least as a most momentous event. The circumstances which attended the corona- tion were extraordinarily simple, almost accidental, according to Einhard. It so happened that hostile elements had driven Pope Leo III out of

Rome, whence he had fled to Charlemagne's court to enlist his aid in recovering his authority. Charlemagne took up Leo's cause, hurried down to the Eternal City and, after investigating the charges brought against the pope, permitted him to clear himself with his oath. Two days later, on Christmas day in the year 800, as Charlemagne was kneeling before the altar after mass, the pope placed a crown upon his head and the assembled throng shouted enthusiastically: "To Charles Augustus, crowned of God, great and pacific emperor of the Romans, life and victory." Einhard concludes his account with the astonishing information that so distasteful did Charlemagne find the incident, that he confessed "had he known the intention of the pope, he would not have entered the Church on that day, great festival though it was."

Did Charlemagne Object? The event has stirred considerable controversy. One group of scholars accepts Einhard's statement regarding Charlemagne's displeasure. This they attribute to the fact that Charlemagne was negotiating with the Byzantine Empire over just such a step. The pope's hasty action might endanger not only eastern acceptance of an emperor in the west, but might also disrupt negotiations over the projected marriage of Charlemagne's daughter to the Byzantine emperor. Several scholars argue on the basis of the bitter controversy which developed two hundred and seventy-five years later between pope and German emperor, that Charlemagne feared the pope would use the precedent of the coronation as basis for his claim, not only to crown the emperor, but even to select him. At most they insist the pope contrived this on his own initiative in order to honor the man to whom he owed his office, and whose loyal protection he hoped to insure for the future. A larger group of scholars doubt Einhard's accuracy when he speaks of Charlemagne's irritation. If Charlemagne had actually made the statement Einhard attributes to him, these scholars maintain it must have been in the nature of a modest disclaimer which recipients of high honors are wont to make. These scholars also point to the smoothness with which the coronation ceremony proceeded to raise doubt as to Charlemagne's ignorance of the preparations. They similarly doubt that the pope would have dared to take such a revolutionary step without first assuring himself of Charlemagne's approval. In view of Charlemagne's tremendous prestige on the one hand, in fact, and, on the other, the strong tradition still surviving in the west concerning the sacred and eternal character of the Roman Empire, his coronation may be considered inevitable.

Significance of the Coronation. If Charlemagne anticipated Byzantine hostility to his coronation, he guessed correctly. However in 813 Michael I recognized his title upon Charlemagne's surrender of the lands he had conquered along the northern and eastern coasts of the Adriatic (Istria, Venetia, and Dalmatia). Furthermore, if Charlemagne feared the pope might make a dangerous precedent of his coronation, he sought to reduce that danger by having his son Louis crown himself. Yet these are actually passing reflections. Far weightier considerations attach to Charlemagne's coronation as Roman emperor. That act signalled, for instance, the formal severing of east and west in the political and, to a lesser degree, in the ecclesiastical spheres. With this act, the west unilaterally set up its own Roman Empire, independent of Byzantine sanction. By this act, the Roman pontiff proclaimed the termination of his physical dependence upon the Byzantine state, and, by the same token, his refusal to respect any further attempts at interference from that government. It officially confirmed the mission Pepin had already assumed for the Frankish kingdom, that of defending western Christianity and protecting the papacy. It thus symbolized the wedding of the western church to the Frankish kingdom, the logical sequel to the Donation of Pepin. It also proved a harbinger of the schism of 1054, which was to divide Christendom into eastern and western churches. One may discover a direct link between Augustine's *City of God* which Charlemagne deeply revered, and his coronation as Roman emperor. Without the imperial character, he could not perform, either properly or effectively, the role he must have been convinced God had reserved for him. "For him," says Professor Ganshof, "the imperial dignity magnified and glorified the royal authority."

Charlemagne and the Church

Charlemagne's Concept of his Position. Even in an age when kings generally accepted a positive responsibility for furthering the kingdom of God, Charlemagne's own efforts on behalf of the church must be considered unique. No king before or since appears to have held so lofty a view of his spiritual mission, or to have devoted so much of his time and resources toward accomplishing that mission. His wars were crusades, his enemies the tools of the devil. His government came as close to a theocracy as Europe has ever witnessed. His spiritual authority he insisted superseded that of the pope. In his claims and actual handling of church-state problems, he went considerably beyond the Caesaro-papism of Justinian. Where Justinian sought to bend the pope to his wishes, Charlemagne simply instructed him what to do; where Justinian, or at any rate his successors, worked for religious uniformity in order to strengthen their regimes, Charlemagne employed church and state to promote the cause of Christianity. Charlemagne held himself responsible to no man or to any authority under God. His mission was directly to heaven. As Alcuin, the most eminent scholar in Charlemagne's circle, expressed this view, the king's royal dignity exceeded that of the other two Christian powers, the papacy and the Byzantine empire, since Christ had charged the Frankish king personally with the leadership of a Christian commonwealth.

No Distinction between Church and State. For this reason Charlemagne did not distinguish in practice between his position as head of the Frankish state and as head of Christendom, between his political and his religious responsibilities, between his ecclesiastical and civil officials, or between the punishment of moral and civil offenses. On the occasion of Leo's accession, he admonished him as a father would a son, to be a good pope, and he reminded him that as it was the king's responsibility to govern and defend the church, it was the pope's to pray for its well-being. He appointed or controlled the selection of all important officials, whether bishop, abbot, or count, and he expected these to assist one another in advancing both the material and spiritual welfare of the realm. He felt as ready to correct irregularities among the clergy as to instruct his stewards in the supervision of his estates. Half of his capitularies pertain directly to church matters. Neither Charlemagne, nor his subjects for that matter, considered it at all incongruous for the king to admonish the clergy against drunkenness and immorality, or to issue decrees concerning liturgy and chant, or even to convene church councils. Though no pope in a position to protest, which Leo III was not, could have accepted such pretensions, actually few popes did more than Charlemagne to advance the cause of Christianity in western Europe. It is true that the western European of the ninth century, and this included Charlemagne, was far from being a model Christian. For all his piety and sincere devotion to the cause of the church, Charlemagne apparently considered the commandment which condemned adultery as intended for others. Yet before he died, Charlemagne had given western Europe what it had lacked, namely, a Christian conscience.

Alliance between Church and State. Under Charlemagne the alliance between the western church and the Franks, which dated back to Clovis, was brought to fruition. Charlemagne's father Pepin had nurtured it by protecting the missionaries working among the eastern Germans and by furthering reform within the church. Charlemagne's grandfather, Charles Martel, had earlier served the Frankish church in similar fashion. Boniface, the apostle of the Germans, acknowledged the great debt he owed Martel. He wrote: "I can neither rule the people of the church nor defend priests, deacons, monks, or nuns; nor am I strong enough to suppress the rites of the pagans and the sacrileges of idols in Germany, without the assistance of the Prince of the Franks, without his rule and the fear he instils." Even more could have been written of Charlemagne's contribution. Such solicitude on the part of these Carolingians can be attributed to two motives, neither exclusive of the other: first, their sincere interest in supporting the missionary efforts of the church among the pagan Frisians and Saxons; second, their conviction that unless these Germans accepted the Christian ethic, their subjugation would prove impermanent if not impossible. So hardly had the din of battle died down before Charlemagne sent in his priests and bishops to complete through spiritual persuasion the total assimilation of the fallen enemy. On the one hand he proscribed such pagan practices as the eating of horse flesh, while on the other he imposed the death penalty on those who refused baptism. The stubborn Saxon must have puzzled over the incongruity of warriors ramming the Christian message of love down his throat. Yet Charlemagne's rigorous methods eventually bore fruit, and in time the Saxon nation took its place in the vanguard of Christian Germans pushing eastward against the pagan Slav.

Charlemagne's Government

A Simple Government.   Somewhat surprising, in view of the heavy mark Charlemagne left upon other institutions of the time, was the meager contribution he made to medieval government. That he provided western Europe its most effective rule since Clovis and for several centuries to come must be attributed principally to his immense prestige, to his industry and persistence, and to his great store of common sense, not to innovations. He took the system he had inherited from his father and made it work as it had never worked before or was ever to work afterwards. Charlemagne's administrative system was almost primitive in its simplicity, so elementary, in fact, that only Charlemagne's constant vigilance and encouragement kept it from foundering. In a rather general way the Carolingian state recognized three responsibilities: the advancement of the church, the defense of the empire, and the establishment of law and order. All three obligations Charlemagne discharged in an admirable degree, an accomplishment all the more impressive in view of the crude machinery and institutions with which he had to work. This constitutes his greatest achievement. His greatest failure was the converse of this: he did not devise those improvements or techniques which would have enabled a monarch of lesser ability to rule successfully. In fact, the inherent weakness of his government began to reveal itself in his declining years, and when he died at seventy-two, the Frankish state was also in decline.

Carolingian Finances.   The Carolingian state was a personal affair, and in no place was this more manifest than in its fiscal operations. The revenues which the king might require to administer his kingdom, he must derive from his own resources. Like a man in any other profession or walk of life, the king was expected to "live of his own." It is true that

Charlemagne did collect considerable booty in his war against the Avars. He was also entitled to the bulk of the fines levied in the royal courts, and he might also receive gifts from those noblemen who attended the meeting of the assembly. Still these sources of revenue were at best inconsiderable and irregular. It was from his own estates, and those of Charlemagne were happily extensive, that he drew the bulk of his revenues. Actually the fortunes of the medieval monarch for several centuries to come would rise and fall with the extent of his crown lands and the efficiency with which these were administered. Of this fact Charlemagne was acutely aware, and the most valuable document which time has preserved from his reign is his detailed directive to his stewards concerning the proper management of his estates. (Reading 49) Yet even though we can be certain that Charlemagne realized more from his estates than any of his predecessors or immediate successors, this would not have sufficed except in an age such as his, when the functions of government were so few and when these few were the responsibility of so many. In the ninth century, every able-bodied man was subject to military service for the three summer months, and he brought weapons in keeping with his rank and means. Great lords came with their horsemen, while men too poor to come individually armed pooled their resources and sent one of their number. Every freeman was expected to attend the sessions of the judicial assemblies in his community. Each community maintained its own roads and bridges, or at least, should have. In an age of no inns, royal officials were expected to put up the king and his retinue as he progressed about the realm. Government was a direct and personal charge in those days, from king on down to ordinary citizen.

Charlemagne's Officials. Charlemagne's capital was itinerant. He did spend more time at Aachen than at any other city, probably because of the proximity of the warm baths. But government in Charlemagne's age meant only men, not buildings or cities or even institutions. The officials who made up his court and provided him counsel and administrative assistance included the following: the seneschal, who supervised the crown estates; the chamberlain, who was responsible for financial operations; the butler, who managed the royal cellar; the marshall or constable, who was in charge of the military establishment. The most important courtier was perhaps the chaplain. He was ordinarily a bishop or abbot, and served not only as confessor, but chief consultant as well. He also handled all legal matters and the keeping of records. There was also the assembly, composed of the more influential men of the kingdom, which met traditionally in the spring or early summer. This assembly functioned partly as a council, partly as a means of publicizing such decrees or capitularies as Charlemagne chose to announce. These capitularies were more in the nature of administrative directives than statutes, although they ordinarily applied to the entire empire. Apart from the light these capitularies throw upon Charlemagne's handling of affairs, they demonstrate most strikingly his wide concern with almost every phase of contemporary life, whether it be administrative, military, religious, or cultural.

Counts, Margraves, Missi Dominici.   The chief administrative unit of the empire was the county, of which there were several hundred. Larger counties, called marches, lay along the frontier. The rulers of these provinces, counts and margraves respectively, enjoyed almost unlimited authority over the people within their jurisdictions. They summoned the men to arms in the spring for the summer campaigns, they held general court three times a year for the adjudication of important civil and criminal cases, and they maintained the peace. Because their remoteness and powerful position might tempt them to rebellion, Charlemagne annually sent out two *missi dominici*, that is, "messengers of the lord (king)," to check on their loyalty. The *missi* also investigated the efficiency and justice of their administrations. It was customary for Charlemagne to pair a bishop or abbot and a civil official as *missi dominici*, since they were "to report to him any inequality or injustice . . . and to render justice to all, to the holy churches of God, to the poor, to widows and orphans and to the whole people." Their instructions also included the inspection of monastic communities where they were to make careful inquiry concerning the proper observance of the Rule of St. Benedict. To reduce the danger of corruption and collusion, the *missi* visited a different group of counties each year and always with a different partner. They gathered their information, not from counts and margraves so much as from the people, whom they would summon to general assemblies and there question concerning the administration. The *missi* reveal on the one hand the rudeness of the Frankish government, on the other Charlemagne's empiric approach to the problems of royal administration.

The Carolingian Renaissance

Decline of Letters.   In the opinion of modern writers, the most enduring phase of Charlemagne's work proved to be the stimulation he afforded to the study of letters. To judge the merit of this, the so-called Carolingian Renaissance, it will be necessary to take a look at the history of learning since the decline of Roman civilization. We have noted how Roman cultural life had waned from the third century onward with the decline of political and economic life within the empire. The advent of the German invaders aggravated conditions already unfavorable to the Muses. City life, which had provided a physical and social nourishment for intellectual interests, was gradually replaced by a dulling provincialism and isolation. The intelligentsia, which had approximated the social and political aristocracy in Roman times, had been supplanted by a German nobility which had at best no knowledge of, at worst a contempt for, the more refined things of life. For the masses, the hard reality of life, that of making a living, shut out all other considerations. Even the tradition of learning was gradually forgotten among those whose ancestors had once been educated. To repeat again the lament which Gregory of Tours had voiced in the sixth century: "Alas! for these our days, for the study of letters is perished amongst us."

Decline not Universal. Yet conditions were not equally unpropitious to learning all over western Europe. In several areas of the west, classical civilization had not suffered so grievously as in Gregory's France. An echo of former vigor lived on well into the sixth century, for example, in north Africa and Italy. In distant Ireland a real brilliance glowed until the late eighth century. In France, even after Visigoth and Vandal had passed through the country, a bishop of Auvergne, Apollinaris Sidonius (d. 489), could describe an enclave at Toulouse where the pursuit of letters and scholarly attainments was still possible. We have seen the keen interest of Theodoric, the Ostrogoth, in keeping schools in operation. Unfortunately, much of what he had preserved of the past was swept away during the subsequent wars between the Ostrogoths and Justinian's armies and during the invasions of the semibarbarous Lombards. Fortunate, on the other hand, was the fact that these Lombards were denied the conquest of the major cities of Italy, so that here at least cultural life never ebbed so low as in France.

The Role of the Church. What proved the most vital factor in the preservation of culture was the Christian church. It was the only organization which continued to function after all other institutions in the west had disintegrated and disappeared. The church employed Latin in its liturgy and literature and retained the substance of the classical curriculum in its schools. A sufficient number of churchmen actually delved so deeply into classical literature as to arouse the criticism of their more puritanical contemporaries. For many of the faithful questioned the propriety and value of pagan learning and literature, however classical it might be. So great a scholar as Tertullian (*ca.* 200) could ask: "What has Athens to do with Jerusalem, what concord is there between the Academy and the Church?" Tertullian's position was, fortunately, an extreme one. Most Roman Christians found little incompatibility between their faith and the educational system in which they had been reared. They continued to read Cicero and Caesar, Vergil, Horace, and the lesser poets much as children of all creeds use the same books in our public schools. Even the most conservative churchmen had to admit the necessity of preserving the educational curriculum and the Latin language itself for use in the liturgy and Scriptures. Yet how could this be accomplished outside the province of the classical tradition? So Augustine's position generally prevailed, which was to "study poets and philosophers in order to sharpen the intellect and make it better able to explain the mystery of the Divine Word, thereby depriving the Egyptians of their treasure in order to erect the tabernacle of the Lord."

Loss of Greek Learning.   It was the misfortune of the west, however, that the roots of this tradition had never penetrated so deeply as in the east. It was also the west's misfortune to bear the brunt of the Germanic invasions. Moreover, even that which was salvaged in the west lacked the most substantial elements in the classical tradition, that is, Greek philosophy and science. Because the Roman scholar of the first and second centuries had been able to read Greek, he felt no compulsion to translate the writings of Hellenic philosophers and scientists. The turbulent third century was not conducive to the translation of Greek works or even to the learning of Greek for that matter. By the fourth century most scholars were Christians, few of whom showed much interest in the learned writings of the pagan Greeks or devoted much time and patience to the process of translating them. By the fifth century, great scholars like St. Augustine could not handle Greek with facility. The consequence was that the heart of the classical tradition was gradually lost to western scholarship. It was this fact, as much as the Germanic invasions themselves and the disruptive expansion of Islam, which accounts for the dismal contrast between the brilliance of the Byzantine and Islamic learning which had incorporated Greek philosophy and science, and the barrenness of western scholarship which had not.

Boethius.   The first scholar in the west who had an appreciation of the gravity of the situation and who worked zealously to preserve the old intellectual order was Boethius (d. 524). Thoroughly schooled in the classical tradition, Boethius had a premonition of how superficial western learning must inevitably become if deprived of its Greek foundation. So he set himself the impossible task of translating into Latin "every work of Aristotle . . . and all the dialogues of Plato, and to evoke a certain concord between them." Though he fell far short of ·that goal, he did provide western Europe with translations of two of the logical treatises of Aristotle, together with a commentary on Aristotle's *Categories* by Porphyry. He also prepared studies on most of the liberal arts. Oxford University was still using his treatise on music in the seventeenth century. Boethius is unique among the transmitters of classical learning in that he was the only layman in the group. He was also the only one whose dedication to learning sprang less from the love of God than from love of learning for its own sake. His most famous work, the *Consolation of Philosophy*, which he wrote in prison awaiting execution, contains no reference to Christianity.

Cassiodorus.   Boethius' contemporary, Cassiodorus (d. 580), like him a high official at the court of Theodoric, was more typical of the scholars of the era. His writings scarcely ever stray from the central theme of God. After forty years at the Ostrogothic court, he removed to one of the monasteries in Calabria which he had founded, and devoted his remaining thirty years to spiritual and intellectual pursuits. Cassiodorus' principal contribution to learning was undoubtedly that of introducing monasticism to what proved two of its major functions in the preservation of knowledge: first, the preparation of compilations and studies based on the writings of the past; second, the transcribing of ancient manuscripts in the monastic *scriptorium*. His was probably the first *scriptorium* to be established in the west. "Of all the work that can be done by manual labor," he affirmed, "nothing pleases me so much as that of copyists—if only they will copy correctly!" His own writings were voluminous: theological treatises, commentaries on the Scriptures, many letters, and a history of the Goths, which, however, survives only in Jordanes' unscholarly compendium. The title of his most influential book, *An Introduction To Divine and Human Readings*, reveals its contents. He discusses the proper method of studying the Scriptures, the writings of the fathers, and the seven liberal arts. To this he appended some practical advice on the copying of manuscripts, on textual criticism, and on the organization of a library. For his interest in the learning of the past, Cassiodorus represents the best of his age. In that he restricts himself to commentaries on this learning, to preserving it rather than adding to it, he reveals to what level learning had fallen. That his works were revered as the best available during the next three hundred years, suggests how much farther learning was still to deteriorate. (Reading 55)

Capella, Donatus, Priscian, Orosius, Gregory of Tours. The writings of several less distinguished scholars of this period enjoyed high repute during the book-starved early Middle Ages. Among these was Martianus Capella whose *Marriage of Philology and Mercury* proved the most popular treatment of the seven liberal arts. Donatus and Priscian composed invaluable grammars which helped keep alive the knowledge of Latin. Equally popular though undeservedly so was Orosius' *Seven Books Against the Pagans*. Orosius, a disciple of St. Augustine, owed his great fame in the Middle Ages to the direful tale he told of the calamities of pagan antiquity. An apologist rather than historian, he convinced his readers in far more devastating a manner than his scholarly mentor had done in the *City of God*, that the ancient pagan world had suffered more than its share of catastrophes. Gregory of Tours (d. 594) wrote his *History of the Franks* in less acceptable Latin than Orosius had employed, and his approach to evidence was hardly more critical. Yet where the history of Orosius is possibly the most inferior account of the ancient world that has come down to us, Gregory's is the only one and hence the best to treat of the early Merovingians. So modern historians reverence him and ignore Orosius. While Gregory enjoyed a distinguished career as bishop of Tours, he would be the first to protest any listing of him here with the transmitters of classical learning. On his own admission, and an admission which his writing does not belie, he had found it impossible to acquire an adequate knowledge of Latin grammar because of the decadence of the times. Still the job needed doing and he had assumed that responsibility, since there could not be found "any grammarian sufficiently competent in the art of writing to relate, either in prose or verse, what had happened in the land of the Franks." (Reading 44)

Isidore of Seville. Far-off Spain, which had managed to retain something of the intellectual lustre of earlier centuries, produced the leading light of the early seventh century. This was Isidore, the learned and influential bishop of Seville (d. 636). Isidore had at hand much of the learning of classical Rome, but he applied himself to its assimilation with greater enthusiasm than discrimination. The result could be lugubrious, as it was in the case of much of the scientific lore he preserved. Though his ultimate source was Pliny's *Natural History* (see page 18), he contented himself with a compilation made by a late classical writer who had been more concerned with the bizarre in Pliny than the conventional. Isidore composed treatises in all the fields of learning which interested the medieval mind: history, literature, theology, and science. He is best known for the encyclopedia of knowledge he prepared toward the close of his life. To this he gave the title *Etymologies*, since he claimed to find in the derivations (often absurd) of the words he catalogued, both their meanings and their essence. (Reading 54) The *Etymologies* constituted the principal source of knowledge for the west until the twelfth century, and was second in popularity only to the *Vulgate* itself. While no brief can be held for its scholarship, Isidore's *Etymologies* has at least this virtue, that of revealing the depth to which scholarship had fallen in the west and the uncritical manner in which learning was purveyed and accepted.

Golden Age of Irish Learning. Only in faraway Ireland had the early Middle Age no need to apologize for the decadence of letters. Ireland of the sixth and seventh centuries was truly the land of "saints and scholars." For the central fount of that island's golden age we must go back to St. Patrick and his fellow missionaries, who introduced Ireland to the classical traditions of the western empire before the rough Germans had shattered them. And as good fortune would have it, no Germans ventured so far west until the Vikings plunged the land into darkness in the early ninth century. (See page 262.) For several hundred years, something akin to the learning of the ancient Christian Rome of the fourth century lightened the skies of that distant land. Scores of monasteries, including famous centers of learning at Bangor and Armagh, took root and flourished. All these have long since passed into oblivion. About all that remains as a reminder of a glorious past, gone almost without trace, is the superbly illuminated copy of the Bible known as the Book of Kells. From Ireland, fiercely zealous missionaries carried Christianity and learning to Scotland and northern

Book of Kells

England, even to Iceland and the islands of the northern Atlantic. Along the forbidding west coast of Scotland, Columba (d. 597) founded a famous monastery at Iona. From Iona, hundreds of monks went forth to establish monasteries throughout Scotland and northern England, including the renowned center of learning at Lindisfarne on the North Sea. From Scotland and Britain in turn, restless Irish monks carried their crosses and books to France, thence to Germany, and even northern Italy. Columbanus (d. 615), a disciple of Columba, sought to convert and reform France almost single-handedly. When the Merovingian court exiled him for his outspoken attacks on its debauchery, he made his way back through Germany and Switzerland. Three of medieval Europe's most celebrated monastic centers: Luxeuil in Gaul, St. Gall in Switzerland, and Bobbio in northern Italy where he closed out his career, owe their origins to the zeal of this indefatigable missionary and scholar.

Anglo-Saxon Monks: St. Boniface. Irish monasticism had pretty well spent itself with Columbanus. The future lay with the better organized Benedictine monks who were closer to Rome and who enjoyed papal support. These established a major center of activity in southeastern England, an area which the Irish had left untouched. This enterprise began with Pope Gregory the Great when in 597 A.D. he sent "The servant of God, Augustine, and with him several other monks, who feared the Lord, to preach the word of God to the English nation." Other eminent missionaries and scholars followed. Theodore of Tarsus, the first archbishop of Canterbury (669), staffed the school there with scholars from the continent and therewith laid the foundation of its future intellectual eminence. By the late seventh century, Anglo-Saxon monks were ready to join, and gradually to supersede, Irish monks in the work of converting and educating France and Germany. This fact was unofficially announced in 664, at the synod of Whitby, when Irish churchmen accepted Roman authority in matters of liturgy and discipline. With Whitby the Irish appear to have lost interest in further missionary activity eastward and to have surrendered the field to the Anglo-Saxons. The foremost of these missionaries was St. Boniface (d. 755). Modern Germans still hail him the "Apostle of Germany" because of the effectiveness of his missionary zeal. It has been said of Boniface that no Englishman ever exerted more influence upon Germany. Not only did he personally convert thousands of pagans in the lands east of the Rhine, but he reorganized and reformed the demoralized Christianity of France, established papal supremacy there, and founded bishoprics, monasteries, and nunneries. Among the monasteries he established was Fulda, destined to become the leading center of learning and missionary activity in medieval Germany. Boniface's missionary zeal never let him rest. As an old man, he resigned his post as archbishop of Mainz to work in the land of the Frisians, where he died a martyr at the age of seventy-four. (Reading 45)

The "Venerable" Bede. Boniface has been called the "morning star" of the Carolingian Renaissance although his religious activities almost blot out his interest in books and learning. The monk whom history ranks first among all the scholars of western Europe in Boniface's century was the "Venerable" Bede (d. 735). Bede represents the finest product of the commingling of the learning of Ireland with that from Italy (through Augustine, Theodore of Tarsus, and others). Bede confessed that "It has ever been my delight to learn or teach or write," and for most of his life he devoted himself to these scholarly pursuits in the friendly atmosphere of Jarrow in northeastern England. This monastery was gifted with one of the best libraries in western Europe. Here during a long and active life, Bede proceeded to assimilate and then reproduce the totality of knowledge available in western Europe. He was acquainted with most of the Latin poets, he knew Greek, and he could read Hebrew. Except for a translation of St. John's gospel into Anglo-Saxon, his works are in Latin, and in a Latin which is almost classical. His writings consisted principally of textbooks and commentaries, and were intended for use by monastic students. Especially valuable to his time were his grammatical, scientific, and exegetical works. We are most grateful, however, for his *Ecclesiastical History of the English People*, without which almost the whole of English history from the early fifth century to the eighth would be a blank page. His care in noting the written records he used, what he had gleaned from conversations with older men, and what he had gathered by hearsay, together with his determination to tell the truth, which, as he wrote, "the true rule of history requires," earn for him the title of the "first great modern historian." His most enduring contribution to modern civilization is the practice of reckoning chronology from the birth of Christ. (Reading 46)

Charlemagne's Achievement. In this series of transmitters of classical and patristic learning which extends from Boethius to Bede, there are names of Italian scholars, of Spanish, Irish, and British. The name of but one native of France (Gallo-Roman) appears, that of Gregory of Tours, and he is in the list more by chronological courtesy than by scholarly merit. His own intellectual deficiencies testify to the low level of French letters, to the fact that the Frankish kingdom was the darkest intellectually in western Europe. It is partly this dismal backdrop which lends the so-called Carolingian Renaissance much of its brilliance. In a more cultured age or country, Charlemagne's efforts in the cause of learning would have won him appreciably less renown. In the France of his day they appeared so spectacular that his patronage of the arts has ever remained his most abiding claim to fame. To accomplish what he set out to do for letters and learning, Charlemagne was obliged to import scholars into his kingdom. His ability to do this; the success of these scholars and his success in elevating French scholarship to a position comparable with that of other lands of western Europe; the generations of scholars who were the direct and indirect products of his renaissance and who assumed and retained the intellectual leadership of western Europe for the duration of the Middle Ages—these constitute Charlemagne's achievement in the field of scholarship and learning.

Foreign Scholars at Aachen. The principal instrument of Charlemagne's renaissance was the palace school at Aachen. His father Pepin had anticipated him in inviting scholars to be his guests, but Charlemagne far outdid him in the impressive circle he was able to gather at his palace. From England he enticed its finest scholar, Alcuin, at the time director of the cathedral school at York. For fifteen years Alcuin graced Aachen with his presence, at which time Charlemagne finally permitted him to retire to Tours as its abbot. Alcuin produced a plethora of studies on the liberal arts and commentaries on the Scriptures. Yet it was not Alcuin's scholarship which constituted his major contribution to learning. It was rather the enthusiasm for education with which Alcuin was able to fire his students, and which bore vigorous fruit in the generations to come. From Spain came the poet Theodulf, whose magnificent processional *Gloria, Laus et Honor* (Glory, Laud, and Honor) can still be heard sung in many of the churches of Christendom. From Ireland came Dungal. Italy sent two grammarians, Peter of Pisa and Paulinus of Aquileia, and the chronicler Paul the Deacon. Paul the Deacon spent several years at Aachen before retiring to Monte Cassino where he wrote his valuable, though not completely trustworthy, *History of the Lombards.* The leading Frank at Aachen was Einhard, who came there in search of an education. His *Life of Charlemagne* remains one of the most readable of all the biographies of illustrious men. That Einhard chose Suetonius for his model serves to demonstrate the classical inspiration behind so much of the scholarly effort put forth at Charlemagne's palace school. (Reading 47)

Charlemagne's Education. Charlemagne liked nothing better than to mingle with the scholars at Aachen. If his erudition was modest, his enthusiasm was enormous. Einhard provides us an indelible picture of his intellectual curiosity.

He was ready and fluent in speaking, and able to express himself with great clearness. He did not confine himself to his native tongue, but took pains to learn foreign languages, acquiring such knowledge of Latin that he could make an address in that language as well as in his own. Greek he could better understand than speak. Indeed, he was so polished in speech that he might have passed for a learned man.

He was an ardent admirer of the liberal arts, and greatly revered their professors, whom he promoted to high honors. In order to learn grammar, he attended the lectures of the aged Peter of Pisa, a deacon; and for other branches he chose as his preceptor Albinus, otherwise called Alcuin . . . the most learned man of the day, with whom the king spent much time in learning rhetoric and logic, and more especially astronomy. He learned the art of determining the dates upon which the movable festivals of the Church fall, and with deep thought and skill most carefully calculated the courses of the planets.

Charles also tried to learn to write, and used to keep his tablets and writing book under the pillow of his couch, that when he had leisure he might practice his hand in forming letters; but he made little progress in this task, too long deferred and begun too late in life.

Charlemagne's Other Efforts in the Interest of Education. If Charlemagne failed to acquire a legible hand in an age when only professional clerks could write, that can be accounted no great loss to posterity. But western Europe would have lost heavily had it not been for his efforts in the cause of learning. In addition to establishing Aachen as a center of learning, he addressed a series of capitularies on the subject of education to his bishops and abbots, the elementary and high school principals of the age. He instructed those who had schools to improve them, those who were without schools to establish them. He directed these prelates not to restrict their schools exclusively to priests and novices, but to make them available to the boys of the neighborhood. "Let there be reading schools for children," he announced in a capitulary of 789. "In every monastery or bishop's seat let them learn psalms, notes, singing, computus, grammar. Let every monastery and every abbey have its school, where boys may be taught the psalms . . . singing, arithmetic, and grammar; and let the books that are given them be free of faults, and let care be taken that the boys do not spoil them either when reading or writing." Charlemagne encouraged his bishops and abbots to build up their libraries; to emend the corrupt manuscripts in their possession and to make copies of these; to prepare grammars; even to improve upon the near-illegible script they had inherited from Merovingian times. Charlemagne provided the revival of learning a final boost by showing his favor to scholars. He rewarded Alcuin with an abbey, to Theodulf he gave a bishopric. (Reading 50)

Results of Charlemagne's Efforts. Though Charlemagne is said to have ordered the old Germanic tales written down, the salient facet of the Carolingian Renaissance for modern scholars was its humanistic interest. Thanks to Charlemagne's encouragement and the efforts of contemporary scribes, most classical manuscripts which were available in the west in his day were carefully preserved and copied. It is no accident that the great bulk of ancient and early medieval manuscripts extant today either date from the Carolingian period or are copies of manuscripts copied in Carolingian *scriptoria*. Abbot Angilbert of St. Riquier, who owed his appointment to Charlemagne, is said to have kept three hundred monks engaged in reproducing manuscripts. An important by-product of the Carolingian Renaissance was the restoration to vulgar Latin of many elements which had been lost since the classical period. (See page 599.) Most of the scholars at Aachen tried their hand at classical poetry, therewith initiating a distinguished tradition that carried on down (sometimes haltingly) through Petrarch to the humanists of the fifteenth and sixteenth centuries. The Carolingian revival served as a powerful stimulus to the intellectual life of such monasteries as Corbie, St. Gall, Reichenau, Fulda, and Regensburg. It was in monastic centers such as these where scholarship remained alive after Charlemagne had died and when barbarous Vikings and Magyars (see page 264), seemed determined to have western civilization die with him. As Professor Dawson writes: "It is impossible to exaggerate the importance of the Carolingian abbey in this history of early mediaeval civilization. Here was an institution which was based on a purely agrarian economy and yet embodied the highest spiritual and intellectual culture of the age. The great abbeys, such as St. Gall and Reichenau, Fulda and Corbie, were not only the intellectual and religious leaders of Europe, but also the chief centres of material culture and of artistic and industrial activity. In them there was developed the traditions of learning and literature, art and architecture, music and liturgy, painting and calligraphy, which were the foundations of mediaeval culture."*

Maurus and Strabo. The Carolingian Renaissance produced its richest fruit a generation after Charlemagne's death. Foremost among the new scholars was Hrabanus Maurus (d. 856), a pupil of Alcuin, who helped make Fulda the leading intellectual center of medieval Germany. Because of his intense interest in learning, his tremendous energy, his numerous essays on education and the liberal arts, and his exhaustive commentaries on the Scriptures, he has been called the "first teacher of Germany." Hrabanus' pupil, Walafrid Strabo, is honored as the brightest literary light of the ninth century. In addition to hymns, he composed poems on lighter themes such as the *Hortulus* (little garden) which provides us a glimpse of the medieval monk enjoying the beauties of nature in the quiet of monastic surroundings. Strabo's most important work was an interpretative study of the Bible, which was recognized as the standard reference of its kind until early modern times. This interest of the Carolingian scholars in the Scriptures must be emphasized. Despite the classical interests of many of the scholars of the ninth century, their prime concern was always the Bible. Such was also Charlemagne's motive in encouraging the study of grammar in the schools of his empire, namely, to insure an accurate understanding of the Scriptures and the writings of the fathers.

The Disintegration of the Carolingian Empire

Inherent Weakness of the State. When death removed Charlemagne's powerful hand, his empire rapidly melted away. It had been largely his

* *The Making of Europe*, pp. 231-232.

creation, and only his vigorous personality had kept it an empire. These were difficult years for any government. There was no nationalism to bind the people of a state together and enlist their common sympathies. No systems of transportation or communications existed which might have counteracted political and economic localism. Economic resources necessary to support a strong government were either nonexistent or inaccessible. Ever at hand was a proud, rapacious landed aristocracy eager to exploit the first show of weakness on the part of the ruler in order to advance its own independence. After Charlemagne's death, the use of the *missi dominici* lapsed. Without a feared monarch able to deal summarily with delinquent or disloyal counts, the device became an empty gesture. Though Charlemagne might have dismissed counts and denied their sons the succession, he usually did not, and his successors dared not.

Louis the Pious and his Sons. And they dared not because they were not of the stuff of Charlemagne. Charlemagne's son, Louis, earned the title, "the Pious," and he probably deserved it. His private morals, at any rate, were a marked improvement over those of his father. Yet the men Louis had to deal with respected force, not piety. Then to aggravate his own difficulties, Louis decided in 817 to associate his eldest son, Lothair, with him as co-emperor and to assign Aquitaine to Pepin and Bavaria to Louis, his younger sons. Up to this time the Carolingian kingdom had happily escaped the evil working of the Salic principle of succession. Now Louis was precipitating the issue long before it became necessary. As might be expected, Louis' first division pleased only Lothair. The birth of another son, Charles, to his second wife, further complicated Louis' problem. Now there were four sons to satisfy. The result was almost continuous warfare among Louis and his sons with only the aristocracy the victors. The nobles sold their services to the highest bidder, and the usual price was greater autonomy and crown lands. Pepin died in 838, Louis in 840, but the wars went on. Lothair's momentary ascendancy in 842 drew Louis and Charles together and at Strasbourg they formalized their alliance with the famous "Strasbourg Oaths." Louis stood before the French-speaking retainers of Charles and swore a holy oath to be his ally, while Charles swore his in a language which Louis' German followers could understand. The oaths have no political significance although philologists treasure them as among the oldest specimens of Old French and Old German.

Treaty of Verdun. Finally in 843, the Frankish bishops were able to persuade the three brothers to accept a settlement known in history as the Treaty of Verdun. According to this agreement, Louis received Saxony, Franconia, Swabia, and Bavaria. These approximated all the lands east of the Rhine with the exception of Frisia (Low Countries), which went to Lothair. To the latter also went the western Rhinelands, Alsace, Burgundy, Provence, and central and northern Italy. The areas to the west were assigned to Charles (the Bald). The manner in which the sons reached this settlement is significant. They simply divided into three portions all the crown lands and ecclesiastical properties which owed payments to the king. The result was particularly unfortunate in the case of Lothair. His portion consisted of a narrow strip of territory some 1000 miles in length, which extended all the way from the North Sea down to southern Italy. Although his share included both Rome and Aachen, all the laws of geography, economics, and nationality protested against this political monstrosity. A more disastrous consequence of the partition at Verdun and one which affected all three kings alike, was the sharp reduction in individual resources with which each might carry on effective government. The Treaty of Verdun possesses a very real historical interest. It marks the formal birth of France and Germany, and of the debatable territories in between, neither wholly French or German, over which the two nations have so frequently quarrelled.

The Last Carolingians. As might be expected, Lothair's country was the first to crumble. Within a few years of his death, the greater portion had fallen to the two other brothers. Shortly after the deaths of Louis and Charles (877), the former empire of Charlemagne tended to break up into dozens of smaller states, with the Carolingian successors exercising hardly more than nominal control over the areas beyond their immediate reach.

These successors were a most undistinguished lot. When the times called for men with titles of "the Valiant" and "the Cruel," we find instead such kings as Charles the Fat and Charles the Simple. The last Carolingian to reign (not rule) in Germany died in 911, while the final representative of the illustrious dynasty in France, Louis V (the Sluggard), ended his inglorious career in 987.

The Coming of the Northmen. While the factors noted above had brought the Carolingian state far on its way toward dismemberment, what hastened that process immeasurably were the invasions of the Vikings from the north and west, of the Saracens from the south, and of the Magyars from the east. The most numerous and destructive of the invaders were the Vikings. So little did Europeans know of them, that they simply called them the Northmen (Norsemen, Normans) or Vikings (men of the fiords). Charlemagne had already been obliged to erect defences against them along the northern coasts of Gaul and Germany, and the chronicler relates how as an old man he had wept bitterly at the thought of all the woe his people would have to suffer at their hands, when he learned that they were seen as far south as his Mediterranean port of Narbonne. Historians can only guess at the motives which impelled the Northmen to leave their unproductive homelands in such numbers in the ninth century. One factor may have been over-population, another the efforts of stronger jarls to extend their domains, as the Norwegian Harold the Fairhaired had done in 872. Such efforts caused rival jarls and their followers to seek their fortunes elsewhere, and to plunder lands of whose existence they had earlier learned as traders. The first desultory raids came as early as 787 in the case of the British Isles. By the second quarter of the ninth century, these raids had swelled to a veritable flood, and all the coastal regions of western Europe were suffering the evils of destructive invasions. (Reading 52)

The Savagery of the Northmen. What little is known of the civilization of these Scandinavians suggests close affinity with the Germans of the fourth century. But they were infinitely more savage and destructive. The names of their leaders bespeak their ferocious character: Erik Blood-Ax, Harold Bluetooth, Thorkill the Skullsplitter. These Vikings had never known the tempering influence of more civilized neighbors and they came as plunderers rather than as settlers. Their ruthless pillaging from across the sea resembled most that of the fierce Saxons who had harassed the eastern shores of England in the late fourth century. Drawing upon the sea for fish, for trade, and for loot, these Northmen developed into the hardiest and most fearsome mariners the world has ever produced. In their open boats, sixty to eighty feet long, which carried from twenty to forty warriors, they scoured the coasts and rivers of western Europe and Russia, the shores of the Caspian, Mediterranean, and Black Sea, and even ventured across the wild Atlantic to North America. The widely scattered graves of hundreds of Scandinavian jarls reveal how ubiquitous and profitable was their plundering. Traders at first, the European chroniclers hardly noticed them until they had turned raiders, at which profession they had no equals. Their shallow draft boats would carry them far up the rivers of Germany and France. After pillaging the communities along the shores, they would round up horses and roam the countryside, a trail of rapine and desolation marking their terrible progress. If dangerous opposition finally developed, they simply took to their boats and were off to areas which were unaware of their proximity. Monasteries were a favorite target of their raids because of their relative helplessness and wealth—and village communities too; and what these savages could not carry off, they destroyed or slaughtered. Almost all of western Europe felt their scourge, and almost every town in France was burned to the ground. Cities such as Seville, Bordeaux, Tours, Orleans, Paris, Utrecht, and Bremen, were sacked on one or more occasions. At first the Northmen came only in the summer. About the middle of the ninth century, they began to operate from permanent bases on islands in the mouths of larger rivers, from which they gradually expanded to carve out new homelands for themselves. (Reading 51)

Their Raids and Settlements. The Swedes, because of their interior location, penetrated the south shore of the Baltic. Thence they moved into Russia to which they gave their name (Byzantine writers referred to them as Russ), and down the rivers of that vast country to the Black and Caspian Seas. The more numerous but badly disorganized Slavs could offer them no resistance. These Swedes proved the least ferocious of the Scandinavians, and from the beginning appeared as much bent on trade as on plunder. Under their leader Ruric, they first established themselves at Novgorod (962), thence moved southward on the Dnieper to Kiev. After several futile attempts to take Constantinople, they had finally to content themselves with a highly lucrative trade with the Byzantine Empire. The Byzantine emperors meantime had developed a deep respect for their prowess, and for over a hundred years recruited the famous Varangian Guard from among the tall and powerfully built Swedes. The Danes and Norwegians harassed the British Isles, Germany, and France. Lindisfarne and Jarrow were among the multitude of smoking monastic centers they left in their wake. All England would have fallen to them but for the prowess of Alfred, who managed to confine them to the Danelaw (roughly the northeastern half of England). A hundred years later, however, they did take over all England under Cnut. (See page 443.) From the foothold the Northmen established in Frisia they were eventually dislodged, but under Rollo in 911, they secured the permanent cession of Normandy. (Reading 77) Ireland suffered its worst raids in the early ninth century, and soon Danish settlements began to appear at Dublin, Cork, and Limerick. The Danish kingdom at Dublin survived until 1014. Northmen occupied Iceland in 874. From there they sailed westward to Greenland, and under Leif Ericsson to Vinland on the North American continent (*ca.* 1000). For all their tremendous energies and destructiveness, they proved extraordinarily assimilable. Only a few place names attest to their presence in northeastern England, and not one word attests to their presence in the dialect spoken in Normandy.

The Moslems.　Southern France and Italy suffered little from the Northmen, but a great deal from the Moslems. These came from Tunis especially, but also from Spain and far-off Crete. In a renewal of Mohammedan expansion in the western Mediterranean (*ca.* 825), the Moslems attacked Christian shipping and Christian communities all along the northern shores of the Mediterranean. Sicily was overrun and conquered, Marseilles was plundered, the suburbs of Rome were sacked, and St. Peter's Outside the Walls was left a burning ruin. Moslem footholds gradually appeared on the continent, notably along the southern coast of France and above Naples. From these strongholds they directed pillaging expeditions into the surrounding areas, the famous Benedictine monastery at Monte Cassino suffering destruction in 884. Moslem raids carried across most of Italy and as far north as southern Germany. From a peak which guarded St. Bernard Pass, they preyed upon travelers and merchants, their depredations earning that height the name Teufelsberg or Devil's Mountain. Had it not been for internal rivalries, there is no telling what calamitous destruction southern Europe might have suffered. Succour appeared from an unexpected quarter, from Constantinople and from Byzantine possessions in southern Italy. By the close of the ninth century, the Moslems had been forced out of Italy, although they were not entirely dislodged from Sicily until the eleventh.

The Magyars.　About the time Moslem raids were dwindling in force and frequency, a new menace appeared from the east in the person of the terrifying Magyar. In fact, along the banks of placid Lake Geneva, Moslem and Magyar clashed over the right of pillaging the helpless countryside. The Magyars were related to the earlier Huns, whence the name Hungarian by which their descendants are known today. These descendants prefer the name Magyar, however, which means men. Toward the end of the ninth century, these Magyars had made their way into the plains of Hungary, whence powerful chargers carried them and their bows and arrows on devastating raids as far west as Spain. Northern Italy suffered severely, as did the Rhine country as far as Flanders. We shall later note their eventual defeat and absorption into the family of Christian nations of western Europe. Now it will suffice to announce the collapse of the organized states of the Carolingians at the hands of Northmen, Moslems, and Magyars, and the opening of the feudal era.

READINGS

No. 44. The Conversion of Clovis

(Gregory of Tour's *History of the Franks*. Migne, *Patrologia Latina*, **LXXI**, 1849. Translation.)

The Conversion of Clovis (pp. 225-227)

The queen [Clotilda] never ceased her efforts to persuade him (Clovis) to acknowledge the true God and abandon his idols. But in no way could he be led to the faith until the time he made war on the Alamans, when necessity forced him to recognize what his heart had up to that time denied. For when the two armies clashed, a terrible slaughter ensued and the army of Clovis was on the point of being completely destroyed. When Clovis saw this, he lifted his eyes to heaven, his heart being touched, and with his eyes filled with tears, he spoke: "Jesus Christ, Clotilda has assured me that you are the son of the living God, and that you give aid to the needy and bestow victory upon those who hope in you. I ask you humbly for your mighty help. If you grant me now the victory over my enemies, and I thus experience that power which the people who honor your name claim to have proved, I will believe in you and have myself baptized in your name. For I have appealed to my gods, yet, as I see, they have forsaken me. I conclude, therefore, that they are without power since they do not come to the aid of those who serve them. On you I now call, and I desire to believe in you. Only first snatch me from out the hands of my adversaries." And as he was yet saying this, the Alamans turned their backs and began to flee. When they saw their king slain, they surrendered to Clovis, saying, "We beseech you, do not permit more of our people to be destroyed, for we are now your men." He therefore put an end to the battle and having brought the people under his authority, returned home in peace. To the queen, however, he reported how he had called on the name of Christ and how he had thus won the battle. This happened in the fifteenth year of his reign.

Whereupon the queen secretly summoned the bishop of Reims, the holy Remigius, and instructed him to teach the word of salvation to the king. The bishop had the king come to him in secret and then began to importune him to accept the true God, the creator of heaven and earth, and to turn away from the idols who could help neither him nor anyone else. But he answered: "Gladly would I hearken to you, holy father, but one thing still makes me hesitate, and that is that the people who follow me will not permit me to foresake their gods. But I will go and speak to them according to your word." As he was approaching his people, they all called out to him at the same time, even before he had opened his mouth, since the divine power had preceded him: "We are abandoning our mortal gods, gracious king, and are prepared to accept the immortal God whom Remigius preaches." This was reported to the bishop who with great joy gave orders to prepare the baptismal font. The streets were now decorated with colored coverings, the churches adorned with white hangings, the baptismal font prepared, scented things scattered about, sweet-smelling candles burned brightly, and the entire temple around the baptismal font was filled with a heavenly fragrance. Indeed such graces did God bestow upon those who were present, that they felt they were transported into the fragrances of paradise. First the king asked the bishop to be baptized. Then he stepped forward like a second Constantine to the baptismal font to be washed clean of the old leprosy and to purge himself with fresh water of the foul stains which he had carried from his youth. As he approached to be baptized, the saint of God addressed him in these eloquent words: "Meekly bow thy head, Sicamber, honor what thou hast persecuted, persecute what thou has honored." . . . Whereupon the king confessed God Almighty as the Trinity and was baptized in the name of the Father, of the Son, and of the Holy Spirit, and was anointed with the holy oil with the sign of the cross of Christ. Of his followers more than three thousand were baptized.

The Death of Sigibert and His Son (pp. 237-238)

While Clovis was staying at Paris, he sent secretly to the son of Sigibert, saying: "See your father is old, weak of foot and lame. If he were to die, you would of right inherit both his realm and our friendship." Thus was the son seduced by ambition and he began to plot to kill his father. When Sigibert left Cologne and crossed the Rhine in order to walk about in the forest of Buchau, while he was sleeping in his tent at noon, his son had assassins attack him and kill him so that he might have the kingdom for himself. But God is just, and the son himself fell into the grave that he had shamefully prepared for his father. He sent messengers immediately to King Clovis who informed him of the death of his father. They reported: "My father is dead, and his kingdom and treasure are mine. Send several of your people to me, and I shall willingly send you what you may like of the treasure of my father." But he [Clovis] replied: "I thank you for your good will. When my people come to you, I ask you to show them everything, but keep it all for yourself." And when they came, he opened the treasure of his father for them to see. As they were looking at this and that, he said; "In this chest my father used to keep his pieces of gold." "Stick your hand down to the bottom," they told him, "so that you can show us everything." He did this and as he was bending down, one of them raised his axe and clove him through the skull. Thus did the same fate befall him as that he had wickedly prepared for his father.

When Clovis learned that Sigibert had been slain and his son as well, he came to the place and called the people together. "Hear ye," he said to them, "what has happened. While I was sailing on the Scheldt, Choloderic, the son of my cousin, was plotting to seize the realm of his father, and convinced him that I wanted him slain. As his father, therefore, was fleeing through the woods of Buchau, he sent murderers after him who killed him. After this he was himself killed, by someone unknown to me, as he was showing his father's treasure. In all this am I wholly without guilt, for the blood of my kindred could I not have shed and infamous would have been the act had I done it. But now that it has happened this way, I give you the following advice: If it pleases you, come into my kingdom and live in security under my protection." At these words they shouted a cry of joy, clashed their shields, raised him up on a shield, and acclaimed him their king. So did Clovis secure the kingdom of Sigibert together with his treasure, while his subjects accepted his dominion. But God day by day humbled his enemies before him and enlarged his kingdom, because he walked before Him with an upright heart and did that which was pleasing in His sight.

No. 45. How Boniface destroyed the oak of Thor

(From Willibald's *Life of Boniface*. Robinson's *Readings*, p. 106.)

Many of the people of Hesse were converted [by Boniface] to the Catholic faith and confirmed by the grace of the spirit: and they received the laying on of hands. But some there were, not yet strong of soul, who refused to accept wholly the teachings of the true faith. Some men sacrificed secretly, some even openly, to trees and springs. Some secretly practiced divining, soothsaying, and incantations, and some openly. But others, who were of sounder mind, cast aside all heathen profanation and did none of these things; and it was with the advice and consent of these men that Boniface sought to fell a certain tree of great size, at Geismar, and called, in the ancient speech of the region, the oak of Jove [i.e. Thor].

The man of God was surrounded by the servants of God. When he would cut down the tree, behold a great throng of pagans who were there cursed him bitterly among themselves because he was the enemy of their gods. And when he had cut into the trunk a little way, a breeze sent by God stirred overhead, and suddenly the branching top of the tree was broken off, and the oak in all its huge bulk fell to the ground. And it was broken into four parts, as if by the divine will, so that the trunk was divided into four huge sections without any effort of the brethren who stood by. When the pagans who had cursed did see this, they left off cursing and, believing, blessed God. Then the most holy priest took counsel with the brethren: and he built from the wood of the tree an oratory, and dedicated it to the holy apostle Peter.

No. 46. Bede's *History*

(The Venerable Bede's *Ecclesiastical History of England*, tr. J. A. Giles. London, 1890.)

Book I. Preface

To the most glorious king Ceolwulph, Bede, the servant of Christ and Priest.

I formerly, at your request, most readily transmitted to you the Ecclesiastical History of the English Nation, which I had newly published, for you to read, and give it your approbation; and I now send it again to be transcribed, and more fully considered at your leisure. And I cannot but commend the sincerity and zeal, with which you not only diligently give ear to hear the words of the Holy Scripture, but also industriously take care to become acquainted with the actions and sayings of former men of renown, especially of our own nation. For if history relates good things of good men, the attentive hearer is excited to imitate that which is good; or if it mentions evil things of wicked persons, nevertheless the religious and pious hearer or reader, shunning that which is hurtful and perverse, is the more earnestly excited to perform those things which he knows to be good, and worthy of God. Of which you also being deeply sensible, are desirous that the said history should be more fully made familiar to yourself, and to those over whom the Divine Authority has appointed you governor, from your great regard to their general welfare. But to the end that I may remove all occasion of doubting what I have written, both from yourself and other readers or hearers of this history, I will take care briefly to intimate from what authors I chiefly learned the same.

My principal authority and aid in this work was the learned and reverend Abbot Albinus; who, educated in the Church of Canterbury by those venerable and learned men, Archbishop Theodore of blessed memory, and the Abbott Adrian, transmitted to me by Nothelm, the pious priest of the Church of London, either in writing, or by word of mouth of the same Nothelm, all that he thought worthy of memory, that had been done in the province of Kent, or the adjacent parts, by the disciples of the blessed Pope Gregory, as he had learned the same either from written records, or the traditions of his ancestors. The same Nothelm, afterwards going to Rome, having, with leave of the present Pope Gregory [III], searched into the archives of the holy Roman Church, found there some epistles of the blessed Pope Gregory, and other popes; and returning home, by the advice of the aforesaid most reverend father Albinus, brought them to me, to be inserted in my history. Thus, from the beginning of this volume to the time when the English nation received the faith of Christ, have we collected the writings of our predecessors, and from them gathered matter for our history; but from that time till the present, what was transacted in the Church of Canterbury, by the disciples of St. Gregory or their successors, and under what kings the same happened, has been conveyed to us by Nothelm through the industry of the aforesaid Abbot Albinus. They also partly informed me by what bishops and under what kings the provinces of the East and West Saxons, as also of the East Angles, and of the Northumbrians, received the faith of Christ. In short I was chiefly encouraged to undertake this work by the persuasions of the same Albinus. In like manner, Daniel, the most reverend Bishop of the West Saxons, who is still living, communicated to me in writing some things relating to the Ecclesiastical History of that province, and the next adjoining to it of the South Saxons, as also of the Isle of Wight. But how, by the pious ministry of Cedd and Ceadda, the province of the Mercians was brought to the faith of Christ, which they knew not before, and how that of the East Saxons recovered the same, after having expelled it, and how those fathers lived and died, we learned from the brethren of the monastery, which was built by them and is called Lastingham. What ecclesiastical transactions took place in the province of the East Angles, was partly made known to us from the writings and tradition of our ancestors, and partly by relation of the most reverend Abbot Esius. What was done towards promoting the faith, and what was the sacerdotal succession in the province of Lindsey, we had either from the letters of the most reverend prelate Cunebert, or by word of mouth from other persons of good credit. But what was done in the Church throughout the province of the Northumbrians, from the time when they received the faith of Christ till this present, I received not from any particular author, but by the faithful testimony of innumerable witnesses, who might know or remember the same; besides what I had of my own knowledge. Wherein it is to be observed, that what I have written concerning our most holy father, Bishop Cuthbert, either in this volume, or in my treatise on his life and actions, I partly took and faithfully copied from what I found written of him by the brethren of the Church of Lindisfarne; but at the same time took care to add such things as I could myself have knowledge of by the faithful testimony of such as knew him. And I humbly entreat the reader, that if he shall in this that we have written find anything not delivered according to the truth, he will not impute the same to me, who, as the true rule of history requires, have laboured sincerely to commit to writing such things as I could gather from common report, for the instruction of posterity.

Bk. II. Ch. XIII. The Conversion of Northumbria

The king [Edwin of Northumbria whom Bishop Paulinus had exhorted to become a Christian], hearing these words, answered, that he was both willing and bound to receive the faith which he taught; but that he would confer about it with his principal friends and counsellors, to the end that if they also were of his opinion, they might all together be cleansed in Christ the Fountain of Life. Paulinus consenting, the king did as he said; for, holding a council with the wise men, he asked of every one in particular what he thought of the new doctrine, and the new worship that was preached? To which the chief of his own priests, Coifi, immediately answered, "O King, consider what this is which is now preached to us; for I verily declare to you, that the religion which we have hitherto professed has, as far as I can learn, no virtue in it. For none of your people has applied himself more diligently to the worship of our gods than I; and yet there are many who receive greater favours from you, and are more preferred than I, and are more prosperous in all their undertakings. Now if the gods were good for anything, they would rather forward me who have been more careful to serve them. It remains, therefore, that if upon examination you find those new doctrines, which are now preached to us, better and more efficacious, we immediately receive them without any delay."

Another of the king's chief men, approving of his words and exhortations, presently added: "The present life of man, O king, seems to me, in comparison of that time which is unknown to us, like to the swift flight of a sparrow through the room wherein you sit at supper in winter, with your commanders and ministers, and a good fire in the midst, whilst the storms of rain and snow prevail abroad; the sparrow, I say, flying in at one door, and immediately out at another, whilst he is within, is safe from the wintry storm; but after a short space of fair weather, he immediately vanishes out of your sight, into the dark winter from which he had emerged. So this life of man appears for a short space, but of what went before, or what is to follow, we are utterly ignorant. If, therefore, this new doctrine contains something more certain, it seems justly to deserve to be followed." The other elders and king's counsellors, by Divine inspiration, spoke to the same effect.

But Coifi added, that he wished more attentively to hear Paulinus discourse concerning the God whom he preached; which he having by the king's command performed, Coifi, hearing his words, cried out, "I have long since been sensible that there was nothing in that which we worshipped; because the more diligently I sought after truth in that worship, the less I found it. But now I freely confess, that such truth evidently appears in this preaching as can confer on us the gifts of life, of salvation, and of eternal happiness. For which reason I advise, O king, that we instantly abjure and set fire to those temples and altars which we have consecrated without reaping any benefit from them." In short, the king publicly gave his license to Paulinus to preach the Gospel, and renouncing idolatry, declared that he received the faith of Christ: and when he inquired of the high priest who should first profane the altars and temples of their idols, with the enclosures that were about them, he answered, "I; for who can more properly than myself destroy those things which I worshipped through ignorance, for an example to all others, through the wisdom which has been given me by the true God?" Then immediately, in contempt of his former superstitions, he desired the king to furnish him with arms and a stallion; and mounting the same, he set out to destroy the idols; for it was not lawful before for the high priest either to carry arms, or to ride on any but a mare. Having, therefore, girt a sword about him, with a spear in his hand, he mounted the king's stallion and proceeded to the idols. The multitude, beholding it, concluded he was distracted; but he lost no time, for as soon as he drew near the temple he profaned the same, casting into it the spear which he held; and rejoicing in the knowledge of the worship of the true God, he commanded his companions to destroy the temple, with all its enclosures, by fire.

No. 47. Weakness of the later Merovingian kings

(From Einhard's *Life of the Emperor Charles*. Robinson's *Readings*, pp. 120-121.)

The Franks in olden times were wont to choose their kings from the family of the Merovingians. This royal line is considered to have come to an end in the person of Childeric III, who was deposed from the throne by command of Stephen, the Roman pontiff; his long hair was cut off and he was thrust into a monastery. Although the line of the Merovingians actually ended with Childeric, it had nevertheless for some time previously been so utterly wanting in power that it had displayed no mark of royalty except the empty kingly title. All the resources and power of the kingdom had passed into the control of the prefects of the palace, who were called the "mayors of the palace," and who employed the supreme authority. Nothing was left to the king. He had to content himself with his royal title, his flowing locks, and long beard. Seated in a chair of state, he was wont to display an appearance of power by receiving foreign ambassadors on their arrival, and, on their departure, giving them, as if on his own authority, those answers which he had been taught or commanded to give.

Thus, except for his empty title, and an uncertain allowance for his subsistence, which the prefect of the palace used to furnish at his pleasure, there was nothing that the king could call his own, unless it were the income from a single farm, and that a very small one, where he made his home, and where such servants as were needful to wait on him constituted his scanty household. When he went anywhere he traveled in a wagon drawn by a yoke of oxen, with a rustic oxherd for charioteer. In this manner he proceeded to the palace, and to the public assemblies of the people held every year for the dispatch of the business of the kingdom, and he returned home again in the same sort of state. The administration of the kingdom, and every matter which had to be undertaken and carried through, both at home and abroad, was managed by the mayor of the palace.

No. 48. The conquest of the Saxons

(From Einhard's *Annals*. Robinson's *Readings*, pp. 129-131.)

At the beginning of the year [782], when supplies were plentiful and the army could be led into the field, the king decided to go into Saxony and to hold there a general assembly, as he was used to do every year in Francia. He crossed the Rhine at Cologne, and with the whole Frankish army came to the source of the Lippe, where he made a camp and remained for many days. He there heard and dismissed the ambassadors sent by Sigfried, king of the Danes, and those who had come from Caganus and Juggurus, chiefs of the Huns, to seek peace.

When the Assembly was dissolved, and he had betaken himself across the Rhine into Gallia, Widukind, who had fled to the Northmen, returned to his fatherland, and with vain hopes aroused the Saxons to rebellion. In the meantime it was reported to the king that the Sorabi Slavs, who inhabit the region between the Elbe and the Saale, had invaded the lands of the Thuringians and Saxons, their neighbors, on a plundering expedition and had sacked and burned several places. He immediately summoned his three ministers—Adalgis, his chamberlain; Geilo, his constable; and Woradus, the head of the palace—ordered that they should take with them East Franks and Saxons and chastise forthwith the audacity of the unruly Slavs.

When the leaders of this force learned, upon entering the Saxon territory, that the Saxons, by Widukind's advice, were about to wage war on the Franks, they abandoned the campaign against the Slavs, and with the forces of the East Franks pushed forward to the place where they had heard the Saxons were massed. Count Theodoric, a kinsman of the king, hastened to join them in Saxony with all the forces he could collect hurriedly in Ripuaria after news reached him of the Saxon revolt. . . .

Then they all pushed forward to a mountain [situated on the southern bank of the river Weser] called Suntal. The camp of the Saxons lay on the northern side of this mountain. In this place Theodoric pitched his camp, while the leaders of the East Franks crossed the Weser and encamped on the river bank, to the end that they might easily join the forces of Theodoric and so surround the mountain.

Then did the leaders of the East Franks take counsel together: for they feared that the glory of victory might be given to Theodoric, if they had him with them in this battle. So they decided to attack the Saxons without him. They accordingly armed themselves, and each man rushed forward with his utmost speed, as fast as his horse could carry him, as if they were pursuing and plundering a fleeing foe rather than attacking an enemy drawn up in line of battle.

But the Saxons stood before their camp ready to meet the onslaught; and because the attack was ill planned it was ill fought. When they gave battle the Franks were surrounded by the Saxons and almost all of them were slain. Those who made good their escape fled for refuge, not to the camp whence they had gone forth, but to the camp of Theodoric, which was on the other side of the mountain. The Frankish loss was greater than mere numbers, for two of the ambassadors, Adalgis and Geilo, were killed, also four counts, and twenty other noble and distinguished men, together with those who followed them, because they would rather die with them than live after them.

When the king heard of this disaster he decided not to delay, but made haste to gather an army, and marched into Saxony. There he called to his presence the chiefs of the Saxons, and inquired who had induced the people to rebel. They all declared that Widukind was the author of the treason, but said that they could not produce him because after the deed was done he had fled to the Northmen.

But the others who had carried out his will and committed the crime they delivered up to the king to the number of four thousand and five hundred; and by the king's command they were all beheaded in one day upon the river Aller in the place called Verden. When he had wreaked vengeance after this fashion, the king withdrew to the town of Diedenhofen for winter quarters, and there he celebrated the Nativity of our Lord and Easter as he was wont to do.

No. 49. The capitulary *de Villis*

(Robinson's *Readings*, pp. 137-139.)

We desire that each steward shall make an annual statement of all our income, giving an account of our lands cultivated by the oxen which our own plowmen drive and of our lands which the tenants of farms ought to plow; of the pigs, of the rents, of the obligations and fines; of the game taken in our forests without our permission; of the various compositions; of the mills, of the forest, of the fields, of the bridges and ships; of the free men and the districts under obligations to our treasury; of markets, vineyards, and those who owe wine to us; of the hay, firewood, torches, planks, and other kinds of lumber; of the waste lands; of the vegetables, millet, panic; of the wool, flax, and hemp; of the fruits of the trees; of the nut trees, larger and smaller; of the grafted trees of all kinds; of the gardens; of the turnips; of the fish ponds; of the hides, skins, and horns; of the honey and wax; of the fat, tallow, and soap; of the mulberry wine, cooked wine, mead, vinegar, beer, and wine, new and old; of the new grain and the old; of the hens and eggs; of the geese; of the number of fishermen, workers in metal, sword makers, and shoemakers; of the bins and boxes; of the turners and saddlers; of the forges and mines—that is, of iron, lead, or other substances; of the colts and fillies. They shall make all these known to us, set forth separately and in order, at Christmas, so that we may know what and how much of each thing we have.

The greatest care must be taken that whatever is prepared or made with the hands—that is, bacon, smoked meat, sausage, partially salted meat, wine, vinegar, mulberry wine, cooked wine, garum, mustard, cheese, butter, malt, beer, mead, honey, wax, flour—all should be prepared and made with the greatest cleanliness.

Each steward on each of our domains shall always have, for the sake of ornament, peacocks, pheasants, ducks, pigeons, partridges, and turtle-doves.

In each of our estates the chambers shall be provided with counterpanes, cushions, pillows, bedclothes, coverings for the tables and benches; vessels of brass, lead, iron, and wood; and irons, chains, pothooks, adzes, axes, augers, cutlasses, and all other kinds of tools, so that it shall never be necessary to go elsewhere for them, or to borrow them. And the weapons which are carried against the enemy shall be well cared for, so as to keep them in good condition; and when they are brought back they shall be placed in the chamber.

For our women's work they are to give at the proper time, as has been ordered, the materials—that is, the linen, wool, woad, vermillion, madder, wool combs, teasels, soap, grease, vessels, and the other objects which are necessary.

Of the kinds of food not forbidden on fast days, two thirds shall be sent each year for our own use—that is, of the vegetables, fish, cheese, butter, honey, mustard, vinegar, millet, panic, dried and green herbs, radishes, and, in addition, of the wax, soap, and other small products; and let it be reported to us, by a statement, how much is left, as we have said above; and this statement must not be omitted as in the past, because after those two thirds we wish to know how much remains.

Each steward shall have in his district good workmen, namely, blacksmiths, a goldsmith, a silversmith, shoemakers, turners, carpenters, sword makers, fishermen, foilers, soap makers, men who know how to make beer, cider, perry, or other kind of liquor good to drink, bakers to make pastry for our table, net makers who know how to make nets for hunting, fishing, and fowling, and other sorts of workmen too numerous to be designated.

No. 50. Charlemagne's capitularies concerning education

(Robinson's *Readings*, pp. 144-146.)

Be it known, therefore, to your Devotion pleasing to God, that we, together with our faithful, have considered it to be expedient that the bishoprics and monasteries intrusted by the favor of Christ to our government, in addition to the rule of monastic life and the intercourse of holy religion, ought to be zealous also in the culture of letters, teaching those who by the gift of God are able to learn, according to the capacity of each individual; so that just as the observance of the monastic rule imparts order and grace to moral conduct, so also zeal in teaching and learning may do the same for the use of words, so that those who desire to please God by living rightly should not neglect to please him also by speaking correctly. For it is written, "Either from thy words thou shalt be justified, or from thy words thou shalt be condemned."

Although it is better to do the right than know it, nevertheless knowledge should precede action. Therefore, each one ought to study what he would accomplish, so that the mind may the better know what ought to be done, if the tongue utters the praises of omnipotent God without the hindrances of errors. For if errors should be shunned by all men, so much the more ought they to be avoided, as far as possible, by those who are chosen for the very purpose that they may be the servants of truth.

Yet, in recent years, when letters have been written to us from various monasteries to inform us that the brethren who dwelt there were offering up in our behalf holy and pious prayers, we noted in most of these letters correct thoughts but uncouth expressions; for what pious devotion dictated faithfully to the mind, the tongue, uneducated on account of the neglect of study, was not able to express without error. We, therefore, began to fear lest perchance, as the skill in writing was wanting, so also the wisdom for understanding the Holy Scriptures might be much less than it rightly ought to be. And we all know well that, although errors of speech are dangerous, far more dangerous are errors of the understanding.

Therefore, we exhort you not only not to neglect the study of letters, but also with most humble mind, pleasing to God, to pursue it earnestly in order that you may be able more easily and more correctly to penetrate the mysteries of the divine Scriptures. Since, moreover, figures of speech, tropes, and the like are found in the sacred pages, it cannot be doubted that in reading these one will understand the spiritual sense more quickly if previously he shall have been fully instructed in the mastery of letters. Such men truly are to be chosen for this work as have both the will and the ability to learn and a desire to instruct others. And may this be done with a zeal as great as the earnestness with which we command it.

(Excerpt from an "admonition" on same subject issued in 789.)

Let the ministers of the altar of God adorn their ministry by good manners, and likewise the other orders who observe a rule, and the congregations of monks. We implore them to lead a just and fitting life, just as God himself commanded in the gospel. "Let your light so shine before men, that they may see your good works, and glorify your Father which is in heaven," so that by our example many may be led to serve God. Let them join and associate to themselves not only children of servile condition, but also sons of freemen. And let schools be established in which boys may learn to read. Correct carefully the Psalms, the signs in writing, the songs, the calendar, the grammar, in each monastery or bishopric, and the Catholic books; because often men desire to pray to God properly, but they pray badly because of the incorrect books. And do not permit mere boys to corrupt them in reading or writing. If there is need of writing the Gospel, Psalter, and Missal, let men of mature age do the writing with all diligence.

No. 51. Northmen attacks on France

(*Annals of St. Vaast.* Robinson's *Readings*, pp. 163-168.)

(882) . . . The Northmen in the month of October intrenched them-selves at Condé, and horribly devastated the kingdom of Carloman, while King Charles with his army took his stand on the Somme at Barleux. The Northmen ceased not from rapine and drove all the inhabitants who were left beyond the Somme. . . .

[King Carloman gave them battle] and the Franks were victorious and killed nigh a thousand of the Northmen. Yet they were in no wise dis-comfited by this battle. . . . They went from Condé back to their ships, and thence laid waste the whole kingdom with fire and sword as far as the Oise. They destroyed houses, and razed monasteries and churches to the ground, and brought to their death the servants of our holy religion by famine and sword, or sold them beyond the sea. They killed the dwellers in the land and none could resist them.

Abbot Hugo, when he heard of these calamities, gathered an army and came to aid the king. When the Northmen came back from a plundering expedition . . . he, in company with the king, gave them chase. They, however, betook themselves to a wood, and scattered hither and yon, and finally returned to their ships with little loss. In this year died Hinckman, archbishop of Rheims, a man justly esteemed by all.

(883) . . . In the spring the Northmen left Condé and sought the coun-try along the sea. Here they dwelt through the summer; they forced the Flemings to flee from their lands, and raged everywhere, laying waste the country with fire and sword. As autumn approached, Carloman, the king, took his station with his army in the canton of Vithman at Mianai, oppo-site Lavier, in order to protect the kingdom. The Northmen at the end of October came to Lavier with cavalry, foot soldiers, and all their baggage. Ships, too, came from the sea up the Somme and forced the king and his whole army to flee and drove them across the river Oise. The invaders went into winter quarters in the city of Amiens and devastated all the land to the Seine and on both sides of the Oise, and no man opposed them; and they burned with fire the monasteries and churches of Christ. . . .

(884) . . . At this time died Engelwin, bishop of Paris, and the abbot Gauzelin was put in his stead. The Northmen ceased not to take Christian people captive and to kill them, and to destroy churches and houses and burn villages. Through all the streets lay bodies of the clergy, of laymen,

nobles, and others, of women, children, and suckling babes. There was no road nor place where the dead did not lie; and all who saw Christian people slaughtered were filled with sorrow and despair.

Meanwhile, because the king was still a child, all the nobles came together in the city of Compiègne to consider what should be done. They took counsel, and decided to send to the Northmen the Dane Sigfried, who was a Christian and faithful to the king, and the nephew of Heoric the Dane, that he might treat with the nobles of his people and ask them to accept tribute money and leave the kingdom.

He accordingly undertook to carry out the task assigned to him, went to Amiens, and announced his mission to the leaders of the Northmen. After long consultations and much going to and fro, these decided to impose upon the king and the Franks a tribute of twelve thousand pounds of silver, according to their manner of weighing. After both parties had given hostages, the people who dwelt beyond the Oise were secure in some degree. They enjoyed this security from the day of the Purification of St. Mary until the month of October.

The Northmen, however, made raids in their accustomed manner beyond the Scheldt, and laid waste all things with fire and sword, and totally destroyed churches, monasteries, cities and villages, and put the people to slaughter. After the holy Easter festival the collection of the tribute began, and churches and church property were ruthlessly plundered. At last, the whole sum being finally brought together, the Franks assembled with a view of resisting the Northmen should they break their pledges, but the Normans burned their camp and retreated from Amiens. . . .

No. 52. Northmen attacks on England

(Anglo-Saxon Chronicle, tr. J. A. Giles. London, 1890.)

A.D. 787. This year king Bertric took to wife Eadburga, king Offa's daughter; and in his days first came three ships of Northmen, out of Haeretha-land [Denmark]. And then the reve [sheriff] rode to the place, and would have driven them to the king's town, because he knew not who they were: and they there slew him. These were the first ships of Danishmen which sought the land of the English nation.

A.D. 793. This year dire forewarnings came over the land of the Northumbrians, and miserably terrified the people; these were excessive whirlwinds, and lightnings; and fiery dragons were seen flying in the air. A great famine soon followed these tokens; and a little after that, in the same year, on the 6th before the Ides of January, the ravaging of heathen men lamentably destroyed God's church at Lindisfarne through rapine and slaughter. And Siga died on the 8th before the Kalends of March.

A.D. 794. This year Pope Adrian and king Offa died; and Ethelred, king of the Northumbrians, was slain by his own people on the 13th before the Kalends of May; and bishop Ceolwulf and bishop Eadbald went away from the land. And Egfert succeeded to the Mercians and died the same year. And Eadbert, who by a second name was named Pren, obtained the kingdom of Kent. And Ethelherd the ealdorman died on the Kalends of August; and the heathens ravaged among the Northumbrians, and plundered Egfert's monastery at the mouth of the Wear; and there one of their leaders was slain, and also some of their ships were wrecked by a tempest; and many of them were there drowned, and some came on shore alive, and they were soon slain at the river's mouth.

A.D. 851. This year Ceorl the ealdorman, with the men of Devonshire, fought against the heathen men at Wembury, and there made great slaughter and got the victory. And the same year king Athelstan and Elchere the ealdormen fought on shipboard, and slew a great number of the enemy at Sandwich in Kent, and took nine ships, and put the others to flight; and the heathen men, for the first time, remained over winter in Thanet. And the same year came three hundred and fifty ships to the mouth of the Thames, and the crews landed and took Canterbury and London by storm, and put to flight Berthwulf, king of the Mercians, with his army, and then went south over the Thames into Surrey; and there king Ethelwulf and his son Ethelbald, with the army of the West-Saxons, fought against them at Ockley, and there made the greatest slaughter among the heathen army that we have heard reported to the present day, and there got the victory.

A.D. 865. This year the heathen army sat down in Thanet, and made peace with the men of Kent, and the men of Kent promised them money for peace; and during the peace and the promise of money the army stole away by night, and ravaged all Kent to the eastward.

No. 53. The Donation of Constantine

(*The Treatise of Lorenzo Valla on the Donation of Constantine*, tr. Christopher B. Coleman. New Haven, 1922. By permission of the Yale University Press.)

The Emperor Constantine the fourth day after his baptism conferred this privilege on the Pontiff of the Roman church, that in the whole Roman world priests should regard him as their head, as judges do the king.

In this privilege among other things is this: "We—together with all our satraps, and the whole senate and my nobles, and also all the people subject to the government of glorious Rome—considered it advisable, that as the Blessed Peter is seen to have been constituted vicar of the Son of God on the earth, so the Pontiffs who are the representatives of that same chief of the apostles, should obtain from us and our empire the power of a supremacy greater than the clemency of our earthly imperial serenity is seen to have conceded to it, choosing that same chief of the apostles and his vicars to be our constant intercessors with God. And to the extent of our earthly imperial power, we have decreed that his holy Roman church shall be honored with veneration, and that more than our empire and earthly throne the most sacred seat of the Blessed Peter shall be gloriously exalted, we giving to it power, and dignity of glory, and vigor, and honor imperial. And we ordain and decree that he shall have the supremacy as well over the four principal seats, Alexandria, Antioch, Jerusalem, and Constantinople, as also over all the churches of God in the whole earth. And the Pontiff, who at the time shall be at the head of the holy Roman church itself, shall be more exalted than, and chief over, all the priests of the whole world, and according to his judgment everything which is provided for the service of God and for the stability of the faith of Christians is to be administered. . . .

"Wherefore, in order that the supreme pontificate may not deteriorate, but may rather be adorned with glory and power even more than is the dignity of an earthly rule; behold, we give over and relinquish to the aforesaid our most blessed Pontiff, Sylvester, the universal Pope, as well our palace [Lateran], as has been said, as also the city of Rome, and all the provinces, places and cities of Italy and the western regions, and we decree by this our godlike and pragmatic sanction that they are to be controlled by him and by his successors, and we grant that they shall remain under the law of the holy Roman church. . . ."

No. 54. The *Etymologies* of Isidore of Seville

(Migne, *Patrologia Latina*, LXXXII, 1850. Translation.)

Book IV. Medicine

Ch. 1. Of Medicine: Medicine is that which protects or restores the health of the body, and its subject matter concerns diseases and wounds. To this subject, therefore, pertains not only those matters which the art of those reveal who are properly called physicians, but food as well, and drink and clothing; that is, all those things which serve to defend and protect our body against blows and accidents.

Ch. 2. Its Name: It is thought that the word medicine is derived from *modo,* that is, in moderation, so that not sufficient but a little be used. For nature is grieved by excess whereas she rejoices in moderation. Whence those who drink herb juices and antidotes in volume and constantly, suffer injury. For all immoderation brings not welfare but danger.

Ch. 3. The Founders of Medicine: The Greeks called Apollo the author and founder of the art of medicine. This science his son Aesculapius enlarged by his fame and work. When Aesculapius was killed by a thunderbolt, the work of curing, it is said, was prohibited and the art disappeared with its author and remained unknown for almost five hundred years until the time of Artaxerxes, king of the Persians. It was then that Hippocrates, the son of Asclepius, born on the island of Cos, revived the art.

Ch. 4. Of the Schools of Physicians: These men, therefore, founded three schools. The first, *Methodica,* was established by Apollo, and it deals in remedies and magical formulas. The second, *Empirica,* that is, using experience, was founded by Aesculapius, which considers not the evidence of signs but only experience. The third, *Logica,* that is, the school of reason, was founded by Hippocrates. For this last, having considered the qualities of ages, districts, and diseases, pursued the art in a rational manner. For the *empirici* consider only experience; the *logici* add reason to experience; the *methodici* observe not the conditions of the elements or the times, age, or causes, but only the diseases themselves. . . .

Book IX. Languages, Peoples, Kingdoms, Officers, Officials, Relationships

Ch. 1. The Languages of Peoples: The diversity of languages arose from the building of the tower [of Babel] after the flood, for prior to the time when the pride of that tower had divided human society into different languages, there was but one tongue for all nations, which is called Hebrew, which the patriarchs and prophets used, not only in their sermons but also in their sacred writings. But while in the beginning there were as many tongues as there were peoples, there came in time to be more people than tongues, since from one language many peoples have risen.

Ch. 2. But languages are used in this place instead of words which came about through language, in that manner of speaking by which a person calls what results, by the name of that which brings it about: thus *mouth* is customarily used instead of *words,* as *hand* is for *writings.*

Ch. 3. There are three sacred languages: Hebrew, Greek and Latin, which excel most throughout the world. For it was in these three languages that the inscription was written which Pilate placed above the cross of our Lord. Whence it is that because of the obscurity of the sacred scriptures a knowledge of all three languages is necessary, so that one may turn to another language if one encounters doubt as to the meaning of a word or passage.

Ch. 4. The Greek language is held to be clearer than any other language; for it is more beautiful than Latin and all other languages. Its branches will be considered under five headings, of which the first is called *koine*, that is, mixed or common, because all use it.

Ch. 5. The second Attic, that is, of Athens, which almost all Greek authors use; the third, Doric, which the Egyptians and Sicilians use; the fourth, Ionic; the fifth, Aeolian, which is spoken by the Aeolians. In the use of the Greek language certain distinctions are observed, for their speech is so diverse.

Ch. 6. Some say there are four Latin tongues, namely, Ancient, Latin, Roman, and Mixed; *Ancient* is that language which was used by the oldest Italic peoples under Janus and Saturn—rude as they say were the songs of the Salii (college of priests); *Latin*, which they spoke under Latinus and the other kings of Etruria in Latium, in which the Twelve Tables were written.

Ch. 7. *Roman,* which dates from the expulsion of the kings by the Roman people, in which Naevius, Plautus, Ennius, Virgil, poets, Gracchus, Cato, Cicero, and other orators composed their writings; *Mixed*, which was carried after the fall of the empire throughout the Roman state with its mores and peoples, its purity being corrupted by solecisms and barbarisms.

No. 55. Cassiodorus on *The Arts and Disciplines of Liberal Studies*

(Migne, *Patrologia Latina*, LXX, 1847. Translation.)

Preface

The preceding book, which we completed with the help of God, contains instruction for the reading of divine writings. This book is known to consist of thirty-three chapters, a number believed to correspond with the age of the Lord, when he bestowed eternal life on a world dead in sin and granted eternal reward to those who believe in him. Now is the time for us to present the text of a second book in seven additional chapters which will deal with secular reading: a number which continuously repeats itself week after week, extending itself to the very end of time.

For it is quite evident that holy scripture frequently expresses with that number something which it intends to be understood as constant and perpetual. Thus as David said: "Seven times each day have I praised you" (Psal. XCVIII, 164); while at other times he promised: "I shall bless the Lord at all times; his praise shall ever be in my mouth." (Psal. XXXII, 2). And Solomon: "Wisdom built herself a house; she has hewn out seven columns." (Prov. IX, 1). In Exodus also where the Lord spoke to Moses: "You will make seven lamps and place them on a candlestick to give light over against." (Exodus, XXV, 37). The same number is constantly mentioned in the Apocalypse in various meanings. (Apoc. I, 4, 11, 12). That number which leads us to eternal life can surely have no defect. Justifiably then is it always used when perpetuity is intended. . . .

Let us enter upon the beginnings of the second volume which we should consider somewhat more diligently. It is our intention to write briefly of the grammatical art, whether rhetorical or related to some other discipline; with which principles it is necessary for us to begin, for it should be first said of grammar, which is the origin and foundation of liberal studies.

The word book (*liber*) is said to be derived from free (*liber*), that is, the bark freed and liberated from a tree, upon which the ancients wrote their verses before there was an abundance of papyri. For we must know, as Varro explains, that the principles of all the arts exist for some usefulness.

Indeed it is called art because it keeps (*artet*) and restrains us with its rules. Others say the word is derived from the Greek *apo tes aretes*, that is, from the virtue of learning which learned men call the science of every good thing.

Second of rhetoric, which because of the splendor and richness of its eloquence, especially in civil matters, is considered particularly necessary and honorable.

Third of logic, which is called dialectic. This science secular teachers declare enables one to separate the true from the false in the most subtle disputations.

Fourth of mathematics, which includes four disciplines, namely, arithmetic, geometry, music, and astronomy. We can call this mathematics a theoretical study in the Latin manner of speaking, by which name it is permitted to designate all studies whatever they teach, but which common name mathematics, because of its excellence, has justly earned for itself; as when a poet is mentioned, Vergil is understood; when an orator, Cicero; however many poets and orators were taught the Latin language; which is also true of Homer and Demosthenes when Greece celebrates eloquence.

Mathematics is indeed the science which considers abstract quantity. Abstract quantity is that which, separated by our intellect from matter or from other accidents, we study by means of reason alone.

7

FEUDALISM

A not uncommon practice since the eighteenth century when the word *feudal* came into use has been that of speaking loosely of the Middle Ages as the feudal period. A similarly careless practice has involved the confusing of the two terms, *feudalism* and *manorialism*, although feudalism relates properly to the aristocratic classes, manorialism to commoners. (For manorialism, see following chapter.) Both unfortunate practices have served to complicate the subject of feudalism, which was already one of the more complex phases in the study of medieval life. This complexity sprang principally from the diversity of feudal practices. Because feudalism was powerfully influenced by local conditions, feudal institutions and practices varied significantly not only from country to country, but frequently even from province to province. Despite feudalism's diversity, however, a sufficient number of common denominators can be extracted from provincial feudalism to reveal the nature of the more common feudal institutions, practices, and traditions. Initially the problem of analyzing feudalism will be simplified if we define feudalism as a system of government. Feudalism also possessed personal and proprietary elements, which when fused with governmental in the tenth, eleventh, and twelfth centuries produced the feudal period proper. Already with the thirteenth century feudalism gave evidence of decline, a fact a few modern writers overlook when they charge feudalism with irrationalities which were actually practices and conventions surviving as anachronisms long after the twelfth century when feudalism had served its purpose.

Origins of Feudalism

Definition. Feudalism has been defined as a system of private government, that is, a political system in which certain basic powers normally possessed by a central authority are exercised by a class of large landowners commonly referred to as the feudal aristocracy. As a system, feudalism took form slowly, molded by a variety of forces and practices, some of which had begun to operate as early as the decline of the Roman Empire in the third century. As a matter of fact, it is to the conditions which contributed to the weakening and eventual disintegration of the state that one must look for the origins of that system. While feudalism has been superficially defined as organized anarchy, it did emerge only as the functioning of a centralized government on a national scale became increasingly difficult and finally impossible. In the preceding chapter we have seen how during Merovingian and Carolingian times government had become an enormously difficult operation; how the success of Clovis and Charlemagne simply proved that only rulers of extraordinary talents could cope with the powerful centrifugal forces which threatened to subvert the state; and how this subversion had finally come to pass in the tenth century as a consequence of the savage assaults of Vikings, Saracens, and Magyars.

Developments Conducive to Feudalism. In order to trace from their origins those forces which conspired to destroy the state, we must go back to the military anarchy which had almost wrecked the Roman Empire in the third century. The civil wars and invasions of that period pretty well shattered the imperial administrative system. It left municipal rule which had been the backbone of Roman bureaucracy thoroughly demoralized if not crushed. Gradually the larger landowners, if not by default, then by usurpation, fell heir to the responsibility of maintaining order over the countryside. The third century also witnessed the extinction of much of the loyalty which had earlier stirred the hearts of the Roman citizenry and bound them to the empire. This was not replaced in the new Germanic kingdoms with any similarly cohesive national sentiment. Furthermore, the commercial ties which had lent the empire a measure of unity and stability began to weaken even before the third century. They grew ever feebler, even disappeared, and would not revive again prior to the eleventh century when feudalism had become a fact. As roads fell into disrepair and the movement of merchants and goods ceased, each community settled down to an isolated social and economic existence of its own. A powerful landed aristocracy, a popular indifference to administration, an economy of agrarian self-sufficiency, all these helped create an atmosphere scarcely conducive to the effective functioning of government.

No Taxation, No Militia. The rough German invader found the operation of the Roman imperial fiscal system beyond his capabilities. From necessity, therefore, but also because his own traditions so dictated, he early laid down the principle that the king, like any other landowner, must live of his own. Since this left the king with wholly inadequate resources with which to maintain a royal bureaucracy, he was obliged to surrender precious crown properties into the hands of covetous counts in order to secure their administrative cooperation. But as the king continued to alienate crown lands, he progressively weakened himself, since these lands constituted his chief source of revenue. A contemporary development aggravated his worsening position. By the eighth century the virile militia of which Tacitus had written had been largely submerged with the rise of a Germanic nobility. Even where the peasant had not completely lost his freedom, he had proved himself unreliable as a fighter except in his own immediate vicinity. Furthermore, the coincident trend away from foot soldiers toward the use of expensive horsemen deprived the king of his last opportunity of building his throne on the broader base of popular support. Instead he was forced to fall back for soldiers upon the landed aristocracy, upon men, therefore, whose financial and military resources were frequently the equal of his own.

Other Factors Leading to the Disintegration of the State. Many of these developments were economic. As such they remained beyond the efforts of any individual or group of individuals who might seek to retard or correct. Among the factors which contributed to the debilitation of the crown during Merovingian and Carolingian times were several of a more personal and accidental nature. A particularly disastrous one was the Frankish practice of parcelling out the realm among the sons of the king upon the latter's death. The bloody, ruthless competition among the sons of Clovis for more than their share of the royal domain was repeated under his Merovingian and Carolingian successors when a king was so unfortunate as to leave more than one son. Thus the death of a king almost regularly signalled the outbreak of civil war. That among the sons of Louis the Pious, as we have seen, led to a permanent tripartite division of the Frankish kingdom. Such wars proved a boon only to the nobility who sold their services to the son who bid highest in terms of crown lands and autonomy. Finally toward the close of the eighth century began that series of terrible invasions from the north, south, and east on the part of the Vikings, Saracens, and Magyars, which might well have overwhelmed regimes more sturdy and secure than those existing in western Europe.

Patrocinium. These, then, were the principal economic and political factors which in enfeebling the state prepared the way for the rise of feudalism. Since feudalism emerged as centralized authority crumbled, a glance now at the measures which society adopted in order to cope with the evils consequent upon the state's weakening should reveal the institutional origins of feudalism. And such is the case. The first of these institutions in point of time was *patrocinium*. Already in the third century powerful landowners found it easy, if not necessary, in view of the veritable collapse of the imperial administrative system, to assume responsibility for the protection of the people living on their estates or villas. Diocletian and subsequent emperors tended to legitimize this trend by freezing the peasants, now known as *coloni*, to the land, and by giving the landowner virtually exclusive administrative control over them. The resulting relationship between the wealthy landowner and the unfree peasant was called patrocinium (from the Latin *pater* meaning father), since it resembled the earlier association between the Roman patron and his client. This relationship between the aristocratic landlord and his helpless tenant hardly prefigured the later feudal association between lord and vassal who were social equals. Yet it does demonstrate how early began the practice by those men who possessed extensive tracts of land, of exercising considerably more than economic control over the lives of the people occupying their estates. The landowner not only protected these tenants from brigands and hostile elements; he settled their disputes as well, taxed them, and even provided them a priest to administer to their spiritual wants. And while the degree of authority each medieval landowner might enjoy would vary with the efficiency of the royal administration, his extralegal jurisdictional powers scarcely terminated anywhere in western Europe prior to the close of the Middle Ages.

Commendation. A second institution whose analysis will shed light on the origins of feudalism is that of commendation. In late Roman times, but especially under the weak Merovingian kings, it became common for free farmers to commend themselves, that is, to offer their lands and their services to a powerful landed proprietor in their vicinity, usually a count or duke, in return for the protection he could afford them against lawless elements with which the government was powerless to cope. The noble landowner was pleased to accept the land of the freeman and his services since these made him correspondingly stronger. Yet he would customarily leave the commendee the possession, that is, the usufruct of his land, together with his personal freedom. It also happened that landless men who had nothing to offer other than services similarly applied to the nobleman for protection. As this was a time when land was cheap and manpower at a premium, the lord would welcome these landless men into his service on relatively the same terms as those who had property to bring with them. It is not difficult to see how in some instances the man who commended himself might eventually find himself slipping down to the level of a serf (unfree peasant) particularly if he were of humble status, while given more favorable circumstances he might rise, because of the value of his services, to the position of a social equal. It is in the latter case that commendation clearly contributed to the evolution of the feudal system. (Reading 56)

Precarium and Benefice. In this exchange of land or services or both for protection, several additional terms offer themselves for consideration. The grant of land which the landed proprietor or lord, as he eventually came to be known, returned or gave to the one seeking his favor and protection was called *precarium* or *precaria*. The terms are derived from the Latin verb *precor*, meaning to ask, and the land thus granted was held on precarious tenure, that is, it might be reclaimed by the lord at his will. In actual practice, however, such lands were ordinarily given for a definite period, usually for the life of the man, and they might even be taken over by his son upon his death. Often used interchangeably with *precarium* was the term *benefice* (boon or favor), although benefice is more properly employed when referring to a precarious grant of land made by a monastery or bishopric.

Immunity. A distinctly political development, and one which probably advanced the cause of feudalism above that of any other single factor, was the granting of immunity. Such grants extended to the person thus favored exemption for his domain from the interference or jurisdiction of the royal officials. While grants of immunity appear in late Roman times, they only became common during the Merovingian period. The earliest grants of immunity were those which the king made to an abbey or bishopric as a mark of his esteem. A privilege which was first granted rarely and only to prelates came in time, however, to be bestowed upon or secured by the more influential or aggressive lay lords. That such grants of immunity frequently amounted to simple usurpation on the part of the lords who enjoyed them, only demonstrated more forcibly the helplessness of many monarchs to prevent such arrogations. All that might be left for the king to do was to put the face of legality upon such usurpations by extending formal grants of immunity. However immunity was acquired, the domains so privileged constituted autonomous enclaves within the kingdom. So common did grants of immunity become that by the close of the ninth century taxes over most of western Europe were being collected, justice administered, and troops recruited, not by the crown officials but by the local lords who enjoyed immunity. (Readings 58, 77)

The Vassal. The term which came to be the most common in feudal parlance was that of *vassal*. In the seventh century it was ordinarily applied to men of humble status who had commended themselves to a lord. As such they were known as *vassi dominici* (servants of the lord). As the loyalty and cooperation which the early Carolingians could expect of their crown officials grew ever more uncertain, they came to place increasing reliance upon these *vassi* or vassals since they were in their personal service. Because of their greater dependability, they began to entrust them with responsible duties and to send them rather than members of the royal officialdom on important missions. Since these missions commonly involved considerable expense, the king found himself obliged to bestow *precaria* upon his *vassi* inasmuch as he had little actual money of his own to give them. Once the king began to hand out lands in this fashion to the non-aristocratic *vassi* of his household, the aristocratic elements in the kingdom indicated their eagerness to become royal vassals too, and the king was pleased to accept them as such. For by making these noblemen his vassals, the king hoped to gain the same personal ascendancy over them that he enjoyed over his nonnoble *vassi*. In fact, by the ninth century the king was requiring his officials to accept the status of vassal, that is, when he was sufficiently strong to induce them to accept that status. The consequence was that the king's counts, dukes, and other aristocratic officials came to be bound to him in a personal relationship considerably stronger because more specific, than the traditional king–subject association.

Military Developments. Thus far no account has been taken of the military considerations which frequently accompanied the agreement between the landed proprietor and the man who commended himself. Actually the reason which most often urged the lord to respond favorably to the person who was commending himself was his need for additional retainers. With the breakdown of law and order in late Roman times, prominent men began organizing their more loyal and robust clients into a guard to provide themselves and the villa a measure of protection against hostile intruders. A contemporary development saw the appearance of captains commanding groups of semicivilized tribesmen (*bucellarii*), such as those which Justinian's generals had pressed into personal service in order to make sure of their loyalty. (See page 144.) The Germans in Merovingian times took quite naturally to this sort of personal service, since it reminded them of their own traditional institution, the *comitatus*. This was the warrior band described by Tacitus, which was composed of youthful warriors who had voluntarily pledged themselves to serve a leader. Whatever the origins of the practice, there could be found in the service of many counts and dukes of the eighth and ninth centuries bands of armed retainers who were ready to challenge the authority of the king unless he happened to be as energetic and feared a man as Charlemagne.

The Use of Horses. Had these armed retainers been foot soldiers, it is entirely possible that the other lines of development which scholars associate with the evolution of feudalism would never have coalesced. Unfortunately for the head of the state who would have preferred an army of infantry, these retainers were horsemen or knights (from the German *Knecht*). For cavalry had become a necessity to western Europe already by the early eighth century. Charles Martel had found it impossible to conduct any kind of offensive against the mounted Moslems who had crossed the Pyrenees from Spain until he put more of his men on horses. The powerful cavalry charges of the Avars and Lombards proved similarly irresistible until the Franks began to use horses. Yet horses were extremely costly, the value of one horse being roughly the equivalent of the value of two dozen oxen. Since the ordinary peasant would have done well to own more than a single ox, he found economics excluding him from the business of war—its expense had vaulted utterly beyond his means. The impact of this change in the art of war upon western governments was far-reaching. To their dismay the early Carolingians learned that recruiting an army had become a far more complicated and costly operation than one of simply summoning the freemen to appear with their weapons. Unless the soldier had a mount, he was hardly a soldier. The Carolingians were forced, accordingly, to fall back upon their own lands and those of the church when theirs proved inadequate, to provide their vassals the means to equip themselves with horses and armor. They also required the great landed proprietors who might have been slow to do so, to maintain similar groups of horsemen of their own. Once this stage in the development of feudalism had been reached, that is, when powerful proprietors had become the king's vassals, when they were enjoying immunity, and when they were recruiting and commanding armed horsemen of their own, the feudal system as we know it had all but evolved.

Fusing of the Ingredients of Feudalism. For purposes of clarifying these different developments, it may be useful to single out for special emphasis the two dominant ingredients present in feudalism, namely, the personal relationship existing between the king and vassal, and the use of land as a means of securing services. With the first ingredient may be associated such institutions or practices as the *comitatus*, commendation, and, especially, vassalage; with the second, feudal land tenure, may be associated *patrocinium*, *precarium*, and immunity. In fact, at the danger of oversimplifying the process, one may date the birth of feudalism to the fusing in the ninth century of these two ingredients, vassalage and land tenure. From another point of view, the feudal system may be conceived of as a practicable means of employing land, which was the chief form and source of wealth, to secure services, when an adequate supply of money was lacking and before a sense of obligation to an impersonal state had come into existence. This land held under feudal tenure had meantime acquired the name fief (from the Latin *feudum*, whence the term feudalism), in place of the earlier *precarium*, *precaria*, and benefice. (Reading 59)

Final Steps in the Evolution of the Feudal System. Certain final developments, most of them occurring in the ninth century, completed the evolutionary processes leading to feudalism. It gradually became traditional for *precaria* to pass from father to son, and while the lord collected a fee (relief) from the son to remind him of his subordination, the grant of land had in fact become hereditary. As such it was known as a fief. And once a fief, it was well-nigh impossible for the king or lord to recover possession of it. Only if the family holding the fief died out could the lord reclaim the estate, in which case the fief was said to escheat to him. Or he might repossess the fief (usually only by force) by declaring it forfeit, on the grounds that the vassal had not fulfilled his obligations. A fief was ordinarily a landed estate, although it might be a source of revenue such as the right to certain ecclesiastical tithes, or a duty such as that of holding the English king's head should he become nauseated on the trip across the

Channel. Since the vassal as fief-holder owed certain services to his lord, the rule of primogeniture came to be adopted lest a division of the fief jeopardize such services. (Reading 76)

Subinfeudation. The vassals of the king, particularly those administering extensive fiefs, learned that, with the fief they held of their lord, they had inherited many of the same problems which vexed him, problems such as that of maintaining law and order and of having their authority accepted throughout their jurisdiction. It happened frequently, as a consequence, that their fiefs suffered a division into administrative parcels similar to that which the king's realm had experienced. Contributing powerfully to this further division of the original fief into smaller fiefs was the military charge upon the vassal of supplying his lord a number of knights. Thus if as vassal of the king he was required to furnish him six knights when the occasion demanded, the simplest manner of raising such knights was for him to parcel out portions of his own fief to six men, each man under obligation to give him knight service. This parcelling out of the original fief into smaller fiefs is what is known as subinfeudation. An inevitable extension of subinfeudation was the appearance of multiple vassal engagements, by which one and the same vassal might hold fiefs from a number of lords, to each of whom he pledged his loyalty. The usual example of what confusion such a practice could lead to is that afforded by the count of Champagne who held fiefs of nine lords, among them the king of France and the German emperor. While the king could hardly have prevented subinfeudation had he wished, each additional subdivision of his country left him just so much farther removed from the subjects who lived on these lower fiefs. His jurisdiction was limited to his vassals, their authority to their vassals, and so on. Appearing with the practice of subinfeudation was the idea that a vassal's obligations toward his king or lord bore a rough relationship to the size of his fief. From this it was an easy step to the conclusion that the lord, who was often no stronger or richer than his vassals, had obligations of his own to those vassals. Thus was born the principle of a mutual contract between king and vassals, a principle most dramatically invoked by King John's rebellious vassals when they forced him to accept *Magna Charta*. (See page 453.)

Feudalism Not Destructive of State. Feudalism has traditionally been associated with the disintegration of the state. As the latter waned, the feudal system took shape; as the king grew increasingly less capable of exercising the powers of government, a feudal aristocracy moved forward to assume or usurp these powers for itself. Yet to say that feudalism emerged as the state declined is one thing, to hold feudalism responsible for this decline is another. It is true that such genuinely feudal practices as subinfeudation were of their very nature subversive of the state. Yet this much must be said in behalf of feudalism, on trial, as it were, for attempting to destroy the state. In the first place, the feudal aristocracy came by most of its powers by default, not seizure. Feudalism as such did not cause a weakening of the state. The state was weak and growing weaker for reasons largely independent of the intent of a feudal aristocracy. Feudalism was not a system of government so much as a political situation to which students have given the name feudalism. It evolved, it was not introduced. At worst, feudalism was a passive agent in the decline of the state; at best, it helped preserve the state. It provided one means and, under the circumstances, about the only one short of the appearance of a Charlemagne, capable of enlisting the cooperation of powerful men who might otherwise have established wholly independent regimes. In France during the reign of Hugh Capet, for example, such feudatories as the duke of Normandy or the count of Flanders could have declared themselves as independent in law as they were in fact. The king was incapable of offering them any resistance. What deterred them from proclaiming their independence was partly the force of tradition, partly the anxiety of the church which sought to keep the concept of a state alive, but partly also the lord-vassal relationship of feudalism. This established a tie, tenuous but real, between the king and the various parts of France when almost all other links had been broken and when the territorial princes would not have countenanced anything stronger. Finally, as feudal government matured and in time developed rules and traditions, it furnished shrewd kings in France and England the means of creating the first modern states.

The Feudal Contract

The Act of Homage. One of the most traditional practices which came to be associated with feudalism and one which reflected above all others the strong personal features it embodied was the act of homage. Even before vassalage had become an honorable institution, the vassal would usually perform some formal act of subjection, such as that of taking an oath, to signify his dependence upon the king. Once feudalism had emerged as a reasonably mature institution with its own peculiar procedures, regulations, and ceremonials, the act of homage did indeed become the foremost ceremonial. In this ceremony the vassal became the man (Latin *homo*) of the lord, thereby officially establishing the lord-vassal relationship. The ceremony was simple, though impressive, and it was the lord's hope that these qualities would serve to remind the vassal always of the pledges he had given. In the act of homage, the vassal knelt before his lord, bareheaded and without weapons in order to symbolize his dependence, placed his clasped hands between those of his lord and repeated the formula: "I become your man of the fief I hold of you, and faith to you will bear of life and members and earthly worship, and faith to you shall bear against all folk who can live or die." (Reading 60)

The Oath of Fealty. The oath of fealty followed immediately. After making his homage, the vassal rose and, with his hand on the Bible or a reliquary containing relics, took an oath of fealty or fidelity to carry out the obligations he was assuming with his vassalage. That the vassal took his oath standing signified that his act was a voluntary one and that his duties were not inconsistent with his dignity as a free man. The oath itself invoked the sanction of God upon the promises made by the vassal. After the act of homage and the oath of fealty, it was customary for the lord to confirm the obligations undertaken by the vassal by giving him a ceremonial kiss. Finally, the lord might formally invest the vassal with the fief by handing him a bit of turf, a stick, or similar object, symbolic of the transfer of the property. (Reading 61)

General Obligations of the Vassal. The obligations which the vassal assumed in the act of homage varied somewhat from country to country, but came to be fairly standardized by the close of the ninth century. The feudal formula which expressed in general terms these obligations of the vassal to his lord was that of giving him *consilium et auxilium* (counsel and aid). Actually feudalism was content with this general statement of the vassal's obligations except in the matter of military service. This was counted in terms of a specific number of knights, the number usually bearing a direct relationship to the value of the fief. The service of these knights was limited to a period of forty days once a year. Should the lord require their services beyond that time, he must assume the expense of maintaining them. Less sharply set down than military service, though no less fundamental, was the charge of court service. The vassal was required to present himself, ordinarily in company with the other vassals, wherever and whenever the lord might summon him, to give counsel and discuss matters of national concern. While such summonses might be irregular and even arbitrary, they gradually assumed a pattern as did other feudal practices. In England, for instance, the king's vassals assembled for meetings of what was called the great council at Easter, Pentecost, and Christmas. A third major duty incumbent upon the vassal, although more implicit than formal, was that of administering the fief. This included the responsibility of maintaining law and order and of providing a system of courts for the common people. The success of the feudal monarchy depended upon the faithful cooperation of the vassals in the discharge of these obligations. (Readings 62, 67, 73)

Feudal Aids and Incidents. In addition to these general obligations owing the lord, feudal custom permitted him to exact payments from his vassals or their fiefs on certain occasions or under certain circumstances. There were traditionally three occasions when an aid was required of the vassal: when the lord's eldest son was knighted, when his eldest daughter was married, and when the lord himself was held for ransom. All three were occasions of great expense and the vassals were obliged to come to the lord's assistance. Similar instances of heavy expense, such as going on a Crusade or building a castle, provided the lord justification for demanding an aid. Rights governing the transfer of fiefs were known as incidents, and several of these proved highly lucrative to the lord. Possibly the most profitable incident to the lord and, conversely, the most odious to the vassal was the relief. This was the fee an heir paid when taking over a fief upon the death of the vassal. Not only might this be a substantial fee; it also served to remind the vassal of the distasteful fact that he only possessed the fief, that is, he had the use of it; the lord as proprietor continued to own it. Wardship conferred upon the lord the right to the income of the fief during the minority of the deceased vassal's son (or daughter), on the theory that until the boy had come of age he was incapable of rendering the services required. The incident of marriage gave the lord the right to select a husband for the fief's heiress when she chose to marry or when the lord decided she should marry. This right rested upon the principle that the husband of the heiress would be the lord's vassal and owe him military service, wherefore the lord should have control over whom she might select. This right appears less unreasonable when one remembers that political considerations rather than Cupid ordinarily dictated the choice of mates among the feudal aristocracy. Should the heiress prefer to marry a husband of her choice, she paid the lord a fee. Thus an English heiress turned over to the royal exchequer a sizeable sum for "license to marry where she wishes, so long as she does not marry herself to any of the enemies of the king." The lord also claimed certain perquisites such as the right of hospitality (French *droit de gîte*). There were few inns during the feudal period, and if the lord found no monastery conveniently at hand at nightfall, he was free to avail himself of a neighboring vassal's hospitality. Since such hospitality was also shared by the lord's retinue which might number a score or more, this right came in time to be as carefully circumscribed as military service. The lord also had the right to the income of an ecclesiastical fief in the interval between the death of one prelate and the selection of his successor. Since the lord often appointed the time for the election of a successor if he did not actually control the selection, there was always the temptation to delay such action beyond a length of time that was fitting. Particularly notorious in this respect was William Rufus, king of England. When he died he held in his possession, so the chronicler laments, "the archbishopric of Canterbury and the bishoprics of Winchester and Salisbury and eleven abbacies, from all of which he was drawing revenues." (Readings 63-70)

The Lord's Obligations. The obligations of the king or lord to his vassals were less clearly defined. On the occasion when the vassal bound himself by formal act of homage and solemn oath of fealty to be faithful to his lord, the latter reciprocated with no oaths or promises of his own. In fact, he never officially abdicated any of the theoretical absolutism which his predecessors had claimed. The turbulent conditions which prevailed generally throughout western Europe in the tenth century completely obliterated, however, any notion of royal absolutism which might have lingered on in theory. The powerful feudatories of France would never have elected Hugh Capet king in 987, or anyone else for that matter, had they not been confident that as king he would be content to reign, not rule, in his kingdom. In terms of effective power, Hugh Capet as king of France enjoyed a position hardly superior to that he held as count of Paris. Since the feudal monarch was no more than the equal of his vassals, feudal law prescribed that he treat them as social equals, that he leave them undisturbed on their fiefs so long as they respected their feudal obligations to him, that he protect them from their enemies, and that he accord them the right of judgment by their peers, that is, by their fellow vassals. That king was only courting revolt who sought by means of crown officials and royal courts to recover some of the prerogatives his historical predecessors may have enjoyed over their subjects; who erected castles outside his own particular domain; who laid any assessments upon his vassals beyond the three traditional aids. (Readings 57, 62)

The Feudal Pyramid. From out of the confusion of feudal practices and precedents, there gradually emerged what has been described as the feudal pyramid. At the top of the feudal hierarchy stood the king, properly known as suzerain, who reigned but did not rule. Feudal custom accorded him only superior, not supreme authority. He was no sovereign. He ruled only those people who lived on his own domain, and, of course, within the limits of the feudal contract, his immediate vassals. The king's chief vassals, ordinarily dukes and counts, had vassals of their own who were called the king's rear or sub vassals. These in turn might have other vassals of their own, while nothing, as we have seen, normally prevented the individual vassal from holding fiefs of several lords. The process of subinfeudation, in theory at least, could proceed down the feudal ladder until the portion of land constituting the fief produced just enough income to support a knight, a so-called knight's fee. With the exception of some territories called allodial lands or allods (Reading 71), which were not held under feudal tenure, much of the land of western Europe represented so many fiefs, and France, for instance, represented not one country but scores of small states. All the members of the feudal aristocracy could be lords excepting only the knight who owned but a single knight's fee. All might be vassals with the exception of the king. Yet in actual practice, it happened that kings were vassals of foreign lords, as was the king of England of the king of France in his capacity as duke of Normandy.

How Did Feudalism Work? How did feudalism work as a system of government? Much depended upon the ability and resources of the particular king involved. A suzerain of the stature of William the Conqueror could exercise real authority, although the feudalism he introduced into England in 1066 was of a sterner order than that which was maintained on the continent. Where the suzerain had limited resources and less ingenuity, he might end up as did Charles the Simple (d. 923), in the dungeon of one of his vassals. The heart of the feudal monarch's weakness lay in his dependence upon the very group whom he wished to humble. In theory his disputes with his vassals and their disputes with each other should have been adjudicated in his court. But it was almost impossible to compel attendance on the part of any vassal who feared an adverse judgment, and only those would accept an unfavorable ruling who were too weak to dispute it.

The traditional feudal monarch lacked an army of his own and a people to whose patriotism he could appeal. He lacked a national bureaucracy. Above all else, he lacked money. He could exercise no authority over the bulk of his subjects since these lived on the fiefs of his vassals. The more he found himself able to correct these weaknesses, the less a feudal monarch he became. In tenth- and eleventh-century France, powerful lords such as the duke of Normandy and the count of Champagne conducted themselves as heads of state with all the prerogatives the king himself might claim. The feudal knight was a fierce and most sensitive individualist, no less prone than modern man to confuse interests with rights and to question the justice of any hostile decision, and he was as quick as the more reckless prospectors during the California Gold Rush to settle his differences by an appeal to arms. The result was what has been euphemistically called the right of private warfare. Though the feudal knight possessed no such right, he never recognized and seldom found any restraints which hindered his exercising it. In France he encountered no effective restraints before the late twelfth century. In England any appeal to this "right" might cost him his head after 1066.

Feudal Warfare

Feudal Warfare not Sanguinary. Yet while many of the feudal king's vassals took the law into their own hands to avenge real or presumed wrongs, to win new fiefs, or to advance some other material ambitions, feudal warfare was never the universal scourge commonly believed. Actually a smaller percentage of the total population fell victim to war during the feudal period than is the case today. Feudal armies were necessarily small since the feudal monarch lacked the power and prestige to compel many men to support him. The large aggregations of the late Middle Ages with their thousands of foot soldiers bearing bows, arrows, and pikes, were no longer feudal armies. Feudal warfare was ordinarily waged by knights, who were necessarily limited in number. Furthermore, these knights were protected by armor of relatively high efficiency. They were also less anxious to kill their opponents than to capture them. It was through the ransom he might be able to collect from his prisoner, that many a knight hoped to secure some compensation for the service he was rendering his lord. That such captures took place with some regularity is evident from ransom being counted one of the three feudal aids. A spirit of fraternity occasionally deterred one knight from killing another, and, no doubt, even the fear of God served at times as a check. Since a knight owed service for but forty days, that of itself restricted the amount of fighting. Feudal warfare consisted for the most part of skirmishes, with the handful of combatants riding off in their several directions after a few exchanges with lance and sword. Even when wars were fought in which kings were engaged, they were not bloody, says Professor Painter. In the decisive battle of Lincoln in 1217, where some six hundred knights on one side fought eight hundred on the other, only one knight was killed.

The Knight's Weapons. The knight was born to fight and spent his whole life doing little else. One reason why he liked nothing better than fighting was the pride and confidence he had in his weapons and armor. For offensive weapons he depended first upon his lance, which when directed with accuracy and power could unhorse his adversary forthwith, unless the blow were parried as dexterously as it had been delivered. If more fighting was required, the knight would close in with battle-axe or mace, then with short sword or dagger. In the eleventh century the knight's protective weapons consisted of a shield, a shirt of chain mail, and a conical helmet (see Bayeaux Tapestry cut). As the penetrating power of certain weapons such as the crossbow increased, so had perforce the defensive qualities of the knight's protective covering. By the fifteenth century such protective devices left him completely encased in plated steel, so skillfully shaped as to cause missiles to glance off rather than pierce. Since several squires and pages normally attended the knight to assist and service him with weapons and new mounts, his effectiveness as a soldier can be readily appreciated. Not without reason has he been likened to a modern tank. His armor was almost as expensive, and an inevitable consequence of the need for the knight to put on more and costlier armor was a steady decline in his numbers.

The Castle. To the castle, even more than to his weapons, did the knight owe his dominant position in feudal society. The first castles appeared during the troubled times of the ninth century. Then they were welcomed as bulwarks of society against lawless elements and cruel invaders. In the fourteenth and fifteenth centuries, peaceful men cursed them as strongholds of feudal misrule and tyranny. The early castle was scarcely better than a blockhouse. Whenever possible it was erected on some naturally defensible site such as a hill or bluff, and surrounded by a palisade of timbers and a deep ditch or moat. As the feudal aristocracy learned how vital strong castles were to its existence and ambitions, more elaborate and extensive fortresses came to replace these earlier structures. The wooden castle was fast disappearing by the close of the eleventh century, even before Crusaders had gained first-hand knowledge in Syria of the vast superiority of stone fortifications. The largest castles enclosed several acres within their walls, often space enough to furnish protection to the peasantry of the surrounding area and much of their livestock in time of danger. The principal features of these later castles included the citadel, called the donjon or keep, which might rise to a commanding height of two hundred feet; the turreted wall of enormous thickness supported with bastion towers so as to provide the defenders an unbroken view of the exterior of the wall; the huge drawbridge which could be lowered across the moat; and the portcullis or iron gate which provided additional protection to the entrance. Because of the tremendous size of some of these castles, the ingeniousness of their defenses, and the difficulty of maintaining an adequate besieging force before them for any extended period of time, they remained practically impregnable until the introduction of artillery in the fifteenth century. Of the manifold obstacles in the path of ambitious monarchs, the castle proved by all odds the most formidable.

Peace of God and Truce of God. War even at best is bad, and while feudal warfare might not involve the death of many knights, its evils frequently fell heaviest upon those least able to defend themselves. If one's adversary had managed to hole himself up in his castle and from the safety of its battlements fling defiant taunts at his enraged attacker, what would prevent the latter from venting his fury on the helpless villagers in the vicinity by firing their homes and slaughtering them and their stock? Even the legions of robbers and outlaws which infested the countryside were no greater curse than the knights with their so-called right of private warfare. Since most feudal monarchs of the period were powerless to maintain peace, no other recourse suggested itself except the forlorn one of appealing to the conscience of the times. Actually this was not an entirely wild hope in view of the astonishing success of the Cluniac and other reform movements of the tenth and eleventh centuries which had mightily stirred the religious sensibilities of western Europe. (See page 496.) Two movements took form in southern France which were aimed

Bayeux Tapestry

at curbing the violence of the times and which rested their sanction on the fear of God. These were the Peace of God and the Truce of God, the first appearing in the late tenth century, the second, early in the eleventh. Both were bolstered and given direction by the decrees of a number of diocesan and provincial synods. The Peace of God essayed to invest peasants, merchants, travelers, pilgrims, the clergy, and holy places with a special immunity from molestation and attack. The Truce of God sought to reduce private warfare by anathematizing fighting on days which were hallowed by the church or during periods when peace was essential to the farmers. The first days thus set aside were Sundays and holy days. Then Saturday afternoons were added and, finally, the entire period from Wednesday evening until Monday morning. Lent was declared a season closed to fighting and similarly Eastertide, both times of year coming when peasants were busy sowing their fields. Fighting was also banned during the interval between the feast of the Assumption of the Blessed Virgin Mary (August 15) and St. Martin's Day (November 11) to enable the peasants to harvest their crops. Of the two movements, the Truce of God was the better respected, although the acceptance of neither was encouraging, despite the efforts of occasional lords to enforce them within their domains. (Reading 72)

Liege Homage. There were additional deterrents to feudal warfare. One was the oath of fealty which the vassal swore to his lord. The feudal age set unusually high regard on one's plighted word. This virtue, together with ecclesiastical anathemas and the fear of hell which God would mete out to anyone guilty of a false oath, was not without its restraining influences. The requirement of liege homage did some good. This consisted of swearing a special oath of prior loyalty to one particular lord on the part of a vassal who held fiefs of several. If a king could require liege homage from all vassals, both immediate and rear, as did William the Conqueror,

Giraudon

Battle of Hastings

he would possess at least the legal authority to proscribe private warfare throughout his realm. By the close of the twelfth century private warfare among petty nobles was no longer common, although it must be admitted that this happy development was due less to the fear of God than to the fear of vigorous monarchs who had overcome the enfeebling forces of feudalism. (Reading 75) Some progress meantime was even achieved toward reducing warfare among kings, this principally through the efforts of popes who deplored such strife as prejudicial to the work of the church in general and to the success of the Crusading movement in particular. (See page 405.) Mention should be made here of the indirect contribution of the Crusades themselves to the cause of peace in western Europe in drawing off its more contentious elements to war against the Moslems. We shall see later how Pope Innocent III sought unsuccessfully to persuade all Christian kings of Europe to become his vassals. As the supreme suzerain of Europe he could have claimed the right to require belligerent vassals to cease fighting and accept the arbitrament of his feudal court. (For Pope Innocent's Christian commonwealth, see page 518.)

Prowess: A Chivalric Ideal. It is a law of human society for men of a particular class or profession to recognize certain rules or ideals which that group considers essential to its well-being and to the proper performance of its functions. Sportsmen have their ideals, so also do physicians and teachers. Even robbers are generally agreed what "virtues" a superior robber should possess. So it was with the feudal knights of the tenth and eleventh centuries. The body of ideals to which they subscribed, collectively if not individually, is what is known as chivalry or the institution of knighthood. Since the knight was a warrior by preference and profession, the first virtue which he admired above all others and which he considered the *sine qua non* of his calling was courage. He must be daring, he must have prowess, he must be valiant. "Be valiant," was the admonition tradi-

Caernarvon Castle, Wales

tionally given the youth when he was struck the ceremonial blow that made him a knight. And before the act of knighting had become part of an elaborate ritual following upon a formal period of training, young men were ordinarily knighted on the field of battle after some conspicuous act of prowess. (Readings 79, 80)

Loyalty. Second only to prowess in importance among chivalric ideals was that of loyalty. No society can function successfully unless the members of that group are willing to recognize their obligations to each other and to abide by their mutual promises. That the feudal aristocracy enjoyed a commendable record on this score is suggested by the absence of anarchy in France during the ninth and tenth centuries despite the nonexistence of an effective monarchy. What contributed significantly toward preventing society from dissolving into chaos during those trying times was the general readiness of vassals to honor their oaths to their lords. This loyalty to one's pledged word had a long history. It might extend as far back as the *comitatus* described by Tacitus, in which young warriors bound themselves to serve a captain they admired. Less remote was the oath of loyalty which the early Carolingians exacted from their *vassi dominici.* A craven knight was an abomination, but one who broke his word was almost as bad. The most famous example of how a knight should honor his word was that provided by King John the Good. Captured by the English during the Hundred Years War, he had been released to return to France before his ransom had been fully paid, upon his son's agreeing to take his place as a hostage. When the English permitted the young man to visit a shrine in Brittany, only to have him decide to remain in France with his wife, King John, true to his word, came back to England.

Generosity.   Prowess and loyalty were the original chivalric ideals and always remained the most fundamental. Due to the softening influences of Christianity and of such literature as the courtly romance, additional knightly virtues of a less martial nature came to make their way into the code of chivalry. Already by the close of the eleventh century the rule of generosity was requiring the feudal noble to be a gracious host and to send his guests away with rich gifts; to be liberal to suppliants who sought his aid and to pilgrims who happened by; to be ungrudging in his support of religious establishments, particularly to those located within his domains. One of the distant antecedents of this feudal generosity might be the extraordinary hospitality which Tacitus had admired in the early Germans. The same openhandedness keeps appearing in the literature of the Germans, notably in the *Nibelungenlied*, where it is carried to such lengths that it leaves the reader to wonder how so much could possibly have been given away at a time when there was so little. Wandering minstrels never missed the opportunity of singing the beneficence of the true knight, especially since their livelihood depended upon his generosity. Even when the nobility had surrendered its preeminence of wealth to the merchant princes and bankers of the late Middle Ages, it never permitted them to deprive it of its tradition of largesse.

Courtesy.   A fourth chivalric ideal appeared soon after the heritability of fiefs in the tenth century had led to the rise of a closed and class-conscious noble estate. This was the ideal of courtesy. Since it composed a small and in its opinion, a superior group which derived its eminence from its own peculiarly noble blood, the feudal aristocracy must observe conventions which set it above the rude masses. Therefore the members of this class should deal fairly with one another. They must fight to win, but not to kill. No two knights should ever attack a single foe. The true knight refused to press his attack once his adversary was unhorsed; neither did he assault him when he chanced upon him without weapons. The knight treated his captured enemy as an equal—even the unvirtuous William Rufus would not keep his noble prisoners in chains but released them on parole—and a captive knight did not flee his captors, although he might permit himself to be rescued. This chivalric ideal of courtesy was gradually extended to the women of the upper classes on the theory that if knights were noble, surely their wives and daughters shared that nobility. What also probably advanced this development was troubadour poetry which exalted the love of woman as exerting an ennobling influence upon man.

Glory and the Service of God. To be a perfect knight, the knight must acquire the reputation of a distinguished warrior. The physical accomplishment of overcoming a dangerous foe was itself most convincing, but such fighting should preferably be done in a worthy cause, and no cause was more worthy than that of the Crusades. That so many knights joined the Crusades can be attributed in part to this desire to gain glory. But in most instances this motive was associated with a higher consideration, that of striving in a noble cause. If Christianity was capable of recruiting thousands of men and women to serve as priests and religious in the struggle for souls, surely there must have been an equally large number willing to test its prowess against the unbeliever on the field of battle. That many knights joined the Crusades because their reputation as good knights demanded it can hardly be questioned, but this only demonstrates more forcibly how much the religious ideal had become a part of chivalry. The good knight should also be ready to protect the weaker members of society—women, widows, children, the poor—although contemporary sources provide as many illustrations of his indifference, even contempt, for these people as of his solicitude.

The Feudal Noble A Constructive Force. Such chivalric ideals as loyalty to one's pledged word must have exercised a sobering influence upon the combativeness of the knight. This was also checked by the church with a richly symbolic ritual with which it clothed the conferring of knighthood, with its tirades against private warfare, and with its appeal to the knight that he dedicate his arms to the service of God and the weaker elements of society. Yet all evidence points to the conclusion that it was easier to induce the knight to direct his bellicose impulses at targets outside Christian Europe, than it was to get him to hang up his sword. This the strong monarch and the headsman's axe accomplished, a combination of which the knight stood in greater awe than he did of the church's threat of eternal damnation. Yet if the devil deserves his due, so does the medieval knight. While many knights were a law unto themselves and a terror to the countryside, there were others who recognized the responsibilities that accompanied the right to bear arms. Much of the evil reputation which clings to the feudal noble was actually the work of the robber baron whom lawful agencies were long powerless to suppress. To his villagers, the local lord was a guardian of the law and a protector. He worshiped with the commoners in the village church; he occasionally took part in their festive gatherings; his wife might supervise the care of their sick, and in times of scarcity he might suffer with them or seek to ease their shortages from the surplus in his own granaries—if any existed there. As years passed by with the same family occupying the dominant position in the community, from father to son down through many generations, there frequently grew up a feeling of responsibility on the one hand and attachment on the other to fashion a strong bond between the manor house and the villagers.

The church might fulminate against the knight's depredations which often despoiled both civilians and clergy alike. Still there were knights who proved generous benefactors to churches and monasteries. Knights frequently put aside their weapons temporarily to join pilgrim groups on their way to Canterbury, Jerusalem, or to the shrine of St. James at Compostella. Others exchanged their arms permanently for a monk's cowl. The originator of the Cluniac reform movement was a nobleman, while a youthful warrior who had once been captured in a feudal skirmish founded the Franciscan order. For all his roughness, the medieval knight may claim the distinction of having established a number of rules which continue to be recognized as the marks of a gentleman: that a man honor the binding force of engagements freely agreed upon; that he repudiate an order which is incompatible with the diginity of a free man; that he be courteous to women. "The ideal knight of feudal chivalry was the lineal descendant of the heroes of Germanic legend and the ancestor of the modern gentleman."*

Social Life of the Castle

Before taking a brief glance at social life in the castle, two observations are in order: first, that the visions of magnificence which the word castle conjures up in romantic minds today may find some basis in fact in the stately chateaux erected in the sixteenth century to serve as residences of the aristocracy, but scarcely any in the fortress-like homes of the feudal nobility of the Middle Ages; second, that though material conditions in the medieval castle might appear appallingly primitive today and hardly suitable for comfortable living, the lord and his lady did not think so, for they knew nothing better. What one age enjoys as luxuries, a later welcomes as conveniences, a third demands as necessities. Human happiness within reasonable limits has always been largely a matter of the mind and of making the most of one's circumstances.

Furnishings and Food. The early castles grew progressively more comfortable with the abating of turbulency in the late tenth century and the return of Crusaders with commodities and ideas of better living from the eastern Mediterranean. The first castles were rude structures usually consisting of two rooms: the one a large hall which served as living quarters during the day and as a bedroom for most of the castle's occupants at night, the other a small sleeping room for the lord and his immediate family. Marked improvement in the castle's appearance and advance in its facilities date from the early twelfth century. By the fourteenth century the

* Sidney Painter, *French Chivalry* (Baltimore, 1940), p. 28.

castle had grown into a commodious establishment, with glass windows replacing wooden shutters, and rugs and carpets serving as floor covering in place of the earlier straw and reeds. The importation of tapestries from the East helped immeasurably in combating the cold and damp which were among the most disagreeable features of the medieval castle. Equally welcome in the thirteenth century was the introduction of chimneys to carry off the choking smoke and fumes. From the use of chimneys the tenants of the castle progressed quickly to the use of fireplaces. Furniture was functional. It included benches and chests, a huge table of planks which filled the center of the main hall, and a large bed for the lord and his lady which was curtained for privacy and against drafts. The woolen clothes of the nobleman differed from those of the peasant chiefly in their finer quality and colorfulness, but they were just as difficult to keep clean. From modern standards the diet of the castle was remarkable chiefly for the huge quantity of wine consumed and for the abundance and variety of meat. On many occasions during the year, the visitor might find beef, mutton, venison, boar, and various kinds of birds and fowl gracing the boards of the more prosperous lords. Since the feudal noble usually lived a considerable distance from his closest aristocratic neighbor, he ordinarily proved a most hospitable host who insisted that his visitors remain his guests for weeks on end. If his own wine cellar and larder ran low, there were the supplies of his villagers to fall back on.

Amusements.   Since the feudal noble was by profession and avocation a warrior, when he was not at war he liked nothing better than to play at war. He might engage in single combat with a visiting friend, or as a member of one group of horsemen trade blows with a second group, or he might take part in a tournament. The tournament appeared in the eleventh century and soon proved a popular and regular means of providing knights diversion at their favorite sport as well as training for the field of battle. It was not uncommon for tournaments of the twelfth century to assume the character of pitched battles, with the end of the afternoon's contest including a few fatalities along with a goodly number of maimed bodies and fractured skulls. Ladies began to appear among the spectators in the thirteenth century, and between them and the strictures of theologians the tournament gradually lost its earlier function as a proving ground for war. By the fifteenth century tournaments had degenerated into mere pageants attended by banquets and dances.

The noble's second passion was the hunt. Game was plentiful in the Middle Ages and of an interesting variety, ranging from the vicious boar and majestic stag to the elusive deer and fox. Hunting remained throughout the Middle Ages the monopoly of the nobility. Whereas most of the privileges which the aristocracy enjoyed could claim some reasonable origin and measure of justification, it was nothing but sheer selfishness that denied the poor peasant even the humble rabbit and pigeon. Among

the most serious blots which besmirch the records of the early feudal monarchs of England was their practice of appropriating extensive forest lands
as royal preserves. According to his chronicler, William the Conqueror
"set apart a vast deer preserve and imposed laws concerning it. Whoever
slew a hart or a hind was blinded. He forbade the killing of boars even as
the killing of harts. For he loved the stags as dearly as though he had been
their father. Hares, also, he decreed should go unmolested." Falconry
counted as many enthusiasts among the ladies as among the men. As indoor amusements might be enumerated backgammon, chess, dice, listen-
ing to the songs of itinerant minstrels and the tales of pilgrims, feasting,
drinking, and dancing. In an age when almost every lady was an heiress
whose hand carried with it wealth and estates, and when most lords were
not content with the one wife permitted them by the church, conversation
must have approached in zest and popularity the character of an indoor
sport.

Feudalization of the Church

The feudalization of Europe during the ninth and tenth centuries did
not stop with the state; it engulfed the church as well. By feudalization of
the church is meant the control of church property and church appointments by the feudal aristocracy. To attribute this development wholly to
feudalism is not entirely fortunate since it rests upon two incorrect implications: first, that lay control of the church was new, which it was not;
second, that some principle inherent in feudalism as an institution led to
the inevitable feudalization of the church. Actually it was rather that those
same factors which brought about the disintegration of the state and the
rise of feudalism caused the ecclesiastical organization of the church to
crumble at the same time and led to the appropriation of control over its
component parts by the local aristocracy.

Lay Control Prior to the Ninth Century. Lay control of the church in a
sense extends as far back as Constantine, who inaugurated the practice of
conferring rights of jurisdiction in civil affairs upon bishops. As the episcopal office attained increasing prominence in both secular and ecclesiastical spheres, the efforts of the state to control its incumbents grew proportionately greater. Because of the political stability of the Byzantine Empire
and its religious maturity, the imperial government's interest in influencing church policy and selecting its personnel seldom extended to the
point where it interfered with the proper functioning of the ecclesiastical
organization. It was unusual for the emperor to interfere in the selection

of prelates below the rank of patriarch, and ordinarily such interference was not injurious to the church. But in the Merovingian west it was a different story. There both political stability and religious maturity were wanting, and what was more ominous for the church, the crown and aristocracy were poorer, and, to a corresponding degree, more rapacious than in Byzantium. "See how poor our treasury is!" complained King Chilperic (d. 584). "Look how the churches have drained our riches away!" Chilperic might have added too how powerless to interfere was the pope at Rome, for the temptation proved irresistible under the circumstances, and kings and counts everywhere laid greedy hands on bishoprics and monasteries and placed their friends and henchmen in control. How unhappy conditions became we have recorded in Boniface's despairing testimony to the pope: "Religion is trodden under foot. Benefices are given to greedy laymen or unchaste and publican clerics. All their crimes do not prevent their attaining the priesthood; at last rising in rank as they increase in sin they become bishops, and those of them who can boast that they are not adulterers or fornicators, are drunkards, given up to the chase, and soldiers, who do not shrink from shedding Christian blood."

Protection of Crown Necessary to Church. If conditions were already bad for the church, in what way could the rise of feudalism have caused them to deteriorate? Actually conditions were not so bad generally in western Europe as Boniface described them to be in France, and even in France they improved appreciably during the late eighth and early ninth centuries through the cooperation of kings like Pepin the Short and Charlemagne. This suggests one reason why the rise of feudalism, more precisely why the appearance of those factors which paralyzed the state, had such deleterious consequences for the church. For in undermining the power of the king, these factors destroyed the one man who was at once the protector of the church and who, in addition, was the only person able to maintain that peace and stability essential to the well-being of the church. How completely the papacy of the ninth century depended upon the support of the Carolingian monarchs became painfully manifest soon after the death of Charles the Bald in 877. Charles was the last Carolingian king capable of exercising effective authority in the west. Charles, in fact, felt strong enough to march down to Rome to lend Pope John VIII assistance against the Moslems who were harassing the papal territories. Five years after Charles' death, Pope John was murdered, and with his death the papacy fell overnight from a position of dictating to princes to one of complete helplessness. Since the Carolingian king to succeed Charles was king only in name and unable to interpose a helping hand, the papacy became at once the pawn of dark factional strife in Rome. Seventy-five years later it was rescued from the mire of Italian politics by Otto I who was, significantly, the first strong king to appear in central Europe after the death of Charles the Bald.

Seizure of Church Properties.   Strong kings were indispensable to the church in the ninth and tenth centuries, but not even the few who appeared could prevent the gradual secularization of ecclesiastical control and property at the hands of the local aristocracy. This secularization started with the seizure of church lands and ended with the actual appropriation of church offices. Already in the early eighth century, landed proprietors were finding the occupation of church properties desirable, even necessary, now that the change in the art of war from foot soldiers to horsemen had caused the business of war to become so enormously expensive. Even a prince as friendly to the church as Charles Martel felt constrained to seize extensive church lands and turn these over to his followers so that they might equip themselves with horses and armor. Everywhere local lords were laying hands on church properties and revenues. To prevent the complete impoverishment of the church, Charlemagne and Louis the Pious decreed that at least one farm be left each parish, but even this modest order proved futile. After Louis the Pious and his sons, no king appeared who was willing or able to block the avarice of the aristocracy, and since the pope had lost his voice at the same time, there was not even the threat of protest from that direction to deter it. The result was a fairly general seizure of the control of bishoprics, monasteries, and parishes by the local aristocracy. A large amount of church property was confiscated outright; incomes such as tithes were appropriated, and relatives and friends were often given direct possession by arranging for their appointment as bishops and abbots. This last step became increasingly common once the bishopric had acquired the status of a fief owing the usual feudal services to its lord. (Reading 78)

The Evils of Secularization.   Several evils followed upon feudalization of the church. The most serious was lay control of the offices of bishop and abbot. Since the bishop had become a vassal with military obligations, it was a matter of first importance to the king that he be a friend, preferably a close relative. Otto I made his brother archbishop of Cologne and a natural son archbishop of Mainz. Under the circumstances, not the spiritual qualifications of the man recommended him for high office in the church, but his political acceptability to the king. This abuse is what is known as lay investiture. Its suppression became the prime objective of the religious reformers of the eleventh century, since worldly bishops and abbots tended necessarily to corrupt the priests and monks in their charge. (For lay investiture, see page 513.) A second consequence of the feudalization of the church was marriage of the clergy. Until the ninth century clerical celibacy had been the rule in the west, after which time the marriage of the clergy became fairly general. A married clergy increased perceptibly the involvement of the church in the feudal system, and led inevitably to the alienation of church properties to the families of the priests. Marriage did not extend to the monasteries or to the upper clergy, and the suppression of the practice was one reform which kings supported, even Henry IV, who fought the church tooth and nail over the issue of lay investiture. Another abuse which can be linked with the feudalization of the church was that of simony or the purchase of church offices. Simony was not unknown before the rise of feudalism, but it grew to be common practice when church property became feudalized and when its value was assessed in terms of knights, aids, and incidents. Thus arose the practice for the bishop upon being invested by the lord with his office, to pay over to him a fee similar to the relief exacted from the son of a deceased vassal when he acquired legal possession of his father's fief. Other church offices were customarily dispensed in the same fashion.

Church Lands the Reason for Feudalization. The basic reason for the feudalization of the church, that is, for secular interests to appropriate for themselves control of church property and offices, lay principally in the estates and revenues belonging to the church. Most churchmen were aware of this, but they were also agreed that the cure for such lay interference was more painful than the disease itself. In a moment of desperation Pope Paschal II (d. 1118) offered, in the course of negotiations with the king of Germany over the issue, to surrender all properties and incomes to which the German monarchy might have some claim. The proposal evoked a horrified protest not only from churchmen who were not prepared to live lives of apostolic poverty, but from the aristocracy as well who saw only the king benefiting from so revolutionary a move. In a period of natural economy when land was almost the sole source of wealth, only a St. Francis could have had the vision to conceive that an institution as far-flung in its activities as the church and so highly organized, had no need for lands to provide it a regular income. Since Paschal's proposal came to naught, feudalization of the church continued a vexatious problem even after the decline of feudalism, when its heritage simply merged with the larger issues of church and state relations.

 READINGS

No. 56. A Frankish formula of commendation (seventh century)

(Translations and Reprints, IV, No. 3, pp. 3-4.)

Who commends himself in the power of another: To that magnificent lord . . . , I , . . . Since it is known familiarly to all how little I have whence to feed and clothe myself, I have therefore petitioned your piety, and your good will has decreed to me that I should hand myself over or commend myself to your guardianship, which I have thereupon done; that is to say in this way, that you aid and succor me as well with food as with clothing, according as I shall be able to serve you and deserve it.

And so long as I shall live I ought to provide service and honor to you, suitably to my free condition; and I shall not during the time of my life have the ability to withdraw from your power or guardianship; but must remain during the days of my life under your power or defence. Wherefore it is proper that if either of us shall wish to withdraw himself from these agreements, he shall pay . . . shillings to his peer and this agreement shall remain unbroken.

Wherefore it is fitting that they should make or confirm between themselves two letters drawn up in the same form on this matter; which they have thus done.

No. 57. Capitulary concerning freemen and vassals (A.D. 816)

(Translations and Reprints, IV, No. 3, p. 5.)

If anyone shall wish to leave his lord and is able to prove against him one of these crimes, that is, in the first place, if the lord has wished to reduce him unjustly into servitude; in the second place, if he has taken counsel against his life; in the third place, if the lord has committed adultery with the wife of his vassal; in the fourth place, if he has wilfully attacked him with a drawn sword; in the fifth place, if the lord has been able to bring defence to his vassal after he has commended his lands to him, and has not done so; it is allowed to the vassal to leave him. If the lord has perpetrated anything against the vassal in these five points it is allowed the vassal to leave him.

No. 58. Grant of immunity for the lands of a bishopric

(*Translations and Reprints*, IV, No. 3, pp. 11-12.)

We believe that it increases the great memorial of our realm, if with benevolent deliberation we concede opportune benefits to the places of the churches . . . under the protection of the Lord, and write them down to endure in stability. Therefore, may your zeal know that we have seen fit upon petition to grant such a benefit, for our eternal reward, to that apostolic man, lord . . . , bishop of . . . ; that in the vills of the church of that lord, which in recent times, or in ours, or by the gift of any one, he is seen to have or which in the future godly piety shall wish to amplify in the right of that holy place, no public judge shall at any time presume to enter for the hearing of causes or for the exaction of payments, but the prelate himself or his successors for the name of the Lord shall be able to rule over this under the name of a complete corporation. We require, therefore, that neither you nor your subordinates nor your successors nor any public judicial power should presume at any time to enter into the vills of the same church anywhere in our kingdom, either those granted by royal bounty or by that of private persons or those which shall in future be granted; either for the sake of hearing altercations or to exact fines for any causes, or to obtain sureties. But whatever the Treasury could expect either of fines or other things either from freemen or from servants and other nations who are within the fields or boundaries or dwelling upon the lands of the aforesaid church; by our indulgence for our future welfare, shall be profitable for the expenses of the same church by the hand of those ruling it, forever. And what we for the name of God and the remedy of our soul and that of our progeny who shall follow us have granted from full devotion, let not the royal sublimity, in the reckless cupidity of any of the judges be tempted to break. And, in order that the present authority may, by the aid of God, remain inviolate in present as in future times we have ordered this to be corroborated below by the subscription of our hand.

No. 59. Grant of fiefs

(Translations and Reprints, IV, No. 3, pp. 15-17.)

Grant of a fief. A.D. 1200 (p. 15)

I, Thiebault, count palatine of Troyes, make known to those present and to come that I have given in fee to Jocelyn d'Avalon and his heirs the manor which is called Gillencourt, which is of the castellanerie of La Ferte sur Aube; and whatever the same Jocelyn shall be able to acquire in the same manor I have granted to him and his heirs in augmentation of the fief. I have granted, moreover, to him that in no free manor of mine will I retain men who are of this gift. The same Jocelyn, moreover, on account of this has become my liege man, saving however, his allegiance to Gerard d'Arcy, and to the lord duke of Burgundy, and to Peter, count of Auxerre.

Grant of a fief. A.D. 1167 (pp. 15-16)

In the name of the Holy and Undivided Trinity, Amen. I, Louis, by the grace of God, king of the French, make known to all present as well as to come, that at Mante in our presence, Count Henry of Champagne conceded the fief of Savigny to Bartholomew, bishop of Beauvais, and his successors. And for that fief the said bishop has made promise and engagement for one knight and justice and service to Count Henry; and he has also agreed that the bishops who shall come after him will do likewise. In order that this may be understood and known to posterity we have caused the present charter to be corroborated by our seal; done at Mante, in the year of the Incarnate Word 1167; present in our place those whose names and seals are appended: seal of count Thiebault, our steward; seal of Guy, the butler; seal of Matthew, the chamberlain; seal of Ralph, the constable. Given by the hand of Hugh, the chancellor.

Grant of a fief of money. A.D. 1380. (p. 17)

We, Regnault de Fauquemont, knight, lord of Bournes and of Sitter, make known to all by these presents, that we have become liege man of the king of France, our lord, and to him have made faith and homage because of 1000 livres of Tours of income which he has given to us during our life, to be drawn from his treasury at Paris. And we have promised to him and do promise by these presents to serve him loyally and well in his wars and otherwise against all who can live and die, in the form and manner in which a good and loyal subject ought to serve his sovereign lord.

No. 60. Homage and fealty to count of Flanders (A.D. 1127)

(Translations and Reprints, IV, No. 3, p. 18.)

Through the whole remaining part of the day those who had been previously enfeoffed by the most pious count Charles, did homage to the count, taking up now again their fiefs and offices and whatever they had before rightfully and legitimately obtained. On Thursday the seventh of April, homages were again made to the count being completed in the following order of faith and security.

First they did their homage thus, the count asked if he was willing to become completely his man, and the other replied, "I am willing"; and with clasped hands, surrounded by the hands of the count, they were bound together by a kiss. Secondly, he who had done homage gave his fealty to the representative of the count in these words, "I promise on my faith that I will in future be faithful to count William, and will observe my homage to him completely against all persons in good faith and without deceit," and thirdly, he took his oath to this upon the relics of the saints. Afterward, with a little rod which the count held in his hand, he gave investitures to all who by this agreement had given their security and homage and accompanying oath.

No. 61. Legal rules for homage and fealty (St. Louis)

(Translations and Reprints, IV, No. 3, pp. 20-21.)

If any one should hold from a lord in fee, he ought to seek his lord within forty days, and if he does not do it within forty days the lord may and ought to seize his fief for default of homage, and the things which should be found there he should seize without return, and yet the vassal would be obliged to pay to his lord the redemption. When any one wishes to enter into the fealty of a lord, he ought to seek him, as we have said above, and should say as follows: "Sir, I request you as my lord, to put me in your fealty and in your homage for such and such a thing situated in your fief, which I have bought." And he ought to say from what man, and this one ought to be present and in the fealty of the lord; and whether it is by purchase or by escheat or by inheritance he ought to explain; and with his hands joined, to speak as follows: "Sir, I become your man and promise to you fealty for the future as my lord towards all men who may live or die, rendering to you such service as the fief requires, making to you your relief as you are the lord." And he ought to say whether for guardianship, or as an escheat, or as an inheritance or as a purchase.

The lord should immediately reply to him: "And I receive you and take you as my man, and give you this kiss as a sign of faith, saving my right and that of others," according to the usage of the various districts.

No. 62. Bishop Fulbert of Chartres on mutual duties of vassals and lords (A.D. 1020)

(Translations and Reprints, IV, No. 3, pp. 23-24.)

Asked to write something concerning the form of fealty, I have noted briefly for you on the authority of the books the things which follow. He who swears fealty to his lord ought always to have these six things in memory; what is harmless, safe, honorable, useful, easy, practicable. Harmless, that is to say that he should not be injurious to his lord in his body; safe, that he should not be injurious to him in his secrets or in the defenses through which he is able to be secure; honorable, that he should not be injurious to him in his justice or in other matters that pertain to his honor; useful, that he should not be injurious to him in his possessions; easy or practicable, that that good which his lord is able to do easily, he make not difficult, nor that which is practicable he make impossible to him.

However, that the faithful vassal should avoid these injuries is proper, but not for this does he deserve his holding; for it is not sufficient to abstain from evil, unless what is good is done also. It remains, therefore, that in the same six things mentioned above he should faithfully counsel and aid his lord, if he wishes to be looked upon as worthy of his benefice and to be safe concerning the fealty which he has sworn.

The lord also ought to act toward his faithful vassal reciprocally in all these things. And if he does not do this he will be justly considered guilty of bad faith, just as the former, if he should be detected in the avoidance of or the doing of or the consenting to them, would be perfidious and perjured.

No. 63. Authority of lord over marriages of vassals (A.D. 1151)

(Translations and Reprints, IV, No. 3, p. 25.)

Then the young man Aegidius, son of Gerard Maufialtre married a wife, Bertha by name, half-sister of Count Baldwin of Hainault and took her without his assent. The count, extremely angry at this, immediately took up arms against him at the beginning of the month of October. Thus from the time in which he had married her till Whitsunday, with or without consent, he kept her closely by force and arms at his house. But Aegidius having been attacked by a severe fever, which troubled him sharply every day, compelled by the counsel of his friends, who had helped him honorably in all things in his war, dismissed and openly abjured her; and peace was restored with the count, and the land was peaceful which had been long troubled by wars.

No. 64. Fees for license to marry (A.D. 1140-1282)

(Translations and Reprints, IV, No. 3, pp. 25-26.)

Ralph son of William owes 100 marks as a fine, to be allowed to marry Margery who was wife of Nicholas Corbet who held of the king *in capite*, and that the same Margery may be allowed to marry him.

Walter de Cancy renders account of 15 pounds to be allowed to marry a wife as he shall choose.

Wiverona wife of Iverac of Ipswich renders account of 4 pounds and 1 mark of silver that she may not have to take any husband except the one she wishes.

Hawisa, who was wife of William Fitz Robert renders account of 130 marks and 4 palfreys that she may have peace from Peter of Borough to whom the king has given permission to marry her; and that she may not be compelled to marry.

Geoffrey de Mandeville owes 20,000 marks to have as his wife Isabella, countess of Gloucester, with all the lands and tenements and fiefs which fall to her.

No. 65. Wardship, relief, and aids

(*Translations and Reprints*, IV, No. 3, pp. 26-28.)

Thomas de Colville renders an account of 100 marks for having the custody of the sons of Roger Torpel and their land until they come of age.

William, bishop of Ely, owes 220 marks for having the custody of Stephen de Beauchamp with his inheritance and for marrying him where he wishes.

Walter Hait renders an account of 5 marks of silver for the relief of the land of his father.

Walter Brito renders an account of 66 pounds, 13s. and 4d. for the relief of his land.

Richard of Estre renders an account of 15 pounds for his relief for 3 knights' fees which he holds from the honor of Mortain.

Next it is proper to see the chief aids of Normandy, which are called chief because they should be paid to the chief lords. In Normandy there are three chief aids. One is to make the oldest son of his lord a knight; the second, to marry his oldest daughter; the third to ransom the body of his lord from prison when he is taken in the Duke's war.

Aid granted to the king (Henry III) for the knighting of his eldest son, that is to say from each fee 40s. The sheriff (of Hereford) renders account of 40s. from John de Balun for one fee, and of 30 pounds from John de Munemul for fifteen fees; the bishop of Hereford renders account of 30 pounds for fifteen fees.

No. 66. Acknowledgment of military duty (A.D. 1212)

(*Translations and Reprints*, IV, No. 3, pp. 29-30.)

William, by the grace of God bishop of Auxerre to all who shall see these presents, greeting in the Lord. Know that we acknowledge that we owe to our lord Philip, illustrious king of the French, military service, as is the common service of bishops and barons; and this for the future we will perform through our knights, as others. For the same lord king has released our person from the service of the army so long as we live.

No. 67. St. Louis on military obligations of vassals

(Translations and Reprints, IV, No. 3, p. 30.)

The baron and all vassals of the king are bound to appear before him when he shall summon them, and to serve him at their own expense for forty days and forty nights, with as many knights as each one owes; and he is able to exact from them these services when he wishes and when he has need of them. And if the king wishes to keep them more than forty days at their own expense, they are not bound to remain if they do not wish it. And if the king wishes to keep them at his expense for the defence of the realm, they are bound to remain. And if the king wishes to lead them outside of the kingdom, they need not go unless they wish to, for they have already served their forty days and forty nights.

No. 68. Dispute over military obligation

(Translations and Reprints, IV, No. 3, p. 30.)

Then Louis, king of the French, in order to escape from the pestilence which was raging with great severity in the camp (before Avignon), betook himself to a certain abbey called Montpensier, which was not far distant from the siege works, till the city should be captured. There came to him at that place Henry, count of Champagne, who had passed forty days at the siege, asking license to return to his own possessions, according to the custom of France. When the king refused his permission the count replied that when his military service of forty days had been performed, he was not bound nor was he willing to remain longer. The king, however, was so inflamed by anger at this that he declared with an oath that if the count should withdraw then he would devastate his whole land with fire.

No. 69. Condemnation by a feudal court (A.D. 1249)

(Translations and Reprints, IV, No. 3, pp. 33-34.)

Raymond by the grace of God count of Toulouse, marquis of Provence, to the nobleman Arnold Atton, viscount of Lomagne, greeting.

Let it be known to your nobility, by the tenor of these presents, what has been done in the matter of the complaints which we have made about you before the court of Agen; that you have not taken the trouble to keep or fulfill the agreements sworn by you to us, as is more fully contained in the instrument drawn up there, sealed with our seal by the public notary; and that you have refused contemptuously to appear before the said court for the purpose of doing justice; and otherwise committed multiplied and great delinquencies against us. As your faults have required, the aforesaid court of Agen has unanimously and concordantly pronounced sentence against you, and for these matters has condemned you to hand over and restore to us the chateau of Auvillars and all that land which you hold from us in fee, to be had and held by us by right of the obligation by which you have bound it to us for fulfilling and keeping the said agreements.

Likewise it has declared that we are to be put into possession of the said land and that it is to be handed over to us, on account of your contumacy, because you have not been willing to appear before the same court on the days which were assigned to you. Moreover, it has declared that you shall be held and required to restore the said land in whatsoever way we wish to receive it, with few or many, in peace or in anger, in our own person, by right of lordship. Likewise it has declared that you shall restore to us all the expenses which we have incurred or the court itself has incurred on those days which were assigned to you or because of those days, and has condemned you to repay these to us.

Moreover, it has declared that the nobleman Gerald d'Armagnac, whom you hold captive, you shall liberate, and deliver him free to us. We will moreover, by right of our lordship that you liberate him.

We call, therefore, upon your discretion in this matter, strictly requiring you and commanding that you obey the aforesaid sentences in all things and fulfill them in all respects and in no way defer the fulfillment of them. For making the announcement, the demand and the reception of these things, we have appointed as our representatives our beloved and faithful nobleman Gaston de Gontaud and R. Bernard de Balencs, promising that whatever shall be done by them in the aforesaid matters, we will hold as settled and firm forever. In testimony of which we have caused these present letters to be corroborated by the strength of our seal. Similar letters, divided through the alphabet, for a perpetual memory of this matter we have caused to be retained with us. Given at Agen, the third of the Kalends of July, A.D. 1249.

No. 70. Forfeiture

(*Translations and Reprints*, IV, No. 3, p. 36.)

It is presented by the jurors above named that the manor of Chinnore along with the hamlet of Sydenham was held of old, from the time of the Conquest, from the lord king of England, by a certain man who was named Walter de Vernon, as one knight's fee; and because the said Walter de Vernon refused to perform his due service from the said manor to the lord king John in the time of the war which sprang up between the lord king John and the king of France, the lord king John with the advice of his council seized that same manor with its appurtenances and removed the said Walter de Vernon, on account of his ingratitude from the possession of the aforesaid manor forever. And the lord king John granted that same manor with its appurtenances for the services that to the same king was due from it to Saer de Quincy formerly earl of Winchester, to hold to himself and his heirs *in capite* from the lord king as one knight's fee; and the heirs of the said Saer held the aforesaid manor in succession, and still hold it, except the hamlet of Sydenham, which the abbot of Thame holds as a gift from Roger de Quincy.

No. 71. From allodial to feudal holding

(Robinson's *Readings*, pp. 176-177.)

To all who shall see the present letters, the Official of Auxerre, greeting. Let all know, that standing in our presence William de la Foret, knight, and Agnes, his wife, asserting firmly that they hold and possess in free allod the property noted below; viz: the arpent of vines situated in the vineyard of Chablis, in the place which is called the Close, between the vines of William Berner, on the one side and the vines of the late Pariot, on the other, [together with other vineyards, meadow and arable land, certain houses, and rents in wine and grain], also all other things which they possessed and held in free allod, as they said, and still hold and possess within the boundaries of Chablis, of Chichiac, of Milli, of Ponche, of Bena and of Chapelle, the direct and hereditary holdings of the same Agnes wherever they may be within the same boundaries, and whatsoever, by their common consent and will, after previous deliberation, they have placed altogether in the fee of the church of St. Martin of Tours, and for the future have wished to hold and possess firmly in fee from the said church.

They promise on their fealty offered by their bodies, that they hold and will hold the things aforesaid and expressed above, with all other things which they hold and possess within the said boundaries wherever they may be and whatsoever, for the future, from the said church in fee, and to the same church in future, by reason of the same property will provide feudal service as they ought to provide it, just as others holding in fee are accustomed to hold and are bound to give or provide. Given A.D. 1267, Wednesday after the Ascension of the Lord.

No. 72. Truce of God for the diocese of Cologne (A.D. 1083)

(*Translations and Reprints*, I, No. 2, pp. 9-12.)

Inasmuch as in our times the church, through its members, has been extraordinarily afflicted by tribulations and difficulties, so that tranquility and peace were wholly despaired of, we have endeavored by God's help to aid it, suffering so many burdens and perils. And by the advice of our faithful subjects we have at length provided this remedy, so that we might to some extent re-establish, on certain days at least, the peace which, because of our sins, we could not make enduring. Accordingly we have enacted and set forth the following: having called together our parishioners to a legally summoned council, which was held at Cologne, the chief city of our province, in the Church of St. Peter, in the 1083d year of our Lord's Incarnation, in the sixth indiction, on the XII day before the Kalends of May, after arranging other business, we have caused to be read in public what we proposed to do in this matter. After this had been for some time fully discussed "pro and con" by call, it was unanimously agreed upon, both the clergy and the people consenting, and we declared in what manner and during what parts of the year it ought to be observed:

Namely, that from the first day of the Advent of our Lord through Epiphany, and from the beginning of Septuagesima to the eighth day after Pentecost and through that whole day, and throughout the year on every Sunday, Friday and Saturday, and on the fast days of the four seasons, and on the eve and the day of all the apostles, and on all days canonically set apart—or which shall in the future be set apart—for fasts or feasts, this decree of peace shall be observed; so that both those who travel and those who remain at home may enjoy security and the most entire peace, so that no one may commit murder, arson, robbery or assault, no one may injure another with a sword, club, or any kind of weapon, and so that no one irritated by any wrong, from the Advent of our Lord to the eighth day after Epiphany, and from Septuagesima to the eighth day after Pentecost, may presume to carry arms, shield, sword or lance, or moreover any kind of armor. On the remaining days indeed, viz., on Sundays, Fridays, apostles' days and the vigils of the apostles, and on every day set aside, or to be set aside, for fasts or feasts, bearing arms shall be legal, but on this condition, that no injury shall be done in any way to any one. If it shall be necessary for any one in the time of the decreed peace—i.e. from the Advent of our Lord to the eighth day after Epiphany, and from Septuagesima to the eighth day after Pentecost—to go from one bishopric into another in which the peace is not observed, he may bear arms, but on the condition that he shall not injure any one, except in self-defence if he is attacked; and when he returns into our diocese he shall immediately lay aside his arms. If it shall happen that any castle is besieged during the days which are included within the peace the besiegers shall cease from attack unless they are set upon by the besieged and compelled to beat the latter back.

And in order that this statute of peace should not be violated by any one rashly or with impunity, a penalty was fixed by the common consent of all; if a free man or noble violates it, i.e. commits homicide or wounds any one or is at fault in any manner whatever, he shall be expelled from our territory, without any indulgence on account of the payment of money or the intercession of friends, and his heirs shall take all his property; if he holds a fief, the lord to whom it belongs shall receive it again. Moreover, if it is learned that his heirs after his expulsion have furnished him any support or aid, and if they are convicted of it, the estate shall be taken from them and given to the king. But if they wish to clear themselves of the charge against them, they shall take oath with twelve, who are equally free or equally noble. If a slave kills a man, he shall be beheaded; if he wounds a man, he shall lose a hand; if he does an injury in any other way with his fist or a club, or by striking with a stone, he shall be shorn and flogged. If, however, he is accused and wishes to prove his innocence, he shall clear himself by the ordeal of cold water, but he must himself be put into the water and no one else in his place; if, however, fearing the sentence decreed against him, he flees, he shall be under a perpetual excommunication; and if he is known to be in any place, letters shall be sent thither, in which it shall be announced to all that he is excommunicate, and that it is unlawful for any one to associate with him. In the case of boys who have not yet completed their twelfth year, the hand ought not to be cut off; but only in the case of those who are twelve years or more of age. Nevertheless if boys fight, they shall be whipped and deterred from fighting.

It is not an infringement of the peace, if any one orders his delinquent slave, pupil, or any one in any way under his charge to be chastised with rods or cudgels. It is also an exception to this constitution of peace, if the Lord King publicly orders an expedition to attack the enemies of the kingdom or is pleased to hold a council to judge the enemies of justice. The peace is not violated if, during the time, the duke or other counts, advocates or their substitutes hold courts and inflict punishment legally on thieves, robbers and other criminals.

The statute of this imperial peace is especially enacted for the security of those engaged in feuds; but after the end of the peace, they are not to dare to rob and plunder in the villages and houses, because the laws and penalties enacted before the institution of the peace are still legally valid to restrain them from crime, moreover because robbers and highwaymen are excluded from this divine peace and indeed from any peace.

If any one attempts to oppose this pious institution and is unwilling to promise peace to God with the others or to observe it, no priest in our diocese shall presume to say a mass for him or shall take any care for his salvation; if he is sick, no Christian shall dare to visit him; on his deathbed he shall not receive the Eucharist, unless he repents. The supreme authority of the peace promised to God and commonly extolled by all will be so great that it will be observed not only in our times, but forever among our posterity, because if any one shall presume to infringe, destroy or violate it, either now or ages hence, at the end of the world, he is irrevocably excommunicated by us.

The infliction of the above mentioned penalties on the violators of the peace is not more in the power of the counts, centenaries or officials, than in that of the whole people in common; and they are to be especially careful not to show friendship or hatred or do anything contrary to justice in punishing, and not to conceal the crimes, if they can be hidden, but to bring them to light. No one is to receive money for the release of those taken in fault, or to attempt to aid the guilty by any favor of any kind, because whoever does this incurs the intolerable damnation of his soul; and all the faithful ought to remember that this peace has not been promised to men, but to God, and therefore must be observed so much the more rigidly and firmly. Wherefore we exhort all in Christ to guard inviolably this necessary contract of peace, and if any one hereafter presumes to violate it, let him be damned by the ban of irrevocable excommunication and by the anathema of eternal perdition.

In the churches, however, and in the cemeteries of the churches, honor and reverence are to be paid to God, so that if any robber or thief flees thither, he is by no means to be killed or seized, but he is to remain there until by urgent hunger he is compelled to surrender. If any person presumes to furnish arms or food to the criminal or to aid him in flight, the same penalty shall be inflicted on him as on the criminal. Moreover, by our ban we interdict laymen from punishing the transgressions of the clergy and those living under this order; but if seized in open crime, they shall be handed over to their bishop. In cases in which laymen are to be executed, the clergy are to be degraded; in cases in which laymen are to be mutilated, the clergy are to be suspended from office, and with the consent of the laymen they are to suffer frequent fasts and floggings until they atone.

No. 73. Summons for military service (A.D. 1072)

(J. H. Round, *Feudal England*. London, 1895, p. 304. Translation.)

William, king of the English, to Athew', abbot to Evesham, greeting. I command you to summon all those who are under your charge and authority that they shall have ready before me at Clarendon on the octave of Pentecost all the knights that they owe me. You, too, shall appear on that day and bring with you the five knights which you owe me for your abbey. Given at Winchester, 1072.

No. 74. Summons to meeting of great council

(William Stubbs, *Select Charters*, Oxford, 1895, pp. 282-283. Translation.)

King [John] to the bishop of Salisbury. We command and pray you that, without any excuse or delay, as you love us and our honor, you come to us at London on the Sunday preceding the Ascension of our Lord, to discuss with us important and difficult matters and the common welfare of our kingdom. And since, concerning those demands which have been made upon us by the king of France through his and our messengers, we hope, with the grace of God, that good fortune will result, it is expedient that we have your counsel and that of the other magnates of our country whom I have ordered summoned at the same time and place. You will on our and your part summon the abbots and conventual priors of your entire diocese, to present themselves at the said council, as they love us and the common good of the realm.

No. 75. Law of Frederick II abolishing wager of battle

(Translations and Reprints, IV, No. 4, pp. 21-22.)

We will that the single combat, or duel as it is commonly called, shall never be adjudged between men subject to our jurisdiction, except in a few specified cases; for it cannot be called so much a real proof as a sort of divination, which is not in accord with nature but is opposed to universal law and inconsistent with just reason. For it is almost if not quite impossible for two champions to come together so equally matched that the one is not wholly superior to the other in strength or does not excel him in some other way by greater vigor and courage or at least in cleverness. But we exclude from the benefit of this humane edict murderers who are charged with having caused the death of others by using poison or some other secret means; and even against these we do not sanction the wager of battle at the beginning of the trial, but command that ordinary proofs be first adduced against them if there be any such at hand, and that only then, as a last resort, when the crime cannot be fully established by other proofs after a thorough investigation by the officials of the court, resort may be had to the judgment of battle to decide the above charges: and we wish all these things to be arranged through the medium of a judge fully cognizant of the proceedings, that he may carefully and diligently investigate the proofs brought out by the inquisition. And if the charges shall not be proved as stated let him grant the accuser permission to offer battle, if nothing was brought out in court prejudicial to the accuser's right. But if the accuser should first offer to prove the crime by witnesses and their testimony should be insufficient, the trial shall not take place by the double method of inquisition and battle, but the defendant, not being convicted of guilt and being presumably innocent, shall be set free; because we wish the same law to be observed among all, both Franks and Lombards, and in all cases. In our new constitution, indeed, wager of battle has been sufficiently recognized in the case of the knights and nobles of our kingdom and of others who are able to offer battle. For we except the crime of treason, respecting which we preserve the judicial duel. Nor is it strange if we subject traitors, secret murderers and poisoners to the duel (though not so much as a method of judgment as to terrify them); not because our Serenity deems that just in their case which it has declared unjust in others, but because we desire that such homicides as have not feared to lay secret plots against human life, which God's power alone can call into existence, should be publicly subjected to this terrible method of proof in the sight of all men as a punishment and an example to others. Those also we exclude from the terms of our leniency who do not hesitate to plot against our peace in which the peace of all the rest is involved.

No. 76. Hereditary character of fiefs recognized in Capitulary of Kiersey (A.D. 877)

(Thatcher & McNeal, *Source Book*, pp. 355-356.)

If a count whose son accompanies us shall die during our absence, our son with the advice of our faithful subjects shall appoint one of the near relatives of the deceased count to govern the county with the aid of the officials of the county and the bishop in whose diocese it is, until we are notified of the case and have an opportunity to give the son of the count his father's honors. But if the deceased count shall leave a minor son, that son shall govern the county with the aid of the officials and the bishop in whose diocese it is, until the death of the said count has been brought to our notice and we endow the son with his father's honors. But if the count shall not leave a son, our son with the advice of our faithful subjects shall appoint someone to govern the county with the aid of the officials of the county and the bishop, until our commands in respect to it are made known. And no one shall feel aggrieved, if we give the county to another than the one who governed it up to the time of our appointment. The same procedure shall be observed in regard to our vassals; and the bishops, abbots, and counts of our kingdom, and our other faithful subjects, shall do the same toward their men.

(Charles the Bald issued this decree when he left France for Italy.)

No. 77. Appropriation or grant of fief? Treaty of St. Clair-sur-Epte (A.D. 911)

(R. G. D. Laffan, *Select Documents of European History*, I. New York, 1930, pp. 14-15. By permission of Methuen & Co. Ltd. Publishers.)

The king hastily sent Archbishop Franco to Rollo, offering to give him the coastland from the river Epte to the boundaries of Brittany, together with his daughter, Gisela, if he would become a Christian. . . . At the stated time they came to the appointed place, called St. Clair—the king with Robert, Duke of the Franks, on the far bank of the Epte, and Rollo on this side, surrounded by their troops. . . . At first the king wished to give him the province of Flanders to live on; but Rollo refused it because of its marshy character. Then Rollo refused to kiss the king's foot on receiving the duchy of Normandy from him. The bishops said, "He who receives such a gift ought to salute the king's foot with a kiss." "Never," said he, "will I bend my knees before anyone, nor will I kiss the foot of any Frank." Moved, however, by their prayers, he ordered one of his warriors to kiss the king's foot. The latter promptly seized the king's foot, carried it to his mouth and kissed it standing, thus throwing the king on to his back. At that there was a roar of laughter and a great disturbance amongst the spectators. However, King Charles and Robert, Duke of the Franks, with the counts and magnates, bishops and abbots, swore an oath of the Catholic faith to the patrician Rollo, on their lives and members and the honour of the whole kingdom, that he should hold and possess the aforesaid territory and transmit it to his heirs. . . .

The king joyfully returned home, while Rollo went with Duke Robert to Rouen in the year 912. And there he was baptized in the sacred font by Archbishop Franco in the name of the Holy Trinity. Robert received him from the font and gave him his own name. The pagans, seeing their leader become a Christian, abandoned their idols, accepted the name of Christ and all came forward for baptism.

No. 78. Feudalization of the church

(Roger of Wendover's *Flowers of History*, tr. J. A. Giles, I., London, 1892, pp. 496-497.)

A.D. 1143. Pope Lucius died, and was succeeded by Eugenius, who sat eight years, four months, and twenty-one days. The same year king Stephen besieged Lincoln, and began to build another tower opposite the castle, which was held by Ralph earl of Chester; but about eighty of his men being slain by the earl, the work was abandoned. The same year Robert Marmiun, a warlike knight, who had expelled the monks of Coventry from their monastery, and turned the church into a castle, was slain one day in front of the monastery, as he was fighting against his enemies, though he was in the midst of his gang of robbers, and no one was hurt but himself: as he died excommunicate, he has death for his portion for ever. At the same time Geoffrey earl of Mandeville, who had perpetrated the same act of wickedness in the monastery of Ramsey, was pierced with an arrow by a low foot-soldier and died: this event happened in front of the same church, as the earl was fighting in the midst of his troops; and the church, whilst it was made use of as a castle, sent forth blood in abundance from its walls, in manifestation of the divine displeasure. Arnulf, also, son of the same earl, who, after his father's death, held the church as a castle, was taken by the king and banished the kingdom, and the leader of his troops fell from his horse and expired on the spot. Reiner, also, commander of the infantry, who was in the habit of burning and destroying monasteries, was sentenced to exile, and, whilst he was crossing the sea, his ship suddenly remained motionless in the water, and when the sailors drew lots, the lot three times fell upon Reiner, whereupon he was put into a little boat with his wife, his children, and all that he had; the boat immediately sank and all the wretched family perished: whilst the ship sailed over the tranquil sea without difficulty or hindrance. The same year Geoffrey count of Anjou was received in due form by the citizens of Rouen, and from that time had the title of duke of Normandy.

No. 79. The ritual of knighthood

(*The Book of the Ordre of Chyualry*. A translation by William Caxton of Ramon Lull's *Le Libre Del Orde De Cauayleria* put into Modern English. By courtesy of the Council of the Early English Text Society. No. 168, 1926, pp. 62-78.)

Of the Examining of the Squire that will enter into the Order of Chivalry or Knighthood

A knight should stand in greater fear of public censure and dishonor than of death itself, and should give greater drive to his courage than hunger, thirst, heat, or cold give to his body. That the squire be made aware of all the perils before he be knighted, let him know that the responsibilities of chivalry cannot be discharged without the necessary equipment which the knight requires, nor without the means to sustain the honorable costs and expenses which chivalry demands. For that squire who is without such equipment and without the means to bear these expenses, if he be a knight, might be tempted to become a robber, thief, traitor, liar, burglar, or acquire some other vices which are inconsistent with chivalry. In similar fashion, a lame man or one overly large or fat, or one who suffers any other unfortunate handicap which would prevent him from fulfilling the office of chivalry, is not qualified to be a knight. For it would not be in keeping with the order of chivalry were she to accept a man to bear arms which were blemished, defiled, or not powerful. For so very noble and high is the honor of chivalry that a squire who is lame in any member, however noble and rich and high born he may be, is not fit nor worthy to be received into the order.

Inquiries should next be made of the squire who is a candidate for knighthood, if he was ever guilty of falseness or treachery which are contrary to the order of chivalry. For he may have been guilty of such conduct, and yet have never realized that he is therefore not worthy to be enrolled in the order of chivalry, nor to become an associate of those who maintain that order. If a squire be vainglorious of that which he does, he is not worthy to be a knight. For vainglory is a vice which destroys and nullifies the merits and blessings which flow from the benefits of chivalry. A squire who flatters brings discord to the order of chivalry. For a man who is a flatterer corrupts good intentions, and the nobility which pertains to the courage of a knight is thereby destroyed. A squire who is proud, evil taught, full of wicked words, of base courage, avaricious, a liar, untrue, slothful, a glutton, perjured, or who is afflicted with any similar vice is not acceptable to chivalry. For if chivalry should accept those that are not fitted for the order, one would have to conclude that in chivalry that which is in keeping with its principles and that which is not, are one and the same thing. And since such chivalry is required of the order of valor, therefore every squire should be examined before he is made a knight.

In what Manner a Squire ought to be received into the Order of Chivalry

Before a squire enters the order of chivalry, it is necessary that he confess the sins which he has committed against God, and that he be determined to serve God who is glorious in the same manner as chivalry. After he is cleansed of his sins, he should receive his Saviour [Communion]. The squire should be knighted on some great feast such as Christmas, Easter, Whitsunday, or similarly solemn day, since many people will be gathered together at that place because of the feastday, who should adore God and pray that He give him the grace to live in accord with the order of chivalry. The squire should fast on the vigil of that feast in honor of the saint whose feastday it is, and he should go to church and pray to God, and ought to remain awake during the night and be in his prayers, and hear about the word of God and about the responsibilities of chivalry. Otherwise, if he should hear jongleurs and ribald fellows talk about unchastity and sin, he would then begin to dishonor chivalry. On the morning of the feast in which he is to be knighted, the squire should have a solemn Mass sung. He should come before the altar and swear to the priest who is the representative of God, his oath of fealty to the one to whom he owes this, and promise to uphold the honor of chivalry to the best of his ability. That same day a sermon should be preached about the twelve articles upon which the Catholic faith is founded, the ten commandments, and the seven sacraments of the holy church, together with other matters that pertain to the faith. The squire should most diligently take heed of and retain these words, so that he remember those elements of chivalry which pertain to the faith. [Here follows a discussion of the articles of faith, the commandments, and sacraments.] And all these things and others that pertain to chivalry, the preacher should make mention of in the presence of the squire, who should pray most devoutly that God give him His grace and His blessing so that he be a good knight all the days of his life.

When the preacher will have discussed all these things which pertain to his office, let the prince or baron who will knight the squire himself possess the virtues of chivalry. For if the knight who does the knighting is not virtuous, how can he give that which he has not? Such a knight is even in worse condition than the plants, for plants have the power to give their natures to others, and beasts and fowls in like manner. But this the knight is unable to do. Such a knight is evil and false who will thus irregularly increase his order. He does wrong and brings disgrace to chivalry. For he will be doing that which is not becoming, and while he should be honoring chivalry, he will be injuring and dishonoring it. Through the fault of such a knight, it happens on occasion that the squire who is knighted by him receives less assistance and grace from God, and less virtue and chivalry than he would had he been knighted by a good and loyal knight. For that reason such a squire is a fool and all others too who receive the order of chivalry from such a knight.

The squire ought to kneel before the altar and lift up his corporal and spiritual eyes to God and his hands to heaven; and the knight then should gird him with his sword, the sign of chastity, justice, and of charity. The knight ought to kiss the squire and give him a palm to remind him of what he has received and promised, of the heavy charge with which he is obliged and burdened, and of the great honor that he has received in the order of chivalry. After the knight spiritual, that is, the priest, and the knight terrestrial will have performed that which pertains to their offices concerning the making of the new knight, the new knight should ride through the town and show himself to the people, so that all men may know and see that he has been newly knighted and know that he is now obligated to maintain and defend the high honor of chivalry. Thus will he have much greater cause to refrain from doing evil. For the knowledge that people know him to be a knight, will lead him to be the more concerned lest he sin against the order of chivalry. On the same day he should provide a great feast, give fair gifts and rich dinners, joust and sport, do other things that pertain to the order of chivalry, and bestow gratuities upon the kings of arms and the heralds as is the ancient custom. The lord who confers the knighthood should give the new knight a present, while the new knight should give him one in return on that same day. For whosoever receives so great a gift as the order of chivalry honors not his order if he gives not in return in keeping with his power to give. All these things and many others which I will not now discuss because of the shortness of the time pertain to chivalry.

Of the Significance of the Arms of the Knight

The vestments with which the priest clothes himself when he sings Mass have some significance which are in accord with his office. The office of the priesthood and of chivalry have much in common. Therefore, the order of chivalry requires that all those things which are necessary to the knight in the fulfillment of his office have some significance. By this means is revealed the nobleness of chivalry and of the order. The knight is given a sword which is made after the manner of the cross, to signify how our Lord God vanquished on the cross the death of humanity with which He was laden for the sin of our first father Adam. In like manner the knight ought to vanquish and destroy the enemies of the cross by the sword. Chivalry is required to dispense justice, and for that reason the sword has two cutting edges to signify that the knight ought to maintain chivalry and justice with it. The knight is given a spear to signify truth. For truth is a thing right and even, and that truth ought to go before falseness. The iron or head of the spear symbolizes strength which truth ought to have above falseness. The pennant signifies that truth reveals faith to all and has no fear or dread of depravity or treachery. Virtue is sustained by hope and by other things as well, which are symbolized by the spear of the knight. The helmet of steel or iron is given the knight to signify the dread of shame. Without that dread the knight may not be faithful to the order of chivalry. [Ramon Lull then explains the symbolism involved, and goes on to note the spiritual significance which attaches to the rest of the knight's weapons, to his defensive gear, even to the equipment which his horse carries.]

No. 80. John of Salisbury on the responsibilities of the knight

(From the *Policraticus*. Migne, *Patrologia Latina*, CXCIX, 1855 Translation.)

> Bk. VI. Ch. 8. The military service is bound by necessity to religion, like that which is consecrated among the clergy in the divine services; that the name of soldier is one of work as much as of honor.

Consider the words of the oath itself, and you will discover that military service, no less than the spiritual, is bound by the requirements of its official duties to religion and the worship of God, since soldiers owe obedience to the prince and ever-watchful loyalty to the state, faithfully and according to the will of God. Wherefore, as I have said, those who are not elected nor sworn, even though they are classified as soldiers, are no more soldiers in truth than priests or clerks whom the church has not called to orders. For the name soldier is one of service as much as of honor. No one, indeed, takes this honor upon himself, but only he who is called by the Lord (*Hebr.* v) may glory in the honor conferred.

Moses and the leaders of the faithful people selected men who were courageous and experienced in battle when it was necessary to oppose an enemy. For these virtues qualify one for selection. That one, on the other hand, who forces himself into the army without being summoned, provokes against himself the sword which he usurps by his own imprudence. For he runs afoul of the eternal decree that declares whoever takes up the sword shall perish by it. (*Matt.* xxvi.) If indeed the word of Cicero is to be applied to him, he is to be classified not as a soldier but as an assassin. For in the writings of the ancients, those men are called assassins and robbers who carry arms without being authorized to do so by law. For the arms which the law does not employ are used against the state.

The sacred text of the Gospel declares that two swords are sufficient to the Christian realm. All others belong to those who came with swords and clubs to take Christ and to destroy His name. For what do they have in common with a soldier, who although they are called do not obey the law according to their oath, but rather believe that the real glory of military service consists in ridiculing the priesthood, in vilifying the authority of the Church, in extending the dominion of man by reducing that of Christ, in flattering and extolling themselves with false commendations, imitating the braggart soldier to the derision of the crowd. Their courage shows itself principally in this, that with their tongues or their spears they stab the clergy and the unarmed citizenry.

What is the office of the duly ordained soldiery? To protect the Church, to oppose treachery, to venerate the priesthood, to protect the poor from injury, to pacify the country, to shed their blood for their brothers as the oath requires, and, if need be, to lay down their lives. The praises of God are in their throats, the two-edged swords are in their hands, to punish nations and to rebuke the people, to bind their kings in chains and the nobles in iron fetters. (*Psal.* cxlix)

But for what purpose? So that they might serve rage, vanity, and avarice, and their own personal whims? Not at all. That they execute rather the judgment entrusted to them (*ibid.*) in that each does not his will but the will of God, of the angels, and of men in accordance with justice and the common good. I say they should do this, since just as it is the function of judges to pronounce judgments, so it is their duty to perform their office by executing it. Surely this honor have all His saints. (*Ibid.*) For soldiers who do conduct themselves in this fashion are saints, and the more zealously they keep the faith of God, the more faithful are they to their prince; and the more faithfully they seek the honor of God in all things, the more success-fully will they advance their own honor.

Ch. 10. Concerning the privileges of soldiers; that by oath they are bound to serve the Church; why the sword is offered on the altar.

It is right that soldiers enjoy many privileges, which is quite evident in ancient law. For they are more free and enjoy more privileges. They are exempt from villanage and extra service (boon work), and from all base service. They are also permitted to plead ignorance of the law, and al-though they are subject to the authority of another, they may dispose by will of their military earnings. Above all, because this is essential to the public good, they are not permitted to want. There are many other privi-leges of this kind which they enjoy but which are too many to enumerate. While there are some who do not consider themselves bound by solemn oath to serve the church, since by custom many do not take an actual oath, there is no one who is not responsible to the Church either by tacit or formal oath. And perhaps the formality of the oath has been dispensed with because every obligation of the office and the sincerity of faith suggest and require this. Wherefore the solemn practice has already been estab-lished that on that very day on which a man is girt with the belt of a sol-dier, he goes solemnly to church, and having placed his sword on the altar, offers it, and, as if by way of solemn profession, pledges himself to the serv-ice of the altar and promises God the perpetual obedience of his sword, that is, his service.

8

THE MEDIEVAL MANOR

A chapter dealing with the medieval manor logically follows the one on feudalism. For manorialism, that is, the agrarian system which prevailed over much of western Europe in the Middle Ages, has been called the "lower side" of feudalism. Medieval feudalism constituted the political and administrative structure of Europe for a large portion of the Middle Ages; manorialism its economic and social system. Both were intimately related, although not entirely coterminous in time. The manor developed somewhat earlier and as an institution was the first to decline, even though the countryside of some sections of western Europe today retains a number of the agricultural arrangements and traditions peculiar to the medieval manor. Both institutions, feudalism and manorialism, took root in a period of noncapitalistic land economy, and so long as that condition persisted, both thrived. The fief of the lord normally comprised a number of manors, the lord providing government and protection, the people of the manor, food, goods, and services. The lord and peasant complemented one another, and together with the clergy provided all that Christians of the Middle Ages believed a heaven-oriented society required: a clergy, the first estate, to pray; an aristocracy, the second estate, to fight and govern; a common class, the third estate, to perform the physical work necessary to satisfy the material needs of the medieval population. As Raymond Lull wrote in his *Book of the Order of Chivalry:* "It is seemly that the men should plow and dig and work hard that the earth may yield the fruits from which the knight and his horse will live; and that the knight who rides and does a lord's work should get his wealth from the things on which his men are to spend much toil and fatigue."

Most People Farmers. These toilers of the soil constituted the largest element in the population of the Middle Ages. This may appear strange to us who find it difficult in this machine age of ours to visualize a time when most people lived on the land and drew their sustenance directly from the soil. Yet that was generally the pattern of economic life throughout the world until less than a hundred years ago. During antiquity and the Middle Ages, the great majority of men and women lived as farmers or food raisers of one kind or another. According to the Domesday Book survey which William the Conqueror ordered made for England in 1806 (see page 445), more than 95 per cent of England's population lived on the land or in village communities at the close of the eleventh century. The only country of western Europe which could claim an appreciably lower percentage of land residents would be Italy. There were, to be sure, a few people who belonged to the third estate or commoner class who were not farmers. They lived in towns and were engaged in industry or commerce. But these constituted only a fraction of the population in antiquity and an even smaller percentage in Europe from the fifth to the eleventh centuries. As we have noted, already during the last centuries of the Roman Empire a strong trend toward agrarian self-sufficiency had set in, particularly in the western provinces. That trend had been accelerated with the coming of the Germans who had never known town life. The disruption of Mediterranean commerce by the Moslems, the political instability of the west from the fifth century onward, the deterioration of roads and bridges remaining from Roman times, the extreme shortage of bullion and fluid capital, these and other factors conspired to fasten an agrarian economy upon western Europe in the early Middle Ages.

Manorialism. A large part of the farm population of western Europe in the Middle Ages lived on what are known as manors. The manor (from the Latin *manere* meaning to dwell) might best be defined as an agricultural estate, held by a lord, and consisting of a village community or communities, together with the surrounding acres from which its occupants drew their sustenance. That all medieval farmers did not live on manors was simply because the manor was the product of local conditions, chiefly soil and climate. Since western Europe from Gibraltar to Novgorod offers a wide variation of climate, topography, and quality of soil, no uniform system of agriculture could possibly have evolved over that two-thousand mile expanse. The medieval agricultural community which we know as the manor or manorial village was fairly typical of England, France, and Germany. It did not take root in Scotland or Wales, nor in the mountainous regions of Spain, southern France, or Italy. These areas maintained only scattered homesteads and developed more specialized economies such as stock raising or vine and olive cultures. The manor flourished only in the grain-producing areas of western and eastern Europe which could sustain a comparatively large population.

Origins of Manorialism. While the manor, much like feudalism, was the natural product of the times, it had historical órigins nonetheless. In part it was the answer of the early Middle Ages to the breakdown of communications and growing provincialism which can be traced back to Roman times. There are, consequently, Roman roots to this peculiarly medieval institution. From the third century onward, more and more of the farmers of the western half of the Roman Empire were finding themselves the semifree *coloni* working the large estates of the Roman aristocracy. As we have seen, the Roman landowner directed not only the economic lives of these *coloni*, but he assumed as well the responsibility of maintaining law and order over his estates which they worked. When the German invader appropriated many of these estates for himself, he was ordinarily content to continue the arrangement which had prevailed between the *coloni* and their Roman lord. The medieval manor also had German roots. These are best to be found in northern France, in England, and in Germany, where Roman institutions had either not established themselves or had been submerged during the Germanic invasions. Here the German free village had become the typical agrarian unit. At one time the bulk of its members had been free farmers or herdsmen who lived a communal sort of life guided largely by custom. Yet surely as early as the sixth century, when the local Germanic chieftains began to arrogate to themselves political powers once shared with the freemen, the latter discovered that their economic freedom was likewise gradually waning. By the close of the Merovingian period the German villager had become socially and economically depressed in status and could no longer be distinguished from the semifree farmers on "Roman" manors. And those farmers who might earlier have escaped the experience of both the Roman *colonus* and the German villager, found no choice in the turbulent times of the eighth and ninth centuries but to subordinate themselves and their acres to the will of a lord.

Differences between Villa and Manor. While many manors of western Europe were sprung from earlier Roman landed estates or villas, there were significant differences between these Roman villas of the late empire and the medieval manor. The proprietor of the Roman villa might view his estates as an investment from which he could derive profit. The manor, on the other hand, was by nature noncapitalistic. When it ceased being noncapitalistic in the twelfth century, it ceased being a true manor in terms of our definition. For where the villa tended toward economic self-sufficiency, often by choice, the manor had no choice to be other than self-sufficient. Its economy was closed, it had few sources of commodities outside itself, it had no outlets for its own products beyond the manorial limits. Because the medieval manor was cut off from competitive forces and produced only for its own people, a natural regression occurred for a time in the methods employed, since there was no longer any premium upon increasing the land's yield. Futhermore, since population stagnated, if it did not actually decline, from the fifth to the tenth century, many communities found they had more tillable soil available than they needed. Consequently, land ceased being a source of profit and became purely a means of subsistence. For this reason the manor may be conceived of as more a social institution, the villa as primarily an economic institution. The personal arrangment between the lord and *colonus* determined the latter's status on the villa. The status of the serf, on the other hand, and manorial procedure in general, were determined largely by tradition, by custom that "since the time whereof the memory of man runneth not to the contrary." Thus on the villa the lord's word was law, on the manor custom and tradition often determined manorial routine. Yet while the lord of the manor encountered greater limitations than the Roman proprietor in his economic exploitation of his estates, his political control over the people living on the manor was virtually unlimited.

Physical Appearance of the Manor. The medieval village presented a picture of unprepossessing tranquillity. The first impression the traveler would receive would be that of its isolation. The manor lived a sleepy life of its own. If it lay athwart a road, the road was at best only a trail which would connect by horseback with some remote village or town. The first structure in the village to catch the eye of the visitor would be the castle, if this happened to be a large community; otherwise the manor house where the lord put up for a month or so each year to eat up the produce of his estates. The manor house would reflect the eminence of its occupant in its location upon the highest ground in the community and by its stately proportions. Also somewhat above the general drabness of the scene would be the village church on which the community would have expended its best structural efforts. All the other buildings would consist of the plain, thatched cottages of the villagers, one as unattractive as the next, with garden plot adjoining and usually a cowshed and hayrick. The remaining structures of the community would include the mill where the grain was ground, and barns and granaries in which grain, hay, and other materials were stored. A mill pond fed by a stream would pretty well complete the physical inventory of the village. (Reading 85)

The Manorial Community

The uniformity which characterized the physical appearance of medieval manors did not extend to the people who dwelled thereon. These enjoyed or suffered, as the case might be, a most confusing diversity of rights and obligations. Of course, the lord of the manor, if he happened to live in the nearby castle or manor house, presented no problem. His duties were largely external: to provide the community protection. In other respects he was quite expendable, since custom, as suggested above, not his word, directed the economic and social life of the community. In any event, he had manorial officials whose business it was to make sure that he would not be defrauded of what was rightfully his. Considerably more vital to the community was the priest who administered to the spiritual needs of the villagers. The priest's ties with the community would probably be close, since he was normally of peasant stock himself and might even have been a member of that manor since birth. Having disposed of these single representatives of the first and second estates, we are left to analyze the condition of those representatives of the third estate who made up more than ninety-nine per cent of the community. It was not their physical appearance nor their social relationships which account for the difficulty of classifying them since these reflected then even less than today the varied income distribution of the members of the village community. It was rather their economic status as members of the manor with respect to the lord which presents scholars the chief problem associated with the manor.

Importance of Custom. Since the manor existed ultimately to provide the lord with the resources necessary to fulfill his role in society, the rights and obligations of its members existed largely in relation to him. On the one hand, the lord was in fact and virtually in law the owner of the lands the villagers tilled, of the homes in which they lived, even of their very freedom of action. On the other hand, so powerful were the customs and traditions which had grown up over a period of centuries touching the status and rights of the inhabitants of the village, that only arrogant or imprudent lords would dare defy these conventions and make arbitrary judgements contrary to the general approval of the community. Consequently, it was more often heredity and circumstance rather than the will of the lord that determined the particular economic condition and personal status of the members of the community. By heredity we mean that the son of a freeman was a freeman, that of a slave a slave, the son of a serf or semifree villager a serf. By circumstance we mean such possibilities as that of a freeman endangering his free status by acquiring lands subject to servile tenure or simply that of living as a member of a very small minority among a community of serfs.

The Freeman. At the top of the manorial community was the freeman. Their number varied sharply from country to country, from century to century. Twelve per cent of the people classified in the Domesday survey referred to above were listed as freemen. These included freeholders who held land in their own right and free tenants who paid a rental which had been fixed by personal arrangement with the lord rather than by custom. The nonfeudal officials of the manor such as the steward and bailiff were freemen. While a sprinkling of freemen might be found on many manors, in terms of total number the great majority of freemen during the manorial period lived in wholly free communities over which the lord had either never exercised manorial control or had relinquished it. Such free villages might be degraded overnight by fiat of a lord as William the Conqueror had done with most of the Saxon communities when he took over England.

At best the line dividing the freeman from the unfree was a narrow one, since the freeman shared in many of the servile activities of the manorial community. He might labor alongside the serf on the lord's land and in the lord's service, although not for so long a period nor at such onerous jobs. He could also give his daughter in marriage without securing the lord's permission, he could appeal, at least in theory, beyond the ruling of the lord, and he could dispose of his holdings and leave the village if he chose. Still because he belonged to a group so very small among a much larger servile company, and since one's status on the manor merged almost imperceptibly with that of the villagers just below, it was easy for him to slip into the more general class of the serf beneath him.

The Medieval Slave. This same tendency, on the other hand, worked to the advantage of the slave who found himself at the lowest rung of the manorial ladder. He had nowhere to go but upward, and there he tended to gravitate. Stronger pressures, in fact, forced him upward in status than those which operated to degrade the freeman. The slave in the ancient sense of a person possessing no rights of any kind was an incongruity in western Europe during the Middle Ages. No medieval writer could have classified slaves as did the respected Roman scholar Varro: dumb implements (plow), semidumb (cattle), and talking (slaves) implements. Medieval society accepted the principle that slaves had souls, even though occasional slaveholders could always be found who refused to honor this principle. Yet it was less this moral consideration than the fact that slavery generally was uneconomical and unnecessary that contributed to its disappearance during the Middle Ages. Since the lord was assured the services of the members of the manor whether slave or serf, he would normally prefer to give the slave a hut and plot of ground for himself, thereby relieving himself of any personal responsibility for feeding and clothing him. Once the lord had done this, the slave ceased being a slave and became a serf. Domesday Book classifies nine per cent of England's population as slaves, but this number decreased rapidly. By 1200 the legal slave had disappeared from western manors (not from western cities). (Readings 84, 89-92)

Many Classes of Serfs. With the freeman on top of the manorial social ladder and the slave at the bottom both vanishing minorities, it becomes clear why most members of the manor are simply classified as serfs or villeins. The terms serf and villein are not entirely synonymous, but fact if not law left them substantially the same. If we were to consider differences so fine as this, we could easily lose sight of the most basic fact about the people on the manor, which was, that conditions and circumstances forced them all into pretty much the same uniform mold whatever the nuances of their particular status. At the head of the unfree population of the manor was the free villein as he was called, who rented his land but could not leave the manor without the lord's permission. The lowliest serf was the cottar who could claim little beyond his rude dwelling and a garden plot. Between the free villein and cottar, many gradations of servile status might be found, although from the lord's point of view and our own vantage point, the commoners on the manor appeared so close together in terms of servile obligations that we shall consider all of them as simply serfs.

Tradition Protected Serf's Rights. Let us examine first the serf's rights, for rights he possessed despite the medieval lawyer's judgment that the will of the lord against him was unlimited. If this was correct, it was so only in a narrowly juristic sense. Over a period of generations if not centuries, custom and tradition had provided the serf certain guarantees before which the will of the lord had to bend. Furthermore, if this unwritten law would not of itself have restrained the lord from putting his hands to the "rights" which the serf had technically usurped, self-interest warned the lord it would be folly to do otherwise. Furthermore, in this consideration of the serf's rights and the lord's claims, we must never lose sight of the fact that the manor was noncapitalistic. Consequently, when the lord became conscious of his legal rights, real or presumed, over his serf, when he began to require more from his subjects than tradition permitted him, he was in fact living in a new age, in a capitalistic era. And capitalism and the manor were incompatible in terms of our definition of the manor. On the true manor, the lord would have had no economic incentive to defy tradition at the expense of his serf's traditional rights.

Right to Remain on the Manor. Perhaps the greatest boons the serf possessed were the equity he held in the land of the manor and his right to remain a member of that community. Though the lord owned all the land and could dispose of the manor as a unit, he could normally not deprive the serf of his acres or force him off the manor. One might compare the serf on the manor to the tenant of an apartment who has a long-term lease extendible at the discretion of the tenant. This right to a place on the manor was a greater blessing than we might appreciate in our days when opportunities elsewhere so often lure us away from our parental homes. For the serf of the ninth and tenth centuries, there was no place to go. Once he left the manor he was an outlaw and treated as such. Thus it was imperative that society should not permit the lord to exercise a right he might legally have possessed, namely, that of expelling the serf. Thus custom assured the serf a home and the protection of a powerful lord at a time when both home and protection were at a premium. In like manner, the acres which the serf had inherited from his father to cultivate had come into the family at a time when the element of profit was absent. Here again society required the lord to recognize the serf's right to farm these acres indefinitely, even when in the course of time they had acquired real economic value.

Other Rights. The serf had the right to use the manorial court against other members of the community (not against his lord). From medieval records it would appear that there was nothing he enjoyed doing better. The serf also enjoyed the right to a family life, although some lords were loath to accept the church's position that the sacrament of matrimony was also intended for commoners. Similarly the church sought, and usually with success, to have the serf released from labor obligations on Sundays and holy days. The number of holy days bulked large in the Middle Ages. In addition to single days such as Ascension Day, the Beheading of St. John the Baptist, and Michaelmas, there were extended periods of festivity at Christmas, Epiphany, Easter, and Pentecost, which were celebrated as holidays. The serf also had the right to share in the dead wood and mast of the forest and in the use of the common pasture and waste lands, although frequently only for a fee. Finally, so long as the serf performed his part of the unwritten agreement with his lord, the lord could not reduce his holdings nor increase his obligations.

The Serf's Obligations. The medieval serf's classification as semifree sprang principally from two limitations: first, he could not dispose of the equity he held in terms of lands and rights in the community; second, he could not leave the manor. A consideration of the origin of these curious restrictions will throw some light on their justification. They hearken back to a time when the manor was almost wholly a social unit, when the protection afforded by the manor was the chief desideratum, and when this protection required both the proximity of a great lord and the cooperation of the members of the community. Then the men were needed as much to defend the community from its enemies as to produce the food the villagers consumed. Consequently, since the serf's presence was required if the community was to survive, custom forbade him to leave. That the serf could not marry his daughter off the manor without the lord's consent may be traced back to this same concern about maintaining all available manpower. Actually this restriction that the serf not leave the manor, did not grow onerous until several hundred years of manorial history had elapsed. As pointed out above, to have a place one could call home was a real boon in the troublesome years of the eighth, ninth, and tenth centuries. And where exactly could the serf who was not content with his surroundings have gone during those centuries except to another manor where he would have been without friends and equity, that is, if he could even have reached there alive? To deny the serf the right to leave his manor in the ninth and tenth centuries was as academic as to deny shore leave to a soldier on a tiny islet in the Pacific a thousand miles from nowhere. With the rise of towns, however, and the appearance of new manors along the frontier which offered the promise of a higher economic status, this restriction upon the serf's freedom of movement became a most galling one. Still even then we read how the lord's right to recover a vagrant serf lapsed after a year and a day.

Other Limitations on the Serf's Freedom. The serf must secure his lord's permission to marry his daughter off the manor (*formariage* in France, *merchet* in England). Since the lord normally required a heavy fee for such a concession, one may assume few serfs found wives elsewhere unless an exchange of brides could be arranged. That manors were not close to one another and that parents loomed as large a factor in marriage arrangements as romance, would also militate against the frequency with which such permission would be requested. The serf paid a small annual capitation or poll tax (*chevage*) as a mark of his servile status. A more odious tax was the *taille* or tallage which might be a personal tax or one based on produce or tenure. What made this tax especially obnoxious was the lord's right to levy it when he chose and for the amount he wished. To take over their deceased father's title to land and cottage, the children paid a *heriot* or *mainmorte* which might include all chattels or at least the best animal. The serf was also obligated for the tithe or tenth of his produce which he paid, in theory, to the church, more often to the lord. The serf paid fees called banalities for the use of such of the lord's properties as his wine press, bake-oven, mill, or brewery. At one time since only the lord could afford such facilities, it was reasonable that others who might use them should pay a fee. Because these payments had grown traditional before the wine press and similar devices had come within the reach of the ordinary peasant, the serf paid the fee whether he availed himself of the lord's equipment or not. And if Christmas and Easter were days of spiritual joy and social rejoicing, they were also expensive. The lord of the manor might require a fat goose or hen from each of his serfs to help him feed guests who happened in. Most if not all these fees were paid in produce, in pigs, chickens, eggs, sheep, grain, bread, wine, wool, vegetables, and so on.

Labor Charge. Onerous though the sum total of such obligations must have been, the heaviest charge against the serf was that of working for his lord. The serf had fallen victim to the requisitions described above partly by accident or circumstance. As such they might linger on as traditional obligations long after the manor as an institution had disappeared. The demand on the serf's labor, on the other hand, was fundamental to the manorial economy. When this had lapsed or had been transformed, the manor would have ceased to exist. As with the fees assessed against the serf, his labor charges (*corvées*) rested upon real situations. Since the lord owned (or claimed) all the land of the manor, and since he did no physical labor of his own, what was more reasonable than that he require those to whom he had granted lands to work the acres he had reserved to his own use? The acres of the lord were called his demesne. They comprised roughly one third the total attaching to the manor. From this land the lord derived the bulk of his food and produce by means of the labor of the serfs of the community. How much labor the ordinary serf would give his lord might vary from as few as two days a week to as many as five, with three being the average. The labor would be done in crews under the watchful supervision of a manorial official and would cover the entire agricultural cycle from plowing, harrowing, sowing, through harvesting. During the harvest time the lord would require additional days of labor called boon days or boon work. Whether the serf considered this additional burden an unqualified evil would depend in measure on the quantity of spirits the lord had at hand to wash down the food he had provided. When farm work did not pre-empt the serf's labor, he might be engaged on the repair of roads, on the fortifications of the castle, in hauling goods, cutting wood, or in one of the other sundry jobs necessary to maintain the manor. If he showed some particular ingenuity he might spend the bulk of the time he owed his lord as a mason, carpenter, smith, leatherworker, or miller. It should be noted that the serf's workday ordinarily ran for no more than five or six hours, that is, a long forenoon or an afternoon. (Readings 81, 88)

Court Duty. The least onerous of the serf's obligations was attendance at the manorial court. This would convene with some regularity about once a month or when occasion demanded, and the place of meeting would be the main hall of the manor house or the church in winter and on the village green in summer. The lord of the manor might preside if he chose, but it was usually his representative, the bailiff, who did so. The chief business turned about property rights, the claims of the lord against the members of the manorial community, or those of the villagers against one another. With such an abundance of parcels of land and an infinitude of rights and obligations, the docket must have been a full one. The court also considered such minor criminal transgressions as theft, trespassing, cursing, and similar infractions of the moral law. Though the villagers were expected to advise as to what custom or right reason dictated in the adjudication of these matters, it might be difficult to block the lord's will with an appeal to "that contrary to which memory serveth not." And if the lord did not ordinarily have his way in the decisions of the court, he had his way at least with the fees and fines the court assessed. (Reading 82)

Medieval Agriculture

Since the manor constituted a largely self-sufficient economic unit concerned almost exclusively with the problem of raising enough food for its livelihood, the majority of the inhabitants were necessarily engaged in agriculture. In fact, one of the most striking contrasts between the medieval community of the eighth to the twelfth century and that of today is that whereas most workers today are occupied with tasks aimed principally at satisfying man's less essential material and aesthetic wants, medieval man pretty well limited himself to the hard task of raising food. Medieval society, of course, needed other goods as well, such as those provided by carpenters, smiths, and tailors, but these always represented a fraction of the whole population. When this small number which served man's needs other than food began growing markedly in volume and importance, the manor was well on its way to breaking up.

Size of the Manor. Since the raising of food was the manor's chief economic concern, its arable land constituted its most valuable asset. Actually the amount of tillable soil directly controlled the size of the manor. The manor would have to have sufficient land for the community's food needs. Because there was ordinarily no outlet for surplus produce, this minimum often constituted the maximum as well. Few manors had fewer than a thousand acres of arable land for food production, which amount of acreage would provide for a community of approximately twenty households. Manors might run considerably larger, as high as twenty-five thousand acres in fact, although two thousand could have been an average. Most of this land medieval man had wrung by dint of hard toil from the solid mass of forest which stretched from Gibraltar into central Russia. One might draw an interesting parallel, indeed, between the march of European civilization northward and eastward during the medieval period and that of American civilization in the seventeenth and eighteenth centuries—how each kept pace to the sound of the axe.

Two-field System. Ancient man learned early that land kept under continuous cultivation for a number of years tends to decline in productivity. He also learned the value of crop rotation and of the application of animal manure, ashes, and marl. Unfortunately, of fertilizers he had an insufficient amount, and to the practice of crop rotation and the plowing under of certain crops he preferred the less scientific but less laborious two-field system. This system was based on his knowledge that if land is permitted to lie idle for a time, it recovers its fertility, particularly when cultivated meantime to keep down the growth of weeds. This combination of enforced idleness (fallow) and cultivation permitted the soil to recapture its fertility through chemical action, an explanation of which he was unaware. He may also have been unaware of the fact that land handled in this fashion tended to store up a greater moisture content, not an unimportant consideration in areas of marginal rainfall. Whatever the explanation ancient man gave the phenomenon, he began to alternate the use of his soil, cultivating half of it one year, the other half the following year, with one half always lying fallow. This is what is known as the two-field system.

The Three-field System. The medieval farmer of France, England, and Germany was blessed with more fertile land than the ancient Italian had to work with and more rainfall as well. He learned in time that his better soil could produce crops two years out of every three. The result was the rise of the three-field system in many parts of western Europe where soil and climate permitted. The arable soil, according to the three-field system, was divided into three parts, two parts being farmed each year, a third left to lie fallow. The usual sequence called for one field to be sown in the spring in a legume or cereal, a second sown in the fall in wheat or rye, a third to lie fallow. The field in which the spring crop was sown was left to lie fallow the second year, the field which had not been cropped would be put to wheat in the fall, while the field which had produced wheat was sown in oats, barley, or one of the spring crops. The children's verse, "oats, pease, beans, and barley grow," has been traced back to this spring planting. The three-field system offered distinct advantages over the two-field. In the first place, one sixth more of the tillable acreage was put to productive use. In the second place, since the fallow field would normally be plowed at least twice to keep down the weeds, the three-field system actually entailed less plowing. The following table showing the cultivation of a manor of nine hundred acres will illustrate these two advantages.

Two-field system	*Three-field system*
450 acres in crop—one plowing	300 acres in wheat—one plowing
450 acres in fallow—two plowings	300 acres in barley—one plowing
Total of 1350 acres plowed to produce	300 acres in fallow—two plowings
450 acres of productive land.	Total of 1200 acres plowed to produce
	600 acres of productive land.

Open-field System. If the three-field system originated in the Middle Ages, so did the open-field system. This was, indeed, a peculiarly medieval practice. Many factors have been suggested to account for its origin, but first we must have an explanation of how the system operated. The name derives from the fact that none of the three fields, not even the holdings of the individual serf, was fenced or hedged. Actually since fences were intended primarily to keep stock in or out, there was little need for them. The manorial period boasted very little stock, and what there was was kept within the immediate vicinity of the village in the care of the younger members of the community. Only after the crop had been harvested was the stock permitted out into the fields. Yet it was not so much the absence of stock which accounted for the absence of fences, as the manner in which the three fields were divided. For a closer look at each field would reveal that they consisted, not of compact plots of thirty or more acres, but rather of a network of strips, each strip usually no more than an acre or half acre in size. Had the serf held contiguous strips, he might conceivably have fenced in his land had he wished. Since the thirty strips which constituted the average holding of a serf were scattered about the three fields, this was impractical, so instead of fences, simple ribbons of unplowed turf or balks separated one serf's strip from his neighbor's, whence the name, the open-field system.

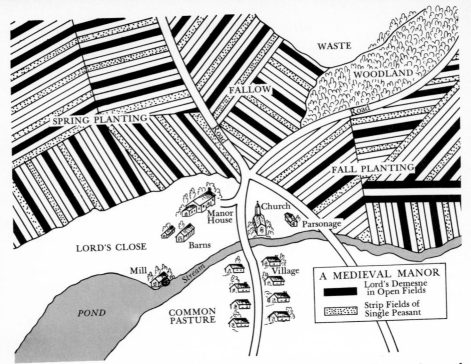

A MEDIEVAL MANOR

- Lord's Demesne in Open Fields
- Strip Fields of Single Peasant

Origin of Open-field System.   Several explanations have been advanced to explain the use of strips in the manorial fields. It has been suggested that when the village had originally been settled, the clearing off of the fields had been accomplished through cooperative effort with each family sharing in the land as the work progressed. As the village grew and additional lands were developed, again through cooperative effort, these also were parcelled out piecemeal. That the quality of soil can vary sharply even in areas no more extensive than a manor also offers some explanation for the open-field system. Only by assigning strips from every portion of the three fields could the community hope to equalize the productivity of each serf's allotments. To have given the members of the community compact holdings would have benefited some at the expense of others, in their walk to and from work from the village where they all lived. The fact that so much of the work of putting in, cultivating, and harvesting the crop required cooperative effort lent itself to the open-field system. The medieval plow, for example, was too large and unwieldy for one man to handle efficiently. Furthermore, since it would tax the strength of as many as eight oxen to pull the plow through the heavy soil, serfs had to help one another in getting their strips plowed since few of them could claim more than one beast. Finally, to have applied cooperative work to compact holdings would occasionally have resulted in a few serfs having all their crop safely in with unusually severe spring rains delaying or endangering the seeding of others.

Manorial Cooperation. While much of manorial agriculture involved cooperative effort, as for example in plowing or doing boon work for the lord, this communal activity must not be confounded with communism. Each man harvested what he grew on his own strips; there was no common granary upon which to draw. True, the amount of the serf's holdings in strips usually determined the extent of other rights. The number of sheep, goats, or cattle he might permit to roam on the waste lands and commons would depend upon the extent of his holdings in strips. As the traditional rule read when enacted: "None shall oppress or overcharge the commons or waste by putting more goods thereon in summer than they can, out of the profits of their farms and tenements, keep in winter." The serf also shared in a proportionate manner in the use of the meadow from which he cut his small but precious reserve of hay. The number of hogs he could let run in the woods would also depend upon his strip holdings. Manorial cooperation extended beyond mere physical effort. Barring the louder voice of the lord's reeve, it was the community that decided when plowing was to begin and where, what would be raised, when the crop would be harvested, when the fields would be thrown open to the village livestock. Partly because common counsel determined much of the manor's methods, partly because of the inflexible character of the open-field system, partly because of the force of tradition, change came very hard to the medieval manor. Yet the medieval farmer was no exception in this respect. The farmer has traditionally been counted society's most conservative member, that is, until the present generation which finds so many farmers' sons putting to test the ideas they learn in agricultural colleges.

Manorial Livestock. The poverty of the medieval manor, by American standards at any rate, was best revealed in the small number and inferior quality of its livestock. The most important beast was the ox, the chief draught animal. Until the horse collar came into use, the horse was used only for riding and, consequently, was a luxury only the lord of the manor could afford. And medieval man could always eat the ox when it had grown old and useless, but not his horse. The ox and the milk cow of the Middle Ages were scrawny animals. In medieval sketches they appear no larger than overgrown calves. No wonder it required eight oxen to draw a plow! Nothing more robust could be expected from the indiscriminate breeding on the fenceless manor and from inadequate and inferior provender. Hay was made of native grasses whose growth was never luxuriant. Because of the meager supply, the older and weaker animals were slaughtered in the fall. The little milk the medieval cow produced normally found its way into cheese. Even today most Europeans shun milk. The manor was most successful in raising swine because these could be left in the woods for most of the year to fend for themselves. Though they proved able to contend with the elements and the wild animals of the forest, the product of that harsh struggle was a far cry from the succulent animal modern farmers bring to market. Other animals on the manor included sheep, goats, chickens, geese, ducks, and the ubiquitous pigeon. Still only the lord might have a dovecot and he might also insist that the sheep be folded on his ground in order to garner as much of the small supply of fertilizer as possible. Little fertilizer, less hay, and no grain for animal consumption, meant little meat on the peasant's table. Yet unlike today's Chinaman who also eats little meat, for medieval man it was not a teeming population that made cereal production inevitable. His meatless fare can be traced rather to his inability to produce tame grasses, to combat such stock diseases as murrain, and to his failure to improve the quality of his stock. (Reading 93)

Medieval Progress in Agricultural Implements. While the farmer of the sixteenth century inherited a sorry lot of implements from his medieval predecessor, they were significantly superior in quality and variety to what the latter had been left by the ancient husbandman. One need but compare the meager progress achieved during the millenia of antiquity with the thousand years of the Middle Ages to grasp some notion of the depressing effect of slave labor upon ancient economy. The curse of the ancient world, an enormous supply of cheap and inefficient labor, was unknown during the medieval period. Actually the opposite, a shortage of labor, on occasion struck western Europe. This occasional labor stringency, together with the increasing population after the tenth century and the rise of towns which we shall consider in the following chapter, all conspired to provide the incentive for labor-saving devices which human ingenuity has always proved itself capable of providing when the need arose. This story is told of the Roman Emperor Vespasian (d. 79 A.D.). An engineer approached him one day with a plan to reduce the amount of labor required in building roads. "But what would I do with my poor people?" asked the emperor. The medieval farmer was poor, to be sure, but the competition of thousands of slaves did not leave him helpless and hopeless.

Implements. The Roman farmer had used a light plow consisting of little more than a beam to which a digging stick (occasionally of iron) had been attached. This primitive tool had proved suitable since most of the soil of the Mediterranean world is light and porous, although cross-plowing was necessary. Now this plow actually never went out of use in medieval times. Where the soil permitted, it was preferred, since it was easy to handle and required no more than a yoke of oxen to pull. As early as the second century A.D., a bulkier wheeled plow came into use in such areas of heavy soil as the Po and Upper Danube valleys. This plow carried a cutting edge of iron to pierce the stubborn sod and a moldboard to turn the soil. Such a plow cut sufficiently deep to eliminate the need for cross-plowing, but as many as eight oxen might be required to pull the heavy implement. This wheeled plow became fairly standard on the manors of

France, England, and Germany. The harrow which was used to break up the clods after plowing was a medieval invention. It consisted of a heavy framework into which pegs of wood or iron were fixed. About the tenth century the Middle Ages saw the introduction of the horse as a draught animal. The manner in which ancient man had harnessed the horse, with a leather band about the body behind the forelegs and another about the neck, had left the animal ill-suited for draught purposes. The harder the horse pulled, the deeper would the strap about its neck cut into the windpipe. The horsecollar, on the other hand, concentrated the pressure about the horse's shoulders and thus introduced an innovation which in time revolutionized draught power on the farm. The ox remained, however, the more common draught animal during the Middles Ages even though it was so much slower than the horse and had always to be used in pairs. The draught horse was limited to the more productive areas of west central Europe where the peasant could better afford the greater investment and where he raised sufficient grain to share some of it with his beast. Tandem harness and the horseshoe also date from about the tenth century, as do barrels, tubs, skis, cranks (to turn grindstones), wheelbarrows, scythes, gears, and flails (to thresh grain). Windmills do not appear in western Europe before the close of the twelfth century, although water power was already being exploited by the miller to grind grain and by the fuller to beat his cloth.

Medieval Measurements.   A brief glance at medieval measurements will prove rewarding since several of these have become the stock in trade of the western world. As with so many other human conventions, they were the result of accident and use, rather than design. The acre, for instance, was the usual size of a serf's strip, forty rods in length by four rods in width. Forty rods was the distance the oxen pulling the plow could walk without halting for a rest, whence the term furlong or furrow long. The rod corresponded in length to that of the ox goad, sixteen and a half feet, long enough to reach the head pair of a group of eight oxen. The rod in turn was five and a half times the length of a cloth unit called a yard. The strip of land was four rods wide because the acre, four rods by forty rods, was as much as the oxen could plow in a long morning (*Morgenland,* as the word acre still appears in German). Since no hay was available for the oxen, they would have to be let out to graze in the afternoon. Our two-hundred and twenty yard dash was first run in the Middle Ages, that is, the length of an acre strip, and also our four-forty, the length of a furrow and back. It would be a mistake, however, to suppose any great degree of standardization of measurements in a period of such rampant provincialism as the Middle Ages. And we can only be grateful that such medieval measures as "as far as a tame hen can go at a single flight" have happily not stood the test of time.

Social Life on the Manor

Though Lord Acton may have said that "The great historian now takes his meals in the kitchen," we know less of the social life of the manor than we do of the monastery, the town, or the castle. The "great unwashed" have become fit topics for the historian only within the last half century. Medieval writers pay the peasant short shrift, and a rather contemptuous one at that. For the peasant at best was "such a stupid lout." Write about the nobility the medieval chronicler would, and of chivalry, of the clergy, of miracles and strange lands, but why of such uninteresting folk as the peasantry. Were there a lower station on the social ladder to which they could sink, there they would surely gravitate. And though the serf, as pointed out above, was no slave, a tremendous gap yawned between him and his "betters." The medieval peasant could not tell us of himself since he could not write, and none of his "betters" who knew how to write considered him worth writing about.

The Serf's Dwelling.   The villager's house consisted of wattle and straw or wattle and mud over a rough framework of tree branches. Stone huts could be found in areas where the necessary materials were abundant. The floor of the cottage was of ground or clay, the roof thatched, with a hole to permit egress of the smoke. Fireplace and chimney date from the thirteenth century. If the cottage had a window it was not glassed in until the fourteenth century at the earliest. A hearth of stone provided the base for the fire over which several pots might be suspended. The peasant could afford no candles, but he could not have read had he had candles to read by. He rose with the sun and retired when it grew dark. His one-room cottage might have a small loft, but privacy was at a premium and the cottage might have to be shared with the married children until these found homes of their own, and with such smaller stock as goats and chickens. Furniture was rough and painfully functional. A wooden frame marked off the bed, which was mattressed with straw. The peasant ate from a table of planks, sat on a stool or bench, and kept his few clothes and belongings in a chest which might also serve as a bench. Most of the home's utensils and receptacles were earthenware, a few were of wood or horn, though one or two iron pots and frying pans were fairly common. (Reading 83)

The Peasant's Clothing and Food.   The peasant's clothes were homespun, of wool or linen, and very limited in number. They included a tunic which was bound about the waist and reached almost to the knees; a cap; long hose, the upper parts of which were in time sewed into breeches or trou-

sers; wooden clogs or foot covering of leather or hide. Shirts and under-
clothing came into use in the fourteenth century. Night apparel he needed
not at all since he slept in his clothes. As simple as was his clothing so also
was the peasant's fare. The bulk of what he ate he grew. He ate rye rather
than wheat since it was cheaper, and baked it into a form of black bread or
ate it as porridge. From his garden plot he drew a variety of vegetables,
including peas, beans, cabbage, and turnips (not potatoes). Eggs and cheese
provided much of his proteins, although salt pork was not uncommon, and
even a fowl might grace his humble board on feast days. If he were fortunate enough to live near a body of water he could hope to vary his monotonous fare with fish. How much he might poach upon the forest for game
would depend on the efficiency of the lord's game wardens. The harshness
of the penalty for poaching, which was mutilation or death, suggests a difficulty in apprehending culprits. Honey proved as indispensable to medieval man's table as it had to the Roman's, but he might have butter which
the Roman had lacked. The use of some spirituous beverage such as wine,
beer, or mead was almost universal. In fact, even today's teetotaler might
find himself tempted to take a bit of wine with his water had he lived in
the Middle Ages in order to make the latter more palatable.

Life on the Manor.   Measured by the yardstick of modern conveniences,
the life of the medieval peasant is apt to appear intolerable. His home had
only a floor of earth; it lacked windows; his diet was monotonous and
often unsavory, with only salt to add a bit of flavor; his wardrobe was
primitive. Still before we commiserate too deeply with his lot, we should
remind ourselves that he was as well off as the ancient Athenian or Roman
peasant. Medieval man knew no better, and it is ordinarily the knowledge
of material deficiencies, not their absence without that knowledge, which
makes men unhappy. Each generation is inclined to sympathize with an
earlier one for having lacked certain advances in the arts or in material
goods which the succeeding era has seen introduced. Yet are we uncomfort-
ably aware of our inability to share in the conveniences to be ushered in
by the atomic age? Quite the contrary, we actually enjoy cutting ourselves off from civilization on occasion and "roughing it" for several weeks
at a time. And the modern Arab, much like his ancestor of Ibn Khaldun's
day (see page 211), still prefers to tether his camel in the modern
dwelling some western nation may have provided for him while he passes
his life in contentment in the tent of his forefathers.

Dark Side of Manorial Life.   It was not the lack of central heating systems and running water which made life hard in the Middle Ages. The importance of these and similar conveniences, at least from the standpoint of
mental tranquillity, is largely psychological. Yet whatever man's mentality,
it is impossible to live without food. Famine was the first bane of medieval
existence, at least until the twelfth century. Scholars designate fully half
the years in each century, from the ninth through the eleventh, as famine

years for many localities in western Europe. Though these famines, because more localized, did not carry off the millions those of India and China have been known to do in recent centuries, they were attended by widespread suffering and malnutrition. Warfare was the medieval peasant's second bane. The peasant did not ordinarily participate directly in hostilities, but this did not prevent brigands or hostile knights from plundering his village, driving off his stock, and possibly killing him in the process. (Reading 184) Froissart (see page 684), tells how a Scottish expedition invaded England while an English army advanced into Scotland, each army avoiding contact with the other, each bent only on pillaging and ravaging the countryside. A third bane was disease, against which the Middle Ages was almost helpless. (See page 578.) The Black Death of 1348, the most disastrous and famous of several plagues that have been identified, carried off from one fourth to one third the population of western Europe. Well might the faithful cry to their God in the Litany of the Saints: "From plague, famine, and war, O Lord, deliver us!"

Village Amusements.   One evil commonly attributed to the Middle Ages which medieval man did not suffer was boredom. There are those who wonder what earlier generations did for recreation when there was no automobile, radio, or television. Actually man has never been at a loss for diversions which are enjoyable regardless of age, clime, or standard of living. Most men and women find nothing more interesting than the society of other men and women. Medieval man in his isolated little community was thrown into the company of relatives and friends and met life in its completely human interplays much more frequently than modern man in his huge urban centers. Sundays and holy days were days of relaxation and festivity and provided medieval man more holidays than most workingmen of the western world enjoy today. Weddings were occasions of general community celebration. Ale feasts, sometimes at the expense of the lord, and benefits for this or that purpose, provided occasions of general mirth and rejoicing. Pageants, religious plays, traveling minstrels, acrobats with trained monkeys or bears, cock fighting, and similar diversions could be expected to break the even tenor of village life from time to time. Music, folk singing, and dancing were popular in medieval villages, often too popular to judge from ecclesiastical censures. A visit to the market in a neighboring manor was certain to prove exciting, a trip to the fair positively enchanting. Medieval children knew many games. Pieter Brueghel painted a picture of villagers at play at games he knew in his day (*ca.* 1550). More than seventy of these have been identified. Since most of them have come down to the twentieth century unchanged, it is a safe assumption that the Middle Ages had first played them. No, life has been reasonably interesting, or depressing, much as the individual has chosen to make it, ever since paleolithic times.

The Decline of the Manor

Much of the difficulty attending an analysis of the medieval manor arises from the fact that the manor was not static. The manor was the natural product of certain economic conditions, and when these changed, so did the manor. While all change, whether social, political, or economic, came more slowly to the Middle Ages than it does in the twentieth century, it came, nonetheless, particularly after the tenth century. As we shall see in some detail in the following chapter, Europe in the eleventh century began to experience a marked increase in population, began to note the first positive signs of a revival of trade, and began to welcome the appearance of industrial communities, towns, as they are to be called, alongside the traditional manorial village. The impact of these developments upon the manor was immediate and, in time, revolutionary in scope. So altered did these factors leave several of the most fundamental features of the manor that already by the close of the thirteenth century, in countries such as England and France, the manor as we have described it was well on its way to disappearance.

Effect of Town upon Village. The rise of the town struck directly at the bases of manorial life in two ways. In the first place it afforded the manor the opportunity of divesting itself of its self-contained character. Since townspeople who engaged in industry and trade did not raise their own food, they made demands upon the manor for commodities which the isolated manorial economy had heretofore never experienced. The manor would now begin to produce surpluses, since it had found a place to dispose of them, and in so doing it would gradually transform its character. The rise of the town affected the manor in yet another way. Until the eleventh century the prohibition upon the serf not to leave the manor had been largely academic—he had no place to go. But now towns both nearby and on the frontier beckoned. New towns such as Lorris which Louis VI established (see page 437), would offer house and lot for a nominal fee, to any serf who would reside there for a year and a day. Then if unclaimed by a lord and a free man, he would be completely exempt from servile exactions, taxes, military service, and *corvées*. The chance to better his lot, at least to change it, was now presented to the serf, and many took advantage of it. It is significant that the manorial economy began first to crumble in areas where towns appeared first and in greatest number, as in Flanders and in northern Italy.

The Medieval Frontier. These towns were largely produced and nourished by the marked population increase Europe experienced from the eleventh to the thirteenth centuries. Yet it was not only by way of towns that this rise in population affected the manor. It also stimulated a frontier movement suggestive of that in American history. All along the periphery of civilization was felt the pressure to push settlement outward. More of Europe's forests were cleared, marshes and swamps were drained, while east of the Elbe the Slavs were forced backward by the encroaching Germans. This frontier movement may be viewed in general simply as the natural consequence of a growing population. In eastern Europe it was expedited by lords who were anxious to increase their feudal holdings. The frontier also moved in the wake of monastic expansion. The Cistercians, for example, who located their monasteries just beyond the limits of civilization, transformed through hard work "much of northern England from a wilderness into a sheep run," and in so doing prepared the area for settlement. Since the bulk of the new settlers who would move into these new areas must come from the manor, the effect of the frontier upon manorial life can be readily appreciated. To attract peasants to their new manors lords would hold out the offer of a freeman's status and as much land as the serf could clear, all to be his own except for a modest quitrent. We even hear of lords hiring promoters to advertise the blessings of these newer settlements. And for the serf who refused, or was forbidden, to listen to the blandishments of these promoters, it frequently became necessary for the lord to ameliorate his servile status at home. (Reading 86)

Manorial Change. There were other developments in the eleventh and twelfth centuries which struck at manorial isolation. One such was the Crusades which afforded the serf the opportunity to escape during the absence of his lord. Whatever the factors, manorial life in large areas of western Europe altered perceptibly during the eleventh and twelfth centuries. Few manors remained unaffected. Many serfs fled to towns or to manors along the frontier which offered a higher status. Because of the rise of towns and the revival of trade, those who stayed on the older manors found they could dispose of surplus crops and commodities, and these began to appear as if by magic. Now that the serf had an incentive to work, he began to work hard for the first time in his life. With his fellow serfs he might add more acres to the three fields. So much new land was opened to cultivation in England in the thirteenth century that parliament sought to regulate the amount by legislation. Manors changed from the two- to the three-field system where this was found feasible. Money came to take the place of services or payments in kind, as plunder brought back from the eastern Mediterranean by Crusaders together with the output of silver mines in Germany eased the bullion drought in western Europe. Even agricultural specialization became possible now that the manor was not entirely dependent upon its own resources. Certain areas began to give some thought to the exploitation of such geographical or natural advantages as they might enjoy. Under the encouragement of an enterprising lord, this or that manor might devote itself to the raising of wheat or rye where those crops were in demand, or to sheep raising where a ready market for wool existed.

Rent for Services. The most revolutionary result consequent upon the factors noted above was the commutation of labor services for a money rent. As population increased and the number of landless serfs on the manor rose, the lord learned that he could get a great deal more work from the day laborers he might employ on his demesne than from serfs who owed him the traditional labor service. Indeed, economists have suggested that a day laborer who could be dismissed if his work were not satisfactory would accomplish three times as much as the serf putting in his customary time on the lord's demesne. So the lord was anxious to find an arrangement by which he could replace the serf and his "forced labor" with agricultural workers. And the serf was most happy to oblige. For the serf reasoned that once free to devote his whole work week, not just half of it, to his own strips, he could not help but profit handsomely. So the lord of the manor worked out an agreement whereby the serf would pay the lord as much for the days he owed him as it would cost the lord to hire a laborer in his stead. The serf now paid rent instead of personal services. He had become a tenant. In fact, once the basic labor service had disappeared, other marks of servile status were also soon to disappear. By the end of the thirteenth century the children of many former serfs were free to go as they wished, to sell their property if they chose, and to marry whom they preferred.

Peasant Revolts. This trend away from serfdom toward a free peasantry, however, slowed perceptibly in the fourteenth century, and in certain areas was even reversed. Actually the tendency to move away from the servile manorial system toward a free agricultural economy had not been at all universal. Even in England and France, large areas had remained unaffected. Before the serfs in such regions would gain their freedom, in fact, before the newly emancipated serf on the more progressive manors had finally established his free status, much bitterness and suffering would have to be endured. So intense, indeed, did agrarian discontent grow that it broke out into open rebellion in Flanders in the early fourteenth century, in England in 1381, and sporadically in France during both the fourteenth and fifteenth centuries in the so-called *Jacquerie*. (Jacques was the traditional name of the French peasant.) The Peasant Revolt in Germany reserved its horrors for the sixteenth century. (Reading 87)

Causes for Discontent. A variety of factors contributed to this agrarian discontent of the late Middle Ages. Basic perhaps was the tendency of the population to level off. The frontier stopped moving after the thirteenth century, no new towns took root, and old ones remained stagnant. The economic bustle of the twelfth and thirteenth centuries did not carry over into the fourteenth, at least not in western and central Europe. There was less demand for the peasant's commodities. Rather than attribute this to the general economic sluggishness of the times which he could not appreciate, the peasant blamed it on more immediate grievances which were clearly visible. For example, the rent he had agreed to pay a century or two earlier, the lord now sought to raise. Actually due to inflation, the lord was partially justified in demanding a higher rent. But the peasant, who knew no more about inflation than the lord, protested strenuously against the higher rent as unwarranted and as beyond his means. Where rents did not go up, the lord of the manor might seek to reimpose a servile status upon his tenants. When labor shortages appeared as after the Black Death, which agricultural workers might conceivably have exploited, the government stepped in as in England with a Statute of Laborers to prevent them from doing so. In some areas profit-minded lords of the manor enclosed the common and waste lands for the exclusive use of their own sheep, thereby denying the villagers a small but crucial source of food for their stock. Finally, some lords, often the more wealthy ones, and ecclesiastical landlords who were less concerned about money rents, proved adamant against the demands of the serf for his freedom. (Reading 94)

Medieval Agricultural Progress.   Despite areas of agrarian discontent and suffering, a survey of the medieval countryside should give us cause to close on a happier note. What a harrowing picture of modern farm life, for instance, would the uncritical observer receive who accepted without qualification the plaints expressed in certain farm journals in an election year? So also was it with the medieval farmer. Though islands of agrarian discontent might erupt here and there in the late Middle Ages, history reveals that peasant protests have been heard almost continuously up to the present time. Furthermore, the peasant revolts of the Middle Ages have grown in the telling. That in England affected barely more than four eastern counties and faded into history within a few weeks. The *Jacquerie* in France, the most spectacular of medieval peasant uprisings, were local affairs which might be as readily ascribed to the miseries consequent upon the Hundred Years' War as to agricultural maladjustments. And in Poland and eastern Europe we hear of no revolts principally because there was no agrarian discontent.

Rather than dwell too long on these signs of agrarian unrest, the student should recall rather such significant achievements claimed for the medieval peasant as the horsecollar and horseshoe, the introduction of new grains such as rye and oats, of new eatables like butter, a marked improvement in the breeding of sheep and horses, and a slow but steady advance in the size of grain yields. Above all, the student should bear in mind the tremendous acreage opened up to cultivation after the eleventh century. While the trend away from serfdom had been neither smooth nor continuous, by the close of the Middle Ages the serf had pretty well disappeared from the countryside west of the Rhine. And one must not forget that for all its hard work and suffering, medieval manorialism constituted a way of life considerably richer in human values than our own modern rural life because it was largely untouched by the dehumanizing influences of an industrial civilization. This unique way of life modern technology and good roads have destroyed. For better or for worse, fewer Europeans live on the land today than in the Middle Ages. Of the homesteads once pertaining to Tavistock Abbey in southwestern England, for example, and once moving with human life, "Today Milemead is in ruins; Pixon and Stileweek are mere barns; a cowshed alone remains at Blackmoorham."*

READINGS

No. 81. Manor of Bernehorne, Sussex (A.D. 1307)

(Translations and Reprints, III, No. 5, pp. 8-13)

Extent of the manor of Bernehorne, made on Wednesday next after the feast of St. Gregory the Pope, in the thirty-fifth year of the reign of King Edward, in the presence of Brother Thomas, keeper of Marley, John de la More, and Adam de Thruhlegh, clerks, on the oath of William de Gocecoumbe, Walter le Parker, Richard le Knyst, Richard the son of the latter, Andrew of Estone, Stephen Morsprich, Thomas Brembel, William de Swynham, John Pollard, Roger le Glide, John Syward and John de Lillingewist, who say etc., that there are there all the following things:

The jurors say that the principal messuage and its garden with the herbage and curtilage are worth yearly 6s.8d.; and the dovecote is worth yearly 5s.; and the windmill is worth yearly 20s.

And there are there 12 acres of thick undergrowth whence the pannage and herbage are worth yearly 2s.

And there are there 42 acres of maritime land in a certain place called Scotsmarsh, each acre of which is worth yearly 12d., the sum being 42s.

And there are there 7 acres and 1 rood of maritime land in a certain place called Aldithewisse; and 47 acres and 3 roods of maritime land in a certain place called Flittermarsh, each acre of which is worth yearly 12d. the sum being 55s.

And there are there 22 acres of maritime land in two places called Pund-

* H. P. R. Finberg, *Tavistock Abbey* (Cambridge, 1951, pp. 52-53).

fold and Longrech; and 7 acres of maritime land in a certain place called Wyssh, and 8 acres and 3 roods of maritime land in a certan place called Upcroft marsh, and 3 acres and a half of maritime land in a certain place called Redewysshe; and each acre is worth yearly 12d.: the sum being 41s. 3d.

And there are there 19 acres, 1 rood of maritime land in a certain place called Berghamsmarsh, and 7 acres in a certain place called Pammarsh, and 3 acres and 1 rood of maritime land beyond the wall of Flittermarsh and Longreche; and each acre is worth yearly 12d.: the sum being 29s. 6d.

And there are there 15 acres of marshy land in a certain place called Swynhamme and 66 acres of marshy land in a certain place called Hoobrokes, each acre of which is worth now 4d. a year; and the foresaid marshy lands, if they should be properly drained will be worth 10d. per acre yearly; the sum being 4£. 4s. 2d.

And there are there 18 acres of waste land in the fields called Welleland and Hammes, and 21 acres of land in the fields called Panden and Panylond, each acre of which is worth yearly 6d.: the sum being 19s. 6d.

And there are there 24½ acres in the field of Berghamme, and each acre is worth yearly 6d.: the sum being 12s. 3d.

And there are there 34 acres of land in a certain place called Swynhamme, and 56 acres of land in a certain field called Hoolonde, of which each acre is worth yearly 3d. and the sum is 22s. 6d.

And there are there 30½ acres of land in the fields called Eldeton and Furneyslland, and 12 acres of land in the fields called Pleme and Schebbecroft and Robertsmarsh, and each acre is worth yearly 3d.: the sum being 10s. 7½d.

And there are there 6 acres and 1 rood of meadow in a certain place called Hoolonde, and 6 acres of meadow in a certain place called Robertsmarsh, and 1 acre of meadow near Robertswood, otherwise called Rokeswood, each acre of which is worth 18d. a year; and the sum is 19s. 10½d.

The total of the acres of woods is 12 acres. The total of the acres of arable land is 444 acres and 3 roods, of which 147 acres 4 roods are maritime land, 101 acres marshy land, 180 acres waste ground. The total of the acres of meadow is 13 acres 1 rood. The total of the whole preceding extent 18£. 10s. 4d.

John Pollard holds a half acre in Aldithewisse and owes 18d. at the four terms, and owes from it relief and heriot.

John Suthinton holds a house and 40 acres of land and owes 3s. 6d. at Easter and Michaelmas.

William of Swynhamme holds 1 acre of meadow in the thicket of Swynhamme and owes 1d. at the feast of Michaelmas.

Ralph of Leybourne holds a cottage and 1 acre of land in Pinden and owes 3s. at Easter and Michaelmas, and attendance at the court in the manor every three weeks, relief and heriot.

Richard Knyst of Swynhamme holds 2 acres and a half of land and owes yearly 4s.

William at Knelle holds 2 acres of land in Aldithewisse and owes yearly 4s.

Roger le Glede holds a cottage and 3 roods of land and owes 2s. 6d. at Easter and Michaelmas.

Alexander Hamound holds a little piece of land near Aldewisse and owes 1 goose, of the value of 2d.

The sum of the whole rent of the free tenants, with the value of the goose, is 18s. 9d.

They say moreover that John of Cayworth holds a house and 30 acres of land, and owes yearly 2s. at Easter and Michaelmas; and he owes a cock and two hens at Christmas, of the value of 4d.

And he ought to harrow for 2 days at the Lenten sowing with one man and his own horse and his own harrow, the value of the work being 4d.; and he is to receive from the lord on each day 3 meals, of the value of 5d., and then the lord will be at a loss of 1d. Thus his harrowing is of no value to the service of the lord.

And he ought to carry the manure of the lord for 2 days with one cart, with his own 2 oxen, the value of the work being 8d.: and he is to receive from the lord each day 3 meals of the price as above. And thus the service is worth 3d. clear.

And he shall find one man for 2 days for mowing the meadow of the lord, who can mow, by estimation 1 acre and a half, the value of the mowing of an acre being 6d.: the sum is therefore 9d. and he is to receive each day 3 meals of the value given above; and thus that mowing is worth 4d. clear.

And he ought to gather and carry that same hay which he has cut, the price of the work being 3d.

And he shall have from the lord 2 meals for 1 man, of the value of 1½d. Thus the work will be worth 1½d. clear.

And he ought to carry the hay of the lord for 1 day with a cart and 3 animals of his own, the price of the work being 6d. And he shall have from the lord 3 meals of the value of 2½d. And thus the work is worth 3½d. clear.

And he ought to carry in autumn beans or oats for 2 days with a cart and 3 animals of his own, the value of a work being 12d. And he shall receive from the lord each day 3 meals of the value given above: and thus the work is worth 7d. clear.

And he ought to carry wood from the woods of the lord as far as the manor for two days in summer with a cart and three animals of his own the value of the work being 9d. And he shall receive from the lord each day 3 meals of the price given above, and thus the work is worth 4d. clear.

And he ought to find 1 man for 2 days to cut heath, the value of the work being 4d. and he shall have 3 meals each day of the value given above; and thus the lord will lose, if he receives the service, 3d. Thus that mowing is worth nothing to the service of the lord.

And he ought to carry the heath which he has cut, the value of the work being 5d. And he shall receive from the lord 3 meals at the price of 2½d. And thus the work will be worth 2½d. clear.

And he ought to carry to Battle twice in the summer season, each time half a load of grain, the value of the service being 4d. And he shall receive in the manor each time 1 meal of the value of 2d. And thus the work is worth 2d. clear.

The total of the rents, with the value of the hens is 2s. 4d. The total of the value of the works is 2s. 3½d.; owed from the said John yearly.

William of Cayworth holds a house and 30 acres of land and owes at Easter and Michaelmas 2s. rent. And he shall do all customs just as the foresaid John of Cayworth.

William atte Grene holds a house and 30 acres of land and owes in all things just as the said John.

Alan atte Felde holds a house and 16 acres of land, (for which the sergeant pays to the court of Bixley 2s.) and he owes at Easter and Michaelmas 4s., attendance at the manor court, relief and heriot.

John Lyllingwyst holds a house and 4 acres of land and owes at the two terms 2s., attendance at the manor court, relief and heriot.

The same John holds one acre of land in the fields of Hoo and owes at the two periods 2s., attendance, relief and heriot.

Reginald atte Denne holds a house and 18 acres of land and owes at the said periods 18d., attendance, relief and heriot.

Robert of Northehou holds 3 acres of land at Saltcote and owes at the said periods attendance, relief and heriot.

Total of the rents of the villeins, with the value of the hens, 20s. Total of all the works of these three villeins, 6s. 10½d.

And it is to be noted that none of the above named villeins can give their daughters in marriage nor cause their sons to be tonsured, nor can they cut down timber growing on the lands they hold, without license of the bailiff or sergeant of the lord, and then for building purposes and not otherwise. And after the death of any one of the foresaid villeins the lord shall have as a heriot his best animal, if he had any; if however he have no living beast the lord shall have no heriot, as they say. The sons or daughters of the foresaid villeins shall give for entrance into the holding after the death of their predecessors as much as they give of rent per year.

Silvester the priest holds 1 acre of meadow adjacent to his house, and owes yearly 3s.

Total of the rent of tenants for life, 3s.

Petronilla atte Holme holds a cottage and a piece of land and owes at Easter and Michaelmas, attendance, relief, and heriot.

Walter Herying holds a cottage and a piece of land and owes at Easter and Michaelmas 18d., attendance, relief, and heriot.

Isabella Mariner holds a cottage and owes at the feast of St. Michael 12d., attendance, relief, and heriot.

Jordan atte Melle holds a cottage and 1 acre of land and a half and owes at Easter and Michaelmas 2s., attendance, relief, and heriot.

William of Batelesmere holds 1 acre of land with a cottage and owes at the feast of St. Michael 3d., and 1 cock and 1 hen at Christmas, of the value of 3d., attendance, relief, and heriot.

John Werthe holds 1 rood of land with a cottage and owes at the said term 18d., attendance, relief, and heriot.

Geoffrey Caumbreis holds half an acre and a cottage and owes at the said term 18d., attendance, relief, heriot.

William Hassok holds 1 rood of land and a cottage and owes at the said term 18d., attendance, relief, and heriot.

The same man holds 3½ acres of land and owes yearly at the feast of St. Michael 3s. for all.

Roger Doget holds half an acre of land and a cottage which were those of R. the miller, and owes at the feast of St. Michael 18d., attendance, relief, and heriot.

Thomas le Brod holds 1 acre and a cottage and owes at the said term 3s., attendance, relief, and heriot.

Agnes of Cayworth holds a half acre and a cottage and owes at the said term 18d., attendance, relief, and heriot.

Agnes of Badlesmere holds 1 acre of land and a cottage and owes at the said term 3s., attendance, relief, and heriot.

William atte Whaunne holds one acre of land and owes at Easter and Michaelmas 2s., and relief.

Total of the rents of the said cottages, with the value of the hens 34s., 6d.

And it is to be noted that all the said cottagers shall do as regards giving their daughters in marriage, having their sons tonsured, cutting down timber, paying heriot, and giving fines for entrance just as John of Cayworth and the rest of the villeins formerly mentioned.

Note, fines (rents rather than penalties) and penalties, with heriots and reliefs are worth yearly 5s.

No. 82. Manorial court rolls, Halmote (A.D. 1345-1383)

(Translations and Reprints, III, No. 5, pp. 24-30.)

(The following items are extracted from the records of the successive courts held by the Steward, Bursar, or Terrar of the Priory of Durham. Three courts a year seem to have been held in each of the fifteen manors belonging to the convent, besides more frequent meetings, at the call of the reeve. The word "halmote" or "halimote" is frequently applied to the manor court meetings, and is generally considered to be equivalent to a meeting in the hall or manor house.)

First Tourn of the Halmotes of the Priory of Durham, beginning at Fery, July 6th, A.D. 1345, before lords William of Chareton and Robert of Benton, Terrar and Bursar, and Simon Esshe, Steward.

Spen, 1345. Agnes widow of Adam of Mora has taken a house and 50 acres of land which her husband Adam formerly held, paying annually for her life 33s. 4d. And there is remitted to her 16s. 8d. a year from the old rent on account of her age and weakness of mind.

Billingham, 1345. Agnes daughter of William Nouthird has taken a cottage with the curtilage, which the said William her father formerly held, to be held on payment of 6d. a year and 20 autumn works in the manor of Billingham, provided she has food. Fine, 2s.: pledges J. of Stokton and Alexander son of Gilbert.

The reeve and jurors complain and present that certain persons named below do not hold land by reason of which they have any right to have part in the common pasture, and yet they feed their cattle on the pasture of the vill to the injury of those who hold land. It is therefore required that they remove their animals from the pasture so that for the future they shall not thus overstock the pasture; under penalty of half a mark.

Billingham, 1364. It is enjoined upon all the tenants of the vill that none of them grind his grain outside of the domain so long as the mill of the lord prior is able to grind, under penalty of 20s.

Newton Bewley, 1365. From John of Baumburg for his transgression against Adam of Marton, in calling him false, perjured, and a rustic; to the loss of the same Adam of Marton 40d., penalty 13d.

Mid-Merrington, 1365. From Richard, son of Thomas, because he has not recalled his son from school (doubtless a villein who was violating the law by endeavoring to have his son trained to be a priest) before the feast of St. Michael as enjoined upon him at the last Halmote, penalty 40d. It is enjoined upon all the tenants of the vill that none of them insult the pounder while fulfilling his duty, nor swear at him.

Coupon, 1365. From Agnes Postell and Alice of Belasis, for breaking the assize of ale, 12d. From Alice of Belasis, for bad ale, and moreover because the ale which she sent to the Terrar was of no strength, as was proved in court, 2s.

Ackley, 1365. It is ordained by common consent that no one permit colts, calves, young steers or any other animals within the field in which grain is sowed until the grain is cut and carried off, under penalty of half a mark.

Fery, 1365. It is ordained by common consent that Robert Todd should keep his sheep from feeding on the grain of his neighbors and on the cow-pasture, under penalty of 40d.: and moreover that each tenant keep his pigs, cows, horses, and other animals from feeding on the grain or treading it, and that the cottagers should keep their cattle within the common pasture, under the penalty foresaid.

Billingham, 1368. It is enjoined upon all the tenants of the vill that none of them cut the balks before the next court.

Coupon, 1368. John Pulter and Robert Fauks were elected ale-tasters, and were sworn.

Newton Bewley, 1368. From Alice, servant of Adam of Marton, for leyr (incontinence), 6d. From Thomas, servant of the same for drawing his knife to strike John Smith, penalty 40d., by grace 12d.

Wallsend, 1368. It is enjoined upon all the tenants of the vill that each of them come on the summons of the reeve to discuss the common business touching the profit of the vill.

Heworths, 1370. It is enjoined upon all the tenants of the vill that they have the common forge and the common oven repaired.

Wallsend, 1370. It is ordained by common consent that each tenant should come to the making of the hay of the common meadow when they shall be warned, under penalty of losing their part and even under penalty of heavy fine.

Mid-Merrington, 1371. It is enjoined on all the cottars and laborers that they work with the farmer of the manor for suitable wages.

Hesilden, 1376. It is ordained by common consent that all things collected within the field, as well as herbage, be carried openly through the middle of the vill and not behind the gardens, in secret. It is enjoined upon all the women of the vill that they restrain their tongues and that they do not quarrel nor swear at anyone.

Billingham, 1378. It is ordained by common consent that at the blowing of the horn of the Reaper, they should come for the gathering of the peas, and when he blows his horn again they all withdraw from the said peas, under penalty of 6d.: and moreover that no one collect except in his own place, unless he is poor.

West Raynton, 1378. A day is give to that vill that they inquire and present whether John Hunting and Cecilia his wife beat Margaret the widow or not, at the next court, under penalty of half a mark. From John Hunting because he did not close his front, so that his animals trampled and destroyed the cabbages of Margaret the widow.

Monkton, 1379. It is enjoined upon Thomas Lane that he cause to be rebuilt before the feast of St. Michael, a barn which was burned in his tenure, under penalty of 40s.

Pittyngton, 1379. It is enjoined upon all the tenants of the vill that they heat up the oven, each one of them when his turn shall come, under penalty of paying 12d.

East Merrington, 1381. It is ordained by common consent that each tenant should keep the animals when his turn comes, and for the day in which he has their custody, he should respond and give satisfaction for injuries made in the grain or herbage to the one or ones who have had the losses, under penalty of paying 4d.

Fery, 1383 It is enjoined upon all tenants of the vill that they should have boundary marks, under penalty of half a mark, and moreover that they should pay the common shepherd his wages, and that they should not speak ill to the said shepherd, under penalty of 40d.

No. 83. Manor house at Chingford, Essex (A.D. 1265)

(Translations and Reprints, III, No. 5, p. 31.)

He received (with the manor) also a sufficient and handsome hall well ceiled with oak. On the western side is a worthy bed, on the ground, a stone chimney, a wardrobe and a certain other small chamber; at the eastern end is a pantry and a buttery. Between the hall and the chapel is a side-room. There is a decent chapel covered with tiles, a portable altar, and a small cross. In the hall are four tables on trestles. There are likewise a good kitchen well covered with tiles, with a furnace and ovens, one large, the other small, for cakes, two tables, and alongside the kitchen a small house for baking. Also a new granary covered with oak shingles, and a building in which the dairy is contained, though it is divided. Likewise a chamber suited for clergymen and a necessary chamber. Also a hen-house. These are within the inner gate.

Likewise outside of that gate are an old house for the servants, a good stable, long and divided, and to the east of the principal building, beyond the smaller stable, a solar for the use of the servants. Also a building in which is contained a bed; also two barns, one for wheat and one for oats. These buildings are enclosed with a moat, a wall, and a hedge. Also beyond the middle gate is a good barn, and a stable for cows and another for oxen, these old and ruinous. Also beyond the outer gate is a pigsty.

No. 84. Manumission of a villein (A.D. 1278)

(Translations and Reprints, III, No. 5, pp. 31-32.)

To all the faithful of Christ to whom the present writing shall come, Richard by the divine permission abbot of Peterborough and the Convent of the same place, eternal greeting in the Lord. Let all know that we have manumitted and liberated from all yoke of servitude William, the son of Richard of Wythington whom previously we have held as our born bondman, with his whole progeny and all his chattels, so that neither we nor our successors shall be able to require or exact any right or claim in the said William, his progeny, or his chattels. But the same William with his whole progeny and all his chattels will remain free and quit and without disturbance, exaction, or any claim on the part of us or our successors by reason of any servitude, forever. We will moreover and concede that he and his heirs shall hold the messuages, land, rents and meadows in Wythington which his ancestors held from us and our predecessors, by giving and performing the fine which is called merchet for giving his daughter in marriage, and tallage from year to year according to our will,— that he shall have and hold these for the future from us and our successors freely, quietly, peacefully, and hereditarily, by paying thence to us and our successors yearly 40s. sterling, at the four terms of the year, namely; at St. John the Baptist's day, 10s., at Michaelmas, 10s., at Christmas, 10s., and at Easter, 10s., for all service, exaction, custom, and secular demand; saving to us nevertheless attendance at our court of Castre every three weeks, wardship and relief, and outside service of our lord the king, when they shall happen. And if it shall happen that the said William or his heirs shall die at any time without an heir, the said messuage, land, rents, and meadows with their appurtenances shall return fully and completely to us and our successors. Nor will it be allowed to the said William or his heirs the said messuage, land, rents, meadows, or any part of them to give, sell, alienate, mortgage, or in any way encumber by which the said messuage, land, rents, and meadows should not return to us and our successors in the form declared above. But if this should occur later their deed shall be declared null and what is thus alienated shall come to us and our successors. In testimony of which duplicate seals are appended to this writing, formed as a chirograph, for the sake of greater security. These being witnesses, etc. Given at Borough for the love of lord Robert of good memory, once abbot, our predecessor and maternal uncle of the said William, and at the instance of the good man brother Hugh of Mutton, relative of the said abbot Robert. A.D. 1278, on the eve of Pentecost.

No. 85. Return from Domesday for Ely

(Adams & Stephens, *Select Documents of English Constitutional History*. New York, 1914, pp. 2-3.)

Here is written down the inquest of lands, in what manner the king's barons have made inquisition, namely, by oath of the sheriff of the shire, and of all the barons and of their Frenchmen and of the whole hundred, of the priest, the reeve and six villeins of each vill. Next the name of the manor, who held it in the time of King Edward, who holds it now; the number of hides; the number of plows on the demesne, the number of those of the men; the number of villeins; the number of cotters; the number of serfs; the number of freemen; the number of sokemen; the amount of forest; the amount of meadow; the number of pastures; the number of mills; the number of fishponds; how much it has been increased or diminished; how much it was all worth then; and how much now; how much each freeman and sokeman held and holds there. All this three times over, namely, in the time of King Edward, and when King William gave it, and as it now is, and if more can be had than is had.

No. 86. Otto III forbids unfree to attempt to free themselves (A.D. 1000)

(Thatcher & McNeal, *Source Book*, pp. 545-546.)

There is need of careful legislation because the princes of the empire, both lay and clerical, rich and poor, the higher as well as the lower, make frequent complaints that they are not able to obtain from their unfree subjects those services to which they have a right. For some falsely declare that they are free because their lords, in many cases, cannot prove the servitude which they [their unfree subjects] are trying in a dishonest way to escape. Others are trying to rise to the honor of freedom because their lords have, for a long time, been hindered from knowing anything about their unfree subjects, and hence the latter have not been kept in their accustomed state of servitude, nor are they forced to pay a tax as a proof of their unfree state. So on this account they declare that they are free and boast that they have lived in freedom, because for a short time they have not fulfilled their servile duties. Therefore we have issued this imperial law: 1. If a serf, led by his desire for liberty, says that he is free, his lord may settle the case by a duel with him, fighting either in person or by his champion [representative], as he may wish. The lord is given this privilege because of the great difficulty there is in proving such things in the regular way. The unfree man may secure a champion for himself if, because of age or disease, he is unable to fight. 2. In order that the unfree may not hide his real condition by avoiding his duties for a time, we decree by this our edict, which, with the help of God, shall be valid forever, that hereafter each one shall show his servile condition by paying a denar of the ordinary currency every year on the first of December to his lord or to the agent whom he shall appoint for this purpose. 3. The children of the free shall begin to pay this tax as a proof of their servile condition in their twenty-fifth year and at the appointed time. And no matter how long they may avoid paying this tax, they shall not thereby become free. 4. If any unfree man belonging to the church shall disobey this edict, he shall be fined one half of all his goods and he shall be reduced to his former unfree condition. For an unfree man of the church may never become free. We strictly forbid the unfree of the churches to be set free, and we order all those who have, by any device, been freed to be reduced to servitude again.

No. 87. Ordinance concerning laborers and servants (A.D. 1349)

(Adams & Stephens, *Select Documents*, pp. 114-115.)

The king to the sheriff of Kent, Greeting. Because a great part of the people, and especially of workmen and servants, late died of the pestilence, many seeing the necessity of masters, and great scarcity of servants, will not serve unless they may receive excessive wages, and some rather willing to beg in idleness, than by labor to get their living; we, considering the grievous incommodities, which of the lack especially of ploughmen and such laborers may hereafter come, have upon deliberation and treaty with the prelates and the nobles, and learned men assisting us, of their mutual counsel ordained:

1. That every man and woman of our realm of England, of what condition he be, free or bond, able in body, and within the age of three score years, not living in merchandise, nor exercising any craft, nor having of his own whereof he may live, nor proper land, about whose tillage he may himself occupy, and not serving any other, if he be required to serve in convenient service, his estate considered, he shall be bounden to serve him which shall so him require; and take only the wages, livery, meed, or salary, which were accustomed to be given in the places where he oweth to serve, the twentieth year of our reign of England, or five or six other common years next before. Provided always, that the lords be preferred before others in their bondmen or their land tenants, so in their service to be retained: so that nevertheless the said lords shall retain no more than be necessary for them; and if any such man or woman, being so required to serve, will not do the same, that proved by two true men before the sheriff, bailiff, lord, or constable of the town where the same shall happen to be done, he shall anon be taken by them, or any of them, and committed to the next jail, there to remain under strait keeping, till he find surety to serve in the form aforesaid.

5. Item, that sadlers, skinners, whitetawers, cordwainers, tailors, smiths, carpenters, masons, tilers, boatmen, carters, and all other artificers and workmen, shall not take for their labor and workmanship above the same that was wont to be paid to such persons the said twentieth year, and other common years next before, as afore is said, in the place where they shall happen to work; and if any man take more, he shall be committed to the next jail, in manner as afore is said.

6. Item, that butchers, fishmongers, hostelers, brewers, bakers, pulters, and all other sellers of all manner of victual, shall be bound to sell the same victual for a reasonable price, having respect to the price that such victual be sold at in the places adjoining, so that the same sellers have moderate gains, and not excessive, reasonably to be required according to the distance of the place from whence the said victuals be carried.

No. 88. The obligations of the serf

(From *Life in Medieval France* by Joan Evans, p. 32, revised and newly illustrated edition 1957. By courtesy of the Phaidon Press, London.)

In June the peasants must cut and pile the hay and carry it to the manor house. In August they must reap and carry in the convent's grain; their own grain lies exposed to wind and rain while they hunt out the assessor of the *champart* and carry his share to the barn. On the Nativity of the Virgin the villein owes the pork-due, one pig in eight; at St. Denis' Day the *cens*; at Christmas the fowl, fine and good, and thereafter the grain-due of two *sétiers* of barley and three quarters of wheat; on Palm Sunday the sheep-due; at Easter he must plough, sow, and harrow. When there is building the tenant must bring stone and serve the masons; he must also haul the convent's wood for two deniers a day. If he sells his land, he owes the lord a thirteenth of its value: if he marries his daughter outside the seigniory, he pays a fine. He must grind his grain at the seigneurial mill and bake his bread at the seigneurial oven, where the customary charges do not satisfy the attendants, who grumble and threaten to leave his bread unbaked.

No. 89. Henry I frees a serf (A.D. 926)

(Thatcher & McNeal, *Source Book*, pp. 546-547.)

In the name of the holy and undivided Trinity. Henry, by the divine clemency king. Let all our faithful subjects, both present and future, know that at the request of Arnulf, our faithful and beloved duke, and also to increase our eternal reward, we have freed a certain priest, named Baldmunt, who is our serf, born on the land of the monastery of Campido. We freed him by striking a penny out of his hand in the presence of witnesses, according to the Salic law, and we have thereby released him entirely from the yoke of servitude. And by this writing we have given a sure proof of his freedom and we desire that he shall remain free forever. We ordain that the said Baldmunt, the reverend priest, shall enjoy such freedom and have such rights [that is, have the same legal status] as all those have who up to this time have been set free in this way by the kings or emperors of the Franks.

No. 90. Henry III frees a female serf (A.D. 1050)

(Thatcher & McNeal, *Source Book*, pp. 547-548.)

Henry, etc. Let all our faithful Christian subjects, both present and future, know that we, at the request of a certain nobleman, named Richolf, have freed a certain one of his female serfs, named Sigena, by striking a penny out of her hand. We have freed her from the yoke of servitude, and have decreed that the said Sigena shall in the future have the same liberty and legal status as all other female serfs have who have been freed in the same way by kings or emperors.

No. 91. Recovery of fugitive serfs (A.D. 1224)

(Thatcher & McNeal, *Source Book*, pp. 548-549.)

Henry [VII], etc. . . . When a quarrel arose between our cities of Elsass and the nobles and ministerials of the same province in regard to the serfs who had run away and gone to the cities, or might hereafter do so, . . . it was settled by the following decision: If a serf belonging to a noble or ministerial runs away and goes to one of our cities and stays there, his lord may recover him if he can bring seven persons who are of the family of the serf's mother, who will swear that he is a serf, and belongs to the said lord. If the lord cannot secure seven such witnesses, he may bring two suitable witnesses from among his neighbors, who will swear that before the serf ran away the said lord had been in peaceable possession of him,

. . . and he may then recover his serf. We also decree and command that all nobles and ministerials who wish to recover their serfs may enter a city for this purpose with our permission and protection, and no one shall dare injure them. At their request a safe-conduct shall be furnished them by the *Schultheissen* and council of the city.

No. 92. Rank of children born of mixed marriages (A.D. 1282)

(Thatcher & McNeal, *Source Book*, p. 549.)

We, Rudolf, by the grace of God king, Augustus, wish by this writing to inform all that while we were holding court at Germersheim on Ash-Wednesday our faithful and beloved subject, Adolf, count of Monte, presented the following question for an official decision: If free peasants contract marriage with unfree, or with others whether of a higher or lower social status, what shall be the status of the children born of such mixed marriages? And all who were present declared that children should always have the rank of that one of its parents who has the lower social status. And by this writing we confirm this decision as a reasonable one.

No. 93. Duties of manorial officers (thirteenth century)

(*Walter of Henly's Husbandry*, tr. Elizabeth Lamond. London, 1890, pp. 85ff.)

The Office of Seneschal

The seneschal of lands ought to be prudent and faithful and profitable, and he ought to know the law of the realm, to protect his lord's business and to instruct and give assurance to the bailiffs who are beneath him in their difficulties. He ought two or three times a year to make his rounds and visit the manors of his stewardship, and then he ought to inquire about the rents, services, and customs, hidden or withdrawn, and about franchises of courts, lands, woods, meadows, pastures, waters, mills, and other things which belong to the manor and are done away with, without warrant, by whom, and how: and if he be able let him amend these things in the right way without doing wrong to any, and if he be not, let him show it to his lord, that he may deal with it if he wish to maintain his right.

The seneschal ought, at his first coming to the manors, to cause all the demesne lands of each to be measured by true men, and he ought to know by the perch of the country how many acres there are in each field, and thereby he can know how much wheat, rye, barley, oats, peas, beans, and dredge one ought by right to sow in each acre, and thereby can one see if the provost or the hayward account for more seed than is right, and thereby can he see how many ploughs are required on the manor, for each plough ought by right to plough nine score acres, that is to say: sixty for winter seed, sixty for spring seed, and sixty in fallow. Also he can see how many acres ought to be ploughed yearly by boon or custom, and how many acres remain to be tilled by the ploughs of the manor. . . .

The seneschal ought, on his coming to each manor, to see and inquire how they are tilled, and in what crops they are, and how the cart-horses and avers, oxen, cows, sheep, and swine are kept and improved. And if there be loss or damage from want of guard, he ought to take fines from those who are to blame, so that the lord may not lose. The seneschal ought to see that each manor is properly stocked, and if there be overcharge on any manor more than the pasture can bear, let the overcharge be moved to another manor where there is less stock. . . .

The seneschal ought, on his coming to the manors, to inquire about wrong-doings and trespasses done in parks, ponds, warrens, conygarths, and dove-houses, and of all other things which are done to the loss of the lord in his office.

The Office of Bailiff

The bailiff ought to be faithful and profitable, and a good husbandman, and also prudent, that he need not send to his lord or superior seneschal to have advice and instruction about everything connected with his baillie, unless it be an extraordinary matter, or of great danger; for a bailiff is worth little in time of need who knows nothing, and has nothing in himself without the instruction of another. The bailiff ought to rise every morning and survey the woods, corn, meadows, and pastures, and see what damage may have been done. And he ought to see that the ploughs are yoked in the morning, and unyoked at the right time, so that they may do their proper ploughing every day, as much as they can and ought to do by the measured perch. And he must cause the land to be marled, folded, manured, improved, and amended as his knowledge may approve, for the good and bettering of the manor. He ought to see how many measured acres the boon-tenants and customary-tenants ought to plough yearly, and how many the ploughs of the manor ought to till, and so he may lessen the surplus of the cost. And he ought to see and know how many acres of meadow the customary-tenants ought to mow and make, and how many acres of corn the boon-tenants and customary-tenants ought to reap and carry, and thereby he can see how many acres of meadow remain to be mowed, and how many acres of corn remain to be reaped for money, so that nothing shall be wrongfully paid for. And he ought to forbid any provost or bedel or hayward or any other servant of the manor to ride on, or lend, or ill-treat the cart-horses or others. And he ought to see that the horses and oxen and all the stock are well kept, and that no other animals graze in, or eat their pasture. . . .

The Office of Provost

The provost ought to be elected and presented by the common consent of the township, as the best husbandman and the best approver among them. And he must see that all the servants of the court rise in the morning to do their work, and that the ploughs be yoked in time, and the lands well ploughed and cropped, and turned over, and sown with good and clean seed, as much as they can stand. The provost ought to see that the corn is well and cleanly threshed, so that nothing is left in the straw to grow in thatches, nor in manure to sprout. The husks, and the trampled corn, and the refuse of the winnowing, may be put together and threshed, and then winnowed and put with the other. And the provost must take care that no thresher or winnower shall take corn to carry it away in his bosom, or in tunic, or boots, or pockets, or sacks or sacklets hidden near the grange. . . .

The Office of Hayward

The hayward ought to be an active and sharp man, for he must, early and late, look after and go round and keep the woods, corn, and meadows and other things belonging to his office, and he ought to make attachments and approvements faithfully, and make the delivery by pledge before the provost, and deliver them to the bailiff to be heard. And he ought to sow the lands, and be over the ploughers and harrowers at the time of each sowing. And he ought to make all the boon-tenants and customary-tenants who are bound and accustomed to come, do so, to do the work they ought to do. And in haytime he ought to be over the mowers, the making, the carrying, and in August assemble the reapers and the boon-tenants and the labourers and see that the corn be properly and cleanly gathered; and early and late watch so that nothing be stolen or eaten by beasts or spoilt. . . .

No. 94. A view of peasant life from Langland

(From *The Vision of Piers Plowman*, in the modern English version of Henry Wells, published by Sheed & Ward Inc., New York, 1945, pp. 50, 87, 92.)

"Can you serve," he said, "or sing in churches,
Or cock hay in my harvest, or handle a hay-fork,
Mow or mound it or make sheaves or bindings,
Reap, or be an head reaper, and rise early,
Or have an horn and be an hayward, and be out till morning,
And keep my corn in my croft from pickers and stealers?
Or make shoes, or sew cloth, or tend sheep or cattle,
Or make hedges, or harrow, or drive geese, or be swineherd?
Or can you work at any craft which the commune calls for,
To be means of livelihood to the bed-ridden?" (p. 50)

"I have no penny," said Piers, "to buy pullets,
Nor geese nor pigs, but two green cheese,
A few curds of cream, a cake of oatmeal,
Two loaves of beans and bran, baked for my children;
And, by my soul, I swear I have no salt bacon,
Nor cook to make collops, I take Christ to witness!
But I have parsley and pot herbs and a plenty of cabbages,
And a cow and a calf, and a cart mare
To draw my dung afield till the drought is over.
There is the little we must live on till the Lammas season.
And then I hope to have my harvest in the garner.
And then I may spread your supper to my soul's content."
So all the poor people fetched peascods,
And brought him beans and baked apples by the lapful,
Ripe cherries, chervils and many small onions,
And offered Piers the present to please Hunger. (p. 87)

The needy are our neighbours, if we note rightly;
As prisoners in cells, or poor folk in hovels,
Charged with children and overcharged by landlords.
What they may spare in spinning they spend on rental,
On milk, or on meal to make porridge
To still the sobbing of the children at meal time.
Also they themselves suffer much hunger.

They have woe in winter time, and wake at midnight
To rise and to rock the cradle at the bedside,
To card and to comb, to darn clouts and to wash them,
To rub and reel and to put rushes on the paving.
The woe of these women who dwell in hovels
Is too sad to speak of or to say in rhyme.
And many other men have much to suffer
From hunger and from thirst; they turn the fair side outward,
For they are abashed to beg, lest it should be acknowledged
At their neighbours what they need at noon and even.
I know all this well; for the world has taught me
What befalls another who has many children,
With no claim but his craft to clothe and feed them,
When the mouths are many and the money scarce.
They have bread and penny ale in place of a pittance.
And cold flesh and cold fish for venison from the butcher.
On Fridays and fast days a farthing worth of mussels,
Would be a feast for such folk, with a few cockles.
It were an alms to help all with such burdens,
And to comfort such cottagers and crooked men and blind folk. (p. 92)

9

THE REVIVAL OF TRADE; THE RISE OF TOWNS; THE CRUSADES

The Revival of Trade

More fundamental in its influence upon western civilization than either feudalism or manorialism was the trade which began to revive late in the tenth century. Feudalism and manorialism declined once they had served their purpose. By the close of the Middle Ages only memories remained of the period when these two institutions had dominated medieval social, economic, and political life. Industry and trade, on the other hand, and the towns and urban institutions which they produced, introduced a civilization which became and remained the dominant feature of western life. Until the twelfth century, the west had lagged far behind Byzantium and Islam in the production and consumption of material goods. Yet already by the close of the thirteenth century western Europe had gained the industrial leadership of the world which it has never relinquished. The rapid development of industry and commerce in the west was all the more extraordinary since it had no ancient traditions upon which to build. Industry and trade had never flourished in the western Roman Empire. What trade had existed had been conducted by Syrians and other easterners. Think of a Roman and one can readily visualize a farmer (early Republic), a soldier, a statesman, but never a trader. But if the peasant or monk or knight were representative figures of medieval society, quite as typical was the burgher. Like the monk and knight, the medieval burgher had no historical ancestor. Therefore, the traditional phrase, "The Revival

377

of Trade," is not an entirely felicitous one. By implication it does more than justice to the trade of the Roman Empire, while it gives less than due recognition to the commercial revolution which took place in the Middle Ages.

The Dark Age of Trade. From less promising antecedents medieval trade could hardly have sprung. As early as the second century A.D., the economy of the Roman Empire had begun to sag. As we have seen, the emperors from Nerva to Marcus Aurelius (96-180) had earned the classification of Good Emperors partly as a result of their efforts to relieve depressed areas and segments of the population. The imperial economy which had sagged in the second century, all but collapsed under stress of military anarchy in the third. While Diocletian was able to right the state almost as it appeared about to dissolve, the reforms which he introduced, together with those of his successors, failed to revive the economic life of the empire. The intrusion of large numbers of semicivilized Germans in the late fourth century and the fifth served to accelerate the trend toward an agrarian economy. The political instability of the sixth century brought no relief, while the expansion of Islam in the seventh which permanently shattered the economic unity of the Mediterranean world seriously aggravated the factors already depressing industry and trade. Urban life decayed to the point of disappearance, population suffered a sharp decline, the flow of money practically ceased, and roads and bridges fell into disrepair because there was little need to keep them up. Finally, in the late eighth century, the Vikings began their destructive raids on western Europe, followed by the Magyars and Saracens who dealt further blows to what remained of the European economy.

Always Some Trade. Yet trade and industry did not disappear, not entirely. A minimal movement of goods never ceased, both within the confines of western Europe as well as between Europe and the Levant. We read how Charlemagne relieved a famine in one part of his realm with food from another. Such movement of goods must have occurred with some regularity in view of the frequency of food shortages. Furthermore, few manors were ever so self-sufficient as not to require some imports, if not of wine, at least of iron and salt. Once areas such as Flanders had established a reputation for some specialty—in the case of Flanders for textiles—a distinct broadening of the base we associate with industry and trade came into existence. Over and beyond the local markets which offered the products of manorial production for sale, fairs where goods from a considerably wider area were available are heard of as early as the fifth century. Scattered Merovingian and Carolingian coins attest to the existence of that medium of exchange even during the "Dark Ages." From the Levant, principally from Constantinople, a small but steady trickle of goods, such as spices, silks, papyri, and liturgical articles, continued to dribble in through the Byzantine ports of Naples, Amalfi, and Venice. Venice was actually something of an anomaly for the times. When cities and industry and trade all about it were in decline, Venice prospered. Islam never quite succeeded in severing that city's connections with Constantinople.

Factors in the Revival of Trade. Yet though industrial economic life was not entirely dead, it was hardly better than moribund prior to the latter half of the tenth century when trade and commerce began to quicken. What caused this revival scholars have difficulty explaining. Surely one of the more fundamental causes was the rise in population. This rise proved all the more stimulating a factor since population had reached its nadir about 950, as a result of the invasions of the Northmen, Magyars, and Saracens. From about the middle of the ninth century, a very perceptible demand for more goods and more food to clothe and feed a growing population became evident. Between the years 1000 and 1300 the population of western Europe probably doubled and rose to approximately sixty millions. What occasioned this remarkable increase is not easy to say, although the fact that life generally held fewer hazards after 950 when the Saracens had been expelled from south-central Europe and when most of the Northmen and Magyars had been converted, must have proved a contributing factor. In addition to the rise in population, the assimilation of the seafaring Vikings into the civilization of western Europe must have encouraged the flow of trade. With Normans established in England, in north-western France, and in southern Italy, and with still others seeking to gain control of the Greek littoral to Constantinople, greater commercial activity was bound to come. The relative peace of the eleventh century and the political stabilization of Germany, England, and France, were conducive to trade. A more immediate stimulus to the revival of Italian commerce came with the clearing of Moslem ships from the Adriatic by Venice in 1002, and the expulsion of Moslems from all Italian waters in 1087 by the Genoese and Pisans. The people of these cities, in fact, followed up their successes by wresting a foothold in Tunis and forcing trade concessions from the Saracens there. Then at the very close of the eleventh century, the tremendous Crusading movement to the Holy Land got under way. This was to prove, on all counts, the most powerful single stimulant to the growth (not the rise) of trade.

Trade Routes. The first strong evidence of a trade revival appeared in Italy. There feudalism with its attendant provincialism had never firmly taken root; in Italy more cities had managed to preserve a measure of their former size; above all, Italy was nearest to Constantinople and the Levant and Venice was actually a Byzantine dependency. For it is to this trade between the eastern Mediterranean and the Italian cities that the revival of western trade must be traced. As the circles of trade widened, Italian merchants began to carry their goods northward through the Alpine passes into Germany and France. From Venice they moved through the Brenner Pass to Augsburg and Nuremberg, thence to the cities of eastern Germany and Poland; or from the Brenner Pass they moved eastward to Regensburg and Vienna on the Danube. The goods which converged on Milan moved northward through Septimer and St. Gotthard Passes to Basel and the Rhine cities, or westward through Great St. Bernard and Mont Cenis Passes to the thriving cities of the Rhone valley. Much of the trade out of Pisa and Genoa moved by water to the mouth of the Rhone and thence northward, or by an old Roman coastal road to Marseilles. Since river transport was cheaper, safer, and faster, trade followed rivers wherever possible. (Europeans still make extensive use of inland waterways for reasons of economy). By a happy circumstance, a series of navigable rivers, the Loire, Seine, Rhine, Weser, Elbe, and Oder, all flow in a generally northerly direction from the Alpine passes to make connection with the English Channel, the North Sea, and the Baltic. These three bodies of water proved as vital to northern commerce as the Mediterranean to that of southern Europe and the Near East.

Routes to and Products from the East. The commodities which the Italian cities imported from the seaports of the eastern Mediterranean and which provided the fuel for the revival of trade, hailed not only from Byzantium, Syria, and Egypt, but also from India and China, and from the tropical regions of Africa. From Constantinople a route ran eastward through the Black Sea and the Sea of Azov, to Sarai on the Volga, thence overland to Turkestan and beyond. Another route cut directly eastward from Trebizond on the Black Sea through Armenia and Persia toward the east. Traders from Syrian ports passed through Damascus along ancient caravan routes to the Euphrates, then down the Persian Gulf to India; or to Baghdad on the Tigris where extensive bazaars displayed goods from almost every corner of the known world. From Alexandria, a caravan could make its way across the Sinai peninsula and down the Arabian coast, or by ship down the Red Sea to tap the tropical products of the Punt or proceed on to India. The commodities and wares which ultimately made their way to Italy over these routes from the largely unknown east, were nothing short of fabulous. They included silk, cotton and dyestuffs; sugar, rice, lemons, oranges, apricots, and melons; perfumes, drugs, and incense; ivory, precious stones, furniture, rugs, tapestries, and glass mirrors. Of special importance among these imports and something Europe was never able to produce, were spices. From the Visigoths who demanded 3,000 pounds of pepper as ransom from Rome back in 410 A.D., to Edward I's England which spent almost $100,000 on condiments in 1300, western Europe displayed a prodigious appetite for spices. It was the lure of spices in fact that sent Vasco da Gama around Africa and Columbus to America during the closing years of the Middle Ages.

European Products. Yet the majority of Europeans were strangers to these eastern commodities and wares. These products of the east were luxuries beyond their reach. Had the revival of trade been limited to them

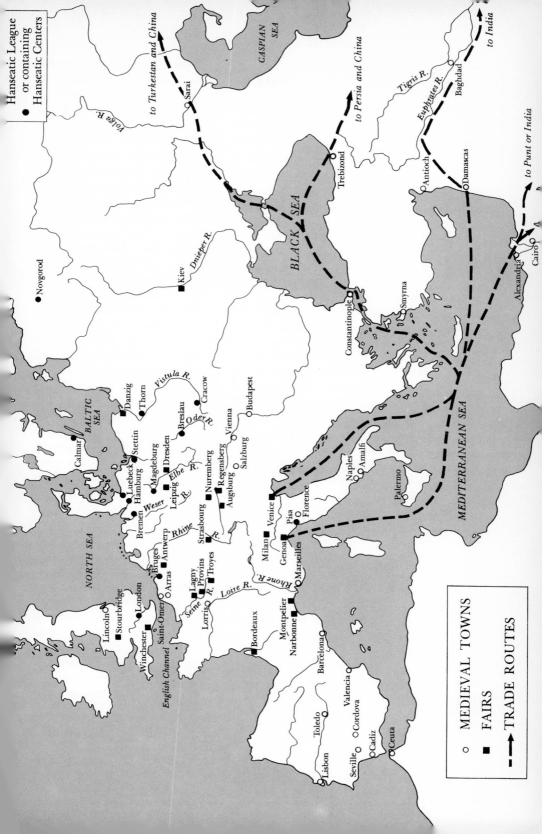

Hanseatic League
or containing
Hanseatic Centers
●

CASPIAN SEA

Volga R.

to Turkestan and China

Sarai

to Persia and China

Tigris R.

Euphrates R.

Baghdad

to India

Dnieper R.

Trebizond

Antioch

Damascus

to Punt or India

Novgorod

BLACK SEA

Kiev

Smyrna

Alexandria

Cairo

Constantinople

Vistula R.

MEDITERRANEAN SEA

Danzig

Thorn

Cracow

Breslau

Budapest

Oder R.

Stettin

Vienna

BALTIC SEA

Magdeburg

Dresden

Salzburg

Calmar

Luebeck

Hamburg

Leipzig

Nuremberg

Regensburg

Augsburg

Naples

Elbe R.

Amalfi

Palermo

Bremen

Weser R.

Milan

Venice

Rhine

Strasbourg

Pisa

Florence

Genoa

Antwerp

R.

Marseilles

Bruges

Lagny

Provins

Rhône R.

Arras

Troyes

Saint-Omer

Lorris

Seine R.

Loire R.

Lincoln

Stourbridge

Winchester

London

NORTH SEA

Montpelier

Narbonne

English Channel

Bordeaux

Barcelona

Valencia

Toledo

Cordova

Cadiz

Ceuta

Seville

Lisbon

MEDIEVAL TOWNS ○

FAIRS ■

TRADE ROUTES ▬▬▶

and to those able to afford them, Europe would not have advanced beyond the modest development of industry and trade of Roman times. Fortunately, this eastern trade proved but the prelude to the development of a truly continental trade. No sooner had the Italian merchant crossed northward beyond the Alps with his store of eastern wares, than he was met by the German and Scandinavian with the products of central and northwestern Europe. These products were of an entirely different sort from what the Italian merchant had to exchange. They were bulky and heavy, and usually of low value, and had it not been for easy water-transport, shipping costs would have made their shipment prohibitive. The commodities of the north included timber, tar, furs, hides, tallow, grain, herring, wine, amber, wool, beer, salt, copper, and iron. The herring was almost as much a staple in the trade of northwestern Europe as spices were in that of the east. While much of the North Sea was fished, there has probably never been so popular a haunt for fishermen as the sound between Denmark and Sweden in the later Middle Ages. Almost as vital as the herring trade to northwestern Europe was that of wine to France. Southwestern France was the heaviest producer, England was possibly the heaviest imbiber, for that country was importing wine to the tune of a gallon a head by 1400. Salt was always a major item of trade in an age of no refrigeration and expensive spices. It was found in many places, in marshes along the seacoast, or mined as at Salzburg (salt mountain). Wool production was similarly widespread. The highest quality wool and the largest quantity to move in trade was that which England shipped to the Low Countries.

Industrial Centers.   Most of these commodities required little processing. Where this was necessary as in the case of metals, the processing was done near the site of origin because of the bulk of the raw materials. Wool, while not bulky, required several operations between raw material and finished cloth. Consequently, in contrast to other production, the textile industry tended to become concentrated in certain areas which enjoyed some significant advantages. The greatest textile area was Flanders which owed its prosperity to its favorable location. It was the natural converging point for trade from England, from the Baltic, from southern France, and from the Rhine. Though the area was not suited to general farming, it proved ideal for sheep raising. So rapidly did the textile industry develop, that within a short time the local supply of wool could not keep the hungry looms working, and heavy imports became necessary from England. (England developed its own textile industry in the fourteenth century). Second in importance to Flanders as a textile center was northern Italy, particularly the city of Florence, where the coarser woolens from the north were reprocessed into finer cloth. Italy, because of its proximity to the Levant, was the first country to introduce certain technical processes from the east. Its geographical advantage enabled it to eventually replace that area in the production of glass, silk, cotton, and luxury wares. In time particular cities became famous for certain specialties: Cordova for leather, Montpellier for dyes, Dinant for copper, Nuremberg for wooden wares. Sweden's reputation as a major source of excellent iron and steel dates back to the Middle Ages, while southwestern England was able to preserve its ancient reputation as an important source of tin throughout the medieval period. All of western Europe, from Italy to Scotland, from Gibraltar to Russia, was sharing in the development of an industry and commerce which was rivaling that of Byzantium and the Mohammedan world by the close of the thirteenth century.

Obstacles to Trade. Yet danger lurks in giving too glowing an account of medieval industrial and commercial expansion. The west actually became industrialized during the nineteenth century, so all the Middle Ages achieved was a strong beginning. Major obstacles hampered economic expansion other than those that only the scientific and technological discoveries of subsequent centuries could remove. Probably the greatest bane to the medieval merchant was the brigand and the robber baron. Until well beyond the close of the Middle Ages, merchants were obliged to travel in armed groups in countries such as Germany where local governments were powerless to cope with lawlessness (also in France during the period of the Hundred Years' War). The Peace of God, together with repeated ecclesiastical fulminations against brigandage, proved ineffective. The absence of roads represented a similarly serious obstacle to trade. Roman roads which could have been used by traders in antiquity but were not, could not be used by the medieval merchant because of their advanced state of disrepair. The building and upkeep of roads was a local concern, which in effect meant nobody's concern. So goods moved normally by pack horse or mule until the fifteenth century when wagons became fairly common. The lack of bridges posed a major obstacle because of the great expense involved in building and maintaining them. So desperate, in fact, did the problem become, that the church indulgenced bridge-building as spiritually meritorious, and religious orders such as the Order of Bridge Brothers dedicated themselves to such work. Most odious of the man-made obstacles to trade were the frequent tolls exacted from the merchant by the lord who owned the road, bridge, ferry, and market which the trader might wish to use. The merchant paid seventy-four tolls on the Loire, sixty on the Rhone. (Reading 101) It was to suppress this practice, to eradicate brigandage, and to halt the arbitrary interference of powerful feudatories, that merchants and towns everywhere supported the growth of strong monarchies.

Sea Travel. Similarly vexing problems harassed the merchant who wished to ship his merchandise by sea. Ships were small, the ocean was often rough, and pirates and Moslems dangerous. For these reasons, the sea captain avoided travel during the winter months and hove close to shore, frequently too close for safety. Most expeditious were the galley ships used in the Mediterranean, but a crew of a hundred oarsmen left little room for cargo. More satisfactory for carrying purposes were the sailing vessels which the Genoese and Venetians developed during the twelfth and thirteenth centuries, which vessels had two or three decks and were a hundred feet long and almost half that wide. These ships were used extensively in transporting Crusaders and their necessities to and from the Holy Land. Because of the phenomenal expansion of the ship-building industry and the constant demand for more goods, significant and steady progress was achieved from the twelfth century onward in the construction of ships and in the mariner's art in general. The rudder and compass came into use in the thirteenth century. (The compass may have been a western invention). Once European mariners had acquired knowledge of tacking, sailing ships quickly forced galleys off the sea because of the greater space they left for cargo. Experience brought improvements in ballasting and cargo-stowing. Wharves and cranes greatly facilitated the loading and unloading of goods, while buoys and lighthouses aided ships in sailing through perilous waters. By the fourteenth century, if not earlier, ship captains could consult *portolani* or sea charts for the best and safest courses between major seaports. Mention should be made of the gradual acceptance of maritime codes which afforded the ship owner and his cargo protection when he visited foreign waters and shores. Because of these advances in the mariner's art, sailors were venturing hundreds of miles westward into the Atlantic and far down the coast of Africa by the late thirteenth and early fourteenth centuries. (See page 769.)

Medieval Fairs.   One of the commercial developments concomitant with the revival of trade was the fair. For its origins, Sidonius Apollinaris takes us back at least to 427 A.D., when he describes those held in the county of Champagne in northeastern France. The first fairs may have risen in connection with religious festivals, when enterprising peddlers would take advantage of the large gathering of people to display their wares. Suggestive of this origin is the word *kermesse* (*ker*, church and *messe*, mass) by which the people of Brittany and Flanders still designate a fair. Most fairs appeared in the twelfth and thirteenth centuries when they developed more often than not out of a village or country market. Such a market was normally a weekly affair, when produce and wares of the locality were offered for sale. It would happen that this or that market prospered either because of its geographical location or the encouragement of the local lord who would guarantee merchants his protection. Markets thus favored often developed into fairs. (Reading 100) Fairs were held annually, or sometimes twice a year. They might last for as long as seven weeks, but three weeks was customary. Although most of the goods displayed at fairs were sold at wholesale to other merchants, a considerable amount of retail purchasing was done, particularly by the aristocracy. Fairs provided an impetus to the evolution of banking methods, since a large quantity of money normally changed hands, much of it of strange denominations. Merchants and bankers commonly settled their accounts at the fair, often in foreign exchange, and arranged for credits at future fairs which they planned to attend. Because fairs were held consecutively throughout the greater part of the year, they came to function as clearing houses for international trade, a role they continued to perform until superseded in the fourteenth century by urban emporia which could perform the job on a permanent basis. The counts of Champagne were quick to recognize the material benefits such fairs would bring them and their province, and zealously promoted their growth. Since the county of Champagne proved the logical meeting ground for assembling goods from northern and western Europe and from the Mediterranean world, the Champagne fairs became the most popular in the Middle Ages. Early in the fourteenth century their prosperity began to wane, however, because of a heavy tax which the king of France levied on goods coming from Flanders. About the same time Venice decided to send the bulk of its exports to central Europe in the so-called Flanders fleet by way of Gibraltar and the Atlantic. Few fairs outlived the Middle Ages, although those of Leipzig, Nuremberg, and Dresden have enjoyed a continuous history down to the present. Much money was spent at fairs and a great quantity of goods changed hands. But what attracted most people—people who came with more curiosity than money—was the store of rich and bizarre (from bazaar) wares they could expect to see, also the travelers from strange lands, aristocratic visitors, and the fortune tellers, minstrels, clowns, jugglers, and similar entertainers who have always been found where people are apt to gather.

The Rise of Towns

The Medieval Town: Definition. Contemporary with the revival of trade was the rise of towns. One might indeed ask what came first, trade or town? Could there have been a revival of trade without towns where people produced wares for export? On the other hand, would towns have risen where people were engaged in surplus production without trade to dispose of these products? We must conclude that trade and town were mutually interactive, trade fostering the rise of towns and towns stimulating the flow of trade, both developing alongside each other. By definition, as has already been suggested, a medieval town was an industrial center, in contrast to the village or manorial community which was agricultural. Yet no hard line need be drawn between the two. A village might number among its inhabitants smiths and artisans who produced more wares than the community could absorb, while in the environs of cities such as Paris would be found farmers and tillable acres. In a narrow sense, as will be explained later, a town was not a town until it had received a charter. Still the occupational distinction between farmers and artisans is the better one and has general validity.

Sites of Towns. A look at the location of towns and at the advantages which first attracted settlers to their sites will shed light on their origins. First and foremost among all considerations was the site's superiority with respect to trade and communications. Every town lay on a trade route. Villages not so advantageously placed never developed into towns. Not all communities, of course, which lay along trade routes developed into towns. Those that did usually possessed some quality beyond that of commercial utility, which contributed to their growth. Administrative centers like Lincoln and Derby in northern England from which the Danes had ruled that part of the country, grew into towns because of their favorable location. The original nucleus about which some towns developed was a monastery to which people had flocked for reasons of protection. Cathedral seats often grew into towns, at least those within the confines of the old Roman Empire, since they were ordinarily situated in important communities. Cathedrals might also offer a measure of protection, even the possibility of employment in view of the size of the establishments and the large body of personnel associated with them. Some towns such as Cologne and Canterbury, grew up at the sites of ancient cities. The frequency with which one encounters the suffix *burg* (*burgh, bourg, borough*) in the names of towns, (Magdeburg, Strasbourg, Peterborough, Bourgos), suggests how many of them took root at fortified places (*burg*, German, and *burough*, English). By the twelfth century, those people whose ancestors had made their homes near a fortress (faubourg, meaning outside the *burg*, or suburb, close to the *burg*) were called burghers, burgesses, or bourgeoisie, words quite devoid of any military connotation. A number of towns reveal the reason for their origin in their names: Oxford, where oxen forded the stream; Cambridge, where there was a bridge over the river; Bruges, simply the bridge. Lastly, there was the *ville neuve* or "new town" which a king or lord might create in the hope of tapping some of the wealth which was to be had in towns. One of the earliest of "new towns" was Lorris, which Louis VI of France founded early in the twelfth century. Few "new towns" took permanent root or prospered in the older parts of Europe, demonstrating the fact that towns, while composed of men, were not entirely man-made. The most successful "new towns" were located in the largely undeveloped east, towns like Breslau, Dresden, Luebeck, and Berlin, where the best sites commercially speaking had not already been appropriated. (Reading 102)

Rise of Industrial Centers. Because of the close relationship between trade and towns, many of the same factors which were operative in the revival of trade also contributed to the rise of towns. Thus the growing population of Europe after 950 and the relative stability and tranquillity of the next century or two, surely encouraged the rise of towns. A factor equally instrumental in the rise of towns and the revival of trade was the development of manufacturing. Industrial centers appeared almost by magic after the tenth century in areas which were blessed by an abundance of raw materials or which enjoyed a fortunate location regarding trade. Such was the case, for instance, with Flanders, which enjoyed one of the most favored locations in Europe with respect to trade, while having, at the same time, ready access to a large supply of local wool. As soon as a demand for textiles made itself felt, a textile industry took root there and flourished, attracting thousands of immigrants to the area. In fact, Flanders, which was almost empty of population in the tenth century, had become the adopted home of some three million people by 1300, and large bustling textile centers such as Ghent, Ypres, Arras, Bruges, and Saint-Omer dotted the countryside. While many of the citizenry of such towns would be occupied with the usual tasks which were necessary to the general well-being of a medieval community, the great majority would be engaged in one or the other of the many processes involved in the manufacture of textiles: cleaning and carding the wool, spinning the thread, weaving, fulling and dyeing the cloth. Normally, it was industrial centers as strategically located as those of Flanders and as close to a supply of raw materials, that grew into the most prosperous and influential towns of the Middle Ages.

Town Charters. In economic terms, the village was an agricultural, the town an industrial and commercial community. In a legal sense, the village remained, to all intents and purposes, just another manorial community, regardless of subsequent industrialization, until the lord granted it a charter. The charter officially created the town. The initiative in securing a charter was assumed by the townspeople. If the traditional manorial obligations of corvée and banalities were odious to an agricultural community of the twelfth century, then to industrial settlements they were intolerable. Consequently, with the wealthier and ambitious residents taking the lead, the townspeople would approach their lord with a request for a charter. They would make three requests of him: that he release them from their personal servile obligations; that he permit them to select their own officials and maintain their own courts and law-enforcement agencies; that he surrender to them the control and administration of the economic life of the community. Such privileges the feudal lord was ordinarily loath to grant, at least at first. These concessions would, in effect, revolutionize the social and economic pattern of medieval society. Extensive readjustment would be necessary before the three traditional classes of clergy, aristocracy, and peasantry could accept the presence of a fourth and wholly distinct class. More immediately, the lord by granting such privileges would be abdicating a great deal of his authority. So lords were slow to respond to the appeal of the burghers. The king usually proved himself readiest to take the step, although he preferred to grant charters to communities on the borders of his lands where they would cause him the least, and his vassals the most, anguish. What induced him and, after him, many more lords to stomach the loss of power involved in the granting of charters, was the money the townspeople were ready to pay for such charters. Kings were always in need of money and most feudal lords were equally impecunious. Most reluctant to grant concessions were the more powerful lords and especially ecclesiastical corporations, monasteries and bishoprics, which had less need for ready money. It frequently required the threat of force before these were ready to capitulate. A few never did, at least not during the Middle Ages. The rights of the monastery of Peterborough were not even extinguished by the Reformation, but were preserved by the dean and chapter down into the nineteenth century. Actually few charters were granted after 1300, and many of those that had been granted, particularly in France, were later modified to the prejudice of town privileges. (Readings 95-97)

Town Air was Free Air.   Whatever the particular rights which the lord granted the town in the charter, they uniformly incorporated the principle that town air was free air. Any serf who remained in a town for a year and a day, without his lord challenging his presence there, was legally a free man. Many of the towns in Italy and France were known as communes, on the theory that there it had been the town as a collective legal personality which had secured the charter or had established its autonomy. Still the distinction between the town and the commune was more technical than real. In the last analysis, the rights and autonomy of each depended upon the power of the king. Where the king was weak as in Italy and Germany, the towns were strongest, almost sovereign. Chartered towns often owed the equivalent of knight's service to the lord granting the charter, a service which was more feudal than manorial. Yet the fee which the town paid annually in exchange for this charter covered servile obligations. While the term charter customarily suggests democratic rule, medieval town government, however, was far from democratic. Control was usually vested in the hands of a financial oligarchy.

The Medieval Gild

Origins of the Gild.   The charter which the lord granted the town frequently provided that an official group of merchants, known as the merchant gild, should supervise the sale and purchase of goods within the environs of that town. Like the town itself, this gild was a peculiarly medieval institution. It is true that a group such as the gild of boatsmen at Paris might claim a continuous history from Roman times when it was a college. (See page 26.) Still such an ancient association was at best accidental, not institutional. The medieval gild had no ancient antecedents. The earliest gilds were probably of religious origin. They might trace their activities back to a time when their members were social confreres in some spiritual confraternity. A more general origin might be discovered in the practice of merchants of a town to travel together because of brigands, when business took them to distant cities. Such expeditions would require planning, and this cooperation might lead in turn to the mutual working out of further problems, such as that of securing recognition as a gild. Gilds began to appear in the late eleventh century, and attained the peak of their importance and affluence in the thirteenth. The first gilds were probably merchant gilds. As industry expanded and grew more specialized, it was inevitable that the members of a particular trade should organize their own independent craft gild. This tendency was all the stronger since men working at the same trade customarily lived in the same neighborhood.

Purpose of the Gild. The first purpose of the gild was to preserve for its members the exclusive right to buy and sell in the community. Merchants who were not members of the gild might buy and sell, but only for a fee. Some exceptions to this rule were permitted. Country folk could bring their produce into town without paying a toll. The same privilege might be extended to foreign merchants who wished to sell at wholesale. In neither instance would the members of the gild suffer any competition. It was to safeguard the advantages of this monopolistic position for themselves that membership in the gild came in time to be strictly limited. In addition to eliminating competition from without, the gild sought to prevent any competition within the gild itself. All members paid the same sum for materials, all paid the same wages, all gildsmen worked the same number of hours, all those in the same craft sold their commodities or services at the same prices. Should a member happen upon a labor-saving device, that, too, would have to be shared without compensation with the other members of the gild—that is, if the device itself was adopted. No merchant might advertise his wares in such a manner as to attract the customers of other members. Certain practices were outlawed: engrossing, that is, cornering the market; forestalling, the purchase of goods on the way to market in order to procure them more cheaply; regrating, the purchase of commodities in the market and their sale again at a higher price without adding any utility to them, that is, buying goods and selling the same for a profit.

Gild Obligations. In return for this monopoly, the gild assumed the responsibility for providing the community with commodities of reasonably good quality. Elaborate rules were laid down by the gild which governed the quality of the materials to be used and the standards to be observed in the processing of these materials. Inspectors employed by the gild made regular tours of investigation to insure the proper observance of these rules, to check upon measurements used by the gildsmen, on the number of threads in the cloth used by tailors, or on the suppleness of the leather in the shoemaker shops. Members of the gild were obliged to do their work in the front part of their shops where it would be difficult to hide shoddy operations. No night work was permitted, since work by candle light was apt to be inferior. Infractions of gild regulations were reported by the representatives of the gild to the town authorities, as in the case of one John Welburgham, who was charged with selling two pieces of fish which were "rotten, foul, and unwholesome for man." John was found guilty and his sentence provided that after returning to the unhappy purchaser the money he had accepted for the fish, he should have the punishment of the pillory for one hour of that day, and that the said fish should then be burned beneath him. (Readings 98, 99)

Gild Education. The most effective means the gild employed to insure the production of quality goods was by means of a system of industrial education. The training program of the gild constituted, in fact, its most constructive and substantial contribution to medieval society. Depending somewhat on the nature of the trade, but usually at about the age of fourteen, a father would apprentice his son to a master gildsman. In return for a financial consideration, the master would engage to teach the boy his trade, and during the period of his apprenticeship to keep him as a member of his own household and raise him as his own son, in effect, to provide him "suitable clothing, shoeing, board, bedding, and chastisement." When the boy, now a young man, had completed his apprenticeship, probably at the age of nineteen, he would be classed as a journeyman and work by the day (from the French *journée*, meaning day). How long the years of his journeymanship lasted depended upon circumstances to a considerable degree. If he were fortunate and a talented worker, and if the gild had room for him, he might rise to the position of master after as little as three years. But he must first accumulate sufficient capital to set himself up with tools, materials, and a shop of his own. Above all, he must have proved his competency to the gild officials by presenting for their examination a masterpiece worthy of a master.

The Just Price. A second responsibility was implicit in the gild's right to exercise monopolistic control over the buying and selling in the town. This was the requirement that its members sell their goods at a "just price." This "just price" entitled the merchant to no more than the cost of his materials plus his time, which he was permitted to sell for enough to enable him to live at the standard traditional to his particular profession. In essence, therefore, the "just price" was the market price. Being a market price, the "just price" might vary with supply and demand, although any action which might cause it to fluctuate was forbidden, wherefore the outlawing by the gild of such practices as engrossing and forestalling. A merchant who cornered the market could not only sell his goods at a price above what was justified, but in doing so he would also make it impossible for the other members of his gild to secure a just price for their goods. Because the gild was in a position to regulate the market price of its commodities, the obligation to sell at a just price placed a dual responsibility upon the gild and its members: not to sell above the market price, and not to interfere in any way with this market price. Actually the principle of the "just price" is not so foreign to our way of thinking as might be supposed. Wherever a monopoly exists today, as for example in the telephone industry, the government interferes and permits the company to sell its services only at what the government considers a reasonable or just price.

The Logic of the Just Price.   The medieval "just price" differed from the modern "reasonable rate" in two respects: it was set by the gild rather than by the state; it was a principle dictated as much by the economics of the medieval situation as by ethical considerations. What made the "just price" an entirely logical and almost necessary practice during the years when the gild flourished, was the noncapitalistic character of medieval economy at that time. Like the manor, the gild evolved at a time when communities were still largely isolated and when a self-sufficient economy generally obtained throughout western Europe. Just as manorial production was geared to the needs of the village community, so was the production of the gilds to those of the town. Take as an illustration the butchers' gild, which provided the townspeople with the meat they required. Because there existed outside the town no demand which the gild might supply, it tended to limit both its production of meat as well as the number of butchers to the needs of the community. Since the market the gild could serve was fixed, since its membership was stable, its place in the economy of the community established, and since this economy in turn was also unchanging, the gild could not easily increase its prices beyond the point custom considered reasonable without disrupting the entire community. It was convention and circumstance, therefore, as much as Christian choice which lay at the basis of the "just price."

Capitalism and the Gild.   This explains why the rise of capitalism and the expansion of trade shook the gild institution to its foundations. Capitalism, which involved the use of goods and the means of production by individuals for profit, goes back no farther than the twelfth century. Until then one cannot readily speak of a bourgeoisie, the social class with which we associate capitalism, or the existence of that small group of men who by way of thrift, fortune, or unscrupulousness, have been able to accumulate a workable amount of capital. The revival of trade and the rise of towns introduced a form of economy with great potentialities for making profits

and amassing fortunes, in short, for the rise of capitalism. For some generations, however, these potentialities could not be exploited, since the revival
of trade had not proceeded sufficiently far to break down the relative isolation of the towns. Therefore, an institution as noncapitalistic as the gild
could emerge, based upon principles of no competition, equal wages, the
sharing of inventions, a fixed standard of living, and a "just price." Still
one should not conclude that a large element of altruism was present in
the birth of the gild. It was designed by wealthy merchants intent on securing for themselves the control of the business of the community. During
the first century or two of the gild's existence these masters were content
with sharing alike the modest benefits of the system, that is, until the
growth of trade had attained such proportions that far greater profits came
within their reach. As pointed out above, the "just price" was a natural
concomitant of the gild system in its early period when a non-capitalistic
economy prevailed. By the fourteenth cenutry when capitalism had developed sufficiently far to have affected a great part of western industry
and commerce, the philosophy "what the traffic will bear" threatened to
supplant the principle of the "just price." Because of the great wealth their
control of business could bring them, masters now carefully restricted
membership in their circle to their close relatives and friends. The ordinary
journeyman could no longer find room at the top. We hear that love of
money is the root of all evil: the history of the decay of the medieval gild
is a case in point.

The Expansion of Trade and the Gild. The expansion of trade affected
the gild adversely, above and apart from capitalism in general. The gild
operated successfully in local trade; it had been organized expressly for
that purpose. When trade developed interregional and international ramifications, the gild generally found it difficult, if not impossible, to adjust
itself to the new situation. How serious was the impact of such trade upon
the gild system can be illustrated by what happened in the textile industry.
Because this industry was concentrated in Flanders and northern Italy, it
not only demanded widespread markets to absorb its products, but it required more capital to finance the extensive operations involved than the
masters of the gild normally had at their command. Control of the textile
industry gravitated inevitably into the hands of big businessmen who were
financiers and capitalists, rather than manufacturers. In Florence, for instance, the famous banking family of the Medici invested heavily in the
industry and eventually gained control. These financiers then would assume the responsibility for purchasing the wool; they would arrange with
masters, or with journeymen directly, to have it processed into cloth, and
then would sell the finished products in the markets of Europe and the
Near East. Most industries which engaged in trade beyond the immediate
locality experienced the same fate as the textile industry, and gradually
fell into the hands of a few financiers. Many masters who lacked the neces-

sary funds or influence, slipped to the position of what might be called foremen today, while journeymen sank to the level of proletariat labor. The most flourishing centuries in the history of the gild were the twelfth and thirteenth. Its history during the two succeeding centuries is marked by bitterness, riots, and insurrections, particularly in Flanders and northern Italy. One note of caution: these last two were also centuries of economic sluggishness, which would have tried a system more "modern" than the gild.

The Gild not a Failure.   Most gilds did not suffer so severely from the impact of capitalism and foreign trades as did those in the textile industry. Transportation costs militated against the organization of most industries on a basis broader than that of the immediate vicinity. Neither were those gilds greatly affected which were composed of highly skilled craftsmen engaged in the production of luxury goods for a limited clientele. These continued to function quite successfully up into modern times. A few are still in existence today. Certain trades continue to employ the system of industrial training set up by the gild, that is, the apprentice, journeyman, and master organization. The medieval gild has attracted unusual attention from modern scholars. It has also recruited champions among idealistically minded men, who are on the lookout for a social and economic system that will function with fewer of such evils as unemployment and industrial strife, which they consider inherent in the capitalistic organization of the economy. These advocates of gild socialism, as it is called, may be accused of a considerable amount of wishful thinking in their insistence that something like the gild system of the Middle Ages would usher in a modern industrial utopia. Yet there is no denying their claims of the excellence of the gild's educational system. The work of the artisans who made the stained glass windows of the Middle Ages or did the wood carving, for example, has scarcely been surpassed. Even more striking are the sculptures which grace Europe's medieval cathedrals, which were the products not of highly paid artists but of humble gildsmen.

Medieval Towns

Their Political Importance.   Because of their growing wealth and population, towns played an increasingly important role in the political history of Western Europe in the late Middle Ages. As early as the closing decades of the thirteenth century, the English king began to bring representatives of the towns into parliament in order the better to tap the wealth of the bourgeoisie. In France they appear in the first meeting of the Estates General in 1302, alongside the powerful first and second estates. Representatives of the towns actually took their place in the cortes in Leon in the late twelfth century. The relations between towns and monarchs were generally friendly, for what benefited the one ordinarily benefited the other also. Towns looked to the king for the peace they wanted for themselves and their business, a peace to which a powerful and irresponsible feudal aristocracy was the greatest threat. Because the king was also interested in humbling the aristocracy, the alliance between town and king proved a natural one. In Spain, as we shall note, the towns played a major part in the rise of royal absolutism, while in both France and England they contributed significantly to that end. Even more immediately appealing to the king than the help the towns might ultimately afford him against the nobility, was their considerable wealth, from which he hoped to derive a handsome and steady source of revenue. Already by 1300, Edward I was realizing a greater volume of revenue from trade than from all his other regular sources combined. So kings took an interest in encouraging trade, and even inaugurated policies which would eventually develop into the full-blown mercantilism of later centuries. Only in Germany and Italy did the towns prove indifferent or hostile to the rise of monarchy. In these countries the towns were already so powerful that their interests frequently coincided with those of the feudality in keeping the king weak.

Their Importance in Medieval History. Medieval towns added a new class to the social structure of western Europe, the urban middle class or bourgeoisie. It is no exaggeration to state that it was this element above all others which laid the foundations upon which western Europe established its commercial, industrial, and political leadership of the world for the next five hundred years and more. The bourgeoisie owed its influence to its wealth. This it amassed in a volume hitherto hardly conceived possible. Because this wealth constituted the bulk of the fluid capital available at the time, it carried unusual weight in the councils of government. Individual members of the urban middle class became the most trusted advisers of kings; they married their daughters into the nobility; they even purchased titles for themselves. The bourgeoisie took the lead in the advance of science and technology in the late Middle Ages. It even contributed with its patronage to the cultural development of the west in the fifteenth and sixteenth centuries. Every town of any importance had schools in the twelfth century. Town clerks and notaries composed the first lay administrative personnel of the west since the disappearance of the Roman bureaucracy. The bourgeoisie represented a great new secular force in medieval life, potentially more dangerous to both state and church than the nobility because of its wealth and numbers. The towns helped kings achieve absolutism by the close of the Middle Ages at the expense of the nobility, but if we were to follow their fortunes beyond that point, we might find them eventually conspiring to destroy the kingship as well. As for the impact of the rise of the bourgeoisie upon the church, it may be significant that no major heresy struck western Europe until the twelfth century when the towns of southern France and northern Italy bred two inimical movements. (See page 519.) The rise of the mendicant orders, the Franciscan and Dominican, may be explained in part by the demand (or need) of the bourgeoisie for a more active and self-sacrificing clergy.

Jacques Coeur. The most spectacular example of the degree of wealth and influence a member of the medieval bourgeoisie could aspire to is that provided by the French merchant prince, Jacques Coeur (d. 1456). Jacques' father had been a merchant too, but Jacques' rise can be traced to his membership in a group to which Charles VII of France had leased the privilege of minting money in Bourges and Paris. That Coeur kept more than his legitimate share in these operations, only his friends will deny. He also realized a huge profit in his trade in metals, shipping silver to the east and bringing back gold. His mercantile enterprises were enormous. He owned a fleet of ships, warehouses in several French cities, and a string of three hundred factories which stretched from southern France to the North Sea. Money brought him favor everywhere, including Rome, where he received special dispensation from the pope to trade with the Moslems, presumably in articles which might be classified as noncontraband. He rose high in the favor of Charles VII, became a member of his council, and treasurer of the royal household. Impecunious nobles found him a ready creditor, and so did the king, although at interest rates ranging as high as fifty per cent. A large portion of the tidy profits Coeur realized from loans to the government he expended on the successful effort of the French to drive the English out of Normandy. For his contribution to the happy conclusion of the Hundred Years' War, which was a significant one, he earned a title for himself. Coeur's wealth proved his ruin in the end. Several of his creditors among the nobility gained the ear of the king, and he was arraigned on the preposterous charge of poisoning the king's favorite mistress and of embezzling public funds. The latter charge stuck—probably a miscarriage of justice even if some had thought it long overdue. Coeur's properties were confiscated and he was condemned to be hanged. With the help of papal agents, he managed to escape his dungeon, and died a few years later (probably a natural death) on a naval crusade which the pope had organized against the Turks. Charles VII subsequently rescinded the judgment of the court against Coeur, and restored much of the father's fortune to his children. Coeur's palatial dwelling rivalled that of the French king, and remains today one of the most princely establishments of the Middle Ages.

Physical Appearance of Towns. The towns and cities in which the bourgeoisie lived were as distinctive in their physical appearance as the castle of the lord and the manorial village of the peasant. To the eye of a modern traveler, their most arresting feature would be the wall or walls with which the community was surrounded, tokens of both the instability of the times and the tendency of the town to grow. Except in "new towns" which had been laid out before the people moved in, the streets which took the visitor to the center of town were narrow and crooked and dark. Buildings, some seven stories tall, with the upper floors projecting beyond the lower in the interest of space, almost blocked out the sunlight. Some communities made a practice of sending a horseman through the streets with his lance across his knees. Any projection which impeded his progress was ordered removed. The streets were unpaved except for the public square which was the show place of the town. Here stood the major structures, the gild and town halls together with the cathedral or similar great church. These were the pride of the townspeople, and upon them the gilds lavished their wealth and ingenuity in order to leave them the envy and admiration of travelers from neighboring towns. Here in the public square the community held its gala festivals, the church its magnificent processions; here the town aldermen met distinguished visitors. The wealthier burghers lived in pretentious stone dwellings, whose high steep roofs were resplendent in their bright tiles. The poorer people occupied areas not greatly different from the slum districts which disgrace our larger cities today. The shopping district consisted of the streets of the gilds, whose shops served alike as factories and stores.

Population and Cleanliness. The population of these medieval towns is difficult to estimate. A community above 50,000 hardly existed unless it were Venice or Paris. London probably never exceeded 25,000; the cities of Flanders were somewhat larger, but most towns numbered but a few thousand. In view of their own limited number, however, and the wide areas of scattered villages they served, medieval towns enjoyed an importance far greater than modern cities of considerably larger population. A great deal has been written about the dirtiness of medieval towns, and this on scanty evidence. Much of the unfavorable comments rests upon the popular though fallacious premise that progress has been inevitable and continuous since the beginning of modern times (1500). Consequently, many people reason, as Professor Thorndike has expressed it, "If Islip is still a stinking village today, think what it must have been when it was the birthplace of Edward the Confessor"* (eleventh century). Numerous town ordinances attest to medieval efforts to keep the streets clean. London could boast of subsurface sewers as early as the twelfth century. It is probable that medieval man was not so sensitive to malodors as we are today, yet the Parisians of the Middle Ages bathed more frequently than do the modern denizens of that city. Not dirt, but fire and plague, were the chief hazards of urban life in the Middle Ages, although firewalls between dwellings were common, and statistics do not reveal any heavier mortality from plagues in urban areas than in villages. (Reading 104)

* *Speculum,* Vol. III (1928), p. 192.

Money and Banking

Coins. The revival of trade and the rise of towns brought about a remarkable development in the use of credit and banking facilities. This was
all the more extraordinary in view of the hopeless monetary confusion
which obtained in the late ninth and tenth centuries. During this period
most feudal lords had usurped the right to coin their own money. The result was enough variety to defy the efforts of the most ingenious money-
changer at the fair to detect the actual content of gold or silver many coins
might possess. The few universally accepted gold coins which still circulated or were being hoarded in the tenth century, included the Arabic
dinar and the Byzantine bezant. As trade began to revive, the demand for
a sound monetary medium grew increasingly insistent. Venice began to mint
a silver penny in the twelfth century. The first gold coin was the one called
augustale which Frederick II had minted in 1231. Genoa and Florence followed a few years later with gold coins of their own. By the close of the
thirteenth century, both Venice and Florence were issuing gold coins
(ducats and florins) which were generally accepted as standard in eastern
and western Europe respectively. Several Western European nations established currencies of their own. The penny of Tours and the sterling
(penny) of England long remained popular in Northwestern Europe.

Evolution of Financial Devices. As trade grew in volume and more goods
began to move along the routes between cities and countries, commercial
banking gradually came into existence. The men who took the lead were
the Italians, who were most heavily engaged in trade and, at the same time,
were operating over a wide territory. To meet the demand for a simpler
and safer method of transacting large financial operations than sending
the actual money, they established agencies in the most important commercial centers of western Europe and the Near East, where importers and
exporters could handle their business expeditiously and without risk. Thus
a merchant in Bruges who wished to make a purchase of silk in Florence,
would purchase a letter of credit in Bruges and take it, rather than the
money, to Florence. There the Florentine representative of the commercial
banker who had sold the letter of credit, would pay him the money with
which to buy the silk. Or if a merchant of Florence owed a bill in Bruges, he
could deposit the amount with a local commercial banker, who would then
arrange for his agent in Bruges to pay the creditor there. When financial

transactions involved merchants in cities as important as Florence and Bruges, however, they would ordinarily be handled in one of the banking houses that began to appear in the thirteenth century. Fairs often served as clearing houses. Merchants who converged there from the major cities of Europe to buy and sell, would use the opportunity to balance accounts with one another and for other merchants for whom they served as agents. By the late fourteenth century we hear of drafts which would empower a banker to pay a certain sum to a third person. By the close of the Middle Ages clearing houses, bills of exchange, drafts, letters of credit, even insurance on cargoes, were well known and were greatly facilitating industrial and commercial expansion.

Rise of Banking.   As financial transactions of this kind grew more regular, more numerous, and, accordingly, more profitable, banking as we know it today slowly emerged as a formal business. The first bankers, moneylenders strictly speaking, were Jews. Partly because the Biblical prohibition against charging interest did not apply to Hebrews when dealing with Gentiles, partly because Jews were among the few traders who could still be found during Merovingian and Carolingian times, they were for many years the only people who had money to lend to straitened lords and ecclesiastics. With the rise of industry and trade, demands for loans grew enormously, and Christians entered the ranks of moneylenders with enthusiasm. By the thirteenth century, they had largely replaced the Hebrew except in more isolated areas. Partly because of interest rates which today would be considered outrageous, the lot of neither the Hebrew nor the Christian moneylender was a happy one. This was especially true of the Hebrew who was already the victim of racial and religious prejudice. Popular conviction that the wealth of Hebrews was immense and at the same time ill-gotten, led to physical attacks on individuals and their properties, if not to occasional pogroms. Kings could usually be found on the side of the Jews against mob violence, but at the price of fleecing them periodically of their savings. Hebrews were, in fact, known as the "king's sponges." Christian bankers often fared no better with kings, who were the worst risks in Christendom. The most important bankers of the fourteenth century, the Bardi and Peruzzi, made the mistake of lending to Edward III and both went bankrupt when he repudiated his obligations. The wily Medici profited by their misfortune and not only amassed the largest family fortune of the Middle Ages, but used their wealth to gain control of Florence and to exert powerful influence in the political and ecclesiastical affairs of fifteenth-century Europe. Their coat of arms still enjoys an undignified existence as the colophon of modern pawnbrokers.

The Church and Capitalism.   What attitude did the church assume toward capitalism, an economic development that promised to revolutionize the static, largely self-sufficient economy of medieval society? To appreciate the church's position, which might appear unrealistic to the modern world, one must bear in mind that medieval theologians were for a long time unaware of the rise of or the nature of capitalism. Their chief mistake, if mistake it was, lay in continuing to apply the ethics of an agrarian society, which had always existed, to the new world of industry and trade which was introducing practices hardly compatible with traditions and institutions hallowed by time and Christian acceptance. Thus in the matter of buying and selling, Aquinas voiced the accepted view of most theologians when he warned: "Trade is rendered lawful . . . when one seeks a moderate gain in trading for the sustenance of his own household or for the relief of the indigent, or when one trades in the interest of the public good lest those things be lacking which are essential to the existence of his country, and when he seeks gain, therefore, not as an end but as the reward for his labor." (Reading 140) For the merchant to earn a reasonable return on his labor was one thing, to make a profit over and beyond that necessary to maintain himself as a member of his profession ("just price") was quite another. Charging more than what was his due would be necessarily at the expense of his neighbor, and, consequently, be a sin against the law of justice. That one person could make a profit and grow prosperous without injuring anyone else was inconceivable to medieval economists. Medieval theologians objected to profit for another reason, namely, that it tempted one to avarice and thus left the door open to ultimate damnation. Christ himself had warned that it was easier for a camel to pass through the eye of a needle, than for a rich man to enter heaven.

The Church on Interest.   The medieval theologian was similarly opposed to the charging of interest. To be entirely accurate, the term usury should be employed here rather than interest. The latter term came into use only when theologians and economists finally came to realize that the interest which financiers of the late Middle Ages wished to charge was not the usury condemned by the Bible. This distinction they were understandably slow in perceiving. Had not the Bible clearly forbidden Hebrews to charge other Hebrews interest? Had not the Koran placed a similar injunction upon Mohammedans? Christian theologians were simply maintaining an ancient and time-honored rule when they denounced the charging of interest as sinful. All these prohibitions, the Judaic, Islamic, and Christian, rested upon the same moral principle, namely, that to charge a man interest constituted a violation of the law of justice, and this for two reasons: first, the borrower needed the money to buy food or shelter; second, to charge for the use of money was stealing since money had no earning powers. To the Bible, the Koran, and to Christian moralists, all loans were consumptive in character. Such loans were the only kind of loans early societies recognized or understood.

The rise of capitalism introduced an entirely new type of loan. Man in the past had borrowed money in order to buy food. Now as the rise of industry and expansion of trade presented unheard of opportunities, he might borrow to invest the money in some profitable enterprise. Indeed, capitalism has been defined as the use of money to make money. A capitalistic loan, therefore, is fundamentally different from a consumptive loan, although it required time before theologians were able to appreciate the essential difference. Nevertheless theologians must have been aware for some time that a loan to a merchant or a lord was unlike a loan to a poor man who needed food for his family. While they did not permit the creditor of a merchant to charge him formal interest until the closing decades of the Middle Ages, they did countenance certain practices which effectively circumvented the prohibition. The creditor might demand a sum over and above the principal lent to cover the risk he had suffered; or he might collect the income of the property with which the debtor had secured his loan. Actually the position taken by the medieval theologian on the issue of interest is not so foreign to our way of thinking as we might suppose. None of us feels as free, for instance, to charge a destitute friend interest for the money we lend him, as we do with the Building and Loan Incorporated with whom we deposit our savings. Finally, it would be difficult to prove that the medieval church's hostility toward capitalism in general and the charging of interest in particular dampened men's ardor for profits. Since the names of churchmen appear prominently among the famous borrowers and lenders of the Middle Ages, one must conclude that the church's opposition was more theoretical than real.

The Hanseatic League

Before concluding this discussion of medieval trade, note should be taken of the most illustrious commercial organization of the Middle Ages, the Hansa of North German Cities or the Hanseatic League. The term *hansa* or its equivalent appears in a number of medieval languages. It means simply a gild or confederacy of merchants. There were other hansas, one of the Rhine cities, for instance, which operated as early as the twelfth century. (Reading 103) The famous Hansa originated about the middle of the thirteenth century, in an alliance between Luebeck and Hamburg for the purpose of policing the rivers and roads in that part of Germany. Other German cities soon joined in this project, since they could expect no help from the impotent German king against brigands and pirates. (Readings 105, 106) From this cooperation against lawlessness, the Hanseatic cities went on to extend to each other reciprocal trading privileges, finally, to secure for themselves a monopoly of the trade of the Baltic. The first official mention of the Hansa appears in 1358 when it numbered some fifty cities. The membership fluctuated constantly as towns joined or withdrew pretty much as they chose. At its peak it may have numbered as many as ninety cities, with colonies in various foreign countries, as at Bruges, London (Steelyard), Novgorod, and Bergen. Though the Hansa was fundamentally interested in commerce, it eventually assumed the character of a political union, with its own flag, diplomatic representatives, and navy, and with regular meetings of the League diet. It scored its greatest success in a victorious war against Sweden. According to the terms of the Peace of Stralsund in 1379, Sweden agreed to permit the Hansa free trade in Danish territory and free passage through Danish waters. The League preferred economic boycott to war, since it found economic boycott generally effective against unfriendly princes or recalcitrant cities. Its monopoly of the herring trade and northern products in general, made the Hansa a formidable power in northwestern Europe in the fourteenth century. Decline set in about the middle of the next century. Dissension and commercial rivalry among the members, notably between Luebeck and Danzig, was inevitable and constant, and occasionally even threatened the existence of the League. A graver threat was that posed by nascent mercantilism on the part of Holland, France, and England, which countries found the Hansa's extensive trading privileges incompatible with their national interests. Even the herring turned against the League by abandoning the friendly Danish waters for those off the coast of Holland. Maybe the herring knew that the future of European trade lay with the cities along the Atlantic seaboard. The passing of Venice in the south (see page 773), at any rate, and the Hanseatic League in the north, heralded as strikingly as did the discovery of America and the all-water route around Africa, the end of one era and the advent of another.

The Crusades

Once trade had begun to revive and towns to spring up in western Europe, nothing so stimulated their further expansion and growth as the Crusades. This is perhaps the principal importance of the Crusades for medieval Europe, that is, the impetus they afforded economic developments of almost every kind, from trade and improved shipping to financial operations and maritime law. Yet to place such emphasis upon the economic aspects of the Crusades is almost to dishonor what must be recognized as among the noblest projects man has ever conceived and undertaken. Few would today endorse the use of military force as the proper method of securing free access to holy places, even if modern society were to consider this important. Still to the great majority of westerners in the Middle Ages, war was a wholly commendable means of achieving so worthy a goal. To the bulk of those thousands upon thousands of knights and foot soldiers who turned their faces eastward on the fearful journey to Jerusalem, this was a holy cause and one which God had enjoined. Perhaps historically the first importance of the Crusades is that of revealing in most vivid fashion the character of the medieval mind in the age of faith. No other age in history has witnessed a similar undertaking. Nevertheless, something of the motivation which impelled the Crusades lives on. We continue to sanctify our wars as crusades for Christianity, even though our religious convictions today are but pallid reminders of the tremendous emotions once evoked in the contest between the crescent and the cross.

Definition of Crusade.   The word *Crusade* is derived from the Latin *crux,* meaning cross. Pope Urban II instructed the knights who engaged to march eastward on the First Crusade against the Moslems to sew a cross on their garments as a reminder to themselves and others that they fought for Christ. The term Crusades pertains traditionally to the military operations undertaken by the Christian West between 1096 and 1270 to secure possession of Jerusalem and the holy places for the use of Christians. In this sense of the word, it has been customary to list seven Crusades, although recent scholars may insist upon eight. Those who count eight distinguish between the expedition of 1218 and the one which Frederick II undertook somewhat belatedly nine years later. Since the number seven has at least been hallowed by time, we shall use that enumeration. Whatever the enumeration preferred, that should not obscure the fact that fierce engagements between Christian and Moslem occasionally broke the relative calm between Crusades, and that a rather constant flow of knights moved eastward to Syria between the Crusades proper for the purpose of strengthening the garrisons which fortified the territories taken on the First Crusade.

Other Contests between Christian and Moslem.   There is a tendency on the part of modern scholars to associate these Crusades, which had as their object the conquest of Palestine and Syria, with the contests between Christian and Moslem which were erupting in Spain and the middle Mediterranean. In Spain, the king of Leon and Castile, with the help of fief-hungry knights from France and the blessing of the pope, was pushing southward into territory long held by the Mohammedan. In Italian waters, Genoa and Pisa had collaborated to drive the Moslem from Sardinia and from Sicily (1091). They even carried their offensive into north Africa to capture Tunis and to force valuable commercial concessions from its emir. That there was an element of a religious crusade about both these operations cannot be denied. Thus the king of Castile remonstrated with missionaries who had come to Spain to preach the Crusades, saying, "Here we are always on a crusade." (Spaniards have been exempted from the law which forbids the use of meat on Fridays to Catholics, in recognition of their century-long crusade against the Moslem.) Yet for all the appeals to religion as motive with which the Spaniard and Italian might have clothed their crusades, one finds it difficult to give second place to national and commercial factors, as is possible with the Crusades in the east. One link between these contests in the west and those in the eastern Mediterranean may be established without fear of contradiction, that is, that by the eleventh century western Europe had finally attained to such military power as to wage offensive warfare against the mighty world of Islam.

Motives. As suggested above, the major factor which inspired the Crusades against the Moslems in Palestine and Syria was religious: to drive them from lands and places held sacred by the west, and to open these to free passage for the thousands of pilgrims who wished to go there. That hard-bitten knights like Bohemond, the disinherited son of Robert Guiscard, fell into step with the host moving eastward on the First Crusade in the hope of carving out solid fiefs for themselves, no one can deny. That the Italian cities supported the Crusades for the economic windfall they hoped to realize in terms of trade and transport is amply demonstrated by the manner in which Venice prostituted the Fourth Crusade to serve its ends. That many knights hoped to make or mend their fortunes in Palestine is undoubtedly true. Pope Urban even whetted their material appetites by reminding them how poor western Europe was compared to that land "flowing with milk and honey." Yet why did ambitious, realistic monarchs such as Philip Augustus of France and Richard of England undertake the Third Crusade? The third king to join them on this Crusade, the aged Frederick Barbarossa of Germany, could scarcely have harbored worldly ambitions which only a campaign in Syria would satisfy. For certain leaders the inconvenience and danger of a Crusade appeared less disagreeable than the shame of remaining at home. Yet it is probable that men as un-Christian as Richard could have been carried away by momentary gusts of religious enthusiasm. Conrad III of Germany, for example, who was one of the leaders of the ill-fated Second Crusade, was ready to acclaim St. Bernard a saint, because no one but a saint could have persuaded him to take up the cross. And, no doubt, the promise of indulgences led many to join the later Crusades. (Reading 112)

The rank and file Crusader could scarcely have hoped for more than the capture of Jerusalem and a safe return home. If he had not permitted preachers like Peter the Hermit to convince him that it was his duty to go, public opinion had insisted that it was. Few illusions blinded him to the dangers that lay ahead. If an Englishman, he made a will before he left, so problematical was his return. Of the hardships attending the 2500 mile march to Jerusalem (from Paris) he could have learned from pilgrims who had been there before, or, after 1100, from bedraggled Crusaders who had managed to return alive from the First Crusade. Yet Crusaders were not saints, whatever the stirring of religious sentiment, and a path of plunder marked their progress eastward. The archbishop of Bulgaria likened their passage through his country to an invasion. The modern reader who peruses the enthusiastic accounts of eyewitnesses concerning the slaughter of Moslems in Syria and Palestine may wonder whether these were indeed Christian Crusaders, although few Crusaders themselves would have doubted for a moment that the massacre of the "infidel" was a thing pleasing to God.

The Pope's Motives. Let us consider the motives of Pope Urban who proclaimed the First Crusade. There we should be able to uncover some of the more immediate, if not fundamental, factors which called forth the Crusades. In 1094 the Byzantine emperor, Alexius Comnenus, sent an urgent appeal to Pope Urban to send aid toward the recovery of Syria and those portions of Asia Minor which the Moslem Turks had overrun. It was in November of the following year that Urban made his dramatic speech in which he proclaimed the Crusade to the thousands of assembled clergy and feudality gathered at Clermont in southern France. (Reading 108) The connection between the emperor's appeal and the pope's proclamation is unmistakable. The plight of the Byzantine Empire was surely the proximate, if not one of the major, causes for the Crusade. This plight dated back to the annihilation of the Byzantine army by the Seljuk Turks at Manzikert in 1071. These Turks were a new and, for a time, an explosive force in the Near East and Asia Minor. Late in the tenth century, one of their chiefs, Seljug ibn Takah, and his followers, had taken service with certain Moslem princes in Persia. They shortly after accepted the religion of their employers and soon took over their power as well. In 1055 they captured Baghdad, from which capital their leader ruled as sultan over an ever widening empire. In 1076 they captured Jerusalem. Though this event alerted the west to the new danger, the power of the Seljuks began to wane almost immediately thereafter, and the Turkish empire broke up within a few years into a number of petty Moslem kingdoms. Alexius hoped to exploit this ebbing of Turkish power and recover his lost provinces, and it was this desire which prompted his appeal to the pope.

Other Considerations. The pope had additional reasons for intervening in the east. Foremost was his desire to free Jerusalem and the Holy Places from Moslem control, so that the thousands of pilgrims wont to go there annually could do so without molestation. This they had formerly been able to do. The Moslems had, in fact, encouraged such devotion and had maintained a benevolent guardianship over the Christian shrines, since it meant business for them. This friendly policy had terminated with the intrusion of the Seljuk Turks, partly because of their fanaticism, partly because their ascendancy to rule disrupted the precarious peace of the area. Stories kept coming back west with returning pilgrims of mistreatment, enslavement, and worse. That these tales lost nothing in the telling goes without saying, but whether true or exaggerated, the issue of the pilgrims proved a decisive one, both in Pope Urban's own motivation as well as in that of the thousands who hearkened to his appeal. The mistreatment of pilgrims, real or alleged, provided the emotional factor which every war requires before a people can be galvanized into action. By a Crusade, Pope Urban may also have hoped to heal the schism by coming to the aid of the Byzantine Empire. He may also have wished to further the cause of peace at home by siphoning off thousands of bellicose knights, or to enhance the prestige of the papacy in its quarrel with Henry IV. (See page 514.)

Leaders of the First Crusade. Contrary to Pope Urban's plans and wishes, several months before the actual Crusade got under way in the summer of 1096, the so-called Peasant Crusade set its tragic course toward Jerusalem. This Peasant Crusade consisted of a number of undisciplined groups led by such popular preachers as Peter the Hermit and Walter the Penniless. (Reading 107) Most of the groups were cut to pieces by furious Hungarians and Bulgarians whom they pillaged on their way eastward. The few who did manage to reach Constantinople Alexius had hurried across the straits into Asia Minor where they were annihilated by the Turks. If peasants expected God to cause Turkish might to melt away at the mere sight of Christian westerners, however poorly armed, the pope had no such illusions. The expedition he organized would have done credit to a great general. His choice of commander, Bishop Adhemar of Puy, proved an admirable one. Only a man of consummate tact, which the bishop was, and one able to command their respect, could have won the cooperation of the feudal leaders of the different crusading contingents, who were among the most haughty individualists of history. These included French lords above all: Robert of Normandy, Robert of Flanders, Godfrey of Bouillon, Stephen of Blois, and Raymond of Toulouse. Bohemond, son of Robert Guiscard, led a group from southern Italy. No kings accompanied the Crusade, and little wonder. William II of England was hardly better than a reprobate, Philip I of France had been excommunicated because of his gross immorality, while Henry IV had his own pope in Germany! Most of the knights who attached themselves to this or that leader were Frenchmen, whence the standard classification by the Moslems of all Crusaders as "Franks."

The Victorious March of the First Crusade. Alexius and Constantinople welcomed the westerners with considerable uneasiness. The emperor had hoped for a strong body of knights who would put themselves under his command in his campaign to recover Asia Minor. Instead he found his city inundated by an obstreperous host, led by bold feudal chieftains who had more contempt than respect for Byzantium. Alexius fortunately possessed all the traditional Byzantine diplomacy, and with the help of Adhemar of Puy, managed to elicit an oath from the western lords that they would turn over to him those territories they might conquer which had belonged to his empire. The first victory over the Turks opened the way to Nicaea which Alexius promptly occupied. Then because of the scarcity of food and water, it was decided that the crusading army split into two groups, a decision which almost proved fatal. At Dorylaeum the Turks attacked one body of Crusaders and would certainly have destroyed it had not the other group come up, almost by accident, just in the nick of time. Near destruction was turned into a great victory, and nothing now blocked the road to Antioch. There good fortune and treachery came to the assistance of the Crusaders, and this key city fell to them in June 1098 after a harrowing siege of eight months. Then of a sudden the Crusaders found

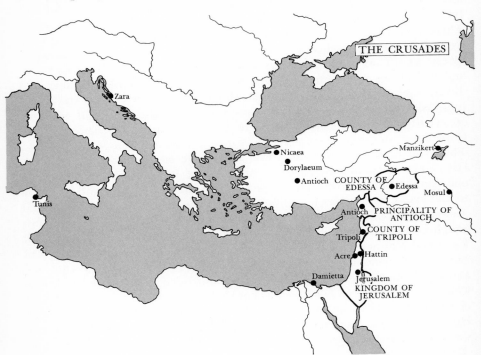

themselves the besieged rather than besiegers, when a huge Turkish army came up belatedly from Mosul to relieve the erstwhile defenders. Fortune had, however, not deserted the Crusaders, and a sally which Bohemond directed at a crucial moment drove off the attackers. Godfrey then led the army on to Jerusalem which fell after a siege of six months on July 15, 1099. A powerful Moslem thrust up from Egypt was met and thrown back at Ascalon in August, and the Christians were in Palestine to stay. (Readings 109, 110)

The Christian States. The territory which the Crusaders conquered for themselves from the Turks stretched like a narrow ribbon some six hundred miles from Edessa in the southeastern corner of Asia Minor southward to almost the outskirts of Egypt. Frightfully vulnerable because of its lack of hinterland and the long distance from friendly allies, this strip of Christian-held territory was further weakened by being divided into four tiny states: the counties of Edessa and Tripoli, the principality of Antioch, and the Kingdom of Jerusalem. These diminutive states were subdivided in turn in the only fashion western Europe knew, into fiefs, which were ruled as virtually independent states. This subinfeudation which contributed immeasurably to the precariousness of the Christian foothold, had one constructive result. It provides scholars an interesting example of what feudatories of the period thought a feudal state should be like. They incorporated their views into the only feudal constitution which time has preserved, probably the only one ever formally drafted, the so called Assizes of Jerusalem. It was fortunate for the Christian states that their lack of unity was counterbalanced by bitter rivalry among the neighboring Moslem chieftains, who could have snuffed out their existence at almost any time had they put their common minds to it.

Religious Military Orders. What proved the principal source of strength to the Christian principalities was the presence of several religious military orders: the Knights of St. John (Hospitalers), the Knights of the Temple (Templars), and the Teutonic Knights. These groups had initially dedicated themselves to the care and protection of pilgrims and crusaders, but had gradually assumed more military functions. Their members lived according to rules which were patterned roughly after those of the monastic orders. The rule which the Templars observed breathed some of the religious fanaticism of its author, St. Bernard. Instead of praying for the furtherance of the City of God, these knights pledged themselves to fight to the death for it. The Templars never surrendered. Saladin, who was respected by friend and foe alike for his humanity (see page 408), had to execute the several hundred Templars and Hospitalers he captured in the battle of Hattin. Though doing yeoman service in maintaining the Christian foothold in Syria and Palestine, the record of these religious military orders is sadly marred by savage feuds which led on occasion to actual alliances with Moslem chieftains against their own kind. Equally crippling to the Christian cause was the criminal competition among the Italian cities for the lion's share of the trade with the crusading states.

Second and Third Crusades. Moslem capture of the city of Edessa in 1444, which protected the northern flank of the Christian foothold in the Near East, called forth the Second Crusade (1147-1149). This crusade was preached by St. Bernard; it was misdirected by Conrad III of Germany and Louis VII of France, and ended up an unqualified failure. The threat to the remaining Christian states did not grow critical, however, until the emergence of Saladin, sultan of Egypt, as leader of the Moslems. Saladin's strong religious motivation and nobleness of character remind one of St. Louis. (See page 440.) Only a man with his unselfish devotion to the cause of Islam could have inspired the warring Moslem chieftains to drop their petty enmities and forge a united front against the Christians. Capitalizing on the factiousness among the Christian feudatories and their allies among the religious military orders, Saladin annihilated a powerful army at Hattin (1187), a battle which only criminal blunders caused the Christians to lose. Jerusalem fell three months later and Europe responded with the Third Crusade (1189-1192). Papal insistence, public opinion, and what crusading sentiments each might have harbored in his breast led three of the most illustrious of medieval monarchs to take up the cross: Richard the Lionhearted of England, Philip Augustus of France, and Frederick Barbarossa of Germany. Saladin could thank Allah that Frederick drowned enroute in Asia Minor. For there is every reason to believe that had Frederick lived, the Third Crusade would have proved even more successful than the First. Frederick was probably the best general of his day, and the army he commanded was undoubtedly the most formidable ever to invade Asia from Europe in the Middle Ages. His greater prestige and age, too, might have enabled him to keep peace between his two quarrelsome co-kings. Even with Frederick dead and the bulk of his army returned to Europe, Richard and Philip succeeded in capturing the mighty fortress city of Acre. Then Philip left, pleading ill health, and Richard knew that though he could hold his own with Saladin, he could never take Jerusalem. Saladin on his part had no great objection to the Christians using Jerusalem, and he also realized that his own Moslem alliance was in grave danger of disintegrating. So a truce was arranged between Richard and Saladin which gave the Christian pilgrims access to Jerusalem. (Reading 111)

Fourth Crusade. Ten years later Pope Innocent III enlisted sufficient recruits from among the powerful feudatories of Europe (mostly French) to organize the Fourth Crusade (1202-1204). (Reading 112) Kings he could not find. Germany was quarreling over who was its rightful king, while the rightful kings of France and England were quarreling over Normandy. Arrangements were made for the Crusaders to converge at Venice, whence the Venetians would transport them to Egypt. When fewer showed up at Venice than had been expected (many Crusaders left by other ports) and when the money contracted for transportation costs could not be raised, Venice was able to persuade the Crusaders to aid in the capture of the Hungarian island of Zara to cover the deficit. Though Hungary was a papal fief, the leaders of the Crusaders felt they had no choice. They took Zara without much difficulty. Next to divert the Crusade from its objective was Alexius, son of Isaac Angelus, recently deposed as emperor by his brother (Alexius III). The son of the deposed Byzantine emperor convinced the Crusaders that it was in their best interests to accept his promise of soldiers and money in return for unseating the usurper—which the Crusaders were successful in accomplishing. Unfortunately, ill-feeling between the Greeks and westerners led to the assassination of Alexius (Isaac had already died) and the Crusaders were forced to take the city a second time. After plundering and looting Constantinople, the Venetians and the Crusaders divided the Byzantine empire between them. Thus ended the inglorious Fourth Crusade. Venice was the only gainer. Its commercial ascendancy in the Mediterranean which endured to the close of the Middle Ages dates from this time. A more enduring reminder of its shameless betrayal of the Fourth Crusade is furnished by the four bronze horses the Venetians took from the Hippodrome at Constantinople to grace the front of their own St. Mark's. Pope Innocent, though chagrined at the turn of events, took some comfort in the thought that the schism had been "healed," and got busy immediately planning a fifth crusade.

Later Crusades. Before Pope Innocent's efforts bore fruit, a distressing episode took place, even more unreasoning than the earlier Peasant Crusade. This one was known as the Children's Crusade. Fortunately, most of the children were persuaded to return to their homes before they had passed beyond southern European ports where some ended up as Moslem slaves. The Fifth Crusade (1218-1221) was unique in that its strategy aimed at taking Jerusalem from the south, by way of Egypt. The Crusade opened auspiciously with the capture of Damietta on the Nile, a reverse which prompted the sultan of Egypt to offer the Crusaders Jerusalem and all Christian prisoners if they would withdraw. The offer was rejected, partly because the sultan had not included fortresses guarding Jerusalem which were considered vital to its defense, partly because the proud papal legate, Pelagius of Albano, who had assumed the direction of the expedition, refused to heed the advice of more realistic Crusaders. As the Crusade's chronicler laments, "Sane counsel was far removed from our leaders." Hardly had the sultan's offer been refused and the Crusaders turned toward Cairo, than the entire Christian army found itself ignominiously trapped by the flooding Nile and forced to surrender. The onus for the debacle of the Fifth Crusade, Pelagius sought to pin on the shoulders of Frederick II who had promised to participate in the enterprise.

Frederick's own expedition finally got under way in 1228. Because the sultan of Egypt felt a war with the Christian army would profit him little and might prejudice his ambitions in Syria, he voluntarily surrendered Jerusalem to Frederick. Several elements in the situation argue against dignifying Frederick's accomplishment as a Crusade. Because of his difficulties back in Italy with the pope (see page 465), Frederick came to the east not as a Crusader but as an excommunicate. Furthermore, what prompted him to come east was not devotion to the cross but the desire to gain the city for his infant son, the "king of Jerusalem." (Readings 124, 125)

The capture of Jerusalem by the Turks in 1244 precipitated the last two traditional Crusades, both Crusades, the Sixth and Seventh, being undertaken by Louis IX of France. The first of these (1248-1254) followed the same course as the Fifth, from the capture of Damietta to the entrapment of the Crusading army. In 1270 Louis undertook his second Crusade, although in such poor health that his biographer, Jean de Joinville, condemned those as criminal who urged him to do so. Louis died in Tunis. Twenty years later (1291), Acre fell to the Turks and with it the last remnant of the imposing stretch of territory the First Crusaders had conquered two hundred years earlier. (The Christians retained Cyprus until the early sixteenth century.)

Christians vs. Ottoman Turks. While the failure of Louis' second expedition in 1270 marks the end of the traditional Crusades, the centuries-old struggle between Christians and Moslems continued on. There was this fundamental difference, however, between the fighting before and after 1270. Until 1270, beginning with Pope Urban's First Crusade, Christian Europe had been on the offensive: western knights had fought for possession of Palestine and Syria. After 1270, western Europe was generally on the defensive, its objective no longer the capture of Jerusalem, but the blunting of Moslem aggressiveness in the eastern Mediterranean and the throwing back of Moslem penetration in the Balkans. Twice, massive Christian and Moslem armies clashed in this area in the late Middle Ages. (See page 774.) As with the early Crusades, popes were generally in the forefront of these later efforts to contain Islam. Several papal expeditions were actually launched, such as the one on which Jacques Coeur died. (See page 395.) It was a pope, Pius V, who inspired the last great joint effort undertaken by Christian powers against the Moslems, the one which resulted in the naval victory at Lepanto in 1571. With the battle of Lepanto, the era of the Crusades might well be considered ended. Turkish power waned sharply after this defeat, and within a few years the crescent ceased being a threat to Christian Europe.

Economic Effects of the Crusades. While the Crusades cut a deep swath through the Middle Ages and left hardly any phase of medieval life unaffected, few modern historians ascribe to them all the far-reaching consequences commonly attributed to them up to a few generations ago. Until recent years, for example, it was customary to trace the origins of important political, social, economic, and military developments of the late Middle Ages to stimuli afforded by the Crusades. Today's scholars are more reserved in their judgments. They credit the Crusades less with originating developments than with powerfully influencing them. Thus the rise of the Italian cities cannot be attributed to the Crusades, but their abrupt emergence to positions of commercial and political eminence in the twelfth century cannot be explained except as resulting from the Crusades. Venice certainly owed its commercial leadership to its ability to exploit opportunities presented by the Crusades. Again, the rise of towns and the revival of trade were well on their way before 1096, but both processes were mightily accelerated by the Crusades. The evolution of more satisfactory methods for handling money and credit was surely expedited by the Crusades. Contributing to this evolution were the doughty Templars of Crusading fame, who shortly after their expulsion from Syria gained somewhat dubious fame for the scope and efficiency of their banking operations. If many more Europeans wore cotton and muslin in 1250 than a hundred and fifty years earlier, if their diet included lemons and apricots, if they spiced their food with cinnamon and cloves, if they walked on rugs and carpets, these changes were due principally to the Crusades.

Religious Consequences. In areas other than the economic the impact of the Crusades is less readily discernible. Whether they served to enhance the leadership and prestige of the papacy remains a moot question. What Rome gained in respect by the success of the First Crusade was largely lost in the failure of those that followed. That the Crusades strengthened Christian faith is equally doubtful. They attest to, they did not necessarily deepen that faith. St. Bernard, stunned by the miserable failure of the Second Crusade—his crusade—wrote: "We have fallen on evil days, in which the Lord, provoked by our sins, has judged the world, with justice indeed, but not with his wonted mercy. The sons of the Church have been overthrown in the desert, slain with the sword, or destroyed by famine. The judgments of the Lord are righteous, but this one is an abyss so deep that I must call him blessed who is not scandalized therein."* The Crusades came closest to producing the image of chivalric perfection in the heroic figure of the Templar or the Knight of St. John. The Crusades probably stirred western Europe to greater missionary activity with St. Francis leading the way with his fruitless visit to the sultan of Egypt. Raymond Lull, who was as convinced as Francis that the sword was not the proper weapon for spreading the City of God, died a martyr among the Moslems of North Africa. Franciscan friars, John of Plano Carpini and William of Rubruquis, carried the Christian message to the Moslems of Africa and to the Mongols of far away China where a third Franciscan, John of Monte Corvino (d. 1328), became the first archbishop of Peking. (Reading 190) On the other hand, the unfortunate Fourth Crusade completed the final estrangement of the eastern half of Christendom from Rome. The Crusades undoubtedly fostered the extension of the use of indulgences. With the passage of time the Crusade also came to be used as a weapon popes employed against European monarchs in the thirteenth century.

Political Effects. What constituted the major political consequence of the Crusades is a matter of conjecture. Would the Byzantine Empire have been able to stave off Moslem engulfment in the twelfth or thirteenth centuries without the indirect aid the west provided with their Crusades against Islam? It is not easy to say. But all scholars are agreed that the

* Quoted in Dana C. Munro, *The Kingdom of the Crusaders* (London, 1935), p. 136.

Fourth Crusade dealt the Byzantine Empire a crippling, almost fatal, blow. When the Byzantine Empire recovered control of Constantinople after the brief existence of the Latin Empire which the Crusaders had set up (1204-1261), it proved little more than a shadow of its former self. (See page 773.) One may count the growth of towns which the Crusades stimulated as a political consequence, in view of the greater influence of the bourgeoisie in European affairs. This is particularly true of the north Italian cities, which had already assumed prominent roles in political affairs by the close of the twelfth century. The history of many town charters dates from the Crusades. They were wrung from nobles who needed money either to take up the cross or to recoup their fortunes upon their return from the east. The feudal aristocracy in general found itself weakened by losses of life and fortune sustained during the Crusades. Robert of Normandy, for instance, mortgaged Normandy to his brother William II, and never got it back. The Crusades furnished the kings of England and France their first opportunity to levy an income tax, a means of raising money which they never forgot. Partly because of the hard lessons learned in Syria, the wooden castle disappeared from western Europe and was replaced by impregnable stone fortresses which scorned the futile efforts of attackers until the invention of artillery. A Crusader, Richard the Lion Hearted, constructed what was probably the most formidable castle ever built in Europe. The walls of his Chateau Gaillard in Normandy, he boasted, could be held against any foe even were those walls constructed of butter. No longer could generals dismiss the footsoldier as obsolete after the vital service of infantry in Syria and Palestine, where the footsoldier protected the armored knight from the speedy Moslem horsemen.

Least controversial of the results which can be attributed to the Crusades is that they inspired some of the best historical writing of the Middle Ages. The *History of Deeds Done Beyond the Sea* by William, archbishop of Tyre, ranks with the finest historical literature of the period, while Villehardouin's *Chronicle of the Fourth Crusade* and Joinville's *Life of St. Louis* have never lost their popularity.

READINGS

No. 95. Charter of Henry II to Lincoln

(Translations and Reprints, II, No. 1, pp. 7-8.)

Henry, by the grace of God, king of England, duke of Normandy and Aquitaine, count of Anjou, to the bishop of Lincoln, justiciars, sheriffs, barons, officers and all his faithful, French and English, of Lincoln, greeting. Know that I have conceded to my citizens of Lincoln all their liberties and customs and laws, which they had in the time of Edward and William and Henry, kings of England; and their gild merchant of the men of the city and of other merchants of the county, just as they had it in the time of our aforesaid predecessors, kings of England, best and most freely. And all men who dwell within the four divisions of the city and attend the market are to be at the gilds and customs and assizes of the city as they have been best in the time of Edward, William and Henry, kings of England. I grant to them moreover, that if anyone shall buy any land within the city, of the burgage of Lincoln, and shall have held it for a year and a day without any claim and he who has bought it is able to show that the claimant has been in the land of England within the year and has not claimed it, for the future as before he shall hold it well and in peace, and without any prosecution. I confirm also to them, that if anyone shall have remained in the city of Lincoln for a year and a day without claim on the part of any claimant, and has given the customs, and is able to show by the laws and customs of the city that the claimant has been in existence in the land of England and has not made a claim against him, for the future as in the past he shall remain in peace, in my city of Lincoln, as my citizen. Witnesses, E., bishop of Lisieux; Thomas, chancellor; H., constable; Henry of Essex, constable. At Nottingham.

No. 96. Charter of Henry II to Wallingford

(Translations and Reprints, II, No. 1, pp. 8-9.)

Henry, by the grace of God, King of England, Duke of Normandy and Aquitaine, and Count of Anjou, . . . I command you that my burgesses of Wallingford shall have my secure peace through my whole land of England and Normandy, wherever they may be. And know that I have given and conceded to them forever all their liberties and laws and customs well and honorably, just as they had them best and most honorably in the time of King Edward, and in the time of my great grandfather King William, and of his son, the second King William, and in the time of King Henry, my grandfather; that is to say, that they should have freely the gild merchant with all its customs and laws, so that neither my bailiff nor any justice of mine should meddle with their gild; but only their own alderman and officer. And if my officers or any justice shall have brought suit against them in any plea or for any occasion or shall have wished to lead them into a suit, I forbid it, and require that they should not make defense in any manner, except in their own proper portmote. And if the reeve himself shall implead them on any occasion without an accuser, they shall not respond, and if on account of any transgression, or by a right judgment any one of them shall have made forfeiture by a right consideration of the burgesses, to the reeve shall he pay it. I forbid, moreover, and require that there shall be no market in Crowmarsh, nor any merchant, unless he is in the gild of the merchants; and if anyone goes out from the borough of Wallingford and lives from the merchandise of the same Wallingford, I command that he should make the right gild of the merchants with the same burgesses, wherever he may be, within the borough or without. Know moreover, that I have given and conceded forever to all the men of Wallingford full quittance from my yearly rent, which they were accustomed to pay from the borough of Wallingford; that is to say, from that which pertains to me in the borough. All these laws and customs and liberties and quittances I give to them and concede forever, and all others which they are able to show that their ancestors had, freely, quietly, and honorably, just as my citizens of Winchester ever had them at the best; and this on account of the great service and labor which they sustained for me in the acquisition of my hereditary right in England. I concede to them, moreover, that wherever they shall go in their journeys as merchants, through my whole land of England and Normandy, Aquitaine and Anjou, "by water and by strand, by wood and by land," they shall be free from toll and passage fees, and from all customs and exactions; nor are they to be troubled in this respect by any one, under a penalty of £10. I forbid, moreover, and require under the same penalty, that the reeve of Wallingford shall not make any fine of scotale or New Year's gift from any one, and that he shall not establish any custom in Wallingford which shall injure the burgesses of the town. Of this grant and concession, the witnesses are Theobald, archbishop of Canterbury and others. Given at Oxford, the first day before the Ides of January.

No. 97. Charter of John to Chester

(*Translations and Reprints*, II, No. 1, p. 10.)

Know that I have conceded and by this my present charter confirmed to all my citizens of Chester that no merchant should buy or sell any kind of merchandise which has come to the city of Chester by sea or by land, except these my citizens of Chester themselves and their heirs, or in accordance with their will; except in the established fairs, that is on St. John the Baptist's day and at the feast of St. Michael. . . . Likewise, I have conceded and by this my present charter confirmed to my said citizens of Chester, to have and to hold their gild merchant, as freely, quietly and honorably as they held it in the time of my uncle, lord Ralph, earl of Chester and Lincoln.

No. 98. Ordinances of the gild merchant of Southampton

(*Translations and Reprints*, II, No. 1, pp. 12-17.)

In the first place, there shall be elected from the gild merchant, and established, an alderman, a steward, a chaplain, four skevins, and an usher. And it is to be known that whosoever shall be alderman shall receive from each one entering into the gild fourpence, the steward, twopence; the chaplain, twopence; and the usher, one penny. And the gild shall meet twice a year: that is to say, on the Sunday next after St. John the Baptist's day, and on the Sunday next after St. Mary's day.

And when the gild shall be sitting no one of the gild is to bring in any stranger, except when required by the alderman or steward. And the alder-men shall have a sergeant to serve before him, the steward another sergeant, and the chaplain shall have his clerk.

And when the gild shall sit, the alderman is to have, each night, so long as the gild sits, two gallons of wine and two candles, and the steward the same; and the four skevins and the chaplain, each of them one gallon of wine and one candle, and the usher one gallon of wine.

And when the gild shall sit, the lepers of La Madeleine shall have of the alms of the gild, two sesters (approximately eight gallons) of ale, and the sick of God's House and of St. Julian shall have two sesters of ale. And the Friars Minors shall have two sesters of ale and one sester of wine. And four sesters of ale shall be given to the poor wherever the gild shall meet.

And when the gild is sitting, no one who is of the gild shall go outside the town for any business, without the permission of the steward. And if any does so, let him be fined two shillings, and pay them.

And when the gild sits, and any gildsman is outside of the city so that he does not know when it will happen, he shall have a gallon of wine, if his servants come to get it. And if a gildsman is ill and is in the city, wine shall be sent to him, two loaves of bread and a gallon of wine and a dish from the kitchen; and two approved men of the gild shall go to visit him and look after his condition.

And when a gildsman dies, all those who are of the gild and are in the city shall attend the service of the dead, and the gildsmen shall bear the body and bring it to the place of burial. And whoever will not do this shall pay according to his oath, two pence, to be given to the poor. And those of the ward where the dead man shall be ought to find a man to watch over the body the night that the dead shall lie in his house. And so long as the service of the dead shall last, that is to say the vigil and the mass, there ought to burn four candles of the gild, each candle of two pounds weight or more, until the body is buried. And these four candles shall remain in the keeping of the steward of the gild.

And when a gildsman dies, his eldest son or his next heir shall have the seat of his father, or of his uncle, if his father was not a gildsman, and of no other one; and he shall give nothing for his seat. No husband can have a seat in the gild by right of his wife, nor demand a seat by right of his wife's ancestors.

And no one of the city of Southampton shall buy anything to sell again in the same city, unless he is of the gild merchant or of the franchise. And if anyone shall do so and is convicted of it, all which he has so bought shall be forfeited to the king; and no one shall be quit of custom unless he proves that he is in the gild or in the franchise, and this from year to year.

And no one shall buy honey, fat, salt herrings, or any kind of oil, or millstones, or fresh hides, or any kind of fresh skins, unless he is a gildsman: nor keep a tavern for wine, nor sell cloth at retail, except in market or fair days; nor keep grain in his granary beyond five quarters, to sell at retail, if he is not a gildsman; and whoever shall do this and be convicted, shall forfeit all to the king.

If any gildsman falls into poverty and has not the wherewithal to live, and is not able to work or to provide for himself, he shall have one mark from the gild to relieve his condition when the gild shall sit. No one of the gild nor of the franchise shall avow another's goods for his by which the custom of the city shall be injured. And if any one does so and is convicted, he shall lose the gild and the franchise; and the merchandise so avowed shall be forfeited to the king.

And no private man nor stranger shall bargain for or buy any kind of merchandise coming into the city before a burgess of the gild merchant, so long as the gildsman is present and wishes to bargain for and buy this merchandise; and if anyone does so and is convicted, that which he buys shall be forfeited to the king.

The common chest shall be in the house of the chief alderman or of the steward, and the three keys of it shall be lodged with three discreet men of the aforesaid twelve sworn men, or with three of the skevins, who shall loyally take care of the common seal, and the charters and of the treasure of the town, and the standards, and other muniments of the town; and no letter shall be sealed with the common seal, nor any charter taken out of the common-chest but in the presence of six or twelve sworn men, and of the alderman or steward; and nobody shall sell by any kind of measure or weight that is not sealed, under forfeiture of two shillings.

No one shall go out to meet a ship bringing wine or other merchandise coming to the town, in order to buy anything, before the ship be arrived and come to anchor for unlading; and if any one does so and is convicted, the merchandise which he shall have bought shall be forfeited to the king.

No. 99. Articles of the spurriers of London (A.D. 1345)

(Translations and Reprints, II, No. 1, pp. 21-23.)

Be it remembered, that on Tuesday, the morrow of St. Peter's Chains, in the nineteenth year of the reign of King Edward III, the articles under-written were read before John Hammond, mayor, Roger de Depham, recorder, and the alderman; and seeing that the same were deemed befitting, they were accepted and enrolled in these words.

In the first place,—that no one of the trade of spurriers shall work longer than from the beginning of the day until curfew rung out at the Church of St. Sepulchre, without Newgate; by reason that no man can work so neatly by night as by day. And many persons of the said trade, who compass how to practice deception in their work, desire to work by night rather by day; and then they introduce false iron, and iron that has been cracked, for tin, and also they put gilt on false copper, and cracked. And further,—many of the said trade are wandering about all day, without working at all at their trade; and then, when they have become drunk and frantic, they take to their work, to the annoyance of the sick, and all their neighborhood, as well by reason of the broils that arise between them and the strange folks who are dwelling among them. And then they blow up their fires so vigorously, that their forges begin all at once to blaze to the great peril of themselves and of all the neighborhood around. And then, too, all the neighbors are much in dread of the sparks, which so vigorously issue forth in all directions from the mouths of the chimneys in their forges. By reason thereof it seems unto them that working by night should be put an end to, in order such false work and such perils to avoid: and therefore the mayor and the aldermen do will, by the assent of the good folks of the said trade, and for the common profit, that from henceforth such time for working, and such false work made in the trade, shall be forbidden. And if any person shall be found in the said trade to do the contrary hereof, let him be amerced, the first time in 40d., one-half thereof to go to the use of the Chamber of the Guildhall of London, and the other half to the use of the said trade; the second time, in half a mark, and the third time in 10s., to the use of the same Chamber and trade; and the fourth time, let him forswear the trade forever.

Also that no one of the said trade shall hang his spurs out on Sundays, or any other days that are double feasts; but only a sign indicating his business: and such spurs as they shall so sell, they are to show and sell within their shops, without exposing them without, or opening the doors or windows of their shops, on the pain aforesaid.

Also, that no one of the said trade shall keep a house or shop to carry on his business, unless he is free of the city; and that no one shall cause to be sold, or exposed for sale, any manner of old spurs for new ones, or shall garnish them or change them for new ones.

Also, that no one of the said trade shall take an apprentice for a less term than seven years, and such apprentice shall be enrolled according to the usages of the said city.

Also, that if any one of the said trade, who is not a freeman, shall take an apprentice for a term of years, he shall be amerced as aforesaid.

Also, that no one of the said trade shall receive the apprentice, serving-man or journeyman of another in the same trade, during the term agreed upon between his master and him; on the pain aforesaid.

Also, that no alien of another country, or foreigner of this country, shall follow or use the said trade, unless he is enfranchised before the mayor, alderman and chamberlain; and that by witness and surety of the good folks of the said trade, who will undertake for him as to his loyalty and his good behavior.

Also, that no one of the said trade shall work on Saturdays, after None has been rung out in the City; and not from that hour until the Monday morning following.

No. 100. Otto III grants a market (A.D. 999)

(Thatcher & McNeal, *Source Book*, p. 581.)

In the name of the holy and undivided Trinity. Otto by the clemency of God emperor, Augustus. If we grant the petitions of our faithful subjects we shall no doubt make them more faithful to us. Therefore, we wish all our subjects, present and future, to know that, at the request of the noble duke, Hermann, we have given our count, Bertold, full authority to establish a market, with a mint, tolls, and public jurisdiction, in a certain place called Vilungen, in the county of Bara, over which count Hildibald has jurisdiction. And by royal decree we make this a legal [and regular] market, with all the functions of a market. And no one shall be permitted to interfere with it. All who wish to come to this market may come and go away in security and peace. No unjust charges shall be levied on them, but they may buy and sell and do everything else that belongs to the business of a merchant. And if anyone tries to violate or break this concession, he shall pay the same fine as one who should violate the market at Constance or Zuerich. He shall pay this fine to count Bertold, or to his representative. The aforesaid count shall have the right of holding, changing, granting, and making any arrangement in regard to this market, as he pleases. . . .

No. 101. Tolls

(From *Life in Medieval France* by Joan Evans, p. 38, revised and newly illustrated edition 1957. By courtesy of the Phaidon Press, London.)

"I, Landru the Fat, seduced and tempted by the greed that often creeps into the hearts of worldly men, admit that I have stopped the merchants of Langres who passed through my domain. I took their merchandise from them and kept it until the day when the Bishop of Langres and the Abbot of Cluny came to me to demand reparation. I had kept for myself a part of what I had taken and restored the rest. The merchants to obtain this remainder, and to be able in the future to cross my land without fear, consented to pay me a certain sum for tribute. This first sin suggested to me the idea of a second, and I undertook to impose and to cause to be imposed by my officers, an exaction called a toll on all those who crossed my territory for business or for pilgrimage. The monks of Cluny, knowing that my predecessors had never levied a tax of this kind, complained strongly and asked me, through my brother Bernard, *Chambrier* of their abbey, to give up this unjust exaction, hateful in the eyes of God. To buy it off and assure safety to travellers, they have given me the sum of three hundred sous."

No. 102. Chartering a *ville neuve* (new town)

(From *Life in Medieval France* by Joan Evans, p. 44, revised and newly illustrated edition 1957. By courtesy of the Phaidon Press, London.)

"Know all men by these presents that I, Henry Count of Troyes, have established the customs defined below for the inhabitants of my Ville Neuve near Pont-sur-Seine between the highways of the bridges of Pugny: every man dwelling in the said town shall pay each year twelve deniers and a measure of barley for the price of his domicile; and if he wishes to have an allotment of land or meadow, he shall pay four deniers an acre as rent. The houses, vines, and fields can be sold or disposed of at the will of the buyer. Men dwelling in the said town shall neither go with the army in the field nor on any expedition if I do not myself lead them. I further accord them the right to have six echevins, who shall administer the common business of the town and shall assist my provost in hearing his pleas. I have decreed that no lord, knight or other, shall take away from the town any of its new citizens, for any reason whatsoever, unless the citizen be his 'homme de corps,' or unless he be in arrears with his *taille*. Signed at Provins, 1175."

No. 103. Alliance of German towns (A.D. 1253)

(Robinson's *Readings*, p. 413.)

We hereby make known to all men, now and in the future, that because of the manifold dangers to which we are constantly exposed, of capture, robbery, and many other injuries, we have, by common counsel and consent, decided to unite in a perpetual confederation under the following terms, and we have mutually given and received word and oath:

First, that if any man shall take captive one of our citizens or seize his goods without just cause, we will altogether deny to him opportunity to trade in all our cities aforesaid. And if the castellan of any lord shall be the author of an injury that has been done, the afore-mentioned privileges shall be altogether withheld from the lord of that castellan, and from all his soldiers and servants, and all others dwelling with him in his castle. . . .

If any robber has taken goods from one of our citizens . . . and the injured man shall go to any one of our [federated] cities seeking counsel and aid, in order that justice may be done upon the malefactor, the citizens of that city shall act as they would be obliged to act if executing justice for a similar crime committed against one of their own fellow-citizens.

And if any of our burgesses shall chance to go to any of our cities and fear to go forth because of peril to life and property, the burgesses of that city shall conduct him to a place whence his fellow-citizens can receive him in safety.

If a knight shall be denounced to us on reasonable grounds as a violator of faith and honor, we will denounce him in all our cities, and will by mutual consent withhold from him all privileges in our cities until he shall pay the whole debt for which he broke his word.

If any one of us shall buy goods taken from any of our confederates by theft or robbery, . . . he shall not offer the goods at retail anywhere and shall be held guilty with the thief and robber.

No. 104. A husband's instructions to his Paris housewife (fourteenth century)

(From "The Menagier's Wife" in Eileen Power's *Medieval People*. Anchor, 1954. By permission of Methuen & Co., Ltd. Publishers.)

Know, dear sister (a term of affectionate respect) that if you wish to follow my advice you will have great care and regard for what you and I can afford to do, according to our estate. Have a care that you be honestly clad, without new devices and without too much or too little frippery. And before you leave your chamber and house, take care first that the collar of your shift, and of your *blanchet, cotte* and *surcotte*, do not hang out one over the other, as happens with certain drunken, foolish or witless women, who have no care for their honour, nor for the honesty of their estate or of their husbands, and who walk with roving eyes and head horribly reared up like a lion, their hair straggling out of their wimples, and the collars of their shifts and *cottes* crumpled the one upon the other, and who walk mannishly and bear themselves uncouthly before folk without shame. . . . Have a care that your hair, wimple, kerchief and hood and all the rest of your attire be well arranged and decently ordered, that none who see you can laugh or mock at you, but that all the others may find in you an example of fair and simple and decent array. . . . When you go to town or to church go suitably accompanied by honourable women according to your estate, and flee suspicious company, never allowing any ill famed women to be seen in your presence. And as you go bear your head upright and your eyelids low and without fluttering, and look straight in front of you about four rods ahead, without looking round at any man or woman to the right or to the left, nor looking up, nor glancing from place to place, nor stopping to speak to anyone on the road. . . . (pp. 105-106)

Cherish the person of your husband carefully, and, I pray you, keep him in clean linen, for 'tis your business. And because the care of outside affairs lieth with men, so must a husband take heed, and go and come and journey hither and thither, in rain and wind, in snow and hail, now drenched, now dry, now sweating, now shivering, ill-fed, ill-lodged, ill-warmed and ill-bedded; and nothing harms him, because he is upheld by the hope that he has of his wife's care of him on his return, and of the ease, the joys and the pleasures which she will do to him, or cause to be done to him in her presence; to have his shoes removed before a good fire, his feet washed and to have fresh shoes and stockings, to be given good food and drink, to be well served and well looked after, well bedded in white sheets and night-caps, well covered with good furs. . . . Certes, fair sister, such service maketh a man love and desire to return to his home and to see his goodwife and to be distant with other women.

And therefore I counsel you to make such cheer to your husband at all his comings and goings and to persevere therein; and also to be peaceable with him and remember the rustic proverb, which saith that there be three things which drive the goodman from home, to wit, a dripping roof, a smoking chimney and a scolding woman. . . . (pp. 109-110)

In summer take heed that there be no fleas in your chamber nor in your bed, which you may do in six ways, as I have heard tell. For I have heard from several persons that if the room be scattered with alder leaves the fleas will get caught therein. Item, I have heard tell that if you have at night one or two trenchers of bread covered with birdlime or turpentine and put above the room with a lighted candle set in the midst of each trencher, they will come and get stuck thereto. Another way which I have found and which is true: take a rough cloth and spread it about your room and over your bed and all the fleas who may hop onto it will be caught, so that you can carry them out with the cloth wheresoever you will. Item, sheepskins. Item, I have seen blankets placed on the straw and on the bed and when the black fleas jumped upon them they were the sooner found and killed upon the white. But the best way is to guard oneself against those which are within the coverlets and furs and the stuff of the dresses wherewith one is covered. For know that I have tried this, and when the coverlets, furs or dresses in which there be fleas are folded and shut tightly up, in a chest straitly bound with straps or in a bag well tied up and pressed, or otherwise compressed so that the said fleas are without light and air and kept imprisoned, then they will perish and die at once. . . . (pp. 116-117)

No. 105. Decrees of the Hanseatic League (A.D. 1265)

(Thatcher & McNeal, *Source Book*, pp. 611-612.)

We wish to inform you of the action taken in support of all merchants who are governed by the law of Luebeck. 1. Each city shall, to the best of her ability, keep the sea clear of pirates, so that merchants may freely carry on their business by sea. 2. Whoever is expelled from one city because of a crime shall not be received in another. 3. If a citizen is seized [by pirates, robbers, or bandits] he shall not be ransomed, but his sword-belt and knight shall be sent to him [as a threat to his captors].

4. Any merchant ransoming him shall lose all his possessions in all the cities which have the law of Luebeck. 5. Whoever is proscribed in one city for robbery or theft shall be proscribed in all. 6. If a lord besieges a city, no one shall aid him in any way to the detriment of the besieged city, unless the besieger is his lord. 7. If there is a war in the country, no city shall on that account injure a citizen from the other cities, either in his person or goods, but shall give him protection. 8. If any man marries a woman in one city, and another woman from some other city comes and proves that he is her lawful husband, he shall be beheaded.

9. If a citizen gives his daughter or niece in marriage to a man [from another city], and another man comes and says that she is his lawful wife, but cannot prove it, he shall be beheaded.

This law shall be binding for a year, and after that the cities shall inform each other by letter of what decisions they make.

No. 106. Decree of the Hanseatic League (A.D. 1265)

(Thatcher & McNeal, *Source Book*, p. 611.)

We ought to hold a meeting once a year to legislate about the affairs of the cities. 5. If pirates appear on the sea, all the cities must contribute their share to the work of destroying them.

No. 107. Peter the Hermit

(From Guibert of Nogent's account. *Translations and Reprints*, I, No. 2, p. 20.)

Therefore, while the princes, who felt the need of many expenses and great services from their attendants, made their preparations slowly and carefully; the common people who had little property, but were very numerous, joined a certain Peter the Hermit, and obeyed him as a master while these affairs were going on among us.

He was, if I am not mistaken, from the city of Amiens, and we have learned that he had lived as a hermit, dressed as a monk, somewhere in Upper Gaul. After he had departed from there—I do not know with what intention—we saw him going through the cities and towns under a pretense of preaching. He was surrounded by so great throngs of people, he received such enormous gifts, his holiness was lauded so highly, that no one within my memory has been held in such honor.

He was very liberal in the distribution to the poor of what he had received. He restored prostitutes to their husbands with gifts. By his wonderful authority he restored everywhere peace and concord, in place of discord. For in whatever he did or said it seemed as if there was something divine, especially when the hairs were snatched from his mule for relics. We do not report this as true, but for the common people who love novelties. He wore a woolen shirt, and over it a mantle reaching to his ankles; his arms and feet were bare. He lived on wine and fish; he hardly ever, or never, ate bread.

No. 108. Pope Urban's address at Clermont

(As reported by Robert the Monk. Robinson's *Readings*, pp. 312-316.)

In the year of our Lord's Incarnation one thousand and ninety-five, a great council was celebrated within the bounds of Gaul, in Auvergne, in the city which is called Clermont. Over this Pope Urban II presided, with the Roman bishops and cardinals. This council was a famous one on account of the concourse of both French and German bishops and of princes as well. Having arranged the matters relating to the Church, the lord pope went forth into a certain spacious plain, for no building was large enough to hold all the people. The pope then, with sweet and persuasive eloquence, addressed those present in words something like the following, saying:

"Oh, race of Franks, race from across the mountains, race beloved and chosen by God,—as is clear from many of your works—set apart from all other nations by the situation of your country as well as by your Catholic faith and the honor which you render to the holy Church: to you our discourse is addressed, and for you our exhortations are intended. We wish you to know what a grievous cause has led us to your country, for it is the imminent peril threatening you and all the faithful which has brought us hither.

"From the confines of Jerusalem and from the city of Constantinople a grievous report has gone forth and has repeatedly been brought to our ears; namely, that a race from the kingdom of the Persians, an accursed race, a race wholly alienated from God, 'a generation that set not their heart aright, and whose spirit was not steadfast with God,' has violently invaded the lands of those Christians and has depopulated them by pillage and fire. They have led away a part of the captives into their own country, and a part they have killed by cruel tortures. They have either destroyed the churches of God or appropriated them for the rites of their own religion. They destroy the altars, after having defiled them with their uncleanness. . . . The kingdom of the Greeks is now dismembered by them and has been deprived of territory so vast in extent that it could not be traversed in two months' time.

"On whom, therefore, is the labor of avenging these wrongs and of recovering this territory incumbent, if not upon you,—you, upon whom, above all other nations, God has conferred remarkable glory in arms, great courage, bodily activity, and strength to humble the heads of those who resist you? Let the deeds of your ancestors encourage you and incite your minds to manly achievements:—the glory and greatness of King Charlemagne, and of his son Louis, and of your other monarchs, who have destroyed the kingdoms of the Turks and have extended the sway of the holy Church over lands previously pagan. Let the holy sepulcher of our Lord and Saviour, which is possessed by the unclean nations, especially arouse you, and the holy places which are now treated with ignominy and irreverently polluted with the filth of the unclean. Oh, most valiant soldiers and descendants of invincible ancestors, do not degenerate, but recall the valor of your progenitors.

"But if you are hindered by love of children, parents, or wife, remember what the Lord says in the Gospel, 'He that loveth father or mother more than me is not worthy of me.' 'Every one that hath forsaken houses, or brethren, or sisters, or father, or mother, or wife, or children, or lands, for my name's sake, shall receive an hundredfold, and shall inherit everlasting life.' Let none of your possessions retain you, nor solicitude for your family affairs. For this land which you inhabit, shut in on all sides by the seas and surrounded by the mountain peaks, is too narrow for your large population; nor does it abound in wealth; and it furnishes scarcely food enough for its cultivators. Hence it is that you murder and devour one another, that you wage war, and that very many among you perish in intestine strife.

"Let hatred therefore depart from among you, let your quarrels end, let wars cease, and let all dissensions and controversies slumber. Enter upon the road to the Holy Sepulcher; wrest that land from the wicked race, and subject it to yourselves. That land which, as the Scripture says, 'floweth with milk and honey' was given by God into the power of the children of Israel. Jerusalem is the center of the earth; the land is fruitful above all others, like another paradise of delights. This spot the Redeemer of mankind has made illustrious by his advent, has beautified by his sojourn, has consecrated by his passion, has redeemed by his death, has glorified by his burial.

"This royal city, however, situated at the center of the earth, is now held captive by the enemies of Christ and is subjected, by those who do not know God, to the worship of the heathen. She seeks, therefore, and desires to be liberated and ceases not to implore you to come to her aid. From you especially she asks succor, because, as we have already said, God has conferred upon you above all other nations great glory in arms. Accordingly, undertake this journey eagerly for the remission of your sins, with the assurance of the reward of imperishable glory in the kingdom of heaven."

When Pope Urban had urbanely said these and very many similar things, he so centered in one purpose the desires of all who were present that all cried out, "It is the will of God! It is the will of God!" When the venerable Roman pontiff heard that, with eyes uplifted to heaven, he gave thanks to God and, commanding silence with his hand, said:

"Most beloved brethren, today is manifest in you what the Lord says in the Gospel, 'Where two or three are gathered together in my name, there am I in the midst of them'; for unless God had been present in your spirits, all of you would not have uttered the same cry; since, although the cry issued from numerous mouths, yet the origin of the cry was one. Therefore I say to you that God, who implanted this in your breasts, has drawn it forth from you. Let that then be your war cry in combats, because it is given to you by God. When an armed attack is made upon the enemy, let this one cry be raised by all the soldiers of God: 'It is the will of God! It is the will of God!' [Deus vult! Deus vult!]

"And we neither command nor advise that the old or feeble, or those incapable of bearing arms, undertake this journey. Nor ought women to set out at all without their husbands, or brothers, or legal guardians. For such are more of a hindrance than aid, more of a burden than an advantage. Let the rich aid the needy; and according to their wealth let them take with them experienced soldiers. The priests and other clerks, whether secular or regular, are not to go without the consent of their bishop; for this journey would profit them nothing if they went without permission. Also, it is not fitting that laymen should enter upon the pilgrimage without the blessing of their priests.

"Whoever, therefore, shall determine upon this holy pilgrimage, and shall make his vow to God to that effect, and shall offer himself to him for sacrifice, as a living victim, holy and acceptable to God, shall wear the sign of the cross of the Lord on his forehead or on his breast. When, indeed, he shall return from his journey, having fulfilled his vow, let him place the cross on his back between his shoulders. Thus shall ye, indeed, by this twofold action, fulfill the precept of the Lord, as he commands in the Gospel, 'He that taketh not his cross, and followeth after me, is not worthy of me.' "

No. 109. Rude manners of Crusaders in Constantinople

(From the *Alexiade* of Anna Comnena. Robinson's *Readings*, pp. 320-321.)

When the Franks had all come together and had taken an oath to the emperor, there was one count who had the boldness to sit down upon the throne. The emperor, well knowing the pride of the Latins, kept silent, but Baldwin approached the Frankish count and taking him by the hand said, "You ought not to sit there; that is an honor which the emperor permits to no one. Now that you are in this country, why do you not observe its customs?" The insolent count made no reply to Baldwin, but said in his barbarous language, as if talking to himself, "This must be a rude fellow who would alone remain seated when so many brave warriors are standing up." Alexis noted the movement of the man's lips and called an interpreter in order to learn what he had said; but when the interpreter had told him he did not complain to the Franks, although he did not forget the matter.

When the counts came to take leave of the emperor he retained this haughty knight and asked him who he was. "I am a Frank," he replied, "of the most high and ancient nobility. I know but one thing, and that is that there is in my country a church built at the crossroads where all those betake themselves who hope to show their valor in single combat, and there make their prayer to God while they await an enemy; I remained there a long time without anybody daring to measure swords with me."

Alexis was on his guard against accepting this challenge. "If you then waited without being able to show your bravery," he said to him, "you now have a chance to fight; and if I may give you a word of advice, it will be not to put yourself either at the head nor rear of the army but in the middle. The experience which I have had of the way in which the Turks make war has convinced me that that is the best place." (Note: Anna noted later in her account with satisfaction that the knight had been killed.)

No. 110. Letter of Godfrey of Bouillon to the Pope

(Robinson's *Readings*, pp. 325-329.)

Multiply your supplications and prayers in the sight of God with joy and thanksgiving, since God has manifested his mercy in fulfilling by our hands what he had promised in ancient times; for after the capture of Nicaea the whole army, made up of more than three hundred thousand soldiers, departed thence. And, although this army was so great that it could in a single day have covered all Romania and drunk up all the rivers and eaten up all the growing things, yet the Lord conducted them amid so great abundance that a ram was sold for a penny and an ox for twelve pence or less. Moreover, although the princes and kings of the Saracens rose up against us, yet, by God's will, they were easily conquered and overcome.

Because, however, some were puffed up by these successes, God opposed to us Antioch, impregnable to human strength. And there he detained us for nine months and so humbled us in the siege that there was scarcely a hundred good horses left in our whole army. God then opened to us the abundance of his blessing and mercy, and led us into the city, and delivered the Turks and all of their possessions into our power.

Inasmuch as we thought that these had been acquired by our own strength, and did not worthily magnify God who had done this, we were beset by so great a multitude of Turks that no one dared to venture forth at any point from the city. Moreover hunger so weakened us that some could scarcely refrain from eating human flesh. It would be tedious to narrate all the miseries which we suffered in that city. But God looked down upon his people, whom he had so long chastised, and mercifully consoled them. Therefore, he at first revealed to us, as a recompense for our tribulation and as a pledge of victory, his lance, which had lain hidden since the days of the apostles. Next, he so fortified the hearts of the men that they who from sickness or hunger had been unable to walk, now were indued with strength to seize their weapons and manfully to fight against the enemy.

After we had triumphed over the enemy, as our army was wasting away at Antioch from sickness and weariness and was especially hindered by the dissensions among the leaders, we proceeded into Syria, stormed Barra and Marra, cities of the Saracens, and captured the fortresses in that country. And while we were delaying there, there was so great a famine in the army that the Christian people now ate the putrid bodies of the Saracens. . . .

And after the army had suffered greatly in the siege [of Jerusalem] especially on account of the lack of water, a council was held, and the bishops and princes ordered that all should march around the walls of the city with feet bare, in order that he who entered it humbly in our behalf might be moved by our humility to open it to us and to exercise judgment upon his enemies.

God was appeased by this humility, and on the eighth day after the humiliation he delivered the city and his enemies to us. It was the very day, indeed, on which the primitive Church was driven thence and on which the festival of the Dispersion of the Apostles is celebrated. And if you desire to know what was done with the enemy who were found there, know that in Solomon's Porch and his temple our men rode in the blood of the Saracens up to the knees of their horses.

No. 111. Richard defeats Saladin at Arsur (Arsulf)

(From documents quoted by Charles Oman in *A History of the Art of War*. London, 1898, pp. 306-314 *passim*.)

The Christian *Itinerarium* describes Turkish tactics as Richard's army marched southward along the coast toward Arsur:

"The Infidels, not weighed down with heavy armour like our knights, but always able to outstrip them in pace, were a constant trouble. When charged they are wont to fly, and their horses are more nimble than any others in the world; one may liken them to swallows for swiftness. When they see that you have ceased to pursue them, they no longer fly but return upon you; they are like tiresome flies which you can flap away for a moment, but which come back the instant you have stopped hitting at them: as long as you beat about they keep off: the moment you cease, they are on you again. So the Turk, when you wheel about after driving him off, follows you home without a second's delay, but will fly again if you turn on him. When the king rode at them, they always retreated, but they hung about our rear, and sometimes did us mischief, not unfrequently disabling some of our men."

The Muslim chronicler, Boha-ed-din, admires the steadfastness of the Crusaders in not breaking rank against which Richard had warned them, despite the harassing tactics of Saladin's skirmishers:

"The enemy moved in order of battle: their infantry marched between us and their cavalry, keeping as level and firm as a wall. Each foot-soldier had a thick cassock of felt, and under it a mail-shirt so strong that our arrows made no impression on them. They, meanwhile, shot at us with crossbows, which struck down horse and man among the Moslems. I noted among them men who had from one to ten shafts sticking in their backs, yet trudged on at their ordinary pace and did not fall out of their ranks. The infantry were divided into two halves: one marched so as to cover the cavalry, the other moved along the beach and took no part in the fighting, but rested itself. When the first half was wearied, it changed places with the second and got its turn of repose. The cavalry marched between the two halves of the infantry, and only came out when it wished to charge. It was formed in three main corps: in the van was Guy, formerly King of Jerusalem, with all the Syrian Franks who adhered to him; in the second were the English and French; in the rear the sons of the Lady of Tiberias and other troops. In the centre of their army there was visible a waggon carrying a tower as high as one of our minarets, on which was planted the king's banner. The Franks continued to advance in this order, fighting vigorously all the time: the Moslems sent in volleys of arrows from all sides, endeavouring to irritate the knights and to worry them into leaving their rampart of infantry. But it was all in vain: they kept their temper admirably and went on their way without hurrying themselves in the least, while their fleet sailed along the coast parallel with them till they arrived at their camping-place for the night. They never marched a long stage, because they had to spare the foot-soldiery, of whom the half not actively engaged was carrying the baggage and tents, so great was their want of beasts of burden. It was impossible not to admire the patience which these people showed: they bore crushing fatigue, though they had no proper military administration, and were getting no personal advantage. And so they finally pitched their camp on the farther side of the river of Caesarea."

The opportunity to attack a disorganized foe which Saladin had hoped for never came, and so to prevent Richard from reaching Jaffa, he finally made his move from behind cover of a thick wood at Arsulf. The *Itinerarium* continues:

"All over the face of the land you could see the well-ordered bands of the Turks, myriads of parti-coloured banners, marshalled in troops and squadrons; of mailed men alone there appeared to be more than twenty thousand. With unswerving course, swifter than eagles, they swept down upon our line of march. The air was turned black by the dust that their hoofs cast up. Before the face of each emir went his musicians, making a horrid din with horns, trumpets, drums, cymbals, and all manner of brazen instruments, while the troops behind pressed on with howls and cries of war. For the Infidels think that the louder the noise, the bolder grows the spirit of the warrior. So did the cursed Turks beset us before, behind, and on the flank, and they pressed in so close that for two miles around there was not a spot of the bare earth visible; all was covered by the thick array of the enemy."

Nevertheless, the Crusaders' line never wavered, following Richard's strict instructions, for he wanted Saladin to commit himself irrevocably all along the front before giving the signal to counterattack. Finally, the pressure became so great, that all of a sudden the entire Crusading cavalry swung forward and attacked. Boha-ed-din writes:

"On a sudden we saw the cavalry of the enemy, who were now drawn together in three main masses, brandish their lances, raise their war-cry, and dash out at us. The infantry suddenly opened up gaps in their line to let them pass through."

According to Boha-ed-din, the Crusaders scored a brilliant victory:

"On our side, the rout was complete. I was myself in the centre: that corps having fled in confusion, I thought to take refuge with the left wing, which was the nearest to me; but when I reached it, I found it also in full retreat, and making off no less quickly than the centre. Then I rode to the right wing, but this had been routed even more thoroughly than the left. I turned accordingly to the spot where the Sultan's bodyguard should have served as a rally-point for the rest. The banners were still upright and the drum beating, but only seventeen horsemen were round them."

The *Itinerarium* summed up the victory: thirty-two emirs and seven thousand rank and file Muslims to the loss of one Christian lord and seven hundred men.

No. 112. Innocent III's privileges to Crusaders

(Robinson's *Readings*, pp. 338-340.)

In order that nothing relating to Christ's business may be neglected, we wish and command patriarchs, archbishops, bishops, abbots, and others who have charge of souls, to set forth zealously to those committed to their care the word of the cross, exhorting in the name of the Father, Son, and Holy Ghost,—the one only true and eternal God,—kings, dukes, princes, marquises, counts, barons, and other magnates, also the communities of cities, towns, and villages, who do not go in person to the aid of the Holy Land, to send a suitable number of warriors, with the necessary expense for three years according to their individual means, for the remission of their own sins,—all which is stated in our general letters, and is also stated below, for the greater surety.

Of this remission we wish that not only those who furnish their own vessels should be partakers, but also those who may have striven to build ships for this purpose. Moreover let it be sternly announced by apostolic authority to those who refuse—if perchance any shall be so ungrateful to our Lord God—that they are to understand that for this they will have to answer to us on the last day of strict judgment before an awful judge. Nevertheless let them first consider with what conscience or what security they will be able to appear before the only begotten Son of God, Jesus Christ, into whose hands the Father gave all things, if they shall refuse in this matter, which is peculiarly fitting for them, to aid him who was crucified for sinners, by whose bounty they live, by whose kindness they are maintained,—nay, more, by whose blood they have been redeemed.

Since it is certainly right that those who give their allegiance to the heavenly Emperor should enjoy a special privilege, when the time of the expedition shall exceed one year in length the crusaders shall be free from collections, tallages, and other taxes. And we have taken their persons and property, after the assumption of the cross, under St. Peter's and our own protection, and we have decided that their defense shall be entrusted to the archbishops, bishops, and all the prelates of the Church. We have also appointed officers of our own especially for their protection, in order that their property may be kept intact and uninjured until their death or return is known with certainty. And if anyone attempts any attack upon their property, he shall be restrained by ecclesiastical censure.

If any of those setting out thither are bound by oath to pay interest, we command that their creditors shall be compelled by the same means to release them from their oaths and to desist from the exaction of interest. But if any creditor shall compel them to pay interest, we order that he shall be forced, by a similar chastisement, to pay it back. . . . Moreover let the prelates of the Church who are proven to be negligent in doing justice to the crusaders and their families, understand that they shall be severely punished.

Therefore, trusting in the mercy of omnipotent God and in the authority of the blessed apostles Peter and Paul, by that power of binding and loosing which God has conferred on us, although unworthy, we grant to all who undergo the difficulties in their own person and at their own expense, full remission of the sins of which they have truly repented with contrite hearts and which they have confessed with their mouths; and at the retribution of the just we promise an increase of eternal salvation. To those also who do not go thither in person but yet, according to their ability and means, send suitable men at their expense, and to those likewise who go in person, although at the expense of others, we promise full remission of their sins. We also will and grant that, according to the kind of their aid and the depth of their devotion, all shall partake of this remission who minister fitly from their property to the aid of that land, or furnish opportune counsel and assistance. Also on all who piously proceed in this task, this general council bestows in common the aid of all its benefits, that it may worthily conduce to their salvation. Amen.

10

THE RISE OF
FEUDAL MONARCHIES

The Feudal Monarchy

Feudal Monarch Did Not Rule.   We have seen how the onslaughts of the Northmen, Magyars, and Saracens completed the dismemberment of the Carolingian world. When these invasions had subsided and the Saracens had been expelled and the Northmen and Magyars had been converted, western Europe settled down to a period of recovery. How this period of relative peace contributed to the rise of towns has been described in the preceding chapter. Here we shall consider the evolution of constitutional institutions and the course of political history during this same period which covered roughly the three centuries beginning about 950. The feudal kingdom, as we saw in an earlier chapter, was apt to be a thoroughly decentralized state. Though the map will show France of the year 1000, for example, as a compact unit, and the Holy Roman Empire an imposing solidarity stretching from the North Sea to Naples, appearances could hardly be more deceiving. Each of these countries had a king, but he was only a suzerain, not a sovereign. He reigned, not ruled. He shared the control of his country with dozens of feudal lords, whose effective authority might be as great as his own. The lords stood between him and his people, and he could do little in his own kingdom without their consent. With no army of his own, with no administrative bureaucracy which was responsible to him, with only a pitifully inadequate revenue to support himself, there was little reason to expect the future to restore him to the position Charlemagne had once enjoyed. He was king in, not of, his country.

Factors Favorable to Kingship. There were present in the situation, however, elements which favored the growth of royal power. Foremost among these was the church. In theory the king was the church's protector. The church strove to make him one in fact. She used her moral influence to temper the brutal excesses of rapacious lords, while her ministers preached of a happy future when peace would come to the distraught countryside through the instrumentality of a strong king. The church made the coronation ritual of the king a most elaborate one. She claimed therewith to invest the king with a sacrosanct character especially sanctified by God. In an age which respected God's anointed, such claims were not wasted. Medieval history reveals the names of few regicides. One of John of England's barons who was warring on the king forbade his crossbowmen to fire on the king, even though John was perhaps the most hated monarch in English history. The title which the medieval king bore, though frequently an empty one, gave him a moral ascendancy which set him sharply above his most powerful vassals. Once circumstances would prove more favorable, this title would serve to lift him above them in fact as he was now only in theory. To help him achieve this goal, towns and merchants would soon be eager to lend him their enthusiastic support. Even feudalism itself, by retaining the notion of kingship, prevented the extinction of the institution of monarchy and helped preserve it for a better day.

The French Feudal Monarchy

Happy Fortune of French Monarchy. France of the late tenth and eleventh centuries presents a good illustration of what the usual feudal monarchy was like. Curiously enough, given another two hundred years, France would similarly reveal how far a little foresight on the part of its kings, coupled with a happy set of circumstances, could carry this same feudal monarchy toward real power. Historians have customarily emphasized the luck of the French monarchy, and this was indeed remarkable. First there was the fortunate location of the capital at Paris in the economic and strategic center of the country. Then by a quirk of history, every king from Hugh Capet in 987 until Louis X in 1316 left a son. France consequently suffered none of the dynastic breaks which impeded the growth of monarchy in Germany during the formative period. By another quirk of fortune, only once was the crown prince (dauphin) not of age when his father died. Even in this solitary instance, not a futile regency, but the resourceful Blanche of Castile, mother of the youthful Louis IX, stepped into the breach, and no forward motion was lost. The reigns of the first

MEDIEVAL FRANCE

The map shows locations including: DUCHY OF BRABANT 1430, Rhine R., FLANDERS, Calais, Courtrai, ARTOIS, Bouvines, Agincourt, Crecy, HAINAULT, DUCHY OF LUXEMBURG 1451, AMIENS, PICARDY, VERMANDOIS, CHAMPAGNE, ENGLISH CHANNEL, NORMANDY 1184, Seine R., Paris, Domremy, DUCHY OF LORRAINE 1475, BRITTANY 1184, MAINE 1184, Orleans, Lorris, ANJOU 1184, Chinon, Loire R., DUCHY OF BURGUNDY 1363, COUNTY OF BURGUNDY 1384, Bourges, Poitiers, AQUITAINE (GUIENNE), Bordeaux, Rhone R., LANGUEDOC, GASCONY, Bayonne, TOULOUSE, KINGDOM OF NAVARRE, KINGDOM OF ARAGON

seven kings beginning with Hugh Capet in 987 averaged almost 34 years, a record never before or since equalled. One result was that the election of the king became a formality and Philip Augustus (d. 1223) was able to dispense with it entirely. And here a little foresight proved helpful. The French kings facilitated the acceptance of the hereditary principle by nominating their sons to succeed them during their own lifetime. Finally, whether by design or necessity, the French kings of the tenth and eleventh centuries avoided interfering in the business of their more powerful vassals. Only when they could speak with real authority did they begin to take a hand in French affairs outside their own domains. Until then they were content to grow old and fat.

Louis VI. The first four Capetians, beginning with Hugh in 987, amounted to very little. The rise of the French monarchy begins with Louis VI, who ascended the throne in 1108. What entitles him to this recognition was his ability to establish himself as master in his own house, in the Ile de France. No French king could hope to have a voice in national affairs until this had been accomplished. Louis humbled the arrogant local officialdom of the royal domain who had flouted his authority and terrorized the countryside and townspeople. With Louis dates the alliance between crown and bourgeoisie which was to prove such a bulwark of strength to the French monarchy. To a number of communities he granted charters, while others, such as Lorris, he brought into existence as "new towns" through a liberal grant of privileges. So strong did Louis make his position at home that he was the first Capetian capable of making his royal authority felt in several of the major French fiefs. To contemporaries, his crowning success was the marriage of his son to the richest and most talented heiress in Christendom, to Eleanor, the daughter of the duke of Aquitaine. That the duke had entrusted his daughter into Louis' keeping when he felt his death drawing near, is best proof of how far Louis had raised the royal prestige. A good share in Louis' noteworthy achievement was owing to Suger, the abbot of St. Denis. Suger, who was of peasant birth, became a monk, distinguished himself as a scholar, and was appointed Louis' tutor. He eventually rose to become Louis' chief minister. Suger was the first in a long line of illustrious French clerical ministers and the only one who could justify his ecclesiastical preferment by his merits as a churchman. The reverse was ordinarily the case. The king would simply promote to high office in the church the clerk who had proved his worth as a councilor. Such preferment both honored the recipient and, at the same time, relieved the crown of the expense of supporting him. (Reading 113)

Louis VII. Historians have been divided in assessing the accomplishments of Louis VII (1137-1180). His warm personal qualities, his success in gaining the support of the pope whom he befriended, his success in keeping Toulouse from falling to the English, even his strong policy in favor of the towns, have been obscured by what proved a capital error, namely, his divorce of Eleanor. Time has served to lend an unmerited glamor to Eleanor's name. Louis knew her for what she was, an intensely frivolous and self-willed young woman. What was more serious in his eyes was her inability to give him a son. As long as Suger lived, he managed to keep husband and wife together. After his death and after fifteen years of fruitless quarreling, their union was annulled on the grounds of consanguinity. Louis was glad to see Eleanor go, and he did not greatly mind the loss of Eleanor's dowry, Aquitaine, since his authority there as duke had not been appreciably greater than his theoretical one as a king. But he minded very much two months later when Eleanor became the wife of his most powerful vassal, Henry, duke of Normandy. Henry was also count of Anjou and

Maine, and two years later was to become king of England. Louis could hardly accept the fact that one of his vassals ruled more of France than he. The long rivalry between England and France, which proved more enduring than any in the history of nations, dates from the marriage between Eleanor and Henry. Louis managed to hold his own against his more talented rival by using the sons that Eleanor gave Henry to war against their own father. Louis' part in the Second Crusade which failed has been noted above. (See page 407.)

Philip Augustus: His Character and Minor Accomplishments. There may be some question regarding the achievement of Louis VII; there is none concerning that of his son Philip II (Augustus) (1180-1223). Historians universally acclaim him one of France's two greatest medieval kings, the other being his grandson, Louis IX. Unlike his sainted successor, Philip was crafty if not treacherous, and easy with the promises he broke whenever it served his interest to do so. On the other hand, to those who were his friends and whom he trusted, he proved himself loyal and generous. In romantic literature he suffers from comparison with his valiant rival, Richard of England, although he was no mean warrior himself and was even something of a military engineer. From the age of fourteen when he assumed control, he drove himself with tireless ambition, often beyond the capacities of his frail constitution. Philip may claim the honor of chartering the university in Paris. He beautified the city of Paris with many fine structures, including the cathedral of Notre Dame, and gave it one of Europe's first paved streets. Part of the key to his remarkable success was the huge volume of revenue he managed to channel into the royal coffers. A large portion of this came from the towns to which he granted many privileges and who responded generously with money and soldiers. He employed burgesses as officials, and entrusted the great seal and the royal treasury to six Parisian merchants when he left on the Third Crusade.

He Enlarges the Capetian Domain. Philip's most spectacular achievement was that of tripling the size of the Capetian domain. The first territory he annexed was the rich fief of Artois, his wife's dowry. To this he added the upper Somme valley including Vermandois and Amiens after a short war with the new count of Flanders. Rich as was Artois, it was inconsequential alongside the extensive areas he acquired at the expense of the king of England. This quarrel he had inherited from his father. Against Henry II he had been content to continue his father's method of sowing dissension between Henry and his sons, which was not difficult. When Richard succeeded to the throne, the two kings patched up a truce and left together on the Third Crusade. When Philip learned of his father-in-law's death, he pleaded illness to hurry home to secure his wife's dowry. He respected his holy oath to Richard not to molest Richard's French possessions only until he had Artois firmly in hand. Yet what he gained at Richard's expense through the duplicity of Richard's brother, John, he had eventually to surrender. Richard was more than a match for Philip in warfare.

Philip and John. Against John, however, Philip achieved complete and permanent success. True, his efforts to advance the claims of Arthur who was the son of the deceased Geoffrey, John's eldest brother, came to naught. But when John captured Arthur and murdered him, or so at least it was believed, most of John's vassals in Normandy and Brittany abandoned him for Philip. (Some of his vassals were less concerned about John's wickedness than they were impressed by his efficiency.) John had already furnished Philip a strong legal case to use against him. In an age which viewed betrothment as a contract binding in law and religion, and when feudal marriages were arranged in terms of dowry rather than romance, it was no light matter to steal the fiancee of a lord. This John had done. When Philip summoned him to answer the charges brought by the aggrieved vassal, only to have John ignore the summons, he forthwith declared his fiefs forfeit. This judgment Philip proceeded to carry out, and John soon found himself dispossessed of almost all his continental possessions save Aquitaine. To retrieve his losses he enlisted the support of Otto, the Holy Roman Emperor, and a number of Philip's disgruntled vassals who resented his growing power. In the battle of Bouvines fought in July 1214, Philip was able to deal the hostile coalition a decisive defeat (John had been defeated a few days earlier), assuring himself of both the possession of the English fiefs north of the Loire, and of the submission of his rebellious vassals as well. When Philip died in 1223 he was not only the largest landowner in France, but the wealthiest and most powerful as well. (Reading 114)

Philip and the Growth of Royal Government. Philip's second great achievement lay in the realm of government where he supplied the crown the bases of a centralized bureaucracy. The best Philip could boast of in the way of royal officials upon his accession were the *prévôts* whom he had inherited from the earlier Capetians. These proved more a liability than an aid to the growth of royal power. Given charge of the royal estates from which the king should have derived the bulk of his precious revenue, the *prévôts* had proved corrupt and insubordinate, inclined to view their positions as hereditary, and to take more from the people than they should have and turning over to the king less than they owed. Philip proceeded to curb their irregularities and to reduce their power with the appointment of a new official, the *bailli*. To the *bailli* he entrusted full judiciary and military authority over the district to which he was assigned, together with complete responsibility for the collection of the royal revenues. But he paid him a salary and moved him to a new district every few years. The *bailli* was generally drawn from the lower nobility or bourgeoisie, while his counterpart in southern France, the seneschal, because of the greater distance from Paris and the proportionate weakness of royal government, was usually a member of the nobility. These officials and their administrative assistants were appointed and paid by the crown. They served the king so long as they served him well. The consequence was the growth of a loyal and efficient bureaucracy dedicated to the crown and to the advancement of its interests.

Blanche of Castile. The reign of Philip's son, Louis VIII, was remarkable chiefly for its brevity. It covered but three years (1223-1226). Louis anticipated the policy of his more renowned son, Louis IX, by dismissing several royal officials who had served the crown too tyrannically. The name of Louis VIII remains associated with the Albigensians (see page 521), against whom he led two crusades, one as dauphin. His intervention in southern France paved the way for the ultimate absorption of Languedoc into the Capetian domain. When Louis died, England and several of Louis' restive vassals sought to exploit the opportunity which had been created by the fact that a twelve year old boy, Louis IX, had ascended the throne. However, they miscalculated the capabilities of Blanche of Castile, Louis VIII's energetic wife, who served as regent for her son. With the loyal support of the towns, particularly of Paris, she met their challenge with vigor and quashed this and subsequent revolts. She forced the count of Toulouse, a friend of the Albigensians, to accept a treaty giving the Capetians that part of his feudatory already conquered, and marking the remainder to come as a dowry accompanying his daughter when she married Louis' brother. Blanche was never popular. She was a foreigner and inclined to be imperious and stern. She was as strict with her son, Louis, as with all others. She treated her daughter-in-law shabbily, and Joinville tells how "she would not suffer, in so far as she could help it, that her son should be in his wife's company, except at night when he slept with her." Yet Louis had a deep and abiding love for his mother, and remained inconsolable for three days when he learned of her death.

Louis IX: His Character. Louis IX (1223-1270) stands forth from the recesses of time as no other French king of the Middle Ages. For this we are indebted to Jean de Joinville, a French nobleman of Champagne, who accompanied him on the Crusade. According to this biographer, Louis was a perfect Christian who lived his Christianity both as man and as king. Joinville was not sure but that he even carried his religion too far. He surely did not approve his washing the feet of the poor or waiting upon lepers. Louis loved the poor. For them he built almshouses, a home for fallen women, another for the poor blind of the city, as well as constructing hospitals and orphanages. Though a king, he lived as a mystic. Under his royal robes he wore a hair shirt. His fare was frugal; he found time for much devotional reading, and he rose during the night to recite the Divine Office. Laugh he could and did, but not on Fridays. He enjoyed himself most in conversation at the dinner table. His love of justice and honest government was what his subjects most appreciated. Fraudulent and tyrannical officials he disciplined with an iron hand, and for those of his subjects who found it impossible to secure justice, he himself presided informally under the oak trees at Vincennes. Feudal warfare shocked his love of peace. In an age which upheld the right of private warfare, he forbade his vassals to bear arms or to settle their differences in trial by combat. France was never so peaceful again before the seventeenth century. He had eleven children by his devoted though strong-willed wife. While he has been judged unfeeling in his attitude toward his family, it was not that he loved them less but that he "loved all manner of people who had faith in God and loved Him." As he admonished his son on his deathbed: "I say to thee to make thyself beloved of the people of thy kingdom; for truly I would rather that a Scot should come out of Scotland and govern the people of the kingdom well and equitably than that thou shouldst govern it ill in the sight of all men." (Reading 115)

His Justice in Foreign Affairs. In foreign affairs where even upright rulers customarily employed expediency, Louis used only justice and wisdom. He might have pushed England and his brother-in-law Henry III right off the continent, and he had sufficient provocation to have done so. But this would have invited war. So he added territories of his own to round out those the English held in the southwest (roughly Guienne), in return for Henry's formal abandonment of claims north of the Loire (chiefly Normandy and Anjou). With the king of Aragon he made a similar arrangement. Louis relinquished any claims south of the Pyrenees, Aragon to any north of the mountains. Philip Augustus would have capitalized upon the bitter struggle between the papacy and Frederick II, the Holy Roman Emperor (see page 467), but not Louis. Not until Frederick was dead and his heir as well, did Louis finally listen to the overtures of the pope and permit his brother, Charles of Anjou, to lead French troops into southern Italy. Saint though Louis was, he did not side with the pope in his feud with Frederick, since he considered their controversy political. He also refused to use the civil arm to force excommunicates to make their peace with the church, unless he were first permitted to pass on the justice of the sentence. Louis' wide reputation for justice attracted a number of appeals to his arbitrament, the most famous the quarrel between Henry III and his nobles. (See page 454.)

The Growth of Royal Government. Louis would have considered his greatest work the two Crusades he undertook, both equally forlorn hopes. (See page 410.) Equally fruitless was the mission of the Franciscans whom he sent to China to convert the khan and his Mongols. Of primary importance, however, was his contribution to the evolution of royal administrative machinery. Much of this growth was surely inevitable in view of the increasing knowledge of law and the problems of government. Much of the groundwork, too, had already been prepared by Philip Augustus. Yet the first evidence of the breaking up of the king's court, the *curia regis,* into specialized departments became visible in Louis' day. During his reign members of the *curia regis* who had a special interest in, or aptitude for, finances, began to devote themselves principally to fiscal matters. They came to be identified in time as the *chambre des comptes* (chamber of accounts). A comparable departmentalization took place in the administration of justice consequent upon the huge increase in appeals to the royal courts. The central court at Paris which handled such judicial business was known as the *parlement de Paris*. The law there applied was theoretically custom, but Louis and his legal advisors accepted the principle of Roman law which made the king the ultimate interpreter of this customary law. Other members of the *curia regis* Louis sent out as *enquêteurs* (inquisitors) to investigate the conduct of the *baillis* and seneschals, to hear complaints, and to hold inquests. This last appointment emphasizes Louis' deep interest in just government, and his ability to furnish his people just administration constitutes his greatest contribution to the rise of the French monarchy. Until Louis' reign, the crown had been feared or ignored. Now for the first time people began to love their king, to respect royal government, to look to the crown for protection and justice. Thus Louis' work complemented that of Philip Augustus. The achievement of the one without that of the other could hardly have proved enduring.

The English Feudal Monarchy

Early Anglo-Saxon Period. Before turning to feudal England, let us glance briefly at the early history of Britain. We last saw England as a province of the Roman Empire, being invaded from the north in the fifth century by Picts and Scots, and from the continent by the Angles, Saxons, and Jutes. Much of the province was lost to civilization, and, since England had no contemporary historian like Gregory of Tours, lost also to history. We know preciously little about these violent times. This was the time when King Arthur fought so valiantly against the Germanic invaders, but he and his exploits are no more substantial than other scattered information the sources have preserved. Celtic civilization retained a foothold only in the mountainous areas of Wales and Cornwall, but here Roman civilization had never rooted itself. The consequence was that Roman culture was swept from the island. It is true that Rome's most important contribution, Christianity, lingered on in the western fringes of the island until it was revived by missionaries from Ireland. And the Roman roads provided the island better thoroughfares in Saxon times than the seventeenth century Stuarts enjoyed. Until the early seventh century when seven kingdoms emerge—Northumbria, Mercia, East Anglia, Wessex, Sussex, Essex, and Kent—England was torn with the strife of dozens of petty states.

Alfred.   The most distinguished name in Anglo-Saxon England is that of Alfred (871-900). Alfred's fame is linked with the coming of the Danes. These Vikings began to harass the island about the time the kings of Wessex gained their ascendancy, that is, the close of the eighth century. Alfred earned his title of "the Great" by his success against these fierce invaders. To accomplish this he reorganized the unreliable militia, the fyrd; he laid the historical foundations at least of the British navy; and he prevailed upon the aristocracy to ride against the speedy invader. Despite initial disheartening reverses, he finally gained the upper hand and forced the Danes to accept a treaty which limited them to the Danelaw, roughly the northeastern half of England. Since the Danes were racially first cousins of the Angles and Saxons, and since they agreed to become Christians, their early assimilation was assured. Alfred's peacetime activities centered largely about the task of repairing the havoc left by the Danish invasions. Monastic life was almost extinct, and with it the religious and intellectual soul of England. To establish a source of scholars and trained administrators, Alfred organized a school at his court to which he invited the few scholars still surviving in England. He encouraged the well-born to send their children to school, and he contemplated an educational system which would serve all his people and even provide training in the vocational arts. Those books whose learning "was most needful for every man to know," he had translated—books like Pope Gregory's *Pastoral Rule*, Bede's *Ecclesiastical History*, and Boethius' *Consolation of Philosophy*. Posterity would not have missed his translation of Orosius' history, although it has found his own comments on the text interesting, e.g. "A man will not be better because he hath a well-born father, if he himself is naught. The only thing which is good in noble descent is this—that it makes men ashamed of being worse than their elders." Alfred reformed the church, codified the law, and established the first centralized monarchy in English history. The records which he instructed monasteries to keep developed into the *Anglo-Saxon Chronicle*.

Edward the Confessor and William the Conqueror.   Alfred's son and grandson reconquered the Danelaw, but the Danes continued to make forays across the North Sea. In 1013 Swein Forkbeard, king of Sweden, landed with an army and conquered almost the whole island for his more famous son Cnut (Canute). Though a foreigner and a pagan, Cnut proved a popular monarch. His reign (1016-1035) was one of peace and prosperity, his rule just, and he preserved the traditions and institutions of the Saxons. Had Cnut's sons inherited the talents of their father and established a dynasty, England might have oriented itself toward Scandinavia in the Middle Ages, rather than toward France. They proved incompetent, however, and in 1042 the Anglo-Saxon aristocracy hailed Edward, the brother of their last native king, as monarch. Edward, known as the Confessor, had been reared at the court of his uncle, the duke of Normandy. His Norman ways and the friends he brought with him from Normandy irritated native sensibilities, and soon a strong Saxon party was born headed by Godwin, earl of Wessex. When the childless Edward died, the Saxon aristocracy immediately proclaimed Godwin's son, Harold, as king. Unfortunately for Harold, two other aspirants appeared who contested his claim. One was Harold Hardrada, king of Norway, who announced himself Cnut's heir. The other was William, duke of Normandy. Both advanced shadowy claims, but neither would probably have been heard from again had not Harold the Anglo-Saxon found himself caught in the middle. He first met and destroyed Harold of Norway's army in the north at Stamford Bridge, then by forced marches hurried south to oppose William's army at Hastings. Late on the afternoon of October 14, 1066, Harold fell dead from an arrow, and Anglo-Saxon England passed into history. (Reading 116)

The Introduction of Norman Feudalism. The Norman Conquest rates second in importance in the history of England only to the severing of the land link with the continent which took place back in prehistoric times. Had some nameless adventurer killed Harold at Hastings and assumed control, the degree of change would probably have been small. But William was duke of Normandy, the most powerful lord in France. Since William retained his duchy in France, in fact, considered England less important than his French possessions, England was wedded to the continent for the balance of the medieval period. What this would entail in terms of warfare with France lay in the future. Immediately for Anglo-Saxon England, the Norman Conquest brought important changes: the replacement of a native nobility with one from France (this extended even to the hierarchy once the Saxon bishops had died); the substitution of French as the language of the court and the literate (in addition to Latin); the introduction of a strongly centralized government in place of one almost subservient to a landed aristocracy; the introduction of feudalism. These last two changes, a centralized government and feudalism, may appear incompatible, and they surely were in France in William's day. The feudalism that William introduced, however, served as a means, not of dissipating, but of strengthening royal power. Certain rights which continental vassals had commonly usurped, William retained, such as the coinage of money, the building of castles, and the punishment of such crimes as treason and murder. William also announced that all England belonged to him, and that all fief-holders, as a consequence, owed him direct loyalty. William's feudalism had an unusually favorable climate in which to function. As long as the Normans were a detested minority, they could ill afford the luxury of revolting; furthermore, all fief-holders were known to William and had personally received their fiefs from him.

William's Government. On the other hand, there were certain Anglo-

Saxon institutions and practices which William's shrewd eye convinced him were worth preserving. The fyrd or local militia was of that character, although it did not figure prominently in the growth of royal power. Of greater value was the Anglo-Saxon judicial system of hundred and shire (county) courts. William retained both, the hundred court meeting once a month to handle local problems, the shire court convening twice a year with jurisdiction not only over important cases, but over pleas of the crown as well, and even over disputes between vassals of different lords. The man who presided over the shire court William also retained, namely, the sheriff. William made him his representative and agent in the shire, and empowered him to administer all fiscal, military, and judicial matters pertaining to the crown. The sheriff provided William a powerful counterpoise against the local aristocracy. William continued the collection of the Danegeld which had originated as tribute to buy off the Danes. The Anglo-Saxon custom for the community of raising a hue and cry and following in pursuit of any criminal, he also preserved. To assist in the ferreting out of those guilty of crime, the king reserved the right to summon the leading men of the community to give information. So successful were his efforts against lawlessness, "that a man of any substance could travel unmolested throughout the country with his bosom full of gold." For the Anglo-Saxon witan (wise men) who had advised the king, William substituted the traditional feudal *curia regis*. What was neither of Norman nor Anglo-Saxon origin was the Domesday Book which William had compiled. According to the *Anglo-Saxon Chronicle*, "there was not a 'hide' of land in England which he did not know who held it and how much it was worth; and these particulars he set down in his survey." The purpose of the survey was to furnish William a record of all the landed property in England and what was owing the king of its value. That no other king of his day could even have contemplated conducting such a survey confirms William's reputation as an energetic, feared, and statesmanlike king. "How to deal with men he learned, when to smite and when to spare." (Reading 117)

William II and the Accession of Henry I.   William's last act of shrewdness was to give England to his second eldest son, William. His first-born, Robert, he rightfully judged too gentle for the job. William Rufus (the Red) was anything but gentle. A contemporary writes how when William went about his kingdom, his people took to the hills. He did keep the proud nobility under his heel, which was what his father most wanted. Toward the church he showed himself equally harsh. It was his wont to keep bishoprics and monasteries vacant for extended periods in order to siphon off the income for himself. When William was killed on a hunting trip, there was no investigation, as one writer has expressed it. Least interested in the cause of William's death was his younger brother Henry, who hurried to Winchester to seize the royal treasury. To bolster his throne, Henry married an Anglo-Saxon princess, granted London the first town charter in English history, invited the saintly Anselm, archbishop of Canterbury, back from exile where he had gone when he found William intolerable, and issued a charter of liberties in which he promised to avoid the illegal acts of his brother. Though Henry frequently failed to honor these promises, this "Charter of Liberties" bears some significance as the first formal acknowledgement by a king of England that his rule was not absolute.

Henry's Work. Henry proved himself a credit to his father. He was as much a statesman as William the Conqueror, and he displayed equal interest in strong and efficient government. His reign of thirty-five years witnessed, accordingly, a continuous expansion of the royal administrative machinery. The bulk of the work of government was transacted through the *curia regis*, but not so much by the large unwieldy body of noblemen which met two or three times a year, as by a small group of advisers who followed the king wherever he went. The chief of these advisers included the justiciar, who acted as the king's representative and as regent in his absence; the chancellor, who had charge of the great seal and who supervised all legal documents, the keeping of records, and correspondence; and the treasurer, who directed the king's fiscal business. These, together with several other officials, supervised the general business of the government. When they attended to financial matters, they would sit around a table which was covered with a checkered cloth, somewhat resembling an abacus, to facilitate computations. From this evolved the term exchequer as the name of the English treasury. To simplify the problem of securing royal justice, Henry began to send out members of the *curia regis* as itinerant justices with authority to handle judicial business reserved to the king. In 1107 Henry anticipated with the Compromise of Bec substantially the same settlement as would be worked out between the papacy and Germany over investiture at Worms in 1122. (See page 515.)

Matilda and Stephen. In one major concern Henry was not successful. That was the problem of succession. His son William, who had married the daughter of the count of Anjou, drowned in the Channel. So to preserve the goodwill of Anjou, his deadliest enemy in France, Henry persuaded his widowed daughter Matilda to marry the count's son. Next he secured holy oaths from all his vassals in both Normandy and England, that they would accept Matilda as queen when he died. Yet all to no avail. Most of the feudal lords preferred the good-natured Stephen of Blois, grandson of the Conqueror through the latter's daughter, who was not associated with the hated Angevins (from Anjou), and who did not promise to be so resolute a ruler as Matilda. The result was nineteen years of disastrous civil war. "Never did heathen men do worse than they did. Men said openly that Christ and His saints slept." Finally in 1153 a compromise was arranged by which Stephen should rule until his death, when Henry, the son of Matilda, would succeed. Stephen died ironically within the year.

Henry II: His Character.   Henry II (1154-1189) began the Plantagenet or Angevin dynasty. Though he spent no more than a third of his thirty-five-year reign in England, many scholars consider him the greatest of all English monarchs. He was a man of marked physical and psychological characteristics: red-faced, raw-boned, bow-legged, stocky, strident of voice, a bundle of nervous energy, strong-willed, given to blasphemous furies,

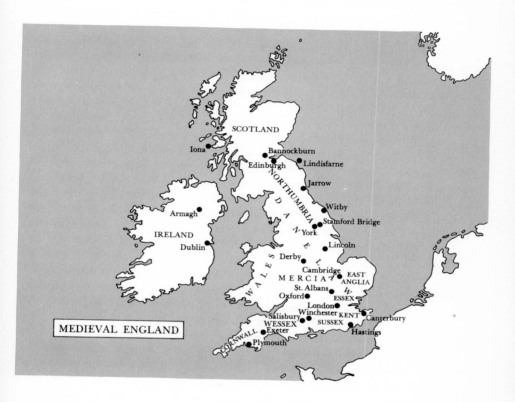

MEDIEVAL ENGLAND

ambitious, and shrewd. Though a hard husband toward Eleanor, she would have crushed a weaker person. Their four sons, a human wolf-pack, and three daughters rounded out perhaps history's most quarrelsome royal house. Henry had an unusual memory and a driving ambition to acquire any knowledge that he could use to make his government more efficient and his rule more effective. Though a notoriously unfaithful husband and no great credit to Christianity, the bishops he selected were able men. Most impressive to contemporaries was the extent of his domains which ranged from the Scottish highlands to the Pyrenees. In addition to England, he held the western half of France including Normandy, Brittany, Anjou, and Aquitaine (the latter through his marriage to Eleanor). He claimed suzerainty over Wales and Scotland, and carved out an enclave about Dublin known as the English Pale. His daughters he used to secure family alliances with the rulers of Saxony, Sicily, and Castile. Because of the size of his domains, his far-flung interests, and, particularly, his wealth, no king before or after Henry during the medieval period raised England to greater prestige in continental eyes. He was plagued throughout his reign by rebellious sons whose hatreds and jealousies were fanned by the French kings who feared him. Though frequently confronted with dangerous revolts, he was able to rally the powerful support of his loyal baronage, the English church, and his own people and officials. He died on the battlefield, his last moments saddened by news that even John, the son whom he had always considered faithful, had deserted him.

Henry's Revenue. If Henry's contemporaries were most impressed with the extent of his domains, Henry had a truer sense of values. He realized that a king's power rose and fell with his income. There was no substitute for a well-filled purse. Confronted with the same insolvable problem which vexed all medieval monarchs—an inelastic income saddled upon the principle that the king live of his own—Henry, nevertheless, achieved gratifying success in expanding his revenues. So extensive, indeed, became the operations of the royal treasury during his reign, that before Henry died the exchequer had developed into the most highly organized branch of the government. We even have a valuable description of this office from the pen of Richard Fitz-Neal, one of Henry's treasurers, entitled *Dialogue of the Exchequer*. Henry's chief source of revenue was always his own estates, but he realized a considerable amount from other sources as well. Especially lucrative were feudal aids and incidents for which he held his barons to a strict account and at unusually stiff rates. Geoffrey de Mandeville, for example, paid 20,000 marks—a king's ransom—for the right to marry Isabella of Gloucester and take over her lands. The Danegeld yielded some revenue before Henry replaced it with a much more substantial tallage which he assessed against his own tenants and against boroughs. On a number of occasions he collected scutage from his vassals in lieu of the military service they owed him. He greatly preferred to use their money to hire troops whom he could control, than to be forced to rely upon the cumbersome and more independent feudal levy. There was, furthermore, always the possibility of unexpended funds remaining after the war needs had been met. Henry sold charters to many towns and forced contributions from the church and from Jews with some regularity. In 1188 he collected a tax based upon income and property known as the Saladin tithe. Though the crusade for which this tax was collected never materialized (Henry died during the preparations), the tax itself proved a convenient method for succeeding kings to employ to meet extraordinary expenses (which then, as now, had a way of becoming increasingly regular). Finally, there were the fees and fines collected through the instrumentality of an efficient system of justice. Though Henry's barons might chafe and protest at his financial practices, none dared call a halt. They were afraid of Henry.

Henry's Great Project. Henry's chief contribution to English history came in the realm of law. Henry had an extensive knowledge and apprecia-tion of law. He was convinced that an efficient and equitable adminis-tration of justice held the key to his ultimate success as king. The smooth functioning of a broad system of royal courts would mean a steady flow of revenue by way of fees and fines. A firm though just enforcement of the law would also provide the best assurance against revolt, while at the same time prove a most persuasive means of gaining the respect and loyalty of his subjects. For these reasons Henry adopted and put to regular use de-vices and practices which the Normans both in England and in Normandy had earlier employed on occasion, and which he was convinced would accomplish his ends. This expansion of royal justice impinged, of course, upon the traditional jurisdictions of the baronial and shire courts, and the church courts as well. Since the superiority of the law constituted in the final analysis the power to rule, Henry's expansion of royal justice repre-sented a fundamental growth of royal power at the expense of the two institutions which mainly blocked royal supremacy, namely, the feudality and the church. That most people were bringing the majority of their disputes to the royal courts when Henry died is a convincing barometer of the success of his great project. That his system of courts laid the ground plan of the English judicial system as it has persisted to the present day further reveals the excellence and solidity of his work.

Itinerant Justices. Henry's steps toward his goal were slow but certain. First he restricted the adjudication of certain crimes to his own royal jus-tices on the plea, that, due to local negligence or even collusion, dangerous criminals were not being punished. Crimes specifically restricted to the royal courts were murder, larceny, robbery, and the harboring of criminals. To these four offenses were later added forgery and arson. To have staked off the adjudication of these offenses for the exclusive jurisdiction of the royal courts would have proved an empty gesture, however, had not Henry expanded the activities of the itinerant justices. They had formerly been sent out, somewhat as the occasion demanded, to meet with the shire court in matters touching taxation and justice. Now they were organized on a permanent basis into five circuits, three justices to each circuit, and were empowered to hold inquests into the commission of the crimes noted. Since this might still involve long delays because of the length of the cir-cuits, Henry set up a permanent court at Westminster, known as the *Capi-talis Curia Regis*, to which plaintiffs could have recourse at any time. Not long after Henry's death this central court split up into three distinct courts: Common Pleas, to try private civil cases; the Court of the Ex-chequer, to handle financial cases to which the government was a partner; King's Bench, chiefly for criminal cases.

Jury of Presentment.   The next step in the progress of royal justice saw the introduction of an improved method of ferreting out criminals. This was accomplished through what is known as the jury of presentment. The origins of the jury (from the Latin meaning to swear) can be traced back to Carolingian and Anglo-Saxon times when responsible men of the community were called upon by the royal officials to furnish information. The reasonableness of the practice appealed to the Normans, but it remained for Henry to make it a regular procedure. As it functioned, the sheriff would impanel a jury composed of twelve "lawful" men from every hundred and four men of each manor, and instruct them to reveal the names of those persons in the neighborhood whom they felt were under suspicion of crime. (Reading 119) When the itinerant justice arrived on circuit, the men so accused were summoned to stand trial. The ordinary method of trial was the ordeal of cold water. Henry shared the general doubt concerning the efficacy of the method, and he made a practice of exiling any person, even though "proved" innocent by the ordeal, who was "of very bad reputation and publicly and disgracefully spoken ill of by the testimony of many and lawful men." (Reading 120) The ordeal itself was permanently discarded as a means of ascertaining guilt soon after 1215, when the church forbade the clergy to participate in its administration.

The Petit Jury and Common Law.   Long before this happened, Henry was experimenting with the jury as a method of judging the evidence itself. The need for something superior to the ordeal had grown particularly urgent in property disputes, since the ordinary method employed to determine justice in these cases was trial by combat. Even at a time when most land was owned by a relatively few lords, trial by combat made no sense. Now when the majority of disputants in property cases were ordinary freemen who were forced to procure the services of professional champions to represent them in a trial by combat, the device was ridiculous. Henry accordingly arranged for the itinerant justice to impanel a group of men who were acquainted with the land in dispute, to give their opinion as to the justice in the case. On the basis of their assertions, the itinerant justice would give judgment. Because this method promised a much more reasonable, impartial, and expeditious method of handling disputes, litigants were happy to purchase the necessary writ to take their case to the royal court. From trying civil disputes, it was just a short step before this same kind of jury was being asked to weigh the evidence in criminal cases. Soon after Henry's death the use of the petit jury in both civil and criminal cases became general throughout England. Also generally uniform throughout the land were other features of the judicial process, such as the manner in which disputes were settled, and the nature of the fines and punishments assessed. This uniformity came as a natural consequence of the fact that itinerant justices were of the same body (the *curia regis*), that they tried the same cases, and that they received their instructions from the same authority. While the itinerant justice considered local custom in his circuit about the country, he gradually came to depend more and more upon precedent, that is, upon judicial decisions made earlier, of which a record had been carefully preserved on the court rolls. The product of the work of the itinerant justice is known as common law, a law which became common for England. Several commentaries dealing with law contributed significantly to the standardization of legal processes. Most noteworthy among these were a *Treatise on the Laws and Customs of England* by Ranulf Glanvil, one of Henry II's judges, and somewhat later Henry Bracton's *On the Laws and Customs of England.*

Henry and Becket. Henry also sought to take over some of the business of the church courts as part of a wider plan to reduce the independence of the English Church. He argued that until the reign of the quiescent Stephen, the crown had exercised the right of approving any appeal to Rome, of participating in the election of bishops, even of passing upon the excommunication of high officials. Provisions which would restore these rights to the crown, together with others pertaining to church-state problems, he had incorporated in a document known as the Constitutions of Clarendon. (Reading 118) These he presented to the new archbishop of Canterbury for approval. Since this archbishop was Thomas à Becket, his close friend and until recently his most resourceful and loyal chancellor, Henry anticipated no difficulty. Thomas, however, had warned Henry when the king suggested that he accept the archbishop's office, that as archbishop he would consider it his first duty to serve the church rather than the state. And so it proved. Basing his opposition on the provision which would have entrusted the punishment of criminous clerks to the state, Thomas refused to ratify the Constitutions. His intransigeance led to exile, to a hollow reconciliation, to more recriminations, in the end to murder. Henry who had one of the most famous tempers in history, had expressed somewhat thoughtlessly in one of his paroxysms of rage the wish that some one might rid him of this obstinate archbishop. Four knights took him at his word. They cut Thomas down in his own Canterbury cathedral where he had taken refuge. Henry was as horror-stricken as the rest of Christian Europe, and did abject penance for his indirect part in the tragedy. The incident served to compromise Henry's position in his struggle with the church, and he was obliged to sacrifice a considerable portion of his Constitutions. He did secure the right for his courts to adjudicate all disputes involving property, even church property, and England acquired its most honored saint and shrine.

Richard. Perhaps the most curious paradox in English history is the great fame of Richard (1189-1199). He made no contribution to the growth of English government. Of his ten-year reign, he spent no more than ten months in England. He spoke French, considered himself a Frenchman, and preferred France. What his reign did accomplish was to demonstrate how well his father Henry had done his work, that for ten years it could support a monarch so indifferent to the country's advancement as was Richard. Yet Hubert Walter, the archbishop of Canterbury, deserved great credit for handling affairs so efficiently during Richard's long absences.

John.   Richard's brother John (1199-1216) was another matter. England never missed Richard, but after John, England was never the same again. Yet England today cherishes the memory of Richard, while the less said about John the better. John is probably the only "bad man" in history whose image no ambitious scholar has attempted to furbish. There is so little constructive to work with. True, John had talent and for what he wanted, strong government and all England's traditional possessions in France, no one could attack him. He lacked, however, the necessary industry, persistence, and self-discipline to see anything through. Few monarchs have had weaker characters. He has been described as cruel, lecherous, treacherous, unscrupulous, superstitious, tyrannical, and vindictive. The word "mean" might best fit his character. No scruples of conscience ever disturbed his mind, and he gave others credit for no more principles than he had. He trusted no one and no one trusted him except perhaps his father, who died of a broken heart when told that even his favorite John had turned against him. His older brother Richard whom he tried to keep immured in a German jail treated him "with a half-contemptuous affection and never seemed to take him and his plottings quite seriously."[*]

John's Misgovernment.   John's reign was an unqualified failure from his point of view. He lost most of his French possessions to Philip Augustus (see page 439), he was forced to recognize Stephen Langton as archbishop of Canterbury (see below), to accept the barons' ultimatum and affix his seal to *Magna Charta* (Great Charter), and he died with the knowledge that Philip Augustus' son Louis was in England leading British rebels against him. The most momentous of these developments for England was the granting of *Magna Charta*. This grew ultimately out of John's efforts to recover Normandy. To raise the necessary money and troops, John assessed scutage after scutage, demanded untraditional aids, and exacted frequent and excessively high incidents. He seized the lands and castles of some lords who failed to meet his demands, he held hostage the families of others, while a few he imprisoned and kept without trial. After the defeat of John's hopes at the Battle of Bouvines in 1214 (see page 439), baronial opposition came to a head. The man chiefly responsible for directing this opposition and bringing John to his knees was the learned and disinterested Stephen Langton. He convinced the more powerful and selfish barons to subordinate their personal grievances to a general program of baronial relief, and in so doing gained the revolt sufficient support to assure its success. When London opened its gates to the barons, John's cause was lost.

[*] John T. Appleby, *John, King of England* (New York, 1959), p. 4.

Magna Charta or the Great Charter. At Runnymede (just outside London) in June 1215, one of the most memorable events in all English history took place when John capitulated to the baronial demands. Even his protest that he was a Crusader and the pope's vassal met no response. No clash in English history ever found the king standing so much alone. John's promise in *Magna Charta* to respect the rights of the church was innocuous enough. The royal promises that followed established principles, however, which would in time provide the legal and historical bases for several of England's most cherished rights and liberties. By promising not to levy any but the traditional aids without consent of the council, John helped lay the basis for parliamentary control of taxation, the keystone to the rise of parliamentary government. His promise not to imprison or punish arbitrarily, but only "by the legal judgment of his peers or by the law of the land," implied recognition of the principle of due process of law and our concept of personal freedom. In affirming the contractual nature of John's relations with his vassals, *Magna Charta* simply reaffirmed feudal custom and law. In promising to respect the rights of the king's free men, his nonfeudal subjects, *Magna Charta* went somewhat beyond the feudal concepts of the day. It is true that the full import of the most basic of these commitments was not appreciated or pressed until the seventeenth century. It is also true that John subsequently repudiated his submission at Runnymede. Yet the privileges or rights recognized by the crown in *Magna Charta* were reaffirmed on later occasions by several of John's successors. This together with other factors helped establish the tradition that the English king was beneath the law, that he was a limited monarch. This is the major significance of *Magna Charta*. Yet glorious though the memory of *Magna Charta* remains in English hearts, these sobering considerations will not down: first, that John was no more cruel nor tyrannical than many of the barons at Runnymede; second, that possibly the real issue which produced *Magna Charta* was the growth of royal government for which Henry II was principally responsible. The barons at Runnymede rebelled against John's misgovernment in particular, against royal government in general. Given the alternative of the supremacy of the feudal aristocracy, the growth of royal government in the thirteenth century cannot be counted other than a blessing. (Reading 121)

Henry III. John's son, Henry III (1216-1272) succeeded at the age of nine. Much is known about Henry's personal characteristics, his mannerisms, his clothing, his extraordinary interest in building, and the variety and huge quantity of wine consumed during his reign at Windsor Castle. Yet Henry himself was such a pallid ruler after so many colorful predecessors, that he even lacks a biographer. Where Henry's father, John, had absolutely no sense of loyalty to family—or to anyone else for that matter— Henry had too much, and had an abundance of relatives to be loyal to. Although good-hearted and unusually pious—he attended at least three masses daily—Henry became the object of another baronial revolt. He was too French and too pro-papal, the barons declared, and too extravagant. The greed and aggressiveness of the leaders of the revolt, notably Simon de Montfort, however, leave one a bit dubious concerning the unselfishness of their motives. Be that as it may, the revolt succeeded at least initially, and Henry was captured. Still, kings were not executed in the Middle Ages, least of all one so harmless as Henry, and he eventually escaped. Though the revolt was finally quashed, the experience profited Henry little. His son, Edward I, however, learned a great deal, but that story is part of a later development, the rise of parliament.

Feudal Germany

Obstacles Peculiar to the Rise of German Monarchy. The German monarchy which emerged after the disintegration of the Carolingian Empire faced somewhat different problems than did the French, and evolved under different circumstances. In Germany feudalism had not advanced so far as in France. While extensive administrative units were as difficult to maintain there as in France, political fragmentation never proceeded so far as to destroy such early ethnic groupings as the Saxon, Franconian, Swabian, and Bavarian nations. The presence of these nations served to prevent complete feudalization of Germany. Their existence similarly proved a major obstacle to the subsequent centralizing efforts of the German king. In fact, the ethnic consciousness of several of these tribes has carried on down into the twentieth century. It is true that the dukes of Saxony, Bavaria, Franconia, and Swabia, were royal officials, at least in theory, and that on rare occasions the king was able to remove them. Yet even when the king appointed men of his own choosing, and this included his closest relatives as well, almost inevitably would these appointees identify themselves with native autonomous sentiment and seek to rule like little kings in their domains. Another major obstacle to the rise of a more powerful German monarchy was the inclusion of much of Italy within the domain of the Holy Roman Emperor. Had successive German monarchs concentrated their efforts on Germany, they might conceivably have established a powerful state there. Their title of Holy Roman Emperor tempted them to dissipate their energies in fruitless Italian campaigns. Furthermore, interference in Italy usually bred difficulties with the pope who was fearful of his independence, and wanted no powerful king on his doorstep. Though the pope had no formidable army of his own, there were always aristocratic elements in Germany and in northern Italy who were eager to fight the pope's battles, since they saw eye to eye with him on the question of a strong king. Finally, the German monarchy had nothing like the French luck in maintaining a long, unbroken sequence of fathers and sons. Almost every hundred years a dynastic break would occur, terminating one family's attempt at building up the monarchy with the assumption of that slow, painful process by another. Thus the elective principle remained alive in Germany, when in England and France it fell into disuse. As a result of these factors, the German kings, who were generally the most able of all the kings of Europe, failed to establish a strong centralized state while their French and English contemporaries succeeded.

The First German Monarchs. The first of the German monarchs, after the extinction of the eastern branch of the Carolingian line in 911, need not detain us long. Conrad I (911-919), duke of Franconia, was chosen king, and at his death Henry I (919-936), duke of Saxony, succeeded him. The latter bears the interesting sobriquet, "the Fowler," derived, so the story goes, from the fact that the messenger who came to announce his election as king of Germany frightened away the king's quarry, much to the royal disgust. If the story is true, it reveals how inconsequential Henry regarded that office to be. At any rate, both he and his predecessor made little pretense to be more than kings in their own duchies. It was without the assistance of the other dukes of Germany that Henry campaigned against the Slavs and Magyars, and erected a series of fortified camps (*Burgen*) to protect the eastern frontier. While Henry's successes were noteworthy, particularly against the Magyars, they are thrown into shadow by the greater exploits of his son, Otto I (936-973). We must take a closer look at Otto, both because he was known as "the Great," and also because his career followed the pattern of most German monarchs during the period. (Reading 122)

Otto and the German Church. Otto's first problem was that of reducing his rebellious dukes. These dukes invariably tested the strength of a new king in the hope of rendering their own positions more independent. Though Otto managed this first hurdle and even placed a brother, a son, and a son-in-law at the head of three of the German duchies, these dynastic dukes proved no more submissive in the end than nonrelatives. Otto greatly advanced the policy initiated by his father of freeing the bishops and abbots of ducal control, and making them his own trusted agents, officials, and advisors. He granted these ecclesiastics additional lands, political powers, and rights over tolls, mints, markets, and justice, in the hope of erecting an effective counterpoise against the autonomous inclinations of the hereditary aristocracy. How vital the loyalty of these ecclesiastics was to the king becomes evident when one bears in mind that almost one third of Germany comprised church lands, which furnished the king more than one half the imperial army. The king could hope to control these ecclesiastics since their offices were not hereditary. Otto made his brother Bruno archbishop of Cologne, and an illegitimate son William, archbishop of Mainz.

The Eastern Frontier. Otto interfered diplomatically in French affairs to the extent of keeping the last Carolingians weak. This would help to insure from attack his western frontier, which he had extended to include most of the old middle kingdom of Lothair. He fought the Czechs of Bohemia and forced them to recognize his overlordship. Otto's greatest single military feat was the breaking of Magyar power at the battle of Lechfeld in 955. Their defeat led to the early conversion of the Magyars and their acceptance into the family of Christian nations. North of the Magyars lay the enormously populous Slavic peoples. Against these Otto directed several expeditions and entrusted others to his eastern vassals. Their common efforts resulted in the exclusion of the Slavs from most of the area between the Elbe and Oder. The land was opened to German colonization, and several bishoprics, including Magdeburg, were established. Shortly after Otto's death the Slavs came swarming back in, and a new drive which began in the twelfth century was required before the permanent exclusion of the Slavs from that area was accomplished.

Otto's Italian Policy. Otto gained most fame from his activities in Italy. Several motives impelled him to project himself into Italian affairs. First was the annexation of that prosperous and populous land to his domains. We are inclined today to rate Italy as far inferior to Germany in wealth and general importance. In Otto's time, of the two countries, Italy was much further advanced culturally and commercially. Otto's interest lay in the latter, in the wealth which the possession of Italy might provide him. What made this wealth doubly inviting was the fact that Italy had less powerful dukes to contest his control than those with which he had to contend in Germany, together with factious cities whose differences he might be able to exploit. By moving into Italy, Otto could also nip any ambitions the ruler of Burgundy might entertain about establishing a powerful state on his southwestern flank which would include north Italy. It has, furthermore, been suggested that Otto came to Italy to take a hand in papal affairs, in order to insure his episcopal policy in Germany against attack from the hands of an unfriendly pope. Actually it was Pope John XII who invited Otto to come to Italy to protect him against the imperialistic pretensions of a petty Italian ruler. When the pope quickly realized that Otto, whom he crowned Roman Emperor, would prove far more dangerous than any petty Italian prince, he repudiated his policy of cooperation. Whereupon Otto replaced Pope John with a pope of his own choice, and exacted a promise from the Romans that "they would never again elect or ordain any Pope without the consent and choice of the Emperor Otto and his son Otto II."

Otto's Achievement. It is difficult to overestimate Otto's achievement. In Germany he enjoyed a position of power hardly equalled by any of his

CENTRAL EUROPE
AND ITALY *ca.* 1300 A.D.

medieval successors. He annexed considerable areas to the west, the east, and the south. He provided Germany's *"Drang nach Osten"* its first powerful stimulus since the time of Charlemagne, and conquered the territory between the Elbe and Oder. The century-old menace of the Magyars he finally destroyed and added that people to the family of European nations. He incorporated north and central Italy, including Rome, into his domains, an annexation which would eventually bring Germany more woe than weal. When he placed his own appointee on the papal throne, he inaugurated nearly a hundred years of German domination of the papacy. This assured the German kings uninterrupted control of the German church, which was the major base of royal power in Germany. For the church, German interference meant a healthier papacy, one extricated from Roman factional politics and soon able to resume its leadership in the ecclesiastical affairs of Europe. Again, only time would reveal how this new papacy would contribute significantly to the weakening of the German monarchy. Otto's acquisition of the title of Holy Roman Emperor provided him a position of prestige and leadership in European affairs far beyond the warrant of the German king's actual power. This empire is known historically as "The Holy Roman Empire of the German Nation." Less extensive than Charlemagne's, it proved more enduring and it played a more important role in European affairs. Its long and tortuous history only came to an end in 1806 at the hands of Napoleon. Finally, when Otto arranged that his son should gain the hand of Theophano, a Byzantine princess, he was able to leave to young Otto the prospect of rounding out his Italian possessions to the south.

Otto II and Otto III. Otto II (973-983) found it impossible to make good his claims to the southern Italian duchies. His one enduring act was that of severing from Bavaria what became the East March or Austria, in order to weaken that duchy. His son Otto III (983-1002) proved an unusual, but not an able monarch. He was elected king despite his tender age of three years. Such an unprecedented event in the history of elective monarchs must be attributed to the attachment of the German hierarchy to the crown. Otto was reared by his Byzantine mother in the Byzantine manner. From her he must have conceived the idea of building a palace in Rome, there to cooperate with the pope in bringing Charlemagne's vision of the "City of God" to fruition. To assure himself of that cooperation, he placed his tutor, Gerbert, the most learned man in the west, on the papal throne as Sylvester II. Otto lived out his short life of twenty-two years in Italy. A chronicler says he had Charlemagne's tomb opened in the year 1000 and took a ring off the dead monarch's finger to wear on his own. Contemporaries may have referred to him as the "Wonder of the World," but his reign was disastrous for the German monarchy. The Slavs recovered much of the territory taken from them by Otto's Saxon predecessors, while the German dukes recovered the powers that these kings had also wrested from them.

Henry III. Otto's successor, Henry II (1002-1024), earned his title "Saint" chiefly for the sincere interest he took in church reform. He repaired in part the effects of the negligence of Otto III by defeating the Poles and forcing them to accept his overlordship. When Henry died, so did the Saxon dynasty on the male side. The electors chose Conrad, duke of Franconia, whose dynasty, the Salian or Franconian, lasted a century (1024-1125). Both Conrad II (1024-1039) and his son Henry III (1039-1056) pursued vigorous policies in both Italy and Germany. Some scholars are tempted to designate Henry III as the German monarch who enjoyed the greatest amount of imperial power in the Middle Ages. They point to his suzerainty over Poland, Bohemia, and Hungary, to the relative peace of Germany during his reign, and to his ability to appoint three popes, the last the great reforming Leo IX. The genuineness of Henry's success, however, does not pass too close a scrutiny. He did not rule in Poland, Bohemia, and Hungary. He reigned there as he did in most of his empire except in those parts of Franconia and Saxony nearest the royal castles. While he was able to place his men in the papacy, these men did more for the church than for Germany. Three years after Henry's death, the Papal Electoral Law of 1059 formally excluded the voice of the German king in papal elections. (See page 513.) Henry's power was based upon the support of the German church and the personal loyalty of his nobles, both exceedingly tenuous bases as his son Henry IV was soon to discover. What the king most needed was an imperial bureaucracy. Since 911 when Conrad I had assumed the crown, nothing which proved of a permanent nature had been accomplished toward that end.

Henry IV. The inherent weakness of the German monarchy came to the surface during the minority of Henry IV (1056-1106). Since Henry was but a boy of six when his father died, the great nobles did as they chose. Their only concern was their own aggrandizement at the expense of royal rights and properties. Henry was reared in an atmosphere of deceit, unscrupulousness, and power politics. When he grew up, his early training left him with only ambition, not principles or ideals. The painful experiences of his minority convinced him of the inherent weakness of the German monarchy. So when he took over at the age of eighteen, he set as his immediate goals the building up of a compact domain which would furnish him a steady flow of revenue and troops, and the creation of a royal bureaucracy which would do his bidding. He began to acquire additional crown lands in southern Saxony and to erect castles there to protect them. For a bureaucracy he made increasing use of *ministeriales* who were members of the servile class whom several of his predecessors had employed on occasion in administrative work. What Henry found appealing about these *ministeriales* was the fact that their careers depended upon royal favor, which they could only keep and advance as long as they were loyal and efficient. They promised to prove far more dependable than the powerful German ecclesiastical princes. But Henry, who had a clearer concept of what the German monarchy needed than any of his predecessors, moved too fast and too aggressively. The German princes, as we shall see (page 514), threw their support to the pope in the bitter contest over investiture, because they had a very real fear that Henry would accomplish his end and force their subordination to the crown. Henry might gain the upper hand momentarily in the civil war that raged in Germany, but in the end his own son joined the princes and forced him to abdicate.

Guelfs and Ghibellines. Though the despicable son, Henry V (1106-1125), adopted the policies of his father, they proved no more successful in the end. The principal event of his reign was not of his doing. This was the Concordat of Worms of 1122, which affected a compromise in the investiture conflict between church and state in Germany. (See page 515.) When Henry died without a male heir, the German princes chose Lothair, duke of Saxony, precipitating a civil war with the Hohenstaufen duke of Swabia who was the nearest of kin. The adherents of the Swabian dukes came to be known as Ghibellines, from the Italian name of their favorite castle in Swabia. Their opponents took the name Guelfs, from Welf, the family name of the duke of Bavaria who was Lothair's son-in-law. In time the Guelfs were identified as the champions of the feudal aristocracy and of decentralization, against the Ghibellines who posed as advocates of imperialism and royal centralization. Because of the aggressive policies the Ghibellines pursued in Italy, they enjoyed the traditional enmity of the papacy. A later German Hohenstaufen emperor, Frederick II, when informed that a friendly cardinal had been elected pope, is said to have exclaimed: "No pope can be a Ghibelline."

Frederick Barbarossa: The Man. When Lothair died, most of the princes gave their vote to Conrad of Swabia even though he was a Hohenstaufen, since the Guelf candidate, Henry the Lion, duke of Bavaria and Saxony, was the more formidable of the two. Civil war raged, however, until Conrad's death and the election of his nephew, Frederick. Since Frederick's father was a Hohenstaufen and his mother a Guelf, his candidacy was acceptable to both factions. Actually Frederick's choice was almost unanimous, so distinguished was his fame throughout Germany. Frederick Barbarossa (1152-1190), as the Italians called him because of his reddish beard, was one of the most powerful characters of the Middle Ages and the greatest German monarch of the medieval period (after Charlemagne, whom the French also claim). He was ambitious and energetic, at the same time shrewd and prudent, and seldom caught in endeavors which were beyond his means. One mistake many historians feel he did make: he sought to emulate the seemingly glorious career of Otto the Great, only to fail as had Otto in seeking to rule both Germany and Italy. Yet no one could have accomplished more in Germany and Italy toward strengthening the imperial position under the circumstances. His manly bearing and powerful physique, together with the courage he displayed on the battlefield and as a Crusader (Second), established him in the eyes of sympathetic contemporaries as the embodiment of the knightly ideal. To many Italians, however, who knew him as a harsh, if not brutal, conqueror, he appeared as something less. When Frederick died on the Third Crusade, an old man of sixty-eight, he was respected and feared in both Christendom and Islam. (For his part in the Third Crusade, see page 408.) His statue was erected by German nationalists of the nineteenth century as representing the most likely of all German medieval monarchs to arouse the latent nationalism of their people.

Frederick and Germany. Frederick began his reign on a conciliatory note. He permitted Henry the Lion of Saxony who was the leader of the Guelfs, to take over Bavaria, and thereby assured Germany greater peace than that country had enjoyed for generations. More direct measures which he took to reduce turbulency, such as proclamations banning warfare and penalizing those breaking the peace, proved ineffectual. In general, he left the German princes undisturbed in their territories, although he insisted upon a careful collection of all feudal dues and demanded recognition of feudal services owing the crown. Over the German episcopacy he exercised a control reminiscent of the days before the Concordat of Worms, and he assured himself of the support of the Rhineland cities by granting them commercial concessions and protection. Like his predecessors, he appreciated the real and potential value of *ministeriales* as loyal agents of royal power, and employed them wherever possible. The actual bases of his power were the imperial domains in Swabia and along the Rhine, which he sought by every means to enlarge and consolidate. Because of his marriage to a Burgundian heiress, he had as great power in that southwestern kingdom as any medieval German monarch enjoyed. Frederick encouraged the introduction of feudal practices into Germany because of his conviction that feudalism, when carefully directed as by his contemporary Henry II of England, held greater promise for the growth of royal power than did the ill-defined position of the German king. Two factors, however, largely neutralized the effectiveness of his measures: first, the fact that his own princes were aping his measures in consolidating their regimes; second, the fact that the German princes were strong enough to force him to give out again fiefs which he had acquired. In contrast to the French king, therefore, the destruction of a disloyal vassal did not mean for Frederick the absorption of his fief, but its bestowal upon another—whose loyalty might prove no more dependable. When Henry the Lion ignored his summons in 1179 to submit answers to the grievances of his neighbors and also to Frederick's that he had not appeared at Legnano with his army, Frederick defeated him and deprived him of Bavaria and Saxony. Yet while he broke up the two duchies he could not keep them for himself, but had to give them out again to new vassals. Had he been able to retain them, the history of Germany might have followed the pattern of France.

Frederick, Italy, and the Papacy. Two years after his accession (1154), Frederick was on his way to Italy. That he spent as much thought and energy during the next twenty-five years on establishing his rule south of the Alps as in Germany, makes it evident that his goal was not so much to rule Germany as to rule the Holy Roman Empire. Of course, his plans for Germany would require time before they bore fruit, while an Italian venture might bring immediate results. On this first trip Frederick learned more than he accomplished. He learned how wealthy were the north Italian cities and, what was equally pleasing to him, how divided they were, both internally and among themselves. He did cooperate with Pope Adrian IV in destroying Arnold of Brescia who had made himself virtual dictator of Rome as head of a communal revolution. The emergence of communal governments in many cities of central and north Italy at this time urged, in fact, an alliance between pope and emperor, since the communes had taken over largely from lords who had been friendly either to pope or emperor. Yet while Adrian and Frederick might agree in opposing the rise of these communes, this is as far as their goals conformed. Each recognized in the other his principal adversary. If Adrian found the anticlerical communes distasteful, he feared Frederick as a positive menace. Frederick for his part quickly saw that Adrian was as shrewd as he was courageous, and that he would bitterly oppose any increase of imperial power in central Italy. (Reading 123)

Battle of Legnano.   Frederick forced the issue in 1158 when he crossed the Alps with a powerful army in order to establish his claims in Italy. These he formally proclaimed at the diet of Roncaglia, where he was attended by lawyers schooled in the imperial traditions of Roman jurisprudence. He announced that he would not be content with reigning as imperial suzerain; he must be accorded regalian rights, that is, the right to levy tolls and customs, to control coinage, and to appoint the chief official, the *podesta,* of the cities. Italy's answer was a general insurrection headed by Milan. A siege of three years reduced Milan to starvation, whereupon the city surrendered and was razed. Milan's fate left Italy quiet for the moment but not resigned. Under the inspiration of the new pope Alexander III (Frederick supported an antipope), the cities of north Italy buried their long-standing animosities, organized the Lombard League, and erected a mighty fortress in northern Italy, named Alessandria after Pope Alexander, to block Frederick's inevitable return from Germany. This the fortress and the Lombard League succeeded in doing, and in 1176 dealt Frederick such a disastrous defeat at Legnano that he gave up the battle for Italy. By making separate settlements with the pope and the Lombard cities, however, he did manage to salvage something more for himself than an empty title. In 1183, with the Peace of Constance, he surrendered all claims to appointing *podestas* and collecting taxes in north Italy, in return for a large annual payment from each city and recognition of his imperial title.

Success or Failure?   Six years later fortune bestowed upon Frederick at one stroke almost as great a victory in southern Italy as he had lost in the north. To the consternation of most Italian princes and the pope, William II, king of Sicily, died in 1189 at the age of thirty-four and childless, leaving his kingdom to his niece Constance, the wife of Frederick's son, Henry. Thus when Frederick set out on his last campaign, the Third Crusade, his once valiant opponent in Germany, Henry the Lion, was but a petty nobleman, while his son Henry was about to become king of all Italy. Modern historians may picture Frederick as a failure; his contemporaries thought quite differently.

Henry VI (1190-1197). When Frederick's son Henry succeeded to the throne in 1190, his empire stretched from the Baltic to the Mediterranean and included the whole of Germany and all of Italy. Henry had to fight for his dowry which he did successfully, against a powerful coalition that included the pope, the cities of northern Italy, the Norman lords of the south, and the rebellious Guelf lords in Germany. In his schemes and campaigns, he put to good use the huge ransom he extracted from England for the release of Richard the Crusader who had fallen into his hands. Good fortune appeared to smile on any project Henry undertook; nothing seemed to be beyond the capabilities of this cold, calculating monarch. Some historians believe he contemplated as his next goal, now that Germany and Italy were firmly in his grasp, the addition of the Byzantine Empire. Whatever Henry's ultimate objectives, all of his luck ran out abruptly in 1197 when he died at the premature age of thirty-two.

The Emergence of Frederick II. Eighteen years of dispute and civil war followed Henry's death. The choice of the Guelf faction was Otto, son of Henry the Lion and brother-in-law of King John of England. The Hohenstaufens supported the ambitions of Henry VI's brother Philip, since Henry's son Frederick was but an infant. On the basis of past Guelf opposition to the imperialistic designs of the Hohenstaufens, Pope Innocent III quite logically preferred Otto and so let it be known. However, the German princes gradually swung around to Philip, who would most certainly have succeeded to the throne had he not been assassinated in 1208. This cleared the way for Otto who was promptly crowned and who just as promptly over-reached himself. As if to prove that, given the opportunity, Ghibelline and Guelf would react in similar fashion, no sooner was he ensconced on the imperial throne than he laid claim to papal territories which he had previously recognized as unalterably papal and prepared to conquer Sicily. Innocent thereupon repudiated him and endorsed with some misgiving the aspirations of Henry VI's son Frederick. Now a boy in his late teens, Frederick had been reared as a ward of the papacy inasmuch as Sicily, of which he was heir, was a papal fief. Before consenting to his candidacy, Innocent elicited from his youthful ward a sacred promise to respect all papal rights in his territories, not to rule over both southern Italy and the Empire, and to go on a Crusade. Since several German princes had meantime turned against Otto, and since Philip Augustus of France was urging the selection of someone more acceptable than the brother-in-law of the English king, Otto's game was up. His fate was finally and decisively decided on the battlefield of Bouvines.

Frederick's Character. Frederick II (1215-1250) was probably the most talented, surely the most interesting, monarch to sit on any throne in the

Middle Ages. And he also remains one of the most controversial. Rare indeed was the medieval scribe who wrote with an unprejudiced pen, and equally rare was the king, ecclesiastic, or prince, who did not exhaust his vocabulary of all its odious terms in referring to the villainies of his adversary. (Readings 124, 125) His contemporaries who did not like him called Frederick a heretic, a constitutional perjurer, even "the baptized Sultan." Arabs he did have among his counselors and Saracen troops in his army; he kept a harem guarded by black eunuchs and regaled himself and his court with dancing girls from Egypt. The menagerie, too, which followed him on his travels was largely gathered from or beyond the Islamic world: a lion, leopard, elephant, apes, peacocks, dromedaries, and several animals such as a giraffe which were the gifts of the sultan of Egypt. A contemporary chronicler hailed him, partly from wonderment, partly from consternation, the "amazement of the world" (*stupor mundi*), less to be sure because of Frederick's exotic tastes and the vagaries of his private life than for his extraordinary talents and his enormous store of knowledge. The pages of history reveal no more versatile monarch. Frederick proved himself an able general and an even greater administrator. He knew six—or was it nine—languages, composed poetry which drew Dante's attention and surrounded himself with scholars and scientists with whom he conversed as an equal. He could ride and fence with skill, produced the most authoritative book ever written on the subject of falconry, and even found time to devote to the study of agriculture and stock-breeding.

Frederick's life, unfortunately, had a dark side, that is, over and above the emperor's harem which outraged western sensibilities. Mistresses kept somewhat in the background were one thing; quite another was the flaunting of an institution tolerable only in the polygamous east. Frederick's private morals even apart from his harem were dissolute, and his treatment of his first three wives was hardly better than cruel. Cruelty, indeed, seemed inherent in Frederick's nature. In the Inferno, Dante has his Hypocrites walking about in gilded copes lined with lead "so heavy that Frederick's cloaks by contrast would seem light as straw." The reference was to Frederick's practice of having traitors wrapped in lead cloaks which were then melted over a fire. Frederick's arrogance, too, was excessive, but it was his cynicism, his skepticism, even agnosticism, which most disturbed his age. Pope Gregory IX warned Christian Europe, "In truth this pestilential king maintains, to use his own words, that the world has been deceived by three imposters, Jesus Christ, Moses, and Mohammed: two of these died in honor, the third was hanged on a tree." That Frederick ever made this statement is doubtful, but that many of his contemporaries could have believed that he did was condemnation enough. (Reading 153)

Frederick and the Papacy. If Pope Gregory was disposed to believe that Frederick had made the statement about the three impostors, no one could blame him. He had good reason to believe the worst of the emperor. For ever since the death of Pope Innocent III (1216), Frederick had been a thorn in the side of the papacy. Innocent died too soon after Frederick's accession to have prevailed upon him to fulfill his promise to go on a Crusade. His successor, Honorius III (1216-1227), although quite as anxious for a Crusade as Innocent, was an old, kindly man and inclined to accept the good faith of anyone, even of a person as dangerous as Frederick. Understandably, all he got from Frederick for his anxieties and prayers were excuses and new promises. He waited and watched as the emperor used the valuable years he should have spent cooperating with other Crusaders, strengthening instead his position in Italy. "What ships, dearest son, what galleys have you made ready?" queried the patient Honorius. When Honorius died and was replaced with Gregory IX (1227-1241), the tone of papal importuning assumed a sharper note. "For five years men have been expecting your Crusade," Gregory warned Frederick. "We will spare you no longer. If you still neglect your duty, we will excommunicate you in the face of the Christian world."

Gregory was clearly no long-suffering Honorius. Quite the reverse. Like his uncle, Innocent III, he confronted opponents with courage and persistence. His choice of names suggests, too, that he was expecting trouble and that he anticipated as bitter a contest with Frederick as Gregory VII had fought with Henry IV over the rights of the church. For only one conclusion could be drawn from Frederick's actions during the ten years of Honorius' pontificate, and that was that the emperor had every intention of retaining both the empire and Sicily for himself despite his pledge to the contrary. Thus the Papal States were caught in a vise, between the jaws of Frederick's domains to the north and to the south. The emperor's principles, ambitions, and resources being what they were, Pope Gregory fully appreciated the gravity of the situation for his state and for the independence of the church. Frederick must be made to take up the cross —as much to get him out of Italy as to recover Jerusalem itself.

Frederick's Crusade. Actually by 1227 when he was satisfied, at least for the moment, with his position in Italy and Germany, Frederick was quite ready to go on a Crusade. Not from any religious motivation, of course; that would have been entirely out of character. He would go to Jerusalem to take over his latest kingdom. In 1225 Pope Honorius had arranged Frederick's marriage to Yolanda, the heiress of the kingdom of Jerusalem, in order to provide the emperor additional incentive for taking up the cross. Therefore, to Jerusalem Frederick was willing to go, although he would choose his own time for going, and he would also choose his own method for securing Jerusalem. For driving the Turks out of the city he had no stomach; he hoped rather to obtain the cession of the holy places through negotiation, and such negotiations might take time. However, he assured the exasperated Gregory that he would leave that year (1227), and he did indeed sail from Brindisi in September. But cholera struck his fleet three days out and Frederick himself fell ill, so he put back to port and disbanded the expedition. The furious Gregory promptly excommunicated Frederick since he had no reason to believe that the emperor's latest excuse for not going was any more genuine than the score of earlier ones which had been false.

Papal excommunication in the Middle Ages could be quite effective when leveled at men in the humbler walks of life. Against kings, however, especially kings like Frederick who punished anyone daring to respect such censures, it frequently proved no more than a nuisance. This excommunication by Gregory, and several subsequent ones, occasioned Frederick some annoyance, particularly later in Jerusalem where he had to crown himself when no prelate would oblige, but it did not deter him from proceeding with his Crusade now that he had set his mind on going. So in defiance of papal anathemas and under the ban of the church, he sailed in June, 1228, and some months later secured from the sultan of Egypt by the treaty of Jaffa possession of Jerusalem, Bethlehem, and Nazareth. Meantime Pope Gregory had sent papal troops into Frederick's southern kingdom and called upon Europe's kings for aid. Though the papal armies were initially successful, once Frederick returned from the east the situation was rapidly reversed. In July, 1239, pope and emperor saw fit to patch up their differences.

Frederick and Germany. For a few years, relations between Pope Gregory and Frederick remained relatively friendly, but only for a few years. New difficulties appeared with Frederick's victories in Germany and north Italy. The trouble started with the revolt of the emperor's son, Henry, who had been placed in nominal control of Germany. It was not that Frederick wanted much from Germany. Actually royal power had declined so far during the troubled years of strife between Philip of Swabia and Otto (IV) when both had bartered crown lands and regalian rights for the support of German nobles, that there was no hope of retrieving the situation. Even the royal *ministeriales* were forgetting their humble origins and conducting themselves as hereditary vassals. Since Frederick found his imperial power in north Italy and Sicily also in jeopardy, he decided to concentrate on establishing his power there and be content in Germany with simple recognition of his authority. He was, furthermore, more of an Italian than a German, and the weather of Germany appalled him. To assure himself of the support of the German princes, both lay and ecclesiastical, he conceded on several occasions such privileges, the last in 1231, as to leave the more powerful lords practically independent. After 1231 Frederick never saw Germany.

Cortenuova. While Frederick did not hope to rule Germany, he could not tolerate the revolt of his son. The Lombard cities came to Henry's aid, but Frederick had little difficulty crushing the rebellion and imprisoning his son. Then he marched against these north Italian cities, the same cities which in 1176 had thwarted his grandfather, Frederick Barbarossa, in his attempt to subjugate them. Now it was a different story. In 1237, at Cortenuova, Frederick won a smashing victory over Milan and its allies, and they, rather than the imperial army, lay crushed. Caution and moderation might have given the emperor mastery of Italy; instead overweening pride and vindictiveness lost him his one and only opportunity. His harsh demand of unconditional surrender aroused new life in the hearts of the despairing cities. "We fear your cruelty," they told him, "which we have experienced; so we prefer to die under our shields by sword, spear, and dart, than by trickery, starvation, and fire."

Frederick and the Papacy Again. Frederick blamed Pope Gregory for inciting the Lombard cities against him, a charge the pope denied. Still after the emperor's victory at Cortenuova, Gregory felt he must throw in his lot openly with Frederick's enemies. For in his elation, Frederick was speaking of reviving the Roman Empire and of making Rome its capital. And he appeared to be moving toward that goal when he married his illegitimate son, Enzio, to the daughter of the ruler of Sardinia (a papal possession) and declared him king. In 1239 Gregory excommunicated the emperor once again, and persuaded Venice and Genoa to join forces with the Lombard cities. Then in order to broaden the campaign against Frederick by enlisting the assistance of Europe, he summoned the prelates of Christendom to meet in Rome at Easter in 1241. The unofficial purpose for convening the council was to depose Frederick, of which fact the emperor was fully aware. So he issued a warning to the princes and prelates of the west that he would not permit the council to assemble, a threat he made good. Some one hundred church dignitaries, including three cardinals, fell into his hands when he intercepted a papal convoy on its way from Genoa to Rome. The emperor hurried the prelates off to filthy prisons in Pisa.

Frederick's sacrilegious audacity in thus capturing a church council horrified all Europe. Pope Gregory never recovered from the shock and died a few months later (aged 98). Louis IX of France shared the general horror at Frederick's action, although the only action he took was to protest against the imprisonment of French prelates. These Frederick released in time and then the others, in order to gain some good will with the cardinals gathered in conclave to select a new pope. (Celestine IV had been elected immediately after Gregory's death, but had died within three weeks.) The cardinals did actually choose a prelate who at one time had been counted a friend of Frederick's, a Genoese bishop who took the name of Innocent IV. Though Frederick was gratified over Innocent's election, he could have entertained no real hope that papal policy would abruptly shift in his favor. When it became evident that Innocent would continue Gregory's anti-imperial policy unaltered, the emperor is said to have observed: "No pope can be a Ghibelline." So the war between Frederick and the papacy and the papacy's allies in north Italy continued on, more bitter than before. Fortune now smiled on Frederick, now on his foes, until his death from dysentery in December, 1250.

Frederick and Sicily. While Frederick's turbulent career closed on this futile note, a truer picture of the man's capabilities comes out of Sicily. That was the country Frederick loved, and he loved not only its climate and scenery, but its political organization as well and his own autocratic position there. He ruled, not just reigned in southern Italy and Sicily, an area which historians have styled "the first modern state." For the origins of this remarkable state we must go back to the Norman knights who happened to pass through the country in the early eleventh century on their way home from the Holy Land, and who stayed on for the promise the region offered. At first they were content to take service as mercenary soldiers. The unsettled condition of the land, however, made it inevitable that men as ambitious and aggressive as the Normans should eventually take over the country. This the sons of Tancred of Hauteville accomplished, notably Robert Guiscard and Roger who conquered southern Italy and Sicily respectively from their Byzantine, Saracen, papal, and feudal lords. Roger and his son Roger II laid the foundations of this "modern" state. When most rulers of western Europe had peripatetic capitals, they ruled from Palermo, one of the most beautiful, cultured, commercially active, and largest cities of the west. When contemporary lords depended on unreliable feudal levies for troops and upon the inadequate income of their own estates for their financial resources, these Norman rulers drew upon a rich flow of revenue from tariffs and taxes to hire a powerful army of mercenaries. They even owned outright silk, iron, salt, tar, and hemp industries. In place of the traditional officialdom drawn from an independently minded aristocracy, they maintained a most efficient bureaucracy which they recruited where they could find the best talent, whether Greek, Moslem, Latin, or native. A Thomas Brown headed the exchequer. They experienced no difficulties with the church, since as permanent papal legates they controlled it. Frederick's own contribution was that of systematizing the practices and precedents of his predecessors and of establishing what in its day was the most centralized and bureaucratic secular government in Europe. The Constitutions of Melfi which he issued in 1231 and which incorporated his legal and administrative enactments, has been called the most constructive piece of statecraft in the Middle Ages. Frederick also issued the first gold coin in the west (1231) and was the first ruler to invite members of the bourgeoisie to serve as royal councilors.

The German Monarchy in 1250. Frederick's death marked the virtual end of the house of Hohenstaufen and of German rule in Italy. His son Conrad IV reigned for four years and then Frederick's natural son

Manfred succeeded him. But the pope's fear and hatred of the family proved implacable. In response to a papal appeal, Charles, count of Anjou and brother of Louis IX, invaded Sicily in 1266. Manfred fell in battle, Conradin, son of Conrad IV, was hunted down and executed. Yet though the papacy won its contest with the Hohenstaufens, the cost of papal victory came high. The constant employment of ecclesiastical censures against Frederick sadly lowered papal prestige, since most of Europe, including St. Louis, felt these spiritual weapons had been used in a political, if not personal, struggle. And in the end, the pope learned that the French in southern Italy showed no more respect for papal rights than had the Germans. Germany also suffered grievously. When Frederick II surrendered his imperial rights to the feudal aristocracy, he destroyed the last faint hope for German centralization in the medieval period. Had Frederick and his predecessors allied themselves with the rising towns of Germany and encouraged industry as did Henry the Lion, the history of the German monarchy might have reflected something of the growth of those in England and France. Where those countries by 1250 had advanced far along the road toward bureaucratic centralization, the German monarchy was even worse off than in 911. It was beyond repair. Small but vigorous states such as Brandenburg, Bavaria, Saxony, and Austria, had grown sufficiently strong to block any future attempts at centralization. It was with these states rather than with the German monarchy that the future of Germany lay.

⬢ READINGS ⬢

No. 113. How Louis VI, with aid of Suger, asserted the authority of the crown

(Robinson's *Readings*, pp. 199-200.)

The young hero, Prince Louis, gay, gracious, and so friendly to all that he passed with some for a person of no force, had hardly come to man's estate when he proved himself an illustrious and courageous defender of his father's realm. He provided for the needs of the Church, and strove to secure peace for those who pray, for those who work, and for the poor. And no one had done this for a long time.

Now it came to pass at this time that certain disputes arose between Adam, the venerable abbot of St. Denis, and a nobleman, Burchard, lord of Montmorency [his vassal], concerning certain customs. The controversy waxed so hot and reached such extremes of irritation that all ties of homage were broken between vassal and lord, and the two disputants betook themselves to arms, war, and fire.

When the affair came to the ears of Lord Louis he was sorely vexed. He delayed not, but ordered the aforesaid Burchard, duly summoned, to appear before his father in the castle of Poissy for judgment. Burchard lost his cause, but refused to submit to the judgment. He was not taken prisoner, for that is not the custom of the French, but having withdrawn to his estates, he straightway learned what manner of injury and calamity the king's majesty can inflict on his disobedient subjects. For this famous youth [Prince Louis] carried arms thither against him and his criminal allies, Matthew, count of Beaumont, and Dreux of Mouchy-le-châtel, vigorous and warlike men. He laid waste the land of Burchard with fire, famine, and the sword; and overthrew all the defenses and buildings, except the castle itself, and razed them to the ground. When his enemies undertook to defend themselves in the castle he besieged them with the French and the Flemish troops of his uncle Robert, as well as with his own. By these and other means he brought the humiliated Burchard to repentance, bent him to his will and pleasure, and satisfactorily adjusted the dispute which had given rise to the trouble.

Matthew, count of Beaumont, had long cherished hatred against Hugh of Clermont, whose daughter he had married. This Hugh was a noble man, but simple and easy to lead. His son-in-law laid hold upon a castle called Luzarches (a share in which was his by right of marriage), and took it altogether, and left nothing undone in strengthening the tower with arms and soldiers.

What could Hugh do but hasten to the defender of the kingdom, throw himself at his feet, and beg him with tears to have compassion on an old man and succor him, for he was grievously oppressed. "I would rather, O dearest Lord," he said, "that thou shouldst have all my land, because I hold it of thee, than that my unnatural son-in-law should have it. If he robs me of it, I wish to die." His sad misfortune smote the king to the heart. He gave the old man his hand in friendly wise and promised to aid him, and so he sent him forth gladdened by hope. And his hope was not vain. For straightway messengers went forth from the court, who sought the count and commanded him, by authority of Hugh's defender, to restore to Hugh the estate of which he had been illegally despoiled; and they summoned him to appear at the court, upon a day appointed, to defend his cause.

The count did not obey this summons, so the defender made haste to execute vengeance. He gathered a great army and went forth against the rebel. He fell upon the castle and attacked it with arms and fire. By hard fighting he stormed and took it; he then placed a strong guard in the keep, and after he had fortified it he restored it to Hugh just as he had promised to do. . . .

A king, when he takes the royal power, vows to put down with his strong right arm insolent tyrants whensoever he sees them vex the state with endless wars, rejoice in rapine, oppress the poor, destroy the churches, give themselves over to the lawlessness which, and it be not checked, would flame out into ever greater madness; for the evil spirits who instigate them are wont cruelly to strike down those whom they fear to lose, but give free rein to those whom they hope to hold, while they add fuel to the flames which are to devour their victims to all eternity.

Such an utterly abandoned man was Thomas of Marle. While King Louis was busied with many wars, he laid waste the territories of Laon, Rheims, and Amiens, devouring like a raging wolf. He spared not the clergy—fearing not the vengeance of the Church—nor the people for humanity's sake. And the devil aided him, for the success of the foolish does ever lead them to perdition. Slaying all men, spoiling all things, he seized two manors, exceeding rich, from the abbey of the nuns of St. John of Laon. He fortified the two exceeding strong castles, Crécy and Nogent, with a marvelous wall and very high towers, as if they had been his own; and made them like to a den of dragons and a cave of robbers, whence he did waste almost the whole country with fire and pillage; and he had no pity. . . .

And the king was moved by the plaints . . . and led an army against him right quickly. He had the clergy, to whom he was ever humbly devoted, in his company, and marched straight against the castle of Crécy. Well fortified was it; yet he took it unprepared because his soldiers smote with an exceeding strong hand; or rather, because the hand of the Lord fought for him. He stormed the strongest tower as if it were the hut of a peasant, and put to confusion the wicked men and piously destroyed the impious. Because they had no pity upon other men, he cut them down without mercy. None could behold the castle tower flaming like the fires of hell and not exclaim, "The whole universe will fight for him against these madmen."

After he had won this victory, the king, who was ever swift to follow up his advantage, pushed forward toward the other castle, called Nogent. . . . When he had taken it he destroyed it utterly, and thus brought peace to the realm. He fulfilled most worthily the duty of a king who beareth not the sword in vain, and he deprived the wicked Thomas and his heirs forever of the lordship over that city. . . .

King Louis spent freely both of money and the sweat of his brow to relieve the sufferings and oppressions of many. He was used to make many such expeditions throughout the country for the relief of churches and of the poor, but we must pass over these, as it would but weary the reader to narrate them. . . .

No. 114. Philip Augustus seizes Normandy

(From Rigord's account. Robinson's *Readings*, pp. 209-212.)

The king of the French summoned John, king of England, as his liegeman, holding from him the counties of Poitou and Anjou and the duchy of Aquitaine, to come two weeks after Easter to Paris to give a satisfactory answer to the charges which Philip made against him. But since the king of England, instead of coming in person on the day indicated, did not even send a satisfactory reply, the king of the French, with the advice of his princes and barons, assembled an army, entered Normandy, and took the little fort of Boutavant, which he destroyed. Orgueil, Mortemer, and all the land which Hugh of Gournay held soon fell into his power. At Gournay he made Arthur [John's brother] a knight and delivered to him the county of Brittany, which had fallen to him by hereditary right. He even added the counties of Anjou and of Poitou, which he had acquired by right of arms. Lastly, he gave him the support of two hundred knights, with a considerable sum of money. Then the king received Arthur as his liegeman. The latter, with the king's permission, left him in July.

A few days later Arthur rashly advanced with a small troop of men into the territory of the king of England, who suddenly came upon him with a vast multitude of armed men, defeated him, and carried him away prisoner with Hugh le Brun, Geoffrey of Lusignan, and several other knights. King Philip, having learned this news, immediately abandoned the siege of the castle of Arques and appeared with his army before Tours, took the town, and set fire to it. The king of England, on his side, arrived, at the head of his troops, after the departure of the king of France and destroyed the same city with its castle.

A few days after, the king of England took the viscount of Limoges and carried him off with him. Although Hugh le Brun, viscount of Thouars, Geoffrey of Lusignan, and the viscount of Limoges were all liegemen of the king of England, nevertheless they allied themselves with the king of the French, both by oath and through hostages. For King John had perfidiously carried off the wife of Hugh le Brun, daughter of the count of Angouleme, and this outrage, added to other grievances of the same lords of Poitou, alienated their fidelity to King John. The following winter the two kings discontinued their war after having guarded their fortress, without, however, concluding either peace or a truce. . . .

The last day of the same month the king of France assembled an army and besieged Rodepont. In about a fortnight, having raised about the place his movable wooden towers and set up his other machines of war, he took the town. He secured as prisoners twenty knights who had bravely defended themselves, a hundred squires, and thirty crossbowmen.

When he had recovered his strength and that of his army he laid siege to Castle Gaillard, in the month of September following. This was a strong fortress which King Richard had constructed upon a high rock which dominated the Seine near the island of Andelys. The king of the French and his army were delayed by the siege of this place for five months, for they were unwilling to undertake an assault lest much blood should be spilled and they might damage the walls and the tower. They hoped to force the besieged to surrender through hunger and deprivation. [Later the king decided upon an attack and successfully took the fortress by assault.] . . .

In the year of our Lord 1203, Philip, king of the French, having assembled his army, entered Normandy on the 2d of May, took Falaise, a very strong castle, Domfront, and a very rich town which the people call Caen. He also brought under his control all the neighboring districts as far as Mont St. Michel. The Normans then came to ask for mercy and delivered up the towns which had been confided to their protection,—Coutances, Bayeux, Lisieux, and Avranches, with their castles and suburbs. As for Evraux and Séez, he already had them in his power. Of all Normandy there only remained Rouen,—a very rich town, full of noble men, the capital of all Normandy,—and Verneuil and Arques, strong towns well situated and well defended. Returning from Caen, the king, having left garrisons in the various cities and castles, laid siege to Rouen.

The Normans, seeing that they could not defend themselves, nor could expect any aid from the king of England, began to think of surrender; nevertheless they judiciously took precautions in order to remain faithful to the king of England. They humbly asked the king of the French to grant a truce of thirty days, which should close at the feast of St. John, for their own city [Rouen] and for Verneuil and Arques, which were in league with Rouen. In this interval they might be able to send to the king of England and ask for aid in so pressing a danger. If he should refuse, the Normans agreed to place their goods and persons, the city and the said castles, in the hands of the victorious Philip, king of the French, and to give as hostages sixty sons of the burghers of Rouen.

At the feast of St. John, the burghers, having received no aid from the king of England, fulfilled their promise and delivered to the king of the French their city of Rouen, a rich town, the capital of all Normandy, with

the two castles of which we have spoken above. Three hundred and sixteen years had elapsed since this city and all Normandy had ceased to
belong to the kings of France. The Northman Rollo, who had come with
his pagan followers, had taken it by right of arms in the time of Charles
the Simple.

No. 115. St. Louis

(*The Memoirs of the Lord of Joinville,* tr. Ethel Wedgwood. London,
1906.)

In the name of Almighty God, I, John, Lord of Joinville, Seneschal of
Champagne, do cause to be written the life of our Saint Louis, that which
I saw and heard during the space of six years that I was in his company on
the pilgrimage over seas and after we returned. And before I tell you of his
great deeds and knightliness, I will tell you what I saw and heard of his
holy words and good teachings, so that they may be found in sequence, to
the edification of those that shall hear them.

The love he bore his people—appeared in what he said to his son during
a sore sickness he had at Fountainebleau;—"Fair son," quoth he, "I pray
thee, win the love of the people of thy kingdom. For truly, I would rather
that a Scot should come out of Scotland and rule the people of the kingdom
well and justly, than that thou shouldst govern them ill-advisedly."

The holy man so loved truth that he would not play even the Saracens
false, as hereafter you shall hear.

Touching his mouth he was sober, for never in my life did I hear him
discourse of dishes, as many rich men do; but contentedly he ate whatever
his cooks set before him. In words he was temperate, for never did I hear
him speak ill of others, nor ever hear him name the Devil; the which is not
common throughout the kingdom, and thereat, I trow, God is ill pleased.
His wine he tempered moderately, according as he saw that the wine could
bear it. He asked me in Cyprus: why I put no water to my wine? and I
told him; it was the physicians' doing, who told me, that I had a thick
head and a cold belly, and that it was not in me to get drunk. And he
said: They deceived me; for unless I used myself whilst young to drink it
watered, if, when old, I desired to do so, I should be seized with gouts and
stomach complaints and never have my health: whereas, if in old age I
were to take my wine neat, I should be drunk every evening, and that it
was a passing foul thing for a gallant gentleman to get drunk. (Pp. 9-10)

He asked me: Whether I washed the feet of the poor on Maundy Thursday? "Sorrow take it Sir!"—said I—"the feet of those wretches will I never

wash!" "Truly," quoth he, "that was ill said; for you should not despise that which God did for our instruction. Wherefore I pray you, for the love of God and of me, that henceforth you will accustom yourself to wash them." (p. 13)

Many a time it chanced in summer, that he would go and sit in the forest of Vincennes, after mass, and all who had business would come and talk with him, without hindrance from ushers or anyone. Then he would ask them with his own lips: "Is there anyone here, that has a suit?"—and those that had suits stood up. Then he would say:—"Keep silence, all of you; and you shall be dealt with in order." Then he would call up my lord Peter of Fontaines and my lord Geoffrey of Villette, and say to one of them: "Despatch me this suit!"—and if, in the speech of those who were speaking on behalf of others, he saw that a point might be better put, he himself would put it for them with his own lips. I have seen him sometimes in summer, when to hear his people's suits, he would come into the gardens of Paris, clad in a camel's-hair coat, with a sleeveless surcoat of tiretaine, a cloak of black taffety round his neck, his hair well combed and without a quoif, and a white swansdown hat upon his head. He would cause a carpet to be spread, that we might sit round him; and all the people who had business before him stood round about, and then he caused their suits to be despatched, just as I told you before about the forest of Vincennes. (pp. 21-22)

Before he went to bed, he used to send for his children, and would tell them stories of the deeds of good kings and emperors; and he used to tell them that they must take example by people such as these. He would tell them too, about the deeds of wicked rich men, who by their lechery and their rapine and their avarice, had lost their kingdoms. "And these things," he used to say, "I tell you as a warning to avoid them, lest you incur the anger of God."

He had them taught the Hours of Our Lady, and caused the Hours for the Day to be repeated to them, in order to give them the habit of hearing their Hours when they should come into their estates.

The King was so liberal an almsgiver, that wherever he went throughout his kingdom, he made gifts to poor churches, to lazar-houses, to almshouses, to asylums, and to poor gentlemen and gentlewomen.

From his childhood up, he was compassionate towards the poor and the suffering; and it was the custom that, wherever he went, six score poor should always be replenished in his house with bread and wine, and meat or fish every day. In Lent and Advent, the number was increased, and many a time the King would wait on them, and place their meat before them, and would carve their meat before them, and with his own hand would give them money when they went away. Likewise on the high vigils of solemn feasts, he would serve the poor with all these things, before he either ate or drank.

Besides all this, he had every day old broken-down men to dine and sup with him, and had them served with the same food that he himself was eating. And when they had feasted, they took away with them a certain sum of silver. . . .

Some of his kindred used to grumble at his liberal almsgiving, and because he spent so much on this kind of thing; but he used to say: "I would much rather be extravagant in alms, for the love of God, than in the pomp and vainglories of this world." (pp. 358-363)

No. 116. The Battle of Hastings

(From William of Malmesbury's *History of the English Kings*. Robinson's *Readings*, pp. 224-226.)

The courageous leaders mutually prepared for battle, each according to his national custom. The English, as we have heard, passed the night without sleep, in drinking and singing, and in the morning proceeded without delay against the enemy. All on foot, armed with battle-axes, and covering themselves in front by the juncture of their shields, they formed an impenetrable body which would assuredly have secured their safety that day had not the Normans, by a feigned flight, induced them to open their ranks, which till that time, according to their custom, had been closely compacted. King Harold himself, on foot, stood with his brothers near the standard in order that, so long as all shared equal danger, none could think of retreating. This same standard William sent, after his victory, to the pope; it was sumptuously embroidered with gold and precious stones, and represented a figure of a man fighting.

On the other hand, the Normans passed the whole night in confessing their sins, and received the communion of the Lord's body in the morning. Their infantry, with bows and arrows, formed the vanguard, while their cavalry, divided into wings, was placed in the rear. The duke, with serene countenance, declaring aloud that God would favor his as being the righteous side, called for his arms; and when, through the haste of his attendants, he had put on his hauberk the hind part before, he corrected the mistake with a laugh, saying, "The power of my dukedom shall be turned into a kingdom." Then starting the song of Roland, in order that the warlike example of that hero might stimulate the soldiers, and calling on God for assistance, the battle commenced on both sides, and was fought with great ardor, neither side giving ground during the greater part of the day.

Observing this, William gave a signal to his troops, that, feigning flight, they should withdraw from the field. By means of this device the solid phalanx of the English opened for the purpose of cutting down the fleeing enemy and thus brought upon itself swift destruction; for the Normans, facing about, attacked them, thus disordered, and compelled them to fly. In this manner, deceived by a stratagem, they met an honorable death in avenging their country; nor indeed were they at all without their own revenge, for, by frequently making a stand, they slaughtered their pursuers in heaps. Getting possession of an eminence, they drove back the Normans, who in the heat of pursuit were struggling up the slope, into the valley beneath, where, by hurling their javelins and rolling down stones on them as they stood below, the English easily destroyed them to a man. Besides, by a short passage with which they were acquainted, they avoided a deep ditch and trod underfoot such a multitude of their enemies in that place that the heaps of bodies made the hollow level with the plain. This alternating victory, first of one side and then of the other, continued so long as Harold lived to check the retreat; but when he fell, his brain pierced by an arrow, the flight of the English ceased not until night.

In the battle both leaders distinguished themselves by their bravery. Harold, not content with the functions of a general and with exhorting others, eagerly assumed himself the duties of a common soldier. He was constantly striking down the enemy at close quarters, so that no one could approach him with impunity, for straightway both horse and rider would be felled by a single blow. So it was at long range, as I have said, that the enemy's deadly arrow brought him to his death. One of the Norman soldiers gashed his thigh with a sword, as he lay prostrate; for which shameful and cowardly action he was branded with ignominy by William and expelled from the army.

William, too, was equally ready to encourage his soldiers by his voice and by his presence, and to be the first to rush forward to attack the thickest of the foe. He was everywhere fierce and furious; he lost three choice horses, which were that day killed under him. The dauntless spirit and vigor of the intrepid general, however, still held out. Though often called back by the kind remonstrance of his bodyguard, he still persisted until approaching night crowned him with complete victory. And no doubt the hand of God so protected him that the enemy should draw no blood from his person, though they aimed so many javelins at him.

No. 117. King William's Domesday Book

(Anglo-Saxon Chronicle, tr. J. A. Giles. London, 1890, pp. 458-459.)

At midwinter the king was at Gloucester with his witan; and he held his court there five days; and afterwards the archbishop and clergy held a synod during three days; and Maurice was there chose to the bishopric of London, William to that of Norfolk, and Robert to that of Cheshire; they were all clerks of the king. After this the king had a great consultation, and spoke very deeply with his witan concerning this land, how it was held and what were its tenantry. He then sent his men over all England, into every shire, and caused them to ascertain how many hundred hides of land it contained, and what lands the king possessed therein, what cattle there were in the several counties, and how much revenue he ought to receive yearly from each. He also caused them to write down how much land belonged to his archbishops, to his bishops, his abbots, and his earls, and, that I may be brief, what property every inhabitant of all England possessed in land or in cattle, and how much money this was worth. So very narrowly did he cause the survey to be made, that there was not a single hide nor a rood of land, nor—it is shameful to relate that which he thought no shame to do—was there an ox, or a cow, or a pig passed by, and that was not set down in the accounts, and then all these writings were brought to him.

No. 118. Constitutions of Clarendon

(Adams & Stephens, *Select Documents*, pp. 11-14.)

In the year 1164 from our Lord's Incarnation, the fourth of the pontificate of Alexander [III], the tenth of Henry II, most illustrious king of the English, in the presence of the same king, was made this remembrance or acknowledgment of a certain part of the customs, liberties, and dignities of his ancestors, that is of King Henry his grandfather, and of others, which ought to be observed and held in the realm. And owing to strifes and dissensions which had taken place between the clergy and justices of the lord the king and the barons of the realm, in respect of customs and dignities of the realm, this recognition was made before the archbishops and bishops and clergy, and the earls and barons and nobles of the realm. . . .

Now of the acknowledged customs and dignities, of the realm a certain part is contained in the present document, of which part these are the chapters:—

1. If controversy shall arise between laymen, or clergy and laymen, or clergy, regarding advowson and presentation to churches, let it be treated or concluded in the court of the lord the king.

3. Clerks cited and accused of any matter shall, when summoned by the king's justice, come into his own court to answer there concerning what it shall seem to the king's court should be answered there, and in the church court for what it shall seem should be answered there; yet so that the king's justice shall send into the court of holy Church to see in what way

the matter is there treated. And if the clerk be convicted, or shall confess, the Church must not any longer protect him.

4. Archbishops, bishops, and persons of the realm are not allowed to leave the kingdom without licence of the lord the king; and if they do leave, they shall, if the king so please, give security that neither in going nor in staying, nor in returning, will they seek the ill or damage of the lord the king or realm.

7. No one who holds of the king in chief, and none of his demesne officers are to be excommunicated, nor the lands of any one of them to be put under an interdict unless first the lord the king, if he be in the country, or his justiciar if he be outside the kingdom, be applied to, in order that he may do right for him; and so that what shall appertain to the royal court be concluded there, and that what shall belong to the church court be sent to the same to be treated there.

8. In regard to appeals, if they shall occur, they must proceed from the archdeacon to the bishop, and from the bishop to the archbishop. And if the archbishop fail in showing justice, they must come at last to the lord the king, that by his command the dispute be concluded in the archbishop's court, so that it must not go further without the assent of the lord the king.

16. Sons of villeins ought not to be ordained without the assent of the lord on whose land they are known to have been born.

No. 119. Jury of presentment

(The Assize of Clarendon. Adams & Stephens, *Select Documents,* pp. 14-17.)

Here begins the Assize of Clarendon, made by King Henry II with the assent of the archbishops, bishops, abbots, earls and barons of all England.

1. In the first place, the aforesaid King Henry, with the consent of all his barons, for the preservation of the peace and the keeping of justice, has enacted that inquiry should be made through the several counties and through the several hundreds, by twelve of the most legal men of the hundred and by four of the most legal men of each vill, upon their oath that they will tell the truth, whether there is in their hundred or in their vill, any man who has been accused or publicly suspected of himself being a robber, or murderer, or thief, or of being a receiver of robbers, or murderers, or thieves, since the lord king has been king. And let the justice make this inquiry before themselves, and the sheriffs before themselves.

2. And let any one who has been found by the oath of the aforesaid, to have been accused or publicly suspected of having been a robber, or mur-

derer, or thief, or a receiver of them, since the lord king has been king, be arrested and go to the ordeal of water and let him swear that he has not been a robber, or murderer, or thief, or receiver of them since the lord king has been king, to the value of five shillings, so far as he knows.

12. And if any one is captured who has in his possession the fruits of robbery or theft, if he is of bad reputation and has an evil testimony from the public, and has not a warrant, let him not have law. And if he shall not have been publicly suspected, on account of the possession which he has let him go to the water.

13. And if any one shall have acknowledged robbery or murder or theft or the reception of them in the presence of legal men or of the hundreds, and afterwards shall wish to deny it, he shall not have law.

14. The lord king wills moreover that those who make their law and shall be absolved by the law, if they are of very bad testimony, and publicly and disgracefully spoken ill of by the testimony of many and legal men, shall abuse the lands of the King, so that within eight days they shall go over the sea, unless the wind shall have detained them; and with the first wind they shall have afterward they shall go over the sea, and they shall not afterward return into England, except on the permission of the lord king; and then let them be outlawed if they return, and if they return they shall be seized as outlaws.

15. And the lord king forbids any vagabond, that is a wandering or an unknown man, to be sheltered anywhere except in a borough, and even there he shall be sheltered only one night, unless he shall be sick there, or his horse, so that he is able to show an evident excuse.

16. And if he shall have been there more than one night, let him be arrested and held until his lord shall come to give securities for him, or until he himself shall have secured pledges; and let him likewise be arrested who has sheltered him.

No. 120. Pleas of the crown and Henry II's attitude toward the ordeal

(Assize of Northampton. Adams & Stephens, *Select Documents*, pp. 20-21.)

These are the assizes made at Clarendon and afterwards revised at Northampton.

1. If any one shall have been accused before the justices of the lord king of murder or theft or robbery or of harboring men who do such things or of forgery or arson, by the oath of twelve knights of the hundred, or if knights are not present, by the oath of twelve freemen, lawful men, and by

the oath of four men from each vill of the hundred, he shall go to the ordeal of water, and if he is undone he shall lose one foot. And at Northampton it was added for rigorous justice that he shall likewise lose his right hand with his foot, and he shall abjure the realm and within forty days he shall leave the kingdom. And if he shall have been to the water whole he shall furnish sureties and remain in the kingdom, unless he has been accused of murder or other infamous felony by the community of the county and of the lawful knights of the country, of which if he has been accused in the said manner, although he has been to the water safely, nevertheless within forty days he shall depart from the realm, and take with him his chattels saving the rights of his lords, and at the mercy of the lord king he shall abjure the realm. . . .

No. 121. The Great Charter *(Magna Charta)*

(Adams & Stephens, *Select Documents*, pp. 42-53.)

John, by the grace of God, king of England, lord of Ireland, duke of Normandy and Aquitaine, count of Anjou, to the archbishops, bishops, abbots, earls, barons, justiciars, foresters, sheriffs, reeves, servants, and all bailiffs and his faithful people, greeting. Know that by the suggestion of God and for the good of our soul and those of all our predecessors and of our heirs, to the honor of God and the exaltation of holy church, and the improvement of our kingdom, by the advice of our venerable fathers Stephen, archbishop of Canterbury, primate of all England and Cardinal of the Holy Roman Church, Henry, archbishop of Dublin . . . of the noblemen William Marshall, earl of Pembroke, William, earl of Salisbury . . . and others of our faithful.

1. In the first place we have granted to God, and by this our present charter confirmed, for us and our heirs forever, that the English church shall be free, and shall hold its rights entire and its liberties uninjured; and we will that it thus be observed; which is shown by this, that the freedom of elections, which is considered to be most important and especially necessary to the English church, we, of our pure and spontaneous will, granted, and by our charter confirmed, before the contest between us and our barons had arisen; and obtained a confirmation of it by the lord Pope Innocent III; which we will observe and which we will shall be observed in good faith by our heirs forever.

We have granted moreover to all free men of our kingdom for us and our heirs forever all the liberties written below, to be had and holden by themselves and their heirs from us and our heirs.

2. If any of our earls or barons, or others holding from us in chief by military service shall have died, and when he has died his heir shall be of full age and owe relief, he shall have his inheritance by the ancient relief; that is to say, the heir or heirs of an earl for the whole barony of an earl a hundred pounds; the heir or heirs of a baron for a whole barony a hundred pounds; the heir or heirs of a knight, for a whole knight's fee, a hundred shillings at most; and who owes less let him give less according to the ancient customs of fiefs.

12. No scutage or aid shall be imposed in our kingdom except by the common council of our kingdom, except for the ransoming of our body, for the making of our oldest son a knight, and for once marrying our oldest daughter, and for these purposes it shall be only a reasonable aid; in the same way it shall be done concerning the aids of the city of London.

13. And the city of London shall have all its ancient liberties and free customs, as well by land as by water. Moreover, we will and grant that all other cities and boroughs and villages and ports shall have all their liberties and free customs.

20. A free man shall not be fined for a small offence, except in proportion to the measure of the offence; and for a great offence he shall be fined in proportion to the magnitude of the offence, saving his freehold; and a merchant in the same way, saving his merchandise; and the villein shall be fined in the same way, saving his wainage, if he shall be at our mercy; and none of the above fines shall be imposed except by the oaths of honest men of the neighborhood.

21. Earls and barons shall only be fined by their peers, and only in proportion to their offence.

23. No vill or man shall be compelled to make bridges over the rivers except those which ought to do it of old and rightfully.

30. No sheriff or bailiff of ours or any one else shall take horses or wagons of any free man for carrying purposes except on the permission of that free man.

39. No free man shall be taken or imprisoned or dispossessed, or outlawed, or banished, or in any way destroyed, nor will we go upon him, nor send upon him, except by the legal judgment of his peers or by the law of the land.

40. To no one will we sell, to no one will we deny, or delay right or justice.

61. Since, moreover, for the sake of God, and for the improvement of our kingdom, and for the quieting of the hostility sprung up lately between us and our barons, we have made all these concessions; wishing them to enjoy these in a complete and firm stability forever, we make and concede to them the security described below; that is to say, that they shall elect twenty-five barons of the kingdom, whom they will, who ought with

all their power to observe, hold, and cause to be observed, the peace and liberties which we have conceded to them, and by this our present charter confirmed to them; in this manner, that if we or our justiciar, or our bailiffs, or any one of our servants shall have done wrong in any way toward any one, or shall have transgressed any of the articles of peace or security; and the wrong shall have been shown to four barons of the aforesaid twenty-five barons, let those four barons come to us or to our justiciar, if we are out of the kingdom, laying before us the transgression, and let them ask that we cause that transgression to be corrected without delay. And if we shall not have corrected the transgression or, if we shall be out of the kingdom, if our justiciar shall not have corrected it within a period of forty days, counting from the time in which it has been shown to us or to our justiciar, if we are out of the kingdom; the aforesaid four barons shall refer the matter to the remainder of the twenty-five barons, and let these twenty-five barons with the whole community of the country distress and injure us in every way they can; that is to say by the seizure of our castles, lands, possessions, and in such other ways as they can until it shall have been corrected according to their judgment, saving our person and that of our queen, and those of our children; and when the correction has been made, let them devote themselves to us as they did before.

63. . . . It has been sworn, moreover, as well on our part as on the part of the barons, that all these things spoken of above shall be observed in good faith and without any evil intent. Witness the above named and many others. Given by our hand in the meadow which is called Runny-mede, between Windsor and Staines, on the fifteenth day of June, in the seventeenth year of our reign.

No. 122. Election of Otto the Great

(From Widukind's *Deeds of the Saxons.* Robinson's *Readings,* pp. 249-250.)

When Henry [I], the father of his country and the greatest and best of kings, was dead, all the people of the Franks and Saxons chose as their chief Otto, his son, whom his father had wished to have them choose. They decided to hold the general election at the palace of Aix-la-Chapelle. . . . When they were come thither the dukes and chief counts and soldiers came together in the portico of the basilica of the great Charles, and put the new king on a throne built there, and gave him their hands, promising to be faithful to him, and pledging him their aid against their enemies. So they made him king after their custom.

While these things were done by the dukes and the other magistrates, the chief pontiff [of Germany, i.e. the bishop of Mainz], with all the priests and the people, awaited below in the basilica the coming of the new king. When he came toward them the pontiff met him and touched the king's right hand. Now the bishop was clad in linen and was adorned with a stole and pallium and bore a staff in his right hand; and he went forward among the people and stood at the altar. He then turned toward the people who stood around that all might see him. "Behold," he said, "I present to you Otto, chosen by God, and previously designated by Henry, lord of this realm, and now made king by all the princes. If this choice is pleasing to you, signify it by raising your right hands toward heaven." And all the people raised their right hands on high, and with a mighty voice prayed for the prosperity of their new ruler.

Then the king, clad according to the Frankish custom in a close tunic, marched with the bishop behind an altar on which lay the royal regalia, —the sword with the belt, the mantle and bracelets, the staff with the scepter and diadem. . . . Then Hildebert, bishop of Mainz, came forward to the altar, took the sword and belt, and turning to the king said: "Take this sword, that thou mayst cast out all the adversaries of Christ, all barbarians and false Christians, by the divine authority given to thee, by all the power of the whole empire of the Franks, to the lasting peace of Christendom."

Then he took the mantle and bracelets and put them upon him: "As the border of this mantle flows to the ground, be thou admonished that thou shouldst glow with the zeal of faith and that thou shouldst endure to the end to maintain peace." Then he took the scepter and staff: "By these tokens be thou admonished that thou shouldst reprove thy subjects with fatherly chastisement and that thou shouldst above all things extend the hand of mercy to the ministers of God and to widows and orphans. And may thy head never lack the oil of compassion, that thou mayst be crowned now and hereafter with an eternal reward."

And he was anointed with the holy oil and crowned by the pontiffs, Hildebert and Wicfried [archbishop of Cologne], with a golden crown. When the consecration was accomplished according to the law, the king was led by those same bishops to the throne, which was built between two marble columns and was reached by a winding stairway, whence he could see all and be seen by all.

When the divine praise had been sung and the mass solemnly celebrated, the king descended to the palace. There he drew near a marble table adorned with royal pomp, and seated himself with the bishops and all the people; and the dukes ministered to him.

No. 123. Lombard towns during the reign of Frederick Barbarossa

(From Otto of Freising's *Deeds of Frederick*. Robinson's *Readings*, pp. 303-305.)

[The Lombards after their arrival in Italy] gradually laid aside their fierce barbarian customs and intermarried with the natives. Thus their children have derived from the mothers' race, and from the character of the country and the climate, something of Roman culture and civilization, and retain the elegance and refinement of Latin speech and manner.

In the government of the cities and in the management of civil affairs they also imitate the skill of the ancient Romans. Furthermore they love liberty so well that, to guard against the abuse of power, they choose to be ruled by the authority of consuls rather than by princes. They are divided into three classes, namely, "captains," vavasors, and the people. To prevent the growth of class pride, the consuls are chosen from each class in turn, and, for fear that they may yield to the lust of power, they are changed nearly every year.

It has come to pass that almost the whole country belongs to the cities, each of which forces the inhabitants of her territory to submit to her sway. One can hardly find, within a wide circuit, a man of rank or importance who does not recognize the authority of his city. . . . In order that there shall be no lack of forces for tyrannizing over their neighbors, the cities stoop to bestow the sword-belt and honorable rank upon youths of inferior station, or even upon laborers in despised and mechanical trades, who, among other peoples, are shunned like the pest by those who follow the higher pursuits. To this practice it is due that they surpass all other cities of the world in riches and power; and the long-continued absence of their ruler across the Alps has further contributed to their independence.

In one respect they are unmindful of their ancient nobility and betray their barbarian origin; for, although they boast of living under law, they do not obey the law. They rarely or never receive their ruler submissively, although it is their duty to show him willing and respectful obedience. They do not obey the decrees that he issues by virtue of his legal powers, unless they are made to feel his authority by the presence of his great army. Although, in a civilized state, the citizens should submit to law, and only an enemy should be coerced by force, yet they often greet with hostility him whom they ought to receive as their own gracious prince, when he comes to demand his own.

This situation brings double evil on the state. The prince's attention is occupied with gathering together an army to subdue the townsmen, and the citizens, though forced to obey the prince, waste their resources in the struggle. The fault, in such a case, lies wholly in the insolence of the people; the prince, who has acted under necessity, should be absolved before God and man.

Among all these cities Milan has become the leading one. . . . It must be regarded as more powerful than any of the others, in the first place, on account of its size and its multitude of brave men, and, secondly, because it has brought the two neighboring cities of Como and Lodi under its sway. Led on by Fortune's smiles, as is the way of this fleeting world, Milan has become so puffed up with pride that she has dared not only to incur the enmity of all her neighbors, but, fearing not even the majesty of the emperor himself, she has recently courted his anger. How this came about I shall presently relate. . . .

No. 124. Crusade of Frederick II (his own account)

(Translations and Reprints, I. No. 4, pp. 22-24.)

Frederic, by the grace of God, the august emperor of the Romans, king of Jerusalem and Sicily, to his well-beloved friend Henry, king of the English, health and sincere affection.

Let all rejoice and exult in the Lord, and let those who are correct in heart glorify Him, who, to make known His power, does not make boast of horses and chariots, but has now gained glory for Himself, in the scarcity of His soldiers, that all may know and understand that He is glorious in His majesty, terrible in His magnificence, and wonderful in His plans on the sons of men, changing seasons at will, and bringing the hearts of different nations together; for in these few days, by a miracle rather than by strength, that business has been brought to a conclusion, which for a length of time past many chiefs and rulers of the world amongst the multitude of nations, have never been able till now to accomplish by force, however great, nor by fear.

Not, therefore, to keep you in suspense by a long account, we wish to inform your holiness, that we, firmly putting our trust in God, and believing that Jesus Christ, His son, in whose service we have so devotedly exposed our bodies and lives, would not abandon us in these unknown and distant countries, but would at least give us wholesome advice and assistance for His honor, praise, and glory, boldly in the name set forth from Acre on the fifteenth day of the month of November last past and arrived safely at Joppa, intending to rebuild the castle at that place with proper strength, that afterwards the approach to the holy city of Jerusalem might be not only easier, but also shorter and more safe for us as well as for all Christians. When, therefore, we were in the confidence of our trust in God engaged at Joppa and superintending the building of the castle and the cause of Christ as necessity required, and as was our duty, and whilst all our pilgrims were busily engaged in these matters, several messengers often passed to and fro between us and the sultan of Babylon; for he and another sultan called Xaphat, his brother, were with a large army at the city of Gaza, distant about one day's journey from us; in another direction in the city of Sichen, which is commonly called Neapolis, and situated in the plains, the sultan of Damascus, his nephew, was staying with an immense number of knights and soldiers also about a day's journey from us and the Christians.

And whilst the treaty was in progress between the parties on either side of the restoration of the Holy Land, at length Jesus Christ, the Son of God, beholding from on high our devoted endurance and patient devotion to His cause, in His merciful compassion of us, at length brought it about that the sultan of Babylon restored to us the holy city, the place where the feet of Christ trod, and where the true worshippers adore the Father in spirit and in truth. But that we may inform you of the particulars of this surrender each as they happened, be it known to you that not only is the body of the aforesaid city restored to us, but also the whole of the country extending from thence to the sea-coast near the castle of Joppa, so that for the future pilgrims will have free passage and a safe return to and from the sepulchre; provided, however, that the Saracens of that part of the country, since they hold the temple in great veneration, may come there as often as they choose in the character of pilgrims, to worship according to their custom, and that we shall henceforth permit them to come, however, only as many as we may choose to allow, and without arms. . . .

No. 125. Crusade of Frederick II (a hostile view)

(From Matthew Paris. *Translations and Reprints*, I, No. 4, pp. 25-29.)

Gerold, patriarch of Jerusalem, to all the faithful, greeting.

If it should be fully known how astonishing, nay, rather deplorable, the conduct of the emperor has been in the eastern lands from beginning to end to the great detriment of the cause of Jesus Christ and to the great injury of the Christian faith, from the sole of his foot to the top of his head no common sense would be found in him. For he came, excommunicated, without money and followed by scarcely forty knights, and hoped to maintain himself by spoiling the inhabitants of Syria. He first came to Cyprus and there most discourteously seized that noble man John of Ibelin and his sons, whom he had invited to his table under pretext of speaking of the affairs of the Holy Land. Next the king, whom he had invited to meet him, he retained almost as a captive. He thus by violence and fraud got possession of the kingdom.

After these achievements he passed over into Syria. Although in the beginning he promised to do marvels and although in the presence of the foolish he boasted loudly, he immediately sent to the sultan of Babylon to demand peace. This conduct rendered him despicable in the eyes of the sultan and his subjects, especially after they discovered that he was not at the head of a numerous army which might have to some extent added weight to his words. Under the pretext of defending Joppa, he marched with the Christian army towards that city, in order to be nearer the sultan and in order to be able more easily to treat of peace or obtain a truce. What more shall I say? After long and mysterious conferences and without having consulted any one who lived in the country, he suddenly announced one day that he had made peace with the sultan. No one saw the text of the peace or truce when the emperor took the oath to observe the articles which were agreed upon. Moreover, you will be able to see clearly how great the malice was and how fraudulent the tenor of certain articles of the truce which we have decided to send to you. The emperor for giving credit to his word wished as a guarantee only the word of the sultan, which he obtained. For he said among other things that the holy city was surrendered to him.

He went thither with the Christian army on the eve of the Sunday when "Oculi mei" is sung [third Sunday in Lent]. The Sunday following, without any fitting ceremony and although excommunicated, in the chapel of the sepulchre of our Lord, to the manifest prejudice of his honor and of the imperial dignity, he put the diadem upon his forehead, although the Saracens still held the temple of the Lord and Solomon's temple, and although they proclaimed publicly as before the law of Mohammed—to the great confusion and chagrin of the pilgrims.

This same prince, who had previously very often promised to fortify Jerusalem, departed in secrecy from the city at dawn on the following Monday. The Hospitalers and the Templars promised solemnly and earnestly to aid him with all their forces and their advice, if he wanted to fortify the city, as he had promised. But the emperor who did not care to set affairs right, and who saw that there was no certainty in what had been done, and that the city in the state in which it had been surrendered to him, could be neither defended nor fortified, was content with the name of surrender, and on the same day hastened with his family to Joppa. The pilgrims who had entered Jerusalem with the emperor, witnessing his departure, were unwilling to remain behind. . . .

This is what the emperor did, to the detriment of the Holy Land and of his own soul, as well as many other things which are known and which we leave to others to relate. May the merciful God deign to soften the results! Farewell.

11

THE CHURCH OF THE HIGH MIDDLE AGES

The most influential and most peculiarly medieval institution of the Middle Ages was the Christian church. Never before or since have so many different peoples and states in the west accepted the same religious creed or have lived within the same ecclesiastical system. The Christian church calmed the fierce individualism of the Viking and Magyar as it had conquered the wild Frank and Saxon. To all peoples, whether Scandinavian, Italian, or Welsh, it furnished a common faith, moral code, and set of ideals. So thoroughly did its influence pervade their mores and institutions, that it left a deep mark not only upon their civilization but upon that of their descendants as well. The Christian heritage of these centuries has transcended far in time and space the limits of medieval Europe, and even today it constitutes much of the substance of what is known as Western Civilization. The church met the child at his birth, accompanied him through life, and attended him on his deathbed. Kings acknowledged the source of their authority to be the Christian God, and in accordance with his laws as defined by the Christian church they promised to direct their energies. Almost as characteristic of the countryside of western Europe as the ubiquitous forest were shrines, crosses, and churches. Everywhere, in art, song, and literature, in school and hospital, in the city and wilderness, medieval man was confronted with the presence of the church. There is no danger that our secular mind will exaggerate the role of the church and of religion in the Middle Ages.

Organization of the Church

Papal Authority. It has been said that the medieval church owed its stability and effectiveness above all else to its organization. This organization had developed essentially along the lines suggested in the early centuries. At the head of the hierarchy stood the pope. Though not recognized by Eastern Christendom after 1054, his authority in the west in the twelfth and thirteenth centuries was being more vigorously asserted and successfully maintained than in the early Middle Ages. He began to call himself the "vicar of Christ," a title descriptive of the position he claimed as the successor of St. Peter. As Peter's representative he recognized no responsibility in either the spiritual or the temporal sphere to anyone save God. Only the pope could summon a general church council, and only those decisions of the council which he approved and proclaimed were recognized as binding upon the faithful. The pope issued decrees called decretals, supervised the administration of the church, and served as the final authority in controversies arising among churchmen over matters of faith and morals, discipline, and jurisdiction. Few kings could outshine the popular awe in which he was held, for even kings knelt before him and kissed his foot. His court rivaled theirs in magnificence, and princes courted his favor as zealously as that of monarchs.

Control of the Hierarchy. Papal claims to spiritual supremacy found easier acceptance, however, than papal efforts to implement such claims among those whom the papacy considered subordinates. The tradition of ecclesiastical obedience to a superior was slow in emerging. It ran counter to human nature; it frequently clashed with the wishes of the local lord, and it had also the problem of poor communications and long distances to overcome. But all popes viewed the fulfillment of their claims to supremacy as both logical and necessary, and were constantly on the search for means which would expedite their acceptance. Monasteries lent them every encouragement, as did reformers, and even occasional lords. Of great assistance, in that it provided a favorable legal climate for these claims, was church or canon law, whose principles were rooted in the imperialistic traditions of Roman law. While never able to control the selection of bishops, the pope did secure by 1300 the right to confirm their appointment, without which confirmation the selectee could not be consecrated. No archbishop might discharge the duties of his office until he had received the pallium from Rome, which was the symbol of his office. In an effort to maintain closer liaison with the hierarchy, the papacy required prelates to make periodic visits to Rome. Periodically also the papacy sent representatives or legates to visit the different Christian countries and conduct investigations. While in those countries, their authority took precedence over that of the resident hierarchy. The papal court opened its services to progressively more types of cases, while it reserved the adjudication of an increasing number to its sole jurisdiction. By the close of the fourteenth century perhaps the majority of parish appointments were being cleared through the papal curia.

Roman Curia.   Providing the machinery for the exercise and extension of papal power was the Roman curia. This consisted of the advisors, assistants, and clerks, ranging in rank from cardinal to office boy, who collected themselves about the person of the pope and who carried on the actual business of the church. At least as early as the twelfth century, the same centralizing tendencies are visible here in the papal curia as in secular governments. These included the assumption of wider responsibilities and the assertion of more extensive claims, with the inevitable mushrooming of personnel and a gradual division into departments. And as might be expected, the growth of the papal curia aroused a storm of protest among churchmen similar to that which the advance of royal bureaucracy had evoked from the aristocracy, possibly even greater indignation because of the superior efficiency of papal administration.

Departments.   The major departments of the curia were the chancery and the camera. The chancery handled all routine correspondence, issued formal pronouncements called bulls (from *bulla* or seal), and conducted most of the judicial business of the curia. The camera was the papal treasury. Its principal task was the unenviable and increasingly difficult one of raising new revenues as the cost of papal government mounted. The feudal principle that the lord was to live of his own also applied to the church, and the opposition of bishops to any marked departure on the part of the papacy from this rule proved scarcely less stubborn than that offered a monarch by his vassals. The largest item in papal revenues was the income from papal estates. Gifts and legacies from pious men and women were also considerable, although they probably did little more than offset constant seizures of money and outright confiscations of church properties by grasping lords. To supplement the income from his estates, the pope could count a variety of revenues whose number was more impressive than the amount realized. These included fees assessed for the settlement of disputes and the granting of dispensations; contributions called annates which priests and bishops paid upon appointment or confirmation to new offices; feudal dues from states such as Hungary and Aragon which were fiefs of the papacy; and Peter's Pence, an annual tax paid by the faithful of several countries. On occasion tithes might be assessed the clergy and even outright subsidies upon authorization of the local hierarchy, although the latter were not common. The king ordinarily permitted such levies only if he received the lion's share, which in England amounted to ninety per cent. There were a few additional sources of revenue, but even when added to the others, they told the same story as that revealed in the exchequers of all medieval kings: never enough.

Cardinals. The men who normally headed the various departments and bureaus of the papal curia were cardinals. These men had first come into prominence in 1059, when as administrators of the most important churches in Rome, they had been designated as the electors of the pope. As a group they formed the college of cardinals. While they had originally been drawn from Rome, by the thirteenth century many were of non-Italian origin, although all were expected to take up their residence in the Eternal City upon receiving the red hat. They might number over fifty, although there were usually fewer, and only the pope could create them. They were the pope's chief advisors. Because of their position and experience, as well as the aristocratic associations of many of the members, they exercised strong influence over the conduct of papal affairs. The cardinalship, however, was a strictly honorary rank and one which enjoyed no special prerogatives other than the privilege of electing a new pope.

The Archbishop. Next to the pope in the hierarchical scheme stood the archbishop or metropolitan. His jurisdiction extended over an area known as the province, which consisted of a number of individual dioceses of which his own was usually the most important. In addition to his ordinary duties as bishop of his diocese, he normally consecrated his suffragan bishops, summoned and presided over provincial synods, and accepted appeals from the episcopal courts. His earlier pretensions to exercise an exclusive jurisdiction over his suffragan bishops, similar to that which the feudal count enjoyed over his own vassals to the prejudice of the king, had been successfully challenged by Pope Nicholas I against Hincmar, archbishop of Reims, back in the ninth century. On the other hand, the determination of the bishops to concede nothing more to the archbishop than a higher dignity, clashed with the traditional right of the metropolitan to visit the dioceses within his province and to investigate their administration. The result was a long and bitter controversy between bishop and archbishop over their respective rights, which was not terminated until the Council of Trent in the sixteenth century.

The Bishop. The persistence of these differences between archbishop and bishop rose principally from the inherent eminence of the latter's office. The bishop was the acknowledged successor of the apostles. He insisted, therefore, that his position in his diocese was entirely analogous to that of the pope for the whole of Christendom. Furthermore, the bishop was a lord, a vassal of the king. Because of the great influence he wielded in both the spiritual and temporal spheres, the filling of his office was frequently a matter of as grave concern to the state as to the church. (See page 512.) This held serious implications for the well-being of the church, since its vitality depended in the last analysis upon the zeal and administrative efficiency of the bishop. The bishop's duties were manifold. His basic function was administrative: the supervision or promotion of the spiritual welfare of the faithful of his diocese through the instrumentality of his priests and religious. To accomplish this task he made periodic visits through the diocese to check first-hand upon clerical discipline and efficiency. Once a year or more frequently if he chose, he summoned the diocesan clergy to a synod where administrative problems and questions of faith and morals were considered. The bishop's jurisdiction extended to the monasteries which lay within the diocese, unless these were directly under papal control. Only the bishop could administer the sacraments of confirmation and holy orders. (See page 505.) A vast amount of business was handled by the episcopal court, from disputes to which the clergy were partners, to matrimonial problems of the laity and the probation of wills. The bishop was required to make regular visits to Rome and to administer the estates of the diocese. In addition to, yet strictly separate from, these ecclesiastical responsibilities were the bishop's feudal obligations to his suzerain.

The Priest. Lowest in the hierarchy stood the priest. His province was the parish, the smallest administrative unit in the territorial organization of Christendom. While the manor or village community was ordinarily coterminous with the parish, their number in towns and cities often varied with the physical size of the churches. Thus the cathedral and collegiate churches (from the colleges in which the resident priests were organized) served large sections of the city, with an inevitable loss of spiritual contact between clergy and laity. The priest's duties consisted primarily of providing his parishioners with divine services on Sundays and holy days, and of administering the sacraments. He did much more preaching than scholars commonly believed a generation ago. Robert Grosseteste, bishop of Lincoln (d. 1253) warned his priests that the only alternative they had to preaching was hell-fire. Since the priest was usually the only one on the manor who had a smattering of education, he frequently served as the village schoolmaster. It was also his duty to relieve the indigent and to minister to the sick, for which charitable purposes a fourth or larger fraction of the tithe was earmarked. He blessed the homes, farms, and animals of the villagers, and served as their guide and comfort in times of trouble and distress.

It is difficult to speak in precise terms of the preparation and worthiness of the priest, since conditions varied so sharply with century and country. A constitution issued by Archbishop Lanfranc of Canterbury in the eleventh century specified two requirements which the candidate must meet: he must be able to read the Latin of the Mass, and he must be able to sing. The Fourth Lateran Council of 1215 required every bishop to maintain a training school for priests. That this bore some fruit is sug-

gested by the fourteenth century report which a bishop's investigating com-
mittee made to him concerning a candidate's qualifications: that he was
"free, legitimate, honest, worthy, somewhat more than thirty years of age,
having his first tonsure, and unbeneficed." On the other hand, the rise of
the friars (see page 499), was fundamentally a direct answer to the
failure of at least the town clergy to do a competent job. This excerpt from
Chaucer's *Canterbury Tales* speaks that poet's view of what the good priest
was like and what he was not like:

> A holy-minded man of good renown
> There was, and poor, the Parson to a town,
> Yet he was rich in holy thought and work.
> He also was a learned man, a clerk,
> Who truly knew Christ's gospel and would preach it
> Devoutly to parishioners, and teach it.
> Benign and wonderfully diligent,
> And patient when adversity was sent
> (For so he proved in great adversity)
> He much disliked extorting tithe or fee,
> Nay rather he preferred beyond a doubt
> Giving to poor parishioners round about
> From his own goods and Easter offerings.
> He found sufficiency in little things.
> Wide was his parish, with houses far asunder,
> Yet he neglected not in rain or thunder,
> In sickness or in grief, to pay a call
> On the remotest whether great or small
> Upon his feet, and in his hand a stave.
> This noble example to his sheep he gave,
> First following the word before he taught it,
> And it was from the gospel he had caught it.
> This little proverb he would add thereto
> That if gold rust, what then will iron do?
> For if a priest be foul in whom we trust
> No wonder that a common man should rust;
> And shame it is to see—let priests take stock—
> A [soiled] shepherd and a snowy flock.
> The true example that a priest should give
> Is one of cleanness, how the sheep should live.
> He did not set his benefice to hire
> And leave his sheep encumbered in the mire
> Or run to London to earn easy bread
> By singing masses for the wealthy dead,
> Or find some Brotherhood and get enrolled.
> He stayed at home and watched over his fold
> So that no wolf should make the sheep miscarry.
> He was a shepherd and no mercenary.
> Holy and virtuous he was, but then
> Never contemptuous of sinful men,
> Never disdainful, never too proud or fine,
> But was discreet in teaching and benign.

His business was to show a fair behavior
And draw men thus to Heaven and their Saviour,
Unless indeed a man were obstinate;
And such, whether of high or low estate,
He put to sharp rebuke to say the least.
       I think there never was a better priest.
He sought no pomp or glory in his dealings,
No scrupulosity had spiced his feelings.
Christ and His Twelve Apostles and their lore
He taught, but followed it himself before.*

The Regular Clergy

A study of the Church's ecclesiastical organization reveals a machinery equal to the task of supplying adequate administrative leadership in the work of saving souls. More was required than officials and bureaus, however, to capture and hold the spiritual loyalty of men. Ideals and the inspiring example of dedicated men and women were needed. Due partly to the low moral tone of the times, partly to the interference of the secular arm, many churchmen were not a credit to their high vocation. They were either unable or unwilling to assume the responsibilities of their offices. Furthermore, even assuming that the majority of priests and bishops were reasonably able and worthy men, the burden of administrative duties provided those who were disinclined to make the effort some justification for not nurturing their own spiritual growth. For those who were not fitted for their work, the frequent contacts with the world operated to make the spiritual life they were expected to grace appear all the more uninviting and unrewarding.

Monasticism: A Reform Movement. It is because of the indifferent record of the secular clergy in the Middle Ages that monasticism has been called the right arm of the church. Had it not been for the assistance, and particularly the inspiration, of the regular clergy, the church of the Middle Ages, far from accomplishing the Christianization of Europe, might have foundered in the attempt. Monasticism represented the ideal in Christian living. Without the more ascetical lives of monks and friars to provide the secular clergy an example of the life of self-abnegation and sacrifice which the Christian God demanded of them, there can be little doubt that the standards of clerical morality would have been appreciably lower. Furthermore, inherent in monasticism is a congenital urge to reform. What Christianity accepted as a general rule of spiritual life—that man's physical

* *Chaucer: The Canterbury Tales*, tr. Nevil Coghill (Penguin Books), 1952, pp. 38-39. By permission of Penguin Books Ltd.

nature tempts him constantly to compromise with the flesh—monasticism was much more acutely aware of and more concerned about neutralizing. It is no accident that the history of reform in the church begins with the rise of monasticism, and that all subsequent reform movements in the history of the medieval church had their inception, and found their motivation, in either the reform of existing monastic orders or in the appearance of new ones. It should be pointed out, finally, that monasticism, through a periodic reform of itself and of the church, tended to implant within the institution the notion of reform. Thus through occasional monastic reform movements and especially the founding of new orders, monasticism was able to absorb movements of protest against clerical corruption, which might otherwise have led to the establishment of independent ecclesiastical organizations.

Monastic Developments of the Ninth and Tenth Centuries. One of the first men to attempt a reform of monasticism was Benedict of Aniane (d. 821). His zeal aroused the admiration of Charlemagne and his ideas of reform earned the enthusiastic support of Louis the Pious. Benedict preached a return to the Rule of the first Benedict. He laid stress upon physical work in the field, on silence, and on the isolation of the monastic community from the world. But the chaotic ninth century was not favorable to the greater centralization he had advocated as the only check against monastic corruption. Such centralization came in the early tenth century with the rise of the Cluniac reform movement. The movement traced its origin back to 910 when Duke William of Aquitaine established a new kind of monastery at Cluny in Burgundy. What made this monastery different was that the duke declared it to be entirely free to direct its own affairs as it wished, subject only to papal jurisdiction. This represented a sharp departure from the practice of the time which found most monastic establishments under the control of a feudal lord or a feudalized bishop who was frequently no better.

Cluniac Reform Movement. Under the leadership of a series of great abbots, Cluny gained renown for its sanctity and zeal, and attracted the attention of other monasteries which asked to become affiliated. The result was the formation of the Congregation of Cluny which included over three hundred houses by the twelfth century. Though the Cluniac movement represented in essence but a stricter observance of the Rule of Benedict, it departed significantly from that Rule in the matter of organization. For in contrast to the autonomy of earlier Benedictine monasteries which according to some critics had opened the door to the relaxation of the Rule by individual communities, the Cluniac houses accepted the continuing supervision of the abbot of Cluny who also appointed their superiors (priors). The most striking manifestation of the strength of the movement is found in the large number of monasteries and churches erected during the tenth and eleventh centuries. It was not uncommon for rougher members of the aristocracy who had been touched by the reform movement, to furnish the means for such building in order to appease God's anger for their crimes. So much construction of the times was monastic in fact, that the term "Monastic" is occasionally employed to classify the style of architecture which was characteristic of the period, rather than Romanesque. (See page 623.) The Cluniac movement marks, if it did not bring about, the rise of monasticism to a commanding position in the affairs of the Christian church. To this reform movement may be attributed a powerful impetus to the correction of such clerical abuses as simony and concubinage, and it was principally the influence of Cluny which made possible the revival of the papacy in the eleventh century and the restoration of papal rule over western Christendom in the twelfth.

Hermits and Carthusians.   The tenth and eleventh centuries witnessed the appearance in the west of a number of anchoritic establishments. Because of its rigorous austerities, the early anchoritism of eastern monasticism had never spread to the west. Yet now in the wake of the spiritual revival which the Cluniac reform movement had induced, an unusually large number of men elected to take up the life of a hermit. These monks did not isolate themselves quite so completely from their fellowmen as did the original hermits, but lived rather in individual cells within reach of a common chapel and the restraining hand of a superior. Among the most famous of these western hermits was Romuald (d. 1000), son of a prominent Ravenna family. So fiercely did the love of God burn in Romuald's heart that he hated everything about himself which was not of God, and he only sought the company of other men in order to change them into anchorites.

The best known of these anchoritic orders was the Carthusian, so named from the location of the first community at Chartreuse in the wilder Alps of southeastern France. The Carthusians practiced the strictest silence, subsisted on the barest minimum of food, and divided their time between private contemplation, prolonged communal prayer and worship, the exercise of austerities, work in the fields, study, and the copying of manuscripts. The Carthusian lived each day as his last and he slept in his coffin. So much did austerity become and remain the mark of the order, that the Carthusians have never required reforming.

The Cistercians.   The aim of the Carthusians was to revive the Rule of St. Benedict in its original vigor. There were other monastic orders that appeared at this time which had the same objective, the most notable of these being the Cistercian. The name of the order is derived from Citeaux (*Cistercium*), on the upper Rhone where the first house was established in 1098. The order was founded by St. Robert of France, given its constitution by St. Stephen Harding of England, and owed its fame and popularity to St. Bernard, whose sanctity was so immense that to identify him with any kingdom under heaven would be almost sacrilegious. The Cistercians applied literally Benedict's admonition to isolate themselves from society.

They chose the remotest areas for their houses. Like the Carthusians, they ate the plainest food, wore only the coarsest cloth, and worshipped in plain, unadorned structures. They shunned all contact with the lay world as defiling, and carefully restricted the use of their schools to members of the community. This education must be thoroughly religious, since nothing else counted but the sanctification of their souls and the glory of God. In one respect they broke with Benedict's Rule. All houses, though independent, were obliged to accept inquisitorial visitation by the abbot of Citeaux, who might himself be removed for laxity by the abbots of four specially designated abbeys. Despite the vigorous asceticism of the order and its signal contribution to the spiritual life of Europe, modern man remembers the Cistercians principally for their material contributions to western civilization. They reclaimed much land from marsh, they cleared forests, they produced the best sheep in England. They have been credited with making first use of the pointed arch in the development of Gothic architecture. Most of the physical labor on the monastic estates of the Cistercians was performed by lay brothers (*conversi*) who were usually serfs who lacked the necessary education and often even the spiritual motivation to aspire to the lowly rank of the monk. Most of the orders of this period welcomed the lay brother, although occasionally to their own ultimate harm. The lay brother gradually took over the physical labor of the monk, a change many reformers deplored, while his low spiritual development often contributed to the deterioration of the standards of the monastic community.

St. Bernard of Clairvaux. The Cistercians were the most prominent order of the twelfth century, their monk St. Bernard (d. 1153) the most influential man of western Europe during the first half of that century. This poses one of the paradoxes of monasticism and of the world too, for that matter, that frequently those men who renounce the world with the greatest finality are sought out with the greatest eagerness by the world which they would renounce. So utterly devoted to God and the sanctification of souls was Bernard, that he would have made every man a monk and turned the world into one vast monastery. He came to Citeaux with thirty others whom he had persuaded to join with him. So manifest was the sincerity of his faith, that men accepted without resentment his biting denunciations of their failings. For through the violence of his asceticism and the sharpness of his censure, shone his deep love for men and his passionate longing for the salvation of their souls. He preached the Second Crusade, ended a papal schism, reformed the French court at Paris, prepared a rule for the Knights Templar, hunted down Arnold of Brescia who would have subjected the church to the civil authority, and was instrumental in forcing the most brilliant intellectual of his age, Abelard, to curb his rationalism. "He would deprive men of the merit of Christian faith," thundered Bernard, to whom all the philosophical knowledge under heaven was not equal in worth to the faith of a peasant. (For his position regarding scholasticism, see page 557.) Scarcely able to spend one hour in the quiet solitude of Clairvaux which he loved, when he was not running about France and Italy on missions of reform he was engaged in the writing of mystical literature or occupied with his huge correspondence. Dante acknowledged him as the supreme mystic of the Middle Ages, as the man most capable of fathoming the mysteries of the supernatural, by making him his guide in the empyrean. (See page 693.) (Reading 135)

The Friars. The Cistercian order marks the appearance of the last of the traditional monastic organizations. A canon of the Fourth Lateran Council (1215) decreed that no new monastic rules, only modifications of existing ones, would be permitted. Yet it is impossible to view the new orders of friars which flourished in the thirteenth century as anything less than a fundamental departure from traditional monasticism. The word friar, from the Latin *frater* meaning brother, suggests the basic difference involved. The monk dedicated himself to a lonely life of personal sanctification in the relative isolation of his monastery. While it was fortunate for western Europe that many monks did not remain in their monasteries, but carried their faith and learning to the outside world, the new orders of friars frankly announced their conviction that the times called for a more direct apostolate. They sought to combine the role of the priest with that of the monk. While not abandoning the contemplative and ascetical practices of the latter, they hoped to unite these with an active ministry among the laity. Instead of selecting some remote wilderness as the site of their community, the friars settled in the cities, with the people among whom they would labor. Since such a location would deprive them of the lands whence monastic communities derived their sustenance, and since lives of apostolic poverty were more in keeping with Christ's charge to his disciples that they have neither "two coats, nor shoes, nor a staff," the new communities depended directly upon the charity of the laity. They were known as mendicant or begging orders.

St. Francis of Assisi. The founder of one of the two most famous of these mendicant orders was St. Francis of Assisi (d. 1226). Francis was the son of a prosperous merchant who had ambitions to make his son an illustrious warrior. Francis was anything but warlike. His jovial, warm-hearted nature, together with his talents as a singer and poet, won him many friends among the youth of Assisi. More a knight errant than soldier, he was captured in a clash with troops from the neighboring town of Perugia, and lodged in prison for several years. There in confinement and during an attack of the fever that followed his release, he began to reflect upon his life and upon God. He rose from his sick bed a different man though not entirely transformed. He never lost the natural cheerfulness of his disposition, his optimism and amiability, nor his love of song and nature. But for his earlier life of leisure and pleasure, he had only regret and shame. Within an extraordinarily short time he acquired an intense love for God and, because they were made by the all-loving Almighty, for his fellowmen as well, even for animals and inanimate objects. Yet while he lavished love upon others, for himself he had no pity. Lady Poverty became his bride, for had not Christ by his example and his exhortations recommended that life to those who loved him? He abandoned his patrimony, lived briefly as a hermit, then took to ministering to that most unfortunate and despised group in medieval society, the lepers. What remained of his pride he destroyed by living off the crusts men threw him—men cynical and contemptuous at first, then respectful and awestruck. His father who had once disowned him as a disgrace to the family, came to revel in the high honor pope, prince, and pauper paid his son. Even the sultan of Egypt whom Francis visited in order to convert, could not help but admire the depth of the saint's faith and devotion. St. Francis died at the age of forty-four. His body was unequal to the burden of mortifications his love of God led him to place upon it. (Reading 137)

The Early Franciscans. Francis' example inspired other men to join him in his life of poverty and charity. Pope Innocent III gave reluctant approval to Francis' plea that he recognize his band as a formal religious community, dedicated to prayer and poverty, and to serving the spiritual and material needs of the poor and unfortunate. The pope was disturbed at the fact that Francis was a layman, and his love of efficiency rebelled at the absence of a more elaborate rule or organization. But this lack proved a strong attraction to souls as truly good as Francis, who agreed with him that the eight beatitudes were sufficient rules for men to live by. Francis and his friars abode in hovels which no beggar would have taken from them; they begged for their own food and for that which they distributed to the poor; they preached the word of God to those who would listen only to men who lived what they preached. Never in medieval times in the west were so many hearts stirred by the ideas of one man. The Franciscan order or Order of Friars Minor as it came to be called, grew to be the largest and most influential in Christendom. Paralleling it was the Order of Poor Clares, an order of women, founded by Clare, a devoted admirer and confidant of Francis. Another group, known as the Third Order or Tertiaries, was composed chiefly of laymen and laywomen who pledged themselves to practice Franciscan principles of Christlike living in their everyday lives.

The Dominicans. The founder of the second great mendicant order of the early thirteenth century, the Order of Preachers, was a Spaniard known in history as St. Dominic (d. 1221). Dominic was a well educated priest who found inspiration for his future career during his labors among the Albigensian heretics of southern France. So convinced was he that the cause of this defection from orthodox Christianity was to be found in a lax, illiterate clergy, that he set out to establish a new order which would produce a different kind of priest. What he wanted was an educated, eloquent zealot, who by word and example would eradicate error where it had taken root. Herein lay the chief contrast between the Dominican and Franciscan orders. Both believed in leading lives of poverty and personal sanctity, but where the Franciscans devoted their efforts first to the materially unfortunate, the Dominicans labored principally among those who required spiritual enlightenment. The Dominicans were, above all else, teachers and preachers. But because they had to know before they could teach others, the Dominicans maintained a vigorous educational system in their convents and flocked to the universities in enthusiastic numbers. So much did preaching become the *raison d'etre* of the organization, that the Dominican rule permitted the relaxation of such regulations as attendance at conventual exercises whenever the higher end of preaching was served. The order became famous for its learning and counted among its brightest luminaries men like Albert the Great and Aquinas. Because of their learning, Dominicans were recruited to advise the courts of the Inquisition, a role which has left them somewhat suspect in modern eyes which view concern about religious regularity as peculiarly unmodern. The modern mind, however, would find much to commend in the democratic procedures employed by the Dominicans in the selection of the prior, and in their use of the representative principle in administering the affairs of the community and those of the organization.

The Achievement of the Mendicants.   Despite varying points of emphases in their origins, the Franciscan and Dominican movements tended to converge even before the middle of the thirteenth century. It is possible therefore, to evaluate in general terms their contribution to church and society. By preaching through word and example the spiritual values of poverty, the friars served to counteract the strong materialistic drift which rising capitalism and secularism were giving to medieval life. The friars assumed the burden of converting the non-Christian which had been earlier borne by the Benedictines. Dominicans and Franciscans could be found laboring among the heathen of eastern Europe, among the Mohammedans of North Africa and the Near East, even among the Mongols of far-off China. This zeal for the souls of foreigners promoted the study of Oriental languages, while the interest of the friars in the care of the sick stimulated the study of medicine. It was the diligence of the mendicants which accounted for the flowering of scholasticism in the thirteenth century. They can also claim credit for much of the medieval accomplishment in science and political thought. Friars composed most of the great hymns of the thirteenth century. Perhaps their principal achievement was the spiritual reformation they worked among the secular clergy. The influence of groups such as the Carthusian and Cistercian was necessarily limited in view of the isolated existence they led. Not so that of the mendicants, whose example and popularity with the laity could not but compel the secular clergy to improve their own lives. They also won the admiration of zealous bishops like Grosseteste of Lincoln who used them as parish priests in order to combat clerical apathy and corruption. There is a famous painting by Giotto which shows St. Francis shoring up the foundation of the church of St. John Lateran which Innocent III dreamed was about to collapse. But Giotto was hardly giving the Dominicans and the other orders of friars (Augustinians and Carmelites) their due. The artist might have improved historically upon his theme had he painted simply a friar, rather than St. Francis, in the role of savior.

The Christian and His Religion

The Central Role of Religion. What must the Christian believe, what must he do in order to be saved? These questions were the most grave, or should be, so medieval theologians insisted, with which the Christian was to concern himself. For of nothing else were the Middle Ages quite so convinced as of this, that the present life was but the testing ground for a future eternity. As Christ had warned: "What doth it profit a man if he gain the whole world and suffer the loss of his soul?" Actually the medieval mind was inclined to be exclusive in its application of this principle. Since God made all things, all things had a divine purpose. All men therefore, and all human conventions and institutions as well, must justify their existence and their behavior in that premise. Not just men as individuals, but corporate societies, governments, even businesses, acknowledged their responsibilities to God. It is this recognition of God as the why and wherefore of the world and of all that is in it, that sets off medieval man and society most sharply from our own.

What the Christian Believed. The Christian was required to believe there was but one God. This God was almighty, omniscient, and omnipresent, just, merciful, and, because of these qualities, incomprehensible. This God had created the universe, including man, not because he had need of man, but that man might love him and share an eternity of bliss with him. But the first man, Adam, broke God's command, wherefore all mankind, because of this transgression, had forfeited heaven. Yet God in his mercy had relented. He sent his own son who by his death on the cross redeemed man, thereby enabling him again to qualify for a happy thereafter in heaven. Still the sin of Adam left man spiritually weakened, his mind darkened, his will to good replaced by concupiscence. As a consequence, salvation would not come easy but be beset by numerous pitfalls and temptations, for "the enemy like a roaring lion goeth about seeking whom he may devour." To assist the Christian in this struggle for heaven,

Christ had given him the church, which would guide and admonish him, and help him gain God's grace through the Mass and sacraments. Without these powerful spiritual aids, the struggle against the powers of darkness would be well-nigh hopeless.

Importance of Church. This left the church indispensable in God's scheme of redemption, and so the faithful were taught. The church worshipped God for and with him, it provided him grace through the instrumentality of the mass and sacraments, it told him what he must believe and do in order to save his soul. The faith it required him to accept originated from three sources: the Bible, the teachings of the fathers or tradition, and revelation. But the biblical text was not always easy to comprehend, the teachings of the fathers not entirely consistent, and what form was divine revelation to take or how was it to be recognized? If individual Christians were permitted to disseminate without official authorization what they claimed to have received by way of private disclosures from above, would not the body of faith be fatally compromised and hopelessly confounded? Yet what was the church? Was it the pope or the hierarchy or the whole of Christendom? This question was more difficult to answer in theory than in practice, and medieval man, quite realistic for all his otherworldly beliefs, was content to accept the church as the voice of his spiritual superiors, much as the ordinary citizen today may refer to any federal official as a "government" man.

The Trinity and Mysteries. A fundamental matter of faith required of the Christian in the Middle Ages was the acceptance of the Trinity. According to this doctrine, God, though one, was composed of three individual persons, each complete and identical in itself, yet constituting but one God *in toto*. First in honor, not in time, was God the Father, the Creator. Next came God the Son, who is in his human nature Jesus Christ, and, finally, God the Holy Spirit, the incarnate love between the first two persons, so intense and perfect as to constitute a separate person. The Christian was assured that the Trinity was the greatest of mysteries, and that he would never be able to comprehend it, at least not while on earth. There were other mysteries as well, such as the ability of Mary to become the mother of God. Yet the medieval mind made no objection to accepting mysteries, since it recognized the infinite superiority of God. Would it not, in fact, be unreasonable for man to presume to fathom with his finite mind the incomprehensible depths of the divine? As St. Paul exclaimed: "O the depth of the riches of the wisdom and of the knowledge of God! How incomprehensible are His judgments, and how unsearchable His ways!"

Heaven, Hell, Purgatory. The medieval Christian never harbored any real doubt about heaven and hell, although he might entertain weird ideas as to what each was like. He might also postpone perilously long, in the opinion of his spiritual superiors, any serious consideration about attaining the one and escaping the other. Those men and women who died neither so corrupted as to merit hell, nor so undefiled as to qualify for immediate entrance into heaven, medieval man consigned to purgatory. This was but a temporary place or state, and would cease to exist once all souls had been purified and had entered heaven. The faithful in the Middle Ages also accepted without protest the church's warning that one must live virtuously if he hoped to gain heaven. The doctrine of predestination which proposed that God from all eternity had designated certain favored souls for heaven and other unfortunate ones for hell, with complete disregard for how they might conduct themselves while on earth, had never seriously troubled any minds except those of occasional theologians. Yet medieval man, who accepted the indispensable character of good works, frequently relied more heavily upon the mercy of God to cover his wrongdoings, than did the dour Calvinist of the sixteenth century who accepted predestination.

The Church as the Distributor of Grace. As important as the church's role of defining and preserving doctrine was its function of furnishing the faithful, through the hands of a sanctified priesthood, such powerful spiritual aids to salvation as the mass and the sacraments. Of these means the mass was surely the more common, if not the more important, since in the one act it performed the two essential purposes of religion: first and foremost, that of honoring God; second, that of sanctifying mankind. Because the mass was the central act of Christian worship in the Middle Ages, and because such worship was considered the *sine qua non* of religion, all the faithful were required to assist at that service on each Sunday and holy day of the year.

The Mass. The dual character of the mass is clearly reflected in the prayers of the service. The introductory prayers consisted largely of acknowledgements of sinfulness and repentance on the part of the participants. These sentiments reached their climax in the *Kyrie Eleison* (Lord have mercy on us) which was repeated several times alternately by priest and people. This phrase has an interesting history in that it remained the only Greek reminder to westerners that their liturgy originated in the east. Having acknowledged their unworthiness, priest and people proceeded next to offer their gifts of bread and wine to God the Father. These the priest asked God to accept and to transform into the body of his own beloved son by means of a miracle known as transubstantiation. According to medieval Christians this miracle took place when the priest spoke the solemn words: "This is my body" and "This is my blood." Next the priest asked God to accept this gift, his son, which, finally, in the communion service, was partaken of by the priest and by those of the faithful who wished to receive. The son then became God the Father's gift to mankind. Thus the mass served to memorialize Christ's sacrifice of himself upon the cross to his father for the sins of mankind, the merits of which the father in return extended to man in the form of grace and ultimate salvation.

The Laity and the Mass. Since the prayers of the mass were recited in

Latin, the extent of popular participation in the mysteries as they unfolded was problematical. While manuals which contained a translation of the service in the vernacular were frequently available, the faithful ordinarily said prayers of a simpler sort. Or they might pass the time gazing at the statues or at the figures and themes portrayed on the walls and in the stained-glass windows, or they might simply bide their time in distracted silence. In the larger churches on Sundays and holy days, the liturgy was embellished by the singing of portions of the mass service. Most common of these were the *Gloria*, a prayer extolling the majesty of Christ, and the *Credo*, a profession of the articles of faith. Thoughtful participation in the mass service was asked of the laity although it was not considered essential, since the act of the mass of its very nature was acceptable to God. Still the priest was under special obligation to acquaint his parishioners with the gospel story of the Sunday. This varied from Sunday to Sunday, according to a carefully planned liturgical calendar, and followed Christ from his birth, through his parables and miracles, to his death. Whatever his knowledge of the deeper significance of the mass, medieval man did appreciate the meaning of transubstantiation. For in most of the chapels and churches of Christendom, however humble their appointments, could be found on the altar a repository which contained the sacred elements—to the faithful, Christ himself. This belief in the real presence, that God in corporeal form was actually and constantly in their midst, provided a tremendous stimulant to the faithful of the Middle Ages.

Baptism, Confirmation, and Penance.   Second to the mass as a source of grace were the sacraments. These have been defined as outward signs instituted by Christ to give grace. By the twelfth century their number had become standardized at seven. The first sacrament, baptism, was the most fundamental, since it removed the sin of Adam, known as original sin, and in so doing made the person again a child of God and heir of heaven. Material witness to the importance of this sacrament is provided by the pretentious baptistries which often adjoined the main church edifice. The sacrament of confirmation strengthened the faith bestowed in baptism through special gifts from the Holy Spirit. This sacrament was administered when the recipient was sufficiently mature to appreciate the significance of the rite. Penance provided the machinery for removing sins committed after baptism. Since even a good man might sin seven times seven each day, recourse was had more frequently to the saving graces of this sacrament than to those of the other six combined. Private confession after the manner of the Irish monks became customary after the tenth century. Several elements must be present to make the reception of the sacrament of penance efficacious. The penitent must reveal all his mortal sins, that is, those which were considered so offensive to God as to be deserving of eternal punishment. The penitent must above all else be sorry for his sins and be firmly resolved to avoid them and their occasion in the future. After the priest had pronounced the formula of absolution, the penitent was obliged to perform the penance his confessor had assigned him. For though God had agreed to absolve the sinner of his guilt—"whose sins you forgive they will be forgiven them"—theologians maintained that divine justice still required the sinner to make some atonement for his crimes. Thus the penance meted out by the priest was intended to fit the crime. It might vary from a few prayers for ordinary transgressions, to a pilgrimage to the Holy Land for murder.

Indulgences. From this theory, that God's justice required something beyond the sorrow of the penitent and the absolution of the priest, there developed the doctrine of indulgences. Not only could the ordinary Christian expect to die with a number of venial or minor sins unshriven, but, in addition, he could die with still a measure of satisfaction owing God for penances never performed or performed without proper devotion. Until sufficient satisfaction had been rendered God to cover this temporal punishment (in contrast to the eternal punishment of hell), the soul must languish in purgatory. In order to reduce this waiting period in purgatory, the pope began to grant indulgences of varying lengths, basing his authority to do so on Christ's promise that "whatsoever thou shalt loose on earth, shall also be loosed in heaven." The faithful could gain these indulgences by a variety of means: by reciting certain prayers, visiting shrines, giving alms to the poor, supporting missionaries, participating in a Crusade against the infidel. The practice of granting indulgences extends back as far as the tenth century and grew increasingly popular during the later Middle Ages. It does not require much imagination to conceive of how readily the practice could lend itself to abuse, particularly in the Middle Ages when purgatory conjured up horrors only less fearful than those which would be the lot of the damned in hell.

The Other Sacraments. The sacrament of the eucharist or communion was received but irregularly by the laity. At her trial Joan of Arc affirmed that as a girl she had confessed once a year and received the Eucharist during the Easter season. The Fourth Lateran Council decreed that the faithful must communicate at least once a year, which must have become customary by that time or a canon so binding in character would not have been issued. In the very early church, communion under both species was common. Because of the danger of spilling the wine or contaminating it, communion came to be restricted to the bread in the fourth century in the west. The sacrament of extreme unction was administered to persons in grave danger of death. The purpose of the sacrament was to bolster the recipient spiritually against the last desperate efforts of the evil spirit to capture his soul. The sacrament of holy orders was administered to candidates for the priesthood by the bishop as the successor of the apostles. It imparted the power to forgive sins and to change the bread and wine at mass into the body and blood of Christ. Matrimony sanctified the union between husband and wife. In this particular instance, the contracting parties were themselves the administrants of the sacrament, the priest simply presiding at the ceremony and according it ecclesiastical sanction. The ritual here reminded the woman that she must be subject to her husband, but that the husband must love his wife as Christ loved the church, of which this connubial union should be a reflection.

Role of Sacraments Exaggerated. A word of caution might be in order here by way of retrospect concerning the role of the sacraments in the spiritual life of the Middle Ages. Because so much space is normally devoted to their clarification, the student not unnaturally betrays a tendency to attach greater importance to them than they deserve. Five sacraments—baptism, confirmation, extreme unction, holy orders, and matrimony—could or, in the normal course of events, would be received only once in a lifetime. As concerns the two remaining sacraments of penance and holy eucharist, few Christians in the Middle Ages confessed their sins or received communion more frequently than two or three times a year. In the daily pattern of personal sanctification, therefore, the role of the sacraments has usually been exaggerated. Most essential from the point of view of official conformity, was attendance at mass on Sundays and holy days. Most popular and spiritually rewarding from the individual Christian's point of view was his personal devotion to God or to the saints and angels. While too much religious devotion has been credited by sentimental souls to this period as the "age of faith," this exaggeration is closer to the truth than the effort to picture salvation before the sixteenth century as a largely mechanical process involving the distribution of saving graces through formal attendance at mass and reception of the sacraments.

Shrines and Devotion to Mary. If the Middle Ages is deserving of the title, the "age of faith," material evidence of this is furnished by the great number of pilgrims that roamed about Europe, visiting shrines and churches which the association of some saint had made holy. England claimed the illustrious shrine of the martyred Thomas à Becket at Canterbury. Thousands of pilgrims travelled to Spain to pray at the shrine of St. James of Compostella. The most popular of all shrines was outside of Europe, in Palestine. Almost with the announcement of toleration began the flow of pilgrims to Jerusalem and vicinity. The eleventh century witnessed a trek of more than seven thousand pilgrims from Germany alone, a truly phenomenal demonstration of faith in view of the two thousand miles of largely roadless country one had to traverse to reach the holy places. Most medieval communities could claim one saint or more, whose fame they perpetuated by dedicating the village church to his honor or by giving their children his name. The saint most venerated was Mary. Devotion to her transcended local preferences. It had spread from the early church in the east and became so diffused throughout Christendom in time as almost to rival the worship of God himself. While mention of the church of Notre

Dame may suggest a specific edifice to the art- and travel-conscious twentieth century man, in the Middle Ages it frequently reminded the faithful of their own church. Mary was so approachable, so appealing. Her beauty, virginity, motherhood, even her sorrows and anguish awakened responses in the hearts of most men and women. No church was complete without her statue, at least one window must reflect her image or an incident in her life. Stories of her miracles and appeals to her intercession abound in the literature of the day, from the lowly verses of such simple tales as the *Juggler of Notre Dame* to the magnificent meters of the *Ave Maris Stella* and *Stabat Mater*.

Faith or Superstition? Was all this religious devotion faith or superstition? This is a delicate question. To the atheist, even faith in God is superstition. Yet even the medieval theologians would have been the first to condemn the excesses to which the veneration of saints and relics was carried. In this the twentieth century, ecclesiastical authorities have found it necessary to remove candle stands from the churches in Italy because of the universal abuse associated with them. Simple minds, then as now, had difficulty distinguishing between veneration and worship, since the powers they mistakenly attributed to saints and to relics encroached on the divine. They could almost be excused for not appreciating the fact that relics possessed no inherent power in view of the enormous, even criminal, efforts made by cities and occasional prelates to secure control of a saint's bones. The people living in the region where Romuald practiced his austerities planned to murder him when they learned he was about to leave their locality, in order to have at least his corpse to ward off evil! Of course, that was the tenth century, and considerable advance in the development of true religion marks the progress of medieval centuries, particularly after the appearance of the friars and the improved quality of the secular clergy from the early thirteenth century. Yet the common people of the Middle Ages never quite sloughed off that deep, unreasoning faith one might associate with relatively simple civilizations. They had learned too little to recognize superstition, although they had also remained sufficiently unsophisticated to have retained their idealism.

Church and State

Church and State in the Ancient World. Almost as enduring as the conflict which goes on in each individual between the promptings of his spiritual and his material natures, is the one which has embittered church and state relations over the question of priority in man's loyalties. Yet though this struggle between church and state has constituted one of the most persistent themes in history, it antedates the Christian era only by way of exception. The ancient state conceived of itself as a sort of theocracy. Its ruler was invariably either descended from the gods directly or had been designated by them as their earthly representative. In the case of the Athenian state, it was the state in its corporate character which directed the destiny of the citizen in accord with the laws of the immortal gods. Because the demands of the gods, as interpreted by the ancient state, were, on the one hand, neither numerous nor exacting, and men's religious views, on the other, neither highly developed nor unyielding, one meets but rarely any instance of conflict over this issue. During most of antiquity church and state were one and the same, and despite all their bickering and quarrels, the gods of paganism were never so jealous or so powerful as to insist upon strict conformity to their particular creed, whatever this might have been.

The State and Christianity. But the God of the Christians was the Jehovah of the Hebrews who had proclaimed: "I am the Lord thy God; thou shalt not have strange gods before me." Therefore, once the Roman state recognized Christianity for the puritanical sect that it was, its reaction was immediate and hostile and remained so until the time of Constantine. Constantine's edict of toleration is unique in that it represented an acknowledgement by the head of an ancient state that a citizen might accept an authority other than that of the emperor in the spiritual order. Constantine, of course, anticipated little grief over Christianity's newly won freedom, since he could conceive of no important issue which would find churchmen leagued against him. For what had aroused their opposition against his pagan predecessors had been the efforts of the state to obstruct them in the practice of their religion. Constantine's attitude was probably not far removed from that of more recent rulers who have vigorously protested that they have nothing against religion, but that they must insist that religious groups restrict themselves to matters of religion and not attempt to apply to social, political, and economic issues the principles of their faith.

Constantine and the Church. Constantine may have doubted the wisdom of his act of toleration when he found the Christian community breaking up into warring factions. These were aggravating, rather than tranquilizing the political disunity he had hoped religious freedom would correct. Therefore, consistent with Roman traditional policy which accorded the emperor supremacy in all matters, whether political or spiritual, he convened the bishops of Christendom at Nicaea and instructed them to iron out their differences. His interest, though compelling, was nothing more than political. He cared not what solution the bishops might reach, just so they reached one. As we have seen (see page 160), Constantine's position vis-à-vis the church came to be the prevailing one in Constantinople. The continued interference in religious affairs by the Byzantine emperors had ordinarily little motivation beyond the hope that a united church would afford stability to their troubled regimes.

Uniqueness of Church-State Struggle in the Middle Ages. The relationship between the medieval church and the state has been productive of a vast amount of literature chiefly because that relationship was so unique. It was markedly different from the situation that had obtained in antiquity, which found state and church usually one and the same institution. It is different from the situation today which finds either a state which is frankly secular in its philosophy and, accordingly, indifferent to the activities of any religion so long as it restricts itself to "religious" affairs; or a state which favors a particular religious denomination to the prejudice or exclusion of all others. Now this last situation comes closest to that which prevailed in the Middle Ages, with several noteworthy exceptions. In the first place, the modern state, whether indifferent to religion or favoring one in particular, exercises final authority in determining what the rights of the religious sect or sects shall be. The medieval church by contrast was so influential, or conversely, the medieval state so weak, that the Christian church could wield powers which today might be considered inconsistent with national sovereignty. Furthermore, the medieval problem was grievously complicated by the fact that the key figure in the ecclesiastical organization, that is, the bishop, was also a vital link in the political hierarchy: he was usually the king's vassal. There is also this difference which makes the medieval situation so unique. In the Middle Ages both church and state felt they had a mandate from God to promote the cause of Christianity. Consequently, there was never any conflict over ultimate objectives as might be the case today, but simply over jurisdiction: should this or that phase of medieval man's activities be supervised by the state or by the church?

The Gelasian Doctrine. This concept of society as a unity under God possessing two coordinate heads—the church in the spiritual sphere, the state in the temporal, both doing his will in their respective orbits—was given official sanction by Pope Gelasius I (d. 496). The occasion of his pronouncement was the attempt on the part of the Byzantine emperor to force acceptance of his imperial judgment in a matter of doctrine. Basing his argument on Christ's exhortation: "Render therefore to Caesar what is Caesar's, and to God what is God's," Gelasius insisted that the spiritual as well as the temporal power drew its authority from God. While each, church and state, was supreme in its own sphere and responsible only to God in the conduct of affairs which fell strictly within its respective province, if either exceeded its province, it was obliged to respect the prior authority of the other. Furthermore, each was under constraint to assist the other in the exercise of its duties. Thus the church preached obedience to constituted civil authority and introduced prayers into the liturgy for the well-being of the ruler and his family. The state in turn punished persons who violated churchmen or their property, undertook crusades against the non-believer, and suppressed heresy as in the case of the Albigensians and Lollards when the situation got beyond the control of the church. (Reading 126)

Gelasian Doctrine Not a Solution. The Gelasian doctrine provided the rule which generally governed church-state relations during the Middle Ages, with minor modifications to suit individuals and circumstances involved. What made such modifications inevitable was the unfortunate fact that jurisdictional matters did not fall into two clearly defined areas quite so conveniently as the Gelasian statement implied. The reverse was frequently the case. Few acts or rights actually are so clearly the state's or the church's as the mapping of strategy against an invader, for example, or the administration of the sacraments. Should the state punish criminous clerks and probate wills as Henry II of England averred, or should the church do so, as Thomas à Becket maintained? Scores of problems of this sort which offered arguments to both contestants were not peculiar to the Middle Ages. Modern society finds itself vexed, for instance, over conflicting claims in the realm of education and social welfare. Because of this middle area, which was neither clearly the church's nor the state's, the line separating the two spheres kept constantly shifting during the Middle Ages. Now it advanced in favor of the church during the aggressive pontificate of a Pope Gregory VII, now it receded at the expense of the church before the forthright attack of a Philip IV. (See page 672.) As we have seen, Henry II justified his claim to broader jurisdiction in this middle area on the plea that, during the reign of the conciliatory Stephen, the church had appropriated the powers he now wanted restored.

The Influential Position of the Bishop. The most sensitive point where claims of church and state to jurisdiction most frequently collided was over the selection of the bishop. This ecclesiastical official found himself clearly within the debatable area over which church and state fought because of the enormous influence he wielded in both religious and secular affairs. For that reason the early Merovingians had already insisted on exercising control over the selection of bishops, a claim advanced since by many states, even as late at the twentieth century. The medieval state was further concerned over the identity of the bishop because of the practice of monarchs in employing prelates in advisory and administrative capacities. There were good reasons for this. In the first place, such men were normally the most competent the king could find. Furthermore, being as a rule less ambitious for wealth and power and better suited to serve as ministers than members of the greedy, haughty, and oftentimes brutal aristocracy, the king would be inclined to place more trust in them. They acted as regents; they supervised the care and education of the king's children; to them were entrusted the keys to the king's iron box when he was away.

Finally, by appointing a bishop as chancellor or justiciar, the king was in effect transferring the burden of supporting him to the diocese, thereby relieving himself of the expense.

The Bishop a Vassal. The most compelling reason, however, why the state demanded a voice, if not sole authority, in the selection of the bishop arose from the fact that the bishop was much more than the most important member of the ecclesiastical hierarchy. He was also a feudal vassal, comparable in power to the count and duke. This he had become during the chaotic ninth and tenth centuries when western Europe had been feudalized. Feudalism, as will be recalled, was based upon land tenure. On the theory that all land belonged to the lord, those vassals holding of his land owed him a number of feudal services, the most important of which was military. Since the lands pertaining to the diocese were frequently extensive, the bishop became automatically one of the king's most powerful vassals. We have seen how the German kings built up the domains of their bishops as an indirect means of strengthening their own positions. Other feudal monarchs were equally aware of the military importance of the bishop. For example, about the only vassal Edward I could count upon in his wars against the Scots was Bishop Bek of Durham, his appointee.

Papal Sovereignty. Yet another facet of the problem of church and state remains to be considered. That was the ambition of the papacy to enjoy the status of a sovereign state. It is difficult to prove that the popes of the sixth through the eighth centuries were desirous of becoming both the official and actual rulers of Rome during this period of Byzantine decline. Once papal temporal sovereignty, with the aid of the Frankish kings, had become a fact, however, there is no question that popes fought to retain, even to enhance, their position. While it is undeniable that motives other than unselfish ones operated in the bosoms of some popes, the fact that every pontiff without exception, whether saint or somewhat less, pursued the same identical policy in this regard, clearly reveals how they all viewed political sovereignty as the necessary prerequisite to spiritual independence. That kings everywhere were selecting men of their choice, frequently relatives, to fill bishoprics and monasteries, served to convince the popes that they could safely pursue no other policy.

Loss of Papal Independence. Of this fact they had become poignantly aware during the unhappy century that followed the death of Pope Nicholas I (d. 867). We have seen how Charlemagne treated the pope as though he were a Frankish bishop, and how he assumed the right to issue capitularies which dealt with such strictly ecclesiastical matters as liturgy and monastic reform. What Charlemagne had done was undoubtedly to the best interests of the church, but the church preferred to do this for itself. Consequently, during the reign of Charlemagne's gentle son, Louis the Pious, the papacy was quick to recover supremacy in ecclesiastical affairs. It even attained such prominence under Nicholas I that it proclaimed the excommunication of the Byzantine emperor for having deposed the patriarch of Constantinople, and forced a Carolingian king to take back his repudiated wife. Almost immediately after Nicholas' death in 867, came collapse for the papacy and the sorriest hundred years in papal history. As we have seen, the onslaught of the Vikings, Saracens, and Magyars not only destroyed organized government, but the ecclesiastical system as well, and the papacy became the football of local Italian politics. A new era dawned for the papacy when Otto I marched into Rome in 962 in answer to a papal plea for aid, thereby inaugurating what was to be roughly a century of domination from the north. While German intervention, in the opinion of many scholars, saved the papacy from dissolution, and while the choice of popes made by Otto and his successors included such extraordinarily capable men as Gerbert and Leo IX, the principle that a lay ruler could designate the head of Christendom was anathema to all reformers. For all men anxious about reforming the church were unanimous in putting their finger on lay control as the prime source of ecclesiastical corruption. To them the logical place to start reform was in Rome—to free the papacy from lay interference.

Papal Electoral Decree of 1059 and Pope Gregory VII. That step was taken in 1059 when a papal decree announced that future popes would be elected by the cardinal clergy of Rome and would be hailed immediately thereafter by the Roman populace. In this instance, what was not said spoke loudest. There was no provision made for imperial approval. Behind this bold move to eliminate the interference of the king of Germany may be seen the hand of Hildebrand, the doughtiest warrior ever to enter the lists in the struggle between church and state in the Middle Ages. Hildebrand was born the son of Italian peasants, but neither the humbleness of his birth nor his small frame and weak voice, could thwart the force of his indomitable will and his fanatical devotion to the cause of reform. He united in his person all the zeal of the Cluniac reform movement, and he drove himself as though he must accomplish its goal singlehandedly in the space of his own lifetime. For almost forty years he guided papal policy toward reform, the last twelve years in his own right as Gregory VII. (Reading 127)

Outbreak of the Investiture Controversy. With papal independence established, the next goal of the reformers—and a far more difficult one— was that of establishing the freedom of episcopal elections. The bitter struggle that ensued between church and state over the question of episcopal succession is known as the investiture controversy. The word investiture is derived from the ritual attending the formal investing of the bishop with the insignia of his office. In the eleventh century when the investiture controversy broke, this investing was being performed by the king. There was nothing reprehensible from the church's point of view for the king to invest the bishop with the usual feudal marks of vassalage, such as a bit of turf and the scepter. The pope might not even have objected too strenuously to the king's also investing his ecclesiastical vassals with the spiritual symbols of their office, in the case of the bishop with ring and crozier, were it not for the fact that the men so invested were ordinarily the king's appointees, not the church's. For what lay at the root of the investiture conflict was the right to select the bishop. Was the king to control this, or was it to be handled canonically, that is, was the bishop to be elected by the clergy of the cathedral? (Reading 128)

Henry IV vs. Gregory VII. As would be expected, the battle over investiture broke out first with the German king. He was the greatest offender in this respect, since he had made control of the German episcopacy a major bulwark of his power. He was also closest to Rome and claimed imperial lordship over the city. In 1075 in a synod held at Rome, Pope Gregory solemnly denounced lay investiture as unlawful. (Reading 129) The same year Henry IV filled the vacant see of Milan with an archbishop of his choice. When called upon by Gregory to withdraw his appointee (Reading 130), Henry convened instead a council of German bishops at Worms which officially declared Gregory deposed. Of this judgment of his bishops, Henry wrote to Gregory in these words: "Henry, King not by usurpation but by God's grace, to Hildebrand, henceforth no Pope but false monk: Christ has called us to our kingdom, while He has never called thee to the priesthood. . . . I, Henry, King by the grace of God, with all of my bishops, say unto thee, 'Come down, come down.' " (Reading 131) Gregory's reply was equally uncompromising. He summoned a synod at Rome, which formally excommunicated and deposed Henry, and sent an appeal to the German princes to carry out the decree. (Reading 132) This the majority of German nobles were only too eager to do, since they had real reason to fear the ambitions of Henry. They therefore suspended Henry for a year, and warned him that if he failed to win papal remission of his sentence of excommunication by February 1077, they would depose him. Henry saw immediately that the combination of pope and feudality was too formidable, and that he would have to submit. So he hurried south with only his wife and son and a few attendants. He found the pope behind the protecting walls of the castle of the Countess Matilda at Canossa, where he had taken refuge at the news of Henry's approach. There took place one of the most dramatic incidents in history, and one that has been most frequently distorted. Though the barefoot Henry, according to Gregory's own account, stood outside the castle walls for three days in the snow begging for forgiveness, it was actually the pope who was the more uncomfortable of the two. For Gregory suspected Henry to be the constitutional liar that he was, and he must have been sorely tempted to deny Henry's plea, particularly since to accept it and revoke the sentence of excommunication would destroy the common front of German nobles against Henry. Fortunately for

Henry, Gregory's conscience prevailed, and he removed the ban of excommunication. (Reading 133)

The Denouement. Despite the pope's action, the German princes proceeded to go through with their plans and depose Henry. (They had actually placed guards at the Alpine passes to prevent the king from going south to make his peace with the pope.) Three years later, when it became manifest that Henry would never surrender his claims to lay investiture, Gregory came to the support of the German princes with a second excommunication of Henry. Henry proved himself equal to the crisis. After suffering a disastrous defeat by the princes, he made an amazing recovery, and soon was crossing the Alps again, this time not as a suppliant, but at the head of an army. Gregory took refuge in the castle of St. Angelo, where he was relieved by Robert Guiscard and his Normans from the south. Though Henry was forced to withdraw, Guiscard's army, which included thousands of Saracens, plundered Rome so savagely that Gregory thought it prudent to leave with Guiscard in order to escape the wrath of the Romans. He died shortly after in 1085 at Salerno, sorely depressed and with only the conviction that he had done God's will to sustain him. His dying words, so the story goes, were: "I have loved justice and hated iniquity; therefore I die in exile."

Concordat of Worms. Though Gregory died in exile, he accomplished much more than he had suspected. Never again was lay investiture carried on so wantonly. It is not that the issue was ever resolved. The best was a compromise agreed to at Worms in 1122, known as the Concordat of Worms. According to the formula accepted by representatives of the church and state, the bishop's election was to be in accordance with the prescriptions of canon law, that is, he was to be elected by the canons of the cathedral. But the election was to be held in the presence of the king or his representative, which meant that the king could always prevent the election of a candidate he did not want. Neither side was entirely happy about the settlement, which in itself was a good indication that it was a fair compromise. As long as the bishop was also a vassal of the king and owed military service, a clear victory for either church or state would have been unreasonable. Probably for a number of reasons, but surely due in part to the manner in which Pope Gregory had dramatized the issue, the caliber of prelates after Canossa was significantly higher than it had been before. (Reading 134)

Innocent III. Gregory's greatest accomplishment was that of again making the papacy the power in European life it had been back in the ninth century under Nicholas, before feudalism had almost smothered it. Because of Gregory's work, it was possible within slightly more than a hundred years of his death, for a more successful pope to exalt the church to the peak of its influence in the Middle Ages. This pope was Innocent III, the youngest man ever to wear the papal tiara. What recommended him to his electors was his profound knowledge of law, his administrative acumen, and his deep spirituality. Innocent's fame rests principally upon the success he attained in his dealings with the great monarchs of Christendom. This is unfortunate for two reasons: first, because that success was not so unqualified as is usually assumed; second, because it obscures his greater achievement in the realm of administrative and disciplinary reform, and in the clarification and preservation of Christian orthodoxy. So brilliant were his knowledge and application of law, that students delighted to attend sessions of the curia when he presided. As soon as he became pope (1198), he proceeded to sweep away the bureaucratic dead wood in the curia and presently made it the most efficient administrative system in the world. Yet this same pope could compose beautiful religious poetry and express the contemplative thoughts of a true mystic (e.g. *On the Contempt of the World*).

The Fourth Lateran Council. Innocent considered the Fourth Crusade his greatest work. Though unhappy about its sequel—the capture of Christian Constantinople rather than Moslem-held Jerusalem—he consoled himself with the thought that God may have preferred the union of Eastern and Western Christendom to the recovery of the Holy Land. The Fourth Lateran Council which he convened in 1215, reveals his comprehensive grasp of the problems besetting the church and the eminently practical fashion in which they were handled. For many months before the bishops convened, Innocent had committees study the different problems in a long agenda and have reports prepared for the consideration and approval of the council. The council was, therefore, largely his work. This, the Fourth Lateran Council, was one of the largest ever convened. More than four hundred bishops, including the patriarchs of Constantinople and Jerusalem, gathered at Rome to lend its decisions the broadest acceptance. Included among the canons which Innocent proclaimed were the following: the dogma of transubstantiation was defined; annual reception of the sacraments of penance and the Eucharist was required of the faithful; bishops were directed to establish schools for the proper training of priests; clerical and monastic abuses were denounced; the clergy was forbidden to participate in ordeals. The council also took steps in preparation for another Crusade against the Moslems, and approved of Frederick II's election as Holy Roman Emperor.

Stephen Langton. It was not for this that Innocent has been called the greatest of the medieval popes, but rather for his success against several of the most powerful monarchs of Europe. First there was King John of England, who refused to accept Stephen Langton as archbishop of Canterbury. This problem grew out of a disputed election at Canterbury. Upon the death of the last archbishop, the younger monks held a secret election and sent their candidate off to Rome to secure Innocent's blessing. When news of this reached John he was furious, and within a short time another candidate, this one John's choice, was also on his way to Rome. Innocent persuaded all parties, that is, all except John, to compromise on Stephen Langton, a noted English scholar and theologian, but John was adamant. To bring him to heel, Innocent was obliged to employ the three spiritual weapons in the papal arsenal: excommunication, interdict, and deposition. A sentence of excommunication excluded the person involved from Christian society and barred him from the reception of the sacraments and attendance at divine services. Interdict was a ban forbidding the clergy to perform any religious service or to administer any sacraments other than baptism and extreme unction for the faithful of a specified community or area. In an age which took spiritual life seriously, an interdict could generate considerable pressure against the party responsible for the prohibition. Deposition speaks for itself, and Innocent was forced to this when John effectively prevented the employment of the other two weapons. Even the sentence of deposition would have proved fruitless had not the king of France, who was entrusted with the papal crusade to unseat John, given every indication of being able and willing to do this, with the cooperation of the English barony. Before this threat, John capitulated. He even went a step farther. Upon Innocent's request he became his vassal, not so much to please Innocent, as for the protection his character as a papal vassal would afford him against his rebellious barons.

Innocent and Philip Augustus. Innocent's difficulties with Philip Augustus of France were of a more personal nature. Philip had put away his wife Ingeborg, a Danish princess, on the false charge of too close a blood relationship, and subsequently married Agnes of Meran, daughter of a Bavarian duke. The protests of Innocent's aged predecessor in the papacy, Philip had simply ignored, but Innocent spoke a stronger language. Yet it required fifteen years of argument and pressure, including another interdict as futile as the one against John, before Philip reinstated Ingeborg. What left Innocent's victory somewhat hollow was the tardiness of Philip's submission and the fact that Agnes had meantime died. Philip also hoped to qualify as leader of the papal crusade against John, which he could scarcely do as an excommunicate.

Innocent and Germany. Innocent won a third resounding victory, so it is commonly said, in the case of Germany, where he was able to place his ward, Frederick, on the throne in 1215. As we have seen, there were two claimants to the throne after the death of Henry VI, one Philip of Swabia, the other Otto of Brunswick. Of the two, Innocent preferred the latter, since he was a Guelf and traditionally anti-imperialist, and so he declared for him. Yet when a majority of the German princes finally swung around to Philip, Innocent had perforce to follow. Before Philip could actually take over the throne, however, he was cut down by an assassin, which left the road open to Otto. This was a happy turn for Innocent, or so he thought until he learned that Otto, far from returning the papal fiefs taken by Henry VI, was planning to add the pope's own Sicily to the imperial possessions. Innocent therefore excommunicated him and reluctantly joined Philip Augustus in sponsoring the candidacy of Henry VI's son, the future Frederick II. (See page 463.)

Innocent's Position Regarding the State.   It will be noted that in none of these instances did Innocent's stand prove decisive. Had it not been for fortunate circumstances over which the pope had no control, John would not have accepted Langton, Philip Augustus would not have taken back Ingeborg, and the German princes would have had Philip of Swabia as their king. Why then have these three episodes been distorted to appear as smashing victories for Innocent at the expense of the state? Two explanations suggest themselves: first, the wish to show how drastically papal power had waned by contrast in the fourteenth century under Pope Boniface VIII (see page 671); second, the need of historians to offer concrete results to prove Innocent's presumed extravagant claims in the temporal order. Yet Innocent's claims were much more modest than customarily maintained. Actually his position vis-à-vis the state represented nothing beyond an extension of the old Gelasian doctrine of two distinct powers sovereign in their respective spheres, expressed somewhat more positively by Innocent because of his own legal astuteness, the growth of canon law, and the acceptance of such documents as the Donation of Constantine.   (See page 240.)   Innocent never claimed supremacy in the temporal order. He did insist, however, that under certain conditions, he had the right and obligation to dictate to kings and to interfere even in purely civil matters. Thus when a monarch defied the moral law, as had Philip Augustus in putting away his wife, the pope might depose him if he remained obdurate. He might arbitrate a disputed election as that between Otto and Philip of Swabia, since the church, so Innocent claimed, had been responsible for transferring the Empire from the east to the west, and because the pope had crowned the emperor and formally invested him with his imperial authority. (This claim was based upon the forged Donation of Constantine.) Innocent would also have justified his interference in the disputed election on the grounds that here was a situation not covered by civil or feudal law. Consequently, lacking a higher temporal court which could pass judgment, that prerogative devolved upon the highest spiritual authority in existence. For this reason, Innocent agreed to legitimize the natural children of Philip Augustus because, as he explained, though this was a civil matter, there remained no higher authority in the temporal order to which Philip might have appealed.

Innocent and World Government.   Did Innocent aspire to the establishment of a world government with himself as head? There is considerable evidence to support a positive answer to this question. It is all the more convincing since such a view would be consistent with Innocent's faith in the rule of law on the one hand, and his conviction, on the other, that all monarchs are responsible to the same God for their actions. Innocent sought to persuade all the kings of Christendom to follow the lead of the rulers of England, Portugal, Aragon, Sicily, Hungary, and Poland, and become his vassals. While the annual tribute these kings would pay into the papal coffers would not be unwelcome, his principal object in being recognized as feudal suzerain was to erect that kind of world organization which the logic of the medieval situation recommended, namely, a commonwealth of Christian nations under the leadership of the pope. War among Christian nations was a complete miscarriage of the will of God, who wished them to live with one another in harmony and devote their common energies toward the advancement of the City of God against Moslem and pagan. A combination of his power as feudal suzerain with that based upon his spiritual prerogatives in the civil order, would enable Innocent to speak with more authority and success in the attainment of these goals.

An Appraisal. For all of Innocent's high-flown theories and hopes of a Christian world which would do the will of God under his direction, he actually accomplished little toward the attainment of that objective. The kings of England and France largely ignored him until it was to their advantage to accept a settlement. Neither was his position decisive in the selection of a German king. Twice Innocent was forced to flee his own papal states. The Fourth Crusade which he inspired and organized did not even reach Syria. Nevertheless, one must admit that when Innocent died, Stephen Langton was archbishop of Canterbury, Ingeborg was queen of France, and the pope's ward, Frederick, was on the German throne and pledged to undertake a Crusade. A less persistent, more patient pontiff would not have achieved so much, nor would have one with a less clear appreciation of the gap between theoretical rights and actual power. Therein lay the answer to Innocent's success in the temporal order. He never permitted the high prerogatives which canonists insisted were his to blind him to the realities of the political situation, a mistake which cost his successor of a hundred years later, Boniface VIII, so grievously. (See page 671.)

Heresy and the Inquisition

Rise of Heresies. Similar to this gap between the powers which the pope might claim in theory and those he could exercise in practice, was the one which frequently yawned between the lives the clergy were expected to lead and those they actually did. Part of this was entirely natural. Even St. Paul confessed to being buffetted by an "angel of Satan," and one may safely assume that many of Paul's medieval representatives did not measure up to that apostle's strength in resisting the blandishments of the evil spirit. As pointed out above, the most persistent theme in the history of monasticism is that of decline and reform. Only zealots of the mettle of a St. Bernard could remain adamant to the temptation of relaxing the rigor of monastic constitutions. Yet this again was nothing unusual, and monastic decline would not of itself have contributed to the rise of heretical movements. However, it was symptomatic of a general deterioration which affected the spiritual life of medieval Europe in the last half of the twelfth century, when the Cluniac reform movement had spent itself and before the friars had appeared to correct the situation. It was during this interval that two heretical movements arose which, in large measure, represented protests against the clerical apathy and laxity of the times.

The Waldensians. These two heresies, the Waldensian surely, the Albigensian less so, were essentially reform movements in their inception. Peter Waldo, who gives his name to the Waldensian heresy, reminds one of St. Francis. Peter was a rich merchant of Lyons who was impelled by love of God and his less fortunate fellowmen to distribute his wealth among the poor. His piety attracted other men much as had that of St. Francis, and the early Waldensian community which he organized, paralleled that of the Franciscans in its practice of austerities and charity. Unlike the Franciscans, however, Waldo had a deep interest in the Bible, parts of which he translated into the vernacular. He also encouraged his followers to study the New Testament and to preach its lessons to the people. Laymen engaged in corporal works of mercy were one thing, quite another were laymen who preached and preached controversially. So, at any rate, thought the pope, and he refused to confirm Waldo's group as a formal religious community. He did finally give qualified permission to him and his followers to preach: they must always obtain authorization from the ordinary of the diocese. This authorization, Waldo and his "Poor Men of Lyons" as they were called, became careless about securing, being convinced that they knew more about the Bible than the bishop in the first place, and, in the second, that their lives of poverty and self-denial were more Christ-like than his and those of his clergy. The inevitable happened. Preaching without permission, and being occasionally unorthodox and frequently anticlerical in what they preached, they provoked papal condemnation in 1181, whereupon what had begun as a reform movement swiftly drifted into revolutionary channels. The more radical Waldensians rejected the priesthood and with it the mass, sacraments, and the church as a divinely instituted institution. Any good man, even woman, might preach so they insisted, since all that a Christian had to believe was in the Bible, and the Bible was sufficiently clear to be interpreted by anyone. It is interesting to note to what degree the Waldensians anticipated the doctrines of the Protestants of the sixteenth century. In their repudiation of oaths and in their pacifism, they were the medieval precursors of the Quakers.

The Albigensians. A more dangerous heresy because of the larger numbers affected and because of its basically un-Christian doctrines, was that of the Albigensians. This movement derived its name from its chief center at Albi in southern France. The sect may be traced back to the Manichaean heresy of the third century (see page 70), but its long association with Christianity left the movement a puzzling confusion of bizarre tenets and practices. One of its peculiarities was the fact that it owed its popularity to two paradoxical features, the one, a puritanical clergy, the other, the offer of a frankly sensual code for the laity. Appealing to the dualistic principle of the Manichaeans that all material was evil, the "perfect" from whom the clergy were recruited, were required to lead celibate lives of austere asceticism. For the rest, though the same rule applied that all flesh was evil, the "believers" need have little concern about surrendering to the weaknesses of the flesh, provided they "believe" what the ideal was and that they receive "consolation" before death. Once they had received this "sacrament," essentially the laying on of hands, they joined the ranks of the "perfect" and must abide by the rigorous regimen required of this group. Lest one backslide after receiving "consolation," suicide was strongly recommended. The clergy might even feel it their duty to facilitate such "suicides" by means of suffocation, should the newly initiated give evidence of weakness. Marriage came in for special condemnation, since it constituted a formal defiance of the Albigensian rule against procreation. Since no such Christian deterrents to immorality existed for the masses as the fear of purgatory or hell, and since if the worst happened and the person died without "consolation" he would simply be reincarnated and be given another opportunity, the lives of most Albigensians hardly bore out the claim that theirs was a reform movement.

Church and State Hostile to Heresy. Yet whether the original motivation of such movements as the Waldensian and Albigensian was reform or revolt, the reaction of both church and state was bitterly hostile. It had been so since the time of Constantine, although the church fathers generally condemned the Christian emperors for inflicting the death sentence for heresy. Even Innocent III and the Fourth Lateran Council did not recommend it, although by the middle thirteenth century it was generally accepted as both necessary and logical. If counterfeiting was punishable by death, argued Aquinas, why not the man who counterfeits truth, since truth is so much more important. And the state was not far behind. The "modern" Frederick II ferreted out heretics and executed them with a zeal which would have done credit to a Crusader. He did this because church and state were so closely-knit in medieval society and both derived their sanctions from the same divine authority, that to attack one would be to endanger the other. One is reminded of the abhorrence felt toward anarchism by both church and state in the nineteenth century and in many countries against Communism in the twentieth. If there was any hesitancy on the part of the medieval state to appreciate the peril to itself inherent in heresy, the ecclesiastical authorities were quick to enlighten it. Thus Pope Gregory XI instructed the archbishop of Canterbury to make it clear to Edward III how the "highly dangerous errors" of John Wyclif "threatened the destruction of the entire state." (Readings 138, 139)

The Albigensian Crusade. Though the church feared the heretic and abominated his heresy, its first aim was that of convincing him of the falsity of his views and of winning him back to orthodoxy. Failing this, since such a source of spiritual infection could not be tolerated, his confinement or death became necessary. Until the thirteenth century, the eradication of heresy was part of the bishop's ordinary responsibility of preserving the integrity of the faith in his diocese. This method proved hopelessly inadequate in the early thirteenth century, however, when large numbers joined the Waldensian and Albigensian movements. Pope Innocent considered the situation a desperate one, particularly since many feudal lords in the affected areas revealed a sympathy for the heresies. Such was the case with Count Raymond VI of Toulouse, whose province was a hotbed of Albigensianism. When the count's agents murdered the papal legate who had excommunicated him, Innocent proclaimed the Albigensian crusade (1209-1229). This proved successful in destroying Albigensianism, although the culture and prosperity of the area suffered almost as seriously.

The Inquisition. Though the Albigensian stronghold had been destroyed, scattered islands of heresy still existed, and men and women tainted with Albigensian and Waldensian views could be found in many places in Italy and France. To cope with this situation, Gregory IX established in 1233 what is known as the Court of the Inquisition or more popularly, the Inquisition. This court, while under the nominal control of the bishop, operated as a direct arm of the papacy. It was staffed with Franciscan and Dominican friars who had been trained to detect heretical views, as well as to convince those charged with heresy of the error of their ways. The court followed a simple routine. A month before it moved into an area, announcement would be made to that effect, coupled with a warning to those under suspicion to clear themselves during that period. When the month of grace had elapsed, the inquisitor and his assessors appeared and examined all persons charged with heretical views. Those who were found guilty and who confessed their errors, were given sentences commensurate with the seriousness of their crimes. Those who refused to admit their guilt in the face of strong evidence, might be tortured in order to force a confession. Those who remained obdurate and defiant, together with any relapsed persons who might have been apprehended, were turned over to the civil arm to be executed.

In Retrospect. Much of the odium attaching to the Inquisition arises from the failure of modern observers to judge it in the historical context of the times. The Middle Ages, in fact western society until well into the nineteenth century, were generous in meting out the death sentence. To the Middle Ages, heresy was the greatest of all crimes. Heresy even outranked premeditated murder in point of heinousness. The heretic was to the Middle Ages what the anarchist was to the nineteenth century. Medieval society did not accept the principle of freedom of conscience or of worship for Christians, since no doubt existed in the minds of ecclesiastical and civil authorities as to what God wanted men to believe. The use of torture to elicit confessions was more Roman than medieval. The practice can almost certainly be linked with the introduction of Roman Law and legal machinery into western Europe in the twelfth and thirteenth centuries. Two final observations may be pertinent: first, when the state failed to cooperate against heresy as in the case of the English government and John Wyclif (see page 679), the church was helpless; second, the number of heretics executed was small. The most violent of all inquisitors, Bernard Gui (d. 1331), turned over forty-five people to the civil arm for execution during his fifteen years of office.

READINGS

No. 126. The Gelasian Doctrine

(Robinson's *Readings*, pp. 72-73.)

There are two powers, august Emperor (Anastasius), by which this world is chiefly ruled, namely, the sacred authority of the priest and the royal power. Of these, that of the priests is the more weighty, since they have to render an account for even the kings of men in the divine judgment. You are also aware, dear son, that while you are permitted honorably to rule over human kind, yet in things divine you bow your head humbly before the leaders of the clergy and await from their hands the means of your salvation. In the reception and proper disposition of the heavenly mysteries you recognize that you should be subordinate rather than superior to the religious order, and that in these matters you depend on their judgment rather than wish to force them to follow your will.

If the ministers of religion, recognizing the supremacy granted you from heaven in matters affecting the public order, obey your laws, lest otherwise they might obstruct the course of secular affairs by irrelevant considerations, with what readiness should you not yield them obedience to whom is assigned the dispensing of the sacred mysteries of religion. Accordingly, just as there is no slight danger in the case of the priests if they refrain from speaking when the service of the divinity requires, so there is no little risk for those who disdain—which God forbid—when they should obey. And if it is fitting that the hearts of the faithful should submit to all priests in general who properly administer divine affairs, how much the more is obedience due to the bishop of that see which the Most High ordained to be above all others, and which is consequently dutifully honored by the devotion of the whole Church.

No. 127. Papal Electoral Law of 1059

(Thatcher & McNeal, *Source Book*, pp. 128-131.)

Most beloved brothers and fellow-bishops, you know, since it is not hidden even from the humbler members, how after the death of our predecessor, Stephen of blessed memory, this apostolic seat, which by the will of God I now serve, suffered many evils, how indeed it was subject to many serious attacks from the simoniacal money-changers, so that the column of the living God seemed about to topple, and the skiff of the supreme fisherman [Peter] was nearly wrecked by the tumultuous storms. Therefore, if it pleases you, we ought now, with the aid of God, prudently to take measures to prevent future misfortunes, and to provide for the state of the church in the future, lest those evils, again appearing, which God forbid, should prevail against it. Therefore, fortified by the authority of our predecessors and the other holy fathers, we decide and declare:

1. On the death of a pontiff of the universal Roman church, first, the cardinal bishops, with the most diligent consideration, shall elect a successor; then they shall call in the other cardinal clergy [to ratify their choice], and finally the rest of the clergy and the people shall express their consent to the new election.

2. In order that the disease of venality may not have any opportunity to spread, the devout clergy shall be the leaders in electing the pontiff, and

the others shall acquiesce. And surely this order of election is right and lawful, if we consider either the rules or the practice of various fathers, or if we recall that decree of our predecessor, St. Leo, for he says: 'By no means can it be allowed that those should be ranked as bishops who have not been elected by the clergy, and demanded by the people, and consecrated by their fellow-bishops of the province with the consent of the metropolitan.' But since the apostolic seat is above all the churches in the earth, and therefore can have no metropolitan over it, without doubt the cardinal bishops perform in it the office of metropolitan, in that they advance the elected prelate to the apostolic dignity [that is, choose, consecrate, and enthrone him].

3. The pope shall be elected from the church in Rome, if a suitable person can be found in it, but if not, he is to be taken from another church.

4. In the papal election—in accordance with the right which we have already conceded to Henry and to those of his successors who may obtain the same right from the apostolic see—due honor and reverence shall be shown our beloved son, Henry, king and emperor elect [that is, the rights of Henry shall be respected].

5. But if the wickedness of depraved and iniquitous men shall so prevail that a pure, genuine, and free election cannot be held in this city, the cardinal bishops with the clergy and a few laymen shall have the right to elect the pontiff wherever they shall deem most fitting.

6. But if after an election any disturbances of war or any malicious attempt of men shall prevail so that he who is elected cannot be enthroned according to custom in the papal chair, the pope elect shall nevertheless exercise the right of ruling the holy Roman church, and of disposing of all its revenues, as we know St. Gregory did before his consecration. . . .

I, Nicholas, bishop of the holy Catholic and apostolic church, have subscribed this decree which has been promulgated by us, as said above. I, Boniface, by the grace of God bishop of Albano, have subscribed. I, Humbert, bishop of the holy church of Silva Candida, have subscribed. I, Peter, bishop of the church of Ostia, have subscribed. And other bishops to the number of seventy-six, with priests and deacons.

No. 128. The *Dictatus* of Gregory VII

(Robinson's *Readings*, pp. 274-275.)

The Roman church was founded by God alone.
The Roman bishop alone is properly called universal.
He alone may depose bishops and reinstate them.

His legate, though of inferior grade, takes precedence, in a council, of all bishops and may render a decision of deposition against them.

He alone may use the insignia of empire (on basis of Donation of Constantine).

The pope is the only person whose feet are kissed by all princes.

His title is unique in the world. (This is the first distinct assertion of the exclusive right of the bishop of Rome to the title of pope, once applied to all bishops.)

He may depose emperors.

No council may be regarded as a general one without his consent.

No book or chapter may be regarded as canonical without his authority.

A decree of his may be annulled by no one; he alone may annul the decrees of all.

He may be judged by no one.

No one shall dare to condemn one who appeals to the papal see.

The Roman church has never erred, nor ever, by the witness of Scripture, shall err to all eternity.

He may not be considered Catholic who does not agree with the Roman church.

The pope may absolve the subjects of the unjust from their allegiance.

No. 129. Papal decree forbidding lay investiture

(Robinson's *Readings*, pp. 275-276.)

Inasmuch as we have learned that, contrary to the ordinances of the holy fathers, the investiture with churches is, in many places, performed by lay persons, and that from this cause many disturbances arise in the Church by which the Christian religion is degraded, we decree that no one of the clergy shall receive the investiture with a bishopric, or abbey, or church, from the hand of an emperor, or king, or of any lay person, male or female. If he shall presume to do so, let him know that such investiture is void by apostolic authority, and that he himself shall lie under excommunication until fitting satisfaction shall have been made.

Following the ordinances of the holy fathers, as we decreed in our former councils held by the mercy of God concerning the regulation of ecclesiastical offices, so also now by apostolic authority we decree and confirm: that, if any one shall henceforth receive a bishopric or abbey from the hands of any lay person, he shall by no means be reckoned among the bishops and abbots; nor shall any hearing be granted him as bishop or abbot. Moreover we further deny him the favor of St. Peter and entrance to the Church, until, coming to his senses, he shall surrender the position that he has appropriated through criminal ambition and disobedience—which is the sin of idolatry. We decree, moreover, that the same rule be observed in the case of inferior ecclesiastical positions.

Likewise if any emperor, king, duke, margrave, count, or any secular dignitary or person shall presume to bestow the investiture with bishoprics, or with any ecclesiastical office, let him know that he is bound by the bonds of the same condemnation. And, furthermore, unless he come to his senses and relinquish her prerogatives to the Church, let him feel, in this present life, the divine wrath both in body and estate, in order that at the Lord's coming his soul may be saved.

No. 130. Gregory's letter upbraiding Henry for ignoring his decrees

(Robinson's *Readings*, pp. 276-279.)

For we cannot but hesitate to send thee our benediction when we seriously consider the strictness of the Judge to whom we shall have to render account for the ministry intrusted to us by St. Peter, chief of the apostles. For thou art said knowingly to associate with men excommunicated by a judgment of the apostolic chair and by sentence of a synod. If this be true, thou thyself dost know that thou mayest not receive the favor of the divine, nor of the apostolic benediction, unless those who have been excommunicated be separated from thee and compelled to do penance, and thou, with condign repentance and satisfaction, obtain absolution and pardon for thy misdeeds. Therefore we counsel thy Highness that, if thou dost feel thyself guilty in this matter, thou shouldst seek the advice of some devout bishop, with prompt confession. . . .

In the next place, it seems strange to us that although thou dost so often send us such devoted letters; and although thy Highness does show such humility in the messages of thy legates . . . yet in conduct and action thou dost show thyself most stubborn, and in opposition to the canonical and apostolic decrees in those matters which the religion of the Church deems of chief importance. For, not to mention other things, in the affair of Milan the acutal outcome shows with what intent thou didst make, and how thou didst carry out, the promises made through thy mother and through our brothers the bishops whom we sent to thee. And now, indeed, inflicting wound upon wound, thou hast, contrary to the rules of the apostolic chair, given the churches of Fermo and Spoleto—if indeed a church can be given or granted by a mere man—to certain persons not even known to us, on whom, unless they are previously well known and proven, it is not lawful regularly to perform the laying on of hands. . . .

In this year a synod was assembled about the apostolic chair, over which the heavenly dispensation willed that we should preside, and at which some of thy faithful subjects were present. Seeing that the good order of the Christian religion has now for some time been disturbed, and that the chief and proper methods of winning souls have, at the instigation of the devil, long been neglected and suppressed, we, struck by the danger and impending ruin of the Lord's flock, reverted to the decrees and teachings of the holy fathers,—decreeing nothing new, nothing of our own invention. (For decrees, see preceding document.)

Lest these things should seem unduly burdensome or unjust to thee, we did admonish thee, through thy faithful servants, that the changing of an evil custom should not alarm thee; that thou shouldst send to us wise and religious men from thy land, to demonstrate or prove, if they could, by any reasoning, in what respects, saving the honor of the Eternal King and without danger to our soul, we might moderate the decree as passed by the holy fathers, and we would yield to their counsels. Even without our friendly admonitions it would have been but right that, before thou didst violate apostolic decrees, thou shouldst reasonably have appealed to us in cases where we oppressed thee or infringed thy prerogatives. But how little thou didst esteem our commands or the dictates of justice is shown by those things which thou afterwards didst.

But since the long-suffering patience of God still invites thee to amend thy ways, we have hopes that thy understanding may be awakened, and thy heart and mind be bent to obey the mandates of God: we exhort thee with paternal love to recognize the dominion of Christ over thee and to reflect how dangerous it is to prefer thine own honor to his.

No. 131. Henry's defiant reply to Gregory

(Robinson's *Readings*, pp. 279-281.)

Henry, King not by usurpation but by holy ordination of God, to Hildebrand, now no Pope but false monk:

Such greeting as this hast thou merited through thy disturbances, for there is no rank in the Church but thou hast brought upon it, not honor but disgrace, not a blessing but a curse. To mention a few notable cases out of the many, thou hast not only dared to assail the rulers of the holy Church, the anointed of the Lord,—archbishops, bishops, and priests,—but thou hast trodden them under foot like slaves ignorant of what their master is doing. By so crushing them thou hast won the favor of the common herd; thou hast regarded them all as knowing nothing,—thyself alone as knowing all things. Yet this knowledge thou hast exerted, not for their advantage but for their destruction; so that with reason we believe St. Gregory, whose name thou hast usurped, prophesied of thee when he said, "The pride of the magistrate commonly waxes great if the number of those subject to him be great, and he thinks that he can do more than they all."

We, forsooth, have endured all this in our anxiety to save the honor of the apostolic see, but thou hast mistaken our humility for fear, and hast, accordingly, ventured to attack the royal power conferred upon us by God, and threatened to divest us of it. As if we had received our kingdom from thee! As if the kingdom and the empire were in thy hands, not in God's! For our Lord Jesus Christ did call us to the kingdom, although he has not called thee to the priesthood: that thou hast attained by the following steps.

By craft abhorrent to the profession of monk, thou hast acquired wealth; by wealth, influence; by influence, arms; by arms, a throne of peace. And from the throne of peace thou hast destroyed peace; thou hast turned subjects against their governors, for thou, who were not called of God, hast taught that our bishops, truly so called, should be despised. . . .

Thou hast further assailed me also, who, although unworthy of anointing, have nevertheless been anointed to the kingdom, and who, according to the traditions of the holy fathers, am subject to the judgment of God alone, to be deposed upon no charge save that of deviation from the faith,—which God avert! For the holy fathers by their wisdom committed the judgment and deposition of even Julian the Apostate not to themselves but to God alone. Likewise the true pope, Peter, himself exclaims: "Fear God. Honor the king." But thou, who dost not fear God, art dishonoring me, his appointed one. Wherefore, St. Paul, since he spared not an angel of heaven if he should preach other than the gospel, has not excepted thee, who dost teach other doctrine upon earth. For he says, "If any one, whether I, or an angel from heaven, shall preach the gospel other than that which has been preached to you, he shall be damned."

Thou, therefore, damned by this curse and by the judgment of all our bishops and ourselves, come down and relinquish the apostolic chair which thou hast usurped. Let another assume the seat of St. Peter, who will not practice violence under the cloak of religion, but will teach St. Peter's wholesome doctrine. I, Henry, king by the grace of God, together with all our bishops, say unto thee: "Come down, come down, to be damned throughout all eternity!"

No. 132. Gregory's deposition of Henry IV

(Robinson's *Readings*, pp. 281-282.)

O St. Peter, chief of the apostles, incline to us, I beg, thy holy ear, and listen to thy servant, whom from infancy thou hast nurtured, and whom, until this day, thou hast shielded from the hand of the wicked that hated me, and do hate me, for my faithfulness to thee. Thou and my lady, the Mother of God, and thy brother, St. Paul, are witnesses for me among all the saints that thy holy Roman church placed me in control against my will; that I had no thought of violence in ascending to thy chair, and that I should rather have ended my life as a pilgrim than by worldly means to have gained thy throne for the sake of earthly glory.

Therefore, through thy grace and through my own merit, I believe that it has been and is thy will that the Christian people especially committed to thee should obey me. To me, in particular, as thy representative and the recipient of thy favor, hast God granted the power of binding and loosing in heaven and earth. In this confidence, therefore, for the honor and security of thy Church, in the name of Almighty God, Father, Son, and Holy Ghost, by thy power and authority, I withdraw from Henry the king, son of Henry the emperor, a rebel of incredible insolence against thy Church, his right to rule over the whole kingdom of the Germans and over Italy. And I absolve all Christians from the bonds of the oath which they have taken to him or which they shall in future take; and I forbid any one to serve him as king.

For it is fitting that he who strives to lessen the honor of thy Church should himself lose the honor which seems to belong to him. And since he has scorned to obey as a Christian, and has not returned to God whom he has deserted, but has had intercourse with the excommunicated; practiced manifold iniquities; spurned the counsels which, as thou art witness, I sent to him for his own salvation; separated himself from thy Church and endeavored to rend it asunder; I bind him, in thy stead, with the chain of the anathema. Relying upon thee, I bind him, that the people may know and prove that thou art Peter, and upon thy rock the Son of the living God hath built his Church, and the gates of hell shall not prevail against it.

No. 133. Gregory's account of Henry's penance at Canossa

(Henderson's *Historical Documents*, pp. 385-387.)

Bishop Gregory, servant of the servants of God, to all the archbishops, bishops, dukes, counts, and other princes of the realm of the Germans who defend the Christian faith, greeting and apostolic benediction.

Inasmuch as for love of justice ye assumed common cause and danger with us in the struggle of Christian warfare, we have taken care to indicate to you, beloved, with sincere affection, how the king, humbled to penance, obtained the pardon of absolution and how the whole affair has progressed since his entry into Italy up to the present time.

As had been agreed with the legates who had been sent to us on your part, we came into Lombardy about twenty days before the date on which one of the commanders was to come over the pass to meet us, awaiting his advent that we might cross over to the other side. But when the term fixed upon had already passed, and we were told that at this time on account of many difficulties—as we can readily believe—an escort could not be sent to meet us, we were involved in no little care as to what would be best for us to do, having no other means of crossing to you.

Meanwhile, however, we learned for certain that the king was approaching. He also, before entering Italy, sent on to us suppliant legates, offering in all things to render satisfaction to God, to St. Peter and to us. And he renewed his promise that, besides amending his life, he would observe all obedience if only he might merit to obtain from us the favour of absolution and the apostolic benediction. When, after long deferring this and holding frequent consultations, we had, through all the envoys who passed, severely taken him to task for his excesses: he came at length of his own accord, with a few followers, showing nothing of hostility or boldness, to the town of Canossa where we were tarrying. And there, having laid aside all the belongings of royalty, wretchedly, with bare feet and clad in wool, he continued for three days to stand before the gate of the castle. Nor did he desist from imploring with many tears the aid and consolation of the apostolic mercy until he had moved all of those who were present there, and whom the report of it reached, to such pity and depth of compassion that, interceding for him with many prayers and tears, all wondered indeed at the unaccustomed hardness of our heart, while some actually cried out that we were exercising, not the gravity of apostolic severity, but the cruelty, as it were, of a tyrannical ferocity.

Finally, conquered by the persistency of his compunction and by the constant supplications of all those who were present, we loosed the chain of the anathema and at length received him into the favour of communion and into the lap of the holy mother church, those being accepted as sponsors for him whose names are written below. And of this transaction we also received a confirmation at the hands of the abbot of Cluny, of our daughters Matilda and the countess Adelaide, and of such princes, episcopal and lay, as seemed to us useful for this purpose. . . .

No. 134. Concordat of Worms

(Robinson's *Readings*, pp. 292-293.)

I, Bishop Calixtus, servant of the servants of God, do grant to thee, beloved son Henry, by the grace of God emperor august of the Romans, permission to hold the elections of the bishops and abbots of the German realm who belong to the kingdom, in thy presence, without simony or show of violence; with the understanding that, should any discord arise among those concerned, thou, by the counsel and judgment of the metropolitan and the suffragan bishops, shalt give support and aid to the party which appears to have the better case. Moreover the one elected may receive the regalia from thee through the scepter, subject to no exactions; and he shall perform his lawful duties to thee for them.

He who is consecrated in other parts of the empire [i.e. in Burgundy or Italy] shall, within six months and subject to no exactions, receive the regalia from thee through the scepter, and shall perform his lawful duties for them, saving all rights which are known to pertain to the Roman Church. In whatever cases thou shalt make complaint to me and ask my help, I, as my office requires, will furnish thee aid. I grant, moreover, to thee, and to all those who are or have been of thy party during this conflict, a true peace.

In the name of the holy and indivisible Trinity, I, Henry, by the grace of God emperor august of the Romans, for the love of God and of the holy Roman Church and of our lord, Pope Calixtus, and for the cleansing of my soul, do surrender to God and to the holy apostles of God, Peter and Paul, and to the holy Catholic Church, all investiture through the ring and the staff; and do agree that in all churches throughout my kingdom and empire there shall be canonical elections and free consecration. . . .

And I grant a true peace to our master, Pope Calixtus, and to the holy Roman Church, and to all those who are or have been on its side. In matters where the holy Roman Church shall seek assistance, I will faithfully render it, and whensoever it shall appeal to me I will see that justice is done.

No. 135. Letters of St. Bernard of Clairvaux

(From *Life and Works of Saint Bernard, Abbot of Clairvaux*, ed. Dom John Mabillon, tr. S. J. Eales I. London, 1889.)

No. 1. (To his cousin Robert who had withdrawn from the Cistercian order to Cluniac. Bernard recalls, with wonderful gentleness and affection more than fatherly, Robert, his relative; who, induced either by shrinking from a very severe Rule, the attraction of a freer life, or the blandishments and cunning suggestions of others, had withdrawn from the Cistercian Order to the Cluniac.)

I have waited long enough, my dear son Robert, perhaps too long, [hoping] that the grace of God might deign to visit both your soul and mine, inspiring you with salutary contrition and me with joy for your repentance. But since my hope is so far not fulfilled, I am no longer able to hide my grief or suppress my anxiety. . . . I do not ask why you went away. I complain only because you have not returned. I speak not of the causes of your departure, but of the delay of your return. Return only, and there shall be peace. Return, and it shall suffice, and I will sing with joy, "He was dead and is alive again; he was lost and is found!" (St. Luke xv, 32)

Surely it was my fault that you departed. I was rigid to a delicate youth; I was severe, and treated harshly a sensitive mind. When you were here you were wont, as far as I remember, to murmur against me, and since, as I have heard, you do not cease to blame me, though absent. It shall not be laid to your charge. I might, perhaps, allege that it was my duty to restrain the passions of petulant youth, and that those harsh beginnings of strict discipline are needful in early years, as the Scripture bears witness: "Chasten thy son with a rod, and thou shalt deliver his soul from death" (Prov. xxiii. 13); and again, "Whom the Lord loveth he chasteneth, and scourgeth every son whom he receiveth" (Heb. xxi, 6); and that "More wholesome are the wounds of a friend than the kisses of an enemy" (Prov. xxvii, 6).

But let it be, as I said, that it was by my fault you went away; only let there be no contention about the offence to hinder the amends for it. I have, perhaps, sometimes in some matters acted unwisely towards you, but never have I been ill-disposed. Therefore, spare the penitent, or at least have consideration for one who speaks frankly to you. If you fear for the future you shall find me not what I was, because I think that you are not what you were. A changed person yourself, you shall find me changed, and him whom you before feared as a master you may safely embrace as a companion. Therefore, whether you withdrew by my fault, as you think and I do not dispute, or by your own, as many think, although I do not maintain it, or by our common fault, as I incline to think, if for this reason you demur to return, you alone shall be without excuse. . . . Now, if you are unwilling to return, seek some other excuse wherewith to flatter your conscience, for henceforth there will be no reason for you to dread the severity of my rule. You need not fear that I shall be too severe to you when you are here, seeing that I abase myself with my whole heart to you when absent, and am bound to you by entire affection. I practise humility, I promise love, and do you still fear? You have fled from a stern [ruler]; return to a gentle one. Let my lenity recall you, since my severity drove you away. . . . (Pp. 107-109.)

> No. 102. (To a certain abbot. Bernard advises that all possible means should be tried to correct a refractory monk, but that, if incorrigible, he should be expelled, lest he should infect others by his company.)

Respecting the brother who is disorderly and disorders others, nor respects the authority of his superior, I give you brief but faithful advice. It is the occupation of the devil to go about in the House of God and seek whom he may devour; on the other hand, it is the task committed to your watchfulness, never as far as you are able, to give place to the devil. The more efforts he makes then to separate from the flock a poor little sheep that he may draw it away the more easily whither there will be none to deliver it from him, the more strenuously, as far as in you lies, ought you to resist, that the enemy may not be able to snatch it from your arms, and say I have prevailed against him. Have recourse, then, in order to save that brother, to every office of charity; spare neither kindnesses, good advice, private reprimands, nor public remonstrances, even sharp correction of words and, if necessary, blows, but, above all, what is usually more efficacious, the pious intercessions of yourself and your brethren to God for him.

But if, when you have done all these things you have no success, you are bound to follow the counsel of the apostle when he says, "Put away from among yourselves that wicked person" (I Cor. v. 13). Let the wicked man be taken away, that he may not make others wicked, for an evil tree can bear only evil fruit. I say that he should be taken away, but not in the manner that he himself wishes; nor should he suppose that he can be permitted to live with your license away from the community, against his profession avoiding obedience, under his own authority, and that according to the law and with conscience wrongly at ease; but he should be cut off, as a diseased sheep is parted from the flock, as a gangrened limb from the body; and in going forth he should be made to know for certain that he will be held by you as a heathen man and a publican. And do not fear that you will act against charity if you provide for the peace of many by the expulsion of one—of one whose malice may easily destroy the peace of many brethren who dwell together. Let that declaration of Solomon console you, "No one can correct that person whom God leaves alone" (Eccles. vii. 13), and that of the Saviour, "Every plantation which My Father hath not planted shall be rooted up" (St. Matt. xv. 13), and that of S. John the Evangelist concerning schismatics, "They went out from us, because they were not of us" (I. S. John ii. 19), and that from the Apostle, "If the unbelieving depart, let him depart" (I Cor. vii. 15). Otherwise the rod of the wicked ought not to be left over the lot of the righteous, lest the righteous put forth their hand unto wickedness. For it is better that one member should perish than the whole community. (Pp. 343-345.)

No. 136. Hugh of St. Victor, the "leading theologian of the twelfth century"

(From *Hugh of Saint Victor on the Sacraments of the Christian Faith*, tr. Roy J. Deferrari. Cambridge, 1951. By permission of the Mediaeval Academy of America.)

On the mystery of light; why it was made first (p. 14)

Therefore, God in beginning to accomplish His works made light first, that afterwards he might make all things in light. For He signified to us that He does not like works which are done in darkness, because they are evil: "For every one that doth evil hateth the light, and cometh not to the light, that his works may not be reproved, for they are evil." (John III, 20. The last phrase is apparently from end of John III, 19). "But he that doth truth, cometh to the light, that his works may be made manifest, because they are done in God." (John III, 21). Therefore, He himself who was to do truth, did not wish to work in darkness; but He came to light and made light, that He might make Himself manifest through light. For He did not make light that He himself might see by light, but that He might make His works manifest by light, because they were done in God. "And" so "God saw all the things that he had made, and they were very good." (Gen. 1, 31). It was necessary for me to state this by way of introduction to give the reason why God made light first.

That man was placed, not created in paradise (p. 117)

Therefore, man was placed and not created in such a place filled with such delights, that he might impute the blessing of God not to nature but to grace, as it is written: "The Lord God took a man, and placed him in a paradise of pleasure." (Cf. Gen. 2, 8.) For he whom He is said to have taken and afterwards placed in paradise, is clearly shown to have been created elsewhere, and to have been removed thence to be placed here.

Why one was created (p. 117)

Therefore, God created first one man, that the beginning of the human race might be one, so that in this the pride of the devil also might be confounded, and the humility of human nature glorified by the likeness of the divine image. For the devil had desired to be another beginning from God, and, that his pride might on this account be the more confounded, man received that in gift which the devil wished perversely to seize and could not obtain; so that the image of God appeared in man in this, that just as God was the beginning of creation for all things, so man would be the beginning of generation for all men, and all men, because they would know that they were from one and were one, would all love one another as if one.

Why woman was made from man, and why from the side (p. 117)

But afterwards as a help to generation woman was made from man himself, since, if she had been made from another source, surely the beginning of all men would not have been one. Now she was made from the side of man that it might be shown that she was created for association in love, lest perhaps, if she had been made from the head, she would seem to be preferred to man unto damnation, or, if from the feet, to be subject unto slavery. Since, therefore, she was furnished to man neither as a mistress nor a handmaid but as a companion, she had to be produced neither from the head nor the feet but from the side, in order that he might realize that she was to be placed beside him, whom he learned had been taken from his very side.

Why the rib was taken from man in sleep (pp. 117-8)

The rib, indeed, from which the body of woman might be fashioned was taken from man in sleep rather than in wakefulness, lest in this he should be thought to have felt some punishment, and that at the same time the marvelous work of divine power might be proven, which opened the side of man while asleep, and yet did not arouse him from the repose of slumber. But, so far as pertains to the spiritual interpretation, the first Adam in sleep furnished from his side the material whence his spouse might be created, because the second Adam afterwards, overcome by the sleep of death on the cross that His spouse the Church might be formed, supplied sacraments by shedding blood with water from His side.

Furthermore, that the body of woman is said to have been made from the rib of man must be understood thus, that from the substance alone of the rib itself, multiplied by the divine power in it, without any extrinsic addition, the same body is believed to have been made, by that miracle indeed whereby afterwards with five loaves of bread multiplied in the hands of Jesus by heavenly benediction five thousand men were filled.

No. 137. The will of St. Francis

(Robinson's *Readings*, pp. 392-395.)

God gave it to me, Brother Francis, to begin to do penance in the following manner: when I was yet in my sins it did seem to me too bitter to look upon the lepers, but the Lord himself did lead me among them, and I had compassion upon them. When I left them that which had seemed to me bitter had become sweet and easy.

A little while after I left the world, and God gave me such faith that I would kneel down with simplicity in any of his churches, and I would say, "We adore thee, Lord Jesus Christ, here and in all thy churches which are in the world, and we bless thee that by thy holy cross thou hast ransomed the world."

Afterward the Lord gave me, and still gives me, so great a faith in priests who live according to the form of the holy Roman Church, because of their sacerdotal character, that even if they persecuted me I would have recourse to them, and even though I had all the wisdom of Solomon, if I should find poor secular priests, I would not preach in their parishes against their will. I desire to respect them like all the others, to love them and honor them as my lords. I will not consider their sins, for in them I see the Son of God, and they are my lords. I do this because here below I see nothing, I perceive nothing corporeally of the most high Son of God, except his most holy body and blood, which the priests receive and alone distribute to others.

I desire above all things to honor and venerate all these most holy mysteries and to keep them precious. Wherever I find the sacred names of Jesus, or his words, in unsuitable places, I desire to take them away and put them in some decent place; and I pray that others may do the same. We ought to honor and revere all the theologians and those who preach the most holy word of God, as dispensing to us spirit and life.

When the Lord gave me the care of some brothers, no one showed me what I ought to do, but the Most High himself revealed to me that I ought to live according to the model of the holy gospel. I caused a short and simple formula to be written, and the lord pope confirmed it for me.

Those who presented themselves to follow this kind of life distributed all they might have to the poor. They contented themselves with one tunic, patched within and without, with the cord and breeches, and we desired to have nothing more. The clerics said the office like other clerics, and the laymen repeated the paternoster.

We loved to live in poor and abandoned churches, and we were ignorant, and were submissive to all. I worked with my hands and would still do so, and I firmly desire also that all the other brothers work, for this makes for goodness. Let those who know no trade learn one, but not for the purpose of receiving the price of their toil, but for their good example and to flee idleness. And when we are not given the price of our work, let us resort to the table of the Lord, begging our bread from door to door. The Lord revealed to me the salutation which we ought to give: "God give you peace!"

Let the brothers take great care not to accept churches, habitations, or any buildings erected for them, except as all is in accordance with the holy poverty which we have vowed in the Rule; and let them not live in them except as strangers and pilgrims. I absolutely interdict all the brothers, in whatsoever place they may be found, from asking any bull from the court of Rome, whether directly or indirectly, in the interest of church or convent, or under pretext of preaching, nor even for the protection of their bodies. If they are not received anywhere, let them go of themselves elsewhere, thus doing penance with the benediction of God.

I firmly desire to obey the minister general of this brotherhood, and the guardian whom he may please to give me. I desire to put myself entirely into his hands, to go nowhere and do nothing against his will, for he is my lord. Though I be simple and ill, I would, however, have always a clerk who will perform the office, as it is said in the Rule. Let all the other brothers also be careful to obey their guardians and to do the office according to the Rule. . . .

And let the brothers not say, "This is a new Rule"; for this is only a reminder, a warning, an exhortation; it is my last will and testament, that I, little Brother Francis, make for you, my blessed brothers, in order that we may observe in a more Catholic way the Rule which we promised the Lord to keep.

Let the ministers general, all the other ministers, and the custodians be held by obedience to add nothing to and take nothing away from these words. Let them always keep this writing near them beside the Rule; and in all the assemblies which shall be held, when the Rule is read, let these words be read also.

I interdict absolutely by obedience all the brothers, clerics and laymen, to introduce comments in the Rule, or in this will, under pretext of explaining it. But since the Lord has given me to speak and to write the Rule and these words in a clear and simple manner, so do you understand them in the same way without commentary, and put them in practice until the end.

And whoever shall have observed these things, may be crowned in heaven with the blessings of the heavenly Father, and on earth with those of his well-beloved Son and of the Holy Spirit, the Consoler, with the assistance of all the heavenly virtues and all the saints.

And I, little Brother Francis, your servitor, confirm to you, so far as I am able, this most holy benediction. Amen.

No. 138. Penances for reconciled Lollards

(Register of William Courteney, archbishop of Canterbury, 1381-1396, folios 144-145. A.D. 1389. Translation.)

On the Sunday following their return home, they [William Smith, Roger Dexter and his wife, Alice] will lead the procession in the collegiate church of St. Mary's in Newark, William carrying an image of St. Catherine in his right hand [William had admitted breaking up a statue of St. Catherine for firewood], Roger and Alice with crucifixes, each carrying a candle weighing one-half pound in his left hand, each bareheaded and barefooted, William and Roger in their undershirts and drawers, Alice in her shift; thrice during the course of the procession, that is, once at the beginning, again at the middle, and lastly at the end, they will genuflect and devoutly kiss these same images in reverence to the cross, in memory of His passion, and in honor of the Virgin. After they enter the church with the procession, they will stand in front of a crucifix while the high mass is being sung, holding the images and candles in their hands. At the close of the mass the said William, Roger, and Alice will make an offering to him who celebrated the mass. Furthermore, on the following Saturday in the open market place of the town of Leicester, the said William, Roger, and Alice, in their under-garments as before and with no additional clothing and with the same images in their right hands, will genuflect and kiss these images three times, once at the entrance to the market place, again in the middle, and for a third time at the farther end. William, because he has had some education, will recite an antiphon and the collect of the feast of St. Catherine, while Roger and Alice, because they are unlettered, will recite a Pater Noster and an Ave Maria with devotion. On the Sunday immediately following they will stand and do in the parish church of that same village what they had done the preceding Sunday in the collegiate church aforesaid. At the close of the mass they will, with humility and reverence, offer the candles they had been holding to the priest or chaplain who read the mass. In view of the present cold weather, lest the penitents contract some bodily injury from standing so long uncovered, we so moderate our rigor to the extent of permitting them to put on what additional clothing they may require while hearing mass after entering these churches, provided, however, that their head and feet remain bare.

No. 139. The burning of heretics (Lollards)

(The statute "De Haeretico." Adams & Stephens, *Select Documents*, pp. 168-171.)

Whereas it is showed to our sovereign lord the king on the behalf of the prelates and clergy of his realm of England in this present parliament, that . . . divers false and perverse people of a certain new sect . . . do perversely and maliciously in divers places within the said realm under the color of dissembled holiness, preach and teach these days openly and privily divers new doctrines, and wicked heretical and erroneous opinions, contrary to the same faith and blessed determinations of the holy church; and of such sect and wicked doctrine and opinions, they make unlawful conventicles and confederacies, they hold and exercise schools, they make and write books, they do wickedly instruct and inform people, and as much as they may excite and stir them to sedition and insurrection, and maketh great strife and division among the people . . . by which sect and wicked and false preachings, doctrines, and opinions of the said false and perverse people, not only most greatest peril of the souls, but also many more other hurts, slanders, and perils, which God prohibit, might come to this realm, unless it be the more plentifully and speedily holpen by the king's majesty in this behalf; especially since the diocesans of the said realm cannot by their jurisdiction spiritual, without aid of the said royal majesty, sufficiently correct the said false and perverse people, nor refrain their malice, because the said false and perverse people do go from diocese to diocese, and will not appear before the said diocesans, but the same diocesans and their jurisdiction spiritual, and the keys of the church with the censures of the same, do utterly contemn and despise; and so their wicked preachings and doctrines doth from day to day continue and exercise, to the utter destruction of all order and rule of right and reason. Upon which novelties and excesses above rehearsed, the prelates and clergy aforesaid, and also the commons of the said realm being in the same parliament, have prayed our sovereign lord the king, that his royal highness would vouchsafe in the said parliament to provide a convenient remedy; the same our sovereign lord the king graciously considering the premises . . . for the conservation of the said catholic faith . . . and prosperity and honor of all his said realm, and for the eschewing of such dissensions, . . . and that this wicked sect, preachings, doctrines and opinions should from henceforth cease and be utterly destroyed, by the assent of the great lords and noble persons of the same realm, being in the said parliament, hath granted, stablished, and ordained, from henceforth firmly to be observed, that none within the said realm, or any other dominions, subject to his royal majesty, presume to preach openly or privily, without the license of the diocesan of the same place first required and obtained, . . . that none from henceforth anything preach, hold, teach, or instruct openly or privily, or make or write any book contrary to the catholic faith or determination of the holy church, nor of such sect and wicked doctrines and opinions shall make any conventicles, or in any wise hold or exercise schools, . . . and that all and singular having such books or any writings of such wicked doctrine and opinions, shall really with effect deliver or cause to be delivered all such books and writings to the diocesan of the same place within forty days from the time of the proclamation of this ordinance and statute. And if any person . . . from henceforth do or attempt against the said royal ordinance . . . then the diocesan . . . such person may by the authority of the said ordinance cause to be arrested. . . . And if any person in any case above expressed, be before the diocesan of the place or his commissaries canonically convicted, then the same diocesan may cause to be kept in his prison . . . as long as to his discretion shall seem expedient. . . . And if any person . . . be before the diocesan of the same place or his commissaries convict by sentence . . . do refuse duly to abjure, or . . . after the abjuration made by the same person be pronounced relapsed, . . . then the sheriff of the county of the same place, . . . shall receive, and them before the people in an high place cause to be burnt; that such punishment may strike in fear to the minds of others, whereby no such wicked doctrine and heretical and erroneous opinions . . . which God prohibit, be sustained or in any wise suffer. . . .

12

MEDIEVAL THOUGHT AND LEARNING

The Seven Liberal Arts

One of the most basic and enduring of the institutions of western civilization is that of the liberal arts. Wonderful indeed has been the manner in which this intellectual core of what the west insists makes a man educated, has withstood the corrosive effects of passing centuries and the vain attacks of "progressive" educators. The Middle Ages honored the liberal arts with one of its most revered numerals, the number seven. This enumeration Capella, Cassiodorus, and Isidore of Seville hallowed in their treatises on the subject. During the Carolingian era the division of the seven into the trivium and quadrivium became common. The trivium, that is, the three ways to learning, included grammar, rhetoric, and dialectic; the quadrivium (four ways) consisted of arithmetic, geometry, astronomy, and music. While the liberal arts can be traced back to Cicero and Plato, their orientation in the Middle Ages was fundamentally different from that given them in classical times. Where the Roman sought an education to be better informed and to become articulate about matters of general interest, in short, to be educated, the student of the Middle Ages saw in his education the means to a greater knowledge of God. If this education did not advance medieval man's spiritual development, official opinion, at any rate, was apt to hold it sterile. So Sulpicius Severus (d. 400 A.D.) raised the query: "Will Latin grammar save an immortal soul?" Fortunately most church fathers were less inclined to question the propriety of classical learning, principally because they had themselves been educated in classical schools, without apparent hurt to their immortal souls. Because of the serious decline of learning, however, where a liberal education had served as the badge of the freeman in classical times, in the Middle Ages it remained until very late almost the exclusive mark of the clergy. Thus an apprehended criminal found able to read and write (Latin) was ordinarily lodged in the bishop's jail.

Grammar. For a period as unsettled and as extended as the Middle Ages, it is impossible to speak of a standard curriculum with respect to quality of content. Perhaps a look at the liberal arts during the Carolingian era will provide a rough average between their content during the centuries immediately preceding the ninth when it was worse, and their content in succeeding centuries when it grew significantly better. The trivium enjoyed more attention than the quadrivium and of its three subjects grammar was most universally studied. After all, grammar made one articulate. As Alcuin defined the subject, it was the "science of letters and the guardian of right speech and writing." With grammar Alcuin included not only what passes for grammar today, but "stories and history" as well. Yet if medieval grammar retained some of the literature of classical times, this literature was studied, not so much for its own cultural values, but rather as a means of facilitating the study of case endings, conjugations, and other elements of simple grammar. In the study of grammar the student would proceed from an elementary introduction to the Latin language to the study of Donatus, Capella, Priscian, and the compilations of Bede. Next he would turn to the Bible, particularly to the Book of Psalms, then to the writings of the church fathers for his "literature." Such reading provided him practical exercise in the study of grammar. If and when he had proved himself sufficiently mature both spiritually and scholastically, he might be allowed to read Vergil, Cicero, Livy, and Ovid. For most contemporary teachers would have agreed with Alcuin, that few students should be permitted to advance beyond the Christian writers, to the "dangerously smooth style" of Vergil for example.

Rhetoric and Dialectic. In Cicero's day, rhetoric had been the most popular of the liberal arts. It was the ambition of every aspiring politician in the last century of the Republic to employ the skill he might acquire in the school of the rhetor as a springboard to political office. The fall of the Republic cost rhetoric its chief motivation, although Cassiodorus in the sixth century could still define that subject as the "art of speaking well on civil questions." How unsubstantial, however, had this rhetoric become by the time of Cassiodorus is evident from his own elementary treatment of the subject. Probably the principal value deriving from its study in the Middle Ages was the knowledge it afforded in the proper drafting of letters and documents. If the greatest period in the history of rhetoric lay behind it, that of dialectic beckoned, but not before the eleventh century. Until then, except for a premature scholar like John the Scot (see page 548), dialectic consisted of what logic could be gleaned from such simple manuals as that prepared by Alcuin. And these manuals were but superficially studied and imperfectly understood. Until the medieval mind took to questioning its authorities, which it only commenced doing in the eleventh century, dialectic served little practical purpose.

The Quadrivium. After mastering in the trivium the tools of learning, the student was prepared to take up the subject matter contained in the quadrivium. In general the content of the quadrivium proved even less substantial than that of the trivium. Arithmetic was studied in order to facilitate the problem of computing the date of Easter. The principal authorities on the subject were Boethius, Isidore, and especially Bede. It was Bede, in fact, who was largely responsible for establishing the birth of Christ as the basis of our chronology. Arithmetic before the introduction of Arabic numerals in the twelfth century could not have been anything but severely elementary. The Greeks and Romans had done what they could by using the letters of the alphabet to express numerical values, but so cumbersome a method had discouraged, rather than advanced, the science. One medieval improvement over antiquity was the introduction of the abacus from the east, although what this device netted the Middle Ages was frittered away in an unprofitable attempt to analyze the supposed properties of numbers. Of geometry the amount was so pitifully small that it could hardly be dignified as part of the curriculum before the discovery of Euclid by the west in the twelfth century. What passed as geometry was mostly geography. Setting the date of Easter was also a major concern of astronomy. What explained the considerable attention medieval scholars devoted to the study of stars and planets, however, was the conviction they had inherited from antiquity that the heavenly bodies influenced men's lives. While they accepted the basic fallacy of the Ptolemaic system, that the earth was the center of the universe, medieval scholars as early as Bede were convinced that the earth was round. Music was limited for the most part to actual practice in the singing of liturgical music. For those who wished to study theory, there existed the treatises of Augustine, Boethius, and Cassiodorus, to mention the best known.

Medieval Schools

Schools of the Early Middle Ages. Equally as elementary as the curriculum were the educational facilities provided in the early Middle Ages (Dark Ages). In Italy, lay schools surely survived as late as the seventh century; some scholars believe they never wholly disappeared in that part of Europe. Generally speaking, however, education by and for the laity was uncommon before the eleventh century. It is possible that given Charlemagne's vigorous encouragement, the church council of the ninth century which decreed, "Let every man send his son to learn letters, and let him remain until he is well instructed," was not voicing an entirely empty hope. A measure of education was, of course, provided by monastic and cathedral schools for those young men who aspired to become monks and priests. From the time of Charlemagne, even boys who were not marked for the religious life might attend the "exterior" schools maintained by occasional monasteries. The palace school of the Carolingian age was usually a lay school, but one which ordinarily limited itself to training the young man in such skills as he would find useful in the council chamber or on the battlefield. Parish schools also existed in this early period where the local priest might provide the children of the community some rudimentary training in reading, writing, and singing.

Lay Schools.   The rise of towns in the eleventh century heralded a sharp advance in medieval education. As town population grew, as their wealth increased, and as burghers came to value education for the prestige it promised and for the practical skills it might impart, schools on both the elementary and secondary levels gradually made their appearance. While the education they furnished was neither free nor compulsory, neither was it so spiritually oriented as the subject matter in monastic and cathedral schools. There is ample evidence of the existence of a substantial number of lay schools even in small towns and villages as early as the twelfth century. We read of elementary schools in thirteenth-century Florence with more than 8,000 boys and girls in attendance; of six "abacus" schools which trained some 1,000 boys for business careers; and of four "high schools" where 500 pupils studied grammar and logic. Although records pertaining to medieval education are neither numerous nor conclusive in their testimony, the fact that universities flourished from the thirteenth century presupposes a system of lower schools. Possibly the name of the first "school-marm" of the western world is that which appears on a Parisian tax roll in 1292.

Monastic Schools.   Monastic schools, which were the best schools western Europe could boast before the year 1000 A.D., date from the very origins of monasticism. All monastic rules, including that of St. Benedict, required the members of the community to acquire sufficient knowledge to read the prayers of the mass and the divine office. (Lay brothers who frequently lacked this ability represent a later monastic development.) Beyond this minimum, monastic education was loath to go. Certain houses, such as those at Lorsch, St. Gall, Bobbio, and Fulda did gain renown as intellectual centers, but such fame was accidental and not the product of a general system of educational endeavor. The reputation of this or that monastic center came usually by chance—the presence there of some scholar or a tradition of learning based upon the activities of earlier scholars. Thus it was possible, although not common, for a monastery like Bobbio to gain distinction as a center of music, and for Fulda to win recognition for the skill of its scribes and the beauty of their script. Monastic schools were ordinarily content to preserve learning, not to add to it, and superiors were generally agreed that for monastic life to be vigorous, it must restrict its schools to religious learning. It is significant that the powerful Cluniac reform movement which revitalized the spiritual life of tenth-century monasticism contributed to the shift of intellectual leadership away from the monastic to the less conservative cathedral school.

Cathedral Schools. Explanations for the rise of the cathedral school to leadership in the field of education after 1000 A.D. are not difficult to find. As just suggested, the cathedral school was less conservative, less tied to tradition than the monastic center. Its location in towns left the cathedral school more sensitive to new interests and developments than was the case with the isolated monastery. The cathedral school's devotion to other-worldly pursuits was not so exclusive. Cathedral schools must train men to work in the world, to consort with kings, to perform the varied tasks of clerks and notaries. Cathedral schools felt a greater responsibility than did the monastic centers to find answers to the questions the new learning from Byzantium and Islam was raising, and to attempt to assimilate this new learning into the traditional content of western thought. Thus, from the year 1000 A.D. the most active schools were such cathedral centers as Reims, Paris, Orleans, Chartres, Tours, and Laon. How intellectual the atmosphere at the most advanced cathedral schools might be is suggested by what one of its students writes of Canterbury in the twelfth century: "In the house of my lord, the archbishop, are most scholarly men, with whom is found all the uprightness of justice, all the caution of providence, every form of learning. They, after prayers, and before meals, in reading, in disputing, in the decision of causes, constantly exercise themselves. All the knotty questions of the realm are referred to us, and when they are discussed in the common hearing, each of us sharpens his wits to speak well upon them."

Intellectual Awakening of the Eleventh and Twelfth Centuries

Books During the Dark Ages. The rise to prominence of the cathedral school in the eleventh century announced the dawn of the intellectual awakening of the west. As we shall find, a principal key to the impressive achievement of this intellectual awakening was books. One is not to conclude, of course, that prior to the eleventh century western Europe was without books, even though Ammianus Marcellinus might lament as early as the fourth century: "The libraries, like tombs, are closed forever." Many books, indeed, had been lost. As explained earlier, roughly one half of the books used in the Rome of the pagan emperors had been in Greek. When the knowledge of Greek disappeared some time during the fifth century, these books became closed books and, for the most part, lost books. Yet Latin classics continued to enjoy high respect despite the aversion of occasional Christian scholars to anything pagan. Augustine and Jerome, —and actually the majority of western scholars—provide eloquent evidence in their own writings of intimate acquaintance with classical literature. While many books suffered destruction during the troubled Dark Ages, many more were preserved, copied, and recopied. From the time of Cassiodorus, the "first librarian of the Latin West," who had encouraged his monks to copy manuscripts monasticism had generally assumed responsibility for preserving the literature of earlier centuries. Alcuin admonished his monks at Tours: "It is better to copy books than to cultivate vines."

As many as three hundred monks busied themselves reproducing manuscripts at St. Riquier in the ninth century. Most of what was copied was of a religious character, to be sure, but secular volumes were not ignored. Among other evidences attesting to the deep interest displayed in these centuries in the classical treasures of ancient Rome is this excerpt from a letter of Lupus of Ferrieres (d. 862) to another classically minded scholar at St. Gall: "Sallust's Cataline and Jugurtha and the books of the Verrine orations (Cicero), and whatever others you know we have either in imperfect shape or not at all, be good enough to bring to us so that through your kindness the defective ones may be corrected, and those which we do not have and cannot have except through you may be acquired all the more gratefully because unexpectedly."*

The Study of the Classics. The classical tradition which barely survived the turbulencies of the "Dark Ages" received a sharp stimulus during the Carolingian period. Scholars like Hrabanus Maurus and Strabo composed respectable Latin poetry in the ninth century, while the tenth even welcomed a Latin playwright, the nun Hrosvitha of Gandersheim. That no plays were available other than the unedifying comedies of Plautus and Terence disturbed the saintly Hrosvitha, so she tried her hand at composing plays in which virtue (and usually the ascetic life) triumphed. Particularly noteworthy were the scope and excellence of the classical studies carried on at such cathedral schools as Chartres, Paris, and Orleans. Under Fulbert (d. 1028), Chartres became the leading center for classical study in the Christian west. Its brightest luminary was John of Salisbury (d. 1180), undoubtedly one of the most distinguished classical scholars of the Middle Ages. He was also probably the best educated man of his age. Although a pupil of the scintillating Abelard, he turned his back on

* Quoted in James Westfall Thompson, *The Mediaeval Library* (Chicago, 1939), p. 94.

dialectic as essentially sterile, and pursued instead the study of the classics, which he found so intellectually rewarding. Copious citations in his writings suggest that he was as familiar with Cicero and Ovid as with Deuteronomy and the Gospels. (Reading 144) For all of John's brilliance, however, the bloom of this twelfth-century humanism was doomed to be brief. Yet it could claim a significant accomplishment before being forced to surrender first place in the schools to the study of dialectic and rational theology. This classical renaissance of the twelfth century, as it has been called, contributed to the establishment of medieval Latin as a clear, standardized language, capable of meeting the growing demands of an advancing civilization. It proved a godsend, for example, to the study of dialectic and of law, disciplines which placed a premium upon clarity of expression. It also added to the heritage from the classical past verse so "classical" in tone and meter as to have been long mistaken as the product of the ancient past.

Revival of Dialectic. Since the eleventh century, humanism had been sharing the attention of scholars with another subject, that of dialectic, which was destined to submerge it. Dialectic, as we have seen, had always been a member of the liberal arts family. Yet like so much of the material studied in that curriculum, its content had been superficial and its achievement inconsequential. Now in the eleventh century, when scholars began to return to the more basic works available in that field, a remarkable revival ensued, which appears all the more impressive for the gloom of the centuries preceding. We have seen, for instance, how Boethius back in the sixth century had contemplated making all of Plato and Aristotle available in translation to the west, together with commentaries which would bring these two philosophers into agreement. Because of his appreciation of how vital to Christian faith the corpus of pagan Greek philosophy would prove, and of his efforts to further that end, Boethius has sometimes been called "the first of the scholastics." Still Boethius fell far short of his goal, and instead of something akin to the revival of the twelfth century which the completion of his project might conceivably have fathered, his death ushered Europe into the "Dark Ages." Merovingian anarchy all but blotted out scholarship, as the lamenting Gregory of Tours has already noted for us. Except for an occasional philosophical treatise by Bede, Alcuin, or Hrabanus Maurus, there is almost a complete blank from Boethius to the eleventh century.

John Scotus Erigena. Yet all was not dark. Clearly visible through the general intellectual gloom of that period are the forms of at least two eminent scholars, John Scotus Erigena (d. 880) and Gerbert (d. 1003). John the Scot was a refugee from Ireland (Erigena for Erin), who fled to the court of Charles the Bald to escape the invading Norwegians. He brought with him a knowledge of Greek which was quite rare in France, and a penetrating mind which was equally unique. John was without question the greatest scholar of his age and "one of the most original thinkers of the Middle Ages." In an age as subservient to tradition and authority as was his, his originality impresses us as all the more extraordinary. If John's contemporaries had difficulty understanding him, that is easy to appreciate in view of the low level of scholarship obtaining at the time. For even today scholars are at variance in assessing his position regarding such a fundamental problem as the relationship between faith and reason. About all modern scholars can agree upon is that John is obscure! And it was probably fortunate for John that he was also too profound or too obscure for his age. His major work entitled, *On the Division of Nature,* in which he sought to wed Christianity to Neoplatonism, was condemned for heresy three hundred and fifty years after his death. The charge against John was that he had proposed a pantheistic interpretation of the universe. It is true that in his speculations he does appear to equate God with nature and philosophy with religion. On the other hand, Professor Gilson insists that in John's famous statement: "It is, therefore, certain that true religion is true philosophy, and conversely, that true philosophy is true religion," he is simply repeating Augustine. One might say that John Erigena could not imagine a faith which was opposed to reason, nor a true authority which could oppose reason. "True authority never opposes sound reason," he wrote, "nor sound reason true authority, inasmuch as . . . they both flow from a single source, to wit, the divine wisdom." John was a master of dialectic. His critical approach was unique in his day and for a hundred years to come. John also produced the first great system of knowledge in the Middle Ages.

Gerbert. The second scholar to break through the uncritical gloom which hung like a pall over western Europe from Boethius until the eleventh century was Gerbert of Aurillac. Like John the Scot before him, he was also "the most learned man of his century." Learning and learning alone accounted for his rise from the level of humble monk to that of tutor of Otto III, abbot, archbishop, and pope (Sylvester II). Despite a full lifetime of service to the church, he found time to absorb all there was to learn in the western Europe of his day. He studied philosophy at Reims, and it was there as teacher that he exerted his greatest influence upon medieval civilization. Though Gerbert was a fine classical scholar, his reputation for learning rested upon his knowledge of astronomy and mathematics which he had learned in Spain. His students, who included the scholar Fulbert, never tired of singing his praises as a teacher. How they marveled over his armillary sphere by means of which he illustrated the movements of the constellations; and his abacus, the most advanced computing instrument western Europe had ever seen! While the curiosity he stimulated in his students concerning the scientific subjects of the quadrivium bore permanent fruit in coming generations of students, his chief influence was felt in the area of dialectic. With characteristic thoroughness he turned away from the elementary study aids on the subject to Boethius' treatises themselves, to his commentaries on Porphyry's *Isagoge* (an introduction to the study of philosophy), and to those of Aristotle's logical works which Boethius had translated. It was partly through Gerbert's influence that dialectic became the most popular subject in the curriculum in the eleventh century.

Importance of Dialectic. The importance of the study of dialectic to the intellectual development of western Europe can hardly be overestimated. Without dialectic to chart a path which would guide scholars in their search for truth and in their organization of knowledge, nothing approximating the phenomenal advance of the twelfth and thirteenth centuries could have been accomplished. By dialectic, the Middle Ages of the eleventh century meant logic, a study which embraced both the science or art of reasoning and the study of certain concepts as well, such as genus, species, substance, property, and difference, the study of which concepts are necessary to the pursuit of truth. Thus dialectic provided the means of arranging in logical and systematic fashion the knowledge preserved in the west since the time of Boethius, however disparate and disjointed this might be. Yet scarcely would dialectic have completed this accomplishment than it would be called upon to undertake the infinitely more difficult task of harmonizing with Christianity the knowledge of the ancient Greeks and the Islamic world which was to become available during the twelfth and thirteenth centuries. Without the rules of logical analysis and synthesis, of deduction and induction to guide them, western scholars could hardly have succeeded in assimilating this pagan, yet profoundly fundamental, body of knowledge into the structure of Christian thought. The ardent champions of logic would make even greater claims for their science. They insisted that if its rules were strictly applied, many hitherto rationally insoluble problems would be resolved and an increasing volume of subsidiary truths could be deduced from the basic truths derived directly from revelation. The boon to the study of theology would be tremendous.

Scholasticism

Scholasticism Defined. The term generally employed to describe this application of logic or reason to Christian truth is scholasticism. The word scholasticism has also invited broader interpretation and application. It has been equated with medieval philosophy and theology. Some scholars have defined it as the educational system of the medieval school. Others understand it to be the particular method employed by university—or schoolmen (singular, *scholasticus*)—in the application of Aristotelian logic to theological problems. Since medieval thinkers, without exception, conceived of all knowledge as leading ultimately and necessarily to the knowledge of God, scholasticism has also been defined as the systematic organization of all knowledge into one coherent system subordinate to theology. Still, the essential function of scholasticism was to reconcile faith and reason, in broader terms, to harmonize the tenets of philosophy with those of theology.

Rational Theology Not New.   By the eleventh century many churchmen were willing to concede that learning had advanced sufficiently far that an effort should be made to understand, not merely to accept blindly, the truths the church required the faithful to believe. Even the saintly Anselm of Bec declared: "It is negligence if we make no attempt to understand what we believe." As for philosophy, of its very nature it was concerned with many of the same fundamental questions which harassed theologians: viz., the origin, nature, and purpose of the world and of man. Yet while this newly awakened interest in reason and philosophy in the eleventh century was to lead to a vast increase in man's understanding of God and of the universe, one must not conclude that this application of reason to Christian faith was something new in the history of the church. The majority of the early church fathers, particularly those of the east, had been well versed in Greek philosophy. They had consistently worked to establish the rational acceptability at least of Christian faith. St. Augustine went far beyond this point. As Aquinas later said of Augustine's application of reason and philosophy in his presentation of Christian faith: "Whenever Augustine, who was imbued with the doctrine of the Platonists, found in their teaching anything consistent with faith, he adopted it; and those things which he found contrary to faith he amended."

Faith, Reason, and Berengar.   Yet neither Augustine nor other early Christian thinkers drew a clear distinction between the provinces of faith and reason, between philosophy and theology. To them these simply represented two ways by which God spoke to man's intelligence. They might have argued that all that was true must necessarily emanate from God, either by way of reason or by revelation. The thinkers of the eleventh century urged, however, that a careful distinction be made between the two. They had a sharper appreciation of the difference between reason on the one hand and faith on the other, no doubt because for so long a time there had been little attempt to rationalize one's belief. To many western scholars of the eleventh century the possibilities of reason in aiding them in their search of truth seemed enormous. Several scholars even permitted their enthusiasm for the new science to carry them into unorthodoxy. Such a one was Berengar, a pupil of Fulbert at Chartres. Fulbert took the position that since man was a rational person, he must first comprehend what he is to believe. "It is a part of courage to have recourse to dialectic in all things, for recourse to dialectic is recourse to reason, and he who does not avail himself of reason abandons his chief honor, since by virtue of reason he was made in the image of God." This position appeared acceptable enough until Berengar applied its implications to the doctrine of transubstantiation. Berengar pointed out that what looked like bread and wine before consecration looked exactly the same after consecration. Consequently, he argued, reason must insist that no change in substance had taken place. Immediately the threat to faith in an untrammeled appeal to reason was made manifest. Fortunately for traditional faith and for medieval dialectic too, for that matter, a contemporary scholar, Lanfranc, was able to answer Berengar's argument in a rational manner, logically acceptable, at least, to the medieval mind. He simply drew a distinction between the substance of the bread and wine on the one hand and their accidents on the other. He reasoned that while the accidents of bread and wine, that is, their physical appearance, their taste, color, and smell, might remain unchanged after consecration, their substance had, nevertheless, been altered, whence the term transubstantiation. While Lanfranc was thus able to use dialectic to meet a dialectical attack, other churchmen like Peter Damian were ready to ban dialectic forthwith as an invention of the devil. Damian argued that only faith was necessary, even proper, for Christians. Had God wished man to apply his reason to matters of faith, Christ would have chosen philosophers, not fishermen to be his apostles. "God have mercy on the souls of those monks," he wrote, "who neglect the rule of St. Benedict to follow the rules of Donatus."

Anselm of Bec. A happy medium between Berengar's worship of dialectic, on the one hand, and Peter Damian's denunciation of it on the other, was struck by Anselm of Bec (d. 1109). Anselm, who was the first great original thinker since John the Scot, believed that because truth was so vast and inexhaustible, reason must retain a legitimate role despite the work already accomplished by the church fathers. The more men understood their faith, he averred, the closer did they draw to the sight of God. Anselm is famous for a number of scholastic formulas, possibly the most basic being the phrase, *"credo ut intelligam,"* that is, "I believe in order that I may understand." This expresses substantially the position assumed by the great majority of scholastics. Concerning the role of reason in the ascertainment of truth, Anselm would start, therefore, with those matters the church required Christians to accept on faith. With the assurance that, since the church could not err, he must be on the right path, he could then seek to establish a rational basis for this faith. Faith, in effect, sought understanding. But Anselm dropped a word of caution to those who might depend too heavily upon reason. "No Christian," he wrote, "ought in any way to dispute the truth of what the Catholic Church believes in its heart and confesses with its mouth. But always holding the same faith unquestioningly . . . he ought himself, as far as he is able, to seek the reason for it. If he can understand it, let him thank God. If he cannot, let him not raise his head in opposition but bow in reverence." Anselm's philosophy has been aptly called "Christian rationalism." Many call him "the father of scholasticism," not because he was the first to make use of philosophy in matters of theological speculation, but because he was the first to attempt the formulation of a thoroughly logical system of theology. However, Anselm was a monk first and foremost, and second only a dialectician. (Reading 141)

Problem of Universals.   Anselm was a participant in that most persistent and controversial of issues to vex medieval scholastics, the problem of universals. In its simplest terms, this problem concerned the relation of genera and species to individuals. What were the nature and function of general terms like "man" and "animal" in the actual world of individual men and animals? Were they merely mental concepts (words), or did they really exist (things)? This problem antedated the Middle Ages. As a philosophical question it had originated with Plato. Plato maintained that the world is composed of general ideas or universals which were subsistent entities possessing true reality, all subordinated to the supreme idea of the good. To Plato these general ideas had existed from all eternity. They, therefore, had preceded in time the appearance of physical things (*ante rem*). According to Plato, these ideas have an existence independent of all minds—they exist in an intelligible world. Plato would hold that such ideas as justice, whiteness, roughness, and goodness possessed true reality, that we classify an act as just, a house as white, and so on, only because of the prior existence of the general idea of justice, of whiteness. Since Plato's influence dominated philosophical thought in the Middle Ages until the thirteenth century through the media of the writings of Plotinus, Porphyry, and Augustine, most scholastics of the twelfth century were inclined to agree with Plato. They were called realists, that is, they held the general idea or universal to possess reality. During the twelfth century, however, more and more scholastics came to question Plato's position on ideas as unreasonable, and to posit, in opposition, Aristotle's contention that the general idea always followed the material object in point of time (*post rem*). Agreeing with Aristotle, they maintained that it was only after the mind had perceived similar objects and had abstracted what qualities they had in common, did the idea itself come into being. Even then, however, it lacked true reality and was but a word or name to conjure by. These latter scholars were accordingly called nominalists, from the Latin *nomen*, meaning word or name.

Basic Nature of Problem.   As thus expressed, the problem of universals appears simple enough and hardly deserving of all the acrimonious debate it precipitated. The difficulty lay rather in the application of the two positions. For example, are we human by virtue of our membership in the human species, or is this species wholly fictional and unreal? Did the general idea of mankind exist before man? If humanity is just a name or a word, how is it that we inherit the sin of Adam, the father of the human race? Is there such a thing as humility over and above particular acts of humility? Is there such a thing as justice, or are there only just acts? If there are only just acts, how is it we call them just? How do we know whether an act is just or unjust? Is there not some idea of justice which helps us form our standards in determining whether an individual act is just or not? Does there exist an ideal beauty which guides man in his appreciation of the attractiveness of a physical object? Are there universal principles, and if so, do these have an existence apart from the acts or processes they describe or are they merely abstracted from experience? Do general ideas have an objective existence, independent of change in the physical world and of human wishes, or are they subject to change? Which is more important, the principle or the individual? What has priority by nature, the individual or society? Can we attach any kind of validity, legal or spiritual, to ideas such as church, state, or society?

Roscelin and Extreme Nominalism.   It will be readily seen that issues such as these would be considered fundamental in the Middle Ages when so much of Christian faith was founded upon theological concepts. Fortunately for medieval orthodoxy, though the philosophical issue between realism and nominalism engendered much argument, very few representatives of this or that school carried their logic to the point of heresy. It was only the extreme realist or extreme nominalist who was apt to overstep the bounds of orthodoxy. Thus the extreme realist, if he carried his world of ideas too far, with all his universals ultimately leading to the absolute universal, stood in some peril of becoming a pantheist. Conversely, the nominalist, in his contempt for ideas and concepts, was just as apt to become a materialist, a character quite as repugnant to the medieval church as the pantheist. Such an extreme nominalist was Roscelin of Compiegne (d. 1122), a contemporary of Anselm. He described universals as sounds, which merely signified words. In contemplating the doctrine of the Trinity, Roscelin protested that, consistent with his nominalism, he could see three persons, Father, Son, and Holy Spirit, quite distinctly, but that the Trinity existed apart from these three as a subsistent entity he refused to accept. Anselm, accordingly, took him to task for what he said amounted to idolatry, and he advised that "those dialecticians, or rather dialectical heretics of our time, who think that universal substances are nothing but words . . . should be wholly excluded from the discussion of theological questions." Incidentally, Roscelin, as well as Berengar before him, was forced to retract his radical statements.

Abelard: His Career.   The scholar who worked out a compromise between the conflicting positions of the realists and nominalists which most later scholastics found acceptable was Abelard (d. 1142). We might describe Abelard's position as that of moderate realism. But before considering this point and Abelard's contribution to scholasticism, a few words are appropriate about his career, which proved as spectacular and stormy as that of any medieval celebrity. Abelard, who became the dominant intellectual figure of his day, was the eldest son of a member of the lower nobility of Brittany. So strong was his enthusiasm for education, however, that he abandoned his inheritance and took up the life of a wandering scholar. His search for knowledge led him to the nominalist Roscelin and eventually to William of Champeaux, who was teaching an extreme realism at the cathedral school in Paris. Although he came to learn, the astute but proud and disputatious Abelard soon turned to ridiculing. His fellow students styled him the "indomitable rhinocerus" (*rhinocerus indomitus*). With their encouragement he set up his own school, where he inspired them with the brilliance and clarity of his lectures and regaled them over the bad logic of their other lecturers. When these lecturers had him expelled from the city, he decided to learn some theology. His new teacher, Anselm of Laon, he found as hopelessly befogged as his earlier masters who had tried to teach him dialectics. "When he lighted a fire," Abelard wrote of Anselm, "he filled the house with smoke." For all his obnoxiousness, Abelard's admitted talents eventually won him a place in the cathedral school at Paris. There is no telling to what heights he might have climbed had it not been for his unfortunate affair with Heloise. He started as the tutor of this pretty, gifted girl and ended as her husband. Heloise, who loved Abelard more than Abelard loved himself, if that were possible, suggested keeping their marriage a secret in order to enable him to continue his career. This her uncle would not countenance, and the upshot was that Abelard took monastic vows while Heloise became a nun. From now on misfortune seemed to dog Abelard's footsteps wherever he turned, whether as monk, abbot, or recluse. His students persuaded him to open another school near Paris, but there he ran afoul of Bernard of Clairvaux for his lectures on the Trinity. Under papal prohibition to teach further, he closed out his tragic career within the friendly walls of Cluny, dying, as its pious abbot wrote Heloise, in the odor of sanctity. (Reading 142)

Abelard's Conceptualism.   As pointed out above, Abelard's own position in the realist-nominalist controversy was one of moderate realism. The sharpness of his intellect convinced him that neither position on the question of universals was entirely tenable. Abelard agreed with the nominalist that the universal had no inherent reality since it can be predicated of several things. A thing is only itself and can be nothing else. Yet he agreed with the realist in insisting that the universal was more than just a word. While it existed only in the mind, still it had a basis or ground in reality. Abelard explained that we arrive at this universal by considering a number of objects from which our mind then abstracts that which they have in common. This concept, though not intrinsically real, does possess intellectual reality. "The astonishing genius of Abelard was that before the translations of Aristotle made by the Arabs had become available in the West, and with only what had filtered down through Porphyry, he concluded that universals exist not before the thing nor after the thing, but in the thing: *non ante rem, nec post rem, sed in re.* They have a real existence, but only in "particulars."* Abelard's solution has been called conceptualism.

Abelard's Sic et Non. Abelard probably exerted his chief influence upon contemporary thought through his provocative *Sic et Non.* This treatise was largely an exemplar of dialectic. Such, at least, was the purpose of the author as stated in the prologue: "The first key to wisdom is this, constant and frequent interrogation. For by doubt we are led to question, by questioning we arrive at the truth." Abelard then proceeded to list 158 theological questions, each followed by passages from Scriptures and the church fathers, some in support of the proposition (*sic*), others opposed (*non*). Included among the propositions were such as: that God is threefold and the contrary; that God is a substance and the contrary; that it is lawful to lie and the contrary. Abelard was the first to admit that some of the quotations he used from Scriptures and the fathers to prove or disprove a proposition were taken out of context, and that a closer scrutiny of the conflicting evidence would reveal it to be less contradictory than it appeared at first glance. But it was not his intention to teach—he did not even bother to give answers to his propositions. What he wanted to do was to stimulate questioning, for neither Scriptures nor the fathers were in complete agreement, or not seemingly so at least. Though the *Sic et Non* infuriated such good mystics as St. Bernard, it did encourage speculation. It also helped to establish the dialectical method in theology, which consisted of marshalling conflicting testimony and argument in support of and against a thesis, followed by that conclusion which reason would seem to dictate. (Reading 143)

Abelard's Position on Reason. Because of Abelard's glorification of the rationalizing process and his deprecation of an excessive devotion to authority, several scholars have classified him as a rationalist. This he was not, at least not in the modern meaning of the term. Abelard never questioned the authority of the church nor divine revelation. As he wrote to Heloise: "I do not want to be a philosopher if it means resisting St. Paul; I do not wish to be Aristotle, if it must separate me from Christ." Abelard's principal error, in the judgment of certain contemporaries, was that of attempting to rationalize the most sacred mysteries of the faith. "He is trying to destroy the merit of Christian faith," warned Bernard, "when he thinks himself able by human reason to comprehend God altogether. He ascends to the heavens and descends even to the abyss. Nothing may hide from him in the depths of hell or in the heights above. . . . He sees nothing as an enigma, nothing as in a glass darkly, but stares at every-

* Anne Fremantle, *The Age of Belief* (A Mentor Book), 1955, p. 99.

thing face to face." It should be noted that Abelard was as unpopular with his fellow teachers as he was popular with his students. The vehemence of Bernard's attack may have been partially due to misrepresentation of what Abelard maintained by colleagues who detested or misunderstood him.

St. Bernard and Scholasticism.   St. Bernard of Clairvaux deserves mention in a discussion of scholasticism, if for no better reason than for the unfriendly attitude he took concerning its value. While his position was not so hostile as Peter Damian's, he belonged to that group which Professor Gilson refers to as those who believe that "since God has spoken to us, it is no longer necessary for us to think." Bernard was a mystic, possibly the greatest the medieval church produced. As a mystic, he rejected the value of reason to faith, and maintained rather that the love of God constituted a surer means of attaining the knowledge of God, the admitted end of all learning, than reliance upon our imperfect natural powers. God was the fount of all truth and wisdom. To those who approached him with love and humility, he would prove a most generous dispenser. In contrast to the moderate scholastic's formula of *credo ut intelligam* (I believe in order that I may understand), and the more radical Christian rationalist's *intelligo ut credam* (I understand in order that I may believe), the mystic St. Bernard would posit *amo ut intelligam* (I love in order that I may understand). The mystic was content to accept without question the body of truth required by the church. The cogency of any doctrine which might puzzle him, he could ascertain through contemplation.

End of Early Scholasticism.   The death of Abelard marks a major point of departure in the history of scholasticism. As perceptive as was Abelard's intellect, there was little farther he could go with the philosophical materials available in the west. The one major philosophical problem remaining for dialecticians of the twelfth century, that of universals, while not solved, had been pretty well worked over. To appreciate how increasingly barren philosophical disputation had become, we have the caustic testimony of John of Salisbury. He tells how a visit to the schools of Paris after an absence of twelve years found the dialecticians there still debating the same sterile questions in the same unproductive manner. Yet he should not have given twelfth-century scholasticism such short shrift. It proved more than just a bright (though short) interlude in the history of medieval scholarship. Its accomplishment, and a very real one this was, was that of preparing the medieval mind for the proper reception and profitable use of the store of learning which was to flood the west during the one hundred and fifty years following Abelard's death. This store, which included the bulk of the philosophical, mathematical, and scientific knowledge of the Byzantine and Islamic worlds, proved so vast that there was no longer any danger of the scholastic mill running short of philosophic grist again.

Learning from the East.   The scholarly treasure of the Near Eastern worlds came principally by way of Moslem hands, either from Spain or from Sicily where Islamic scholars had been poring over learned manuscripts for centuries. A few important works hailed directly from Constantinople. We read of western agents being sent into Spain in the twelfth century, particularly to Toledo, in search of Arabic manuscripts. However procured, these manuscripts included most of what Aristotle had written: his *Ethics, Politics, Rhetoric, Poetics, Metaphysics, Physics, On Animals,* and his more advanced logical works. In addition, there were Ptolemy's *Almagest* and Galen's encyclopedic medical writings, the works of Hippocrates and Discorides, several of Plato's *Dialogues,* Euclid's *Elements of Geometry,* the trigonometry, algebra, and arithmetic of Al Khwarizmi, and the scholarly commentaries and treatises of such Moslem savants as Avicenna, Al Farabi, and Averroës. Already being studied in Sicily and Italy by the close of the eleventh century was the *Corpus Juris Civilis* of Justinian. Almost as numerous were Arabic treatises dealing with astrology and alchemy.

Translators. These writings of ancient and Islamic learning were in Greek and Arabic, both strange languages to the west. If Greek was almost unknown, Arabic was even more a mystery, lacking as it did a formal grammar, and bearing, in addition, the stigma of the infidels' language. Under the circumstances, the task of translation, even from the Greek, proved a formidable one. When the Byzantine emperor sent a manuscript of the Greek Discorides to the caliph at Cordova in the tenth century, he had a Greek scholar accompany the document. Nevertheless, the work of translation was undertaken with an enthusiasm that amounted to hysteria. Where ordinarily today the job of translation is considered a thankless task and left to unsung heroes, in the medieval twelfth and thirteenth centuries even eminent scholars like Albert the Great, Robert Grosseteste, or Roger Bacon lent a hand. How universal was the activity of these translators is reflected in the names of several of the more prominent: Adelard of Bath, Rudolf of Bruges, Hermann of Carinthia, Gerard of Cremona, John of Seville. Western scholars generally preferred Arabic translations from the Greek to the original Greek itself because of sundry emendations, additions, and criticisms the former frequently included. Unfortunately, many of these Arabic translations were faulty, a source of no end of trouble in the case of Averroës' translations of Aristotle. It was at this time and because of these Arabic translations that Islam exerted such a strong influence upon western thought. So covetous, indeed, was the west of anything the Islamic world had to offer, that even the Koran ended up in translation!

Aristotle's Importance. It was, then, the introduction of this new knowledge into the west during the last half of the twelfth and early thirteenth centuries that accounted for the break between the scholasticism of Abelard and that of Aquinas. Of this new knowledge, the writings of Aristotle were the most influential. In fact, the tremendous impact of Aristotle's works upon medieval thought can scarcely be imagined. Never before nor since has the Greek philosopher's esteem been so high. Dante referred to him in the *Divine Comedy* as "the master of the men who know." To Aquinas and most medieval scholastics, he was simply "the Philosopher." There were, to be sure, voices raised in protest against this deep reverence for the ancient Greek, particularly from amongst the ecclesiastical authorities. After all, Aristotle was a pagan. Several of his fundamental views could not possibly be reconciled with Christianity. Aristotle had asserted, for example, that the world was eternal, not created. To Aristotle, God was hardly more than a hypothetical term he used to explain change. Aristotle denied that man had a supernatural destiny. Because of the misgivings such views engendered, the study of Aristotle's metaphysics and natural philosophy was prohibited for a time early in the thirteenth century at Paris. The great majority of scholars showed little reticence, however, in tapping what they considered a veritable gold mine of extraordinarily advanced knowledge in almost every field of learning in which they were interested. Some scholars carried their enthusiasm for Aristotle to the extreme of proclaiming him always right and definitive, on every subject in which he had expressed himself. Such were the so-called Latin Averroists. They assumed essentially the same position on Scripture and faith as Averroës' study of Aristotle had forced him to accept with regard to the Koran. With their leader, Siger of Bribant, the Latin Averroists insisted that what is true philosophically may not be true theologically—the principle of the double truth.

Albert the Great.   It was fortunate for the future of scholasticism that men like Siger were in the minority. Had they been in the majority among scholars, scholasticism might well have withered in the face of a hostile and uncompromising church. Not only were those but few who carried their admiration of Aristotle to the point of heterodoxy, but there appeared eminent scholars who disagreed with them, who were able to fit Aristotle into his proper place in the Christian order and render him acceptable to the official church. The first such great scholar was Albert the Great (Albertus Magnus) (d. 1280). In fact, for all of Albert's unusual erudition, modern scholars consider this his greatest achievement, that of putting Aristotle into the good graces of the ecclesiastical authorities. Albert found much to admire in Aristotle and in his fellow-pagan philosophers as well. He wrote: "though shorn of the light of the faith, they have none the less spoken in a wonderful manner of the Creator and His creatures. Virtue and vice they knew, and a great number of truths which faith as well as reason announce from on high." Albert was the first scholastic to master the whole of Aristotle's writings. His commentaries, which fill twenty-one volumes, he dedicated to the task of incorporating into the Christian structure of faith all that could be harmonized from Aristotle's writings. Yet Albert was what one might call a cautious admirer of Aristotle. Though he was the teacher of Aquinas, the scholastic who would shortly incorporate a great deal more of Aristotelianism into Christianity, Albert himself preserved much of the Augustinian and Neoplatonist tradition in his writing. He marks a point in transition between the scholasticism of Abelard (and Anselm) and that of Aquinas. We should also note that Albert was one of the first scholastics to recognize philosophy as a separate science, independent of theology, but of significant value to its study.

Thomas Aquinas: His Life. Albert won the title, "the Great," from his contemporaries. His true greatness has since been obscured by the mammoth shadow cast by his renowned pupil Thomas Aquinas (d. 1274). Thomas was the son of the local count of Aquino. Against the most determined, even criminal, efforts of his own family to deter him, he became a member of the lowly Dominican order. As a boy he was taught by the Benedictine monks at Monte Cassino. He attended the university at Naples, moved next to Paris, where he met Albert whom he followed to Cologne. As a teacher of theology which he considered his primary vocation, he taught at several universities and occupied one of the two chairs allotted the Dominicans at Paris. He was held in high esteem by the pope and was on his way to attend the council at Lyons under papal instructions, when he died prematurely at the age of forty-nine. Physically a large and heavy man, he was shy by nature, humble, and magnanimous. His reserve as a student earned him the dubious sobriquet, the "Dumb Ox." But his mentor, Albert, who was more perceptive than Aquinas' fellow-students, chided them: "You call him a Dumb Ox. I tell you this Dumb Ox shall bellow so loud that his bellowings shall fill the world." Part of Aquinas' reserve was nothing more than deep absorption with his own thoughts. The story is told how on one occasion he was seated in the banquet hall of Louis IX, deep in thought and completely oblivious of the king and the chattering company about him, when of a sudden he shocked the assembly of courtiers and their ladies into horrified silence by striking the table with his ponderous fist and thundering, "That will answer the Manichees."* (For the Manicheans, see page 521.) Aquinas' biographers say he enjoyed mystical experience. After saying mass in December 1273, he told his secretary that he would write no more since "all I have written seems to me like so much straw compared with what I have seen and with what has been revealed to me."* His monumental work, the *Summa Theologiae*, was never completed.

Aquinas and Aristotle. Because of the sublimity of his thought, Aquinas has been called the "Angelic Doctor." We might attribute his profundity first to his own brilliance of intellect. As the agnostic Huxley exclaimed: "His subtlety of intellect seems to be almost without parallel." Aquinas' scholarly achievement next owes a tremendous debt to Aristotle. Of all the scholastics he was most successful in analyzing Aristotle's erudition and in fitting those elements which Christianity could use into the pattern of

* Quoted in G. K. Chesterton, *St. Thomas Aquinas* (New York, 1933), pp. 115, 172.

Christian thought. Aquinas' particular approach to Aristotle is important to note: he fits Aristotle to Christianity, not the reverse. For though Aquinas is inclined to detect more sympathetic implications in Aristotle's philosophy than most Christian scholars, he is not an apologist for the pagan. Actually his approach is both thoroughly orthodox and scholarly. What he found in Aristotle that was rationally true, he was convinced was in complete harmony with faith. When he discovered Aristotle maintaining a seemingly logical position which was unacceptable to Christianity, he traced the fault to Aristotle's premises. For Aquinas was supremely confident on this one score, that since God is the author of truth and the creator of the world, He could not teach anything in the natural or rational order that contradicted what He taught in the supernatural. The inability of our intellects to comprehend such mysteries as the Trinity simply betrayed the inadequacy of human reason. But reason can establish their reasonableness. Thus with Aquinas, no conflict exists between faith and reason. They are complementary. Reason reigns supreme in the natural order where God's natural laws hold sway, but in the supernatural realm reason must yield to faith.

His Common Sense and Optimism. What is perhaps most distinctly Aristotelian about Aquinas is his insistence that much of our knowledge comes by way of experience. This opposed the Platonic view that knowledge was derived from our intellect—that we simply recollect knowledge already present in our souls before we were born. Aquinas followed Aristotle in declaring that our minds could extract knowledge from our sense experience which extended beyond the limits of the world of sense. For this position Aquinas has been called the philosopher of common sense. Yet he posited revelation for Aristotle's intuition, as the second source of our knowledge. And where the problem of motion or becoming was Aristotle's central metaphysical problem, for Aquinas his principal concern was the problem of being. Aquinas has also been called the "Apostle of Optimism." In contrast to the Augustinian tradition that held man so corrupted by original sin as to leave him with a natural bent toward evil, Aquinas asserted man was naturally good. To Thomas the world and all that was in it was wholly rational. This issue enjoyed more than academic importance in the thirteenth century in view of the Albigensian heresy which was equating evil with all things material. Aquinas maintains, nevertheless, that for all of man's natural virtues, he is unable to fulfill his deepest aspirations without God's grace. To guide man in the proper use of his faculties, Aquinas prepared the first complete system of Christian ethics based upon reason. Aquinas' position regarding the interpretation of the Scripture is important. Not only did he insist that many passages are difficult to understand; he also declared that a literal interpretation which clashes with an obvious fact must be considered false.

The Summa Theologiae. Aquinas' fame rests principally upon his two encyclopedic works, the *Summa Theologiae* and the *Summa contra Gentiles*. The *Summa Theologiae* provides a complete synthesis of Christian faith and morals based upon Scripture, tradition, and the teachings of the church, and sanctioned by reason. Aquinas' systematic organization and clarity of expression are superb and his reasoning compulsive. Once the reader accepts Aquinas' premises, he is carried with inexorable logic to accept his conclusions. The *Summa contra Gentiles* is concerned primarily with answering problems raised by Islamic and Jewish philosophers. Much of the content is necessarily philosophical, since a cardinal rule with Aquinas is always to debate issues in terms which the disputants will accept. The eighteen folio volumes of writings which Aquinas has left (with the aid of secretaries) also include commentaries on most of the books of the Old and New Testament, on the *Sentences* of Peter Lombard which his own *Summa Theologiae* was to supersede, on most of the writings of Aristotle, together with sermons and treatises on a variety of philosophical and theological questions. Some notion of the immensity of his industry is suggested by the fact that he poses some 600 questions in the *Summa Theologiae*, advances some 10,000 objections, and refutes all of these. Though Aquinas suffered something of an eclipse after his death, the Council of Trent (1545-1563) rehabilitated him and declared his work to be definitive. It has ever since been regarded as the most authoritative source of Catholic theology. (Reading 140)

St. Bonaventure. Aquinas' friend, the Franciscan Bonaventure (d. 1274), though always a theologian and mystic, ranks, nonetheless, as one of the most profound of the scholastics. Completely humble and self-effacing, his absorbing interest in God earned him the title of the "Seraphic Doctor." (Of the choirs of angels, the seraphim were believed to be closest to God.) Bonaventure found convincing proof of God's existence in nature, in the natural goodness of man, in the consciousness each human being has of himself. This Aquinas could not do. Bonaventure, in strict Augustinian tradition, further objected to the independent role Aquinas would assign reason. He insisted rather that faith must always guide reason, even in the rational and natural order where Aquinas had held reason sufficient to itself. Through Adam's sin, man lost his capacity to contemplate God directly; it now required an effort of the will which could only be moved and sustained by grace. On the other hand, though as great a mystic as Bernard, Bonaventure assigned an honored and important role to knowledge, where Bernard was apt to be fearful of the intellectual pride such scholarly search might induce. And Bonaventure even departed from one of the cardinal principles of his revered founder, Francis of Assisi, when he encouraged his fellow friars to pursue advanced studies in the universities. He himself occupied the Franciscan chair of theology at Paris. Yet one must never forget that the only knowledge Bonaventure defended—for that matter, the only knowledge most scholastics recommended—was that which pertained directly or indirectly to God. Bonaventure's most important theological work was his commentaries on the *Sentences of Peter Lombard*; his most important mystical writing, the *Journey of the Mind to God*.

Duns Scotus.   For all of Bonaventure's admitted profundity, the Franciscans selected the scintillating Duns Scotus (from Scotland) (d. 1308) as their greatest scholastic representative. That he won this recognition is all the greater tribute to his unusual intellectual powers since Scotus found himself in the same unenviable position as all scholastics after Aquinas. So scholarly and supremely thorough was Thomas' synthesis, that all subsequent scholars had perforce to assume the secondary role of critic, and so also did Scotus. How valid were some of Scotus' criticisms and what was his particular position on certain fundamental issues he raised remain matters of dispute to this day. That they will remain at least until the authenticity of writings ascribed to him has been established. To his contemporaries, in their fondness for honorific titles, he was the "Subtle Doctor." To less friendly critics who felt his subtleties were so finely drawn as to pass beyond the realm of the significant, he was the "dunce." Yet his penetrating mind simply detected illogicalities and *non sequiturs* which escaped the vision of less perceptive scholars. Perhaps his greatest point of difference with Aquinas lay in the major role he attributed to the will in the attainment of the knowledge of God, rather than to the intellect. While continuing the Augustinian-Franciscan tradition, Scotism reflects important influences from Aristotle and his Arabic commentators. Scotus ushered in the critical and somewhat barren turn scholasticism was to take in the fourteenth century.

William of Ockham.   The last important scholastic of the Middle Ages was the English Franciscan William of Ockham (d. 1349). We shall meet him later as a political theorist on the side of the German emperor against the papacy—and as a scientist. Here we are concerned with his scholasticism, which made a sharp break with the rational theology of Aquinas. On the fundamental question of the relationship of faith to reason, Ockham took a revolutionary position and one which proved fatal for scholasticism. Where Aquinas had held faith and reason mutually supplementary and wholly consistent one with another, Ockham considered faith so far superior to reason and so all-persuasive of itself, that the application of reason to theological questions was as unnecessary as it was unreasonable. Ockham left faith intact, to be sure, but for the earnest efforts of Albert the Great, of Aquinas, and of the earlier scholastics to provide matters of faith a rational basis, he had only scorn. Just as faith must be accepted without question and investigation, so natural truth might be pursued free of theological considerations. Together with Scotus, Ockham maintained not that God willed only things which were good, rather that things were good only because God commanded them. The former position invited rational and metaphysical analysis of God's mind and of what was good and true; but in the latter case God's will being without limitations, almost repelled such study as futile. The result was less concern about God and more about man and his justification. Because of this development in theology, together with the tendency to split hairs in logic over inconsequential maters, the study of scholasticism fell into disrepute in the closing centuries of the Middle Ages. Yet modern logic finds much of value in the logic of Ockham and of his contemporaries.

The Rise of Universities

Origins of the University. The flowering of scholasticism after the middle of the twelfth century, which produced the galaxy of Albert the Great, Aquinas, Bonaventure, and Duns Scotus, also brought forth the university. Whether the scholasticism of the earlier part of the twelfth century, that is, of Abelard's day, would have given rise to the university is doubtful. Surely the university would have come in time. Still it was the influx of philosophical and scientific works from the Islamic and Byzantine worlds during the late twelfth century which provided scholasticism with intellectual materials of a high order, and which, in turn, produced the university. For it is to books, in the last analysis, that we must look for the origins of the medieval university. The works of Aristotle, of Galen and Ptolemy, and of other ancient Greek and more modern Islamic scholars, provided the subject matter which revolutionized the level of instruction in the cathedral school. Today one can most easily discover the basic difference between the secondary school and the university by examining their respective libraries. In similar fashion, it was this higher learning from the east which gave birth to the university, one of the most unique and most enduring of the contributions of the Middle Ages to western civilization.

Additional Factors. It is true that books of themselves do not tell the entire story of the rise of the medieval university. Unless books are welcomed, unless they are read and studied, they represent so much unlocked learning. Had these books entered western Europe during the eighth or ninth centuries, the impulse they would have given scholarship would have been negligible. Coming as they did in the twelfth and thirteenth centuries, just when the western mind was eagerly searching after the information they had to provide, their impact was immediate and far-reaching. For books on law, on medicine, but especially, on philosophy, did the west stretch out eager hands. A third factor, in addition to books and to this interest in books, helped to produce the first universities. That was the fame which had come to a particular school because of its tradition of scholarship or the presence there of a famous scholar or scholars. In short, that school which enjoyed a reputation for providing instruction above the level of the traditional monastic or cathedral school, developed into a university. Finally the increasing population and prosperity of towns in the thirteenth century, together with the intellectual and religious vigor of the friars, notably the Dominicans, provided additional stimuli to the rise of universities.

From Cathedral School to University. It might be well to suggest a fourth factor in the rise of universities. This was the great demand for a higher education in the twelfth and thirteenth centuries. So large was the number of students who sought an education, that it forced the rise of an institution substantially different from the old cathedral or monastic school. The majority of these students came from the towns which were growing more populous, more prosperous, more robust. That the cathedral school was normally located in the city, accounts in large measure for the evolution of the university from it rather than from the monastic center. Furthermore, as we noted earlier, cathedral schools had proved themselves more responsive to the needs of a changing society, the monastic schools holding themselves, by contrast, more strictly to purely monastic business. A cathedral school which because of its fame or its varied offerings could attract students from longer distances acquired the name of *studium generale*, literally a "general school." Because the heavy influx of students to these centers almost immediately led to the formation of corporations or associations of students or masters, the phrase "university of students" or "university of masters" early replaced the *studium generale* as the accepted title of such schools. The Latin word *universitas*, from which the English "university" is derived, simply meant any such organization and was commonly employed by craft gilds. Possibly because of the fame of these students gilds, partly because other gilds soon began to use vernacular equivalents, the academic gild eventually appropriated the word "university" for its own use.

University Organization. The organization of the early university was quite simple. The cathedral school which was the parent organization had been directed by the chancellor of the cathedral chapter. With the appearance of these "universities" of students and masters, the chancellor gradually found himself deprived of the substance of control. His authority to grant the license to teach became a formality, and his real authority was transferred, in the case of the university of Paris, first to a proctor, then to a rector who was also dean of the arts faculty. At Oxford a university chancellor held the post of chief executive from the early thirteenth century. While no organization became standard for all medieval universities, fairly uniform was the dominant position enjoyed by the general assemblies of the masters. It is interesting to note that the faculties of many universities today still enjoy that powerful position. The larger universities such as Paris were traditionally organized into four faculties (we now would employ the term college or school), those of the arts, law, medicine, and theology. At Paris, the students who were enrolled in the arts course, which was the most numerous group, were divided for administrative purposes into four nations: the French which included students from southern Europe; the Norman; the Picard which included students from the Low Countries; and the English which included those from northern and eastern Europe. In general, the northern and eastern universities followed the example of Paris where the gilds of masters were dominant, where clerical influence was strong, and where the study of theology dominated the curriculum. The universities of southern Europe, by contrast, followed the example of Bologna. There, because of the large number of mature law students, the atmosphere was more professional (less clerical), and the student gilds remained powerful. Instead of masters laying down regulations for students, we occasionally read of the reverse. Thus at Bologna, the gild of students required masters to cover a certain amount of material in a systematic manner, to be present at all times unless specifically excused, and to begin and to terminate their lectures on time! Bologna can be classified as a lay university, a rarity in the Middle Ages.

Purpose of University Gilds. The reference to the character of instruction at Bologna suggests that one of the purposes for the organization of student gilds was the improvement of the quality of teaching. This was unusual, however, even for the Middle Ages. More material and immediate, ordinarily, were the objectives of the gild: reasonable rentals, better food, protection against discrimination, real or imagined, on the part of the local authorities, who, the students were confident, showed them more firmness than sympathy. Something had to be done for those students who were not citizens of the particular university city and therefore, lacked the protection of the law. The university community discovered early that more cooperation could be elicited from the municipal authorities by working through their gild organizations. Failing to secure satisfaction by this method, the students and masters might simply "migrate" to a more friendly city. It is said that almost half of the medieval universities represent migrations from older institutions. The university of Oxford owed its birth to a secession of English students from Paris in 1167 (upon orders of Henry II), Cambridge from Oxford, and Padua from Bologna. Migration would, of course, be impossible today, but not in the Middle Ages of the twelfth and thirteenth centuries when universities consisted essentially of masters and students, not of laboratories, libraries, and dormitories.

University Privileges. Less primitive methods soon replaced migration or its threat to bring redress of injuries. Both church and state showed commendable alacrity in protecting the new institutions, once they recognized them as such. The state accorded the students the so-called benefit of clergy, which carried exemption from taxes, military service, and freedom from local civil jurisdiction. The church (pope) customarily granted the university an autonomous status with respect to the local bishop's authority, and placed it directly under his own. This was a boon eagerly sought after by the masters, since it left the licensing of teachers and granting of degrees under university control. In time, the university might grow so independent as even to resent papal interference. Thus the chronicler writes in shocked tones how when a papal bull was announced at Oxford critical of that university's failure to silence Wyclif, the university authorities "were for a long time undecided whether they should receive the papal bull with honor, or with dishonor wholly ignore it." One can only marvel at the care with which both church and state respected the "liberties" of the medieval university. No modern university enjoys the independence, influence, and respect, that the university of Paris did in the Middle Ages. (Readings 145, 146)

Bologna, Paris, and Other Universities. Salerno, just below Naples, enjoyed a reputation as a medical center as early as the middle of the eleventh century. Yet because it remained principally, if not exclusively, a medical school, it may not be classified as the first university. That distinction is ordinarily given to Bologna. Bologna's history as a law center has been traced back to a Pepo in the eleventh century. It probably had a tradition of legal scholarship extending as far back as Roman times although its real fame dates from the days of the great Irnerius (d. 1125), who was the first to apply the jurisprudence contained in the *Digest* in his commentaries on law. Equally important was the work of Gratian, the next big name at Bologna. In his *Decretum* (*ca.* 1140), Gratian set up canon (church) law as a discipline distinct from theology in general, and applied to it certain principles drawn from the *Corpus Juris Civilis.* Frederick Barbarossa conferred formal rights on the scholarly community in 1158, the act which marks the official birth of the university. The university of Paris may be as old as Bologna. We hear of students flocking there in the early twelfth century to hear Abelard. Its nucleus was the cathedral school of Notre Dame, whence it spread across to the left bank of the Seine to the Latin Quarter (so-called because of the language spoken there). Paris, the most respected of all medieval universities, dated its official foundation from 1200. That was the year when Philip Augustus granted a charter in order to mollify the irate masters and students who were threatening to migrate over the brutal manner in which the local authorities had handled a student riot. The origins of Oxford remain obscure. The time of the secession of students from Paris in 1167 noted above may be as good a date as any. The first chancellor was the renowned scholar, Robert Grosseteste, whose tenure began in 1214. Cambridge University bears the birth date of 1209. Salamanca, the oldest of the Spanish universities, was founded in 1220. This university and that of Naples, which Frederick II established in 1224, are examples of universities which did not evolve, but were founded. From the late thirteenth century, formal founding became the usual method of establishing a university. Prague was chartered by Charles IV in 1347; Heidelberg, the oldest university of Germany, was chartered in 1385. By the close of the Middle Ages some eighty universities were in existence, about half by papal charter, the other half by imperial or princely foundation.

Degrees. Originally the medieval university was a teachers' college: the goal of the student was to teach. The first degree was simply the *licentia docendi* (license to teach), which the chancellor of the cathedral school had already conferred. With their rise the gilds of masters assumed the right to determine qualifications for teaching and for degrees. All degrees were originally teaching degrees. The bachelor's degree, which today marks the termination of academic life for the vast majority of students, was primarily a qualifying degree in the Middle Ages. It marked the completion of four years of study, after which the student was qualified to do some elementary teaching while he continued on to a master's degree. One might consider it the equivalent of a journeyman's rank in a craft gild. The master of arts degree, which corresponded to the old *licentia docendi*, normally required six years of study in the arts. After passing his examination and successfully defending his thesis, that is, his masterpiece, the student would be formally admitted into the masters gild. Now he could teach if he found a room he could use for classes and if he could attract students. By the middle of the thirteenth century, the establishment of endowed chairs tended to limit such opportunity to the select few. Yet this dampened few ambitions since by that time many students were earning degrees simply for the prestige these carried or to qualify for employment in the service of church, state, or commune. Many undoubtedly found employment teaching in what would be called secondary schools today. The degrees of doctor, professor, and master were largely synonymous. The degree in theology was the most difficult to attain. It required some dozen years of study beyond the master's degree and a minimum age of thirty-five. Paris' disturbing experience with Abelard may have had something to do with thus limiting the teaching of theology to mature scholars.

University Curricula. Only a few of the largest universities could boast the full four curricula of arts, theology, civil and canon law, and medicine. A knowledge of Latin was presupposed, if the university did not make certain of this competency by entrance examination. To state simply that the arts course constituted the seven liberal arts would be misleading. Considerably less attention was paid to the quadrivium than to the trivium, and much less to grammar and rhetoric than to logic. Logic dominated the curriculum, while the scholastic method of beginning with a proposition, examining the arguments pro and con, and drawing thence the most reasonable conclusion, was common to all study. As might be expected, Aristotle provided the core of the arts subject matter, particularly his philosophical and scientific works. After completing the arts course (law students were frequently exempted), the student was ready to embark on one of the professional fields. If he chose theology, and few did because of the difficulty of the course and the long years of study involved, he would study the Bible, commentaries on the Bible, the writings of the church fathers, and Peter Lombard's *Sentences*. This latter served as the standard text in theology until the adoption of Aquinas' *Summa*. If the student chose law, and most students who went beyond the arts course did so, he might limit himself to Gratian's *Decretum*. If he wished to exploit to the fullest the demand for lawyers and jurists, he would study both canon and civil law. The study of the latter rested preeminently upon the *Digest*. The medieval university was most successful in training lawyers, partly because "law is a form of scholasticism," partly because the lack of laboratories and instruments did not hamper his study of legal literature. As Rashdall, the leading authority on the medieval university, writes: "In many respects the work of the School of Bologna represents the most brilliant achievement of the intellect of mediaeval Europe." Finally, if the student chose to study medicine, he read Galen, Hippocrates, and the commentaries of Avicenna and other Islamic scholars. Here, by modern notions, he made least progress. Surgical observation (not practice), which might pass as laboratory, was itself severely restricted, and the microscope was still far in the future. (Reading 147)

The Medieval University Student. What kind of student enrolled in the medieval university? That is not so easy a matter to determine as it is of today's student. For one thing, colleges and universities are more uniform today in organization and curriculum than in the Middle Ages. For another thing, the age distribution of students in the Middle Ages was considerably greater. Many boys enrolled at the age of fifteen, although friars and monks, who made up a significant percentage of the student body, were five to ten years older. Let us hope it was the younger element about whom all the stories are told of wandering from school to school, of roistering and brawling. Those surely were vigorous times! An Oxford statute forbade students from carrying bows and arrows, and universities' records make regular mention of sanguinary contests between "town and gown!" (All students wore the clerical garb.) Yet Professor Stephenson's observation is probably a safe one, always allowing, of course, for the less even course of life in the Middle Ages, that "the average student was law-abiding and conscientious, although his wilder brethren were always the more conspicuous." What has helped make the latter more conspicuous has been a rich heritage of beautiful and rollicking verse he has left behind. (See page 603.) As university life became more standardized, student life grew correspondingly less ebullient. A major factor in channeling the more unruly proclivities of the student came with the establishment of the college. The first famous college was one founded by Robert of Sorbon, confessor of St. Louis. He established a house at Paris to provide lodging and food for sixteen needy theological students. An amazing number of similarly philanthropically minded donors caused colleges to be built during the late Middle Ages, almost seventy growing up around the university of Paris. (Reading 148)

Medieval vs. Modern University. It will be of interest to draw some contrasts between medieval and modern universities. That such contrasts are marked and many is true, even though one modern scholar has described the university as that medieval institution which, second only to the church, has perhaps changed the least. Even a cursory glance will disclose that theology is no longer considered the "queen of the sciences"; that the medieval university boasted no sports, no dramatics, no history or social sciences, no libraries, no laboratories, even no buildings for a long time, no schools of engineering, pedagogy, journalism, business, and agriculture, no foreign languages, no boards of trustees, nor extracurricular activities which consume so much of the modern student's time. Where the medieval university used logic, the modern relies upon the laboratory. There was much more discussion and debate in the Middle Ages. As Robert of Sorbon would have it: "Nothing is known perfectly which has not been masticated by the teeth of disputation." A medieval thesis was a thesis, never a statistical study of evidence. More medieval students came from the lower classes than is the rule today, and where the financially straitened student today waits tables for his meals, his medieval predecessor might beg for his or copy parts of books, keeping for himself one copy and a bit of money. Class-cutting was more common in the Middle Ages, this despite the fact that it was a rare week indeed that did not boast a holiday (holy day). It may come as a surprise to some to learn that academic freedom was not born with Jefferson and the University of Virginia. It was highly regarded in the Middle Ages. The university of Oxford objected strenuously to papal attempts to silence one of its masters, Wyclif, partly because they considered such interference an impertinence. And the English ecclesiastical authorities were willing that Wyclif air his revolutionary theories so long as he kept them within the ivied halls of Oxford. The greatest contrast between the medieval and modern university lies in the character of the student body. Not only did girls and women not attend the medieval university; the clergy practically monopolized the lecture halls. Henry VIII's decrees had the effect of transforming Oxford and Cambridge from clerical schools to preserves of the aristocracy.

Yet the medieval university, like its modern counterpart, offered courses of study, issued degrees, maintained faculties, conducted examinations, and engaged in the pursuit of higher learning in an organized fashion. As the late Professor Haskins pointed out, our universities, like those of the Middle Ages, "are still associations of masters and scholars leading the common life of learning." Finally, both medieval and modern university represent the most powerful influences upon the intellectual life of their times.

Medieval Science

In no field of endeavor have the Middle Ages received less their due than in science and technology. Even the term "medieval" is occasionally heard as a synonym for that which is irrational and unscientific. Yet no similar stigma attaches to the term "ancient," even though Ancient History, for all its millenia can boast but a handful of Greek scientists and an unimpressive record of technological progress. This leads one to suspect that the misconception of the unscientific character of the Middle Ages must flow from the venerable fallacy that it was only with the sixteenth century, the first of the "modern" centuries, that man began to make real progress in art, in technology, in science, and in intellectual pursuits in general. Happily with each passing year, scholarly research makes more manifest how "unscientific" is this view of the Middle Ages, and how so much for which "modern" man has earned commendation was already old when Columbus discovered America. Illustrative of this redressing of the record of medieval, at the expense of modern, science is the case of the obscure Italian Mariano of Siena, whose early fifteenth-century sketches of guns and projectiles have only recently received any attention. "No one who has looked at these drawings can fail to realize that they anticipated a great deal for which the famous Leonardo da Vinci (one of the first "modern" men) has usually received the sole credit."*

Medieval Technology. "The origins of modern science are to be found at least as far back as the thirteenth century."† So writes Professor Crombie. The record of man's ingenuity, however, of science as applied to material things, began with human history. And in the preparation of this record, medieval man, even before the thirteenth century, contributed his share. As we have seen, something as fundamental to civilization as the horsecollar and horseshoe date from the tenth century. The inventors of

---

* Carl Stephenson, *Mediaeval History* (New York, 1935), p. 488.
† A. C. Crombie, *Augustine to Galileo* (London, 1952), p. xiv.

these devices remain nameless, as do the legions of ingenious farmers, craftsmen, and artisans who accounted for most of man's technological progress prior to the nineteenth century. We have noted what was accomplished in the way of agricultural implements (see page 348), and we have described the skill of the medieval gildsman. (See page 393.) In the chapter following we shall read of the extraordinary skill of the medieval architect, whose cathedral, from point of view of engineering and beauty, can vie with the architectural monuments of any age. The sculptures of these great churches, their stained-glass windows, the stone masonry and bricklaying that went into their building, all attest to the nimbleness of medieval hands and wits. Without the aid of formal chemistry, western smiths learned to make fine steel and to fashion this into marvelously wrought weapons and form-fitting armor. Western artisans learned to mold beautiful vessels of gold, silver, and pewter, to work ivory, glass, and leather. Chimneys and furnaces which the warm Mediterranean world of antiquity had not needed, cranes, water-screws, siphons, mechanical clocks, glass windows, spectacles, and the rudder—these and other significant marks of material progress bear witness to the vigor of medieval craftsmanship. While the west could not have accomplished all this without major assistance from Byzantium and Islam, not sufficient credit has been paid western skill and persistence in bringing many eastern ideas to fruition. "Such techniques were perfected through long and obscure experimentation, as were the making of fine fabrics, the designing of musical instruments, the grinding of lenses (whether for eye-glasses or for telescopes), and the mining, smelting, and working of metals. The technological advance of western Europe between 1000 and 1500 is just beginning to be appreciated."*

Compass, Gunpowder, Power, Printing Press. Perhaps the four most momentous of all technological changes or inventions ever to affect western civilization were contributions of the medieval west: the exploitation of nonhuman power, the magnetic compass, the gun, and the printing press. (Western claims to the invention of the compass and gunpowder are not finally established and may never be in view of the paucity of evidence.) In the use or development of these four, western Europe has singularly excelled, and by their means has been able to Europeanize much of the world. The compass opened the way to the discoveries and explorations of the late medieval and early modern periods; the gun enabled the westerner to hold what he had discovered or to acquire what he coveted; the use of power in the production of goods provided the west that material superiority over the rest of the world which it has never relinquished; the printing press supplied it the means of flooding the world with its views. Artillery was employed in the early fourteenth century, hand-guns in the fifteenth, which century also found the Hussites fighting effectively with

* Carl Stephenson, *ibid.*

history's first tanks. The magnetized needle which we know as the compass is found described in twelfth-century manuscripts by western and Islamic writers. Our eternal search for more power goes back to the Middle Ages, which witnessed an amazing exploitation of animal, wind, and water power, a phenomenon quite foreign to slave-ridden antiquity. So extensively, indeed, did English fullers exploit water power, that within two centuries after the eleventh, the entire industry had shifted from the plains of southeastern England to the hills of the northwest where water power was available. The invention of the printing press consisted essentially of the use of moveable metal type in place of separate blocks for each individual page. Two westerners lay claim to this invention, John Gutenberg of Mainz being customarily awarded the honor over Lourens Coster of Haarlem. Gutenberg's press began printing, a few years before 1450, Bibles and religious literature for the most part. The impact of the printing press upon civilization has received sharply conflicting assessments. The skeptical critic points out that most people could not read before the nineteenth century, and today, as in the past, most readers limit themselves to what is entertaining or to reading views to which they already subscribe. Yet while the printing press may not have worked the intellectual wonders its champions have claimed for it, it has surely come to revolutionize the leisure time of millions.

Scientific Knowledge of Early Middle Ages.   Though medieval man was able in time to make a worthy contribution to the history of the scientific method and to theoretical science, his first efforts in that direction were not encouraging. Like the Islamic and Byzantine scholar, he built upon the Greek achievement. Yet before the twelfth century, all that was available to him was what he could find in Pliny's voluminous though uncritical *Natural History*. To this "vast thesaurus of ancient knowledge, true and false," Boethius and the other transmitters of classical learning whom we have seen (see page 251), turned for most of their scientific (and unscientific) summaries. This is all the west had to work with before the twelfth century when it finally gained direct access to the ancient Greek and later Islamic stores of knowledge. It was this development which ushered in the age of modern science. Nevertheless, western Europe even before the twelfth century could boast a few scientific minds, could point to men who used their powers of observation as man has always been wont to do. Thus Bede, in writing about tides, supplemented the formal knowledge at hand concerning that phenomenon with what he himself had observed. Yet in science as in philosophy, the west was generally content to accept and listen in these early centuries, when facilities for study were so elementary and when life itself was so frequently in peril.

Barriers to Progress.   Several blind spots, a few of ancient origin, obstructed scientific progress in the Middle Ages. Among these was the influence of Neoplatonism which had emphasized the perfection of the world of ideas and the corresponding imperfection and inadequacy of the world which we see. Such a philosophy had discouraged scholars like Augustine, for example, from taking a closer look at nature. The Middle Ages gave general acceptance, too, to the claims of ancient astrology, magic, and superstition, and added to these a rich store of its own. Christian belief that such supernatural agencies as angels and saints could interfere with the natural course of human fortunes usually invited a growth of superstition. The Christian love of symbolism which held natural phenomena to be, above all else, merely symbols of deeper religious significance, frequently led scholars to limit their study of nature and the physical world to the discovery of spiritual applications. Thus Roger Bacon, whose name is the most distinguished in the history of medieval science, among other justifications for the study of mathematics, recommended it as a means of advancing our understanding of God. He wrote: "Mathematics should aid us in ascertaining the position of paradise and hell, and promote our knowledge of Scriptural geography and sacred chronology, help us visualize the ark, tabernacles, and temple, so that from an accurate ascertainment of the literal sense, the true spiritual meaning may be deduced."

Adelard of Bath. The scholar who might be singled out as the first true scientist of the Middle Ages was Abelard's contemporary, Adelard of Bath (d. 1150). We have a record of his presumed conversation with his nephew, in which he sought to impress upon the young man the superiority of knowledge based on observation and experiment to knowledge accepted on authority. While Adelard recognized God's creation of all things, he insisted that "nature is not confused and without system, and so far as human knowledge has progressed it should be given a hearing. Only when it fails utterly should there be recourse to God."* It is an interesting coincidence how these two contemporaries, with the similarly sounding names, Abelard and Adelard, should have been among the very first to advocate the same rational approach in the acquisition of knowledge, whether it be metaphysical or natural. To Professor Crombie, Adelard's position marks the "great watershed that divides the period when men looked to nature to provide illustrations for moralising, from that in which men began to study nature for its own sake."†

Compilers of Scientific Lore. Less original than Adelard, though worthy of our attention, were a number of compilers of scientific information. One such encyclopedist was Alexander of Hales (d. 1245), an Englishman, who had the distinction of being the first Franciscan to occupy a chair at the university in Paris. Though his work, the first *Summa Theologiae*, dealt principally with theology, it did contain much material based upon Aristotle's physics and natural history. Voluminous it was without doubt.

---

* Quoted in Crombie, *op. cit.*, 13.
† Crombie, *ibid.*

Roger Bacon says it "weighed about as much as one horse could carry." More comprehensive was the scientific content in Alexander of Neckham's (d. 1217) work entitled *On the Nature of Things*, a potpourri of fact and fancy drawn principally from his reading, partly from his own observations. Although Alexander of Neckham was primarily concerned with drawing moral instruction from natural phenomena, he was generally well informed and not unappreciative of the scientific spirit. (Reading 149) The most important compiler of medieval scientific lore was Vincent of Beauvais (d. 1264). The title of his massive work was *Speculum Maius* (greater mirror), which, according to the modest claim of its author, reflected, as in a mirror, "whatever has been made or done or said in the visible and invisible world from the beginning until the end, and also of things to come"! The worth of this and similar compilations to contemporary scholars is questionable. It would be a lucky scholar, indeed, who could have isolated that information which was correct from the accompanying mass of superstition and misinformation. These *summae* do attest, however, to the intellectual activity of the times. They illustrate how studiously scholars worked to assimilate the vast amount of learning that was coming in from the east.

Albert the Great. Among the first medieval scholars to make a positive contribution to knowledge beyond the strictly dialectical and theological was Leonard of Pisa (d. 1245). In his *Book of Abacus* and his treatise *On the Practice of Geometry*, he introduced the west to Hindu-Arabic numerals and the zero. He also presented alongside the contribution of Islam, significant additions of his own in the field of practical arithmetic, trigonometry, and algebra. Albert the Great, the scholastic, was also a leading scientist of the thirteenth century. Though an enthusiastic student of Aristotle, he proved no slavish purveyor of that ancient philosopher's views. Particularly original and noteworthy were his observations on the fauna of western Europe, running the gamut as they did from bees and spiders to hawks and whales. Of whales he rejected all lore except what he himself had confirmed and he dismissed stories of harpies and griffins as sheer fabrications. He observed the habits of beavers and eels, and proved to his own satisfaction that sea turtles did not drink salt water nor did ostriches eat iron. When he describes the manner in which the female shepherd dog teaches her cubs to kill wolves he sounds every inch an experienced dog-trainer. And he warns the falconer in treating the diseases of his birds that "experience is the best teacher."

Robert Grosseteste. Perhaps the greatest of all medieval scientists was the learned Robert Grosseteste (d. 1253), first chancellor of Oxford and distinguished bishop of Lincoln. Although of obscure birth, his force of intellect and character raised him to such eminence that all men, including king and pope, respected and feared him. On one occasion the pope was threatening to discipline him for his refusal to approve the provision of the pope's nephew to a benefice in the diocese of Lincoln. One of the cardinals remonstrated with the pope: "He is esteemed as a great philosopher, learned in Greek and Latin literature, zealous for justice, a reader in the schools of theology, a preacher to the people, and active enemy of abuses. . . . He is a catholic and a holy man, a better man than we are.* Despite a crowded career capped by almost twenty years as an outstanding prelate, Grosseteste drove himself to produce a staggering quantity of scholarly work, which included treatises on philosophical and scientific questions, commentaries on the Bible and on Aristotle, sermons, and even allegories. To his devoted disciples he strongly recommended the study of languages and of mathematics, the study of languages to open up the wealth of Islamic learning, the study of mathematics to facilitate the pursuit of scientific study. Harassed by the presence of faulty translations from the Greek, he invited Greek scholars to come to England and made many translations of his own. Grosseteste appears to have been the first medievalist to go systematically into the problem of the role of experiment in scientific inquiry. The first wave theory of light has been credited to him, and he has been called "the original architect of the Gregorian Calendar of 1582." His experiments with lenses contributed to the development of the first spectacles. His most valuable contribution to science, however, was the impetus he gave to scientific study. Both the reputation of medieval Oxford as a center of scientific studies and the reputations of disciples of his like Roger Bacon, rest squarely upon his work.

Roger Bacon. Roger Bacon (d. 1292) was the most notable of Grosseteste's pupils. Of obscure birth like his mentor, he studied at Oxford and Paris and joined the Franciscan order, attracted probably more by the advantages a religious life would have for study than by the monastic ideal itself. For by temperament he was utterly unfitted for community life, being as caustic in his criticism of others as he was bombastic about his own talents. "Puerile vanity" is how he dismissed the profound treatises of Aquinas. It was these deficiencies of character, rather than the scientific views he expressed, that got him into difficulties with his superiors. He did suffer ecclesiastical censure for his writings on astrology, and it was his ensuing "imprisonment" which long gave him unmerited fame as the first martyr to the cause of science. His predictions of ships which would be driven by machines faster than any group of rowers could propel them; of cars that would move with amazing speed without benefit of draught animals; of flying machines with wings like a bird; these and other prophecies as to what science and technology promised in the future, have earned him similarly greater recognition than they actually warranted. Yet Bacon did have a fierce zeal for learning, and not learning of the traditional scholastic kind, but for linguistics, mathematics, astronomy, optics, and chemistry. His major work, the *Opus Maius*, he wrote at the request of Pope Clement

* Quoted in *Robert Grosseteste*, ed. D. A. Callus (Oxford, 1955), p. 194.

IV who had come to his defense. It consisted of a prospectus of what might be accomplished, as he explained to the pope, if adequate financial assistance were provided. Unfortunately the pope died, and nothing beyond this prospectus ever materialized. Bacon did advance somewhat beyond his teacher Grosseteste, especially in optics, but hardly more than could be expected of a diligent scholar. History is finally placing Grosseteste and Bacon in their proper relationship, giving the one a higher niche than scholars had earlier accorded him, the second a significantly lower one. (Reading 150)

Other Scientists: An Evaluation.   There were contemporaries of Bacon such as Peter of Abano who was probably the most learned man living around the year 1300, and many more scholars in the fourteenth and fifteenth centuries who continued to study mathematics and the sciences. Their work has passed largely unnoticed, partly because their findings were not spectacular, partly because of the shadow which has only recently been lifting from the record of medieval scholarship. Yet their contribution was nonetheless significant. It prepared the necessary groundwork upon which the more sensational discoveries of the seventeenth century became possible. Between men like Oresme (d. 1382) whose study of falling bodies may have anticipated some of the work of Galileo, and whose analytical geometry foreshadowed that of Descartes—between Oresme of the late Middle Ages and the scientists of the seventeenth century, there is a direct link which the humanists of the fifteenth and sixteenth did not quite succeed in severing. On the other hand, medieval scientists were still working largely in the dark. Professor Durand's evaluation of Oresme's scientific achievement—"a texture of 'hunches,' with all the good and bad that the term implies, shrewd common sense, a knack of focussing the dispersed ideas of other minds, a certain prophetic vision, and a considerable arbitrariness in disposing of facts"*—might be applied to other men of science in the late medieval and early modern periods. But again quoting Professor Durand, what was common to Oresme and to these other scientists was "the passion with which they strove to reduce man's search for knowledge to a principle of unity leading to mastery of Nature."

Astronomy and Optics.   Now to take a brief glance at what the Middle Ages believed and contributed in the sciences. The west joined Islam and Byzantium in accepting the Ptolemaic system which held the earth to be the center of the universe. Yet there were western scholars, and Islamic as well, who entertained grave misgivings concerning the validity of the system. In both worlds, agitation was voiced for a reform of the calendar. Of course, most people accepted the sphericity of the earth. The study of astronomy led to further development of trigonometry and optics. Light was considered the first form of material things and the first principle of motion and efficient causation, which explains the great amount of study

* *Speculum*, XVI (1941), p. 184.

scholars devoted to optics. A practical result of this interest was the invention of spectacles. On the other hand, western scholars wasted much study on the presumed influence of stars and planets upon human health. Such a misconception was fairly common. According to Roger Bacon, the physician who lacked a knowledge of astronomy had nothing but "chance and fortune" to help him in the treatment of disease.

Alchemy and Biology. In chemistry or alchemy western Europe did not proceed appreciably beyond Islamic scholarship. The alchemist, for all his preposterous search for an elixir of life or the means to transmute baser metals into gold, did learn much about chemical reactions, about distillation, about the properties of different elements, and the nature of various substances. Perhaps no more industrious and dedicated scientist do the pages of scholarship reveal than the alchemist. With untiring zeal, he pressed his experiments despite the dark and sometimes dangerous suspicions of his fellow citizens, and in the face of almost complete lack of success and encouragement. One of the most interesting manuscripts in the field of biology to come from the medieval period is the work on falconry by Frederick II. This versatile monarch was thoroughly scientific in his approach to his subject. He read all that could be found in Greek and Moslem sources, reserving always the right to dismiss ancient views as "lying" and inferior to his own observations. His manuscript contains some 900 pictures of individual birds, as finely drawn as those which appear in modern books of ornithology. We have referred to Albert the Great's interest in biology. He probably knew more about the animal and insect kingdom than any scholar of his day.

Medicine. In the field of medicine the medieval contribution was meager. Some modern critics, of course, would dismiss all medical progress antedating Pasteur as inconsequential. Actually a great amount of intensive study was carried on at such medical centers as Salerno, Montpellier, Bologna, Padua, and Paris. Medieval physicians used herbs and drugs to fight disease, some such as castor oil and camphor still being the stock in trade of the modern drug store. The medieval physician could induce a kind of anaesthesia with the use of a liquid consisting chiefly of opium. Though he accepted the influence of the heavenly bodies upon disease and the interference of the supernatural, his approach beyond this was quite scientific. He was able to make some astonishingly accurate diagnoses. Where he failed almost completely was in the curing of the maladies he was able to diagnose. Yet if he was not the first to recognize the principle of infection, he was the first to apply it scientifically. Leprosy had become almost extinct by the close of the Middle Ages, although at one time as many as one person in every two hundred had been afflicted with the dread disease. We also read of hernia operations, the grafting of skin, and the filling of dental cavities with gold leaf. We would prefer not to hear so much about "blood-letting," which seems to have been a common method of purging the body of that same kind of constitutional lethargy which more recent generations felt would better respond to doses of sulphur and molasses. All reputable physicians recognized the essential nature of the study of anatomy in the treatment of bodily disorders. Though such study was hampered by the authorities, it was not forbidden. Perhaps the most important single contribution of the Middle Ages in the field of medicine was the charitable hospital.

 READINGS

No. 140. On the ethics of buying and selling

(From the *Summa Theologiae* of St. Thomas Aquinas. Translation.)

To the fourth article we proceed in this manner. It appears that in carrying on business, one may not sell a thing at a higher price than was paid for it.

1. For Chrysostom says on *Matt.* xxii, 12: "Whoever buy anything that he may sell it, intact and unchanged, at a profit, is the merchant who is cast out of the temple of God." And similarly does Cassiodorus write on *Ps.* lxx, 15: "Because I have not known learning or business according to another version." "What," he asks, "is trading except to buy cheaply in order to sell at a high price?" And he adds: "It was such traders whom the Lord drove out of the temple." Yet no one is driven from the temple except one who has sinned; therefore such business is sinful.

2. Furthermore, it appears from the above, that it is contrary to justice to sell goods at a higher price, or to purchase them for a lower price than they are worth. For he who in trading sells a thing at a higher price than he paid, must either have bought it for less than it was worth or have sold it at a price above its value. Therefore, this act cannot be without sin.

3. Furthermore, Jerome declares: "Flee that trading cleric like the pest who once poor has grown rich or once unknown has become famous." For it seems that trading ought not to be forbidden clerics unless it be sinful. Therefore, for traders to buy at a low price and to sell at a higher is sinful.

[Objection] But opposed to this Augustine writes on *Ps.* lxx, 15: "Because I have not known learning. The trader, grasping for gains, curses his losses, and lies and perjures himself over the value of his goods. Yet these are sins of a man, not of the trade, which can be conducted without these sins." Therefore, trading is in itself not illicit.

[Answer] I reply that to devote oneself to the exchange of goods is the business of traders. As the Philosopher writes (*Polit.* I, 3): "The exchange of things is of two kinds. The one is indeed natural and necessary, by means of which one thing is exchanged for another or goods for money, in order to meet the exigencies of life. And such trading does not properly pertain to merchants but more to domestic servants or civil officials whose duty it is to provide those things essential to the well-being of the house or the state. Another kind of exchange is of money for money or of any goods for money, not because the things are necessary for life but for the sake of gain. And indeed it appears that this trading pertains properly to merchants. According to the Philosopher, the first kind of exchange is commendable, because it serves a natural need; the second, on the other hand, is justly censured, since considered in itself, it serves merely the lust for gain which knows no end but continues on into infinity. And therefore trading, considered in itself, has a certain censure, since by its very nature it does not suggest a good or necessary end.

Nevertheless gain which is the end of trading, while by its nature not implying anything good or necessary, still does not imply anything evil or contrary to virtue. For which reason there is nothing which prohibits gain from being directed to some necessary or good end. Thus is trading rendered lawful. Thus when one seeks a moderate gain in trading for the sustenance of his own household or for the relief of the indigent, or when one trades in the interest of the public good lest those things be lacking which are essential to the existence of his country, and seeks gain not as an end but as the reward for his labor.

To the first argument I answer that the position of Chrysostom must be understood to refer to trading whose purpose is gain; which appears to apply particularly in the case of him who sells at a higher price goods which has not undergone any change. For if he sell at a higher price goods that has undergone change, it would appear that he is receiving a reward for his labor. Nevertheless, this gain also can be legitimately intended, not as the ultimate end but because of another necessary or good end, as has been said.

To the second argument I answer that not everyone who sells at a higher price than he bought is a trader, but only he who buys with the hope that he can sell at a higher price. For if he buy a thing not to sell but to keep, and later for some reason decides to sell, this is not trading even though he may sell at a higher price. For this he can do legitimately either because he has improved the thing in some way, or because the price of the goods has changed due to change of place or time, or because in transferring it from one place to another he has exposed himself to danger, or in having it transferred. In this case neither the buying nor the selling is unjust.

To the third argument I reply that clerics ought not only to abstain from those things which are in themselves evil but even from those which have the appearance of evil. Indeed, this happens in trading because it is ordered to earthly gain of which clerics ought to be contemptuous and because of the frequency with which traders sin; as Ecclesiasticus (xxvi, 28): "with difficulty can the trader avoid sins of the lips." There is yet another reason and this is that trading involves the soul too deeply in secular cares and draws it, consequently, away from spiritual matters. Wherefore the Apostle (II *Tim.* ii, 4) declares: "No one fighting for God entangles himself in worldly pursuits." Nevertheless clerics are permitted to engage in the first kind of business which is appointed to serve the necessities of life, either by buying or selling.

No. 141. Anselm's ontological argument for the existence of God

(The *Proslogium* of St. Anselm, tr. Sidney Norton Deane. The Open Court Publishing Co., La Salle, Illinois, 1958.)

After I had published, at the solicitous entreaties of certain brethren, a brief work (the *Monologium*) as an example of meditation on the grounds of faith, in the person of one who investigates, in a course of silent reasoning with himself, matters of which he is ignorant; considering that this book was knit together by the linking of many arguments, I began to ask myself whether there might be found a single argument which would require no other for its proof than itself alone; and alone would suffice to demonstrate that God truly exists, and that there is a supreme good requiring nothing else, which all other things require for their existence and well-being; and whatever we believe regarding the divine Being. . . . (P. 1.)

I do not endeavor, O Lord, to penetrate thy sublimity, for in no wise do I compare my understanding with that; but I long to understand in some degree thy truth, which my heart believes and loves. For I do not seek to understand that I may believe, but I believe in order to understand. For this also I believe, that unless I believed, I should not understand.

And so, Lord, do thou, who dost give understanding to faith, give me, so far as thou knowest it to be profitable, to understand that thou art as we believe; and that thou art that which we believe. And, indeed, we believe that thou art a being than which nothing greater can be conceived. Or is there no such nature, since the fool hath said in his heart, there is no God? (Psalms xiv. I) But, at any rate, this very fool, when he hears of this being of which I speak—a being than which nothing greater can be conceived—understands what he hears, and what he understands is in his understanding; although he does not understand it to exist.

For, it is one thing for an object to be in the understanding, and another to understand that the object exists. When a painter first conceives of what he will afterwards perform, he has it in his understanding, but he does not yet understand it to be, because he has not yet performed it. But after he has made the painting, he both has it in his understanding, and he understands that it exists, because he has made it.

Hence, even the fool is convinced that something exists in the understanding, at least, than which nothing greater can be conceived. For, when he hears of this, he understands it. And whatever is understood, exists in the understanding. And assuredly that, than which nothing greater can be conceived, cannot exist in the understanding alone. For, suppose it exists in the understanding alone: then it can be conceived to exist in reality; which is greater.

Therefore, if that, than which nothing greater can be conceived, exists in the understanding alone, the very being, than which nothing greater can be conceived, is one, than which a greater can be conceived. But obviously this is impossible. Hence, there is no doubt that there exists a being, than which nothing greater can be conceived and it exists both in the understanding and in reality.

And it assuredly exists so truly, that it cannot be conceived not to exist. For, it is possible to conceive of a being which cannot be conceived not to exist; and this is greater than one which can be conceived not to exist. Hence, if that, than which nothing greater can be conceived, can be conceived not to exist, it is not that, than which nothing greater can be conceived. But this is an irreconcilable contradiction. There is, then, so truly a being than which nothing greater can be conceived to exist, that it cannot even be conceived not to exist; and this being thou art, O Lord, our God.

So truly, therefore, dost thou exist, O Lord, my God, that thou canst not be conceived not to exist; and rightly. For, if a mind could conceive of a being better than thee, the creature would rise above the Creator; and this is most absurd. And, indeed, whatever else there is, except thee alone, can be conceived not to exist. To thee alone, therefore, it belongs to exist more truly than all other beings, and hence in a higher degree than all others. For, whatever else exists does not exist so truly, and hence in a less degree it belongs to it to exist. Why, then, has the fool said in his heart, there is no God (Psalms xiv, I), since it is so evident, to a rational mind, that thou dost exist in the highest degree of all? Why, except that he is dull and a fool? (Pp. 6-9)

No. 142. Abelard's autobiography

(Robinson's *Readings*, pp. 447-449.)

[Abelard explains first why he gave up his inheritance and went out in search of an education.]

Consequently I traversed the various provinces, engaging in disputation and visiting all those places where I heard that the art of logic flourished. I came finally to Paris, where this art was wont to be most cultivated, to William of Champeaux, my preceptor, who at that time was quite justly famous in his profession. I remained with him for a time and was at first favorably received; later he came to dislike me heartily, when I attempted to oppose certain of his opinions. I began frequently to argue against him, and sometimes appeared to get the better of him in debate. Moreover those among my fellow-students who stood highest were especially indignant with me, since I was reckoned of slight consequence owing to my youth and the brief period I had been studying. Here my calamities had their beginning and they still continue.

[Abelard next tells of setting up his own school, then how he was expelled from Paris by other lecturers whom he had attacked for their bad logic. He decided to go to Laon to study theology under Master Anselm, then a famous lecturer in that subject.]

I accordingly betook myself to this old man, but found that he owed his name rather to mere tradition than to any special ability. If one applied to him, uncertain as to some question, one left him still more uncertain. He was marvelous in the eyes of those who merely listened, but contemptible to those who asked questions. He enjoyed an astonishing facility in words but was despicable in his understanding and fatuous in his reasoning. . . . When I discovered that he was like a tree full of leaves but without fruit, I did not spend many days lying idle in his shade. I went more and more infrequently to his lectures. Some of the most prominent among his students took this ill, since I seemed to despise their great master.

[One day Abelard's fellow-students, who regarded him as very ill prepared for the study of theology, asked him jokingly what he thought of the reading of the Scriptures. Abelard replied that he believed that any one who could read ought to be able to understand the writings of the saints without a long course under a master.]

Those who heard laughed and asked if I would presume to interpret the

Scriptures myself. I said that if they wished to try me I was ready. They then exclaimed, amid renewed laughter, that they gladly assented.

[They agreed upon a very obscure passage in Ezekiel. Abelard insisted upon the students coming on the morrow, although they advised him to take more time to think over the passage.]

I said indignantly that it was not my custom to reach my goal by long practice but by my wits. I added that they should either let me off altogether or come to my lecture when I wished them to come.

At my lecture few were present, since it seemed absurd to them all that I, hitherto almost wholly inexperienced in the Scriptures, should undertake the task so suddenly. However, all who came were so pleased that, one and all, they praised my words and urged me to proceed with my comments according to my interpretation. As the affair became known, those who had not been present at the first lecture began to come in great numbers to the second and third. All were, moreover, eager to make notes from the very beginning, upon the explanation which I had given the first day.

No. 143. Abelard's *Sic et Non*

(Robinson's *Readings*, pp. 450-451.)

There are many seeming contradictions and even obscurities in the innumerable writings of the church fathers. Our respect for their authority should not stand in the way of an effort on our part to come at the truth. The obscurity and contradictions in ancient writings may be explained upon many grounds, and may be discussed without impugning the good faith and insight of the fathers. A writer may use different terms to mean the same thing, in order to avoid a monotonous repetition of the same word. Common, vague words may be employed in order that the common people may understand; and sometimes a writer sacrifices perfect accuracy in the interest of a clear general statement. Poetical, figurative language is often obscure and vague.

Not infrequently apocryphal works are attributed to the saints. Then, even the best authors often introduce the erroneous views of others and leave the reader to distinguish between the true and the false. Sometimes, as Augustine confesses in his own case, the fathers ventured to rely upon the opinions of others.

Doubtless the fathers might err; even Peter, the prince of the apostles, fell into error; what wonder that the saints do not always show themselves inspired? The fathers did not themselves believe that they, or their companions, were always right. Augustine found himself mistaken in some cases and did not hesitate to retract his errors. He warns his admirers not to look upon his letters as they would upon the Scriptures, but to accept only those things which, upon examination, they find to be true.

All writings belonging to this class are to be read with full freedom to criticize, and with no obligation to accept unquestioningly; otherwise the way would be blocked to all discussion, and posterity be deprived of the excellent intellectual exercise of debating difficult questions of language and presentation. But an explicit exception must be made in the case of the Old and New Testaments. In the Scriptures, when anything strikes us as absurd, we may not say that the writer erred, but that the scribe made a blunder in copying the manuscripts, or that there is an error in interpretation, or that the passage is not understood. The fathers make a very careful distinction between the Scriptures and later works. They advocate a discriminating, not to say suspicious, use of the writings of their own contemporaries.

In view of these considerations, I have ventured to bring together various dicta of the holy fathers, as they came to mind, and to formulate certain questions which were suggested by the seeming contradictions in the statements. These questions ought to serve to excite tender readers to a zealous inquiry into truth and so sharpen their wits. The master key of knowledge is, indeed, a persistent and frequent questioning. Aristotle, the most clear-sighted of all the philosophers, was desirous above all things else to arouse this questioning spirit, for in his *Categories* he exhorts a student as follows: "It may well be difficult to reach a positive conclusion in these matters unless they be frequently discussed. It is by no means fruitless to be doubtful on particular points." By doubting we come to examine, and by examining we reach the truth.

[Next follow 158 questions or theses, among them:]
Should human faith be based upon reason, or no?
Is God one, or no?
Is God a substance, or no?
Does the first Psalm refer to Christ, or no?
Is sin pleasing to God, or no?
Is God the author of evil, or no?
Is God all-powerful, or no?
Can God be resisted, or no?
Has God free will, or no?
Was the first man persuaded to sin by the devil, or no?
Was Adam saved, or no?
Did all the apostles have wives except John, or no?
Are the flesh and blood of Christ in very truth and essence present in the sacrament of the altar, or no?
Do we sometimes sin unwillingly, or no?

No. 144. John of Salisbury's attack on scholasticism

(From *Frivolities of Courtiers and Footprints of Philosophers*, tr. Joseph B. Pike. Minneapolis, 1938. By permission of the University of Minnesota Press.)

An Attack on Scholasticism and a Plea for Humanistic Studies.

Consider the leading teachers of philosophy of our own day, those who are most loudly acclaimed, surrounded by a noisy throng of disciples. Mark them carefully; you will find them dwelling on one rule, or on two or three words, or else they have selected (as though it were an important matter) a small number of questions suitable for dispute, on which to exercise their talent and waste their life. They do not however succeed in solving them but hand down to posterity for solution by their disciples their problems, with all the ambiguity with which they have invested them.

In their lecture room they invite you to battle with them, become pressing, and demand the clash of wit. If you hesitate to engage, if you delay but for a moment, they are upon you. If you advance and, though unwillingly, engage them and press them hard, they take refuge in subterfuge; they change front; they torture words; with tricks of magic they transform themselves until you marvel at the reappearance of the slippery, changing Proteus. But he can be trapped more easily if you insist on understanding his meaning and intention despite his voluble and erratic language. He will finally be vanquished by his own meaning and be caught by the words of his mouth, if you can grasp their significance and hold it firmly.

The points of dispute of our modern Proteus however are as useless as they are trivial. If in disgust over time wasted on such trifles you press your attack he again has recourse to evasion. As if taking refuge in the bosom of Mother Earth like Antaeus, he strives to recover his strength in the element in which he was born and brought up. Such a roundabout way; so many detours! As though it were necessary to traverse a labyrinth to reach the common place! . . .

If therefore you hoist them with their own petard you may well pity them their poverty in almost every capacity. Some seem to excel in details; others offer for sale all branches of philosophy, and yet in the details they are without the proper philosophic background. There are some who hope to attain perfection as the result of excellence in one branch; there are others who devote their energy to the whole field though they lack the knowledge of its parts. I find it hard to say which are in greater error, since perfection is not derived from one and no one has the power to devote himself faithfully to all. However he who seeks perfection in all from one is the more absurd, while he who claims proficiency in all is the more arrogant. It is the mark of the indolent to occupy himself with one thing to the exclusion of all else, of the dilettante to embrace them all. . . .

All reading should be done in such a way that some of it when finished should be disregarded, some condemned, and some viewed *en passant,* that the subject matter be not entirely unknown; but above all careful attention should be given to those matters which lay the foundation of the life of the state, be it by the law of the state or else by ethical principles, or which have in view the health of body and soul. Since then the chief branch [grammar] among the liberal arts, without which no one can teach or be taught properly, is to be merely greeted *en passant* and as it were from the door, who can imagine that time should be devoted to other branches which being difficult to understand or impractical and harmful do not conduce to the betterment of man? For even those things that are required for man's use prove very harmful if they occupy his attention to the exclusion of all others.

Does anyone doubt the desirability of reading the historians, the orators, and the authorities on approved mathematics, since without a knowledge of them men cannot be, or at least usually are not, liberally educated? Indeed those who are ignorant of those writers are termed illiterate even if they can read and write. But when such writers lay claim to the mind as though it belonged exclusively to them, although they praise learning they do not teach; rather they hinder the cultivation of virtue. This is the reason that Cicero when dealing with the poets, to make his remarks more effective, burst out, "The shout of approbation of the populace, as though it were some great and wise teacher qualified to recommend, puts the stamp of genius upon whom it wishes. But they who are so lauded, what darkness do they spread, what fears engender, and what passions inflame!" . . . Elsewhere however Cicero highly commends writers. He says, "He alone who fears no contempt himself casts contempt upon poets and writers in other branches of artistic literature, as well as upon the historians. They know what virtue is and offer the material for philosophic study, for they brand vices; they do not teach them. Their works are attractive too on account of the help and pleasure they give to the reader. They make their way amid dangers which threaten character, with the intention of securing a foothold for virtue." . . . I myself am of the opinion of those who believe that a man cannot be literate without a knowledge of the authors. Copious reading, however, by no means makes the philosopher, since it is grace alone that leads to wisdom. . . .

It may be assumed that all writings except those that have been disapproved should be read, since it is believed that all that has been written and all that has been done have been ordained for man's utility although at times he makes bad use of them. For the angels too were, so to speak, ordained on account of the soul, but the corporeal world, according to the statement of the fathers, for the use of the body. . . . Just so in books there is something profitable for everybody provided, be it understood, the reading is done with discrimination and that only is selected which is edifying to faith and morals. There is matter which is of profit to stronger minds but is to be kept from the artless; there is that which an innately sound mind rejects; there is that which it digests for character-building or perfecting eloquence; there is that which hardens the soul and causes spiritual indigestion in matters of faith and good works. There is scarcely a piece of writing in which something is not found either in meaning or expression that the discriminating reader will not reject. The safe and cautious thing to do is to read only Catholic books. It is somewhat dangerous to expose the unsophisticated to pagan literature; but a training in both is very useful to those safe in the faith, for accurate reading on a wide range of subjects makes the scholar; careful selection of the better makes the saint. . . .

No. 145. Privileges granted to students by Frederick Barbarossa

(Robinson's *Readings*, pp. 452-453.)

After a careful consideration of this subject by the bishops, abbots, dukes, counts, judges, and other nobles of our sacred palace, we, out of our piety, have granted this privilege to all scholars who travel for the sake of study, and especially to the professors of divine and sacred laws, namely: that they may go in safety to the places in which the studies are carried on, both they themselves and their messengers, and may dwell there in security. For we think it fitting that, so long as they conduct themselves with propriety, those should enjoy our approval and protection who, by their learning, enlighten the world and mold the life of our subjects to obey God and us, his minister. By reason of our special regard we desire to defend them from all injuries.

For who does not pity those who exile themselves through love for learning, who wear themselves out in poverty in place of riches, who expose their lives to all perils and often suffer bodily injury from the vilest men— yet all these vexatious things must be endured by the scholar. Therefore, we declare, by this general and ever-to-be-valid law, that in the future no one shall be so rash as to venture to inflict any injury on scholars, or to occasion any loss to them on account of a debt owed by an inhabitant of their province,—a thing which we have learned is sometimes done, by an evil custom. And let it be known to the violators of this decree, and also to those who shall at the time be the rulers of the places where the offense is committed, that a fourfold restitution of property shall be exacted from all those who are guilty and that, the mark of infamy being affixed to them by the law itself, they shall lose their office forever.

Moreover, if any one shall presume to bring a suit against them on account of any business, the choice in this matter shall be given to the scholars, who may summon the accusers to appear before their professors, or before the bishop of the city, to whom we have given jurisdiction in this matter. But if, in sooth, the accuser shall attempt to drag the scholar before another judge, even though his cause is a very just one, he shall lose his suit for such an attempt.

We also order this law to be inserted among the imperial constitutions under the title, *ne filius pro patre, etc.*

Given at Roncaglia, in the year of our lord, 1158, in the month of November.

No. 146. Statutes of Gregory IX for the University of Paris (A.D. 1231)

(Translations and Reprints, II, No. 3, pp. 7-11.)

Gregory, the bishop, servant of the servants of God, to his beloved sons, all the masters and students at Paris—greeting and apostolic benediction. . . . Concerning the condition of the students and schools, we have decided that the following should be observed: each chancellor, appointed hereafter at Paris, at the time of his installation, in the presence of the bishop, or at the command of the latter in the chapter at Paris—two masters of the students having been summoned for this purpose and present in behalf of the university—shall swear that, in good faith, according to his conscience, he will not receive as professors of theology and canon law any but suitable men, at a suitable place and time, according to the conditions of the city and the honor and glory of those branches of learning; and he will reject all who are unworthy without respect to persons or nations. Before licensing any one, during three months, dating from the time when the license is requested, the chancellor shall make diligent inquiries of all the masters of theology present in the city, and of all other honest and learned men through whom the truth can be ascertained, concerning the life, knowledge, capacity, purpose, prospects and other qualities needful in such persons; and after the inquiries, in good faith and according to his conscience, he shall grant or deny the license to the candidate, as shall seem fitting and expedient. The masters of theology and canon law, when they begin to lecture, shall take a public oath that they will give true testimony on the above points. . . .

Moreover, the chancellor shall promise to examine in good faith the masters in medicine and arts and in the other branches, to admit only the worthy and to reject the unworthy.

In other matters, because confusion easily creeps in where there is no order, we grant to you the right of making constitutions and ordinances regulating the manner and time of lectures and disputations, the custom to be worn, the burial of the dead; and also concerning the bachelors, who are to lecture and at what hours, and on what they are to lecture; and concerning the prices of the lodgings or the interdiction of the same; and concerning a fit punishment for those who violate your constitutions or ordinances, by exclusion from your society. And if, perchance, the assessment of the lodgings is taken from you, or anything else is lacking, or an injury or outrageous damage, such as death or the mutilation of a limb, is inflicted on one of you, unless through a suitable admonition satisfaction is rendered within fifteen days, you may suspend your lectures until you have received full satisfaction. And if it happens that any one of you is unlawfully imprisoned, unless the injury ceases on a remonstrance from you, you may, if you judge it expedient, suspend your lectures immediately.

We command, moreover, that the bishop of Paris shall so chastise the excesses of the guilty, that the honor of the student shall be preserved and evil deeds shall not remain unpunished. But in no way shall the innocent be seized on account of the guilty; nay rather, if a probable suspicion arises against any one, he shall be detained honorably and on giving suitable bail he shall be freed, without any exactions from the jailors. But if, perchance, such a crime has been committed that imprisonment is necessary, the bishop shall detain the criminal in his prison. The chancellor is forbidden to keep him in his prison. . . .

Also, the vacation in summer is not to exceed one month, and the bachelors, if they wish, can continue their lectures in vacation time. Moreover, we prohibit more expressly the students from carrying weapons in the city, and the university from protecting those who disturb the peace and study. And those who call themselves students, but do not frequent the schools, or acknowledge any master, are in no way to enjoy the liberties of the students. . . .

No. 147. Statutes of Robert de Courcon for the University of Paris (A.D. 1215)

(Translations and Reprints, II, No. 3, pp. 12-15.)

Robert, servant of the cross of Christ, by the divine mercy cardinal priest with the title of St. Stephen in Monte Celio and legate of the apostolic seat, to all the masters and scholars at Paris—eternal safety in the Lord.

Let all know, that having been especially commanded by the lord pope to devote our energy effectively to the betterment of the condition of the students at Paris, and wishing by the advice of good men to provide for the tranquillity of the students in the future, we have ordered and prescribed the following rules:

No one is to lecture at Paris in arts before he is twenty years old. He is to listen in arts at least six years, before he begins to lecture. He is to promise that he will lecture for at least two years, unless he is prevented by some good reason, which he ought to prove either in public or before the examiners. He must not be smirched by any infamy. When he is ready to lecture, each one is to be examined according to the form contained in the letter of lord P. bishop of Paris (in which is contained the peace established between the chancellor and the students by the judges appointed by the lord pope, approved and confirmed namely by the bishop and deacon of Troyes and by P. the bishop, and J. the chancellor of Paris).

The treatises of Aristotle on logic, both the old and the new, are to be read in the schools in the regular and not in the extraordinary courses. The two Priscians, or at least the second, are also to be read in the schools in the regular courses. On the feast-days nothing is to be read except philosophy, rhetoric, *quadrivialia* (subjects belonging to the quadrivium), the Barbarisms (Donatus), the Ethics (of Aristotle), if one so chooses, and the fourth book of the Topics (Boethius). The books of Aristotle on Metaphysics or Natural Philosophy, or the abridgements of these works, are not to be read, nor "the doctrine" of master David de Dinant, of the heretic Almaric, or of Maurice of Spain.

In the inceptions and meetings of the masters and in the confutations or arguments of the boys or youths there are to be no festivities. But they may call in some friends or associates, but only a few. We also advise that donations of garments and other things be made, as is customary or even to a greater extent, and especially to the poor. No master lecturing in arts is to wear anything except a cope, round and black and reaching to the heels—at least, when it is new. But he may well wear a pallium. He is not to wear under the round cope embroidered shoes and never any with long bands.

If any one of the students in arts or theology dies, half of the masters of arts are to go to the funeral, and the other half to the next funeral. They are not to withdraw until the burial is completed, unless they have some good reason. If any master of arts or theology dies, all the masters are to be present at the vigils, each one is to read the psalter or have it read. Each one is to remain in the church, where the vigils are celebrated, until midnight or later, unless prevented by some good reason. On the day when the master is buried, no one is to lecture or dispute.

We fully confirm to them the meadow of St. Germain in the condition in which it was adjudged to them.

Each master is to have jurisdiction over his scholars. No one is to receive either schools or a house without the consent of the occupant, if he is able to obtain it. No one is to receive a license from the chancellor or any one else through a gift of money, or furnishing a pledge or making an agreement. Also, the masters and students can make among themselves or with others agreements and regulations, confirmed by a pledge, penalty or oath, about the following matters: namely, if a student is killed, mutilated or receives some outrageous injury and if justice is not done; for taxing the rent of *Hospitia;* concerning the dress, burial, lectures and disputations; in such a manner, however, that the university is not scattered nor destroyed on this account.

We decide concerning the theologians, that no one shall lecture at Paris before he is thirty-five years old, and not unless he has studied at least eight years, and has heard the books faithfully and in the schools. He is to listen in theology for five years, before he reads his own lectures in public. No one of them is to lecture before the third hour on the days when the masters lecture. No one is to be received at Paris for the important lectures or sermons unless he is of approved character and learning. There is to be no student at Paris who does not have a regular master.

In order moreover that these may be inviolably observed, all who presume contumaciously to violate these our statutes, unless they take care, within fifteen days from the date of the transgression, to correct their presumption in the presence of the university of masters and scholars, or in the presence of some appointed by the university, by the authority of the legation with which we are entrusted, we bind with the bond of excommunication.

Done in the year of grace 1215, in the month of August.

No. 148. Jacob Vitry on the life of the students at Paris

(*Translations and Reprints,* II, no. 3, pp. 19-21.)

Almost all the students at Paris, foreigners and natives, did absolutely nothing except learn or hear something new. Some studied merely to acquire knowledge, which is curiosity; others to acquire fame, which is vanity; others still for the sake of gain, which is cupidity and the vice of simony. Very few studied for their own edification, or that of others. They wrangled and disputed not merely about the various sects or about some discussions; but the differences between the countries also caused dissensions, hatreds and virulent animosities among them, and they impudently uttered all kinds of affronts and insults against one another.

They affirmed that the English were drunkards and had tails; the sons of

France proud, effeminate and carefully adorned like women. They said that the Germans were furious and obscene at their feasts; the Normans, vain and boastful; the Poitevins, traitors and always adventurers. The Burgundians they considered vulgar and stupid. The Bretons were reputed to be fickle and changeable, and were often reproached for the death of Arthur. The Lombards were called avaricious, vicious, and cowardly; the Romans, seditious, turbulent and slanderous; the Sicilians, tyrannical and cruel; the inhabitants of Brabant, men of blood, incendiaries, brigands and ravishers; the Flemish, fickle, prodigal, gluttonous, yielding as butter, and slothful. After such insults from words they often came to blows.

I will not speak of those logicians before whose eyes flitted constantly "the lice of Egypt," that is to say, all the sophistical subtleties, so that no one could comprehend their eloquent discourses in which, as says Isaiah, "there is no wisdom." As to the doctors of theology, "seated in Moses' seat," they were swollen with learning, but their charity was not edifying. Teaching and not practicing, they have "become as sounding brass or a tinkling cymbal," or like a canal of stone, always dry, which ought to carry water to "the bed of spices." They not only hated one another, but by their flatteries they enticed away the students of others; each one seeking his own glory, but caring not a whit about the welfare of souls.

Having listened intently to these words of the Apostle, "If a man desire the office of a bishop, he desireth a good work," they kept multiplying the prebends, and seeking after the offices; and yet they sought the work decidedly less than the preeminence, and they desired above all to have "the uppermost rooms at feasts and the chief seats in the synagogue, and greetings in the market." Although the Apostle James said, "My brethren, be not many masters," they on the contrary were in such haste to become masters, that most of them were not able to have any students except by entreaties and payments. Now it is safer to listen than to teach, and a humble listener is better than an ignorant and presumptuous doctor. In short, the Lord had reserved for Himself among them all only a few honorable and timorous men who had not stood "in the way of sinners," nor sat down with the others in the envenomed seat.

No. 149. Alexander Neckam's *On the Nature of Things*

(Robinson's *Readings*, pp. 439-440.)

The eagle, [Neckam tells us] on account of its great heat, mixeth very cold stones with its eggs when it sitteth on them, so that the heat shall not destroy them. In the same way our words, when we speak with undue heat, should later be tempered with discretion, so that we may conciliate in the end those whom we offended by the beginning of our speech.

The wren is but a little bird, yet it glories in the number of its progeny. Who has not wondered to hear a note of such volume proceeding from so trifling a body? The smaller the body, indeed, the greater the sound, it would seem. But such things we are taught that the virtues of little things should not be scorned. . . . They say, moreover, that when the body of the wren is put upon the spit and placed before the fire it need not be turned, for the wren will turn itself, not forgetful of its royal dignity.

The stratagem by which, according to a fabulous story, it gained the royal power among birds is well known. The birds had agreed among themselves that the glory of the supreme power should be allotted to the one who should excel all others by flying highest. The wren seized its opportunity and hid itself under the eagle's wing. When the eagle, who attains nearest to Jove's gates, would have claimed the supremacy among its fellows, the little wren sallied forth and perching on the eagle's head declared itself the victor. And so it obtained its name of Regulus (i.e. "ruler").

This fable touches those who enter upon the words of others and presumptuously appropriate the credit due elsewhere. As the philosopher says, "We are all like dwarfs standing upon giants' shoulders." We should therefore be careful to ascribe to our predecessors those things which we ought not to claim for our own glory, and not follow the example of that wren which, with little or no effort of its own, claimed to have outdone the eagle. . . .

The sailors, as they sail over the sea, when in cloudy weather they can no longer profit by the light of the sun, or when the world is wrapped in the darkness of night, and they are ignorant whither the ship's course is directed, touch a needle to the magnet; the needle will then whirl around in a circle until, when its motion ceases, its point is directed to the north.

No. 150. The *Opus Maius* of Roger Bacon

(*The 'Opus Majus' of Roger Bacon*, ed. John Henry Bridges. Oxford, 1897, pp. 167-172. Tr.)

1. With the fundamental principles of the wisdom of the Latins set forth in the areas pertaining to languages, mathematics, and optics, I wish now to reveal the foundations of experimental science since without experience nothing can be sufficiently understood. For there are two ways to learning, that is, through reasoning and through experience. Reason

proposes and forces us to accept a conclusion, although it does not guarantee that conclusion nor does it remove all doubt to such an extent that our minds rest confident in the possession of truth, unless experience also supports this truth. While many may possess proofs of discernible things, their lack of experience causes them to neglect these, with the consequence that they neither avoid what is injurious nor follow that which is good. For if some one who has never seen fire has been able to prove to himself through adequate reasoning that fire burns, injures, and destroys objects, yet never will his mind be entirely satisfied nor will he avoid fire before putting his own hand or something combustible into fire, so that by experience he might confirm what reason had taught. Yet once he has had this experience with fire, his mind is convinced and rests in the splendor of truth. Therefore, reasoning does not suffice, but only experience.

This is evident in mathematics where demonstration is most persuasive. Indeed, that person who has received the most convincing demonstration of the equilateral triangle, without experimental illustration, never accepts the conclusion, nor does he use this knowledge but neglects it, until experience is provided through the intersection of two circles, from either intersection of which two lines may be drawn to the extremities of the given line. Then the man accepts the conclusion without protest. What therefore Aristotle says concerning proof, that it is reasoning which causes us to know, is to be so understood only if experience accompanies it and not of simple proof itself. Also, what he says in the first book of his *Metaphysics*, that those who know the reason and cause are wiser than those who have empiric knowledge, he means those who have only this knowledge but do not know the cause. But I am speaking here of the man who knows the reason and in addition has arrived at the cause through experience. These men are perfect in their knowledge, as Aristotle indicates in his sixth book of *Ethics*, and their simple statements must be accepted as though they were offering proof, as he says in the same place.

Wherefore he who is inclined to accept with deep satisfaction the truth of statements without proof being offered, must realize what he lacks by not having this experience. This can be readily illustrated by examples. For authors write many things which the crowd accepts on the basis of reasoning which lacks the proof only experience can afford, and which are wholly false. It is a common belief, for example, that diamonds cannot be broken except by a goat's blood, and philosophers and theologians accept this opinion blindly. Yet it has not once been proved that the blood of a goat will break a diamond although men have attempted this; and without that blood a diamond can be easily broken. For I have seen this with my own eyes and this is important, since gems cannot be shaped without pieces of this diamond. . . . Then it is stated that warm water in a vessel will freeze faster than cold water, for it is argued that opposites are excited by opposites as enemies are attacked by others. Nevertheless, it is certain to one who makes the experiment that cold water freezes faster. They ascribe this position to Aristotle in his second book of *Meteorology*. Yet Aristotle certainly does not say this, although he does say something similar to this which has tended to confuse them, namely, that if cold and hot water are poured on a cold surface, as upon ice, the hot water will freeze more quickly, and this is true. Still if hot and cold water are placed in separate containers, the cold water will freeze more quickly. Wherefore everything ought to be made certain through experience.

2. Because this experimental science is totally unknown to ordinary students, I have been unable to persuade them of its utility unless I reveal at the same time its virtue and its proper signification. This science alone knows how to test perfectly what can be done by nature, what by the industry of art, what by fraud, what the songs, conjurations, invocations, prayers, and those sacrifices which belong to magic, wish and dream, and of what is in them, so that all falsehood is removed and only the truth of art remains. This science alone teaches how to view all the absurdities of magicians, not that they may be confirmed, but rather that they may be avoided, as logic examines sophistical reasoning.

THE LITERATURE AND ARTS OF THE HIGH MIDDLE AGES

For the most convincing criteria of any period's cultural maturity, the scholar turns to its literature, art, and music. It is these accomplishments which best reveal man's intellectual and spiritual capabilities. It is the picture of the reindeer which paleolithic man painted in polychrome on the walls of his cave, almost before the dawn of history, that provides conclusive proof that men, not sub-humans, did this painting. Homer's *Iliad* and *Odyssey* force the otherwise skeptical scholar to admit that the Greeks of the ninth century B.C. must have enjoyed a remarkably high culture, even when what little physical evidence remains suggests a people who had still much to learn. Today we are frequently reminded, to our embarrassment, that our ability to fashion the fastest airplanes, construct the highest buildings, and achieve the longest life expectancy are not absolute marks of culture. How advanced was the culture of the Middle Ages? It had advanced to a much higher plane than we with our modern preconceptions are often able to appreciate. Actually to the student who wishes to judge their cultural maturity, the Middle Ages can reveal a genuinely characteristic literature, a religious art which in scope and quality has never been approached, and a musical achievement to whose principles and melodies a large number of our own must be traced. The haunting strains of Chopin's nocturnes, for instance, might never have been composed, had not that artist chanced into a church and heard melodies which were born in the Middle Ages.

Literature

The literature of the Middle Ages reveals the intellectual and artistic capacity of that period. It is true that the depth of medieval literary thought and its richness of expression may not be immediately apparent to the modern reader. Several walls, as it were, separate the world of medieval people from our own. Their spiritual orientation was different and infinitely more pervasive of their culture. Their knowledge of the physical world was less scientifically accurate than ours, but being less finite, it proved more conducive to poetic thought. The social and political patterns of life which their literature reflects are frequently foreign to us and to our way of thinking. Some of the favorite literary genres of the Middle Ages appear strange today. The allegory, which ran riot in medieval literature, is apt to seem naive in the light of our more materialistic philosophy, even if we are not annoyed by the greater intellectual exercise such an oblique presentation of ideas demands. This lack of "modernity" in medieval literature contributes to the notion that the Middle Ages were also deficient in artistry of expression. Yet Santayana says that medieval thought itself was more inherently poetic than more recent thought. The bulk of medieval literature was poetical, a style of writing considerably more sensitive to the subtleties of artistic expression than prose. And much of medieval poetry was presented to the accompaniment of melody. Even of the robust epics which many modern readers might find especially nonintrospective, one critic writes: "Nothing in medieval literature is more important than the revival of imagination through the influence of barbaric myths and legends."* Recent literary criticism is finally discovering the greatness of medieval literature (that is, beyond the acknowledged giants Dante and Chaucer), thus paralleling the discovery made a generation or more ago about medieval art and scholasticism by modern art historians and philosophers.

Medieval Latin Literature

Medieval Latin. The literature of all modern nations of Europe, such as that of the French, German, English, and Italian, had its roots in the

* W. P. Kerr, *The Dark Ages* (London, 1911), p. 44.

Middle Ages. The one literature which did not outlive the period was the non-national Latin literature. To many students it will come as a surprise to learn that the Middle Ages produced a Latin literature. Of the epochal writings of Cicero, Vergil, and Horace they would have heard, but not of Medieval Latin literature, because this literature was not classical. Medieval Latin literature employed a Latin which until recent years most classicists considered decadent and rude. It is true that the origins of this Medieval Latin go back to the Vulgar Latin spoken in the late second, third, and fourth centuries of the Christian era by the common people of Rome, by soldiers, bakers, and carpenters. Until about 800 A.D., this Vulgar Latin continued to grow and change almost as the common people chose, and most rapidly after 550 A.D. when the early Christian scholars who had enjoyed a classical education were dead. Even these church fathers, men like Ambrose, Augustine, and Jerome, preferred on occasion to sacrifice the rules of grammar and versification in order to enhance the popular appeal of their sermons and poetry. Thus St. Augustine composed a long doctrinal poem, the *Abcdarius*, which was to be sung by his congregation, not only with complete disregard for the norms of classical versification, but even with occasional incorrect forms in order the better to reach the people. Gregory of Tours, who unlike St. Augustine could write only Vulgar Latin, tells how a vision of his deceased mother reassured him that God was pleased with his use of Vulgar Latin, since it would be more intelligible to the people. Vulgar Latin's period of natural growth, or perhaps more accurately, deterioration, continued on pretty well unchecked until the time of Charlemagne, when he and his circle of court scholars made a valiant effort to restore classicism to Latin. Though their efforts fell far short of complete success, they did so improve Latin that the people could no longer understand it, and church councils felt compelled to order the clergy to use Vulgar Latin (*lingua Romana* or *rustica*) when preaching. From the time of Charlemagne the revised interest in formal grammar and rhetoric in the monastic and cathedral schools restored still more of the classical element to Latin. And since Latin remained now the exclusive preserve of the schooled, its period of growth ceased. This Latin of the eleventh and twelfth centuries is what is known as Medieval Latin.

   Medieval vs. Classical Latin.   By the close of the twelfth century when Medieval Latin had become fairly standardized, what major differences could one detect between it and the Latin of Cicero? The most striking difference would, probably, be that of vocabulary. In the area of vocabulary the Medieval Latin was vastly more extensive. Imagine Shakespeare's bewilderment were that bard called upon to read a modern newspaper. Cicero would have encountered equal difficulty understanding a scholarly work of the thirteenth century, because of all the strange terms he had never seen before and of the new meanings old words had acquired since his day. In addition to this richer vocabulary, Medieval Latin had a simpler grammar.

The medieval scholar usually did not feel grammar so essential and only an occasional one possessed the talent to express himself in the majestic periods Cicero so loved. As Tertullian protested in an oft-quoted statement: "We do not speak eloquently; we live." So the medieval scholar used a language with a syntax closer to our sequence of subject, verb, and predicate. Significant changes in orthography also divided the two Latins. For example, the medieval scribe wrote *e* for *ae* (e.g. *puelle* for *puellae*) and syncopated an interior unaccented syllable (e.g. *saeculum* became *saeclum*). Medieval Latin showed a most unscholarly unconcern about the proper use of the different cases (e.g. dative for genitive, accusative, and ablative), revealed no more fastidiousness in the use of the tenses (e.g. perfect for imperfect), and expressed purpose with the infinitive (e.g. he went to the store *to buy* bread). Cicero might shudder at these and other changes; the humanists of the fifteenth century would sneer; but Medieval Latin's greater flexibility of form and greater willingness to meet new demands made it significantly superior to classical Latin for general use. It continued to live and to do the work of a living language until the humanists of the fifteenth century killed it by insisting upon a "pure" (classical) Latin.

Latin Prose Literature. Apart from the mass of religious, ecclesiastical, legal, and scholarly writing, one encounters a deluge of prose in Medieval Latin, but prose which may pass as literature only under the broadest definition of the term. Of this, the largest class is hagiography or lives of the saints. No literature was more popular before the thirteenth century, when the *Golden Legend* of James of Voragine (d. 1298), most famous of medieval collections of lives of the saints, appeared. (Reading 151) The appeal of such literature must have been well nigh irresistible. First, this was the "age of faith," for which the lives of heroic unselfishness that pious men and women spent in the service of God held a powerful attraction. Besides, people have always enjoyed reading about the marvelous, and to people who accepted the miraculous what could be more marvelous than miracles? In addition to hagiography, Medieval Latin prose furnished a host of tales of every variety, some romantic, others dealing with adventure, some coarse, others inspiring. Among these stories one catches glimpses of the animal stories which would later develop into the famed Renard epic (see page 614): viz., the account of the desperate plan of the rats to hang a bell about the neck of their mortal enemy, the cat. A curious group of medieval tales in Latin are classified under the title *Gesta Romanorum* or *Deeds of the Romans*. What is most curious about these tales is that the sole element which is Roman is usually the fictitious Latin name given the emperor, who often did no more than establish the period (equally fictitious) of the story. Among the *Gesta Romanorum* is the story of a knight who fell in love with the daughter of Emperor Celestinus (!). To gain the favor of a visit with his beloved, he borrowed money and gave his flesh as surety that the amount would be repaid at a certain hour. Of course he was late in returning the money, and so the unromantic creditor demanded his flesh. Whereupon the heroine of the story cut her hair, dressed up in men's clothes, and successfully defended her knight before the bar by employing a variant of the same argument that Shakespeare used in his *Merchant of Venice*. However innocuous these stories might be, they always presumed to teach a moral, although a hard-pressed author on occasion might suggest to the reader that he propose his own. (Reading 152)

Chronicles. Considerably greater claim to literary excellence may be advanced for the treatises which flowed from the industrious pens of medieval scholars from Bede down to the close of the Middle Ages. The language of the discourses of Anselm, for instance, or the letters of Bernard, is clear and forceful and not without literary grace. John of Salisbury wrote prose which was perhaps the best which was written in the Middle Ages. Even the classicists of ancient Rome would have approved. Only an occasional post-Roman phrase betrays Gerbert to have been a medieval writer, not a Ciceronian. Yet as a rule, this type of writing was too scholarly or too meager of literary quality to pass for literature. No greater claim to literary merit can be made by the annals and chronicles of monastic scribes. The simple annals of the ninth and tenth centuries, with a few exceptions, had scarcely even historical interest to commend them. They usually consisted of a mere cataloging of local minutiae. The majority of monastic chronicles were much more informative. They did have the bad tradition of beginning their accounts with Adam, and what they finally got down to telling about their own times was often lacking in accuracy and organization. Much of the chronicler's information came by way of hearsay, and this he was not above coloring for the greater glory of God or the confusion of some disagreeable nobleman. Nevertheless, a monastery with a tradition of eminent chroniclers such as St. Albans, did produce excellent chronicles. St. Albans was strategically located just north of London, and proved a favorite stopping-over place for notables on their way to and from the city. With the help of the news such visitors would bring, the monastic scribe could write, not as a recluse, but almost like a London reporter. The finest account, for example, of the Mongols of Genghis Khan (see page 766), is that preserved in the fascinating pages of the sharp-tongued St. Albans chronicler, Matthew Paris (d. 1259). (Readings 153, 191) On the continent, perhaps the best historical writing in Latin was done by Otto of Freising. His *Chronicle of Two Cities*, which was inspired by St. Augustine's *City of God*, represents medieval interpretative history at its best. (Reading 123) The only medieval historian to dispute Otto's pre-eminence would be William, Archbishop of Tyre. (See page 412.)

Medieval Latin Poetry. If one must admit to some reservations concerning the literary quality of Medieval Latin prose, there is no question whatsoever about the high quality of its poetry. Medieval Latin poetry, in fact, merits recognition on two counts: first its excellence; second, its signal contribution to the evolution of poetical techniques. It is not a simple matter to establish the claim of any poetry to be called excellent. Yet a noted literary critic has described that most famous of Medieval Latin poems, the *Dies Irae,* as "the greatest of all hymns and one of the greatest of all poems." (Reading 154) The fact that almost two hundred and fifty poets have tried their hand unsuccessfully at translating its matchless rhythm and thought, would appear to bear out this critic's judgment. The contribution of Medieval Latin poetry to poetical technique, being a less subjective matter, is easier to demonstrate. Actually the work of medieval poets amounted to a veritable revolution. They, not Homer or Vergil, are the founders of modern poetry. Their most far-reaching innovation was to replace the classical quantitative verse with something closer to spoken Latin and, consequently, more popular. Where classical verse had depended upon an elaborate schematization of long and short vowels to create rhythm, the medieval poet substituted accentual verse with the rhythm produced by a sequence of accented and nonaccented syllables. Actually the substitution of accentual verse for quantitative became a logical and inevitable step in view of the phonological changes Latin underwent in late Roman times. Here again the common people were responsible. So strongly did they accentuate the stressed syllable in a word, that any distinction between those vowels which were long and those short was obscured and gradually forgotten. While this accentual verse was certainly sung by ordinary folk in late Roman times, it remained for the Middle Ages to dignify it as poetry. A second medieval development in poetry was the insistence upon regularity in the number of syllables to the line. A third introduction was rhyme, again so natural a device it must surely have antedated the Middle Ages, but again only among the meaner folk whom classical writers ignored. Thus, at least two of the most important elements in modern poetry, accentual verse and rhyme, are both products of medieval origin.

Hymn Writers. The church father, Ambrose, holds the title of "Father of Latin Hymnody." He was the first to express pious sentiments in the simple accentual rhythm of popular poetry. Though he did not abandon quantity, he wrote with a conscious syllable count, and he intended that accent should provide the rhythm for his verse. He composed for congregational singing, for common folk, therefore, who were accustomed to accentual verse. Actually the bulk of Medieval Latin poetry, whether religious or secular, was intended to be sung, and to be sung, not by a small group of specially trained clerics or entertainers, but by the people. After Ambrose, hymn writers appear in a fairly constant stream down to the close of the Middle Ages when humanism stifled forever the voice of Medieval Latin song. Popes, kings, cardinals, bishops, statesmen, monks, and devout laymen, all helped fill the pages of the fifty-eight volume modern collection of medieval hymns. Among the names of the early writers whose compositions found their way into the liturgy of the Christian church were Sedulius,

Prudentius, Fortunatus, and Theodulf. One meets with surprise the name of Abelard whose real artistic talents history has almost overlooked. The anonymity of such favorite hymns as the "Jesus, the Very Thought of Thee" is regrettable. Pope Innocent III contributed the *Veni Sancte Spiritus* (Come, Holy Spirit), Aquinas a number of great Eucharistic hymns (e.g. *Lauda, Sion, Salvatorem,* or Praise, Sion, Your Savior). For the moving beauty of his verse, Adam of St. Victor has earned acclaim as the "best of Latin hymn-writers," if not the "greatest poet of the Middle Ages." Thomas de Celano composed the magnificent verses of the sombre *Dies Irae,* a poem descriptive of the Last Judgment and the soul's fears on that "day of wrath." Finally, mention should be made of the tenderest hymn of the Middle Ages, the *Stabat Mater* of Jacopone da Todi. The poet tells of the sorrowing mother before the body of her crucified son, and of the plea sinful man makes for her powerful intercession.

> At the cross her station keeping,
> Stood the mournful mother weeping
> Close to Jesus to the last.

Christian quantitative poetry, however, which attempted to follow strictly classical standards, remained still-born. It lacked popular appeal—even the church did not want it.

Secular Latin Poetry. Composing with equal artistry and with the same accentual verse and rhyme as the composer of religious verse, were a group of Goliardic poets of the Latin Middle Ages. But how different was their theme! The hymnist sang of Mary, the sorrowing mother. The Goliard boasted of his waywardness: "Down the broad way do I go, young and unregretting." The term Goliard is commonly used to designate the composer of this secular verse, from Golias, the legendary patron of all uninhibited Latin poets of the twelfth and thirteenth centuries. We know little about the composers of this secular verse. One can think of good reasons why they might have wanted to remain anonymous: so much of what they rhymed about lay on or just beyond the periphery of respectability, even for the Middle Ages. Not all the poems are irreverent, ribald, blasphemous, and gibing, but a goodly number are. As one indignant churchman observed: "I believe that the devil is in these poets." Yet if the Goliard was a devil, he also knew how to compose beautiful verse, and about softer themes as well, about love and romance, about the joys of spring, about home. It is assumed that most of the poets were university students. Only these could have composed in Latin; only university students could have had the imagination, or the devil-may-care attitude of these Goliards; only university students could have parodied or satirized churchmen in such scholarly fashion; only university students could have left so large a store of convivial, love, and drinking songs. (Reading 155) One Goliard song still heard sung on university campuses is the *Gaudeamus Igitur.*

Let us live then and be glad
While young life's before us!
After youthful pastime had
After old age hard and sad,
Earth will slumber o'er us.

Vernacular Literature

The Rise of Vernacular Languages. Before embarking upon a discussion of vernacular literature, we should consider, for a moment, the rise of vernacular languages. The word vernacular is derived from a Latin root meaning native or indigenous. What pass, therefore, as the vernacular languages of Europe in the Middle Ages are the various Celtic, Slavic, Germanic, and Romance tongues, to mention the most important groupings. From one or the other of these families are descended various dialects, all of them native, all of them proclaiming more manifestly than other cultural facets the common intermingling of different national strains. It is nothing short of amazing, for example, how men from the Arctic Circle to Sicily and from Gibraltar to the Urals, employ phonologically related sounds to designate father and mother, regardless of nationality, culture, and creed. The philologist, that is, the scholar who studies the origins and formation of languages, has discovered many other facts about the speech of medieval (and modern) Europe. Yet there are so many more facts which still elude his grasp. This he attributes to the fact that certain dialects never did produce a script, to the tardiness with which many peoples developed one of their own, to the paucity of examples of early writing when this did finally appear. Among the most treasured of these last are the Gothic Bible of Ulfilas which is the earliest extensive record we have of any Germanic language, and the Strasbourg oaths taken in 842 A.D. by the kings of the West and East Franks. (See page 260.)

Vernacular Languages. Irish, one of the Celtic languages, was possibly the first of medieval tongues to produce a written language, probably because it developed free of competition with Latin. But Irish as a language was too far removed from the continent to exert any appreciable influence eastward except in the British Isles. While Celtic themes, as we shall see, played an important role in the rise of the romance, Celtic literature remained too aloof from western Europe to share in later developments there. It remained largely primitive in its themes. The Slavic languages, particularly those of the Balkans, reflect strong Greek influences.

In contrast to the Celtic, they produced no literature of note until after the medieval period. The Germanic tongues reflect in number and diversity the extensiveness of the area over which they were spoken and the disparate character of the influences which affected their evolution. Slavic influences are visible but inconsequential, due to the traditional antipathy between the two nationalities. Latin influences were most important, although never so powerful as to transform a speech except in the case of English. Although Anglo-Saxon was as Germanically pure as the Scandinavian dialects, the English were using a speech at the close of the Middle Ages which had absorbed possibly one-half the Latin vocabulary. The Romance tongues bear that classification because of their direct origin in the Latin of early medieval times, from which they had branched off and become clearly established languages by the year 1000 A.D. They are, consequently, less indigenous than the Germanic and Celtic, but became just as much the speech of the people. Their different modern forms—for example, French, Spanish, Italian, Portuguese, and Rumanian—owe less to the diversity of foreign influences with which the Latin (vulgar) speaking natives may have come into contact, than to the introduction of new words and new pronunciations (mispronunciations). The only Romance language which reflects important Germanic influences is that of northern France. This dialect, partly because it was that spoken in Paris, won out over the Provençal used in most of southern France. The bulk of the vernacular literature of the Middle Ages appeared in one or the other of the Germanic and Romance languages.

Epic Poetry. The oldest monuments of vernacular literature are in poetic form. Men learned early that matter can be more readily and accurately passed on by word of mouth when it is in rhythmic form. Prose is the product of a higher civilization and usually emerges only hundreds of years after poetry. It seems highly probable that early verse was sung as frequently as it was recited, although the line separating recitation and song must have been a narrow one. The earliest large class of poetry which has come down to us in European vernaculars is the epic. Epic poetry tells a story of heroic and noble deeds, in stately, solemn verse. It may present characters who are engaged in extraordinary episodes which are important in the founding of a nation. Frequently an element of the tragic is present. The larger portion of this early verse was probably lost and forgotten before it could be recorded. Some of this loss was due to the vicissitudes of time, some to intent. We read how Louis the Pious gave orders that the old Germanic poems which his father Charlemagne had preserved be destroyed because their pagan character disturbed him. While the oldest manuscripts containing these epic poems date from the eleventh century, the poems themselves must have lived through many previous centuries in recitative form.

Beowulf.   The oldest of the Germanic epics is the Anglo-Saxon *Beowulf.*
Beowulf was a Swedish hero who came to the aid of the king of Denmark
and slew three monsters: Grendel, Grendel's dam, and a dragon. The tale is
relatively simple, although various minor interludes accompany the central,
powerful theme. The names of the hero, the monsters, and the other characters in the story are pagan, and the talk is of wild places and storms, a
primitively terrifying world. Yet the author of the poem was surely an educated Christian. While he took a wild folktale for his plot, his Beowulf
becomes almost a Christian knight and the brutal animals he slays the
symbols of diabolical evil. The poem possesses high literary artistry and its
moral and spirit has been matched by only a few poets.

Nibelungenlied and Sagas.   Somewhat more native is the pagan atmosphere of the best known German epic, the *Nibelungenlied* (*Song of the
Nibelungs*). Though the written version of the twelfth century contains
talk of masses: "What good priests were at his (Siegfried's) funeral!"—
more in keeping with the pagan spirit of the narrative is the frightful
vengeance Kriemhild perpetrated against the dastardly Hagan for stabbing
her Siegfried in the back. In the *Nibelungenlied* we have an example of
how some solid historical reference occasionally protrudes above the mass
of legend and folklore which make up the body of epic narratives. In the
Song of the Nibelungs, hardly recognizable yet certainly present is the story
of the massacre of the Burgundians by the Hunnic allies of the Romans in
435 A.D., together with such figures as Attila the Hun and Theodoric, king
of the Ostrogoths. (Reading 156) In the oldest versions of the *Nibelungenlied,* which are found in the Eddic poems of Scandinavia and Iceland, there
is portrayed in its purest form the savage barbarism of Teutonic paganism.
These Eddic poems appeared between the eighth and tenth centuries. They
are older than the Scandinavian sagas (thirteenth century), more elemental
in the passions they describe, more primitive in their ethics and in their
way of drawing people. The sagas tell in terse, unadorned prose, tales of
the hard life of the north, made even more harsh by war and blood-feuds.
In the story of *Burnt Njal,* by popular acclaim the greatest of the sagas,
Hallgerda tells her servant Brynjolf that Atli is working in the wood.
"What shall I do to him," he asks. "Thou shalt kill him," says she. Brynjolf
finds Atli making charcoal, but Atli sees him not. Brynjolf gives him a
stroke on the head with his axe. Said one: "Hallgerda does not let her
housecarles die of old age." Some of the sagas contain a significant amount
of history, others are wholly fictional as far as can be determined. It is intriguing to note how Christian influences slowly and painfully force their
way into the thoroughly pagan climate of the saga. (Reading 157)

Poema del Cid.   Medieval Spain boasted a famous epic, the *Poema del
Cid* (*Poem of the Cid*). Cid is Arabic for "lord," the lord and hero of the
poem being the renowned Castilian warrior Rodrigo Diaz de Bivar (d.
1099), who worked prodigious feats of arms against the Moslems in the

cause of Spain and Christianity. So at least runs the story in what has been called the finest poem in the Spanish language. It is surely the national epic of Spain, and

> Sought by Navarre and Aragon for queens his daughters twain;
> And monarchs of his blood today upon the thrones of Spain.

In actual life the Cid was not adverse to raising his trusty right arm to lend the Infidel assistance against men of his own faith when he found the inducement sufficiently attractive. Still it is more romantic to remember him as the peerless warrior: "Before the lances of my Cid the fray became a flight;" "No perfidy was ever found in the Perfect One." The *Poem of the Cid* introduces an element normally absent from the epic, when it sings at some length of the Cid's daughters. They were married to two noblemen, who shortly after the weddings, repudiated their brides because of their low birth. Two princes of royal blood, however, proudly claimed the girls' hands, and the two craven noblemen suffered the punishment and ignominy their crime merited. The poet voices the indignant sentiment of his readers:

> He who a noble lady wrongs and casts aside, may he
> Meet like requital for his deeds, or worse if worse there be.

French Epic. The French epic, one of France's great contributions to medieval literature, provides the first example of a distinctly Christian epic. The literary maturity of the French *chansons de geste* (songs of great deeds) springs principally from their later appearance (not much before the twelfth century) and to the fact that members of the clergy together with professional minstrels or jongleurs may have had most to do with their authorship. That the clergy contributed the bulk of the historical and legendary matter, and that the French epics flourished principally along pilgrim routes, notably that leading to the popular shrine of St. James Compostella in Galicia (northwest Spain), are plausible, though not fully established, theories. The stories centered about the exploits of some knight or group of knights, such as those associated with the court of Charlemagne or that of his son Louis the Pious. No truer mirror does medieval literature provide of the traditions of feudal life than these French epics, in their glorification of courage, devotion to the faith, and loyalty to one's lord.

> Men for their lords great hardship must abide,
> Fierce heat and cold endure in every clime,
> Lose for his sake, if need be, skin and hide.*

---

* This passage and the two following from *The Song of Roland*, tr. Dorothy L. Sayers (Penguin Books), 1957, pp. 95, 94, 116.

Song of Roland. This idea of loyalty is expressed vividly in the most famous of French epics, the *Chanson de Roland*. The poem consists of 4002 assonated verses. The historical kernel which survives, though distorted, is of an incident which took place upon Charlemagne's return from a campaign against the Moslems in Spain. While his army was making its way through a narrow defile in the Pyrenees known as Roncesvalles, the Christian Basques fell upon the rear guard, destroying the baggage train it was protecting and killing Roland, the captain in command. In the *Song of Roland*, this becomes an attack by Moslems, made possible through the black treason of Ganelon, Roland's step-father. Roland and his tiny band find themselves about to be overwhelmed by a horde of Moslems, and his advisers beg him to sound his horn, Olifant, in order to summon Charlemagne.

> Quoth Oliver: "Herein I see no blame:
> I have beheld the Saracens of Spain;
> They cover all the mountains and the vales,
> They spread across the hillsides and the plains;
> Great is the might these foreigners display,
> And ours appears a very small array."

But Roland considers this weakness and refuses:

> "I thirst the more," quoth Roland, "for the fray.
> God and His angels forbid it now, I pray,
> That e'er by me fair France should be disfamed!
> I'd rather die than thus be put to shame;
> If the King loves us it's for our valour's sake."

So they fight, and most successfully, so that of the enemy "of hundred-thousand scarce two will fight again." Nevertheless, total numbers tell in the end. With most of his men dead, Roland finally sees no alternative, and blows "with all his might" a blast on his horn so powerful that Charlemagne hears "thirty great leagues" ahead. But Roland's tremendous effort "burst the veins of his temple outright." He places his sword Durandal beneath him when he finds himself too weak to break it, confesses his sins, and dies. Charlemagne returns to destroy the Infidel. Aude, Roland's betrothed, falls dead when she learns of his death, while Ganelon is tied to four horses and torn to pieces. So runs the most famous of medieval epics. Almost no place is reserved for the expression of softer sentiments such as love. Roland's thoughts when he dies are of Charlemagne, of God, and of France, not of Aude. Most unusual, for so early a period in the Middle Ages, is the introduction of a note of nationalism. The poet speaks of "fairest France," and he has the Moslems cry:

> "French Fatherland, be curst of Mahomet!
> Your sons are bravest of all the sons of men."

The Romance: Origins. What was probably the most popular form of literature in the Middle Ages, the romance, shared several of the features of the epic. It dealt with marvelous deeds, always a popular motif in the Middle Ages, which loved marvels; there is present a small core of historical fact, or, at least, what may have passed as history with contemporaries; and its verse rings with the clang of doughty swords and battle-axes. Wherein is the romance so different as to warrant classifying it separately from the epic? It is, first of all, longer than the epic, and its tale is more complex. More important, it bases its interest as much upon romantic love as upon valor. And where in the epic the hero holds the center of interest and makes the action, in the romance what happens does so because of the story. The origins of this type of literature have been traced back to the interest of the twelfth century in classical antiquities. The first romances were largely adaptations in the vernacular of themes found in such ancient writers as Vergil and Homer. The oldest group of these romances, in fact, those of the matter of Rome, include stories drawn ultimately from the tragedies of Sophocles, Homer's *Iliad* and *Odyssey,* and Vergil's *Aeneid.* Regardless of origin, however, love above all else must be served, and in the medieval romance, the story of the *Aeneid* becomes essentially a tale of the tragic love between Aeneas, the wandering Trojan hero, and Dido, the queen of Carthage.

King Arthur and the Round Table. Of a large variety of romances, some based upon folktales such as Robert the Devil who died a saint, others upon alleged historical incidents as far distant as Byzantium; by far the most popular was that associated with King Arthur and the Round Table. If Arthur was not a wholly legendary figure, he may have been a Romanized Celtic hero of the sixth century. Bede makes no mention of him. Whatever his historical authenticity, he owed his fame and his introduction into cultivated continental literature to Geoffrey of Monmouth who included him in his *Historia Regum Brittaniae (ca.* 1137) (*History of the Kings of Britain*). A French poet, Wace, added to Geoffrey's account the story of the Round Table, while the Englishman Layamon in his *Brut* furnished the motivation behind the illustrious deeds of the members of this peerless circle—they vie for precedence at the Table. The origin of this matter of Arthur and the Round Table is believed to have been Celtic, harkening back to older stories about quarrelsome Irish warriors and to Celtic wars and to the Celtic otherworld. As adapted by French writers, the knight of the epic who fought for king and God becomes in the romance the chivalrous warrior who will dare the incredible to please his lady. Furthermore, in place of the simple, harsh assonance of the epic, the romance as fully developed was recited in rhymed couplets which were more harmonious to sophisticated ears.

Chretien de Troyes. The first poet to combine successfully the different elements in the romance and to set the pattern of its love motif was a Frenchman, Chretien de Troyes (*ca.* 1180). Chretien, who was a poet at the court of the sympathetic countess of Champagne, brought to his work a broad knowledge of love literature which extended from the ancient poems of Ovid to the romantic songs of contemporary troubadours. (See page 611.) A favorite among his extremely popular romances was that of Tristan and Iseult. (Chretien's own version is lost.) The dauntless Tristan had agreed to go to Ireland to bring back the young and ravishingly beautiful Iseult to be the bride of his elderly lord, King Mark of Cornwall. Lest the discrepancy in their ages blight the happiness of their marriage, Iseult's mother prepared a love potion for Mark and her daughter. As fate would have it, instead of being drunk by Mark and Iseult, the potion was taken by mistake by Tristan and Iseult. This left the two young people bound together in a bond of deathless love which for many years passed by the notice of the generous-minded and somewhat senile Mark. In the end tragedy cut off the tumultuous lives of the two lovers, although King Mark agreed that their bodies be placed in the same tomb.

German Writers of Romance. More in keeping with the Christian and chivalric ideals of the Middle Ages, which would have been offended by Tristran's adultery as well as by his breach of faith with his lord, was the story of Parceval. As a callow and erring youth, Parceval sets out to find the Holy Grail, which to later poets becomes the cup Christ used at the Last Supper. In the hands of the greatest of German writers of romance, Wolfram von Eschenbach, it appears to be a stone of wondrous virtue which symbolizes man's spiritual purification through atonement. So through sorrow and suffering, Parzival (the name of Wolfram's hero) finally emerges a heroic figure fit to become king of the Grail. One other German, Gottfried of Strassburg, achieved high fame as a writer of romance. His version of the Tristan-Iseult story is recognized as the best of the series. Gottfried's influence is clearly visible in the works of Wagner, Tennyson, and Swinburne. But the romance in general evokes modest interest among modern readers, unless they are able to pierce through the story itself to the ideas and symbolism there hidden. While admiring the skill with which the best poets of romance managed to fit an amazing amount of subordinate action into their plots, they are apt to find monotonous the description of a constant flow of amazing feats, the flat characterization, and the adherence to stereotyped chivalric patterns.

Marie de France. The composer of a simpler type of romance was the poetess Marie de France (d. 1189). Her composition is called a lay (French *lai*), which may be defined as a romantic tale of Celtic origin comprising melody and narrative. For her themes, Marie drew upon the same rich store as the romance, that is, Celtic tales, of which, as she writes, "Many a one, on many a day, the minstrel has chanted to my ear." Her stories were shorter than the usual romance, but showed no greater variety nor deeper interest in character portrayal. Because of their greater concern with love and less with martial feats, the lays were particularly popular with the ladies. As one near-contemporary wrote: "These lays are wont to please ladies, who listen to them with delight, for they are after their own hearts."* They surely delighted to read about love potions, about heroines who swooned for love, and who, on occasion, even died of broken hearts! What woman, for instance, would not nod approval to the bits of warning wisdom Marie would let fall for her feminine readers: e.g. "Great is that woman's folly who puts her trust in man;" or "Better is the love of an honest man, so he be of sense and worth, than that of a prince or king, with no loyalty in him."

Aucassin and Nicolette. Mention should be made here of one of the most appealing of medieval stories, that of Aucassin and Nicolette. It is not easy to find a place for this charming tale in the usual classifications of medieval literature. Perhaps it deserves to be kept in a class all its own. Though not a play, it was probably presented by two persons, a narrator reciting the prose, a singer chanting the verse. Aucassin, the son of a Christian lord, falls in love with Nicolette, a Saracen ex-slave. The girl's religion establishes an impassable barrier between the two in the opinion of Aucassin's parents. This is not so for Aucassin, who is even willing to go to hell with Nicolette rather than live without her. After all, as he reassures himself, the most interesting people go to hell. Nicolette flees with Aucassin after her. Unusual adventures meet the two lovers at every turn. All ends happily in the end when Nicolette proves to be a high-born damsel. Some parody of contemporary institutions appears intended in such incidents as Aucassin, a knight, falling off his horse when he becomes too absorbed in thoughts of Nicolette; or when he bestirs himself to fight only when he realizes that if captured and beheaded, he will no longer be able to talk to his beloved. Yet the story is really a romance, one of the most human and delightful tales of romantic love to come out of the Middle Ages.

Troubadour Poets and Lyric Poetry. The love element in the romance surely owed some of its inspiration to the lyric poetry which appeared in southern France in the early part of the twelfth century and flourished at the turn of the thirteenth. By lyric verse is generally understood poetry which expresses emotion in the first person, in contrast to epic verse which is narrative or descriptive of event and incident. Lyric verse seems to have been sung to the accompaniment of a lute or stringed instrument, and the music was as important as the words themselves. The origins of lyric poetry are obscure. They may be traced to the festive gatherings of peasants when they joined to celebrate the coming of spring, or the month of May, or a wedding. This lyric poetry of the common folk never disappeared, although

* *Lays of Marie de France* (Tr. Eugene Mason, New York, 1954, p. xi).

as such it seldom found its way into formal literature. What did enter formal literature was the adaptation of its melodies and sentiments in a literary form more ·suited to the tastes of the aristocratic classes. This latter lyric poetry was first sung in southern France, in the Provence, whence its popularity carried it to other countries. The composer of this kind of lyric verse, and of the music that accompanied it, was known as the troubadour. William IX, duke of Aquitaine (d. 1127), enjoys the honor of being the first troubadour. (Some literary critics go so far as to acclaim William the father of modern poetry.) The names of some five hundred troubadours have been preserved, the greatest of the Provençal poets being Bernard de Ventadour. At least Bernard was ready to claim his pre-eminence, for he sang: "It is no wonder that I sing better than any other singer; for my heart draws me more than others toward Love, and I am better made for his commandments." Troubadours who were not blessed by such fortune as William of Aquitaine lived off the patronage of kings and princes and their ladies. For the presentation of his verses, the troubadour depended upon a joglar or minstrel. The jongleur of northern France might be both composer and performer. Such was the most famous of all troubadours, Walther von der Vogelweide (d. 1228), the German minnesinger (he sang of love or *Minne*). Walther sang his own verses as he trudged from castle to castle, and his plaint, "Many a man and woman have I made glad—might I so have gladdened myself," must have echoed the melancholic thoughts of many a wandering medieval minstrel. (Reading 158)

Troubadour Themes. Walther sang of love. He also voiced on occasion his own political views, for which he has been called the first patriot of German literary history. And he could be bitterly satirical. In these moods he was not a typical troubadour, however. For the troubadour thought only of love, but a love of a very particular sort. Courtly love it has been called. The question of the origins of this courtly love remains a problem. Arabic, classical, even liturgical influences among others, have been suggested. It remains a love apart from any in the long catalog of loves about which poets have written verses. Courtly love was not carnal, nor was it platonic. It stopped at a point somewhere between. The troubadour accepted the premise that the sole ennobling force in man's life was the sexual love of a woman. Yet it must be the love of a woman who was superior in worth, for only then would the love of the troubadour for her refine his emotions and exalt his sentiments. The object of the lover's affections must reciprocate his love for unrequited love was injurious, even dabasing. William of Aquitaine speaks of the great influence of love in one of his poems: "Through joy (originating from her) the sick man can grow well, and through sadness (originating from her) the healthy man can die, and the wise man become a fool, and the handsome man alter his good looks, and the most courtly become vile and the completely base become courtly."

Classes of Troubadour Poetry. This appeal to love was the most common kind of troubadour song and was called the *chanso*. There were others of a less artificial cast, which in time came to be expressed according to carefully regulated schematizations of meters and rhymes. Among the more popular were the *tenso* or debate, which found two singers arguing over such questions as whether it were better to see one's beloved dead than married to another; the *sirventes*, which was political in character, and if favorable to the local lord, might have been suggested to the troubadour by the lord himself in order to enhance his popularity; the *pastourelle*, which sang of the amorous knight who happened upon a beautiful shepherdess; the *alba* or dawnsong, which told how a friendly guard or a nightingale would warn two lovers that daybreak was near. Whatever the particular type of lyric or theme, troubadour verse remained the poetry of polite society. Its theme was generally of knights and ladies; the troubadour was himself frequently of that class, while the joglar who sang the verses depended upon the lord of the castle for his livelihood. (In northern France, the troubadour and joglar became the trouvere and jongleur.)

The Fabliaux: Their Character. There was something unreal about the classes of vernacular literature considered thus far. The epics told of supermen locked in combat with dragons, of indomitable warriors who slew thousands of the foe. Even the realistic saga has the dead Gunnar sing a song from his grave (*Story of Burnt Njal*). In the romance, the extraordinarily valiant hero overcomes, with consummate regularity and monotony, all obstacles which seek to bar him from his devastatingly beautiful damsel. The troubadour sang of an unreal love; its appeal was always esoteric. A reaction to these stories about things which could hardly have happened, and of men and women who could hardly have lived, was bound to come. It came with the *fabliaux*. The *fabliau* was the antithesis of fantasy, of refinement, and sophistication. It was ordinarily a rough, frankly human, humorous story, told in rhymed verse. As a literary form it flourished especially during the thirteenth century. Scholarly research finds a link between its appearance and the twelfth-century revival of interest in the old Latin comedies of Plautus and Terence. Be that as it may, the *fabliaux* are essentially folktales, the kind that have a way of reappearing, generation after generation, with such characters as fit them to each new age and environment. For Plautus' braggart soldier and clever slave, the *fabliaux* present the prosperous merchant who is regularly deceived, and the unprincipled clerk who usually does the deceiving. More gross than satirical, the *fabliaux* aimed at arousing boisterous laughter, rather than contempt for the persons vilified. The *fabliaux* found few women who were virtuous, and fewer priests who were saints.

A Fabliau. A *fabliau* that turns about a kind of rude cleverness tells of a peasant who liked to beat his wife. To get revenge, she went to the king and told him that her husband was in reality a great physician, but an unusually modest one, who would not admit his medical competency short of being pommeled to death. It chanced some time later, that a bone became lodged in the throat of the king's daughter. The king immediately summoned the peasant, ordered him to cure his daughter, and, of course, was forced to have him beaten before he "confessed" he was a physician. By means of buffoonish grimaces and antics, the peasant, now doctor, was able to make the girl laugh so hysterically, that she coughed up the bone. However, the king did not dismiss the peasant. Instead he assembled all the sick of the kingdom and directed the physician to heal them. Never at a loss, the "physician" had a huge fire built, and then announced that all would be cured of their maladies if the person who was sickest among them would walk into the blaze. But everyone whom he approached and questioned concerning his health assured him that he had never felt better in his life. And thus twice the peasant displayed an ingenuity with which the *fabliaux* did not ordinarily credit him.

Fables. Next come a group of poems called fables. In these stories animals play the part of human characters, though still retaining their own physical characteristics. The best known of ancient fable writers was Aesop, although it is to Aesop's Latin imitator, Phaedrus, that the medieval fable is traced. Here we meet Marie de France again, this time as the most productive author of fable stories. She has more than one hundred to her credit. Like the ancient fables, these of the Middle Ages possessed a moral, such as the story of the ass which sought to gain its master's affection in the same manner his little dog had been doing—by rushing forward eagerly to meet him when he came home and pawing him! Note might be made here of medieval bestiaries. These were stories about animals, some as legendary as the unicorn, which included a description of the animal and its traits, followed by an attempt to discover some symbolic significance. Lapidaries attempted to achieve the same spiritual end by using precious stones instead of animals as their theme, with even more bizarre results as concerned accuracy.

The Romance of Renard. Distinct from the fable is the collection of stories associated with Renard, that most ingenious and cunning of foxes. Where the fable had a moral, the stories about Renard did not; neither were they originally satirical. Their appeal was similar to that of the *fabliaux*. The usual animal characters bear standard names: Renard the fox, Isengrin the wolf, Tybert the cat, Bruin the bear, Bernard the ass, Chanticleer the cock, Noble the lion. For the origins of this literary genre, such stories as that of the raven with the cheese suggest ancient sources, although tales existing in earlier medieval folklore must have provided the bulk of the episodes. The *Romance of Renard (Roman de Renart)* consists of some 30,000 verses. These are arranged in a series of twenty-seven branches, each branch dealing with a separate episode. The first branch appeared about the middle of the twelfth century. How popular they proved is revealed by the fact that *renard* replaced the common noun *goupil* in the French vocabulary for fox. And their popularity was not limited to medieval times. Professor Holmes believes that so similar are some of Joel Chandler Harris' Uncle Remus stories to the Renard cycles, "that it seems almost impossible to imagine anything but collusion."* Thus the plot of "How Brer Rabbit lost his great big bushy tail" may be a nineteenth-century adaptation of the medieval tale which describes how Renard taught Isengrin, the wolf, how to catch fish: all he need do was to tie a bucket to his tail and lower it through a hole in the ice. Of course, while Renard busied himself stirring up the fish as he promised, the wolf's tail became frozen in the ice, and that was the end of the tail! Renard always got the better of the other animals, even at his funeral. He had been apparently vanquished by the more powerful (but slower witted) Isengrin, but only feigned death. Carried off to be buried, he effected his escape before they got him safely interred. Toward the close of the thirteenth century, satire tended to become the dominant note in the stories, and Renard lost most of his earlier popularity. (Reading 159)

The Romance of the Rose: The Plot. A fairly constant idea that appears and reappears in medieval literature is that of allegory. We meet it in such epics as *Beowulf*, for instance, where the contest between good and evil is symbolized in the clash between Beowulf and the dragon. The romances made constant use of allegory, the most striking example being the quest for the Holy Grail, which was generally conceived of as a symbol of sanctification. In a later chapter we shall meet with Dante's *Divine Comedy*, which is fundamentally a grand allegory of man's search for God. A purer type of allegory, in the sense of presenting ideas by means of forms not entirely lifelike (e.g. Patience), is provided by the thirteenth-century poem entitled *The Romance of the Rose*, the most widely read medieval composition. More than two hundred manuscript copies have survived the Middle Ages, although today's interest in the poem is negligible. This very long poem of some 22,000 lines, had two authors, one quite unlike the other. William of Lorris composed the first part, probably before 1237, while Jean of Meun, a Parisian bourgeois, wrote the second part about forty years later. The only element which gives unity to the two parts is the general theme of love. The author falls asleep:

> 'Twas in my twentieth year of age,
> When Love doth all young hearts engage
> To pay him toll, that on my bed
> I lay one night, as custom led,
> Asleep, when o'er my spirit fell
> A wondrous pleasant dream. . . .

---

* U. T. Holmes, *A History of Old French Literature*, New York, 1948, p. 212.

He dreams how he came upon a garden into which Hatred, Wickedness, Avarice, and other vices barred him access. But Gladness, Generosity, and Nobility come to his assistance, while arrows from the bow of the God Love leave him a willing slave of love. His object now becomes a rose (the Lady) which is enclosed within a garden. He is about to possess himself of the rose, when Jealousy, Shame, Fear, and Slander interfere. They remove the precious bud to the security of a strong wall, at which melancholic turn William of Lorris breaks off his account. Jean of Meun takes up the thread of the story and has Reason remonstrate with the lover who is about to die of grief and despair. Reason's arguments about the vanity of love prove unavailing. Eventually with the help of Venus, Genius, and Nature, the lover is able to penetrate the fortress and win the rose. The poet concludes: "It was day and I awoke."

William of Lorris' Part.   The poem is one of those all-embracing compositions, like Dante's *Divine Comedy*, which provides an almost panoramic view of the times. As one literary critic writes of *The Romance of the Rose* "the thirteenth century lies before us." The first part, that by William of Lorris, constitutes a psychological study of love. It is thus similar to the sentimental philosophizing of the troubadour. William writes of "Love's gentle art," of the beauties of nature, of the song of birds.

> The bullfinch piped beneath, above
> I heard the crooning turtle-dove
> Near by, the sweet-voiced tiny wren
> While high in air, beyond my ken,
> The skylark soared.

In this idyllic setting, the Lover pledges his abject submission to Love:

> Whatso you deem
> Most fitting e'en though good it seem
> To you to prison me or slay
> Speak but the word, and I obey.
> My life is yours to waste or save,
> I render me your bounden slave.

Jean of Meun's Part.   The modern historian is more interested in what Jean of Meun takes such an interminable time in telling. Not only does this poet feel obliged to continue, if not expand, the service of Love, but he misses no opportunity to display an astonishing amount of erudition and a great store of his worldly wisdom for the edification of his reader. If Jean of Meun was not one of the foremost poets of the thirteenth century, he was surely the best informed—and the most verbose. One wonders how an ordinary layman could have acquired so much knowledge of science, of classical literature and mythology. The modern reader is especially interested in the poet's asides, in which he speaks out about his own times. Of kings, he protests:

> No! No! the heavenly powers deign not
> More to note deaths of king I wot
> Than those of honest churls, nor are
> King's bodies dead, one dab of tar
> More worth than those of clerk and squire,
> Or honest men who work for hire.

What mades a man noble is not his birth—

> An upright heart
> Doth true nobility impart,
> But mere nobility of birth
> I reckon of little worth.

Jean of Meun is sharp with the friars, but against womankind he fairly lets himself go. His excoriation of that sex ranks with the most eloquent denunciations of women with which medieval literature, both religious and secular, abounds. Women are not to be trusted, he writes:

> For in five minutes woman's tongue
> May to a dozen tunes be rung,
> And thousands of evasive phrases
> She mingles with her sophistries,
> For than a woman none lie
> More sweetly or more hardily.

The *Romance of the Rose* reveals in the pen of Jean of Meun the growing assertiveness and critical spirit of the rising bourgeoisie.

Medieval Drama: Mystery Plays. Like ancient Greek drama, that of the Middle Ages had its roots in religion. Christian drama developed from the trope, which is defined as a textual interpolation into the liturgy of the mass for the purpose of clarifying its meaning. From there, the trope was transferred to the Divine Office, where it was gradually expanded and in time rendered partly dramatic by having individual members of the clergy sing or recite the parts spoken by the characters represented in the trope. The first trope of which there is any record is the tenth-century Easter play called the *Quem Quaeritis* (Whom do you seek?). These are the words which the angel addressed to the holy women who came to visit Christ's sepulchre. Soon a Christmas trope appeared, and a little later even dramatized pieces about popular saints like St. Nicholas and St. Catherine were in evidence. The inclusion of materials dealing with the lives of the saints permitted both a greater fictionalizing and the introduction of a much more human element. As these dramatizations grew more elaborate, the church proved too confining, and the mystery play, as it came to be called, moved out in front of the church or to the village commons. Here the use of costumes, scenery, and additional characters prepared the way for the pageants of the late Middle Ages which might portray all of religious history from the creation of the angels down to the Last Judgment. The Passion Play of Oberammergau represents a modern survival of these medieval pageants. One of the best known of mystery plays was the Play of Adam (*Jeu d'Adam*). (See page 658.) Though the play is in French, the Latin of the stage directions indicates that priests or clerks made up the cast of characters. Yet this clerical participation was exceptional once the play had moved outside the church. All clerical participation was formally forbidden by the Fourth Lateran Council in 1215. (Reading 160)

Miracle and Morality Plays.   The term miracle play is usually given to a dramatic presentation which involved saints and their miraculous achievements, in contrast to mystery plays which were drawn from the Bible. In the fifteenth century the morality play appeared, in which the themes were presented chiefly by allegorical figures such as personified virtues and vices. The most famous morality play, *Everyman* (mankind), is assigned to the very close of the Middle Ages. Morality plays did not remain inspirational. Many of the late medieval presentations were as secularized as the dramatic farces noted below. A famous group of fourteenth-century plays was the *Miracles of Notre Dame*. Mary, the Mother of God, consistently appears in the role of miraculously extricating some grievous sinner from the clutches of Satan. Thus in the *Nun Who Left Her Abbey*, Mary takes the place of a nun who had fled her convent to take up a life of sin. Years later the ex-nun returns to her village home incognito and is astonished to learn that she is still supposed to be at the convent where she is leading a life of heroic sanctity. When she discovers that it is Mary who is impersonating her, she repents, returns to the convent, where in time she impresses all with her virtue.

Dramatic Farce.   Plays of this sort were extremely popular in the late Middle Ages. They presented much opportunity for wealth of incident and character. In fact, the dramatic or secular farce of the fourteenth and fifteenth centuries probably grew out of homely, humorous episodes in the mystery and miracle plays, such as the tavern scene in the *Play of St. Nicholas*. Farces were short, simple, comic stories which based their humor on the rich store of human frailties. Almost every medieval character, from priest to bourgeois, knight, and peasant, came in for use and abuse. "There are no heroes and no heroines, no brave actions and no leaders; but plenty of rogues and fools, whose guile and folly give rise to those situations which picaresque literature swarms with and which had once delighted the makers of the *fabliaux*." The best of those extant is *The Farce of Master Pierre Patelin*. One critic has observed that Louis XI of France, who was something of a rogue himself (see page 747), would have enjoyed a farce like *Pierre Patelin*. "We may imagine his laughter as he saw one rascal outwit another, until a mere lout, a 'sheep in clothing,' outwits them all. That was something after his own heart." (Reading 161)

Medieval Art

Medieval Art was Religious. Medieval art expresses the spirit of the Middle Ages quite as eloquently as does medieval literature. For the illiterate who could not appreciate the written word, that spirit spoke even louder by means of stained glass windows, mosaics, and sculpture, whose messages he could understand. As Pope Gregory argued in the controversy over the use of images: "Painting can do for the illiterate what writing does for those who can read." Medieval art reflects more forcibly than other phases of the period's civilization, the central and all-pervading influence of Christianity. Until the close of the Middle Ages, the art student must restrict himself in the study of medieval architecture almost exclusively to churches. In the field of sculpture, illuminated manuscripts, mosaics, and what are called the minor arts, he finds little which is not an expression of religious inspiration. Only in the late Middle Ages, when the rise of a wealthy urban middle class made it possible, are there structures, paintings, and sculpture of a secular nature. Yet these still remain in the minority. Today, medieval people are no more, their literature is rarely read, their philosophy is ignored, their political institutions so altered as to be hardly recognizable, their agricultural and commercial practices completely superseded. Medieval ideas and concepts, it is true, provide the warp and woof of our modern civilization, but in their naked forms they are largely submerged. The one facet of medieval civilization which continues to speak convincingly of "the age of faith" that was, is Romanesque and Gothic art.

The Pagan Roman and Christian Basilica. For the forerunner of the Romanesque and Gothic church, we must go back to late Roman times, to the spacious, rectangular type of structure known as the basilica. The term basilica is derived from the Greek word meaning royal, that is, a structure majestic in its proportions. It was the structure which the early Christians found best suited to their needs, much more so than the Roman temple which, although occasionally a very stately edifice, served more the function of a shrine outside which the pagan citizenry might gather for ceremonial exercises. The Christians required, as we found in the Byzantine east (see page 166), a building sufficiently commodious to house many people, and to keep them protected from the elements while they participated in a rich liturgical service. For such purposes, the Ulpian basilica in the forum of Emperor Trajan would have required little alteration. The Christian basilica kept the main central area for the nave, and even the two aisles on either side of the nave might be retained in the larger churches (e.g. St. Paul's Outside the Walls). The semicircular area at one end of the main hall became the apse in the Christian church, and an altar was placed where once a pagan judge presided. The corresponding semi-circular area at the other end of the main hall was replaced by doors. These doors were usually to the west, as the Christian church was traditionally oriented toward the east, the altar being in the end closest to Jerusalem. The Christian basilica was usually supplied with transepts, which amounted to a nave set at right angles to the axis of the church and inserted between the apse and the nave proper. In their general arrangements and proportions

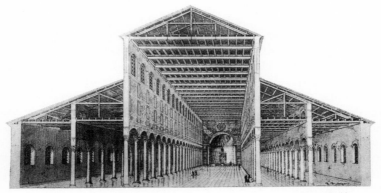

From Dehio

Perspective Section of St. Paul's Outside the Walls

the pagan and Christian basilicas were otherwise similar. Two rows of columns which ran the length of the nave and defined its breadth, sup-ported the walls of the clearstory. Most of the light for the interior made its way into the building through the windows in the clearstory walls. The Christian architect retained the simple timber roof of the Roman basilica, since he found this cheaper to construct and easier to erect than stone vaulting.

The most evident differences between the earlier Roman and later Chris-tian basilicas were in their interior decoration, and even here a second look might be necessary to detect them. Thus a first glance at the heavy mouldings which divided the wall surfaces of the nave into horizontal planes would give the same rich effect. A closer scrutiny, however, would reveal the work in the Christian church as less carefully done. The same technical inferiority would be visible in the columns of the Christian church, unless these happened to have been taken from an earlier pagan building. The exquisite symmetry and delicacy of detail in the columns of S. Maria Maggiore (432 A.D.), for example, clearly identify them with products of an age long before the fifth century. In contrast to the Roman structure, the Christian basilica made increasingly greater use of mosaics, frequently covering the entire wall surface of the nave and apse. Christian decorative figures and symbols tended to be simple, partly because more delicate work was beyond the ability of artists after the second century,

Santa Maria Maggiore

partly because the artist was less interested in beauty than in truth. Greater detail had to be sacrificed in the interest of sharpness and clarity of representation. Little difference would be reflected between the richly coffered ceilings of the more pretentious pagan and Christian edifices. Similarly, whether pagan or Christian, the horizontal mouldings, together with the vista of oft-repeated columns, tended to carry the eye forward toward the apse and gave the interior an illusion of great length.

Early Christian Art. In its broader aspects, early Christian architecture reflects no significant evidence of deterioration from classical standards. Yet the technical inferiority of Christian interior decoration just noted

The Good Shepherd

suggests that Christian sculpture and the minor arts would show a comparable lack of excellence, and such is the case. The Christian artist had stronger motivation, and he revealed considerably greater originality and diversity in the subjects he portrayed, than did his pagan predecessor. But in workmanship, foreshortening, sharpness of detail, correctness of form, and symmetry, Christian artists were deficient. The principal examples of their work have been uncovered in the catacombs. Frescoes and *graphiti* which date back to the close of the second century have been found on the walls of these subterranean galleries. Among the subjects most frequently depicted are figures from the Old Testament like Adam and Eve, Abraham, Noah, and Jonah. Jonah was a particularly popular character, since his emergence from the belly of the sea monster was held to prefigure the resurrection of Christ from the tomb. The same interest in symbolism is revealed in early Christian statuary (e.g. the Good Shepherd), in the elaborate carving on sarcophagi, in mosaics, in the ivory panels covering reliquaries and pyxes, and in the illustrated pages of manuscripts. Christian symbolism in general discouraged naturalism, since the significance of the idea or incident portrayed was so much more important than the excellence of its artistry. Actually symbolism possessed real functional values. Certain abstract ideas could only be expressed by means of symbols, or could not have been expressed in any other way more effectively or economically. Symbolism invests early Christian art with its principal appeal and together with an inherited aversion to images, explains the use of the flat, frontal representation so characteristic of the period.

Western Art from 500 A.D. to 1000 A.D.　After 500 A.D. and until approximately 1000 A.D., western art, with the possible exception of that of Italy, passed into something of the same eclipse which afflicted learning during that period. Because of the turbulency of the times, no clear and uniform art forms had opportunity to emerge. It was the Dark Ages. Still it was not a moribund or static period. Actually if one quality can be singled out as fairly common to the art of the period it is vigor. This is exemplified best in the marvelous intertwining and interlacing of flowers, birds, and dragons, against a bewildering background of complicated patterns of lines and colors, which type of work serves as the field for so much of the sculpture and painting (illuminated manuscripts) of German and Celtic Europe. The most important structure was Charlemagne's sixteen-sided church at Aachen, which he had patterned after the sixth-century church of San Vitale in Ravenna. (See page 167.) It was the marvel of its day, as witness the many contemporary comments it provoked. Illuminated manuscripts emanating from Aachen and monastic centers like St. Gall reveal, on the one hand, strong influences from the Byzantine world, on the other, the emergence of native patterns and art forms. The Book of Kells (see page 253), which is the most magnificent illuminated manuscript of the western world, dates from this period. Wood carvings, wrought iron, and such art pieces as the Bayeux Tapestry which constitutes a valuable historical source for William's invasion of England in 1066, attest to the artistic vigor and imagination of the period. A striking example of both these qualities is provided by the scenes engraved on the bronze doors of the church of Hildesheim (*ca.* 1000 A.D.). The panel which shows God accusing Adam, Adam charging Eve, and Eve in turn shunting the blame for their sin off on the devil, tells its story perhaps more forcibly because the proportions of the figures are not so skillfully done as to distract attention from the theme.

Romanesque Architecture.　The first great art style of the west which may properly be called medieval is the Romanesque. By this is meant an art which was neither predominantly classical nor Christian nor Germanic, but rather one in which these and other elements had attained a fusion after the general pattern of medieval civilization. This is not to say that the art of certain areas did not continue to reflect more immediate influences, including the Byzantine and Celtic. Such diversity has always characterized the art of western Europe, and a large amount of variety should be expected of the Romanesque period. For the period when Romanesque flourished (*ca.* 1000-1200 A.D.), while not so turbulent as the Dark Ages just ended, was one, nevertheless, in which many lords were seeking by force to establish their dynasties and to consolidate their power. Among the more powerful factors which counteracted local tendencies and invested Romanesque architecture with a high degree of similarity of form was the

Photo-Wehmeyer

Bronze Doors of Hildesheim

fact that the bulk of construction was monastic. So many churches of the period were abbeys, indeed, that the term "Monastic" is at times preferred to Romanesque. Monastic influence upon Romanesque architecture is visible in the enlarged choir, which became necessary to accommodate a large number of monks. For the same reason, the apse in the Romanesque church was extended by the addition of the *chevet*, essentially a series of chapels with connecting ambulatory. Furthermore, the subdued light of the Romanesque interior produced an atmosphere many would have considered more conducive to monastic contemplation and to a thoughtful recitation of the Divine Office.

Romanesque Vaulting. The principal factor, however, which controlled all Romanesque construction and forced it into a fairly regular mold was the particular kind of roof the Romanesque architect preferred to construct. For nothing is more basic to architecture, neither spires, façade, windows, floor plan, or decoration, than the manner in which the roof is

Sketches of Medieval Vaulting   Scientific American, *November 1961, p. 146*

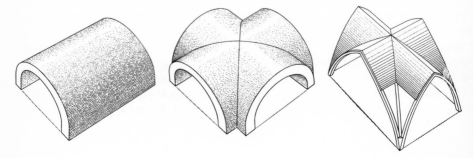

adjusted to the walls of the building. The heavy stone vault which covered the nave of the Romanesque church made Romanesque what it was. The use of the stone vault may have been actuated by the desire to reduce the fire hazard present in the timber roof of the basilica or to provide more permanent covering. It may simply have been the result of an inherently human urge to "have something different." In any event, the Romanesque architect was the first in the Middle Ages to employ stone vaulting over nave and aisles. To span these areas he used two different vaults, the barrel and the intersecting. The use of the latter kind he found feasible only over the narrow aisle space since this could be readily divided into squares. The oblong space above the nave presented a major difficulty. The use of an intersecting vault appeared out of the question, since the Romanesque architects employed only semicircular vaults. Two vaults of unequal height would therefore have resulted; the vaults above the shorter sides of the oblong surface to be vaulted being lower than those above the longer sides. To vault the uneven area which would result was too complicated an operation to be practicable.

The Romanesque architect chose, therefore, to span the nave with a barrel vault. As it turned out, this was not an entirely happy solution, since it forced the elimination of large clearstory windows. For to absorb the pressure of the tremendous weight of the stone vault and its powerful thrust outward, it was necessary to make the walls of the clearstory strong and massive, which meant proportionately less area for windows. The most the Romanesque architect felt safe in doing was to cut windows of very modest size into the walls to let in a little light. Larger windows would have caused the walls to buckle. In time he learned that the pressure of the vault could be appreciably reduced and the problem of construction simplified by first spanning the nave area with transverse and intersecting arches, then filling in the intervening space with lighter stone. He also experimented with extra buttresses under the aisle roofs to take up some of the thrust of the nave vault. When he did this he discovered that he could elevate the nave roof somewhat higher and enlarge slightly the windows in the clearstory walls. He also discovered the principle of the ribbed vault by introducing diagonal ribs at the lines of intersection of the vault. But here he halted his experimentation, leaving the Gothic architect to take the next logical step forward. The Romanesque architect stopped with a solidly constructed church, one with a darkened interior whose columns had become piers, with interior decoration held to a minimum since it could not be readily admired, and with the role of decoration in breaking the monotony of space being assumed by the ribbed arches of the nave vault and the light and shadow which filtered from out the triforium recesses. (The triforium was the gallery above the aisle which opened upon the nave.) The first and most enduring impression of Romanesque is one of strength and solidity. A church built according to the unusually heavy Norman style

Southwell Minster, England

National Buildings Record

Marburg—Art Reference Bureau

Buttressing in Church of the Trinity, Caen

almost resembled a fortress; only a few small windows relieved the unbroken stretch of massive wall and tower.

Romanesque Sculpture. Romanesque sculpture is as distinctly Romanesque as the heavy walls of the Romanesque church. Characteristic is the subordination of its function to architecture: it is decorative. A second characteristic of Romanesque sculpture, at least in the beginning, is the

evident limitation in the technical skill of the sculptor. A third characteristic is its didactic purpose. It restricted itself to figures, stories, or
ideas taken from the Bible, which the faithful would find instructive. These
qualities of Romanesque sculpture are revealed in the sculpture on the
façade of the Modena cathedral which portrays the sin of Adam and Eve. It
would be difficult to find art more simple and unsophisticated, yet so unmistakable in its message. Considerably superior in a technical sense and
also on a higher level intellectually, are the figures which appear in the
tympanum above the lintel of the twelfth-century church of St. Trophime
at Arles. The seated Christ is shown surrounded by his evangelists in the
guise of their traditional symbols. Matthew is represented as a winged man
since his gospel traces in its opening sentences the human descent of Christ.

Photo-Jean Roubier

St. Sernin, Toulouse

The eagle symbolizes John whose gospel soars as if on the wings of an
eagle to the throne of heaven. Luke is represented by an ox since he places
so much emphasis upon the sacrificial nature of Christ's death. Mark is the
lion: he opens his gospel with a description of John the Baptist as the
voice of one crying in the wilderness, which was the haunt of the lion.
Romanesque sculpture at its best (or is it Gothic?) is presented in the
series of figures, the Ancestors of Christ, which flank the west portal of the

Church of St. Pierre, Moissac

Modena Cathedral, façade

Ancestors of Christ: Chartres

St. Trophime in Arles, façade

cathedral of Chartres. The figures are elongated almost to the point of becoming columnar, and as firmly fitted into the wall as the columns which separate them. Yet the spiritual function of the figures is not thereby obscured. Though the bodily proportions are deformed, the spiritual effect is heightened, and the ideal embodied in the figures becomes the more readily intelligible.

Gothic Architecture. The crowning architectural glory of the Middle Ages was the Gothic. This style emerged in the late twelfth century in northern France about Paris, flourished in the thirteenth, and remained the dominant art of western Europe, except in Italy, up into early modern times. The Italian architects of the fifteenth and sixteenth centuries (Renaissance) rebelled against such non-Roman features as its pointed arches, its spires, and the tracery of its windows, and stigmatized it as Gothic or barbarous. Happily this parochial view is no more, and no odium attaches any longer to the term Gothic. Those magnificent Gothic cathedrals of western Europe which have survived the Middle Ages now revel in the name Gothic, as each summer they welcome thousands of visitors who come to marvel at their wonders. These wonders include a perfect harmony of sculpture and architecture; the soaring vertical lines of the interior which carry the eye to the extraordinary height of the nave vault; the graceful ribbing of the vault; the rich, deep light that streams in through the stained glass windows. One feature, more extraordinary than the others, is not immediately apparent, and that is the marvelous engineering which alone made such structures possible. In this last respect, Gothic architecture has never been surpassed. By most careful, even daring, use of balance and counterbalance, of thrust and pull, of weight and counterweight, the Gothic architect erected an edifice so economical in terms of stone and support, as seemingly to defy the laws of gravity. And he did this, not to flaunt his ingenuity, but to enable him to replace the stone walls of the clearstory with glass. Because he succeeded in accomplishing this, and because the clearstory walls of the Gothic cathedral, as a consequence, consist in the main of great windows divided by tracery or by piers that carry from the floor to the vault, the Gothic church has been likened to a greenhouse or a bird cage. The abundance and diversity of figures, incidents, and ideas presented in the sculpture and stained-glass windows of the Gothic cathedral (there are 6,000 painted and sculptured figures in Chartres), the wealth of symbolism that pervades it, the rich ritual of its ceremonies, have caused it to be called the school of the Middle Ages. There medieval man could learn almost all that was known about heaven and about his own world, and there the modern scholar can learn almost as much about medieval man.

Superiority of Rib Vault. For all its glory, Gothic represents nothing more revolutionary than an extension or fulfillment of principles of construction already implicit in Romanesque. The Romanesque architect had already crossed the nave area with transverse and intersecting spans, he was using ribbed vaulting over the aisle, and he had introduced buttresses in the triforium area in order to permit greater elevation of the nave vault and the introduction of somewhat larger windows in the clearstory walls. As we have noted, he had not attempted to employ the intersecting or rib vault over the nave because of the difficulty of covering an area marked off by arches of different height. Now this is what the Gothic architect set out to do, that is, to span the nave with a rib vault. If he could use a rib vault there, he could erect a loftier nave and at the same time expand enormously the portion of the clearstory walls he could appropriate for windows. For the great advantage of the rib vault over the barrel vault is this, that whereas the combined pressure of weight and thrust of the barrel vault is continuous all along the wall at the base of the vault, in the rib vault this pressure is concentrated at and limited to four points which rest upon the piers. Therefore, while the continuous pressure of the wall upon the barrel vault made it foolhardy for the Romanesque architect to pierce this with large windows, the Gothic architect had no misgivings about removing the entire wall space between the piers which supported the legs of the rib vault, and replacing this with windows as high as the apex of the vault, once he got his rib vault into place.

Pointed Arch and Flying Buttress. How did the Gothic architect accomplish this, a feat which the Romanesque had never attempted, either because he had considered it beyond his ingenuity or because he had been entirely satisfied with the very real beauty of Romanesque? He did it by introducing two innovations, one surely new in design, that is, the flying buttress, a second, surely new in its application, the pointed arch. These furnished the keys to the emergence of Gothic, and they appeared within

Sainte-Chapelle

such a short space in the late twelfth century, that, almost with the suddenness with which men tunneling through a mountain break out into the daylight, these architects were able to present to the world a strikingly different style of architecture, so different from the Romanesque in proportions and atmosphere, indeed, as almost to obscure its parentage. By moving the buttress out from under the aisle roof and making it "fly," the Gothic architect found that he could raise his vault as high as the inherent structural qualities of stone would permit. Then by pointing his round arches and bringing them all to a common level, he discovered that he could employ the rib vault just as satisfactorily to cover the oblong areas of the nave as the square areas above the aisle. Thus was Gothic born.

Popularity of Gothic. The most impressive of the Gothic churches were cathedrals. They are as characteristic of the late twelfth century and thirteenth, as the Romanesque abbey church was of the eleventh and early twelfth. While the monks did much of the construction work on their churches, cathedrals were usually the products of the towns. Because of the wealth accumulating there, because of the pride of the burghers in erecting the most pretentious cathedral within traveling distance, because of the ambition of bishops to grace their dioceses with the most imposing churches within their powers, western Europe embarked on the greatest period of church building which the history of ecclesiastical art has ever

French Government Tourist Office

Amiens

Ground Plan of Amiens

Athlone Press, London

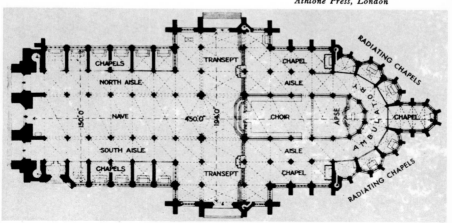

recorded. France especially, then England, Germany, and the Low Countries, were attracted to the style. Gothic was indigenous to France—contemporaries called it the "French Style." It may have been that fact or the greater wealth of France and its more numerous cities—whatever the explanation, France erected the most distinguished Gothic churches and the largest number. Henry Adams says that during the hundred-year period

Laon Cathedral   Lincoln Cathedral window

from 1170 to 1270, France built eighty cathedrals and nearly five-hundred churches of comparable size, thereby expressing "an intensity of conviction never again reached by any passion, whether of religion, of loyalty, of patriotism, or of wealth."* Only universal popular cooperation could have evoked so much building. One is reminded of the mass sentiment expressed on the occasion of the First Crusade. The construction of Chartres in 1149 drew this observation from the archbishop of Rouen: "The inhabitants of Chartres have combined to aid in the construction of their church by transporting the materials . . . the faithful of our diocese and of other neighbouring regions have formed associations for the same object; they admit no one into their company unless he has been to confession, has renounced enmities and revenges, and has reconciled himself with his enemies. That

* Henry Adams, *Mont-Saint-Michel and Chartres* (Mentor, 1961), p. 98.

Notre Dame: note flying buttresses

done, they elect a chief, under whose direction they conduct their wagons in silence and humility."*

Gothic Sculpture. There is a small, though significant, step from Romanesque to Gothic sculpture. Some of the splendor of the Gothic cathedral seems to have rubbed off on its statuary. The figures of the Romanesque stand almost imbedded in the wall. Those of the Gothic church begin to leave the masonry. They rest on platforms with canopies above their heads. The Romanesque figures commonly assume a frontal pose. Those of the Gothic cathedral are less stereotyped, they turn a bit in their places, their heads suggest an attempt at individualization. In place of the solemn visage of the Romanesque saint which conforms with the darker, more ascetic atmosphere of the Romanesque abbey, the Gothic saint at times almost ventures a smile—when this is appropriate! Though the Gothic sculptor fared no better than the Romanesque in articulating legs with torso, there was greater evidence of a human body underneath the hard exterior of his statues, and the folds of their garments are looser and fall more naturally. To identify his characters, the Gothic sculptor made an earnest attempt to go beyond the mere introduction of physical objects such as keys in the case of Peter or a bag of money for Judas. He gave his figures different poses, even varied their facial expressions, their beards and hair. Yet his

* Henry Adams, *op. cit.*, p. 106.

Amiens: Apostles

Beau-Dieu of Amiens

Amiens: West Front

naturalism, greater than that of the Romanesque, never tempted the Gothic sculptor to shed the element of the abstract and spiritual which hovers about the Gothic church and diffuses itself throughout its structure. The *Beau-Dieu* of Amiens cathedral shows Christ as a man, and as God too. The expression of the face and the lines of the figure are sufficiently life-like to bring out his manhood, but not so natural as to obscure his godli-ness. His pose is dignified and solemn. In his left hand he holds the Book of the Law, while he raises his right in benediction upon those who respect his laws. Beneath his feet lie crushed the adder and the basilisk, symbols of the forces of evil which he has vanquished. Had the sculptor carried his skill any farther and made his figure more natural, which he could not, he would have destroyed the atmosphere which invests Gothic sculpture with its peculiarly spiritual appeal.

The Bible in Stone. The Gothic cathedral remained always the house of God. The sculpture of the cathedral of Amiens has been called "the Bible in stone." The cathedral was the abode of the patriarchs, of saints and angels, of Christ and the Trinity, and especially of Mary. "Nearly every great church of the twelfth and thirteenth centuries belonged to Mary," until in France one asks for the church of Notre Dame as though it means cathedral. Even the figures of knights, of peasants, of gildsmen with their hammers and trowels, of shepherds and their sheep, which appear in the stained glass windows and the sculpture of the Gothic cathedral, could justify their presence there. At Semur, as Joan Evans writes, "one window given by the corporation of clothmakers, is entirely taken up with pictures of the processes of cloth making, and no saint or religious scene appears in it . . . yet it was in no way incongruous with a religious edifice. In this congruity with every side of life lay the true greatness of the religious art of the Middle Ages." Work was spiritually ennobling; it was a form of

Bourges: typanum

prayer. Here was portrayed the manner in which the clothmakers were working out their salvation. One last feature of Gothic art should not pass unnoticed. That is the fact that the names of almost all sculptors, glassmakers and architects remain buried in the collectivity of their respective gilds. Those very few whose names have been recorded, received no greater acclaim from their contemporaries than does the skilled bricklayer or plasterer today.

Medieval Music

Origins. One of the most precious legacies we have from the Middle Ages is our music. Music is as old as man, but ours goes back no farther than the Middle Ages. From its origins, medieval music was a handmaid of the Christian church, and actually remained faithful to the service of religion even longer than medieval art and drama. The music of the Middle Ages can be traced back to a number of sources, surely the most influential being the Hebrew. Since the first Christians were Hebrews, they quite naturally retained much of the Hebrew liturgy. We read how Christ and his apostles sang a hymn at the Last Supper, how Paul encouraged the singing of spiritual songs, and how Pliny the Younger found the Christians still singing hymns in his letter to the Emperor Trajan. (See page 81.) Two of the most traditional phrases in the Christian liturgy were taken over directly from the Hebrew, the one, the Alleluia, without change, the second, the "Holy, Holy, Holy," in translation. Other eastern influences, such as Greek, Syrian, and Byzantine, had a share in the evolution of medieval music. The singing of hymns was recommended by the early church fathers in the east as a means of combating the popularity of religious songs such heretical groups as the Gnostics were using. St. Augustine is our authority for the view that it was St. Ambrose who introduced the hymn to the west. Ambrose's purpose in doing so was to help the faithful pass the time more pleasantly as they maintained guard in the church in Milan which the Arians hoped to appropriate. "Then it was first instituted that after the manner of the Eastern Churches, Hymns and Psalms should be sung, lest the people should wax faint through tediousness of sorrow: and from that day to this the custom is retained . . . congregations throughout other parts of the world following herein."

Plain Chant. The position of the church fathers regarding the spiritual value of music to the church was neither uniform nor enthusiastic. Augustine expresses a number of reservations on the subject, and appears finally to have taken a conservative stand. "That mode seems to me safer," he wrote, "which I remember to have been often told me of Athanasius, bishop of Alexandria, who made the reader of the psalm utter it with so slight inflection of voice, that it was nearer speaking than singing." This was and remained substantially the mind of the medieval church on the role of music in the divine services, namely that the melody should never be permitted to grow overly elaborate, and that it should always be carefully subordinated to the liturgy. The name given this music, that is, plain song or chant, reveals how successful the church proved in keeping it simple. This chant, which was destined to prove the most important in the development of Western music started out as a kind of sonorous prose in which the psalms were recited. The singing was in unison, often antiphonal, with the Christian cantor leading the group. So "plain" was this chant that it lacked both sharps and flats, employed only a modest range of notes, and ordinarily assigned an individual syllable to each note. It followed no measured intervals of time, but was guided by the natural rhythm of the text. A number of tones evolved in time, such as solemn, joyous, spirited, and funereal, to fit the liturgy of the occasion. Because Pope Gregory the Great, with characteristic efficiency, introduced some system into contemporary musical practices, plain song usually goes by the name of Gregorian chant, although the exact nature of Gregory's contribution is not known. This Gregorian or Roman chant became general throughout western Europe largely through the instrumentality of the Benedictine monks. We hear of Charlemagne asking the pope to send instructors to train his Franks in the chant. The Golden Age of plain song was the seventh century, but it dominated the field of music until 1000 A.D.

Polyphony. Modern music, which is based essentially upon harmony, can be traced back to the ninth and tenth centuries, when the first recorded steps were taken away from monomelody toward polyphony. This began with the practice called *Organum*, that is "organized" melody. To accompany the principal tone which was sung by the tenor (from the Latin, *tenere*, to hold), a second voice would be introduced, singing the same melody and observing the same timing, but four or five tones, or even an octave, higher or lower as the case might be. A second development followed quickly, that of free *organum* or descant, when the accompanying voices would deviate from the melody, that is, they would not necessarily follow the tenor as he rose to a higher or dropped to a lower note. From descant the next step was counterpoint, which dates from the thirteenth century, where the second melody is related "note against note" to that of the principal melody, but yet has a melody of its own. The harmonius effect which the combination of different though consonant tones would produce awakened medieval composers to the potentialities inherent in counterpoint, and led to harmony, the chief characteristic of Western music. Concomitant with the development of polyphonic music was the introduction of musical notation, staffs, clefs, sharps, and flats. In this development, the work of Guido of Arezzo (d. 1050), a Benedictine monk, who introduced the four-line staff and square notes, is especially to be noted. One other name deserves mention in this brief sketch of medieval music, even though the person died long after the Middle Ages. This was Palestrina (d. 1594), director of the Sistine Chapel choir, who composed masses and motets which preserved the essential simplicity yet grandeur of medieval liturgical music against the threat of overelaborateness which had begun to transform it in some quarters.

Secular Music. Some of the influences which produced polyphonic music were secular. The origins of secular music are shrouded in deeper gloom than those of religious music. About all we know concerning it is by way of the denunciations of ecclesiastical censors who would send it back to the devil whence it came. Of course, it was not the melodies so much as the vulgarity of secular music which provoked these attacks. Secular music reflected the variety sprung from a vigorous imagination on the one hand and the absence of organized control on the other. Songs of every sort have come down to us: love, drinking, boating, reaping, hunting, even victory songs. We also encounter a wealth of musical instruments—an astounding number of stringed instruments, some played with a bow, others strummed; together with horns, trumpets, cymbals, drums, tambourines, and dulcimers. Organs were fairly common by the year 1000 A.D. What most secular melodies were like, is lost in the dust of time, although some of them were surely captured by the composers of religious hymns. The chief composers of secular music were jongleurs and joglars, while the ability to play the fiddle which was the most popular musical instrument of the late Middle Ages, was as traditional in certain areas as guitar playing was among the cowboys of the cattle country. Mention should be made of the contribution of the rondel to polyphonic music. This was the prototype of our own round, the "Three Blind Mice." The earliest and most quoted rondel is the thirteenth-century English refrain, "Sumer Is Icumen In."

Sumer is icumen in,	Summer is come in,
Lhude sing cuccu!	Sing loud, cuckoo!
Groweth sed and bloweth med	Seed grows and meadow blooms
and springeth the wude nu.	and the woods now bursts forth.
Sing cuccu!	Sing cuckoo!
Awe bleteth after lomb,	Ewe bleats after lamb,
Ihouth after calue cu,	Cow lows after calf,
Bulluc sterteth, bucke uerteth.	Bullock leaps, buck [jumps].
Murie sing cuccu!	Merry sing, cuckoo!
Cuccu, cuccu,	Cuckoo, cuckoo,
Wel singes the cuccu.	Well do you sing, cuckoo.
ne swik thu nauer nu!	Cease thou never now!
(Refrain)	(Refrain)
Sing cuccu nu, Sing cuccu!	Sing cuckoo now, Sing cuckoo!
Sing cuccu, Sing cuccu nu!	Sing cuckoo, Sing cuckoo now!

READINGS

No. 151. The Golden Legend of James of Voragine: Saint Longinus

Longinus was the centurion who with other soldiers was ordered by Pilate to stand guard at the cross of the Lord, and who pierced His side with a lance. The signs that he saw take place then, that is, the darkening of the sun and the quaking of the earth, caused him to become a Christian. What convinced him above all else, some writers declare, was that his eyes had become very poor either because of a malady or age, but that he had suddenly recovered his sight when some of Christ's blood which had run down the shaft of his lance accidentally touched his eyes. He thereupon abandoned the life of a soldier, received instruction from the apostles, and for twenty-eight years led the life of a monk in Caesarea of Cappadocia, converting many to the faith by his word and example.

In time he was haled before the governor of the province, and when he refused to sacrifice to the gods, the governor had his teeth torn out and his tongue cut off. Nevertheless, Longinus did not lose the power of speech, but, seizing an axe and proceeding to smash and break the idols, he exclaimed: "We shall see if these are gods!" The demons fled the idols and entered into the bodies of the governor and his companions, and raging and howling cast themselves at the feet of Longinus. Longinus said to the demons: "Why do you make your home in idols?" They answered: "Whenever the name of Christ is not invoked and where his sign does not appear, there we make our home." Meantime the governor was beginning to lose his mind and his sight as well. And Longinus said to him: "Know that you will not be cured unless you have me put to death. For just as soon as I have been slain by you, I shall pray for you and I shall obtain health for your body and your soul." The governor therefore had him beheaded forthwith, and then, falling down on his corpse, he wept and did penance. And immediately he regained his sight and his health, and lived out the remainder of his life doing good works.

No. 152. *Gesta Romanorum*

(*The Early English Versions of the Gesta Romanorum* by Sidney Herrtage. London, 1879. Modern English Translation.)

Polemius An Emperor (pp. 238-240)

Polemius, an emperor in the city of Rome, had three sons whom he loved very much. One night as he lay in his bed the thought struck him that he should dispose of his empire, and he decided to leave it to the laziest of his sons. Whereupon he summoned his sons and said to them: "He that is the laziest of you and is the most slothful shall inherit my kingdom after my death." "Then shall I have it," replied the eldest son, "for I am so lazy and so much given to sloth that I would rather let my foot burn in the fire when I am sitting near a blaze, than pull it away and save it." "No," protested the second son, "I am lazier than you. For if a rope were about my neck and I was to be hanged, and if my two hands were free and in one I held the end of the rope and in the other a sharp sword, I would prefer to die and be hanged rather than move my arm to cut the rope and save my life." "It is rather I," insisted the third son, "who shall reign after my sire, for I surpass you both in sloth. If I were lying in bed with both my eyes wide open and the rain were to come pelting down on my eyes, I would prefer to let the rain wash them right out of my head than bother to turn my head either to the right or to the left." Thereupon the emperor bequeathed his realm to the third son as being the laziest.

The Moral

Dear Friends: The emperor is the devil, the king and father of all the children of pride. By the first son is understood the man who lives in a city or place whose wickedness lights a flame of fire, that is, of sin in him; yet he would rather burn in sin with the devil than remove himself from his company. By the second son is understood that person who realizes that he is being throttled by the cords and bonds of sin and yet will not drive sin away with the sword of his tongue and be shriven here, but prefers to be hanged for it in hell. By the third son upon whose eyes, both right and left, water is dripping, is understood he who hears the doctrine concerning the joys of paradise and the pains and torments of hell, yet because of the weakness of his will turns his head neither to the right, that is, to abandon sin because of the joys of heaven, nor to the left, that is, to leave off sinning for fear of the pains of hell, but goes on sinning without ceasing. These people shall inherit the kingdom of hell, not the kingdom of heaven.

May the Ruler who reigns always by right deliver us from this [hell] and lead us to that [heaven]. Amen.

No. 153. Matthew Paris, the chronicler

(Matthew Paris's English History from the Year 1235 to 1273, tr. J. A. Giles, I. London, 1852.)

How the fame of the emperor Frederick was dimmed (pp. 157-158)

In the course of the same year, the fame of the emperor Frederick was clouded and stained by his envious enemies and rivals; for it was imputed to him that he was wavering in the Catholic faith, or wandering from the right way, and had given utterance to some speeches, from which it could be deduced and suspected that he was not only weak in the Catholic faith, but what was a much greater and more serious crime, that there was in him an enormity of heresy, and the most dreadful blasphemy, to be detested and execrated by all Christians. For it was reported that the emperor Frederick had said (although it may not be proper to mention it), that three conjurers had so craftily led away their contemporaries as to gain for themselves the mastery of the world: these were, Moses, Jesus, and Mahomet; and that he had impiously put forward some wicked and incredible ravings and blasphemies respecting the most holy eucharist. Far be it, far be it, from any discreet man, much less a Christian, to unlock his mouth and tongue in such raving blasphemy. It was also said by his rivals, that the emperor agreed and believed in the law of Mahomet more than that of Jesus Christ, and that he had made some Saracen harlots his concubines. A whisper also crept amongst the people (which God forbid to be true of such a great prince), that he had been for a long time past in confederacy with the Saracens, and was more a friend to them than to the Christians; and his rivals, who were endeavouring to blacken his fame, attempted to establish this by many proofs. Whether they sinned or not, He alone knows who is ignorant of nothing.

No. 154. The *Dies Irae*

(*Lyra Catholica,* tr. Edward Caswall. London, 1849, pp. 241-244.)

Dies irae, dies illa
Solvet saeclum in favilla
Teste David cum sibylla.

Quantus tremor est futurus,
Quando judex est venturus,
Cuncta stricte discussurus!

Tuba, mirum spargens sonum
Per sepulcra regionum
Coget omnes ante thronum.

Mors stupebit et natura
Cum resurget creatura,
Judicanti responsura.

Liber scriptus proferetur,
In quo totum continetur,
Unde mundus judicetur.

Judex ergo cum sedebit
Quidquid latet, apparebit:
Nil inultum remanebit.

Quid sum miser tunc dicturus?
Quem patronum rogaturus,
Cum vix justus sit securus?

Rex tremendae majestatis,
Qui salvandos salvas gratis,
Salva me, fons pietatis.

Recordare, Jesu pie,
Quod sum causa tuae viae:
Ne me perdas illa die.

Quaerens me, sedisti lassus:
Redemisti Crucem passus:
Tantus labor non sit cassus.

Juste judex ultionis,
Donum fac remissionis
Ante diem rationis.

Nigher still, and still more nigh
Draws the Day of Prophecy,
Doom'd to melt the earth and sky.

Oh, what trembling there shall be,
When the world its Judge shall see,
Coming in dread majesty!

Hark! the trump, with thrilling tone,
From sepulchral region lone,
Summons all before the throne:

Time and Death it doth appal,
To see the buried ages all
Rise to answer at the call.

Now the books are open spread;
Now the writing must be read,
Which condemns the quick and dead.

Now, before the Judge severe
Hidden things must all appear;
Nought can pass unpunish'd here.

What shall guilty I then plead?
Who for me will intercede,
When the Saints shall comfort need?

King of dreadful Majesty!
Who doest freely justify!
Fount of Pity, save Thou me!

Recollect, O Love divine!
'Twas for this lost sheep of thine
Thou thy glory didst resign.

Satest wearied seeking me;
Sufferedst upon the Tree:
Let not vain thy labour be.

Judge of Justice, hear my prayer!
Spare me, Lord in mercy spare!
Ere the Reckoning-day appear.

Ingemisco, tamquam reus:
Culpa rubet vultus meus:
Supplicanti parce, Deus.

Lo! thy gracious face I seek;
Shame and grief are on my cheek;
Sighs and tears my sorrow speak.

Qui Mariam absolvisti,
Et latronem exaudisti,
Mihi quoque spem dedisti.

Thou didst Mary's guilt forgive;
Didst the dying thief receive;
Hence doth hope within me live.

Preces meae non sunt dignae:
Sed tu bonus fac benigne,
Ne perenni cremer igne.

Worthless are my prayers, I know;
Yet, oh, cause me not to go
Into everlasting woe.

Inter oves locum praesta,
Et ab haedis me sequestra,
Statuens in parte dextra.

Sever'd from the guilty band,
Make me with thy sheep to stand,
Placing me on thy right hand.

Confutatis maledictis,
Flammis acribus addictis:
Voca me cum benedictis.

When the curs'd in anguish flee
Into flames of misery;
With the Blest then call Thou me.

Oro supplex et acclinis,
Cor contritum quasi cinis:
Gere curam mei finis.

Suppliant in the dust I lie;
My heart a cinder, crush'd and dry;
Help me, Lord, when death is nigh!

No. 155. Goliardic verse

(From *Wine, Women, and Song* by John Addington Symonds.)

A Wandering Student's Petition

I, a wandering scholar lad,
Born for toil and sadness,
Oftentimes am driven by
Poverty to madness.

Literature and knowledge I
Fain would still be earning,
Were it not that want of pelf
Makes me cease from learning.

These torn clothes that cover me
Are too thin and rotten;
Oft I have to suffer cold,
By the warmth forgotten.

Scarce I can attend at church,
Sing God's praises duly;

Mass and vespers both I miss,
Though I love them truly.

Oh, thou pride of N———,
By thy worth I pray thee
Give the suppliant help in need,
Heaven will sure repay thee.

Take a mind unto thee now
Like unto St. Martin;
Clothe the pilgrim's nakedness,
Wish me well at parting.

So may God translate your soul
Into peace eternal,
And the bliss of saints be yours
In His realm supernal.

The Confession of Golias (selected stanzas)

Carried am I like a ship
Left without a sailor
Like a bird that through the air
Flies where tempests hail her;
Chains and fetters hold me not,
Naught avails a jailer;
Still I find my fellows out
Toper, gamester, railer.

Down the broad road do I run,
As the way of youth is;
Snare myself in sin, and ne'er
Think where faith and truth is,
Eager far for pleasure more
Than soul's health, the sooth is,
For this flesh of mine I care,
Seek not ruth where ruth is.

Prelate, most discreet of priests,
Grant me absolution!
Dear's the death whereof I die,
Sweet my dissolution;
For my heart is wounded by
Beauty's soft suffusion;
All the girls I come not nigh,
Mine are in illusion.

In the second place I own
To the vice of gaming:
Cold indeed outside I seem,

Yet my soul is flaming:
But when once the dice-box hath
Stripped me to my shaming,
Make I songs and verses fit
For the world's acclaiming.

In the third place, I will speak
Of the tavern's pleasure;
For I never found nor find
There the least displeasure;
Nor shall I find it till I greet
Angels without measure,
Singing requiems for the souls
In eternal leisure.
In the public-house to die
Is my resolution;
Let wine to my lips be nigh
At life's dissolution:
That will make the angels cry,
With glad elocution,
"Grant this toper, God on high,
Grace and absolution!"

No. 156. The *Nibelungenlied*

(*The Nibelungenlied,* tr. William Lettsom. New York, 1901.)

Fifteenth Adventure: How Siegfried was Betrayed (pp. 143-157 *passim*)

Then Hagan, Lord of Trony, as had before been plann'd,
Went to take leave of Kriemhild ere yet they left the land.

"Ah! well is me," said Kriemhild, "that I've a lord who lends
Such firm assistance ever to back my dearest friends,
As now does my brave Siegfried for my brethren's sake;
Therefore," said the fair lady, "good courage will I take.

"My good friend, Sir Hagan, bear in remembrance still
How much I love my kinsmen, nor ever wish'd them ill.
For this requite my husband, nor let me vainly long;
He should not pay the forfeit, if I did Brunhild wrong.

"My fault," pursued she sadly, "good cause had I to rue.
For it I have far'd badly; he beat me black and blue;
Such mischief-making tattle his patience could not brook;
And for it ample vengeance on my poor limbs he took."

"You'll be friends together," said he, "some other day.
But, Kriemhild, my dear lady, tell me now, I pray,
At my hands to your husband what service can be done,
Fain would I do it, lady, better love I none."

The noble dame made answer, "Fear should I not at all,
That by the sword of any my lord in fight would fall,
But that he rashly follows his fiery martial mood.
Else could no harm befall him the noble knight and good."

"Lady," then answer'd Hagan, "since thus you harbor fear
Lest hostile force should slay him, let me yet further hear,
What best may serve our purpose the warrior to defend.
On foot, on horse, I'll watch him, his guardian and his friend."

Said she, "Thou art my cousin, and I alike am thine;
To thy good faith commend I this dearest lord of mine.
That thou wilt tend his welfare, assurance firm I hold."
Then told she him the secret far better left untold.

She said, "My husband's daring, and thereto stout of limb
Of old, when on the mountain he slew the dragon grim,
In its blood he bath'd him, and thence no more can feel
In his charmed person the deadly dint of steel.

"Still am I ever anxious, whene'er in fight he stands,
And keen-edg'd darts are hailing from strong heroic hands,
Lest I by one should lose him, my own beloved make.
Ah! how my heart is beating still for my Siegfried's sake!

"So now I'll tell the secret, dear friend, alone to thee
(For thou, I doubt not, cousin, will keep thy faith with me),
Where sword may pierce my darling, and death sit on the thrust.
See, in thy truth and honor how full, how firm my trust!

"As from the dragon's death-wounds gush'd out the crimson gore,
With the smoking torrent the warrior wash'd him o'er.
A leaf then 'twixt his shoulders fell from the linden bough.
There only steel can harm him; for that I tremble now."

Then said the Chief of Trony, "A little token sew
Upon his outer garment; thus shall I surer know
The spot that needs protection as in the fight we stand."
She thought his life to lengthen, the while his death was plann'd.

Said she, "Upon his vesture with a fine silken thread
I'll sew a secret crosslet; by this small token led
Thy hand shall guard my husband, as through the press he goes,
And in the shock of battle confronts his swarming foes."

"So will I do," said Hagan, "my honor'd lady dear."
She thought her lord to profit, and keep from danger clear,
But all she did to aid him serv'd but to betray.
Leave then took Sir Hagan, and joyous strode away.

What he had learn'd from Kriemhild his lord then bade him show
"Put off this march," said Hagan, "and let us hunting go;
Now have I all the secret; now in my hand is he;
Could you but contrive it?" "For that," said Gunther, "trust to me."

The false king and his courtiers to hear his words were fain.
I ween, so base a treason knight ne'er will do again,
As then was done by Hagan, when to his faith for aid
So fair a lady trusted, and so foully was betrayed.

Sixteenth Adventure: How Siegfried was Slain

Gunther and Hagan, the warriors fierce and bold,
To execute their treason, resolv'd to scour the world,
The bear, the boar, the wild bull, by hill or dale or fen,
To hunt with keen-edg'd javelins; what fitter sport for valiant men?

In lordly pomp rode with them Siegfried the champion strong.
Good store of costly viands they brought with them along.
Anon by a cool runnel he lost his guiltless life.
'Twas so devis'd by Brunhild, King Gunther's moody wife. . . .

Then rode they thence, and hasten'd to a wildering forest drear.
Many a bold knight, on pastime intent and merry cheer,
In the train of Gunther and Siegfried took his way.
Stout Gernot and young Giselher at home preferr'd to stay.

Many a well-laden sumpter before them cross'd the Rhine,
That for the fellow-hunters carried bread and wine.
And flesh and fish in plenty, with every dainty thing
That might become the table of such a mighty king. . . .

The hunting now was over for the most part at least;
Game was brought in plenty and skins of many a beast
To the place of meeting, and laid the hearth before.
Ah! to the busy kitchen what full supplies they bore!

Then bade Gunther summon the noble hunting crew
To the royal breakfast; a horn a huntsman blew
That far and wide re-echoed, and told to all around
That by the tryst-fire ready the king was to be found. . . .

Down in a flowery meadow sat they right merrily.
Ah! what dainty viands cheer'd that proud company!

Still delay'd the attendants the ruddy wine to pour.
Never else were warriors better serv'd before.
But for the heinous treason with which they fram'd their plot,
All that choice band of champions were free from blame or blot.

Then said the noble Siegfried, "I needs must wonder here,
That joyous wine is wanting with such abundant cheer.
When so o'erflows the kitchen, how is't the cellar's dry?
Treat merry hunters better, or hunt no more will I.

"I have deserv'd in Rhineland more hospitable care."
Then answering from the table spoke Gunther false and fair.
"This fault shall soon be mended, and reason done you first.
For this we may thank Hagan, who makes us die of thirst." . . .

Then spake the Chief of Trony, "Ye noble knights and bold,
I know just to our wishes a runnel clear and cold
Close by, so be not angry, but thither let us go."
Th'advice brought many a champion sorrow and mortal woe. . . .

The noble knight Sir Siegfried with thirst was sore opprest,
So earlier rose from table, and could no longer rest,
But straight would to the mountain the running brook to find,
And so advanc'd the treason his faithless foes design'd. . . .

Cool was the little runnel, and sparkled clear as glass.
O'er the rill King Gunther knelt down upon the grass.
When he his draught had taken he rose and stepp'd aside.
Full fain alike would Siegfried his thirst have satisfied.

Dear paid he for his courtesy; his bow, his matchless blade,
His weapons all, Sir Hagan far from their lord convey'd,
Then back sprung to the linden to seize his ashen spear,
And to find out the token survey'd his vesture near;

Then, as to drink Sir Siegfried down kneeling there he found,
He pierc'd him through the crosslet, that sudden from the wound
Forth the life-blood spouted e'en o'er his murderer's wee.
Never more will warrior dare so foul a deed.

Between his shoulders sticking he left the deadly spear.
Never before Sir Hagan so fled for ghastly fear,
As from the matchless champion whom he had butcher'd there.

No. 157. The Icelandic saga

(*The Story of Burnt Njal*, tr. G. W. Dasent. Edinburgh, 1861, pp. 241-246.)

Gunnar's Slaying

Gunnar's hall was made all of wood, and roofed with beams above, and there were window-slits under the beams that carried the roof and they were fitted with shutters. Gunnar slept in a loft above the hall, and so did Hallgerda and his mother.

Now when they were come near to the house they knew not whether Gunnar were at home, and bade that some one would go straight up to the house and see if he could find out. But the rest sat them down on the ground. Thorgrim the Easterling went and began to climb up on the hall. Gunnar sees that a red kirtle passed before the windowslit, and thrusts out the bill, and smote him on the middle. Thorgrim's feet slipped from under him, and he dropped his shield, and down he toppled from the roof. Then he goes to Gizur and his band as they sat on the ground. Gizur looked at him and said:

"Well, is Gunnar at home?"

"Find that out for yourselves," said Thorgrim; "but this I am sure of, that his bill is at home," and with that he fell down dead.

Then they made for the buildings. Gunnar shot out arrows at them, and made a stout defence, and they could get nothing done. Then some of them got into the outhouses and tried to attack him thence, but Gunnar found them out with his arrows there also, and still they could get nothing done. So it went on for a while, then they took a rest, and made a second onslaught. Gunnar still shot out at them, and they could do nothing, and fell off the second time. Then Gizur the White said:

"Let us press on harder; nothing comes of our onslaught."

Then they made a third bout of it, and were long at it, and then they fell-off again.

Gunnar said, "There lies an arrow outside on the wall, and it is one of their shafts; I will shoot at them with it, and it will be a shame to them if they get a hurt from their own weapons."

His mother said: "Do not so, my son; nor rouse them again when they have already fallen off from the attack."

But Gunnar caught up the arrow and shot it after them, and struck Eylif Aunund's son, and he got a great wound; he was standing all by himself, and they knew not that he was wounded.

"Out came an arm yonder," says Gizur, "and there was a gold ring on it, and took an arrow from the roof, and they would not look outside for shafts if there were enough in doors; and now ye shall make a fresh onslaught."

"Let us burn him house and all," said Mord.

"That shall never be," says Gizur, "though I knew that my life lay on it; but it is easy for thee to find out some plan, such a cunning man as thou art said to be."

Some ropes lay there on the ground, and they were often used to strengthen the roof.

Then Mord said: "Let us take the ropes and throw one end over the end of the carrying beams, but let us fasten the other end to these rocks and twist them tight with levers, and so pull the roof off the hall."

So they took the ropes and all lent a hand to carry this out, and before Gunnar was aware of it, they had pulled the whole roof off the hall.

Then Gunnar still shoots with his bow so that they could never come, nigh him. Then Mord said again that they must burn the house over Gunnar's head. But Gizur said:

"I know not why thou wilt speak of that which no one else wishes, and that shall never be."

Just then Thorbrand Thorleik's son sprang up on the roof, and cuts asunder Gunnar's bowstring. Gunnar clutches the bill with both hands, and turns on him quickly and drives it through him, and hurls him down on the ground.

Then up sprung Asbrand his brother. Gunnar thrusts at him with the bill, and he threw his shield before the blow, but the bill passed clean through the shield and broke both his arms, and down he fell from the wall.

Gunnar had already wounded eight men and slain the twain [Thorgrim Easterling and Thorbrand]. By that time Gunnar had got two wounds, and all men said that he never once winced either at wounds or death.

Then Gunnar said to Hallgerda: "Give me two locks of thy hair, and ye two, my mother and thou, twist them together into a bowstring for me."

"Does aught lie on it," she says.

"My life lies on it," he said; "for they will never come to close quarters with me if I can keep them off with my bow."

"Well!" she says, "Now I will call to thy mind that slap on the face which thou gavest me; and I care never a whit whether thou holdest out a long while or a short."

Then Gunnar sang a song:

> Each who hurls the gory javelin
> Hath some honour of his own,
> Now my helpmeet wimple-hooded
> Hurries all my fame to earth.
> No one owner of a war-ship
> Often asks for little things,
> Woman, fond of Frodi's flour (gold),
> Wends her hand as she is wont.

"Every one has something to boast of," says Gunnar, "and I will ask thee no more for this."

"Thou behavest ill," said Rannveig (Gunnar's mother), "and this shame shall long be had in mind."

Gunnar made a stout and bold defence, and now wounds other eight men with such sore wounds that many lay at death's door. Gunnar keeps them all off until he fell worn out with toil. Then they wounded him with many and great wounds, but still he got away out of their hands, and held his own against them a while longer, but at last it came about that they slew him.

No. 158. Poetry of the troubadours

(Robinson's *Readings,* pp. 436-438.)

A Song of *Vidal*

Oh, 'tis good and fair
When the trees all wear
Fresh green leaves,—the air
Sweet with flowers new,
   Song birds, here and there,
   Chanting full in view,
   While gay lovers sue,
   Amorous and true;
Loved and lover I would be,
Yet such answers to my plea
It hath been my lot to find
That I've nearly lost my mind.

Strength and heart and mind,
Lovingly inclined,
I have all resigned
To my lady fair;
   Glad new life I find
   Like the boughs that wear
   Fruit again,—birds air
   All their music there;
Springing leaves and blossoms new
In my heart I ever view,
And this joy will ever be
Mine, for she hath heard my plea.

A Song by *Bernard de Ventadorn*

Whene'er the lark's glad wings I see
Beat sunward 'gainst the radiant sky
Till, lost in joy so sweet and free,
She drops, forgetful how to fly,—
   Ah, when I view such happiness
   My bosom feels so deep an ache,
   Meseems for pain and sore distress
   My longing heart will straightway break.

Alas, I thought I held the key
To love! How ignorant am I!
For her that ne'er will pity me
I am not able to defy;
   My loving heart, my faithfulness,
   Myself, my world, she deigns to take,
   Then leave me bare and comfortless
   To longing thoughts that ever wake.

A Song by *Walther von der Vogelweide*

When from the sod the flow'rets spring,
And smile to meet the sun's bright ray,
When birds their sweetest carols sing
In all the morning pride of May,
   What lovelier than the prospect there?
   Can earth boast anything more fair?
   To me it seems an almost heaven,
   So beauteous to my eyes that vision bright is given.

But when a lady, chaste and fair,
Noble and clad in rich attire,
Walks through the throng with gracious air,
As sun that bids the stars retire,—
　　Then, where are all thy boastings, May?
　　What hast thou beautiful and gay
　　Compared with that supreme delight?
　　We leave thy loveliest flowers, and watch that lady bright.

Wouldst thou believe me,—come and place
Before thee all this pride of May;
Then look but on my lady's face,
And, which is best and brightest? say:
　　For me, how soon (if choice were mine)
　　This would I take, and that resign!
　　And say, "Though sweet thy beauties, May,
　　I'd rather forfeit all than lose my lady gay."

No. 159. Reynard the Fox

(*The History of Reynard the Fox,* turned into English verse by F. S. Ellis.
London, 1897.)

XII. How Reynard Was Shriven on His Way to the Court

The twain [Reynard and Grymbert Dachs, Reynard's sister's son] had fared
　　but little while
When Reynard said: "I feel how vile
My sins have been, and surely know
That now in jeopardy I go
To lose my life. I sore repent
The unholy way in which I've spent
So many years: no priest is here
To give me shriving, therefore, dear
And worthy Nephew, unto thee
Will I confess me—contritely;
Assured I feel, that were I shriven,
I less should dread to go to Heaven."

Said Grymbert: "Eme, if thou a mind
For shriving hast, thou must behind
Thee leave all lust to rob and steal."

Quoth Reynard: "That I deeply feel,
And so, *Confiteor tibi Pater*
A heap of evil deeds, and later
Will tell them fully, one by one,
And shrift received, and penance done,
Shall wend lighthearted." Grymbert said:

"If thou the slough of sin wouldst shed
Through shrift, then English speak, I pray."

Said Reynard: "Much I grieve to say,
Few men have done more wickedness
Than he who humbly doth confess
To thee his sins, and penance craves.
A many beasts have found their graves
Through my misdeeds. Mine Eme, the Bear,
With honeycombs did I ensnare;
And Tybert Cat, with hope of mice.
Then Chanticlere did I entice
From out his yard, with specious tale,
And ate his children. Time would fail
To go through all my crimes. The King
and Queen I slandered with a string
Of vilest falsehoods, which will stick
For ever by them. Many a trick
On Isegrym the Wolf I've played:
A monk of Eelmare was he made
By my assistance, where I too
Donned monkish hood and gown. He drew
Therefrom small profit. When he sighed
To ring the bells, I tightly tied
The bell-rope round his feet, and soon
He rang therewith so wild a tune,
That, mazed and scared, folk ran to see
Who made such hideous minstrelsy.
And when 'twas found that Isegrym
Rang out the chime, they fell on him
With sticks and staves, till helpless left,
Half dead he lay, of sense bereft.
Another time the dullard sought
Fishing to learn of me, and bought
His knowledge dearly. . . .

The Wolf another time I led
To rob a henroost, where I said
A cock and seven fat hens arow
Sat on a perch. As down below
We stood and watched, a high fall-door
I pointed out, and said: 'The floor,
Where sit the birds, is just behind
That door, climb up, and ye shall find
Your heart's desire.' He laughing went,
Suspecting nought, but all intent
On plenteous feasting; here and there
He snuffed about, then cried: 'Some snare
I fear ye set, or jape ye play,
Dear Nephew;' softly quoth I, 'Nay!
The man, dear Eme, who good will win
Must something venture: further in

The birds are roosting,' then a shove
I gave, and lo! the door above
Fell with a thundering noise adown,
That well might rouse a spell-bound town.

As through the house the clatter rang,
The slumberers started up, and sprang
From out their beds in wild affright,
Shrieking aloud, 'A light! a light!'
And when they found 'twas Isegrym
Who caused this fear, they set on him,
And strook his body nigh to death."

"Dear Nephew, shame admonisheth
My tongue to leave some things untold
That scarce were fitting to unfold
To youthful ears, but deeply I
Repent my past carnality.
Here ends this woful roll of crimes
That stain the memory of past times,
And breed remorse within my breast:
But now, unburdened and confessed,
My mind feels easier, shrift I pray
At thy kind hands, to drive away
The clouds that hover o'er my soul,
Thy healing words shall make me whole."

Grymbert, who subtle was, and wise,
Replied: "Dear Eme, this tree supplies
The means of penance," straight he broke
A slender twig, of fair grown oak,
And said, "Dear Uncle, wouldst thou quite
Absolve thy soul, thy body smite
Three times with this small rod, then bound
Three times across it on the ground:
Thou must not stumble, but keep straight
Thy legs, if thou wouldst expiate
Thy crimes: then take the rod in hand
And three times kiss it, this will stand
For token of obedience meek.
No further penance need ye seek,
But count your sins as wiped away,
From childhood's hour till this same day."
The Fox was glad. Then Grymbert said:
"Dear Eme, henceforward be ye wed
To holy works, read well your psalms;
Keep fasts and holy days; give alms;
Frequent the Church; forthon leave sin,
And theft and treason, so within
Due time ye may to Heaven attain."
The Fox declared his heart right fain
Of holy counsel, and content
Seemed Grymbert—straight they Courtward went.

No. 160. A mystery play

(*Adam, a Religious Play of the Twelfth Century*, tr. Edward Noble Stone. Seattle, 1926. By permission of the University of Washington Press.)

(Let Paradise be set up on a somewhat lofty place; let there be put about it curtains and silken hangings, at such an height that those persons who shall be in Paradise can be seen from the shoulders upward; let there be planted there sweet-smelling flowers and foliage; let diverse trees be therein, and fruits hanging upon them, so that it may seem a most delectable place. . . .

Whoever shall speak the name of Paradise, let him look back at it and point it out with his hand. Then let the Lesson begin "In the beginning God created the heaven and the earth." And after this is ended let the choir sing: "And the Lord God formed man." And when this is ended, let the Figure God say: "Adam!" and let him answer: "Lord!")

> Figure: Out of earthly clay I fashioned thee.
> Adam: I know it, yea!
> Figure: A living soul to thee I gave
> In thee my likeness did I grave
> Mine earthly image making thee.
> Never must thou rebellious be.
> Adam: Not I! but I will trust thee aye,
> And my Creator I'll obey.
> Figure: A fitting fere I've given thee
> (Eve is she hight) thy wife to be—
> Thy wife to be and partner,
> And thou must ever cleave to her,
> Do thou love her, let her love thee;
> So shall ye both be blest of me.
> Let her thine own commands obey,
> And both be subject to my sway.
> From thy rib-bone her form I wrought;
> No stranger she, but from thee brought.
> Out of thy body I shaped her frame;
> From thee, not from without, she came.
> Govern her, then, with counsel wise,
> Nor let dissent betwixt you rise,
> But love and mutual service great.
> Such is the law of wedlock's state.
> Figure: (To Eve) Now will I speak to thee, O Eve.
> Take heed, nor lightly this receive;
> If thou to do my will art fain,
> Thy heart its goodness will retain;
> Honour and love to me accord,

Thy Maker and acknowledged Lord;
To serve me be thy heart inclined
With all thy might and all thy mind.
Love Adam, hold him dear as life;
He is thy husband, thou his wife;
Ever to him submit thy heart
And from his teaching ne'er depart;
Serve him and love, with willing mind;
Therein is wedlock's law defined.
If thou art proved a helper meet
I'll set you both in glory's seat.

. . . . .

(Then let the Figure go to the church, and let Adam and Eve walk about, innocently delighting themselves in Paradise. In the meantime, let the demons run to and fro through the square, making fitting gestures; and let them come, one after another, alongside of Paradise, shewing Eve the forbidden fruit, as if entreating her to eat thereof. Then let the Devil come unto Adam; and he shall say unto him.)

Devil: How liv'st thou, Adam?
Adam: In felicity.
Devil: Is it well with thee?
Adam: There's nothing vexeth me.
Devil: It can be better.
Adam: Nay, I know not how.
Devil: Then wouldst thou know?
Adam: It recks me little now.
Devil: I know, forsooth!
Adam: What boots it to me to learn?
Devil: And why not, pray?
Adam: Naught doth it me concern.
Devil: Concern thee 't will
Adam: I know not when.
Devil: I'll not make haste to tell thee, then.

. . . . .

(Then shall the Devil, sadly and with downcast countenance, depart from Adam and he shall go even unto the gates of Hell, and he shall hold converse there with other demons. Thereafter, he shall make an excursion among the people; but presently he shall draw near to Paradise, on the side where Eve is, and, approaching Eve with a cheerful countenance and much blandishment, he thus accosteth her:)

Devil: Eve, hither am I come, to thee.
Eve: And prithee, Satan, why to me?
Devil: Seeking thy weal, thine honour, too.
Eve: God grant it!
Devil: Then, thy fears eschew.
Long since, I've mastered by my pains
Each secret Paradise contains;
A part of them to thee I'll tell.
Eve: Begin, then, and I'll listen well.
Devil: Thou'll hearken to me?

Eve: Hearken? — yea,
  Nor vex thy soul in any way.
Devil: Thou'll keep it hidden?
Eve: Yea, in truth.
Devil: Nor publish it?
Eve: Not I! forsooth.
Devil: Then, to this contract I'll agree,
  Nor further pledge require of thee.
Eve: Might'st safely trust my promise, though.
Devil: Thou'st been to a good school, I trow!
  Adam I've seen—a fool is he.
Eve: A little hard.
Devil: He'll softer be;
  But harder now than iron is.
Eve: A noble man!
Devil: A churl! I wis.
  Thought for himself he will not take;
  Let him have care, e'en for thy sake.
  Thou art a delicate, tender thing,
  Thou'rt fresher than the rose in spring;
  Thou'rt whiter than the crystal pale,
  Than snow that falls in the icy vale.
  An ill-matched pair did God create!
  Too tender thou, too hard thy mate.
  But thou'rt the wiser, I confess;
  Thy heart is full of cleverness;
  Therefore 'tis good to treat with thee.
  To thee I'd speak; have faith in me.
  Let none know of it.
Eve: Who should know?
Devil: Not Adam even.
Eve: Be it so.
Devil: Now will I speak; do thou give ear.
  None, save us twain, is present here,
  And Adam yon, who hath not heard.
Eve: Speak up! He'll not perceive a word.
Devil: I'll shew thee, then, what crafty plot
  Was 'gainst you in this garden wrought:
  The fruit God gave you to possess
  Hath in it little goodliness,
  But in the fruit to you forbidden
  Exceeding virtue lieth hidden;
  Therein is found of life the dower,
  Dominion, mastery, and power.
  Knowledge of evil and of good.

. . . . .

(Then shall the Devil depart from Eve and shall go unto Hell; but Adam shall come unto Eve, being sore displeased because the Devil hath spoken with her, and he shall say unto her:)

Adam: Say, wife, what thing of thee inquired
  That evil Satan?—what desired?

. . . . .

No. 161. A medieval farce

(*The Farce of Master Pierre Patelin,* Englished by Richard Holbrook. Boston, 1905, Excerpts.)

(Patelin, an un-prosperous barrister, is berated by his wife, Guillemette, for his inability to buy her some cloth. He promises to bring home enough to make both of them a suit. When his wife gibes him and asks how he plans to do this, he replies:)

Patelin: That's telling! If I fail, my dear, to fetch you cloth enough for both of us, and to spare, then I'm a fibber! [Playfully surveying his wife.] What colour suits you best? A greenish grey? Or Brussels cloth? Or some other sort?

(He goes off to Draper Guillaume Joceaulme, renowned for his penny-pinching thrift, and greets him with a beguiling smile.)

Patelin: My worthy sir, God bless you!
Draper: And give you joy!
Patelin: I have been really longing to see you, Guillaume. How is your health? You're feeling tiptop, eh?

(He continues to flatter the draper, and recalls in glowing words the sterling qualities of the draper's deceased father.)

Patelin: Ah, he was a knowing man!—your father was, I mean. God rest his soul! [Scanning the Draper with amazement.] When I look at you, I can't believe I'm not looking at him! What a good merchant he was! And clever? . . . [Waving his hand in such a way as to suggest the almost limitless ability of the elder Joceaulme.] I swear, your face is as like his as a regular painting. . . . If God ever took pity on any being, may he grant your father his soul's pardon! [Takes off his hat and glances piously toward heaven. The Draper follows suit.]

(Patelin gradually breaks down the draper's suspicions, and finally persuades him to sell him six ells of cloth—on credit—that is, for an hour or two, long enough for the draper to finish his day's business, close his shop, and hurry to Patelin's house for the money, some wine, and "a bit of that goose my wife [Guillemette] is roasting!")

Draper: [Aside]: The man drives me mad. [Aloud] Go on! Away! I will follow you then and bring the cloth.
Patelin [nimbly seizing the bundle of goods]: Nothing of that sort! How will it burden me? Not a whit, beneath my elbow . . . so.
Draper [trying to recover his property]: No indeed, sir! it would be better for me to bring it.
Patelin [tucking the cloth into his long gown]: I'll be hanged if you go to such

pains! See how snug it lies, here, under my elbow. What a jolly hump it will give me! Ah! now it's all right! [With mock hilarity.] We'll have a fling before you leave.

(Much ill at ease, the draper sees the cloth depart under Pierre's arm, and follows after in anxious haste once he closes his shop. Patelin meantime had hurried home, where he suggested a stratagem to his bewildered wife how they might hold on to the cloth without paying the money they did not have.)

Patelin: He is coming to eat some goose—on a wild goose chase, I mean. Now here's our game. Of course he will be braying to get money on the spot; so I've hatched out a nice arrangement. I'll simply lie on my bed, and play sick; then, when he comes, you will say, "Oh, do speak low!" Then you must groan and pull a long face. "Alas!" (you'll say) "he fell sick these two months past,"—or say six weeks,—and if he cries, "that's all flim-flam, for he has just been at my shop," you must say, "Alas! this is no time to romp!" Then let me pipe him a little tune, for music is all he shall get.

(The stratagem works. Patelin carries on as though he were delirious, his wife pretends to expect his death at any moment, and the draper finally leaves in a state of confused shock, sure only that someone had swindled him out of his six ells of cloth. The story now introduces a shepherd who comes to Patelin to seek legal advice. His employer, this same draper, had caught him red-handed stealing his sheep and slaughtering them. Because the shepherd gives the appearance of being an unusually dull-witted fellow, Patelin advises him that his only hope of escaping just punishment for his crime is to answer ba-a to each and every answer put to him in court.)

Patelin: Here is the trick! As soon as they call on you for trial, answer nothing but *ba-a-a* [mimicking a sheep's bleat], whatever they say to you. And if they happen to curse you, saying, "Ha, stinking fool! a pox on thee, villain! Art thou flouting the court?" go *ba-a*. "Oh!" I'll say, "he is half-witted; he thinks he is talking to his sheep!" But even if they split their heads with roaring, not another word! Beware!
Shepherd: I take it to heart, and truly I will be wary, and I will do it properly, I promise and affirm . . . call me fool outright if I utter today another word, to you or to any one, whatsoever they say to me, but only *ba-a*, as you have taught me.

(All went well, even better than Patelin had planned. When the draper saw Patelin and recognized him as the scoundrel who had stolen his cloth, he became highly excited and correspondingly incoherent in his addresses to the judge. The judge for his part was finding the shepherd's constant *ba-a*'s most disconcerting.)

Judge [to the shepherd]: Step forward. Speak.
Shepherd [shambling forward and looking very dull]: *Ba-a!*
Judge: Hoity-toity! Here's a mess! What is this *ba-a*? Am I a goat? Speak to me!
Shepherd: *Ba-a!*
Judge: A murrain on you! Ha! Are you flouting us?

Patelin [to the judge]: Believe me, he is crazy, or stupid, or he fancies he's among his sheep.

Draper [wildly to Patelin]: Damn me, if you are not the very man that took it—my cloth, I mean. [To the judge]: Oh, you can't imagine, sire, by what deceit. . . .

Judge [threatening]: Hold your tongue! Are you an idiot? Leave that matter alone, and let's to the point!

Draper: True, your Worship; but the circumstance concerns me; yet on my faith I'll not utter another word about it. Another time it may be different. I shall have to swallow it whole. Well, as I was saying, I gave six ells [the Judge starts up] . . . I mean, my sheep . . . pray, sir, forgive me . . . this nice master [Patelin] . . . my shepherd, when he ought to have been in the fields . . . [Shaking his fist at Patelin and appealing frantically to the Judge]. He told me I should have six crowns in gold, as soon as I came . . . [as the Judge threatens] . . . I mean, three years ago my shepherd gave me his word that he would watch over my flock loyally and do me no damage to it, nor any villainy, and then . . . [seeing Patelin] now he denies me outright both cloth and money. [To Patelin]: Oh, Master Patelin, truly . . . [Catches a warning frown from the Judge.] That scoundrel robbed me of the wool of my sheep; and healthy though they were, he killed them, and made them die by pounding out their brains . . . [Again Patelin distracts his attention.] When he had tucked my cloth under his arm-pit he hurried off, saying I should go and get six crowns at his house.

(The proceedings finally reach such a pass, the distraught judge dismisses the case. Patelin is happy—until he comes to collect his fee from the shepherd.)

Patelin: Say, Lambkin!

Shepherd: *Ba-a!*

Patelin: The plaintiff's gone, now. Cease thy *ba-a*: it's no longer needed. [Winsomely.] Didn't I trounce him? Didn't I counsel thee just right?

Shepherd: *Ba-a-a!*

Patelin: Come, come! Nobody will overhear you. Speak right out. You needn't fear.

Shepherd: *Ba-a!*

Patelin: It is time for me to be going. Pay me!

Shepherd: *Ba-a!*

Patelin: Why ba-a? It's not needed any longer. [Holds out his hand.] Come! Pay me well and nicely.

Shepherd: *Ba-a!*

(And the story ends with Patelin, now the creditor, receiving nothing but *ba-a*'s from his none too dull-witted client.)

14

RELIGIOUS AND CULTURAL DEVELOPMENTS OF THE LATE MIDDLE AGES

The Decline of the Medieval Church

Among the topics which traditionally conclude a survey of medieval history is that of the "Decline of the Medieval Church." With so much that was distinctly medieval in decline, such as the manor, feudalism, and the gild, it is little wonder that the institution most peculiar to the Middle Ages, the Catholic Christian church, should also have declined. Like the decline of these other institutions, that of the church raises a number of problems. If there was a decline in the vigor of Christian life, was this so serious as to approach a positive deterioration of faith and morals? Assuming a decline, did this decline affect both head and members or only the church's leadership? If it was the papacy that declined, was it the spiritual character of the papacy that waned or was it its influence or both? If the state grew stronger in the late Middle Ages as we shall discover was the case, then in view of the constitution of medieval society, we should expect significant decline in the church's influence in medieval life. Yet should this decline be viewed as anything more than relative on the part of the church? If papal power within the church organization grew more compulsive and ecclesiastical administration more centralized as they did in the late Middle Ages, shall these trends be deprecated as evidences of decline when similar tendencies on the part of contemporary secular governments are generally commended? Would this topic, the decline of the church, traditionally close a survey of medieval civilization had the sixteenth century not produced a Protestant Reformation? (The church's condition had not been healthy during earlier periods like the tenth and late twelfth centuries.) While these questions have evoked differing replies, there is no disagreement among scholars over the serious impact upon the church of such late-medieval developments as the Avignonese Residence, the Great Schism, and the conciliar movement.

Growth of the Papal Curia. Whether the growing centralization of the church in the late Middle Ages redounded to its ultimate well-being or decline, it was very much a fact. Actually the tendency toward bureaucratic proliferation had been visible since the accession of Innocent III and even beyond. Part of the growth of papal government came with the expansion of spiritual activities such as missionary work; part was the result of the curia's efforts to assume fuller direction of ecclesiastical affairs; part of this growth simply represented the tendency of most administrative systems in the late Middle Ages to expand in order to handle the needs of an advancing civilization. The practice of papal provisions illustrates two ways in which the business of the Roman curia expanded. In order to secure means of support for the members of the curia who were employed in Rome, the papacy reserved to itself the right of appointment to an increasing number of benefices (e.g. parishes and canonries). At the same time, many clerks, among them university students who hoped to continue their studies or to secure appointments after graduation, appealed to the popes for benefices. The judicial business of the curia experienced tremendous expansion. Almost unlimited was the right of appeal to Rome, and almost as unlimited were the disputes which kept rising between the regular and secular clergy over such matters as the spiritual care of the laity, between patrons over rights of presentation to benefices, between bishops and deans and between bishops and archbishops over questions of jurisdiction. The papal camera or treasury witnessed considerable expansion. Since the cost of papal government, like that of secular states, was rising, and since the traditional incomes from the papal states were dwindling, it became necessary to develop new sources of revenue and to exploit those already in existence with greater efficiency. Actually it was principally the camera's financial policies which provoked such universal clerical attack on papal corruption during the Avignonese Residence. This suggests why the growth of centralization in the church must be viewed as both a blessing and a curse. What was gained for the church through the greater efficiency which centralization effected, was partly lost in good will in the resentment aroused over the cost and slowness of papal administration and the heavier taxation the burgeoning papal bureaucracy necessitated.

The Papacy of the Late Middle Ages. Until recent years it has been customary to lay major responsibility for the decline of the church in the late Middle Ages to the low character of the popes. This view is no longer generally accepted. The Avignonese popes (1305-1377) were above average in the acceptance of their responsibilities, and the popes of the fifteenth century were not far behind. The corrupt pontificates of an Innocent VIII (1484-1492) or Alexander VI (1492-1503) have served to obscure the constructive work of a Nicholas V (1447-1455) and Callistus III (1455-1458). Because of the religious upheaval of the sixteenth century which has been traced to the failure of the popes of the fifteenth century to carry out a thoroughgoing reform of the church, the seriousness of other problems confronting the papacy during that period has not been appreciated. History proves that reform should have been the first and last concern of the popes during those years, but that was scarcely evident before the fact. What aroused deepest anguish for the popes during the fifteenth century was the ominous march of the Ottoman Turks up the Danube. Their first concern always was to organize crusades in order to halt that progress. From 1378 until 1415 the Great Schism almost precluded the consideration of other problems. After 1415 and until 1450 successive popes gave earnest thought to thwarting the conciliar movement which they regarded as a deep threat to both themselves and to the church. During the later Middle Ages the turbulency of the Papal States and the dangerous rivalries among the despots of northern Italy posed serious problems for the papacy. (Reading 171) What did not deserve the attention several popes paid it, in view of the urgency of other matters, was the advance of humanism. Yet though little real reform was achieved by the popes of the fifteenth century, it was not because of a complete absence of conscientious effort. A prerequisite to the success of papal efforts to reform the church was the cooperation of cardinals, hierarchy, and clergy, and of the kings and aristocracy of western. Europe as well. That the record of the Council of Constance in the matter of reform was hardly more impressive than that of the popes serves to reveal the complexity of the problem.

The College of Cardinals in the Late Middle Ages. The times called for a series of popes of the caliber of Innocent III, but that would have been expecting too much of the college of cardinals. As a group, the cardinals were distinguished less for their learning and piety than for the luxuriousness of their lives. A goodly number owed their positions to the eminence of their family connections. Since the pope played or attempted to play an influential role in political affairs, why should not kings and princes insist that they have a representative in the college of cardinals who would protect and favor their interests. Lorenzo the Magnificent's second son, Giovanni, the future Pope Leo X, became a cardinal at the early age of fourteen to make sure the Medici fortunes were represented in Rome. In the hope of strengthening his position in the faction-ridden Papal States, the pope occasionally raised to the cardinalate men whose only qualifications were their family relationship with him. Political considerations consequently divided cardinals gathered in conclave to select a new pope as often as did differences over the fitness of a candidate to fill the office of St. Peter. The action of the cardinals in 1378 in repudiating their election of Urban VI because his policies endangered their position speaks eloquently of their selfishness. That they could elect a man as pope in 1492 who had had a malodorous private life and who may have assured his election through bribery (Alexander VI), suggests that the ensuing one hundred years had not effected much improvement in their character.

The Clergy of the Late Middle Ages. The clergy of the late Middle Ages were better educated, did more preaching, and were probably freer of clerical irregularities than during the centuries preceding. Monks and friars could be found in appreciable numbers in attendance at the universities. Thus the constitutions of Benedict XII (1334-1342) which were several times reaffirmed, required monasteries to send five per cent of their monks to the university. The larger monastic orders maintained houses of study at the leading universities, while friaries frequently sought to reduce the cost of university instruction by establishing art courses of their own. Attention shall presently be drawn to the inspiring preaching and writing of a number of Dominican mystics who contributed to the spread of lay piety in the late Middle Ages. The remainder of the clerical picture, however, is not encouraging. A few new monastic orders appeared, although none acquired the renown or showed the vigor of the earlier Franciscan and Dominican orders. The Hundred Years' War and the Black Death reduced the number of monks within the monastery walls and the number of peasants working the lands without, to a point where both the spiritual and material foundations of many institutions were endangered. Though England did not suffer so severely as did France from the crippling effects of the Hundred Years' War, it is impossible to discount entirely the harsh strictures which Langland, Wyclif, and Chaucer leveled at the lives of the clergy. Despite the efforts of several popes to revitalize monasticism, the institution upon which the very existence of the church had at times depended, the "rhythm of monastic life shows a slow but continuous tendency to slacken."* The unseemly quarreling among monks, friars, and secular clergy over questions of property, theology, and pastoral responsibilities and rights, served to stultify spiritual life within the ranks of the clergy while it scandalized the laity without. For the failure of many of the clergy to live up to the ideals of their high vocation, the rise of anticlericalism in the late Middle Ages provides the most convincing proof.

Lay Piety in the Late Middle Ages. The uninspiring record of the clergy stands out sharply before the astonishing vigor of popular piety in western Europe, particularly in Germany and the Low Countries, in the late Middle Ages. Some scholars attribute this upsurge of lay piety to the horrors of

* Dom David Knowles, *The Religious Orders in England* (Cambridge, 1955), p. 6.

the Black Death and the Hundred Years' War which led men to think more deeply of their last end. Others trace it to the eloquent preaching of men like the Dominican Master Eckhart and his associates. Actually lay piety was not a new phenomenon; witness the thousands of pilgrims who had trekked annually to their favorite shrines in Europe and Palestine since the tenth century. The most striking manifestation of lay piety in the late Middle Ages took the form of lay religious organizations. The most popular of these, the Brethren of the Common Life, closely resembled the Franciscan movement of the thirteenth century. Its founder, Gerard Groote (d. 1384) of Deventer, a layman, attracted thousands through his preaching and example to join his order which eventually adopted the Augustinian rule. (The Augustinians were one of the orders of friars.) Though organized into communities, the Brethren of the Common Life took no formal vows. The members who dedicated themselves to lives of poverty, celibacy, and prayer, worked among the poor and preached the goodness of God and the love of neighbor. Perhaps the Brethren of the Common Life made their most permanent contribution to western civilization through the copying of manuscripts (chiefly of a devotional character) and the establishment of schools. Thomas à Kempis, Luther, and Erasmus are numbered among illustrious Europeans who attended these schools.

Less numerous than the Brethren of the Common Life were the Beghards and Beguines which were associations of laymen and women respectively. These groups engaged in teaching and in caring for the sick, while seeking to exemplify in their own lives the virtues of the eight beatitudes. The most active organization to labor among the sick and poor was the Order of the Holy Ghost which numbered more than 400 establishments in France in the fifteenth century. The Friends of God who appeared in the middle fourteenth century sought to combat the secularistic tendencies of the times through edifying lives of virtue and the achievement of a closer union with God through prayer and contemplation. Other religious communities, such as the Brethren of the Free Spirit and the Fraticelli, were inclined to carry their admiration for apostolic poverty and their devotion to the interior life to lengths which the medieval church judged heretical.

The Rhineland Mystics and Kempis. There were other pious men in addition to Groote who attained fame as mystics in the late Middle Ages. Among the more prominent of these men of the fourteenth century were the Dominican Master Eckhart (d. 1327) and his friar disciples John Ruysbroeck, John Tauler, and Henry Suso. The general theme of these mystics was that of living in the presence of God. God lives in all of us, the mystic would assert, but His presence is felt only in proportion to man's ability to suppress his sensual inclinations and to make God's will his will. God assists man with His grace, but man must reciprocate with faith and love. Eckhart stressed the importance of obedience, self-denial, patience, and prayer to spiritual growth, but he best revealed the depth and intensity of his own faith when he wrote directly of God. Eckhart said man must become so permeated with the divine presence that "he may radiate that Presence without working at it." The best known of the fifteenth century mystics is the Augustinian friar, Thomas à Kempis (d. 1471), whose *Imitation of Christ* ranks second only to the Bible in popularity among Christians. Kempis' affirmation, "I would rather feel compunction than be able to define it," reflects the preference of the late Middle Ages for an emotional rather than for the intellectual approach of scholasticism to the knowledge of God. (Readings 162, 163)

Late Medieval Mysticism and Protestantism.   Because most Protestant groups of the sixteenth century tended to subordinate, if not dismiss, the organized church with its sacramental system as unimportant in God's plan of sanctification and placed emphasis upon personal prayer instead, many writers have established a direct link between the lay piety and mysticism of the late Middle Ages with Protestantism. It is true that groups such as the fraticelli, whom the pope excommunicated for their extreme views on apostolic poverty, and the Flagellants, who taught that sin could be cleansed by thirty-three days of flogging, wasted no love on the medieval church as the agent of God's grace. Furthermore, the pietist tendencies of the Beghards and Beguines drew upon themselves the supicions of orthodox theologians. And that the writings of several of the Rhineland mystics left a deep impression upon the Reformers of the sixteenth century we have Luther's own testimony. Of Tauler he wrote: "I have found in him more solid and true theology than is to be, or can be found in all the scholastic doctors of the universities." Yet the fact remains that not one of the leading mystics of the late Middle Ages was heretically inclined. If the orthodoxy of an occasional statement could not pass rigid inspection, such deviation was unintended. As Eckhart protested: "I may err but I may not be a heretic—for the first has to do with the mind and the second with the will!" Thomas à Kempis concluded his *Imitation* with a long chapter on the Eucharist, in which sacrament this mystic felt the Christian should logically conclude his search for God. St. Catherine of Siena (d. 1380), a simple Italian girl who scaled the heights of mystical experience, fought most valiantly for the preservation of the papacy. Three of the leading mystics of the sixteenth century: St. Teresa of Avila, St. Ignatius of Loyola, and St. John of the Cross, were not Protestants. This much, however, may surely be said for the relationship between the lay piety of the late Middle Ages and the rise of Protestantism: that had not so many people derived so much more spiritual solace from their own prayers than from the ministration and example of the clergy, the acceptance and spread of Protestantism would not have been so rapid.

Capitalism, Humanism, Individualism vs. Christianity.   Though lay piety attained noteworthy proportions in the late Middle Ages particularly in the valley of the Rhine, is was not so pervasive a movement that it transformed the popular mentality of western Europe. In fact, certain contemporary developments which were by nature inconsistent with or hostile to Christianity may have blunted the faith of as many people as the ideas of Groote, Eckhart, and others had stirred. The expansion of capitalism, for example, and the rise in the standard of living which it eventually effected militated against the appeal of the gospel of Christianity which extolled the virtues of self-abnegation and condemned the vanity of material comforts. The manner in which the masters of the gilds exploited their position in the late Middle Ages reveals how readily medieval men succumbed to the lure of material gain once this came within reach. Then there was the rise of humanism which acclaimed the superiority of the pagan civilization of Greece and Rome and which, in general, bestowed an unmedieval blessing upon the enjoyment of life. Humanism of this sort was certainly incompatible with the spirit of Christian mortification, at least as preached by its loudest devotees. Thus Lorenzo Valla lamented: "Would that man had fifty senses, since five give such delight!" Yet such extreme humanism affected only a few. Pope Nicholas V demonstrated the fact that the same person could be a generous patron of humanism and at the same time a credit to the highest traditions of his holy office. Finally, there were the Italian despots, the leading exponents of the cult of the individual which has so impressed sympathetic students of the Italian Renaissance. This cult held up man, not God or eternal verities, as the criterion of what was good. The arrogant, supremely confident expression on Verrochio's Colleoni (page 701) provides a striking illustration of this type. However, it is questionable whether this form of excessive individualism actually affected more people in the fifteenth century than it had in the twelfth. And it would have been difficult to find any late-medieval individualists who were more ruthless and unprincipled than the feudal aristocracy of the eleventh and twelfth centuries. The effects of these "isms," therefore, of capitalism, humanism, and individualism, upon Christianity in the late Middle Ages have probably been more frequently overstated than the reverse.

The Rising Threat of the State. Thus far our examination of developments in the realm of religion has not uncovered any startling weakness or change which might have accounted for the decline of the church, real or alleged, in the late Middle Ages. It is true that neither the papacy, hierarchy, nor clergy exhibited any strong evidence of moral and spiritual leadership. Also disquieting was the presence of a measure of anticlericalism, implicit in the rise of lay religious movements. The rise of humanism tended to abet this anticlericalism, as did the expansion of capitalism which accompanied it. Still all this was not serious. What did hold grave implications for the church, however, especially for papal leadership, were four other developments: the Avignonese Residence, the Great Schism, the conciliar movement, and, above all else, the rise of the national or, better, the dynastic state. While the effects of the first three developments proved damaging to the spiritual health of the church and to the prestige of the papacy, these effects were largely temporary. What placed the stamp of permanency upon the decline of the church in the late Middle Ages was the rise of the state. Pope Callistus (1455-1458) pleaded earnestly with the rulers of Christendom to undertake a crusade against the Ottoman Turks who had just captured Constantinople. Only Genoa responded and not without selfish motives, but Aragon promptly attacked the Genoese expedition—so sadly had papal leadership of Christian Europe waned since the pontificate of Innocent III! Yet even Innocent could not have prevented a sharp readjustment in the relationship between church and state in favor of the latter. The church had never been stronger than the state, even under Innocent III. Nevertheless, until the late Middle Ages, the church could hope to challenge the policies of ambitious monarchs. She could usually enlist the sympathies of a powerful feudality which was equally averse to the emergence of a strong king. Furthermore, until the late Middle Ages national consciousness remained too diminutive a force to be of any use to the crown, nor for that matter had the machinery of state advanced to a point where it could have provided the king the means of effective rule. By the fourteenth century the situation had changed. The feudality had grown weaker; the people were awakening to nationalism, and royal administrations were reaching for new powers while administering old ones more effectively. In this development lies the true decline of the church in the late Middle Ages. In many respects the fourteenth and fifteenth centuries were centuries of transition from medieval to modern times. In no respect was this more evident than in the relationship between church and state. A change was inevitable; even an Innocent III could not have prevented it.

Boniface VIII and the Taxation of the Clergy.   The new era in church-state relations broke with the turn of the fourteenth century. The cast of characters in the drama which announced the change included three men, each quite unlike the others. Representing the papacy was Boniface VIII, a renowned canon lawyer, who as a young man had been ambitious, proud, and aggressive. Now Boniface was seventy-seven and growing older, more unbending, more committed to blocking any encroachment by the state upon what he considered the church's prerogatives. Representing the state were Edward I of England and Philip IV of France. Edward was a true Christian. His zeal for the recovery of the Holy Land reminds one of the enthusiasm which the First Crusade had evoked two hundred years earlier. There was no more of the anticlerical about Edward than about St. Louis. Philip's whole character still eludes the historian. The little that is revealed is not reassuring. Be that as it may, both Edward and Philip were agreed that the state had the right to tax the clergy. They needed the revenue and, ironically enough, for the same purpose—to prosecute their war against one another in Gascony. On occasion, earlier popes had winked at such taxation, even though Innocent III's Fourth Lateran Council had anathematized the practice. When Edward's successive demands passed beyond what the archbiship of Canterbury considered reasonable, that prelate appealed to Boniface for assistance. This Boniface furnished him in the famous bull *Clericis Laicos* (1296). (Bulls are known by their opening words.) While Boniface had canon law and tradition to sustain him, prudence recommended a less forthright affirmation. For in his *Clericis Laicos* he reiterated in somewhat stronger language the condemnation expressed by earlier canons against lay taxation of the clergy, and threatened with excommunication any lay person who made such demands or any clerk who acquiesced thereto "without the expressed permission of the papal chair." Edward's reply outdid Boniface's warning in directness. On the principle that those who did not support the government could not look to it for protection, he summarily outlawed the clergy and confiscated the possessions of those who refused to pay what he demanded. Philip embargoed the shipment of money from his dominions. Since the alternative was bankruptcy and the collapse of his Italian ambitions, Boniface capitulated. Within the year he rescinded the force of *Clericis Laicos*, annouced that the state could tax the clergy in an emergency, and authorized the state itself to decide when such an emergency existed. (Reading 164)

Boniface and Philip. This terminated Boniface's difficulties with Edward. English-papal relations in fact continued generally amicable until the reign of Henry VIII, and English kings learned that more could be accomplished by working with than against the pope. Philip IV remained hostile. One is puzzled at what lay behind his next move—whether he hoped to exploit Boniface's discomfiture and force new concessions from the papacy, or whether he simply wished to humiliate him further. Philip's chief advisers, Pierre Flote and William of Nogaret, were men of little honor and even less love for the papacy. Both Nogaret's father and mother had been burned at the stake for heresy, and Nogaret hated Boniface with the vehemence of a paranoiac. Philip precipitated the new quarrel by seizing Bernard de Saisset, bishop of Pamiers, on the charge of being "disrespectful, blasphemous, and seditious." He then demanded that Boniface degrade the bishop so that he could be punished for his treason. Because this was clearly contrary to medieval practice, and since the bishop had earlier served as papal legate, Boniface refused, and instructed Philip instead to release the bishop and send him on to Rome for trial. At the same time he announced the summons of a council to Rome which would consider charges brought against Philip. Philip countered with the first meeting of the Estates General (1302), before which body Flote read a garbled version of Boniface's latest bull which left the impression that Boniface claimed to be both spiritual and civil lord of France. The pope in turn replied with the most famous bull ever issued in the history of the

papacy, the *Unam Sanctam*, which enunciated in most emphatic language
the papal position vis-à-vis the state. The bull's salient points were three:
that there is but one church outside of which no salvation is possible; that
the spiritual authority is supreme and may judge the temporal *ratione
peccati* (i.e. when the latter sins); that whosoever resists the highest spiritual power, resists God. Wherefore it concluded: "It is altogether necessary
to salvation for every human creature to be subject to the Roman Pontiff."
(Reading 165) Philip's answer was the convening of a great council at
Paris before which Nogaret aired all possible charges against Boniface and
a number that were not possible. He accused Boniface of being an idolater,
a sorcerer and a murderer; he claimed further that Boniface kept a demon
as a pet whom he consulted before making any decision; that despite his
eighty-five years he led a most foul and vicious private life. Assured of the
support of the council, Nogaret left for Italy to bring Boniface by force
to Paris to stand trial. The night before Boniface was to release a bull ex-
communicating Philip and freeing his subjects from their allegiance,
Nogaret together with the leaders of the Colonna faction and about two
thousand troops occupied Anagni where Boniface was staying, seized the
pope, and held him prisoner for three days. To what extent Boniface
was maltreated remains a question. The citizens of Anagni finally bestirred
themselves and drove out the intruders. Boniface returned to Rome where
he died within the month, his death no doubt hastened by the indignities
he had suffered. Though Europe recoiled at the outrage, no one lifted a
hand to succor the papacy. So passed the papacy of Innocent III, never to
return. Philip went on to new victories.

The Avignonese Residence, Great Schism, and Conciliar Movement

The Avignonese Residence.   The tragic struggle between Boniface and
Philip might not have marked a turning point in the history of the papacy
had it not been for the Avignonese Residence that followed. During this
period, 1305-1377, the popes made their residence principally at Avignon
rather than Rome. (Clement actually moved to Avignon only in 1309.)
Because of that Residence, the papacy, instead of recuperating its fortunes
or at least fortifying what remained of its position, suffered the loss of
additional power and prestige. The Avignonese Residence had an innocent enough beginning. In 1305 the cardinals elected the archbishop of
Bordeaux who took the name of Clement V. Clement got as far as Avignon
on his way to Rome and stopped. At Avignon also remained his successors
for the next seventy years. What prompted Clement to go no farther was the

dangerous situation in Rome where such factions as the Colonna and Orsini had converted the city into a veritable no man's land. Hesitation led to delay and delay took on the character of permanency when Clement's successor began the construction at Avignon of luxurious quarters for himself and his curia.

Evils of the Avignonese Residence. For the papacy, the consequences of the Avignonese Residence proved disastrous. First, there was the charge that the Avignonese popes were subservient to the French crown. French they were and most of the cardinals, too. Avignon, though itself not French territory, was an enclave within a French sea. Yet Philip IV was actually the only French king sufficiently strong during this period to have bent the papacy to his will. The most regrettable instance of this influence was papal dissolution of the Knights of the Temple to whom Philip was heavily in debt and whose wealth he coveted. (See page 736.) The influence of Philip's successors, however, could hardly have been anything but negligible since they were almost without influence in their own country. Possibly the worst consequence for the church of the Avignonese Residence was the strain which the sharp increase in papal exactions placed upon the loyalty of the clergy. The cost of the new papal capital had to be met, while the loss of the bulk of papal revenues realized in the past from the Papal States had to be covered. Furthermore, whether new revenues or old ones, all were being collected with unaccustomed efficiency and with a vigor born of desperate need. Everywhere the reaction of the clergy was bitter. The clergy of Cologne protested: "In consequence of the exactions with which the Papal Court burdens the clergy, the Apostolic See has fallen into such contempt, that the Catholic faith in these parts seems to be seriously imperiled. The laity speaks slightingly of the Church, because, departing from the custom of former days, she hardly ever sends forth preachers or reformers, but rather ostentatious men, cunning, selfish, and greedy. Things have come to such a pass, that few are Christian more than in name." The magnificence of the papal palace and those of the cardinals at Avignon appeared to belie the honest needs of the popes and furnished material instead for the charge that the papacy was greedy, selfish, and corrupt. Petrarch called the city "the false, guilt-laden Babylon, the forge of lies, the horrible prison, the hell on earth," whence the term "Babylonian Captivity" to stigmatize the period as one during which the French had imprisoned the papacy at Avignon. Petrarch was but voicing Italian resentment at the absence of the pope which cost Italy and Rome much in terms of prestige and revenue. Yet many people could not but consider it scandalous, whatever the justification, that the pope had abandoned the see of Peter. The Great Schism, the most serious consequence of the Avignonese Residence, was to come later.

The Attack of Political Theorists. Recent scholarship has absolved the Avignonese papacy of most of the odium which has attached to it since the fourteenth century. Of the six popes to follow the first Clement at Avignon, only Clement VI failed to take an active interest in missionary expansion, disciplinary reform, the promotion of peace (particularly between England and France), the restoration of papal rule in the Papal States, the organization of a crusade against the Ottoman Turks, and the suppression of heresy. It was fortunate for the papacy that the Avignonese popes were of reasonably high caliber. Not only did its location at Avignon and its financial policies invite harsh criticism from the clergy and laity, but its traditional position of leadership within the church organization came under heavy attack at the hands of several of the most vocal critics of the church in the Middle Ages. Among these were the so-called Spiritual Franciscans, the minority group among the Franciscans which had fiercely opposed any relaxation of St. Francis' prohibition against the acceptance of property by the order. In their uncompromising insistence upon complete poverty, the Spiritual Franciscans gradually came to attack all clerical wealth as sinful, since, as they maintained, Christ and his apostles had practiced absolute poverty. Although most of these Franciscans eventually returned to the order, an irreconcilable group known as the Fraticelli took the revolutionary step of repudiating papal authority when Pope John XXII (1316-1334) condemned several of their views as heretical. Several of those who fled the ecclesiastical authorities found a haven at the court of the German emperor, Louis the Bavarian, who was having his own quarrel with the pope. It was here that William of Ockham, whom we met earlier, prepared a lengthy treatise in which he attacked papal authority and the traditional medieval view of the relationship between church and state. Ockham declared that the pope was fallible in matters of faith, and that truth could be found only in the Bible as interpreted by the wise. He also maintained the superiority of the general council to the pope, denied the pope any practical authority in temporal affairs, and accorded the emperor authority to depose an unworthy or heretical pope.

Marsiglio of Padua.   The most virulent attack on papal power came from the pen of Marsiglio of Padua, one of Ockham's recruits. In collaboration with John of Jandun, another scholar from the university of Paris, Marsiglio published in 1324 the most revolutionary political treatise to appear in the Middle Ages. In this, his *Defensor Pacis* (Defender of Peace), he announced that the state, not the church, was the superior authority and dominant force in society, but that the state was subject to the people, that is, to its more responsible elements, wherein resided the highest authority. In the spiritual sphere, the supreme authority was not the pope but the community of believers. "The assumed supremacy of the bishop of Rome," Marsiglio declared, "is without foundation." Marsiglio insisted that the clergy lead lives of relative poverty and that they limit themselves to strictly spiritual services, principally to preaching and to administering the sacraments. The church was to be shorn of all coercive authority such as excommunication and interdict, and questions of orthodoxy were to be determined by society. Marsiglio would, in effect, make the church little more than a department of the state. For all his fine theories, however, Marsiglio did not lose contact with reality. When he fled Paris for the court of Louis of Bavaria, he revised his position on what was the highest authority and substituted the imperial power for popular sovereignty. (Reading 166)

Dubois and Wyclif. Among the lawyers who counseled Philip IV on how to raise money and how to deal with the papacy was one Pierre Dubois. In a treatise entitled "On the Recovery of the Holy Land," Dubois proposed that the only way peace could be brought to Christendom and a successful crusade waged against the Moslems was for the French king to extend his rule over all the west. In order to facilitate the accomplishment of this end, the French king should be free to confiscate all church property. Though legally entitled to rule the Papal States on the basis of the Donation of Constantine, the pope should abdicate his authority since he was manifestly incapable of ruling these effectively. Dubois was the leading medieval representative of that popular French school which holds the French to be superior to all other people since they are endowed by nature with greater logic and, consequently, never oppose themselves to right reason. Dubois suggested as good a reason for this alleged superiority as did any of his numerous successors. He attributed French preeminence to the stars which had a way of shining with greater beneficence over France than elsewhere. More indicative of the maturity of Dubois' thought was his advocacy of public education for both sexes, which should include instruction in foreign languages, engineering, and agriculture. In his early writings, John Wyclif (d. 1384) devoted considerable attention to the question of church-state relations. On the theory that the right of dominion came from God and that in losing God's grace unworthy churchmen forfeited this right, Wyclif proposed that temporal lords confiscate the property of sinful priests, bishops, and popes. Wyclif also attacked the "Caesarian clergy," and urged that church and churchmen be excluded from political life.

The End of the Avignonese Residence. The Avignonese popes were under constant pressure to return to Rome. Sincere reformers implored them to do so; delegations from Rome begged them to return; Dante and Petrarch led the *literati* in demanding a return. Much of the justification for avoiding Rome was removed after the vigorous work of Cardinal Albornoz who re-established papal control in the Papal States. Conversely, the tranquillity of Avignon became less Arcadian with the collapse of French arms in the Hundred Years' War, when "free companies" began to pillage the area and even lay siege to the papal palace. Other considerations urged return too, such as the serious disrepair of many buildings in Rome and the real fear that the Papal States would themselves be lost should the Avignonese Residence be extended. Perhaps most instrumental in effecting the end of the "Babylonian Captivity" were the earnest entreaties of two saintly women, St. Brigid of Sweden and St. Catherine of Siena, who warned the popes that it was God's will that they return. In 1369 Urban V (d. 1370) returned briefly to Rome, and in January, 1377, Gregory XI permanently terminated the Avignonese Residence.

The Great Schism.   No sooner had the church weathered one crisis than an infinitely more serious one broke. Pope Gregory XI died in 1378, and the cardinals gathered in Rome for one of the shortest though most momentous conclaves in the history of the papacy. The French cardinals commanded a large majority, but they could not agree on one of their number. Without much difficulty, however, they compromised on the archbishop of Bari, a Neapolitan, who took the name of Urban VI. All would have been well but for two circumstances. In the first place, the Roman populace in its anxiety to insure the election of a Roman pope who would be less likely to return to Avignon, shouted and rioted for the election of a Roman. In the second place, Urban proved to be considerably less than the excellent choice anticipated. "Of a rather sanguine, impulsive and pugnacious nature, he was prone to outbursts in which he used most abusive and vituperative words about the cardinals and other high dignitaries assembled around him."* This unfortunate trait, together with his decision to initiate reform of the church forthwith, starting with the college of cardinals, and, finally, his refusal to share the control of the church with these cardinals, provoked what is known historically as the Great Schism. As Cardinal Robert of Geneva warned Urban: "Unlike your predecessors, Holy Father, you do not treat the cardinals with that honour which you owe to them. You are diminishing our authority, but verily I tell you that we will do our best to diminish yours."* Scarcely two months after their unanimous election of Urban, the cardinals withdrew to Anagni where they repudiated Urban's election as noncanonical since carried out under duress, and announced their selection of Robert of Geneva who took the name of Clement VII.

Division of Europe.   Now there were two popes, Urban at Rome, Clement at Avignon. This was not the first occasion when the west had experienced a schism, but it was the first time when one of the rival popes was not clearly the creature of a German king, for instance, and when both popes could claim so large a number of sincere supporters. This support split generally along lines of nationality. France and its friends—Naples, Sicily, and Scotland—adhered to the popes at Avignon; England, Flanders, Scandinavia, Hungary, Poland, and most of Italy and Germany, acclaimed Urban. A closer look at allegiances, however, would have revealed dioceses divided over the issue and monasteries with two hostile abbots. Saints were among those confused. Sts. Vincent Ferrer and Colette upheld the cause of Clement; Sts. Catherine of Siena and Brigid of Sweden that of Urban. Even

* Walter Ullmann, *The Origins of the Great Schism* (London, 1948), pp. 45, 48.

the cardinals may have been able to rationalize the honorableness of their action, although St. Catherine berated them and their deed: "If I look at your lives, I look in vain for the virtue and holiness which might deter you . . . from falsehood."*

Council of Pisa. Though Europe was divided in its allegiance to Rome and Avignon, it was of one mind as to the immediacy with which the schism should be terminated. The evils which the schism generated were too manifest: a general loosening of disciplinary controls; the surrender by the warring popes of ecclesiastical privileges to secular princes in order to gain their support; above all, the destruction of the fundamental principle of the Petrine succession upon which the western ecclesiastical system had been founded. Now that the church had two visible heads, people might eventually conclude that there was nothing God-ordained about the papacy, and that they might all have churches of their own. Critical though the situation was, plan after plan to heal the schism ran afoul of the intransigency of the two popes, who refused to permit a council to scrutinize their titles on the grounds that such a move would admit the possible illegitimacy of their claims. The first move to heal the schism proved a mistake. Following the advice of such distinguished theologians as John Gerson and Peter d'Ailly of the University of Paris, the cardinals of the respective popes (Urban and Clement had each a successor by this time), convened at Pisa in 1409, declared both popes deposed, and elected a new pontiff who took the name of Alexander V. This ill-advised action, however, only compounded the confusion, for as neither the Roman nor Avignonese pope accepted the ruling at Pisa, there were now three popes instead of two. Neither did most of Europe accept the Pisan pope, since tradition and canon law had it that a council to be genuine must be convoked by a pope. Finally, Emperor Sigismund, an adherent of the Pisan pope, now John XXIII, persuaded John to summon a general council to meet in Constance in Switzerland in the fall of 1414. Constance was considered neutral territory and acceptable to French, Italian, and German interests. When the council convened, the Roman pope, Gregory XII, notified Sigismund that he would abdicate if first permitted to convoke formally the council. Upon the council's acceptance of Gregory's offer, its success was assured.

Council of Constance: 1414-1418. With the blessing of two of the three popes, at least initially, the Council of Constance proceeded to write a memorable page in the history of church councils. Its most important accomplishment was that of terminating the schism. Gregory resigned as agreed, but John fled the council when he saw his hopes of being recognized as pope vanish. Thereupon the council formally deposed him, together with the Avignonese pope when the last of the latter's political adherents (the Spanish kingdoms) withdrew their support. This reveals one of the more revolutionary features of the Council of Constance, namely,

* Quoted in Ullman, *op. cit.*, p. 68.

the important role played by the heads of several of the ruling states of western Europe. Actually the decisions made by the council were not reached on the basis of the individual votes of prelates, but rather by nation—German, English, French, Italian, and Spanish—in order to neutralize the large number of Italian ecclesiastics. Once all three popes had resigned or had been deposed, the council elected a Colonna cardinal who took the name of Martin V (1417-1431). Less impressive was the achievement of the Council of Constance in the matter of reform, a problem second in importance on the council's agenda only to the ending of the schism itself. It is significant that the eighteen paltry reforms which ·the assembled prelates could agree upon to present to the new pope for ratification were concerned solely with papal abuses. Neither bishops nor cardinals would accept any restriction on practices of their own which others might consider reprehensible—so difficult is it for men to recognize as objectionable faults to which they have grown accustomed!

John Wyclif. A third objective of the council was the suppression of heresy. Two heretical movements, Lollardy in England and Hussitism in Bohemia, required attention. Lollardy, though almost suppressed, demanded formal condemnation, together with the heretical theses of John Wyclif, who was believed to have been Lollardy's principal inspiration. John Wyclif was a learned Oxford scholar who had come into prominence in February, 1377, when he appeared at St. Paul's, London, to answer to charges of heresy. The attempt of the English hierarchy on that occasion and again a year later to discipline him came to naught because of the intervention of John of Gaunt, uncle of the boy king, Richard II. Why Gaunt interfered to save Wyclif remains something of a mystery, although his motives were probably personal. In any event he did not countenance Wyclif's heretical views, and he was surely partner to the government's order to Wyclif in 1378 that he cease his attacks on the church. Shortly thereafter Wyclif left Oxford, probably under pressure to do so, and retired to his parish at Lutterworth where he died in 1384. Like most heretic-reformers, Wyclif's first criticisms of the church took the form of attacks on clerical abuses and irregularities. From these relatively unimportant targets, he gradually turned his assault upon such fundamental doctrines and practices as transubstantiation, the papacy, religious orders, indulgences, and pilgrimages. Since the pope could teach heresy, so Wyclif maintained, he appealed to the Scriptures as the source of truth. In his voluminous writings which ranged over almost the entire field of faith and morals, Wyclif laid down the broad lines of attack on the church which the Reformers of the sixteenth century did little more than develop.

Lollardy. Wyclif's exact relationship with Lollardy has not been definitely established. The chronicler speaks of "poor priests" whom Wyclif sent out to disseminate his views, and Englishmen of the late fourteenth century would have been hard pressed to distinguish between these "poor priests" and simply vagrant priests like John Ball who preached revolt against the established order in both church and state. Still, Wyclif was a member of the squirearchy and could never have endorsed the social and economic levelling which the Lollards generally advocated. Neither did the Lollard leaders at Oxford have much sympathy for the nonreligious objectives of Lollardy. This fact principally accounts for the growing radicalism of Lollardy once William Courteney, the archbishop of Canterbury, eradicated its intellectual headquarters at Oxford. For by so doing he deprived Lollardy of both the respectability and conservatism which might otherwise have enabled it to play an important role in English history. As it was, Lollardy never affected more than an "insignificant minority," and shortly after the government had authorized the death penalty for Lollards in 1401, what was left of the movement went underground. If it ever reappeared, it was never adopted by the Anglicans of the sixteenth century who would have been horrified at its "radical" program, but rather by the later Brownists and Independents. (Reading 167)

John Hus. The Council of Constance had no difficulty with Wyclif. He was already conveniently dead and his sympathizers were scattered and impotent. So after a careful study of his works, the council simply ordered his writings to be burned and his "bones dug up and cast out of consecrated ground, provided they could be distinguished from those of Christians buried near-by." John Hus proved a tougher problem. His doctrines, which were not substantially different from Wyclif's, had become the rallying point for Bohemian nationalism. Some of his ideas surely came from Wyclif. Many Bohemians had studied at Oxford during the early eighties and had brought back with them to Bohemia some of Wyclif's writings and a lively admiration for his theories. Among these Bohemian scholars was Jerome of Prague. John Hus was a distinguished professor at the university of Prague. Being a peasant by origin, he was able to gain the support of the lower classes, something which Wyclif had never been able to do. Hus's criticism of established tradition and authority, which were principally German, actually assured him the enthusiastic adherence of all classes in Bohemia. Emperor Sigismund hoped to cripple this nationalist movement by having Hus recant, and he persuaded him to come to Constance on an imperial safe-conduct. Hus came willingly enough, for he was convinced he could persuade the assembled theologians of the orthodoxy of his views. There he was thrown into prison after the protesting Sigismund had been assured that a safe-conduct to a heretic had no binding force. Sigismund had less difficulty rationalizing his action when he learned that Hus maintained that unworthy monarchs could be deposed. Hus was ordered to retract thirty-nine statements taken from his writings which the council judged heretical. When he refused to do this until proved in error from Scripture, the council reluctantly declared him an obdurate heretic and ordered him burned. Jerome of Prague was executed in the following year. But neither church nor empire was able to extinguish the national and religious revolt the doctrines of these two men had fired.

Conciliarism. The Council of Constance marked a signal victory for conciliarism, that is, the movement supported by a growing number of ecclesiastics and theologians in the late fourteenth and early fifteenth centuries which would have made the general church council superior to the pope. Ockham and Marsiglio had planted the seeds of conciliarism, but without the incidence of the Great Schism these seeds would never have matured. The schism forced hostile theologians to view conciliarism as something more than just a distasteful theory, and then even to adopt it when it proved the ultimate means of healing this schism. The champions of conciliarism capitalized on this victory by having the council at Constance enact two decrees. The first, *Sacrosancta*, affirmed the doctrine of conciliar supremacy. The second decree, *Frequens*, required the pope to call a general council in five years and at regular intervals thereafter. Martin V had other notions, however, and after giving qualified acceptance to the decrees, he announced that "no one may appeal from the supreme judge, this is, the Apostolic see or the Roman Pontiff, Vicar on earth of Jesus Christ, or may decline his authority in matters of faith." The council was too tired and too divided to offer effective protest. (Readings 168,169)

Council of Basel and the End of Conciliarism. Without enthusiasm Pope Martin called a council at Pavia in 1423 (within the five years decreed at Constance). Only a few delegates put in an appearance and nothing was accomplished. Seven years later, in 1431, a council convened at Basel in Switzerland. The achievement of this council would also have proved negligible but for the war which had broken out in Bohemia and the victories of the Hussites over the imperial armies. The new pope, Eugenius IV, had practically ignored the council until he learned that it had invited the Calixtines, that is, the moderate Hussites, to send representatives to Basel in a move to drive a wedge between them and the more extreme Taborites. The Calixtines derived their name from their demand that the laity be permitted to receive communion from the chalice (Lt. *calix*). They had other demands too, such as the abolition of the temporal power of the church, but demanded nothing so radical as the Taborites who advocated a church quite similar to sixteenth-century Calvinism. Because of the council's willingness to deal with the Calixtines, Eugenius declared the council dissolved. The pope's action proved most imprudent, however, for it served to revive conciliarism which had been steadily losing momentum during the years since Constance. Instead of meekly adjourning, the council bluntly informed the pope that only the council could dissolve itself, and so unfavorable was the political reaction to the pope's stand, that he felt obliged to rescind his order ending the council. Now it came the turn of the conciliarists to be imprudent. Emboldened by the pope's discomfiture, they proceeded to draw up a series of harsh measures which would have emasculated the papacy. The result was the alienation of the majority of the conservatives at Basel. This development emboldened the pope in turn to move the council to Ferrara where papal influence was stronger, ostensibly to accommodate Byzantine representatives from Constantinople who were coming west to discuss the healing of their schism with Rome. Only the radical element refused to budge from Basel. Left to themselves, they grew ever more extreme and ended by deposing Eugenius and setting up a pope of their own. With this rash act the conciliarists destroyed conciliarism. Not only had the princes of Europe already cooled to conciliarism when they learned they could secure greater concessions from one pope than from a divided council, but if there was one point upon which all western Europe could agree it was the folly of another schism. Universally spurned by both political and ecclesiastical Europe, the Basel group finally recognized in 1449 the futility of further gestures; they accepted the resignation of their pope, and adjourned.

It might be mentioned by way of obituary, that conciliarism left but a dismal record of achievement. Because of its lack of homogeneity, the general council proved as inept at approving and carrying out reforms as had the papacy. Even reforms proposed at the expense of the papacy did not gain acceptance easily. Representatives of the university of Paris, for instance, protested vigorously against the move to ban papal provisions since many of its students depended upon that form of papal assistance to finance their studies. Conciliarism's only real success was in effecting a compromise with the moderate Hussites, but this was at the cost of theological principles which Aquinas would never have accepted. Pius II formally interred conciliarism in 1460 with his bull *Execrabilis* in which he anathematized any appeal to a general church council rather than to the pope. (Reading 170)

Literary Figures of the Late Middle Ages

Medieval literature attained its full maturity in the fourteenth and fifteenth centuries. Granting the vigor of the epic of *Beowulf* and the *Chanson de Roland*, granting the originality and depth of thought reflected in the courtly romance, troubadour song, and allegory, all of these still represented, however, a native talent as yet largely unsophisticated and untrained. Balance in presentation and organization, artistry of expression, and, especially, portrayal of character, had not reached by 1300 the high level great literature normally demands. Furthermore, medieval literature prior to the fourteenth century was apt to find its appeal restricted to a special class or age. This is not so of the vernacular literature of the late Middle Ages which is as timeless as that of ancient Greece and the Elizabethan age. Dante, Chaucer, Boccaccio, and Villon are as well-known in the English-speaking world today as Homer, Sophocles, Horace, and Goethe. In the late Middle Ages individual writers move out in front of the company of men and women, largely nameless, who contributed the earlier epics and *fabliaux*. Together with a galaxy of eminent painters and sculptors whom we shall presently note, they make manifest the fact that the Middle Ages had culturally come of age.

Villon. The leading French poet of the late Middle Ages was François Villon (d. 1463?). His surname was that of the priest who adopted him, then gave him a fine education, and sent him off to the university of Paris where he earned a master of arts degree and proceeded on to the study of theology. In the course of acquiring an education, however, Villon also acquired a taste for carousing and related vice. The student body at the university in his day harbored criminal elements who "matriculated" simply for the cover the benefit of clergy would provide their villainies. Villon's weakness of character caused him to gravitate toward this group. He became a member of a fraternity of unprincipled men, killed at least one person in the course of his brawls, spent some time in jail for robbery, and was last seen hurrying from Paris to escape the gallows. What he did thereafter is unknown; considering his record, it could hardly have been commendable. All this we learn from his poetry, and what "an idle, dissipated, unbalanced, rhyming scholar, without pride and without shame" he was. His low moral and material estate he is inclined first to lay to his own deficiencies, and next perhaps to women. If the kind of woman that ennobles was to be found in the taverns of Paris, it was Villon's misfortune to discover there the other kind. So he writes:

> Love now and wenches I forswear;
> War to the knife to them I mete
> For death (and not a rap they care)
> Through them treads hard upon my feet.

Be that as it may, whether Villon is singing witty, clever verses, whether he revels in coarse, brutal expression, whether he rises to a sublimity all the more beautiful for the inelegance of his preceding thought, he expresses himself in lyrics which are among the most beautiful in the history of poetry. The world will forgive much the poet who penned a prayer to the Mother of God in order to please his own mother. The opening lines of this poem read:

> Lady of Heaven, Regent of the earth,
> Empress of all the infernal marshes fell,
> Receive me, Thy poor Christian, 'spite my dearth,
> In the fair midst of Thine elect to dwell:
> Albeit my lack of grace I know full well.

Villon's ballads he intersperses with the more ordinary meters of his two works, the *Petit Testament* and the *Grand Testament*. In these "last wills and testaments" he disposes of all the qualities and possessions he has and some he has not—the sword he leaves to a roistering companion is still at the pawnshop—while he expresses at the same time his own ideas about himself and about life. These last the modern reader finds provocative and surprisingly fresh. One might, in fact, venture the thought that over and above Villon's acknowledged talents, what inspires some of the present-day sympathy for the poet is the assumption that, not only his artistry, but his moral degeneracy as well, and his candor in acknowledging it, are so much more modern than they are medieval. (Reading 176)

Froissart and Commines. The leading chroniclers of the late Middle Ages were two Frenchmen, Jean Froissart (d. 1410) and Philip de Commines (d. 1509). Froissart was the chronicler of the age of chivalry which was closing, Commines the historian of royal absolutism that was opening. Froissart suffers in comparison with Commines for his lack of objectivity, and for his failure to show more interest in and sympathy for the bourgeoisie and peasantry. That he moved among the aristocracy all his life and had met many of the great personages he introduces to his readers may account for part of the imbalance in his narrative. He does consider causes, motives, and effects, but it is at best time which he is loath to take from the more romantic recounting of the courageous deeds of gallant knights clashing in chivalrous combat. As he announces in the opening paragraph of his *Chronicles*, he is recording "the noble adventures and deeds of arms, performed in the wars between England and France . . . to the end that brave men taking example from them may be encouraged in their well-doing." (Readings 182, 183) In the case of Commines, the reader finds no pageantry; instead a great deal of realism. Commines appears to have absorbed some of the cynicism of his master, Louis XI. Like him, he too was not misled by courtly manners and resplendent robes. In his *Memoirs* of the reigns of Louis XI and Charles VIII, Commines is continually searching for personal motives, for he was sure that selfishness and ambition accounted for most of men's actions. He admired unscrupulous, treacherous kings like Louis XI who got things accomplished; he despised chivalrous men like Charles the Rash of Burgundy who were fools. Commines recommended the study of history since "it holds the master key to all types of frauds, deceits, and perjuries." His cynicism was not of the Middle Ages which was passing, but of the realistic, unchivalrous era which was beckoning. (Reading 185)

Langland. Late medieval England witnessed the flowering of a native literature which the Norman Conquest had blighted three hundred years earlier. The greatest examples of this literature appeared in the dialects spoken in the Midlands (Mercia), whose Anglo-Saxon base had been considerably modified by several hundred years' association with Norman French. One of the most popular of contemporary poets to compose in this speech was William Langland (d. 1400?). Many problems remain unsolved concerning both Langland's identity and his poetry. He may have been a priest; at least he possessed a great store of theological learning. His poem, *The Vision of Piers Plowman,* is an allegory, and like *The Romance of the Rose* it opens with the poet falling asleep. In the first of a series of visions, he sees a great field flanked by the Tower of Truth (heaven) and a dark Dungeon (hell), the field itself being covered with all manner of people, most of them "too busy at their various jobs and jobberies" to take much notice of either tower or dungeon:

> A fair field full of folk I found between them,
> With all manner of men, the meanest and the richest,
> Working and wandering as the world demanded.
> Some put them to the plough and practised hardship
> In setting and sowing and seldom had leisure;
> They won what wasters consumed in gluttony.
> Some practised pride and quaint behaviour,
> And some disguised in clothes and features.
> Prayer and penance prevailed with many.*

Holy Church appears and explains the purpose of life, which is to seek God through Truth and Love. Next comes Lady Meed, the symbol of wealth, who is given dominion over the Seven Deadly Sins. These describe in turn their sinful wonts which Reason and Repentance are able to bring them to deplore. The penance assigned them is to seek Truth, but they soon discover that only a simple farmer, Piers Plowman, who is the symbol of Christian living, is able to show them the way. Next the poet considers the proper characters of Do Well, Do Better, and Do Best, which symbolize respectively the lay or active life, the priestly or contemplative life, and the episcopal or governing life. In the poet's search for these, he meets different psychological personifications such as Thought, Wit, Clergy, and Scripture, whom he questions about Do Well since his salvation depends on knowing this. Further instruction in the rule of life comes with the introduction of Abraham, the symbol of Faith, and Moses the symbol of Hope. But Abraham and Moses represent the Old Law of Judaism and as such prove inadequate. This is not true of Charity which enters in the guise of the Good Samaritan and who represents the New Law of Christianity; for Charity proves true to its character and tends a man fallen among robbers as Faith and Hope take to their heels. The Good Samaritan proceeds to explain to the dreamer that the person who fell among robbers is sinful mankind, and only a God incarnate (God plus man) will be able to redeem it. Whereupon Langland beholds another vision. He imagines he is in Jerusalem on Palm Sunday and sees someone who now looks like the Good Samaritan, now like Piers Plowman riding upon an ass. Faith assures him it is Christ in His human nature, about to go on to His death and to His

* This and the following passage from *The Vision of Piers Plowman,* in the modern English version of Henry Wells, published by Sheed & Ward Inc., New York, 1945, pp. 3, 284.

resurrection which follows. The last section of the poem shows Piers, now the successor of St. Peter, building a great barn, that is, Holy Church. But the good which the cardinal virtues (prudence, justice, fortitude, and temperance) accomplish is largely undone by Anti-Christ. Conscience in desperation calls upon Nature for help, and Nature sends plagues with which to instil in men the fear of God. Yet Anti-Christ is not overcome and even corrupts some inside the Holy Church. Contrition begins to waver. All appears lost. Still Conscience, though sorely tried, refuses to despair:

"By Christ," said Conscience, "I will become a pilgrim
And walk as wide as all the world endures
To seek Piers the Plowman; by him shall Pride perish.
He shall find friars a maintenance who flatter as beggars
Grieving me, Conscience;—grant Nature to avenge me
And send good hap and good health till I have Piers the Plowman."
So he cried for grace, till I began to waken.

The poem is partly a moral survey of mankind, partly a discussion of the nature of Christianity, partly a reflection upon important theological problems. Langland presents a detailed view of the evils of the time and of the failings of men, of commoners, officials, and churchmen. He supplements this with a pattern of repentance which will correct these failings, but a regimen which will involve penance and good works rather than pardons and indulgences. Even famine and unemployment, the twin economic curses of the day, will respond to hard work. Because the poet considers theological questions which no longer interest society and because he makes extensive use of allegory which is occasionally difficult to comprehend, the poem is not easy to read. Yet the poet's deep sincerity, his ability to analyze the weaknesses of human nature, the power and ruggedness of his expression, make his work one of the immortal pieces of English literature. (Reading 94)

Chaucer. Chaucer (d. 1400), Langland's contemporary and countryman, was quite unlike the solemn poet of allegory. The setting of Chaucer's chief work, *The Canterbury Tales*, is religious to be sure. It is a pilgrimage group on its way to England's most celebrated shrine, the tomb of St. Thomas à Becket at Canterbury. Yet this religious background serves only to provide the poet a literary device around which to tell a series of tales. Where Langland wrote in an intensely serious vein, Chaucer wrote principally to amuse and entertain. Langland saw little in life he would not have changed; Chaucer does judge life, but frequently so unobtrusively that it is easy to miss his barbs and ironies. So little is known of Langland's life; even his grave remains a mystery. Fame and honor, on the other hand, were Chaucer's constant companions, and he gives his name to the Poets' Corner in Westminster Abbey. As the son of a moderately well-to-do vintner, Chaucer received a good education, became a favorite valet of Edward III, saw active diplomatic service, held such offices as comptroller of the customs and justice of the peace for the county of Kent, and at length became a member of parliament. Like Wyclif, he owed most of his preferments to the friendship of John of Gaunt, his brother-in-law. Two trips to Italy on the king's business contributed measurably to his literary development. It was his preference for the English spoken in the London circles in which he moved that helped establish that dialect as the basis of modern English.

The body of the *Tales* consists of stories which most of the twenty-nine assorted pilgrims exchanged at The Tabard Inn at Southwark where they had gathered before proceeding on their way to Canterbury. They include, among others, stories by the Knight, Lawyer, Prioress, Monk, Physician, Pardoner, Friar, Squire, Merchant, Franklin, and the Wife of Bath. The tales which Chaucer has his characters tell he drew from a variety of sources: from *fabliaux*, chivalric epics, and chronicles, and from Petrarch. Some of the stories are humorous, others boisterous, a few chivalrous. They reveal Chaucer as a writer with an amazing store of information and a broad knowledge of human nature. What assures *The Canterbury Tales* literary immortality is their mastery of language, the vivid accuracy of descriptive detail, the poet's charming wit and subtle irony, and the deftness of character delineation. Several of his characters have become almost legendary because of the exquisite finesse with which he drew them:

the "elegant Abbess Madam Eglantyne"—

> At meat her manners were well taught withal
> No morsel from her lips did she let fall,
> Nor dipped her fingers in the sauce too deep . . .

the Monk—

> His head was bald and shone as any glass,
> So did his face, as if it had been greased.
> He was a fat and personable priest;
> His bright eyes rolled, they never seemed to settle,
> And glittered like the flames beneath a kettle . . .

the Clerk—

> Long given to Logic, longer than was prudent;
> The horse he had was leaner than a rake,
> And he was not too fat, I undertake,
> And had a hollow look, a sober air;
> And thread upon his overcoat was bare.

Even Chaucer's animals reval the artist's touch. Here is his barnyard rooster about to crow:

> This Chanticleer stood high upon his toes,
> He stretched his neck, his eyes began to close,
> His beak to open; with his eyes shut tight
> He then began to sing with all his might.*

No one has ever questioned Chaucer's poetical talents. But how his-

* *Chaucer: The Canterbury Tales*, tr. Nevill Coghill (Penguin Books), 1952, pp. 28, 30, 33, 252. By permission of Penguin Books Ltd.

torical are the portraits Chaucer paints? One may well wonder. Chaucer's Knight is a "most distinguished man" who from his youth "followed chivalry, truth, honor, greatness of heart and courtesy." There may have been a few knights in Chaucer's day who approached that picture, but they were certainly not typical of the brutal, rapacious aristocracy which was the bane of God and society. Chaucer has only commendation for members of society at his own level or above. The Yeoman is a "sturdy citizen," the Merchant "an excellent fellow," the Franklin a "model among landed gentry," the Lawyer "wary and wise." It is when Chaucer dips below his own social level that he can afford to be caustic. The Miller is a "master hand at stealing grain," the Skipper even worse. "Few were the rules his tender conscience kept." Still this is mild chiding compared to the devastating assault he makes upon members of the clergy, always fair game in the Middle Ages. Only the Parson escapes with his reputation. The most loathsome of body and despicable of soul among Chaucer's characters are the Summoner and Pardoner, but the Monk and Friar are not far behind. Monks and friars and pardoners much as Chaucer describes them might be found in fourteenth-century England, but they were no more typical of their kind than Chaucer's Knight was of his. Perhaps Chaucer in his own way was a reformer after all. Open criticism of the aristocracy, he might have argued, would have jeopardized his career, while, who knows, a few lords might be drawn to emulate the virtues of his "ideal" Knight. Showing the Monk and Friar as negations of the ideal, on the other hand, might serve to arouse the wayward religious to correct their lives.

Dante. The proverb "Never an ill wind that does not blow someone good" was never truer than in the case of Dante (d. 1321). Had it not been for the boiling over of the political caldron that was Florence in the early fourteenth century, which brought the faction known as the Blacks into power and forced the Whites of which Dante was a member into exile, politics might conceivably have absorbed the amazing talents of this genius and the world would never have seen the *Divine Comedy*. For Dante had risen to membership in the six-man magistracy that ruled Florence. Under ordinary circumstances he could have looked forward to an active and distinguished career as one of that city's most honored citizens. All this was ended with his exile at the age of thirty-seven. He lived out the remaining twenty years of his life for the most part in relative poverty and sadness, separated from his wife and family; and far away from the beautiful city he loved. Now this Italian city became his home, now that. In time, between wealthy patrons whom his poetry won him and his own lectures on literary subjects, he acquired sufficient means to close out his last years in reasonable comfort at Ravenna. There reunited with his children he composed the *Paradiso*, the happiest part of his great poem. He died and was buried at Ravenna where his bones still lie, despite the desperate efforts repentant Florence has made to recover its most illustrious citizen.

Beatrice. Two incidents in Dante's life call for comment since both influenced his writing. The first was his chance meeting with Beatrice. He tells how this happened—he was nine years old, she but eight—yet so deeply did the sight of her stir him, that, as he confessed later: "Behold a god stronger than I, that is come to bear rule over me." Dante saw Beatrice on occasion thereafter, but he never courted her. She became the wife of another and died at the early age of twenty-four. She always remained for Dante the embodiment of chaste womanhood which ennobles man. In the *Divine Comedy*, as we shall see, Beatrice becomes the symbol of God's grace: as Dante, the man, is happy in her presence, so the human soul, which the Dante of the poem symbolizes, is happy in the love of God. The other incident that colored his writings was the arrival of Henry VII, the Holy Roman Emperor, in Italy in 1310. Dante hoped that the emperor might restore peace to that distracted peninsula and indirectly make possible his return to his beloved Florence. That hope proved vain, and Dante was fated to take his place with so many other illustrious men in history who have died with their fondest dreams unrealized.

The Vita Nuova, Convivio, De Monarchia, De Vulgari Eloquentia. Dante's catholicity of scholarly interests stands revealed in a variety of writings. His *Vita Nuova*, that is, the "new life" which his admiration of Beatrice had engendered in him, earned him his first acclaim as a poet. It is the story of his love for Beatrice, in which he interrupts his prose narrative with beautiful lyrics in her honor.

> So gentle and so modest doth appear
> My lady when she giveth her salute,
> That every tongue becometh, trembling, mute;
> Nor do the eyes to look upon her dare.

This piece reflects the influence of Provençal lyric poetry, although Dante's love for his Lady is much more sublimated than was that of the traditional troubadour. In his *Convivio* (banquet) Dante planned to introduce the layman to scholastic philosophy and science by means of fourteen courses. He never got beyond the fourth. Again as in the *Vita Nuova*, prose and verse are interspersed with personal references. The *Convivio* reveals the mature student thoroughly committed to the scholastic synthesis as based upon Aristotle and adapted and refined by Aquinas. The *Convivio* was the first scholarly work to appear in Italian. Dante's *De Monarchia* presents the author's political views on the relationship between church and empire. Dante maintained that God expected both church and state to advance his work, but as independent partners. The empire had its authorization directly from God. While Dante opposed any interference in politics by the church as being bound to corrupt that institution, he did insist that the only effective bar to the inevitable tyranny of the state was the acceptance of Christian principles as taught by that church. Yet the state was divinely appointed to exercise control over all temporal matters, even those pertaining to the church. In the *De Vulgari Eloquentia* (On the Use of the Vernacular), also written in Latin so that scholars would read it, Dante argued the cause of the Italian vernacular as an eminently satisfactory vehicle for scholarly expression. He recommended his own Tuscan dialect as superior to the other thirteen then in use in Italy.

Divine Comedy. Dante's greatest work is the *Divine Comedy*. The title may appear strange. Dante called it simply *Commedia,* which meant a story with a happy ending. There is nothing humorous about the *Divine Comedy*, although the story has a happy ending, the happiest, in fact, that any medieval story could have—the admittance of the human soul into the presence of God. For the theme of the *Divine Comedy* is the sanctification of the human soul. It is symbolic of the soul's journey from a state of spiritual misery to one of holy bliss. As Dante explained to his friends: "The whole work was undertaken, not for a speculative, but for a practical end—to remove those who are living in this life from the state of wretchedness and to lead them to a state of blessedness."* Dante's purpose was to show why and how God punishes those who insist upon having their own way, and how he rewards those who choose rather to do his will. Dante seeks to reveal something of the nature and function of hell, purgatory, and heaven. The *Divine Comedy* is the profoundly moving story of man's spiritual regeneration from a condition bordering on unregeneracy, to one of such spiritual excellence that he is able to behold the sight of the Beatific Vision. It is this higher message which caused later generations to join the word "Divine" to Dante's original *Commedia*.

Three-fold Division of the Divine Comedy. The *Divine Comedy* is divided into three parts: the *Inferno* (hell), *Purgatorio* (purgatory), and *Paradiso* (heaven). The story begins with hell: Dante enters hell; he passes through the infernal regions and climbs up to purgatory; then he rises up to heaven. Of course, as the medieval Christian believed, once a soul entered hell, there was no returning. Dante was fully aware of this, and he has inscribed above the frowning portals of hell those awful words so expressive of the horror of hell: "Leave hope behind all ye who enter here." But for the sake of the story Dante must make an exception to the rule of hell. Actually Dante who makes this journey is more than just Dante, the poet, the exile from Florence. He is also the symbol of the human soul, of a soul so lost to sin that nothing short of the revolting and terrifying experience of hell itself can awaken it to the hideousness of sin.

The Inferno. Dante conceives hell as a huge funnel, its top at the earth's surface, its point at the center of the earth. This huge hole Lucifer made when he fell from heaven, and Dante places the prince of devils at the very bottom of the hole, at the center of the earth. Hell is organized into a series of circles, and as Dante climbs down its precipitous sides the atmos-

* Quoted in *The Divine Comedy* (Carlyle-Wicksteed—The Modern Library, 1952), p. 607.

phere grows ever darker, more suffocating and blacker, the stench more oppressive, the noise more deafening. The story begins with Dante lost in a woods, the symbol of the human soul lost in sin.

> I awoke to find myself in a dark wood
> Where the right road was wholly lost and gone.

He spies a mountain, Mount Purgatory, and is about to attempt to climb it, when several ravenous beasts obstruct his way, the beasts symbolizing his own sins externalized. Vergil now appears, sent by Beatrice, as he explains, to help Dante in his extreme peril. Beatrice is here the symbol of God's grace, Vergil the symbol of reason. Dante is presumably so mired in sin that faith can no longer touch him. God hopes that reason may exert some influence, and for that end sends Vergil to become his guide. Vergil tells Dante that before he can scale Mount Purgatory he must go through hell, there to acquire some appreciation of his own depravity and the ugliness of sin. Whereupon Dante and Vergil move on through the gates of hell. They first come to the Limbo of unbaptized souls who may not enter heaven but who suffer none of the punishments of hell. Here Dante sees Socrates and Aristotle, the "master of those that know"; Homer and Horace; and Caesar "with the falcon eyes." The reader might expect to find Caesar farther down on one of the lower levels of hell in view of his manifold crimes, but to Dante, Caesar is the symbol of the Holy Roman Empire. From Limbo the path falls off abruptly and passes down past souls who are being punished for sins that grow progressively more offensive the deeper Dante and his guide proceed toward the center of the earth. The punishments inflicted on the sinners suggest the nature of their sins. Thus the gluttonous wallow in stinking mire, warriors and murderers are immersed in a river of boiling blood, hypocrites stagger about bowed down in gilded cloaks which are lined with lead and which make physical progress as difficult in hell as their hypocrisy made spiritual progress impossible on earth. Down Dante and Vergil move, down to the very pit of hell where they find Satan gnawing in his three mouths the bodies of the three archtraitors of the world: Judas who betrayed Christ, the founder of the church; Brutus and Cassius who betrayed Caesar, the founder of the Empire.

Purgatorio. Dante and Vergil crawl down Satan's hairy legs and pass out through a tunnel, emerging in the southern hemisphere at the base of Mount Purgatory. This mountain was also produced by the impact of Lucifer's fall and corresponded in size and shape to the funnel of hell. Its main levels are seven, each associated with one of the seven deadly or capital sins from which the soul is purged in its progress up the mountain. Hell served to instil in Dante, that is, the human soul, a horror of sin; purgatory serves to eradicate the roots from which sin grows. The names of these sins are inscribed upon Dante's forehead by the porter who guards the gates of purgatory as he gives him admittance. On the first level Dante and Vergil meet the proud who are bent double by an enormous stone on their backs, their bodies unequal to its burden—to symbolize how inferior they were in life to the exalted position to which they had presumed in their pride. After traversing this level, the angel of humility appears and erases the sign of pride from Dante's forehead. On the next level, the vice of envy is purged, the angel of generosity in turn wiping from Dante's forehead the mark of envy—and so on. As Dante and Vergil mount higher in purgatory, in contrast to the darkness and stench of hell which grew ever thicker as they descended, and the scowls and blasphemies which the impenitent hurled at them, the atmosphere now grows lighter, the birds begin to sing, and smiles and benedictions greet them from the penitents they meet. After passing the seventh level, Dante enters the Earthly Paradise, which "was empty now because of her fault who gave ear to the Serpent." Dante drank of two rivers before leaving Purgatory, the first, the Lethe, the mythological river of forgetfulness, in order to erase all memory of evil and sin; the second, the Eunoe, that is, the water of Good Remembrance, to restore so much of the memory of sin as was necessary to stimulate the soul to further spiritual progress, and to symbolize God's power to turn even sin to serve his purpose.

Heaven.   Leaving the earthly Paradise, Dante begins his ascent through the different spheres of the heavens, but now with another guide. Vergil must be left behind since he is unbaptized. Vergil, too, as the symbol of reason, would be helpless before the mysteries of heaven. Beatrice, who is the symbol of faith and revelation, comes forward to serve as Dante's new guide and interpreter. She answers those of Dante's many queries which she can; other problems she assures him will be clarified as they make further progress in their ascent. Dante notices as he ascends that he feels no bodily weight any longer, and Beatrice explains that since he is in heaven he is now subject to the gravitational pull of God and necessarily moves upward. Dante and Beatrice pass through the spheres of the moon, the sun, and the different planets, each sphere possessing its own spiritual significance and symbolism. Thus in the sphere of Mars they encounter such medieval warriors as Charlemagne and Roland who fought for Christianity. In the sphere of Saturn, who was the Roman god of the golden age of simplicity, they meet St. Benedict and other distinguished monks. They see St. Thomas Aquinas, the Dominican, who speaks to them of the heroic sanctity of St. Francis of Assisi; then Bonaventure, the Franciscan, who discourses upon the spiritual wisdom of St. Dominic. Dante places souls at different levels in their relationship to God, even though as saints they all enjoy his presence, in order to show how they vary in their capacity to penetrate the mysteries of heaven. Yet regardless of the proximity of the blessed to God, they are all completely happy and content, for such is the rule of heaven. Where discord and hate prevail in hell, in heaven harmony and love are supreme. Once Dante and Beatrice ascend to the ninth heaven,

St. Bernard takes over as guide. Bernard, the mystic renowned on earth for his love of God, is here the symbol of divine wisdom which alone is capable of penetrating the mysteries of the upper heavens before which Beatrice, the symbol of faith, is impotent. But Bernard in turn must eventually give place to Mary, the mother of God, who is alone able to prepare Dante for the ultimate vision of him who is the "love that moves the sun and the other stars." Now that Dante has attained the sight of the Beatific Vision, of God Himself, his journey is over, his sanctification is completed, and so is his story. The glories of God are so transcendent that not only do direct words fail, but the use of symbols to convey meaning becomes futile, and Dante grows silent.

In the midst of presenting the soaring theme of the *Divine Comedy*, Dante stoops now and then to express his views on more mundane questions. We hear echoes of the argument of the *De Monarchia*, even of the *De Vulgari Eloquentia*. Dante gains a measure of revenge over several of his political enemies by consigning them to hell, although artistic honesty forces him to meet an occasional friend there too. The avarice of the papacy comes in for criticism as well as the worldliness of those Franciscans who no longer led the self-effacing life of their sainted founder. The reader who cannot appreciate the beauty of the poetry is most impressed by the poet's extraordinary erudition. So recondite, in fact, are many of the classical allusions, so fine the theological lessons drawn, so extensive the amount of medieval philosophy and science woven into the story, that it must be read with the help of a commentary. Withal the *Divine Comedy* represents the greatest piece of scholarly artistry ever produced. The richness and delicacy of Dante's imagery have scarcely ever been equalled; the rhythm of his superbly beautiful Italian remains untranslatable. His most recent translator confesses: "when Dante chooses to be sheerly beautiful, he writes not like a man but like an angel."* Dante's brilliance of characterization, his economy of language, the architectural grandeur of his theme have drawn the reverent praise of many poets. Perhaps no other work of literature has aroused so much admiration in so many countries and so many readers as the *Divine Comedy*.

Petrarch. Petrarch (d. 1374) was another exile from Florence. He planned initially to become a lawyer, but gave this up for the priesthood, probably less from spiritual motives than for the greater leisure that life would leave him for study. At any rate, he was no credit to the church. His most famous poems are exquisitely beautiful love sonnets penned in honor of Laura, a married woman. Yet he assumed on occasion the role of religious critic and, despite the sensuality of his verse, revealed a genuine attraction to asceticism. Petrarch was among those few illustrious poets who have won acclaim in their own lifetimes. Feted by the aristocracy and crowned poet laureate of Italy, he protested his inability to account for this unbounded

* Dorothy Sayers, *The Comedy of Dante Alighieri: Hell* (Penguin, 1951), p. 64.

admiration. "They may know why, I certainly do not," he said. He surely did not assess his Italian poetry in the manner posterity has, and in time turned away from the vernacular to devote his remarkable talents instead to the barren composition of classical Latin verse. (See page 707.) His fame, needless to say, rests upon some three hundred sonnets in Italian which rank with literature's finest lyrics. Perhaps no other medieval poet exerted as much influence upon later literary developments as did Petrarch. He remains one of the truly great literary figures of the Middle Ages. (Reading 173)

Boccaccio. Boccaccio (d. 1375) was Petrarch's disciple and admirer. He completes the most celebrated trio of writers any city ever produced within so short a space of time. He was the son of a Florentine merchant, dabbled for a time in French literature, and composed a series of poetical pieces in honor of his Fiametta ("little flame"). All thought of becoming a poet evaporated, however, when he read Petrarch's matchless sonnets. Instead he turned to prose and with the *Decameron* earned for himself the title of "father of Italian prose." The setting of the *Decameron* is a castle in which a company of seven young women and three young men isolate themselves during an outbreak of the Black Death. In the process of providing this setting, Boccaccio has left posterity the most graphic and accurate medieval account of that dread plague. The tales, a hundred of them, which the young men and women exchange to while the time away, are new only for the graceful and clever style in which they are written. The themes are old for the most part, and go back to classical sources and to the *fabliaux*. As in the *fabliaux*, womankind and the clergy are the butts of most of the humor. Like Petrarch, Boccaccio expended his talents during his last years on the study of the classics. (Reading 174)

Art in the Late Middle Ages

The late Middle Ages witnessed significant developments in the fields of painting, sculpture, and architecture. Art like literature was coming of age, that is, it was beginning to reflect the aesthetic interests of a civilization well on its way to cultural maturity. Of these late-medieval developments we may single out first the introduction of secularism into art. Until the fourteenth century, the church had absorbed most of the efforts of architects, painters (illuminated manuscripts), and sculptors. Now the growing affluence of the aristocracy and bourgeoisie enabled secular elements to bring forward their claims to a share of the work of these artists. The student of late-medieval art must study not only churches, but gild halls, civic buildings, colleges, and palaces as well; and he will find many paintings and sculptures of nonreligious subjects to hold his attention along with those of a traditionally religious nature. As ever greater demands came to be made upon medieval artists by an increasingly diversified group of patrons with tastes and ideas of their own, art showed a tendency not only to expand enormously, but to separate into its major component branches of architecture, painting, and sculpture. Another development of the late Middle Ages followed inevitably once the individualism inherent in the arts was given free rein. This was the emergence of actual painters, sculptors, and architects from out of the anonymity of the gild. The history of art in the late Middle Ages is almost a history of artists. As the late-medieval artist developed greater skill and experience, he was able to demonstrate finally his ability to portray his subjects more truthfully and to invest them with greater character than had been possible since ancient Greek times. A final development in late-medieval art was the appearance of a neoclassical art in Italy, which was largely a reflection of the Italian interest of the fifteenth century in classical antiquity. (See page 703.)

Architecture.   The late Middle Ages witnessed two major developments in the field of architecture. The first was the tendency of Gothic to become more elaborate. This late Gothic is known as Decorated in England, as Flamboyant in France. A second development was the appearance of a neoclassic style, notably in Italy, which for want of a better term is known as Renaissance style. The trend toward an embellished Gothic is strikingly exemplified in the two spires of the cathedral at Chartres. (See picture, page 696.) The spire on the left (facing the cathedral) dates from the early sixteenth century, some three hundred and fifty years after the spire on the right was constructed. Its richer ornamentation marks the only direction toward which Gothic could turn. Complicated tracery and lace-like stonework, particularly on the façade and spires, reveal the tendency of late

Right: Palazzo
Strozzi, Florence
Left: Bruges
Town Hall
*Official Belgian
Tourist Bureau.*

King's College Chapel, Cambridge   Chartres

Gothic to divorce decoration from construction. Where in classical Gothic
statues had been secured in the masonry, now they are standing free and
complete in themselves. Even the vaults above the nave and aisles reflect
the preference for greater ornateness. One of the most impressive examples
of this trend is that provided by the fan vault of King's College Chapel, in
Cambridge. (See picture, page 696.)

The architecture of late-medieval Italy reveals a style almost as distinctive as Romanesque. Its birth in Italy may be explained by the presence
of many classical ruins, especially in Rome, and the failure of Gothic to
spread south of the Po. Hot, sunny Italy had little love for the glass walls
of the Gothic church. Yet paradoxically, the first important edifice to suggest the new classical tendencies was the Gothic cathedral of Florence.
Brunelleschi (d. 1446) had been commissioned to construct its tremendous
dome despite his stubborn refusal to reveal his plans to the board of direc-
tors lest he be given less than full credit for his achievement—striking
testimony to the passing of the old order which had obscured the talents
of individual architects in the collectivism of the gild. Before proffering his
services, Brunelleschi had made a thorough study of the Roman Pantheon,
the largest domed building from classical antiquity. The dome he erected
for the Florence cathedral was consequently not pure Gothic. Its structural
facts are subordinated to formal effect, and the essential buttressing is
buried in the masonry. Where Gothic owed much of its artistic beauty to
the close correlation between structural lines and decoration, in the Renaissance structures of late-medieval Italy the engineering facts are generally
hidden under an effective covering of classical decorative motifs and
devices. The Palazzo Strozzi and Medici-Riccardi Palace in Florence are

prime examples of Renaissance architecture, not because of their construction, which is quite conventional, but because of the manner in which interior and exterior surfaces are covered. Horizontal mouldings mark different levels in elevation of the walls; windows are outlined by classical columns or pilasters, arches, and architraves, while facing the top of the structure is the ornate crowning cornice of the roof. Pilasters, coffered panels and ceilings, rosettes, round arches, and entablatures embellish the interiors. More basically classical construction is provided by the mammoth barrel vaults, round arches, and tremendous dome of such grandiose structures as St. Peter's church.

Sculpture. Significantly new developments in medieval sculpture were presaged as early as the thirteenth century in the work of Nicola Pisano (d. *ca.* 1278). Pisano studied ancient Roman sarcophagi in the hope of recapturing the lost art of representing men, women, and nature more truthfully. So successful were his efforts that he was able to show the form of the human body underneath its exterior drapery, and more than any of his contemporaries to give it a natural and relaxed pose. That Pisano was not alone in his endeavors to achieve greater realism is evident from the sculptured figures of Ekkehart and Uta in the Gothic cathedral of Naumburg (*ca.* 1260). Ekkehart and Uta are portrayed as actual persons who could have looked in life essentially as they now appear in stone. Interest in greater naturalism and accuracy of detail moved steadily forward and

Florence Cathedral

Italian State Tourist Office

Doors of Paradise: Ghiberti   St. Peter's

attained a new level of eminence in the late fourteenth-century work of
the Netherlander Claus Sluter (d. 1405). Sluter's Moses is no pallid echo,
but the living image of the venerable patriarch of the Hebrews whose
untiring solicitude and adamantine will alone preserved his people from
destruction. The most illustrious medieval sculptors were the great Florentine trio of Ghiberti (d. 1455), Donatello (d. 1466), and Verrochio (d. 1488).
Ghiberti distinguished himself as a master of relief sculpture. The bronze
doors which he executed for the Baptistry of San Giovanni in Florence
were acclaimed by Michelangelo as worthy to serve as the gates of paradise.
It was Ghiberti's knowledge of the laws of perspective which enabled him
to add a degree of naturalism to his figures that had never before been
achieved by any medieval sculptor. The genius of Donatello, the greatest
of all medieval sculptors, stands best revealed in his ability to individualize
his subjects and to invest them with personality. His David is the first
unclothed figure of monumental character of the period. By leaving off
the clothes Donatello could demonstrate most convincingly his ability to
portray the human body exactly as the historical circumstances of the
subject demanded. Verrochio incorporated in his condottiere Colleoni
something of the nervous energy which characterized the ebullient life of
north Italy in the fifteenth century.

Painting. The most spectacular developments in the realm of art in the
late Middle Ages came in the field of painting. The fact that the medieval
painter, unlike the sculptor, had no classical models from which to work,
makes his achievement all the more impressive. The artist who inaugurated a new epoch in painting and thereby won for himself the title of
"father of modern painting" was Giotto (d. 1337). His "revolution" con-

Giraudon

Limbourg Bros: Les Très Riches Heures du Duc de Berry (month of June)

sisted in securing greater naturalism in his subjects than that attained by any of his contemporaries, an achievement made possible through his earnest study of Byzantine paintings and mosaics. Though these were typically flat and rigid in their appearance, they did provide him an introduction to the principle of foreshortening and revealed a shading and mixture of colors far superior to anything known in the west. Giotto achieved his objective of informing his figures with life and emotion by working out a scheme of light and shadow. The figures in his *Lamentation* are human beings, not just human representations. They feel, move, and express the emotions of living men and women. This trend toward naturalism which Giotto initiated received powerful encouragement from Masaccio (d. 1428), a veritable genius, who died before he had completed his twenty-eighth year. Masaccio was able to invest his figures with such truthfulness of expression and movement that the renowned trio of early sixteenth-century artists, Leonardo da Vinci, Michelangelo, and Raphael, turned to his famous work, *The Tribute Money*, to learn how to invest their own paintings and sculptures with the quiet simplicity of this genius.

Oil Painting.   The artist's search for the means to achieve complete truthfulness of expression came appreciably nearer success with the introduction of oil painting. The great advantage of oil over other liquids for the purpose of binding the colored powder into a kind of paste was that

Right: Gattamelata by Donatello (detail)

Below: Gattamelata by Donatello

Right: Colleoni by Verrochio

Left: Presentation by Niccolò Pisano

oil set less quickly, thus permitting the artist more time in which to shade colors into each other. The invention of oil painting has been ascribed to Jan van Eyck (d. 1441), the leading representative of the Flemish school of painting. For van Eyck a slow-drying paint was indispensable, since he sought to create the illusion of depth, not through the use of perspective and foreshortening as in Italy, but by means of elaborate detail, delicately colored and carefully arranged as to spacial relationships. His *Arnolfini and His Wife* portrays two people who possess distinct personalities, who display emotions, who even appear a bit self-conscious over the presence of the painter. The room in which they stand contains a number of incidental objects, all of them exquisitely drawn, even to the grain in the wood flooring, yet all the details are carefully subordinated so as not to destroy the unity of the picture which demands that husband and wife remain the center of attention.

Late Medieval Developments in Painting. With his knowledge of anatomy, foreshortening, and perspective, and his possession of a rich variety of colors, the late-medieval painter was able to produce a wealth of pictures whose colorful attractiveness, delicate shading, and intriguing themes appear all the more engaging for the suddenness with which this art evolved. Several developments which were new to the painter's art call for comment. One was the large number and variety of incidental objects such as rocks, grass, trees, scarfs, jewelry, flowers, and furniture, which the painter drew into his picture. Another was the appearance of portraits of living men and women, actually sat for and purchased by wealthy members of the bourgeoisie and aristocracy, who wanted them for their homes. A third departure from earlier conventions was the omission of religious symbolism from pictures of saints and angels. A fourth was the occasional introduction of subjects drawn from classical mythology such as Botticelli's the *Birth of Venus*, an echo of humanism which was influencing the intellectual life of Italy at the time.

An observation which frequently suggests itself on the basis of these developments is that painting was no longer the handmaid of the church it had once been and that even religious art itself was not so religious any more; that rising secularism and a growing indifference to religion were stirring in men a uniquely nonmedieval interest in the world about them. Such an analysis may possess a measure of validity, but it is apt to lose sight of less subjective factors which might better account for these developments. The lack of symbolism in religious paintings, for instance, can be adequately explained in the artist's wish to inform his subject directly with spirituality by having facial expression and posture convey this impression rather than falling back upon such "crutches" as halos and Bibles. The appearance of subjects drawn from mythology does not necessarily reflect a spirit hostile to Christianity. As we shall presently see, popes were frequently in the forefront of the humanism which bred this interest in pagan antiquities. The inclusion of landscape and natural objects into pictures simply reveals the continuing interest of the Middle Ages in the things of nature. Natural objects also provided the artist a particularly challenging opportunity to display his talents, since the hues which nature employs are generally more subdued and more delicate in their shading than those of man-made objects. That late-medieval men desired portraits of themselves should occasion little surprise. Such a longing men have always entertained since paleolithic times. But medieval man did not sit for a portrait before the fifteenth century, not because of his earlier presumed preoccupation with things eternal, but because all the artist could have given him at any time previous would have been a flat representation of the species *homo sapiens* with his own name inscribed beneath. The fact remains, finally, that the great majority of sculptures and paintings of the fifteenth century continued to be of religious themes.

Italian Humanism

The reappearance of classical art forms in Italy during the closing centuries of the Middle Ages accompanied or reflected a parallel revival of interest in classical literature and thought on the part of Italian humanists. The father of this late medieval humanism was Petrarch, and it was also Petrarch who fathered the idea of a "renaissance," the term frequently used to identify the transitional centuries between the high Middle Ages and modern times. What was reviving and being restored to life in Petrarch's opinion was the classical culture of Greece and Rome which had lain dormant since the fourth century. Petrarch and his humanist contemporaries branded the centuries intervening since the decline of Rome as "dark ages," as it was their fond conviction that here in their own fourteenth century they were rekindling the lights of that splendid world of Cicero, Vergil, and Livy. No passing fancy was this, and so vigorous and sustained proved this fascination for the classical past, that it induced writers as distinguished as Petrarch and Boccaccio to abandon brilliant careers in vernacular literature in order to devote their time and talents to this new passion.

Earlier and Italian Humanism. This humanism of the late Middle Ages shared that admiration for the style of Cicero and Vergil which had stirred earlier humanists like John of Salisbury. Like this earlier humanism, that of Italy in the fourteenth and fifteenth centuries produced a scattering of poets, essayists, and letter-writers who sought to emulate the literary excellence of classical authors with compositions of their own. If the products of this Italian humanism were not appreciably superior to those of an

Fra Lippi: Madonna and Child

earlier middle age, its failure was not due to lack of motivation. For this new group of humanists would not stop with the literary beauty of classical literature; they hoped to recapture its spirit, in fact discover in its richness and variety the secret of that urbanity and cultural sophistication which they believed had marked the Roman gentleman of classical times. These humanists of the late Middle Ages were laymen for the most part or priests and bishops who thought and wrote as laymen, whereas the representatives of earlier humanism were exclusively religious. And the number of late medieval humanists far exceeded that of earlier centuries as they far outshone them in their enthusiasm. Nevertheless, despite the great

Masaccio: Tribute Money

attention some modern scholars have paid it, Italian humanism touched only a small group of intellectuals, real and assumed, and was limited for its recruits to the aristocracy, clergy, and wealthy bourgeoisie and to the few beneath this level who were fortunate to find patrons. Scarcely before 1500, that is several generations after the introduction of humanistic studies into the schools, did this circle of humanists widen sufficiently to constitute a representative portion of society.

Humanism and Education. Surely its influence upon education must be counted Italian humanism's most enduring contribution to Western thought. The first schools to broaden the study of grammar and bid welcome to literature and history were what might be called the secondary schools of the day. By the close of the Middle Ages many communities could boast of such "Latin" schools. Though universities refused to break with their theology-oriented curriculum before the Protestant Reformation, humanistic studies did manage to effect an entry, and at the turn of the century Martin Luther was studying Vergil, Ovid, and Juvenal at the university of Erfurt. The leading centers of humanistic studies in the late Middle Ages, however, were privately supported "academies," such as that maintained by the Medici in Florence. By 1500, because of the influence of humanism, liberal education with its more secular philosophy and greater emphasis upon language and literature had acquired in large measure the character it has today.

Classical Manuscripts. Perhaps the most visible witness to the activities of Italian humanists in the late Middle Ages was their avid search for classical manuscripts. This search carried them to places as distant as Crete and Denmark, although the majority of the manuscripts brought to life turned up in medieval monasteries like Bobbio and St. Gall. (Reading 175) The accumulation of manuscripts led inevitably to the establishment of libraries, and renowned institutions as the Vatican and Laurentian

(Medici) libraries date from this period. A status symbol of the aristocracy of the fifteenth century, indeed, was the possession of a number of classical manuscripts. The science of textual criticism was born of the need to produce correct editions of classical works, and spectacular fruit of the new critical approach came with the humanist Lorenzo Valla's announcement that he had proved the Donation of Constantine a forgery. Not only books, but coins, gems, medals, and statuary were lovingly collected, and one might assign the birth of archaeology to the year 1462 when the humanist Pope Pius II forbade further use of the Colosseum and Rome's other historic monuments as "quarries."

Humanism's Literary Achievement.   The literary production of humanism was impressive in volume but in little else. Few literary ages have left so meager a legacy for the instruction and entertainment of future generations —and this is understandable. Because humanists sought to revive, at best recapture, not create, imagination and originality which are the marks of great literature are wanting in their writings. Theirs also lacked any stylistic pre-eminence, since the best Latin they wrote fell short of Cicero's and Vergil's. Only Petrarch's humanist friends agreed with him in ridiculing the Italian poetry which had brought Dante high fame. "Who indeed could excite envy in me," boasted Petrarch, "who do not envy Vergil?" No work

Giotto: Lamentation

Alinari—Art Reference Bureau

of this period better reveals the dedication of Italian humanism to the goal of reviving the classical past, nor the immense labors expended on a task which was apt to be literarily sterile, than Petrarch's own long, heavy, uninspiring epic entitled *Africa*. (Its hero is the great Scipio.) And the irony of it all was that in their growing intolerance toward the use of any Latin word which failed of listing in a Ciceronian concordance, the humanists killed the very language they were worshipping.

More successful was the historical writing which the study of Livy and Tacitus prompted many humanists to undertake. No longer the rambling narrative of medieval "Christian" chroniclers, but an organized, style-conscious, rationalistic presentation of past politics and wars, which was still not modern history but more professional even though less interesting.

Revival of Greek Studies. The revival of Greek studies was the principal feature of fifteenth century humanism. Petrarch, in the forefront of the movement, could only admire, not read, the few Greek manuscripts that came into his hands, but by the end of the Middle Ages a knowledge of Greek was no longer rare in Italy, and Greek manuscripts graced the libraries of many humanists. The Byzantine scholar Manuel Chrysoloras was the only teacher of Greek in Italy at the beginning of the fifteenth century, but more came with the councils of Ferrara and Florence, others with the fall of Constantinople, while the enthusiasm of some humanists carried them to Greece to learn the language. Plato rather than Aristotle appealed to the humanists, and poetry, history, and oratory, rather than science. While earlier medieval thought was impregnated with Platonism, particularly in the form of Neoplatonism, the scholastics of the universities had almost nothing of Plato himself to study. Now all of Plato's important writings became available, although what most intrigued the humanists was the Greek philosopher's superb style and his idealism. Even the fact that Plato could be more easily reconciled with Christianity on such fundamental points as the immortality of the soul recommended him to certain humanists. The most prominent center of Platonic studies was the Academy at Florence which the Medici maintained, and to which the fame of its distinguished luminary Marsilio Ficino attracted many students from outside Italy. The leading "philosopher" of this Academy was Pico della Mirandola. His attempt to produce a synthesis of the world's wisdom from Christian, pagan Greek, Arabic, Hebrew, and Persian sources, expressed the broadened perspective most humanists claimed they were employing in their study of mankind.

Humanism and Medieval Christianity. What impact did humanism have upon medieval Christianity? With interests and philosophies so opposite, should not one expect the history of their relationship in the fourteenth and fifteenth centuries to have been one of friction and estrangement? That is true, but only had the popes of the period been St. Bernards, for St. Bernard would not have countenanced anything which was not positively Christian. As it was, the popes of the fourteenth and fifteenth centuries either viewed humanism with indifference or like Nicholas V and Pius II contributed to the eventual transfer of the capital of humanism from Florence to Rome. Even the ambition of some humanists to develop a non-Christian system of ethics based upon Cicero and Seneca posed no threat to religion, since few humanists recognized any essential conflict between their obligations to God and their cultural interests. The humanist citizen envisaged by Pico della Mirandola in his *Oration on the Dignity of Man* would still have observed the Ten Commandments and have hearkened to the instructions of the church. A free-thinking humanist like Valla had humanist friends who were devout Christians, while between these extremes moved the great majority of their fellows, neither the better nor the worse for their humanism. Some of the humanist interest in Plato, as noted above, sprang from the conviction, earlier emphasized by St. Augustine, that Platonists were closest to Christianity. Actually humanist interest in the classical past had also extended to a study of the church fathers. Humanism was no foe of Christianity, although a bitter critic of scholastic domination of the world of the intellect. Because of this latter antagonism and of its success in winning this contest, humanism did contribute measurably to the gradual secularization of culture and to the passing of the old medieval order.

Claus Sluter:
The Well of Moses

Monuments Historiques des Caisse Nationale

READINGS

No. 162. Thomas à Kempis' *Imitation of Christ*

The Imitation of Christ, tr. Leo Sherley-Price. Penguin Books, 1952.
(By permission of Penguin Books Ltd.)

Ch. 1. Counsels on the Spiritual Life (pp. 27-28)

"He who follows Me shall not walk in darkness," says Our Lord.

In these words Christ counsels us to follow His life and way if we desire true enlightenment and freedom from all blindness of heart. Let the life of Jesus Christ, then, be our first consideration.

The teaching of Jesus far transcends all the teachings of the Saints, and whosoever has His spirit will discover concealed in it heavenly manna. But many people, although they often hear the Gospel, feel little desire to follow it, because they lack the spirit of Christ. Whoever desires to understand and take delight in the words of Christ must strive to conform his whole life to Him.

Of what use is it to discourse learnedly on the Trinity, if you lack humility and therefore displease the Trinity? Lofty words do not make a man just or holy; but a good life makes him dear to God. I would far rather feel contrition than be able to define it. If you knew the whole Bible by heart, and all the teachings of the philosophers, how would this help you without the grace and love of God? "Vanity of vanities, and all is vanity," except to love God and serve Him alone. And this is supreme wisdom—to despise the world, and draw daily nearer the kingdom of heaven.

Is it vanity to solicit honours, or to raise oneself to high station? It is vanity to be a slave to bodily desires, and to crave for things which bring certain retribution. It is vanity to wish for a long life, if you care little for

709

a good life. It is vanity to give thought only to this present life, and to care nothing for the life to come. It is vanity to love things that so swiftly pass away, and not to hasten onwards to the place where everlasting joy abides.

Keep constantly in mind the saying, "The eye is not satisfied with seeing, nor the ear filled with hearing." Strive to withdraw your heart from the love of visible things, and direct your affections to things invisible. For those who follow only their natural inclinations defile their conscience, and lose the grace of God.

Ch. 23. A Meditation on Death (pp. 56-59)

Very soon the end of your life will be at hand: consider, therefore, the state of your soul. Today a man is here; tomorrow he is gone. And when he is out of sight, he is soon out of mind. Oh, how dull and hard is the heart of man, which thinks only of the present, and does not provide against the future! You should order your every deed and thought, as though today were the day of your death. Had you a good conscience, death would hold no terrors for you; even so, it were better to avoid sin than to escape death. If you are not ready to die today, will tomorrow find you better prepared? Tomorrow is uncertain; and how can you be sure of tomorrow?

Of what use is a long life, if we amend so little? Alas, a long life often adds to our sins rather than to our virtue! Would to God that we might spend a single day really well! Many recount the years since their conversion, but their lives show little sign of improvement. If it is dreadful to die, it is perhaps more dangerous to live long. Blessed is the man who keeps the hour of his death always in mind, and daily prepares himself to die. If you have ever seen anyone die, remember that you, too, must travel the same road.

Each morning remember that you may not live until evening; and in the evening, do not presume to promise yourself another day. Be ready at all times, and so live that death may never find you unprepared. Many die suddenly and unexpectedly; for at an hour that we do not know the Son of Man will come. When your last hour strikes, you will begin to think very differently of your past life, and grieve deeply that you have been so careless and remiss. . . .

Keep yourself a stranger and pilgrim upon earth, to whom the affairs of this world are of no concern. Keep your heart free and lifted up to God, for here you have no abiding city. Daily direct your prayers and longings to Heaven, that at your death your soul may merit to pass joyfully into the presence of God.

No. 163. Meister Eckhart

(*Meister Eckhart's Mystische Schriften*, tr. into modern German by Gustav Landauer. Berlin, 1903, pp. 165-168. Translation.

Concerning Detachment

I have read many books, both by pagan authorities and by prophets, and read also the Old and the New Testament, and with earnestness and complete diligence have I endeavored to learn what the best and highest virtue is which can draw man closest to God, or possessing which man would be most like to the image God had of him before Creation when there was nothing [like sin] to separate him from God. And were I to search all remaining literature and study and examine it to the best of my ability, I should find nothing other than pure detachment, that is, detachment from all creatures. That is why our Lord said to Martha: "one thing is necessary," which meant nothing more than that whoever wishes to be untroubled and pure must possess one virtue, that is, the virtue of detachment.

Teachers indeed praise love highly, as for example St. Paul when he says: "Whatsoever I might do, if I have not love, I have nothing." Yet I extol detachment more than love. My first reason is that what is good about love is that it forces me to love God. Now it is far better that I force God to come to me than that I force myself to go to God. And this is true because my very salvation depends upon this, that I am united with God. But God can more readily adapt Himself to me and join me than I Him. Detachment brings God to me, which I can demonstrate in this way: everything prefers indeed its natural condition. Now the natural condition of God is simplicity and purity: these spring from detachment. Therefore God must of necessity give Himself to the soul that is detached.

A second reason why I place detachment above love is that love obliges me to accept everything that pleases the will of God, while detachment obliges me to be sensitive to nothing except to God. Now it is far better to be sensitive to nothing other than God than it is to suffer all for the sake of God. For when one suffers, one takes one look as it were at the creature who has caused him to suffer. Detachment, on the other hand, is completely divorced from the consideration of all creatures. That such detachment is sensitive to God alone I prove by arguing that what is experienced must in some way be experienced. But detachment is so close to Nothing, that there is nothing so precious that it can make a place for itself in a detached heart.

The authorities also praise humility above many other virtues. I place detachment above humility and for this reason. Humility can exist without detachment; detachment, on the other hand, cannot exist without humility. For perfect humility has as its goal self-abasement. Yet detachment comes so very closely to Nothing that nothing can get between it and Nothing. For this reason there can be no perfect detachment without humility, and two virtues are always better than one.

The other reason why I prefer detachment to humility is this, that perfect humility denies itself before all creatures. Yet in the very act of self-denial, the person pays some attention to other creatures. Detachment, however, remains in itself. For never can any self-abasement reach such a point that self-containment cannot rise still higher. Perfect detachment concerns itself with nothing; it considers itself neither below nor above any creatures; it neither desires to be below or above; it wants to remain within itself, being neither a source of affection or of sorrow to anyone; it wills neither equality nor inequality, to have neither this or that in common with any creature; it wants nothing other than to be alone. Therefore nothing of any kind will be troubled by it.

I also prefer detachment to mercy, since mercy is nothing else than that a person goes outside himself upon the complaint of a fellow-man and permits his heart to be disturbed. Detachment is free from this, remains in itself, and permits itself to be affected by nothing. In short, when I examine all virtues, I find none so free of deficiencies and so tending toward God than detachment.

No. 164. *Clericis Laicos*

(*Translations and Reprints*, III, No. 6, pp. 21-23.)

Bishop Boniface, servant of the servants of God, in perpetual memory of this matter. Antiquity shows us that the laity has always been exceeding hostile to the clergy; and this the experience of the present time clearly demonstrates, since, not content with their limitations, the laity strive for forbidden things and give free reign to the pursuit of illicit gain.

They do not prudently observe that all control over the clergy, as well as over all ecclesiastical persons and their possessions, is denied them, but impose heavy burdens upon the prelates of the churches, upon the churches themselves, and upon ecclesiastical persons both regular and secular, exacting talliages and other contributions from them. From such persons they require and extort the payment of a half, a tenth, a twentieth or some other quota of their property or income, and strive in many other ways to subject the churchmen to slavery and bring them under their control.

And (with grief do we declare it) certain prelates of the churches and ecclesiastical persons, fearing where they ought not to fear, and seeking a temporary peace, dreading to offend a temporal more than the eternal majesty, do, without having received the permission or sanction of the Apostolic See, acquiese in such abuses, not so much from recklessness, as want of foresight. We, therefore, desiring to check these iniquitous practices, by the council of our brothers, do, of our apostolic authority, decree that whatever prelates and ecclesiastical persons, whether monastic or secular, whatever their order, condition or status, shall pay, or promise or agree to pay to laymen, any contributions or talliages, tenths, twentieths or hundredths of their own, or their churches' revenues or possessions, or shall pay any sum, portion or part of their revenues or goods, or of their estimated or actual value, in the form of an aid, loan, subvention, subsidy or gift, or upon any other pretense or fiction whatsoever, without authority from this same Apostolic See,—likewise emperors, kings and princes, dukes, counts, barons, podesta, captains, officers, rectors, whatever their title, of cities, castles or other places wherever situated, or any other persons, whatever their rank, condition or status, who shall impose, exact or receive such payments, or who shall presume to lay hands upon, seize or occupy the possessions of churches, or of ecclesiastical persons deposited in the sacred edifices, or who shall order such to be seized or occupied, or shall receive such things as shall be seized or occupied,—likewise all who shall consciously lend aid, council or support in such undertakings, either publicly or privately,—shall, by the very act, incur the sentence of excommunication; corporations, moreover, which shall show themselves guilty in these matters, we place under the interdict. . . .

No. 165. *Unam Sanctam*

(*Translations and Reprints*, III, No. 6, pp. 19-21.)

That there is one Holy Catholic and Apostolic church we are impelled by our faith to believe and to hold—this we do firmly believe and openly confess—and outside of this there is neither salvation or remission of sins. . . .

In this church and in its power are two swords, to wit, a spiritual and a temporal, and this we are taught by the words of the Gospel, for when the Apostles said, "Behold, here are two swords," (in the church, namely, since the apostles were speaking), the Lord did not reply that it was too many, but enough. And surely he who claims that the temporal sword is not in the power of Peter, has but ill understood the word of our Lord when he said, "Put up thy sword in its scabbard." Both, therefore, the spiritual and the material swords, are in the power of the church, the latter indeed to be used for the church, the former by the church, the one by the priest, the other by the hand of kings and soldiers, but by the will and sufferance of the priest. It is fitting, moreover, that one sword should be under the other, and the temporal authority subject to the spiritual power. For when the apostle said, "there is no power but of God and the powers that are of God are ordained," they would not be ordained unless one sword were under the other, and one, as inferior, was brought back by the other to the highest place. . . . It behooves us, therefore, the more freely to confess that the spiritual power excels in dignity and nobility any form whatsoever of earthly power, as spiritual interests exceed the temporal in importance. All this we see fairly from the giving of tithes, from the benediction and sanctification, from the recognition of this power and the control of these same things. For the truth bearing witness, it is for the spiritual power to establish the earthly power and judge it, if it be not good. Thus, in the case of the church and the power of the church, the prophecy of Jeremiah is fulfilled: "See, I have this day set thee over the nations and over the kingdoms"—and what follows. Therefore, if the earthly power shall err, it shall be judged by the spiritual power, if the lesser spiritual power err, it shall be judged by the higher. But if the supreme power err, it can be judged by God alone and not by man, the apostles bearing witness saying, the spiritual man judges all things but he himself is judged by no one. Hence this power, although given to man and exercised by man, is not human, but rather a divine power, given by the divine lips to Peter, and founded on a rock for Him and his successors in Him [Christ] whom he confessed; the Lord saying to Peter himself, "Whatsoever thou shalt bind" etc. Whoever, therefore, shall resist this power, ordained by God, resists the ordination of God, unless there should be two beginnings, as the Manichaean imagines. But this we judge to be false and heretical, since, by the testimony of Moses, not in the beginnings, but in the beginning, God created the heaven and the earth. We, moreover, proclaim, declare and pronounce that it is altogether necessary to salvation for every human being to be subject to the Roman Pontiff. . . .

Given at the Lateran the twelfth day before the Kalends of December, in our eighth year, as a perpetual memorial of this matter.

No. 166. Marsiglio's own conclusions from his *Defensor Pacis*

(Thatcher & McNeal, *Source Book*, pp. 318-323.)

1. The one divine canonical Scripture, the conclusions that necessarily follow from it, and the interpretation placed upon it by the common consent of Christians, are true, and belief in them is necessary to the salvation of those to whom they are made known.

2. The general council of Christians or its majority alone has the authority to define doubtful passages of the divine law, and to determine those that are to be regarded as articles of the Christian faith, belief in which is essential to salvation; and no partial council or single person of any position has the authority to decide these questions.

3. The gospels teach that no temporal punishment or penalty should be used to compel observance of divine commandments.

5. No mortal has the right to dispense with the commands or prohibitions of the new divine law; but the general council and the Christian "legislator" alone have the right to prohibit things which are permitted by the new law, under penalties in this world or the next, and no partial council or single person of any position has that right.

6. The whole body of citizens or its majority alone is the human "legislator."

7. Decretals and decrees of the bishop of Rome . . . have no power to coerce anyone by secular penalties or punishments, except by the authorization of the human "legislator."

8. The "legislator" alone or the one who rules by its authority has the power to dispense with human laws.

10. The election of any prince or other official . . . is determined solely by the expressed will of the "legislator."

13. No prince . . . has full authority and control over other persons, laymen or clergy, without the authorization of the "legislator."

14. No bishop or priest has coercive authority or jurisdiction over any layman or clergyman, even if he is a heretic.

16. No bishop or priest or body of bishops or priests has the authority to excommunicate anyone or to interdict the performance of divine services, without the authorization of the "legislator."

17. All bishops derive their authority in equal measure immediately from Christ, and it cannot be proved from the divine law that one bishop should be over or under another, in temporal or spiritual matters.

19. No mortal has the authority to permit marriages that are prohibited by the divine law, especially by the New Testament. The right to permit marriages which are prohibited by human law belongs solely to the "legislator. . . ."

21. The "legislator" alone has the right to promote to ecclesiastical orders, and to judge of the qualifications of persons for these offices, by a coercive decision, and no priest or bishop has the right to promote anyone without its authority.

27. The human "legislator" has the right to use ecclesiastical temporalities for the common public good and defence, after the needs of the priest and clergy, the expenses of divine worship, and the necessities of the poor have been satisfied.

32. The general council of all Christians alone has the authority to create a metropolitan bishop or church, and to reduce him or it from that position.

33. The Christian "legislator" or the one who rules by its authority over Christian states, alone has the right to convoke either a general or local council of priests, bishops, and other Christians, by coercive power. . . .

37. It is always permitted to appeal to the "legislator" from a coercive decision rendered by a bishop or priest with the authorization of the "legislator."

No. 167. Lollard doctrines condemned in 1382

(Translations and Reprints, II, No. 5, pp. 9-11.)

1. That the material substance of bread and of wine remains, after the consecration, in the sacrament of the altar.

2. That the accidents do not remain without the subject, after the consecration, in the same sacrament.

3. That Christ is not in the sacrament of the altar identically, truly and really in his proper corporal presence.

4. That if a bishop or priest lives in mortal sin he does not ordain, or consecrate, or baptize.

5. That if a man has been truly repentant, all external confession is superfluous to him or useless.

6. Continually to assert that it is not founded in the gospel that Christ instituted the mass.

8. That if the Pope is foreordained to destruction and a wicked man, and therefore a member of the devil, no power has been given to him over the faithful of Christ by any one, unless perhaps by the Emperor.

10. To assert that it is against sacred scripture that men of the church should have temporal possessions.

11. That no prelate ought to excommunicate any one unless he first knows that the man is excommunicated by God.

15. To assert that it is allowed to any one, whether a deacon or a priest, to preach the word of God, without the authority of the apostolic see, or of a Catholic bishop, or of some other which is sufficiently acknowledged.

16. To assert that no one is a civil lord, no one is a bishop, no one is a prelate, so long as he is in mortal sin.

17. That temporal lords may, at their own judgment, take away temporal goods from churchmen who are habitually delinquent; or that the people may, at their own judgment, correct delinquent lords.

18. That tithes are purely charity, and that parishioners may, on account of the sins of their curates, detain these and confer them on others at their will.

21. That saints who have instituted any private religions (religious orders) whatever, as well as those having possessions as of mendicants, have sinned in thus instituting them.

22. That religious persons living in private religions are not of the Christian religion.

23. That friars should be required to gain their living by the labor of their hands and not by mendicancy.

24. That a person giving alms to friars, or to a preaching friar, is excommunicate; also the one receiving.

No. 168. The decree *Sacrosancta*

(Robinson's *Readings*, pp. 511-512.)

In the name of the Holy and Indivisible Trinity, of the Father, Son, and Holy Ghost. Amen.

This holy synod of Constance, constituting a general council for the extirpation of the present schism and the union and reformation of the Church of God in head and members, legitimately assembled in the Holy Ghost, to the praise of omnipotent God, in order that it may the more easily, safely, effectively, and freely bring about the union and reformation of the Church of God, hereby determines, decrees, ordains, and declares what follows:

It first declares that this same council, legitimately assembled in the Holy Ghost, forming a general council and representing the Catholic Church militant, has its power immediately from Christ, and every one, whatever

his position or rank, even if it be the papal dignity itself, is bound to obey
it in all those things which pertain to the faith, to the healing of the
schism, and to the general reformation of the Church of God in head and
members.

It further declares that any one, whatever his position, station, or rank,
even if it be the papal, who shall contumaciously refuse to obey the
mandates, decrees, ordinances, or instructions which have been, or shall be,
issued by this holy council, or by any other general council legitimately
summoned, which concern, or in any way relate to, the above-mentioned
objects, shall, unless he repudiate his conduct, be subjected to condign
penance and be suitably punished, having recourse, if necessary, to the
resources of law. . . .

No. 169. The decree *Frequens*

(Robinson's *Readings*, pp. 512-513.)

A frequent celebration of general councils is an especial means for cultivating the field of the Lord and effecting the destruction of briers, thorns,
and thistles, to wit, heresies, errors, and schism, and of bringing forth a
most abundant harvest. The neglect to summon these fosters and develops
all these evils, as may be plainly seen from a recollection of the past and a
consideration of existing conditions. Therefore, by a perpetual edict, we
sanction, decree, establish, and ordain that general councils shall be celebrated in the following manner, so that the next one shall follow the close of
this present council at the end of five years. The second shall follow the
close of that, at the end of seven years, and councils shall thereafter be
celebrated every ten years in such places as the pope shall be required to
designate and assign, with the consent and approbation of the council, one
month before the close of the council in question, or which, in his absence,
the council itself shall designate. Thus, with a certain continuity, a council will always be either in session, or be expected at the expiration of a
definite time.

This term may, however, be shortened on account of emergencies, by the
supreme pontiff, with the counsel of his brethren, the cardinals of the holy
Roman Church, but it may not be hereafter lengthened. The place, moreover, designated for the future council may not be altered without evident
necessity. If, however, some complication shall arise, in view of which such
a change shall seem necessary, as, for example, a state of siege, a war, a pest,
or other obstacles, it shall be permissible for the supreme pontiff, with the
consent and subscription of his said brethren, or two thirds of them, to

select another appropriate place near the first, which must be within the same country, unless such obstacles, or similar ones, shall exist throughout the whole nation. In that case, the council may be summoned to some appropriate neighboring place, within the bounds of another nation. . . .

No. 170. The bull *Execrabilis*

(Thatcher & McNeal, *Source Book*, p. 332.)

The execrable and hitherto unknown abuse has grown up in our day, that certain persons, imbued with the spirit of rebellion, and not from a desire to secure a better judgment, but to escape the punishment of some offence which they have committed, presume to appeal from the pope to a future council, in spite of the fact that the pope is the vicar of Christ and to him, in the person of St. Peter, the following was said: "Feed my sheep" [John 21:16] and "Whatsoever thou shalt bind on earth shall be bound in heaven" [Matt. 16:18]. Wishing therefore to expel this pestiferous poison from the church of Christ and to care for the salvation of the flock entrusted to ús, and to remove every cause of offence from the fold of our Saviour, with the advice and consent of our brothers, the cardinals of the holy Roman church, and of all the prelates, and of those who have been trained in the canon and civil law, who are at our court, and with our own sure knowledge, we condemn all such appeals and prohibit them as erroneous and detestable.

No. 171. The "political papacy" of the fifteenth century

(*History of Florence* by Niccolo Machiavelli. New York, 1901.)

During these events in Lombardy, the pope [Sixtus IV] sent Lorenzo to invest Citta di Castello, for the purpose of expelling Niccolo Vitelli, the place having been abandoned to him by the League, for the purpose of inducing the pontiff to join them. During the siege, Niccolo's troops were led out against the papal forces and routed them. Upon this the pope recalled the Count Girolamo from Lombardy with orders first to recruit his army at Rome, and then proceed against Citta di Castello. But thinking afterward, that it would be better to obtain Niccolo Vitelli as his friend than to renew hostilities with him, an arrangement was entered into by which the latter retained Citta di Castello, and the pope pacified Lorenzo as well as he could. He was induced to both these measures rather by his apprehension of fresh troubles than by his love of peace, for he perceived dissensions arising between the Colonnesi and the Orsini.

In the war between the king of Naples and the pope, the former had taken the district of Tagliacozzo from the Orsini, and given it to the Colonnesi, who had espoused his cause. Upon the establishment of peace, the Orsini demanded its restoration by virtue of the treaty. The pope had frequently intimated to the Colonnesi that it ought to be restored; but they, instead of complying with the entreaties of the Orsini, or being influenced by the pope's threats, renewed hostilities against the former. Upon this the pontiff, unable to endure their insolence, united his own force with those of the Orsini, plundered the houses they possessed in Rome, slew or made prisoners all who defended them, and seized most of their fortresses. So that when these troubles were composed, it was rather by the complete subjugation of one party than from any desire for peace in the other. . . .

Upon the decease of the pontiff, Rome was immediately in arms. The Count Girolamo withdrew his forces into the castle; and the Orsini feared the Colonnesi would avenge the injuries they had recently sustained. The Colonnesi demanded the restitution of their houses and castles, so that in a few days robberies, fires, and murders prevailed in several parts of the city. The cardinals entreated the count to give the castle into the hands of the college, withdraw his troops, and deliver Rome from the fear of his forces, and he, by way of ingratiating himself with the future pontiff obeyed, and retired to Imola. The cardinals, being thus divested of their fears, and the barons hopeless of assistance in their quarrels, proceeded to create a new pontiff, and after some discussion, Giovanni Batista Cibo, a Genoese, cardinal of Malfetta, was elected (1484), and took the name of Innocent VIII. By the mildness of his disposition (for he was peaceable and humane) he caused a cessation of hostilities, and for the present restored peace to Rome.

No. 172. Petrarch's reputation as a literary critic

(From a letter of Petrarch's. Robinson's *Readings*, pp. 526-527.)

It is after all but a poor consolation to have companions in misery. I should prefer to be ill by myself. Now I am involved in other's ill fortune as well as in my own, and am hardly given time to take breath. For every day letters and poems from every corner of our land come showering down upon my devoted head. Nor does this satisfy my foreign friends. I am overwhelmed by floods of missives, no longer from France alone, but from Greece, from Germany, from England. I am unable to judge even my own work, and yet I am called upon to be the universal critic of others.

Were I to answer the requests in detail, I should be the busiest of mortals. If I condemn the composition, I am a jealous carper at the good work of others; if I say a good word for the thing, it is attributed to a mendacious desire to be agreeable; if I keep silence altogether, it is because I am a rude, pert fellow. They are afraid, I infer, that my disease will not make way with me promptly enough. Between their goading and my own madness I shall doubtless gratify their wishes.

But all this would be nothing if, incredible as it may seem, this subtle poison had not just now begun to show its effects in the Roman curia itself [at Avignon]. What do you think the lawyers and doctors are up to? Justinian and Aesculapius have palled upon them. The sick and the litigious cry in vain for their help, for they are deafened by the thunder of Homer's and Virgil's names, and wander oblivious in the woody valleys of Cirrha, by the purling waters of the Aonian fountain. But it is hardly necessary to speak of these lesser prodigies. Even carpenters, fullers, and plowmen leave the implements of their calling to talk of Apollo and the Muses. I cannot say how far the plague, which lately was confined to a few, has now spread.

No. 173. Sonnets of Petrarch

(*One Hundred Sonnets of Petrarch Together with His Hymn to the Virgin*, tr. Albert Crompton. London, 1898.)

I. To the Reader (p. 9)

O ye whose ears have caught in scattered strain
An echo of the sighs that erewhile fed
My heart, in maze of youthful error led,
—How different from the man I now remain—
Where one is found who doth of Love complain
I shall win grace, or pity in its stead
For all the notes of varying passion bred,
Wherein I range 'twixt hopes and sorrows vain.
But well I now can see how common bruit
Made me a byword, whence with shame unfeigned

At my own self myself am oft aglow.
Shame is alas my fitful folly's fruit,
And penitence and knowledge dearly gained
That all the world's applause is empty show.

II. Sweet-Looking p. 11

'Twas on the day when the sun's golden round
Sickened in pity of his Maker's woe,
That I was ta'en, and failed defence to show,
Since, Lady, to thine eyes I lay fast bound.
At such a time me thought there need be found
No special fence against my lurking foe,
All careless and secure I chanced to go,
And hence my griefs the general mourning crowned.
And so Love took me all unarmed, the way
Through my poor eyes direct unto my heart,
Where tears within had breach and entrance rent.
But little honor gained the god that day,
To wound me, all defenceless, with his dart,
While 'gainst thy arms his bow he never bent.

VI. A Distant Hope (p. 19)

If life so long continue, in despite
Of bitter sorrow and protracted woes,
That I should see before its final close
Of my loved lady's eyes the fading light;
The golden tresses silvered, and bedight
No more garlands, yea behold the rose
Forsake the face which in my sorest throes
Abashes lamentations, mine by right;
May Love with boldness then my tongue inspire,
That I may tell her how the years have past,
The days and hours of my hidden fire;
For, come what may, my hope remaineth fast,
That, though the time suit not with soft desire,
Her sighs, how late soe'er, will help at last.

XIII. Time the Disenchanter (p. 33)

As I draw nearer to the fatal day,
Which doth abbreviate all mortal woe,
I see Time's courses still more swiftly flow,

And all my hopes from him fade fast away.
We do not long, unto my thoughts I say,
Of Love conversing now, for well I know
Our earthly burden melts like summer's snow,
And then the peace is ours for which we pray.
With Time those expectations disappear,
Which made us cheat ourselves, then smiles and pain
And passion cease, then lamentation dies.
Then is it given to see in prospect clear,
How oft our dread becomes the source of gain,
How often uselessly we waste our sighs.

Hymn to the Virgin (p. 213)

Virgin most fair! sunclad, with stars encrowned,
Who of the highest Sun has earned such praise
That in thy form he hid his majesty;
To thee Love urges me my hymn to raise,
But ah! without thy help my tongue is bound,
And failing his whose love was laid in thee.
Her I invoke, who hears most readily
  Whoso in faith does call:
  O Virgin! if for all
Of mortal woes thou hast felt sympathy,
Hearken my prayer, from heart most contrite given,
  And help me in the fray,
Though I be clay, and thou the Queen of Heaven.

No. 174. Boccaccio's *Decameron*

(The Decameron of Giovanni Boccaccio, tr. J. M. Rigg. London. Excerpts.)

I say, then, that the years of the beatific incarnation of the Son of God had reached the tale of one thousand three hundred and forty-eight, when in the illustrious city of Florence, the fairest of all the cities in Italy, there made its appearance that deadly pestilence, which, whether disseminated by the influence of the celestial bodies, or sent upon us mortals by God in His just wrath by way of retribution for our iniquities had had its origin some years before in the East, whence, after destroying an innumerable multitude of living beings, it had propagated itself without respite from place to place, and so, calamitously, had spread into the West.

In Florence, despite all that human wisdom and forethought could devise to avert it, as the cleansing of the city from many impurities by officials appointed for the purpose, the refusal of entrance to all sick folk, and the adoption of many precautions for the preservation of health; despite also humble supplications addressed to God, and often repeated both in public procession and otherwise, by the devout; towards the beginning of the spring of the said year the doleful effects of the pestilence began to be horribly apparent by symptoms that shewed as if miraculous.

Not such were they as in the East, where an issue of blood from the nose was a manifest sign of inevitable death; but in men and women alike it first betrayed itself by the emergence of certain tumours in the groin or the armpits, some of which grew as large as a common apple, others as an egg, some more, some less, which the common folk called gavocciolo. From the two said parts of the body this deadly gavocciolo soon began to propagate and spread itself in all directions indifferently; after which the form of the malady began to change, black spots or livid making their appearance in many cases on the arm or the thigh or elsewhere, now few and large, now minute and numerous. And as the gavocciolo had been and still was an infallible token of approaching death, such also were these spots on whomsoever they shewed themselves. Which maladies seemed to set entirely at naught both the art of the physician and the virtues of physic; indeed, whether it was that the disorder was of a nature to defy such treatment, or that the physicians were at fault—besides the qualified there was now a multitude both of men and of women who practiced without having received the slightest tincture of medical science—and, being in ignorance of its source, failed to apply the proper remedies; in either case, not merely were those that recovered few, but almost all within three days from the appearance of the said symptoms, sooner or later, died, and in most cases without any fever or other attendant malady.

Moreover, the virulence of the pest was the greater by reason that intercourse was apt to convey it from the sick to the whole, just as fire devours things dry or greasy when they are brought close to it. Nay, the evil went yet further, for not merely by speech or association with the sick was the malady communicated to the healthy with consequent peril of common death; but any that touched the clothes of the sick or aught else that had been touched or used by them, seemed thereby to contract the disease. . . .

In which circumstances, not to speak of many others of a similar or even graver complexion, divers apprehensions and imaginations were engendered in the minds of such as were left alive, inclining almost all of them to the same harsh resolution, to wit, to shun and abhor all contact with the sick and all that belonged to them, thinking thereby to make each his own health secure. Among whom there were those who thought that to live temperately and avoid all excess would count for much as a preservative against seizures of this kind. . . . Others, the bias of whose minds was in the opposite direction, maintained, that to drink freely, frequent places of public resort, and take their pleasure with song and revel, sparing to satisfy no appetite, and to laugh and mock at no event, was the sovereign remedy for so great an evil. . . . Thus, adhering ever to their inhuman determination to shun the sick, as far as possible, they ordered their life. In this extremity of our city's suffering and tribulation the venerable authority of laws, human and divine, was abashed and all but totally dissolved, for lack of those who should have administered and enforced them, most of whom, like the rest of the citizens, were either dead or sick, or so hard bested for servants that they were unable to execute any office; whereby every man was free to do what was right in his own eyes.

Not a few there were who belonged to neither of the two said parties, but kept a middle course between them, neither laying the same restraint upon their diet as the former, nor allowing themselves the same license in drinking and other dissipations as the latter, but living with a degree of freedom sufficient to satisfy their appetites, and not as recluses. They therefore walked abroad, carrying in their hands flowers or fragrant herbs or divers sorts of spices, which they frequently raised to their noses, deeming it an excellent thing thus to comfort the brain with such perfumes, because the air seemed to be everywhere laden and reeking with the stench emitted by the dead and the dying, and the odours of drugs. . . .

Tedious were it to recount, how citizen avoided citizen, how among neighbours was scarce found any that shewed fellow-feeling for another, how kinsfolk held aloof, and never met, or but rarely; enough that this sore affliction entered so deep into the minds of men and women, that in the horror therefrom brother was forsaken by brother, nephew by uncle, brother by sister, and oftentimes husband by wife; nay, what is more, and scarcely to be believed, fathers and mothers were found to abandon their own children, untended, unvisited, to their fate, as if they had been strangers. . . .

It was the common practice of most of the neighbours, moved no less by fear of contamination by the putrefying bodies than by charity towards the deceased, to drag the corpses out of the houses with their own hands . . . and to lay then in front of the doors, where any one who made the round might have seen, especially in the morning, more of them than he could count; afterwards they would have biers brought up, or, in default, planks, whereon they laid them. Nor was it once or twice only that one and the same bier carried two or three corpses at once; but quite a considerable number of such cases occurred, one bier sufficing for husband and wife, two or three brothers, father and son, and so forth. And times without number it happened, that, as two priests, bearing the cross, were on their way to perform the last office for some one, three or four biers were brought up by the porters in rear of them, so that, whereas the priests supposed that they had but one corpse to bury, they discovered that there were six or sometimes more. Nor, for all their number, were their obsequies honored by either tears or lights or crowds or mourners; rather, it was come to this, that a dead man was then of no more account than a dead goat would be today. From all which it is abundantly manifest, that that lesson of patient resignation, which the sages were never able to learn from the slight and infrequent mishaps which occur in the natural course of events, was now brought home even to the minds of the simple by the magnitude of their disasters, so that they became indifferent to them.

As consecrated ground there was not in extent sufficient to provide tombs for the vast multitude of corpses which day and night, and almost every hour, were brought in eager haste to the church for interment, least of all, if ancient custom were to be observed and a separate resting-place assigned to each, they dug, for each graveyard, as soon as it was full, a huge trench, in which they laid the corpses as they arrived by hundreds at a time, piling them up as merchandise is stowed in the hold of a ship, tier upon tier, each covered with a little earth, until the trench would hold no more. . . .

How many grand palaces, how many stately homes, how many splendid residences, once full of retainers, of lords, of ladies, were now left desolate of all, even to the meanest servant! How many families of historic fame, of vast ancestral domains, and wealth proverbial, found now no scion to continue the succession! How many brave men, how many fair ladies, how many gallant youths, whom any physician, were he Galen, Hippocrates, or Aesculapius himself, would have pronounced in the soundest of health, broke fast with their kinsfolk, comrades and friends in the morning, and when evening came, supped with their forefathers in the other world!

No. 175. Poggio, the humanist, finds a manuscript

(Quoted in John Addington Symonds, *The Revival of Learning*. New York, 1888, pp. 135-136.)

(The account which Poggio, a leading humanist, gave of his visit to the monastery of St. Gall in a Latin letter to a friend. After describing the wretched state in which the "Institutions" of Quintilian had previously existed, he proceeds as follows:)

I verily believe that, if we had not come to the rescue, he [Quintilian] must speedily have perished; for it cannot be imagined that a man magnificent, polished, elegant, urbane, and witty could much longer have endured the squalor of the prison-house in which I found him, the savagery of his jailers, the forlorn filth of the place. He was indeed right sad to look upon, and ragged, like a condemned criminal, with rough beard and matted hair, protesting by his countenance and garb against the injustice of his sentence. He seemed to be stretching out his hands, calling upon the Romans, demanding to be saved from so unmerited a doom. Hard indeed it was for him to bear, that he who had preserved the lives of many by his eloquence and aid, should now find no redresser of his wrongs, no saviour from the unjust punishment awaiting him. But as it often happens, to quote Terence, that what you dare not wish for comes to you by chance, so a good fortune for him, but far more for ourselves, led us, while wasting our time in idleness at Constance,* to take a fancy for visiting the place where he was held in prison. The Monastery of S. Gall lies at the distance of some twenty miles from that city. Thither, then, partly for the sake of amusement and partly of finding books, whereof we heard there was a large collection in the convent, we directed our steps. In the middle of a well-stocked library, too large to catalogue at present, we discovered Quintilian, safe as yet and sound, though covered with dust and filthy with neglect and age. The books, you must know, were not housed according to their worth, but were lying in a most foul and obscure dungeon at the very bottom of a tower, a place into which condemned criminals would hardly have been thrust; and I am firmly persuaded that if any one would but explore those *ergastula*† of the barbarians wherein they incarcerate such men, we should meet with like good fortune in the case of many whose funeral orations have long ago been pronounced. Besides Quintilian, we exhumed the three first books and a half of the fourth book of the *Argonautica* of Flaccus, and the *Commentaries* of Asconius Pedianus upon eight orations of Cicero.

No. 176. From the poems of François Villon

(*The Poems of Master Francis Villon of Paris*, tr. John Payne. London, 1881.)

The Greater Testament (pp. 26-29)
XXII

My time of youth I do bewail,
That more than most lived merrily,
Until old age 'gan me assail,
For youth had passed unconsciously.
    It wended not afoot from me,
    Nor yet on horseback. Ah, how then?
    It fled away all suddenly,
    And never will return again.

---

* Poggio was attending the council of Constance as apostolic secretary.
† Penitentiaries or jails.

XXIII

It's gone, and I am left behind,
Poor both in body and in wit,
Sad and forlorn and weak as wind;
Coin, land and goods, gone every whit.
   And all my kindred to me knit,
   Forgetting natural affect,
   To disavow me have seen to fit,
   Finding my every fortune wrecked.

XXIV

Yet have I not my living spent
On gourmandise or gluttony
Nor through love that I repent:
None is there can reproach it me,
   Except he rue it bitterly;
   I say, without untruthfulness—
   From this you cannot make me flee—
   Who's done no wrong should none confess.

XXV

True it is I have loved whilere
And willingly would love again:
But aching heart and paunch that ne'er
Doth half its complement contain
   The ways of Love allure in vain.
   But none but those its sweets may prove
   Whose well-filled stomach wags amain;
   Hunger was fatal aye to love.

XXVI

If in my time of youth, alack!
I had but studied and been sage
Nor wandered from the beaten track,
I had slept warm in my old age.
   But what did I? As bird from cage,
   I fled the school; and now with pain,
   In setting down this on the page,
   My heart is well-nigh cleft in twain.

XXVII

I have construed what Solomon
Intended, with too much largess,
When that he said, 'Rejoice, my son,
In thy fair youth and lustiness:

But still to wisdom thee address;
For youth and adolescence be'
(These are his words, nor more nor less)
'But ignorance and vanity.'

XXVIII

Like as the loose threads on the loom,
Whenas the weaver to them lays
The flaming tow, burn and consume,
So that from ragged ends (Job says)
   The web is freed,—even so my days
   Have fled and vanished past recall.
   Nor pain nor travail me affrays,
   For death shall set me free from all.

XXIX

Where are the gracious gallants now
That of old time I did frequent,
So fair of fashion and of show,
In song and speech so excellent?
   Stark dead are some, their lives are spent;
   There rests of them nor mark nor trace:
   May they in Heaven find content;
   God have the others in His grace!

XXX

Some, Christ-a-mercy, have become
Masters and lords and great of grace;
Some beg barefoot and see no crumb
Of bread save in some window-place;
   Others the tonsure did embrace,
   That now fat lives in convent spend,
   Well shod and clad and sleek of face;
   Of some of them this is the end.

15

POLITICAL DEVELOPMENTS OF THE LATE MIDDLE AGES

The Decline of Feudalism and the Growth of Monarchy

Two major political developments, the decline of feudalism and the growth of strong monarchy, hold our attention during the fourteenth and fifteenth centuries. Feudalism rose, as we have seen, during the ninth and tenth centuries as monarchies weakened and the state began to disintegrate. Now the trend was in the opposite direction. From at least the twelfth century in France and somewhat earlier in England, kings tended to grow stronger and the state more stable, while the feudality began to experience a gradual diminution of power. Of course, the rise of monarchy was neither uninterrupted nor universal throughout Western Europe. Henry III of England was not so strong a king as his grandfather Henry II; the German monarchs of the late thirteenth century commanded fewer resources than had Otto I and Frederick Barbarossa. Yet with the exception of the king of Germany, whose situation was unique, time and circumstance appeared to favor the ambitions of strong monarchs, while they frowned upon the political fortunes of the feudal aristocracy. In the ninth century conditions seemed to conspire against the kingship; from the thirteenth century onward they generally worked in its favor. Even during the dark days of the French and English monarchies in the fifteenth century (see below), the question was not whether the kingship would disappear—of which there had been a distinct possibility in the tenth and eleventh centuries—the question was rather who would take possession of the kingship and use it to rule.

A Reversal of Earlier Factors. Many of the factors which nourished the rise of the monarchy at the expense of the feudality during the later Middle Ages were only the reversal of similar factors which had earlier contributed to the debilitation of the state. These included the disappearance of urban life and the decline of trade; the rise of a natural economy that forced the king to rely upon his own personal and inadequate resources; the king's dependence upon officials whose hereditary position left them virtually independent in view of the absence of roads and other communications; a change in the art of war which neutralized the effectiveness of a militia and gave rise to a haughty knightly class; and the Salic principle of succession. By the fourteenth century these factors were largely nonoperative or were to become so shortly. Towns began to appear toward the close of the tenth century, trade to revive, and Western Europe gave encouraging signs of throwing off the economic lethargy which had helped reduce government to a minimum. By the fourteenth century advancing capitalism was providing the king rich sources of revenue with which to hire mercenary soldiers to fight his wars and professional civil servants to administer his affairs. Political stabilization and developing economic ties encouraged the stirring of a sense of national consciousness which was sympathetic of the aims of the monarchy. In the eighth century a change in the art of war had immobilized the infantry. But in the twelfth and succeeding centuries further developments in warfare tended to rehabilitate the foot soldier while depriving the knight of his invincibility. In place of the earlier Salic principle according to which a kingdom was parceled out among all the sons of a deceased monarch, the rule of inheritance from the tenth century on was that of primogeniture. Therefore, once the king had established his position as hereditary, which he had accomplished in England and France by the twelfth century, the son could plan to build his power upon the foundations his father had left him.

Developments in the Art of War. What proved a most critical development favoring the rise of the monarchy and the decline of feudal power was a change in the art of war. Back in the eighth century the foot soldier had demonstrated his helplessness against the cavalry charges of Moslems and Avars, and had given way to the knight on horseback. The infantry became obsolete—but not for long. In the Third Crusade foot soldiers proved themselves indispensable in slowing the fierce attacks of the speedy Saracen horsemen. Even earlier at the battle of Legnano (1176), and again later at Bouvines (1214) and Courtrai (1302), the infantry showed itself a decisive factor. The weapon the foot soldier found most effective was the crossbow, which discharged its missile with such dreadful force that if it did not kill, it horribly mangled, its target. A more humane though more lethal weapon was the long bow which made its appearance on the continent during the Hundred Years' War. This could shoot more accurately and more rapidly than the crossbow, actually at the rate of an arrow every ten seconds in the hands of a skilled archer. So tremendous was its thrust, that it could pierce armor at two hundred yards, as the French knights learned to their woe in successive disastrous defeats at the hands of the English. The hardy Swiss mountaineers had meantime fashioned a weapon of their own, the pike, which they used with deadly effect against horsemen who dared invade their hills. The pike ranged to some twenty feet in length and was topped with a wicked barb. In their well-organized formations, the Swiss spearmen proved themselves capable of breaking up cavalry charges and of maneuvering successfully on the offensive as well. To meet these growing threats, the knight's armor went through a gradual process of evolution, from links to rings, to chains, and, finally, to plate armor. By 1400 the knight and his mount were almost encased in armor. Except against well-placed shots they had become practically invulnerable, but their protection cost them their mobility. Once unhorsed the knight was apt to find his heavy armor a death trap. By the fifteenth century heavy cavalry was scarcely effective except on the offensive and under the most ideal conditions. Yet the death knell of knightly military might only sounded with the crash of artillery during the first half of the fifteenth century. While its success on the field of battle was still severely limited, against castles artillery proved wonderfully destructive. Within a few months the French demolished some sixty Norman castles during the closing years of the Hundred Years' War and ejected the English unceremoniously from the land they had held for generations. By the close of the Middle Ages the noble's castle had become nothing more than a chateau.

The King and His Army. Even before the knight's vincibility on the field of battle had become manifest, even before his castle had come tumbling down upon him, his military indispensability to the king had been materially reduced. Already in the twelfth century, Henry II of England had made considerable use of scutage, that is, he had permitted his vassals to substitute a money payment for the knight service they owed him. With the money they paid him, he raised a force of mercenaries, placed middle-class captains in command, and as a result emancipated himself measurably from dependence upon the feudal levy. This removed a particularly serious obstacle from the path of ambitious monarchs, for the feudal levy had proved a most undependable force: it served for but forty days after which it might evaporate; it was directed by independent-minded, self-seeking lords who were tempted to leave off fighting whenever it was to their interest to do so. By the close of the thirteenth century it had become customary in England for the king to accept a sum of money and release his vassals from knight service. The royal army consisted then principally of infantry, supported by what knights the king had of his own and others whom he might hire. While a king's vassals felt under no restraint to raise similar armies of their own unless forbidden to do so by the occasional king strong enough to enforce his will, their means were usually not equal to the expense. Only a king or wealthy German prince or prosperous Italian town could afford such a mercenary army. Two factors, therefore, each associated with military developments, collaborated to undermine the position of the feudality in favor of that of the monarch: the first, changes in the art of war itself; the second, the ability of the king to equip an army of his own and the inability of the feudal lord to do so.

Role of the Middle Class. This ability of the king to equip his own army can ultimately be traced back to the revival of trade and the rise of towns. The urban middle class which trade and towns had brought forth turned over to the crown the money needed to achieve its pre-eminence. They purchased charters from him; they manufactured, imported, and exported goods upon which he collected duties; they voted him taxes; they lent him direct assistance with troops of their own and with others which they hired. All this they were pleased to do for him, partly in return for the commercial and political favors he extended to them, partly because the alternative to royal rule was feudal misrule. Feudalism, like manorialism and the gild, was an institution whose proper province was a condition of natural economy. All three institutions were doomed with the rise of capitalism. Where the feudality in both England and France had fought the crown in the twelfth and thirteenth centuries in order to preserve or enhance its position, in the late Middle Ages the members of the feudality fought among themselves to gain control of the monarchy. Yet so powerful had the royal position grown by the fifteenth century, that regardless of which feudal faction emerged triumphant, the king it installed in the palace eventually made himself its master.

Feudality in Partial Eclipse. Had the feudal aristocracy been able to close ranks against the king in the late Middle Ages, it could have emasculated the monarchy. But that would be asking tigers not to fight. Once the monarchy had attained a position of power, the days of feudal independence were numbered, as much because of the aristocracy's own selfish pride as because of forces from without. Yet though the kings of England, France, and Spain had deprived the feudality of the substance of its power by the close of the Middle Ages, that feudality retained the appearance thereof well up into modern times. Politically, the count, duke, and earl continued as before to fill the most important posts in the royal household, although normally in a private capacity rather than as representatives of a self-conscious feudality. The feudality monopolized the higher offices in the army and foreign service as well. Because the feudal aristocracy held on to the bulk of the land long after the close of the Middle Ages, it managed to exercise controlling influence in such representative bodies as the House of Commons in England. As a matter of fact, the crown would require time, patience, and force, before it could convince the feudality that ownership of land no longer carried the traditional prerogative of regulating the lives of the people on the land as it had in the earlier Middle Ages. The feudal lord did not pay taxes since this was the mark of the ignoble classes, although he might be asked to vote subsidies. Socially the aristocracy dominated Europe almost into the twentieth century. And though knighthood as an institution charged with real responsibilities to society had become a closed chapter long before the end of the Middle Ages, the pomp and circumstance of chivalry grew progressively more brilliant as if to hide the hollowness underneath. The most exclusive knightly orders of the Middle Ages appeared in the closing hours of chivalry: the Order of the Golden Fleece in Burgundy, the Order of the Garter in England, the Order of the Star in France. What the feudal aristocracy found most difficulty in obscuring was its impoverishment. Except for the fortunate few who had the foresight to turn their lands to commercial agriculture or to marry heiresses with more wealth than pedigree, the majority found that cheapening money and mounting expenses left the old manorial and feudal revenues hopelessly inadequate.

The Growth of Royal Power. The power of the king waxed as that of the feudal aristocracy waned. It had already grown significantly at the expense of the church. We have seen how in the early fourteenth century the kings of England and France had obliged the pope to permit them to tax clerical wealth. From that time onward few conflicts disrupt relations between church and state. The state had become so strong that it left the king in an overwhelmingly favorable position in negotiations with the papacy. Short of a demand impinging upon doctrinal orthodoxy, the pope had little choice but to yield. It is for this reason that legislation such as the Statute of Provisors enacted by the English parliament in 1356 proved so barren of results. Though the statute was directed officially at the pope, the chief culprit in the matter of provisions was the king, who consistently demanded and received the lion's share in appointments to ecclesiastical benefices. If the pope was making more appointments than parliament approved, it was only because the king had given his consent, and that for a price. The Pragmatic Sanction of Bourges which Charles VII issued in 1438 provided the king of France a double-edged sword to use against pope and feudal hierarchy. By means of this decree in which the crown appropriated control over certain revenues and appointments which had been traditionally the pope's, the king could assure himself of papal cooperation by dangling before the pope the bait of abolishing the Sanction, while at the same time using the threat of doing so to make certain of the support of the local bishops who benefited by the limitation of papal interference.

The position of the Hapsburg rulers of Germany and the Spanish monarchs was similarly strong. Having forced the pope to become a willing or unwilling ally, and already enjoying the active cooperation of the bourgeoisie, the Western monarch was well on his way toward absolutism by the close of the Middle Ages. As royal revenues rose, so did the size and officiousness of the royal bureaucracy. Lawyers trained in the imperialistic traditions of Roman law stepped forward to provide legal justification for royal claims. Nascent national consciousness worked in favor of the crown, although the attitude of the people toward the king continued to be too personal to equate entirely with nationalism. His state was more dynastic than national. As Louis XI was wont to affirm: "I am France." But whatever the state was, it was no longer medieval. There was something fundamentally incongruous between medieval traditions on the one hand and on the other kings with the absolutist proclivities of a Ferdinand of Spain, a Henry VII of England, or a Louis XI of France.

France and the Hundred Years' Wars

Philip the Fair. After the death of Louis IX in 1270, the French monarchy never again produced a saint, but it could boast of men as statesmanlike as Philip Augustus. Louis' son Philip III (1270-1285) was not one of these, although he had the sagacity to insure the annexation of Navarre and Champagne to the royal domain by betrothing his son to their heiress. The next king, Philip IV (1285-1314), is the most unpleasant figure in French medieval history. His soubriquet, "the Fair," he owed to his handsome appearance, not to his sense of justice. Of this last he had none. What he contributed to the discussions with the group of able though unscrupulous councilors who had his ear, remains a mystery. But history holds him responsible for approving and executing what they advised. The most reprehensible measures the crown undertook sprang from Philip's need for money. Feudal aids and incidents became almost unfeudal in the efficient manner and regularity with which they were collected; towns suffered successive assessments for tallage; the French clergy after Boniface's tragic end was practically helpless before his demands; and sales taxes were levied on such staples as wheat, wine, and salt. On several occasions Philip employed the dangerous tactic of debasing the coinage and more frequently the criminal one of extorting money from wealthy subjects by "judicial" process. By these and other means he managed to stave off bankruptcy, but at the cost of the popular esteem Louis IX had won the French monarchy.

Suppression of the Templars. Several incidents touching individuals or groups who balked his will or who had money he wanted reveal Philip's brutal rapaciousness. The sordid business involving Pope Boniface was discussed in the preceding chapter. He summarily expelled from the country Jews and Italian bankers who had advanced him huge sums and seized their accounts, which he collected for himself. Against the Knights Templars he had to move cautiously because of the power and prestige of the order. Nogaret had assured him that the order was immensely wealthy, which Philip could easily believe since he owed them tremendous sums himself. So he directed his lawyers to "justify" his coming suppression of the order. This was no simple matter despite the fact that the Templars had drawn censure for their luxurious living and generally purposeless existence. Besides all this, the most illustrious of the Crusading orders was now famous for the banking activities in which it was deeply engaged. Still its only real crime was its wealth which Philip wanted together with the return of his promissory notes. Nogaret who was a past master at trumping up charges did himself particularly proud in this instance. First he managed to browbeat Pope Clement V into authorizing proceedings against the order. With the aid of torture Nogaret was able to force confessions from a goodly number, only to have these repudiate their confessions when re-examined by papal agents. But Philip would have his way as he had with Boniface. With the use of troops he overawed a church council which had been convened to try the order, and eventually blackmailed the pope into suppressing the organization. Pope Clement salved his conscience to the extent of directing that the order's properties be turned over to the Hospitalers with which the Templars had earlier been advised to combine. Philip had other plans. After "proving" the guilt of several scores of Templars by burning them at the stake for heresy, he seized and kept all of the order's wealth which he could find in France. The story is told how the grand master, protesting his innocence as he burned at the stake, called upon God to summon all three principals in the crime, the pope, Nogaret, and Philip, before His judgement seat within the year. They were all dead in six months. Philip's expulsion of the Jews and bankers, his suppression of the Templars, together with his debasement of the coinage and repressive taxation had a depressing effect upon the nation's economy. Among the casualties were the Champagne fairs which his taxes blighted.

Growth of Royal Government. A more attractive phase of Philip's reign was its contribution to French constitutional history. This followed principally from the marked increase in the business of the royal government which caused the *curia regis* to break up further into special groups or commissions, each with its own duties and personnel. Part of this expansion was inevitable as the ways and needs of society grew more advanced. But the French government had a special cause for expansion, beyond that of England for instance; for France was a confused assortment of provinces, often with individual customs and privileges. Common law, as we have seen, came naturally to England. France presented by contrast almost the heterogeneity of a United Nations. As the size of the royal bureaucracy and

EUROPE
ca. 1500 A.D.

FINLAND

DOMAIN OF TEUTONIC KNIGHTS

Novgorod

Moscow

Dnieper R.

L I T H U A N I A

WEST PRUSSIA

Tannenberg

Vistula R.

KINGDOM OF POLAND

Cracow

GALICIA

Dniester R.

RUTHENIA

Danube R.

Varna

BULGARIA

Constantinople

Nicomedia

Nicaea

Angora

Gallipoli

Antioch

Nicopolis

KINGDOM OF HUNGARY

SERBIA

CROATIA

CORINTHIA

Luebeck

BRANDEN-BURG

Oder R.

AUSTRIA

Vienna

KINGDOM OF BOHEMIA

Elbe R.

SAXONY

STYRIA

CARNI-OLA

VENETIAN REPUBLIC

PAPAL STATES

KINGDOM OF THE TWO SICILIES

Bremen

Cologne

Trier

Rhine R.

Mainz

Danube R.

BAVARIA

SWITZER-LAND

Milan

DUCHY OF MILAN

Genoa

REPUBLIC OF GENOA

Venice

Po R.

Pisa

Florence

REPUBLIC OF FLORENCE

ARCHDUCHY OF

Rhone R.

SCOTLAND

IRELAND

ENGLAND

Seine R.

Loire R.

FRANCE

Ebro R.

PORTUGAL

SPAIN

the responsibilities it assumed expanded, a significant transformation took place in the character of its personnel. Men of the commoner class who had earned degrees in civil law in the university began to make their way into the royal service and, because of their greater efficiency and dependence upon the crown, to replace gradually the traditional aristocratic element there. These new men had no sympathy for the feudality as they brought to their work a legal philosophy founded upon the imperialistic principles of Roman law.

The Estates General. The most interesting institutional development of Philip's reign appeared with the first meeting in 1302 of what came to be called the Estates General. Similar groups had met previously but only on a provincial basis. This occasion in 1302 was the first when the king's vassals and rear vassals (upon consent of their immediate lords), lay and ecclesiastical, convened at Paris together with representatives of the towns. This Estates General may be viewed as a glorified *curia regis* since the formal purpose of its convening was to give counsel to the king, one of its traditional feudal obligations. Even the presence of the towns represented little break with tradition, since they were classified as corporate vassals of the king. Philip's prime motive in summoning this first meeting of the Estates General was chiefly to make certain that this, the ruling and articulate element of France, would accept his version of the struggle with Pope Boniface. The purpose of the second meeting of the Estates General in 1308 was similar, to prepare "public opinion" to accept Philip's liquidation of the Templars. At the third meeting of the group in 1314 the crown sought and received authorization to raise money by negotiation with the various provinces in order to prosecute the war in Flanders more vigorously. Some suggestion that a future beckoned for the Estates General comparable to that which lay before the English parliament is revealed in the crown's bowing before the criticism voiced during the second meeting of the States in 1308 against the debasing of the coinage and against a proposed tax. Yet France was too extensive, the burden of traveling to Paris too onerous, and the demands of the different groups represented not sufficiently uniform to augur well for the evolution of an effective body to check the crown. Furthermore, the provinces preferred to do business individually with the royal agents in the expectation that they could secure greater concessions in private negotiation than simply as members of a national body.

The Hundred Years' War

Causes. As it happened, these constitutional developments bore no immediate fruit. That they failed to prepare the way for further royal aggrandizement during the century following was due principally to the outbreak of the Hundred Years' War (1337-1453). There were times in fact during this long conflict when the French monarchy itself appeared about to go under and France to dissolve into a number of independent states. The causes for this war are not difficult to find. Fundamental was the continued existence of English possessions in France over which the two countries had already fought for well on to two hundred years. These possessions were now narrowed down to Guienne, since England under Henry III had formally renounced claims to any territory north of the Loire (primarily Normandy) in exchange for a clear title to the southwest. Additional irritants were present to embitter relations between the two countries, such as the intermittent clashes between English and French traders and fishermen in the Channel and North Sea. A sore point too was the pro-English sentiment of the burghers of Flanders whose heavy imports of English wool assured them of England's sympathy against their count who was pro-French. There was, finally, the alliance between Scotland and France which actually provoked the struggle. For it was Philip VI's decision in 1336 to send troops to aid the Scots who were opposing Edward III's attempt to conquer them, that precipitated the conflict. Philip's interference convinced Edward of the advisability of first solidifying his hold on Guienne before becoming too deeply embroiled in Scotland.

Edward's Claim.   What was not a cause for the war was the claim which the king of England, Edward III, advanced for the French throne. He put forward this claim in order to provide his war aims a legal base and also to protect the Flemish. The Flemish had recently deposited a large sum of money with the pope as surety that they would not again rebel against the king of France. By claiming to be the rightful king of France, Edward could protect them from violating their pledge and forfeiting their surety. Edward did have a claim to the French throne, a weak one. His mother was the daughter of Philip IV (the Fair). Philip had been succeeded by his three sons, Louis X, Philip V, and Charles IV in rapid succession, all three sons dying without male issue. When the last son, Charles IV, died in 1328, the senior branch of the Capetian house became extinct in the male line. In view of Edward's relationship through his mother, this development might have occasioned some anxious moments had it not been for the precedent set when Louis X died in 1316. An assembly of notables had declared at that time that although Louis left a daughter, "a woman cannot succeed to the kingdom of France." Consequently, upon the death of Charles IV, the crown was immediately proffered to the son of Philip IV's brother who is known in history as Philip VI (1328-1350). Upon Philip's coronation, Edward had formally acknowledged him as his overlord for Guienne. Ten years later he revoked his action on the plea that while his mother could not succeed to the French throne because of the "incompetency of her sex," she might serve as a "bridge and plank" by which the succession would pass to him.

Why the War Lasted so Long. The term "Hundred Years' War" is misleading. It tends to obscure the fact that England and France had already had a long history of war over English possessions in France. It also suggests an uninterrupted period of warfare. This was happily not the case, and extended truces intervened, even treaties of peace. Still for much of France it mattered little whether actual war prevailed or formal peace, so powerless was the French government to prevent unemployed soldiers from looting and pillaging the countryside. The war lasted so long a time because England, the nation that won the victories, lacked the resources to exploit its successes. England was attempting to defeat, even conquer, a nation five times more populous and many times wealthier. It was, therefore, almost a foregone conclusion that the war would eventually produce a French victory, but because of France's unwillingness to accept the fact that a change in the art of war had taken place, this victory came late, very late. The war lasted so long too because neither nation was able to bring anything approaching its full potential to bear on the conflict. For the English this is understandable, since they viewed the struggle as almost a foreign war. They would be happy to win, but not at the price in taxes and men required. Chance, against whose unscrutable twists and turns Thucydides had warned all those who go to war, also had a major hand in prolonging the war. For almost thirty years of Charles VI's long reign (1380-1422), France was cursed with an insane king, while England suffered its turn under Henry VI (1422-1461), who though mad for shorter periods than Charles (his maternal grandfather from whom he inherited the disease), proved hardly more astute as a ruler in his lucid intervals. The war ended with the English pushed off the continent except for Calais. But there was no treaty of peace. Most of England's kings for the next hundred years planned to or did resume hostilities.

Edward III and the Opening of the War. The English had the more able king when the war started in 1337. Edward III (1327-1377) reminds one of Richard the Lion-Hearted. He was popular and he knew a great deal about fighting. Had he evinced less interest in pleasure and more in governing, he might have left a mark upon English history. As it is, his epitaph should read: "He lived too long." France's king, Philip VI (1328-1350), had not even military prowess to commend him. The first important development of the war was the revolt of the Flemish burghers under the leadership of Jacob van Artevelde, a wealthy cloth merchant. The count of Flanders had prohibited commercial relations with England in order to destroy the strong economic ties between the two areas, only to force the burghers into open alliance with the English in 1339 when the latter promised military aid and a steady flow of wool. In the main the history of the first part of the war simply set the pattern for that to follow. Neither nation had any money; surely not the English. Edward, for instance, had made such a military display at Coblentz to impress the German emperor into accepting an alliance, that he had exhausted his funds and had to return home. The new crown which he had optimistically made to grace his early coronation as king of France he had to pawn to raise money. Even the name of his second son, John of Gaunt, reveals his perennial lack of funds. Edward owed the burghers of Ghent so much, that they would not permit the royal family to return to England, but kept his son and pregnant wife as sureties while he returned alone to raise funds.

Crecy (1346). The first major engagement of the war was an accident. Edward had landed an army in Normandy not quite sure what his objective was other than conducting a major raid through enemy territory. After capturing and plundering Caen, he continued on to the Seine where he learned of the approach of Philip with a large force. He immediately turned northward hoping to reach the Channel, but found himself caught from behind at Crecy by an army overwhelmingly his superior. Actually had it not been for his numerical inferiority Edward would have been defeated. In the emergency he had no choice but to rely upon his despised longbowmen, who, as much to his surprise as that of the French, riddled the attacking French knights and turned certain defeat into a butchery. Yet despite the annihilation of the French army, all Edward could do after his crushing victory was to return to England. He lacked the men and money to garrison the country. (Reading 182)

The Black Death. A calamity more grievous than war befell France and England in 1348. This was the Black Death or bubonic plague. Its source has been traced to grain ships from the Crimea which tied up at Italian and southern French ports, the germs themselves being carried by rats and probably distributed by fleas. The plague derives its name from the dark blotches that appeared on the body, which with boils and swollen glands in the neck, armpits, and groin, were its chief symptoms. Nothing proved effective against the dread disease save flight. The scourge of 1348-1350 was only the worst of several visitations Western Europe suffered in the course of the fourteenth and fifteenth centuries. Outbreaks were, in fact, recorded as late as the eighteenth century, and the Black Death still remains a menace in the Orient. Villages appeared to suffer as severely as cities, and occasional monasteries were decimated. The Cistercian monastery in Devonshire counted but the abbot and two monks after the terrible scourge had passed through that community of twenty-three, while the village of Givry in France recorded more deaths in four months in 1348 than in the twenty years preceding. Where tax rolls are available they show a radical decrease; in other places where they had been kept, they often ceased altogether. It is estimated that between one fourth and one third the population of Western Europe was carried off. In the past it was customary to attribute a number of important consequences to the Black Death, such as the decay of manorial economy and the decline of the church. Recent scholarship is inclined to question the conclusiveness of the evidence. (Readings 174, 186)

Battle of Poitiers. The Black Death had no known effects upon the war, but it may have contributed to a constitutional upheaval in France which would have transformed that nation's history had it proved permanent. What precipitated this upheaval was a catastrophe suffered by French arms at Poitiers in 1356, a catastrophe in many ways similar to the slaughter at Crecy ten years earlier. Edward III's eldest son Edward, the Black Prince (he wore black armor), was in command of the English and Gascon forces; King John II (1350-1364) the Good (he was a good fellow) was in command of the French. The Black Prince, though hardly the paragon of chivalry that contemporaries regarded him, was far superior to John who "had as yet given proof of nothing but gallantry and military incompetence."* In fact, that is all he ever gave evidence of. The Black Prince found himself in much the same predicament as had his father at Crecy, in that he unexpectedly came upon a much larger French army. The French in their confidence brushed aside his frantic appeal for an armistice and decided to crush his army. As at Crecy, because of their numerical inferiority, the English were forced to "resort to stratagems unworthy of knights: concealment along hedges, ambushes in woodland, fire of the Welsh archers which decimated the enemy's horses, feints to lure on their various 'battles' one by one."* The result was the annihilation of the French army. Among the host of proud captives the English took back with them to England was King John himself.

Marcel and the Jacquerie. France was in a state of near anarchy. The king was a prisoner, the dauphin, the future Charles V, seemingly nothing more than a shiftless young man. The estates seized the opportunity to make an assertion of leadership. Already several months before the disaster at Poitiers, many of them had gathered at Paris and had drawn up a program of reform calling for a royal council under their control. They demanded that the estates convene at regular intervals, and that the administration of taxes, the raising of troops, and the making of peace rest in their hands. What they wanted in substance was a constitutional monarchy, and so shaken was the crown by the debacle at Poitiers that the estates prevailed upon the dauphin to accept the changes. The element principally instrumental in forcing through these constitutional reforms had been the Parisian burgesses under the leadership of Etienne Marcel, provost of the merchants of the city. Unfortunately for the success of the program, the peasants of several provinces chose this inopportune time to revolt. These peasant uprisings, called Jacquerie after the traditional name of Jacques for the French peasant, began to erupt in May 1358. What provoked them were the cruel devastations of the war and the pillaging by

* Edouard Perroy, *The Hundred Years War* (New York, 1951), pp. 125, 131.

routiers or free companies during peace time, which had made life intolerable for the peasantry. These *routiers* were mercenary troops who lived off the country when unpaid, which was more often than not. The present word brigand had its origin from the kind of protective armor one particular group of these marauding soldiers wore. Another group earned the name *tard-venus* or "latecomers," since they operated over ground already despoiled by earlier marauders. The aroused peasants vented their blind rage on the castles and possessions of the aristocracy who had continued to exact manorial services and taxes even when failing to provide their subjects in return the traditional protection they owed them. These revolts served to rally the terrified aristocracy behind the dauphin who by this time had repudiated the new constitution. The Jacquerie served also to discredit the burgesses and Marcel who were mistakenly believed to sympathize with the peasants. Marcel who had become virtual dictator of Paris was assassinated and royal control restored. (Reading 184)

Charles V. The Treaty of Bretigny (1360) brought a temporary halt to hostilities. On the basis of Crecy and Poitiers, France was obliged to accept the loss of Calais together with English sovereignty over Aquitaine. But like most dictated peaces, once Charles V (1364-1380) felt in a position to do so, he repudiated Bretigny and renewed the war. Charles V fully merited the title "the Wise" which contemporaries bestowed upon him. Industrious, prudent, patient, a student of government and history, he was the first French king who did not lead his own armies, although he revealed much greater knowledge of military tactics than most of his predecessors who did. His success may be attributed in large measure to several permanent taxes which the estates authorized, including a hearth tax and levies on salt, wine, and other merchandise when such merchandise was being moved from province to province. Collected with efficiency and expended with care, the proceeds from these taxes enabled Charles to carry on an unusually effective kind of guerilla warfare against the English. Since he could not suppress all the lawless bands of *routiers* who infested the countryside, he took many of them into his service and placed them under command of Bertrand Duguesclin, one of their captains. Instead of glorious engagements such as Crecy and Poitiers which had ended in inglorious defeat, French warfare now assumed the humble character of raids and skirmishes at which the *routiers* and Duguesclin proved themselves masters. Now the wheel of fortune began to reverse itself and by 1374 French arms, coupled with the dotage of Edward III and the broken health of the Black Prince, managed to reduce English holdings in France to just three seaports, Bayonne, Bordeaux, and Calais. One grave mistake the "wise" Charles did make, although only time would reveal its lamentable consequences. Back in 1361 when the duchy of Burgundy had escheated to the crown, Charles' father, King John, had turned it over as an appanage to his son Philip, Charles' younger brother. At the time he had persuaded the German emperor to add an imperial fief to the duchy, the county of Burgundy or Franche-Comte which adjoined it. Charles now took the dangerous step of further increasing the extent of Philip's possessions by arranging his marriage to the heiress of Flanders. Charles' hope was to build a powerful semi-independent domain to strengthen France against possible enemies toward the east. But Burgundy proved so strong and ambitious in time that it almost encompassed the destruction of France.

Agincourt and the Treaty of Troyes. Trouble developed in the early nineties when Charles VI (1380-1422), already incompetent, suffered his first attacks of insanity. Two factions sprang up to seize control of the throne, the one, the Orleanists, headed by Charles' younger brother Louis, the duke of Orleans, the other, the Burgundian, directed by Charles' uncle Philip, duke of Burgundy. Bitterness between the two factions flared into open war soon after Philip's death when his son, the new duke, John the Fearless, hired some ruffians to assassinate Louis (d. 1407). As bad luck would have it for the French, the English king Henry V (1413-1422) decided the time had come to prosecute with vigor a war which had lagged for almost thirty-five years. He accordingly crossed over to Normandy, marched northward across the Somme, and at Agincourt encountered an army three times the size of his own, under command of Orleanist leaders. (The Orleanists are generally known as the Armagnacs after the count of Armagnac who was the father-in-law of the new duke.) Completely confident in their huge superiority in the number of knights, the French attacked as a "herd of blind buffaloes," only to suffer a disaster even greater than that at Crecy. The French lost 5,000 men; the English less than 100. Henry eventually overran Normandy with the help of John the Fearless, the latter seizing Paris, while the dauphin, Charles, fled south with his Armagnac allies. The severity of the English demands prompted John, however, to consider reaching a settlement with the dauphin, only to be murdered as he knelt to make his abeyance to Charles. His son, Philip the Good, swore revenge on the dauphin, and promptly signed the Treaty of Troyes with the English (1420). According to the terms of this treaty, the insane Charles VI disowned his son, the dauphin, and designated as his heir and regent Henry V who had married his daughter Catherine. Both Henry V and Charles VI died in 1422, but the English and Burgundian armies continued to press their conquest of France. Orleans alone remained the last powerful stronghold loyal to the former dauphin and still uncrowned Charles VII. It appeared that only a miracle could retrieve the situation, and Charles was himself so sunk in lethargy that he seemed wholly indifferent to the possibility of such a miracle. It was at this moment that Joan of Arc entered the picture. (Reading 183)

Joan of Arc. Joan of Arc was born in 1412 of devout French parentage in the hamlet of Domremy on the border of Lorraine. She received no formal education, never learned to read or write, although she revealed during her subsequent trial a remarkably subtle and perceptive mind. As a child she was wont to spend long hours in prayer to her favorite saints, Mary and the virgin-martyrs Catherine and Margaret. On one occasion at the age of fourteen while watching sheep, she had taken shelter from the rain in an abandoned chapel, where she fell asleep, and, according to her later testimony, experienced her first supernatural manifestation. She heard the voices, later saw the figures of Saints Catherine, Margaret, and Michael —"saw them with these very eyes, as well as I see you," she insisted at her trial. Her saints in time gave her her instructions: she was to go to the dauphin Charles and escort him to Reims to be crowned. (France's monarchs were traditionally crowned at Reims.) But Joan refused and for four years remonstrated with her saints: "I am a poor girl. I do not know how to ride or fight." The voices gave her no rest: "It is God who commands," they persisted, "he has had compassion on the French." Joan's parents remained unconvinced, but a cousin agreed to take Joan to the captain of the garrison at Vaucouleurs to seek an escort for the trip to Chinon where Charles was loafing. The captain first roughly rebuffed her but upon her third appeal relented and delegated six men to accompany her through the three hundred miles of enemy-held territory to Chinon. Charles had been apprised of her coming, and to test the girl's sincerity hid his identity, but she picked him out from among the company of courtiers without hesitation. A commission of bishops and theologians whom Charles appointed to examine her, found her an entirely virtuous girl and one who might well serve as God's instrument. Whereupon Charles gave her a white horse and banner. On the banner she ordered inscribed the words "Jesus and Mary."

Joan's Victories and Capture. A transformation meantime had swept the demoralized French soldiery. God had sent Joan to bring them victory! Where before, as the chronicler remarks, two hundred Englishmen could rout five hundred Frenchmen, now the reverse was the case. An attack on the English lines before Orleans proved unexpectedly successful, and after three days fighting the English were in precipitate flight. Yet it required Joan's constant urging to sustain the flagging interest of the king who was by nature lazy, procrastinating, and irresolute, and who even shuddered at the thought of war. A series of victories opened the way to Reims where Charles was crowned on 17 July 1429, just three months after Joan had donned her armor. Joan begged Charles to exploit the enthusiasm which his victories and coronation had evoked, but the king sank back into his lethargy. He preferred to give his ear, particularly because it required less exertion, to treacherous councilors who advised negotiations with Burgundy. In desperation, since her "voices" were warning her that her time was running out, Joan organized a force of her own. While outside the walls of Compiègne to help ward off a large Burgundian force, the drawbridge of the city was pulled up either by treachery or mistake, and she was captured.

The Burgundians turned her over to the English for what today would be somewhat above a half million dollars. The English commanders were most anxious to have Joan in their hands. In order to restore the morale of their soldiers, they must prove her admitted supernatural powers were diabolical rather than divine, and that she was a witch and not God's emissary. Pierre Cauchon, the unscrupulous bishop of Beauvais, whom the French advance had driven from his diocese, proved a ready tool and upon instructions of the English organized and directed one of the most famous mistrials in history. For six weeks Joan defeated the efforts of a battery of sixty trained canonists and theologians who sought to trap this illiterate, counsel-less girl into making statements which might be judged heretical. But her utter guilelessness and sincerity completely baffled their attempts. Thus to the damaging question whether she was in God's grace, to which an affirmative answer would leave her open to the charge of presumption, while a negative one would imply an admission of witchcraft, she answered simply: "If I am not, may God make me so: if I am, may God keep me so."

Joan's Martyrdom. But the duke of Bedford, the English commander, insisted that the court declare her a witch and heretic, which it accordingly did. She was given the choice of confessing the spuriousness of her "visions" or of being burned at the stake. As it developed, it was easier to secure the judgment of the packed court against her than her confession. Yet to execute her without such a confession would simply make her a martyr and leave the English soldiers quite as dispirited as ever. So a variety of promises and threats were employed to bring her to yield, and she was shown instruments of torture and the stake at which she would be burned. Joan's courage appears finally to have given way, at least momentarily. No wonder! For a year now she had been caged in a filthy prison; for a part of that time she had been secured to her bed by chains about her neck, a foot, and a hand, mistreated by her brutal jailors, abandoned by the contemptible Charles who did not lift a finger to save her, and denied the company of friends, of women, and of all spiritual consolation. Joan at length weakened to the extent of affixing her name to some sort of confession which she could not read. Its true import remains a matter of controversy, although the longer confession which has been preserved is manifestly a forgery. At any rate, the morning after making her "confession," she affirmed the authenticity of her visions, declaring, "All that I then said and revoked, I said from fear of fire." This about-face proved fatal, for now she could be classified as a relapsed heretic and summarily sentenced to death. Joan's execution was carried out under circumstances of profound pathos. Even her bitterest enemies were misty-eyed, so the chronicler reports, as Joan died clutching a crucifix and calling upon the name of Jesus. Many of the onlookers must have agreed with the English soldier who exclaimed at the moment when she collapsed: "We are lost; we have burned a saint!" Joan was exonerated of the charges of witchcraft and heresy in a process authorized by the pope in 1456, and in 1920 the Catholic Church declared her a saint. The fame of this illiterate peasant girl has outlived that of any other Frenchman from medieval times!

The End of the War. If the English hoped the death of Joan would revive the confidence of the English troops, they were mistaken. After her death they won no major victories, and while historians are free to doubt the genuineness of Joan's visions, there is no denying the inspiration her death afforded the French cause. A major stroke of fortune was the neutralization of Burgundy. This the English brought upon themselves by their exorbitant demands for French territory which alienated their French allies. The indignant Burgundians instead negotiated the Treaty of Arras in 1435 with Charles, who granted the duchy complete autonomy and exempted the duke from all feudal services and royal taxation. Vital monies were secured through loans from Jacques Coeur and by action of the Estates General which voted the crown in 1439 the right to assess and collect the *taille* in perpetuity and to raise troops and to reorganize the army. (The *taille* fell principally upon the peasantry which had no voice in the Estates General.) Charles resumed the war with vigor in 1449. His new army consisted in time of three branches, the cavalry which was the most important, the infantry which was the least dependable, and the artillery which the Bureau brothers made the best in Europe. Within a few months the French had expelled the English from Normandy, and by the end of 1453 had cleared them from Guienne. All that remained of England's century-old empire in France was Calais. Charles has been called "the Well Served." Surely his success in bringing the Hundred Years' War to a happy conclusion and of raising the fortunes of the French monarchy above that accomplished by any of his predecessors was not so much the achievement of this somewhat mediocre, repulsive prince, as it was the work of Joan and of Coeur among other individuals, of nascent French nationalism and the collapse of royal government in England.

Louis XI. Louis XI (1461-1483) came by his ill-looking physical appearance honestly. His industry and shrewdness on the other hand, even his cynicism and unscrupulousness, were beyond those any of his immediate ancestors could boast or deplore. His unpleasant sobriquet, "the Spider," he earned (and deserved) for the skill and deviousness of his far-flung spying and diplomatic activities. His long thin nose he poked into every nook and cranny of France and so untiring and mobile was he that couriers had difficulty locating him. Parsimonious to the point of being mean, the only luxuries he permitted himself were horses and dogs for hunting. But he knew how to combine business with pleasure as, for instance, when he made his periodic visits to the dungeons where he kept his political prisoners, to make sure these were securely in chains. Not one sou did he waste on gracious living, which he despised. He dressed like a commoner, and he preferred to employ members of the bourgeoisie in the government instead of noblemen since he found them more trustworthy and tractable. He even hired ruffians who were in jail, or should have been, to do his errands. Religion was hardly more than superstitution with him, and he was wont to appeal to the saints whose images he carried on the wide brim of his hat when he needed assistance in one of his projects, whether commendable or criminal. The church he kept in a tight grasp. He was actually in exile when his father Charles died—his father did not feel safe with him around —so anxious was Louis to be king! The man who gave Louis haven, the duke of Burgundy, learned later that Louis as king never permitted sentiment, or principle for that matter, to stand between him and his ambition to be absolute. (Reading 185)

Charles the Rash and the End of Burgundy. This duke was Charles, known as "the Rash" because his ambitions and enterprises usually outran his means. From his father Philip, Charles inherited the richest domain in the West: Holland, Hainault, Brabant, Flanders, and Luxemburg in the north, and the duchy and county of Burgundy along the middle Rhone. His was also the most brilliant court in the West, and he sought to make it the most cultured as well through generous patronage of writers and artists. Two major goals absorbed his efforts: first, to close the territorial gap between the two parts of his domain; second, to become king of Burgundy. There is little question that he would have attained both goals had it not been for Louis XI. History seldom presents two antagonists one so completely the antithesis of the other. Charles was everything Louis was not: handsome, gallant, chivalrous, and a model of Christian morality. But he was also imprudent. Because most of the great nobles in France rightly feared Louis and resented his exclusion of them from the government, they became Charles' ready allies and organized themselves into the League of the Public Weal. Louis had few friends, but a lot of money which he found most effective in making friends, even among the proud French nobility. He did suffer several setbacks in his struggle with Charles, but the bits of territory he ceded he eventually recovered, while the promises and treaties he made, he broke when it was safe to do so. He outlived by accident or design most of the nobles who joined the League and eventually took over their lands. As for Charles, it was his misfortune that his territorial ambitions disturbed too many neighbors who listened willingly to Louis' suspicions and gladly accepted his gold. These neighbors were composed of members of the aristocracy of Alsace and Lorraine and the Swiss. It was the latter whose pikemen defeated Charles in two great battles, leaving him dead in the second with his skull cloven and his Burgundy gone forever. Louis grabbed what he could of Charles' possessions, notably Picardy and the duchy of Burgundy. Two other provinces, Artois and the county of Burgundy he arranged to acquire by betrothing his son to their heiress. When Louis died, of the great medieval French fiefs only Flanders and

Brittany remained outside the royal domain. Thus at the close of the Middle Ages the long painful process which had started in 987 with Hugh Capet was all but completed. The monarchy Louis bequeathed to his son Charles VIII (1483-1498) was no longer medieval because king Charles ruled, not reigned. He had a regular army of his own and a bureaucracy which he appointed and dismissed. Instead of feudal dues, he collected taxes which he could levy as he chose. The members of the French feudal aristocracy were no longer his equals but his subordinates. The new French monarchy had sloughed off its medieval limitations and was ready to move into the modern era, the era of absolutism.

England in the Late Middle Ages

Several interesting parallels suggest themselves between the histories of France and England in the late Middle Ages. The Hundred Years' War affected both countries, of course, although France in a far more disastrous manner than England. Each country suffered the curse of a king who was incompetent if not insane and, at the same time, unusually long-lived, with near-fatal consequences for their respective monarchies. In fact, in both France and England royal absolutism rose triumphant less than a short fifty years after their monarchies had reached the nadir of their fortunes and seemed about to disintegrate. To the rise of this royal absolutism bloody conflicts contributed powerfully in both countries, as, for example, the Hundred Years' War in France, and the War of the Roses in England. Historically the most significant development in France in the late Middle Ages was the emergence of a strong monarchy. Only a moderately powerful aristocracy remained in 1500 which was capable of offering any protest to its domination of the country. In England, even more significant for the future than the emergence of royal absolutism was the rise of parliament. Parliament enjoyed approximately the same position in England vis-à-vis the crown as the French nobility did in France: it was its only check. But here the similarity stopped. Parliament had a glorious history awaiting it, the French aristocracy only decline. While the English parliament was an aristocratic body, it was nevertheless an organized group with rules and traditions, and it did in theory represent the entire nation. France had nothing comparable since the Estates General had written its obituary in 1439 with its grant to Charles VII of sweeping powers over army and taxation.

Edward I. The rise of parliament is linked intimately with the reign of

Edward I (1272-1307), the medieval monarch of whom England can be proudest. In so many respects Edward achieved excellence. His family life was exemplary. He participated in one Crusade and worked earnestly to organize another. He was a man of honor and the epitaph on his tomb, *Pactum Serva* (Honor Thy Pledge), was no servile flattery. Edward's sense of justice, though less personal than St. Louis', was instrumental in providing English jurisprudence with the solid mold it still preserves. His work of reorganizing the English government proved of such a high order that it remains his greatest single contribution to English history. He enlarged the frontiers of his England, always a monarch's most direct road to the hearts of his subjects. He was blessed with an amiable disposition; he was handsome, and he boasted a vigorous physique. "Longshanks" they called him. He might, finally, be considered the first truly English king to occupy the English throne since the death of Edward the Confessor, although like his Norman and Plantagenet predecessors, he spoke French.

Origins of English Parliament. The English parliament had its origins in the *curia regis*, the feudal body which convened two or three times a year upon summons from the king. The business of the *curia regis* included questions of war and peace, disputes between vassals, the clarification of feudal obligations, and trial of its members. Since its fundamental purpose was to give counsel, it was generally called the great council when it convened in full membership. For reasons of convenience, the term *curia regis* applied more narrowly to the smaller group of councilors in regular attendance upon the king. The first significant step from the great council to the evolution of parliament as we know it today was taken during the reign of Henry III. In order to secure a more popular base for his revolt, Simon de Montfort directed each shire and borough to send two representatives to meet with the great council in 1265. Henry III and his son Edward had no choice under the circumstances but to do the same, although they soon discovered that having shire and borough representatives at hand offered definite advantages. As the proceeds from feudal and manorial sources grew progressively less adequate to meet the mounting cost of government, the crown found itself appealing in the thirteenth century with growing frequency to the great council for additional funds, usually a general levy on the personal property of all classes. Since the boroughs and shires controlled an increasing percentage of the country's wealth, the attendance of their representatives at meetings of the great council provided the crown a more convenient and effective method of negotiating with them there in a body than privately and individually. A second development affecting the membership of parliament was in process of crystalization in the thirteenth century. This was the change in personnel from feudal tenants-in-chief who traditionally made up the great council to a smaller more select body of peers. Because of the expense and difficulties of travel, only those vassals attended the meeting of the council who received a personal summons.

Those who received only the general summons issued by the sheriff were inclined to ignore it. Since Edward's parliament which met in 1295 appeared to embody these developments, that is, it included representatives of the boroughs and shires and, at the same time, an aristocratic element limited to those individual peers who had received a personal summons, it came to be hailed by contemporary writers as the Model Parliament. The term parliament itself, which derived from the French word meaning to speak or discuss, gradually replaced the earlier designations of great council and *curia regis.* (Reading 177)

Developments of the Fourteenth Century. The fourteenth century witnessed several additional developments in the evolution of parliament. Edward I would have preferred to rule without benefit of parliament and so would every king who succeeded him. But financial exigencies growing out of his wars with the Welsh, Scots, and French, left him no choice but to appeal repeatedly to the great council for funds. Had the king found his traditional feudal and manorial dues sufficient, there would probably have been no parliament at all or at best a feeble body such as the French Estates General which had been so unwise as to grant the crown permanent control over taxation. For what proved the decisive factor in the rise of parliamentary government was the establishment of the principle that national revenues over and beyond the traditional aids and incidents, in effect, all taxation, must be authorized by parliament. It was parliament's control of the purse strings that enabled it eventually to acquire control over legislation. Since it was their money, directly or indirectly, which was involved, little short of a manifest emergency could induce the members of parliament to vote the king a subsidy. Even then they usually insisted upon making their grant contingent upon the king's promise to redress certain grievances. These the king would then correct either by royal ordinance or, more permanently, by statute, which consisted of formal promulgation by the crown of resolutions agreed upon by parliament. From this negative approach to legislation, it was not long before parliament began to assume a positive role in the enactment of laws. The fourteenth century saw the separation of parliament into two bodies, the houses of lords and commons. The initiative in this move was taken by the burgesses and knights of the shire. In the presence of their aristocratic fellow parliamentarians they had felt ill at ease and had been conspicuous chiefly by their silence. Parliament retained the traditional judicial functions of the original great council, although formal consideration of guilt became the exclusive prerogative of the house of lords. The latter house still remains England's highest court. But parliament succeeded in establishing the principle that the entire body should have control over common law. Yet for all the advance parliament achieved during the late Middle Ages, the fact remains that the king ignored that body when he needed no money. Not until the late seventeenth century when parliament finally recognized its obligation to pay the cost of government through taxation did it actually assume direction of the state. Nonetheless, parliamentary institutions remain medieval England's greatest contribution to Western civilization.

Edward's Wars. Edward's great ambition was to absorb Wales and Scotland and to solidify English possession of Guienne. He initiated his expansionist program with Wales, the northern part of which was ruled by the native prince Llewellyn. The latter's failure to put in an appearance at Edward's coronation furnished Edward pretext for an attack. Though the Welsh made themselves troublesome with their long bows, Edward's campaign was so well organized that it succeeded without much difficulty. Llewellyn found his rule restricted to a small section of northern Wales. A second war broke out almost immediately over the extortionate methods of the English; Llewellyn was slain and all of Wales was annexed. Edward's son, who was born in Wales at the close of the campaign, fell heir to Llewellyn's title of prince of Wales and passed it on to British crown princes after him. With Scotland Edward hoped war would not be necessary. England claimed an ancient overlordship, but none of Edward's predecessors had had the imprudence to put the claim to the test. Edward found an opportunity to do so in 1290 when the Scottish throne fell vacant. Upon his insistence the Scots gave him the privilege of choosing, as king, either Robert Bruce or John Balliol. Edward chose the latter, but when he summoned Balliol for military service in France, the Scottish king repudiated his homage and made an alliance with France. A short war sufficed to discipline Balliol, but a new revolt broke out under William Wallace which required six years of hard fighting to suppress. It was while journeying northward to put down a third revolt, this one inspired by Robert Bruce, that Edward died. Edward's quarrel with Philip IV over Guienne did not come to blows until after his death.

Edward's Legislation. Edward's most constructive and enduring work came in the realm of law. And this was most timely. Almost a hundred years had elapsed since Henry II had prepared the bases of royal judicial administration. During this interval little had been done to extend his work, to systematize developments which had taken place, or to correct abuses which had appeared. Furthermore, the royal power had itself been subjected to heavy and successful attack by the feudality during the reigns of Edward's two predecessors, John and Henry III. The legislation which Edward sponsored was concerned in the main with correcting evils in local administration and in defining and fortifying the position of the crown. Several statutes had as their objective the elimination of such malpractices by royal officials as the levying of excessive fees. Lest the decline of feudalism endanger certain royal feudal revenues and rights, Edward reaffirmed royal claim to such feudal incidents and perquisites as wardship, relief, and escheat. Because lords were making fictitious grants of lands to the church in order to escape the payment of feudal obligations, a statute prohibited transfers of property to the church without royal permission. Edward discovered that the future of the royal judiciary which had looked so bright in Henry II's day had been jeopardized during the feeble reign of Henry III when many baronial courts revived and expanded their jurisdiction. He therefore declared all private courts abolished except where a formal charter authorizing same could be produced. Here he was forced to be content with a partial victory, so threatening was the feudal outcry. Yet those barons who insisted on retaining private jurisdiction he compelled to pay heavily for the privilege. Since subinfeudation tended to splinter feudal obligations to the point of disappearance, Edward sought to discourage the practice by requiring the buyer of any land to assume the same obligations to the king as those the seller had had. Interesting, though of relatively little value, was his attempt to revive the ancient militia by ordering all men between the ages of fifteen and sixty to equip themselves with weapons. But a step of major significance was his move to tap the growing wealth of the bourgeoisie for the crown by imposing custom duties on the export of wool. Even though his banishment of the Jews in 1290 was economically injurious, when Edward died in 1307 the crown was realizing more from customs than from all the older traditional sources of revenue combined. To such a degree did Edward's work tend to regularize English jurisprudence for centuries to come that it earned for him the title of the English Justinian. (Reading 178)

The Peasant Revolt of 1381. The chief misfortune of Edward II's unfortunate reign (1307-1327) was the disastrous defeat of the English at Bannockburn by a Scottish army one-third its size. Robert Bruce's victory assured the independence of the northern kingdom. Edward III (1327-1377) is best known for his part in the Hundred Years' War to which he devoted his not inconsiderable talents. He gave little thought to strengthening the position of the crown and he has left no real mark on English history. Great hopes were entertained of Edward's popular son, the Black Prince, but his death anticipated that of his father by one year. During the minority years of the Black Prince's son Richard II (1377-1399), the latter's uncle, John of Gaunt, served as regent. Richard came out of his minority in dramatic fashion on the occasion of the Peasant Revolt of 1381. The principal agitators of this, England's only peasant rebellion, were irregular priests like John Ball who preached a program of political, economic, social, and religious reform and change that filled most contemporaries with consternation. Though the revolt was triggered by the government's attempt to force payment of a poll tax, the third in four years, it reflected peasant misery less than discontent. Actually the condition of the peasant was appreciably better during the last half of the fourteenth century than it had ever been before, largely because of a shortage of labor which enabled him to secure better terms from his lord. (See page 355.) Yet these concessions only whetted his desire for more, while they served to awaken him to his lowly condition. A popular couplet among the discontents ran:

> When Adam delved and Eve span
> Who was then the gentleman?

Violence broke out in southeastern England in June and spread quickly to London. Since the army was at Plymouth waiting passage to France, the city could not be defended. With the help of sympathizers among the lower classes in the city, the mob took over, seized and beheaded the treasurer and chancellor, and sought vainly for John of Gaunt who was fortunately away in Scotland. They killed his servants and what lawyers they could find, and burned all charters and records that they could unearth in the hope of destroying the legal bases for their serfdom. Richard who had taken refuge in the tower held a conference with the insurgents and promised the peasants an end to personal serfdom, commutation of all services to money rents, together with the abrogation of hostile legislation such as the Statute of Laborers. (See page 356.) During a second conference, Wat Tyler, the gruff leader of the insurgents, was stabbed by the mayor of London when he pulled out his knife. Richard's presence of mind saved the day. Before the milling mob could rush to avenge Tyler's death, he dramatically announced himself their new leader and promptly led them out of the city where they were eventually hunted down and exterminated. "Serfs ye are and serfs ye will remain," Richard retorted when shown promises of liberation he had given the peasants. (Readings 179, 180)

Deposition of Richard. The incident revealed Richard a man of such capabilities that the noble councilors were alarmed. They had more reason for anxiety when Richard proceeded quietly to exclude them from his counsels and transfer his confidence to men of less aristocratic rank. In 1386 the Lancastrian party, that is, the faction headed by John of Gaunt who was the duke of Lancaster, demanded that he dismiss this new group of confidants. Though Richard's first impulse was to declare that at their bidding he would not remove the lowliest scullion in his kitchen, he eventually capitulated upon intimation that it might otherwise be his lot to suffer the same fate as his murdered great-grandfather, Edward II. Within the year, however, he attempted to humble the Lancastrians, only to have them revolt and seize control. The "Merciless Parliament" of 1388 under Lancastrian direction ordered and carried out the execution of a number of Richard's "evil" advisors. This ruthless show of power still did not frighten Richard into passivity. It only made him more cautious. In the late summer of 1397 he struck with a vengeance, executed his chief opponents, and introduced personal rule. Then early in 1399 he made the fatal mistake of seizing John of Gaunt's enormous estates—a fatal mistake because most Englishmen had a greater respect for property than for God.

Revolt broke out under the leadership of Gaunt's son, Henry, who captured Richard, forced him to abdicate, and probably arranged his murder. (Reading 181)

The Lancastrians. Henry IV (1399-1413), the first of the Lancastrians, introduced the most sterile century in English history. Fifty years of fruitless foreign war and another thirty-five of turmoil and strife at home tell the story. Henry's questionable title to the throne did not help. Two dissident movements absorbed his energies, a nationalist uprising in Wales and Lollardy in England. Henry V (1413-1422) proved the ablest and most popular of the Lancastrians, but all his talents were wasted on hollow victories in France. The "Cut-throat," French historians call him for ordering the execution of the aristocratic prisoners taken at Agincourt, an act which proclaimed as loudly as did cultural developments in Italy the passing of the Middle Ages. Henry's son Henry VI (1422-1461) inherited the mental disease of his French grandfather, but whence he inherited his gentle, unsuspecting nature is difficult to say. Neither idiocy, however, nor mildness was fitted to tame the wild passions of men aroused over the losses in France or dim the prospect of exploiting the shakiness of Henry's throne to their own advantage. Almost every baronial family in England was linked with one or the other of the numberless legitimate and illegitimate descendants of Edward III and his sons. A struggle for the throne became inevitable. So hardly had the Hundred Years' War closed than the War of the Roses opened between the Lancastrians (red rose) and the Yorkists (white rose). The latter championed the ambitions of Richard, duke of York, whose claim was as good as that of the Lancastrians. Most formidable of Richard's adherents was his nephew, Richard Neville, earl of Warwick, the richest man in England. The Yorkists eventually defeated their opponents and forced Henry VI into exile. But when Edward, the son of the deceased Richard of York, decided to wed a Lancastrian widow rather than advance his political fortunes by marrying a French princess, Warwick broke with him and placed Henry VI back on his throne. Shortly after, however, the army of Henry went down to defeat and with it the fortunes of the Lancastrians and Warwick. Edward IV (1461-1483) could have been one of England's more distinguished monarchs had he not been so lazy. His popularity, uncommon ability, and the money and resources at his command might have enabled him to establish the absolutism which the Tudors did establish a century later. But he chose the life of a voluptuary and died of overindulgence at the early age of forty. His brother, Richard of Gloucester, the "bad man" of English history, seized the throne, probably murdered Edward's two sons, but for all his machinations was only to fall among the slain on Bosworth Field in 1485 in battle with Henry Tudor.

The Triumph of Crown over Feudality. With Richard III in 1485 on Bosworth Field died medieval England, if it had not died before. Henry VII (1485-1509) went on to prepare the bases for the absolutism which we associate with modern times. The War of the Roses had vastly simplified his task, for in its bloody battles the English feudality virtually destroyed itself. Though the actual number of combatants in the war was small, they included a heavy proportion of the aristocracy, and in the fighting no quarter was given. Those few baronial families which emerged reasonably intact from the war were impoverished. The king by contrast had grown enormously wealthy. The estates of all the different families who had held the throne automatically remained crown property, while the possessions of many other lords including the vast ones of Warwick were confiscated. Furthermore, the king's ownership of these extensive holdings furnished him considerable influence in local affairs. He also received powerful encouragement from the towns and peasantry which abominated the feudal misrule and semi-anarchy of the past fifty years and saw in him a man who could bring peace and order to their troubled country. They were not disappointed.

Germany in the Late Middle Ages

We have seen how the histories of the French and English monarchies roughly paralleled one another during the late Middle Ages. In the course of their long Hundred Years' War and the War of the Roses in England, royal power appeared headed for destruction first in France, then in England. Fortunately the long, dark days of the reigns of the French Charles VI and the English Henry VI ended before irreparable damage had been suffered, and subsequent kings proved capable of bringing the monarchy in both countries to the threshold of absolutism. Since the German monarchy of 1250 had approximately attained the political maturity of the other two, one might suppose that its history in the late Middle Ages would continue to follow along comparatively similar lines. Unfortunately for Germany it did not, and the history of the late-medieval German monarchy diverges sharply from that of England and France. Where the governments in those two countries tended generally in the direction of greater centralization and solidarity, in Germany the trend was toward decentralization. Where France and England emerged from the medieval period as powerful, unified states, Germany in 1500 was to all intents and purposes nothing more than a geographical expression. We can trace the history of England and France in the late Middle Ages by following the fortunes of the crown. It would be idle to do so in Germany, for the German monarchy became

in time as unsubstantial as the emperorship itself with which it was identified. Where the kings of England and France had become virtually absolute by 1500, the German kings by contrast were even less promising figures
than their predecessor Conrad had been back in 911. The history of Germany in the late Middle Ages is the history of its component parts, of such
states as Austria, Luxemburg, Bavaria, Brandenburg, and Switzerland,
rather than of Germany itself.

Germany Before and After 1250.   Not only was the history of Germany
in the late Middle Ages radically different from that of France and England, it also offered sharp contrasts with its own earlier history. The principal point of departure in the history of Germany in the Middle Ages is
the year 1250. That year marked the death of Frederick II, the last powerful representative of the imperialist Hohenstaufen dynasty which at one
time had entertained ambitions of ruling both Germany and Italy. The
German kingship which was revived in 1273 was innocent of all such pretensions. Except for a visionary like Henry VII, the German kings of the
late Middle Ages were content with Germany. Partly because of their
exclusion from Italy, partly because German kings after 1250 no longer
insisted upon control of the German hierarchy as in the days of Henry IV,
the history of German-papal relations is no longer the earlier chronicle of
invective and antipopes. We read rather of mutual cooperation against
the Ottoman Turks who posed an equal threat to Christianity and to
Germany. Before 1250 the German monarch was generally concerned with
building up his power; after 1250 he busied himself not at all with re-
habilitating the monarchy. He dedicated his efforts rather toward promoting his own family fortunes. As opposed to the earlier monarchy which
under Frederick Barbarossa had attempted to exploit feudal rights in the
crown's possession, the monarchy after 1231, when Frederick II had surrendered all regalian rights in Germany, had no prerogative to which to
appeal save that founded on the principle of escheat. Yet as fortune would
have it, more was accomplished toward establishing a strong dynastic monarchy on the strength of this last surviving feudal principle than what had
previously been achieved on the basis of manifold feudal rights which
early German monarchs might have pressed.

Germany a Confused State.   Germany in the fourteenth and fifteenth
centuries was a country of the wildest confusion. To attempt a history of
its sixteen hundred principalities, of which about thirty are entitled to
more than a dot on the map, would be foolhardy. Yet all of them were *de
facto* independent. Late medieval France contained hundreds of dukes,
counts, and other noblemen, but these were all rather well subordinated to
the crown. The hundreds of noblemen in Germany on the other hand, many
of them with high-sounding titles that would fill a page, were laws unto
themselves. Illustrative of the rampant particularism characteristic of late-

medieval Germany were the imperial knights, a lawless group of penniless warriors who lived principally by rapine on their tiny fiefs, and admitted no allegiance to anyone except the powerless emperor. In Germany war was the order of the day: between rival claimants to the throne; between princes over inheritances; between Germans and Hussites; between the Swiss cantons and the Hapsburgs who sought to rule them; between Teutonic Knights and pagan Slavs and, later, Christian Poles and Liths; between Lithuania and Poland and Bohemia; between the imperial cities and neighboring princes; between the Hansa and unfriendly towns and principalities; between the occasional German king who lived in the past and the Italian cities which he attempted to dominate; among the scores of petty princes and knights intent only on enlarging their diminutive domains.

The German Diet. The one institution in Germany which might theoretically have abated some of this confusion, that is, the diet, was itself a study in confusion. In its inception it represented the princes and clergy. Then as seven particular states acquired sole right to elect the emperor, these seven constituted a sort of upper house, the remaining lay and ecclesiastical lords a second, with the free imperial cities becoming a third house. The emperor would presumably convene this large, unwieldy body in times of emergency. Yet though emergency was the order of the day in Germany in the fourteenth and fifteenth centuries, nothing was ever accomplished by the diet. The emperor would confer with its membership and if any resolution could be agreed upon, would promulgate a decree which embodied that resolution. This decree then was considered law throughout Germany. Yet only those princes to whose advantage it was to do so enforced it. Hardly a shred of authority was left to the diet. The insuperable gaps which yawned between the ambitions of the rival groups represented in the diet barred the cooperation necessary to its growth. Furthermore, the catalyst which served to stimulate the growth of parliament in England, that is, the fear of the monarchy, was non-existent in Germany. The German monarchy was impotent and unfeared, and the princes were never so foolish as to erect an institution which would only have succeeded in restricting their own authority.

Revival of German Monarchy. Yet not all was confusion in Germany. Above the political wilderness of Germany in the late Middle Ages two developments of particular note protrude: first, the emergence of small, but compact and potentially strong dynastic states; second, the continued extension of German civilization toward the east. The most famous and powerful of the German dynastic states was that of the Hapsburgs. This family's fortunes date from the election of Rudolf of Hapsburg as king of Germany in 1273. His election terminated a period known as the Interregnum (1254-1273), an interval when none of the aspirants to the German kingship commanded sufficient support to secure general acceptance. Though the papacy had but recently accomplished the destruction of the German monarchy (see page 469), it now assumed the initiative in ending the Interregnum. A chaotic Germany could afford little help to a Crusade, while a German king might discourage petty princes from making a mere subject out of the church. The German princes were not averse to the idea of a monarchy, although they made certain of no possible royal inter-ference by electing Rudolf, a small Swabian count. Rudolf (1273-1291) did not fail them. He had no illusions concerning the prerogatives of his new position. He realized fully that it was too late to attempt anything so pre-tentious as his fellow-kings might be minded to do in England and France. Where they had the solid foundation of a firmly entrenched royal adminis-trative machinery upon which to build, he had nothing. Furthermore, the German feudal aristocracy was infinitely more formidable than that of Eng-land and France. So Rudolf prudently ignored Germany, and Italy as well, and busied himself with advancing his own family fortunes. As luck would have it—and there never was so lucky a dynasty as the Hapsburg—the German princes were willing to encourage him in this. The reason was the power of Ottokar of Bohemia which had assumed alarming propor-tions since his absorption of Austria, Styria, Carniola, and Carinthia in 1246. Since the German princes feared Ottokar and since his provinces should theoretically have escheated to the crown in 1246 upon the death of their lord, they gave Rudolf their blessing to seek their recovery. This he accomplished, and ever since, until 1918, the fortunes of the noble city of Vienna have been linked with those of the most famous dynasty in Western history.

Henry VII, Louis IV, and Charles IV. Because of Rudolf's success, the German princes passed over his son Albert and chose Adolf of Nassau (1291-1298), a less dangerous candidate. But Albert overthrew Adolf and inaugurated an aggressive policy of aggrandizement which only ended with his assassination in 1308. The uneasy princes had had enough of the Haps-burgs and turned to the poverty-stricken Luxemburg family. Their choice, Henry VII (1308-1313), permitted the fatuous dream of reviving German power in Italy to lure him south of the Alps where he died. In the civil war that broke out over the succession upon Henry's death, fortune even-tually smiled upon the ambitions of the duke of Bavaria, Louis of Wittles-bach (1314-1347). But Pope John XXII protested that he, rather than the fortunes of war, should decide in a contested election. The pope's somewhat anachronistic stand, reminiscent of the brighter days of Innocent III now long faded away, precipitated the last bitter feud between church and state in the Middle Ages. Among the emperor's stoutest champions in a struggle which the impotence of the pope and the emptiness of the imperial title robbed of any reality, was William of Ockham whom Louis had be-friended. Louis stated his position in the decree *Licet Juris* (1328), which announced that the man whom the princes of Germany elected held both titles, king and emperor, and that he did this without benefit of papal confirmation. (Reading 187) Louis' successor, Charles IV of Bohemia (1347-1378), the ablest and most unscrupulous German monarch of the late Middle Ages, promulgated a more famous decree in 1356, the so-called Golden Bull. This conferred exclusive right to elect the German king upon seven princes: the archbishops of Trier, Cologne, and Mainz, the count Palatine of the Rhine, the king of Bohemia, the duke of Saxony, and the margrave of Brandenburg. Both reason and ambition dictated Charles' step. Because many territories and rights had changed hands during the turbulency of the previous hundred years, the question of who was and who was not entitled to cast a vote were frequently matters of dispute. This confusion was now ended. Furthermore, by settling upon these seven princes, Charles achieved a rough balance between the older states of western Germany and the newer ones to the east. The bull also provided that these seven states remain undivided and undiminished, a provision which Charles hoped would have a stabilizing influence upon Germany and which would also prompt the seven so privileged to look with favor upon the fortunes of his children. (Reading 188)

Sigismund, Frederick III, and Maximilian. This last hope of Charles was fulfilled. Still the only distinction his first son Wenceslas could claim was that of being the most illustrious inebriate in history to lose his job because of drinking. The disgusted princes gave the crown to Ruprecht of the Palatinate (1400-1410), and then to Wenceslas' brother, Sigismund (1410-1437). Sigismund was not nearly so important a man as he supposed, although some adventitious fame came his way because of his part in the council of Constance and the fact that the two counts to whom he gave Saxony and Brandenburg established dynasties, the Wettin and Hohenzollern respectively, which endured until 1918. Sigismund had no son, so his son-in-law, Albert of Austria, fell heir to the extensive domains of the two most powerful dynasties in central Europe, the Hapsburgs and Luxemburgs. This windfall assured the Hapsburgs of the imperial election from now on, since to elect someone else would have invited civil war. The electors also saw the wisdom of selecting a Hapsburg whose family's domains lay athwart the road of Turkish expansion. Albert ruled for only one year, but his son, the extraordinarily incompetent Frederick III, reigned for fifty-three (1440-1493). Though not insane like the long-lived Charles VI of France and Henry VI of England, he might just as well have been. Confusion became even more confounded during this dreadful period when organized society appeared to be tottering on the brink of dissolution. Everyone appeared to be at everybody else's throat: robber barons, Hussites, peasants, free imperial cities, and princes. Landfrieden, that is, regional agreements among local lords to respect the peace of the area, which had earlier been tried and failed, failed again. City leagues proved no more permanent, and even the great Hansa chose this time to disintegrate. The only kind of justice which could be procured was the rough, summary sort meted out in so-called Fehmic courts. Bohemia and Hungary were lost to the empire in 1457, while imperial fiefs went to swell the growing domain of Charles the Rash of Burgundy. The only person these anarchical conditions did not appear to depress was the resourceless and witless Frederick who never lost faith in Austria's destiny, but kept inscribing upon his papers and belongings a cryptic character composed of the five vowels and signifying "Alles Erdreich Ist Oesterreich Unterthan" (the entire earth is subject to Austria). Curiously enough, that is what almost happened. Frederick's son Maximilian married Mary, the heiress of Burgundy, who brought Artois, Franche Comte, and the Low Countries into the empire. Maximilian also inherited Bohemia and Hungary. His son Philip married Joanna, the daughter of Ferdinand and Isabella, the richest heiress in Christendom. So within a generation of Frederick's death, Dutch, Indians, Spaniards, Germans, Czechs, Hungarians, and even Filipinos were paying homage to the house of Hapsburg.

Switzerland. The chief hope of late-medieval Germany lay not in the empire but in such dynastic, seminational states as Bavaria, Saxony, and Brandenburg. The most interesting political entity, however, was not a national state at all, but a union of German-, Italian-, and French-speaking mountaineers who lived in the Swiss Alps. These Swiss were among the oldest subjects of the Hapsburgs. The original nucleus around which the state of Switzerland eventually coalesced was composed of the three forest cantons of Uri, Schwyz, and Unterwalden. These lay about Lake Lucerne between St. Gothard Pass and the Rhine where a number of bustling commercial communities had sprung up. In 1291 these three cantons pledged themselves in the Perpetual Compact to stand together against the threat of subjection by Rudolf of Hapsburg who had brushed aside their protest that they were imperial fiefs and had moved to incorporate them into his family domains. A long history of guerilla warfare ensued, punctuated from time to time by bloody battles such as Morgarten (1315) and Sempach (1386) where the Swiss attacking from strong defensive positions with battle-axe and pike proved capable of destroying strong feudal armies. Only in 1499 in the Treaty of Basel did the Hapsburgs reluctantly recognize the Swiss as independent. Meantime other cantons had joined the original three and by the close of the Middle Ages thirteen Swiss cantons were organized into what was known as the League of Upper Germany. Despite differences in language, friction between peasants and townspeople, and bitterness later over religious issues, the Swiss realized that they could not afford the luxury of falling out among themselves or they would have been overwhelmed by their unfriendly neighbors. The member cantons entrusted to a federal diet regulation of their external affairs, while each retained autonomy in local matters. Their stunning victories over the Hapsburgs and Charles the Rash of Burgundy brought fame to their arms and led to a constant demand for their services as mercenary troops and palace guards during the seventeenth and eighteenth centuries. The only reminder today of this glorious page in the history of Switzerland is the Swiss guard at the Vatican. (Reading 189)

German Expansion Eastward and the Teutonic Knights. The development in late German medieval history with greatest consequences for the future was the extension of German civilization eastward. This movement originated with Charlemagne who established a series of marches along the eastern frontier and succeeded in rolling back the Slavic peoples almost to the Elbe. Otto I pushed them back to the Oder. But the pressure of the prolific Slavs was heavy and constant. No sooner would German vigilance be relaxed than back the Slavs would come swarming over lands from which they had earlier been expelled. During the reign of Frederick Barbarossa individual counts and dukes undertook a new German offensive which resulted in the founding of such states as Luebeck, Mecklenburg, and Brandenburg. Now in the thirteenth century, the German *"Drang nach Osten"* received new impetus and made its greatest advance, first under Danish direction, then under the auspices of two religious-military orders, the Brothers of the Sword and the Teutonic Knights. The latter group had left Syria early in the thirteenth century for Hungary, whence a Polish prince invited them to Poland to assist him against the pagan Prussians. If this Polish nobleman never lived to regret his action, his fellow-countrymen did. For what began as a crusading project rapidly acquired the character of an imperialistic movement as German nobles swarmed into the area to carve out fiefs for themselves. Within a hundred years of their arrival, the Teutonic Knights had erected a state which extended from Pomerania to the Gulf of Finland. In the process they all but exterminated the Prussians, converted the Balts and Slavs in the area, and threw up a barrier against Polish expansion to the Baltic. Even Poland itself seemed threatened with Germanization as large numbers of German merchants began to settle in the country. But the expansionist Knights overreached themselves. When they veered southward to strike at the sprawling empire of Lithuania, they drove the Poles and Liths into alliance. In 1386 Jagiello, Prince of Lithuania, became a Christian and married Jadwiga, the heiress of Poland. Not only did the subsequent conversion of the Liths deprive further expansion of the Teutonic Knights of any religious justification, but the union of the two peoples brought the Knights into conflict with the largest state in Europe. At Tannenberg in 1410 a huge Polish-Lith army broke the back of Teutonic power. Subsequent defeats led to the disastrous Peace of Thorn (1466) which cost the Knights West Prussia and Danzig and left them only East Prussia which they were permitted to retain as a fief of Poland. The Teutonic Order itself disappeared in 1525 when the grand knight, a Hohenzollern, became a Lutheran. Germans continued to dominate the economic and cultural life of the south Baltic until World War II.

Eastern Europe and Scandinavia

Poland. The Poles, the chief beneficiaries of the defeat of the Teutonic Knights, had entered "Western" history with their conversion to Christianity by Bohemian missionaries in 966. Their first great ruler was Boleslav the Brave (992-1025) who earned the title of king on the strength of the large state he erected. This comprised Slovakia, Silesia, Lusatia, Moravia, Pomerania, Ruthenia, and temporarily Bohemia. Upon his death, however, occurred the first partition of Poland when most of these territories were lost and Poland itself became an imperial fief. Early in the twelfth century Boleslav III (d. 1138) recovered Pomerania, but promptly destroyed any future role Poland might fill as a buffer state between medieval Russia and Germany by dividing his country into five principalities for his five sons. Internal dissension was inevitable. In the thirteenth century the Teutonic Knights and Mongols struck savage blows at what was left of the country. For a short time independence itself was lost to Bohemia. In 1333 Poland's leading medieval monarch, Casimir III (d. 1370), known as Casimir "the Great," ascended the throne. Though he conquered Galicia, his efforts were principally devoted to developing his country internally. His liberal immigration policy encouraged many Germans and Jews to enter the country and they brought trade and industry with them. Poland became a vigorous center of Jewish culture. Casimir also abolished serfdom and laid the foundations of the University of Cracow. Yet he and his successors granted dangerous concessions to the already proud nobility, thereby rendering impossible the growth of any kind of effective royal administrative machinery. That several of Poland's kings were concomitantly rulers of either Hungary or Lithuania and inclined to neglect Poland's best interests, also hampered the rise of Poland. Furthermore, the absence of natural frontiers posed as persistent a threat to Poland's existence in the Middle Ages as it has done ever since. With the defeat of the Teutonic Knights and the acquisition of a corridor to the Baltic, the fifteenth century reckoned to be an auspicious one for Poland. Casimir IV (1447-1492) was able to place a son on the throne of Bohemia and Hungary, another on the throne of Lithuania. But a third son, John Albert (d. 1501), who inherited the Polish throne, extended further privileges to the nobles at the expense of kingship, burghers, and peasantry, a policy which could only leave Poland's future a dark one.

Bohemia. The Bohemians who occupied most of Moravia and Bohemia owed their conversion to the Greek Sts. Cyril and Methodius who labored among them in the ninth century. In time German opposition forced the disciples of the two missionaries to leave the area to western monks and the land of Bohemia fell within the pale of Latin rather than of Greek Christianity. What made this Western orientation permanent was the invasion of the Magyars who drove a permanent wedge between the western Slavs of Bohemia, Moravia, and Poland and the south or Yugo Slavs of the Balkans. Otto I conquered the Czechs about 950 and their land remained a feudal principality of the German kingdom throughout the Middle Ages. Ottokar I (1197-1230) secured the title of king during the interval following the death of Henry VI when the rival candidates for the German kingship bid for his favor. The successful candidate, Frederick II, issued the Golden Bull which accorded the Bohemian nobles the right to elect their own king. Czech power and influence reached its peak during the reign of Charles IV (1347-1378), who strove earnestly to promote the native interests of his adopted land. The acquisition of Silesia and Upper Lusatia precipitated a heavy influx of Germans into the country, which stimulated industry and trade but aroused national consciousness as well. Czechs suddenly became aware of the fact that Germans dominated the political, economic, even cultural life of the country. Their protests secured the establishment of Prague as a diocese separate from Magdeburg, and after the death of Charles a number of German masters were forced out of the university of Prague. Yet Czech nationalism only became a threat to the empire with the execution of John Hus for heresy in 1415. Five times in the conflict that followed did the imperial armies suffer defeat through the skillful strategy of John Ziska and his primitive tanks. When the Calixtines, however, permitted themselves to be detached from Hussitism by the concessions offered by the Council of Basel (see page 681), the more radical Taborites were crushed. But religious bitterness and nationalist fears of being absorbed by Hungary kept Bohemia in a ferment into the sixteenth century.

Hungary. The Hungarians, or Magyars as they prefer to be called, proved the most enduring of the mounted nomads to invade Europe from Asia. Late in the ninth century they overwhelmed the Slavs living in the broad plain between the Danube and Carpathians and absorbed remnants of the Avar nation which Charlemagne had recently destroyed. As we have seen earlier, their plundering raids carried them across the Rhine, the Rhone, and into northern Italy. Early in the tenth century the German kings began to curb their pillaging and in 955 Otto I administered a crushing defeat at Lechfeld. For all their barbarous traditions, they proved readily assimilable into the family of Christian nations. In the year 1000, their first king, St. Stephen, received his crown from the hands of the pope and became his vassal. Forsaking its role as the plunderer of Western civilization, Hungary now essayed the role of its defender against the Mongols who overran most of the country in the thirteenth century. It was to bolster the country against similar inroads that the king authorized the aristocracy to erect castles. Further encouragement was afforded the evolution of feudalism in the Golden Bull issued by King Andrew in 1222, which granted the aristocracy wide powers and recognized periodic meetings of the diet or national assembly. So solidly entrenched did these concessions leave the landed aristocracy that it remained a power in Hungarian politics until the Communist conquest of the country in 1945. Several kings of the fourteenth century, notably Louis I (the Great) (1342-1382), adopted a vigorous program of "Westernizing" Hungary's economy and culture. More might have been accomplished along these lines had it not been for the Turkish menace which absorbed all the nation's resources. Some success was achieved against the dreaded foe notably by John Hunyadi whose exploits won election of his son Matthias Corvinus as king in 1458. Yet while Corvinus dealt the Turks several defeats, none proved decisive. Within thirty-five years of his death (d. 1490) the Turks had subjugated his country.

Scandinavia. The histories of the three Scandinavian countries which had sprung from the same fierce Viking brood (see page 262) followed roughly similar courses in the later Middle Ages. Harold Fairhair forced some semblance of centralization upon Norway by 900, although the land owed its conversion and civilization to St. Olaf (1016-1029). Cnut of Denmark drove Olaf from his kingdom and went on to establish an impressive empire which included England. Because the Norwegians lay on the outer circle, they took possession of such island groups as the Faroes and Shetlands and of Iceland and Greenland beyond. Iceland usually enjoyed an independent status. About the year 1000 all of Scadinavia had accepted Christianity, and by the early twelfth century all three countries had advanced sufficiently far to have their own metropolitans. Until then their bishops had been subject to the archbishop of Bremen. All three countries developed some of the features of the feudal system, although fiefs never became hereditary, and allodial lands remained as numerous and extensive as those held directly from the king. The peasantry too was never quite so submerged as in feudal Europe, probably because of Scandinavia's more scattered population. Scandinavia figured prominently in the revival of trade, although Germans, more specifically the Hanseatic League, controlled its fishing industry and largely directed the commercial activity of such centers as Bergen, Wisby, and Stockholm. Waldemar IV (1340-1375), king of Denmark, sought to break Hanseatic control of Danish trade, but was defeated and obliged to accept the Peace of Stralsund in 1370 which guaranteed the Hansa free passage through Danish waters. His ambitious daughter, Margaret, who married the ruler of Norway, then attempted to unite the three Scandinavian countries, which goal she accomplished in 1397 in the Union of Calmar. Though Sweden withdrew from the Union in 1448 and selected its own king, Denmark and Norway remained united until pried apart by the Congress of Vienna (1815). While Sweden had conquered and colonized Finland already by the thirteenth century, none of the three Scandinavian countries approached during the Middle Ages the importance of Poland and Bohemia. An explanation for this failure may be found in the dominant position held by the local aristocracy.

Russia. It was the Swedish Vikings who gave their name to Russia. They began to penetrate its vastness in the eighth century, moving up the rivers which emptied into the Baltic, thence overland a few miles to the Dnieper and Volga, which carried them to the Black and Caspian Seas. Bent first on piracy, then on trade, they made the first of several unsuccessful attacks on Constantinople in 860, and had eventually to be satisfied with a commercial treaty. One of their leaders, Ruric, established a principality at Novgorod in 862, and shortly afterward his followers founded another to the south at Kiev. By the middle of the eleventh century Kiev had grown into the second largest city of Christendom, overshadowed only by Constantinople itself. Perhaps the most significant event in Russian medieval history was the treaty with Byzantium (*ca.* 989) by which the Kievan prince Vladimir agreed to be baptized, to make his people Christian, and to marry the sister of the emperor. As much by reason of this treaty as by laws of geography and economics, Russia remained closely associated with Byzantium in the Middle Ages. From Constantinople it received its religion, while other institutions together with its language and art forms also reflected significant influences from the city on the Bosporus. By the close of the tenth century the huge Slavic population had engulfed the Swedish element, and nobles of Swedish extraction were employing Slavic names. Vladimir's grandfather was an Igor.

The Mongols Invade Russia. Next in importance to the conversion of Russia by Constantinople was the invasion of the country by the Mongols. The Mongols or Tartars, as medieval chroniclers called them, came from Mongolia rather than the Ural-Altaian area which had spawned the earlier nomadic invaders from out of Asia. Still the Mongols were fully as ferocious as, and had an even greater disregard for human life than, the earlier Huns, Avars, and Magyars. The man who made their name a symbol of terror for Eurasia was Genghis Khan (universal lord) (1167-1227), than whom no human being before or since has slaughtered and destroyed on a more staggering scale. His Mongols razed huge cities and massacred populations with no more concern than that of the aroused frontiersmen in our early history who wiped out small Indian villages. The magnificent city of Baghdad with its population of near one million fell to them in 1258 and was obliterated. Their overwhelming numbers, their mobility, and their

deceptive tactics on the battlefield spelled the destruction of scores of enemies from the China Sea to Prussia. At its height the Mongol empire
included all of China, central Asia, Persia, Mesopotamia, Poland, Hungary,
Bulgaria, Serbia, and all of Russia save only Novgorod. (The Mongol
horsemen found the marshlands south of the city more of an obstacle than
hostile armies.) But for a fortunate institution, the kuraltai, the Mongols
might have engulfed the world. This kuraltai involved the periodic meeting of the chief Mongol nobles at Karakorum in faraway Mongolia for the
purpose of electing a successor when the khan died. Many months must
necessarily elapse between the death of one khan and the election of
another. Not only might Mongol power ebb during such intervals, but the
new khan might prove less capable as a general or leader; he might be
faced with trouble at home from rebellious chieftains who refused to
recognize him, or his attention might be diverted elsewhere. (Reading 191-
192)

Emergence of Modern Russia. Russia suffered its first Mongol attack in
1223. Though this attack was completely successful, the Mongols did not
follow it up until 1237. Then it took them but four years to subjugate the
entire country (except Novgorod). While the Mongols left the Russians
their religion and interfered little directly in their economic and cultural
lives, the fact that Russia was cut off from the West for more than a hundred years had important consequences for its progress. The Mongols were
content with the heavy exactions of tribute which they ordered brought to
Sarai, their capital on the Volga. Their first empire was known as the
Golden Horde, from the golden tent of Batu, the grandson of Genghis. As
time went on the hand of the Mongol khan relaxed and the Horde broke
up into smaller units. The city destined to assume the lead in freeing the
land from Asiatics was Moscow. In 1328 the khan appointed Ivan I (d.
1341) its grand prince and entrusted him with the duty of collecting the
tribute from the other princes. Somewhat later the prince of Muscovy
acquired the right to adjudicate disputes among the Russian aristocracy.
In the same century the see of the metropolitan was moved from Kiev to
Moscow. Still, progress came slowly until the reign of Ivan III (1462-1505),
the real founder of modern Russia. He it was who finally drove out the
Mongols, captured Novgorod, expelled the Hanseatic merchants, and conquered most of the territory which Lithuania had held east of the Dnieper.
On the strength of his victory over the neighboring Russian princes, he
assumed the title of "Tzar of All the Russians," while on the strength of
his marriage to the niece of the last Byzantine emperor, he claimed the role
of protector of the Orthodox Church after the fall of Constantinople. And
he preferred to style Moscow the "Third Rome." Yet his signal achievements could not obscure the fact that Russia was still cut off from the
Black Sea by the Turks at the close of the Middle Ages. Many contem-

poraries would indeed have considered Russia's future less bright than that of the combined state of Poland and Lithuania to the west.

Southern Europe

Spain. Strong monarchies failed to evolve in Scandinavia and east-central Europe, but the monarchy which evolved in Spain did not so fail. By the close of the Middle Ages, the king of Spain was virtually absolute. Yet the king's victory was not an easy one. History, topography, and racial diversity militated against national unity. Spain had never been one country, either in Roman times or under Visigothic rule. The Moslems had not been able to conquer the northwestern Asturias, and their own brilliant caliphate of Cordova broke up early in the eleventh century. Still the presence of the Moslems did provide a common cause about which all Spaniards could rally. The Moslem occupation, indeed, proved the most important fact in Spanish medieval history. It helped engender a militaristic, almost fanatic Christianity; it brought hundreds of crusading and fief-hungry knights into the country; it made Spain a country of warriors and the Spaniard the best soldier in Europe in 1500; it provided the theme for the *Poema del Cid*, the leading literary production of medieval Spain. Four Christian states emerged by 1000: Aragon, Navarre, Leon, and Castile, while another, Portugal, separated from Leon about the middle of the twelfth century. When not fighting among themselves, the Christian states warred with the Moslems, who were forced permanently on the defensive after their disastrous defeat of 1212 at Las Navas de Tolosa. Leon merged with Castile in 1230, but more momentous for the future was Aragon's union with Barcelona. As the peninsula's most aggressive state, Aragon established footholds on the north African coast, conquered the Balearic Islands, occupied Sicily in 1282, Sardinia a little later, and Naples and southern Italy in the fifteenth century. Chartered towns made their appearance in Spain as early as the tenth century and leagues of towns called *hermandades* in the thirteenth. These last the crown found helpful in humbling the nobility. The first Spanish *cortes*, a body representing towns and nobility, convened in 1188 in Aragon, more than seventy-five years before a similar body met in England. This cortes and those of other Spanish states acquired wide powers in the field of legislation and taxation before their submergence in the fifteenth century. What proved an event of signal importance in the history of Spain was the marriage of Isabella of Castile and Ferdinand of Aragon in 1469. The united kingdoms snuffed out the existence of Granada, the last of the Moslem states in 1492, while Ferdinand somewhat later rounded out traditional Spain with the conquest of the southern portion of Navarre. Ferdinand and Isabella also laid the groundwork for royal absolutism, in the accomplishment of which they employed the Court of the Inquisition to enforce not only religious uniformity but political subservience as well. Under Ferdinand's stern encouragement, thousands of baptized Jews and Moslems were convicted of heresy and executed by the Spanish Inquisition. Even Ignatius Loyola, the founder of the Jesuits, twice ran afoul of its long, cruel tentacles.

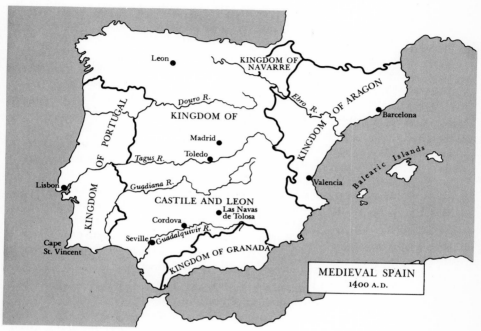

Portugal and Pre-Fifteenth Century Discoveries.   Portugal merits attention apart from Spain primarily because of its role in broadening man's knowledge of the world. Indeed, Portugal discovered and explored more of the earth's surface than any other state in history. Curiosity about what lies just beyond the horizon is as old as man himself, although it has been principally men bent on trade or booty who have gathered most of our geographical knowledge. Partly because these motives were joined to missionary zeal in the Middle Ages, medieval Europe was able to advance its knowledge of the rest of the world far beyond that of antiquity. The first significant step in expanding the medieval world of the West was made by the Vikings. Though the discovery of North America was forgotten, the north Atlantic, Greenland, and Iceland remained permanent additions to the geographical lore of Europe. To this knowledge the Crusades contributed a better acquaintance with the lands of the eastern Mediterranean. In the thirteenth century the interest in converting the fierce Mongols carried to China a number of missionaries who brought back wondrous accounts of the strange civilizations of the Orient. (See page 411.) The most noted account of China was that of the Venetian traveler, Marco Polo. According to Marco Polo's admiring secretary, "from the creation of Adam to the present day, no man, whether Pagan, or Saracen, or Christian, or other, of whatever progeny or generation he may have been, ever saw or inquired into so many and such great things." Marco Polo accompanied his father and uncle on their second visit to China (1271-1295), and it is the description of his experiences, what he saw and what he learned on this trip, that makes his story the most marvelous travel tale ever recorded. Marco Polo has something to say about India, the East Indies, Japan, Ceylon, Tibet, Burma, Madagascar, even Abyssinia, although he did not visit all the places he mentions. Yet there can be little question that had it not been for the disintegration of the Mongol empire soon after the death of Polo's friend, the famous Kublai Khan (d. 1294), followed by the rise of an unfriendly Ming dynasty in China in 1368, the West's knowledge of the Orient would have become so substantial by 1492 that Columbus could not have mistaken the red men he found in the West Indies for Indians. (Reading 192)

Portuguese Discoveries. With the Mings slamming the door in its face in the east, Western Europe turned with greater interest to the west and south. Already in the thirteenth century several attempts had been made to find a way around Africa. In 1270 the Canary Islands were discovered (rediscovered) by a Genoese navigator. By 1351 the Azores and Madeira Islands had been explored. The fifteenth century found Portugal unusually active. Because Italian cities enjoyed a monopoly of Mediterranean trade, Portugal had no choice but to exploit its favorable location on the Atlantic and sail the open sea. King John inaugurated the greatest period of Portuguese activity in 1415 with his capture of Ceuta, a pirate stronghold across from Gibraltar. The most distinguished Portuguese explorer was the third son of King John, known historically as Prince Henry the Navigator (d. 1460), although he did little if any navigating. But his studies in the mariner's art and the school which he organized on Cape St. Vincent proved of invaluable assistance to scores of actual navigators in their voyages into the unknown ocean. Henry was also grand master of the military-religious Order of Christ, and his fondest hope was to carve a Christian state out of northwestern Africa similar to that which the Teutonic Knights had established on the Baltic. Still it was slaves and gold rather, and the possibility of finding an all-water route to the spice-lands of the east, that whetted the appetite of most Portuguese navigators. The first slaves captured in Africa appeared in Lisbon in 1441. Ever farther south the Portuguese ventured until in 1487 Bartolomeo Dias finally reached and rounded the Cape of Good Hope. Though he sailed some five hundred miles northward to assure himself that the continent had been turned, another decade passed before Vasco da Gama ended the century-old quest for a water route to India when his small fleet of four ships dropped anchor in the harbor of Calicut (1498). Portugal went on to establish a fabulous empire among the "Spice Islands" of the East Indies, but that story reaches beyond the confines of the fifteenth century. What does not was the "culminating achievement of Europe's late middle age,"* that is, the discovery of the new world by Christopher Columbus.

Italy. From point of view of political organization, Italy was never more truly a geographical expression than in the closing centuries of the Middle Ages. A hodgepodge of states of confusing variety and shifting fortunes shaped the troubled history of the tormented peninsula. The northern urban states reveled in the power and affluence of the "Age of Despots." The Papal States in the center of the peninsula shared the cultural brilliance of the north, but except for short intervals presented much the same semi-anarchical condition as in preceding centuries. In the south the kingdom of the Two Sicilies, that is, Sicily and the kingdom of Naples, was well-advanced along the road of economic and political decline. A glance at the Papal States and Naples will suffice before we give a longer look at north Italy. The Papal States continued among the worst governed states of Europe despite spasmodic attempts to establish papal power. Their political instability arose from a number of factors, chief among these the elective position of their ruler. Until modern nationalism had awakened in people a love of country and a wish to support its government, only a dynasty could provide a satisfactory substitute. None was possible in this ecclesiastical state. Rome participated, to be sure, in the flowering of Italian culture; in fact, she assumed the lead after the middle of the fifteenth century. But when popes like Sixtus IV (d. 1484) and Alexander VI (d. 1503) essayed the combined role of spiritual leader of Christendom and political lord of the Papal States, they simply proved that one and the same man could not fill the offices of pope and Italian despot in the late Middle Ages without debasing the one or failing in the other. In the south, the kingdom of the Two Sicilies had retrogressed since the advanced rule of the Normans and Hohenstaufens. In 1282 the Sicilians welcomed invaders from Aragon, but rival French factions struggled over control of the kingdom of Naples until it too fell to Aragon in 1435. In 1495 Charles VIII of France led an army into Naples where he had himself crowned king, only to leave precipitately before the threat of capture by the Spanish and Hapsburgs. The close of the Middle Ages did not terminate the turbulency of political life in southern Italy, nor stay its drift toward economic and political bankruptcy.

North Italy: The Age of Despots. In Tuscany and the Po valley, however, control of an effective though despotic nature brought civilization there to its height, both economically and culturally. Of the dozen or more cities which had enjoyed autonomy or independence in the four-

* Hayes, Baldwin, Cole *History of Europe* (New York, 1949), I, 438.

teenth century, just a few remained. Of these the most powerful were Genoa, Florence, Milan, and Venice. These states were all different; yet in certain features they were similar. Trade and industry brought them their prosperity. They were urban states, and the ruling element, whether aristocratic or mercantile, lived within the city walls. Politically they were responsible for giving the period the name, "The Age of Despots." The despot might be a member of an aristocratic family, or he might be nothing more than an adventurer. Venice produced no single despot, although the small group which directed that state's policies exercised autocratic control. But whatever the origin or nature of the despotism, it was above all else efficient, and, at the same time, without scruples as to the means it employed to be efficient. It also patronized the arts. Some despots such as Lorenzo the Magnificent possessed a true appreciation of the beautiful; others encouraged poets and artists as a means of popularizing themselves. The people preferred such despots to the factional strife which had bred them. Despots were usually harsh only toward those they feared, who were not the people, and they even hired professional captains called condottieri and mercenary soldiers to fight their battles rather than call upon the citizenry. Even these battles were ordinarily more exciting and colorful than sanguinary. The word Machiavellian serves to characterize the political philosophy of north Italian despots in the fifteenth century. In his *The Prince* (1513) Machiavelli proposed what all despots knew and practiced, namely, that not justice but success should be the hallmark of the true prince. As Machiavelli answered his own query whether it was better for a prince to be loved than feared: "The reply is, that one ought to be both feared and loved, but as it is difficult for the two to go together, it is much safer to be feared than loved, if one of the two has to be wanting."

Milan, Genoa, Florence, Venice. Milan owed its rise to the trade which moved to and from the city through three Alpine passes to the north and west. During the mortal conflict with Frederick Barbarossa in the twelfth century, Milan had assumed a leadership in northern affairs which it generally retained to the close of the Middle Ages. For almost two hundred years the Visconti family controlled the government. In 1450 Francesco Sforza, a condottiere in the employ of the Visconti, forced the duke to give him his daughter in marriage, thereby facilitating his subsequent seizure of power. Genoa's location on the Mediterranean assured it a leading part in the revival of trade and a major share of the profits accruing from the transport of Crusaders and supplies to Syria. In 1261 it destroyed the Latin Empire at Constantinople whose trade Venice had monopolized, and in 1284 eliminated Pisa, its chief competitor on the west coast of Italy. For a hundred years Genoa vied with Venice for the lion's share of the carrying trade with the Levant and only dropped behind after its defeat in the last of their wars in 1381. Florence owed its prosperity to its great textile industry and to the rise of large banking houses. Under republican forms an oligarchy dominated the city until 1434 when Cosimo di Medici (d. 1464), head of the most famous banking house of the Middle Ages, seized control with the blessing of the people. It was his grandson, Lorenzo the Magnificent (d. 1492), who brought Florence to the peak of its cultural and political eminence. Shortly after Lorenzo's death, Charles VIII of France entered the city, overthrew the Medici, and opened the way for the eventual rise of Savonarola, a Dominican friar, to a position of virtual dictatorship. So deeply did Savonarola's attacks on Medicean and papal corruption and on their own morals fire the emotions of the populace, that for a few months they hailed him as a prophet, only to applaud his execution for heresy in 1498 when the Medici returned to power. The violence of the histories of Florence and Milan leaves the course of events in Venice appear wonderfully placid by contrast. There a close-knit commercial oligarchy kept affairs and government within its iron grasp. Industry was important in the economic life of the city, but all considerations were subordinated to trade. Even territory was acquired only when deemed vital to the city's commercial lifelines. The rise of the Ottoman Turks had a depressing effect upon Venice's prosperity since it disturbed the economy of the area and cost Venice several valuable footholds along the Balkan littoral. But this blow Venice could absorb more readily than it could the Portuguese opening of an all-water route to India which brought spices into Europe at prices Venice could not meet. When news was brought of Vasco da Gama's successful voyage, "all the city of Venice was greatly impressed and alarmed, and the wisest men held that this was the worst news that could ever come to the city."* With the Middle Ages passed also the commercial supremacy of Venice and the Mediterranean. The future lay with the Atlantic and the states to the west.

The Ottoman Turks. Those who proved to be the last and most successful of the Asiatic invaders to set permanent foot upon European soil were the Ottoman Turks. These people had been dislodged from their home in Turkestan by the Mongols, whence they entered Anatolia as mercenaries of one of the Seljuk sultans. Othman or Osman (d. 1326) who gave the tribe its name, set up an independent state early in the fourteenth century. The Turks were an unusually warlike tribe, although the debility of the Byzantine Empire greatly facilitated their expansion. One source of the strength of the Turks was their practice of demanding men from the peoples they subjugated, whom they then trained as soldiers and incorporated into their armies. The most famous of these non-Turkish troops were the Janissaries (new troops), who had originally been Christian, but whom the Turks raised as Moslems and forged into the most feared infantry of the age. The Byzantine Empire, which was torn by civil strife and had never recovered either its possessions or its strength after its revival in 1261, could afford them little hindrance. After overrunning Nicaea and Nico-

* H. M. F. Prescott, *Friar Felix at Large*, New Haven, 1950, p. 5.

media, the Turks pushed into Europe in 1354, captured Gallipoli and shortly after Adrianople which they made their capital. Nothing seemed capable of halting their inundation of the Balkans. They subjugated the Bulgarians and destroyed on the battlefield at Kossovo in 1389 a formidable Serbian nation which under Stephen Dushan (d. 1355) and his successors had conquered the entire area save only Constantinople itself. In panic at the advance of the Turks, the emperor Sigismund gathered a huge army which fought them at Nicopolis in 1396. Sigismund was among the fortunate few who survived the annihilation of the Crusading host. The Turks now prepared to take helpless Constantinople, but had to postpone siege operations when the last Mongol conqueror, Tamerlane or Timur the Lame, appeared in the Near East. Timur had conquered most of central Asia and Mesopotamia, and at Angora in 1402 inflicted a crushing defeat upon an enormous Turkish army. Fortunately for Turkey, Timur's interest was diverted to China, although the Turks were a generation licking their wounds before resuming the attack on Constantinople. Actually certain Christian leaders such as John Hunyadi were able to win scattered victories, against them and even to undertake an offensive here and there. The optimism these successes generated terminated abruptly with the destruction of the Crusading army at Varna on the Black Sea in 1444. Nothing now could prevent the capture of Constantinople. Such factors as the overwhelming superiority in numbers which the Turks enjoyed, their powerful artillery (the best of the period) which broke gaping holes in the city's fortifications, the ships which by means of a wooden track a mile long they were able to bring into the upper harbor and to attack the Byzantine fleet from the rear —all made the fall of the city inevitable. On May 29, 1453, Emperor Constantine XI fell in the fighting, and many of his vanquished troops with him, and with them the city. As the fall of Rome to the Visigoths in 410 had ushered in the Middle Ages, so the fall of the "New Rome" to the Turks in 1453 proclaimed the passing of that era.

READINGS

No. 177. Writs of summons to parliament (A.D. 1295)

(Adams and Stephens, *Select Documents*, pp. 82-84.)

Summons to the Clergy

The King to the venerable father in Christ Robert, by the same grace archbishop of Canterbury, primate of all England, greeting. As a most just law, established by the careful providence of sacred princes, exhorts and decrees that what affects all, by all should be approved, so also, very evidently should common danger be met by means provided in common. You know sufficiently well, and it is now, as we believe, divulged through all regions of the world, how the king of France fraudulently and craftily deprives us of our land of Gascony, by withholding it unjustly from us. Now, however, not satisfied with the before-mentioned fraud and injustice, having gathered together for the conquest of our kingdom a very great fleet, and an abounding multitude of warriors, with which he has made a hostile attack on our kingdom and the inhabitants of the same kingdom, he now proposes to destroy the English language altogether from the earth, if his power should correspond to the detestable proposition of the contemplated injustice, which God forbid. Because, therefore, darts seen beforehand do less injury, and your interest especially, as that of the rest of the citizens of the same realm, is concerned in this affair, we command you, strictly enjoining you in the fidelity and love in which you are bound to us, that on the Lord's day next after the feast of St. Martin, in the approaching winter, you be present in person at Westminster; citing beforehand the dean and chapter of your church, the archdeacons and all the clergy of your diocese, causing the same dean and archdeacons in their own persons, and the said chapter by one suitable proctor, and the said clergy by two, to be present along with you, having full and sufficient power from the same chapter and clergy, to consider, ordain, and provide, along with us and with the rest of the prelates and principal men and other inhabitants of our kingdom, how the dangers and threatened evils of this kind are to be met.

(Identical summons were sent out to the two archbishops and eighteen bishops, and, with the omission of the last paragraph, to seventy abbots.)

Summons of the Barons

The king to his beloved and faithful relative, Edmund, Earl of Cornwall, greeting. Because we wish to have a consultation and meeting with you and with the rest of the principal men of our kingdom, as to provision for remedies against the dangers which in these days are threatening our whole kingdom; we command you, strictly enjoining you in the fidelity and love in which you are bound to us, that on the Lord's day next after the feast of St. Martin, in the approaching winter, you be present in person at Westminster, for considering, ordaining and doing along with us and with the prelates, and the rest of the principal men and other inhabitants of our kingdom, as may be necessary for meeting dangers of this kind.

(Similar summons were sent to seven earls and forty-one barons.)

Summons of Representatives of the Counties and Boroughs

The king to the sheriff of Northamptonshire. Since we intend to have a consultation and meeting with the earls, barons and other principal men of our kingdom with regard to providing remedies against the dangers which are in these days threatening the same kingdom; and on that account have commanded them to be with us on the Lord's day next after the feast of St. Martin in the approaching winter, at Westminster, to consider, ordain, and do as may be necessary for the avoidance of these dangers; we strictly require you to cause two knights from the aforesaid county, two citizens from each city in the same county, and two burgesses from each borough, of those who are especially discreet and capable of laboring, to be elected without delay, and to cause them to come to us at the aforesaid time and place.

Moreover, the said knights are to have full and sufficient power for themselves and for the community of the aforesaid county, and the said citizens and burgesses for themselves and the communities of the aforesaid cities and boroughs separately, then and there for doing what shall then be ordained according to the common counsel in the premises; so that the aforesaid business shall not remain unfinished in any way for defect of this power. And you shall have there the names of the knights, citizens and burgesses and this writ.

(Identical summons were sent to the sheriffs of each county.)

No. 178. Edward I's Statute of Merchants (A.D. 1283)

(Stubbs, *Select Documents*, pp. 72-74.)

Forasmuch as merchants, which heretofore have lent their goods to divers persons, be greatly impoverished, because there is no speedy law provided for them to have recovery of their debts at the day of payment assigned; and by reason hereof many merchants do refrain to come into this realm with their merchandises, to the damage as well of the merchants, as of the whole realm; the king by himself and his council hath ordained and established, that the merchant which will be sure of his debt, shall cause his debtor to come before the mayor of London, or of York, or Bristol, and before the mayor and a clerk, which the king shall appoint for the same, for to acknowledge the debt and the day of payment; and the recognizance shall be entered into a roll with the hand of the said clerk, which shall be known. Moreover, the said clerk shall make with his own hand a bill obligatory, whereunto the seal of the debtor shall be put, with the king's seal, that shall be provided for the same purpose, the which seal shall remain in the keeping of the mayor and clerk aforesaid: and if the debtor doth not pay at the day to him limited, the creditor may come before the said mayor and clerk with his bill obligatory; and if it be found by the roll, and by the bill, that the debt was acknowledged, and that the day of payment is expired, the mayor shall incontinent cause the movables of the debtor to be sold, as far as the debt doth amount. . . .

And to defray the charge of the aforesaid clerk, the king shall take out of every pound one penny. This ordinance and act the king willeth to be holden from henceforth throughout all his realm of England, among all persons whosoever they may be, who shall freely choose to make such recognizance; except Jews, to whom this statute extendeth not.

No. 179. Charter of manumission and pardon to rebels (Peasant Revolt of 1381)

(Translations and Reprints, II, No. 5, p. 19.)

Richard, by the grace of God, King of England and France, and Lord of Ireland, to all his bailiffs and faithful ones, to whom these present letters shall come, greeting. Know that of our special grace, we have manumitted all of our lieges and each of our subjects and others of the County of Hertford; and them and each of them have made free from all bondage, and by these presents make them quit. And moreover we pardon our same lieges and subjects for all kinds of felonies, treasons, transgressions and extortions, however done or perpetrated by them or any of them, and also outlawry, if any shall have been promulgated on this account against them or any of them; and our most complete peace to them and each of them we concede in these matters. In testimony of which thing we have caused these our letters to be made patent. Witness, myself, at London, on the fifteenth day of June, in the fourth year of our reign. (1381)

No. 180. Withdrawal of manumissions

(Translations and Reprints, II, No. 5, pp. 19-20.)

It is ordained that all manner of manumissions, obligations, releases, and other bonds made by compulsion, duress, and threat, in the time of this last rumor and riot against the laws of the land and good faith shall be wholly quashed, annulled and holden for void; and they which have caused to be made or do yet withhold such manumissions, obligations, releases, bonds and other deeds, so made by duress, shall be sent before the king and his council, there to answer of their deed; and further, shall be constrained to make delivery and restitution of the said deeds to them that made the same against their good will, with the copies of the same, if perchance they have thereof made any before in order to use or renew the effect of the same another time, if they may. And likewise, it is accorded that all entries made in lands or tenements, and also all feoffments made in the time of the same rumor by compulsion and menace, or otherwise with force of people, against the law, shall be void and holden for none. And the king straitly forbiddeth to all manner of people, upon pain of as much as they are able to forfeit to him in body and goods, that none from henceforth make nor begin again, in any manner, such riot and rumor, nor other like them. And if any do the same, and this be duly proved, it shall be done concerning him as of a traitor to the king and to his said realm.

No. 181. Deposition of Richard II

(*Chronicon Ade de Usk*, tr. E. M. Thompson. Oxford, 1904, pp. 171-198.)

In the parliament of Shrewsbury, the king got the whole power of the government to be given over to him and to six others to be named by him for the term of his life, where and when he should please. By means of which commission he afterwards condemned the said duke of Hereford to perpetual exile, seizing all his goods. And he passed sentence against the memory of many who were dead. And at length, in an evil hour, he set out for Ireland (29 May, 1398) to subdue it, for, as will hereinafter be seen, his return to his own land was to his injury. . . .

This duke Henry returned from exile in company with Thomas, archbishop of Canterbury, and Thomas, earl of Arundel, the son, who for fear of his life had fled to him in France from the keeping of the duke of Exeter, king Richard's brother: and he landed on the twenty-eighth day of June [1399] with scarce three hundred followers, as above said, at a deserted spot in the northern parts of the land. And there first came to his help the chief forester of his forest of Knaresborough, Robert Waterton, with two hundred foresters; and afterwards the earls of Westmoreland and Northumberland, and the lords Willoughby and Greystock, and, in short, within a few days he stood in triumph, with one hundred thousand fighting men at his back. . . .

King Richard, learning in Ireland of the landing of the duke, set out in full glory of war and wealth, and made for the shores of Wales at Pembroke with a great host, and landed on the day of Saint Mary Magdalene (22 July), sending forward the lord Despencer to stir up his men of Glamorgan to his help; but they obeyed him not. Dismayed by this news coming in from all sides, and acting on the advice of those who I think were traitors, and hoping to be relieved by the succour of the men of North Wales and Chester, he fled in panic at midnight with only a few followers to Caermarthen, on the road to Conway castle in North Wales. Whereupon the dukes, earls, barons, and all who were with him in his great host, according to the text: "Smite the shepherd and the sheep shall be scattered" (Zech. xiii. 7), disbanded, and making their way through by-ways into England were robbed of everything by the country people. And I saw many of the chief men come in to the duke thus stripped; and many of them whom he trusted not, he delivered into divers keepings.

On the eve of the Assumption of the Blessed Virgin (14 August), my lord of Canterbury and the earl of Northumberland went away to the king at the castle of Conway, to treat with him on the duke's behalf; and the king, on condition of saving his dignity, promised to surrender to the duke at the castle of Flint. (Richard was subsequently deposed by order of parliament and removed to the Tower.)

On Saint Matthew's day (21 September), just two years after the beheading of the earl of Arundel, I, the writer of this history, was in the Tower, wherein King Richard was a prisoner, and I was present while he dined, and I marked his mood and bearing, having been taken thither for that very purpose by Sir William Beauchamp. And there and then the king discoursed sorrowfully in these words: "My God! a wonderful land is this, and a fickle; which hath exiled, slain, destroyed, or ruined so many kings, rulers, and great men, and is ever tainted and toileth with strife and variance and envy"; and then he recounted the histories and names of sufferers from the earliest habitation of the kingdom. Perceiving then the trouble of his mind, and how that none of his own men, nor such as were wont to serve him, but strangers who were but spies upon him, were appointed to his service, and musing on his ancient and wonted glory and on the fickle fortune of the world, I departed then much moved at heart. . . .

And now those in whom Richard, late king, did put his trust for help were fallen. And when he heard thereof, he grieved more sorely and mourned even to death, which came to him most miserably on the last day of February (1400) as he lay in chains in the castle of Pontefract, tormented by Sir [Thomas] Swineford with starving fare. . . .

No. 182. Froissart's account of the battle of Crecy

(Robinson's *Readings*, pp. 466-470.)

[Having reached a point near Crècy,] the king of England was well informed how the French king followed after him to fight. Then he said to his company: "Let us take here some plot of ground, for we will go no farther till we have seen our enemies. I have good cause here to abide them, for I am on the right heritage of the queen, my mother, the which land was given her at her marriage; I will challenge it of mine adversary, Philip of Valois." And because he had not the eighth part in number of men that the French king had, therefore he commanded his marshals to choose a plot of ground somewhat for his advantage; and so they did, and thither the king and his host went. . . .

Then [after arranging his army in three divisions,] the king lept on a palfrey, with a white rod in his hand, one of his marshals on the one hand and the other on the other hand. He rode from rank to rank, desiring every man to take heed that day to his right and honor. He spake it so sweetly and with so good countenance and merry cheer that all such as were discomfited took courage in the seeing and hearing of him. And when he had thus visited all his battles [i.e. divisions] it was then nine of the day. Then he caused every man to eat and drink a little, and so they did at their leisure. And afterward they ordered again their battles. Then every man lay down on the earth, his helmet and his bow by him, to be the more fresher when their enemies should come. . . .

The lords and knights of France came not to the engagement together in good order, for some came before and some came after, in such evil order that one of them did trouble another. When the French king saw the Englishmen his blood changed and he said to his marshals, "Make the Genoese go on before and begin the battle in the name of God and St. Denis." There were of the Genoese crossbows about fifteen thousand, but they were so weary of going afoot that day a six leagues armed with their crossbows that they said to their constables, "We be not well ordered to fight this day, for we be not in the case to do any great deed of arms; we have more need of rest." . . .

Also the same season there fell a great rain, and a flash of lightning with a terrible thunder, and before the rain their came flying over both battles a great number of crows for fear of the tempest coming. Then anon the air began to wax clear, and the sun to shine fair and bright, the which was right in the Frenchmen's eyes and on the Englishmen's backs.

When the Genoese were assembled together and began to approach they uttered a great cry to abash the Englishmen, but these stood still and stirred not for all that. Then the Genoese a second time made a fell cry and stept forward a little, but the Englishmen removed not one foot. Thirdly they shouted again and went forth until they came within shot. Then they shot fiercely with their crossbows. Then the English archers stepped forth one pace and let fly their arrows so wholly and so thick that it seemed snow. When the Genoese felt the arrows piercing through their heads, arms, and breasts, many of them cast down their crossbows and did cut their strings and returned discomfited.

When the French king saw them fly away he said, "Slay these rascals, for they shall let and trouble us without reason." Then ye should have seen the men-at-arms dash in among them and they killed a great number of them; and ever still the Englishmen shot where they saw the thickest press. The sharp arrows ran into the men-at-arms and into their horses, and many fell, horses and men, among the Genoese, and when they were down they could not rise again; the press was so thick that one overthrew another. And also among the Englishmen there were certain rascals that went afoot with great knives, and they went in among the men-at-arms and slew and murdered many as they lay on the ground, both earls, barons, knights, and squires; whereof the king of England was after displeased, for he had rather that they had been taken prisoners. . . .

No. 183. Conditions during the reign of Charles VII

(A Contemporary Letter, Robinson's *Readings*, pp. 474-475.)

Charles VI being dead, Charles VII succeeded to his father in the kingdom, in the year of our Lord 1422, when he was about twenty-two years of age. In his time, owing to the long wars which had raged within and without, the lethargy and cowardliness of the officers and commanders who were under him, the destruction of all military discipline and order, the rapacity of the troopers, and the general dissolution into which all things had fallen, such destruction had been wrought that from the river Loire to the Seine,— even to the Somme,—the farmers were dead or had fled, and almost all the fields had for many years lain without cultivation or any one to cultivate them. A few districts might indeed be excepted, where if any agriculture remained, it was because they were far from cities, towns, or castles, and in consequence the constant excursions of the despoilers could not be extended to them. . . .

We have ourselves beheld the vast regions of Champagne, Brie, Chartres, Perche, Beauvais, . . . Amiens, Abbeville, Soissons, Laon, and beyond toward Hainault, well-nigh deserted, untilled, without husbandmen, grown up in weeds and briers. In many places where fruit trees could flourish these had grown up into dense forests. The vestiges of such ruin, unless the divine clemency shall aid mere human endeavor, will, it is to be feared, last for long years to come.

If any kind of cultivation was still carried on in the regions enumerated, it could only be done close to cities, towns, or castles, no farther away than the watch could be seen, stationed on a high lookout, whence he could observe the robbers as they approached. He would then give the alarm by means of a bell, or a hunter's horn, to those in the fields or vineyard, so that they could betake themselves to a place of safety. This happened so frequently in many places that so soon as the oxen and plow animals were loosed, having heard the signal of the watch, they would, taught by long experience, rush to a place of safety in a state of terror. Even the pigs and sheep did the same.

No. 184. The countryside after a battle or raid

(From *Lorrains* as quoted by A. Lucharie in *Social France at the Time of Philip Augustus,* tr. Edward Krehbiel. New York, 1929, p. 261. By permission of the author.)

They start to march. The scouts and the incendiaries lead; after them come the foragers who are to gather the spoils and carry them in the great baggage train. The tumult begins. The peasants, having just come out to the fields, turn back, uttering loud cries; the shepherds gather their flocks and drive them towards the neighboring woods in the hope of saving them. The incendiaries set the villages on fire, and the foragers visit and sack them; the distracted inhabitants are burned or led apart with their hands tied to be held for ransom. Everywhere alarm bells ring, fear spreads from side to side and becomes general. On all sides one sees helmets shining, pennons floating, and horsemen covering the plain. Here hands are laid on money; there cattle, donkeys, and flocks are seized. The smoke spreads, the flames rise, the peasants and the shepherds in consternation fall in all directions.

When the knights have passed, there is nothing left.

In the cities, in the towns, and on the small farms, windmills no longer turn, chimneys no longer smoke, the cocks have ceased their crowing, and the dogs their barking. Grass grows in the houses and between the flagstones of the churches, for the priests have abandoned the services of God, and the crucifixes lie broken on the ground. The pilgrim might go six days without finding any one to give him a loaf of bread or a drop of wine. Freemen have no more business with their neighbors; briars and thorns grow where villages stood of old.

No. 185. Louis XI of France

(From the *Memoires* of Commines. Robinson's *Readings,* pp. 481-485.)

Small hopes and comfort ought poor and inferior people to have in this world, considering what so great a king suffered and underwent, and how he was at last forced to leave all, and could not, with all his care and diligence, protract his life one single hour. I knew him, and was entertained in his service in the flower of his age and at the height of his prosperity, yet I never saw him free from labor and care.

Of all diversions he loved hunting and hawking in their seasons, but his chief delight was in dogs. . . . In hunting, his eagerness and pain were equal to his pleasure, for his chase was the stag, which he always ran down. He rose very early in the morning, rode sometimes a great distance, and would not leave his sport, let the weather be never so bad. And when he came home at night he was often very weary and generally in a violent passion with some of his courtiers or huntsmen; for hunting is a sport not always to be managed according to the master's direction; yet, in the opinion of most people, he understood it as well as any prince of his time. He was continually at these sports, lodging in the country villages to which his recreations led him, till he was interrupted by business; for during the most part of the summer there was constantly war between him and Charles, duke of Burgundy, while in the winter they made truces. . . .

When his body was at rest his mind was at work, for he had affairs in several places at once, and would concern himself as much in those of his neighbors as in his own, putting officers of his own over all the great families, and endeavoring to divide their authority as much as possible. When he was at war he labored for a peace or a truce, and when he had obtained it he was impatient for war again. He troubled himself with many trifles in his government which he had better have let alone; but it was his temper, and he could not help it. Besides, he had a prodigious memory, and he forgot nothing, but knew everybody, as well in other countries as in his own. . . .

The king had ordered several cruel prisons to be made: some were cages of iron, and some of wood, but all were covered with iron plates both within and without, with terrible locks, about eight feet wide and seven high. The first contriver of them was the bishop of Verdun, who was immediately put in the first of them that was made, where he continued fourteen years. Many bitter curses he has had since for his invention, and some from me as I lay in one of them eight months together in the minority of our present king. He also ordered heavy and terrible fetters to be made in Germany, and particularly a certain ring for the feet, which was extremely hard to be opened, and fitted like an iron collar, with a thick weighty chain, and a great globe of iron at the end of it, most unreasonably heavy, which contrivances were called the king's nets. However, I have seen many eminent and deserving persons in these prisons, with these nets about their legs, who afterwards came forth with great joy and honor, and received great rewards from the king. . . .

No. 186. The Black Death

(Walsingham, *Historia Anglicana. Translations and Reprints*, II, No. 5, p. 2.)

In the year of grace 1349, which was the twenty-third year of King Edward, the Third since the Conquest, a great mortality of mankind advanced over the world; beginning in the regions of the North and East, and ending with so great a destruction that scarcely half of the people remained. Then towns once full of men became destitute of inhabitants; and so violently did the pestilence increase that the living were scarce able to bury the dead. Indeed, in certain houses of men of religion, scarcely two out of twenty men survived. It was estimated by many that hardly a tenth part of mankind had been left alive. A murrain among animals followed immediately upon this pestilence; then rents ceased; then the land, because of the lack of tenants, who were nowhere to be found, remained uncultivated. So great misery followed from these evils that the world was never afterward able to return to its former state.

No. 187. The imperial decree *"Licet Juris"* (A.D. 1338)

(Thatcher & McNeal, *Source Book*, pp. 279-280.)

Both the canon and the civil law declare plainly that the dignity and authority of the emperor came of old directly from the Son of God, that God has appointed the emperors and kings of the world to give laws to the human race, and that the emperor obtains his office solely through his election by those who have the right to vote in imperial elections [the electors], without the confirmation and approval of anyone else. For in secular affairs he has no superior on earth, but rather is the ruler of all nations and peoples. Moreover, our Lord Jesus Christ has said: "Render unto Caesar the things which are Caesar's, and unto God the things which are God's." Nevertheless, certain persons, blinded by avarice and ambition, and totally ignorant of the Scriptures, have distorted the meaning of certain passages by false and wicked interpretations, and on this basis have attacked the imperial authority and the rights of the emperors, electors, and other princes and subjects of the empire. For they wrongfully assert that the emperor derives his position and authority from the pope, and that the emperor elect is not the real emperor until his election is confirmed and approved, and he is crowned by the pope. These false and dangerous assertions are clearly the work of the ancient enemy of mankind, attempting to stir up strife and discord, and to bring about confusion and dissensions among men.

In order to prevent this we now declare by the advice and with the consent of the electors and other princes of the empire, that the emperor holds his authority and position from God alone, and that it is the ancient law and custom of the empire that he who is elected emperor or king by the electors of the empire, thereby becomes true king and emperor of the Romans, and should be obeyed by all the subjects of the empire, and has full power to administer the laws of the empire and to perform all the functions of the emperor, without the approval, confirmation, authorization, or consent of the pope or any other person. . . .

No. 188. The Golden Bull of Charles IV (A.D. 1356)

(Thatcher & McNeal, *Source Book,* pp. 283-305.)

Ch. I. 1. We decree and determine by this imperial edict that, whenever the electoral princes are summoned according to the ancient and praiseworthy custom to meet and elect a king of the Romans and future emperor, each one of them shall be bound to furnish on demand an escort and safe-conduct to his fellow electors or their representatives, within his own lands and as much farther as he can, for the journey to and from the city where the election is to be held. . . .

16. When the news of the death of the king of the Romans has been received at Mainz, within one month from the date of receiving it the archbishop of Mainz shall send notices of the death and of the approaching election to all the electoral princes. But if the archbishop neglects or refuses to send such notices, the electoral princes are commanded on their fidelity to assemble on their own motion and without summons at the city of Frankfort within three months from the death of the emperor, for the purpose of electing a king of the Romans and future emperor.

17. Each electoral prince or his representatives may bring with him to Frankfort at the time of the election a retinue of 200 horsemen, of whom not more than 50 shall be armed.

Ch. II. 1. (Mass shall be celebrated on the day after the arrival of the electors. The archbishop of Mainz administers this oath, which the other electors repeat:)

2. "I, archbishop of Mainz, archchancellor of the empire for Germany, electoral prince, swear on the holy gospels here before me, and by the faith which I owe to God and to the holy Roman empire, that with the aid of God, and according to my best judgment and knowledge, I will cast my vote, in this election of the king of the Romans and future emperor, for a person fitted to rule the Christian people. I will give my voice and vote freely, uninfluenced by any agreement, price, bribe, promise, or anything of the sort, by whatever name it may be called. So help me God and all the saints."

3. After the electors have taken this oath, they shall proceed to the election, and shall not depart from Frankfort until the majority have elected a king of the Romans and future emperor, to be ruler of the world and of the Christian people. If they have not come to a decision within thirty days from the day on which they took the above oath, after that they shall live upon bread and water and shall not leave the city until the election has been decided. . . .

Ch. IX. We decree, by this present law, that our successors, the kings of Bohemia, and all the electoral princes, ecclesiastical and secular, shall hold and possess with full rights, all mines of gold, silver, tin, copper, iron, lead, or other metals, and all salt works, both those already discovered and those which shall be discovered in the future, situated within their lands, domains, and dependencies. They shall also have authority to tax Jews, the right to collect tolls already in force, and all other rights which they or their predecessors have possessed to the present day. . . . We extend this right by the present law to all the electoral princes, ecclesiastical and secular, and to their legal heirs, under the same conditions and form.

Ch. XI. 1. We decree also that no count, baron, noble, vassal, burgrave, knight, client, citizen, burgher, or other subject of the churches of Cologne, Mainz, or Trier, of whatever status, condition or rank, shall be cited, haled, or summoned to any authority before any tribunal outside of the territories, boundaries, and limits of these churches and their dependencies, or before any judge, except the archbishops and their judges. . . . We refuse to hear appeals based upon the authority of others over the subjects of these princes; if these princes are accused by their subjects of injustice, appeal shall lie to the imperial diet, and shall be heard there and nowhere else. . . .

2. We extend this right by the present law to the secular electoral princes, the count palatine of the Rhine, the duke of Saxony, and the margrave of Brandenburg, and to their heirs, successors, and subjects forever.

Ch. XXV. If it is proper that the integrity of the ordinary principalities should be preserved, for the better securing of justice and peace for the subjects, it is even more important that the great principalities of the electoral princes should be kept intact in their domains, honors, and rights. Therefore we determine and decree by this imperial edict that the lands, districts, fiefs, and other possessions of the great principalities, namely, the kingdom of Bohemia, the palatinate of the Rhine, the duchy of Saxony, and the mark of Brandenburg, should never under any circumstances be separated, divided, or dismembered. In order that they may be preserved in their integrity, the first-born son in each case shall succeed to them, and shall exercise ownership and dominion in them. . . .

Ch. XXIX. 1. We have learned from records and traditions, that it has been the custom in the past to hold the election of the king of the Romans in Frankfort, the coronation in Aachen, and the first diet in Nuernberg; therefore we decree that in the future these ceremonies shall be held in these places, unless there shall be some legitimate obstacle. . . .

Ch. XXXI. Since the majesty of the Holy Roman Empire has to control the laws and government of diverse nations differing in customs, life and speech, it is right and in the judgment of the wise men expedient that the Princes Electors . . . should be taught the varieties of the different tongues and languages; so that they who assist the Imperial Highness may understand and be understood by the more persons. Wherefore we decree that the sons, heirs and successors of the illustrious Princes Electors, the King of Bohemia, the Count Palatine of the Rhine, the Duke of Saxony and the Margrave of Brandenburg, who may be presumed naturally to know the Teutonic tongue and to have learned it from infancy, shall from their seventh year be instructed in the Italian and Slav languages, so that by their fourteenth year they shall, by God's grace, be learned in those tongues.

No. 189. Beginning of the Swiss Confederation (A.D. 1290)

(Thatcher & McNeal, *Source Book*, pp. 267-269.)

In the name of the Lord, amen. It is a good thing for the public utility if communities agree to preserve order and peace. Therefore let all know that the men of the valley of Uri, and the community of the valley of Schwyz, and the commune of those who live within the mountains of the lower valley [Unterwalden], considering the dangers that threaten them, and in order to be better able to defend themselves and their possessions, have, in good faith, promised mutually to assist each other with aid, counsel, and support, and with their persons as well as their possessions, with all their power and with their best effort, within the valley and without, against each and all who may try to molest, harm, or injure any of us in our persons or in our possessions. Each commune promised to aid the others whenever it should be necessary, and at its own expense to assist the others in repelling the attacks of their enemies and in avenging their injuries. The three cantons took oath that they would do these things without treachery.

We hereby renew the ancient agreement which has existed among us. (1) Each man, according to his condition, shall be bound to obey his lord and to serve him in the proper manner. (2) We unanimously promise, decree, and ordain that in the aforesaid valleys we will not receive any judge who has bought his office in any way, or who is not an inhabitant of the valley. (3) If a dispute arises among us, the more prudent among us shall meet and settle it as seems best to them. If anyone refuses to accept their decision we will all assist in enforcing it. . . . (10) If war [feud] or a quarrel arises between any of us, and one of the parties refuses or neglects to secure its justice or to render satisfaction, we are all bound to defend the other party.

As an evidence that these statutes shall be binding forever this present document was made at the request of the aforesaid inhabitants and sealed with the seals of the three communities.

Done in the year of our Lord 1290, at the beginning of August.

No. 190. The army of Genghis Khan

(From the account of John of Plano Carpini. Richard Hakluyt, *The Principal Navigations, Voyages, Traffiques & Discoveries*, I. Glasgow, 1903, pp. 515-516.)

Chingis Cham divided his Tartars by captains of ten, captains of a 100 and captains of a 1000. And over ten millenaries or captains of a 1000, he placed, as it were, one colonel, and yet notwithstanding over one whole army he authorized two or three dukes, but yet so that all should have especial regard unto one of the said dukes. And when they join battle against any other nation, unless they do all with one consent fall back, every man that flies is put to death. And if one or two, or more of ten proceed manfully to the battle, but the remainder of those ten draw back and follow not the company, they are in like manner slain. Also, if one among ten or more be taken, their fellows, if they rescue them not, are punished with death. Moreover they are enjoined to have these weapons following: two long bows or one good one at the least, three quivers full of arrows, and one axe, and ropes to draw engines withal. But the richer sort have single edged swords, with sharp points, and somewhat crooked. They have also armed horses with their shoulders and breasts defended, they have helmets and brigandines. Some of them have jackes, and caparisons for their horses made of leather artifically doubled or trebled upon their bodies. The upper part of their helmet is of iron or steel, but that part which compasseth about the neck and the throat is of leather. Howbeit some of them have all their foresaid furniture of iron framed in the manner following. They beat out many thin plates a finger broad, and a handful long, and making in every one of them eight little holes, they put thereunto three strong and straight leather thongs. So they join the plates one to another, as it were, ascending by degrees. Then they tie the plates unto the said thongs, with other small and slender thongs, drawn through the holes aforesaid, and in the upper part, on each side thereof, they fasten one small doubled thong unto another, that the plates may firmly be knit together. These they make, as well for their horses caparisons, as for the armour of their men. And they scour them so bright that a man may behold his face in them. Some of them upon the neck of their lance have a hook, wherewith they attempt to pull men out of their saddles. The heads of their arrows are exceedingly sharp cutting both ways like a two edged sword, and they always carry a file in their quivers to whet their arrowheads. They have targets made of wickers, or of small rods. Howbeit they do not (as we suppose) accustom to carry them, but only about the tents, or in the emperors or dukes guards, and that only in the night season. They are most politic in wars, having been exercised therein with other nations for the space of these 42 years. When they come to any rivers, the chief men of the company have a round and light piece of leather, about the borders whereof making many loops, they put a rope into them to draw it together like a purse, and so bring it into the round form of a ball, which leather they fill with their garments and other necessaries, trussing it up most strongly. But upon the midst of the upper part thereof, they lay their saddles and other hard things, there also do the men themselves sit. This their boat they tie unto a horse tail, causing a man to swim before and to guide over the horse, or sometime they have two oars to row themselves over. The first horse therefore being driven into the water, all the other horses of the company follow him, and so they pass through the river. But the poorer sort of common soldiers have every man his leather bag or satchel well sown together, wherein he packs up all his trinkets, and strongly trussing it up hangs it at his horse's tail, and so passes over, in manner aforesaid.

No. 191. A thirteenth-century view of the Mongols

(Matthew Paris's *English History*, tr. J. A. Giles, I. London, 1852, pp. 312-313.)

In this year (1240), that human joys might not long continue, and that the delights of this world might not last long unmixed with lamentation, an immense horde of that detestable race of Satan, the Tartars, burst forth from their mountain-bound regions, and making their way through rocks apparently impenetrable, rushed forth, like demons loosed from Tartarus (so that they are well called Tartars, as it were inhabitants of Tartarus); and overrunning the country, covering the face of the earth like locusts, they ravaged the eastern countries with lamentable destruction, spreading fire and slaughter wherever they went. Roving through the Saracen territories, they razed cities to the ground, burnt woods, pulled down castles, tore up the vine-trees, destroyed gardens, and massacred the citizens and husbandmen; if by chance they did spare any who begged their lives, they compelled them, as slaves of the lowest condition, to fight in front of them against their own kindred. And if they only pretended to fight, or perhaps warned their countrymen to fly, the Tartars following in their rear, slew them; and if they fought bravely and conquered, they gained no thanks by way of recompense, and thus these savages ill-treated their captives as though they were horses.

The men are inhuman and of the nature of beasts, rather to be called monsters than men, thirsting after and drinking blood, and tearing and devouring the flesh of dogs and human beings; they clothe themselves in the skins of bulls, and are armed with iron lances; they are short in stature and thickset, compact in their bodies, and of great strength; invincible in battle, indefatigable in labour; they wear no armour on the back part of their bodies, but are protected by it in front; they drink the blood which flows from their flocks, and consider it a delicacy; they have large and powerful horses, which eat leaves and even the trees themselves, and which, owing to the shortness of their legs, they mount by three steps instead of stirrups.

They have no human laws, know no mercy, and are more cruel than lions or bears; they have boats made of the hides of oxen, ten or twelve having one amongst them; they are skilful in sailing or swimming, hence they cross the largest and most rapid rivers without any delay or trouble; and when they have no blood, they greedily drink disturbed and even muddy water. They have swords and daggers with one edge, they are excellent archers, and they spare neither sex, age, or rank; they know no other country's language except that of their own, and of this all other nations are ignorant. For never till this time has there been any mode of access to them, nor have they themselves come forth, so as to allow any knowledge of their customs or persons to be gained through common intercourse with other men; they take their herds with them, as also their wives, who are brought up to war, the same as the men; and they came with the force of lightning into the territories of the Christians, laying waste the country, committing great slaughter, and striking inexpressible terror and alarm into every one. The Saracens, therefore, desired and begged to be allowed to enter into alliance with the Christians, in order that they might, by multiplying their forces, be enabled to resist these human monsters.

No. 192. The travels of Marco Polo

(*The Book of Ser Marco Polo*, tr. Henry Yule. London, 1903.)

Prologue (I, 1-2)

Great princes, emperors, and kings, dukes and marquises, counts, knights, and burgesses, and people of all degrees who desire to get knowledge of the various races of mankind and of the diversities of the sundry regions of the world, take this book and cause it to be read to you. For ye shall find therein all kinds of wonderful things, and the divers histories of the great Armenia, and of Persia, and of the land of the Tartars, and of India, and of many another country of which our book doth speak, particularly and in regular succession, according to the description of Messer Marco Polo, a wise and noble citizen of Venice, as he saw them with his own eyes. Some things indeed there be therein which he beheld not; but these he heard from men of credit and veracity. And we shall set down things seen as seen, and things heard as heard only, so that no jot of falsehood may mar the truth of our book, and that all who shall read it or hear it read may put full faith in the truth of all its contents.

For let me tell you that since our Lord God did mould with his hands our first father Adam, even until this day, never hath there been a Christian, or Pagan, or Tartar, or Indian, or any man of any nation, who in his own person hath had so much knowledge and experience of the divers parts of the world and its wonders as hath had this Messer Marco! And for that reason he bethought himself that it would be a very great pity did he not cause to be put in writing all the great marvels that he had seen, or on such information heard of, so that other people who had not these advantages might, by his book, get such knowledge. And I may tell you that in acquiring this knowledge he spent in those various parts of the world good six-and-twenty years. Now, being thereafter an inmate of the prison at Genoa, he caused Messer Rusticiano of Pisa, who was in the said prison likewise, to reduce the whole to writing; and this befell in the year 1298 from the birth of Jesus.

Ch. LII (I, 251-252)

Concerning the Customs of the Tartars

Now that we have begun to speak of the Tartars, I have plenty to tell you on that subject. The Tartar custom is to spend the winter in warm plains, where they find good pasture for their cattle, whilst in summer they betake themselves to a cool climate among the mountains and valleys, where water is to be found as well as woods and pastures.

Their houses are circular, and are made of wands covered with felts. These are carried along with them whithersoever they go; for the wands are so strongly bound together, and likewise so well combined, that the frame can be made very light. Whenever they erect these huts the door is always to the south. They also have waggons covered with black felt so efficaciously that no rain can get in. These are drawn by oxen and camels, and the women and children travel in them. The women do the buying and selling, and whatever is necessary to provide for the husband and household; for the men all lead the life of gentlemen, troubling themselves about nothing but hunting and hawking, and looking after their goshawks and falcons, unless it be the practice of warlike exercises.

They live on the milk and meat which their herds supply, and on the produce of the chase; and they eat all kinds of flesh, including that of horses and dogs, and Pharaoh's rats (a kind of kangaroo-rat), of which last there are great numbers in burrows on those plains. Their drink is mare's milk.

They are very careful not to meddle with each other's wives, and will not do so on any account, holding that to be an evil and abominable thing. The women too are very good and loyal to their husbands, and notable housewives withal. Ten or twenty of them will dwell together in charming peace and unity, nor shall you ever hear an ill word among them.

Ch. LIII (I, 256-257)

Concerning the God of the Tartars

This is the fashion of their religion. They say there is a most high god of heaven, whom they worship daily with thurible and incense, but they pray to him only for health of mind and body. But they have also a certain other god of theirs called Natigay, and they say he is the god of the earth, who watches over their children, cattle, and crops. They show him great worship and honour, and every man hath a figure of him in his house, made of felt and cloth; and they also make in the same manner images of his wife and children. The wife they put on the left hand, and the children in front. And when they eat, they take the fat of the meat and grease the god's mouth withal, as well as the mouths of his wife and children. Then they take of the broth and sprinkle it before the door of the house; and that done, they deem that their god and his family have had their share of the dinner.

Book II. Ch. I (I, 331)

Of Kublai Khan and his great Power

Now as I come to that part of our book in which I shall tell you of the great and wonderful magnificence of the Great Khan now reigning, by name of Kublai Khan, khan being a title which signifyeth "The Great Lord of Lords," or emperor. And of a surety he hath good right to such a title, for all men know for a certain truth that he is the most potent man, as regards forces and lands and treasure, that existeth in the world, or ever hath existed from the time of our first father Adam until this day. All this I will make clear to you for truth, in this book of ours, so that every one shall be fain to acknowledge that he is the greatest lord that is now in the world, or ever hath been. And now ye shall hear how and wherefore.

Book II. Ch. VI (I, 348)

And after the Great Khan had defeated Nayan in the way you have heard, he went back to his capital city of Cambaluc and abode there, taking his ease and making festivity. This happened in the month of November, and he remained there during the months of February and March, in which latter month our Easter occurs. And learning that this was one of our chief festivals, he summoned all the Christians, and bade them bring with them the Book of the Four Gospels. This he caused to be incensed many times with great ceremony, kissing it himself most devoutly, and desiring all the barons and lords who were present to do the same. And he always acts in this fashion at the chief Christian festivals, such as Easter and Christmas. And he does the like at the chief feasts of the Saracens, Jews, and Idolaters. On being asked why, he said: "There are four prophets worshipped and revered by all the world. The Christians say their God is Jesus Christ; the Saracens, Mahommet; the Jews, Moses; the Idolaters, Sogomon Borcan (Buddha), who was the first god among the idols; and I worship and pay respect to all four, and pray that he among them who is greatest in heaven in very truth may aid me." But the Great Khan let it be seen well enough that he held the Christian Faith to be the truest and best—for, as he says, it commands nothing that is not perfectly good and holy. But he will not allow the Christians to carry the Cross before them, because on it was scourged and put to death a person so great and exalted as Christ.

Popes of the Middle Ages

Marcellinus	296– 304	John II	533– 535
Marcellus I	308– 309	Agapitus I	535– 536
Eusebius	309– 310	Silverius	536– 537
Melchiades	311– 314	Vigilius	537– 555
Silvester I	314– 335	Pelagius I	555– 561
Mark	336	John III	561– 574
Julius I	337– 352	Benedict I	575– 579
Liberius	352– 366	Pelagius II	579– 590
Damasus I	366– 384	Gregory I (the Great)	590– 604
Siricius	384– 399	Sabinianus	604– 606
Anastasius I	399– 401	Boniface III	607
Innocent I	401– 417	Boniface IV	608– 615
Zosimus	417– 418	Deusdedit	615– 618
Boniface I	418– 422	Boniface V	619– 625
Celestine I	422– 432	Honorius I	625– 638
Sixtus III	432– 440	Severinus	640
Leo I (the Great)	440– 461	John IV	640– 642
Hilary	461– 468	Theodore I	642– 649
Simplicius	468– 483	Martin I	649– 655
Felix III	483– 492	Eugenius I	654– 657
Gelasius I	492– 496	Vitalian	657– 672
Anastasius II	496– 498	Adeodatus II	672– 676
Symmachus	498– 514	Donus	676– 678
Hormisdas	514– 523	Agatho	678– 681
John I	523– 526	Leo II	682– 683
Felix IV	526– 530	Benedict II	684– 685
Boniface II	530– 532	John V	685– 686

Conon	686– 687
Sergius I	687– 701
John VI	701– 705
John VII	705– 707
Sisinnius	708
Constantine I	708– 715
Gregory II	715– 731
Gregory III	731– 741
Zachary	741– 752
Stephen II	752– 757
Paul I	757– 767
Stephen III	768– 772
Adrian I	772– 795
Leo III	795– 816
Stephen IV	816– 817
Paschal I	817– 824
Eugenius II	824– 827
Valentine	827
Gregory IV	827– 844
Sergius II	844– 847
Leo IV	847– 855
Benedict III	855– 858
Nicholas I	858– 867
Adrian II	867– 872
John VIII	872– 882
Marinus I (Martin II)	882– 884
Adrian III	884– 885
Stephen V	885– 891
Formosus	891– 896
Boniface VI	896
Stephen VI	896– 897
Romanus	897
Theodore II	897
John IX	898– 900
Benedict IV	900– 903
Leo V	903
Sergius III	904– 911
Anastasius III	911– 913
Lando	913– 914
John X	914– 928
Leo VI	928
Stephen VII	929– 931
John XI	931– 935
Leo VII	936– 939
Stephen VIII	939– 942
Marinus II (Martin III)	942– 946
Agapitus II	946– 955
John XII	955– 964
Leo VIII	964– 965
Benedict V	964– 966
John XIII	965– 972
Benedict VI	972– 974
Benedict VII	974– 983
John XIV	983– 984
John XV	985– 996
Gregory V	996– 999
John XVI (antipope)*	997– 998
Silvester II	999–1003
John XVII	1003
John XVIII	1003–1009
Sergius IV	1009–1012
Benedict VIII	1012–1024
John XIX	1024–1032
Benedict IX	1032–1044
Silvester III	1045
Gregory VI	1045–1046
Clement II	1046–1047
Damasus II	1048
Leo IX	1049–1054
Victor II	1055–1057
Stephen IX	1057–1058
Benedict X (antipope)	1058–1059
Nicholas II	1058–1061
Alexander II	1061–1073
Gregory VII	1073–1085
Victor III	1086–1087
Urban II	1088–1099
Paschal II	1099–1118
Gelasius II	1118–1119
Callixtus II	1119–1124
Honorius II	1124–1130
Innocent II	1130–1143
Celestine II	1143–1144
Lucius II	1144–1145
Eugenius III	1145–1153
Anastasius IV	1153–1154

* Majority of antipopes not listed.

Adrian IV	1154–1159	Benedict XI	1303–1304
Alexander III	1159–1181	Clement V	1305–1314
Lucius III	1181–1185	John XXII	1316–1334
Urban III	1185–1187	Benedict XII	1334–1342
Gregory VIII	1187	Clement VI	1342–1352
Clement III	1187–1191	Innocent VI	1352–1362
Celestine III	1191–1198	Urban V	1362–1370
Innocent III	1198–1216	Gregory XI	1370–1378
Honorius III	1216–1227	Urban VI	1378–1389
Gregory IX	1227–1241	Clement VII (Avignon)	1378–1394
Celestine IV	1241	Boniface IX	1389–1404
Innocent IV	1243–1254	Benedict XIII (Avignon)	1394–1423
Alexander IV	1254–1261	Innocent VII	1404–1406
Urban IV	1261–1264	Gregory XII	1406–1415
Clement IV	1265–1268	Alexander V (Pisa)	1409–1410
Gregory X	1271–1276	John XXIII (Pisa)	1410–1415
Innocent V	1276	Martin V	1417–1431
Adrian V	1276	Eugenius IV	1431–1447
John XXI	1276–1277	Nicholas V	1447–1455
Nicholas III	1277–1280	Callixtus III	1455–1458
Martin IV	1281–1285	Pius II	1458–1464
Honorius IV	1285–1287	Paul II	1464–1471
Nicholas IV	1288–1292	Sixtus IV	1471–1484
Celestine V	1294	Innocent VIII	1484–1492
Boniface VIII	1294–1303	Alexander VI	1492–1503

Kings of France

(Capetian)

Hugh Capet	987– 996
Robert II	996–1031
Henry I	1031–1060
Philip I	1060–1108
Louis VI	1108–1137
Louis VII	1137–1180
Philip II (Augustus)	1180–1223
Louis VIII	1223–1226
Louis IX	1226–1270
Philip III	1270–1285
Philip IV (the Fair)	1285–1314
Louis X	1314–1316
Philip V	1316–1322
Charles IV	1322–1328

(Valois)

Philip VI	1328–1350
John II (the Good)	1350–1364
Charles V	1364–1380
Charles VI	1380–1422
Charles VII	1422–1461
Louis XI	1461–1483
Charles VIII	1483–1498

Kings of England

William I (Conqueror)	1066–1087
William II (Rufus)	1087–1100
Henry I	1100–1135
Stephen	1135–1154
Henry II	1154–1189
Richard I	1189–1199
John	1199–1216
Henry III	1216–1272
Edward I	1272–1307
Edward II	1307–1327
Edward III	1327–1377
Richard II	1377–1399
Henry IV	1399–1413
Henry V	1413–1422
Henry VI	1422–1461
Edward IV	1461–1483
Edward V	1483
Richard III	1483–1485
Henry VII	1485–1509

Kings of Germany

Conrad I	911– 918	Frederick II	1215–1250
Henry I (the Fowler)	919– 936	Conrad IV	1250–1254
Otto I (the Great)	936– 973	*Interregnum*	1254–1273
Otto II	973– 983	Rudolf	1273–1291
Otto III	983–1002	Adolf	1292–1298
Henry II	1002–1024	Albert	1298–1308
Conrad II	1024–1039	Henry VII	1309–1313
Henry III	1039–1056	Louis IV	1314–1347
Henry IV	1056–1106	Charles IV	1347–1378
Henry V	1106–1125	Wenceslas	1378–1400
Lothair	1125–1137	Rupert	1400–1410
Conrad III	1138–1152	Sigismund	1410–1437
Frederick I (Barbarossa)	1152–1190	Albert II	1438–1439
Henry VI	1190–1197	Frederick III	1440–1493
Philip of Swabia and		Maximilian	1493–1519
Otto IV of Brunswick*	1198–1214		

* claimants

Bibliography

Historical Atlases: E. W. Fox & H. S. Deighton, *Atlas of European History* (New York, 1957); Hammond's *Historical Atlas* (Maplewood, N.J.); R. R. Palmer, *Atlas of World History* (Chicago, 1957); *Penguin Atlas of Medieval History* (Penguin); W. R. Shepherd, *Historical Atlas* (New York, 1956). *Cambridge Medieval History* (8 vols., Cambridge, 1911–1936); C. P. Farrar & A. P. Evans, *Bibliography of English Translations from Medieval Sources* (New York, 1946); W. E. Lunt, *History of England* (New York, 1947); L. J. Paetow, *Guide to the Study of Medieval History* (New York, 1931. Does not include England); C. W. Previté-Orton, *The Shorter Cambridge Medieval History* (2 vols., Cambridge, 1952).

CHAPTER 1.

Paperbound: J. B. Bury, *History of the Later Roman Empire* (Dover); J. Carcopino, *Daily Life in Ancient Rome* (Yale); M. Cary and T. Haarhoff, *Life and Thought in the Greek and Roman World* (Barnes & Noble); S. Dill, *Roman Society: From Nero to Marcus Aurelius* (Meridian); S. Dill, *Roman Society in the Last Century of the Western Empire* (Meridian); E. Gibbon, *Decline and Fall of the Roman Empire* (3 vols., Washington Square); S. Katz, *The Decline of Rome and the Rise of Mediaeval Europe* (Cornell); F. Lot, *The End of the Ancient World* (Torch); H. Mattingly, *Roman Imperial Civilization* (Anchor); *Meditations* of Marcus Aurelius (several editions); H. S. Moss, *The Birth of the Middle Ages* (Oxford); Pliny's *Natural History,* Lloyd Haberly, ed. (Frederick Ungar Publishing Co.).
   Clothbound: R. F. Arragon, *The Transition from the Ancient to the Medieval World* (New York, 1936); C. Bailey, *The Legacy of Rome* (Oxford, 1936); *Cambridge Ancient History,* X, XI, XII (Cambridge, 1934–1939); M. Cary, *A History of Rome Down to the Time of Constantine* (New York, 1954); H. Mattingly, *The Man in the Roman Street* (London, 1947); M. Rostovtzeff, *The Social and Economic History of the Roman Empire* (2 vols., Oxford, 1957).

CHAPTER 2.

Paperbound: St. Augustine's *City of God* (several editions); St. Augustine's *Confessions* (several editions); C. N. Cochrane, *Christianity and Classical Culture* (Galaxy); H. Daniel-Rops, *The Church in the Dark Ages* (2 vols., Image); E. S. Duckett, *The Gateway to the Middle Ages: Monasticism* (Ann

Arbor) ; A. Fremantle, *Treasury of Early Christianity* (Mentor) ; H. M. Jones, *Constantine and the Conversion of Europe* (Collier) ; H. Marrou, *Saint Augustine and His Influence through the Ages* (Men of Wisdom) ; J. McCann, *Saint Benedict* (Image) ; *New Testament* (several editions) ; H. Pope, *Saint Augustine of Hippo* (Image) ; E. K. Rand, *Founders of the Middle Ages* (Dover) ; *Rule* of St. Benedict (several editions) ; H. O. Taylor, *Emergence of Christian Culture in the West: The Classical Heritage of the Middle Ages* (Torch) ; H. Waddell, *Desert Fathers* (Ann Arbor) ; J. Weiss, *Earliest Christianity* (Torch).

Clothbound: A. Alfoeldi, *The Conversion of Constantine and Pagan Rome* (Oxford, 1948) ; S. Baldwin, *The Organization of Medieval Christianity* (New York, 1929) ; E. C. Butler, *Benedictine Monasticism* (London, 1919) ; *Cambridge Medieval History,* I ; C. H. Dawson, *Religion and the Rise of Western Culture* (London, 1950) ; L. E. Elliott-Binns, *The Beginnings of Western Christendom* (London, 1948) ; M. L. Laistner, *The Intellectual Heritage of the Early Middle Ages* (Ithaca, 1957) ; J. Lebreton and J. Zeiller, *The History of the Primitive Church* (2 vols., New York, 1942–47) ; C. C. Richardson, *Early Christian Fathers* (Philadelphia, 1953).

CHAPTER 3.

Paperbound: W. C. Bark, *Origins of the Medieval World* (Anchor) ; C. H. Dawson, *The Making of Europe* (Meridian) ; S. Dill, *Roman Society in the Last Century of the Western Empire* (Meridian) ; A. F. Havighurst, *The Pirenne Thesis* (Heath) ; F. Lot, *The End of the Ancient World and the Beginnings of the Middle Ages* (Torch) ; H. S. Moss, *The Birth of the Middle Ages* (Oxford) ; H. Pirenne, *Mohammed and Charlemagne* (Meridian) ; R. E. Sullivan, *Heirs of the Roman Empire* (Cornell) ; Tacitus, *On Britain and Germany* (Penguin) ; J. M. Wallace-Hadrill, *The Barbarian West* (Torch).

Clothbound: J. B. Bury, *The Invasion of Europe by the Barbarians* (London, 1928) ; *Cambridge Medieval History,* I ; M. Deanesley, *A History of Early Medieval Europe, 476–911* (London, 1960) ; A. Dopsch, *The Economic and Social Foundations of European Civilization* (New York, 1937) ; F. Dvornik, *The Slavs: Their Early History and Civilization* (Boston, 1956) ; R. H. Hodgkin, *History of the Anglo-Saxons* (Oxford, 1953) ; E. Thompson, *A History of Attila and the Huns* (Oxford, 1948).

CHAPTER 4.

Paperbound: N. H. Baynes & H. Moss, eds., *Byzantium: An Introduction to East Roman Civilization* (Oxford) ; J. B. Bury, *History of the Later Roman Empire from the Death of Theodosius I to the Death of Justinian* (Dover) ; R. Guerdan, *Byzantium* (Capricorn) ; J. M. Hussey, *The Byzantine World* (Torch) ; S. Runciman, *Byzantine Civilization* (Meridian) ; A. A. Vasiliev, *History of the Byzantine Empire* (Wisconsin).

Clothbound: E. Barker, *Social and Political Thought in Byzantium, from Justinian I to the Last Palaeologus* (Oxford, 1957) ; N. H. Baynes, *The Byzantine Empire* (London, 1946) ; *Cambridge Medieval History,* II, IV; C. Diehl, *History of the Byzantine Empire* (Princeton, 1925) ; C. Diehl, *Byzantium: Greatness and Decline* (New Brunswick, 1957) ; G. Ostrogorsky, *History of the Byzantine State* (Oxford, 1956).

CHAPTER 5.

Paperbound: T. Andrae, *Mohammed: The Man and His Faith* (Torch); *Arabian Nights* (several editions); E. Dermenghem, *Muhammad and the Islamic Tradition* (Men of Wisdom); H. A. Gibb, *Mohammedanism: An Historical Survey* (Galaxy); G. E. von Grunebaum, *Medieval Islam: A Study in Cultural Orientation* (Phoenix); A. Guillaume, *Islam* (Penguin); P. K. Hitti, *Arabs: A Short History* (Gateway); B. Lewis, *The Arabs in History* (Torch); *Koran* (several editions).
    Clothbound: T. W. Arnold, *The Preaching of Islam* (London, 1935); T. W. Arnold & A. Guillaume, *The Legacy of Islam* (London, 1947); *Cambridge Medieval History*, II, IV; P. K. Hitti, *History of the Arabs* (New York, 1956); R. Levy, *The Social Structure of Islam* (Cambridge, 1957).

CHAPTER 6.

Paperbound: Bede, *A History of the English Church and People* (Penguin); J. Brønsted, *The Vikings* (Penguin); C. N. Cochrane, *Christianity and Classical Culture* (Galaxy); S. C. Easton & H. Wieruszowski, *The Era of Charlemagne* (Anvil); *Einhard, Life of Charlemagne* (Ann Arbor); W. P. Ker, *The Dark Ages* (Mentor); H. Pirenne, *Mohammed and Charlemagne* (Meridian); E. K. Rand, *Founders of the Middle Ages* (Dover); R. E. Sullivan, *The Coronation of Charlemagne, What Did It Signify?* (Heath); H. O. Taylor, *Emergence of Christian Culture in the West* (Torch); J. M. Wallace-Hadrill, *The Barbarian West, A.D. 400–1000* (Torch); R. Winston, *Charlemagne: From the Hammer to the Cross* (Vintage).
    Clothbound: E. Brehaut, *An Encyclopedist of the Dark Ages:* Isidore of Seville (New York, 1912); *Cambridge Medieval History*, II; M. Deanesley, *A History of Early Medieval Europe, 476–911* (London, 1960); S. Dill, *Roman Society in Gaul in the Merovingian Age* (London, 1926); A. Dopsch, *The Economic and Social Foundations of European Civilization* (London, 1937); E. S. Duckett, *Alcuin, Friend of Charlemagne* (New York, 1951); H. Fichtenau, *The Carolingian Empire* (Oxford, 1957); Gregory of Tours, *History of the Franks* (2 vols., tr. O. Dalton, Oxford, 1927); M. L. Laistner, *The Intellectual Heritage of the Early Middle Ages* (Ithaca, 1957); M. L. Laistner, *Thought and Letters in Western Europe, A.D. 500–900* (London, 1957); H. O. Taylor, *The Medieval Mind* (2 vols., Cambridge, Mass., 1949).

CHAPTER 7.

Paperbound: F. L. Ganshof, *Feudalism* (Torch); R. S. Hoyt, *Feudal Institutions: Cause or Consequence of Decentralization?* (Holt, Rinehart & Winston); C. W. Oman, *The Art of War in the Middle Ages* (Cornell); S. Painter, *French Chivalry* (Cornell); S. Painter, *Mediaeval Society* (Cornell); R. W. Southern, *The Making of the Middle Ages* (Yale); D. M. Stenton, *English Society in the Early Middle Ages* (Penguin); C. Stephenson, *Mediaeval Feudalism* (Cornell).
    Clothbound: M. Bloch, *Feudal Society* (London, 1960); *Cambridge Medieval History*, VI; W. S. Davis, *Life on a Medieval Barony* (New York, 1923); G. Tellenbach, *Church, State, and Christian Society at the Time of the Investiture Controversy* (Oxford, 1940); A. Luchaire, *Social France in*

the Time of Philip Augustus (New York, 1912); B. Lyon, *From Fief to Indenture: The Transition from Feudal to Non-Feudal Contract in Western Europe* (Cambridge, Mass., 1957).

CHAPTER 8.

Paperbound: H. S. Bennett, *Life on the English Manor* (Cambridge); G. G. Coulton, *Medieval Village, Manor, Monastery* (Torch); U. T. Holmes, *Daily Living in the Twelfth Century: Based on the Observations of Alexander Neckam in London and Paris* (Wisconsin, 1952); S. Painter, *Mediaeval Society* (Cornell); E. Power, *Medieval People* (Anchor); R. W. Southern, *The Making of the Middle Ages* (Yale); D. M. Stenton, *English Society in the Early Middle Ages* (Penguin).

    Clothbound: P. Boissonade, *Life and Work in Medieval Europe* (New York, 1927); *Cambridge Economic History of Europe,* I (J. H. Clapham, ed., Cambridge, 1941); H. Heaton, *Economic History of Europe* (New York, 1948); G. C. Homans, *English Villagers of the Thirteenth Century* (Cambridge, Mass., 1941); A. Luchaire, *Social France in the Time of Philip Augustus* (New York, 1912); N. Neilson, *Medieval Agrarian Economy* (New York, 1936).

CHAPTER 9.

Paperbound: H. L. Adelson, *Medieval Commerce* (Anvil); J. J. Jusserand, *English Wayfaring Life in the Middle Ages* (Barnes & Noble); J. H. Mundy & P. Riesenberg, *Medieval Town* (Anvil); R. A. Newhall, *The Crusades* (Holt, Rinehart and Winston); S. Painter, *Mediaeval Society* (Cornell); H. Pirenne, *Economic and Social History of Medieval Europe* (Harvest); H. Pirenne, *Medieval Cities* (Anchor); E. Power, *Medieval People* (Anchor); H. F. Prescott, *Friar Felix at Large* (Yale); S. Thrupp, *Merchant Class of Medieval London* (Ann Arbor); Villehardouin and de Joinville: *Memoirs of the Crusades* (Everyman).

    Clothbound: P. Boissonade, *Life and Work in Medieval Europe* (New York, 1927); *Cambridge Economic History,* II (Cambridge, 1952); *Cambridge Medieval History,* IV, V; Joan Evans, *Life in Mediaeval France* (Oxford, 1925); Fulcher of Chartres, *Chronicle of the First Crusade* (tr. M. E. McGinty, Philadelphia, 1941); H. Heaton, *Economic History of Europe* (New York, 1948); R. Latouche, *Birth of Western Economy* (New York, 1960); R. S. Lopez & I. W. Raymond, *Medieval Trade in the Mediterranean World* (New York, 1955); D. C. Munro, *The Kingdom of the Crusaders* (New York, 1935); S. Runciman, *A History of the Crusades* (3 vols., Cambridge, 1951–1954); *A History of the Crusades* (ed. K. M. Setton, 2 vols., Philadelphia, 1955–1962); R. C. Smail, *Crusading Warfare* (Cambridge, 1956); J. W. Thompson, *Economic and Social History of the Middle Ages* (New York, 1928); William, Archbishop of Tyre, *A History of Deeds Done beyond the Sea* (tr. E. A. Babcock & A. Krey, New York, 1943).

CHAPTER 10.

Paperbound: P. H. Blair, *Introduction to Anglo-Saxon England* (Cambridge); J. Bryce, *Holy Roman Empire* (Schocken); E. S. Duckett, *Gateway* to the Middle Ages: France and Britain (Ann Arbor); A. Kelly, *Eleanor of Aquitaine and the Four Kings* (Vintage); S. Painter, *The Rise of Feudal Monarchies* (Cornell); S. Runciman, *The Sicilian Vespers* (Penguin); G. O. Sayles, *Medieval Foundations of England* (Perpetua).

Clothbound: G. Barraclough, *The Origins of Modern Germany* (Oxford, 1947); Z. N. Brooke, *A History of Europe, 911–1198* (London, 1951); *Cambridge Medieval History,* III, V, VI; R. Fawtier, *The Capetian Kings of France* (London, 1960); E. Kantorowicz, *Frederick II* (London, 1931); F. Kern, *Kingship and the Law in the Middle Ages* (Oxford, 1939); C. Petit-Dutaillis, *The Feudal Monarchy in France and England* (London, 1936); A. L. Poole, *From Domesday to Magna Carta, 1087–1216* (Oxford, 1955); F. M. Stenton, *The First Century of English Feudalism* (Oxford, 1961); J. W. Thompson, *Feudal Germany* (Chicago, 1928).

CHAPTER 11.

Paperbound: M. W. Baldwin, *The Mediaeval Church* (Cornell); G. K. Chesterton, *St. Francis of Assisi* (Image); H. Daniel-Rops, *Cathedral and Crusade: Studies of the Medieval Church, 1050–1350* (Image); E. S. Duckett, *Gateway to the Middle Ages: Monasticism* (Ann Arbor); J. Jorgensen, *St. Francis of Assisi* (Image); H. C. Lea, *The Inquisition of the Middle Ages* (Citadel); J. B. Morrall, *Political Thought in Medieval Times* (Torch); *Readings in Church History* (ed. C. J. Barry, vol. I, Newman); S. Runciman, *Mediaeval Manichee* (Compass).

Clothbound: M. W. Baldwin, *The Medieval Papacy in Action* (New York, 1940); S. Baldwin, *The Organization of Medieval Christianity* (New York, 1929); R. F. Bennett, *The Early Dominicans* (Cambridge, 1937); *Cambridge Medieval History,* V, VI; E. Emerton, *The Correspondence of Pope Gregory VII* (New York, 1932); J. Evans, *Monastic Life at Cluny* (Oxford, 1931); B. S. James, *Saint Bernard of Clairvaux* (New York, 1957); B. Jarrett, *Life of St. Dominic* (London, 1924); D. Knowles, *The Religious Orders in England* (2 vols., Cambridge, 1950–1955); C. McIlwain, *The Growth of Political Thought in the West* (New York, 1932); S. R. Packard, *Europe and the Church under Innocent III* (New York, 1927); R. W. Southern, *The Making of the Middle Ages* (New York, 1953); G. Tellenbach, *Church, State, and Christian Society at the Time of the Investiture Controversy* (Oxford, 1940); W. Ullmann, *The Growth of Papal Government in the Middle Ages* (London, 1955); W. Williams, *St. Bernard of Clairvaux* (Manchester, 1953).

CHAPTER 12.

Paperbound: Thomas Aquinas, *Summa Theologiae* (several editions of selections); G. K. Chesterton, *St. Thomas Aquinas* (Image); F. C. Copleston, *Medieval Philosophy* (Torch); F. C. Copleston, *Aquinas* (Penguin); F. C. Copleston, *A History of Mediaeval Philosophy* (2 vols., Image); A. C. Crombie, *Medieval and Early Modern Science* (2 vols., Anchor); A. Fremantle, *The Age of Belief* (Mentor); E. Gilson, *Heloise and Abelard* (Ann Arbor); E. Gilson, *Reason and Revelation in the Middle Ages* (Scribner's); C. H. Haskins, *Renaissance of the 12th Century* (Meridian); C. H. Haskins, *Rise of Universities* (Cornell); G. Leff, *Medieval Thought from St. Augustine to Ockham* (Penguin); *Selections from Medieval Philosophers* (ed. R. McKeon, 2 vols.,

Scribner's) ; R. W. Southern, *The Making of the Middle Ages* (Yale) ; H. Waddell, *Peter Abelard* (Compass) ; M. de Wulf, *Philosophy and Civilization in the Middle Ages* (Dover).

Clothbound: F. B. Artz, *The Mind of the Middle Ages* (New York, 1958) ; *Cambridge Medieval History,* VI; A. C. Crombie, *Robert Grosseteste and the Origins of Experimental Science* (Oxford, 1953) ; A. C. Crombie, *Augustine to Gallileo* (London, 1952) ; C. G. Crump & E. F. Jacob, *The Legacy of the Middle Ages* (Oxford, 1938) ; E. Gilson, *History of Christian Philosophy in the Middle Ages* (New York, 1955) ; C. H. Haskins, *Studies in Medieval Culture* (New York, 1958) ; H. F. Jolowicz, *Historical Introduction to Roman Law* (Cambridge, 1952) ; H. Rashdall, *The Universities of Europe in the Middle Ages* (3 vols., Oxford, 1936) ; H. O. Taylor, *The Mediaeval Mind: A History of the Development of Thought and Emotion in the Middle Ages* (Cambridge, Mass., 1949) ; L. Thorndike, *History of Magic and Experimental Science* (4 vols., New York, 1923–1934) ; L. Thorndike, *University Records and Life in the Middle Ages* (New York, 1944) ; P. Vinogradoff, *Roman Law in Medieval Europe* (Oxford, 1929).

CHAPTER 13.

Paperbound: Henry Adams, *Mont-Saint-Michel and Chartres* (Anchor, Mentor) ; *Aucassin and Nicolette and Other Medieval Romances* (Everyman) ; E. Auerbach, *Introduction to Romance Languages and Literature* (Capricorn) ; J. Bedier, *The Romance of Tristan and Iseult* (Anchor) ; *Beowulf* (Penguin, California) ; Chrétien de Troyes, *Ywain* (Ungar) ; *Everyman and Medieval Miracle Plays* (Everyman) ; *Sir Gawain and the Green Knight* (Penguin) ; Geoffrey of Monmouth, *History of the Kings of Britain* (Everyman) ; N. L. Goodrich, *The Medieval Myths* (Mentor) ; A. Hauser, *The Social History of Art* (vol. I, Vintage) ; E. Holt, *A Documentary History of Art* (2 vols., Anchor) ; *Icelandic Saga* (Bison) ; W. P. Ker, *The Dark Ages* (Mentor) ; W. P. Ker, *Epic and Romance* (Dover) ; *Medieval and Tudor Drama* (ed. J. Gassner, Bantam) ; *Medieval Mysteries, Moralities, and Interludes* (Barron's Educational Series) ; *Njal's Saga* (Penguin) ; E. Panofsky, *Gothic Architecture and Scholasticism* (Meridian) ; *Parzival by Wolfram von Eschenbach* (Vintage) ; *The Poem of the Cid* (Barron's Educational Series, California) ; N. Pevsner, *An Outline of European Architecture* (Penguin) ; *The Romance of the Rose* (Everyman) ; *Song of Roland* (several editions) ; A. Temko, *Notre-Dame of Paris: The Biography of a Cathedral* (Compass) ; *Tristan of Gottfried von Strassburg* (Penguin) ; *Volsunga Saga* (Collier) ; H. Waddell, *The Wandering Scholars* (Anchor) ; T. H. White, *The Bestiary* (Capricorn).

Clothbound: *The Anglo-Saxon Chronicle* (Everyman) ; *Arthurian Romances* (Everyman) ; C. G. Crump & E. F. Jacob, *The Legacy of the Middle Ages* (Oxford, 1938) ; J. Evans, *Art in Medieval France* (London, 1948) ; *The Fall of the Nibelungs* (Everyman) ; *Heimskringla: The Norse King Sagas* (Everyman) ; M. Helin, *A History of Medieval Latin Literature* (New York, 1949) ; U. T. Holmes, *A History of Old French Literature* (New York, 1948) ; W. T. Jackson, *The Literature of the Middle Ages* (New York, 1960) ; Marie de France, *Lays of Marie de France and Other French Legends* (Everyman) ; C. Morey, *Medieval Art* (New York, 1942) ; F. J. Raby, *A History of Secular Latin Poetry in the Middle Ages* (Oxford, 1957) ; F. J. Raby, *A History of Christian Latin Poetry from the Beginnings to the Close of the Middle Ages* (Oxford, 1953) ; G. Reese, *Music in the Middle Ages* (New York, 1940) ;

J. A. Symonds, *Wine, Women, and Song* (London, 1925); M. Valency, *In Praise of Love* (New York, 1958); H. Waddell, *Medieval Latin Lyrics* (London, 1933); K. Young, *The Drama of the Medieval Church* (2 vols., Oxford, 1933).

CHAPTER 14.

Paperbound: B. Berenson, *Italian Painters of the Renaissance* (Meridian); Boccaccio's *Decameron* (several editions); J. Burckhardt, *Civilization of the Renaissance in Italy* (2 vols., Torch); Chaucer's *Canterbury Tales* (several editions); *Cloud of Unknowing* (Penguin); Dante's *Divine Comedy* (several editions); J. N. Figgis, *Political Thought from Gerson to Grotius: 1414–1625* (Torch); *Meister Eckhart, A Modern Translation* (tr. R. Blakney, Torch); *Master Eckhart and the Rhineland Mystics* (ed. J. Ancelet-Hustache, Men of Wisdom); John Froissart, *The Chronicles of England, France, and Spain* (Everyman); M. P. Gilmore, *The World of Humanism* (Torch); Walter Hilton, *The Ladder of Perfection* (Penguin); J. Huizinga, *Waning of the Middle Ages* (Anchor); T. Kempis, *Imitation of Christ* (several editions); P. O. Kristeller, *Renaissance Thought* (Torch); William Langland, *Piers the Ploughman* (Penguin); K. B. McFarlane, *John Wycliffe and the Beginnings of English Nonconformity* (Collier); *The Portable Renaissance Reader* (J. B. Ross & M. M. McLaughlin, eds., Viking); G. Sarton, *The Appreciation of Ancient and Medieval Science during the Renaissance* (Perpetua); G. C. Sellery, *The Renaissance: Its Nature and Origins* (Wisconsin); J. A. Symonds, *Revival of Learning* (Capricorn); *The Complete Works of François Villon* (Bantam).

Clothbound: H. Baron, *The Crisis of the Early Italian Renaissance* (2 vols., Princeton, 1955); L. E. Binns, *Decline and Fall of the Mediaeval Papacy* (London, 1934); *Cambridge Medieval History*, VII, VIII; J. M. Clark, *The Great German Mystics: Eckhart, Tauler, and Suso* (Oxford, 1949); E. K. Chambers, *English Literature at the Close of the Middle Ages* (Oxford, 1945); J. Evans, *English Art, 1307–1461* (Oxford, 1949); A. C. Flick, *The Decline of the Medieval Church* (2 vols., London, 1930); W. K. Ferguson, *The Renaissance in Historical Thought* (Boston, 1948); D. Hay, *The Italian Renaissance in Its Historical Background* (Cambridge, 1961); M. Spinka, *John Hus and the Czech Reform* (Chicago, 1941); B. Tierney, *Foundations of the Conciliar Theory* (Cambridge, 1955); W. Ullmann, *Origins of the Great Schism* (London, 1948); K. Vossler, *Mediaeval Culture: An Introduction to Dante and His Times* (2 vols., New York, 1929).

CHAPTER 15.

Paperbound: J. Beevers, *Saint Joan of Arc* (Image); E. P. Cheyney, *The Dawn of a New Era: 1250–1453* (Torch); John Froissart, *The Chronicles of England, France, and Spain* (Everyman); G. L. Haskins, *Growth of English Representative Government* (Perpetua); J. Huizinga, *The Waning of the Middle Ages* (Anchor); *Joan of Arc: Self-Portrait* (Collier); N. Machiavelli, *History of Florence and of the Affairs of Italy* (Torch); Marco Polo, *Travels* (several editions); A. R. Myers, *England in the Late Middle Ages* (Penguin); J. Nohl, *The Black Death* (Ballantine); C. W. Oman, *The Art of War in the Middle Ages* (Cornell); R. Pernoud, *Joan of Arc* (Evergreen); H. Pirenne,

Economic and Social History of Medieval Europe (Harvest) ; F. Schevill, *The Medici* (Torch) ; J. A. Symonds, *The Age of Despots* (Capricorn).

Clothbound: S. Baldwin, *Business in the Middle Ages* (New York, 1937) ; C. R. Beazley, *The Dawn of Modern Geography* (3 vols., New York, 1949) ; *Cambridge Economic History*, II, III; *Cambridge Medieval History*, VII, VIII; O. Cartellieri, *The Court of Burgundy* (New York, 1929) ; F. Dvornik, *The Making of Central and Eastern Europe* (London, 1949) ; L. Fabre, *Joan of Arc* (New York, 1954) ; V. H. Green, *The Later Plantagenets: A Survey of English History between 1307 and 1485* (London, 1955) ; H. Heaton, *Economic History of Europe* (New York, 1948) ; E. F. Jacob, *The Fifteenth Century, 1399–1485* (Oxford, 1961) ; A. B. Kerr, *Jacques Coeur* (New York, 1928) ; G. H. Kimble, *Geography in the Middle Ages* (London, 1938) ; J. H. Mariéjol, *The Spain of Ferdinand and Isabella* (New Brunswick, N.J., 1961) ; M. McKisack, *The Fourteenth Century, 1307–1399* (Oxford, 1959) ; E. Perroy, *The Hundred Years War* (London, 1951) ; E. Power, *The Wool Trade in English Medieval History* (London, 1941) ; C. W. Previté-Orton, *A History of Europe: 1198–1378* (London, 1948) ; F. Thompson, *A Short History of Parliament, 1295–1642* (Minneapolis, 1953) ; J. W. Thompson, *Economic and Social History of Europe in the Later Middle Ages, 1300–1530* (New York, 1931) ; G. Vernadsky, *The Mongols and Russia* (New Haven, 1953) ; W. T. Waugh, *A History of Europe: 1378–1494* (London, 1932).

Index